# The Routledge Handbook of Counterterrorism and Counterinsurgency in Africa

This book illustrates how Africa's defence and security domains have been radically altered by drastic changes in world politics and local ramifications.

First, the contributions of numerous authors highlight the transnational dimensions of counterterrorism and counterinsurgency in Africa and reveal the roles played by African states and regional organisations in the global war on terror. Second, the volume critically evaluates the emerging regional architectures of countering terrorism, insurgency, and organised violence on the continent through the African Union Counterterrorism Framework (AU-CTF) and Regional Security Complexes (RSC). Third, the book sheds light on the counterterrorism and counterinsurgency (CT-COIN) structures and mechanisms established by specific African states to contain, degrade, and eliminate terrorism, insurgency, and organised violence on the continent, particularly the successes, constraints, and challenges of the emerging CT-COIN mechanisms. Finally, the volume highlights the entry of non-state actors – such as civil society, volunteer groups, private security companies, and defence contractors – into the theatre of counterterrorism and counterinsurgency in Africa through volunteerism, community support for state-led CT-COIN Operations, and civil-military cooperation (CIMIC).

This book will be of use to students and scholars of security studies, African studies, international relations, and terrorism studies, and to practitioners of development, defence, security, and strategy.

**Usman A. Tar** is Distinguished Endowed Professor of Defence and Security Studies at the Nigerian Defence Academy, and Director of the Academy's flagship Centre for Defence Studies and Documentation (CDSD).

# The Routledge Handbook of Counterterrorism and Counterinsurgency in Africa

*Edited by Usman A. Tar*

LONDON AND NEW YORK

First published 2021
by Routledge
2 Park Square, Milton Park, Abingdon, Oxon OX14 4RN

and by Routledge
52 Vanderbilt Avenue, New York, NY 10017

*Routledge is an imprint of the Taylor & Francis Group, an informa business*

© 2021 selection and editorial matter, Usman A. Tar; individual chapters, the contributors

The right of Usman A. Tar to be identified as the author of the editorial material, and of the authors for their individual chapters, has been asserted in accordance with sections 77 and 78 of the Copyright, Designs and Patents Act 1988.

All rights reserved. No part of this book may be reprinted or reproduced or utilised in any form or by any electronic, mechanical, or other means, now known or hereafter invented, including photocopying and recording, or in any information storage or retrieval system, without permission in writing from the publishers.

*Trademark notice*: Product or corporate names may be trademarks or registered trademarks, and are used only for identification and explanation without intent to infringe.

*British Library Cataloguing-in-Publication Data*
A catalogue record for this book is available from the British Library

*Library of Congress Cataloging-in-Publication Data*
A catalog record has been requested for this book

ISBN: 978-1-138-57539-4 (hbk)
ISBN: 978-0-367-50612-4 (pbk)
ISBN: 978-1-351-27192-9 (ebk)

Typeset in Bembo
by MPS Limited, Dehradun

To the victims of terrorism and their families for bearing the cost of madness, and to humanitarian relief workers who provide succor and hope to the victims of terrorism across the world.

We eulogize four distinguished scholars of African Defence and Security who either contributed a chapter or provided suggestions for improving the book manuscript, but did not live to see this *Handbook* – Professor Haruna Wakili, Professor Chukwuma Osakwe, Professor Moses Tedheke, and Professor Habu Galadima. In their mentorship and scholarship of engagement, they bequeathed a legacy that lives on.

# Contents

Contents

Contents

# Acknowledgements

In the course of working on this book project, I have incurred debts of appreciation to a number of people and organisations who provided selfless support. First, my employers – the Nigerian Ministry of Defence (MOD) and Nigerian Defense Academy (NDA) – granted me exceptional institutional support to see this manuscript completed. The Commandant, Major General Jamil Sarham proved himself as a pro-intellectual and pro-knowledge enterprise Chief Executive Officer of the Academy. I am equally grateful to the following senior colleagues in the Academy for their invaluable support and patience while we were working on this project: Professor Isa Garba, the Academy Provost; Professor Azubike Sonny Nwankwo; Prof OE Tangban, Prof CN Ubah, Prof AO Ahmed, Prof SC Osuala, Prof SA Ochoche; Prof DO Alabi, Prof IO Mbachu, Prof MEU Tedheke, Prof Usman Mohd, Prof YA Umar; Prof Mohammed Onimisi; Prof IA Imam, Prof CC Osakwe, Prof Ayuba Kwasau, Prof Joel Ajibua, Prof MS Abdulsalam, Prof JK Aremu, Prof Terzungwe Nyor, Prof Joshua Okpanachi, Prof Suleiman Saad, Dr VS Akran and Air Cdr (Prof) PA Agashua.

I offer my sincere appreciation to the following external colleagues, some of whom read portions of this volume and made valuable suggestions: Prof Alfred Zack-Williams (University of Central Lancashire, UK), Prof Kenneth Omeje (University of Johannesburg South Africa), Prof Usman Gbla (Fourah Bay College, University of Sierra Leone); Prof Rita Abrahamsen (University of Ottawa, Canada); Prof Ebenezer Obadare (University of Kansas, USA), Prof Cyril Obi (Social Science Research Council, USA), Prof Usman Gbla (Fourah Bay College, University of Sierra Leone); Prof Celestine Oyom Bassey (University of Calabar, Nigeria), Prof Rauf Ayo Dunmoye (ABU, Zaria, Nigeria), Prof Paul Pindar Izzah (ABU, Zaria, Nigeria), Prof Kayode Omojuwa (ABU, Zaria, Nigeria), Prof Aja Akpuru-Aja (Abia State University, Uturu, Nigeria), Prof Sam Egwu, Prof Nanven Audu Gambo (University of Jos, Nigeria), Prof Habu Mohammed and Prof Umar Pateh (Bayero University of Kano, Nigeria), Prof Albert Isaac Olawale (University of Ibadan, Nigeria), and Prof Yusuf Zoaka, Prof Kabiru Mato and Prof Abdulhamid Suleiman-Ozohu (all of the University of Abuja, Nigeria), Prof OBC Nwolise (University of Ibadan, Abuja), Prof Abdullahi Ashafa (Kaduna State University).

A number of military officers and civilian colleagues, serving and retired, guided us (some even queried some of our assumptions) on issues of defense and security: Air Marshal SB Abubakar; Air Vice Marshal MN Umaru, Major General AM Jibril, Major General GA Wahab, Major General Ahmed Mohammed (Bandit), Major General Adamu Abubakar, Major General Rogers Ibe Nicholas, Major General CO Onwamaegbu, Major General IM Yusuf, Major General A Oyebade, Air Vice Marshal AA Zannah, Air Vice Marshal AS Alao, Major General AA Mshelbawala; Major General AG Aduwuyi, Major General RB Usoro, Major General JN Nwoaga, Major General RC Duru, Rear Admiral KO Komolafe, Rear Admiral HA Babalola, Rear Admiral SI Alade, Air Vice Marshall MY Asimi, AVM MA Mohammed, AVM JON

Ode, Brigadier General SD Bala, Brigadier General JN Temlong, Brigadier General KO Aligbe, Brigadier General SS Ibrahim, Brigadier General S Ibrahim, Col IB Alaya, Col ASM Wase, and Captain Ahmed Chiroma.

I am grateful to the following colleagues at the Department of Political Science and International Relations (PSIR), and Department of Defence and Security Studies (DSS) at the Academy: Dr BE Mijah, Dr NT Mohammed, Col Dr Abiodun Oluwadare, Col AE Odupitan, Dr SM Lawal, Dr AE Bature, Dr Barnabas Ekpo, Dr Sudany Adejoh, Mr Hadiza Abdullahi, Mrs Aisha Ajoke Abdulsalam, Mr Promise Ntagu, Mr NK Achi, Major Auwal Isa, Major IK Gaddafi, Mallam SS Suleiman, Ms Olutayo Ajibade, Mrs Nufaisa Ahmed Garba, Mr Leo Onora, Ibrahim L Ismail, Olayiwola A Richard, Jamaludeen Mohammed Ali, Sulaiman Ali, Mallam Sagir, Mohammed Jibrin, and Daniel Ocheje. I am grateful to my colleagues at the Centre for Defence Studies and Documentation, NDA: Mrs NK Nurudeen, Mr Samuel B. Ayegba, Mr Yekini Bello, Captain Bashir Bala, Mubarak Mashi, Kabiru Zubairu, Mr Solomon Amboh, Mrs Folashade Aregbesola, Babangida Mohammed, and Helen Okpe.

My extended family was incredibly supportive during my regular absence to work on the manuscript. My wife, Fatima, and children – Mustapha, Abubakar, Aisha, Maryam, and Amaal – have been my pillars of support. My parents and siblings prevailed on me to keep going: Hajja Yakaka Mohd Tar, Alhaji Maina Tar, Alhaji Abubakar Akirga, Hajja Yagana Abubakar, Mustapha Tar, Hajja Fanta, Ya Fanta Mohd Tar, Momodu Mohd Tar, Jibrin Mohd Tar, Isa Mohd Tar, Architect Yusuf Abubakar, Prof Prince Sansui Ibrahim, Dr Halimatu Sadiya Ibrahim, Dr Aisha Kana, Navy-Lieutenant Faruk Ahmed, Barrister Hauwa Faruk Ahmed, and ASC Kabiru Yakubu.

Words cannot convey my gratitude to the folks at Routledge Publishers. I missed several deadlines but they encouraged us to keep going. In particular, Leanne Hinves, Routledge's Commissioning Editor, and Editorial Assistant Henry Strang were profoundly patient and understanding.

Finally, to those whose names are inadvertently omitted, my sincere apologies.

# About the Editor

**Usman A. Tar** (PhD) Professor of Political Science and Defence Studies and Distinguished Endowed Chair of Defence and Security Studies (26RC Endowment) at the Nigerian Defence Academy, and Director of the Academy's flagship Centre for Defence Studies and Documentation (CDSD). Prof Tar has held faculty positions in Africa, United Kingdom, and Republic of Iraq. He is a Member of the Board of Social Science Research Council's African Peacebuilding Network (SSRC/APN), New York, USA. He was formerly an Associate Research Fellow at John and Elnora Ferguson Centre for Africa Studies (JEFCAS) at the University of Bradford, UK. He was also an Assistant Professor at the Department of Politics and International Relations and Director of Postgraduate Studies at the University of Kurdistan-Hewler, Northern Iraq. Prof Tar is the author of *The Politics of Neoliberal Democracy in Africa* (London/New York: IB Tauris, 2009); *Globalization in Africa: Perspectives on Development, Security, and the Environment* (Lexington Books, Lanham MD, USA, 2016); *Defence Transformation and the Consolidation of Democracy in Nigeria* (Kaduna: Academy Publishers, 2018); and *New Architecture for Regional Security in Africa: Counter-Terrorism and Counter-Insurgency in the Lake Chad Basin* (Lexington Books, Lanham MD, USA, 2020). Prof Tar has consulted, or consults, for the *Westminster Foundation for Democracy* (WFD, Nigeria), *United Nations Development Programme* (UNDP, Nigeria), *United States Institute for Peace* (Nigeria Office) and *Konrad Adaneur Stiftung* (German Development Fund, Nigeria). He also serves as visiting professor and external examiner to several institutions of higher learning in Nigeria and overseas. Prof Tar was a member of the Nigeria's Presidential Committee to review the country's defence policy (2014-2015), and currently serves as a member the high-powered Ministerial Think Tank to monitor threats to Nigeria's national defence and security. Address: Centre for Defence Studies and Documentation, Nigerian Defence Academy, Kaduna. email: uatar@nda.edu.ng.

# Contributors

**Dauda Abubakar** is a Professor at the Department of African Studies and Political Science, University of Michigan-Flint, USA. Prof Abubakar has extensive teaching and research experience in Africa. His expertise cuts across international politics, comparative politics, federalism, civil society, democratisation, agrarian question, and development studies with a particular focus on Africa. Email: dauda@umflint.edu.

**Sulaiman Saidu Abubakar** is a Lecturer in the Department of Political Science and International Relations, Nigerian Defence Academy, Kaduna. He holds BSc Political Science from the University of Maiduguri, and MSc Political Science from Ahmadu Bello University, Zaria. His areas of academic interest include China in Africa, Terrorism and Counterterrorism, Peace and Conflict Studies, among others. Email: slyjad@gmail.com.

**Oludare Felix Ajiola** is a Lecturer in the Department of History and Strategic Studies, University of Lagos, Nigeria. He is a Doctoral candidate preparing for the viva in the Department of History, at the University of Ibadan, Ibadan, Nigeria. His fields of interest are African Development Studies, and Social and Economic History. Email: dare_felix@yahoo.com.

**Aniche Delight Aniche** is a Lecturer in the Department of Cyber Security, Nigerian Defence Academy, Kaduna. He has a Masters degree in Cyber Security *and had a number of organisational learning and practical roles in the corporate and social sectors in the field of ICT before joining academia in 2014. Delight Aniche is an ICT expert and academic* working at the intersection of technology, entrepreneurship, education, innovation and security. Delight is an astute innovator, social entrepreneur, academic, and a leader with lots of innovations and papers to his credit one of which (CrowdWatch) he presented at the 3rd International Open Data Conference in Ottawa Canada courtesy of the IDRC and the World Bank. His research interests span the field of cybersecurity, network security, privacy, digital skill transfer, and startup entrepreneurship.

**Abdulmalik Auwal** is Associate Professor in the Department of Political Science, Bayero University, Kano. He served in the capacity of Sub Dean and Deputy Dean in the Faculty of Social and Management Sciences and later on Faculty of Social Sciences at the same university. He was a Fulbright visiting scholar at the programme of African Studies, University of Massachusetts Boston, USA; a former state executive and member of Society for Peace Studies and Practice (SPSP) Nigeria; the National Treasurer of Fulbright Alumni Association of Nigeria (FAAN); the North-West Coordinator on National Task Force for the Eradication of Unclassified Films in Nigeria; a member of Social Science Council of

Nigeria (SSCN) and Centre for Research and Documentation, Kano; Director Education, Lameen Humanitarian Foundation, Kano. He has published widely on democracy, civil society, participative security, political parties, ethnoreligious conflict, interfaith dialogue, and conflict management. Email: amauwal1969@yahoo.com

**Samuel Baba Ayegba** (BSc, MSc) is a Lecturer in the Department of defence and security studies; and a research fellow at the Centre for Defence Studies and Documentation (CDSD), Nigerian Defence Academy, Kaduna. He is a candidate for PhD in defence and strategic studies at the Nigerian Defence Academy. He has published extensively on several peer review platforms. His area of specialisation includes Security and Strategic Studies, Environmental Politics, Peace and Conflict Studies. Email: samuel.ayegba@gmail.com.

**Bashir Bala** is a Captain in the Nigerian Army, and a candidate for PhD in Strategy and Security Studies at the University of Exeter, United Kingdom. He graduated from the Nigerian Defence Academy, commissioned at the Royal Military Academy Sandhurst, United Kingdom, and thereafter, attended Shijiazhuang Mechanized Infantry Academy for Basic and Advanced Special Operations Courses, China. He was formerly a tactical commander in several critical Counterinsurgency Operations in the Northeast Region of Nigeria. He is the author (with Prof Usman Tar) of the forthcoming volume *New Architecture for Regional Security in Africa: Counterterrorism and Counterinsurgency in the Lake Chad Basin* (Lexington Books, Lanham MD, USA). Email: basheerbala@gmail.com.

**Al-Hassan Conteh** is Ambassador of Liberia to Nigeria, Benin, Equatorial Guinea, and Liberia's Permanent Representative to the Economic Community of West African States (ECOWAS). He was the former President of the University of Liberia (2004–2008). He served as the Chair of the ECOWAS Permanent Representative Committee and the Mediation and Security Council of ECOWAS at the Ambassadorial level from 2017 to 2018. He is the current Dean of West African Ambassadors and Deputy Dean of African Ambassadors in the Federal Republic of Nigeria. His professional interests and specialisations are in demography, regional systems and policy analysis, strategies of international development, quantitative methods, development economics, economic-demographic interrelations, population geography, higher education management, conflict transformation, and development diplomacy. His research includes "Boundaries and Conflict in the Mano River Region of West Africa," (With (Prof Marilyn Silberfine of Temple University) published in Conflict Management and Peace Science, Vol. 23, No. 4, 343–361 (2006). Ambassador Conteh holds a PhD degree in Regional Science and Demography from the University of Pennsylvania, a Master of Arts degree in Demography from the University of Pennsylvania, a Master of Philosophy degree in Demography from the United Nations Cairo Demographic Center, and a Bachelor of Arts degree in Geography and Demography from the University of Liberia. Emails: alconteh@yahoo.com; alconteh2@gmail.com.

**Nachana'a Alahira David** is Associate Professor at the Department of Political Science and Defence Studies at the Nigerian Defence Academy, Kaduna. She obtained a PhD in Political Science from Ahmadu Bello University, Zaria (Nigeria) and has held a sabbatical position at the Adamawa State University, Mubi. David's research interest covers international organisation, security studies, gender, and rural livelihood. Email: nachanaa29@yahoo.co.uk.

**Marc-Antoine Pérouse de Montclos** is a Senior Researcher at the Institut de recherche pour le développement (IRD) and a Global Fellow at PRIO (Peace Research Institute, Oslo), Marc-Antoine Pérouse de Montclos is a Doctor in political science and taught as a Professor at the French Institute of Geopolitics in the University of Paris 8. A specialist on armed conflicts and humanitarian aid in Africa South of the Sahara, he graduated from the Institut d'études politiques in Paris (IEP), where he also taught and lived during several years in Nigeria, South Africa and Kenya. He published some 80 articles and books, including *Le Nigeria* (1994), *Violence et sécurité urbaines* (1997), *L'aide humanitaire, aide à la guerre ?* (2001), *Villes et violences en Afrique subsaharienne* (2002), *Diaspora et terrorisme* (2003), *Guerres d'aujourd'hui* (2007), *Etats faibles et sécurité privée en Afrique noire* (2008), *Les humanitaires dans la guerre* (2013), *La tragédie malienne* (2013), *Crises et migrations* (2014), *Boko Haram: Islamism, Politics, Security, and the State in Nigeria* (2015), *Violence, statistics, and the politics of accounting for the dead* (2016), *Violence in Nigeria: A qualitative and quantitative analysis* (2016), *Un développement humanitaire ? Les ONG à l'épreuve de la critique* (2016) and *L'Afrique, nouvelle frontière du djihad ?* (2018). Email: marc-antoine.perouse-de-montclos@ird.fr

**Eugene Eji**, DSS, PSC, FDC, MA, PhD, is a Brigadier General in the Nigerian Army. He holds a Master of Arts degree in Security and Intelligence Studies, and a Doctor of Philosophy in International Studies from the University of Buckingham, United Kingdom. Eugene has held strategic appointments such as Principal Staff Officer (Intelligence) at the Office of the National Security Adviser, Abuja, Nigeria. He was also a Deputy Defence Adviser at the Nigeria High Commission, London, where, in line with his job role, he liaised effectively with the British Metropolitan Police. He is a fellow of the Buckingham University Centre for Security and Intelligence Studies, United Kingdom and the National Defence College, Nigeria, among other affiliations. Email: eugeneeji@yahoo.co.uk

**Idamwenhor Napoleon Enayaba** is a development practitioner with experience in Security and Justice Reform; Prevention and Counter Violent Extremism (PCVE); community stability; conflict resolution and public safety and security. He equally has programme management experience, monitoring, evaluation, and learning including far-reaching technical experience in governance and public policy research, evaluation, analysis, and advisory. He is an astute promoter of community all-inclusivity led decision-making process through dialogue that promotes public ownership and legitimisation of policy and initiatives that directly impacts communities. Through inclusive dialogue, Napoleon fosters active communication between the military, other security institutions, and the Nigerian public. Napoleon currently coordinates a broad range of civil society organisations implementing a security and justice reform programme in Nigeria. He holds a masters degree in Conflict, Security and Development and a Bachelor of Arts degree in History. Email: idanapleon@yahoo.com

**Gerald E. Ezirim** is a sabbatical research fellow at the National Defence College, Abuja-Nigeria, and Senior Lecturer in the Department of Political Science, University of Nigeria, Nsukka, from where he received his MSc and PhD. A 2010 Research Fellow with Friedrich-Ebert-Stiftung West African Regional Office on *Oil and Gas Governance in the Gulf of Guinea*, he has written on voter apathy in Nigeria; terrorism and transnational organized crimes in West Africa; election security threats; Small Arms and Light Weapons; energy hegemony and maritime security in the Gulf of Guinea, and oil crimes, national security in Nigeria, in high impact journals and for various organisations. His areas of interest are international relations, security, conflict and peace, democratisation, oil politics, and African politics. He is a member of the Nigerian Political Science

Association (NPSA); Nigerian Institute of International Affairs (NIIA); and Society for Peace Studies and Practice (SPSP). He has been a member of the Editorial Board of many journals such as the *Journal of Liberal Studies, University of Nigeria Journal of Political Economy*, and the *Journal of International Relations and Diplomacy*. Having just ended his tenure as the Director of Research and Publications of the Nigerian Political Science Association, South East Zone, he was recently elected Secretary-General of the Nigerian Political Science Association. In terms of academic leadership, he has supervised more than 40 undergraduates and 25 MSc, and is presently supervising about nine Doctoral candidates. Email: gerald.ezirim@unn.edu.ng

**Audu Nanven Gambo** is a Professor of International Relations and Strategic Studies in the Department of Political Science, University of Jos, Nigeria. He holds a PhD degree in International Relations and Strategic Studies from the University of Jos. He was the Director of Centre for Conflict Management and Peace Studies, University of Jos between 2010 and 2015. He was a Fulbright Fellow for the Study of United States Foreign Policy at the University of South Carolina in 2006. He was also a Visiting Scholar at the University of Amsterdam, Netherlands, in 2011. His scholarship focuses on national defence, Conflict and peace studies, foreign policy, and security studies and he has published nationally and internationally in these areas. Among his recent publications is *Peace Architecture for Jos city, Nigeria* (2013), published by John Archers Publishers in Ibadan. Email: audugmb@gmail.com

**Mesfin Gebremichael** is an Assistant Professor at the Institute for Peace and Security Studies (IPSS), Addis Ababa University (AAU) teaching courses on identity, culture, and conflict as well as peace and security issues of the Horn of Africa to post-graduate students. He is a Director of the African Research Universities Alliance (ARUA) Center of Excellence (CoE) for post-conflict societies hosted by IPSS. He is also Editor-in-Chief of conflict analysis and insight reports published on the IPSS website. His research interest focuses on governance, peace, and development studies of the Horn of Africa. He has extensively engaged in researches related to the political practice and political economy of Ethiopia, public enterprises and development in Ethiopia, federalism and conflict management in Ethiopia, counterinsurgency and counter financing of terrorism in the Horn of Africa. Email: mesfin.g@ipss-addis.org.

**Mnyero Janja Ibn Sheikh Gunda** is a Lecturer at the University of Dodoma, Tanzania. He holds a PhD in Education from University Putra Malaysia. His research focuses on education and knowledge. Some of his publications are Gunda content knowledge among teacher educators in Tanzania (2013), Exploring the Islamic perspective of pedagogical content knowledge among teacher educators in Tanzania (2013) and conceptualising the term of Islamic in Islamic schools: the Tanzanian experience (2016).

**Gambo Maimuna Hammawa** is a Lecturer in Federal College of Education Yola, Adamawa State of Nigeria. She earned a PhD in Political Science from Universiti Putra Malaysia. She has 24 articles published in local and international journals, among which are Women's Rights Organisations (WROs) Effective Agents of Social Change? The Efforts of WROS in Overcoming Challenges in Legislative Advocacy of the Violence against Person Prohibition (VAPP) Act in Nigeria (2018). IOSR *Journal of Humanities and Social Science (IOSR-JHSS), 33 (7)56–61*; Issues and Challenges in Nigeria's democracy of the Fourth Republic: Any Role for Political Science education (2012). *BADALA Journal of Arts and Social Science, 8(6), 134–139*. Hammawa is a member of the Nigerian Political Science Association and her areas of interest are Civil Society Organisation, Peace Studies, and Legislative Politics. email: mg.hammawa@gmail.com

**Anne Uchenna Ibobo-Eze** holds an MSc in Peace and Security Studies from Ekiti State University, Nigeria, where she also obtained BA (Hons) History and International Studies. She is currently the Convener of an NGO, Enterprising Youths Empowerment Initiative (EYEI). She was a Research Fellow at the Centre for Strategic Research and Studies, National Defence College, Abuja (2012– 2018). She was also the Research Assistant to PLO and SA Protocol to the President and Commander in Chief of the Armed Forces of Nigeria (2013–2015). Ibobo-Eze's research interests span Defense and Security Studies, International Relations, Regional/National Security, and Development Studies. Her publications include: Professional Military Education and Defence Transformation: The Role of National Defence College in Nigeria; The Economic and Financial Crimes Commission, Crude Oil Theft and Nigeria's National Security; and Protracted Farmer-Herder Conflict in North Central Nigeria and the Role of Security Agencies: Issues, Effects and Strategies. Email: anne.diplomat@gmail.com.

**Lucky Osagie Imade** is an Associate Professor of International Relations, Director of Model UN Program at the American University of Nigeria, and was a US Fulbright Senior Scholar to Nigeria during the 1999/2000 academic year. Dr Imade has received several awards, grants, and fellowships to travel abroad, conduct research, attend conferences and workshops in an effort to internationalize the campus. He has led the award-winning AUN delegation to participate in both national and international Model UN conferences around the world since 2008. Dr Imade is the author of many scholarly publications and research reports. His research focus is on political transition and economic reform in Africa. Email: lucky.imade@aun.edu.ng

**Hussaini Jibrin** is a Senior Lecturer in the Department of History and War Studies, Nigerian Defence Academy (NDA) Kaduna, Nigeria. He obtained BA History from Bayero University Kano, MA Military History, NDA, Kaduna, and PhD Military History, Usmanu Danfodio University, Sokoto respectively. He has been teaching various courses and supervises research at both undergraduate and postgraduate levels. Dr Hussaini has attended and presented papers at many conferences within and outside Nigeria. These include: Regional Conference on *Peace Building and Reconstruction in the Chad Basin* organized by Centre for Peace and Security Studies, Modibbo Adama University of Technology, Yola in collaboration with the Nigerian Army (September 2016); Postgraduate Conference on *Changing Land Use, Resource Conflicts and Environmental Implications on African* organized by the Department of History, University of Dar es Salam, Tanzania in collaboration with the Department of History, University of Warwick, England *Landscapes* (August 2015); the 1st International Conference on *First World War and Africa 1914–2014*, organized by the Department of History, University of Cape Coast, Ghana (October 2005), among others. Similarly, he contributed a number of articles and chapters in peer-reviewed journals and book projects. With a career spanning over a decade, he has held different academic and administrative responsibilities in Nigerian Universities. He edited two books: *Readings on Peace Studies and Conflict Resolution,* (2016); and (with AM Ashafa) *The Nigeria Army in a Democracy Since 1999: A Professional Demonstration of Military Subordination to Civil Authority: Essays in Honor of Lieutenant General T.Y. Buratai* (2017). Email: babanabbas14@gmail.com.

**Muhammad Sanusi Lawal** is a Senior Lecturer in the Department of Political Science and Defence Studies (PSDS) Nigerian Defence Academy. He joined the services of the Academy in 1997 as a Graduate Assistant. He was Programme Director of the Academy's Masters in

Security Studies and Administration (MASSA) from 2013 to 2015, and Postgraduate Diploma in Public Administration (PGDPA) from 2015 to date. Dr Lawal attended the Ahmadu Bello University Zaria where he obtained his BSc in Political Science and Masters in Public Administration in 1994 and 2004 respectively. He then obtained his PhD in Defence and Strategic Studies from the Nigerian Defence Academy in 2018. Dr Lawal is the Editor (with Prof Usman A. Tar and Dr Mohammed Tafida) of *Securing Nigeria's Democracy: Perspectives on Democratic Control of the Military in a Fragile Democracy* (NDA Press and Yusufu Bala Usman Institute, Zaria, forthcoming).His areas of research interests include Peace and Conflict Studies, Gender, Development and Security Studies. Email: sanusilawal1967@gmail.com

**Taofeeq Olawale Lawal** is a graduate of the University of Ilorin where he had a first degree in History and had his Masters degree in Diplomacy and Strategic Studies at the University of Lagos (UNILAG). He is a member of the Historical Society of Nigeria (HSN) and the Nigerian Institute of Management (NIM).

**Roy Love** is a former Senior Lecturer in Economics at the Universities of Addis Ababa, Botswana and Lesotho, and has had an interest in Ethiopian affairs since the 1970s. His doctorate was on the Ethiopian coffee economy, and he has published in the Review of African Political Economy, African Affairs, Afriche e Orienti, Northeast African Studies, Journal of Southern African Studies, and in Papers and Proceedings of the triennial International Conferences of Ethiopian Studies, the most recent of which was October 2018. He has contributed to the Horn of Africa Programme at Chatham House, London, and prepared expert reports on Ethiopia and Eritrea for UK asylum courts. He is currently an Associate Staff member attached to the Centre for Lifelong Learning at the University of York, UK. Email: roylove439@btinternet.com

**Pamela Machakanja** is an Associate Professor of Peace and Conflict Studies and dean of the College of Business, Peace, Leadership, and Governance at Africa University, Mutare, Zimbabwe. She holds a PhD in Peace and Conflict Studies and MA in Peace and Conflict Resolution from the University of Bradford, United Kingdom; as well as a Masters degree in Educational Psychology and a Bachelor of Education from the University of Zimbabwe. Her research interests include Peace and Conflict Analysis; Peace and Security; Peacebuilding; Transitional Justice; Memory Work; Leadership Development and Gendered Development. She was a recipient and team member of the Social Science Research Council's African Peacebuilding Network's Collaborative Working Group (CWG) Research Grant in 2016–2018. Email: pamelamachakanja@gmailcom

**Jonathan Sule Maiangwa** is a Lecturer at the Department of Political Science, University of Maiduguri, Borno State, Nigeria. He is the author of a book titled, "The Concept of Terrorism in Africa" widely in circulation. He holds a PhD in Political Science from Benue State University, MSc in International Relations, PGDE (Education Psychology) Abuja, and BSc Political Science from the University of Maiduguri. His research interests are in terrorism, counterterrorism/counterinsurgency, local security institutions, defence contractors, governance, and development studies. Email: maiangwajs@gmail.com

**Yusuf Abdullahi Manu** is a Lecturer at Federal University Dutse. He completed his PhD in Defence and Strategic Studies at the Nigerian Defence Academy Kaduna. His area of interest is in peace and security studies. He has published widely in both local and international journals and has contributed chapters in many edited books. Email: ymanugella@gmail.com

**Chpicai Shollah Manuel,** PhD Candidate (DSoc Sci International Migration, Human Security and Border Studies), Master in Peace and Governance, Master in Intellectual Property Law, Bachelor of Social Sciences in Sociology and Economics. Currently affiliated with Africa University as a Lecturer in the area of Peace and Security, Governance, and International Relations. Email: mshollah@gmail.com

**Kyari Mohammed** is a Distinguished Professor of History, and Vice Chancellor of the Nigerian Army University, Biu (NAUB). He was former Vice-Chancellor of Moddibo Adama University of Technology (MAUTECH), Yola, Adamawa State, and served as Chair for Peace and Security Studies at the same institution. Prof Mohammed is one of Nigeria's leading scholars on the ongoing Boko Haram insurgency and counterinsurgency. Mohammed earned his PhD in 1995 at the University of Ibadan (UI), Nigeria, and became a professor in 2007. He then served as Professor of History at Gombe State University between October 2008 and September 2012, and has served in many other offices as well as having authored over 70 publications. Email: kyarix2@gmail.com

**Mala Mustapha** is a Reader and Chair at the Department of Political Science University of Maiduguri, Nigeria. He obtained his MA in International Politics and Security Studies at Bradford Universitym UK in 2003, and was awarded a PhD in Conflict Resolution and Peace Studies by the University of Central Lancashire, UK in 2013. His research interests are the security in the Lake Chad region, the Horn of Africa, and regional security in Africa focusing on themes of resource conflicts, political economy, globalisation and human security, democracy and democratisation in Africa, and terrorism studies. Recently his research focuses on internal displacements (refugee/IDP), humanitarian crisis, and counterterrorism and counterinsurgency studies in the Northeast part of Nigeria and Somalia. He has published widely in peer-reviewed journals and books including the *Review of African Political Economy* and *CODESRIA*. Email: mmustapha@gmail.com

**Chikodiri Nwangwu** is a Lecturer in the Department of Political Science, University of Nigeria, Nsukka (UNN). His research interests include political economy, governance, security studies, and electoral studies. He is a member of Nigerian Political Science Association, Institute for Innovations in Development (IID), Association for Research on Civil Society in Africa (AROCSA), and Association for Research on Nonprofit Organisations and Voluntary Action (ARNOVA). Currently, he is a doctoral student in UNN where he teaches political science in the Department of Political Science. He has published well-researched articles in reputable journals, including the *Japanese Journal of Political Science* and *Journal of Language and Politics*. He has also participated in several national and international conferences.

**Ben U. Nwosu** is currently a senior research fellow at the Institute for Development Studies, University of Nigeria, Enugu Campus, and a Sabbatical Research Fellow at the Centre for Strategic Research and Studies, National Defence College, Abuja, Nigeria. He obtained BSc (Hons) in Political Science and an MSc in the same discipline with a specialisation in International Relations, from the University of Nigeria, Nsukka. He trained for his doctorate in the area of Political theory at the University of Waikato in New Zealand. Ben has a teaching experience of about 15 years comprising two Nigerian Universities and his alma mater in New Zealand. After serving for about 11 years at the Department of Political Science, of the University of Nigeria, he obtained a joint parallel appointment to be a research fellow at the Institute for Development Studies in Enugu Campus. Presently he teaches courses that relate with Development and Policy Practice, Sociology of Development, Civil Society, and Development Processes. He has written several book chapters in works that have appeared in international publishing houses, local and international peer-reviewed journals. His 2012 paper, Tracks of the third wave, published in the Review of African Political Economy was rated by Taylor and Francis as one of the leading works in African studies. His research track includes democratic theory and democratisation, conflict, civil society, governance and public policy. His on-going research is centred on building democracy through participation especially the role of participatory budgeting in actuating citizens interest in governance issues. Email: ben.nwosu@unn.edu.ng

**Francisca Nonyelum Ogwueleka** is a Professor of Computer Science and Cyber Security at the Nigerian Defence Academy, Kaduna. She is currently the Dean of the Faculty of Military Science and Interdisciplinary Studies. Her research focuses on big data, artificial intelligence, cloud security, data mining techniques, steganography, penetration testing solutions, and information security. She has nine published books, two book chapters, and 92 original articles in international and national journals. She is a member of numerous professional bodies, an editorial board, and conference technical program committee. She has been a keynote speaker and conference session chair in several international and national conferences. She has received many academic and professional awards. Professor Ogwueleka is an external examiner for PhD dissertation and MSc thesis evaluation for national and international universities. She was a resource person for the development of Nigeria Undergraduate Curriculum in Cyber Security and Information Technology programmes for National Universities Commission. She has held different academic and administrative positions in the university. She is happily married with children. Email: ogwuelekafn@gmail.com

**C. Nna-Emeka Okereke** is with the Centre for Strategic Research and Studies, National Defence College, Nigeria. He obtained his BSc, MSc, and PhD in Political Science with specialisation in International Relations from the Abia State University (1993), University of Lagos (1999), and the University of Nigeria Nsukka (2007) respectively. In August 2013, Dr Emeka Okereke completed a Fellowship in Higher Defence and Strategic Studies at the National Defence College. Between June 2014 and May 2015, he was a Senior Lecturer in the Department of Political Science/Deputy Dean, College of Social and Management Sciences at the Caleb University Lagos. Presently, he is the Head, Department of Area and Regional Studies at the National Defence College. Dr Emeka Okereke also conducts consultancy researches on Terrorism and Transnational Organised Crimes in Africa for the Intergovernmental Agency against Money Laundering (GIABA), Dakar and the African Centre for the Study and Research on Terrorism, Algiers. Email: emekaokereke@gmail.com

**Rasheed O. Olaniyi** is a Reader/Associate Professor in the Department of History and former Sub-Dean (Postgraduate) Faculty of Arts, University of Ibadan, Nigeria. He earned his PhD from Bayero University, Kano, Nigeria in 2004. He is the author of *Diaspora Is Not Like Home: A Social and Economic History of Yoruba in Kano, 1912–1999* (Muenchen, Germany: Lincom Europa, 2008) and *Community Vigilantes in Metropolitan Kano, 1985–2005* (IFRA Ibadan, 2005) and *History for Senior Secondary Schools* (Ibadan: Bounty Press, 2017). In the summer of 2008, he was a Visiting Scholar of African History at the Kennesaw State University, Georgia, USA. He was Visiting Scholar of African History, Pan African University (PAUWES), Tlemcen, Algeria. Olaniyi has contributed chapters in books and articles in journals on urbanisation, migration, diaspora, forced labour, human trafficking, and civil society movement. Olaniyi is a Fellow of the American Council of Learned Societies (ACLS); Member, CODESRIA, Dakar Senegal; Senior Fellow, French Institute for Research in Africa (IFRA), University of Ibadan and Fellow, Jawaharlal Nehru Institute of Advanced Study, Jawaharlal Nehru University, New Delhi, India. He served as the Acting Dean of Faculty of Arts, Management and Social Sciences while Sabbatical at Kola Daisi University, Ibadan, Nigeria. Email: rasolaniyi@gmail.com; rasolaniyi@yahoo.com.

**Kenneth Omeje** is the Director, Manifold Crown Consulting Services in Bradford, UK; Visiting Professor, Institute for Peace and Security Studies (IPSS) in Addis Ababa University, Ethiopia and University for PEACE (UPEACE) Africa Programme, Addis Ababa; Research Fellow, Centre for African and Gender Studies, University of the Free State, Bloemfontein, South Africa; and Visiting Professorial Fellow, Department of Political Science and Defence Studies, Nigerian Defence Academy, Kaduna, Nigeria. With over 25 years of professional academic experience, Kenneth holds a PhD degree in Peace Studies from the University of Bradford and MA degree in Peace and Conflict Studies from the European University Centre for Peace Studies in Stadtschlaining, Austria. He has previously held the positions of Senior Research Fellow at the John and Elnora Ferguson Centre for African Studies, University of Bradford, UK (2014–2017); Senior Research Associate, Faculty of Humanities, University of Johannesburg, South Africa (2015–2018); and Professor of International Relations at the United States International University in Nairobi, Kenya (2009– 2018). Kenneth is the author of *High Stakes and Stakeholders: Oil Conflict & Security in Nigeria* (Aldershot: Ashgate, 2006); *Extractive Economies and Conflicts in the Global South: Multi-regional Perspective on Rentier Politics* (ed. Ashgate, 2008); *State–Society Relations in Nigeria: Democratic Consolidation, Conflicts and Reforms* (ed. London: Adonis & Abbey, 2007); *War to Peace Transition: Conflict Intervention and Peacebuilding in Liberia* (ed. Lanham-Maryland: University Press of America, 2009); *Conflict of Securities: State and Human Security in Africa* (co. ed. London: Adonis & Abbey, 2010); *Conflict and Peacebuilding in the African Great Lakes Region* (co. ed. Indiana: Indiana University Press, 2013), *The Crises of Postcoloniality in Africa* (edited, Dakar: CODESRIA, 2015), *Peacebuilding in Contemporary Africa: In Search of Alternative Strategies* (edited, London: Routledge, 2019), etc. He has more than 90 publications, including books, book chapters, contributions to international encyclopaedias and articles in well-regarded journals. Kenneth has previously held visiting research fellowship positions at the Centre for African Studies, University of Florida, Gainesville, USA (Spring, 1992); Law Department, Keele University, UK (Spring, 2000); Institute of Higher Education, Comprehensive University of Kassel, Germany (Summer, 2000); Department of International Politics, University of Wales, Aberystwyth (Spring, 2001); and Georg Eckert Institute (GEI) in Braunschweig, Germany (Autumn 2014). He is a Fellow of the West Africa Institute (WAI) in Praia, Cape Verde and a member of the Advisory Board of the African Peacebuilding Network (APN) of the Social Science Research Council (SSRC) of New York. Email: komeje@manifoldcrown.org

**Omona Andrew David** is a Senior Lecturer and Head of Department at Uganda Christian University, a National Coordinator for Religious Leaders' Justice and Peace Network, a Researcher, Transitional Justice Fellow, and a Trainer of Trainers in Peace-building and Conflict Resolution in the East and Greater Horn of Africa. He holds a PhD in Political

Studies/International Relations and Diplomacy, MA International Relations and Diplomacy, MA Theology, BA with Education, and several specialised Diplomas and Certificates. He has done extensive research on conflicts in Africa, the Great Lakes Region and Uganda in particular. His current research interest is in Transitional Justice, Peacebuilding and conflict resolution, and Ethics. He has done collaborative research with people from across the world and still looks forward to getting researchers to collaborate with in his areas of expertise. Email: adomona3@gmail.com

**Freedom C. Onuoha** is a Senior Lecturer in the Department of Political Science, University of Nigeria, Nsukka. He is also the Coordinator of the Security, Violence and Conflict (SVC) Research Group at the University. He received his BSc (Political Science) in 2000; MSc (Political Economy) in 2007; and PhD (Political Economy) 2013, all from the University of Nigeria, Nsukka. Dr Onuoha has also taken courses in higher management of defence, peace support operations, disaster management, and protection of civilians. Prior to joining the University, he spent over a decade as a Research Fellow at the Centre for Strategic Research and Studies (CSRS), National Defence College, Abuja. He was appointed the Head of Department, Conflict, Peacekeeping, and Humanitarian Studies, at the CSRS in January 2014; a position he held until he joined the University. His research and teaching interests focus on diverse aspects of defence and security studies, with emphasis on violent extremism, terrorism, organized crime, state fragility, critical infrastructure protection, and energy security. Dr Onuoha has contributed several dozen articles and essays in both reputable local and international journals and books. He was listed among the top 100 Global Thinkers of 2014 by the *Lo Spazio della Politica* for his ground-breaking studies on the Boko Haram; such as *Why do Youth Join Boko Haram* (Washington DC: USIP, 2014) and *A Danger not to Nigeria alone: Boko Haram's Transnational Reach and Regional Responses* (Abuja: Friedrich Ebert Stiftung Regional Office, 2014). Dr Onuoha has equally participated in several local and international conferences, seminars and workshops, as a guest speaker, panellist and facilitator. He regularly features as a guest analyst on several local and international broadcast and television outlets including, among others, African Independent Television, National Television Authority, Channels Television, Radio Nigeria, Al Jazeera Network, and *Radio France Internationale*. Dr Onuoha consults for several local and international organisations. He is a member of professional bodies such as the Nigerian Political Science Association (NPSA), Society for International Relations Awareness (SIRA), and Alumni Association of National Defence College (AANDEC). Dr Onuoha holds a fellow of defence college (FDC), from National Defence College, Nigeria. Email: chufreedom@gmail.com, chufreedom@yahoo.com.

**Chukwuma CC Osakwe** is a Military Historian plying his craft in the Nigerian Defence Academy and providing professional consultancy services to various military institutions across Nigeria. He earned a PhD in Military History from the City University of New York. He serves as Head, Department of History and War Studies, Nigerian Defence Academy and Director, Centre for the Study of Leadership and Complex Military Operations, Nigerian Defence Academy. Professor Osakwe has amassed extensive research portfolios and writings in military history, war studies, military leadership, security studies, intelligence, and strategy. He is the author of *Leadership and Complex Military Operations* (Academy Press Kaduna, 2016), Studies in Disarmament, Demobilization and Reintegration (Academy Press, Kaduna), *Nigerian Defence and Security* (Academy Press, Kaduna, 2014), and *Perspectives in*

*African Historical Studies: Essays in Honour of Professor CN Ubah* (Academy Press, Kaduna, 2014). Email: lecturec@yahoo.com.

**Merry Omon Osiki** lectures at the Department of History and Strategic Studies, University of Lagos, Nigeria. Dr Osiki obtained two PhDs in Specialised History, and History and Strategic Studies at Nanjing Normal University, Nanjing, China, and the University of Lagos, Lagos State, Nigeria, respectively. His research interests cover international relations, conflict resolution, China-Africa studies, and international migration and human trafficking. Email: oosiki@unilag.edu.ng, omonosiki@gmail.com.

**Abba Gana Shettima** is Professor of Rural Sociology at the University of Maiduguri, Nigeria. He holds a PhD in Sociology with a specialisation in Rural Sociology. He has over 30 years of teaching and research experience at the university level; and has researched into rural resources, livelihoods, and conflict. His current area of research interest is the *Boko Haram* insurgency in North-Eastern Nigeria, as well as understanding the confluence of conflicts in Northern Nigeria: the *Boko Haram* insurgency, farmer-pastoralist conflict and rural banditry. He has widely published in national and international journals. He was a Fulbright Graduate Visiting Researcher, NC State University, USA (2000–2001), a fellow of the Leadership for Environment and Development (LEAD-International), Laureate of the Gender Institute, Council for the Development of Social Science Research in Africa(CODESRIA), and the United Nations University International Leadership Academy(UNU/ILA). He is a member of the International Sociological Association (ISA). He is presently a Professor of Rural Sociology at the University of Maiduguri, Nigeria. Email: agshettima@gmail.com

**Usman A. Tar** is endowed Professor of Defence and Security studies, and Director, Centre for Defence Studies and Documentation at the Nigerian Defence Academy (NDA). Board Member, Social Science Research Council of the Africa Peacebuilding Network (SSRC/APN), New York, USA. Formerly, Associate Research Fellow at John and Elnora Ferguson Centre for Africa Studies, University of Bradford, UK. He is Author of *The Politics of Neoliberal Democracy in Africa* (London/New York: IB Tauris/Bloomsbury, 2009); Editor of *Globalization in Africa: Perspectives on Development, Security, athe nd the Environment* (Lanham, MD, Lexington Books, 2016); *The Palgrave Handbook of Small Arms and Conflict* (Palgrave Macmillan, Forthcoming) and *Defence Transformation and the Consolidation of Democracy in Nigeria* (Kaduna: Academy Publishers, 2017). Prof Tar is Consultant to United Nations Development Programme (UNDP), Westminster Foundation for Democracy (WFD) and Konrad Adaneur Stiftung (the German Development Fund). He is also External Examiner or Resource Person to several higher education and research institutions in Nigeria and overseas. Email: uatar@nda.edu.ng, usmanatar@gmail.com

**Celestine Uchechukwu Udeogu** is a Lecturer and Doctoral candidate in the Department of Political Science, University of Nigeria, Nsukka. His thesis is on *Global Oil Production and the Nigerian Economy*. He majors in International Political Economy with research interests verging on State and Economy, Peace and Conflict Studies, Terrorism and Strategic Studies, Global Governance and Politics, Informal Sector, among others. Udeogu has attended many conferences, in addition to having published many Journal Articles in highly rated journals, including Thomson Reuters indexed journals with high impacts and some Book Chapters in popular books of reading. As a University Lecturer, Udeogu has taught a number of courses of interest, including International Organisations and Institutions within which this current chapter squarely falls. Although a Political Scientist with urbane bias in International Political Economy, Udeogu has been invited as a resource person to a number of workshops, including the just concluded Rivers State Government's workshop on *Governance and Primary Healthcare System*. Udeogu's academic versatility is further manifested in his foray into literary writing, having recently published the fast-selling *Legends of the Great Legacy* (novel) in August 2017. Email: celestine.udeogu@unn.edu.ng

**Emmanuel Idemor Ukhami** is a docotoral candidate in Defence and Strategic Studies at the Nigerian Defence Academy, Kaduna. He is a writer and has authored books, written several articles in journals and newspapers, and contributed in book chapters. Some of his publications include: *Issues in International Relations*; and (with Prof Usman A. Tar) *Nigeria's Foreign Policy in the Fourth Republic: Perspectives on Obasanjo and Yar'Adua Administrations* (Kaduna, PylaMak, 2019). His area of interest is on international relations and security. Email: emmysunny@yahoo.com

**Ubong Essien Umoh** is a Nigerian Defence Academy trained Military Historian plying his craft in various military institutions. He is Associate Professor in the Department of History, University of Uyo, Nigeria. Professor Umoh is associated with The Centre for the Study of Leadership and Complex Military Operations, Nigerian Defence Academy, Kaduna; The Centre for Defence Studies and Documentation, Nigerian Defence Academy, Kaduna; The Air Force War College, Abuja; The National Institute of Policy and Strategic Studies, Jos, among others. Email: ubongumoh@uniuyo.edu.ng

**Caroline Varin** is a Senior Lecturer in International Relations at Regent's University London and Associate Fellow of the Global South Unit at the London School of Economics. She has published four books on violent non-state actors and African security: 'Violent Non-State Actors in Africa (Palgrave 2017); Boko Haram and the War on Terror' (Praeger 2016) and 'Mercenaries, Hybrid Armies and National Security: Private Soldiers and the State in the 21st Century' (Routledge 2014), and Security in Nigeria (pending). Dr Varin is also Director of Professors Without Borders. Email: varinc@regents.ac.uk, cvarin19@gmail.com

**Sharkdam Wapmuk** is Associate Professor at the Dept of Defence and Security Studies, Nigerian Defence Academy. He was a Senior Research Fellow and Head, Division of African Politics and Integration, Nigerian Institute of International Affairs (NIIA). He obtained his PhD in International Relations and Strategic Studies from the University of Jos. He is also a graduate of Universities of Maiduguri and Jos, where he earned his B.Sc Degree Political Science (Second Class Upper Division) and M.Sc in Political Economy and Development Studies. He has over ten years of Academic research experience. He is currently the editor of the *Nigerian Forum: A Journal of Opinion on World Affairs*, published by the NIIA. While his geographic areas of interest include Africa and Asia, his research interests are in the thematic fields of Africa-India relations, cooperation and integration in Africa, African development initiatives, security and development, democratisation, diaspora and development, and roles of think-tanks in national development. He has published a number of journal articles, book chapters and monographs in these areas. He is a member of scholarly bodies, including the Nigerian Political Science Association (NPSA) and Nigerian Society of International Affairs (NSIA). Email: swapmuk@nda.edu.ng, sharksnaw@gmail.com

**Gani Joses Yoroms** is the immediate past Acting Provost of the Centre for Strategic Research and Studies (CSRS) at the National Defence College Nigeria (between October 2016–

August 2017), and a Professor of Political Science at Bingham University Nigeria with research interests in Politics, Defence and Foreign Policy Studies, Geopolitics, Political Economy, Conflict and Security Governance; and Rule of Law. He acquired his PhD at the Ahmadu Bello University in Nigeria (2002). Earlier on he has been an SSRC-MacArthur Fellow at Watson Institute Brown University, USA 1994. Professor Yoroms was a member of GIZ-ECOWAS Centre of Excellence Assessment Team that visited the UN Mission Field in Cote d'Ivoire, 2012 to verify the DDR Programmes in Peacekeeping Mission. Significantly also, he served as a member of ECOWAS Initial High-Level Planning Team for the deployment of troops to ECOWAS, meeting in Abidjan in 2012; and later became a Resource Person for the development of Concept of Operation (CONOPS) for the African-Led International Mission in Mali (AFISMA) in 2013. He has also been a consultant for the National Universities Commission (Nigeria), BOOZ Allen Hamilton/ USAFRICOM, USA, Stuttgart, Germany August 2009 working on Nigerian Military Project. Similarly, he was a consultant with CRISE, Oxford University, UK on 'Inequality, Cultural Identities and Militancy in Nigeria' (January 2007). Also being one of the Consultants of the Programme on Federal Studies (PEFs), the University of Ibadan where he worked on Conflicts in Taraba State, Nigeria. In addition, he was a member of a team of expert in Electoral Security that developed and produced the manual on Electoral Violence Mitigation(EVM) in Nigeria for the Impendent National Electoral Commission(INEC) Electoral Institute(TEI), Abuja, from 2015–2016. He was also a member of Nigeria Vision 2020. Email: yoromsgani@yahoo.com

# Abbreviations

| | |
|---|---|
| AAMA | Association of African Maritime Administration |
| ACBS | African Coastal and Border Security |
| ACCORD | African Centre for the Constructive Resolution of Disputes |
| ACEI | Association for Islamic Education and Culture |
| ACIC | Islamic Cultural Association of Cameroon |
| ACIRC | African Capacity for Immediate Response to Crises |
| ACOTA | African Contingency Operations Training Assistance |
| ACPC | Association of Caribbean and Pacific Countries |
| ACRI | African Crisis Response Initiative |
| ACSR | African Centre for the Study and Research on Terrorism |
| ACSRT | African Centre for the Study and Research on Terrorism |
| ACTED | Agency for Technical Cooperation and Development |
| ADF | Allied Democratic Forces |
| ADIE | State Information Technology Agency |
| AEC | African Economic Communities |
| AFISMA | African-Led International Force in Mali |
| AFRC | Armed Forces Revolutionary Council |
| AFRICOM | Africa Command Trans-Sahara Counterterrorism Partnership |
| AFRIPOL | African Mechanism for Police Cooperation |
| AIAI | Al-Ittihad al-Islamic |
| AIDS | Acquired Immune Deficiency Syndrome |
| AKP | Justice and Development Party (Turkey) |
| ALQIM | Al-Qa'ida in the Lands of the Islamic Maghreb |
| AMIS | African Union Mission in Sudan |
| AMISOM | African Union Mission to Somalia |
| AML | Anti-Money Laundering |
| AML/CFT | Anti Money Laundering/Counter Financing of Terrorism |
| AMLEP | African Maritime Law Enforcement Partnership |
| AMOCI | Association of Orthodox Muslims of Côte d'Ivoire |
| AMSCI | Association of Sunni Muslims of Côte d'Ivoire |
| AMUPI | Malian Association for the Unity and Progress of Islam |
| ANC | African National Congress (South Africa) |
| APC | Action Congress Party |
| API | Adamawa Peace Initiative |
| APSA | African Peace and Security Architecture |
| AQ Core | Al-Qaeda Core |

| | |
|---|---|
| AQIAP | Al-Qaeda in the Arabian Peninsula |
| AQIM | Al-Qaida in the Maghreb |
| AQIMA | Al-Qaeda in the Islamic Maghreb |
| ARLPI | Acholi Religious Leaders Peace Initiative |
| ASF | African Standby Force |
| ATA | Anti-Terrorism Assistance |
| ATMs | Automatic Teller Machines |
| ATPU | Anti-Terrorism Police Unit |
| AU | African Union |
| AU | African Unity |
| AUIMS | African Union's Integrated Maritime Strategy |
| BAKWATA | National Muslim Council of Tanzania |
| BAT | Antiterrorism Brigade |
| BATUK | British Army Training Unit Kenya |
| BH | Boko-Haram |
| BHT | Boko Haram Terrorists |
| BINUCA | United Nations Peace building Office in Central Africa |
| BMATT | British Military Advisory and Training Team |
| BOYES | Borno Youth Empowerment Service |
| BPST | British Peace Support Team |
| CAB | Central African Brothers |
| CAERT | Center for Studies and Research on Terrorism |
| CAR | Central African Republic |
| CBRN | Chemical, Biological, Radiological and Nuclear (proliferations) |
| CCAIM | Committee for the Coordination of Islamic Associations in Mali |
| CDA | Communication Decency Act |
| CDC | Community Development Council |
| CEMZ | Combined Exclusive Maritime Zone |
| CERT | Computer Emergency Response Team |
| CEWARN | Conflict Early Warning and Response Mechanism |
| CEWARU | Conflict Early Warning and Response Unit |
| CEWS | Continental Early Warning System |
| CFIN | Cyber Forensic Institute of Nigeria |
| CFSP | Common Foreign and Security Policy |
| CFT | *Counter-Terrorist* Financing |
| CGPSC | Contact Group on Piracy off the Coast of Somalia |
| CIA | Central Intelligence Agency |
| CIMIC | Civil-Military Co-operation |
| CIRT | Computer Incidence Response Team |
| CISSA | Conference of Committee for Intelligence and Security Services for Africa |
| CJTF | Civilian Joint Task Force |
| CJTF-HOA | Combined Joint Task Force–Horn of Africa |
| CMR | Civil-Military Relations |
| CMRRD | Commission for the Management of Strategic Mineral Resources, National Reconstruction and Development |
| CNMC | Cameroon-Nigeria Mixed Commission |
| COESPU | Center of Excellence for Stability Police Unit |

| | |
|---|---|
| COGWO | Coalition for Grassroots Women Organizations |
| COIN | Counter Insurgency |
| COIN-T | Counter-insurgency Theory |
| CONOP | Concept of Operations |
| COSPNU | Civil Society Organization for Peace in Northern Uganda |
| CPB | Coastal Patrol Boats |
| CR | Country Reports |
| CRESMAC | Regional Centre for Maritime Security in Central Africa |
| CRESMAO | Regional Coordination Centre for Maritime Security in West Africa |
| CSAI | Supreme Council of Islamic Affairs (Chad) |
| CSO | Civil Society Organization |
| CSOs | Civil Society Organizations |
| CT | Counter Terrorism |
| CTC | Counter-Terrorism Committee |
| CT-COIN | Counter Terrorism and Counter Insurgency |
| CTED | Counter-Terrorism Committee Executive Directorate |
| CTF | Counter Terrorism Finance |
| CTITF | Counter-Terrorism Implementation Task Force |
| CTS | Critical Terrorism Studies |
| CVE | Countering Violent Extremism |
| DCAF | Geneva Centre for the Democratic Control of Armed Forces |
| DCU | Microsoft's Digital Crime Unit |
| DDoS | Distributed Denial of Service (attack) |
| DDRR | Demobilization, Disarmament, Reintegration and Rehabilitation |
| DFID | Department for International Development |
| DGSE | Chadian Secret Service |
| DIA | Defence Intelligence Agencies |
| DOD | Department of Defence |
| DOS | Department of State |
| DRC | Danish Refugee Council |
| DRC | Democratic Republic of Congo |
| DSC | A presence in the Kenyan Defence and Staff College |
| DSS | Department of State Security |
| EAC | East African Community |
| EACTI | East African Counterterrorism Initiative |
| EAMWS | East African Muslims Welfare Society |
| EAPC | Euro-Atlantic Partnership Council |
| ECCAS | Economic Community of Central African States |
| ECOMOG | ECOWAS Monitoring Group |
| ECOWAS | Economic Community of West African States |
| EEA | European External Action |
| EEZ | Exclusive Economic Zone |
| EFCC | Economic and Financial Crime Commission |
| EFFORT | Endowment Fund for the Rehabilitation of Tigre |
| EFP | Ethiopian Federal Police |
| EIASC | Ethiopian Islamic Affairs Supreme Council |
| EIJ | Egyptian Islamic Jihad |
| EIMS | ECOWAS Integrated Maritime Strategy |

| | |
|---|---|
| EIPC | Enhanced International Peacekeeping Capabilities program |
| ELF | Eritrean Liberation Front |
| ENDF | Ethiopian National Defence Force |
| EO | Executive Outcomes |
| EPLF | Eritrean People's Liberation Front |
| EPRDF | Ethiopian People's Revolutionary Democratic Front |
| EPRS | European Parliamentary Research Service |
| ESAAMLG | Eastern and Southern Africa Anti-Money Laundering Group |
| ESDI | European Security and Defence Identity |
| ESDL | Ethiopian Somali Democratic League |
| ETFC | Ethiopian Task Force for Counterterrorism |
| EU | European Union |
| EUCOM | European Command |
| EUROROFORCA | European Force in Central Africa |
| EUTAM | European Training Mission |
| FATF | Financial Action Task Force |
| FBI | Federal Bureau of Investigation |
| FCO | Foreign and Commonwealth Office |
| FDI | Foreign Direct Investments |
| FEDEMU | Federal Democratic Movement |
| FIU | Financial Intelligence Unit |
| FLEC | Front for the Liberation of Enclave of Cabinda |
| FMF | Foreign Military Financing |
| FMS | Foreign Military Sales |
| FOBA | Force Obote Back Again |
| FOCAC | Forum on China-Africa Cooperation |
| FSRBs | Financial Action Task Force Regional Bodies |
| GA | General Assembly |
| GABAC | Group d'Action Countre La Afrique Countrale |
| GCC | Gulf Cooperation Council |
| GCCS | Global Center on Cooperative Security |
| GCI | Global Cybersecurity Index |
| GCOIN | Global Counterinsurgency |
| GCTF | Global Counterterrorism Forum |
| GDP | Gross Domestic Product |
| GGC | Gulf of Guinea Commission |
| GHP | Gulu Hope for Peace |
| GIA | Armed Islamic Group |
| GIABA | Intergovernmental Action Group against Money Laundering and Terrorist Financing |
| GNA | Government of National Unity |
| GOG | Gulf of Guinea |
| GPE | Global Partnership on Education |
| GPOI | Global Peace Operations Initiative |
| GSPC | Salafist Group for Preaching and Combat (Algeria) |
| GTI | Global Terrorism Index |
| GUSCO | Gulu Save the Children Organization |
| GWOT | Global War on Terror |

| | |
|---|---|
| HCIM | High Islamic Council of Mali |
| HIPPO | High Level Independent Panel on United Nations Peace Operations |
| HIV | Human Immune Virus |
| HOA | Horn of Africa |
| HRF | Human Rights Focus |
| HRM | Human Rights Monitoring |
| HRW | Human Rights Watch |
| HSM | Holy Spirit Movement |
| HUMINT | Human Intelligence |
| HURIPEC | Human Rights Peace Centre |
| IASC | International Agency Standing Committee |
| ICC | Inter-regional Coordination Centre |
| ICEPCVE | Centre of Excellence in Preventing and Countering Violent Extremism |
| ICG | International Crisis Group |
| ICI | Istanbul Cooperation Initiative |
| ICISS | International Commission on Intervention and State Sovereignty |
| ICJ | International Court of Justice |
| ICPAC | IGAD Climate Predication and Application Center |
| ICPAT | IGAD Capacity Building Program against Terrorism |
| ICPLD | IGAD Center for Pastoral Area and Livestock Development |
| ICRC | International Committee for the Red Cross |
| ICSOs | International Civil Society Organizations |
| ICSP | Instrument contributing to Stability and Peace |
| ICT | Information and Communication Technology |
| ICTs | Information and Communication Technologies |
| ICU | Islamic Courts Union |
| IDI | ICT Development Index |
| IDMC | Internal Displacement Monitoring Center |
| IDP | Internally Displaced Persons |
| IDPs | Internally Displaced Persons |
| IED | Improvised Explosive Device |
| IFS | Instrument for Stability |
| IGAD | Intergovernmental Authority on Development |
| IGADD | Intergovernmental Authority on Drought and Development |
| IMATC | International Mine Action Training Centre |
| IMB-PRC | International Maritime Bureau's Piracy Reporting Centre |
| IMET | International Military Education and Training Program |
| IMF | International Monetary Fund |
| IMO | International Maritime Organisation |
| INTERPOL | International Police |
| INXA | Iskuxirka Nabadaiyo Xuquuqal Adamiga |
| IOM | International Organization for Migration |
| IPOB | Independent People of Biafra |
| IS | Islamic States |
| ISDSC | Inter-state Defense and Security Committee |
| ISIL | Islamic State of Iraq and the Levant |
| ISIS | Islamic State in Iraq and Syria |
| ISMS | Integrated Strategy for Maritime Security |

| | |
|---|---|
| ISPDC | Inter-state Politics and Diplomacy Committee |
| ISSP | IGAD Security Sector Program |
| ISTAR | Intelligence, Surveillance, Target Acquisition and Reconnaissance |
| ISWAP | Islamic State's West Africa Province |
| ITU | International Telecommunication Union |
| IUU | Illegal, Unreported and Unregulated |
| JAES | Joint African -European Strategy |
| JEM | Justice and Equality Movement |
| JMTF | Joint Multinational Task Force |
| JTAB | Joint Terrorist Branch |
| JTF | Joint Task Force |
| JTF-HOA | Joint Task Force Horn of Africa |
| KDF | Kenya Defence Force |
| KICWA | Kitgum Concerned Women's Association |
| KKK | Ku Klux Klan |
| LAS | League of Arab States |
| LCB | Lake Chad Basin |
| LCBC | Lake Chad Basin Commission |
| LDC | Least Developed Countries |
| LEND | Liberation for the Emancipation of Niger Delta |
| LIGS | Liu Institute for Global Security |
| LIMC | Libyan Islamic Movement for Change |
| LNA | Libyan National Army |
| LP | Labour Party |
| LRA | Lord's Resistance Army |
| MACA | Military Aid to Civil Authority |
| MAD | Mutually Assured Destruction |
| MAD | Mutually Assured Destruction |
| MBD | Million barrels per day |
| MCO | Ministerial Committee Organisation |
| MDD | Movement in Defence of Democracy |
| MDF | Movement for the Democratic Force |
| MENA | Middle East and North Africa |
| MENAFA | Middle East North Africa Financial Action |
| MEND | Movement for the Emancipation of the Niger Delta |
| MIDSA | Migration Dialogue for Southern Africa |
| MINUSCA | United Nations Multidimensional Integrated Stabilization Mission in the Central African Republic |
| MISCA | International Support Mission to the Central African Republic |
| MK | Umkhonto we Sizwe |
| MLA | Mutual Legal Assistance |
| MNCs | Multinational Corporations |
| MNJTF | Multi-National Joint Task Force |
| MNLA | National Movement for the Liberation of Azawad |
| MOC | Maritime Operations Centres |
| MONUSCO | United Nations Organization Stabilization Mission in the Democratic Republic of the Congo |

| | |
|---|---|
| MONUSCO | United Nations Organization Stabilization Mission in the Democratic Republic of the Congo |
| MOOTW | Military Operations Other Than War |
| MOU | Memorandum of Understanding |
| MOWCA | Maritime Organisation for West and Central Africa |
| MPLT | Popular Movement in Defence of TChad |
| MSF | Médecins Sans Frontières |
| MSP | Malacca Straits Patrols |
| MSS | Muslim Students Society |
| MTISC-GOG | Maritime Trade Information Sharing Centre for the Gulf of Guinea |
| MUJAO | Movement for Oneness and Jihad in West Africa |
| MUJIWA | Movement for Ones and Jihad in West Africa |
| MUJWA | Movement for Unity and Jihad in West Africa |
| MUNUSMA | United Nations Multidimensional Integrated Stabilization Mission in Mali |
| NACTEST | National Counter Terrorism Strategy |
| NATCC | National Anti-Terrorism Coordination Committee |
| NATO | North Atlantic Treaty Organisation |
| NCC | National Counterterrorism Centre |
| NCSS | National Cyber security Strategy |
| NCTC | National Counterterrorism |
| NDA | Niger Delta Avengers |
| NDPVF | Niger Delta Peoples Volunteer Force |
| NGCERT | Computer Emergency Response Team |
| NGO | Non-Government Organisation |
| NGOs | Non-Governmental Organisations |
| NIF | National Islamic Front |
| NIMASA | Nigeria Maritime Administration and Safety Agency |
| NIS | Nigerian Immigration Service |
| NMLA | National Movement for the Liberation of Azawad |
| NPFL | National Patriotic Front of Liberia |
| NPF | Nigeria Police Force |
| NPLF | National Patriotic Front of Liberia |
| NPO | Non-Profit Organisation |
| NRA | National Resistance Army |
| NRC | Norwegian Refugee Council |
| NSA | National Security Adviser |
| NSCIA | Nigerian Supreme Council for Islamic Affairs |
| NSVAs | Non State Violent Actors |
| NTC | National Transitional Council |
| NTC | National Training Centre |
| NWPPL | Network Women Pioneers for Peace and Life |
| OAU | Organization of Africa Unity |
| ODA | Official Development Assistance |
| OECD | Organisation for Economic Cooperation and Development |
| OEF | Operation Enduring Freedom |
| OHCHR | Office of the Commissioner for Human Rights |
| OHGS | Offensive Hand Gun System |

| | |
|---|---|
| OIC | Organization of Islamic Countries |
| OIN | Niger Islamic Organisation |
| OLF | Oromo Liberation Front |
| ONLF | Ogaden National Liberation Front |
| ONS | Office of National Security |
| ONSA | Office of the National Security Adviser |
| OPDO | Oromo People's Democratic Organisation |
| OPEC | Organization of Petroleum Exporting Countries |
| OPV | Offshore Patrol Vessels |
| OSESS | Office of Special Envoy for South Sudan |
| PAGAD | People Against Gangsterism and Drugs |
| PC | Personal Computer |
| PDP | People's Democratic Party |
| PHRN | Peace and Human Right Network |
| PISCES | Personal Identification Secure Comparison and Evaluation System |
| PLO | Palestinian Liberation Organization |
| PMCs | Private Military Companies |
| PMSCs | Private Military and Security Companies |
| POCDATARA | Protection of Constitutional Democracy against Terrorist and Related Activities Act |
| POTA | Prevention of Terrorism Act |
| POTR | Prevention of Terrorism Regulations |
| PREACT | Partnership for Regional East Africa Counterterrorism |
| PRT | Provincial Reconstruction Team |
| PSAs | UK Public Service Agreements |
| PSC | Peace and Security Council |
| PSCs | Private Security Companies |
| PSI | Pan Sahel Initiative |
| PSOs | Peace Support Operations |
| PSTC | Peace Support Training Centre |
| R2P | Responsibility to Protect |
| RAF | Royal Air Force |
| REC | Regional Economic Community |
| RECAPP | Regional Cooperation Agreement on Combating Piracy and Armed Robbery against Ships in Asia |
| RECs | Regional Economic Communities |
| RISDP | Regional Indicative Strategic Development Plan |
| RISR | Regional Impact Situation Reports |
| RSI | Regional Strategic Initiative |
| RUF | Royal United Front (Sierra Leone) |
| SAA | Secure Anchorage Area |
| SAARC | South Asian Association for Cooperation |
| SADC | South African Development Community |
| SADD | South African Department of Defence |
| *SALT* | Strategic Arms Limitation Talks |
| SALW | Small Arms and Light Weapons |
| SAP | Structural Adjustment Programme |
| SCF | Save the Children Fund |

| | |
|---|---|
| SFA | Security Forces Assistance |
| SGPC | Salafist Group for Preaching and Combat |
| SG | Secretary General |
| SIPO | Strategic Indicative Plan for the Organ |
| SLA | Sudan Liberation Army |
| SLA | Sierra Leone Army |
| SMJTF | Special Military Joint Task Force |
| SNA | Somali National Army |
| SOMS | Straits of Malacca and Singapore |
| SPLA | Sudan People's Liberation Army |
| SPLM | Sudan People Liberation Movement |
| SRF | Sudan Revolutionary Front |
| SRRC | Somali Restoration and Reconciliation Council |
| SSC | Satellite Surveillance Centre |
| SSS | State Security Service |
| STTEP | Specialized Tasks, Training, Equipment and Protection |
| SUPKEM | Supreme Council of Kenya Muslims |
| SWAPO | South West Africa People's Organization |
| TESEX | Live Fire and Tactical Effects Simulation |
| TFG | Transitional Federal Government (Somalia) |
| TIP | Terrorist Interdiction Program |
| TNC | Transition National Council |
| TNG | Transitional National Government |
| TOC | Transnational Organized Crime |
| TPA | Terrorism Protection Act |
| TPB | Terrorism Prevention Branch |
| TPLF | Tigray People's Liberation Front |
| TSCI | Trans-Sahel Counterterrorism Initiative |
| TSCTI | Trans Sahara Counter Terrorism Initiative |
| TSCTP | Trans-Sahara Counterterrorism Partnership |
| TSTI | Transnational Security Threats Initiative |
| TUG | Transnational Unity Government |
| UAE | United Arab Emirates |
| UAVs | Unmanned Aerial Vehicles |
| UCM-CI | Muslim Cultural Union Côte d'Ivoire |
| UFL | Sahel Fusion Liaison Unit |
| UIC | Union of Islamic Courts |
| UK | United Kingdom |
| ULIMO | United Liberation Movement of Liberia for Democracy |
| UN | United Nations |
| UNO | United Nations Organization |
| UNAMSIL | United Nations Mission in Sierra Leone |
| UNCCT | UN Counter-Terrorism Strategy |
| UNCLOS | United Nations Conventions on the Law of the Sea |
| UNCTAD | United Nations Conference on Trade and Development |
| UNCTITF | United Nations Counter-Terrorism Implementation Task Force |
| UNDP | United Nation Development Program |
| UNDPI | United Nations Department of Public Information |

| | |
|---|---|
| UNEP | United Nations Environment Programme |
| UNESCO | United Nations Educational Scientific and Cultural Organization |
| UNGA | United Nations General Assembly |
| UNGCTS | United Nations Global Counter-Terrorism Strategy |
| UNISOM | United Nations Operation in Somalia |
| *UNITA* | *União Nacional para a Independência Total de Angola or National Union for Total Independence of Angola* |
| UNLA | Uganda National Liberation Army |
| UNMISS | United Nations Mission in the Republic of South Sudan |
| UNO | United Nations Organisation |
| UNOCAS | United Nations Office for Central Africa |
| UNOCHA | United Nations Office for the Coordination of Humanitarian Affairs |
| UNODC | United Nations Office on Drugs and Crime |
| UNOMSIL | United Nations Observer Mission in Sierra Leone |
| UNOWAS | United Nations Office for West Africa and the Sahel |
| UNRF I & II | Uganda National Rescue Front |
| UNSC | UN Security Council |
| UNSG | United Nations Secretary General |
| UPDCA | Uganda People's Democratic Christian Army |
| UPDF | Uganda People's Defence Force |
| US | United States |
| US AFRICOM | United States Africa Command |
| US CT-COIN | United States counterterrorism and counterinsurgency |
| US NAVAF | United States Naval Forces Africa |
| USA | United States of America |
| USAFRICOM | US African Command |
| USAID | United States Agency for International Development |
| USCTC | United States Counter Terrorism Center |
| USD | United States' Dollar |
| USSR | Union of Soviet Socialist Republic |
| VNSA | Violent Non-State Actors |
| VOA | Voice of America |
| VP | Vitalite Plus |
| WB | World Bank |
| WEF | World Economic Forum |
| WEU | Western European Union |
| WFP | World Food Program |
| WTC | World Trade Centre |
| WTO | Warsaw Treaty Organisation |

# Part I
# Conceptual perspectives

# 1

# Introduction

## The frontiers of counterterrorism and counterinsurgency in Africa

*Usman A. Tar*

## Introduction

Africa has acquired an ignoble status as "ground zero" in the global resurgence of violent extremism (VE), and an active front in countering violent extremism (CVE). However, Africa is not an isolated domain in the concerted effort to address the symptoms and root causes of VE; it is part and parcel of a global effort at anti-terrorism. A global coalition has emerged to coalesce international efforts to provide collective security against transnational crimes and terrorist activities. In Africa, a plethora of Violent Non-State Actors (VNSAs) – for example *Al-Shabaab, Al-Qaeda in the Maghreb, Boko Haram, Ansaaru Deen* and *Lord's Resistance Army* – have challenged the legitimacy and authority of the state, and created human carnage and loss of life and properties, while also engaging the local state and its armed forces in physical combat. On the other hand, virtual criminality and "ungoverned spaces" have further added a layer of burden and complexity on states' ability to deal with these emerging security challenges. Thus, several anti-terror legislation and strategies have been developed by states, individually, bilaterally and multilaterally, to contain or curtail these threats. At the same time, the state deploys enormous resources to contain the security challenges. However, most African states are bedevilled by "crisis of legitimacy" as a result of poor governance, imprudent management of resources, official corruption, and failure in welfare provisioning. Thus, a number of states have failed to degrade or defeat insurgency and terrorism in their domains. At the same time, the conventional security approach of the state in managing the challenge is both inadequate and overstretched. Armed insurgents and terror organisations have amassed vast instruments of warfare and are challenging the legitimacy and integrity of the state. Indeed, in some states such as Somalia, Nigeria, Uganda, and Kenya, terrorist organisations have curved "ungoverned spaces" which stand out as pockets of "terror(ist) haven" and a groundswell for violence threatening national, regional, and global security. For instance, in the North-Eastern part of Nigeria, and pockets of surrounding regions and states, there is a virtual existence of garrison spaces in which coercion from state and violence from insurgent terrorisms together haunt the security of the citizens. Consequently, massive displacement of the citizens from their places of habitation and sources of livelihood pose multiple challenges to the state and humanitarian community. Beyond terrorist insurgency in the North East of Nigeria, there is also the issue of kidnapping for ransom, increase in the spate of armed robbery, and general criminality that further compound the scourges of insecurity. Across Africa and the world, terrorism, insurgency, and other forms of security challenges are increasing in space, number, and intensity. States' commitment to physical, regime and human securities have become the core preoccupations of governments all over the world, including Africa.

Africa is often portrayed as a breeding ground for terrorism, insurgency, and militancy. Since 9/11, the global community has focused attention on, and channelled resources to, Africa as a peculiar front for the so-called "Global War on Terror" (GWT). The continent has witnessed significant in-flow of Security Sector Assistance (SFA) from the international community in terms of boosting the capacity of the Africa Union (AU), Regional Economic Co-operations (RECs), and security and bureaucratic apparatus of the various individual states to counterterrorism, insurgency, and organised violence in the region. This book illustrates how Africa's defence and security environments have been radically altered by drastic changes in world politics and local ramifications. Recent events – such as the end of the Cold War in 1990, and the terrorist attack on the World Trade Centre on 11 September 2001 – have unleashed new developments on Africa's precarious development and security. Amidst the severe global economic slowdown, majority of African countries are largely plagued by poor economic performance in terms of GDP, GNP, standard and quality of living, industrial output, economic transparency and governance index, etc. Today, in the majority of African countries, large swathes of the population survive on less than two dollars a day. African countries are bedevilled by crises of development and security as evidenced by a plethora of "civil wars" across the continent, while violent extremism, fundamentalism, terrorism and insurgency have exacerbated exponentially. Globalisation is argued to have further weakened the African state and provided an enabling environment for the efflorescence of a bevvy of "virtual security risks" such as cyber-terrorism, cybercrime, perverse effects of new media, and social networking. In addition, globalisation has emboldened terror organisations to frontally confront the local state, overwhelm its armed forces, usurp territory, and literally carve out "ungoverned spaces" (Tar, 2017a, 2017b)

The *Handbook* distinctly illustrates how African states have developed new structures for countering terrorism, insurgency, and organised violence on the continent, as well as showing how they have developed unilateral, bilateral, and multilateral platforms for countering organised and transnational violence. The global support for countering terrorism in Africa appears to be driven by the enlightened motives by the concerned "developed" countries of the global security community to come to the aid of weak African states as a means of making the continent more secure, better governed, and immune from harbouring terrorist groups (Chapters 12–19). The book also shows the efflorescence of new and improvised, seemingly independent, regional architectures for counterterrorism. Examples include the AU's Peace and Security Commission as well as a host of similar initiatives in ECOWAS, SADC, IGAD, COMESA and Maghreb Union, that have led to a new regional architecture for defence and security in the continent (Chapters 20–25). Beyond the strengthening of existing RECs, there are attempts to build newer regional platforms – for instance, in the Lake Chad Basin, which encompasses Western and Central African regions, the formation of the Joint Multinational Task Forces (MNJTF) under the aegis of the Lake Chad Basin Commission (LCBC). LCBC was formed in 1968 to manage the aquatic resources of the Lake Chad but eventually expanded in 1998 to deal with security issues and herald the formation of a collective security framework to confront the transnationalisation of the Boko Haram insurgency in the region (Chapters 25 and 37). The MNJTF was developed to pool together economic and security resources under a novel collective security arrangement to ensure intelligence fusion and coordination of military strategy to confront insurgency and criminality. In addition to regional architecture, there has been a remarkable improvement in the existing municipal strategies for counterterrorism through enhanced and fast-track legislation, infrastructure development, and rejigging of national armed forces' standard operating procedures for countering terrorism and insurgencies at the levels national grand norm, strategy, operations, and tactics. Thus, this volume reveals that African states and regional organisations constitute formidable building blocks for the emerging structures for CT-COIN in Africa. Beyond the regional and national efforts, there appears to be a partnership for security through active participation of civil society organisations and humanitarian agencies (Chapters 11 and 35), as well as, in some particular contexts such as in Nigeria, the emergence of civilian tasks forces to complement the efforts of government forces. As both Nwonsu and Auwal reveal in this *Handbook*, realising the limits of the conventional security provisioning and management, groups within society organize, often with the support of the state, provide volunteer networks for complementary roles that are useful to create a broad security architecture in the state (Chapters 37 and 41). This development draws in civil society and volunteerism into security discourse in at least two senses. First, civil society organisations complement the state as a popular front for CT-COIN and, therefore, a layer of protection against destructive forces. The second point questions security volunteerism of civic groups because civil society bears an essence which questions possible use of coercion in its participation in vigilante groups. Thus, there is a need to examine the dynamic interaction of state and civil society in the containment of insurgency and other security challenges in Africa.

In essence, the *Handbook* highlights a number of novel trends on CT-COIN in Africa. First, it critically highlights the transnational dimensions of counterterrorism and counterinsurgency in Africa, and reveals the roles played by African states and regional organisations in the global war on terror. Second, the volume critically evaluates the emerging regional architecture of countering terrorism and insurgency and organised violence on the continent through the *African Union Counterterrorism Framework* (AU-CTF) and *Regional Security Complexes* (RSCs). Third, the volume distinctly illustrates the CT-COIN structures and mechanisms established by specific African states to contain, degrade, and eliminate terrorism, insurgency, and organised violence on the continent, particularly highlighting the successes, constraints and challenges of these emerging CT-COIN mechanisms. Finally, the volume highlights the entry of non-state actors – such as civil society, citizens' volunteer groups, private security companies, and defence contractors – into the theatre of CT-COIN in Africa through volunteerism, community support for state-led CT-COIN Operations, and civil-military cooperation (CIMIC).

## The frontiers of CT-COIN in Africa – emerging threats and regional security architectures

### Conceptual and contextual contours

Terrorism, insurgency, and CT-COIN are subject to fierce contestations at both conceptual and contextual levels. The conceptual parameters of the debate are thoroughly explored in Chapters 2–11 and will not be discussed here. However, the following analytic synopsis can be offered: first, current conceptualisations are steeped in abstract definitions and contestations, with little attention on local context in Africa. Second, most conceptual analyses are skewed in terms of understanding and addressing the root causes of insurgency/terrorism, especially in Africa. Clearly, Africa is seen as a volatile but fertile ground for terrorism/insurgency, as well as a marginal player in the "global war on terror". Thus, western approaches to countering violent extremism and insurgencies, especially the models of the USA and her allies, appear to be designer models that are aimed at meeting the strategic objectives of the western powers: local dynamics and "national interests" of African states are often placed in the back burner. Finally, the conceptual literature is clearly driven by western scholars and policymakers based on their policy agenda. There is an acute need to place the African experience and "cultural relativity" on the drawing board. It is anticipated that this *Handbook* will provide the much-needed perspectives on how Africa is coping with the challenges of terrorism, insurgency, and CT-COIN based on thorough utilisation of empirical data on local experiences and conjectures.

Africa is often painted, especially in western intelligence and security communities, as the fault line or "ground zero" in the global effort to contain the scourges of hunger and instability. Africa's poor governance and developmental profile support the bleak depiction of the continent: since achieving independence in the 1960s only a few African countries have been able to overcome the precipitous hangover of inherited colonial hangovers – particularly, economic decline and political instability superintended by a praetorian elite that is willing to steal or compromise the national patrimony to nourish its self-centred interest. At the same, while dealing with global aspersions, Africa is also undergoing a phenomenal transformation in regional security and, in particular, is developing a regional architecture for peace and security.

This volume is predicated on – but also deviates from – a number of existing conceptual and contextual literature in the field. A key focus, in this volume, is the emerging architecture for counterterrorism and counterinsurgency in Africa. A key early intervention, perhaps, is *Uniting Africa: Building Regional Peace and Security Systems* by Francis (2006) which leads the debate on why and how African countries are building the structures for "security regionalisation", and are increasingly becoming united in terms of co-operative peace, security, and development in more profound ways in the post-Cold War era (since 1990) than at any other time in Africa's post-colonial history. Moving forward from the failure of the earlier typically idealistic African unity project, the volume demonstrates how peace and security challenges have created the imperative for change. The volume argues that a series of regional peace and security systems are emerging and that states that have participated in practical experiments in regional peace-keeping, peace support operations, conflict stabilization/management, and preventive diplomacy are building *de facto* systems of peace and security that could be institutionalised and extended. The *Handbook* pays particular attention to emerging structures for regional security through the African Union (AU) and Regional Economic Cooperations (RECs). This present volume seeks to illuminate how African countries are developing elaborate structures at municipal, regional and continental and global (multilateral) levels, and how unity is deployed in fine details in building regional, state-centred and society-centred structures for countering terrorism and insurgency on the continent. This *Handbook* further illuminates the challenges of building these structures of countering organised violence in a globalising world where the boundaries of the state are no longer fixed or defensible using coercive, kinetic means. Thus, the volume expounds the efficacy and limits of the conventional kinetic approach – which have become glaring since 9/11 – and the need to balance the conventional approach with the non-conventional non-kinetic approach. This reality is produced by the shift in African battlespace from symmetric conflicts involving state military forces – inter-state wars, irredentist wars, proxy wars, and incendiary civil wars with foreign involvement – to asymmetric conflicts involving conventional militaries and versus violent non-state actors (VNSAs). This fundamental shift in the battlespace appears to have caught African militaries unawares. Since independence, African militaries have, in the fore, been groomed to prepare for conventional war (foreign aggression), with a sprinkle of acquiring the capacity and domain awareness for providing military aid to civil authority.

The rise of violent extremism and global jihadism has increasingly pushed African defence and policy establishment to focus attention on building capacity for counterterrorism and counterinsurgency. A number of materials have focused on these emerging scenarios. For instance, in *Terrorism in Africa*, Martha Crenshaw (1994) provides one of the early analyses of the evolution, imminent rise, and dynamism of terrorism in Africa. Published soon after the Cold War and long before 9/11, the book offers bold pointers to the scourge of terrorism in Africa paying sufficient attention to the local and extra-continental forces behind terrorism in the continent. Another pioneering work is Ali Mazrui's *Nkrumah's Legacy and Africa's Triple Heritage Between Globalization and Counter Terrorism* (Mazrui, 2000). This 72-page pamphlet contains the revised texts of a series of three lectures, the Aggrey-Frazer-Guggisberg Memorial Lectures, delivered by the late Professor Ali Mazuri at the University of Ghana in 2002. The first lecture explores globalisation as the product of religion, ideology, technology, economy, and empire. It postulates that globalisation can be positive or negative, depending upon the values it has realised. Mazrui raised questions such as: how does globalisation impact terrorism and counterterrorism in Africa? How does this relate to the rise of terrorism and counterterrorism on the continent? While making an allusion to "counterterrorism", this modest pamphlet actually offers philosophical reflections rather than the deconstructive diagnosis of globalisation, terrorism and counterterrorism in Africa. In addition, the book is steeped in philosophical talk with a scarce focus on the material dimension of counterterrorism in Africa. Nevertheless, it provides a deep reflection on the transnational dimension of globalisation and CT-COIN, and Africa's experience in this emerging phenomenon.

The comparative dimension of CT-COIN has received attention. What are the experiences of various African countries on terrorism, insurgency and CT-COIN? To what extent do African countries learn from each other's experience of CT-COIN? Some interventions are worth noting here: For instance, in *The Egg Breakers – Counterterrorism in Sub Saharan Africa*, Jacobus Kotze (2013) provides a historical and comparative study on how terrorists and the Security Forces evolved through the years, starting with the Kenyan Mau Mau Movement, the Rhodesian Bush War, and the South African Boer War. The volume provides a robust analysis of the CT-COIN experience in these countries. The author was part of the South African Police Force between 1985–1991 and brought his personal experience to bear in his analysis. A key import of the volume is that in colonial and post-colonial Africa, insurgencies are driven by structural injustice, and were characterised by failure of the state to meet existential needs of the population. In addition, the volume argues the rise of rebellion was usually driven by the middle class with the support of the peasantry. Almost always, these insurgencies are locally constructed and geographically restricted to the state: the risk of transnationalisation of terror was either minimal or non-existent. This contrasts with the current spate of insurgency and terrorism in Africa in 1990s and 2000s where terrorism and insurgency have assumed transnational dimensions, and foreign influence on both sides of the terror divide – insurgent/terror organisations and the state – are as compelling as they are counter-productive. Similarly, *The Battle of the Casbah: Terrorism and Counterterrorism in Algeria, 1955–1957*, Paul Aussaresses (2002) – the infamous "torturer of Algiers" – examines how the state in colonial Africa dealt with the scourge of violent nationalism and organised violence. The book provides a first-hand account of how the colonial Algerian state conducted its CT-COIN operations in the 1950s, particularly the standard of treatment accorded to the so-called terrorists captured as prisoners of war. By using severe torture methods on captured terrorists, the state actually succeeded in further bolstering the resolve of the armed guerrilla. Finally, in *Counterinsurgency in Rhodesia*, Jakkie Cilliers (2016) provides a rich account of insurgency and COIN in colonial Zimbabwe. The book was originally published in 1985 and became one of the earliest scholarly and objective contributions available on the Rhodesian counterinsurgency. It documents and explains why the state of Rhodesia lost the war: its failure to address the root causes of the war of national liberation. In addition to documenting the origins of the national struggle, each chapter of the volume, examines a separate institution or counterinsurgency strategy directly related to the development of the conflict, concluding with a summary view of the Zimbabwean security situation both past and present.

A number of analytic points emerge from the foregoing accounts of insurgency, terrorism, and CT-COIN in colonial and post-colonial Africa. First, insurgency emerged in different nomenclatures – "war of national liberation", "nationalist struggle", "rebellion" – but their objectives include to unsettle the existing *status quo* and, if possible, upturn the structural inadequacies of the state or seek its outright replacement with a narrow (garbed in popular) construction of the state. On its part, the formal state tended to accelerate its coercive response to deal ruthlessly with the rebellion through a kinetic approach and "scorched earth policy" with dire consequences. Thus, the non-kinetic approach (battle for hearts and minds) was often overlooked. Second, until the 1990s, insurgencies in Africa were not as globally connected as they have been afterwards: back then, insurgency and terrorism appeared to be more restricted to local dynamics. This enabled the local state to seek to use local mechanisms – often spearheaded by the armed forces – to muzzle, disarm, liquidate, or dismantle terror infrastructures. Too often, this resulted in heavy clampdown of the terror cells, as well as the leadership, foot soldiers, and local sympathisers of the insurgency organisations across the national space. Finally, the aforementioned experiences reveal that early insurgencies in Africa were driven by clear political and ideological motivations with a clear focus on capturing the state; this contrast, for instance, with the emergence of recent insurgencies with clear religious and sectarian motivations as exemplified by *Al-Shabaab* in Eastern Africa and *Boko Haram* in Western Africa. Others were driven by even narrower but materialist motivations as exemplified by the environmental militancy in the Niger Delta.

Since the 1990s, Africa has been undergoing a paradigm shift on the efficacy of conventional and unconventional dimension (that is, kinetic and non-kinetic alternatives) of CT-COIN. This is predicated on the fact that the continent has been experiencing the efflorescence of varying species of insurgent and terrorist organisations as outlined above. A sample work, in this regard, is *Terrorism and Counterterrorism in Africa: Fighting Insurgency from Al Shabaab, Ansar Dine and Boko Haram* by Solomon (2015) which offers a refreshing critique of traditional counterterrorism approaches, with their emphasis on the military, as a failing model of CT-COIN in Africa. It also pays attention to how African countries are coming to terms with the contradiction associated with using a traditional approach to confront an unconventional enemy. Thus, the limits of conventional approach are demonstrated conspicuously. While Solomon (2015) pays adequate attention to CT-COIN in Nigeria and Somalia, it leaves room for further assessment of other emerging hotspots of terrorism and insurgency elsewhere in Africa. In this *Handbook*, we draw attention to a more holistic diagnosis and prognosis, with an emphasis on multiple alternatives for curbing the scourge of terrorism. The volume pays attention to three case studies (*Al-Shabaab* [Somalia], *Ansaru Deen,* and *Boko Haram* [Nigeria]). It also provides wider comparative analyses and case studies of the regional, state, and societal structures for CT-COIN in Africa.

In Africa, there is a hype about local ownership of governance and policy, including measures for countering terrorism and securing the state and society. This is the more so in countries that have undergone restoration of liberal democracy since the 1990s. But in most of Africa, the praetorian military culture of the state – characterised, for instance, by resorting to an overwhelming force to address public protests, extra-judicial killing, secrecy in defence governance and lack of accountability in procurement and deployment of kinetic force – has continued to undermine the democratic claims of many African countries. Therefore, the tension between democratic renaissance and coercive norms has affected Africa's solution to managing national and regional security. In *Terrorism and Counterterrorism: An African Perspective,* Imobighe and Egwavoen (2016) offer some decent analyses of the evolution and dynamics of terrorism and counterterrorism in Africa, with special focus on Nigeria. Seven Africanist scholars mustered by the *African Strategic and Peace Research Group in Nigeria,* a local private think-tank based in Lagos, here address the threat of terrorism in the context of the global strategic climate. The volume demonstrates, to some extent, local approaches to CT-COIN based on the paradigm of "Africa's solution to Africa's problems". This paradigm shift, rooted in the discourses of the reformed African Union (AU), is crucial because it lays emphasis on the imperatives of "local content" or domestic ownership in CT-COIN at the strategic, operational, and tactical levels. The volume is framed against the background of the altered shape of the global security equation, and the devalued utility of the notion of security through state-centric military preparedness. The authors posit that the failure to grasp the exact nature of terrorism is leading to the spread of terrorist violence to parts of Africa hitherto regarded as relatively safe. Further, the adverse socio-political conditions on the continent have increased Africa's vulnerability. The contributors examine areas where the experiences of other regions are relevant, providing both a regional and global context. While the volume offers a modest attempt to conceptualise and contextualise terrorism and counterterrorism in Africa, it does not provide a balanced analysis of the spectres of terrorism and counterterrorism in Africa. In addition, the volume does not examine the emerging architectures of CT-COIN in Africa from the perspectives of the AU and regional security complexes (Ochoche, 2016). This *Handbook* provides a more robust and current analysis of CT-COIN in Africa from the perspectives of not only RECs but will also offer case analyses of specific African countries.

## Transnational perspectives on CT-COIN in Africa

The international community considers Africa as a major theatre for CT-COIN. African countries consider themselves, at least at the official and bureaucratic contexts, as strategic partners in the global coalition of the willing to confront and defeat terrorist organisations and sleeper cells that are domiciled on the continent. However, African countries have remained weak, and their armed forces have been overwhelmed with the incapacity in dealing with the menace of terrorism. While there may be some consensus on global and African aspiration and strategy for CT-COIN, there appears to be a tension between African and global perceptions regarding the threats of terrorism. The negligence of the "cultural relativity" of violent extremism has had serious implications on any attempt to build a united global front to deal with the menace of terrorism. Often overlooked is the fact that Africa is, itself, a major victim of terrorism: African states are coming to terms with the scourges of terrorism and its humanitarian and security repercussions. What are the policies of global powers and multilateral agencies with reference to countering terrorism and insurgency on the continent? Are these policies driven by objectives realities of Africa? What are the policy thrust, strategic drivers, and operational/tactical approaches of global partners in countering violent extremism and insurgency in Africa? What are the successes and limitations of the global approach to CT-COIN in Africa? Is there a global consensus on countering violent extremism and insurgency in Africa? In Chapters 20–27, contributors consider the role of global actors in CT-COIN in Africa and offer some responses to these questions. The following key points emerge from these chapters. First, an international response to terrorism and insurgency is constructed at bilateral and multilateral levels (Chapters 24–27 dwell on bilateral dimensions; and Chapters 20–23 deal with multilateral dimensions).

Both bilateral and multilateral interventions are underpinned by the national interest of the partnering states, and/or institutional expectations and conditionalities of the multilateral organisations. Second, international interventions tend to be centred on the state at the expense of non-state actors – NGOs, humanitarian agencies, religious organisations, and community-based organisations. In providing support for CT-COIN, international organisations tend to target or cooperate with the local state and RECs often to the exclusion of local population and opinion moulders. This approach fails to recognise the jointed vulnerabilities of, and intricate interconnection between, state and non-state actors. Terrorism targets all members of society; support for countering terrorism ought to target the entire spectrum of state and society. Third, international organisations, especially the UN, EU, and NATO, are overwhelmed by their own institutional limitations in countering the challenges of global (and regional) terrorism. Though these institutions have put in place complex and steady mechanisms for countering violent extremism and insurgency in Africa, their efficacy is heavily constrained by the overwhelming pressure and expectation of their member-states. Most of these organisations are either undemocratic or weak in taking firm actions, especially actions that run contrary to the desires of their member-states. To be sure, international organisations are formed by disparate states each with colliding national interests and aspirations. Therefore, multilateral platforms lend themselves to the push and pull of their member-states: in the final analysis, they may be utterly oblivious of, or insensitive to, the wishes and aspirations of the beneficiaries of SFAs. Finally, international CT-COIN interventions are constrained by the bureaucratic bottlenecks of the recipient local states. Most local states have put in place their own anti-terror legislation, and their armed forces and security agencies are sometimes averse to foreign intervention. The transcendent and complex nature of terrorism and insurgency have frustrated the territorialisation of the security space: it has become politically expedient for African countries to reach to regional and international partners to stem the tide of terrorism across the globe. Therefore, through defence diplomacy, African states are increasingly partnering with global actors to contain violent extremism and insurgencies.

## Regional perspectives on CT-COIN in Africa

The regional dimensions of the threats of terrorism/insurgency in Africa are under-reported in the international media or, even worse, overlooked by policy communities in the global centres of power. The news emanating from Washington and London often depict African states as a "helpless terrorscape" whose weak structures are not able to overcome, much less defeat, terrorist organisations on the continent. Due to the challenges of regional integration and security regionalisation – as a result of an inherited colonial hangover, and the crisis of governance that followed the post-colonial era – African countries are often depicted as unable to forge formidable regional fronts for confronting the scourges of terrorism and insurgency. However, since the 1990s, African countries have developed a continent and sub-regional mechanisms for CT-COIN (Francis, 2006). In this *Handbook,* contributors provide refreshing analyses on specific regional organisations in Africa: African Union (Chapter 20); West Africa (Chapter 21); Horn of Africa (Chapter 22); Southern Africa (Chapter 23); Gulf of Guinea (Chapter 24) and the Lake Chad Basin (Chapter 25). Each chapter in this Section articulates the impetus for security regionalisation as the scaffold for CT-COIN, and outlines the challenges and prospects of regional mechanisms for CT-COIN on the continent.

Some poignant pointers emerge from the regional analysis of CT-COIN in Africa. First, with regards to the AU and most RECs, it is apparent that African countries have defied the odds to develop a relatively robust continental architecture for CT-COIN largely based on common perceptions of threats, well-nurtured regional consensus, and consistent turnover of regional protocols that seek to secure the continent in defiance of the all-too-familiar neo-colonial and post-colonial structural encumbrances. Of the key colonial powers on the continent, France and Britain appear to have maintained a sustained interest in shaping politics in Africa – mainly through reinforcement of existing defence agreements and Security Forces Assistance (SFA) programmes that seek to bolster the capacity of African states that are in needs and regional organisations specific countries to foster collective security. Nevertheless, the interests of specific former colonial powers – especially Britain, Belgium, France, and Italy – are often at odds with that of African states. For instance, recent developments in the AU and RECs have clearly shown that African countries are poised to chart a new course in CT-COIN on the continent. This paradigm shift has given impetus to a new drive on the continent that seeks to reinforce the bond of unity on the continent. However, some former colonial powers have not rested on their oars: they have come up with clandestine initiatives (decoys?) to present dummies that, on face value, appear to promote common interest but actually seek to provide a space for manoeuvrability and outright intervention on the security affairs of the ost state. As the incident of the Lake Chad Basin has shown, France has developed a parallel regional platform – G5 Sahel – to counter the emerging architecture for regional security in the LCB (see Chapters 18 and 25). Thus, it is fair to note that African countries are developing a regional mechanism for CT-COIN in an atmosphere that is both compelling and antagonistic of security regionalisation. The modest successes recorded by most regional organisations covered in this *Handbook* clearly show a resilient resolve on the part of African states to pool their collective energies even on the face of a hostile crisis of post-coloniality. Second the regional CT-COIN initiatives – particularly, the African Union Peace and Security architecture and similar architectures in the RECs; and regional protocols for anti-terrorism – are in tandem with national aspirations, if not a tenuous product of national fear, amongst willing African states. Desperate times call for desperate measures: the suffocating repercussions of terrorism and insurgency have necessitated a coalescence of regional institution building to confront the scourges of terror. A case in point is the establishment of the regional standby forces under the auspices of the AU. The standby forces are designed to be based in each of the major regional security complexes on the continent (see Chapter 20). The contribution of troops and logistics for the standby forces are to come from a member state of the respective RECs, while grand strategy is to be provided by the AU. In addition, troop contribution is to be based on national quota and capacity. Thus, there appears to be some sort of democratisation of CT-COIN on the African continent. Finally, in the regional cases of CT-COIN initiatives, there are clear challenges that are standing in the way of steady progress. These challenges include, among others, inadequacy and disparity of funding from member states, territorialisation of the security space and, specifically, the adversity of some national defence establishments to continentalise and regionalise security in variance with national interest and aspiration; sabotage from international partners and former colonial powers; and decline of global support as a result of the perception of corruption and political instability associated with many African states. Nevertheless, the various analyses in this Section point to a steady prospect for regional CT-COIN on the continent on the ground of shared sense of vulnerability amongst African countries and contingent regional platforms for collective security.

## National perspectives on CT-COIN in Africa

African states are experiencing the threats of terrorism and insurgency both individually and in a shared sense of vulnerability: most African countries are coming to terms with their peculiar local variants of violent extremism – *Boko Haram* in Cameroon, Chad, Niger, and Nigeria; *Interhamwe* in Rwanda and Burundi; Balaka in CAR; and *Al-Shabab* in Somalia, Kenya, and Uganda, among others. Though some of these VNSAs exist in more than one state, their structure, spread, *modus operandi,* and impact differ from one country to another – thus, for instance, Boko Haram casts different spells on Cameroon, Chad, Niger, and Nigeria. In this *Handbook,* cases are provided from nine specific countries to drive home the cultural relativity, national specificity, and uniqueness of the CT-COIN drive of each country (Chapters 26–34). Each of these countries has a story to tell; each has developed its own national architecture for CVE and CT-COIN, and each faces a unique set of challenges. The cases are wide and varying: e.g. Nigeria and Sierra Leone in the western coast of Africa (Chapters 29 and 23); Uganda, Somalia, and Tanzania in Eastern Africa and the Horn (Chapters 26, 27 and 34); and Egypt, Libya, and Algeria in Northern Africa (Chapters 29, 30 and 32). However, there are also commonalities and even bilateral efforts amongst contiguous neighbours to deal with the scourges of violent extremism and insurgency – examples of the bilateral or multilateral drive include cooperation amongst member countries of IGAD (Chapter 22); LCBC (Chapter 25), and SADC (Chapter 23), among others. The chapters presented in this section of the *Handbook* unveil the following imperatives. First, most African countries have been tenuously facing their own local terrorist and insurgency organisations and, in doing so, they have faced some successes and challenges. Second, terrorist and insurgency organisations have established an acute sense of connection to their global and African "peers" in profound ways. The Boko Haram in Cameroon, Chad, Niger, and Nigeria, that was hitherto unknown since 2002, has by 2015 grown enough branches to join forces with the global terror fraternity – the *Islamic State of Iraq and Syria* (ISIS) – to form the *Islamic State in West Africa Province* (ISWAP). Third, several VNSAs in Africa have developed sufficient technological, logistic, and operational momentum to confront regular armed forces and paramilitary agencies in their host states, and overrun significant territory that was eventually classified as "ungoverned spaces" – an aphorism for territories that are no longer under the control of the formal state. Citizens' accounts of life in these "ungoverned spaces" have revealed that the "new sheriffs in town" (VNSAs) have quickly set up some semblance of justice, administration, and taxation which are harsh and cause misery to the captive population. They have also sought to establish social provisioning entities – makeshift clinics, schools, and transport networks. This remained the fate of citizens in "ungoverned space" until they are eventually recaptured by the state forces. Fourth, the experiences in many Africa countries have revealed that state armed forces resorted to the use of kinetic force (coercive means) at the expense of non-kinetic power (persuasion, diplomacy, and material incentives) to undermine, defuse, and defray public anger arising from the crisis of governance and developmental failures that underpin violent extremism and insurgency (see also Tar, 2019 and Yusuf, 2019).

## Alternative perspectives on CT-COIN in Africa

In Africa, regional and national securities are often constructed as an exclusive domain of the state. This state-centric approach was inherited from the Cold War era when nations clashed with one another to promote their national interest and defend their territorial integrity. By extension, the Cold War mindset had privileged the national armed forces as a guardian force exclusively entrusted with the powers to deploy coercive force in defence of the state and the ruling elites – that is, "regime security" at the expense of "human security". Since the end of the Cold War in 1990 and, particularly following 9/11, there has been a paradigm shift on the limits of kinetic force as an exclusive means for defending the state. This was precipitated by the weakening of many states as a result of "crisis of legitimacy" and, conversely, the rise of violent non-state actors seeking to upturn or replace the legal state with its own caricatured construction of the state – this is the more so for VNSAs that confess narrow sectarian ideologies or theocratic construction of the state (see Chapter 38). At the same time, constructive humanitarian and humanitarian agencies have emerged to provide succour and hope to victims of the unconventional battle between the formal state and VNSAs. The laws of armed conflict are put to the test as both parties (state armed forces and VNSAs) fortuitously violate the rules of engagement in seeking to achieve an upper hand (see Chapters 9 and 38). In this section of the *Handbook*, contributors offer refreshing material on the role of non-state actors as fortuitous agents of CT-COIN in Africa – either as perpetrators of the violence or provides of relief. Cases presented include civil society (Chapter 35); humanitarian service providers (Chapter 36); VNSAs (Chapter 38); defence contractors (Chapter 39); private security companies (Chapter 40); civilian volunteers (Chapter 41); child soldiers (Chapter 42); and vulnerable persons (Chapter 43).

Materials presented in this Section raise a number of pertinent issues. First, contrary to the prevailing opinion both in the literature and policy, non-state actors have emerged on both sides of the state-insurgency divides to confront, challenge, or supplement the formal state, as the case may be. Second, those who challenge the state seek to upstage, overwhelm, unseat, or unsettle the state – for instance, VNSAs and child soldiers (when recruited by VNSAs) – with varying degrees of success and failure. On the other hand, it is apparent that humanitarian service providers and civil society organisations who seek to support good causes and, on a neutral level, provide succour to victims of violence, especially in a war-torn terrain characterised by rampant abuse of human rights and humanitarian law, have struggled to provide such services at huge human and material costs. Humanitarian service providers often find themselves in the crossfire, being arrested by agents of the state on austere grounds of guaranteeing their security or to conduct mop-up operations to clear territories hitherto occupied by terrorists, or being abducted by VNSAs in return for a ransom. Thus, the sacrifices of civil society and humanitarian workers in the domains of CT-COIN in Africa have been phenomenal: the spirit of humanitarianism has bolstered these organisations. Third, it is apparent that some non-state actors have provided enormous CT-COIN support to the state, ruling classes and/or private elites who can buy their services – examples include mercenaries as defence contractors, and private security companies. These "service providers" are in the business of selling security – in the form of military hardware, technology, mercenary service or protection of public and private assets and human life – in return for money. Thus, the profit motive and spirit of capitalism play a vital role in CT-COIN in Africa. Other non-state actors such as civilian volunteers are, however, pushed by "existential motive" to support the state. By supporting the armed forces in its CT-COIN drive, civilian Joint Task Forces have successfully negotiated a fortuitous entry into the battlespace – as a support unit of the armed forces. As revealed in Chapter 42, in Nigeria, the recruitment of the civilian volunteers was reluctantly accepted by battle-fatigued armed forces as a force multiplier to confront the Boko Haram insurgency. The armed forces provided basic training in weapon handling, basic regimentation, and battle formation and tactics, while the local state provided the resources to buy vehicles, uniforms and kits for the volunteers. In return for their services, the volunteers were paid a modest wage. A key question is, what happens to the civilian volunteers after the CT-COIN "season"? There are concerns that unless a facility is created for their demobilisation and re-integration to normal society, civilian volunteers shall constitute a *nouveau* source of threat in the post-CT-COIN era. Finally, it is also revealed that an ominous category of the nonstate actors – women, children, and the aged – constitute the violated and neglected victims of CT-COIN. Displaced from their homes and farms and pushed into refugee camps, they are forced to survive on the handouts of humanitarian agencies and what little they muster from begging or menial jobs around campsites. So long as the battle rages, there is no end in sight for this vulnerable category.

## References

Aussaresses, Paul (2002). *The Battle of the Casbah: Terrorism and counter-terrorism in Algeria, 1955–1957.* New York: Enigma Books.

Cilliers, Jakkie K. (1985, reprinted 2016). *Counter-insurgency in Rhodesia.* London: Routledge.

Crelinsten, R. D. (2007). Counterterrorism as global governance: A research inventory. In: Magnus Ranstorp (Ed.), *Mapping terrorism research: State of the art, gaps and future direction* (pp 210–235). Abingdon, Oxon: Routledge.

Crenshaw, Martha (Ed.). (1994). *Terrorism in Africa.* New York: G.K. Hall & Co/ Maxwell Macmillan International.

Pérouse de Montclos M.-A. (Ed.). (2014). *Boko Haram: Islamism, politics, security, and the state in Nigeria.* Ibadan: IFRA-Nigeria. Leiden, African Studies Centre, Waposo Series n°2.

Francis, D. J. (2006). *Uniting Africa: Building regional peace and security systems.* London: Routledge.

Ganor, B. (2005). *The counterterrorism puzzle: A guide for decision makers.* New Brunswick, NJ: Transaction Publishers.

Imobighe, T. A., & Egwavoen, A. N. T. (2016). *Terrorism and counter-terrorism: An African perspective.* Nigeria: HEBN Publishers.

Kotze, Jacobus (2013). *The egg breakers – Counter terrorism in sub Saharan Africa.* North Charleston, SC: Create Space Independent Publishing Platform.

Martin, G. (2003). *Understanding terrorism: Challenges, perspectives and issues.* Thousand Oaks, CA: SAGE Publications.

Mazrui, Ali A. (2000). *Nkrumah's legacy and Africa's triple heritage between globallization and counter terrorism,.* Accra: Ghana University Press.

Ochoche, Sunday A. (2016). Terrorism and counter terrorism: The African experience. In: T. A. Imobighe & A. N. Eguavoen (Eds.), *Terrorism and counter terrorism: An African perspective.* Ibadan: Heinemann.

Okumu, W. (Ed.). (2009). *Domestic terrorism in Africa: Defining, addressing and understanding its impact on human security.* Pretoria: Institute for Security Studies.

Pérouse de Montclos M.-A. (Ed.). (2014). *Boko Haram: Islamism, politics, security, and the state in Nigeria.* Ibadan: IFRA-Nigeria, and Leiden, African Studies Centre, Waposo Series n°2.

Ranstorp, M. (2007). Introduction: mapping terrorism research – challenges and priorities. In: Magnus Ranstorp (Ed.), *Mapping terrorism research: State of the art, gaps and future direction* (pp 1–28). Abingdon, Oxon: Routledge.

Rapoport, D. C. (2004). The four waves of modern terrorism. In: Audrey Kurth Cronin & James M. Ludes (Eds.), *Attacking terrorism: Elements of a grand strategy* (pp 44–73). Washington, DC: Georgetown University Press.

Reich, W. (Ed.). (1998). *Origin of terrorism: Psychologies, ideologies, theologies, states of mind.* Washington, DC: Woodrow Wilson Centre Press.

Schmid Alex, P. & Jongman A. (2005). *Political terrorism.* Piscataway, New Jersey: Transaction Publishers.

Shin, D. (2004). Fighting terrorism in East Africa and the Horn. *Foreign Service Journal* (September), 38–49.

Sinai, J. (2007). New trends in terrorism studies. In: Magnus Ranstorp (Ed.), *Mapping terrorism research: State of the art, gaps and future direction* (pp 31–50). Abingdon, Oxon: Routledge.

Solomon, H. (2015). *Terrorism and Counter-Terrorism in Africa: Fighting Insurgency from Al Shabaab, Ansar Dine and Boko Haram.* New York: Palgrave

Tar, U. A. (2017a). Introduction: The challenges of globalisation in Africa. In: U. A. Tar, B. E. Mijah, & M. E. U. Tedheke (Eds.), Globalisation in Africa: Perspectives of development, security and the environment. Lanhan, MD: Lexington Books.

Tar, U. A. (2017b). Conclusion: The prospects of globalisation in Africa. In: U. A. Tar, B. E. Mijah, & M. E. U. Tedheke (Eds.), Globalisation in Africa: Perspectives of development, security and the environment. Lanhan, MD: Lexington Books.

Tar, U. A. (2019). Dynamics of interagency collaboration in Nigeria: Towards synergy in National Defence and Security. *NARC Journal* (Publication of Nigeria Army Resource Centre), 2(1) (September), 1–20.

Von Hippel, K. (2007). Responding to the roots of terror. In: Magnus Ranstorp (Ed.), *Mapping terrorism research: State of the art, gaps and future direction* (pp 94–105). Abingdon, Oxon: Routledge.

Yusuf, I. M. (2019). Wining hearts and minds in counterinsurgency operations: Operation LAFIYA DOLE in perspective. *NARC Journal* (Publication of Nigeria Army Resource Centre) *2*(1) (September), 21–46.

# 2

# Exploring the concept of terrorism: the morphology of organised violence

*Kenneth Omeje*

## Introduction

As terrorist activities increase in breadth and intensity, the Global War on Terror (GWOT) gathers momentum, the meaning of terrorism tends to be increasingly polemical and pejorative. The connotation of terrorism in contemporary international politics is essentially "polemical" because the post-9/11 global war on terror and the views of its proponents seem to have markedly narrowed the meaning of terrorism to "international Islamist Jihad", culminating in a deepening "civilisational warfare" between the west and the Islamic world. On the other hand, the meaning of terrorism is somewhat "pejorative" because of the pervasive invocation of the ideological cliché by many antagonists of the concept that "one man's terrorism is another man's freedom fighter", which from all intents and purposes, make terrorism seemingly neb-ulous. This chapter critically explores the concept of terrorism from different intellectual perspectives, its meaning, and definitional connotations. The discursive merits and limitations of the various perspectives are analysed as a basis for attempting a systematic reconception aimed at strengthening the explanatory power of the concept.

At the early stages of the US government-led Global War on Terror in the aftermath of the 11th September 2001 terrorist attack in the US, I was privileged to participate in a major US government foreign policy event dominated by discussions of President George W. Bush's (Jr) global war on terror. This event was the February 2004 Senior Leaders Seminar at Washington DC hosted by the Africa Centre for Strategic Studies (ACSS), which is part of the US National Defence University, an affiliate of the Pentagon. The two-week seminar brought together 98 senior military officers, top government officials, and civil society leaders from 43 African countries to discuss security issues in Africa (ACSS, 2004:1). Many high profile speakers graced the occasion including Paula Dobriansky, the US Under-Secretary of State for Global Affairs at the time, and Paul Wolfowitz, an ex-US Deputy Secretary of Defence and then World Bank President. Even though this African foreign policy event was called a "Seminar" (a title ap-parently used as an innocuous euphemism), from its actual design, driving objectives, content, and delivery, however, the programme was framed as an African foreign policy re-development and re-training workshop, designed to ideologically mainstream Africa into the US-led global war on terror. It was an exclusive workshop convened to restructure African foreign policies in the image and likeness of the US government's unfolding agenda of global war on terror. Participants were carefully selected from various targeted institutions and government departments and consequently vetted for approval by the US host institution. The Seminar was extraordinarily generous and flamboyant, all expenses fully paid by the US government. Participants were given a guided tour of the US Foreign and Defence policy establishment in Washington, as well as the 9/11 victims' memorial in the Pentagon. The rationale was to induct participants to the strategic processes of formulating and implementing US foreign/defence policies and to also incense us to the horror of international terrorism. Conscientious efforts were made by the American foreign policy think tank in the two-week "Seminar" to justify the US-led global war on terror and more importantly to sell to the African participants the dominant US discourses on terrorism, including the correlated counterterrorism agenda. In their responses, most African participants were of the view that the US-led global war on terror was informed by the worldwide security interest of the west, especially the United States, and that most African countries have their own more pressing security threats, notably the motley of local insurgencies and civil militia activities that menaced national security and state sovereignty. Even though the African representatives in this Seminar were reluctant about the global war on terror, it did not prevent many African governments from quickly embracing the campaign by reason of the preponderant influence of the US government.

Fast-forward to 2019, many African countries certainly have more compelling practical reasons for counterterrorism and counterinsurgency operations, not necessarily the American version of the war on terror. Why and how are the various African governments securitising terrorism? It suffices to say that the American-led Global War on Terror is primarily aimed at actual and potential threats against the sprawling interests of the US and the west globally, including externally-originated threats capable of being exported or transmitted into the west. Interestingly, foreign and defence policy agendas of the US and the west are always preceded and driven by the robust discourses and theories of their foreign and defence policy intelligentsia. The interests they serve are invariably those of the hegemonic forces controlling the state apparatuses, key home-grown transnational business corporations, and "the military-industrial complex" (Schlosberg, 2017:1). It is the interests of this hegemonic governing coalition in foreign and defence policies that the state often articulates and rationalises as "national interests."

African governments will be doing a great disservice to their people and infraction to their "national interests" if the primary reason for adopting and implementing counterterrorism measures is to backstop the US-led war on terror. At a more academic level, it is apparent that the US anti-terror policies and their underlying intellectual justifications are theories and philosophies that tend to circumscribe and limit the meaning of terrorism to serve the contemporary ideological interest of the west to the disadvantage of the developing world. Many African states have to securitise the war against terrorism, making themselves stakeholders of an externally driven enterprise in which their interests are mostly marginal and incidental. Similarly, the concept of terrorism has been hijacked and re-defined by western right-wing intellectuals serving the interest of the global war on terror. If African states are to securitise the war on terror, it is only fitting that African intellectuals should contest the meaning of terrorism with a view of sufficiently liberating the concept and expanding its definition and scope to accommodate the interests and reality of their people and governments.

An expanded and more inclusive definition of terrorism is considered vital for both intellectual and practical purposes. At the very least, it will help to advance the status of knowledge in the field and also to appropriately refocus any meaningful anti-terrorist campaigns in local, regional, and international systems in a much more legitimate, proactive, and sustainable way. There are diverse theories and perspectives in the conceptualisation of terrorism. These intellectual viewpoints are, strictly speaking, not mutually exclusive. However, for analytical convenience, I have tried to make a theoretical distinction between them. Some of the more crucial perspectives are explored below.

## Socio-psychological conceptions

Classical sociological and psychological theories of deviance, crime, and violence have been the basis for some of the earliest attempts to conceptualise terrorism. These theories have triggered a related chain of multiple-level causation, basically centring on social structures (for most sociologists) and identifiable personality traits (for most psychologists). Scholars like Gurr (1975), Hamilton (1979), Horowitz (1983), Crenshaw (1985), and Lindner (2001) have constructed different theories attributing terrorism or violence in general to [structures of] misery and oppression, humiliation and despair, poverty and exploitation, relative deprivation and frustration, as well as to idle and radical intellectualism (comparatively deemed to have different structural content) in society.

Other exponents of this paradigm go as far as propounding purpose-based typologies of terrorism or constructing a behavioural profile of different categories of terrorists under the assumption that based on their bio-sociological backgrounds some individuals possibly have a 'terrorist personality', a profile analogous to the 'authoritarian personality' found in the literature on political violence (Schmid and Jongman et al., 1988:50–51, 87–96).

Without bothering to chronicle the diverse definitions of terrorism immanent from socio-psychological theories – definitions that apparently no longer exert tremendous weight and influence in contemporary terrorist literature – it suffices to state that issues such as "misery, frustration, grievances, and despair" which exponents argue "lead to terrorism have many roots in international and national political, economic, and social situations affecting the terrorists…" (Schmid and Jongman et al., 1988:63). The latter (root causes) should therefore constitute a more fundamental basis for theorisation than the former (effects). Consequently, the search for a terrorist personality has largely been fruitless and the methodology frequently adopted in the search amounts to crude empiricism. Essentially, the inner motivations of terrorists, as well as "the precise chain of causation of particular acts, cannot be traced with scientific exactitude" (Schmid and Jongman et al., 1988:63). More significantly perhaps, the disposition to terrorism, from all indications, cannot be said to be a permanent human complex and there are no empirical guarantees that some non-terrorists or "normal persons" may not broadly share the key sociological and psychological characteristics of terrorists.

## Legal conceptions of terrorism

Some of the earliest efforts to define terrorism were made from legal perspectives, especially criminal [municipal] law and public international law as the following discussion demonstrates. Moreover, legal conceptions of terrorism have continued to resonate in contemporary policy circles. The first bold and coherent attempt to define terrorism was made by the League of Nations in 1937 through its Draft Convention for the Prevention and Punishment of Terrorism. Although it never came into force, the Convention broadly defined terrorism as "criminal acts directed against a state and intended to or calculated to create a state terror in the minds of particular persons, or group of persons, or the general public" (see UNODCCP, 2001). In the League's definition, the state was conceived as the sole victim or target of terrorism. The Convention was not categorical on the possible mastermind or perpetrator of terrorism but political events contemporaneous to the time, such as the assassinations of a number of European monarchs and diplomats, suggest that radical subnational groups (non-state actors) were the likely unpronounced perpetrators. Some scholars have actually tried to re-inforce to definitional linking of terrorism to violence perpetrated by non-state actors by introducing the Weberian notion of the "legitimate" and "illegitimate use of force" to the conception of terrorism, the "legitimate use of force" corresponding to state actors and the "illegitimate" referring to use of violence by non-state actors (see Jackson and Sinclair, 2012:57). This distinction is, however, not sustainable because of well-documented accounts of state-sponsored terror perpetrated by some of the world's most noted dictators of the last one hundred years, including leaders like Adolf Hitler in German, Josef Stalin in the defunct USSR, Idi Amin in Uganda, and General Pinochet in Chile.

The events of World War II and the mechanisms employed by states in the bi-polar rivalry that followed the war led to the recognition of the state as a key sponsor of terrorism. Introducing the concept of state sponsorship and canvassing for its criminalisation, the United Nations International Law Commission in its 1954 Draft Code of Offences Against the Peace and Security of Mankind defined state-sponsored terrorism as "the undertaking or encouragement by the authorities of a state, or the toleration by the authorities of a state of organised activities calculated to carry out terrorist acts in another state".[1]

In what appears to be the most generic definition ever contemplated, the UN General Assembly adopted a resolution on 9 December 1985 in which it loosely defined [or apparently described] terrorism as "acts which endanger or take innocent human lives, jeopardise fundamental freedoms, and seriously impair the dignity of human beings".[2] This definition basically characterises some effects that tend to be common (but are by no means limited) to terrorist actions.

Without resolving the question of definition, the UN and its specialised agencies have hitherto adopted a variety of treaty provisions on specific aspects of international terrorism, such as conventions aimed at suppressing aircraft hijacking, unlawful acts against the safety of civilian aviation or of airports serving international aviation, unlawful acts against internationally protected persons including diplomatic agents, taking of hostages, theft of nuclear materials, and unlawful acts against the safety of maritime navigation.[3]

At the regional levels, the European Union, Organisation of American States (OAS), Africa Union (AU), South Asian Association for Regional Cooperation (SAARC), the Commonwealth of Independent States, the League of Arab States, and the Organisation of the Islamic Conference (OIC) have all adopted different conventions aimed to combat aspects of terrorism most prevalent in their regions, without expending considerable amounts of energy to proffer a broad-based and inclusive definition of terrorism or of international terrorism, which tends to be the primary concern of some of the organisations.[4]

At the national level, the approaches of most states to terrorism are as equivocal as it proves at the international level. States basically employ the term terrorism to serve their conveniences and interests, often without bothering to provide a definition of the concept. Even where definitions are attempted or anti-terrorist legislations are adopted, the underlying purposes are usually restricted to helping individual states prosecute or solve some terrorist-related problems peculiar to them. Typical examples of some crucial legislative frameworks pre-9/11 include the Republic of Ireland and the UK anti-terrorist legislations directed primarily at the situation in Northern Ireland; the Indian and Pakistani anti-terrorist legislations directed mainly at radical ethnoreligious minority cults and the situation in Kashmir; Australia's and New Zealand's anti-terrorist statutes aimed primarily at de-hospitalising their countries as safe havens for expatriate war criminals and terrorists (Mickolus, 1980; Murphy, 1989).[5]

In the post-9/11 era, the trend has not become radically different. A number of developed countries and major state parties to the International Covenant on the Elimination of All Forms of Racial Discrimination (ICERD), such as the UK, USA, Canada, and Germany, have adopted legislations within the framework of their fight against international terrorism, which provide the impetus for prolonged detention and profiling of suspected terrorists in utter breach of the ICERD. The UK Anti-Terrorism Act 2001 and 2006 and the US Patriot Act 2001 clearly enable the state authorities to detain, for a long or indefinite period, non-nationals without charge, on mere suspicion of them having participated in terrorist activities or having links with terrorist groups (see FIDH, 2002; Hill, 2017). Based on an *a priori* or vague definition of a terrorist as "someone linked to or holding membership of a terrorist group", legal instruments such as the above have been persistently used for ethnic profiling and prolonged incarceration without trials of many young Muslims in the Cuban Island maximum-security prison of Guantanamo Bar by the US government on suspicion of terrorist linkages (see CNN, 2017; FIDH, 2004). The American State Department maintains a constantly reviewed and updated list of most wanted terrorists, terrorist organisations, and state sponsors of terrorism for purposes of travel advice to its citizens and application of various sanctions. A number of developing countries believed to be soft-underbellies of international or home-grown terrorism, such as Algeria, Kenya, Nigeria, Mali, and Uganda have also adopted anti-terrorism legislations and practices.

In many developing countries of Africa and Latin America where typical terrorist activities like the hijacking of aircrafts, kidnappings, assassinations, suicide bombing, or use of explosives have a relatively shorter history, it is common practice to prosecute acts of this nature under applicable criminal codes in the absence of any anti-terrorist legislations. In general, many developing countries are reluctant to invoke international anti-terrorist conventions they have acceded to in, for instance, dealing with suspected cases of international terrorism.

At another level, it is pertinent to observe that perhaps more than any other state in modern international history, the US government has contributed most to the fight against terrorism and the attempts to define the phenomenon. At least ten different US Government Departments and Agencies have over the years proffered different definitions of terrorism (see Schmid and Jongman et al., 1988:32–33; Schmid and Jongman, 2005). Among the different definitions proffered by the American government Departments, the most influential one tends to be the definition contained in Title 22 (Section 265f[d]) of the United States Criminal Code and one that the American government has enforced since 1983. According to the statute(see also Sterba and French, 2003:140):[6]

- The term terrorism means premeditated, politically motivated violence perpetrated against 'non-combatant' targets by subnational groups or clandestine agents, usually intended to influence an audience
- The term international terrorism means terrorism involving citizens or the territory of more than one country
- The term terrorist group means any group practising, or that has significant subgroups that practise international terrorism

"For purpose of this definition", the Statute further illustrates, "the term non-combatant is interpreted to include, in addition to civilians, [the] military personnel who at the time of the incident are unarmed and/or not on duty".[7] In an amended version of its November 2002 definition promulgated on 31st January 2011, the US Department of Defence defined terrorism as "the unlawful use of violence or threat of violence to instill fear and coerce governments or societies.

Terrorism is often motivated by religious, political, or other ideological beliefs and committed in the pursuit of goals that are usually political" (Clark, 2017:81). Boaz Ganor has provided a well-informed critique of the US government's definitions in his articles reviewed below (see the section on "The Boaz Ganor Re-conception").

In general, even though studies and legislations based on the legal perspective have made enormous contributions to the evolution of the study of terrorism, there are at least two major drawbacks associated with the approach. The first is that its conceptions of terrorism are largely problem-specific and, to that extent, limited to the strategic persuasions of the definers. This problem is partly related to the penal character and instrumentality of law itself, which usually gives leverage to the hegemonic group or dominant political classes in society to often foist their normative standards on the legal system with the authoritative backing of state power. In other words, defining terrorism almost solely as a means to enforce legal prosecution, as important as the latter is, will invariably reproduce the material/strategic interests and particularistic view-point of the more powerful in society, some time to the detriment, disaffection, and resentment of the less powerful opponents and subalterns. This phenomenon is apparent in both the local and international systems, not least in the post-9/11 discourses of terrorism and the global war on terror.

Most cases of terrorism, among other things, occur because of people's disillusionment with the institutionalised legal and political frameworks of goal attainment in society. Thus, defining terrorism almost exclusively as a means to enforce legal prosecution within the context of a politico-legal regime perceived to be unjust or to be incapable of rendering justice by a section of the society that resorts to terrorist violence tantamounts to recycling the definitional imbroglio.

The second drawback, which has been elaborated in the section dealing with the expanded definition of terrorism is that, because of their western social and epistemological orientation, most definitions captured under the rubric of the legal framework are substantially limited in scope and therefore do not accommodate a great deal of the representations of the phenomenon in different parts of the world, especially in the developing countries.

## Terrorism as defined in a political context

Different scholars and security experts have tried to define terrorism within a more or less extra-legal context, notably the context of politics. Schmid and Jongman et al. (1988:5–6) in their *magnum opus, Political Terrorism,* have cited and analysed some 109 different definitions of terrorism, which they obtained from an empirical survey of noted pundits in the field. Following their survey of definitions, the authors made at least two significant findings that are relevant to the conceptualisation of terrorism. The first is that they extrapolated some recurring empirical indicators of terrorism arranged in the order they statistically appear in the definitions proposed by respondents. These include *inter alia*:

Second, the authors outlined some crucial issues, which, in the opinion of respondents, remain unresolved in the definition of terrorism. Notable among these issues, some of which have been raised by previous scholars or more emphatically reinforced by subsequent researchers can be paraphrased as follows (cf. Hermon, 2000; Murphy, 1989; Netanyahu, 1986).

i. The boundary between terrorism and other forms of [political] violence.
ii. Distinguishing terrorism from closely related incidents, such as ordinary criminal acts, guerrilla warfare, and war of national liberation, the open war between irreconcilable parties or groups and violent actions resulting from mental illness.

*Table 2.1* Empirical Indicators of Terrorism

| Empirical Indicators of Terrorism | % of Appearance in the Definitions |
| --- | --- |
| Violence, force | 83.5 |
| Political | 65 |
| Fear (emphasis on terror) | 51 |
| Threats | 47 |
| Psychological effects and anticipated reactions | 41.5 |
| Victims – target differentiation | 37.5 |
| Purposive, planned, systematic, organised action | 32 |
| Methods of combat, strategy, tactics | 30.5 |

Source: Schmid and Jongman et al. (1988:29–31).

iii. Whether state terrorism and resistance (anti-state) terrorism are part of the same phenomenon.
iv. Is terrorism a sub-category of coercion?
v. Could terrorism be legitimate and (if so) under what conditions?

Finally, Schmid and Jongman et al. (1988:28) articulated a thoughtful definition of terrorism, stating that:

> Terrorism is an anxiety-inspiring method of repeated violent action, employed by (semi-) clandestine individual, group or state actors, for idiosyncratic, criminal or political reasons, whereby – in contrast to assassination – the direct targets of violence are not the main targets. The immediate human victims of violence are generally chosen randomly (targets of opportunity) or selectively (representative or symbolic targets) from a target population, and serve as message generators. Threat- and violence-based communication processes between terrorist (organisation), (imperilled) victims, and main targets are used to manipulate the main target (audience[s]), turning it into a target of terror, a target of demands, or a target of attention, depending on whether intimidation, coercion, or propaganda is primarily sought.

Undoubtedly, the issues raised in the study by Schmid and Jongman et al. are a useful point of departure in comprehending terrorism. The distinction they make between targets and victims of terrorism in their definition is a useful one, though it will be hard to concede to their view that terrorism is partly carried out "for idiosyncratic and criminal reasons". Accepting such a sweeping assumption would certainly make it difficult if not impossible to distinguish terrorism from ordinary civil crime, such as armed robbery, arson, and rape. If terrorists indulge in armed robbery, arson, and rape in the course of their violent campaign as many have occasionally done, these civil crimes, as heinous as they are, are usually not the primary motivation or goal of the terrorist campaign and thus should not be misrepresented as such. It is also important to emphasise that in circumstances where members of an aggrieved group hold strong perceptions or feelings of deprivations, alienation, and persecution or have been exposed to such a traumatic fate, a derivative terrorist movement has a great propensity of producing heinous bandwagon externalities against the targeted audience, including armed robbery, arson, looting, and rape.

Clearly, of all the aforementioned questions raised by Schmid and Jongman et al., the most critically recurrent in extant literature tends to be the problem of distinguishing terrorism from guerrilla warfare and war of national liberation. Whilst terrorism practically evokes a negative image, guerrilla warfare and war of national liberation tend to attract considerable solidarity and sympathy in the international community. As such, most militant subnational groups engaged in violent campaigns for whatever reasons would, at any rate, define themselves or prefer to be defined as a guerrilla movement (or perhaps more legitimately, freedom fighters) carrying out a war (or more palatably a campaign or protest) of national liberation or probably, of national self-determination.

In an attempt to distinguish terrorism from the war of national liberation or freedom fight, Benzion Netanyahu (1986:27) argues *inter alia*:

> For in contrast to the terrorist, no freedom fighter has deliberately attacked innocents. He has never deliberately killed small children, or passers-by in the streets, or foreign visitors, or other civilians who happen to reside in the area of conflict or are merely associated ethically or religiously with the people of that area ... Consequently, no freedom fighter could stand for violations of man's rights, let alone perpetrate them himself... Yet that is precisely what the terrorist does – and in the most brazen and brutal manner.

Benjamin Netanyahu, the Israeli Prime Minister, and a noted counterterrorism strategist, based his initial definition of terrorism on the above assumption that terrorists do not aim at the "innocents". In Netanyahu's definition (1986:9), "terrorism is the deliberate and systematic murder, maiming and menacing of the innocent to inspire fear for political ends". The renowned Prime Minister in his later publication was to replace the term "the innocent" with another term, "civilians", and revised his definition of terrorism as "the deliberate and systematic assault on civilians to inspire fear for political ends" (1995:8). Although Benjamin Netanyahu's second definition tends to be an improvement on the first in the sense that the term "the innocent" is a more elusive or manipulatable category, the definition is still not inclusive enough to, for instance, capture terrorist attacks on non-human targets. Second, the change in political discourse represented by the re-conception tends to mask an ideological value supportive of state terrorism in the sense that it makes the Israeli state able to define Palestinian attacks on the Jewish settlers in the West Bank as a terrorist attack. However, it is arguable whether civilians that are part of a political project, such as the identification of the Jewish settlers in West Bank, Gaza, and other Palestinian enclaves with the Zionist expansionist project, are "innocents". Many critics would argue to the contrary.

Terrorism is widely recognised by most pundits who espouse different political perspectives as a type of political violence. Wilkinson (1996; 2001), a noted expert, for instance, defines terrorism as "a special kind of political violence designed to create a climate of fear among a wide target group than the immediate victims, usually for political ends". The characteristic objectives of terrorism, writes the author, include: massive and immediate publicity as a result of outrage or a series of atrocities; to inspire followers and sympathisers to further acts of terrorism or insurrection; to provoke the authorities into a repressive over-reaction, which the terrorists can then exploit to their political advantages (Wilkinson, 1996; 2001). Suffice it to simply observe that Wilkinson's definition or conception is overly elitist and construes terrorism as a mere act of violence by a group of subalterns intent on provoking those in authorities. In addition and contrary to historical evidence, the author presumes that states and those in authority do not practice or abet terrorism.

## The Boaz Ganor re-conception

One of the most outstanding contributions to the conceptualisation of terrorism in contemporary time has come from the diverse works of Professor Boaz Ganor, Founder and

23

Director of the International Policy Institute for CounterTerrorism in Herzliya, Israel. Even though Ganor's works are not published in leading western journals or by the big publishing houses in the West, his works are still considered highly significant for at least two reasons. Firstly, they coalesce some of the finest arguments dotting the literature on political violence, with the author further rethinking and weaving them into a persuasive analytical framework. Secondly, given the highly strategic position occupied by the author by virtue of the famous Policy Institute he directs in the Middle East (a region most noted for terrorism) his views on terrorism have greatly found expression among Israeli statesmen, government, and security think-tank, and among a significant cluster of the American and western counterterrorism intelligentsia.[8] Ganor (2001a:1; 2007) expounds a theory of terrorism deduced from accepted international law and principles regarding what behaviours are permitted in conventional wars between states. According to the author, these laws are set out in the Geneva and Hague Conventions, which in turn are based upon the basic principle that the deliberate harming of soldiers during wartime is a necessary evil, and thus permissible, whereas the deliberate targeting of civilians is absolutely forbidden (Ganor, 2001a:1; 2010). He further observes that "according to the international Conventions, any deliberate attack upon civilians in wartime by regular military forces ("the state" – *my emphasis*) is already defined as a war crime; should such an attack be carried out in peacetime, the act is defined by Convention as "crime against humanity" (Ganor, 2001a:2). Since the deliberate use of violence on civilians in both war and peace times by the state has been sufficiently criminalised in international law as war crime and crime against humanity respectively, Ganor refrains from applying the term terrorism to acts of violence perpetrated by the state. In his words, the term "terrorism is superfluous when describing the actions of sovereign states ..." (Ganor, 2001a:2). Hence, he considers the term to be more appropriate in describing a conflict between a non-state organisation and a state.

There is the need to emphasise that the idea of rescuing the term terrorism or deriving a theory of it from such a phenomenon as "war crime" cannot be originally credited to Ganor. Terrorism expert, A. Schmid, earlier in his 1992 Report to the Vienna-based UN Terrorism Prevention Branch canvassed the viewpoint that the existing consensus on what constitutes a war crime should be adopted as a point of departure in defining terrorism (see UNODCCP, 2001). According to Schmid, if the core of war crimes – deliberate attacks on civilians, hostage-taking and the killing of prisoners – is extended to peacetime, we could simply define acts of terrorism as "peacetime equivalents of war crimes" (UNODCCP, 2001).

Having said that, Ganor (2001b:6; 2010) proposes a distinction between guerrilla warfare and terrorism based on the international law-informed distinction he makes between military and civilian targets. The author inveighs the US State Department's definitional hinging of terrorism on "the deliberate use of violence against non-combatants, whether civilians or military personnel", arguing that terror groups cannot only be expected to attack battle-commissioned and ready forces, otherwise "they would lose the element of surprise and be quickly defeated" (2001a:3). This will be practically unacceptable to terrorist organisations, he reasoned. Ganor (1999:2; 2001b:6; 2010) finally proposes a persuasive definition of terrorism for the international community, defining the term as "the intentional use of, or threat to use of violence against civilians or against civilian targets, in order to attain political aims." Ganor has applied the above definition and conceptual framework in analysing diverse contemporary developments in the politics of terrorism.[9]

## A response to Ganor

Undoubtedly, Ganor has made a significant contribution to the construction of a theory of terrorism. He tries to build a useful bridge between the legal and political perspectives by anchoring his theory on accepted international law principles relating to the permissible behaviour of states in wartime. Nevertheless, the author's theory subsumes a number of unsustainable arguments and contradictory logic.

Firstly, Ganor's attempt to make a differentiation between military and civilian targets in his conception of terrorism raises serious conceptual and practical difficulties. A similar difficulty is raised by the author's attempt to distinguish guerrilla warfare and terrorism based on targets chosen by the perpetrators, namely military targets (in guerrilla warfare) and civilian targets (in terrorism). These distinctions blur more than they try to explain. Terrorist targets and activities are much more complex than the simplistic straitjackets that Ganor's taxonomy attempts to create. Both terrorism and guerrilla warfare are rather two complexes, interconnected, and highly dynamic processes that are not mutually exclusive. In other words, whereas the two phenomena might have certain peculiar characteristics, they do share many commonalities, especially in terms of chosen targets and mode of activity. Depending on the specific geopolitical circumstances, both terrorism and guerrilla warfare could be a goal-attainment, violence-inclined strategy in political struggles, widely applied by "terrorist movements", local insurgencies, national liberation movements, or freedom fighters. Some of these groups are also often bound by an extremist ideology. As a goal-attainment, violence-inclined strategy, however, the elements of non-conventional armed struggle and surprise attacks are the core defining characteristics of guerrilla operations (Guevara, 1998), and contemporary terrorist groups are increasingly taking these tactics on board. Similar to guerrilla warfare, terrorism is a tactic often (but not exclusively) devised by the weak in the game of asymmetrical warfare. Both terrorism and guerrilla warfare are in this respect the strategic devices and tactics of the weak. In the context of globalisation and the use of advanced technologies such as the Internet to facilitate and spread the specific brands of terrorist ideology on a worldwide scale, international terrorism could be aptly described as a global form of guerrilla warfare.

It is remarkable that some groups originally described as terrorist movements do, in the course of their struggles, undergo strategic mutations to acquire necessary international legitimacy to become redefined as national liberation or progressive movements or even to be transformed into political parties. Examples include the Palestinian Liberation Organisation (PLO) in Palestine, and Sinn Fein, the traditional republican movement in Northern Ireland that have been respectively reinvented as a national liberation movement and a political party. In the light of these complex interconnections, it will seem illogical to base the existence or definition of either terrorism or guerrilla warfare on the occlusion or total absence of the other.

To further illustrate the nature of the confusion inherent in Ganor's attempt to define terrorism based on the aforementioned conceptual distinctions, it is worthwhile to outline some of his views (2001b:6):

> As noted, terrorism is "a violent struggle intentionally using, or threatening to use, violence against civilians, in order to attain political aims", whereas guerrilla warfare is "a violent struggle using (or threatening to use) violence against military targets, security forces, and the political leadership, in order to attain political aims." Terrorism is thus different from guerrilla warfare in the mode of activity and in the target chosen by the operators.

Based on conventional practice, it is adequate to say that intentional use or threat to use violent attacks on either civilian or military targets are sometimes alternative or simultaneous expressions of a common cause, either related to terrorism or to guerrilla warfare. Typical examples of this abound from the activities of some of the groups more obviously described as terrorist organisations, such as the ELN and FARC in Colombia, Jamaah Islamiyah in Indonesia, al-Gama at al-Islamiyyah in Egypt, Al-Qaida and GIA (Armed Islamic Group) in Algeria, as well as from those guerrilla warfare-oriented freedom fighters like the Kongra-Gel (Kurdish PKK) and the pre-independence Frelimo and Renamo in Mozambique.

A simple examination of the 11 September 2001 (9/11) incident in the US in which some Al-Qaida suicide terrorists crashed four hijacked planes will help to bolster the critique. In the 9/11 incident, two of the hijacked planes were intentionally crashed into the New York World Trade Centre, an undeniably civilian target, which, following Ganor's definition, amounts to terrorism. The third hijacked aircraft was intentionally crashed into Pentagon, an arguably military target, which, following Ganor's definition, would amount to guerrilla warfare. The fourth aircraft, which never reached its target crash-landed in a field in Pennsylvania and this renders its classification rather more problematic. However, the four flights were passenger aircraft with scores of civilians on board whose lives were lost in the dastardly incidents, albeit there is an implicit supposition based on the nature of terrorism itself, that the passengers were not the primary targets. The aircraft could have been non-passenger or non-civilian aircraft, such as in the 1941 Pearl Harbour incident,[10] in which case the apparent conceptual confusion between terrorism and guerrilla warfare in an incident generally believed to be a terrorist onslaught would have become even more pronounced.

By corollary, Ganor's dismissal of the concept of "non-combatant" introduced by the US State Department in its definition of terrorism may not be defensibly rationalised. Deliberate use of violence on non-combatants, such as in the case of the security personnel and top government functionary victims of the 9/11 Pentagon suicide terrorist attack can be nothing short of terrorism. But if in a state of war, non-combatants of the military establishment, such as unarmed or gallivanting soldiers are suddenly attacked, the latter can hardly pass as terrorism as both predictable and surprise attacks on military targets are generally acceptable strategies of war. Hence, although there is a lack of consensus among experts on what constitutes a military target, it is my supposition that military targets should broadly include such disputed defence-related categories as non-combatants of the military establishment, military installations in non-residential areas, and defence headquarters. This is ostensibly a critical conceptual clarification lacking in the US State Department's definition.

Furthermore, Ganor's exoneration of sovereign states from charges of terrorism on the grounds that existing international law amply covers their terrorism-related offences under Conventions on War Crime and Crime Against Humanity is, to say the least, a misnomer. This position will not only obstruct the anti-terrorist stride historically made by the international community but will also make a nonsense of any future international campaign to fight terrorism. The international community has since the 1950s recognised the state as a major perpetrator of terrorism under the concept of "state support and state sponsorship" (cf. Murphy, 1989: 31–43; Quillen, 2000). A great deal of Cold War terrorism in a number of West European countries, including the indiscriminate bombings in Italy between the late 1960s and mid-1980s, which at the time were believed to be the works of right-wing and anti-state terrorist groups, were masterminded by American intelligence services and NATO in collaboration with the local security services (Ganser, 2005). According to Ganser's recent exposition, the reason was to counter the increasing strength of the Italian Communist and Socialist parties, both of which were tasked with weakening NATO from within. Hence, those bombings and massacres, which remain unpunished, because the state cannot convict itself or declare itself responsible for what happened, were supposed to force the Italian public, to turn to the state to ask for greater security (Ganser, 2005).

For clarity, terrorism, unlike war crime, is scarcely associated with a state of mutually consenting or prosecuted war. Crime against humanity, which as Ganor rightly observed, mostly occurs in peacetime, is technically different from terrorism in the sense that it is characteristically linked to organised pogrom and brutality carried out against a population or section(s) of it, usually at a scale that ordinarily could have hardly been possible without the instrumentality or complicity of the state. State support and state sponsorship of terrorism, on the other hand, involves a variety of activities ranging from state terrorism (direct active involvement using personnel and intelligence operatives), direct support (e.g. financial, rhetorical), indirect support (e.g. intelligence, manpower training), diplomatic assets, provision of weapons and explosives, logistic support, territorial hospitality, tacit support or deliberate inaction (foreknowledge of impending terrorist attacks and failure to act), and non-conventional support in high-technology (nuclear, biological, and chemical weapons) (cf. Murphy, 1989:31–43; Quillen, 2000). The above examples of forms of state involvement in terrorism have very little or nothing to do with crimes against humanity.

## Expanding the definition of terrorism

The task of expanding the definition of terrorism is lightened by the preceding analysis of some of the prevalent conceptions and perhaps misconceptions of the phenomenon. Terrorism, as already emphasised above, is both an ideology-bound extremist campaign and a goal-attainment, violence-inclined strategy in political struggles. As a political campaign or movement, terrorism is informed by an extremist ideology and is also goal-oriented, regardless of how irrational, clumsy, and illegitimate the goal might seem to the opponent or to the outsider in general. Fundamentally, the goal or aim of terrorism usually hinges on strong disapproval of some perceived actions, intentions, policies, or inactions of an opponent (not necessarily the target or victim of an attack), and/or to compel the latter to act in some desired manner. The nature of the goal is more or less political in the sense that it is directly or indirectly related to "the agenda of real, *perceived,* or discursive power relations in society" (see Crotty, 1996:204–205). In both theory and practice, the political content of terrorism enables the phenomenon to be more easily distinguished from ordinary criminal acts of violence and from violent actions resulting from a mental abnormality.

As a strategy, terrorism basically relies on the use of unstinted methods of violence or threat of violence in expressing grievances or pressing a claim, regardless of how conceivably absurd or irrational the claim might be deemed to be. The application of violence in terrorism is quite often without proportionality to any established grievances, especially given the fact that the victims of terrorist attacks are not always the core or relevant adversaries. Although terrorism occurs within a wide extent of political struggles, it is important to recognise the peculiar circumstances under which the phenomenon takes place. Terrorism literally occurs in all circumstances short of a mutually declared or a mutually prosecuted war, which may include, in a tense situation, low-intensity conflict situation, or in a state of a unilateral declaration of war. In theory, all these circumstances can still be described as peacetime. In other words, charges of terrorism can hardly be sustained under conditions of openly prosecuted or mutually consenting war between disputant parties even though insurgency campaign by some alleged terrorists such as the Islamic State in Iraq and Syria (ISIS) or Al Qaeda in the Islamic Maghreb (AQIM) in northern Mali could interplay with other forces to precipitate or aggravate a war situation.

Where the activities of some alleged terrorists who are motivated by the allure of state power and its related political demands conspire to precipitate or aggravate a war situation, we are probably no longer dealing with incidents of terrorism but a case or rebel insurrection and political insurgency. Should the same group such as AQIM be unbanned and join the political process in Algeria by putting up candidates for national elections, then we are dealing with a political party as opposed to what has always been perceived and described as a terrorist group. In other words, the focus of analysis should not be so much on the known or perceived designation of a group but on the established pattern of activity it pursues at any given conjuncture. This observation keeps terrorism away from obverting war situations and makes the distinction between terrorism and a war crime, for instance (which is associated with a state of war), more feasible.

Consequently, terrorism is usually an intentional and premeditated act whilst its targets are wide-ranging, excluding perhaps only active combatants (e.g. soldiers in the battlefront or those simply commissioned for a designated military operation) and including, among others, civilians, non-combatant servicemen, military installations and sites, civilian targets and economic investments. Another important dimension of terrorism often overlooked in mainstream literature is the ideological dimension and influence which makes terrorism to be not just a group membership phenomenon but also an individual fantasy. At the ideological level, terrorism is spread, propelled, and reproduced by the power of incitement, propaganda, and indoctrination, which is inadvertently contrived to appeal to one's inner spiritual, psychological, and political self. The ideological dimension of terrorism, which in the contemporary global setting has been particularly enabled and globalised by the help of the Internet is important for understanding why there is a growing number of self-radicalised young Islamist adults in the west who arm themselves with home-made bombs or machete and embark on a solo or joint spread of violent attacks in the streets of London, Manchester, Paris, and Brussels. Similarly, it is this ideological dimension of terrorism that partly accounts for why many self-radicalised young Islamists who were born, raised, and educated in the comfort of modern western societies would embark on the seemingly "suicide mission" of travelling to Syria and Iraq to fight on the side of ISIS or to be married off to ISIS fighters in the case of the radicalised young women. The profile of many of these pro-terrorism voluntarists, as well as other masterminds of terrorist attacks in various Western countries clearly suggest that poverty, illiteracy, and socio-economic deprivation have no practical correlation with radicalisation and the tendency to carry out terrorist assaults as is often contemplated in public discourses. Virtually all the terrorist attacks carried out in the West have been executed by voluntarists of middle-class backgrounds most of whom have a good level of education. Further, at the ideological level, many impressionable young teenage boys and girls have been recruited and brainwashed or conscripted and compelled by radical Islamist groups like Boko Haram in Nigeria and used to carry out a suicide bombing on congested civilian locations such as open markets, churches, and busy streets. Therefore, an acceptable definition of terrorism should be expansive enough to capture the ideological dimension of the phenomenon, among other key elements.

Having said that, terrorism can therefore be defined as the intentional use or threat to use violence against non-combatants (including civilians) and non-human targets in circumstances usually short of 'consenting war' in order to achieve the goal(s) that the attackers feel politically, socially, or spiritually convinced about or conscripted to serve. In terms of structure and content, terrorism has local, regional, and international dimensions, and it could be deployed in pursuit of courses that may bother historical struggles, national politics, religious antagonism, international politics, ethnocultural conflict, global political economy, and the likes.

After elucidating some of the key elements of this definition, it suffices at this juncture to stress that issues of global political economy are a major source of contemporary terrorist politics, which hitherto are largely glossed over by many analysts in their efforts to conceptualise and define terrorism. This is in spite of the growing number of local insurgencies and civil militias in various developing countries employing terrorist strategies (without necessarily turning into a full-blown "terrorist movements") in their various campaigns. Some of these campaigns bother on ethnic nationalism, irredentism, racism, religious fundamentalism, and anti-globalisation. A vicious externality of some of the more destructive campaigns is the growing predation and terrorising of local populations (i.e. extortion, rape, plunder, arson) by insurgents and militias leading to the debate about the primacy of greed versus grievance in local conflicts (see Collier and Hoefller, 2000). Hence, there is a varying range of dimensions of terrorism in some of local resource-based, ethnonational or religious insurgencies in countries like Colombia, Mexico, and Nigeria, which have apparently caused more deaths and economic devastation than the magnitude recorded in the 9/11 US incident. The real import of the observed domestic dimensions in some of the conflict-ridden developing countries is that alongside with ethnic nationalism, irredentism, racism, and religious fundamentalism, trends of globalisation, especially the dynamics of international political economy, play a significant role in both informing and defining the political contexts of contemporary terrorist activities. A more inclusive definition of terrorism should therefore be able to capture the unfolding local and international realities. Consequently, if terrorism, as argued in this chapter, is primarily (but not exclusively) a political phenomenon, a proactive and sustainable solution to it lies greatly in political re-engineering than in military reprisal, albeit the latter cannot be completely ruled out. Notable among the aspects of the proposed political re-engineering are constitutional and institutional reforms, democratisation and governance reforms, constructive engagement with states and communities where terrorism incubates, educational reforms, etc. In the end, the specific solutions to terrorism depend largely on the particular context and circumstance of the case concerned.

## Conclusion

Clearly, this chapter has placed more emphasis on the review and expansion of the definition of terrorism and not necessarily in the delineation of who is a terrorist and which organisation is a terrorist group, as important as these two factors might seemingly be. Whereas the definition of terrorism as an activity, ideology, or methodological device practiced or favoured by diverse individuals, groups, or states has substantial relevance as an analytical concept, the definition of who is a terrorist or which group is a terrorist organisation has a vein of ideological banality, notwithstanding the obvious examples of groups like Al Qaeda in the Islamic Maghreb (AQIM) and Boko Haram in the Lake Chad Basin, two outlawed groups that are notorious for their vicious campaign of terror. Am I endorsing or glossing over vicious groups that are almost universally acclaimed to be terrorist groups? By no means! States and inter-state organisations have established legal and political frameworks for dealing with outlawed clandestine, under-ground, and shadow entities (e.g. political associations, cultural organisations, educational in-stitutions, media organisations, business corporations, political insurgencies, etc.) whether or not they are inclined to terrorism. In other words, the so-called terrorist groups are just one among all other outlawed vicious organisations that modern states contend with, especially fragile post-colonial states in regions like Africa.

However, there is the need to be cautious about attributing some immutability and tran-sitivity to terrorist identity, organisations, and movements because such a definitional preoccupation can be, and has often been, arbitrarily employed as an instrument of discrimination, victimisation, and repression of vulnerable communities by some powerful forces in both the local and international systems. Consequently, it is a definitional predilection that tries to universalise, as a given, the discourses of terrorism held by some hegemonic forces in society (including in the international system), discourses that, at any rate, tend to limit and re-define terrorism.

## Notes

1 See UN Draft Convention for the Prevention and Punishment of Certain Acts of International Terrorism, UN Doc. A/2693, 1972. See also, Quillen (2000).

2 UN General Assembly Resolution 40/61, 40 UNGA Resolution Supplement (No. 53) 301, UN Doc. A/40/53, 1985.

3 See UN Treaty Collection website: http://www.//untreaty.un.org/English/Terrorism.asp for: Convention on the Prevention and Punishment of Crimes against Internationally Protected Persons, including Diplomatic Agents, adopted by the General Assembly of the United Nations on 14 December 1973; International Convention against the Taking of Hostages, adopted by the General Assembly of the United Nations on 17 December 1979; International Convention for the Suppression of Terrorist Bombings, adopted by the General Assembly of the United Nations on 15 December 1997.

4 See UN Treaty Collection website: http://www.//untreaty.un.org/English/Terrorism.asp, for the detailed provisions of the following regional conventions: European Convention on the Suppression of Terrorism, concluded at Strasbourg on 27 January 1977 (deposited with the Secretary-General of the Council of Europe); OAS Convention to Prevent and Punish Acts of Terrorism Taking the Form of Crimes against Persons and Related Extortion that are of International Significance, concluded at Washington, D.C. on 2 February 1971 (deposited with the Secretary-General of the Organisation of American States); OAU Convention on the Prevention and Combating of Terrorism, adopted at Algiers on 14 July 1999 (deposited with the General Secretariat of the Organization of African Unity); SAARC Regional Convention on Suppression of Terrorism, signed at Kathmandu on 4 November 1987 (deposited with the Secretary-General of the South Asian Association for Regional Cooperation); Treaty on Cooperation among States Members of the Commonwealth of Independent States in Combating Terrorism, done at Minsk on 4 June 1999 (deposited with the Secretariat of the Commonwealth of Independent States); Arab Convention on the Suppression of Terrorism, signed at a meeting held at the General Secretariat of the League of Arab States in Cairo on 22 April 1998 (deposited with the Secretary-General of the League of Arab States);Convention of the Organisation of the Islamic Conference on Combating International Terrorism, adopted at Ouagadougou on 1 July 1999 (deposited with the Secretary-General of the Organisation of the Islamic Conference).

5 Murphy (1989:12–14); See also, UK Government Prevention of Terrorism (Temporary Provisions) Act of 1974, cited in Mickolus (1980).

6 See US State Department (1998) "Patterns of Terrorism, 1997". US Department of State, April. http://www.hri.org/docs/USSD-Terror/97/intro.html.

7 See US State Department, (1998) "Patterns of Terrorism, 1997". US Department of State, April. http://www.hri.org/docs/USSD-Terror/97/intro.html.

8 Ganor enjoys a high profile professional career having served as consultant to Israeli government ministries on counterterrorism, and consultant to the Israeli Prime Minister on his book, *Fighting Terrorism*. He currently serves on the trilateral – Palestinian, Israeli, American Committee on "Incitement", established under the Wye Accords and he is a guest/visiting professor in various Israeli and American institutions. See the following websites for more information, https://www.ict.org.il/ Worker.aspx?ID=1; http://powerbase.info/index.php/Boaz_Ganor; and http://www.disted. unomaha.edu/speakers/ganor.htm.

9 Cf. Ganor, B. (2000) "Suicide Terrorism: An Overview" ICT Papers, 15 February http://www. file:///A|/ICT-Counter-Terrorism7_files/articledet.htm; Ganor, B. (2001) "Fundamental Premises for Fighting Terrorism", ICT Papers, 16 September. http://www.file:///A|/ICT-Counter-Terrorism6_files/articledet.htm, Ganor B., K. Von Knop, and C. Duarte eds. (2007) *Hypermedia Seduction for Terrorist Recruiting - Volume 25 NATO Science for Peace and Security Series: Human and Societal*

*Dynamics*. NATO Science for Peace and Security Series No. 25, Eilat: IOS Press; and a host of other articles and monographs published both by ICT and by the Jerusalem Centre for Public Affairs.

10  Clearly, the 1941 Pearl Harbour incident was not a terrorist attack and has therefore not been cited as one. I have only mentioned it as an example of a non-civilian aerial attack, which in all probability could be contemplated by terrorists or in terrorist violence. For a general discussion of the Pearl Harbour attack, see Weber (2002).

# References

ACSS (2004). *Senior Leaders Seminar – Programme Highlights*. A complication by the Africa Centre for Strategic Studies detailing the Senior Leaders Seminar held in Washington DC, 8–20 February. 108 pages.

CNN (2017). Guantanamo Bay Naval Station Fast Facts. CNN 7 March. http://edition.cnn.com/2013/09/09/world/guantanamo-bay-naval-station-fast-facts/index.html

Collier, P. & Hoeffler, A. (2000). *Greed and grievance in Civil War*. World Bank. http://www.worldbank.org/research/conflict/papers/greedgrievance_23oct.pdf.

Crenshaw, M. (1985). The psychology of political terrorism. In M. Hermann (Ed.), *Handbook of political psychology*, 2nd Edition. San Francisco: Jossey Base.

Crotty, M. (1996). *The Foundations of Social Research*. London: Sage Publishers.

FIDH (2002). The FIDH Request the UN Committee on the Elimination of Racial Discrimination for Urgent Procedure on Anti-Terrorist Legislations in the UK, USA and Germany. A Communique released by the Paris-based International Federation of Human Rights (FIDH), 6 March. http://www.fidh.org/communiq/2002/ij0603a.htm.

FIDH (2004). *Thematic Debate: Non-Citizens and Racial Discrimination*. Report Presented at the 64th Session of the Committee on the Elimination of Racial Discrimination, UN Geneva. February. http://www.fidh.org/IMG/pdf/cerd1503a.pdf.

Ganor, B. (1999). Security Council Resolution 1269: What it Leaves Out. (Herzlia: ICT Papers, The International Policy Institute for Counter-Terrorism, The Interdisciplinary Center). 25 October. http://www.file:///A|/ICT-Counter-Terrorism_files/articledet.htm.

Ganor, B. (2001a). Terrorism: No Prohibition Without Definition. (Herzlia: ICT Papers, The International Policy Institute for Counter-Terrorism, The Interdisciplinary Center). 7 October. http://www.file:///A|/ICT-Counter-Terrorism_files/articledet.htm.

Ganor, B. (2001b). Defining Terrorism: Is One Man's Terrorism Another Man's Freedom Fighter? (Herzlia: ICT Papers, The International Policy Institute for Counter-Terrorism, The Interdisciplinary Center), September. http://www.file:///A|/ICT-Counter-Terrorism5_files/articledet.htm.

Ganor, B. (2007). *The counter-terrorism puzzle: A guide for decision makers*. New Brunswick, NJ: Transaction Publishers.

Ganor, B. (2010). Defining Terrorism - Is One Man's Terrorist Another Man's Freedom Fighter? 01/01/2010. (Herzlia: ICT Papers, The International Policy Institute for Counter-Terrorism, The Interdisciplinary Center). https://www.ict.org.il/Article/1123/Defining-Terrorism-Is-One-Mans-Terrorist-Another-Mans-Freedom-Fighter.

Ganser, D. (2005). *NATO's secret armies – Operation Gladio and terrorism in Western Europe*. London: Frank Cass.

Guevara, E. (1998). *Guerrilla Warfare*, 3rd Edition. Lincoln: University of Nebraska Press.

Gurr, T. R. (1975). Theories of violence and the control of intervention. In W. Friedman & J. N. Moore (Eds.), *Law and Civil War in the Modern State* (pp. 70–91). Baltimore: John Hopkins Press.

Hamilton, P. (1979). *Espionage, terrorism and subversion*. Surry: Peter Helms.

Hermon, C. C. (2000). *Terrorism today*. London: Frank Cass & Co.

Hill, Max, (2017). Independent Reviewer on Terrorism Legislation. June. https://terrorismlegislationreviewer.independent.gov.uk/

Hoffman, B. (1999). *Inside terrorism*. New York: Columbia University Press.

Horowitz, I. L. (1983). The routinisation of terrorism and its unanticipated consequences. In M. Crenshaw (Ed.), *Terrorism, legacy and power*. Middletown-Connecticut: Wesleyan University Press, 38–64.

Jackson, R., & Sinclair, S. J. (2012). *Contemporary debating on Terrorism*. New York: Routledge, Chapman & Hall.

Lindner, E. G. (2001). Humiliation as the source of terrorism: A new paradigm. *Peace Research: The Canadian Journal of Peace Studies*, 33/2, 59–69.

MacCauley, Clark (2017). Constructing terrorism: From fear and coercion to anger and jujitsu politics. In Michael Stohl, Richard Burchill, & Scott Howard Englund (Eds.), *Constructions of terrorism: An interdisciplinary approach to research and policy* (pp. 79–90). Oakland: University of California Press.

Mickolus, E. F. (1980). *The literature of terrorism*. Westport: Greenwood Press.

Murphy, J. F. (1989). *State support of international terrorism*. Boulder: Westview Press.

Netanyahu, Benjamin (1986). Defining terrorism. In B. Netanyahu (Ed.), Terrorism: How the West can win. London: George Weidenfeld & Nicolson Ltd.

Netanyahu, Benjamin (1995). *Fighting terrorism*. New York: Farrar, Strauss and Giroux.

Netanyahu, Benzion (1986). Terrorists and Freedom Fighters. In Benjamin Netanyahu (Ed.), *Terrorism: How the West can win*. London: George Weidenfeld & Nicolson Ltd.

Quillen, C. (2000). State-Sponsored WMD Terrorism: A Growing Threat. Discussion Paper – The Terrorism Research Centre, Washington D. C. July. http://www.terrorism.com/analysis/quillen-wmd-terrorism.pdf.

Schlosberg, Justin (2017). The Media-Technology-Military Industrial Complex. https://www.tni.org/files/publication-downloads/stateofpower2017-complex.pdf

Schmid A. P. & Jongman, A. I., et al. (1988). *Political terrorism*. Amsterdam: SWIDOC & Transaction Books.

Schmid, A. P., & Jongman, A. J. (2005). *Political terrorism: A new guide to actors, authors, concepts, data bases, theories, and literature*. New Jersey: Transaction Publishers.

Sterba, J. P., & French, S. E. (2003). *Terrorism and international justice*. New York: Oxford University Press.

UNODCCP, (2001). Definitions of Terrorism. http://www.undcp.org/terrorism-definition.html.

Weber, C. (2002). Flying Planes Can be Dangerous. *Millennium: Journal of International Studies*. 31/1, 129–148.

Wilkinson, P. (1996). Track 11: Security and Terrorism in the 21st Century. Centre for the Study of Terrorism and Political Violence, St. Andrews University. January 13. http://www.st-and.ac.uk/academic/intrel/research/cstpv

Wilkinson, P. (2001). *Terrorism versus democracy: The liberal state response*. London, Frank Cass Publishers.

# 3

# Mapping the contours of terrorism and counterterrorism in Africa

*Eugene Eji*

## Introduction

Africa, the second largest and second most-populous continent in the world, is currently under the threat of complex terrorist situations that have significantly transformed its security landscape. The phenomenon of terrorism is, however, not new in the continent having manifested in various forms during the colonial period and thereafter. The emergence of Al-Qaeda networks such as Al-Qaeda in the Islamic Maghreb (AQIM), Al-Shabaab, and Boko Haram further heightened the threat of terrorism across the continent. These and other terrorist groups have exploited factors such as governance deficit, ethno-religiosity, and other grievances to undermine the authority of African governments and the wellbeing of its citizens. Ironically, initiatives by African governments at national, regional, continental, and global levels in countering terrorism appear not to have achieved the desired result. This chapter reflects on the trend of terrorism in Africa and the counterterrorism efforts of African states at individual and collective levels. It surmises that African governments need to go beyond prescribing standards to pursuing pragmatic and concerted efforts against all forms of terrorism in line with the principle that terrorism in one country is terrorism in all.

Terrorism and the fight against terrorism have assumed such monumental dimensions that no part of the world can claim to be immune, either directly or indirectly. In Africa, terrorism occurs in many guises and locations with the acts justified by a plethora of different ideologies and grievances. The phenomenon is also not new in the continent when viewed from the multiplicity of scholarly perspectives on the subject. Crenshaw (1994: 4), for instance, traces the origin of terrorism in Africa to the colonial period. According to her, terrorism was a feature within resistance movements, military coups, political assassinations, and various intra- and inter-state wars that affected most African states at some point during the continent's transition to independence and subsequent post-colonial period. Accordingly, it could be said that domestic cases of terrorism particularly those perpetrated by perceived marginalised groups, and by the state against the groups in the form of political repression, have been rife across the African continent.

On the other hand, cases of international terrorism in Africa became pronounced from the 1990s particularly in Sudan where Osama Bin Laden was believed to have operated, and where

33

the attempted assassination of Egyptian president Hosni Mubarak was organised (Lyman, 2008: 249–259). The blowing up of the American embassy in Nairobi and Dar es Salaam by Al-Qaeda cells in 1998 was a further indication of the dawn of international terrorism in Africa (Mayer, 2008: 114). In the 2000s, AQIM, Al-Shabaab, and Boko Haram emerged amidst other forms of terrorism in the continent. The activities of these groups further worsened Africa's terrorism situation. For instance, in 2012, Islamists linked to AQIM seized the opportunity of Mali's loss of control over its northern parts to capture key towns.[1] In Somali and its neigh-bouring countries, the Al Shabaab group has continually mounted attacks against citizens, government forces, and international peacekeepers. Similarly, in Nigeria, an Islamic sect po-pularly known as Boko Haram emerged spreading its activities to the neighbouring countries of Niger, Chad, and Cameroon in the Lake Chad region. Further compounding the threat is the growing quest by the Islamic State in Iraq and Syria (ISIS) to expand its influence in Africa as demonstrated by the activities of the Islamic State in Central Africa Province (ISCAP), Islamic State in the Greater Sahara (ISGS) and Islamic State in West Africa Province (ISWAP).

The threat posed by terrorism to the integrity of African states and the wellbeing of their citizens has been enormous thereby leading to its placement in the front burner of the security agenda of many of the affected states. Counterterrorism measures have been put in place by some African governments at the national level, and similar mechanisms have been replicated at the sub-regional/regional and continental levels. For instance, the Nigerian government em-placed a National Cybersecurity Policy and Strategy to contain cyberterrorism as well as the Policy Framework and National Action Plan for Preventing and Countering Violent Extremism to tackle tendencies that breed terrorism. The African Union (AU) has championed a number of protocols and conventions towards collective counterterrorism efforts at the continental level, including harnessing the efforts of the United Nations (UN) and other in-ternational partners. In spite of all these arrangements, terrorism in Africa remains far from being contained implying that the counterterrorism efforts of African governments, both in-dividually and collectively, seem not to have yielded satisfactory outcomes. While the focus of this chapter is on making an overview of the trend of terrorism and counterterrorism in Africa, some pertinent question would need answers, such as: why is terrorism prevalent in Africa, and how has been the conduct of counterterrorism in terms of the implementation of policy, legal, and other frameworks? In line with this is the appropriateness and effectiveness of the strategies adopted by African governments and by extension the way forward for effective counterterrorism in the continent. The Chapter will begin by providing a conceptual and historical overview of terrorism in Africa to facilitate a better understanding of the afore-mentioned issues that the chapter seeks to address.

## Conceptual and historical overview of terrorism in Africa

The word "terrorism" is very popular, dynamic, and controversial. It is a very popular word in terms of frequency of usage; commonly used in the political lexicon as much the same way as the threat of it has become a daily occurrence in many countries of the world today. It is dynamic in the sense that it has changed both in meaning and nature from the French Revolution when it was used as a regime instrument, to a revolutionary, anti-monarchical and anti-anarchist forms; and assuming nationalist, separatist as well as ethno-religious and ideo-logical (particularly anti-West) dimensions (Hoffman, 2006: 3–4). Terrorism is controversial in meaning, and it could be argued that a major issue in conceptualising terrorism is its definitional problem. The general consensus among scholars is that terrorism is a subjective and multifaceted phenomenon that defies a universally accepted definition (Hoffman, 2006: 1–3; Gibbs, 2012: 63). In the light of this, Schmid and Jongman (2005: 6) observed that researchers from various fields "have spilled almost as much ink as the actors of terrorism have spilled blood" and yet have reached no consensus on what terrorism is. They counted 109 definitions of terrorism that covered a total of 22 different definitional elements of the term (Schmid et al., 1988: 5–6). In spite of this, it could be argued that defining terrorism, at least in context-specific terms, is invaluable for the understanding of any discourse on the subject, and as Boaz (2002: 288) also opines, for a successful counterterrorism effort.

In broad terms, terrorism is a tactic involving the use or threat of the use of violence by the individual, group(s), sub-state, or state actor(s) to register their grievances against existing political, economic, or social situations perceived as not favourable to them. They do this with the aim of intimidating or instilling fear into the population, thereby influencing the government to take or not to take a particular course of action. In conceptualising terrorism in Africa, however, the point needs to first be made that the threat of and vulnerability to terrorism differs from continent to continent, sub-region to sub-region, and state to state implying that regions and countries will interpret and react differently based on their unique perception of the threat. It is also worth noting that the notion on whether the person defining terrorism identifies with the victim or the perpetrator as aptly captured by the "one man's terrorist is another man's freedom fighter" cliché that stresses the fact that the definition of terrorism depends on the perspective and world view of the one defining it (Boaz, 2002: 292; Hoffman, 2006: 24–25). Botha (2008: 28) opines that terrorism is not a new threat or concept in Africa, but what is worrying is the application of Western models to the situation in Africa which results in double standards and consequently negatively impacts the understanding of terrorism in Africa. She points to the fact that domestic terrorism presents a more immediate challenge in Africa, and indeed the developing world, than transnational terrorism which is experienced more in the developed world (Botha, 2008: 29). Domestic terrorism in this sense comprises terrorist acts usually conducted by local groups within the state for the purpose of overthrowing a government or achieving local political advantage (Okumu, 2009: 1). It also takes the form of repressive regimes and brutal subjugation of opposition.

The observed trend in Africa is that when a group resorts to violence against a government or segment of society; it is regarded as terrorism, but when the government or security forces use the same (and even worse) methods; this is paradoxically done in the name of state security. However, as Boaz (2002: 293) notes "when a group or organisation chooses terrorism as a means, the aim of their struggle cannot be used to justify their actions." In this context, therefore, there is a need to regard terrorism as politically motivated acts of violence against a civilian population whether there are carried out by a state or a non-state actor.[2] One is therefore content that the AU, perhaps in the realisation of the need to promote an African perspective of terrorism, took on a broad definition of terrorism when in its Act, it defines terrorism as:

> ...any act which is a violation of the criminal laws of a state party and which may endanger the life, physical integrity or freedom of, or cause serious injury or death to any person, any member or group of persons, or causes or may cause damage to public or private property, natural resources, environmental, or cultural heritage and is calculated or intended to:
>
> (i). intimidate, put in fear, coerce or induce any government, body, institution, the general public or any segment thereof, to do or abstain from doing any act, or to adopt or abandon a particular standpoint or to act according to certain principles; or

(ii). disrupt any public service, the delivery of any essential service to the public or to create a public emergency; or

(iii). create general insurrection in a State.[3]

In article 3(1), the AU equally notes that:

(i). The struggle waged by peoples in accordance with the principles of international law for their liberation or self-determination, including armed struggle against colonialism, occupation, aggression and domination by foreign forces, and

(ii). Political, philosophical, ideological, racial, ethnic, religious or other motives shall not be a justifiable defence against a terrorist act.[4]

Conceptualised in this way, Oyeniyi (2010: 34–80) posits that the AU is clear on what terrorism in Africa is, and corroborates the fact that terrorism is not a new development in Africa.

In tracing the history of terrorism in Africa, it could be argued that although scholars such as Crenshaw (2009: 4) view the colonial period as ushering terrorism in the continent, traits of the phenomenon existed much earlier. Before the advent of colonialism, there were organised groups, societies, and kingdoms in Africa that are thought to have employed terrorist tactics of fear, intimidation, violence, and threat of violence against one another. For instance, Oyeniyi (2010: 34–80) points to the existence of socio-cultural and political groups in Nigeria such as *Ndinche, Modewa, Aguren, Eso, Akoda* and *Ilari*. More so, pre-colonial empires such as those of Egypt, Ethiopia, Wolof, and Mutapa are believed to have carried out acts against neighbouring kingdoms as well as quell internal opposition in a manner that would today qualify as state terrorism. Comolli (2015: 15–16) similarly notes that the Sokoto Caliphate employed intimidation and fear in expanding its territorial hold, and in propagating the religion of Islam across the Sahel.

During the colonial era, terrorist tactics of violence, intimidation, and fear were employed by the colonialists to coerce or persuade the local population into accepting regime policies (Oyeniyi, 2010: 34–80). On the other hand, the same tactic of violence and fear was used by some indigenous societies to resist colonial rule and/or fight for independence from the colonial government. An instance of this was the Mau Mau Uprising that emerged from the Kenyan African Union in the early 1950s to organise a militant kind of nationalism against the British colonial government. While the Mau Mau carried out attacks against the white settlers and their loyalists in protest against the colonial regime, the British forces allegedly engaged in torture and mass execution of the Mau Mau activists in a bid to suppress the group (Anderson, 2013: 150–154). It is in the light of this that some scholars such Okumu (2009: 1) view as a state of "official" terrorism the brutal suppression of perceived terror groups by the colonial government, and furthermore believe that colonialism sowed the seed of terrorism in Africa and other post-colonial societies.

The post-colonial era in Africa was characterised by the failure of most states to "settle down" and democratically manage their independence. The socio-political and economic structures handed down by the colonial government were apparently weak and were further weakened by competition for the control of power by the elites mainly along ethnoreligious and other divisive lines. Solomon (2015: 40) observes that ill-defined borders created by the colonial powers left several newly independent African states "with a seething mix of majority and minority ethnic groups" resulting in their having to negotiate "these competing and volatile racial, ethnic and religious identities." Further worsening the situation were the spate of military coups and the tendency of some African leaders to hold tight to the reins of government employing, in the process, brutal subjugation of opposition. These situations contributed to the emergence of violent non-state actors across the length and breadth of the continent. For instance, in North Africa, the Armed Islamic Group (GIA) of Algeria, apparently in the pursuit of an Islamic state after Algerian independence, resorted to kidnapping, assassination, and bombings to destabilise and overthrow the Algerian government.

In the eastern and central parts of the continent, a number of the groups formed to fight for independence either metamorphosed or gave birth to splinter rebel groups that employed terrorist tactics with the aim of controlling or influencing government in their now independent states. Notable examples include the Eritrean Liberation Front (ELF) in Eritrea, Allied Democratic Forces (ADF) in Uganda with bases in the Democratic Republic of Congo (DRC), and the Lord's Resistance Army (LRA) also in Uganda with its activities spread across the DRC, Central African Republic (CAR), and South Sudan.

It is perhaps important to note here that wider political, ethnic, religious, and other grievances are a factor in the nature of terrorism and mode of operation of these terrorist groups. The ADF, for instance, comprise of membership mainly from the Muslim Tabliq Sect considered as self-identified "religious crusader", employed methods of attacks varying from armed assaults and bombings to arson, kidnapping, and hostage-taking of youths, particularly school children (Forest and Giroux, 2011: 5–17). The ADF atrocity was to the extent that its members burnt to death 80 students of the Kichwamba Technical College in Kabarole district of Uganda by setting fire on their locked hostels (Forest and Giroux, 2011: 5–17). The LRA on the other hand is known to operate as an ideologically apocalyptic Christian group. With leadership provided by the Acholi tribe, the group has since its emergence in 1987 carried out widespread assassinations, arson, abductions, and child slavery (Davenport, 2011).

In Southern Africa, ethnic nationalism and race factor feature prominently in the strategic use of terrorism as a weapon by aggrieved groups to express their grievances. South Africa's African National Congress (ANC) military wing, known as *Umkhonto we Sizwe* (MK), between 1961 and 1990 carried out executions, torture, and assault against loyalists of the Apartheid regime as well as bombings of government installations to the extent that it was classified a terrorist organisation by the South African government and the United States. The narrative was similar in Zimbabwe where the nationalists, in pressing home their demand for black majority rule, engaged the then Rhodesian government in violent attacks while the Rhodesian government on its part formed the Selous Scouts that carried out raids, abductions, and bombings of civilian (nationalists) homes (Melson, 2005: 57). What appears to be an irony is that Robert Mugabe, one of the foremost Zimbabwean nationalist who became president of the country in 1980, adopted a sustained campaign of intimidation against political opponents in order to remain in power.

The West African sub-region has also had its share of domestic cases of terrorism in the postcolonial era. The Royal United Front (RUF) of Sierra Leone, which sought to overthrow the government in the 1990s, exemplifies this. The group was known for its assault on the civilian population particularly hacking off limbs to intimidate and spread fear among the population, as well as for its use of child soldiers. It allegedly received financial support and recruited members from neighbouring Liberia.[5] In Liberia itself, there was political instability occasioned by coups and counter-coups and the emergence of rebel armed groups such as the National Patriotic Front of Liberia (NPFL) and the United Liberation Movement of Liberia for Democracy (ULIMO). The armed groups, some of them using Sierra Leone, Cote d'Ivoire, and Guinea as staging areas, launched widespread acts of violence against the Liberian civilian population in attempts to take over the seat of government.

The foregoing discussion reiterates the point that terrorism in Africa has been interwoven in broader conflicts thereby making the phenomena both multifaceted and complex. Although many of the non-state actors originated and operated within specific countries, a number of others took advantage of tribal and socio-cultural affinity particularly among border communities to find safe-havens in neighbouring countries from where they receive logistic support, recruit members, plan, and conduct their activities in the targeted country.[6] Equally, the conditions that foster terrorism – both pull and push factors – appear engendered within the African states and consequently the localisation of the threat posed by terrorism. This, however, changed as the fragile African states became vulnerable to a new wave of terrorism that is transnational, and more often than not, ideologically inspired.

A significant swathe of Africa ranging from the north to the south and east to west of the continent have now become frontlines in a global jihadi movement that often seeks to replace the secular *status quo* with Sharia-based governance (Antwi-Boateng, 2017: 253–284). The situation is grievous to the extent that in the Global Terrorism Index (GTI) ranking for 2016, ten out of the first 20 most terrorised countries in the world are African countries.[7] The countries, as shown in Table 3.1, are fairly distributed across Africa indicating that the threat of terrorism traverses the continent. The major terrorist groups in Africa, as earlier mentioned and shown in Figure 3.1, include AQIM, Al-Shabaab, and Boko Haram with influx of Islamic State elements. They have all been inspired by radical Islamic ideology and, as Solomon (2015: 1–19) notes, are wreaking havoc across the African continent and beyond. It is this new and contemporary form of terrorism in Africa that I now focus on.

*Table 3.1* GTI Top 20 Most Terrorized Countries Ranking for 2016

| Rank | Country | Score |
|---|---|---|
| 1 | Iraq | 9.96 |
| 2 | Afghanistan | 9.444 |
| 3 | Nigeria | 9.314 |
| 4 | Pakistan | 8.613 |
| 5 | Syria | 8.587 |
| 6 | Yemen | 8.076 |
| 7 | Somalia | 7.548 |
| 8 | India | 7.484 |
| 9 | Egypt | 7.328 |
| 10 | Libya | 7.283 |
| 11 | Ukraine | 7.132 |
| 12 | Philippines | 7.098 |
| 13 | Cameroon | 7.002 |
| 14 | Turkey | 6.738 |
| 15 | Thailand | 6.706 |
| 16 | Niger | 6.682 |
| 17 | Democratic Republic of the Congo | 6.633 |
| 18 | Sudan | 6.6 |
| 19 | Kenya | 6.578 |
| 20 | Central African Republic | 6.518 |

Source: Adapted from http://economicsandpeace.org/wpcontent/uploads/2016/11/Global-Terrorism-Index-2016.2.pdf, accessed 29 August 2017.

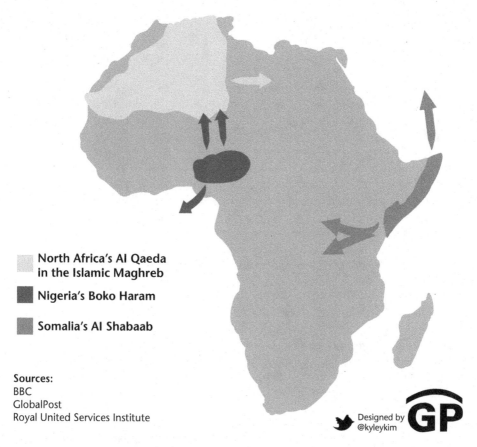

**North Africa's Al Qaeda
in the Islamic Maghreb**

**Nigeria's Boko Haram**

**Somalia's Al Shabaab**

**Sources:**
BBC
GlobalPost
Royal United Services Institute

Designed by
@kyleykim **GP**

*Figure 3.1* Map of Africa Showing Main Terrorist Groups
Source: https://www.google.com.ng/search?q=Map+of+terrorism+in+africa, accessed 29 August 2017.

## Current trends on terrorism in Africa

Africa's security landscape is currently dotted with varying typologies and magnitudes of terrorism. While domestic cases of terrorism have held sway and predated the independence of many of the states, the new wave of transnational terrorism now prevails. The place of Africa in this new and contemporary terrorism is significant in many ways. Significant in this regard is the point that terrorists took advantage of the weak governments and poor security architecture of states in the continent to operate. The freedom of action offered by the ungoverned space enabled the terrorists to launch attacks on Western interests and institutions that could be said to have ostensibly become soft targets by virtue of their location in a continent composed of weak and fragile states. A corollary point to this is the prevalent poverty, famine, and general underdevelopment in the continent that made the ideology of the terrorists (that is essentially *anti-status quo*) appealing to the masses, and in the process attracting membership to terrorist organisations. To this effect, groups whose activities were hitherto localised and categorised as domestic terrorist groups took up the ideology propagated by the transnational groups and in the process became infused into the global jihadi network. More significant is the fact that Africa became a sanctuary for transnational terrorist organisations such as Al-Qaeda. This became evident between 1991 and 1996 when Osama bin Laden shifted the base for his Mujahedeen operations to Sudan (Morell and Harlow, 2015: 13). Here, he established connections and supported both financially and militarily, Islamic jihadi networks in Egypt, Algeria, and Afghanistan.

The Egyptian Islamic Jihad (EIJ) that is allegedly linked to the earlier mentioned attempted assassination of Mubarak, and the GIA which was eclipsed by its splinter faction, the Salafist Group for Preaching and Combat (GSPC), all operated largely as Al-Qaeda cells. In 2006, a foremost EIJ and Al-Qaeda leader, Ayman al-Zawahiri, announced a union of the GSPC with Al-Qaeda and accordingly changed its name to AQIM in 2007 (Forest and Giroux, 2011: 5–17). The activities of AQIM now transcend Algeria to Mali, Burkina Faso, Niger, and to some extent Morocco, Mauretania, Nigeria, and Chad. Alongside AQIM emerged the Boko Haram Islamic sect that rose to become the world's deadliest terrorist group in 2015.[8] The group's area of operation cuts across Nigeria (where it originated) to Niger, Chad, and Cameroon. Extending the contour line of terrorism to the east and horn of Africa is the Al-Shabaab group. Originally a Somali-based group, its foray along the Somali-Kenya border and attacks on the African Union Mission to Somalia (AMISOM) peacekeepers made the group a compelling terrorist threat in the region.

The AQIM, Boko Haram, and Al-Shabaab, alongside their ancillary and splinter groups, as well as Islamic State affiliates are arguably the current most dominant terrorist groups in the continent. Their activities bear marked similarities. For instance, they all engage in an anti-government campaign aimed to establish an Islamic state in place of the existing secular states, which they regard as having been corrupted with Western values. However, remarkable differences exist that are peculiar to their historical, socio-cultural, economic, and political environments necessitating that the nature of the terrorist threat, motivations, mode of operation, and affiliations as espoused by these dominant terrorist groups are better understood by examining them individually. The individual exploration of the emergence and activities of these Sects would also enable a better analysis of the counterterrorism drive of individual countries concerned as well as their regional initiatives.

## Al-Qaeda in the Islamic Maghreb (AQIM)

The AQIM came into being in 2007 when the GSPC announced its allegiance to Al-Qaeda and changed its name to reflect its new status (Chivis and Liepman, 2013: 2–3). The group's ideology is rooted in Salafi-Jihadist doctrine with the political aim of overthrowing the secular governments in the North African states of Algeria, Mauretania, Morocco, Libya, and Tunisia, and replacing them with Islamic-styled governments based on Sharia Law.[9] The AQIM has continued to push its violent activities southwards, deep into the Sahel and West African states of Mali, Burkina Faso, Cote d'Ivoire, and Niger. It carries out armed assault, hostage-taking, and kidnapping for ransom in these countries. Northwards, AQIM has threatened the European countries of Spain and France, which by location are contiguous, being separated only by the Mediterranean Sea. France in particular has continuously received threats of attacks from the AQIM due to the country's historical, political and military ties with the governments of states in the Maghreb and Sahel (Laub and Masters, 2015). Its affiliates, sub-groups cum allies include Ansaru, Ansar Dine, Ansar al-Sharia, Al-Qaeda in the Arabian Peninsula (AQIAP), and the Movement for Oneness and Jihad in West Africa (MUJAO). In March 2017, an AQIM off-shoot in the Sahara announced a fresh merger with Al-Mourabitoun (another AQIM splinter group based mainly in Algeria) and the Mali-based Ansar Dine to form Jama'at Nasr al-Islam wal Muslimi.[10]

## Boko Haram

Also known by its original name, Jama'atu Ahlis Sunna Lidda'awati wal-Jihad, Boko Haram started as a quiet Islamic study group which became popular from 2002 under the leadership of one Mohammed Yusuf (Madike, 2011). The sect propagates an ideology that is highly critical of the Nigerian government and Western civilization. It thus attracted, or was used to easily manipulate the poor and unemployed who felt that their condition was caused by governance failure, corruption, and moral decadence. The group became violent from 2004 after a series of confrontations with the Nigerian security forces (Kyari 2014: 9–32). On 26 July 2009, Boko Haram staged an armed uprising in Bauchi that subsequently spread to Borno, Yobe, Kano, and other states in northern Nigeria. Mohammed Yusuf was arrested and later killed while in police custody (Onuoha, 2010: 54–67). The sect became more devastating under a new leader, Abubakar Shekau. It leveraged on Improvised Explosive Devices (IEDs) to undertake roadside, vehicle-borne, and suicide bombings including attacks on high profile targets such as the Nigerian Police Headquarters and the UN building in Abuja. It also captured an area in the northeast of Nigeria that equalled the size of Belgium (Comolli, 2015: 161).

Furthermore, Boko Haram's activities spilled over to Niger, Chad, and Cameroon. The sect established links with AQIM, Al Shabaab, and in 2015 pledged allegiance to ISIS renaming itself as ISWAP.[11] It employs media propaganda and particularly the Internet to convey its messages. The sect also engages in ISIS-styled beheadings of victims, abductions, and engagement of females (including girls as young as 10 years) for suicide terrorism (Akbar, 2015). On 14 April 2014, Boko Haram abducted about 276 girls from Government Girls' School Chibok, an incident that attracted much global attention (Nti, 2014). In 2016, the Nigerian government claim that its military has decimated Boko Haram to the extent that it can no longer hold territory.[12] However, the sect continues to carry out ambushes and suicide attacks in vulnerable communities particularly in the suburbs of Maiduguri town, Internally Displaced People (IDP) camps, and remote settlements in the northeast of Nigeria as well as in parts of neighbouring countries where there is a thin presence of troops.

## Al-Shabaab

Al-Shabaab is a Somali-based Suni-Jihadi fundamentalist group that emerged as an offshoot of the Islamic Courts Union (ICU) of Somalia. It became prominent after the defeat of the ICU by the Transitional Federal Government (TFG) of Somalia and its Ethiopian allies in 2006 (Solomon, 2015: 39). Shuriye (2012) notes that the group's political ideology is to establish an Islamic state of Somalia and eventually spill-over this ideology throughout the Horn of Africa and perhaps to the East and Central Africa. It, therefore, aims to destabilise and ultimately overthrow the government of Somalia while launching an offensive against Somali's neighbours, AU and UN peacekeepers in retaliation for intervening on the part of the government. Al-Shabaab highly abhors Western values to the extent of banning radio stations from playing music and local video centres from showing foreign matches.[13] It metes out harsh punishments such as the stoning of adulterers and amputating the hands of thieves.[14] Al-Shabaab's use of propaganda has been effective in conveying its messages and recruiting members. Its propaganda machinery includes radio and television broadcasts, and the use of the Internet particularly for twitting and micro-blogging (Odhiambo et al., 2013). The Sect pledged alliance to Al-Qaeda in 2012 and is thought to have links with AQIM, Boko Haram, and the Islamic State of Iraq and the Levant (ISIL).[15] Although the group has lost grounds, having been forced to retreat from major cities to some rural areas, it still carries out sporadic attacks and suicide bombings. The

Westgate Shopping Mall shooting on 21 September 2013, the attack on Garissa University College on 2 April 2015 and the United States military base at Lamu on 5 January 2020 in Kenya as well as on Somali's Af-Urur military base on 8 June 2017, twin truck bomb in Mogadishu on 14 October 2017 and another truck bomb on 28 December 2019 were some of Al-Shabaab's attacks in recent years that left scores of casualties.[16]

## Overview of counter terrorism in Africa

Counterterrorism operations involve offensive measures taken to prevent, deter, pre-empt, and respond to terrorism."[17] In Africa, a lot of initiatives at countering terrorism have been undertaken, but how far the schemes and programmes have translated from theory to practice in terms of implementation remain a concern. Generally, counterterrorism in Africa could be viewed at the levels of national, sub-regional/regional, continental, and global effort.

At their respective national levels, African states have, among other measures, formulated counterterrorism strategies, enacted anti-terrorism legislations, and mobilised their security apparatus to counter the threat posed by terrorism. In terms of regional counterterrorism initiatives, the efforts of the Economic Community of West African States (ECOWAS), Economic Community of Central African States (ECCAS), East African Community (EAC), South African Development Community (SADC), and the Intergovernmental Authority on Development (IGAD) have been significant. These regional organisations, in recognition of the fact that terrorism constitutes a threat to the political and socio-economic development of their respective entities, included counterterrorism among their programmes and plans of action.

The IGAD, for instance, has its counterterrorism pillar with main goals and activities geared towards building the national and regional capacity of countries in the Horn of Africa at countering terrorism, radicalisation, and extremist violence.[18] It partners with individual countries, the AU, and the UN among other organisations in its counterterrorism drive. There are also organisations that cut across regions such as the Lake Chad Basin Commission (LCBC) which comprise the West African states of Nigeria and Niger, the Central African states of Chad, Cameroon, South Sudan, and the Republic of Central Africa as well as the North African countries of Libya and Algeria. The Commission has been at the forefront of collaborations against terrorism in the region, and in the process, setting up joint action to curb insurgency within and across the common borders of the countries.[19]

The AU is the umbrella body for the counterterrorism effort of African states at the continental level. From 2000 when it came into being, the AU sought to depart from the more traditional and narrow defence of the sovereignty of its predecessor, the Organization of Africa Unity, to a more pragmatic conflict resolution mechanism based on the notion that conflict within any African state could affect the whole continent (Lyman, 2008: 249–259). How far this has been achieved, and generally how the counterterrorism effort has been driven by African states remain debatable, as I will highlight in the next segment.

## Counter terrorism in Africa: principles and praxis

The survey of the current trends of terrorism and the overview of counterterrorism in Africa earlier made indicate that although the two phenomena seem to dot the whole of Africa, their "contours" could be described as "high and low" or being in greater dimensions in some parts than others. In terms of counterterrorism, the degree to which initiatives have been implemented and their effectiveness vary from nation to nation and region to region depending largely on the underlying nature of the threat as well as the commitment of the country or countries involved. In mapping the contours of the counterterrorism effort in Africa therefore, a context-specific approach that would account for case-specific or peculiarities of efforts would seem both necessary and appropriate. This will be done here by examining the cases of counterterrorism efforts at the national level using, as an example, Nigeria's effort against Boko Haram, at the sub-regional/regional level using the efforts of countries of the Sahel region against AQIM and then, the AU initiatives at the continental level. I will finally examine the efforts of the international community, that is, global efforts at countering terrorism in Africa.

## National counter terrorism effort: Nigeria versus Boko Haram

Nigeria's commitment to the fight against terrorism remained mainly passive until the 2009 upsurge of Boko Haram terrorist activities that compelled the Nigerian government to deploy the military in a full-scale offensive against the sect. In July 2011, a Joint Task Force (JTF) comprising personnel of the military, intelligence, and security agencies was established in Borno State, and subsequently in the other terrorist affected states in Nigeria.[20] This was complemented by the Civilian Joint Task Forces (CJTF), a vigilante organization established by some youths and able-bodied men to confront the activities of Boko Haram.[21] Furthermore, two army divisions, with the name 7 Division and 8 Task Force Division Nigerian Army, were established in northeastern Nigeria to tackle the terrorists. By mid-2015, many areas of Nigeria's territory seized by the terrorists were reclaimed through the concerted efforts of the Nigerian military, mercenaries hired by the President Jonathan's regime, and the armed forces of Nigeria's contiguous countries.

In terms of legislation, a Terrorism Protection Act (TPA) was enacted by Nigeria's National Assembly in February 2011 and reviewed in June 2013 (Udeh, 2013: 307–333). In January 2011, the government appointed a Presidential Adviser on Terrorism and established a counterterrorism Centre at the Office of the National Security Adviser (ONSA) to facilitate the implementation of counterterrorism strategy and overall coordination of government effort (Dasuki, 2014). The country's National counterterrorism Strategy (NACTEST) was endorsed for implementation in April 2014, and the second edition released in August 2016. Also noteworthy are the bilateral and multilateral engagement efforts of the Nigerian government with organisations and partners such as the UN and the European Union (EU), with states such as the United States, United Kingdom, and France, as well as with contiguous countries of Benin, Cameroon, Chad, and Niger (Udeh, 2013: 307–322).

An assessment of the counterterrorism posture of the Nigerian government reveals the primacy of the conventional military-centric approach, as opposed to the non-conventional approach. This is a major contradiction because countering terrorism and insurgency is essentially asymmetric warfare that can hardly be executed using the conventional approach. However, while evidence on the ground indicates a hard traditional military approach to counterterrorism, comments from the Office of the National Security Adviser (ONSA), that supervises the NACTEST, have often been that Nigeria was disposed to employing a soft approach to counterterrorism (Dasuki, 2014). It is further noted that the terrorists have kept changing tactics in asymmetrical warfare that has challenged the Nigerian military in terms of capacity. Onuoha observes that although the Nigerian military was able to use conventional tactics to recapture territories held by the terrorists, it has been unable to cope with the terrorists' unconventional tactics of suicide bombings, abductions, and guerrilla attacks.[22] Moses (2017) further questions the claims by the Nigerian government that the military has decimated Boko Haram. Also, despite notable successes, the Nigerian military has been associated with human rights abuses which have not only tended to alienate it from the public but also attracted condemnation particularly from human right groups.[23] The allegation of human right abuses has also made it difficult for Nigeria to procure weapons from the United States and other Western countries thereby undermining the capacity of its military in the counterterrorism campaign. In the face of seeming challenges, however, the Nigerian military through operation code-named LAFIYA DOLE and Multi-National Joint Task Force (MNJTF) collaboration, has largely constricted the Boko Haram and ISWAP fighters to their strongholds around the Sambisa Forest, Lake Chad and the Borno State border aeas with neigbouring countries.

## Regional effort: Sahel countries and Al-Qaeda in the Islamic Maghreb

In recognition of the fact that the security threat posed by AQIM in the Sahel is beyond the capacity of individual states to handle, joint counterterrorism efforts were initiated by the affected Sahel states. For instance, the leaders of Algeria, Niger, Mali, and Mauritania agreed in July 2009 to work in concert against AQIM. This led to the formulation of the Tamanrasset Plan which culminated in the setting up of a joint command centre for security, intelligence sharing, and military coordination (Hoskins, 2010). The participating countries also agreed to increase the number of security forces deployed for counterterrorism in the Sahel from 25,000 to 75,000 (Hoskins, 2010). However, this plan remains ineffective due to the sometimes fractious relations between member states.

Furthermore, in their collaboration with the international community, a joint European Union-Africa strategy was adopted in December 2007 (Rugy, 2010: 123). It was designed to promote holistic approaches to security, conflict prevention, and resolution linked to good governance and sustainable development. Similarly, the United States established the Pan Sahel Initiative (PSI) in 2002 which was replaced by the Trans Sahara Counter Terrorism Initiative (TSCTI) in 2005 (Ochoche, 2006: 171). The programmes aimed to improve border control capabilities and enhance regional security among Sahel states cutting across parts of North Africa, West Africa, and Central Africa. It also provided for the training of Special Forces of West African states.

More significant perhaps is the collaboration between the Sahel countries and France which led to France launching its Plan Sahel in Mali, Mauretania, and Niger in 2008. The plan which aimed to fight terrorism and assist local development programmes was complemented with the establishment of a quick reaction force and permanent military bases at Dakar in Senegal and Libreville in Gabon (Chauzal and Damme, 2015). In 2013, France launched Operation Serval against AQIM-backed Tuareg rebels in their self-declared republic of Azawad in northern Mali. France has also been a major driver of the Sahel G-5 countries multinational military force aim to tackle Islamic militants in the Sahel (Sepgupta, 2017). The body was approved by the UN through a resolution passed on 21 July 2017. It comprises French former colonial countries of Burkina Faso, Chad, Mali, Mauritania, and Niger. The Sahel G-5 is expected to operate in coordination with French troops and the UN peace support mission in Mali known as the Multidimensional Integrated Stabilization Mission in Mali (MINUSMA). However, the effectiveness of the force could depend on the willingness of the United States to partner with France and the UN to support it financially and otherwise. This is given the initial reluctance of the United States particularly on the issue of the approval of a broad mandate for the force (Sepgupta, 2017).

## The African Union counter terrorism efforts

The AU's framework for countering terrorism is enshrined in the 1999 AU Convention on the Prevention and Combating of Terrorism and its 2004 Protocol which empowers the Union's

Peace and Security Council (PSC) to coordinate and harmonise continental efforts in the prevention and combating of international terrorism in all its aspects.[24] In 2004, the AU also established the African Centre for the Study and Research on Terrorism (ACSRT) with a view to centralising information and research on terrorism, develop counterterrorism capacity building programmes, and provide a forum for interaction and cooperation among member states and regional mechanisms. In 2011, the AU Assembly adopted the African Model on counterterrorism to assist states to harmonise legislation on terrorism. Similar AU initiatives were undertaken in 2014 which include proposals for the establishment of a counterterrorism Fund, African anti-terrorism Model Law, and specialised joint counterterrorism units at the sub-regional levels within the framework of the African Standby Force (ASF).[25] There were also proposals to enhance inter-state police cooperation, intelligence sharing, and an agreement on the convening of an annual AU Coordination Forum to coordinate efforts on countering terrorism.

Although the AU is credited with the feat of sending African peacekeepers to terrorist and insurgent prone Burundi, Côte d'Ivoire, the DRC, Somalia, and South Sudan, sometimes ahead of the UN, the organization has found it increasingly challenging to effectively implement, let alone sustain most of its lofty initiatives. The large size of the continent comprising 34 of the poorest countries in the world, weak states many of which are experiencing serious unrest, strong historical Islamic presence, and a mosaic of both traditional and clumsy post-colonial societal structures that are little understood present a set of challenges for the AU. Also, political divisions between African nations create an environment of suspicion that hinders necessary cooperation between African states and their commitment to embracing the AU's counterterrorism policy. For instance, it took more than a decade for the Algiers Protocol to come into force, and only 15 member countries had ratified it as at early 2015 with some of the main players in the fight against terrorism in the continent such as Nigeria, Kenya, and Somalia been among those that have not (Allison, 2016). These issues, among others, prevent the AU from developing into a truly effective force.

## Global efforts at countering terrorism in Africa

Global efforts at countering terrorism in Africa are borne out of the realization that the continent is composed of ungoverned spaces that provide safe havens for terrorists to operate with impunity. Many African states are arguably weak and unable to provide safeguards or counter the threat posed by terrorism. Africa is thus thought to provide breeding grounds for terrorists that threaten the rest of the world (Antwi-Boateng, 2017: 253–284). The impact of globalisation and advancement in Information Communication and Technology (ICT) has more than ever before connected events in Africa to the rest of the globe (Forest and Giroux, 2011: 5–17). The mass human exodus of Africans seeking opportunities in Europe , and the Western world's search for investments and opportunities in Africa ensured that the international community could not fold their arms to the terrorism situation in Africa. To this end, countries and organisations such as the United States, United Kingdom, Canada, France, Germany, the EU, and the UN have, among a host of others, been active in providing military, diplomatic, economic, intelligence, law enforcement, and other lines of support to the continent.

The United States counterterrorism efforts in Africa, for example, began as far back as the 1990s in response to Al-Qaeda activities in the continent. In retaliation for the attacks on its embassies, the United States bombed a chemical plant in Sudan and subsequently conducted searches, capturing and killing alleged perpetrators of the attacks (Lyman, 2008: 249–259). The United States counterterrorism efforts in Africa became more pronounced after the September

11 attacks on the country. It combined both hard and soft approaches. In 2002, it established the Combined Joint Task Force-Horn of Africa (CJTF-HOA) in Djibouti. Also, as part of its Department of State's Antiterrorism Assistance (ATA) programme, the country provides training on a wide range of disciplines, including bomb detection and crime scene investigation in countries such as Tanzania.[26]

In countries such as Chad, Niger, and Burkina Faso, the United States Agency for International Development (USAID) is leading efforts to support youth empowerment through education, skills training, strengthening local governance capacity, and improving access to information thereby targeting groups most vulnerable to extremist ideologies. Similar United States' counterterrorism projects in Africa include the counterterrorism Finance (CTF) programme which provides African nations with internal and cross-border financial investigations training and the Global Counterterrorism Forum (GCTF) which focuses on identifying critical civilian counterterrorism needs.[27]

Generally, the United States programmes in Africa could be summed up as involving several components. These include political (led by the Department of State), economic (led by USAID), and military actions complemented by the establishment of a unified Africa Command (AFRICOM) in 2007 to bring together its varied security programmes in Africa. Some scholars and statesmen have however raised concerns that the new Africa Command and other United States anti-terrorism programmes signal an increased militarization of United States policy in Africa.[28] This seems to have become apparent under the new government of President Donald Trump giving the intention of the United States to go on with the sale of Super Tucana jets to Nigeria, increased presence of Predator and Reaper drones in its military bases in Niger, special forces operations in Somalia and bomber strikes against Islamic State extremist in Libya. Clearly, the balance between soft and hard approaches as well as human as opposed to state security in countering terrorism in Africa remains a challenge. The import of all of these is that countering terrorism in Africa has been daunting, and continue to be problematic at the national, regional, continental, and global levels.

## Conclusion

Terrorism visibly dominates the security landscape of Africa presenting a very potent security challenge that is both phenomenal and complex. Terrorism in Africa predates colonialism but became more pronounced in colonial and post-colonial Africa. The domestic type of terrorism appears to have had a longer history and higher occurrences than international terrorism. Even at this, globalisation has made it that events in Africa, including terrorism, resonates at the global level thereby blurring the line between domestic and international terrorism in Africa. Hence, from the 1990s when Osama bin Laden considered Africa a good ground for terrorism, the continent has not had a restive season from the threat of, and the fight against terrorism, attracting not only the concern of African states but the international community as well.

The efforts at countering terrorism in Africa have been at the levels of individual national governments, and collectively at sub-regional/regional and continental. At all of these levels, lofty schemes and programmes have been outlined. However, the commitment of African governments coupled with weak security architecture, ailing economies, political instability, and fractious relations have hampered the desired outcomes in the fight against terrorism in Africa. The African nations have had to rely on the support of the economically and technologically advanced countries including organizations such as the EU and the UN in its counterterrorism effort. This is not without its problems as more often than not, the interests of the advanced countries are brought into play.

Going forward, African countries need to individually and collectively go beyond talk-shops to build capacity and present a united front towards confronting terrorism in the continent. This is with the realisation that terrorism in one country is terrorism in all and that foreign assistance can only be effective if there is a commitment on the part of African states and their emplacement of good governance. The need to deemphasise the military-centric approach to counterterrorism, and emphasise people-centric responses based on democratic best practices, rule of law, and observance of human rights is imperative. Furthermore, is the requirement for all stakeholders, including the international community, to strengthen the AU. This is as it appears obvious that an effective continental counterterrorism framework already exists in the AU, and it is therefore up to member states and the union to implement it with the active support of the international community.

## Notes

1 See United States Department of Defence Country Reports on Terrorism for 2012, published 30 May 2013, online at https://www.state.gov/j/ct/rls/crt/2012/209979.htm, accessed 18 July 2017.
2 Some countries such as the United States and its agencies are silent on the aspect of state actors as perpetrators of terrorism. The Institute for Economics and Peace in its Global Terrorism Index also omitted state actors in its data.
3 See African Union Convention on the Prevention and Combating Terrorism Article 1 (3).
4 Ibid, Article 3 (1).
5 This resulted in the United Nations Security Council passing Resolution 1343 on 7 March imposing a new arms embargo on Liberia for supporting the RUF.
6 The ADF, LRA and ULIMO are examples as earlier mentioned in the text.
7 See Global Terrorism Index Report, *Institute for Economics and Peace*, November 2016, online at http://economicsandpeace.org/wp-content/uploads/2016/11/Global-Terrorism-Index-2016.2.pdf, accessed 29 August 2017. The African countries and ranking in the GTI are Nigeria (3$^{rd}$), Somalia (7$^{th}$), Egypt (9$^{th}$), Libya (10$^{th}$), Cameroon (13$^{th}$), Niger (16$^{th}$), DRC (17$^{th}$), Sudan (18$^{th}$), Kenya (19$^{th}$) and CAR (20$^{th}$).
8 Global Terrorism Index Report, *Institute for Economics and Peace*, November 2015, p. 2. Available online at http://economicsandpeace.org/wp-content/uploads/2015/11/Global-Terrorism-Index-2015.pdf, accessed 30 June 2017.
9 Counter Extremism Project Report, *Al-Qaeda in the Islamic Maghreb*, online at https://www.counterextremism.com/threat/al-qaeda-islamic-maghreb-aqimt, accessed 14 June 2017.
10 See Fox News, 2 March 2017, online at http://www.foxnews.com/world/2017/03/02/3-mali-islamic-extremist-groups-merge-pledge-to-al-qaida.html, accessed 20 August 2017.
11 See Nigeria's Boko Haram pledges allegiance to Islamic State, *BBC News* 7 March 2015, http://www.bbc.co.uk/news/world-africa-31784538, and LudovicaIaccino, "Nigeria: Boko Haram changes name to Islamic State's West African Province after Isis alliance." Online at http://www.ibtimes.co.uk/nigeria-boko-haram-changes-name-islamic-states-west-african-province-after-isis-alliance-1498696..., accessed 15 March 2017. The mainstream Boko Haram still remains under the leadership of Abubakar Shekau..
12 Nigeria's Attorney General and Minister of Justice, Abubakar Malami's speech at the 25th Session of the Commission on Crime Prevention and Criminal Justice in Vienna, Austria on 23 May, 2016. Online at http://www.pulse.ng/local/boko-haram-terrorists-can-no-longer-hold-territory-malami-says-id5070326.html, accessed 15 August 2017.
13 BBC News "Africa's Militant Islamic Groups" 6 December 2013, online at http://www.bbc.com/news/world-africa-24587491, accessed 14 January 2017.
14 Ibid.
15 General Carter F. Ham, AFRICOM Commander's speech during a special session at the Senior Leaders Seminar, hosted by the Africa Center for Strategic Studies on June 25, 2012, in Arlington, Virginia. Available online at http://nigerianssavingnigerians.org/2012/06/27/africoms-ham-says-u-s-interested-in-stable-secure-africa-more-than-ever-by-africa-center-for-strategic-studies/, accessed 23 March, 2017.
16 The reported number of deaths were: Westgate Shopping Mall (about 62), Garissa University College

(about 147), Lamu military base (3 Americans), Af-Urur military base (about 70 persons) as well as about 500 and 79 in the Mogadishu truck bombings of 2017 and 2019 respectively.

17  See US Army Field Manual, 2006, p. 4.

18  Global Centre on Cooperation Security/ISSP project "Strengthening Regional Capacities to Prevent and Counter Violent Extremism in the IGAD Region and the Greater Horn of Africa" publication, January 2015, online at http://www.globalcenter.org/wp-content/uploads/2015/01/22Jan2015-IGAD-CVE-PD.pdf, accessed 18 July 2017.

19  Security Council briefing on the situation in the Lake Chad Basin Region, Under-Secretary-General Jeffrey Feltman, United Nations Department of Political Affairs, New York, 27 July 2016. Online at http://www.un.org/undpa/en/speeches-statements/27072016/lake-chad-basin, accessed 21 August 2017.

20  Interview with Major General J. A. H. Ewansiha, Chief of Training and Operations Nigerian Army, Abuja, 3 March 2014.

21  The emergence of the CJTF was largely due to the over-stretching of government forces and the need to defend towns and villages where there was a deficit in security coverage.

22  Interview of Freedom C. Onuoha, Senior Research Fellow, Centre for African Research Studies Abuja, on 2 June 2015.

23  For example, Amnesty International allegations of extrajudicial killings in their report *Rank on Their Shoulders. Blood in Their Hands* and the United States refusal to sell arms to Nigeria on claims of human right abuses by the Nigerian military that contravenes the Leahy Law.

24  United Nations Office to the African Union Department of Political Affairs Counter Terrorism project outline available online at https://unoau.unmissions.org/counterterrorism, accessed 15 August 2017.

25  Ibid.

26  White House Office of the Press Secretary "Fact Sheet: Partnering to Counter Terrorism in Africa" 6 August 2014. Available online at https://obamawhitehouse.archives.gov/the-press-office/2014/08/06/fact-sheet-partnering-counterterrorism-africa, accessed 23 January 2017.

27  Ibid.

28  For example Solomon, Lyman, Mayer and Botha whose works were cited in this chapter.

# References

Akbar, Jay (2015, July 10). Like master, like servant: Nigerian terror group Boko Haram releases first beheading video since pledging allegiance to ISIS. *Daily Mail Online*. Available online at http://www.dailymail.co.uk/news/article-3156551/Like-master-like-servant-Nigerian-terror-group-Boko-Haram-releases-beheading-video-pledging-allegiance-ISIS.html, accessed 13 February 2017 at 1800hrs.

Allison, Simon (2016, January 26). 26th AU Summit: Why isn't the AU's counter-terrorism strategy working?. *Institute for Security Studies*. Available online at https://issafrica.org/iss-today/26th-au-summit-why-isnt-the-aus-counter-terrorism-strategy-working, accessed 19 August 2017 at 2104hrs.

Anderson, D. (2013). *Histories of the hanged: The dirty war in Kenya and the end of empire*. London: W. W. Norton.

Antwi-Boateng, Osman (2017). The rise of Pan-Islamic terrorism in Africa: A global security challenge. *Politics & Policy*, *45*, 2. Available online at http://library.cqpress.com/cqresearcher/document.php?id=cqresrre2015071000, accessed 3 January 2019 at 2228hrs.

Botha, Anneli (2008). Challenges in understanding terrorism in Africa: A human security perspective. *Africa Security Review*, *17*(2), 28–41.

Chauzal, G. & T. V. Damme (2015, March). The roots of Mali's conflict moving beyond the 2012 crisis. *Clingendael Institute's Conflict Research Unit*. Available online at https://www.clingendael.nl/pub/2015/the_roots_of_malis_conflict/3_a_playing_field_for_foreign_powers/, accessed 12 August 2018 at 1717hrs.

Chivis, Christopher S., & Liepman, Andrew (2013). *North Africa's menace: AQIM's evolution and the US policy response*. Santa Monica, CA: Rand National Defense Research Institute.

Comolli, Virginia (2015). *Boko Haram: Nigeria's Islamist insurgency*. London: Hurst & Co Ltd.

Crenshaw, Martha (Ed.). (1994). *Terrorism in Africa*. Boston: GK Hall & Co.

Crenshaw, Martha. (2009). Intimations of mortality or production lines? The puzzle of "Suicide Terrorism." *Political Psychology*, *30*(3), 359–364.

Dasuki, Sambo Mohammed. (2014, March). *The Roll Out of Nigeria's Soft Approach to Countering Terrorism*. Paper presented at Counter Terrorism seminar, Abuja, Nigeria.

Davenport, David L. (2011). Acholi Clan, Ethnic, and National Identities in Post-Conflict Northern Uganda: A Case Study in Koch Goma Sub-County, Nwoya District. *Independent Study Project (ISP) Collection. Paper 1206*. Available online at http://digitalcollections.sit.edu/isp_collection/1206, accessed 12 March 2019 at 1414hrs.

Forest, James, & Giroux, Jennifer (2011). Terrorism and political violence in Africa: Contemporary trends in a shifting terrain. *Perspectives on Terrorism*. *5*(3–4), 5–15.

Boaz, Ganor (2002). Defining terrorism: Is one man's terrorist another man's freedom fighter?. *Police Practice and Research*, *3*(4), 287–304.

Gibbs, Jack P. (2012). Conceptualization of terrorism. In J. Hogan & K. Braddock (Eds.), *Terrorism studies: A reader*. Abingdon, UK: Routledge.

Hoffman, B. (2006). *Inside terrorism*. New York: Columbia University Press.

Hoskin, Veronica (2010, May 4). Algeria/Mali/Mauritania/Niger: Tamanrasset plan. *Africa Research Bulletin: Political, Social and Cultural Series*, *14*, 156–191.

Kyari, Mohammed (2014). The message and methods of Boko Haram. In Marc-Antoine Pérouse de Montclos (Ed.), *Boko Haram: Islamism, politics, security and the state in Nigeria* (Vol. 2). Leiden: African Studies Centre (ASC) Institut Français de Rechercheen Afrique (IFRA) West African Politics and Society Series.

Laub, Zachary, & Jonathan Masters (2015). *Al-Qaeda in the Islamic Maghreb (AQIM)*. New York: Council on Foreign Relations. Available online at https://www.cfr.org/backgrounder/al-qaeda-islamic-maghreb, accessed 15 June 2019 at 2012hrs.

Lyman, Princeton N (2010). The war on terrorism in Africa. In Donald Rothschild & Edmond Keller (Eds.), *Africa-US Relation: Strategic Encounters*. Boulder, Col: Lynne Rienner.

Madike, Isioma. (2011, June 19). *Boko Haram: Rise of a deadly sect. National Mirror (Nigeria): June 19*.

Melson, Charles D. (2005). Top secret war: Rhodesian special operations. *Small Wars and Insurgencies*, *16*(1), 57–82.

Mayer, Jane (2008). *The dark side: The inside story of how the war on terror turned into a war on American Ideals*. New York: Doubleday.

Morell, Michael, & Harlow, Bill (2015). *The great war of our time*. New York: Twelve.

Moses, Rose (2017, August 5). How decimated is Boko Haram?. *Vanguard Newspaper*. Available online at https://www.vanguardngr.com/2017/08/decimated-boko-haram/, accessed 28 August 2018 at 1726hrs.

Nti, Nana Bemma. (2014). *Silence on the Lambs: The Abducted Chibok Schoolgirls in Nigeria and the Challenge to UNSCR 1325*. Kofi Anan International Peacekeeping Training Centre Policy Brief 3. Available online at http://www.kaiptc.org/Publications/Policy-Briefs/Policy-Briefs/Nana-KAIPTC-Policy-Brief-3---The-Abducted-Chibok-S.aspx, accessed 14 December 2018 at 1233hrs.

Ochoche, Sunday A, (2006). Terrorism and counter-terrorism: An African experience. In T. A. Imobighe & A. N. T. Eguavoen (Eds.), *Terrorism and counter-terrorism: An African perspective*. Ibadan: Heinemann Educational Books.

Ochoche, Sunday A. (2016). Terrorism and counter terrorism: The African experience. In T. A. Imobighe & A. N. Eguavoen (Eds.), *Terrorism and counter terrorism: An African perspective*. Ibadan: Heinemann.

Odhiambo, Elijah O. S., Maito, Thomas L., Kassilly, Janet, Chelumo, Sarah, Onkware, Kennedy, & Oboka, Wycliffe A. (2013). Al-Shabaab Terrorists Propaganda and the Kenya Government Response. Available online at http://ijhssnet.com/journals/Vol_3_No_7_April_2013/14.pdf, accessed 15 May 2018 at 1600hrs.

Okumu, W. (Ed.). (2009). *Domestic terrorism in Africa: Defining, addressing and understanding its impact on human security*. Pretoria: Institute for Security Studies.

Onuoha, Freedom. C. (2010). The Islamist challenge: Nigeria's Boko Haram crisis explained. *African Security Review*, *19*(2), 54–67.

Oyeniyi, A. B. (2010). Terrorism in Nigeria, groups, activities and politics. *International Journal of Politics and Good Governance*, *1*(1), 1–16, available: http://onlineresearchjournals.com/ijopagg/art/42.pdf.

Rugy, V. (2010). The economics of homeland security. In Friedman, et al., *Terrorizing ourselves: Why US counter terrorism policy is failing and how to fix it*. Washington DC: Cato Institute.

Schmid, Alex P., Jongman, Albert J., et al. (1988). *Political terrorism: A new guide to actors, authors, concepts, data bases, theories, and literature.* New Brunswick, New Jersey: Transaction Books.

Schmid, Alex P., & Jongman, A. (2005). *Political terrorism.* Piscataway, New Jersey: Transaction Publishers.

Sepgupta, Somini. (2017). U.N. Security Council Welcomes Deployment of New Counterterrorism Force in Africa. New York Times, 21 June 2017. Available online at https://www.nytimes.com/2017/06/21/world/africa/security-council-sahel-france-united-states.html, accessed 12 August 2018 at 2344hrs.

Shuriye, Abdi O. (2012). Al-Shabaab's Leadership Hierarchy and its Ideology, *Academic Research International*, 2(1), 274–285, available: http://www.savap.org.pk/journals/ARInt./Vol.2%281%29/2012%282.1-32%29.pdf.

Solomon, Hussein (2015). *Terrorism and counter-terrorism in Africa fighting insurgency from Al Shabaab, Ansar Dine and Boko Haram.* London: Palgrave Macmillan.

Udeh, Chinedu S. (2013). Boko Haram and counter terrorism strategy in Nigeria. In O. Mbachu & U. Bature (Eds.), *Internal Security Management in Nigeria: A Study in Terrorism and Counter-Terrorism.* Kaduna: Medusa.

# 4

# Counterterrorism and postcolonial crisis in Africa

*Ubong Essien Umoh*

## Introduction

This chapter is tasked with the intellectual and academic responsibility of illuminating the relationship between counterterrorism and the postcolonial crisis in Africa as a historical process of cause and effect. It is a modest attempt at emphasising aspects of change and continuity in the postcolonial crisis in Africa burdened with superfluous phrases and scornful superlatives. The chapter highlights the postcolonial phase in Africa as crisis-ridden with an emphasis on counterterrorism as only reinforcing a tragic condition made possible by the quality of governance. Engaging the trifecta of democratisation, security, and development, the chapter draws significantly upon the weak state argument which is the basis for terrorism and its twin component, counterterrorism. The chapter identifies two basic styles for countering terrorism in Africa: continental and extra-continental. Both styles overlap and have depended largely upon counterterrorism regimes—sets of implicit or explicit principles, norms, rules, and decision-making procedures for countering terrorism. While the continental approach captures the effort of the Organization of African Unity (OAU)/African Union (AU), the extra-continental approach captures the counterterrorism regimes and practices of the United Nations (UNO, European Union (EU), the United States (US) and its western allies. Both approaches have been intent upon absolving the threat of terrorism by denying it support and sanctuaries in Africa. However, the extent to which this reinforces Africa's overbearing dependency and weakness is an analytic thread that runs through the chapter.

## Evolving a phrase for a phase: post-colonial Africa and its crisis

Postcoloniality in Africa is a phase, albeit a final phase denoting a leap forward from the precolonial and colonial phases. At a glance, it should suggest changes over time, however, distinct continuities from its antecedent phase (colonialism) appear to curtail its quality. As a peculiar and dynamic phase that is magnetic to crises, it has attracted a plethora of phrases from the academic such as "failed state", "failing state", "weak state", "fragile state", "infantilist state", "baby states", "dependent state", "third world state", "crisis state", "vampire state", "predatory state", "developing state", "hell-hole", "shit hole", "political jungle", "warlord state", "juridical (as opposed to empirical) states", "pirate state", "quasi-states", "suspended states", "kleptocratic state", "collapsed states", "weak states", "imported states", and "lame Leviathans", among others. These metaphors of the postcolonial crisis in Africa blow-up images of postcolonial realities and dismiss Africa as the world's most troubled continent and a continent full of surprises. All these expressions fit into Dowden's (2008) description of African states as "altered", surviving by "ordinary miracles", and Meredith's (2006) political commentary on Africa. It also nests into Chinweizu's (1975) pessimistic image of Africa's dependency on the West.

The blend of crises that have embraced states in Africa after the colonial phase has often been argued to be linked to colonial heritage and post-colonial vestigial structures. As Ake (1981) enthused, for the majority of African states, the expression "postcolonial" does not mean that the economy has been decolonized or no longer possesses the features of a colonial economy. Ashcroft (2001a, 2001b) portrays postcolonial as the dynamic ways and means post-colonial African societies have responded to colonial control, revealing the remarkable capacity for change and adaptation. Consequently, the African postcolonial crisis also throws up the elastic relationship between colony and post-colony, colonial and postcolonial as well as colonial crisis and postcolonial crisis. As observed by (Omeje, 2008: 92), "most African states entered the postcolonial phase beleaguered, fractured and straggling." In the array of literature on the postcolonial crisis in Africa, there has been an overall scholarly temptation to analyze the postcolonial crisis in Africa through the filter of Marxist and dependency theorists. The colonial political economy by inference set the background for the "phenomenon of infantilism" where the African state became wholesomely dependent on the West resulting in control and manipulation. For Andre Gunder Frank (1966), the colonial phase arguably set the pace for the development of underdevelopment in Africa; while Walter Rodney (1973) blamed Europe for the underdevelopment of Africa. Claude Ake's (1981) *Political Economy of Africa* was far less polite in submitting that the colonial economy was characterized by disarticulation and incoherence, giving rise to a dependent economy upon independence.

Although the international system is structured to be independent and interdependent, the African condition has been that of more dependence after independence. Indeed, in the African context, interdependence appears to have reinforced dependency. The continuous dependency appears to depict Africa as a "perpetual child" in need of support, assistance, mentoring, supervision, and even guidance from above and without. This portrays Africa as a time-space of infantilism, requiring continuous western propping and chaperoning (Omeje, 2008: 93). Such propping and chaperoning have assumed taxonomies like assist, reform, develop, protect, modernize, liberate, stabilize, emancipate, strengthen, boost, among others.

Africa's postcolonial crises are threefold: the crisis of democratisation, the crisis of security, and the crisis of development; resting on a dominant tripod dimension: political, security, and economic. All these bother on the quality of governance in African states. Counterterrorism in Africa concerns with the second leg of the tripod – security. Consequently, three dual themes appear to have informed the continuous prodding of Western response, interference, and influence in Africa: democracy and democratization, security and insecurity; economic growth and development. This overlaps with the three dimensions to the postcolonial crisis in Africa. The need to enforce democracy on African states, especially during the Cold War period, resulted in the proliferation of splinter groups bearing different manifestoes for the democracy project (Umoh, 2012). Consequently, civil wars blossomed across Africa with dyads employing a wide range of free fall tactics including terrorism. As it turned out, African civil wars became a problem for development, exacerbating Seers' (1969) tripod of poverty, unemployment, and inequality. Within Africa, the postcolonial crisis has been sustained by a compromise and connivance between the ruler and the ruled making for what Clapham (1982) calls "clientelism" and "patronage" or what Joseph (1983, 1987) refers to as "prebendalism" or what Mbembe (2001, 2006) denotes as the "logic of conviviality" and the "intimacy of tyranny" or what Thomson (2008) identifies as "legitimacy through materialism".

African politics in its post-colonial phase have been marred by authoritarianism, corruption, military intervention, and leadership failures amidst a broader socio-economic crisis characterized by poverty. These favorite themes bother on the quality of governance and have made democracy a necessary western prescription for African states. However, peace based on democratic consolidation in Africa has increasingly made the continent more conflict-prone as democratizing states have shown a greater tendency to experience armed conflicts than stable autocracies (Chole & Ibrahim, 1995; O'Donnell & Schmitter, 1986; Söderberg & Ohlson, 2003; Umoh, 2012, 2015). Most manifestations of instability in African states are proceeds from the democratization process. According to van der Walt and Solomon (2014: 72–73):

> The post-9/11 counterterrorism strategies proposed for weak and failing states argue that the promotion of democracy and good governance will result in increasing the legitimacy of the ruling power to exercise control over its territory and population by means of regular, multiparty elections, and by providing a conducive setting for socio-economic reforms (i.e. the alleviation of extreme poverty). Such developments, it is suggested, will in turn allow for the building of state capacity and institutions aimed at combating terrorism, through the training and rebuilding of the security forces – so-called security sector reform.

The quality of democracy in a majority of African states ridicules what democracy represents in theory, substance, and practice. The test run and a trial version of democracy in Africa or what can be aptly called "African democracy" results in an outcome of heat transfer to the security landscape of most post-independence African states. Consequently, the post-independence African space has begged for immediate and sustained external intervention as many states, given their fragile nature, became hotbeds of insurgency and domains of terrorists.

The quality of governance made possible by a malfunctioned leadership is a direct manifestation of weak states in Africa. To this end, weak state capacity has served as one of the significant variables of the postcolonial crisis in Africa. For much of Africa, weak state capacity remains a causal swing between failing state and failed state. Such states, with their litany of ungoverned spaces, hold a number of attractions for terrorist organizations (Takeyh & Gvosdev, 2009). However, as Scott (2017) avers, such states in Africa are in fact failed post-colonies. They are less the failure of existing states and more the failed rooting and institutionalization of imported and reified models of Western statehood (Scott, 2017). This suffices to reinforce the relationship between a colony and colonial, post-colony and post-colonial, as well as post-colony crisis and post-colonial crisis.

Postcolonial as a phrase denoting a period after the colonial setting was preceded by decolonization which in most cases was violent. For the colonial government, most expression and the manifestation of decolonization violence were acts of terrorism attracting counterterrorism responses. A good example was the decolonization process in French Algeria between 1954 and 1962. As submitted by Reid (2012: 328): "One of the most striking features of postcolonial Africa's trajectory has been the proliferation of violent conflict, and what can be termed the militarization of political culture." In most African states, this postcolonial militarized political culture became sustained and viewed as terrorism by the postcolonial African state.

States in Africa have arguably turned into a terrorist menu (Davis, 2010). In most states, criminality has morphed into terrorism. Freedom fighters have acted in the capacity of terrorists, challenging the essence of counterterrorism. For instance, the *Al Shabaab* in Somalia started first as a freedom fighter but was later tagged as a terrorist group when they employed terrorist tactics. The same applied to the Movement for the Emancipaption of the Niger Delta (MEND) after the bombing of the Eagle Square in Abuja, Nigeria, on October 1, 2010.

## Theorising counterterrorism for postcolonial Africa

Unlike terrorism which lacks an internationally recognized definition, counterterrorism can easily be established. Whatever definition terrorism may assume, counterterrorism is its response. However, unlike terrorism, counterterrorism involves a significant dose of speculation. It could be propelled by events that have not yet happened, be a result of speculation on possible threats, and undertaking measures to prevent them through fortifying defenses, bolstering the capability to respond to, and recover from, terrorist attack (Sheehan, 2007). Indeed, the need to prevent and deter future terrorist attacks encompasses the objective of counterterrorism. Consequently, counterterrorism in Africa is not just a response to terrorism but a check to the weight of the crisis that pervades the African landscape. It addresses state security in general and interfaces with its nearest synonym – countering violent extremism (CVE). As such, counterterrorism is often lumped into the CVE literature (see Gow, Olonisakin, & Dijxhoorn, 2013; Ramdeen, 2017).

Counterterrorism, like counterinsurgency, remains one of the few military malpractices (see Osakwe & Umoh, 2013). Some aspects of counterinsurgency have been grouped with counterterrorism and scant literature on the subject has upheld this dilemma (see Sharan, 2016). Hughes (2011) has argued that the confusion between insurgency and terrorism is obstructed by willful acts of conflation, such as the Bush administration's insistence that the invasion and occupation of Iraq was part of the War on Terror. Given the integration of the tactics of terrorism into an insurgency, counterinsurgency operations have interfaced counterterrorism, making it difficult to distinguish between the two. As further enthused by Hughes (2011: 7): "…terrorism often co-exists with other forms of internal conflict, and in practice, it is often difficult to distinguish between counterterrorism and counterinsurgency (COIN). Furthermore, terrorism can also be a by-product of intense civil strife…". This implies that terrorism is elastic, embracing a range of violence subsets which adds to its overall complex outlook.

Consequently, counterinsurgency operations against *Al Shabaab, Ansar Dine,* and *Boko Haram* are also considered counterterrorism operations given the ambiguous employment of terror tactics as well as the amorphous nature of their overall armed activities at the strategic and operational levels. While East Africa has served as a hotbed of the Al-Qaeda terrorist group, North Africa appears to serve as a transit route for terrorists targeting Europe, and West Africa has witnessed an increased propensity to express their rejection of western values through terrorist acts (see Diallo, 2005) carried out by terrorist organisations such as *al-Shabaab, Boko Haram* (and its splinter, the Islamic State in West Africa Province), Al-Qaeda in the Islamic Maghreb (AQIM), and *al-Murabitoun.* In the Sahel, AQIM and *al-Murabitoun* continue to operate in parts of northern Mali and along the border corridor between Mali, Burkina Faso, Cote d'Ivoire, Niger, and Libya.

In terms of the discipline of history's guiding law of cause and effect, Africa's postcolonial crisis is the cause and counterterrorism the effect. Drawing from this, counterterrorism is captured as a response to one of the features of the postcolonial crisis in Africa – terrorism. The relationship between counterterrorism and the postcolonial crisis in Africa props out as a complicated link between association and causality, with counterinsurgency serving as the object of study and the postcolonial crisis in Africa as the subject of study.

## Continental counterinsurgency regimes and practices in postcolonial Africa

Although counterterrorism in Africa has been argued to be a sideshow, compared with the more critical struggles taking place in the strategically important areas of the Middle East (le Sage, 2008), the African context has been deserving of study given the depth of continental attraction and attention. Circumscribed within the continental approach has been the efforts of states at the regional and sub-regional level in propping up regimes to identify, deter, intercept and prevent terrorism – making for what the chapter refers to as counterterrorism regimes. Such regimes at a glance meant an African solution to an African problem.

The first African continental position on terrorism came in 1992 as a response to a wave of violence from Islamist groups in Algeria. The Organization of African Unity (OAU) Resolution 213 on the Strengthening of Cooperation and Coordination among the African States claimed: "...to strengthen cooperation and coordination among African countries in order to circumvent the phenomenon of extremism and terrorism"(http://www.peaceau.org/uploads/algiers-convention-terrorism.pdf). This was followed in 1994 by the Tunis Declaration on a Code of Conduct for Inter-African Relations. The Declaration arguably was characterised by the key counterterrorism principle of *aut dedere aut judicare*, which forces states to either bring terrorist suspects to justice or extradite them (see http://www.un.org/popin/oau/tunisdcl.htm).

More progress was made after the twin bombings of the US embassies in Nairobi and Dar es Salaam in 1998. It accelerated the 1999 Algiers Convention on the Prevention and Combating of Terrorism. The Convention put in place a criminal justice framework for counterterrorism in Africa. The Algiers Convention defined areas of cooperation among states and provided a legal framework for extradition as well as extra-territorial investigations and mutual legal assistance (http://www.peaceau.org/uploads/algiers-convention-terrorism.pdf). In January 2002, a regional summit of East African leaders was held in Khartoum to endorse a resolution against international terrorism. Tunisia launched its counterterrorism law in 2003 – a piece of legislation for dealing with terrorism offenses. The Antiterrorism Brigade (BAT) under the Ministry of Interior's National Police was also set up and became responsible for tactical operations related to counterterrorism and in aiding the Ministry of Interior and Ministry of Defense in detecting, deterring, and preventing acts of terrorism. In Egypt, the 'terrorist entities' law consisting of ten articles was passed by President Abdel Fattah al-Sisi.

In 2004, the AU adopted the anti-terrorism protocol which required 15 states to ratify it before entering into force. In the same year, the South African government enacted the Protection of Constitutional Democracy against Terrorist and Related Activities Act (POCDATARA). In 2007, the Government of Senegal amended its criminal code to establish criminal offenses for terrorist acts as defined in the Organization of African Unity Convention on the Prevention and Combating of Terrorism. Since 2014, military forces in the Lake Chad Basin region, have endeavoured to work together through the Multinational Joint Task Force (MNJTF) to counter *Boko Haram*. Similarly, forces from 11 Economic Community of West African States (ECOWAS) states initially responded to the security crisis in Mali and worked alongside the French military to destroy terrorist safe havens in northern Mali and provide the stability required for the peace process to advance. Senegal has worked to improve its law enforcement capacity by participating in multilateral training events organized by the Global Counterterrorism Forum (GCTF), African Union (AU), and ECOWAS (Maluki, n.d).

## Extra-continental counterterrorism regimes and practices in postcolonial Africa

Extra-continental counterterrorism regimes and practices show that terrorism in Africa is far from being an African problem in need of an African solution. Contemporary globalisation feasting on a system of networks makes terrorism an extra-continental concern and attraction. State and non-state actors beyond the African continent have been involved with counter-terrorism in Africa. The United Nations (UN), the European Union (EU), and the United States (US) have been the most engaging of the extra-continental agents. Throughout Africa, an overview of UN activities in assisting Member States to address terrorism can be gleaned from the various UN General Assembly and Security Council resolutions, hereby identified as regimes. These UN regimes primarily include but are not limited to Security Council resolutions 1267 (1999) and 1989 (2011), 1373 (2001), 1540 (2004) and 1624 (2005), and General Assembly resolution 60/288 on the United Nations Global counterterrorism Strategy (UNGCTS) adopted by the Assembly in 2006 and its subsequent review resolutions. On 21 May 2013, the Security Council considered the challenges posed by terrorism in Africa in the context of maintaining international peace and security.

During the 1990s the Security Council acted against incidents of terrorism by, at the most extreme, imposing economic and diplomatic sanctions in states. This was evident in relation to Libya in 1993 (in response to the Lockerbie bombing) and Sudan in 1996 (in response to the prescient Sudanese government support for Bin Laden and acts of terrorism) (Norman, 2004). The 2006 regime strategy is based upon four pillars: addressing the conditions conducive to the spread of terrorism (Pillar I), preventing and combating terrorism (Pillar II), building the states' capacities and strengthening the role of the United Nations (Pillar III), and ensuring human rights and the rule of law (Pillar IV). All UN African member states signed on to the UN Global counterterrorism Strategy, and African states and sub-regional bodies progressed in making efforts at countering terrorism by adhering to the four pillars of the UN. The regime identifies the capacity building as a central element of global counterterrorism efforts. The International Monetary Fund (IMF) has also provided capacity development advice on anti-money-laundering and countering the financing of terrorism to several Governments in Africa, in-cluding Comoros, Ghana, Morocco, Nigeria, Sao Tomé and Principe, South Sudan, and Sudan.

The European Security Strategy (2003) considered terrorist cells emerging in Africa as a threat to the European Union (EU). However, counterterrorism appeared to have remained a marginal concern as revealed in its Common Foreign and Security Policy (CFSP) regime (Sicurelli, 2010). EU action in countering terrorism is often organised around four objectives: prevention, protection, pursuit, and response. In 2007, the EU established the Instrument for Stability (IfS) and rechristened it as the Instrument contributing to Stability and Peace (IcSP). The Horn of Africa (HOA), the Middle East and North Africa (MENA), and the Sahel (Mali, Mauritania, and Niger) make up the geographical areas under the scope of IcSP (https://ec. europa.eu/europeaid/sectors/human-rights-and-governance/peace-and-security/instrument-contributing-stability-and-peace_en). In Africa, the EU and its member states deal simulta-neously with the African Union (AU), the regional economic communities such as the Southern African Development Community (SADC), the Intergovernmental Authority on Development (IGAD) and the Economic Community of Western African States (ECOWAS), and individual states. Much of EU counterterrorism action in Africa is undertaken within the framework of The Africa-EU Strategic Partnership. The Africa-EU strategic partnership calls for cooperation in many areas, including politics, development, and security (European

Commission/African Union Commission 2007). This partnership provides multiple avenues through which the EU and African states can explore how to pursue counterterrorism while enhancing democracy (Makinda, 2009). In June 2017, the EU pledged to fund a counter-terrorism force made up of troops from Mauritania, Mali, Chad, Burkina Faso, and Niger – known as the Sahel G-5.

The US has been at the forefront of counterterrorism efforts in Africa for obvious reasons. It has been an integral aspect of their foreign policy echoing President Kennedy's Inaugural Address on January 20, 1961, that "... we shall pay any price, bear any burden, meet any hardship, support any friend, oppose any foe, to assure the survival and success of liberty". The bombing of Libya in 1986 by the Reagan administration in response to Libyan sponsored terrorist attacks against US targets in Europe; the US cruise missile attacks on targets in Sudan in 1998 in response to the *Al Qaeda* bombings of US embassies in Kenya and Tanzania point to US counterterrorism posture in Africa before 9/11. However, since the attacks on 11 September 2001, the US and the western world have been engaged in what has been con-troversially called the "war on terror" (Howard, Sawyer, & Bajema, 2009). The "war on terror" and the war on terrorism emerged as an attractive phrase for counterterrorism during the Bush administration. Obama's Administration chose to rebrand the subject of terror and use the expression "oversea contingency operations" (see Whitaker, 2010). As argued by the erstwhile US Secretary of Defense, Robert Gates, what is dubbed the War on Terror, is in grim reality, a prolonged worldwide irregular campaign – a struggle between the forces of violent extremism and moderation. Even when the initial "war on terror" appeared to start and concentrate in Afghanistan and Iraq (see Rogers, 2004), Africa, distanced and reluctant as it was, could not be left out or neglected in Bush's expanded "war on terror." As counterterrorism became spec-ulative and proactive, efforts greatly expanded into Africa. In this regard, US-Africa counter-terrorism relations connote shifting geopolitics in an age of terror (Kraxberger, 2005). By all means, after 9/11, Africa transformed from a continent in need of humanitarian help and aid to a risk continent in need of counter-terror security.

At the strategic level, US counterterrorism in Sub-Saharan Africa is a quad-fold structure (see Dempsey, 2006). The first is kinetic military operations which target hubs and sanctuaries of terrorists in Africa through aerial bombardment and drone strikes. The second is security assistance programs with African regional partners focused on building local state capacity to counter terrorism across African states through logistical support, training missions, and in-telligence assistance. Third, is the expanding scope of extradition agreements and partnerships with law enforcement agencies in Africa, while working with African states and their inter-national organisations to restrict the ability of terrorist groups to operate in the global commons. The fourth is addressing the root cause of terrorism through developmental programming.

The attempt to build a robust partnership in Africa to counterterrorism is seen in the es-tablishment of the Pan Sahel Initiative (PSI), the Trans-Sahel Counterterrorism Initiative (TSCTI), the East Africa Counterterrorism Initiative (EACTI), and the establishment of Joint Task Force-Horn of Africa (JTF HOA) in Djibouti (Dempsey, 2006; Kraxberger, 2005). The US military's Africa Command (AFRICOM) was established in response to Washington's concerns over ungoverned spaces on the continent and their potential for development as safe havens for Al-Qaeda and other transnational terrorist groups. Between 3 and 23 May 2010, AFRICOM oversaw Operation FLINTLOCK, a training exercise in the Sahel involving 600 US troops; 150 Europeans from France, Germany, the Netherlands, Spain, and the UK; and 400 soldiers from Burkina Faso, Chad, Mauritania, Mali, Niger, Nigeria, and Senegal. In 2014, FLINTLOCK brought together more than 1,000 troops from 18 countries, including eight African nations. In 2016, the exercise involved 30 military armies from the African continent and beyond (https://www.economist.com/news/middle-east-and-africa/21693739-americas-fbi-helps-train-new-generation-new-kind-conflict-counterterrorism).

Nigeria has enjoyed robust relations with the US regarding counterterrorism cooperation. The Government of Nigeria, through the help of the US, has an intelligence infusion cell, the Joint Terrorist Branch (JTAB), tasked with streamlining coordination and information sharing on counterterrorism matters among key agencies, which includes the State Security Service (SSS), the intelligence agencies, the national police, and the military. The Nigerian government participates in US counterterrorism capacity programs under the US Department of State's Antiterrorism Assistance program, including the training of members of the Nigeria Police Force in the awareness and capacity to protect and preserve evidence from terrorism crime scenes (Maluki, n.d). Through the Anti-Terrorism Assistant (ATA) program, Nigeria Police, customs officials, and immigration officers also participated in an interagency rural border patrol training to build the law enforcement sector's ability to effectively utilise all agencies in tackling rural border security challenges. With US training and assistance, the government established an Anti-Terrorism Police Unit (ATPU), the Joint Terrorism Task Force (later disbanded), a National counterterrorism Centre, and a National Security Advisory Committee. The US Department of State's Antiterrorism Assistance (ATA) program has also provided the Senegalese government with training and enabling equipment to build investigative and border security capacities. Through the Regional Strategic Initiative (RSI), ATA helped establish a Cyber Crime Investigative Unit with the Senegalese National Police, Criminal Investigative Unit (Maluki, n.d).

## Implications of counterterrorism for postcolonial crisis in Africa

From the standpoint of military history, counterinsurgency in Africa in part manages a post-colonial military problem – that of a professional and modernised African military in terms of force projection, strategy, tactics, and techniques. Terrorist groups and terror cells have taken advantage of the overall weakness of most African states in terms of ungoverned spaces and undisciplined political-military force to sustain their activities. External counterterrorism assistance appears to help curb the ineffectiveness bandwidth of African militaries to respond to terrorist threats and terror tactics. The weapon systems needed to prevent, intercept, and repel terrorism are much higher quality than what the domestic arms industry of most African states can manufacture. For instance, the Offensive Handgun System (OHGS) such as the MP-5 series, Cobra Helicopters, high-tech surveillance and attack drones, Bluetooth communication devices, and a wide range of non-lethal weapons, are force multipliers for counterterrorism that a majority of African militaries lack the local capacity to produce and deploy. It appears that African militaries have become better equipped and updated in the context of counter-insurgency operations. Consequently, it provides a way out of the postcolonial problem of a non-professionalised and non-modernised military in Africa. Although dependency theorists may be quick and apt at identifying the imperial consequences of external military assistance; the skills, knowledge, and confidence made possible by this military interdependence for African militaries cannot be neglected. After all, the lack of military professionalism makes it easier for social entrepreneurs of violence to carry out terrorist attacks on designated targets.

Counterterrorism in Africa has also accelerated the pace of regional and sub-regional integration in Africa. Regional responses from OAU/AU, as well as sub-regional responses from organisations like ECOWAS and SADC, have strengthened the fabric of regional and sub-regional unity and cooperation. Of the various African sub-regional organisations, ECOWAS and SADC stand out as having achieved some measure of security cooperation.

Cooperation in the aspect of intelligence sharing among West African states surged with the abduction of the Chibok girls by *Boko Haram* (see Cline, 2016). Bilateral and multilateral treaties between and among African states have witnessed a surge in the face of counterterrorism commitments. Military cooperation has also redoubled. In October 2014, the Lake Chad Basin Commission (LCBC) member states (Cameroon, Chad, Niger, and Nigeria) and Benin decided to improve their cooperation to counter *Boko Haram*, by pledging troops to the Multinational Joint Task Force (MNJFT) set up in 1998 to combat transnational crime in the Lake Chad region.

However, since counterinsurgency in Africa depends largely on western assistance, it partly reflects a challenge to the sovereignty of African states. Sovereignty remains a key noun in international relations and studies. Colonialism, imperialism, nationalism, separatism, irredentism, neocolonialism, neo-imperialism, pseudo-colonialism, core and periphery, metropole and satellite, north and south, as well as mother and baby, are variations of the theme of sovereignty. Consequently, the degree to which a state perceives its sovereignty threatened in relation to gains made from the international system, determines resistance or acceptance. The sovereignty of postcolonial African states has remained largely contested and externally influenced thereby resulting in continuity rather than change from colonial rule. In Omeje's (2008: 89) words: "the US-led war on terror tends to reinforce the crisis of postcoloniality in Africa by deliberately producing metaphors, images, discourses, doctrines, and policies aimed at magnifying and mainstreaming terrorism scares on the turbulent politico-economic landscape of Africa, as a means to justify imperial governance and supervision".

To this end, while some African states have embraced western initiatives of establishing offshore zones of security hubs in Africa like African Command (AFRICOM) and other similar initiatives, others have appeared to express overwhelming reluctance and others have out rightly resisted it (see Whitaker, 2010). Operation MONOGRAM, the British Ministry of Defence's program for training foreign armies in counterterrorism tactics, received negative press scrutiny in July 2008 that focused on the Kenyan Army's elite unit. Also, the establishment of AFRICOM aroused a generally wary response from African states which explains why its headquarters is still based in Stuttgart, Germany. Nigeria suspects that it is a means of undercutting its regional influence, while South Africa expresses concerns that AFRICOM will destabilise the continent by embroiling it in the War on Terror, thereby undermining the African Union. Consequently, AFRICOM has been portrayed in academic circles as a Trojan Horse for US neocolonialism and as a cover for its commercial, economic, and strategic competition with China and other powers that are developing their own stake in exploiting Africa's resources.

Overlapping with the above position is the contention that counterterrorism in Africa has consequently increased and renewed dependency – the central theme of Africa's postcolonial crisis. African states appear not to have ownership of the counterterrorism programs and policies of various extra-continental counterterrorism regimes which African states are required to implement. Since much of counterterrorism depends on external aid and funding, as argued by Okumu and Botha (2007), the African voice generally has not been adequately represented in global debates on security matters, and on terrorism and counterterrorism in particular. Such dependency further factors into the weak state argument making for continuity rather than a change in Africa's postcolonial crisis. It captures another betrayal of Africa in the tortuous pathway of post-colonial development (Ayittey, 1993). With the continued prevalence of counterterrorism in Africa, another part of the Karl Maier's (2002) "African house" appears to be falling fast.

Given that terrorism in Africa is an outcome of weak state phenomena, counterterrorism in Africa relies upon the Hobbesian Leviathan – a security goliath the west alone can best provide. Consequently, some countries have jumped on board and seized the anti-terrorism rhetoric, others have been reluctant partners, and several have resisted the imposition of the regime (Whitaker, 2010). Indeed, "counterterrorism from above" portrays African states as weak states incapable of independently ensuring their security. These states in Africa are weak because they are dependent and they are dependent because they are weak. Moreover, they can only remain dependent as long as they remain weak – a feature that appears to be self-inflicted and convenient. The weakness is not an unfortunate predicament but a conscious creation that is intent upon attracting agents of foreign interests, making for what Doyle (1986) and Ndlovu-Gatsheni (2007) call "imperialism by invitation." So intense and sustained has been the western prodding of Africa in the guise of a "reluctant sheriff" that it appears difficult to disagree with Englebert's (1997) submission that the contemporary African state is neither African nor state.

The counterterrorism rhetoric appears to have also provided various political regimes in Africa with an opportunity to persecute and liquidate political opposition, including rival ethnonational groups (Omeje, 2008). Most African states have been known to use the rhetoric of counterterrorism to intimidate internal challengers, quash public dissent, and oppress rival political factions (Busher, 2014). Counterterrorism forces have become a threat to the values that democracy upholds. The governments of Mali and Niger have been known to hush and persecute their disgruntled Tuareg minorities and other excluded nomadic groups in the guise of counterterrorism (see Keenan 2004, 2006). In Kenya, Nigeria, Cameroon, and Tunisia, the introduction of emergency measures under the guise of counterterrorism has often resulted in restrictions on human rights, freedom of expression, and outright physical abuses (Comolli, 2017). In Nigeria, the Independent People of Biafra (IPOB) became a proscribed organisation by attaching a terrorist label to it. Complementing the above is the argument that counter-insurgency appears to have increased the militarisation of the African space, making for what Omeje (2008) calls "anti-terror militarisation". Regime change has also featured as a viable counterterrorism strategy serving as continuity rather than change to the persistent postcolonial problem of military coups. To this end, counterterrorism is arguably linked to the abuse of state and political power – a prevailing and thriving manifestation of the postcolonial crisis in Africa.

## Conclusion

The political, security, and economic dimensions of Africa's postcolonial crisis has attracted external responses. Manifest post-colonial crises in Africa have combined to make Africa fertile ground for domestic and international terrorism and its key attraction – counterterrorism. The primary responsibility of preventing and combating terrorism appears to remain with African states and with its sub-regional and regional regimes which further enhances their integration. However, counterterrorism in Africa is highly dependent on external gratification and "help from above", reinforcing external ties that both bind and blind. Given the perpetuity of postcolonial crisis in Africa through an interplay between inside and outside forces, extra-continental counterterrorism regimes and practices have often been considered as arsonists posing as firefighters.

For the majority of postcolonial Africa, counterterrorism has been a response to the weak and slowly collapsing security architecture of most African states resulting in the increased militarisation of the African space from within and beyond. While counterterrorism in Africa is relevant for the African postcolonial crisis, it is important to define the limits of relevance given that counterterrorism has its own politics and economics. Consequently, counterterrorism in

Africa should not just be dismissed as a continuation of foreign adventurism. If there should be a useful meaning to counterterrorism in Africa, it should be a façade for countering failing and weak states in Africa. This would weave seamlessly into countering bad governance and corrupt leadership – twin postcolonial realities that have left African states in an almost permanent state of weakness and dependence. Overall, to discuss counterterrorism in postcolonial Africa is to engage in an unfinished state of uncertainty, as continuity rather than change best explains the postcolonial conditions that combine to create an environment for terrorist organisations to morph and prosper.

## References

Ake, Claude (1981). *A political economy of Africa*. Addison-Wesley: Longman Ltd.
Ashcroft, Bill (2001a). *Post-colonial transformation*. New York and London: Routledge.
Ashcroft, Bill (2001b). *On post-colonial features: Transformation of a colonial culture*. London: Bloomsbury Academic.
Ayittey, George B. (1993). *Africa betrayed*. New York: St. Martin's Press.
Busher, Joel (2014). Introduction: Terrorism and counterterrorism in Sub-Saharan Africa. *Journal of Terrorism Research*, *5*(1), 1–4.
Cawthra, Gavin, & van Nieuwkerk, Anthoni (2004). *Regional renaissance? Security in a globalized world: The Southern African development community. Dialogue on Globalization Briefing Papers*, June, 2–17.
Chinweizu, Ibekwe (1975). *The West and the rest of Us: White predators, black slavers and the African Elite*. New York: Random House.
Chole, Eshetu, & Ibrahim, Jibrin (Eds.). (1995). *Democratisation process in Africa: Problems and prospects*. Dakar: CODESRIA.
Clapham, Christopher (1982). Clientelism and the state. In Clapham Christopher (Ed.). *Private patronage and public order*. London: Pinter.
Cline, Lawrence E. (2016). African regional intelligence cooperation: Problems and prospects. *International Journal of Intelligence and Counterintelligence*, *29*(3), 447–469.
Comolli, Virginia (2017). The Counterterrorism Yearbook 2017: Africa. *The Strategist*, Australian Strategic Policy Institute.
Davis, John (2007). *Africa and the war on terrorism*. London: Ashgate.
Davis, John (2010). *Terrorism in Africa: The evolving front in the war on terrorism*. Lanham: Lexington Books.
Dempsey, Thomas (2006). Counterterrorism in African Failed States: Challenges and Potential Solutions. US Army Strategic Studies Institute.
Diallo, G. (2005). Terrorism in Africa is the new name of the game. *Africa Renaissance*, *2*(1) January/February, 38–49.
Dowden, Richard (2008). *Africa: Altered state, ordinary miracles*. London: Portobello Books.
Doyle, Michael (1986). *Empires*. Ithaca: Cornell University Press.
Englebert, P. (1997). The contemporary African State: Neither African nor state. *Third World Quarterly*, *18*(4), 767–775.
European Commission/African Union Commission The Africa-EU Strategic Partnership: A Joint Africa-EU Strategy. Lisbon, 9 December 2007.
European Security Strategy. (2003). *A secure Europe in a better world*. Brussels, December 12.
European Union. Instrument Contributing to Stability and Peace in Africa. Available at: https://ec.europa.eu/europeaid/sectors/human-rights-and-governance/peace-and-security/instrument-contributing-stability-and-peace_en, Date accessed and retrieved: September 17, 2017.
Ewi, M., & du Plessis, A. (2014). Counter-terrorism and Pan-Africanism. In B. Saul (Ed.). *Research Handbook on International Law and Terrorism*. Cheltenham, UK: Edward Elgar.
Frank, Andre Gunder (1966). The development of underdevelopment. *Monthly Review*. *18*(4), 17–31.
Gow, James, Olonisakin, Funmi, & Dijxhoorn, Ernst (Eds.). (2013). *Militancy and violence in West Africa: Religion, politics and radicalization*. New York: Routledge.
Howard, Russell D., Sawyer, Reid L., & Bajema, Natasha E. (Eds.). (2009). *Terrorism and counterterrorism: Understanding the new security environment*. Boston: McGraw Hill.
Hughes, G. (2011). *The military's role in counterterrorism: Examples and implications for liberal democracies*. Carlisle: Strategic Studies Institute.

Joseph, Richard A. (1983). Class, state and prebendal politics in Nigeria. *Journal of Commonwealth and Comparative Politics, 21*(3), 21–38.

Joseph, Richard A. (1987). *Democracy and prebendal politics in Nigeria: The rise and fall of the second republic.* New York: Cambridge University Press.

Keenan, J. (2004). Terror in the Sahara: The implications of US imperialism for North and West Africa. *Review of African Political Economy, 101*(31), 497–511.

Keenan, J. (2006). Security and insecurity in North Africa. *Review of African Political Economy, 108*(33), 269–296.

Kraxberger, Brennan M. (2005). The United States and Africa: Shifting geopolitics in an 'Age of Terror'. *Africa Today, 52*(1), 46–68.

le Sage, Andre (Ed.). (2007). *African counterterrorism cooperation: Assessing regional and subregional initiatives.* Nebraska: Potamc Books.

Maier, Karl (2002). *This house has fallen: Nigeria in crisis.* London: Basic Books.

Makinda, Samuel M. (2009). *The European Union, the fight against terrorism and its impact on democracy building in Africa.* International Institute for Democracy and Electoral Assistance (IDEA), Australia.

Maluki, Patrick (n.d). Learning from country best practice in Africa: In search of a grand counter terrorism strategy, available at: http://idis.uonbi.ac.ke/sites/default/files/chss/idis/idis/Maluki-LEARNING%20FROM%20COUNTRY%20BEST%20PRACTICE%20IN%20AFRICA-2.pdf. Date accessed and retrieved: September 30, 2017.

Mbembe, Achille (2006). The intimacy of tyranny. In Bill Ashcroft, Gareth Griffiths & Helen Tiffin (Eds.). *The postcolonial studies reader* (pp. 66–70). London and New York: Routledge.

Meredith, Martin (2006). *The state of Africa: A history of fifty years of independence.* London: Free Press.

Ndlovu-Gatsheni, Sabelo J. (2007). Weak states and the growth of the private security sector in Africa: Wither the African state. In Sabelo Genedze (Ed.). *Private security in Africa: Manifestations, challenges and regulations* (pp. 17–38). Pretoria: Institute of Strategic Studies.

Norman, Paul (2004). The United Nations and Counter-terrorism After September 11: Towards an Assessment of the Impact and Prospects of Counter-Terror 'Spill-Over' Into International Criminal Justice Cooperation. Paper presented to British Society of Criminology Conference 6–9th July 2004, University of Portsmouth.

OAU Convention on the Prevention and Combating of Terrorism. Available at: http://www.peaceau.org/uploads/algiers-convention-terrorism.pdf, Date accessed and retrieved: August 21, 2017.

O'Donnell, Guillermo, & Schmitter, Phillipe C. (1986). *Transitions from authoritarian rule: Tentative conclusions about uncertain democracies.* Baltimore: John Hopkins University Press.

Okumu, Wafula, & Botha, Anneli (Eds.). (2007). *Understanding terrorism in Africa: In search for an African Voice.* Pretoria: Institute for Security Studies.

Omeje, Kenneth (2008). The war on terror and the crisis of postcoloniality in Africa. *South African Journal of International Affairs, 11*(2), 89–114.

Omeje, Kenneth (2015). *The crises of postcoloniality in Africa.* Dakar: CODESRIA.

Osakwe, Chukwuma, & Umoh, Ubong Essien (2013). The military and counterinsurgency operations in Nigeria. In Ozoemenam Mbachu & Umar M. Bature (Eds.). *Internal security management in Nigeria: A study in terrorism and counterterrorism* (pp. 391–406). Kaduna: Medusa Publishers.

Ramdeen, Marisha (2017). *Countering terrorism and violent extremism in Africa.* ACCORD Conflict Trends, July (2), 49–56.

Reid, Richard J. (2012). *A history of modern Africa: 1800 to the present* (2nd ed.). West Sussex: John Wiley & Sons.

Rodney, Walter (1973). *How Europe underdeveloped Africa.* Tanzania: Bogle-L'Ouverture Publications.

Rogers, Paul (2004). *A war on terror: Afghanistan and after.* London: Pluto Press.

Scott, Catherine (2017). *State failure in Sub-Saharan Africa: The crisis of post-colonial order.* London: I.B. Tauris & Co.

Seers, Dudley (1969). The meaning of development. *International Development Review, 11*(4), 3–4.

Sharan, Anupama (2016). *Terrorism and counter-terrorism in Africa: Fighting insurgency from Al Shabaab, Ansar Dine and Boko Haram.* Basingstoke: Palgrave.

Sheehan, Michael A. (2007). Foreword. In Yonah Alexander & Michael B. Kraft (Eds.). *Evolution of US counterterrorism policy* (Vol. 1, pp. xv–xvi). Connecticut: Praeger Security International.

Sicurelli, Daniela (2010). *The European Union's Africa policies: Norms, interests and impact.* Surrey: Ashgate.

Söderberg, Mimmo, & Ohlson, Thomas (2003). *Democratisation and armed conflicts in weak states.*

Department for Cooperation with Non-Governmental Organisations and Humanitarian Assistance and Conflict Management, Swedish International Development Cooperation Agency (SIDA).

Takeyh, Ray, & Gvosdev, Nikolas K. (2009). Do terrorist networks need a home? In Russell D. Howard, Reid L. Sawyer & Natasha E. Bajema (Eds.). *Terrorism and counterterrorism: Understanding the new security environment*. Boston: McGraw Hill.

Thomson, Alex (2008). *An introduction to African politics*. New York: Routledge.

The Economist (February 2016), Available from: https://www.economist.com/news/middle-east-and-africa/21693739-americas-fbi-helps-train-new-generation-new-kind-conflict-counter-terrorism, Date accessed and retrieved: September 8, 2017.

Tunis Declaration on Population and Development in Africa. July 1994, Available at: http://www.un.org/popin/oau/tunisdcl.htm, Date accessed and retrieved: August 21, 2017.

Umoh, UbongEssien (2012). Armed conflicts in postcolonial Africa and the democratic peace theory. *Nasarawa Journal of General Studies*, 1(2), 7–25.

Umoh, Ubong Essien (2015). Cameroon, Nigeria and the Bakassi Conflict: Building blocks for a non-democratic peace theory. *Journal of International Relations and Development*, 18(2), 227–247.

van der Walt, Ruan, & Solomon, Hussein (2014). Histories and spaces of terrorism in Africa: The post-9/11 strategic challenge of Somalia's al Shabab. *Afro Eurasian Studies Journal*, 3(1), 71–99.

Whitaker, Beth Elsie (2010). Compliance among weak states: Africa and the counter-terrorism regime. *Review of International Studies*, 36, 639–662.

Young, Crawford (2012). *The post-colonial state in Africa: A half-century of independence, 1960–2010*. Madison: University of Wisconsin Press.

# 5

# Globalisation, terrorism, and counterterrorism in Africa

*Abba Gana Shettima*

## Introduction

The central premise of this chapter is that while all acts of terrorism stem from locally rooted issues, the process of globalisation fuels the growth and spread of terrorism. African-based terrorist organisations such as *Boko Haram* in Nigeria and *Al-Shabab* in Somalia originated in response to local issues, but they have continued to increase in notoriety and gained global visibility. Globalisation aided their spread across regions. The narratives employed by the leadership of *Boko Haram* and *Al-Shabab* to justify their violence and the medium used to disseminate their voice and campaign of violence are all rooted in the modus operandi of global terrorism.

The chapter argues that the process of globalisation, particularly the influence of the Internet, resulted in the rise of international terrorist networks and organisations such as Al-Qaeda and the Islamic State in Iraq and Syria (ISIS), cross-border crime, and the proliferation of small arms. The chapter concludes by arguing that if localised terrorism such as *Boko Haram* and *Al-Shabab* are to be subdued, effective counterterrorism campaigns must be developed to limit the reach of their voice and power to the localities and ultimately defeat them at that level. One concrete suggestion in the chapter is to create an international protocol against the spread of vice and violence of terrorism through internet channels such as YouTube. Another direction is to develop appropriate counter-narratives at both the local and global levels to deny terrorists the appropriation of religious and moral justifications for their brutality.

## Conceptual definitions and debates

Concepts constitute the building blocks of theory and the foundation of any meaningful scientific analysis. As Wallerstein (2000: 156) rightly argued:

> Analysts do not manipulate data, though many of them like to think that is what they are doing. Rather, analysts manipulate concepts. Concepts become our friends, even our children. They take on a certain life of their own, and it is tempting to stretch their usage beyond the purpose for which they were created. This is what reification is about.

Thus, an attempt will be made to define the key concepts in this chapter for a proper grounding of the subsequent discussions. The five key concepts running through this chapter are globalisation, terrorism, insurgency, CounterTerrorism (CT), and CounterInsurgency (COIN).

## Globalisation

Globalisation is a concept that gained currency in the latter decades of the 20th century; some analysts described it as "the buzz word of the last two decades" (*The Economist*, 2013). To be precise, the term became popular in the 1990s, but as a process, globalisation has been happening for centuries. According to Grinin and Korotayev (2013), its beginnings can be traced to either as far back as the first movement of people out of Africa to other parts of the world or to the 3rd Millennium BC, which has been regarded by scholars such as Frank as the beginning of the Modern World System (Frank, 1993).

Some scholars such as Conversi (2010) contend that a projection of globalisation far back into the historical past, called "global primordialism", renders the concept entirely inoperative and useless for political analysis. He argues that we need to know when globalisation started to define what it is precisely. He questions why, for instance, long-distance contacts during late antiquity are regarded as some form of "incipient globalisation" as Harris (2007) did. Conversi's position is that there must be some appropriate historical starting point, which, in his view is not earlier than the "post-1948 international agreements marking the global triumph of American power, and culminating in the demise of the Soviet bloc" (Conversi, 2010: 37).

While it is beyond the scope of this chapter to go into the details of mapping out the historical trajectories of globalisation, it is pertinent to note that globalisation as a process passed through different phases. As outlined by Harlan and Rahschulte (2011), globalisation has passed through three main stages. The first phase, which lasted from the 15th to the 18th centuries was a period characterised by individuals struggling to overcome several barriers mostly natural and man-made obstacles in their quest for material wealth and prosperity. During this epoch, the major impediment to global interconnectedness was territorialism. In the second phase, from the 19th to the 20th centuries, the world witnessed globalisation through advances in industrialisation, transportation, communication, and the technology of mass production, which culminated in the industrial revolution.

In the third and present phase of globalisation corresponding to the 21st century, there has been a massive explosion of information and communication technologies (ICTs), particularly the Internet and satellite television. The world has become more or less borderless in terms of commerce, as well as social and political interaction. The present phase is particularly important for a discussion of globalisation and terrorism, and it will be the central focus of this chapter.

The definition of globalisation is as contested as the history of the concept. Generally, it is apparent in the literature on globalisation that how the concept is defined is determined by where it is placed chronologically. Those who project globalisation into the historical past, for example, consider long-distance contacts between nations, cultures, races, and religions stretching back to centuries as evidence of "globalisation". As earlier argued in line with Conversi (2010), such a long-term historical view of globalisation renders it meaningless, particularly in the context of what it means in the present dispensation. This is why the definition of globalisation adopted in this chapter relates to the realities of the late 20th century; and more profoundly, the 21st century. While several scholars have appropriately defined globalisation in the context of the present (for example, Giddens, 1990; Friedman, 2006), the definition which is considered more relevant within the context of this chapter was the one articulated by Giddens (1990: 64). In Giddens's view, globalisation is "The intensification of worldwide social relations which link distinct localities in such a way that local happenings are shaped by events occurring many miles away and vice versa". Perhaps in no other area is this interconnection of the local with the global more manifest than in the area of the spread of terrorism.

## Terrorism

Terrorism and insurgency are interconnected because both are forms of asymmetrical warfare. Interestingly, however, some scholars such as Kilcullen (2005) contend that the two terms were considered almost synonymous and therefore used interchangeably until the late 20th century. Terrorism is generally defined as the use of violence against the state and civilians by sub-state actors in asymmetrical warfare to create fear, hence "terror", in the targeted population thereby seeking to advance some political, ideological, religious, ethnic, or economic causes. However, the definition of what constitutes terrorism is also subject to historical, political and ideological interpretations. Those who take a long-term historical view of terrorism seek to expand its meaning to include not just sub-state actors but the state itself. Jalata (2011), for example, argued that the spread of terrorism could not be separated from the capitalist world system.

Referring to the works of earlier scholars such as Thornton (1987) and De Las Casas (1992), it is argued that the development of capitalism in 15th century Western Europe, and its expansion to the rest of the world through colonialism, was necessarily accompanied by the spread of state-sponsored terrorism and genocide, as evidenced, for example, in the colonisation, enforced servitude, and expulsion of the Native Americans from their land. Similarly, Africa and many other parts of the Developing World were subjected to brutal acts of terrorism through the Trans-Atlantic Slave Trade and colonialism. Jalata (2011) thus appropriately talks of the occurrence of "terrorism from above" (i.e. state actors) and "terrorism from below" (i.e. non-state actors) and critiques scholars from both the right and left for failing to understand the root causes of both types of terrorism.

## Insurgency

Insurgency is closely related to terrorism though they are not the same. One of the most elaborate distinctions between an insurgency and terrorism was provided by the US Department of Defence (DoD Department of Defence, 2007). Since the United States is at the forefront of the so-called 'war on terror' at the global level, the DoD's conceptualisation of insurgency and terrorism is crucial because it has not just academic implications but broader implications for CounterTerrorism (CT) and CounterInsurgency (COIN). According to the DoD, terrorism involves the deliberate use of violence or threat of violence to instil fear to force governments or societies to yield to some goals of the terrorists bordering on politics, religion or ideology. Insurgency, on the other hand, is a form of an organised resistance movement which relies essentially on a combination of subversion, sabotage, and armed conflict to realise its aims.

Generally, the ultimate objective of insurgencies is to overthrow the existing social order, and thus, reallocate power within a country. Insurgents use ideology to target governments; terrorist target governments and the society at large to advance an ideology. Insurgency is thus a broader political movement which may and often does employ terrorism as a strategy. However, in terms of spread, terrorists are more likely to use global narratives and unleash fear across geographical borders than insurgents who might just focus on their immediate political environment. In this context, a definition of insurgency as articulated by Afzal (1991: 2) provides some valuable insight into the concept: "Insurgency is a form of rebellion in which a dissident group that has the support of a sizeable portion of the population instigate widespread acts of civil disobedience, sabotage, terrorism and wages guerrilla warfare to overthrow a government or to extract political, economic, or social concessions".

## Counterterrorism and counterinsurgency (CT-COIN)

There are several options open to states in terms of responding to the violence perpetrated by non-state armed groups such as rebels and terrorists. In some instances, such as the case of groups seeking some form of political autonomy, states can:

> Simply accede to demands for autonomy, independence, control of government, or significant reforms, they can give concessions, they can also engage, at the simplest level, in one of three ways of countering the insurgency: population-centric, draining-the-sea and counter terrorism (Lopez & Jackson, 2017: 4).

Lopez and Jackson further argue that population-centric (sometimes referred to as winning hearts and minds)˙and draining-the-sea counterinsurgency approaches are both based on the premise that an effective way to counter any form of insurgency is by cutting them off from the rest of the population, which is their primary source of support, supplies, recruitment, and intelligence. Population-centric approaches seek to address the political roots of insurgency, especially governance issues focusing on the provision of essential services and jobs to the citizenry. This not only provides legitimacy to the government but also delegitimises the antics of the belligerent groups. Advocates of draining-the-sea approach also consider the population as the centre of counterinsurgency. Still, unlike the winning-hearts-and-minds strategy, they argue that the community can be cowed into submission by instilling fear through the use of such tactics like mass arrests and deportations, collective punishment and even deliberate killing of civilians (Lopez & Jackson, 2017). Both of these two counterinsurgency approaches contrast sharply with counterterrorism which focuses on the insurgents rather than the population and relies on 'hard' military strategy rather than 'soft' political, economic or psychological strategies. The principal aim of counterterrorism is to use covert and overt military strategies to capture or kill terrorists, as well as destroy their operational base. Hence the U.S. Army "calls its counterinsurgency thrust non-lethal while the term for counterterrorism is lethal targeting" (Anderson, 2010: 1).

From this brief outline of counterinsurgency and counterterrorism, it is apparent that CT and COIN are interconnected. CT is a combination of the various practices, techniques, tactics, and strategies adopted by governments and their security and law enforcement agencies including the police, military, and other similar agencies in response to threats and acts of terrorism, which may be real or probable. COIN, on the other hand, can be defined as "comprehensive civilian and military efforts that are taken to defeat and contain insurgency and address its root causes simultaneously" (U.S. Government Counter Insurgency Guide, 2009). As indicated earlier, terrorism is one of the many strategies employed by insurgents to advance their cause. Hence, counterterrorism can, therefore, be best regarded as a component of counterinsurgency. Thus most wars against terrorism are a combination of both counterinsurgency and counterterrorism, and that in practice, "striking a balance between counterinsurgency and counterterrorism got the best results" (Anderson, 2010: 2).

## Globalisation, terrorism, and counterterrorism in Africa

Having presented some definitions of the key concepts in this chapter (details of which are addressed in specific chapters of this handbook), we now move on to discuss the interconnections between globalisation, terrorism, and counterterrorism in Africa. The premise of the chapter is that most, if not all, terrorist organisations are fuelled by domestic causes but further exacerbated by the process of globalisation. Incidences of domestic injustices are rife across the world but particularly in the third world countries of Africa, Asia, and Latin America. According to Cilliers (2006), such locally rooted injustices "once framed within an appropriate belief system and supported by the right leadership and organisation" can quickly transform "an incipient insurgency" into a terrorist organisation, "particularly if confronted by a strong state such as Israel or the US" Cilliers's argument is that "all terrorism is local—that terrorism largely stems from local issues, whether the perpetrators want to send a message to rulers or advance nationalist, social or religious claims" (Cilliers, 2006: 59–60).

## Local roots of terrorism

In most if not all instances, it is difficult for terrorist organisations to continue to use global rhetoric to justify their domestic violence against the state and innocent citizens. Hence terrorists try to exploit local sources of grievances such as poor governance, injustice, poverty, political, ethnic or religious marginalisation, and other similar forms of perceived or real failures of the state, for example, within the context of Africa, terrorist organisations such as *Boko Haram*, Al-Qaeda in the Islamic Maghreb (AQIM) and *Al-Shabab* all emerged in response to local problems and demands. Indeed, even *Al-Qaeda*, perhaps the best known trans-national terrorist organisation in the contemporary period, started as an essentially domestic response to a domestic problem. Al-Qaeda's justification for global jihad started as a critique of the corruption, injustice, and lack of accountability in the Arab world, and in particular, Saudi Arabia—Osama Bin Laden's country.

*Boko Haram's* emergence and subsequent growth in the North- Eastern region of Nigeria beginning effectively from 2009 has been attributed to a variety of factors, mostly local. It has been argued, for example, that, "poor social and economic conditions in the north, weak state control, and heavy-handed security measures have enabled *Boko Haram* to flourish, recruit and built its support base" (Crowley & Wilkinson, 2013: 100). Similarly, Mohammed (2014: 10) has argued that during the *Dawah* (proselytisation) phase of the rise and development of *Boko Haram* which was focused on "intensive proselytisation, recruitment, indoctrination and radicalisation of its members", the *Dawah* largely centred on criticisms of Nigeria's secular system, the glaring corruption especially among the elites "as well as the conspicuous consumption and opulence of the Western-educated elites amid poverty". Other scholars point to "poor governance, frustration and a sense of injustice among those who live at Nigeria's peripheries, be it geographically or socio-economically" as the critical drivers in the establishment of *Boko Haram* (Perouse de Montclos, 2014: 9).

In Northern Mali, a combination of radical Islamists groups made up of *Ansar Deen*, AQIM, and the Movement for Oneness and Jihad in West Africa (known with its French acronym MUJAO) joint forces together to displace the Touareg rebels in the region, the National Movement for the Liberation of Azawad (MNLA). In so doing, the Islamists exploited the already long-standing local grievances such as economic underdevelopment and central government neglect of Northern Mali. Also, the central Malian state has been weakened by the Touareg rebellion against these grievances (Branson & Wilkinson, 2013).

*Al-Shabaab* emerged as a terrorist organisation in Somalia in 2006. Before then, it was the youth wing of a relatively moderate Islamist organisation known as the Islamic Courts Union (ICU) in Somalia. *Al-Shabaab's* rapid rise to prominence and emergence as one of the most deadly terrorist groups in Africa was aided by local structural and governance factors. Since the overthrow of the Military dictator Mohammed Siad Barre in 1991, Somalia has been entangled in decades of political turmoil and anarchy, which created not only power vacuum in the centre but a state of lawlessness throughout the country. For many years, warlords held sway in Mogadishu until the ICU displaced them. The ICU, mostly characterised by its harsh judgments, became so powerful and gradually spread from the capital to the countryside—providing some security and semblance of law and order in an environment of chaos, but this was short-lived as a result of local resistance and foreign interference.

Ethiopia, Somali's next-door neighbour, felt threatened and in December 2006 invaded Somalia to dislodge the ICU. Thus, the Ethiopian invasion became the immediate spur that led to the rise of *Al-Shabaab* as an insurgency which deployed a full arsenal of terrorist tactics to resist the Ethiopian occupation. However, the long-term factors that gave rise to *Al-Shabaab* are local and rooted in the collapse of the Somalia state, lack of effective governance, soaring poverty, and famines, among many other factors.

It is therefore evident that in Africa as elsewhere in the world where terrorism is rife, locally rooted sources of grievances and discontent are exploited by terrorists not only to justify their violence but use it as the political and ideological platform to recruit and indoctrinate their members. Almost all theoretical postulations of the causes of non-state terrorism or "terrorism from below" point to such locally rooted grievances in the form of cultural, religious, economic and other similar forms of oppression, human rights violations, attacks on human freedoms, etc. However, such grievances do not automatically lead to terrorism.

Such grievances are transformed into acts of terrorism by some aggrieved sections of the population as a result of several intervening factors, including the persistent refusal of the state to address long-standing grievances peacefully and fairly. Other factors include the development of extreme religious or other ideologies and the emergence of leaders and ideologues in the aggrieved population (Jalata, 2011). "Terrorism does not ignite spontaneously. Grievances exist all over the world—and require intense politicisation, leadership, organisation and resources" (Cilliers, 2006: 61). Such leaders often emerge as charismatic individuals who can recruit and mobilise for action against the state, its agencies and symbols of authority and indeed the general public unsympathetic to its cause.

## Globalisation as an impetus to terrorism in Africa

It is, therefore, safe to argue that all terrorism is local in terms of its primary drivers. Still, all terrorism in the contemporary period is also global in terms of modus operandi. Globalisation has a considerable influence not only in the way terrorists operate but also in terms of helping local terrorists connect with other terrorists in distant locations in terms of ideology, recruitment, training, propaganda, and so on. Some analysts argue that the incidence of terrorism has increased in the age of globalisation. For example, according to Stibli (2010: 1), the incidence of terrorism was rare in the Cold War era. Thus between 1968 and 1989, terrorism occurred approximately 1.673 times per year. However, between 1990 and 1996, it has increased to 4.389 times per year, which represents an increase of 162%. This dramatic increase was not unconnected with the rise of globalisation and its attendant consequences, including the rise of religious fundamentalism across the world.

Globalisation has created enormous economic opportunities in many parts of the world, leading to prosperity. However, globalisation has also widened inequality across the globe, especially in the third world. Globalisation has fuelled terrorism in Africa and beyond by widening the social and material contrast between an affluent and culturally different West and a poor, mostly impoverished third world. While local grievances act as the trigger to terrorism, global inequality and injustice provide the moral and political rallying points for most terrorists. In a twisted format, globalisation has fuelled the spread of wars and communal strife through the proliferation of Small Arms and Light Weapons (SALWs), the rise of "Warlords", arms merchants and "War Economies." The dark allies of globalisation have given rise to a new class of people who made their wealth from the blood of others, mostly from the already impoverished global south, thus compounding the rift between haves and haves-not, thereby consolidating existing insurrections and creating new ones.

As the former UN Secretary-General Ban Ki-moon (2017) noted in his message to the 2017 *Global Poverty Reduction and Development Forum*:

> This year [2017] marks the 25th International Day for the Eradication of Poverty. During this quarter-century, the number of people living in extreme poverty has halved and living conditions have improved all over the world. But the fight against poverty is not over. Globalization and technological progress have increased inequalities and left millions of people behind.

The millions of people left behind by the prosperity of globalisation especially in Sub-Saharan Africa and many parts of Asia and Latin America do not have enough food to eat, clean water to drink or access to functional and affordable health care system and qualitative education. They live in despair and hence, vulnerable to the antics of terrorists. Poverty, despondency and religious fundamentalism are a combustible mix that prepares the breeding ground for terrorism.

Some scholars contend that globalisation, particularly the aggressive marketisation that it promotes, leads to the degradation of social existence (Burawoy, 2008; Smith 2008). Degradation is here defined by Smith (2008: 371–372) as "being forcibly pushed down into a lower grade of existence" and represents just one form of humiliation. "Other forms of humiliation include being outrageously entrapped, enslaved, excluded, neglected or killed." Humiliation leads to resentment on the part of the oppressed, as for example, the resentment expressed by the hitherto conquered peoples of Africa and Asia against European colonial empires. Smith argues that while the first moment of humiliation was experienced by those who were hitherto independent but conquered and subjugated by colonialism; the second moment of humiliation is currently being experienced in the world. This type of "humiliation is relegation, being pushed down within the social hierarchy of respectability and worth; in other words, degradation."

Contemporary globalisation has degraded many in this way such as the millions of workers pushed out of steady jobs into casual employment and often, completely out of work, local traders whose fortunes have been grossly reduced by the giant of supermarkets and online stores as well as university graduates condemned to a lifetime of unemployment and under-employment throughout the world. Those who are humiliated response to their situation in different ways. While some may accept it as their fate, others are trying to "do" something to change their situation—and in extreme circumstances, "doing" something about humiliation brought about by the forces of globalisation can, and does include acts of terrorism. "In fact, the actions of the displaced and excluded are profoundly shaping our globalising world. A significant scope for political initiative lies in the hands of the resentful in Eurasia, Africa, and America, North, and South. Not just terrorists, but a multitude of men and women within the urban populations from which they spring" (Smith, 2008: 373).

Perhaps the most fundamental way in which globalisation has exacerbated terrorism especially in Africa is in terms of the sheer power and reach of Information and Communication Technologies (ICTs) particularly the Internet and satellite television. The Internet has been identified as one of the most important and effective channels used by terrorists for the purposes of propaganda (recruitment, radicalisation, and incitement to terrorism), financing, training, planning, execution and cyber-attacks (UNODC, 2012: 3). Thus, the Internet, in particular, has created a communication network with a truly global reach and with little or no barriers. With the aid of the Internet, individuals and groups can communicate with a high level of anonymity, in real-time, and be reaching a limitless audience spread across geographical and political boundaries.

Terrorism, as the term implies, largely depends on inflicting maximum fear through acts of physical and psychological violence. However, beyond the acts of violence, terrorists rely on the Internet and satellite television among other modern mass communication channels to spread their propaganda. Propaganda is the oxygen on which terrorism blossom and come to fruition. The way in which terrorist groups in the world including those in Africa such as *Boko Haram* and *Al-Shaabab* have effectively used the Internet has greatly aided in transforming them from localised nuisance to global nightmares.

For instance, *Boko Haram's* 2014 mass abduction of 276 female students in Chibok, Borno state, Nigeria sparked widespread international attention and condemnation—exactly the sort of global publicity the terrorist group was looking for. The Boko Haram leader Abubakar Shekau subsequently issued several videos on YouTube, taunting not only the Nigerian government but the international community on the abduction of the Chibok girls, describing the girls as their 'slaves' that will be sold in the market. Access to the Internet has given local terrorists a global voice and visibility, thereby emboldening and providing them with a platform for indoctrination and recruitment of new members. It is therefore not surprising that *Boko Haram* repeated this mass abduction of schoolgirls with the further kidnapping of over 100 schoolgirls in Dapchi, Yobe State at the Government Girls' Science and Technical College in February 2018. The abduction of civilians, particularly such mass abductions is now serving a two-pronged purpose for *Boko Haram*, namely generating money through negotiated ransom payments (which the Nigerian government hardly admits) as well as the huge local and international publicity that it receives as a result.

It has been argued quite rightly that the global revolution in communication and transportation technology has made terrorism "easier and deadly" (Black, 2004: 22). It is now easier for terrorists to plan and execute their acts of terrorism across borders due to globalisation and its attendant shrinking of time and space. As illustrated by the terrorist attacks on the United States of America on September 11th, 2001, terrorists can now plan and execute attacks thousands of miles from their home base, a feat that was "literally impossible less than a century earlier" (Black, 2004: 22). Terrorists also share knowledge and experience of their deadly activities online; according to UNODC (2012), the Internet serves as a "virtual training camp" for terrorists who post training materials ranging from online manuals, video clips, information, and advice.

The forces of globalisation, again, particularly the Internet and other communication channels allow locally based terrorist groups in Africa to connect with terrorists elsewhere in the world. In August 2014, at the height of the insurgency, *Boko Haram* took over Gwoza, a major town in Borno state, and declared it the headquarters of its "Caliphate", obviously being inspired by the transnational terrorist network, ISIS. In 2015, *Boko Haram* leader Abubakar Shekau pledged the group's allegiance to ISIS leader and self-proclaimed caliph Abu Bakr al-Baghdadi in an audio message posted over the Internet: "We announce our allegiance to the caliph…and will hear and obey in times of difficulty and prosperity…we call on Muslims everywhere to pledge allegiance to the caliph." This was almost immediately reciprocated by ISIS. Through a spokesman, ISIS accepted *Boko Haram's* pledge of allegiance, who said the aim of establishing a caliphate had now been extended to West Africa. Thus this had bolstered ISIS's image as a trans-national terrorist organisation and projected *Boko Haram's* global ambitions.

Finally, the global incidence of cross-border crime and the proliferation of SALW have in many ways facilitated the growth and spread of terrorism in Africa. Even before the onset of terrorist organisations in Africa, SALW made up of an array of weapons such as machine guns, grenades, rifles, pistols, and others have been used in deadly conflicts in countries such as Sudan, Uganda, Sierra Leone, Liberia, Rwanda, Angola, Democratic Republic of Congo and Somalia. Such weapons are often recycled from one country to another and "their ownership is transferred among fighters, security forces and war profiteers" (Religion for Peace, 2017: 4). In the recent past, the globally inspired *Arab Spring* of 2010–2011 brought political instability in North Africa and parts of the Middle East, with security repercussions for the entire Africa and Middle Eastern regions. The collapse of the Muammar Gaddafi regime in Libya in 2011, for example, led to various splinter rebel groups ransacking the huge Libyan armoury. This had no doubt aided terrorist groups like *Boko Haram* and *Ansar Deen*, AQIM and MUJAO. It is quite plausible to argue that *Boko Haram's* rise in notoriety from 2011 was aided in part by the influx of Libyan SALW through Nigeria's vast and poorly controlled porous borders with Niger, Tchad and Cameroon.

The above discussions show clearly how the various forces of globalisation aid terrorism in Africa. However, it is important to note that just as globalisation is an impetus to terrorism; it also presents opportunities for counterterrorism. First, the same ICTs deployed by terrorists to incite and propagate terrorism can be, and is often used by states to monitor terrorists' plans and activities online. Secondly, it also provides an effective platform for states to exchange information in real-time and cooperate across borders in counterterrorism activities. This point has been well articulated by Black (2004: 22): "while technology enhances opportunities for terrorism by shrinking physical space, it also sows the seeds of terrorism's destruction...technology thus makes terrorism easier and deadlier in the short term, but in the long term it destroys the social geometry on which terrorism depends."

## Conclusion

It has been argued in this chapter that terrorism in Africa emanates from some locally rooted issues. However, the growth and spread of terrorism in the continent has been greatly aided by the forces of globalisation. The power and reach of ICTs particularly the Internet has been effectively exploited by terrorist groups in Africa to project their voice and visibility on the global scale. Globalisation has also aided terrorists in Africa to connect with trans-national terrorist groups such as *Al-Qaeda* and *ISIS*. Globalisation, which is triumphant capitalism, has created prosperity in some parts of the world, in a massive sea of poverty. Thus globalisation has degraded the quality of human existence especially in the third world including Africa. This degradation of the quality of human existence has led to humiliation and resentment on the part of many people in the world. Some of those resenting have resigned to fate. Some have voted with their feet and yet some others have resorted to terrorism, or at least appropriated the narratives of global injustice to justify acts of terror. It is finally concluded that while globalisation has been an impetus to terrorism, it also provides the opportunities for globally collaborative efforts in counterterrorism. For the global collaborative efforts to work, however, there is the need for African states to develop international counterterrorism protocols in the area of military collaboration and in terms of curtailing the voice and visibility of terrorists on the global scale.

# References

Afzal, M. S. (1991). *Insurgency and counter insurgency*. USAWC Military Studies Programme Paper.

Anderson, G. (2010). Counterinsurgency vs. counterterrorism: A civilians view. *Small Wars Journal*, 1–4, available: https://smallwarsjournal.com/blog/journal/docs-temp/375-anderson.pdf (accessed on 13/1/ 2019).

Black, D. (2004). The geometry of terrorism. *Sociological Theory*, *22*(1), 14–25.

Branson, K., & Wilkinson, H. (2013). Analysis of the conflict in Northern Mali. In M. Tremolieres (Ed.), *Conflict over resources and terrorism: Two facets of insecurity* (pp. 87–97). Paris: OECD.

Burawoy, M. (2008). What is to be done? Theses on the degradation of social existence in a Globalising world. *Current Sociology 56*(3), 351–359.

Conversi, D. (2010). The limits of cultural globalisation. *Journal of Critical Globalization Studies*, *3*, 36–59.

Cilliers, J. (2006). Africa, root causes and the 'War on Terror'. *African Security Review*, *15*(3), 57–71.

Crowley, R., & Wilkinson, H. (2013). Boko Haram: A new threat in West Africa. In M. Tremolieres (Ed.), *Conflict over resources and terrorism: Two facets of insecurity* (pp. 99–112). Paris: OECD.

De Las Casas, B. (1992). *A short account of the destruction of the Indies*. Edited and translated by Nigel Griffin. London: Penguin Books.

DoD (Department of Defence). (2007). Source files, available: https://usiraq.procon.org/sourcefiles/InsurgentsvsTerrorists.pdf (accessed on 1/01/2018).

*The Economist* (2013). Available: https://www.economist.com/blogs/freeexchange/2013/09/economic-history-1.

Frank, G. (1993). Bronze age world system cycles. *Current Anthropology*, *32*(4), 383–419.

Friedman, T. L. (2006). *The world is flat: A brief history of the 21st century*. London: Macmillan.

Giddens, A. (1990). *The consequences of modernity*. Stanford: Stanford University Press.

Grinin, L., & Korotayev, A. (2013). The origins of globalization. In J. Sheffield, A. Korotayev & L. Grinin (Eds.), *Globalization: Yesterday, today and tomorrow* (pp. 2–29). Litchfield Park: Emergent Publications.

Harlan, E., & Rahschulte, T. (2011). *History of* . Insights to a Changing World Journal, (2), 18–33.

Harris, A. (Ed.). (2007). *Incipient globalization? Long-distance contacts in the 6th century*. Oxford: Archaeopress.

Jalata, A. (2011). Terrorism from above and below in the age of . *Sociology Mind*, *1*(1), 1–15.

Kilcullen, D. (2005). Countering global insurgency. *Journal of Strategic Studies*, *28*(4), 597–617.

Ki-Moon, B. (2017). *Secretary General's Message on Global Poverty Reduction and Development*. Available: http://www.un.org/sg/en/content/sg/statement/2017-10-09/secretary-generals-message-global-poverty-reduction-and-development (accessed on 20/2/2018).

Lopez, A. M., & Jackson, S. F. (2017). *From Winning Hearts and Minds to Whacking Them in Outhouses: Counterinsurgency and Counter terrorism policy across East and South Asia*. Paper presented at International Studies Association International Meeting, Honk Kong, June 17, 2017.

Mohammed, K. (2014). The message and methods of Boko Haram. In Marc-Antoine Perouse de Montclos (Ed.), *Boko Haram: Islamism, politics and the state in Nigeria* (pp. 9–32). Leiden: African Studies Centre.

Perouse de Montclos, Marc-Antoine (2014). *Nigeria's interminable insurgency? Addressing the Boko Haram crisis*. London: Chatham House.

Religion for Peace (2017). *Small arms and light weapons: Africa a resource guide for religions for peace*. New York: Religions for Peace.

Smith, D. (2008). Globalization, degradation and the dynamics of humiliation. *Current Sociology*, *56*(3), 371–379.

Stibli, F. (2010). Terrorism in the context of globalization. *AARMS*, *9*(1), 1–7.

Thornton, R. (1987). *American Indian holocaust and survival: A population history since 1492*. Norman and London: Oklahoma Press.

UNODC (2012). *The Use of the Internet for Terrorist Purposes*. New York: The United Nations.

U.S. Government Counter Insurgency Guide (2009). Available: https://www.state.gov/documents/organization/119629.pdf.

Wallerstein, I. (2000). *The essential Wallerstein*. New York: The New Press.

# 6

# Saudi Wahhabis and jihadi terrorism in Africa

## Between fairy tales and conspiracy theories

*Marc-Antoine Pérouse de Montclos*

## Introduction

Like Europe, where speculations about a fifth-column of Wahhabi terrorists seem to have replaced the ancient fears of the Turks or the Saracens, there are a lot of rumours about the role played by Saudi Arabia in framing and supporting Jihadism in Africa. These assumptions tend to obscure the local dynamics of conflicts and point to foreign scapegoats to explain insurgencies that result from bad governance, corruption, social injustice, and the brutality of security forces. They also focus on the role of religion and the relevance of de-radicalisation to counter violent extremism. Hence this chapter puts into perspective the Wahhabi influence in Africa and deconstructs the links made between Saudi Arabia and Jihadi Terrorism. First, it argues that Saudi Arabia is a very conservative monarchy and a target of jihadi groups; it is quite different from the Libyan or Syrian type of rogue states that used to support terrorist networks all over the world. Secondly, the analysis shows that so-called radical Islamic ideas do not circulate one way: African Muslim clerics produced their own "theology of liberation" and manipulated foreign doctrines to justify their rebellion. Moreover, it is crucial to clarify confusions related to the misuse of the word "Wahhabi." Finally, many historical and linguistic factors explain why Arabic Salafis failed to re-Islamise the continent South of the Sahara.

The issue is quite controversial.[1] Contrasting theories are used to explain that today's jihadism either results from the irrationality of religious fanaticism or, on the contrary, from the extreme rationality of a vast conspiracy originating from the Arab world to convert Africans to a so-called "radical" Islam. Yet all these hypotheses point to the inherent violence of Saudi puritanism. According to its detractors, the Wahhabi form of Salafism is associated with religious extremism and has become dominant in the Muslim world. It promotes obedience at home and rebellion abroad (Redissi, 2007; Rasheed, 2008). Following this logic, the roots of jihadi terrorism are allegedly in Saudi Arabia, not in sub-Saharan Africa. Therefore, the priority would be to "de-radicalise" the minds and develop counter-narratives against Wahhabi indoctrination to properly deal with insurgent groups such as AQIM (al-Qaeda in the Islamic Maghreb) in Mali, MUJWA (Movement for Unity and Jihad in West Africa) in Mauritania, or Boko Haram in the Lake Chad Basin.

Such reasoning, however, is based on unfounded hypotheses that are analysed in this chapter. The first hypothesis is to suppose that African Muslims are incapable of producing their own "theology of liberation." If we follow this line of thought, jihadists in the Sahel passively waited for permissive ideas from the Middle East to challenge the power of corrupt governments and Sufi brotherhoods in the region. But this vision of Islam as a mere import from Arabia hardly corresponds to the historical record. In the 19th century, the Sufis led jihads in the Sahel and did not wait for the financial support of oil-producing countries in the Gulf to establish Islamic proto-states.

Additionally, we should call into question the indoctrinating potential of the Wahhabi school of thought. Its power of attraction is allegedly so immense that it alone would be enough to convince and mobilise Africans who are supposedly easy to influence and to manipulate because they are gullible, impoverished, idle, and willing to sell themselves to the highest bidder to commit suicide bombings and fight government forces. In practice, the Salafist preaching (*Da'wa*) in Africa is confronted with numerous obstacles related to language issues, the Arabs' racism, conflicts between fundamentalist groups, and the limits of Saudi Arabia's international cooperation — a country that is deeply conservative and legalistic, which is also the target of terrorist attacks. In this respect, we should avoid crediting Wahhabism with an influence which it certainly does not have.

## An imaginary Islamist international

Indeed, speculations about the importance of the Saudi form of Salafism assume that the Arab world occupies a principal place in the dissemination of an ideology that justifies the use of jihad. There are, however, other hubs of Islamist militancy in sub-Saharan Africa.[2] Asia, for example, exports its forms of fundamentalism through the Pakistani missionaries of the *Tablighi Jamaat* (Association for Preaching). As for Iran, its 1979 revolution attracted young activists who converted to Shia Islam, which was formerly confined to Levantine communities on the continent, in Nigeria and Senegal (Leichman, 2015).

Alongside Morocco and Egypt, African countries such as Libya and Sudan also trained Muslim clerics who sometimes became fundamentalists. Muammar Gaddafi granted numerous scholarships to promote Sharia through its World Islamic Call Society (*Jamiyyatal Da'wa al-Alamiyya al-Islamiyya*), which was founded in 1972, and a campus for Sub-Saharans (*Kulliyat al-Da'wa al-Islamiyya*), which opened in Tripoli in 1974. Meanwhile, Khartoum tried to develop an alternative to al-Azhar in Cairo to train Muslim clerics in Omdurman and, later on, in the International University of Africa, which was established in 1992 by Umar Al-Bashir's Islamist junta, on the premises of an older Islamic African Centre (*Merkaz al-Islami al-Ifriqi*).[3]

Saudi Arabia is therefore not the only Muslim country involved in proselytising activities in Africa South of the Sahara. In the Gulf, Oman and Yemen were historically much more connected to Eastern Africa. Saudi Arabia is now getting lots of attention because of its economic power, its messianic ambitions, and the fact that it handles the pilgrimage to Mecca, which is the symbolic centre of a global Islam. Assumptions about the influence of Wahhabism are also justified by operational, theological, rhetorical, and iconographic similarities that can be observed between the various jihadist movements fighting south of the Sahara, from Somalia to Mali. However, instances of mimicry and idealised references to a global revolutionary model do not constitute evidence that there is indeed an Islamist International based in Riyadh or Mecca to plan and coordinate terrorist attacks throughout the world. This so-called "global Islamic terror fraternity" appears to be based on imagination and fear.

Historically, Muslims faced many challenges to transcend geopolitical interests to envision themselves as an imaginary community of believers (*Ummah*). Following a congress organised in Mecca in 1926, attempts were made to unify the Sunnis under the aegis of Riyadh, yet they mostly brought to light the profound cultural divisions of Muslim countries (Kramer, 1986; Landau, 1994). At the institutional level, for instance, many member states of the Organization of Islamic Cooperation (OIC), founded in 1969 and based in Jeddah, have been unable to get rid of the pan-Arabist nationalist ideology of the colonial period. Since 1980, the Muslim Brothers also tried in vain to go beyond interpersonal relations to set up an international organisation (*al-tanzim al-duwali*) and bring together, under the same banner, political parties as diverse as the Islamic Salvation Front in Algeria, Hamas in Palestine, al-Islah in Yemen, Jamaa Islamiyya in Lebanon, the Islamic Action Front in Jordan, the al-Nahda movement in Tunisia, or the Justice and Development Party (AKP) in Turkey (Lacroix, 2017, p. 74). In Sudan too, the éminence grise of Omar el-Bechir's junta, Hassan el-Turabi, failed to build an alternative to the OIC with the various jihadist movements that were fighting throughout the world in the 1990s, from the Philippines to Algeria. Twenty years later, the failures of al-Qaeda or Daesh to organise an Islamist International have been just as significant (Mendelsohn, 2016).

Today, it would be difficult to find a central command or any kind of coordination between jihadist groups which are highly fragmented, with very local agendas. Allegiances to al-Qaeda or Daesh, to which many observers attach so much importance, hardly alter the mode of operation of African terrorist guerrillas. Controlling a given territory is not the preserve of Daesh either, as illustrated by AQIM in northern Mali in 2012 or al-Shabaab in southern Somalia in 2008–2014, which are still affiliated to al-Qaeda.

In this respect, the capacity of African insurgents to instrumentalise external supports should not be underestimated. Undoubtedly, Sahelian jihadists did not need instructions in Arabic to take up arms and get some training in asymmetric wars which were already taught by Marxist revolutionaries. The trust required to sustain clandestine groups was built in the local languages, which have remained the chief means of communication for the recruitment of combatants in Nigeria, Mali, Kenya, and Somalia. In practice, African jihadists have followed local agendas and changed their allegiance depending on their current interests. Examples include dissidents such as Adnan Abu Walid Al-Sahrawi and Abu Musab al-Barnawi. They left al-Qaeda and joined Daesh to escape the authority of al-Mourabitoun in Western Sahara in May 2015 and of Boko Haram in Nigeria in August 2016.

Moreover, affiliations to Arab jihadist movements often correspond to a communication strategy that aims to give the group an international dimension yet has a low operational impact on the ground. Whether foreign connections are real or not does not matter much in the end. In some of his videos, for example, the head of Boko Haram, Abubakar Shekau, paid tribute to both the leaders of al-Qaeda and Daesh despite their rivalries and doctrinal antagonism.[4] His objective was mainly to take advantage of the media to make himself seem important.

## Saudi Arabia as a victim of terrorism

Accusing Riyadh of financing terrorist groups relies on misconceptions. First, Saudi Arabia does not send military advisers to Africa, unlike the United States or the Soviet Union during the Cold War. In the Gulf, the United Arab Emirates is currently the only one to be directly involved in wars on the continent, especially in Libya. On the contrary, Saudi Arabia is a profoundly conservative, legitimist, legalistic, and realistic kingdom. It does not share any of the characteristics of terrorist or rogue states like Sudan, Libya, Iran, and erstwhile Syria. Today, it has little to gain from supporting insurgent fundamentalist movements in Africa, since it is itself the victim of jihadist attacks. As soon as 1979, when Afghanistan was invaded by the Soviet Union and the Islamic revolution triumphed in Iran, the Great Mosque in Mecca was attacked and devastated by a Mahdist commando fighting the corruption of the Saud regime. Al-Qaeda from 2003 and Daesh from 2014 then took over. They blamed the kingdom for its "sacrilegious" alliance with the Great Satan, America, and carried out attacks against security forces and Shiite mosques in Saudi Arabia. In this regard, the monarchy would have been ill-advised to support terrorist movements in Africa: one of the perpetrators of al-Qaeda attacks in Saudi Arabia, for example, was a Chadian national executed by Riyadh in early 2016.

Of course, such a backlash does not absolve Wahhabism of its responsibility in the dissemination of a jihadist ideology across the Muslim world. Saudi puritanism could be compared to a kind of Frankenstein's monster who turned against his creator and the hand that had fed him. This is illustrated by the Taliban and al-Qaeda's mujahedeen in Afghanistan — they were initially funded by Riyadh (and by the CIA) during the struggle against the Soviet occupation. In Saudi Arabia, the leader of the commando that devastated Mecca in 1979, Juhayman al-Utaybi, was also trained by Abd al-Aziz ibn Baz, a controversial Wahhabi judge and, later, Grand Mufti who had recommended the security services to release his former student in 1978. Likewise, in Africa, some preachers educated in the Islamic University of Medina became more radical than their teachers, or protected extremists who eventually criticised them for being too soft. In Northern Nigeria, for instance, a Saudi-trained Sheikh, Jafar Adam, first looked after the founder of Boko Haram, Mohammed Yusuf, before being assassinated in 2007 by killers who allegedly worked for his former student.

There are also the contradictions that any ideology fosters. For example, Protestant capitalists, agriculturalists and traders, some of whom were Quakers, campaigned for the abolition of slavery, which was the source of their prosperity.[5] Similarly, the Saudi dynasty could have propagated an ideology that would ultimately destroy it. To make such a claim, however, we would need to know for sure that Wahhabi indoctrination was indeed the starting point of jihadi terrorism in Africa. Are Islamist pamphlets so mesmerising that they would naturally lead to suicide bombing? Was Adolf Hitler's *Mein Kampf* enough to trigger Nazi fanaticism? Nothing could be less certain. Indeed, Wahhabism touches upon many aspects of private life, including praying. Despite its totalitarian essence, it cannot be reduced to a doctrine that focuses on getting power through armed struggle. It is intrinsically linked to the Saudis' tribal and monarchical history and is thus poorly adapted to internationalist projects. It distinguishes itself from today's jihadists by its scrupulous observation of rites and Sharia. Also, there is no reason Wahhabism should have radicalised the youth in sub-Saharan Africa but not in the Gulf, where the Saudis are one of the least represented nationalities among the foreign combatants of Daesh.

In any case, religious extremism and sectarianism do not necessarily lead to insurgency and terrorism. This does not only apply to Islamist fundamentalists vis-à-vis "misguided" Muslims. In 19th-century Victorian England, for example, Protestants of the Salvation Army wanted to forcibly convert "bad" Christians— without making good on their threats. Today, some African imams also preach hatred and vengeance. Yet their sermons do not always lead to physical clashes. The same causes do not produce the same effects. In Nigeria, for example, the leaders of Boko Haram, radical militants of the Muslim Students Society (MSS), Sheikh Ibrahim al-Zakzaky's Shiite brothers (*Yan Shi'a*) and the most conservative "Izala" factions of the "Society for the Eradication of Evil Innovations and the Re-establishment of the Sunnah" (*Jama'at Izalat al-Bida wa Iqamat al-Sunna*) have all criticised the corruption of the ruling class, the harmful effects of the neo-colonial school, and the shortcomings of a democratic model of Western inspiration. Only the first group has turned to terrorist-type violence after the extra-judicial execution of its spiritual guru, Mohamed Yusuf, by the

Nigerian police in 2009. Because of their repeated provocations, Sheikh Ibrahim al-Zakzaky's followers have faced the repression of security forces and have not (yet?) opted for armed struggle. As for MSS students and "Izala" adepts, they have often become civil servants, sometimes in remarkably high ranks. They have adjusted quite well to the Nigerian state's strategy of co-optation of the most vocal opponents.

There is also no hard evidence showing that African Muslim protesters always need Salafism and some training abroad to be radicalised. In Nigeria, for example, many Muslim activists were already radical before going to Saudi Arabia… or Iran. Thus, the founder of Boko Haram, Mohammed Yusuf, made the pilgrimage to Mecca in early 2004 to escape from security forces because he was an agitator suspected of having supported jihadists in Kanama, a small village on the border of Niger (Pérouse de Montclos, 2015). In the same vein, Ibrahim al-Zakzaky was already one of the fieriest militants of the MSS on the campus of the University of Zaria before converting to Shia Islam and going to Iran. In the predominantly Christian southern regions of Nigeria, Asari Dokubo was also an agitator and a student unionist in the University of Calabar before being seduced by the 1979 Iranian revolution, converting to Islam, going to Tehran, and opting for armed struggle to defend the rights of the Ijaw in the oil-producing areas of the Niger Delta (Pérouse de Montclos, 2008).

## On the limits of religious indoctrination

Now, we should ask ourselves whether indoctrination in mosques or Qur'anic schools constitutes a central and determining factor that leads Muslim protest groups in Africa to turn to violence. Most of the suicide bombings in the world are not motivated by Islamic issues but by the foreign occupation of territory (Pape, 2006). In Europe, it turned out that many jihadists did not have a religious past, did not go to mosque much, and did not participate in preaching (Da'wa).[6] In sub-Saharan Africa, surveys of combatants of al-Shabaab in Kenya, Boko Haram in Nigeria, and AQIM or the Katibat Macina in Mali have also refuted the primary role that had been attributed to radical imams and Qur'anic teachers to explain terrorism (Pérouse de Montclos, 2016, 2018a). Instead of Islamic fanaticism, the vast majority said they took up arms to defend themselves, protect their families, or avenge relatives who had been executed or tortured to death by security forces.

Today's jihadist leaders seem to have little knowledge of religious texts, unlike their elders of the 19th century in the Sahel (Loimeier, 2016, p. 295). This is also the case for foot soldiers. A major UN study revealed that, out of 573 members of al-Shabab, Boko Haram and, to a lesser extent, AQIM interviewed mainly in prisons or rehabilitation centres, about 57% of them did not know or did not understand the suras of the Qu'ran (UNDP, 2017). At a meeting organised by the newspaper Le Monde in Paris on 2 May 2016, the Emir of Kano also confirmed that in Nigeria, Boko Haram fighters had never read Hassan al-Turabi, mentor of the Muslim Brotherhood in Sudan, or Muhammad ibn Abd al-Wahhab, the founder of Wahhabism in Saudi Arabia. Once captured by government forces and interrogated in prison, many even proved to be ignorant of the Qur'an. They indeed did not become terrorists after reading Muhammad ibn Abd al-Wahhab.

Religious texts do not determine actions and only serve to justify violence. In the same vein, most Anarchist or Bolshevik militants at the beginning of the 20th century had not read Pierre-Joseph Proudhon or Karl Marx. Today, the same could be said of the Muslim Brothers. Unlike the Salafists, they are not particularly interested in theological orthodoxy. Their doctrine comes in very various forms from one country to another and reveals a great malleability, which sometimes leans towards a Muslim version of Christian democratic parties. With a strong foothold in national identities, the Muslim Brothers held off the idea of resurrecting a caliphate and reviving pan-Islamism. Being pragmatic, they preferred to make compromises and form alliances with Shiite or Sufi groups.

In Africa, too, political commitments and armed struggles in the name of Islam are not caused by religious beliefs alone. In Somalia, Mali or Nigeria, social inequalities, government failures, abuses by security forces, and feelings of injustice have been much more important in triggering and prolonging jihadi rebellions. Instead of focusing on Wahhabi indoctrination from Saudi Arabia, we need to understand local dynamics that shape the mobilisation of young African Muslims in armed struggles. Could we say that there would have been no jihadist uprisings in Nigeria, Mali, or Somalia without the doctrinal support of Wahhabism and, more rarely, funding from Saudi Arabia? Surely not, if we take a closer look at the genesis of these insurgent movements.

After the annulment of the Islamists' electoral victory in Algeria in 1991, the fighters who later founded AQIM would not have been able to conquer northern Mali without Tuareg rebels who took advantage of the political vacuum left by the collapse of Muammar Gaddafi's regime in Libya in 2011 and the withdrawal of the Malian army because of the 2012 coup in Bamako. In the same vein, the Boko Haram insurgency started and developed in Maiduguri in 2009 because of extra-judicial executions and a confrontation with the police over motorcycle helmets! As for al-Shabaab in Somalia, they prospered on the ruins of a failed state after the collapse of Siad Barre's dictatorship in 1991.

From this point of view, Wahhabism is one ideological resource, among others, which is used to justify politico-religious struggles often tainted by greed. Historically, African Muslims did not need Saudi funding and radical ideas from Arabia to produce their theology of Islamic reform. Although they are now integrated into the establishment, Sufi brotherhoods in the Sahel were the backbone of the prominent jihadist and anti-colonial movements of the 19th century. For example, Usman dan Fodio, who founded the Sokoto Caliphate, was a follower of the Qadiriyya.[7] In this respect, we should rethink the current narratives about an opposition between a Black and syncretic Sufism (seen as tolerant) against an Arab and radical Salafism (seen as terrorist). Both communities have had intense debates on puritanism, the use of violence, disobedience, or political obedience to the authorities.

## Fluid categories and easy confusions

It is difficult to grasp the real significance of Wahhabism in sub-Saharan Africa today. Indeed, the question is too often reduced to a selection of religious practices. Yet the use of the Qur'an to justify social revolts started long before Saudi proselytism. Occasionally, narratives about the "salafization" of politics in Africa are also based on little anecdotes. Some find it surprising, for example, that the authorities of the Republic of Niger open their public speeches by reciting the *Shahada*, the Muslim profession of faith. But this was already the case with the military in power in the 1970s (Triaud, 1982). The proliferation of mosques does not prove a radicalisation of religious practices either. It is mostly a reflection of the demographic growth of Muslims, and it often signals a fragmentation — even a weakening of Islam — when dissident imams found their congregation, like the pastors of evangelical churches.

Similarly, wearing a headscarf that covers the head (*hijab*) or the whole face (*niqab*) is not necessarily a sign of adherence to radical Salafism, as it has also enabled secluded women to leave their homes and occupy public spaces. On a practical level, it can also be used to protect oneself from the desert sands, to hide the fact that the same outfit is being worn repeatedly, or to seduce rich and reputedly pious men (Masquelier, 2009; Nyamnjoh, 2005; Alidou, 2011). In any case, it would be absurd to imagine that wearing a *niqab* would necessarily mean that it would later be accessorised with an explosive belt for a suicide bombing.

The word "Wahhabi" itself refers to all sorts of movements in Africa. It is widely overused, like the term "fascist," which often refers to regimes that are authoritarians but do not claim any ideological link to Benito Mussolini. Historically, the coloniser already found it difficult to differentiate Islamic schools of thought. In West and East Africa, for example, the British as-similated the Mahdist rebels of Sudan to the followers of the Reformed Tijaniyya in Nigeria, who prayed in the same way. Likewise, the Wahhabis of Saudi Arabia and the Ibadis of Oman were both described as "fervent" fanatics (*mutawwia*) although only the former considered it legitimate to kill Muslims they deemed deviant (Wilkinson, 2016, p. 154; Hill, 2013).

Today, confusions happen even more frequently because of the homonymous names of various jihadist movements. Surveys show that Africans tend to consider all these groups to be of the same mould (Benkirane, 2015). Confusions also concern the different Islamic schools of thought. Specialists of de-radicalisation usually understand traditional Sufi orders as an endogenous barrier to Saudi fundamentalism. Yet in the Central African Republic, for example, "Wahhabis" actually means "Sufis" because they are seen as an import.[8] In West Africa too, "Wahhabis" have been given all sorts of names: "deceivers" (*shargidi*) among the Yoruba of Lagos, "dissenters" (*munkirun*, or *munkirai*) among the Hausa of Accra, "Sunnis" (*sunnadunko* or *sunamogo*) among the Soninke and the Bambara of Mali, "ibadis" (*ibadou*) among the Wolof of Senegal or "hypocrites" (*munafiqun*) and "dissidents" (*mahabous*) among the Mousgoum of northern Cameroon. In general, these terms have a pejorative connotation and refer to foreigners (Ménoret, 2004).

The European Counterterrorism Centre also uses keywords to identify Wahhabi imams and map the so-called "radical" (rather than sectarian) Islam in the Sahel. Based on a semantic analysis of their sermons, the strange conclusion was drawn that Wahhabi clerics controlled all official councils representing Islam south of the Sahara.[9] In fact, these organisations serve the interests of governments and include many Sufis. They aim at regulating preaching, monitoring imams, and managing pilgrimages to Mecca, like the Islamic Cultural Association of Cameroon (ACIC, founded in 1963), the Nigerian Supreme Council for Islamic Affairs (NSCIA, founded in 1974), the National Muslim Council of Tanzania (BAKWATA, founded in 1968), the Supreme Council of Kenya Muslims (SUPKEM, founded in 1973) and the Ethiopian Islamic Affairs Supreme Council (EIASC, founded in 1976, officially recognised in 1991, and briefly dissolved after riots in 1995). In Mali, for example, Amupi (the Malian Association for the Unity and Progress of Islam) was founded by the military junta authorities in 1980 to control the expansion of a Wahhabi association, the Union Culturelle Musulmane (Muslim Cultural Union), which had been founded in 1953, banned by Modibo Keita's socialist government at independence, and legalised by Moussa Traoré's regime between 1968 and 1971. After the collapse of the dictatorship in 1991, the CCAIM (Committee for the Coordination of Islamic Associations in Mali) took over before being supplanted by the HCIM (High Islamic Council of Mali) in 2002. Other countries in the region have followed similar paths with the Association Islamique du Niger (Islamic Association of Niger), created by the military junta in 1974 and renamed the Conseil Islamique du Niger (Islamic Council of Niger) in 2003 to supervise fundamentalist groups after riots in 2000, or with the Comité Islamique d'Arbitrage (Islamic Arbitration Committee) established by Chad's dictatorship in 1974 and replaced by the CSAI (Supreme Council of Islamic Affairs) in 1990 (Elischer, 2015).

In this regard, the opposition between Wahhabism and Sufism is not as clear-cut as some observers usually think. Jihadism, first, does not reflect one specific current of Islam and linking it to a particular school of thought would not make much sense. Historically in West Africa, for example, Sufis led the 19th-century jihads. Although they are assimilated to Salafism and Jihadism, the Wahhabis are also criticised by some fundamentalists because of their allegiance to a Saud dynasty that is allied to America. Among other things, purists accuse them of promoting Sharia in a top-down manner, through the government instead of clerics. According to David Commins (2006, 6), Salafism's revivalism in the kingdom is in fact a sign of Wahhabism's diminished authority. It opposes loyalists to the dynasty and zealots who jettison traditional political authority, reacting to a state doctrine that is deemed hypocritical.

Indeed, Wahhabism is both a branch of Salafism and the official ideology of the Saud dynasty, Custodian of the Two Holy Mosques. As they refuse to worship human beings, including the founder of their doctrine Muhammad ibn Abd al-Wahhab (1703–1792), the Wahhabis prefer to call themselves "unitarist" (*muwahhidun*) or "traditionalist" (*ahl al-sunna*).[10] They developed a scriptural and literal approach to the teachings of the prophet, based on the Qur'an and hadiths. At the same time, they criticised the mediation practices of Sufi orders that recognise the authority of charismatic masters in-between God and his followers. Nonetheless, one of the great historical references of the Wahhabis is a cleric, Ahmad Ibn Taimyyah (1263–1328), who was allegedly a member of the Qadiriyya brotherhood.

Categories are thus fluid. In Africa, some fundamentalists align themselves with the glorious past of jihadists trained in the school of a Sufism, yet they reject its syncretism. Conversely, groups considered to be Wahhabi have sometimes taken positions against Saudi Arabia. Sometimes called Wahhabiyya, a terminology that refers to the Sufi brotherhoods of the region, the Izala followers of the "Society for the Eradication of Evil Innovations and the Restoration of Orthodoxy" (*Jama'at Izalat al-Bida wa Iqamat al-Sunna*), founded in 1978 in Nigeria, for example, split over the first Gulf crisis in 1991. One of their factions, a rather large one, in the most populous country in Africa, openly supported Saddam Hussein against Saudi Arabia, a position also adopted by Hassan el-Turabi's Muslim Brotherhood, in power in Sudan after 1989.

Moreover, the Izala do not consider themselves as being Wahhabi. As one of their Nigerian leader from Gombe State said: "the Society doesn't call for revolution in Islam". Whereas Wahhabis rely on the Hanbali school of jurisprudence, he added, the Izala follows the Maliki law (Ben Amara, 2014, p. 133).

A few available surveys also confirm that a rigid understanding of Islam is misleading. In their overwhelming majority, African Muslims do not recognise themselves in any of the currents that Westerners try desperately to categorise under the labels of Sufism, Wahhabism, Salafism, Mahdism, Millenarianism, or Shiism. In general, imams are the ones who claim an affiliation with one school of thought or another. But the majority of Muslims in northern Cameroon and Nigeria, for example, do not say they belong to any particular Islamic tradition (Seignobos & Iyébi-Mandjek, 2000, p. 145).[11] The same goes for Malians in cities like Sikasso (Warms, 1992, p. 494). Therefore, it is almost impossible to quantify the actual influence of Wahhabis in sub-Saharan Africa.

## Obstacles to Wahhabi proselytism

Fundamentalist ideas from the Gulf are hindered by many obstacles in the Sahel, including language issues, Arabs' racism, the resistance of traditionalists, and the limitations of social media in regions that are not connected to the Internet. In contrast with the Sufi brotherhoods, which were the first to truly Islamize the rural masses in Africa, the Wahhabis remained confined, for a long time, to a tiny urban and educated elite. After a few failed attempts in Nigeria in the 1870s, they appeared in the Sahel around 1945 with the so-called *Subbanu* or *Wahhabi* when Malian, Guinean and Gambian students from al-Azhar University created in Bamako a branch of the "Society of Young Muslims" (*Jama'at Shubban al-Muslim*), which was founded by Abd al-Hamid Said in Cairo in 1927 and which extended in Côte d'Ivoire, Sierra Leone, and Upper Volta (Kaba, 1974; 2000, p. 190; Triaud, 1986). But these Wahhabis were soon rejected. They were the victims of "pogroms" in Bamako in 1957 then Ouagadougou in 1973 and they were expelled from mosques in Bouaké in 1952, Gagnoa in 1956, Sifié in 1957, Treichville in 1958, and Man in 1959 (Amselle, 1985; Hiskett, 1980; Miran-Guyon, 1998, p. 10).

In this respect, it is important not to underestimate the deep rift between Arabs, who are seen as foreigners, and the black world of sub-Saharan Africa, where Islam has long been assimilated to raids, looting and slavery because it was associated with conquering groups such as the Fulani, the Tuaregs, or the Somali, i.e. communities with a "fair complexion." Only North Africa was truly arabised by military conquest and colonisation. East Africa was affected by the slave trade with the Gulf but the cultural influence of the Arabic peninsula was rather felt in the development of a lingua franca, Swahili, and the establishment of coastal Arab merchants who got married there. As for West Africa, the trans-Saharan caravan trade did not lead to such mixing, probably because its land was less hospitable and its climate more difficult (Hiskett, 1994, p. 194). In a way, the success of Sufism in the Sahel testified to an Africanization of Islam. Far from the Arabs of the Gulf, many local Muslim clerics thus preferred to refer to black heroes such as Bilal ibn Rabah, a slave of Ethiopian origin and one of the first converts to Islam who was the prophet's Muezzin in Mecca before fighting in Jerusalem in 638 and dying in Damascus in around 641.[12]

Indeed, Muslims in Africa South of the Sahara did not simply follow religious models from the Middle East. For example, they embraced the Maliki rather than the Saudis' Hanbali school of law. Like Ibadism in Oman, the austerity of Wahhabi puritanism slowed down its expansion in Africa, especially when it condemned the worshipping of saints, redemption, the healing powers of the marabouts, beliefs in good fortune (*baraka*), mystic prayers (*dhikr*), the exuberance of religious ceremonies, the celebration of the Prophet's birthday (*mawlid*), the extravagance of funerals, the luxury of marriages, and in general, evil innovations (*bid'a*). In the same vein, not all the young African clerics who trained in the Gulf returned to Africa to spread Wahhabism. Angered by the Arabs' racism, some have preferred to give up their Islamic studies or go back to Sufism.[13]

Combined with strong local resistance, divisions within the Wahhabi movement have also played a significant role. The Association of Orthodox Muslims of Côte d'Ivoire (AMOCI) sheds light on this issue. It was created because the Wahhabis had failed to take control of the Ivorian branch of the Muslim Cultural Union (UCM-CI), founded in 1957 and briefly banned in 1958–1960 before being reclaimed by mainstream clerics. To challenge their Salafist detractors, indigenous Sufi brotherhoods vilified the tactics of foreign agents and Muslim immigrants from Upper Volta, Nigeria, and mostly from Sékou Touré's "socialist" Guinea, a regime that was hostile towards President Félix Houphouët-Boigny in Côte d'Ivoire. They accused them of plotting against the government until the authorities finally allowed, in 1976, the creation of AMOCI and of Wahhabi mosques to be in a better position to control the situation. Such legalisation did not testify to the infiltration of a Saudi fifth column within the civil service.[14] For the authorities, the objective was instead to ease tensions between Muslim communities, especially during the Friday prayers and the main religious celebrations. Torn by internal rivalries and various accusations of embezzlement, AMOCI quickly became lethargic. In 1984, the authorities suspended it for two years. They closed its centre in Abidjan, which paradoxically precipitated the creation of Wahhabi mosques in other Ivorian towns such as Bouake in the north. AMOCI eventually failed to unite its followers when it changed its name and became the Association of Sunni Muslims of Cote d'Ivoire (AMSCI) in 1994.

In general, the language barrier also contributed to slowing down the propagation of Wahhabism. African Muslims still say their prayers (and, for a tiny minority among them, recite the whole Qur'an) in Arabic without being able to speak Arabic. With a few exceptions, preaching and Friday sermons (*khutba*) are still done in vernacular languages, revealing a profound contradiction in the Islamists' call (*Da'wa*). Indeed, fundamentalists regret that the use of Arabic in Africa has become profane, for example, through Al-Jazeera television programs. For them, the language of the Qur'an is sacred, and the Holy Book should not be translated, to avoid mis-understandings and inaccuracies. Only its exegesis could be done in vernacular languages.

As a result, translations of the Qur'an into Wolof, Fulani, Bambara, Yoruba, Zulu, Amharic, or Kikuyu came out exceptionally late, a century after translations of the Bible by Christian mis-sionaries. The most conservative Ulamas had to be convinced first before Saudi Arabia finally accepted to finance translations of the Holy Book, into Hausa by the Izala in Nigeria in 1979 or into Swahili in Kenya in 1969 by a famous Khadi of Mombasa, Sheikh Abdallah Salih al-Farsi.[15] They often had to adapt to the competition of other proselytising organisations such as the Ahmadiyya, a brotherhood of Indian origin, which had already translated the Qur'an into Swahili and had a growing influence in East Africa (Loimeier, 2016, p. 406). After the 1979 Iranian revolution, the objective was also to counter the Shiite propaganda through the distribution of free books.

Instead of supporting preaching in vernacular languages, Saudi Arabia has, however, pre-ferred to focus its efforts on teaching Arabic. This was a considerable challenge because, except for Northern Africa and Sudan, the use of Arabic remained extremely limited on the continent, including in countries where it was recognised as an official language, e.g. Comoros, Chad, Djibouti, Eritrea, Mauritania, and Somalia. In Niger, for example, it is spoken by only about 0.3% of the population over the age of six. However, it is used more than French among people who are literate in the national languages. More generally, illiteracy is still widespread in rural areas of the Sahel. Thus in Northern Nigeria, three-quarters of school-age children cannot read or write a sentence in their preferred language while only one third can add two-single digit numbers on paper correctly (Hoechner, 2018, p. 87). As for neighbouring Chad, it is just as difficult to assess the progress of Arabic since it was granted official language status in 1982 to make it easier to recruit northern Muslims into the state apparatus. Adopted by the 1996 Constitution and implemented in 2010, bilingualism in public education now forces franco-phone southerners to take courses in Arabic to obtain a civil servant position. However, such a policy also aims to control Qur'anic schools better. Because of the lack of qualified teachers, Franco-Arab schools are often managed by marabouts who seek to teach Islam rather than a foreign language (Ladiba, 2011).

We do not know if the proportion of Arab speakers in the Sahel is on the rise. Several elements seem to suggest otherwise. Firstly, the number of Saudi scholarships remains low at the continental level in comparison with the efforts of Western countries to support edu-cation: in fifty years, only about 25,000 Muslims, including a minority of Africans, have gone to school in Medina.[16] Additionally, recent research shows a relative decline in Arab-Islamic education in Nigeria and Senegal and reveals that it has stagnated in Somalia (Aiglepierre & Bauer, 2016, p. 32). On the contrary, some African languages are on the rise. Like Malay or Turkish, Swahili, for instance, was transcribed into the Roman alphabet, as was Hausa, which gradually abandoned its Arab precursor, Adjami. Despite being a member of the League of Arab States and being geographically close to Saudi Arabia, Siad Barre's dictatorship also chose the Roman alphabet to transcribe Somali as a national language in 1972. Such a de-cision is instructive. Although it is still prevalent in some commercial networks across the

Sahara and along the East African coast, Arabic is not associated with notions of progress and development in a global world. Unlike the Islamic University of Say in the Republic of Niger, where Arabic is the sole language of instruction, the Islamic University of Mbale in Uganda had thus to use English to maintain its position in the education market and offer more career opportunities to its students.

In practice, advances in telecommunications, the power of social media, and the development of trade flows do not say much either about trends in cultural interactions between Sub-Saharans and the Arabian Peninsula. Gulf countries often deport undocumented African immigrants. Moreover, Mecca no longer exerts as much influence as it used to when the pilgrimage legitimised Sahelian kingdoms and contributed to fixing settlement in Northern Nigeria or Sudan. Although the number of pilgrims has skyrocketed in the last century, statistics tell a different story. Since the period of independence, the proportion of African Muslims who go to Mecca has been declining (Bianchi, 2004; Pérouse de Montclos, 2018b). There are several reasons for such a trend, starting with Saudi Arabia's quotas to contain illegal immigration and the spread of diseases. Structurally, the entrance to the pilgrimage is also limited by the spatial constraints of a ritual that cannot be spread out over time and which therefore makes it necessary to restrict access to the holy places to avoid stampedes and deadly accidents.

In the countries of origin of African pilgrims, economic crises and the restrictions of the authorities also contributed to reducing the flows. In other words, fewer believers are likely to meet and mingle in Mecca, which, in any case, is not the central intellectual hub where revolutionary Islamic ideas emerged in the 20th century. Of course, we should not draw any hasty conclusions: the relative decline in the number of pilgrims is not an indicator of the secularisation of Muslim societies or radicalisation of the youth in other centres of Islamic education, including the universities of Cairo, Khartoum, Medina or Islamabad. But this forces us to reconsider the influence of Wahhabism and the Saudi state in Africa.

## Conclusion

Despite all the money spent by Riyadh, it is indeed striking to note that the doctrine of Muhammad ibn Abd al-Wahhab has hardly gone beyond the Gulf. Almost no Muslim cleric, whether in Africa or the Middle East, claims a direct affiliation to his school of thought (Devji, 2008, p. 289). His name is quoted mostly by antiterrorism "specialists," but it is seldom mentioned by imams when they debate to approve or condemn jihad. Many analysts thus introduce an element of confusion when they describe as "Wahhabis" groups that do not claim any affiliation to Muhammad ibn Abd al-Wahhab. To understand contemporary jihadist movements through the writings of an 18th-century theologian would be as challenging as trying to "explain al-Qaeda with the Qur'an or the Inquisition with the Bible" (Blin, 2017, p. 32). In practice, it is much more useful to analyse the local political and social conditions that cause insurrections in the name of Islam. Rather than looking for scapegoats abroad, the real question lies in the predatory violence of African states, the failures of development, and the responsibilities of the ruling class in the rise of jihadist-type armed protests. The goal of the fight against terrorism is to prevent conflicts and defuse the causes of discontent, rather than to "de-radicalise" the minds of the protesters afterwards.

## Notes

1  In general, academic literature on Saudi Arabia seldom focuses on its relations with Africa. For a vision of Wahhabism as a supporter of terrorism, see Valentine (2016), Conesa (2016), Redissi (2007), and Gold (2003). Written, respectively, by a French defence adviser and an Israeli diplomat who has

never been to Saudi Arabia, the works of Pierre Conesa and Dore Gold are particularly outrageous. For a more nuanced analysis, yet one that was accused of promoting the regime and its doctrine, see DeLong-Bas (2008).

2  In the same vein, it should be noted that it was Muslims from British India who took over the struggle for the restoration of a caliphate during the interwar period, while Osama bin Laden pledged allegiance to an Afghan, Mullah Muhammad Omar, rather than to a Saudi or an Egyptian cleric.

3  That centre was inaugurated in 1967 in a building that belonged to the spiritual heirs of the Sudanese Mahdi, the *Ansar*, before being closed down by the "socialist" dictatorship of General Gaafar Nimeiry in 1969, then nationalised and reopened in 1977.

4  In the same vein, the Paris attacks in January 2015 were claimed by both Amedy Coulibaly in the name of the Islamic State and by the Kouachi brothers, Chérif and Said, on behalf of AQAP (al-Qaeda in the Arabian Peninsula).

5  It is estimated that over sixty years, from 1808 to 1867, the struggle against the slave trade caused Great Britain to lose nearly 2% of its national income, while its share in the world production of sugar cane collapsed. Traders, industrialists, sailors, and bankers lost substantial market shares while consumers paid more for their sugar and taxpayers shouldered the financial cost of the hunt for traffickers. See Kaufmann and Pape (1999, p. 636).

6  According to investigations conducted in 2014 and 2015, some had recently converted to Islam, and most were second-generation immigrants who had explicitly rejected the traditions and religious culture of their Muslim parents, questioning the actual role of Salafism in their "brainwashing." See Roy (2016).

7  Nehemia Levtzion (1987, p. 33) claims that Wahhabi teachings also inspired him. This hypothesis is highly contested by Loimeier (2010, p. 273) and Hiskett (1994, p. 137).

8  Likewise, in the Maniema region of Kivu in the Democratic Republic of Congo, Sufi brotherhoods are considered to be foreign because they were imported in the 1920s by Arabs from Zanzibar and they preach in Swahili rather than in local languages. See Leinweber (2012).

9  Anonymous interviews with the author, Paris, 2016.

10 First used negatively by its detractors, the term "Wahhabi" spread among its supporters on the Arabian Peninsula towards the end of the nineteenth century. King Abbd al-Aziz then officially prohibited its use in 1929, preferring the term "Salafist". See Mouline (2017, pp. 45&55).

11 See also an excellent survey funded by the Dutch cooperation in Nigeria. http://www.qeh.ox.ac.uk/node/21877.

12 The founder of Boko Haram, Mohamed Yusuf, also referred to Bilal ibn Rabah in one of his sermons in 2006. See Kyari (2014, p. 15).

13 Of the 18 first Nigerian scholarship recipients sent by Saudi Arabia to the Islamic University of Medina in 1968, 16 dropped out and returned home before the end of the academic year. Many of them complained about learning anything and getting bored! See Thurston (2016, p. 80).

14 Miran-Guyon, 1998. For an opposite view, see Haynes (1996, p. 125).

15 Sheikh Abdullah Salih al-Farsi had been the student of another Khadi of Mombasa, Sheikh al-Amin bin Ali al-Mazru'i (1891–1949), who had created a movement for Reformation (*Al-Islah*) in 1931 and followed the teachings of the precursor of the Egyptian Salafism, Mufti Muhammad Abduh (1849–1905). In turn, Sheikh Abdullah Salih al-Farsi became the Chief Khadi of Kenya from 1978 to 1982 and initiated a Puritan movement of Sunnah followers (*Ansar al-Suna*) which, like the Izala in Nigeria, strongly criticised the mysticism of the Sufi brotherhoods.

16 In the case of Mali, for example, the numbers are particularly low in 40 years, with 50 scholarship recipients who often took advantage of their stay on the Arabian Peninsula to find work there instead of going back home (Amselle, 1985, p. 350). For the whole continent, Saudi Arabia accommodated 2,285 Sub-Saharan students in 2009, a figure that included non-religious curricula. Despite an increase in recent years, these numbers cannot be compared to the hundreds of thousands of Sub-Saharans registered in French, American, or British universities, their central countries of destination. Except for Mali, Niger and Mauritania, Saudi Arabia is actually not the first choice of emigration for the educated youth from African Muslim countries; for instance, it ranked ninth for Nigeria in 2015 (Campus France, 2017).

# Bibliography

Aiglepierre, R., & Bauer, A. (2016). Quantifier et qualifier le choix de l'enseignement arabo-islamique en Afrique subsaharienne. *Afrique Contemporaine, 257*, 25–40.

Alidou, O. (2011). *Engaging modernity: Muslim women and the politics of agency in postcolonial Niger.* Wisconsin: The University of Wisconsin Press.

Amselle, J.-L. (1985). Le Wahabisme à Bamako (1945–1985). *Canadian Journal of African studies, 19*(2), 345–357.

Ben Amara, R. (2014). 'We introduced sharia'. The izala movement in Nigeria as initiator of sharia-reimplementation in the north of the country: some reflections. In J. Chesworth & F. Kogelmann (Eds.), *Shari'a in Africa today: Reactions and responses.* Leiden: Brill.

Benkirane, R. (2015). *Rapport sur les perceptions des facteurs d'insécurité et d'extrémisme violent In les régions transfrontalières du Sahel.* Genève: Institut de hautes études internationales et du développement (IHEID).

Bianchi, R. (2004). *Guests of God: Pilgrimage and Politics in the Islamic World.* New York: Oxford University Press.

Blin, L. (2017). Wahhabisme, salafisme et djihadisme. *Les carnets du CAPS, 24*, 29–50.

Campus France. (2017). *La mobilité internationale des étudiants africains.* Paris: Hors Séries n°16.

Commins, D. (2006). *Wahhabi Mission and Saudi Arabia.* London: I. B. Tauris.

Conesa, P. (2016). *Dr. Saoud et Mr. Djihad: la diplomatie religieuse de l'Arabie saoudite.* Paris: Robert Laffont.

DeLong-Bas, N. (2008). *Wahhabi Islam: From Revival and Reform to Global Jihad.* Oxford: Oxford University Press.

Devji, F. (2008). The 'Arab' in global militancy. In M. A. Rasheed (Ed.), *Kingdom without borders: Saudi political, religious and media frontiers.* London: Hurst.

Elischer, S. (2015). Autocratic legacies and state management of Islamic activism in Niger. *African Affairs, 114/457*, 577–597.

Gold, D. (2003). *Hatred's kingdom: How Saudi Arabia Supports the new global terrorism.* Washington, DC: Regnery Publishing.

Haynes, J. (1996). *Religion and politics in Africa.* London: Zed.

Hill, J. (2013). Religious extremism in Northern Nigeria past and present: parallels between the Pseudo-Tijanis and Boko Haram. *The Round Table, 102*(3), 235–244.

Hiskett, M. (1980). The "community of grace" and its opponents, the "rejecters:" a debate about theology and mysticism in Muslim West Africa with special reference to its Hausa expression. *African Language Studies, 17*, 126–130.

Hiskett, M. (1994). *The course of Islam in Africa.* Edinburgh: Edinburgh University Press.

Hiskett, M. (1994). *The Sword of truth: The life and times of the Shehu Usuman dan Fodio.* Evanston, IL: Northwestern University Press.

Hoechner, H. (2018). *Quranic schools in Northern Nigeria: Everyday experiences of youth, faith, and poverty.* Cambridge: Cambridge University Press.

Kaba, L. (1974). *The Wahhabiyya: Islamic reform and politics in French West Africa.* Evanston: Northwestern University Press.

Kaba, L. (2000). Islam in West Africa: Radicalism and the new ethic of disagreement, 1960–1990. In N. Levtzion & R. Pouwels (Eds.), *The history of Islam in Africa.* Oxford: James Currey.

Kaufmann, C., & Pape, R. (1999). Explaining costly international moral action: Britain's sixty-year campaign against the Atlantic Slave Trade. *International Organization, 53*(4), 631–668.

Kramer, M. (1986). *Islam assembled: The advent of the Muslim congresses.* New York: Columbia University Press.

Kyari, M. (2014). The message and methods of Boko Haram. In M.-A. Pérouse de Montclos (Ed.), *Boko Haram: Islamism, Politics, Security, and the State in Nigeria.* Ibadan: IFRA-Nigeria. Leiden, African Studies Centre, Waposo Series n°2.

Lacroix, S. (2017). L'islamisme au prisme des Frères musulmans. In S. Mervin & N. Mouline (Eds.), *Islams politiques: Courants, doctrines et idéologies.* Paris: CNRS.

Ladiba, G. (2011). *L'émergence des organisations islamiques au Tchad: enjeux, acteurs, territoires.* Paris: L'Harmattan.

Landau, J. (1994). *The Politics of Pan-Islam: ideology and organisation.* Oxford: Clarendon Press.

Leichman, M. (2015). *Shi'i Cosmopolitanisms in Africa: Lebanese Migration and Religious Conversion in Senegal.* Bloomington: Indiana University Press.

Leinweber, A. (2012). The Muslim minority of the democratic republic of Congo: from historic marginalisation and internal division to collective action. *Cahiers d'études africaines, 206-207*, 517–544.

Levtzion, N. (1987). The 18th-century: background to the Islamic revolutions in West Africa. In N. Levtzion & J. Voll (Eds.), *Eighteenth-century Renewal and Reform in Islam*. Syracuse, NY: Syracuse University Press.

Loimeier, R. (2010). Africa South of the Sahara to the first world war. In F. Robinson (Ed.), *The New Cambridge History of Islam: Volume 5. The Islamic World in the Age of Western Dominance*. Cambridge: Cambridge University Press.

Loimeier, R. (2016). *Islamic Reform in 20th Century Africa*. Edinburgh: Edinburgh University Press.

Masquelier, A. (2009). *Women and Islamic Revival in a West African Town*. Bloomington: Indiana University Press.

Mendelsohn, B. (2016). *The al-Qaeda Franchise: The Expansion of al-Qaeda and Its Consequences*. Oxford: Oxford University Press.

Ménoret, P. (2004). Le wahhabisme, arme fatale du néo-orientalisme. *Mouvements*, *36*(6), 54–60.

Miran-Guyon, M. (1998, December). Dynamisme urbain d'un islam réformiste en Côte d'Ivoire contemporaine (1960-1996). *Islam et Sociétés au Sud du Sahara*, *12*, 5–74.

Mouline, N. (2017). In S. Mervin & N. Mouline (Eds.), *Les prétentions hégémoniques du wahhabisme*. Paris: CNRS.

Nyamnjoh, F. (2005). Disquettes and thiofs in Dakar. *Africa*, *75*(3), 295–324.

Pape, R. (2006). *Dying to win: The strategic logic of suicide terrorism*. New York: Random House.

Pérouse de Montclos, M.-A. (2008). Conversion to Islam and modernity in Nigeria: a view from the underworld. *Africa Today*, *54*(4), 71–87.

Pérouse de Montclos, M.-A. (Ed.). (2015). *Boko Haram: Islamism, politics, security, and the state in Nigeria*. Los Angeles: Tsehai.

Pérouse de Montclos, M.-A. (2016). A sectarian Jihad in Nigeria: The case of Boko Haram. *Small Wars & Insurgencies*, *27*(5), 878–895.

Pérouse de Montclos, M.-A. (2018a). *L'Afrique, nouvelle frontière du djihad?* Paris: La Découverte.

Pérouse de Montclos, M.-A. (2018b). Pilgrimage to Mecca and "Radical" Islam: new trends from Sub-Saharan Africa. *Journal of the Middle East and Africa*, *9*(1), 273–289.

Rasheed, M. (2008). The minaret and the palace: obedience at home and rebellion abroad. In M. Rasheed (Ed.), *Kingdom without borders: Saudi political, religious and media frontiers*. London: Hurst.

Redissi, H. (2007). *Le pacte de Nadjd ou comment l'islam sectaire est devenu l'islam*. Paris: Seuil.

Roy, O. (2016). Peut-on comprendre les motivations des djihadistes? *Pouvoirs*, *158*, 15–24.

Seignobos, C., & Iyébi-Mandjek, O. (Eds.). (2000). *Atlas de la province Extrême-Nord Cameroun*. Yaoundé: IRD.

Thurston, A. (2016). *Salafism in Nigeria: Islam, Preaching, and Politics*. Cambridge: Cambridge University Press.

Triaud, J.-L. (1982). L'Islam et l'Etat en République du Niger (1974-1981). In O. Carré (Ed.), *L'Islam et l'État In le monde d'aujourd'hui* (pp. 246–257). Paris: P.U.F.

Triaud, J.-L. (1986). Abd Al-Rahman l'Africain (1908-1957). Pionnier et précurseur du Wahhabisme au Mali. In O. Carré & P. Dumont (Eds.), *Radicalismes islamiques. Volume II: Maroc Pakistan, Inde, Yougoslavie, Mali* (pp. 162–180). Paris: L'Harmattan.

UNDP. (2017). *Journey to Extremism in Africa: Drivers, Incentives and the Tipping Point for Recruitment*. New York: UNDP.

Valentine, S. R. (2016). *Force and Fanaticism: Wahhabism in Saudi Arabia and Beyond*. London: Hurst.

Warms, R. (1992). Merchants, Muslims, and Wahhabiyya: The elaboration of Islamic identity in Sikasso, Mali. *Canadian Journal of African Studies*, *26*(3), 485–507.

Wilkinson, J. (2016). *Arabs and the Scramble for Africa*. Sheffield: Equinox.

# 7

# The global war on terror and its African front

*Omon Merry Osiki*

## Introduction

Africa constitutes a significant front in the global war on terror. Understandably, the literature on terrorism in Africa has mainly focused on its financing on the continent (Achi & Tar, 2013), its impact on national development (Osiki, 2014), its connection to globalisation (Maiangwa, 2016; Osiki, 2016; Leonald-Fwa, 2016; Krech, 2011; Obi, 2008), as well as its impact on state-building (Adeniran, 2013), among others. These areas have been better covered because of the attention that the 2001 terrorist attacks on the World Trade Centre and the Pentagon in the United States created across the world (Krech, 2011:125–137). Yet, as Africa remains the earth's oldest and most enduring landmass (Reader, 1997:9), there is no doubt that it represents a large and complex new front in the fight against terrorism. Therefore, Africa's share of terrorist activities has been humongous, ranging from suicide bombings to hostage-taking, kidnappings, assassinations, hijacking and other related activities.

Nevertheless, despite the various studies on Africa's contributions to global terrorist attacks and terrorism prevention efforts, the intellectual input of African scholars to the discourse of terrorism has been relatively negligible compared to the effort of their Western counterparts. Hence, gaps remain in the literature on Africa and the fight against terrorism. Therefore, the current study seeks to shed light on the global war on terror with a focus on its African front, which certainly deserves full attention in the literature on terrorism. It addresses pertinent questions on international terrorism such as: What were the special global war efforts on terror and their implications on Africa? What were the significant contributions of Africa to the global war on terrorism? What mechanism did African states put in place to address the nagging issue of terrorism? Lastly, to what extent did African nations collaborate with the international community in the fight against terrorism?

The chapter begins with this introduction, followed by a conceptual framework on terrorism in Africa, discussions on a few striking global efforts on the war on terror as well as its implications on the war on terror in Africa, and a section on Africa's contributions to the war on terror, followed by a conclusion. The various sections indicate that Africa's response to terrorism has been variegated, based on the limits of its capability and resources.

## Review of relevant literature and conceptualisation of terrorism

Historians, political scientists, sociologists and others agree that groups that assist or directly perpetrate violent political activities as a means to resist or overthrow hegemonic oppression have their precedent in history. In a comprehensive review of the literature on the history of terrorism, Boyns and Ballard (2004:10) argued that the origins of terrorism and political violence stem from the perceived imbalances in power distribution between the powerful and the powerless and their struggle over the symbolic, ideological, economic and political basis of social relations. In the same vein, the trio of Thomas Hobbes, John Locke and J.J. Rousseau devoted a large part of their intellectual erudition to explaining the relationships between the powerful and the weak (Sabine & Thorson, 1973). However, Hodgson and Tadros (2013:497–499) have advised that in defining terrorism we must be guided by the principle of "fair labelling" to avoid the "condemnatory effects" of any proposed definition. They have also suggested the need to identify the "moral core" of terrorism and offer clarification of several "distinct dilemmas" (such as the terrorist purpose, the terrorist action, the terrorist target, the terrorist method, and the terrorist agent) in an attempt to define the concept (Hodgson & Tadros, 2013:498–500). The terrorist purpose indicates that the terrorist act must have a specific purpose. On the other hand, terrorist action refers to "the immediate action that terrorists take to advance their goals" such as killing or maiming the terrorist targets. The terrorist target refers to the identity of victims of the terrorist action, the terrorist method concerns how terrorists aim to achieve their political goals, and the terrorist agent refers to the nature of the terrorist agent performing the terrorist action (Hodgson & Tadros, 2013:499–522).

Terrorism may be seen as the premeditated use or threat to use violence by subnational groups or individuals against non-combatants to obtain socio-political or related objectives through the intimidation of a broad audience beyond that of the immediate victims (Gaibulloev & Sandler, 2011:357). It can also be a systematic or predetermined use of violence by an individual(s) or sub-national groups against communities, governments, or those in power to obtain a political, social, religious, or economic objective through intimidation of a large audience beyond that of the immediate victims (Elu, 2012:345; Enders & Sandler, 2006). In connection, terrorist activities such as bombings, hostage-taking, kidnapping, and armed attacks are intended to raise the anxiety level of citizens (and other concerned persons), so that they pressure their government to concede to the terrorists' demands. Therefore, the motive for any terrorism is for political or social/economic change in a given society. It is in this context that Gaibulloev and Sandler have argued that without the apparent motive of socio-political or economic transformation, "violent acts of bombings, kidnappings, or armed attacks are merely criminal activities for extortion or sociopathic reasons" (Gaibulloev & Sandler, 2011:357).

Moreover, Boyns and Ballard (2004:5–25), like many other writers (also known as "terrorologists") such as Cooper (1978) and Reich (1990), have described terrorism as "political violence" that is also a social problem. They agree with Scott (1990) that terrorism could be seen as a violent response to hegemonic dominance or an attempt to overcome the dominant hegemony by the creation of an alternative and a counter-hegemonic movement (Boyns & Ballard, 2004:10). In that case, terrorism (bottom-up) may be organised by disenfranchised or marginalised groups in an attempt to intentionally contradict hegemonic social configurations within their state (Boyns & Ballard, 2004:10). Lastly, Boyns and Ballard (2004:13) maintain that terrorism signifies a counter-hegemonic response to perceived control and that the actions of terrorists represent a reaction to perceived powerlessness matched with the assumption that "one's way of life has been threatened."

On the other, Juliet Elu (2012:345–357) suggests that in Africa and South Asia, terrorism is a common economic good, which can be elastic. Hence, she means that tackling terrorism would require concerted efforts that would include both reducing underdevelopment and addressing the personal needs of would-be terrorists. While Elu's (2012:354) theorisation of terrorism in Africa between 1980 and 2004 should be commended, her conclusion that terrorism in Africa and South Asia is not motivated by political, existential, or related issues falls short of a comprehensive analysis of the persistence of the activities of groups such as Boko Haram and others in their different enclaves in Africa.

On their part, Gaibulloev and Sandler (2011:357) have distinguished between domestic and transnational terrorism on the one hand and between state terrorism and state-sponsored terrorism on the other. For instance, they have opined that through its perpetrators, victims, audience and influence, domestic terrorism solely involves the venue country where the act of terrorism takes place. This can explain why the assassination of local government officials by a domestic terrorist group is seen as a domestic terrorist event. However, they have demonstrated succinctly that transnational terrorist incidents should have ramifications that extend beyond the venue country. Thus, a terrorist event in which for instance a plane is hijacked in one country and is made to fly to another country should be considered as a transnational terrorist attack (Gaibulloev & Sandler, 2011:357). They have also argued that if the victims or perpetrators in a terrorist incident are from countries other than the host or venue country (such as the Luxor massacre in November 1997, which involved foreign nationals from France, Germany, Japan, Switzerland, the United Kingdom, and elsewhere), then the terrorist attack is transnational (Gaibulloev & Sandler, 2011:357; Jenkins, 1986:773–786).

In the same vein, writers have distinguished between state terrorism (top-down) and state-sponsored terrorism. While state terrorism indicates a situation whereby the government of a state terrorises its citizens or those of other countries through the application of grossly violent (institutional) coercion (Boyns, & Ballard, 2004:10), state-sponsored terrorism occurs when a government clandestinely aids a terrorist group by offering through funding, safe havens, intelligence, training, or by other means (Mickolus, 1989:287–293). Indeed, it has been argued elsewhere that the origin of the concept of terrorism appears to lie in state action to control political opponents (Hodgson & Tadros, 2013:522). For instance, due to the alleged Eritrean government's funding and equipping of Islamic insurgents in Somalia, the U.S. State Department contemplated adding Eritrea to its list of state sponsors of terror. Eritrea allegedly provided safe harbour to the leader of the Council of Islamic Courts, Sheikh Hassan Dahir Aweys, who was believed to be an al-Qaeda collaborator (Isaacson, 2008:8). Similarly, U.N. Security Council Resolution 748 of 31 March 1992 described Libya as a terrorist state and urged it to "cease all forms of terrorist action and all assistance to terrorist groups" (Hodgson & Tadros, 2013:522). Finally, we adopt the definition of terrorism provided by Hodgson and Tadros in our analysis of terrorist activities in Africa because of its holistic consideration of the purpose, target, method and the terrorist agent in the perpetuation of terrorist acts.

## The global war on terror

The events of 11 September 2001 changed the landscape, perception and strategies on the war on terror in the global arena because it pushed the United States to the vanguard of the war against international terrorism (Elu, 2012:345; Wanandi, 2002:184–189; Romaniuk, 2010:591–613). Before the 1980s, the fight against terrorism was primarily within the purview of the Central Intelligence Agency (CIA) and the Department of State. However, from the early 1980s, following some global terrorist activities such as the Iran hostage crisis, the responsibility to investigate terrorism was transferred to the Federal Bureau of Investigation (FBI) (Elu, 2012:345). Furthermore, following the 11 September 2001 terrorist incident, more law enforcement agencies became involved in the processes of investigation, arrest and prosecution of terrorists and terrorist organisations (Boyns & Ballard, 2004:8; Romaniuk, 2010:591–613). Today, the approach to fighting terrorism has mostly changed from reliance on "diplomacy and intelligence" to criminal prosecution and the use of military action (Boyns & Ballard, 2004:9). Specifically, between the Bush and Obama administrations, U.S. involvements in counterterrorism operations in Africa and other parts of the world were pursued under the regimes of the "War on Terror" and "overseas contingency operations." In reality, however, there was no significant change in strategy as far as international efforts on the war on terror in Africa were concerned (Whitaker, 2010:639).

At the global level, the U.N. Counterterrorism Committee (CTC) was created in 2001 to monitor the implementation of Security Council Resolution 1373. The CTC consisted of all 15 members of the Security Council. Its focus was to encourage all U.N. members to ratify all existing U.N. legal instruments on terrorism and related regional agreements. It also enjoined members to enact relevant domestic legislation necessary for the enforcement of the resolution mentioned above. Also, the CTC strategy was to encourage countries to domesticate anti-terrorism provisions and international agreements as well as build a global legal infrastructure against terrorism. Accordingly, national governments were expected to submit periodic reports to the CTC on the three areas of criminalisation, prevention and punishment of terrorism-related activities. On this basis, the Counterterrorism Committee Executive Directorate (CTED) was created in 2004 to provide the CTC with the necessary advice and technical assistance to combat terrorism (Whitaker, 2010:641; Heng & McDonagh, 2008:553–573).

Moreover, U.N. anti-terrorism efforts were complemented at the regional levels. For instance, there was the Inter-American Convention Against Terrorism, the defunct Organisation of African Unity (OAU) Convention on the Prevention and Combating of Terrorism (1999) as well as the commitment of the successor organisation, the African Union (AU), to combat terrorism by establishing a terrorism research centre in Algeria. Others were the Arab Convention for the Suppression of Terrorism (1998), the South Asian Association for Cooperation (SAARC), Regional Convention on Suppression of Terrorism (1987), and the European Convention on the Suppression of Terrorism (1977), which predates the CTC (Whitaker, 2010:642). Indeed, since the 11 September 2001 episode, regional, sub-regional, and national efforts to strengthen anti-terrorism and counter-terrorist financing (CTF) legislation have increased across Africa, Asia, Europe, the Americas, and other parts of the world (Whitaker, 2010:642; Mombo & Mwaluda, 2000:36–41).

## Africa and the age of terror

Africa is one of the continents to have witnessed terrorist activities since the last decade of the 20th century. Leading terrorist groups such as al-Qaeda and its affiliates are believed to have operated in several African countries, especially Comoro, Kenya, Libya, Sudan, Somalia, Tanzania, Mali, Nigeria and others (Lyman & Morrison, 2004:75–86; Gaibulloev & Sandler, 2011:357). In some of these areas, terrorists carried out spectacular incidents such as the "Black Hawk Down" incident against US peacekeeping troops in Mogadishu, Somalia on 3–4 October 1993. There were also the bombings of the US embassies in Nairobi, Kenya, and Dar es Salaam, Tanzania on 7 August 1998 that claimed 224 people, including 12 Americans, and injured 5,000 others (Lyman & Morrison, 2004:75–86). The two incidents were ascribed to al-Qaeda, which later in 2002 also claimed to have been responsible for killing 15 people in an

Israeli-owned hotel near Mombasa in Kenya (Lyman & Morrison, 2004:75). The incidents alarmed the United States and compelled the country to adopt a much more holistic approach to fighting terrorism in Africa. It forced U.S. officials into the realisation that Africa could not be kept at the "back of the queue forever" if U.S. security interests were to be advanced there (Lyman & Morrison, 2004:76). Other related attacks included the Luxor massacre of tourists on 17 November 1997 at Hatshepsut's Temple in Egypt by the Islamic Group, in which 62 people were killed and 24 others injured (Mickolus & Simmons, 2006). In the same vein, the car bombing of the Israeli-owned Paradise Hotel in Mombasa, Kenya on 28 November 2002 by an Al-Qaeda affiliated Somali group, which killed 16 (including 3 suicide terrorists) and injured 8, was intended to cause economic and psychological damage and create panic and apprehension in the process (Gaibulloev & Sandler, 2011:355–371).

Then there was the bombing of tourist sites in Sharm el-Sheikh, Egypt on 23 July 2005. As Isaacson (2008:8) has succinctly noted, owing to the West's continued military presence in the Middle East, al-Qaeda turned its focus to the occupation of new fronts, especially Africa, in its global jihad, the reason being that the continent is deemed a haven for its cells. Furthermore, in recent times, social instability in Mali, Libya and other parts of the Maghreb and West Africa has intensified the presence of al-Qaeda in Africa. In 2007, the Algerian Salafist Group for Preaching and Combat (SGPC) became part of the larger al-Qaeda organisation under the name "al-Qaeda in the Islamic Maghreb" (AQIM) (Isaacson, 2008:8).

All these examples indicate that after 11 September 2001 several terrorist enclaves emerged in Africa. In the Greater Horn of Africa, comprising Djibouti, Eritrea, Ethiopia, Kenya, Somalia, Sudan, Tanzania, and Uganda, for example, al-Qaeda and its affiliates had an undeniable presence. They recorded some horrendous activities in the area (Lyman & Morrison, 2004:76). The closeness of the region to the Middle East, its socioreligious composition, coupled with the factor of its strategic location, made it essential to the US counterterrorism programme.

Similarly, in 2007 security personnel in Nigeria arrested three al-Qaeda suspects, who had allegedly trained with SGPC in Algeria in 2005 (Isaacson, 2008:8). A few of these terrorist groups benefitted from the solidarity dynamics of terrorism (Alexander, 2004; Collins 2004a, 2004b), which encouraged the recruitment and spread of their membership across Africa. For instance, it is believed that the al-Qaeda infrastructure in East Africa was built on "linkages with an Arab-origin minority." Hence, the presence of terrorism in the region was closely linked to their religious radicalisation and their responses to the "effects of deep-rooted (socio-economic and political) problems" (Lyman & Morrison, 2004:76). Similarly, the Lord's Resistance Army (LRA) in Uganda, which was notorious for kidnapping children to serve as soldiers and domestic servants, as well as the Allied Democratic Forces (ADF) also in Uganda, had the intention to spread across the country and neighbouring communities in East Africa. In particular, the LRA's operations were felt in Uganda, South Sudan, the Democratic Republic of the Congo, Central African Republic, and Chad. Similarly, the ADF consisted of dissident troops and extremist Muslim groups, who exploited religious and ethnic sentiments in the recruitment of new members (Whitaker, 2010:653). Similarly, the Al-Shabaab in Somalia exploited the solidarity dynamics of terrorism to establish bases in the Horn of Africa (Whitaker, 2010:653).

Furthermore, in the late 20th and early 21st centuries, Africa and Asia were reported to have hosted the top ten terrorist groups in the world and arguably remain fertile breeding and cultivating grounds for terrorists from and to other continents (Elu, 2012:347). Some of these terrorist groups represented deadly examples of global terrorism. For instance, terrorist groups such as the Boko Haram in Nigeria and AQIM were notorious for seizing territories and sacking villages in Northeast Nigeria, Niger Republic, parts of northern Cameroon and Mali. In particular, like the Lord's Resistance Army, the Boko Haram operated as a transnational terrorist group. Therefore, its attacks were felt in Nigeria, Cameroon, Chad and Niger. It also could extend its activities to other neighbouring West African and Central African countries. While the group's avowed goal and ultimate aspirations were the Islamisation of their area of operation and the creation of an Islamic state (Ousman, 2004:65–105), it was also concerned about religious, political and economic issues (Lyman & Morrison, 2004:79). Some of the non-religious motivations for the group's activities included their dissatisfaction with decades of corruption in Nigeria, economic mismanagement, financial chaos, poverty, political repression and social tensions in the country (Ousman, 2004:77). Besides, the Boko Haram group was openly against the secularisation of the society along with the Western culture. It also disagreed with the promotion of external policies and influences perceived as a menace to the integrity of the Islamic community (Ousman, 2004:66–69; Kruglanski & Fishman, 2006:45–48). This provided the basis for the group's fundamentalist brand of Islam, resulting in the killing and maiming, primarily via bombings, of hundreds of people in the northern part of the country, not least the Northeast of Nigeria.

## Africa's contributions to the war on terror

Different measures have been adopted to fight terrorism in Africa. These include the adoption of global and regional legal frameworks to combat terrorism, efforts of national governments as well as external assistance from governments and non-governmental organisations outside Africa. First, international efforts to combat terrorism in Africa were coordinated by the United States, European countries and other interest bodies (De Vries, 2005:3–9). For instance, in 2002, before the Boko Haram activities became more menacing, the Bush administration singled out Nigeria as a country with "significant impact" and deserving of "focused attention" in the U.S. 2002 National Security Strategy (Lyman & Morrison, 2004:81). Besides, as early as 2000 it was predicted that the emergence of Islamic fundamentalism, together with the rise of inter-religious violence, ethnic nationalism and agitations, and anti-western sentiments could transform Nigeria into an unusual attraction to violent militant Islamists, and consequently, a paradise for terrorist networks (Ousman, 2004:78). The emergence of the Boko Haram group after that as well as militant activities in the Niger Delta area justified some of the predictions.

Expectedly, several countries responded to terrorist activities in Africa. The United Kingdom provided a substantial package of the military, intelligence, and development support to Nigeria to help it tackle the Boko Haram threat. UK military assistance included training of personnel, together with information and intelligence gathering. The UK also assisted in the treatment and rehabilitation of victims of Boko Haram attacks. For instance, in 2014 the UK contributed £1.7 million to the U.N.'s Central Emergency Response Fund and the European Commission's Humanitarian Aid and Civil Protection department programmes in Nigeria to address the effects of Boko Haram activities. The Department for International Development provided additional £1 million to the International Committee of the Red Cross to provide humanitarian assistance to those directly affected by the activities of the terrorists (Foreign and Commonwealth Office, 2015).

Before the 2001 terrorist incident, the United States in 1995 designated Sudan, along with countries such as Iran, Iraq, Syria, Libya, Cuba, and North Korea, as a terrorist state, a haven for global terrorism and a funder and sponsor of international terrorism. This was due to its links to transnational militant Islamist movements such as Iran's Hezbollah, the Palestinian Hamas, and Egypt's Islamic Jihad etc., as well as the fact that it was host to hardline terrorists such as the

Saudi-born Osama bin Laden. Moreover, the country was also alleged to have been involved in the attempted assassination of Egyptian President Hosni Mubarak in 1995 in Addis Ababa, Ethiopia (Ousman, 2004:92; Bremer, 1995:40–42).

In 1997, the U.N. Security Council and the United States imposed trade and financial sanctions against the government of Sudan (Ousman, 2004:92; Mickolus, 1989:287–293). Then in August 1998, following its East Africa embassy bombings, the United States launched retaliatory cruise missile strikes against Khartoum Al-Shifa Pharmaceutical plant. The plant was allegedly used in the manufacturing of chemical weapons to facilitate global terrorism (Ousman, 2004:92–93).

Moreover, the United States in 2002 created the Combined Joint Task Force-Horn of Africa (CJTF-HOA) to combat terrorism in the region. The task force involved 1,800 U.S. soldiers backed by the U.S. Central Command. It was based in Djibouti and charged with the responsibility to "deter, pre-empt, and disable terrorist threats" from Kenya, Somalia, and Kenya (Lyman & Morrison, 2004). A multinational naval interdiction force assisted the CJTF-HOA. Besides, in June 2003 the administration of President George Bush, Jnr. announced a $100 million package of counterterrorism measures to boost the work of the task force (Lyman & Morrison, 2004:77; Heng & McDonagh, 2008:553–573). The strategic, commercial and maritime importance of the region explains the rationale behind the vast U.S. financial commitment to the project. Moreover, it was generally believed that the Greater Horn of Africa should be used as "a frontline region" in the war against terrorism in East and Northeast Africa (Lyman & Morrison, 2004:77; Sperotto, 2014:221–230).

The second point to note is that the different countries in Africa have responded to terrorist activities based on their capability, availability of funds, the relevant strategies and personnel, as well as the amount of international cooperation from which they have benefitted. For instance, the Nigerian government's anti-terrorist security interventions were initially lacklustre and ineffective, especially before 2014. It can be argued that insufficient political will to fight the terrorist group coupled with reported cases of corruption (Omonobi, 2016) affected military operations and sometimes crippled the morale of men and officers deployed to combat the scourge.

More importantly during the period, the Nigerian state seemed to have been bedevilled by political turmoil in addition to its preoccupation with guaranteeing stability and peace across the length and breadth of the country (Bergesen & Lizardo, 2004:38–52). There was also the issue of lack of sufficient support from the global community, especially the initial apparent lacklustre attitude of the authorities of the United States to sell vital weapons to Nigeria. This explains why, among other reasons, there were several terrorist attacks in Nigeria between 2011 and 2014. In 2014, there were increased reports of attacks by the group, thereby prompting the Nigerian government to increase its counterattacks, especially in the northeast area of the country, resulting in the death of thousands of civilians as well as military and Boko Haram members; the abduction of over 270 schoolgirls was, however, the climax of the group's activities (Falode, 2016).

From 2015, onward more efforts were put into combating the Boko Haram pandemic. Indeed, before the 2015 general elections in the country, the government of President Goodluck Jonathan intensified efforts to reverse the unprecedented gains recorded by the group, which seized and occupied a few territories in the Northeast of the country.

Initially, the government encouraged the establishment of the Special Military Joint Task Force (SMJTF) in 2011, comprising personnel from the Nigeria Police Force (NPF), the Department of State Security (DSS), the Nigerian Immigration Service (NIS) and the Defence Intelligence Agencies (DIA) (*Vanguard*, 2011). In addition, the government activated its counterterrorism and counterinsurgency strategies, mobilised its armed forces (totalling 100,000 soldiers) to confront the security challenge and in May 2013 declared a state of emergency in the three north-eastern states of Yobe, Adamawa and Borno mostly affected by the activities of the terrorists (Falode, 2016). Moreover, the Nigerian government also established the Civilian Joint Task Force (CJTF), comprising vigilante groups, youths (male and female), hunters, farmers and other interested groups in the area to complement the efforts of the military in combating the Boko Haram group (Falode, 2016; Hansen, 2015:1–19).

However, there were reported cases of extrajudicial activities and killings by the military and members of the CJTF, thus forcing the international community to be cautious in their assistance to the Nigerian army. For example, in August, Amnesty International and the Channel 4 "Dispatches" programme alleged that Nigerian military personnel and the CJTF had perpetrated extrajudicial killings in their reactions to the Boko Haram attack on Giwa barracks in March 2014 (Foreign and Commonwealth Office, 2015; Dragu & Polborn, 2014:511–525). Nevertheless, the need to legalise the fight against terrorism encouraged the government to fast-track the passage of the Anti-Terrorism Act of 2013, which stipulated death penalty sentences for terrorists and insurgents and the destruction of suspected terrorist enclaves (Hansen, 2015; Erunke, 2013).

The third point to stress is the contribution of the defunct Organisation of African Unity (OAU) and its successor, the African Union (AU), to the war against terrorism. In particular, the OAU Convention on the Prevention and Combating of Terrorism, which was adopted in 1999, emphasised national and regional efforts to combat terrorism in Africa. Moreover, the convention enjoined African states to criminalise terrorist acts by enacting national laws and cooperating in combating terrorism (AU Peace and Security, 2015; Whitaker, 2010:639–662).

On its part, the AU has been able to promote the Counterterrorism and Counterinsurgency (CT-COIN) framework to provide legal and institutional backings to the war on terror. The CT-COIN is complemented by similar institutions such as the Africa Peace and Security Commission, the Continental Early Warning System (CEWS), the African Peace and Security Architecture (APSA), the African Standby Force (ASF) and the African Centre for the Study and Research on Terrorism (ACSRT). In particular, the ACSRT provides intellectual training and the necessary research base for CT-COIN in Africa (AU/PSC, 2015). It was established through the Plan of Action of the African Union High-Level Inter-Governmental Meeting on the Prevention and Combating of Terrorism on 11–14 September 2002 in Algiers, Algeria.

Other anti-terrorism institutions and initiatives at the regional level included the African Model Anti-Terrorism Law, which was adopted at Equatorial Guinea in 2011. It was aimed at providing technical assistance to African states in combating terrorism.

At the level of the Economic Community of West African States (ECOWAS), some counterterrorism measures were designed to combat the menace. These included the development of communication strategies such as radio and television discussion programmes and press conferences to counter radicalisation. It also comprised the organisation of national workshops for religious leaders in West Africa in a bid to strengthen collaboration between government and the inter-religious community, as well as delinking religion from terrorism and underscoring the principle of religious peace and harmony (*Vanguard*, 2017). Other measures included the organisation of counterterrorism training for security personnel in West Africa as well as the enactment of anti-terrorism legislation. In this regard, the Nigerian state was ahead of other countries in the sub-region, mainly because of Boko Haram activities, which put the military capability of the country to test.

In addition, ECOWAS also encouraged inter-regional collaborations in combating terrorism in the sub-region. Nigeria benefitted from these collaborations in the fight against Boko Haram. Moreover, other ECOWAS countries also adopted measures to fight terrorism in the sub-region. For instance, Niger's proximity to Nigeria exposed the country to Boko Haram activities. However, before the Boko Haram menace gained momentum, the government of Niger had in 2000 banned six "fundamentalist-oriented organizations" because they were responsible for disturbing the peace of the country. The organisations were considered too militant to accommodate Westerners and liberals. Specifically, the Association for Islamic Education and Culture (ACEI) and Niger Islamic Organisation (OIN) were accused of spreading anti-Western sentiments and mobilising followers to support Jihad and revolt against the government (Ousman, 2004:87). An example of such anti-Western action occurred when local Islamist groups' threats of a terrorist attack against the 2001 Paris Dakar rally led to the cancellation of the event (Ousman, 2004:87).

Outside ECOWAS, there have also been concerted efforts to combat terrorism in Africa. Specifically, the activities of PAGAD (People Against Gangsterism and Drugs) and its ally Qibla were considered anti-Western in Southern Africa. PAGAD organised protests and campaigns and are believed to have conducted about 189 bomb attacks between 1996 and 2000 against South African authorities, synagogues, gay nightclubs, moderate Muslims, tourist attractions and Western-associated restaurants. Indeed, the 25th August 1998 bombing of the Cape Town Planet Hollywood centre was a significant example of their terrorist activity (Ousman, 2004:83). However, beginning in 2001, the South African authorities and law-enforcement personnel moved swiftly to curtail their activities by prosecuting leading members of the organisation (Ousman, 2004:83).

In East Africa, the war on terror varied from one country to another. For instance, Whitaker's (2010:640) studies have shown that in Uganda government readily signed on to the George Bush administration's "War on Terror" partly to gain support for its struggle against rebels in the north of the country (Whitaker, 2010:651; Stith, 2010:55–66). On the other hand, the Tanzanian government passed some domestic counterterrorism laws to honour international commitments but did little to implement their provisions. In contrast, Kenyan security personnel cooperated with their American counterpart in anti-terrorism operations, even though their parliament was initially reluctant to pass the anti-terrorism legislation (Whitaker, 2010:651).

Nevertheless, the three countries of Kenya, Tanzania, and Uganda benefited from the U.S. $100 million East African Counterterrorism Initiative (EACTI) launched by the Bush administration in 2003 (Whitaker, 2010:651; Haynes, 2005:1321–1339). Specifically, Uganda participated in the Anti-Terrorism Assistance (ATA) programme, which trained local police as well as the Terrorist Interdiction Program (TIP), which provided technology to screen travellers arriving at airports and borders. Uganda also worked with Kenya and Tanzania to harmonise security regulations to forestall terrorist attacks. Besides, the U.S. also funded the Ugandan police in the development of forensic laboratories. On their part, Ugandan authorities in 2002 passed the Anti-Terrorism Act, thereby paving the way for terrorists to be specifically charged with terrorism instead of a treasonable felony as had hitherto been the case (Whitaker, 2010:652). In the aspect of the use of force, Ugandan President Yoweri Museveni launched a major military offensive against the LRA and ADF displacing thousands of Ugandan villagers in the process. While the ADF was easily wiped out, the LRA continued to fight until 2006, when its leaders entered into negotiations with the Ugandan government, leading to the signing of a ceasefire in 2008. Unfortunately, the ceasefire agreement collapsed and another major military offensive, which pushed the LRA out of Uganda into the Democratic Republic of Congo, was launched in late 2008 (Whitaker, 2010:652). Without doubt, Uganda has been very active in the war against terrorism in Somalia and the East African coast generally.

In Tanzania, the Prevention of Terrorism Act was enacted in 2002. The act increased the government's powers to investigate and prosecute terrorism offences and made it illegal to commit, finance, or assist terrorist acts. It also required those with knowledge about terrorist acts to disclose the information to the relevant authorities (Whitaker, 2010:655; Haynes, 2005:1321–1339; Romaniuk, 2010:591–613). Moreover, to tackle terrorism financing, the country passed the Prevention of Money Laundering Act in November 2006. It started its implementation in 2007 with the creation of a Financial Intelligence Unit (FIU) to track suspicious transactions in the country. It also established a National Counterterrorism Centre (NCC) in 2007 as a follow-up to the FIU (Whitaker, 2010:655).

In Kenya's fight against terrorism, the government established a National Counterterrorism Centre, an Anti-Terrorism Police Unit, the Joint Terrorism Task Force, and a National Security Advisory Committee. Furthermore, the United States and Kenyan militaries conducted periodic joint training exercises on how to tackle terrorism and other related crimes. Kenya also benefitted from the US $100 million African Counterterrorism Initiative (Whitaker, 2010:657–8; Haynes, 2005:1321–1339; Mombo & Mwaluda, 2000:36–41).

## Conclusion

An attempt has been made in this chapter to demonstrate that Africa represents a significant front in the war against global terrorism since the pandemic became widespread in the early 1990s. While terrorism in Africa has been ostensibly propelled by socioeconomic and religious considerations, operationalised through the seemingly irrational choices of suicide bombings, hostage-taking, kidnapping and outright battles with state forces, combating the scourge has remained herculean. Although considerable domestic, national, and international resources have been expended to combat terrorism in Africa, it is becoming increasingly clear that these are still lacking. More political will, the strengthening of military strategies, international collaborations, and the adoption of some home-grown strategies would have to be deployed to address the menace.

Moreover, there has to be a considerable shift in the way African countries respond to terrorist threats and activities. Local interest groups must unite to nip terrorist acts in the bud. Besides, some underlying strategic and political factors in the growth of terrorism would need to be addressed promptly to avoid creating uncertainty in the efforts to combat terrorism. Lastly, how Africa would fare in the distant future in the fight against terrorism will depend on how the continent can resolve lingering socio-economic, religious and political crises as well as how it can build lasting solutions to factors that predispose the continent to terrorism.

## References

Achi, N. K., & Tar, Usman A. (2013). Understanding and financing terrorism: Conceptual and empirical issues. *Journal of Defence Studies*, *18*, 171–190.

Adeniran, A. B. (2013). The crisis of legitimacy, terrorism and the imperative of state-building in Nigeria. *Ibadan Journal of Peace and Development*, *2*, 21–42.

Alexander, J. (2004). From the depths of despair: Performance, counterperformance, and 'September 11'. *Sociological Theory*, *22*(1), 88–105.

AU Peace and Security. (2015). *Countering terrorism and violent extremism*. Addis Ababa, Ethiopia: African Union Commission.

Bergesen, A. J., & Lizardo, O. (2004). International terrorism and the world-system. *Sociological Theory*, *22*(1), 38–52.

Boyns, D., & Ballard, J. D. (2004). Developing a sociological theory for the empirical understanding of terrorism. *The American Sociologist*, *35*(2), 5–25.

Bremer, P. L. (1995). Seizing the initiative: The US role in combatting global terrorism. *Harvard International Review, 17*(3), 40–42, 76.

Collins, R. (2004a). Solidarity and security in the wake of terrorist attack. *Sociological Theory, 22*(1), 53–87.

Collins, R. (2004b). *Interaction ritual chains.* New Jersey: Princeton University Press.

Cooper, H. H. A. (1978). Terrorism: The problem of the problem definition. *Chitty's Law Journal, 26*, 105–108.

De Vries, G. (2005). The European union's role in the fight against terrorism: (Opening address-the role of the EU in the fight against terrorism). *Irish Studies in International Affairs, 16*, 3–9.

Dragu, T., & Polborn, M. (2014). The rule of law in the fight against terrorism. *American Journal of Political Science, 58*(2), 511–525.

Elu, J. U. (2012). Terrorism in Africa and South Asia: Economic or existential good?. *The Journal of Developing Areas, 46*(1), 345–357.

Enders, W., & Sandler, T. (2006). *The political economy of terrorism.* New York: Cambridge University.

Erunke, J. (20 February 2013). *Senate okays death penalty for terrorism.* Lagos: Vanguard.

Falode, J. A. (2016). The nature of Nigeria's Boko Haram war, 2010-2015: A strategic analysis. *Terrorism Research Initiative, 10*(1), 41–52.

Foreign and Commonwealth Office. (12 March 2015). *Nigeria-Boko Haram and the fight against terrorism.* United Kingdom: Foreign and Commonwealth Office.

Gaibulloev, K., & Sandler, T. (2011). The adverse effect of transnational and domestic terrorism on growth in Africa. *Journal of Peace Research, 48*(3), 355–371.

Hansen, W. (2015). *Boko haram: Religious radicalism and insurrection in Northern Nigeria. Journal of Asian and African Studies, 52*(4), 1–19.

Haynes, J. (2005). Islamic militancy in East Africa. *Third World Quarterly, 26*(8), 1321–1339.

Heng, Y., & McDonagh, K. (2008). The other war on terror revealed: Global governmentality and the financial action task force's campaign against terrorist financing. *Review of International Studies, 34*(3), 553–573.

Hodgson, J. S., & Tadros, V. (2013). The impossibility of defining terrorism. *New Criminal Law Review: An International and Interdisciplinary Journal, 16*(3), 494–526.

Human Rights and Democracy Report (2014).

Isaacson, M. (2008). Instability: Al Qaeda's inroads into Africa. *Harvard International Review, 29*(4), 8–9.

Jenkins, B. M. (1986). Defense against terrorism. *Political Science Quarterly, 101*(5), 773–786.

Krech, H. (2011). The growing influence of Al-Qaeda on the African continent. *African Spectrum, 46*(2), 76–95.

Kruglanski, A. W., & Fishman, S. (2006). *Terrorism between syndrome and tool. Current Directions in Psychological Science, 15*(1), 45–48.

Leonald-Fwa, K. (2016). Globalisation and Africa's security challenges for the twenty-first century. In: U.A. Tar, Etham B. Mijah & Moses E. U. Tedheke (Eds.), *Globalisation in Africa: Perspectives on development, security and the environment* (pp. 219–237). London: Lexington Books.

Lyman, P. N., & Morrison, J. S. (2004). The terrorist threat in Africa. *Foreign Affairs, 83*(1), 75–86.

Maiangwa, J. S. (2016). Globalisation and new waves of terrorism in Africa. In A. Tar Usman, Etham B. Mijah & Moses E. U. Tedheke (Eds.), *Globalisation in Africa: Perspectives on development, security, and the environment* (pp. 257–269). London: Lexington Books.

Mickolus, E. F. (1989). What constitutes state support to terrorists?. *Terrorism and Political Violence, 1*(3), 287–293.

Mickolus, E. F., & Simmons, S. L. (2006). *Terrorism, 2002–2004: A chronology.* Westport, CT: Praeger Security International.

Mombo, E., & Mwaluda, Samson M. (2000). Relationship and challenge in Kenya and East Africa. *Transformation, 17*(1), 36–41.

Obi, C. I. (2008). West African security in the context of the global war on terror: some reflections. In Ayodeji O. Olukoju & Muyiwa Falaiye (Eds.), *Global understanding in the age of terrorism.* Lagos: University of Lagos Press.

Omonobi, K. (2016). *Systemic corruption affecting war against terrorism in Nigeria-IGP Idris.* Lagos: *Vanguard.*

Osiki, O. M. (2014). The magnitude of Samson option: Militancy, terrorism and national development in Nigeria. *VUNA Journal of History and International Relations, 1*(2), 212–226.

Osiki, O. M. (2016). Globalisation of violence: Terrorism and its impact on (inter)national security. In U. A. Tar, Etham B. Mijah & Moses E. U. Tedheke (Eds.), *Globalisation in Africa: Perspectives on development, security and the environment* (pp. 289–305). London: Lexington Books.

Ousman, A. (2004). The potential of Islamist terrorism in Sub-Saharan Africa. *International Journal of Politics, Culture, and Society, 18*(1/2), 65–105.

Reader, J. (1997). *Africa: A biography of the continent.* New York: Vintage Books.

Reich, W. (1990). *Origins of terrorism: Psychologies, ideologies, theologies, and states of mind.* New York: Cambridge University Press.

Romaniuk, P. (2010). Institutions as swords and shields: Multilateral counter-terrorism since 9/11. *Review of International Studies, 36*(3), 591–613.

Sabine, G. H., & Thorson, T. L. (1973). *A history of political theory* (4th ed.). New Delhi: Oxford and IBH Publishing Co. PVT Ltd.

Scott, J. C. (1990). *Domination and the arts of resistance: Hidden transcripts.* New Haven: Yale University Press.

Sperotto, F. (2014). The future of the American fight against terrorism. *Rivista di Studi Politici Internazionali, 81*(2/322), 221–230.

Stith, C. R. (2010). Radical Islam in East Africa. *The Annals of the American Academy of Political and Social Science, 632*, 55–66.

Vanguard (15 May 2017). *Sierra Leone implementing ECOWAS counter-terrorism strategy-parliamentarian.*

Vanguard (17 June 2011). *Nigeria: FG sets-up joint task force.*

Wanandi, J. (2002). A global coalition against international terrorism. *International Security, 26*(4), 184–189.

Whitaker, B. E. (2010). Compliance among weak states: Africa and the counter-terrorism Regime. *Review of International Studies, 36*(3), 639–662.

White, J. R. (2002). *Terrorism: An introduction* (3rd ed.). Belmont, CA: Thompson/Wadsworth.

Wilkinson, P. (1974). *Political terrorism.* New York: Wiley.

# 8

# Radicalisation, violent extremism, and de-radicalisation in Africa

*Freedom C. Onuoha and Chikodiri Nwangwu*

## Introduction

In a meeting of the Pan-African Parliament in Johannesburg, South Africa, on 11 May 2017, Ambassador Mull Katende, chairman of the Peace and Security Council (PSC) of the African Union, informed legislators that, "the threat of terrorism, violent extremism, and radicalisation continues to grow in certain parts of our continent" (cited in Isilow, 2017). His assertion reflects the growing concern of local communities, African states, regional bodies, and international organisations over the upsurge in radicalisation towards violent extremism and terrorism in different parts of Africa. Over the last decade, the continent has witnessed an exponential increase in the number of fatalities arising out of attacks by extremists. Africa is fast becoming a haven for Islamic extremists, fundamentalist ideologues, violent terrorists, and armed insurgents with dire consequences both for Africa and the world. A recent study has shown that violent extremism in Africa has killed more than 33,000 people between 2011 and early 2016, and caused widespread displacement, creating or aggravating humanitarian crises affecting millions of people and undermining economic prospects across the continent (UNDP, 2017). Consequently, some African states are not only concerned with how to prevent or counter radicalisation and violent extremism but also are making efforts at de-radicalisation as a means of salvaging radicalised individuals or groups.

This chapter, therefore, discusses the phenomenon of radicalisation towards violent extremism and the efforts at de-radicalisation in Africa. To this end, the chapter is framed on the following questions: In what ways are radicalisation, violent extremism and de-radicalisation interlinked? What factors underpin the increase in radicalisation towards violent extremism and terrorism in Africa? What methods do violent extremist groups adopt in radicalising people in Africa? And what efforts are being made concerning de-radicalisation in some African states? Providing answers to these and other related concerns are what this chapter seeks to achieve.

The chapter is organised into seven sections. Following this introduction, the next section provides the conceptual framework of analysis. While the third section overviews the manifestation of violent extremism in Africa, the fourth section discusses the factors contributing to radicalisation in the continent. The fifth section highlights the diverse methods violent extremist groups have adopted in radicalising sympathisers and recruits. The sixth section reflects on recent de-radicalisation efforts in Africa with a focus on Nigeria and Niger, while the last section concludes the chapter.

## Conceptualisation: violent extremism, radicalisation, and de-radicalisation

Before delving into the intricacies of the subject of concern, it is germane to conceptualise some key terms – radicalisation, violent extremism, and de-radicalisation. This will contribute to a shared understanding of their usage in this Chapter *vis-à-vis* their meaning, nature, and linkages in society.

### Radicalisation

The concept of radicalisation has gained significant currency among government officials, media practitioners, scholars, and security officials in discourses on terrorism and violent extremism, especially since the terrorist attacks of 11 September 2001. It is a term commonly used in the quest to understand why people engage in violent acts, and in the processes of countering extremist behaviour (Hinds, 2015). Those who use the term do not agree on a single definition, but a loose consensus has emerged that radicalisation, whether at the individual or group level, involves a process of rejecting the status quo and often democratic ideals; adopting an extreme political, social, or religious ideology; and condoning violence as a means to achieving ideological goals (Onuoha, 2014; Sodipo, 2013; Ashour, 2009). For the purposes of this Chapter, radicalisation is defined as "the process by which an individual or group transitions from passive reception of revolutionary, militant, or extremist views, ideas, and beliefs to the active pursuit of these ideals, especially through promoting, supporting or adopting violence to realise such intentions" (Onuoha, 2014: 3).

Experts believe that radicalisation is the result of a complex overlap of concurring and mutually reinforcing factors, unique to each context and, to a certain extent, everyone. The process of radicalisation begins with changes in self-identification due to grievances, frequently driven by personal or group concerns regarding local issues as well as international events. A grievance is understood to create a sense of alienation or disenchantment that provides a cognitive opening for radicalisation. A radical ideology – an extreme set of ideas – then provides the individual with a new outlook and explanation for the world in which he finds himself. An individual becomes mobilised as he slowly integrates into a community of other like-minded people. Finally, a tipping point – usually a specific event – can push an individual or group from rhetoric to action (Vidino, Pantucci, & Kohlmann, 2010). However, becoming radicalised does not *automatically* mean that a person is engaging, or will engage, in violent or dangerous behaviour (Angus, 2016). However, in some cases and contexts, the drastic change in viewpoints, attitudes, and behaviour inherent in radicalisation lead to acts of violent extremism and terrorism.

## Violent extremism

The usage of the term "violent extremism" in academic and policy circles has increasingly gained traction in recent times. For all the attention that the term has received, there is the absence of a clear and universally accepted definition. The *Living Safe Together* project of the Australian government defines violent extremism "as the belief and actions of people who support or use ideologically-motivated violence to achieve radical ideological, religious or political views" (cited in UNESCO 2016: 11). Similarly, Mirahmadi et al. (2015: 2) define it as "those activities and beliefs which are used to advocate, engage in, prepare, or otherwise support ideologically-motivated violence to further socio-economic and political objectives." It is important to note that such activities or beliefs can also be used in pursuit of religious objectives.

Violent extremism is defined here as the manifestation of activities and beliefs of a person or group who not only promotes or justifies the use of ideologically-motivated violence to achieve religious, ideological, political or social change but also acts accordingly in pursuit of those objectives. It is therefore the ideology that accepts and justifies the use of violence to reach a particular ideological goal. As noted by Angus (2016), violent extremism is an extension of radicalisation from a benign expression of a viewpoint to the use of violence to achieve a particular objective. Thus, violent extremism can be exhibited along with a range of issues, including politics, religion, ideology, and gender relations.

## De-radicalisation

There is no universally held definition of the term "de-radicalisation", and it may have different implied meanings for the variety of stakeholders that are active in the broad area of counterterrorism studies and countering violent extremism. Horgan (2008) defines de-radicalisation as programmes that are directed against individuals who have become radical with the aim of re-integrating them into society or at least dissuading them from violence. Similarly, Clutterbuck (2015: 2) defines it as "the methods and techniques used to undermine and reverse the completed radicalisation process, thereby reducing the potential risk to society from terrorism". In other words, de-radicalisation is a kind of programmed intervention that "seeks to reverse the radicalisation process for those already or partly radicalised or help them to disengage with radical or extreme groups, whether or not they change their ideas" (ISD, 2010: 4). Consistent with the above perspectives, radicalisation is seen here from a "reversal-process" prism to emphasise the distinction with counter-radicalisation, which describes methods to stop or control radicalisation as it is occurring; and anti-radicalisation, which describes methods to deter and prevent radicalisation from occurring in the first place (Clutterbuck, 2015).

Against this backdrop, it is easier to appreciate how radicalisation, violent extremism and de-radicalisation are related. As shown in Figure 8.1, they are phenomena that manifest in society, especially in terrorism-ridden states. Radicalisation reflects that dynamic, non-linear psycho-social process by with an individual or group due to some unmet needs, deep-rooted grievances and coupled with exposure to ideology becomes alienated from society and mobilises towards promoting, supporting or adopting violence to realise some objectives. The resultant situation is violent extremism, which is manifest violence that is inspired or justified by an extremely political, religious, or social ideology. Convinced that such individuals or groups were not "born" violent extremist or terrorists, some states embark on de-radicalisation as a deliberate comprehensive programme that leverages dialogue, counselling, re-orientation, and empowerment to rehabilitate these individuals with the hope of reintegrating them into mainstream society.

In this sense, both radicalisation and de-radicalisation are processes rather than static states. They are also unique to each context, and their logical outcome in a particular case is dependent on the individual or context, or both. Thus, radicalisation as a process may or may not compose of phases depending on the individual or context. Where phases occur in the radicalisation process, they may not necessarily be sequential, and they can also overlap, meaning that a person may skip a stage in reaching militant action or may become disillusioned at any given point and abandon the process altogether (Christmann, 2012). On the other hand, de-radicalisation as a process allows the government to address extremism in individuals or groups that have already committed violence. As a process, it may or may not succeed in helping the recipient to renounce violence. The outcome may depend on the recipient or context, or both.

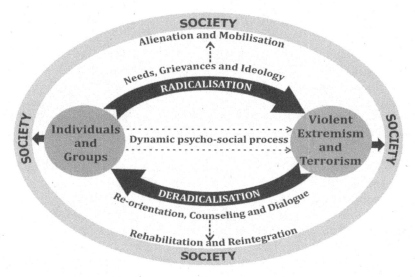

*Figure 8.1* Dynamics of Radicalisation, Violent Extremism and De-radicalisation
**Source**: Authors (2017)

Against this premise, the onward journey by an individual from non-violent life towards violent extremism in society begins with radicalisation, and the backward journey from violent extremism to non-violent life is facilitated through de-radicalisation. The tasks before the government are to ensure that at-risk individuals do not get radicalised in the first place and those that have become radicalised are effectively reoriented to renounce violence. In both cases, the task is herculean and presents a complex challenge in each society.

## Overview of violent extremism in Africa

Since the dawn of the 21ˢᵗ century, several African states have witnessed a significant increase in terrorist attacks by violent extremist groups (Omotosho, 2017). These groups are as diverse as the peculiar socio-economic, political, and geographic environment that laid the foundation for their emergence in Africa. Space will not warrant an exhaustive discussion of their nature and activities but suffice it to note that a survey of the five regions of Africa reveals the existence of several established extremist groups.

In North Africa, for example, the push for democracy made possible by the "Arab Spring" or *Arabellion* has created a domestic security vacuum that terrorist and violent extremist groups are exploiting to establish footprints in places where they hitherto operated or re-establish their foothold where some states had significantly driven them underground in the past. For instance, extremist groups of many stripes have taken advantage of the Western-backed brutal ousting of the regime of Muammar Gaddafi to establish strong footholds in Libya. ISIS's Libya affiliate has launched several terrorist attacks on locations ranging from prisons, and oil facilitates to foreign embassies. Similarly, Algeria continues to witness attacks mounted by domestic and transnational terrorist groups such as the January 2013 siege at the In Amenas Gas Plant, staged by the *Al-Mulathameen* Brigade ("THE Masked Brigade" or "Those Who Sign with Blood"). In total, 685 Algerian workers and 107 of the 132 foreigners working at the plant were freed, while 37 hostages and 32 terrorists were killed during the four-day siege (Onuoha, 2013).

Egypt has not been spared. The rise of Islamic extremism in Egypt hacks back to the 1990s. Still, the spate of terrorist attacks has assumed a worrisome dimension since the emergence of groups that are affiliated with the Islamic State in Iraq and Syria (ISIS), such as the Sinai Province. Their attacks have targeted religious minorities (Coptic Christians), Egyptian security forces, military installations, tourist sites and aviation infrastructure. While Islamists have for decades targeted Egypt's Coptic Christians, deadly attacks on Coptic churches have increased dramatically since 2016. At least 102 Egyptian Christians have been killed in four separate attacks since December 2016. The most devastating attacks saw twin blasts target churches in Tanta and Alexandria on Palm Sunday, killing 28 and 17 people, respectively, in April 2017 (Martin, 2017). Also, about 23 Egyptian soldiers were killed in July 2017 when Islamic State suicide car bombers tore through two military checkpoints in North Sinai.

In East Africa, Somalia, Kenya, and Uganda have been severely hit by terrorism, mostly executed by Somali-based Al-Shabaab and its local affiliates. Somalia has suffered over two decades of lawlessness, invasion, and Islamist militancy since the collapse of the Siad Barre regime in 1991, prompting the African Union to intervene with its 22,000-strong African Union Mission in Somalia (AMISOM). Al-Shabaab has carried out more than 360 attacks in Somalia in the last decade. In September 2015, Al-Shabaab attack on AU's Janale base allegedly killed 50 Ugandan troops. Also, as many as 100 Kenyan soldiers died in an Al-Shabaab attack at their base in El Adde, Somalia, in January 2016 (Ali & Billard-Arbelaez, 2017). Enraged by Uganda's and Kenya's contribution of troops to the AMISOM, Al-Shabaab has equally carried out devastating retributive attacks in these countries. On 11 July 2010, for instance, Al-Shabaab's led twin bombings targeting two groups of soccer fans watching the World Cup games, in Kampala, killed about 79 people and injured many others. The September 2013 attack at the Westgate Premier Shopping Mall, Nairobi, which resulted in the death of 70 people, and the April 2015 massacre of 148 people at the Garissa University College, Garissa, were legendary examples of audacious transnational attacks in Kenya by Al-Shabaab.

Furthermore, the rise of militant extremism in Tanzania is a major concern in East Africa. Tensions between elements of Tanzania's Christian and Muslim communities have escalated, with a handful of outbreaks of acts of domestic terrorism. On 5 May 2013, for instance, 3 people were killed and 67 injured in an improvised explosive devices attack on St Joseph's Roman Catholic Church in Arusha, Tanzania, blamed on Islamist militants with connections to the *Jumuiya ya Taasisi za Kiislam* (Brankamp, 2013). It is feared that transnational terrorist groups such as Al-Shabaab and Al Qaeda may try to exploit the evolving Christian-Muslim tensions to its advantage, by recruiting and radicalising Tanzania's militants into mounting large scale attacks on local or Western targets (LeSage, 2014). Indeed, in the first four months of 2015, Al-Shabaab militants were directly involved in five battles with Tanzanian security forces, resulting in the deaths of eight policemen and soldiers (ACLED, 2015).

In West Africa, terrorist footprints are increasing due to the activities of Al-Qaeda in Islamic Maghreb (AQIM) operating largely in the Sahara-Sahel region; the Movement for Unity and Jihad in West Africa (MUJAO) and Ansar Dine based in northern Mali; and Boko Haram operating in the Lake Chad area. Since September 2006, when the Salafist Group for Preaching and Combat (GSPC) transmuted to AQIM, the group has provided logistical supports to other sleeper terrorist groups operating in North and West Africa (IRIN, 2012). The AQIM has continued to threaten Western interests in the region with kidnappings of westerners for ransom across the vast Sahara-Sahel, generating an estimated US$70 million in ransom payments between 2006 and 2011 (Foster-Bowser & Sanders, 2012). Its ties with Mali Islamists – Ansar Dine and MUJAO – have equally emboldened such groups to mount audacious attacks in Mali. It is estimated that between 9 February and 22 May 2013, Mali experienced twelve suicide attacks in the cities of Timbuktu, Gao, Kidal, Ménaka, and Gossi (Atallah, 2013). Burkina Faso, a neighbouring country to Mali, is another West African country that has seen a surge in violent extremism over the past few years. A January 2016 attack at the Splendid Hotel in Ouagadougou, by gunmen, believed to have ties with AQIM and the Al Mourabitoun left 30 people dead. On 13 August 2017, suspected Islamic extremist opened fire at an upscale Turkish restaurant, Aziz Istanbul, in Ouagadougou killing at least 18 people (Burke, 2017). There is equally the threat posed by the self-proclaimed Islamic State in the Greater Sahara (ISGS) under Adnan Abu Walid al-Sahraoui, which has carried out a handful of attacks in Burkina Faso and Niger, including the Tongo attack of October 2017 that killed five Nigerien soldiers and four US marines.

The growing audacity of the Boko Haram area is one of the many developments that have made West-Central Africa a region of growing terror concern. Following an anti-government revolt, it waged in July 2009, the group's ten-year insurgency has claimed at least 20,000 lives and displaced more than 2.6 million people in Nigeria. As of September 2016, the insurgents have killed at least 1,300 civilians, 120 soldiers and abducted an estimated thousand people in Cameroon. It has carried out several such deadly attacks in Niger and Chad as well.

More recently, Southern Africa has become a region of special interest by the international community given evolving threat of violent extremism and terrorism in Mozambique. The emergence and activities of a group known as the *Al Sunnah wa Jama'ah*, which is remarkably like what was seen with Boko Haram in Nigeria, is behind the growing attention. The group is also known as *Al-Shabaab* (The Youth), even though it has no connections with the Somali terror group, *Al Shabaab*. Mozambique experienced its first jihadi terror attack on 5 October 2017, when 30 militants of the *Al Sunnah wa Jama'ah*, attacked a police station and a military post in the coastal town of Mocimboa da Praia, in Cabo Delgado province (Ahmed, 2018). They killed two policemen, looted arms, and ammunition, and temporarily occupied the town. The group which initially concentrated attacks on security or state interests has shifted to civilians, with the potential to target energy facilities in the future. Since mid-May 2018, some 35 people have been killed in a series of brutal attacks involving beheading and arson blamed on the group (Morier-Genoud, 2018). The state has equally responded forcefully to the evolving threat, by arresting over 300 persons, destroying, or closing some mosques and discouraging the wearing of the hijab. Inappropriate states responses and heavy-handed counterterrorism measures by the state could cause further radicalisation of the group's members, forcing them to establish connections with established transnational jihadist organisations.

Overall, studies have shown that majority of African states have been affected by violent extremism in some way, with Nigeria, Somalia, and Libya the most severely affected in the last few years (Cachalia, Ndung'u, & Salifu, 2016). This brings to the fore concerns on the factors responsible for the radicalisation of people towards violent extremism and terrorism in Africa.

## Factors contributing to radicalisation and violent extremism in Africa

Several factors act as drivers or facilitators of radicalisation towards violent extremism and terrorism in any given society. These factors are often socio-economic, religious, political, and even geographic in nature. Often, these factors are not mutually exclusive but interlinked in diverse ways. It is pertinent to note that an underlying element in the escalation of terrorism is the existence of *perceived, imagined, or real* grievances among an identifiable sub-group of a larger population such as an ethnic or religious group discriminated against by the majority.

Perceived grievances are a feeling of anger that is experienced by a person subjectively and out of proportion to the true nature of the source of concern. For instance, Kenyan security operations against al-Shabaab members and sympathisers within their borders are perceived by many Kenyan Muslims and Somali refugees as discriminatory against their communities and religious activities (Jackson, 2014). The grievances could be said to be real when the threat manifests and directly affects the concerned individuals or groups, such as the ongoing Israeli-Palestinian conflict where young Palestinians continue to support Hamas in its war against Israel's occupation of Palestinian territory (Sheizaf, 2014). The grievances are imagined when the actions of the individual or group in questions were not driven by any real or perceived imminent threat to their values. Against its backdrop, a social movement develops in order to redress these grievances and to gain either equal rights or a separate state; terrorism is then the resort of an extremist faction of this broader movement (Ogundiya & Amzat, 2008).

Across Africa, the failure of some states to address grievances arising from widespread economic deprivation, unemployment and poverty have driven the youth towards violent extremism. Some studies have shown that poverty is associated with violent extremism (Keefer & Loayza, 2008; Krueger, 2008; Denoeux & Carter, 2009). In Africa, mass poverty provides a fertile ground for extremist violence to take root and spread beyond national borders. As the economic situation in Africa worsens, the state has retreated in providing basic services allowing religious actors to become increasingly dominant in shaping people's perceptions of state and society. Increasingly, extremist ideologues in Nigeria, Tanzania, Kenya, Somalia, Egypt, Mali, and Libya, among other places, aggressively challenge not only moderate religious views, but also the authority of the state to govern.

Harsh economic conditions in turn have made young people vulnerable to radical messages and narratives of Islamists and terrorist groups who claim to be fighting injustice and corruption prevalent in the society (Davis, 2007). Many others have fallen prey to extremist recruitment through monetary inducements and other forms of enticement. For example, Al-Shabaab re-cruiters promised monthly salaries of 40,000 Kenyan Shillings (approximately US$385) to some vulnerable Muslim youth in Garrisa to join their *jihad* (Meleagrou-Hitchens, 2012). Thus, individual and group grievances like poverty, unemployment, illiteracy, discrimination, and economic marginalisation are commonly used by sinister groups as mobilising instruments to find support and recruits for terrorist activities (Olojo 2013; Mbah, Nwangwu, & Edeh, 2017).

In addition, discontent with state failure has seen individuals and groups mobilise to challenge their governments in Africa. Authoritarian regimes, in turn, resort to repression to quell discontent. As a result, repressive tendencies by African states with the attendant human rights violations have fuelled the rise of violent extremism and radicalisation in several parts of Africa. Their heavy-handed tactics, extra-legal and militarised measures which usually undermine civil liberties contribute to feelings of grievances and marginalisation that underpin radicalisation and violent extremism (Mbah & Nwangwu, 2014). Hence, African states which are culpable of rights violations are usually correlated with the outbreak of terrorism, from Algeria through Egypt to Nigeria. In Nigeria, for instance, the radicalisation of Boko Haram members is connected to the extra-judicial killing of their leader, Mohammed Yusuf, and other members of the group (Onuoha, 2012). Similarly, Al-Shabaab has skilfully exploited Muslim grievances against repressive tendencies of Kenyan security forces to deepen recruitment and radicalisation in the Eastleigh area of Nairobi (ICG, 2014).

The porosity of Africa's international borders adds another layer to the escalation of violent extremism in the continent. The porosity of borders occurs both in physical and virtual spaces, which will be elaborated upon subsequently. Given the character of colonial Balkanisation of Africa, "most African governments find it extremely difficult to administer international boundaries that divide 177 cultural and ethnic groups" (Okumu, 2010: 22). The situation is compounded by the failure of successive governments to properly administer these borders. As

Okumu (2010: 22) noted, "the high level of insecurity on African borders is largely due to the way they are administered and managed, and less to do with how colonialists drew them." These borders are known for their acute shortage of security and law enforcement officials. The few that are deployed are poorly trained, made to work with inadequate and obsolete equipment, and are sometimes poorly remunerated. Terrorist groups have historically been able to bribe their way into the pockets of unscrupulous security and border officials to receive or traffic weapons across borders in Africa (Young, 2014).

Consequent upon the crisis of governance and border porosity, the proliferation of small arms and easy movement of militants exacerbate the problem of terrorism in Africa. In 2010, it was estimated that 500 million illicit weapons were in circulation globally. Of this number, about 100 million were said to be in sub-Saharan Africa, with eight to ten million concentrated in the West African sub-region (Bah, 2010). Access to such weapons has enabled and emboldened disgruntled groups or radicalised individuals to engage in violent extremism.

In relation to virtual porosity, extensive penetration of foreign religious ideologies, particularly Islam and Christianity, has fostered growing religious intolerance and polarisation in Africa. Both religions are inherently proselytising and have a voracious appetite for new converts. This has led to three related dangerous ubiquitous trends in the practice of religion in Africa. First, the proliferation of denominations and sects; second, the proliferation of "roaming" preachers and religious ideologies; and third, the increasing reliance on interpretations offered by preachers or ideologues rather than on the true injunctions of religious text (Onuoha, 2014). With little or no capacity by the state to rein in these figures, many ideologues have indoctrinated and radicalised impressionable youths with their insidious ideology. More so, decades of externally driven diffusion of religious ideas by well-funded foreign Islamist groups fuels the rise of violent extremism in Africa. The permeation of *Salafi jihadi* ideology from the Gulf States has been the chief culprit. Widespread internet access and increasingly easy travel have made the penetration of foreign ideologies in Africa even faster, deeper, and more extensive in the wake of weak state capacity for physical and virtual monitoring, regulation, and control of borders. Thus, growing proselytisation and manipulation of religion has contributed to the rise of violent extremism in Africa (Trofimov, 2016). How then do extremist ideologues and groups radicalise individuals in the continent?

## Modes of radicalisation by violent extremist or terrorist groups in Africa

Radicalisation towards violent extremism and terrorism is now a growing source of concern in local communities across Africa. This is in addition to the international attention Africa is receiving as a new volatile site for the terrorist activity. Social, economic, political, religious, and psychological factors in each community can increase an individual's vulnerability to radicalisation, which can either manifest as self-radicalisation or structured radicalisation. Although the progress of an individual down this path is often exceedingly difficult to predict or detect in a community, evidence abounds on how terrorist ideologues influence individuals in moving down the path of radicalisation by exploiting diverse methods. The different methods used are first summarised in Table 8.1 and elaborated upon subsequently.

### *Indoctrination*

This is one of the subtle methods of radicalisation adopted by violent extremist or terrorist groups in Africa, as elsewhere in the world. Indoctrination is understood here as the process of inculcating ideas, values, attitudes, or beliefs on an individual or group with the intent of making

*Table 8.1* Some Radicalisation Methods used by Violent Extremist Groups in Africa

| S/No | Mode | Location/ Platforms | Purveyors | Tools |
|---|---|---|---|---|
| 1 | Indoctrination | Religious Centres | Imams, Indoctrinators | Distorted sermons or teachings, Religious Texts, Exercise books |
| 2 | Brainwashing | Camps or Training Facilities | Ideologues | Visual displays, Tapes, Magazines, Spiritual books, etc. |
| 3 | Hypnosis | Camps, Training Facilities | Manipulators/ Spiritualists | Drugs, Black Magic, Charms, Spiritual books |
| 4 | Propaganda/ Exhortation | Internet/Media | Propagandists | Publications, Videos, YouTube, Twitter (social media) |

**Source**: Onuoha, F.C. (2016). "Boko Haram's Recruitment and Radicalisation Methods in Nigeria: An Exposé", *South East Journal of Political Science*, 2(1), 181–203.

them develop a blind and complete agreement with those beliefs (Snook, 1972). It is aimed at influencing people to uncritically embrace newfound ideas, values, or beliefs and to back them up with anything but opinion. The process of indoctrination is often conducted in religious centres (mosques) or training camps of terrorist groups. In relation to religious centres, extremist clerics engage in distorted teachings to influence their audience. In their training facilities such as those of Al Shabaab's military-style Mtwara and Tanga camps, Boko Haram's Camp Zero and 'Camp Abuja' in Sambisa forest, and Sina Province's Abu Hajr al-Masri Camp, indoctrinators rely on manipulative texts to teach recruits to accept a set of beliefs or values without questioning them.

## Brainwashing

This is another method used by extremists and terrorists in their radicalisation drive. Brainwashing refers to the systematic, and often violent, but not always conscious, distortion or conditioning of the mind of another person for selfish or other harmful purposes using operant conditioning (Wilson, 2014). In this method, recruits are brought to training camps, where experienced ideologues then work with them one-on-one to instil a virulent fanaticism and bloodlust toward those described as infidels and apostates. Using videos, sermons and other emotive materials, experienced ideologues then skilfully evoke visions of martyrdom to radicalise recruits into volunteering for an extreme act of violence such as suicide bombing. Pain, stress, or violent intimidation could be applied mostly on incompliant recruits. In the case of Al-Shabaab, for example, Hassan (2009) reported that:

> They brainwash our young boys daily to the extent that they made them a human bomb. They erroneously inform these young men that blowing themselves up for the sake of Islam (which is not true) is one of the surest ways to enter paradise....Al-Shabaab brainwashed our beautiful and innocent young girls to marry an older men from either Afghanistan or Arab countries in order to support the "jihad", as reported repeatedly. In numerous occasions when these courageous young girls refused to marry these ugly and old men, they were raped to terrorize other girls (https://www.hiiraan.com/mop4/2009/july/11510/al_shabab_s_reign_of_terror.aspx)

The essence of applying intimidation or pains is to break or reduce the recruit's adaptive energy or vitality level. Those who are brave enough to refuse such intimidation and other dehumanising treatment such as rape or torture are often subjected to painful death before colleagues to break the resolve of other onlookers.

## Hypnosis

This is another method employed by terrorist groups in Africa to radicalise individuals. Although related to brainwashing, hypnosis is a very deep and subtle alteration or distortion of the brain so that it responds in certain ways. It is a state of inner absorption, suspension of mental and rational consciousness, concentration, and focused attention (American Society of Clinical Hypnosis, 1973). Unlike brainwashing, hypnosis does not need to be coupled with punishments or rewards to be effective or remain viable, and it is usually short in duration (Wilson, 2014). Terror hypnotists or spiritualists make use of substances like mind-bending drugs and voodoo (black magic) to condition the mind of young recruits into carrying out violent activities. In areas where they operate, the Boko Haram has employed hypnosis in radicalising some recruits to carry out violent acts. For instance, one of the two suspected Boko Haram female suicide bombers intercepted in northern Cameroon on 25 March 2016 before she could blow herself was found to be "heavily drugged and therefore not in full control of her senses" (Nwabughiogu, 2016).

## Propaganda

Globally, terrorist organisations place a good deal of emphasis on communicating their messages across a diverse audience. The use of propaganda is a key component of this strategic messaging. The Internet and social media offer platforms for the propagation and sharing of extremist ideology, training materials, explosive making manuals, and sourcing of members. Various tools such as audio and videotapes, recorded sermons, and posting on websites, among others, are used in this regard to achieve diverse objectives. The objectives include, but not limited to, gaining the admiration of its supporters, and catalysing self-radicalisation of sympathisers (Hussain & Saltman, 2014). Exposure to extremist views, sermons, messages, videos, and write-ups by intolerant hate preachers or radical clerics that are accessible online are known sources of self-radicalising influences. Although extremist groups in Africa have embraced social media as part of their radicalising propaganda tool, it is difficult to gauge the level of recruits they have attracted through this means. Going forward, this is an area that needs further investigation by security/intelligence agencies and academics.

## Recent de-radicalisation interventions in Africa

Given that radicalisation is a process that could be facilitated through exposure to certain influences or experiences, some terrorism-ridden African states have turned to de-radicalisation as a means of salvaging radicalised individuals that have committed violent acts. Such individuals may be those who wilfully surrendered or those arrested by state security forces. Hence, a variety of de-radicalisation programme has been initiated in some African countries such as Algeria, Egypt, Kenya, Niger, Nigeria, and Morocco, among others, to change the ideologies held by these extremists and eventually allow for their release from security custody and reintegration into normal society. Across Africa, schemes vary in stages of evolution and approach of delivery. However, there is a lot of debate as to whether they work.

With the escalation of Boko Haram insurgency in much of the Lake Chad area, Nigeria and Niger have initiated different de-radicalisation programmes. While Nigeria runs both a prison-based and military-administered camp models of de-radicalisation, Niger is currently piloting an orientation centre-based de-radicalisation programme.

Nigeria's de-radicalisation programmes have become a key strategy in the government's effort to end Boko Haram insurgency. In 2013, the Office of the National Security Adviser (ONSA) devised a three-pronged Countering Violent Extremism (CVE) approach focusing on "De-Radicalisation, Counter-Radicalisation and Strategic Communication". The De-Radicalisation strand focuses on intervention in the prison for those convicted of terrorism-related offences as well as suspects awaiting trial. Hence, "a regimen of aftercare is embedded as part of the de-radicalisation process, devised for detainees granted amnesty or released by court order as well as those willing to renounce terrorist activities" (QIASS, 2013: 179). A basic de-radicalisation model was adopted for use in Nigerian prisons pilot de-radicalisation programme which began in March 2015. It consists of four stages: engagement; risk assessment; needs assessment; and interventions. The programme drew on the expertise of criminologists and art therapists. It also included sports facilities and literacy and numeracy courses. An assessment of the first eight months of the pilot scheme noted that "the de-radicalisation programme in Kuje prison is already having a positive impact on prisoners, staff and prison management" (Barkindo & Bryans, 2016: 18).

In April 2016, the Nigerian Defence Headquarters (DHQ) announced the establishment of "Operation Safe Corridor" (OSC) programme, with a training camp in Gombe State. The OSC is primarily aimed at de-radicalising, rehabilitating, and reintegrating repentant or surrendering Boko Haram members back into normal life in the society. About eleven agencies of the government are expectedly involved in the programme, which is overseen by the military and headed by a Brigadier-General of the Nigerian Army. The programme is designed to expose them to psycho-social therapy, training on citizenship, and vocational skills acquisition such as carpentry, tailoring, vulcanising, welding, and barbing, among others. Upon completion, successful candidates are expected to be assisted with grants to set up businesses in their various communities. As of March 2017, there were supposedly more than 4,500 Boko Haram members who have surrendered under the OSC initiative and being held in secret detention centres around the country (Anyadike, 2017a). Some view the programme as being overtly militarised, in addition to using a grandiose facility with a significant number of staff but conducting poorly package de-radicalisation session for just six repentant Boko Haram members (Allamin, 2017). Currently, the OSC camp in Gombe is absorbing a myriad of Boko Haram members who are surrendering or being captured due to the intensity of ongoing military operations (NAN, 2017). In July 2017, the OSC reported that five ex-combatants had completed a six-week training programme at the Gombe State camp, with 95 others trained in vocational skills such as tailoring and carpentry. Despite modest success in its training component, the OSC programme has been criticised for lacking in the legal framework that captures the status of repentant fighters, a multitude of secret detention sites that makes profiling and referral of captured militants difficult, poor definition of categories of ex-combatants qualifying for the programme, and the short duration nature of rehabilitation programme. Others are distrust of the military by some Boko Haram members who otherwise would want to surrender, absence of biometric registration of enrolees in the camp, and failure to consult the communities that would receive the ex-combatants (Allamin, 2017; CDD, 2017; and Anyadike, 2017a). In Northeastern Nigeria, many communities deeply affected by the Boko

Haram insurgency and the attendant internal population displacement, have expressed deep scepticism, even resentment, against the OSC. The resentment is rooted in the fact that public resources were committed to the rehabilitation of scoundrels who have caused the destruction of the state, and peoples' livelihood and way of life (Tar, 2017). Similarly, in a workshop focusing on OSC organised by Abuja-based *Centre for Democracy and Development*, held in Maiduguri in July 2016, many participants threatened to take reprisal action against the re-habilitated Boko Haram members once they are returned to society. Members of the Civilian Joint Task Force in Maiduguri indicated their resolve not to allow any ex-Boko Haram combatants to be resettled in their communities. In general, "participants were unanimous in their objection to the reintegration of defecting Boko Haram fighters in the near term. They called for a ten-year window before defecting members can be reintegrated into local communities" (CDD, 2016: 3).

As with Nigeria, Niger is another West African country currently piloting a scheme for the de-radicalisation of ex-Boko Haram fighters. Since 2015 Niger had suffered deadly attacks from the Boko Haram, including recruitment and radicalisation of its citizens by the group. Local authorities in 2016 commenced a project of discreetly approaching families whose children have joined Boko Haram to encourage them to pass on a message of amnesty from the government for those ready to surrender. The government promised to pardon and assist those who surrendered to re-integrate into their communities. Such targeted "secret messaging" has encouraged about 150 Boko Haram members to surrender across the Diffa Prefecture. Encouraged by this, the government of Niger in December 2016 launched a de-radicalisation and reintegration programme for Boko Haram fighters who quit the battlefield. More than 150 people are in the programme, including fighters' "wives" and 28 young boys (Anyadike, 2017b). They were originally kept in Diffa town but later relocated to the Goudoumaria Reintegration Centre, where vocational training and de-radicalisation programmes are to take place over a two-year period (Rackley, 2017). Although the intervention looks promising, the programme is fraught with several challenges, such as the absence of a legal framework for the amnesty, absence of psycho-social support services, poor financing and resourcing of the programme, limited consultation with local communities, possible infiltration of Boko Haram moles disguised as defectors, and inadequate logistics in the event of a spike in the number of defectors.

Although both Nigerian and Nigerien intervention schemes for ex-terrorists and armed insurgents are incipient, the success of these programmes appear to be rooted in the following features: local ownership of the process, adoption of the legal framework for granting of amnesty, well-planned and resourced implementation framework, effective state policing capacity to deal with the fear of reprisals from former colleagues, confidence in state institutions which encourage defection, use of credible individuals in re-orientation and therapy sessions, and adequate consultation of local communities expected to receive de-radicalised terrorists. In fact, failure to integrate local communities in de-radicalisation programmes may explain why at least two of the former Boko Haram members who passed out of the OSC programme in Gombe camp were killed when they returned home (Anyadike, 2017a).

Apart from the foregoing state-centric de-radicalisation programmes in Africa, global and regional groupings, as well as extra-regional actors and preponderant states, have been at the vanguard of promoting similar initiatives in the continent. To this end, the European Union (EU) and its partners assisted the ONSA in developing the prison-based de-radicalisation programme as well as "*The Guide to the De-radicalisation Programme*", as a guidance document for countering violent extremism and laying the fundamental basis for the establishment, implementation and monitoring of de-radicalisation programmes within and outside the prison environment in Nigeria. Similarly, in 2015, the United Nations Office on Drugs and Crime (UNODC), in partnership with the Austrian and Danish governments and Nigerien heads of prison administration organised an interdisciplinary de-radicalisation workshop in the Niger Republic. The workshop which held in Niamey from 28 to 30 April 2015 centred on public safety, alternatives for imprisonment, managing high-risk inmates, and plans for re-integrating prisoners to reduce recidivism.

At the continental level, the African Union (AU) has not formulated any comprehensive regional strategy on de-radicalisation. However, it leverages the African Centre for the Study and Research on Terrorism (ACSRT) in building capacity of member-states' institutions in combating violent extremism and counter-radicalisation. Established in 2004, the Centre is part of the Peace and Security Department of the AU Commission and plays a key role in implementing the AU's counterterrorism framework. The Centre also collaborates with some regional and international partners, especially the EU, UNODC, UN Counterterrorism Committee (CTC), UN Counterterrorism Implementation Task Force (CTITF), and the Global Counterterrorism Forum. On the other hand, the Economic Community of West African States (ECOWAS) supports its member-states with capacity-building programmes designed to boost their CVE initiatives. In 2013, for instance, ECOWAS adopted the *Political Declaration on a Common Position Against Terrorism* which included a Counterterrorism Strategy and Implementation Plan. The document called upon member states to develop de-radicalisation programmes that seek to counter radical ideologies and terrorist propaganda, as well as promote mainstream religious teachings and interfaith dialogue at all levels, broad-based social awareness programmes involving civil society groups, employment and community-based programmes for youth groups, and broad-based participation in political and economic policies and institutions.

## Conclusion

Violent extremism is a growing threat to peace, security, and development in Africa. Most of the terrorist activities across the continent are being carried out by people recruited or radicalised by extremist ideologues or terrorist groups. Reversing the tide of radicalisation is a matter that requires urgent attention and resources from African states. Response to radicalisation have come in diverse ways, but the implementation of de-radicalisation programmes is a notable dimension of a softer approach in counterterrorism measures that is gaining recognition.

While de-radicalisation programmes may succeed in salvaging some radicalised individuals, experiences such as in France have shown that it can also fail in helping bring about behavioural change in others. Some believe therefore that de-radicalisation as a response to radicalisation and violent extremism has limited potency in achieving the desired result, essentially because it deals with symptoms rather than causes of the problem. As radicalisation fuels violent extremism in Africa, it is anticipated that more attention would be paid to de-radicalisation as one of the soft tools in dealing with terrorism. To this end, it is germane that more scholarly attention is devoted to understanding what works and does not work in terms of ongoing de-radicalisation programmes in Africa. This is with a view to identifying lessons learned and uncovering best practices that could help promote success in current and future de-radicalisation programmes in Africa.

Lastly, the need for more investment on measures that would limit the exposure and predisposition of African youths to radicalisation; whether through online contact, familial ties, or social networks, cannot be overemphasised. This is more than ever imperative given the loss of territorial control by ISIS in the Middle East and reliable intelligence report that highly radicalised ISIS members of African origin are heading back home. There is growing apprehension that Africa would become ISIS' battlefield. There is therefore the urgent need for the continental and regional bodies to deepen engagements with member-states to explore avenues for greater collaboration in responding to the evolving threat. Both the AU and the ECOWAS should create or support platforms for the robust exchange of ideas and lessons on the successes and failures recorded in de-radicalisation efforts. This will enable African states to learn from each others' successes, avoid pitfalls in de-radicalisation programmes and improve upon the delivery of de-radicalisation programmes as one of the soft tools of counterterrorism.

## References

ACLED (Armed Conflict Location and Event Data Project). (2015). Al-Shabaab in Tanzania: current status and potential future patterns. In: *ACLED* [online]: http://www.crisis.acleddata.com/al-shabaab-in-tanzania-current-status-and-potential-future-patterns/ (accessed: 5/9/2017 at 0915hrs).

Ahmed, I. (2018). Experts alarmed at rise of Jihadi terrorism in Mozambique. Voice of America [online]: https://www.voanews.com/a/experts-alarmed-at-rise-of-jihadi-terrorism-in-mozambique/4434140.html (accessed: 16/6/2018 at 1215hrs).

Ali, M., & Billard-Arbelaez, S. (2017). Al-Shabaab attacks in Somalia (2006–2017). In: *Al Jazeera* [online]: http://www.aljazeera.com/indepth/interactive/2016/08/al-shabab-attacks-somalia-2006–2016-160830110231063.html# (accessed: 20 August 2017).

Allamin, H. (2017). *Interviewed by the first author at Maidugurithe*. Borno State, 7 September 2017.

American Society of Clinical Hypnosis. (1973). *A Syllabus of hypnosis and a handbook of therapeutic suggestions*. Chicago: American Society of Clinical Hypnosis.

Angus, C. (2016). *Radicalisation and violent extremism: causes and responses. NSW Parliamentary Research Service, e-brief*, No. 1.

Anyadike, O. (2017a). Boko Haram: Nigeria winning the battle but losing the war?. In: *IRIN* [online]: https://www.irinnews.org/feature/2017/05/04/boko-haram-nigeria-winning-battle-losing-war (accessed: 1/9/2017 at 1215hrs).

Anyadike, O. (2017b). How jobs can help Niger win the war against Boko Haram. In: *IRIN* [online]: https://www.irinnews.org/analysis/2017/07/17/how-jobs-can-help-niger-win-war-against-boko-haram (accessed 1/9/2017 at 1215hrs).

Ashour, O. (2009). *Votes and violence: Islamists and the processes of transformation*. London: The International Centre for the Study of Radicalisation.

Atallah, R. (2013). Crisis in the Sahel: Mali terrorism threat growing. In: Online: http://www.acus.org/new_atlanticist/crisis-sahel-mali-terrorism-threat-growing (accessed 5/8/2016 at 1013hrs).

Bah, A. (2010). Micro-disarmament in West Africa: The ECOWAS moratorium on small arms and light weapons. *African Security Review, 13*(3), 33–46.

Barkindo, A., & Bryans, S. (2016). De-radicalising prisoners in Nigeria: Developing a basic prison based deradicalisation programme. *Journal for Deradicalisation, 7.*

Brankamp, H. (2013). Tanzania's Islamist militants: A domestic threat from a domestic context. In: *ThinkAfricapress* [online]: http://thinkafricapress.com/tanzania/tanzanias-militant-islamists-domestic-threat-domestic-context? (accessed: 5/9/2014 at 0915hrs).

Burke, J. (2017). Burkina Faso: At least 18 dead in restaurant attack. In: *Guardian* [online]: https://www.theguardian.com/world/2017/aug/14/terror-attack-restaurant-burkina-faso-many-dead (accessed: 6/9/2017 at 1215hrs).

Cachalia, R. C., Ndung'u, I., & Salifu, U. (2016). *The dynamics of youth tadicalisation in Africa: reviewing the current evidence. Institute for Security Studies Paper, Issue 296.*

CDD - Centre for Democracy and Development. (2017). *Prospect for Transitional Justice Initiatives in the North East.* Abuja: CDD.

CDD - Centre for Democracy and Development. (2016). *Stakeholders' dialogue on government approaches to managing defecting violent extremists, abuja, policy brief.* Abuja: CDD.

Christmann, K. (2012). *Preventing religious radicalisation and violent extremism: A systematic review of the research evidence.* Research Report, London: Youth Justice Board.

Clutterbuck, L. (2015). *Deradicalisation programs and counterterrorism: A perspective on the challenges and benefits.* Washington: Middle East Institute.

Davis, J. (2007). *Africa and the war on terrorism*. United Kingdom: Ashgate Publishing Ltd.

Denoeux, G., & Carter, L. (2009). *Guide to the violent extremism drivers*. Washington, DC: A publication of the United States Agency for International Development.

Foster-Bowser, E., & Sanders, A. (2012). Security threats in the Sahel and beyond: AQIM, Boko Haram and Al Shabaab. In: Online: http://reliefweb.int/sites/reliefweb.int/files/resources/Full_Report_3818.pdf (accessed: 3/9/2016 at 1215hrs).

Hassan, I. (2009). Al-Shabaab's reign of terror. In: *Hiran* [online]: https://www.hiiraan.com/mop4/2009/july/11510/al_shabab_s_reign_of_terror.aspx (accessed 10/8/2017 at 1015hrs).

Hinds, R. (2015). *Role of Development Assistance in Countering Extremism and Terrorism* (GSDRC Helpdesk Research Report 1210). Birmingham, UK: GSDRC, University of Birmingham.

Horgan, H. (2008). Deradicalisation or disengagement? *Perspectives on Terrorism*, 2(4), 1–8.

Hussain, G., & Saltman, E. M. (2014). *Jihad trending: A comprehensive analysis of online extremism and how to counter it*. London: Quilliam.

ISD - Institute for Strategic Dialogue. (2010). *The role of civil society in counter radicalisation and de-radicalisation. PPN Working Paper*.

ICG - International Crisis Group. (2014). *Kenya: Al-Shabaab – closer to home. Africa Briefing* No. 102 Nairobi/Brussels.

IRIN - Integrated Regional Information News. (2012). Mali: holy wars and hostages – Al-Qaeda in the Maghreb. In: *IRIN* [online]: http://www.irinnews.org/Report/95208/MALI-Holy-wars-and-hostages-Al-Qaeda-in-the-Maghreb (accessed: 5/8/2016 at 1215hrs).

Isilow, H. (2017). AU: Terrorism a major challenge for African security. In: *Anadolu Agency* [online]: https://www.aa.com.tr/en/africa/au-terrorism-a-major-challenge-for-african-security/816661 (accessed 10/8/2017 at 1015hrs).

Jackson, T. (2014). Al-Shabaab capitalises on Muslim Grievances in Kenya. *Tony Blair Institute for Global Change*, 3 October, https://institute.global/insight/co-existence/embattled-isis-may-turn-africa (accessed 28/10/2017 at 1215hrs).

Keefer, P. & Loayza, N. (Eds.). (2008). *Terrorism, economic development, and political openness*. New York: Cambridge University Press.

Krueger, A. B. (2008). *What makes a terrorist: Economics and the roots of terrorism (new edition)*. New Jersey: Princeton University Press.

LeSage, A. (2014). *The rising terrorist threat in Tanzania: domestic Islamist militancy and regional threats. Strategic Forum No. 288*.

Martin, D. (2017). Egypt's deadliest terror attacks. In: *Deutsche Welle* (online): http://www.dw.com/en/egypts-deadliest-terror-attacks/g-39702393 (accessed: 13/7/2017 at 1218hrs).

Mbah, P., & Nwangwu, C. (2014). The counter-insurgence operations of the joint task force and human rights abuses in Northern Nigeria, 2011—2013. *Journal of Educational and Social Research*, 4(5), 67–78. 10.5901/jesr.2014.v4n5p67.

Mbah, P., Nwangwu, C., & Edeh, H. C. (2017). Elite politics and the emergence of Boko Haram insurgency in Nigeria. *TRAMES: Journal of the Humanities and Social Sciences*, 21(2), 173–190. https://doi.org/10.3176/tr.2017.2.06.

Meleagrou-Hitchens, A. (2012). Al Shabaab: Recruitment and radicalisation in Kenya. *ICSR Insight* [online]: http://icsr.info/2012/11/icsr-insight-al-shabaab-recruitment-and-radicalisation-in-kenya/ (accessed: 5/11/2013 at 1215hrs).

Mirahmadi, H., Ziad, W., Farooq, M., & Lamb, R. D. (2015). *Empowering Pakistan's civil society to counter global violent extremism*. In: The Brookings Project on U.S. Relations with the Islamic World: U.S.-Islamic World Forum Papers 2014.

Morier-Genoud, E. (2018). *Mozambique's own version of Boko Haram is tightening its deadly grip. The Conversation*, [online]: http://theconversation.com/mozambiques-own-version-of-boko-haram-is-tightening-its-deadly-grip-98087 accessed: 17/6/2018 at 1215hrs.

NAN- News Agency of Nigeria, (2017). 52 repentant Boko Haram members undergoing deradicalisation in Gombe- Army. In *Premium Times* [online]: http://www.premiumtimesng.com/news/more-news/236255-52-repentant-boko-haram-members-undergoing-deradicalisation-gombe-army.html (accessed 29/8/2017 at 1325hrs).

Nwabughiogu, L. (2016). *FG verifying claims of alleged Chibok girl bomber in Cameroon. Vanguard*, 27 March.

Ogundiya, I. S., & Amzat, J. (2008). Nigeria and the threats of terrorism: Myth or reality. *Journal of Sustainable Development in Africa, 10*(2), 165–189.

Okumu, W. (2010). *Africa's problematic borderlines. Africaa.org*, February/March.

Olojo, A. (2013). *Nigeria's troubled North: Interrogating the drivers of public support for Boko Haram.* Hague: International Centre for Counter-Terrorism.

Omotosho, M. (2017). The growing threat of extremist groups in Africa: Issues and challenges. *APSA Africa Workshop Alumni e-Newsletter, 4*(2), 6–11.

Onuoha, F. C. (2016). Boko Haram's recruitment and radicalisation methods in Nigeria: An exposé. *South East Journal of Political Science, 2*(1), 181–203.

Onuoha, F. C. (2014). *Why do youth join Boko Haram. Special Report,* No 348. Washington, DC: United States Institute of Peace.

Onuoha, F. C. (2013). *Westgate attack: Al-Shabaab's renewed transnational Jihadism. Report,* Doha: Al Jazeera Centre for Studies.

Onuoha, F. C. (2012). The audacity of the Boko Haram: background, analysis and emerging trend. *Security Journal, 25*(2), 134–151.

QIASS - Qatar International Academy for Security Studies. (2013). *Countering Violent Extremism: The Counter Narrative Study.* Qatar: Doha.

Rackley, E. (2017). The region in Niger quietly piloting a Boko Haram amnesty. In: *African Argument* [online]: http://africanarguments.org/2017/04/20/region-niger-quietly-piloting-boko-haram-amnesty/? (accessed 10/8/2017 at 1015hrs).

Sheizaf, N. (2014). Why do Palestinians continue to support Hamas despite such devastating losses?, +924 Magazine, 22 July, https://972mag.com/why-do-palestinians-continue-to-support-hamas-despite-such-devastating-loses/94080/ (accessed 28/10/2017 at 1215hrs).

Snook, I. A. (1972). *Concepts of Indoctrination.* London: Routledge and Kegan Paul.

Sodipo, M. O. (2013). *Mitigating radicalism in Northern Nigeria. Africa Security Brief,* No. 26.

Tar, U. A. (2017). *Review comments on the earlier draft of this chapter on 3 October 2017.*

Trofimov, Y. (2016). Islamic State invades vulnerable Africa. In: *Business Day Live,* Online: http://www.bdlive.co.za/africa/africanperspectives/2016/02/10/islamic-state-invades-vulnerable-africa (accessed 6/9/2017 at 1215hrs).

UNDP - United Nations Development Programme. (2017). *Journey To Extremism In Africa: Drivers, Incentives and the Tipping Point for Recruitment.* New York: United Nations Development Programme.

UNESCO - United Nations Educational, Scientific and Cultural Organization. (2016). *A Teacher's Guide on the Prevention of Violent Extremism.* France: UNESCO.

Vidino, L., Pantucci, R., & Kohlmann, E. (2010). Bringing global Jihad to the horn of Africa: Al Shabaab, Western fighters, and the sacralization of the Somali Conflict. *African Security, 3*(4), 261–238.

Wilson, L. (2014). Brainwashing. *The Centre for Development* [online]: http://www.drlwilson.com/Articles/BRAINWASH.htm (accessed 10/8/2017 at 1215hrs).

Young, E. (2014). *Terrorism in Africa.* Being a paper presented to participants of Program in Terrorism and Security studies, at George C. Marshall Center, Garmisch-Partenkirchen, Germany, 14 March.

# 9

# Laws of armed conflicts, counterterrorism and counterinsurgency

## Emerging conceptual and empirical contours in the battle space

*Chukwuma CC Osakwe*

## Introduction

Change and continuity have been known to characterise the nature of warfare even before the adoption of the First Geneva Convention in 1864. The changing nature of war has attracted a host of superlative adjectives such as (ir)regular warfare, (un)conventional warfare, (un)civilised warfare, guerrilla warfare, invisible warfare, invincible warfare, among others. Varying subsets of war have been added to these superlatives which are distinguished for its aloofness and contradictions upon the traditional conceptualisation of war. Insurgency, terrorism, militancy, gangsterism, warlordism, and its armed counter-responses (such as counterinsurgency and counterterrorism) make for some of them that have found exclusive rooms in war's spacious house. They all make for armed conflicts since they circumscribe collective and group violence with a recognisable degree of organisation, sophistication, and sustenance. Warlords leading "unconventional armies" in warfare have emerged in various parts of the world; and in the pursuit of their struggles, they sometimes employ methods that amount to violations of the laws of armed conflict (Edemekong, 2004). This makes for a challenge to existing laws of armed conflict (LOAC). This chapter tries to examine the challenging interpretation, observation, and implementation of LOAC in the context of counterterrorism and counterinsurgency using the *Boko Haram* armed conflict in the North East of Nigeria as a peculiar case study. Consequently, an analysis of *jus ad bellum* (justification of the decision to engage in battle), *jus in bello* (justification for activities carried out in battle), and *jus post bellum* (justification for actions carried out after battle) appear lumped in relative ambiguity.

## International laws designed to govern the moderation of armed hostilities

War is a behaviour that looms so large for all humanity. This has resulted in humanity embarking on ways to provide, amidst the cruelty and barbarity of war, protection for civilians and for those no longer taking part in the fighting; and even place restrictions on violence between combatants (Kalshoven, 2004). Indeed, this human endeavour underpins the basis for LOAC. The rules governing the resort to force form a central element within international law. Together with the principle of territorial sovereignty and the independence of equality of states, they provide the framework for international order (Dinstein, 2005; Gray, 2004; Neff, 2005).

The Geneva Convention for the Amelioration of the Condition of the Wounded in Armies in the Field was adopted in 1864. It was revised and developed in 1906. The laws of war were codified at the Hague Conferences of 1899 and 1907. Another convention, relative to the Treatment of Prisoners of War, was also adopted in 1929. In 1949, after WWII had ended, States adopted the four Geneva Conventions, which remained the cornerstone of LOAC. While the first three Geneva Conventions of 1949 grew out of existing treaties on the same subjects, the fourth Geneva Convention was a novel one, being the first LOAC treaty to deal with the protection of civilians during armed conflict. The death toll among civilians during WWII was one of the reasons for the development and adoption of such a treaty.

In the post-WWII environment, there was a need for rules applicable to wars of national liberation and as well as civil wars. It then became needful to adopt new texts in the form of Protocols additional to the Geneva Conventions, rather than revising the Geneva Conventions. This took place in June 1977 and became known as the Additional Protocols of 1977. To this end, contemporary LOAC concerns and relates to the four 1949 Geneva Conventions, the 1977 Protocols Additional to these Conventions, the 1954 Hague Convention for the Protection of Cultural Property, and the 1980 Weapons Convention. They all make for rules governing wartime relations.

The laws of war imply that there is a legal regulation on the use of force. The concept of the "laws of war" is made possible in order to regulate the conduct of individuals, nations and other agents in war and to mitigate the worst effects of war (Osakwe & Umoh, 2014). To this end, laws of war are intended to mitigate the "evils" of war by protecting both combatants and non-combatants from unnecessary suffering; safeguarding certain fundamental human rights of persons who fall into the hands of the enemy, particularly prisoner of war, the wounded and sick, and civilians; and facilitating the restoration of peace (Dinstien, 2004). Besides bringing wars to a quick end, LOAC help to restrict wars to their political objective and to protect people and property from unnecessary destruction and hardship (Osakwe & Umoh, 2014). LOAC applies from the initiation of armed conflicts and extends beyond the cessation of hostilities until a general conclusion of peace is reached or a peaceful settlement is achieved. Among other issues, the laws of war address declaration of war, acceptance of surrender and the treatment of prisoners of war; military necessity along with distinction and proportionality; and the prohibition of certain inhumane weapons which cause unnecessary sufferings (Solis, 2010). The most important principle in the laws of war is the effort to limit warfare to the combatants and to protect civilians when possible.

The most dramatic weakness of traditional international law has been its admission that states may use force to compel compliance with its will. There exists a paradox that traditional international law while leaving untouched the ultimate right to resort to war, achieved some regulation of the use of force short of war. To an extent, arguable, the war was at best first crime against peace (Jessup, 1958). The necessary condition for war crimes is that, first, there exists a law of armed conflict (Osakwe & Umoh, 2014). The United Nations War Crimes Commission describes the laws and customs of war as "the rules of international law which belligerents have customarily, or by special convention, agreed to comply in case of war". When such "special conventions" under the "rules of international law" are violated, a war crime can be said to have been committed. This implies that every violation of the laws of war is a war crime.

The International Committee of the Red Cross opines that "serious violations of international humanitarian law constitute war crimes". What constitutes "serious violations" continues to undergo serious introspection into its core assumptions. It suggests that some crimes can be committed in wars which are not "serious" enough to be classified as war crimes (Kalshoven, 1987).

## LOAC, "old wars" and "new wars": evolution towards a solution

War in the legal sense is a legal condition which equally permits two or more hostile states to carry out contention by means of armed forces (Wright, 1942: 116–118). This traditional perspective of war appears to throw so many burdens on states as the custodian of the monopoly of armed violence. However, past, and even evolving realities have shown that the manipulation of violence is not the sole preserve of states and indeed state actors. Qualitative changes violent conflict has seduced scholars in the field to think in terms of "new wars". Attempts have been made to put forward a distinction from earlier forms of armed conflict. According to Kaldor (1999), "the new wars can be contrasted with earlier wars in terms of their goals, the methods of warfare and how they are financed." Six variables *cum* arguments have been used to enhance the changing nature of the armed conflict. First, is the main protagonists and units of analysis of war, such as states or non-state actors, public or private actors, terrorist groups, and warlords. Second, we have the primary motives of protagonists, such as ideology, territorial secession, or material aggrandisement. Third, is the spatial context: interstate, "civil", regional, or global spheres. Fourth, is the technological means of violence – the weapons and strategies of war. Fifth, the social, material, and human impact of conflict, including patterns of human victimisation and forced human displacement. Sixth, the political economy and social structure of conflict (see Newman, 2004: 174).

The "new war" argument is sustained by the observation that the spatial context of contemporary wars is within, rather than between, states, albeit with attendant regional spillovers. The central actors in such armed conflicts are insurgency groups, criminal gangs, diaspora groups, ethnic parties, international aid organisations, and mercenaries, as well as regular armies (Newman, 2004: 175). Non-state actors have competed and even shown proficiency in the manipulation of violence. There is also the obvious manifestation of the utility of violence as an opportunity for entrepreneurship and profit – rebellion as a business; making for the primacy of the continuation of violence rather than a military victory. Such environments create a sense of legitimacy for criminal actions which in peacetime would have been punishable by law. The situation where armed conflicts are far more likely to be caused by economic opportunities than by grievance is what Collier (2000) refers to as "economic agenda" in armed conflicts. Fall (1965), Fearon and Laitin (2003), Kalyvas (2005), Kalyvas and Balcells (2010), all agree that most civil conflicts in the post–World War II era share a common type of warfare: insurgency.

With a peculiar relationship with LOAC, "new wars" proponents throw it up as a distinct type of armed conflict characterised by the deliberate targeting and forcible displacement of civilians as a primary objective of violence, and the "importance of extreme and conspicuous atrocity" (Kaldor, 1999). Systematic rape, ethnic cleansing, the use of child soldiers, and a high proportion of civilian casualties are prominent features of new wars. Consequently, "refugee movements are no longer side effects of conflict, but in many cases are central to the objectives and tactics of war" (United Nations High Commissioner for Refugees (UNHCR) 2000: 282). Insurgencies and its counterparts exhibit these wholesale features.

Kaldor (1999) presents the new war thesis as the breaking down of "the distinctions between external barbarity and domestic civility, between the combatant as the legitimate bearer of arms and the non-combatant, between the soldier or policeman and the criminal…" However, the argument that most contemporary armed conflicts now take place within states rather than between states has been challenged. Boot (2013), has shown that armed conflicts between and within states have been constant in the evolving concept of sovereignty. Guerrilla wars, terrorism and insurgencies have been argued by Boot (2013) to be the traditional way of waging war rather than the popular opinion of being the non-traditional way of waging war. Consequently, insurgency, terrorism and its likes have predated David Petraeus, Osama Bin Laden, Hezbollah, Hamas, Entebbe, Rwanda, Ku Klux Klan (KKK), Akkad, the Nihilist, Lawrence of Arabia, and the Tartan Rebellion (see Boot, 2013). In these eras and areas, the six variables outlined by Newman (2004) have been effervescent. Insurgent groups, criminal gangs, diaspora groups, ethnic parties, international aid organisations, and mercenaries, as well as regular armies, have stood out as the central actors in such armed conflicts. The KKK, apart from having a hateful economic agenda, deliberately targeted civilians as a primary objective of violence. Indeed, atrocities have been a feature of all wars since the ambush at Beth-Horon in AD 66. Furthermore, as Newman (2004: 181) argues, forced human displacement – both collateral and deliberate – has also long been a feature of violent conflict, and ethnic cleansing is not peculiar to the wars of the 1990s.

With the changing but continuously blurred distinction between peoples, armies, and governments, LOAC offers more problems than solutions. As Newman (2004: 185) pointed out, it is dependent on changes in approaches, analysis as well as the social reality of war and warfare. The battlefield from the earliest times has often been an asymmetric one in terms of tactics and strategy. The almost exclusive employment of counter value rather than counter-force strategy distinguishes terrorist and insurgent armed violence. The utilisation and manipulation of armed violence in such armed conflicts swing between state militaries answerable to state authority and armed groups answerable to individual authority. In Africa, Asia and Latin America for instance, the historical roots of insurgency go beyond 19th-century doctrines of colonial warfare. Consequently, LOAC has succeeded in evolving much but solving less of the basic problem – an asymmetric battlefield and symmetric application of laws.

## Legal challenges inherent in small wars regulated by big laws

In 1906, Colonel Callwell of His Britannic Majesty's Forces defined "small wars" as a distinct type of warfare which involved "campaigns undertaken to suppress rebellion and guerrilla warfare in all parts of the world where organised armies are struggling against opponents who will not meet them in the open field." In the evolving and changing relationship between laws and wars, LOAC bears the character of big laws – at least for its recognition, coverage, and duration – which covers big wars and small wars. Insurgency warfare shared basic features with guerrilla warfare drawn upon the innovative Spanish methods to withstand and challenge the Napoleonic forces in Spain. Consequently, insurgency best describes a small war amid a big one – the central commentary dignified in the work David Kilcullen (2009). The composition of small wars, or at best war in bits, often makes for the graduate level of war. By 1940, engagement in small wars became a domineering feature of the United States Marine Corps leading to the publication of Small Wars Manual as a leading text on the subject.

The inability of the international community to provide the parties fighting small wars the comparatively extensive and clear legal framework that is in existence for State-versus-State conflict does not appear new. The 1998 Rome Statute provides the clearest convention-based listing of the legal norms applicable to small wars. LOAC has treated the problem and challenges of small wars under non-international armed conflict. However, the basic problem has been the application of LOAC on non-state actors. State actors since 1949 in Geneva, have shown reluctance in allowing the rules of international armed conflict to apply to non-international ones. The devoted attempt by the International Committee of the Red Cross (ICRC) to ensure the equality of such rules appear to be their most obvious frustration. Exceptionally limited success was only achieved with the inclusion of Common Article 3 protections applicable to "conflicts not of an international character." However, states, including post-colonial new states indulged in expressing concern that a treaty regime that provides the same rights as states to non-state opponents - existing and potential - would get the non-State opponents "legitimised".

In the context of international law – the mother rules – war is treated in the context of a tripod where there exists justification for recourse to war (*jus ad bellum*), a justification for actions taken in war (*jus in bello*), and justification for actions taken after the war (*jus post bellum*). To the extent arguable, *jus ad bellum* provides legitimacy to state actors to undertake and engage in wars. While the non-State appears not to have a distinct justification for engaging in armed conflict, but attempt smuggling in through the leakages in the contextual application, they (non-State actors) appear to enjoy the graciousness provided by the composite binary – *Jus in bello,* which applies equally to all participants, State and non-State alike. The legal regulation of non-international armed conflict has also been challenged by the "right authority" clause needed to give legitimacy for engagement in war. For LOAC, international law applies to the subject of international law – States – and the object of international law – non-States.

## Hearts and minds in laws of war

The success of CT-COIN warfare associates purposefully with the winning of hearts and minds of the local population. The Classical School of Counterinsurgency led by Anglo-French military practitioners and theorist such as Robert Thompson (1966), Roger Trinquier (1961) and David Galula (1964) hold the sustained notion that the essence of counterinsurgency involves an armed struggle between an incumbent government and an insurgent movement for the political allegiance of the population. The term *cum* expression "winning the hearts and minds" (WHAM) of the people became the thriving thesis of their treatise. The composite of this is the "enemy-centric" approach which is focused on defeating insurgents and guerrillas militarily. In WHAM, the local population often throws up as a bride to be simultaneously courted by the government forces and non-government armed groups. The insurgent forces hide among the population and in the cover of the population. The government forces indulge the local population to isolate the insurgent forces.

A combination of classic literature on insurgency and counterinsurgency (I-COIN) stress the population-centric nature of the armed contest. Guevara (1961: 2) has argued that "the guerrilla is supported by the peasant and worker masses of the region and of the whole territory in which it acts. Without these prerequisites, guerrilla warfare is not possible." Indeed, the entire body of literature devoted to counterinsurgency has focused on the problem of public support for success and indeed defeat. Tse Tung (1937; 1961) compared the relationship between revolutionaries *cum* insurgents and the local population with the relationship that exists between fishes and water. In his famous submission, "the revolutionaries *cum* insurgents swim among the local population as fishes swim in the water" (Tse Tung, 1966). For Galula (1964), the real task of the counterinsurgent is an armed competition to secure the population against insurgent subversion. To this end, a war against insurgents is 80 per cent political and only 20 per cent military, requiring a reformist impulse and unity of civil-military effort from any incumbent government.

The concepts of war crimes and crimes against humanity seem to have taken a centre stage in the crafting, codification, and implementation of LOAC. In fact, the intersection of crimes against humanity, among others, derives from the nature and character of the peculiar wars of the century which has the "people" as the centre of gravity. In course of the war to win hearts and mind, the wars of counterinsurgency and counterterrorism is fought in "people's" space, by the people, with the people, for the people, and/or amongst the people. Thus, the people are thrust in the vortex of the barbarity of war that they become victims. In military lexicon, they are described as part of the collateral damage.

In counterinsurgency, there appears to be an almost natural process for adhering to the laws of war. This has to do with the need to win or at best influence the hearts and minds of the local population. Keeping to the laws of war improves the confidence of the local population on the counterinsurgency troops. While the insurgent forces might boast to have control of the population and hide in it, the counterinsurgent forces appear bound to regulate its conduct to win over the local population. While hearts and minds cannot be wholesomely won, it can be influenced. Few have argued that WHAM is a misleading notion because the primary problem to be resolved in any counterinsurgency is less the winning of "hearts and minds" than establishing effective security on the ground in a manner that facilitates political progress. A balance needs to be struck between using coercion and seeking co-operation; between "search-and-destroy" missions against guerrilla cadres and mounting "secure-and-hold" operations to protect the target population against insurgent influence.

## Case study: armed conflict and the challenge for LOAC in Nigeria

The *Boko Haram* armed conflict which erupted in 2009 graduated steadily from a local municipal crime in Nigeria into a formidable regional terror organisation with a vast connection to global terror networks. Varied nomenclatures were thrown up by the Nigerian state and civil society to categorise the event. To the extent arguable, internal disturbances and tensions (such as riots and isolated and sporadic acts of violence), although disrupt public order, do not amount to armed conflict because the level of violence is not sufficiently high or because the persons resorting to violence are not organised as an armed group. In practice, LOAC does not apply to situations of violence that do not amount to armed conflict. Consequently, cases of this type are governed by the provisions of human right law and domestic legislation.

The intrinsic object of war is to impose the will of a belligerent state on the enemy by force. It is the purpose of the laws of war to determine the permissible forms, areas, and object of the exercise of physical pressure by belligerents against each other (Schwarzenberger, 1960: 185). LOAC is a compromise between two underlying principles: of humanity and of military necessity. These two principles shape all its rules. The principle of military necessity permits only that degree and kind of force required to achieve the legitimate purpose of a conflict which is the complete or partial submission of the enemy at the earliest possible moment with the minimum expenditure of life and resources. The principle of humanity forbids the infliction of all suffering, injury, or destruction not necessary for achieving the legitimate purpose of conflict.

Military operations in Nigeria's North East appear to lack a designated area of operations. Consequently, the theatre of war is extensive, ambiguous, and expanding. However, a state engaged in armed conflict is free to attack its adversary anywhere in war (see Fleck, 2003: 53). The major sources of LOAC to which, Nigeria is a State-Party, are the Geneva Conventions and their Protocols, and customary international law. In a non-international armed conflict, such as the one in north-east Nigeria, the parties to the conflict are bound to comply with the norms contained in Common Article 3 of the Geneva Conventions, Protocol II to the 1949 Geneva Conventions and customary international law, which consists of rules that are binding on all states. Nigeria acceded to both the Geneva Conventions and their Protocols.

The accuracy in distinguishing between combatants and civilians as well as distinguishing between military targets and the civilian population stands out as a challenge. This has resulted in extensive sufferings for civilians in the conflict area. One basic principle of IHL is that of "distinction" – all measures must be taken to distinguish between military targets and civilians or civilian objects. Although three sets of participants can be easily identified – combatants, civilians and non-combatants – international law regarding persons taking part in, or affected by, an international armed conflict makes a fundamental distinction between combatants and civilians (Fleck, 2003: 65). The use of the term "non-combatants" implies that other members of the armed forces may be excluded from direct participation in hostilities but are only attachments to the armed forces without being members. They are known as "persons who accompany the armed forces". This is however an indication that their primary status is that of civilians. However, persons who do not belong to the armed forces can, under exceptional circumstance, attain combatant status by virtue of an act of their state or through their decision, as is illustrated by the inclusion of police forces in the armed forces or the armed resistance of the civilian population against an invasion. Article 48 states that: "In order to ensure respect for and protection of the civilian population and civilian objects, the Parties to the conflict shall at all times distinguish between the civilian population and combatants and between civilian objects and military objectives and accordingly shall direct their operations only against military objectives" (ICRC, 1977: 34–35)

The protection of the civilian population is the frontline advocacy of LOAC. The civilian population and individual civilians enjoy general protection against dangers arising from military operations. As stated in Article 50, the civilian population comprises all persons who are civilians and the presence within the civilian population of individuals who do not come within the definition of civilians does not deprive the population of its civilian character (ICRC, 1977: 35). Indeed, whenever doubt exists whether a person is a civilian, that person shall be considered a civilian (ICRC, 1977: 35). To this end when *Boko Haram* armed group swim among the local population like Mao's "fish in water", the environment is still considered a civilian population at least by the fact that there is "more water than fishes". Thus, the ratio of *Boko Haram* personnel to the local civilian population typically determines the regulation in the deployment of force by CT-COIN forces. Collateral damages have often soared on the popular commentary of *Boko Haram* armed group using human shields. This has made the Nigerian military CT-COIN progress slow and its success limited. The illusion is complicated by the reality that a circumspect battlefield is hardly ascertained. However, Article 52 infused a clause that provides flexibility to this application. It states that:

> The presence or movements of the civilian population or individual civilians shall not be used to render certain points or areas immune from military operations, in particular in attempts to shield military objectives from attacks or to shield, favour or impede military operations. The Parties to conflict shall not direct the movement of the civilian population or individual civilians in order to attempt to shield military objectives from attacks or to shield military operations (ICRC, 1977: 37).

Consequently, it is the fundamental obligation of combatants to distinguish themselves from the civilian population to increase the protection of the civilian population against the effects of hostilities. The Convention also prohibits an attack on civilian population or civilian by way of reprisals.

Reprisals are coercive measures which would normally be contrary to international law, but which are taken in retaliation by one party to a conflict to stop the adversary from violating international law. Reprisals have been a common feature of the military operation in the battlefield of the North East by both dyads.

The 2013 and 2014 reports of the Amnesty International on North East military operations have shown footage of extensive reprisal attack on the local population consequent upon the suspicion that the local population fell short of being neutral. Such attacks make for indiscriminate attacks in the context of the Convention which include: attacks not directed at a specific military objective as well as attacks which employ a method or means of combat which cannot be directed at a specific military objective. Although reprisal is often factored into military operations of such kind, it should not be directed at civilian populations. The law of reprisals is often closely connected with the principle of reciprocity since it allows one state illegally injured by another to react to the violation of the law by an action which itself would normally breach international legal obligations (see, Kalshoven, 2004). Field evidence from the battle theatre in the North East of Nigeria shows that reprisals have not been necessarily effective in forcing the adverse party to respect the law, since reprisals often produce the contrary effect, tending to prompt a harsher reaction to every new reprisal of the adverse side, thereby setting up a process of escalation (see, Kalshoven 2004; Fleck, 2003: 478).

## Stereotyping the battle space: counterterrorism or counterinsurgency?

Military operations of the Nigerian military in the North East has often assumed the complex phrase "counterterrorism-counterinsurgency", professionally abbreviated CT-COIN. This is in direct response to the assumption and reality of the armed conflict the Nigerian government is arrayed against. The violent activities of *Boko Haram* are often amplified in the narrative of terrorism outside the North East battlefield and amplified in the narrative of insurgency within the battlefield area of the North East. However, the battlefield is not acknowledged to be expanded *strictu sensu* beyond a circumscribed North East. This provides a warped notion of wartime and peacetime occurring together in Nigeria. The usage of the expression "war on terrorism" by the Nigerian state further makes it omnibus as it provides an expanding theatre but a restricted operation. Thus, in the battlefield of the North East, counterterrorism is often factored in a counterinsurgency strategy. Between 2011 and 2012, a counterinsurgency strategy not too distinguished from a counterterrorism strategy was developed and circulated as an official doctrine. Indeed, a clinical separation of counterterrorism and counterinsurgency in the North East of Nigeria appears avoided. Be it as it may, the expression "armed conflict" provides a parallel expression to capture the runaway conceptual confusion. A clear understanding and conceptualisation of the armed conflict engaged in will influence the kind of doctrine, education, or training, necessary for forces deployed to the North East.

By interpretation, LOAC continues to apply in the whole territory of the warring state or in the case of internal conflict, the whole territory under the control of a party, whether actual combat takes place. Do captured personnel of the *Boko Haram* armed group enjoy Prisoner of War (PoW) status? What happens when the PoW status of someone caught in the hostilities is in doubt? LOAC upholds that all persons detained outside an armed conflict are protected by the domestic law of the detaining State and by human rights law. LOAC, however, upholds that when the PoW status of a prisoner is in doubt, a competent tribunal must be established to rule on the issue. In most cases as observable, domestic laws have been used to handle *Boko Haram* members suspected to be involved in acts of terrorism within and outside the conflict zone. Suspected members of the *Boko Haram* armed group have been charged to civil courts in Nigeria.

Gleaned from the Geneva Convention and Additional Protocol, LOAC does not regulate terrorist acts committed in peacetime as such acts are subject to domestic and international law. Persons detained in connection with a non-international armed conflict waged as part of the fight against terrorism are protected by common Article 3, Additional Protocol II when applicable and the relevant rules of customary LOAC. Since the rules of human rights law and domestic law also apply to them, they are entitled to the fair trial guarantees of LOAC and human rights law if they are tried for crimes they might have committed.

While LOAC appears not to provide a definition of "terrorism" it prohibits most acts committed in armed conflict that would be considered "terrorist" by prohibiting "measures" of terrorism and "acts of terrorism LOAC also prohibits hostage-taking. Article 33 of the Fourth Geneva Convention, states that "collective penalties and likewise all measures of intimidation or of terrorism are prohibited." Article 4 of Additional Protocol II prohibits "acts of terrorism" against persons not or no longer taking part in hostilities. Additional Protocols I and II also prohibit acts aimed at spreading terror among the civilian population. It states that "Acts or threats of violence, the primary purpose of which is to spread terror among the civilian population, are highly prohibited" (See Article 51, Paragraph 2, of Additional Protocol I; Article 13, paragraph 2, of Additional Protocol II).

One of the challenges of LOAC in the battlefield of the North East is the clinical determination of the armed conflict carried out. LOAC applies only in situations of armed conflict. It offers two systems of protection: one for international armed conflict (IAC) and another for non-international armed conflict (NIAC). The rules applicable in a specific situation will depend on the classification of the armed conflict. IACs occurs when one or more States resort to the use of armed forces against another State. An armed conflict between a State and an international organisation is also classified as an IAC. Wars of national liberation, in which peoples are fighting against colonial domination and alien occupation and against racist regimes in the exercise of their right of self-determination, are classified as IACs under certain conditions (See Article 1, Paragraph 4, and Article 96, Paragraph 3, of Additional Protocol I).

An NIAC is an armed conflict in which hostilities are taking place between the armed forces of State and organised non-State armed groups, or between such groups. Moreover, for hostilities to be considered an NIAC, they must reach a certain level of intensity and the groups involved must be sufficiently organised. However, in certain situations, several armed conflicts may be taking place at the same time and within the same territory. In such instances, the classification of the armed conflict and, consequently, the applicable law will depend on the relationships between the belligerent. The *Boko Haram* armed conflict in Nigeria's North East throws up a basic challenge for classification. The temptation to tag it a non-international armed conflict is almost apprehended by the frequent diffusion of the conflict into Cameroon, Niger, and Chad.

The definition of NIAC in Additional Protocol II requires that organised non-State armed groups must exercise territorial control "as to enable them to carry out sustained and concerted military operations and to implement this protocol." In this regard, Additional Protocol II develops, extends, and even supplements common Article 3, albeit without modifying its existing conditions of application. In Nigeria's CT-COIN operations in the North East, the extensive and porous borders have seduced and permitted neighbouring state like Chad and Cameroon to engage *Boko Haram* armed groups or act in concert with the Nigerian military under the Multinational Joint Task Force structure. Common Article 3 and Additional Protocol II places this as NIAC between Nigeria and *Boko Haram* on the one hand, and another NIAC between Cameroon and/or Chad and *Boko Haram* on the other hand.

LOAC appears not to recognise any specific categories of person in NIAC. This is because States do not want to give members of organised non-state armed groups the status of "combatants", which entails the right to take a direct part in hostilities. Consequently, there is no "combatant" status in NIAC and as such, there is no prisoner-of-war status either. This makes for *Boko Haram* armed group members in the North East of Nigeria to be prosecuted under Nigeria's domestic law. The only provision given by Common Article 3 and Additional Protocol II is that everyone not actively involved in hostilities, or no longer taking part in them, is entitled to protection.

Steep in the CT-COIN rhetoric, is the manifestation that the Nigerian State considers and treats the *Boko Haram* armed conflict as a security issue. It is framed within the idea of domestic security, albeit a complex one. CT-COIN in the North East is treated both as a single operation and multiple operations in one. In some cases, one operational name supplements another operational name, and in other cases, one operational name complements another. Thus, dotting the landscape of the North East battlefield has been nuances such as Operation Restore Order I (ORO I), Operation BOYONA, Operation Zaman Lafiya, Operation Lafiya Dole, Operation Crackdown, Operation Gama Aiki, and Operation Safe Corridor.

Operation Restore Order was mandated, to "restore law and order to the North-Eastern part of the country with emphasis on Maiduguri." A quick one was added to circumscribe Yobe and named Operation Restore Order III (ORO III). When a state of emergency was declared in 2013, Operation BOYONA was established to cover the states affected by the state of emergency – Borno, Yobe and Adamawa states. Operation Lafiya Dole both complemented and supplemented BOYONA as it handled the overall CT-COIN operations comprising three divisions in more than five states in the North East. This was however complemented with Operation Crackdown mandated to wind down the war against insurgents and clear the remnants of the *Boko Haram* sect in Sambisa Forest. An extension to it was Operation Gama Aiki, which was mandated to serve the same purpose as Operation Crackdown in the northern part of Borno state. A post-military operation - Operation Safe Corridor, was set up to de-radicalise and rehabilitate repentant *Boko Haram* members.

## The footprints insurgency and LOAC legal bandwidth

The legal bandwidth of LOAC appears to flaw Nigerian troops in the North East of extra-judicial killings, torture. Since at least May 2013, the situation in north-east Nigeria has constituted a non-international armed conflict. The Nigerian state has used its military to counter *Boko Haram* rather than law enforcement agencies. Meanwhile, *Boko Haram* has the command structure and capacity to maintain military operations. In this context, *Boko Haram* is bound by LOAC. Members of *Boko Haram* have been involved in war crimes and crimes against humanity, such as torture, rape, sexual violence, sexual slavery, forced marriages and the recruitment of child soldiers. *Boko Haram*'s attacks also constitute a widespread, as well as systematic, attack on the civilian population in furtherance of an organisational policy (Amnesty International Report, 2014).

Leaders and men of the *Boko Haram* armed group are often argued to have received only rudimentary military training. Consequently, their knowledge of LOAC appears very rudimentary to give room for wholesale violation. The same does not apply to government forces and this is what differentiates fighters from soldiers. Thus, while all soldiers are fighters by training, all fighters are not soldiers. However, the fact that one side in an armed conflict violates LOAC does not justify its adversary in disregarding that law. Also, the fact that an armed conflict is labelled "guerrilla warfare" or "insurgency warfare", does not alter the duty to comply with the laws of war (Fleck, 2003).

While the question as to whether armed groups are under an obligation to make full reparation for violations of international humanitarian law is unsettled, practice indicates that such groups are required to provide a measure of appropriate reparation. However, the combination of under-resourcing, low morale and impunity for violations has created an atmosphere in which the security forces have not only repeatedly failed to protect the civilian population from attacks by *Boko Haram*, but have also been involved in rampant human rights violations through extrajudicial execution. A case in point is the mass execution of over 640 recaptured *Boko Haram* detainees from the military detention facility at Giwa Barracks in Maiduguri, Borno state in March 2014 (Amnesty International Report, 2014).

In terms of responsibility, the Nigerian state has responsibility for all violations of LOAC committed by their troops or those acting under their authority in the battlefield of the North East and beyond. This responsibility entails the obligation on the Nigerian state to ensure full reparation for losses or injuries suffered. The Armed Forces Council of Nigeria holds the responsibility for the command and discipline of the armed forces of Nigeria. The President is the Commander in Chief of the Armed Forces which makes him responsible for all military operations as briefed by the Chief of Defence Staff. Although the army does not have a civilian oversight body, the National Assembly provides a general oversight role. This places the issue of responsibility for actions taken in the field in a structural vacuum. Under the Terrorism (Prevention) Act (as amended in 2013), the military has been given wide powers to arrest and detain people. Section 27 allows the arrest and detention of a person "found on any premises or places or in any conveyance" by the "relevant law enforcement officer of any agency until the completion of the search or investigation under the provisions of this act." Under the amended act, anyone who "does, attempts or threatens any act of terrorism", "omits to do anything that is reasonably necessary to prevent an act of terrorism", or "assists or facilitates" an act of terrorism, is guilty of an offence.

Torture has featured as a war crime while obtaining information or extracting a confession from *Boko Haram* members using punishment, intimidation, or coercion. It has been argued that respecting human rights would make it more difficult to defeat *Boko Haram*. However, extrajudicial killings and other abuses of human rights by the *Boko Haram* armed groups do not absolve the Nigerian government of the responsibility to conduct CT-COIN operations professionally in a manner that is fully consistent with their human rights obligations and LOAC rules. Although it is difficult, it is not altogether impossible.

## Conclusion

LOAC has evolved over time and has generated issues, challenges, and debates with the parallel evolution of war. Insurgency and terrorism and its armed counter process hang on the balance challenges of reconciling LOAC tending towards full criminalisation of war and a rapturous embrace of humanitarianism with a sanctimonious military objective of influencing or winning "hearts and minds". The dynamic nature of small wars in the North East of Nigeria has undermined LOAC. There is a lack of consensus as to what law applies in the battlefield of small wars in the North East. The degree to which human right law in the context of LOAC governs and regulate the use of force, the treatment of detainees and the accountability process in internal conflicts leaves both the argument and conclusion open-ended.

The extent to which LOAC can be applied in its entirety to insurgency and terrorism-based warfare in the North East remains contentious. Both the Nigerian state and the international community can best be said to have achieved limited success in coordinating a valid response and solution. This appears to remain so if the small wars of the North East are fought between a state abiding by the laws of war and non-state armed groups that have little regard to these regulations. The *Boko Haram* armed conflict in the North East of Nigeria supports the Marcus Tullius Cicero's aphorism that "in times of war, the laws fall silent" (*silent enim leges inter arma*). For the duration of the war and the activities circumscribed within the radius of the battlefield, humanitarianism appeared to have been left under siege. In all, the extent to which the blood of civilians stains the victory of Nigerian CT-COIN forces in the battlefield of the North East defines the adherence to LOAC.

## References

Amnesty International Report. (2014). *'Our job is to shoot, slaughter and kill' Boko Haram's reign of terror in North-East Nigeria.* London: Amnesty International.

Amnesty International Report. (2015). *Stars on their shoulders, blood on their hands: War crimes committed by the Nigerian military.* London: Amnesty International.

Boot, Max (2013). *Invisible armies: An epic history of guerrilla warfare from ancient times to the present.* New York: Liveright Publishing Corporation.

Collier, Paul (2000). Rebellion as quasi-criminal activity. *Journal of Conflict Resolution, 44*(3), 839–853.

Dinstein, Y. (2005). *Aggression and self-defence.* Cambridge: Cambridge University Press.

Dinstien, Y. (2004). *The conduct of hostilities under the law of international armed conflict.* New York: Cambridge University Press.

Edemekong, Edemekong (2004). *Enforcement of the laws of armed conflict.* Uyo: Ivy Press Ltd.

Fall, B. B. (1965). The theory and practice of insurgency and counterinsurgency. *Naval War College Review, 7*(8), 21–37.

Fearon, J. D., & Laitin, D. D. (2003). Ethnicity, insurgency and civil war. *American Political Science Review, 57*(1), 75–90.

Fleck, Dieter (Ed.). (2003). *The handbook of humanitarian law in armed conflicts.* Oxford: Oxford University Press.

Galula, D. (1964). *Counterinsurgency warfare: Theory and practice.* New York: Praeger Security International.

Gray, C. (2004). *International law and the use of force.* Oxford: Oxford University Press.

Green, L. (2000). *The contemporary law of armed conflict.* Manchester: Manchester University Press.

Guevara, E. (1961). *Guerrilla warfare.* North Melbourne: Ocean Press.

International Committee of the Red Cross (ICRC). (1977). *Protocol additional to the Geneva conventions of 12 August 1949.*

Jessup, Philip C. (1958). *A modern law of nations: An introduction.* New York: The Macmillan Company.

Kaldor, Mary (1999). *New and old wars: Organized violence in a Global Era.* Stanford, CA: Stanford University Press.

Kalshoven, Fritz (1987). *Constraints on the waging of war.* Geneva: International Committee of the Red Cross.

Kalshoven, Fritz (2004). From international humanitarian law to international criminal law. *Chinese Journal of International Law, 3*(1), 151–161.

Kalyvas, S. (2005). Warfare in civil wars. In I. Duyvesteyn & J. Angstrom (Eds.), *Rethinking the nature of war* (pp. 88–108). Nashville, TN: Abingdton.

Kalyvas, S., & Balcells, L. (2010). International system and technology of rebellion: how the end of the cold war shaped internal conflict. *American Political Science Review, 104*(3), 415–429.

Kilcullen, David J. (2009). *The accidental guerrilla: Fighting small wars in the midst of a big one.* New York: Oxford University Press.

Lawrence, T. E. (1927, 1998). *Revolt in the desert.* Chesham: Combined Publishing.

McColl, R (1969). The insurgent state: Territorial bases of revolution. *Annals of the Association of American Geographers, 59*(4), 613–631.

Neff, S. (2005). *War and the law of nations: A general history.* Cambridge: Cambridge University Press.

Newman, Edward (2004). The 'new wars' debate: A historical perspective is needed. *Security Dialogue, 35*(2), 173–189.

Osakwe, Chukwuma C., & Umoh, Ubong Essien (2014). Private military contractors, war crimes and international humanitarian law. *Scientia Militaria: South African Journal of Military Studies, 42*(1), 64–79.

Chukwuma CC Osakwe

Schwarzenberger, Georg (1960). *A manual of international law* (4th ed.). London: Steven and Sons Limited.

Shaw, Malcom N. (2008). *International law.* Cambridge: Cambridge University Press.

Solis, G. D. (2010). *The law of armed conflict: International humanitarian law in war.* Cambridge: Cambridge University Press.

Thompson, Robert (1966). *Defeating communist insurgency.* New York: Praeger Publishers.

Trinquier, Roger. (1961). *Modern warfare: A French view of counterinsurgency.* Paris: Editions de la Table Ronde.

Tse-Tung, M. (1937, 1961). *On Guerrilla warfare.* Champaign: University of Illinois.

Tse-Tung, M. (1938, 1967). *On protracted war.* China: Foreign Language Press.

Tse-Tung, M. (1966). *Quotations from Chairman Mao Tse-tung (The little red book).* Peking: Peking Foreign Language Press.

United Nations High Commissioner for Refugees (UNHCR). (2000). *The state of the world's refugees: Fifty years of humanitarian action.* Oxford: Oxford University Press.

Wright, Quincy (1942). *A study of war.* Chicago: Chicago University Press.

# 10

# Information and communication technology, cyber-security and counterterrorism in Africa

*Francisca Nonyelum Ogwueleka and Aniche Delight Aniche*

## Introduction

Africa is the continent with the largest population of citizens within the youthful age bracket, with 200 million people (UNDP, 2017). Since the early 2000s, the activities and energies of the youth catalyse the demand and uptake in Information Communication Technology (ICT). They upset and create a shifting balance in the socio-economic structure and security configuration of societies across Africa in an unprecedented manner (Symantec and AU Commission, 2016). With poorly managed human and natural resources leaving poverty in its wake, this constellation of youthful energies in drove into the ICT sector – which, in Africa and most of the developing world, remains poorly managed and unregulated – exhibit increasing risk propensity and responsiveness to opportunities giving off a myriad of positive and negative effects, even while ICT development in the continent encounters many challenges on its path to maturity (UNDP, 2017).

While their responsiveness to opportunities is expanding the ICT ecosystem, setting it on its path to natural growth, their risk propensity prompts, as a matter of critical urgency, the close monitoring, understanding, exploration and mitigation of the rapidly evolving global cyber-security and cyber terrorism domains especially as they impact Africa (ITU, 2016). With the virtual lifestyle closing the gap with reality, more aspects of an average life increasingly depend on ICT hence adding more resource to the "Toolbox of Threat Actors" in a violent world, a fact alluded to by former United States President, Barack Obama in his 2015 speech on Cyber Security,

> ...one of the greatest paradoxes of our time is that the very technology that empower us to do great good can be used to undermine us and inflict great harm. The same ICT that help us make our military the most advanced in the world are targeted by hackers from China and Russia who go after our defence contractors and systems that are built for our troops. The same social media we use in government to advocate for democracy and human right around the world can also be used by terrorists to spread hateful ideologies, so these threats are a challenge to our National security (Caiazzo, 2015).

This phenomenon is exacerbated by the vague definitions and interpretations of the various branches of "Security", which are beginning to converge or relate deeply with ICT and Cyber Security (UNDP, 2017). Even with expanding advantage for Threat Actors, thanks to ICT, existing evidence tilts the balance in favour of the enormous benefits of ICT in many other areas. This perhaps crystallises that the only logical path to a solution in the shifting socio-economic structure and security configuration of societies – made possible in part by the emergence of ICT – leads in the direction of living with but guarding against the impact of the expanding advantages of Threat Actors in the digital era through the instrumentality of ICT, cybersecurity and counterterrorism rooted in well-articulated technical principles, policy framework (legislation), and cooperation.

Besides the contribution of ICT to the "Toolbox of Threat Actors", the existing socio-economic structure, power balance and security configurations across Africa are laden with injustice, depravity, ignorance, weak institutions, and leadership failure. These unfortunate but salvageable realities have become, in addition to the potentials of ICT, significant mobilisation instruments towards the endless security misfortunes of most African societies (Yonazi et al., 2014). Appreciating these factors and their roles is critical to expanding the discussion for a meaningful understanding and possible anticipation of the maturity direction of ICT, Cyber Security and Cyber Terrorism ecosystem in Africa, and for viable ICT-driven Counterterrorism and Security approach, policies and norms that can mitigate both physical and virtual threats.

This Chapter presents a conceptualisation of ICT, Cyber Security and Cyber Terrorism to guide the understanding of their rising significance in the 21st century. It also provides a background on ICT, Cyber Security and Cyber Terrorism development in Africa by discussing the emerging ICT and cybersecurity ecosystem in Africa comparing existing infrastructures, architecture, gaps, and geographic maturity to developed countries. The Chapter further reviews existing trends and implications of ICT and Cyber Security in a violent world considering the various instruments of mobilisation as well as the role of different digital platforms in various global security crises. The Chapter also traces the deficits of Science, Technology, ICT and Cyber Security in Africa, highlighting existing whitespaces, anticipated growth and the way forward for Africa's ICT, Cyber Security and ICT-Driven Counterterrorism in a violent world. Finally, the chapter offers some policy blueprints for transforming and improving Africa's preparedness for counterterrorism and counterinsurgency through ICT and cybersecurity. There is scope for ICT to provide a robust platform for boosting Africa's resilience against terrorism, organised violence, and cyber-crime.

## Conceptualisation: ICT, cyber security and cyber-terrorism

The sudden burst of computerisation combined with the rapid spread of the internet and the never-ending pursuit for improved quality of life is continuously revolutionising the way we live. This precipitated a diversity of socio-technical realities and threat vectors unimaginable in the recent past, through the daily online movement of 200 billion devices, fallen entry requirements for cyber threats actors with burgeoning dark web communities, and unending evolution of applications and products with rapid innovation (Matthew, 2014). ICT had been hailed in many quarters as the solution to many challenging developmental problems. Whether or not it has lived up to this reputation is an ongoing debate. However, it has been observed that ICT has catalysed developments along unpredicted paths, which has been influenced by erratic events of different scales and actors of various interests. The wide range of ICT applications and rapid evolution has made its definition and conceptualisation inconsistent to all its fields of application but rather a changing concept continuously shaped by technical development and social context as seen by the different lenses of various stakeholders (Gehem, Usanov, Frinking, & Rademaker, 2015).

Generically, Information and Communication Technologies (ICT) may be defined as an extended-term for Information Technology (IT), which stresses the role of unified communication and integration of telecommunications computers as well as necessary enterprise software, middleware storage, and audio-visual systems enabling users to access, store, transmit, and manipulate information (ITU, 2007). However, a worthy point to ponder is, "how much of these sectors and interests see ICT from the same lens?" Any befitting ICT concept aligns with one or more of its many facets, perceptions, and varying impact on the various society segments. Such an integrated approach fosters an appreciation of technology as a vital socio-cultural concept. It reveals the importance of the growing interest in cybersecurity and cyber terrorism and helps identify the various constructs with which ICT can be characterised or conceptualised (Sawyer & Chen, 2002).

The erratic events such as 911, rapid technological innovation and prototyping and the shifting boundaries of normality as we know them, actors of varying interests such as repressive regimes, state actors, hacktivists, businesses, researchers etc., and societal contexts are factors of enormous influence in the uptake and use of ICT hence the segmented concepts that may be held of ICT. To different professions (stakeholders), the primary objectives or minimum requirements of these representations differ – along the line of events, actors and contexts that influence them. For instance, a government reaching its citizens using ICT and exacting control may view ICT artefacts in the hands of the citizens, as a tool for governance hence will want everyone to have access. The activists venting ideological change often in collision with authorities will appreciate it more as a useful instrument of mobilisation, which everyone should access with enough privacy and anonymity. The cybercriminal will possibly conceptualise it as the channel to extend his/her reach and perpetuate his/her illegality on unsuspecting victims hence may wish that only the vulnerable have access. At the same time, the law enforcement arm of a repressive regime will prefer fewer citizens to have access for fear of utilising it to checkmate government authorities. For every stakeholder, the professional or social domain inclinations of such a stakeholder shape their conceptualisation of what ICT should embody making it difficult to untangle the various conceptual strands without a systematic approach (Sawyer & Huang, 2007; UN, 2011).

In the light of the disparity in what ICT meant and the need for a systematic approach, Sawyer (2000) identified five generalised approaches to representing ICT conceptualisation with sublevel forms or constructs. The characterisations are namely, feature or tool view, functional or ensemble view, proxy view, proof of concept view, and presence/absence view. The *feature* or *tool view* is the common or received view of ICT, which characterises ICT to operate as designed to behave. The *functional* or *ensemble view* is the socio-technical appreciation of ICT. Characterisation of ICT in this view reveals the interdependence of people and specific ICT artefacts connected through roles, use of information and action. The *proxy view* is that some often-quantified surrogates like penetration, spending or awareness, can capture or measure the value of ICT. *Presence/Absence or Nominal View* is an approach were ICT characterisation is implicit. In this view, features, functions, models, and proxy of ICT are not defined but named. *Proof of Concept View* is an approach that characterises ICT as a construct of what it can do.

While most of the western world has projected ICT as an enabler for good governance, many African governments see it as a threat to their tight-fisted regime as seen in the over 40-day internet outage in Cameroun earlier in 2017. Others see ICT as both the key and barrier to development and as a black hole into which every inefficiency can be blamed and every excuse flushed (James, 2017). It is, therefore, essential to note that even in a rapidly changing world with changing socio-cultural context, events and interests; extending beyond our current limitations and expressing the creative potentials in us through and into creative solutions that satisfy our goals are sacrosanct in our characterisation and conceptualisation of ICT.

The word "security" in general usage is synonymous with "being safe", but as a technical term "security" means not only that something is secure, but that it has been secured. Therefore, cybersecurity is concerned with making cyberspace safe from threats, particularly cyber-threats. Cybersecurity is defined as the proactive and reactive processes working toward the ideal of being free from threats to the confidentiality, integrity, or availability of the computers, networks, and information that form part of, and together constitute cyberspace. The authors, however, offer their definition of Cybersecurity as – "A general term that refers to the theatre of possibilities, processes, practices and actions; for organising offensive/pre-emptive ICT enabled strategies against and/or for computer systems, network systems, information systems, people, processes, natural/accidental events and technology, and for organising defensive strategies against natural/accidental occurrences, computer-facilitated/induced violations, abuses, crime and other malicious activities" Cybersecurity is a complex field, combining domains as diverse as information security, network security, system security, cyber hygiene, cyber laws/legislations, social context, critical infrastructure protection, national security, cybercrime, cyber-terrorism and cyber-warfare. Cybersecurity thus encompasses computer security, information security, ICT security, network security, infrastructure protection and more. In line with the notion of information security, cybersecurity is concerned with the protection against threats to the confidentiality, integrity, and availability of information or data. Still, it is not worried about information as a threat in "itself" as such, i.e., with information that poses a risk - *qua* information, such as hate speech or revenge porn. This distinguishes the concept from the broader notion of cyber safety, which also encompasses risks constituted by the informational content of the data processed within cyberspace (Samantha et al., 2015).

Cybersecurity has progressively advanced from the confined realm of technical experts into the political limelight. With events such as the discovery of the nuclear-industry sabotaging *Stuxnet* computer worm, numerous tales of cyber espionage by foreign states, the growing dependence on the "digital infrastructure" along with the sophistication of cybercriminals and the well-publicised activities of hackers' collectives, the impression is created that cyber-attacks are becoming more frequent, more organised, more costly and altogether more dangerous. As a result, a growing number of countries consider cybersecurity to be one of their top security issues (Dunn Cavelty, 2012). After 2010, the tone and intensity of the debate changed even further: the latest trend is to frame cybersecurity in strategic-military terms and to focus on countermeasures such as cyber-offence and cyber-defence, or cyber-deterrence (Dunn Cavelty, 2012).

In current discussions on cybersecurity, there is a focus on critical infrastructure due to increasing dependence of societies on the smooth functioning of all sorts of computer-related applications and ICT artefacts such as software-based control systems – a combination of vulnerabilities, technology and transnational interdependence. There is an increased focus on states as the primary cyber "enemy", coining the term cyber-espionage as well as an increase in "hacktivism", a portmanteau combining hacking and activism and denoting a phenomenon of deliberately challenging the self-proclaimed power of states to keep information considered vital for national security secret (e.g. *Wikileaks*, hacker collectives such as *Anonymous* and *LulzSec*). There is also recognition for what may be described as a process of "cross-fertilisation" of cyber-threats and terrorism, where cyber-threats support the claims to the dangerous nature of the terrorists and the terrorist character of the attacks makes them more worthy of attention (Dunn Cavelty, 2012).

In addition, the public discourses that tout the potential effects of cyber-attacks as disruptive, crippling, and devastating in the increasingly networked societies, interconnected economies and national securities are becoming critical influencer to cybersecurity conceptualisation. A factor of immense impact to the African narrative of cybersecurity conceptualisation is the rapid proliferation of mobile devices that has extended the prevalent traditional fraud of the 90s and the convergence lifestyle they promote (Marco, 2015). This class of economic fraud which got its street name from the 419 Article of the Nigerian Criminal Code that addressed it, is one of the early instances of Social Engineering and is now aided in leaps and bound by the rapid proliferation of mobile devices with little or no compensation in digital education for ICT adopters in Africa. With over 80% mobile penetration between 2000 and 2009 in Africa many previously personal activities have since been taken online and into the mobile devices (Caiazzo, 2015). This in many ways, positively and negatively tints the lens with which we interact with ICT and interpret the concept of cybersecurity considering how convenient and as well vulnerable it makes life especially in the absence of necessary infrastructure, institutions and policies for the ICT user protection characterising the teething African cybersecurity ecosystem (Gehem et al., 2015).

Barry Collin, a senior research fellow at the Institute for Security and Intelligence in California was the first to coin the term "cyber-terrorism" in 1997. He defined it as the convergence of "cybernetics" and "terrorism" (Fischer, Rollins, & Theophany, 2014). Professor Dorothy Denning described it as the convergence of terrorism and cyberspace, and this is by far the most cited definition (Denning, 2000). James Lewis defined cyber terrorism as "the use of computer network tools to shut down critical national infrastructures or to coerce or intimidate a government or civilian population" (Lourdeau, 2004). The US Federal Bureau of Investigation (FBI) defined the whole concept of terrorism as "the unlawful use of force or violence against persons or property to intimidate or coerce; a government, the civilian population, or any segment thereof, in furtherance of political or social objectives" (Jessica, 2016).

Cyber terrorism shares a lot of primary attributes with traditional terrorism. In breaking down the concepts of cyber terrorism to its fundamental elements, there are at least five elements, which must be satisfied to construe cyber terrorism.

i. Political motivation for the cyberattacks and should lead to death or bodily injury.
ii. Fear element and/or physical harm through cyberattack techniques.
iii. Attacks must be severe attacks and against critical information infrastructures such as financial, energy, transportation, and government operations.
iv. Attacks that only disrupts non–essential services are not considered cyber terrorism.
v. The attacks must not primarily be focused on monetary gain.

Cyber terrorism includes warfare attacks against a nation state and forcing ICT infrastructure and assets to fail or to destroy them. The objective is to create fear within a target population where monetary gain is not the focus. Based on the nature of a borderless world, challenges that the authorities may face are a clear line of cyber terrorism activities, technical impediments, legislative aspect, enforcement and prosecution of internet offenders, and public-private partnership (Zahri & Syahrul, 2017).

## ICT and cyber-security in a violent world

The terrorist attacks of key institutions in the United States on 11 September 2001 (popularly known as 9/11) marked a turning point in world history and the beginning of the 'War on Terror'.

The attacks killed an estimated 3000 people, making it the deadliest terrorist incident in human history. Subsequently, the War on Terror led to the invasion of Afghanistan in 2001 and Iraq in 2003. Hitherto, "Terrorism" defined as the use or threat of violence to further a political cause, which historians believe dates back to the days of Judas of Galilee leader of the Zealots and a key influencer on the Sicarii Jewish terrorist organisation in the 1st century AD, was not an issue of critical global attention. Modern terrorism took life after the Second World War as nationalist movements rose across old empires of the European powers and discovered the ability of terrorism to generate publicity for the cause and influence global policy.

From the chart in Figure 10.1, it would be observed that terrorism took centre stage post-9/11 attacks on the World Trade Centre and attempted attacks on the Pentagon and other vital infrastructure in the United States, as terrorism incidents spiked post-9/11. The interconnectedness of the 21st century associated with globalisation exacerbated this outcome by adding a technological capacity to the terrorist arsenal. Terrorists use ICT tools to communicate, recruit, spread terrorist ideology, raise, and move fund etc. without detection or hindrance. Two broad approaches to terrorism are peculiar and defined by ICT and Cyber Security. The first involves the use of ICT in perpetrating terrorist attacks and the second centres on the exploitation of ICT security vulnerabilities in perpetrating terrorist attacks.

Most of the attacks under the first category like the use of ICT to disseminate terrorist propaganda, recruit members, mobilise and move funds, exchange information even to the point of using ICT to build and/or control their instrument of assault may not qualify as cyberterrorism or even cyber threat. For instance, in the 9/11 attack, terrorists used ICT in preparing the attacks and controlling the aeroplanes to crash into the World Trade Centre. On the other

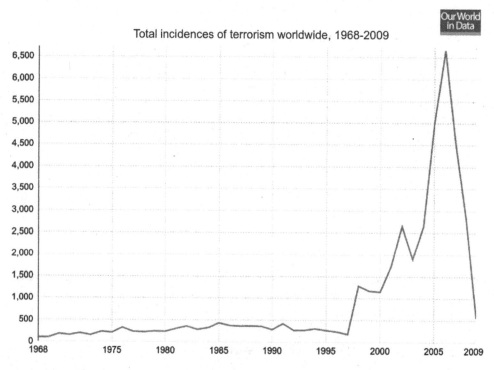

*Figure 10.1* Chart on Global Terrorist Incidences from 1968 – 2009
Source: RAND Database of Worldwide Terrorism Incidents – Our World in Data

hand, most of the attacks under the second category qualify as cyber terrorism, involving the exploitation of security vulnerabilities in information systems often using cyber means. Other means such as social engineering, physical theft or coercion can be employed but solely for advancing the cyber means (Jessica, 2016). Table 10.1 shows the pre and post 9/11 terrorist attacks by country

With pervasive penetration of ICT access around the world as shown in Table 10.2, and increasing dependency in information system over high-speed networks, the cyberspace has become a vital extension of our physical reality and activities in them and their attendant consequences are now more synchronised and inseparable from the physical world. This has amplified the impact of any vulnerability, which of course is intrinsically unavoidable. This brought a very new dimension to the subject of terrorism and violence, which has since gotten many siblings including Religious Extremism and Militancy. ICT permeation and inter-connected societies have so lowered the bar of terrorism that single

Table 10.2 shows the Internet Demographic Data of the interconnected world for 2015.

individual or few groups of people has the capacity to bring a nation on its knee by replacing the requirement for the huge fund, workforce etc., with a few computer and lines of codes, sometimes yanked off the internet.

The emergence of cyberattacks and even the term "cyber-terrorism" predates 9/11. Exploits in this period were motivated initially by the urge to impress (pranks by pranksters) then by financial gains. While the motivation for financial gain still holds sway for hackers, a third and fourth motivating factor has added two more groups to the pile: the "hacktivists" and "ter-rorists". Just like the physical world activists, in pursuing their goal the hacktivists are motivated by the need for change and employs nonviolent tactics such as Denial of Service (DoS), Distributed Denial of Service (DDoS), Website Defacing, Leaking of State Secrets etc. Terrorist and Violent Extremists' tactics focus on the use of violence and are motivated by the urge to destroy, intimidate, and kill. The Global Terrorism Index has also noted that religious ex-tremism has overtaken national separatism to become the main motivation of terrorist attacks around the world (George, 2014; Joshi, Ghafoor, Aref, & Spafford, 2002).

In 2010, a coordinated DDoS used millions of infected zombie computers to attack websites of mainstream media organisations like the Sun News online and they were unavailable for hours. On July 21, 2014, hackers, leaving behind a series of nasty tweets, infiltrated the Twitter

Table 10.1 Pre and Post 9/11 Terrorist Attacks by Country

| Rank | 1970 to 9/10/2001 Country | % of All Attacks | 9/11/2001 to 2008 Country | % of All Attacks |
|------|---------|------------------|---------|------------------|
| 1 | Columbia | 8.8 | Iraq | 25.77 |
| 2 | Peru | 8.35 | India | 9.48 |
| 3 | El Salvador | 7.38 | Afghanistan | 9.03 |
| 4 | Northern Ireland | 5.13 | Pakistan | 7.63 |
| 5 | India | 4.61 | Thailand | 5.84 |
| 6 | Spain | 4.14 | Philippines | 3.85 |
| 7 | Turkey | 3.49 | Russia | 3.65 |
| 8 | Chile | 3.15 | Colombia | 3.22 |
| 9 | SriLanka | 3.03 | Israel | 2.89 |
| 10 | Philippines | 2.96 | Nepal | 2.55 |

Source: RAND Database of Worldwide Terrorism Incidents – Our World in Data.

*Table 10.2* Internet Demographic Data, 2015

| An interconnected world | |
|---|---|
| World population | 7.345 billion (1) |
| Number of Internet users in the world | 3.2 billion (2) |
| Number of Internet users in Africa | 330.9 million (3) |
| Number of mobile devices in the world | 7 billion (4) |
| Internet penetration rate in Europe | 70% (5) |
| Internet penetration rate in Africa | 28.6% (6) |
| Number of cyber-attacks neutralised by Kaspersky in Africa in the first quarter of 2014 | 49 million (7) |
| Number of active Facebook users per month | 1.65 billion (8) |
| Monthly number of Google searches | 100 billion (9) |
| Daily number of Tweets | 500 million (10) |
| Number of mobile subscribers in Africa | 311 million (11) |
| Number of email transactions per day | 215 billion (12) |
| *General Internet and demographic data* | |

*Source:* Cybersecurity in Africa -Facts and Figures.

account of the Kenya Defence Forces (KDF). The hacktivist group "Anonymous" claimed responsibility and broke into the account of KDF spokesperson Maj Emmanuel Chirchir. Earlier, they had defaced the website of the National Environment Trust Fund under the Ministry of Environment (Dipolelo, 2016). In 2015, Anonymous Senegal attacked the sites of the State Information Technology Agency (ADIE) and of the Ministry of Livestock and Animal Production.

The 2015 Security Summit held in Johannesburg – positioned South Africa as the most attacked country on the African continent in 2015 and revealed a 150% DDOS attacks during 2014 – 2015 in Africa – and these attacks occur where multiple compromised systems, usually infected with a Trojan, are used to target a single system causing valuable downtime to assets like websites. Techniques and malware like worms, obfuscators and injectors, backdoors, viruses, trojans, and ransomware were used in these attacks (Serianu Cyber Threat Intelligence Team, 2016). The three levels of cyberterror capability are defined by Monterey Group (Gehem et al., 2015) as simple-unstructured, advanced-structured, and complex-coordinated. Simple-unstructured refers to the capability to conduct basic hacks against individual systems using tools created by someone else. Advanced-structured has the capability to conduct more sophisticated attacks against multiple systems or networks and to modify or create basic hacking tools. Complex-coordinated has the capability for a coordinated attack capable of causing mass disruption against integrated heterogeneous defences including cryptography.

The cyberspace is expanding not only for cyber terrorists who of course pose a serious threat to peace everywhere in the world but also for cybercriminals, whose activities are estimated to be costing the world close to $1 trillion annually. This group employs diverse methods and tools like malware, viruses, hacking, scams, fraud, and theft to prey on their victim (Caiazzo, 2015). According to Microsoft's Digital Crimes Unit (DCU), there are nearly 400 million victims of cybercrime each year. India, followed by Pakistan, Egypt, Brazil, Algeria, and Mexico, have the largest number of infected machines involving malware developed outside Eastern Europe. In Africa, as internet penetration deepens, though there is inadequate availability of data to ac-curately measure the impact or control of cybercrime, a report by the cybersecurity firm

Kaspersky states that more than 49 million cyberattacks took place in the continent during the first three months of 2014, most of them in Algeria, Egypt, South Africa, and Kenya. It is a common notion that the continent is a safe haven for cybercriminals given the high rate of ICT penetration in the continent, the high level of ignorance, the lack of necessary legal framework and institution, and the lack of skilled cybersecurity manpower (Dipolelo, 2016).

The cybersecurity firm Kaspersky Lab in 2015, also detected 884,774 new malware programs. This means a threefold increase in 2014 (285,539). Though the number of new banking trojans has decreased to 16,586, 94,344 unique users were victims of mobile ransomware attacks. This figure is five times higher in 2014 when it was 18,478 (Ponemon Institute, 2016).

## Africa's emerging ICT and cybersecurity infrastructure

It is difficult to think of any sphere of life that is yet to be embedded with ICT. The explosive computerisation of the 21st century is revolutionising humanity in a profound way; shaping creation, access, use, processing and preservation of information and its ancillary resources and rendering traditional approach to these activities inept (Daniel & Samantha, 2016). The digital revolution is possible because of various novel inventions and scientific principles that have perfected the representation, manipulation, and transmission of information. While the developed world is in front of these inventions and innovations and is, therefore, interconnected with a retinue of necessary infrastructure, most of the developing world struggle in this respect. Even at two decades of near-stagnation, Africa's growth performance has also improved hugely, at a faster rate than most developed countries, since the start of the 21st century with a strong medium-term growth prospect at 4.8% and 5.2% in 2013 and 2014 respectively and Africa is home to most of the world's fasters growing economies (Economic Commission for Africa, 2013).

This growth in the continent is no doubt attributable to the expanding middle class and youthful population receptive to an increasingly digitised lifestyle. This was confirmed by the World Bank and the International Telecommunications Union (ITU) estimates which reveal that mobile penetration in the telecommunication segment rose from 16% for urban population at the end of the 1990s to 90% by 2009. Rural coverage came close to 50% within the same period with an average of 63% in 2013, and more than 26.1% of the population as of 2016 are hooked up to the Internet for their everyday activity (Mark, Rebecca, & Michael, 2011; ITU, 2016). ICT is deeply permeating every facet of the society in the continent at an impressive rate with increasing quality of service and price reduction (Randeep et al., 2010).

In an era of the knowledge economy, ICT is seen as the game-changer for Africa with respect to its numerous developmental problems (UN, 2011). Leveraging the youthful demography of the African population, the sector has had an impressive run seeing what was recently considered technological infrastructure for very wealthy organisation become vital social infrastructures. The strides of many African countries especially Kenya and Nigeria with companies like Safaricom, MTN, Globacom, Multi-choice, Konga, Omatek and products like M-Pesa, Interswitch, DSTv, Ushahidi and many more have been remarkable in maturing the African ICT ecosystem (Daniel & Samantha, 2016; Jean & Amzath, 2016). Some of them has gone on to claim a market niche at the global stage.

Experts estimate is that 80% of PCs in Africa are infected with malware of different categories. It is also a fact that 18 adults are victims of cyberattacks every second around the globe amounting to 1.5 million victims annually. The 2012 Symantec Report says that Africa experienced 42% increase in cybercrime with 80% of South African adult population victims of cybercrime making South Africa the third in the number of cybercrime victims globally below Russia and China (Ponemon Institute, 2016).

Over 31% of the cyberattacks in Africa are cyber espionage against small and large businesses and Nigeria is the target and source of most of the malicious cyberattacks and internet activities in Africa with negative ripple effects in other West African countries (Serianu Cyber Threat Intelligence Team, 2016). Other increasing negative trends of expanding digital exposure of the African continent is the internet facilitated kidnapping, financial fraud, cyber-terrorism, and cyber-enabled terrorism (Quarshie & Martin-Odoom, 2012).

These emerging threats have attracted public outcry in many quarters. Recently the Nigerian Minister of Communication Technology added his voice by calling on African leaders to act, warning that if nothing is done, it will have an untold effect on economic growth, foreign investment, and security. The Central Bank of Nigeria has revealed that Nigerian banks lost over N159 billion to electronic fraud and cybercrime between 2000 and 2013, bank customers lost N6 billion in 2014 whereas their South African counterparts lost more than N8 billion (Nigerian Communication Week, 2014).

The adoption of ICT in the planning, coordination, execution, and promotion of terror by terrorist groups in Africa is another disturbing dimension in the negative uptake of ICT and Cybersecurity challenges in Africa. Evidence from an investigation into recent activities of Boko Haram in Nigeria, the Westgate Mall attack in Kenya and Al-Qaeda in Islamic Maghreb (AQIM) in Northern Africa bears credence to this trend (Abdisaid, 2016).

These unchecked and undesirable cyber norms across Africa are making an untold impact on the economy of the region. Many of these negative norms have become normalised and rationalised even by the masses that bear the brunt. It is common for users across Africa to go to the market and buy copies of pirated software, movies, music, or books. The irony is that even software companies and authors working awfully hard on their own products and hoping to make revenue from them are also very guilty of this sin. Hence, Africa has a very booming piracy market with about 73% piracy rate and a revenue loss of over 1.7 billion USD according to a 2011 report by the Business Software Alliance. The pirated unsupported software are major contributors to the malware problems of the region.

To worsen the trend, many governments of African nations with a good level of enthusiasm are stepping up ICT adoption policies and infrastructure development initiatives to respond to the growing demand of ICT uptake with little or no understanding and recourse to the interactions of key factors influencing ICT, Cybersecurity and Cyberterrorism development in their national contexts while many others are doing nothing at all (Mark et al., 2011). This subjective and erratic approach by African leaders to the policy formulation of ICT and Cybersecurity norms is vastly different from the co-ordinated, well-articulated, and integrated strategies of other regions (Marco, 2015). To alleviate this confusion and provide standardised indicators for ICT development, the International Telecommunication Union defined a framework, the ICT Development Index (IDI), for measuring and standardising ICT development in countries and mapping the impact to stakeholders' efforts (ITU, 2016). The composite index is designed to measure the following:

- the level and evolution over time of ICT developments within countries and the experience of those countries relative to others;
- progress in ICT development in both developed and developing countries;
- the digital divide, that is, the differences between countries in terms of their levels of ICT development; and

- the development potential of ICTs and the extent to which countries can make use of them to enhance growth and development in the context of available capabilities and skills (ITU, 2016).

The Index helps depict ICT readiness, reflecting the level of networked infrastructure and access to ICTs, ICT intensity reflecting the level of use of ICTs in the society, and ICT impact reflecting the results/outcomes of more efficient and effective ICT use and is composed of three sub-indices, and eleven indicators;

- *Access sub-index*: This sub-index captures ICT readiness comprising five infrastructure and access indicators (fixed-telephone subscriptions, mobile-cellular telephone subscriptions, international Internet bandwidth per Internet user, households with a computer, and households with Internet access).
- *Use sub-index*: This sub-index captures ICT intensity comprising three intensity and usage indicators (individuals using the Internet, fixed broadband subscriptions, and mobile-broadband subscriptions).
- *Skills sub-index*: This sub-index seeks to capture capabilities or skills, which are important for ICTs comprising three proxy indicators (mean years of schooling, gross secondary enrolment, and gross tertiary enrolment). As these are proxy indicators, rather than indicators directly measuring ICT-related skills, the skills sub-index is given less weight in the computation of the IDI than the other two sub-indices.

Using this index and Global Cybersecurity Index, a graphical representation of the continent's ICT and Cybersecurity development and maturity in comparison to the world is presented. Figure 10.2 illustrates the interaction of the different factors and infrastructure in the ICT ecosystem.

The indicators captured and measured under each of the sub-index.

a). *ICT infrastructure and access indicators*

Indicators included in this group provide an indication of the available ICT infrastructure and individuals' access to basic ICTs and include:

1. Fixed-telephone subscriptions per 100 inhabitants.
2. Mobile-cellular telephone subscriptions per 100 inhabitants.

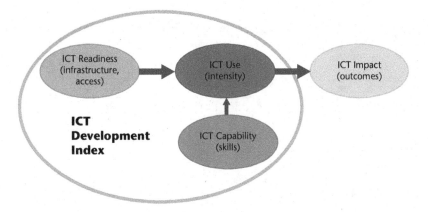

*Figure 10.2*  Three Stages in the Evolution towards an Information Society
*Source:* International Telecommunication Union IDI Conceptual Framework and Methodology

    3.   International Internet bandwidth (bit/s) per Internet user.

    4.   Percentage of households with a computer.

    5.   Percentage of households with Internet access.

b). *ICT use indicators*

    1.   Percentage of individuals using the Internet.

    2.   Fixed-broadband subscriptions per 100 inhabitants.

    3.   Active mobile-broadband subscriptions per 100 inhabitants.

c). *ICT skills indicators*

    1.   Mean years of schooling rate.

    2.   Gross enrolment ratio at the secondary level.

    3.   Gross enrolment ratio in tertiary level.

The indicators were carefully and rigorously normalised and rescale against a reference value as shown in Table 10.3 for straightforward comprehension of the contribution of the various indicators and sub-index in measuring ICT development around the world.

    Africa's ICT development status against developed countries, despite many gains and a growth rate that is highest among other regions, can be best described as extremely poor given its demographic realities. Figure 10.3 illustrates this poor performance by contrasting Africa's performance under various indicators with the rest of the world. Figure 10.4 shows the ICT Development Index scores of various regions including Africa. In Figures 10.5 and 10.6 charts, the national ICT profile of the world ICT best-performing country (Korea) with IDI score of 8.78 and Africa's ICT best-performing country (Mauritius) with IDI score of 5.55 and number 73 globally was shown respectively. Figures 10.7 and 10.8 charts present the national ICT profile of one of the world's largest economy (the United States of America) with IDI score of

*Table 10.3* ICT Development Index – Indicators, Reference Values and Weight

| ICT access | Reference value | (%) |
|---|---|---|
| 1. Fixed-telephone subscriptions per 100 inhabitants | 60 | 20 |
| 2. Mobile-cellular telephone subscriptions per 100 inhabitants | 120 | 20 |
| 3. International Internet bandwith (bit/s) per internet user | 976'696* | 20 |
| 4. Percentage of households with a computer | 100 | 20 |
| 5. Percentage of households with Internet access | 100 | 20 |
| **ICT use** | **Reference value** | **(%)** |
| 6. Percentage of individuals using the Internet | 100 | 33 |
| 7. Fixed-broadband subscriptions per 100 inhabitants | 60 | 33 |
| 8. Active mobile-broadband subscriptions per 100 inhabitants | 100 | 33 |
| **ICT skills** | **Reference value** | **(%)** |
| 9. Mean years of schooling | 15 | 33 |
| 10. Secondary gross enrolment ratio | 100 | 33 |
| 11. Tertiary gross enrolment ratio | 100 | 33 |

ICT access — 40
ICT use — 40
ICT skills — 20

ICT Development Index

*Source:* ITU IDI Conceptual Framework

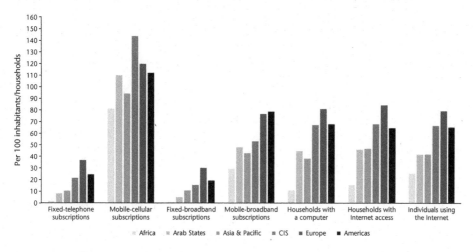

*Figure 10.3*   Chart of ICT Regional Penetration Status 2016
*Source:* ITU Measuring the Information Society Report 2016

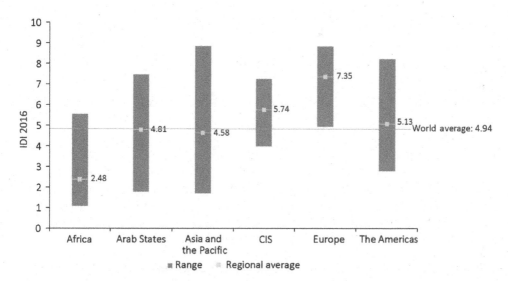

*Figure 10.4*   Chart of IDI Average Score by Region compared with Global Average
*Source:* ITU Measuring the Information Society Report 2016

8.17, number 1 regionally and number 15 globally, and the national ICT profile of one of Africa's largest economy (Nigeria) with IDI score of 2.72, number 14 regionally and 137 globally.

In the cybersecurity front, cyber confidence is an essential prerequisite of a functioning information society based on digital technology and the path to harnessing its transformational power for development. The ITU Global Cybersecurity Index (GCI) Framework identified five areas of activities that are used in combination with the GCI to measure a country's cybersecurity commitment and development. These areas, which forms the basis of cybersecurity indicators, include Legal Measures, Technical Measures, Organisational Measures,

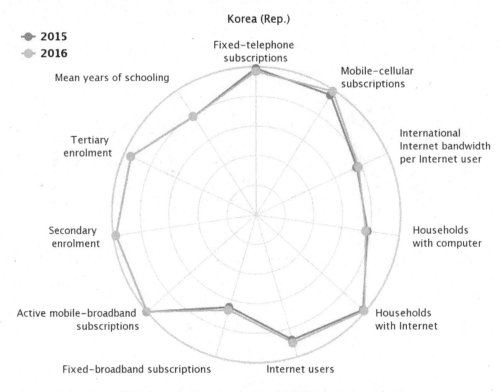

*Figure 10.5* Chart of IDI Country Card for the World ICT Best Performing Country
*Source:* World Telecommunication/ICT Indicators Database 2016

Capacity Building and Cooperation. Under these areas, African nations generally trail behind their counterparts in other regions of the world. The 2014 Global Cybersecurity Index and Cyber Wellness Profile reveal that many African nations lack certain baseline infrastructure: a legislative framework that provides harmonious behaviour and regulation for entities in the cybersecurity ecosystem; national technical institutions, standards and certifications; organisational structure with competent policies, governance roadmap, responsible agency and national benchmarking procedure; capacity-building strategy in cybersecurity and cooperation with other countries. The 2014 GCI scores where the United States led the world with 0.824 GCI score and the best African countries (Egypt and Mauritius) came behind 29 other countries with 0.588 GCI scores each reinforced this condition.

## IT-driven counterterrorism and cyber-security policy in Africa

According to expert estimate, the global cost of cybercrime to the world economy is US $ 500 billion, which is about the GDP of Nigeria (521.8 billion dollars), Africa's largest economy. The Nigerian economy loses heavily to the scourge of cybercrime estimated to be costing the country US $ 500 million every year (Ponemon Institute, 2016; Jean & Amzath, 2016). The United Nation's definition of cybercrime covers any illegal behaviour directed by means of electronic operations targeting the security of computer systems and the data processed by them. This obviously goes beyond the emails scam phenomenon of the notorious "yahoo boys" of Nigeria to a host of other illegal activities using ultra-sophisticated means (Gehem et al., 2015).

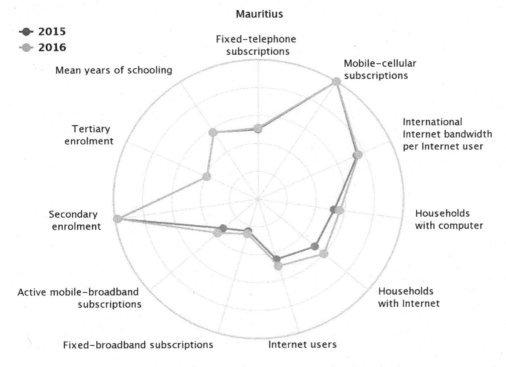

*Figure 10.6* Chart of IDI Country Card for Africa ICT Best Performing Country
*Source:* World Telecommunication/ICT Indicators Database 2016

Following the contours of challenges confronting Africa's distinctive digital cultures, it is easy to recognise that cybersecurity and cyber resilience are not simply technical problems that respond to advanced technical solutions as the case in advanced nations attempt to suggest (Fischer et al., 2014). Contrarily and by comparing data on ICT penetration measured by the proportion of mobile phone subscription in the country and its population, to its GDP per capita for countries like Mali, Malawi and Madagascar on one end of digital penetration ranking in Africa and Ethiopia at the other end, the correlation between ICT penetration and economic growth becomes skewed revealing the unique and unprecedented case of African ICT and Cybersecurity ecosystem inherently shaped by political footprints (ITU, 2016). Without adequate check and balances, increasing securitisation of domestic and international politics and cybersecurity policies may require a costly trade-off of individual and collective freedoms (James, 2017).

Besides the digital divide, the inimitable interaction of the technical, social, and political factors produces distinctive outcomes that foster the many deviations in Africa's ICT and Cyber Security experience. For instance, average internet penetration in Africa in 2015 was 27% while North America was 86%. However, the internet growth rate in Africa from 2000 to 2015 was 6,958% while it was just 187% in North America. When facts like this are transposed with the 38% illiteracy rate reality in the continent, different conceptualisations and approaches like emulation, extraversion and enculturation to ICT and its attendant cybersecurity characterisations begin to emerge (ITU, 2016; Gehem et al., 2015).

Current trends in cybersecurity and counterterrorism drive the maturity of these fields with a more holistic and comprehensive approach etched into National Cybersecurity Strategies of the

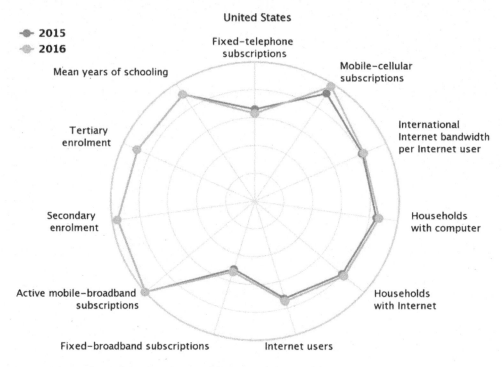

*Figure 10.7* Chart of IDI Country Card for one of the World's Largest Economy
*Source:* World Telecommunication/ICT Indicators Database 2016

given country. Regional communities are not left out as more regional powers like the EU takes the front seat in championing effective cybersecurity and counterterrorism initiatives and policies (Orji, 2013). The Global Cybersecurity Index articulated five standard areas through which cybersecurity development can be guided and/or assessed. They include the Legal domain, Technical domain, Organisational Domain, Capacity Building, and Cooperation.

Using these priorities, a state's effort in cybersecurity development can be measured by looking at the achievements under each indicator. Cybersecurity efforts in Africa are still at the teething stage and stagnated by lack of capacity and political will even as reports suggest that lack of strong cybersecurity strategy is economically bleeding the continent through cybercrime and other nefarious cyber activities by cybercriminals.

The 2015 Global Cybersecurity Index and Cyber Wellness Profile Report depicts the regions cybersecurity efforts as below using the metrics previously defined. Table 10.4 is showing the level of efforts of the top 20 countries in the region in line with our defined metrics under legal, technical, organisational, capacity and cooperation domains with a total index score and ranking.

## Mauritius

Mauritius has the best cybersecurity outlook in Africa with an index score of 0.5882. Under the legal domain, the country has four legislation and two regulatory and compliance instruments. In the technical domain, the country has a functional Computer Emergency Response Team operating under the National Computer Board, a statutory body under the Ministry of

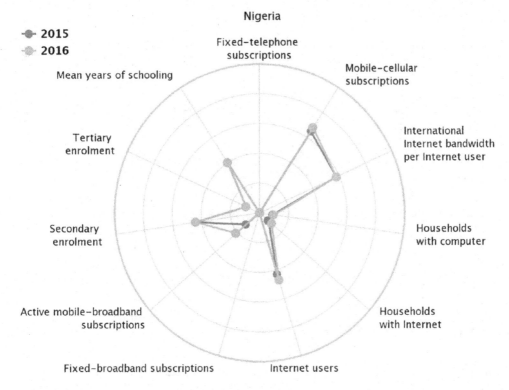

*Figure 10.8* Chart of IDI Country Card for one of Africa's Largest Economy
*Source:* World Telecommunication/ICT Indicators Database, 2016

Technology, Communication and Innovation, and has officially approved national and sector-specific cybersecurity frameworks for implementing internationally recognised cybersecurity standards. Cybersecurity strategy is included in NICTSP 2007–2011 and 2011–2014 and a new national cybersecurity Strategy and Action Plan has been developed. The National Information Assurance and Critical Information Infrastructure Protection Policy provide a national governance roadmap for cybersecurity.

## Nigeria

Nigeria ranks 4th in the regional ranking with an index score of 0.4412. The country has four legislations on cybersecurity but so far, no known regulatory and compliance instrument across the board. There is a functional Computer Emergency Response and Readiness Team under the Office of the National Security Adviser and a second one NGCERT is underway. The technical framework for cyber and information security is the officially recognised national and sector-specific cybersecurity framework for implementing internationally recognised cybersecurity standards. The Legal Framework for CIS Operational Procedure Manual for CIS is underway. The Computer Forensics Institute of Nigeria (CFIN) and the Association of Certified Cybersecurity Policy are the officially approved national cybersecurity frameworks for the certification and accreditation of national agencies and public sector professionals. The Office of the National Security Adviser has produced a draft of National Cybersecurity Strategy and provides National Cybersecurity Roadmap. Ministry of Communication Technology,

*Table 10.4* 2015 Global Cybersecurity Index and Cyber Wellness Profile Report of the Best 20 Performing Countries in Africa

| Country | Legal | Technical | Organisational | Capacity Building | Cooperation | Index | Ranking |
| --- | --- | --- | --- | --- | --- | --- | --- |
| Mauritius | 0.7500 | 0.6667 | 0.6250 | 0.5000 | 0.5000 | 0.5882 | 1 |
| Uganda | 0.7500 | 0.5000 | 0.8750 | 0.2500 | 0.5000 | 0.5588 | 2 |
| Rwanda | 1.0000 | 0.5000 | 0.5000 | 0.3750 | 0.5000 | 0.5294 | 3 |
| Nigeria | 0.2500 | 0.3333 | 0.5000 | 0.5000 | 0.5000 | 0.4412 | 4 |
| Cameroon | 0.7500 | 0.5000 | 0.3750 | 0.5000 | 0.1250 | 0.4118 | 5 |
| Kenya | 1.0000 | 0.3333 | 0.2500 | 0.2500 | 0.5000 | 0.4118 | 5 |
| South Africa | 0.2500 | 0.5000 | 0.6250 | 0.2500 | 0.2500 | 0.3824 | 6 |
| Burkina Faso | 0.0000 | 0.5000 | 0.7500 | 0.0000 | 0.2500 | 0.3235 | 7 |
| Ghana | 0.7500 | 0.3333 | 0.2500 | 0.2500 | 0.1250 | 0.2941 | 8 |
| Togo | 0.0000 | 0.3333 | 0.3750 | 0.2500 | 0.2500 | 0.2647 | 9 |
| Cote d'Ivoire | 0.7500 | 0.3333 | 0.1250 | 0.1250 | 0.1250 | 0.2353 | 10 |
| Liberia | 0.0000 | 0.0000 | 0.2500 | 0.3750 | 0.2500 | 0.2059 | 11 |
| Tanzania | 0.5000 | 0.3333 | 0.0000 | 0.1250 | 0.2500 | 0.2500 | 11 |
| Benin | 0.5000 | 0.0000 | 0.2500 | 0.1250 | 0.1250 | 0.1765 | 12 |
| Botswana | 0.7500 | 0.1667 | 0.2500 | 0.0000 | 0.0000 | 0.1765 | 12 |
| Malawi | 0.0000 | 0.0000 | 0.1250 | 0.3750 | 0.2500 | 0.1765 | 12 |
| Senegal | 1.0000 | 0.0000 | 0.1250 | 0.0000 | 0.1250 | 0.1765 | 12 |
| Zambia | 0.2500 | 0.3333 | 0.1250 | 0.1250 | 0.0000 | 0.1471 | 13 |
| Burundi | 0.2500 | 0.0000 | 0.1250 | 0.1250 | 0.1250 | 0.1176 | 14 |
| Seychelles | 0.7500 | 0.0000 | 0.0000 | 0.0000 | 0.1250 | 0.1176 | 14 |

*Source:* Global Cybersecurity Index

Office of the National Security Adviser, Nigerian Communications Commission, Economic and Financial Crimes Commission, National Information and Technology Development Agency are responsible for implementing the National Cybersecurity Strategy. Nigeria has 4 public sector professionals certified under internationally recognised certification programs in cybersecurity while the Central Bank is the only certified public sector organisation.

## South Africa

South Africa has four legislations on cybersecurity but no regulation and compliance instrument across the board. It has a functional Computer Incidence Response Team CIRT and officially recognised cybersecurity framework for implementing internationally recognised cybersecurity standards through the National Cybersecurity Policy Framework. The officially recognised body for certification and accreditation of public organisations and professionals is absent. South Africa has an officially recognised National Cybersecurity Policy Framework approved by the Cabinet in March 2012, to establish an environment that will ensure confidence and trust in the secure use of ICTs and there is an officially recognised National Cybersecurity Strategy, which the State Security Agency is responsible for implementing. There is no officially recognised benchmarking, standardisation development, workforce development or certified public sector professional or organisation.

## Continental framework: the African Union cybersecurity convention

In the regional front, the African Union Convention on Cyber Security and Personal Data Protection seeking to establish a Legal Framework for Cyber Security and Personal Data

Protection embodies the existing commitments of African Union Member States at sub-regional, regional and international levels to build the Information Society (Dotzauer, 2014). This crystallises the objectives and broad orientations of the Information Society in Africa and strengthens existing legislation on Information and Communication Technologies (ICTs) of the Member States and the Regional Economic Communities (RECs). It goes to address the need for harmonised legislation in the area of cybersecurity in Member States of the African Union, and to establish in each State party a mechanism capable of combating violations of privacy that may be generated by personal data collection, processing, transmission, storage and use; by proposing a type of institutional basis (Dotzauer, 2014). It also seeks substantive criminal law, to modernize instruments for the repression of cybercrime by formulating a policy for the adoption of new offences specific to ICTs, and aligning certain offences, sanctions and criminal liability systems in force in the Member States with the ICT environment (Orji, 2013).

The fact that the AU was able to establish a regional protocol on matters of cybersecurity despite differing opinions and concerns, is a significant development for Africa's digital eco-system given that the continent is often viewed as a safe haven for cybercriminals. The Convention addresses three key areas often seen as inadequately or not regulated at all by the governments in the region. They include electronic transactions, personal data protection, and cybersecurity and cybercrime.

## The deficits of science, technology, ICT and cyber-security in Africa

The incoherent and ineffective ICT, cybersecurity trends and policy drives in Africa are only symptoms of more endemic problems and failures than they are problems of their own. In the light of so much unorthodox ICT and cybersecurity development curve and leapfrogging being experienced in the continent, African ICT and cybersecurity realities defy models and templates obtainable in other climes and can be said to be unique and peculiar to the continent. This has precipitated the need for indigenous solutions devised with relevant local experiences and knowledge for the peculiar African digital technology problems, which in some cases becomes a global standard. With local knowledge, the innovators could leverage peculiar local experiences to provide proper physical identification alternatives and secure financial transaction using other identification documents like a voter's card, driving license, etc. A comparable situation is the case of the BRCK solar-powered Wi-Fi device which provides internet access to dead spots around the world (Jake, 2016).

However, while these examples represent those exceptional cases where the continent exerted her resourcefulness against all odds, the colossal deficit of science and technology in the continent and the attendant lack of applied technical skills and competence has always defeated such breakaway innovations and negated development across Africa. This understanding and the dire need for technological skill and capacities were re-echoed by Demitu Hambissa, the Ethiopian Minister of Science and Technology. She observed that the pace of skills and technological development and innovation has been slow in Africa because of the absence of a critical mass of university-educated manpower skilled in hands-on technology fuelled by the lack of high-quality laboratories and scientific equipment, as well as the unavailability of long-term finance and weak private sector initiative (African Development Bank, 2014).

The Nigerian Minister for Communication Technology at the Future-Sat Africa Summit 2017 held in Abuja on 11 July 2017 also shared a view where he posited that deliberate at-tention must be paid to technology transfer and capacity development in Africa for the con-tinent to have a fair share of the business opportunities provided by the ICT sector. Available evidence shows that while Africa is home to over 15% of the world population, its technology contribution to global productivity is less than 2% as there is less than one technologically skilled professional in every 10,000 compared to the more 20 in 10,000 in the West economies (Elebeke, 2017; World Bank, 2015).

With the slow uptake on science and technology in Africa, the necessary infrastructures and technological capacities needed to support ethical ICT uptake and cybersecurity evolution in Africa are grossly inadequate likewise the social, political, institutional, and cultural developments and awareness required. This is one of the major drawbacks of current Africa infrastructure and economic leapfrogging. Therefore, in the absence of an established efficient, dynamic technological skill, science transfer system, ICT and cybersecurity capacity-building for both users and technology producers takes a hit, giving rise to current policy and technical imbalance that makes sustainable development a difficult reality in Africa.

## Strategic considerations for effective cyber security in Africa: toward a positive cyber hygiene

The digital age is upon us and cybersecurity has since become a global phenomenon. With the awareness of interconnectedness, the enigma of a security chain being as strong as the weakest link in a chain is made clear, hence the rest of the world needs Africa to be aware and ready as a cyber-unsafe Africa in the global cyberspace is a substantial vulnerability to others.

Cyber Security is still a teething domain especially for Africa with little or no existing lessons to learn from, or standard practices to adapt and adopt. Every economy is supposed to invent its own wheel to suit its peculiarities. However, it was observed that several basic cybersecurity principles repeat themselves across economies hence proper documentation, sharing of best practices, and collaboration are strategic factors Africa must consider (WEF, 2014).

In the whitepaper, Global Agenda Council on Cyber Security published by the World Economic Forum in 2014, international fragmentation, international norm-setting and role are part of the key obstacle to robust ICT and cybersecurity development. The whitepaper identified the following factors as strategic considerations, organisations, and individuals should consider when addressing the cybersecurity challenges in Africa:

i. Adopting best practices and cyber hygiene: An important first step is developing policies and procedures that include regularly validating approved hardware and authorised software, establishing security system configurations, timely patching of applications and operating systems, controlling and auditing user privileges, and educating users.
ii. Improved authentication: Organisations must move beyond insecure passwords to mechanisms such as two-factor authentication and continuous authentication technology, which will become increasingly important as more devices connect to the internet.
iii. Preparing for attacks: It is critical that organisations take steps to prepare for eventual attacks, including enhancing forensic capabilities, developing business continuity plans, and developing plans for regaining user trust.
iv. Blended governance approaches: The public and Global Agenda Council on Cybersecurity private sectors must explore new ways of collaboration that would leverage the perspectives of governments, companies, civil society, and academia.
v. Careful government interventions: The public and private sectors must collaboratively construct effective regulations and frameworks that address cybersecurity needs without hampering innovation or diminishing trust.
vi. Independent security organisations: Independent organisations can reward the implementation of best practices and create high-information consumers.

## Conclusion

The conceptualisation of ICT, Cyber Security and Cyber Terrorism guide the understanding of their growing significance in the 21st century. The discussion on the emerging ICT and cybersecurity ecosystem in Africa and the comparison of the existing infrastructures and ecosystem maturity to developed countries show the gaps and efforts being made for greater success. Cyber terrorism aimed at intimidating a government or its people in the continuance of political or social objectives. Positively and negatively, this affects the way with which we interact with ICT and interpret the concept of cybersecurity considering how convenient and vulnerable it makes life especially in the absence of vital infrastructure, institutions and policies for the ICT user protection. This describes the teething African cybersecurity ecosystem and provides an opportunity for huge improvements.

This chapter has also connected the salient though dispersed points to demonstrate that the narrative of security in the cyberspace, as well as the uptake or rejection of ICT in various societies, are not written only with the ink of technology. The significance of the legal and legislative as well as the regulatory and enforcement components for ICT and Cyber Security and their role in Counterterrorism were crystallised. The overlap of military and civil responsibilities in the security of cyberspace reinforces the notion of everyday users being the first line of defence in potential cyber-attacks, cyber terrorism, and/or cyberwar hence the need for investment in practical user cyber hygiene and awareness. Finally, the agenda for the establishment of relevant transparent civilian-led Cyber Security regulatory institutions and the strengthening of existing security and Cyber Security institutions as well as improving the general cybersecurity capabilities of all government agencies are set and prioritised.

## References

Abdisaid, M. A.-K. (2016). *Islamist extremism in East Africa. African Security Brief.* African Centre for Strategic Studies. No. 32.

African Development Bank. (2014). Poor technological capability undermining Africa's growth potential. Retrieved from https://www.afdb.org/en/news-and-events/poor-technological-capability-undermining-africas-growth-potential-13684/ (accessed 20/06/2017).

Caiazzo, P. (2015). *The cyber threat in Africa. The Cipher Brief.* Expert Commentary Oct. 14. Retrieved from https://www.thecipherbrief.com/article/cyber-threat-africa (accessed 21/06/2017).

Dunn Cavelty, M. (2012). The militarisation of cyber security as a source of global tension. In D. Möckli (Ed.), *Strategic trends and analysis: Key developments in Global Affairs.* Switzerland: Center for Security Studies, ETH Zurich. Retrieved from. http://www.css.ethz.ch/publications/pdfs/Strategic-Trends-2012-Cyber.pdf. (accessed 22/06/2017).

Daniel, G. A., & Samantha, K. (2016). Developing the ICT infrastructure for Africa: Overview of barriers to harnessing the full power of the internet. *Hastings Journal of Education for Library and Information Science, 47*(1), 4–16.

Denning, D. E. (2000). *"Cyberterrorism" being a testimony given to the house armed services committee special oversight panel on terrorism global dialogue, autumn 2000.*

Dipolelo, M. (2016). *Cyberattacks on the rise in South Africa. African Brand Link,* 14 June, 2016. Retrieved from http://www.africanbrandlink.com/cyber-attacks-rise-south%C2%A0africa (accessed 21/06/2017).

Dotzauer, Erwin (2014). *African union convention on cyber security and personal data protection. African Union Report.* Retrieved from https://www.au.int/web/en/treaties/african-union-convention-cyber-security-and-personal-data-protection (accessed 20/06/2017).

Economic Commission for Africa. ( 2013). *Making the most of Africa's commodities: Industrializing for growth, jobs and economic transformation. Economic Report on Africa 2013.*

Elebeke, Emmanuel, (2017). *Infrastructure deficit undermines Africa's development, says Shittu. The Vanguard Newspaper.* Retrieved from https://www.vanguardngr.com/2017/07/infrastructure-deficit-undermines-africas-development-says-shittu/ (accessed 13/08/2017).

Fischer, E. A. Liu, Rollins, E., & Theophany, C. J. (2014). *The 2013 cybersecurity executive order: Overview and considerations for congress.* Washington, DC: Congressional Research Service.

Gehem, M., Usanov, A., Frinking, E., & Rademaker, M. (2015). *Assessing Cyber Security: A Meta-Analysis of Threats, Trends, and Responses to Cyber Attacks.* Netherland: The Hague Centre for Strategic Studies (HCSS).

George, A. (2014). *Religious extremism main cause of terrorism, according to report.* The Guardian Tuesday 18 November 2014. Retrieved from https://www.theguardian.com/news/datablog/2014/nov/18/religious-extremism-main-cause-of-terrorism-according-to-report (accessed 25/06/2017).

ITU (International Telecommunication Union). (2016). *Measuring the information society report 2016.* International Telecommunication Union, Geneva Switzerland.

ITU. (2005). *A comparative analysis of cybersecurity initiatives worldwide.* WSIS Thematic Meeting on Cybersecurity Geneva 2005.

ITU. (2007). *Measuring the Information Society 2007: ICT Opportunity Index and World Telecommunication/ICT Indicators.* Geneva: ITU.

Jake, Bright (2016). *A brief overview of Africa's tech industry and 7 predictions for its future.* World Economic Forum on Africa 2016. Retrieved from https://www.weforum.org/agenda/2016/05/a-brief-history-of-africas-tech-industry-and-7-predictions-for-its-future/ (accessed 27/06/2017).

James, A. L. (2017). *Sketching the contours of cyber conflict in Asia.* IAPS DIALOGUE: The Online Magazine of the Institute of Asia & Pacific Studies, March 27, 2017. Retrieved from https://iapsdialogue.org/2017/03/27/sketching-the-contours-of-cyberconflict-in-asia/ (accessed 29/06/2017).

Jessica, S. (2016). *Lessons from terrorists. Explaining Violence.* Retrieved from https://www.bu.edu/today/2016/psychology-of-terrorists/ (accessed 22/06/2017).

Jean, S. & Amzath, F. (2016). Cyber security in Africa: Facts and figures *posted 7 July 2016.* Retrieved from http://www.scidev.net/sub-saharan-africa/icts/feature/cybercrime-africa-facts-figures.html (accessed 24/06/2017).

Joshi, J. B. D., Ghafoor, A. , Aref, W. G. , & Spafford, E.H. (2002). Security and privacy challenges of a digital government. In: W. J. McIver & A. K. Elmagarmid (Eds.), *Advances in digital government. Advances in database systems* (Vol. 26). Boston, MA: Springer. doi: https://doi.org/10.1007/0-306-47374-7_7.

Lourdeau, K. (2004). Congress testimony. Retrieved from http://www.fbi.gov/congress/congress04/lourdeau022404.htm (accessed 13/07/2015).

Mark, D. J., Rebecca, M., & Michael, M. (2011). Africa's ICT infrastructure: Building on the mobile revolution. *Directions in development infrastructure.* Washington DC: A World Bank Publication Series.

Matthew, S. (2014). *The secret world of stolen smartphones, where business is booming.* PUBLICATION of GADGET LAB. 18/12/2014. Retrieved from https://www.wired.com/2014/12/where-stolen-smart-phones-go/ (accessed 20/05/2017).

Marco, O. (2015). *Cyber security challenges & capacity building. Expert Meeting on Cyber Laws and Regulations for Enhancing E-commerce: Including Case Studies and Lessons Learned.* International Telecommunication Union, 25-27 March 2015.

Military Guide to Terrorism in the Twenty-First Century. 15 August 2007. *US Army and Command Doctrine.* US TRADOC G2 Handbook No. 1, Washington, USA. Retrieved from http://www.au.af.mil/au/awc/awcgate/army/guidterr/ch02.pdf. (accessed 21/06/2017).

Nigerian Communication Week, June 23, 2014. Banks lose N159Bn to cyber crimes. Retrieved from https://ncw.com.ng/banks-lose-n159bn-to-cyber-crimes/ (accessed 2/06/2017).

Orji, J. U. (2013). *Cybersecurity law and regulation* (pp. 96–115). Nijmegen, Netherlands: Waolf Legal Publishers (WLP).

Ponemon Institute. (2016). *The cost of data breach study: Global analysis.* Ponemon Institute Research Report

Quarshie, Henry Osborn & Martin-Odoom, Alexander (2012). Fighting cybercrime in Africa. *Journal of Computer Science and Engineering,* 2(6), 98–100. doi:10.5923/j.computer.20120206.03.

Randeep, S., Seth, A., Philippe, D., Arturo, M.-K., & Christine, Z.-W. Q. (2010). Assessing and enhancing country competitiveness. *Global opportunities in IT-based services.* Washington DC: The World Bank.

Samantha, A., Marlou, B., Lorenzo, D., Maša, G., Kaspar, K., Bert-Jaap, K., Ronald, L., Maurice, S., Karine, E. S., & Ivan, Š. (2015). *The governance of cybersecurity: A comparative quick scan of approaches in Canada, Estonia, Germany, the Netherlands and the UK.* WODC, Ministry of Security & Justice. Tilburg University TILT – Tilburg Institute for Law, Technology, and Society.

Sawyer, S. (2000). *The five ways to study computing*. Seattle, WA : School of Information, University of Washington (The lSI/Samuel Lazerow Lecture), December 5.

Sawyer, S., & Chen, T. (2002). *Conceptualizing information technology in the study of information systems: Trends and issues. Submitted for review and possible inclusion at the December, 2002 Barcelona conference of the IFIP8.2 Working Group on Information Systems on Organizations and Society*.

Sawyer, S., & Huang, H. (2007). Conceptualizing information, technology and people: Comparing information science and information systems literatures. *Journal of the American Society of Information Science and Technology, 4*(2), 1436–1447.

Serianu Cyber Threat Intelligence Team. (2016). *Achieving cyber security resilience: enhancing visibility and increasing awareness*. Africa Cyber Security Report.

Symantec and AU Commission. (2016). *Cyber crime and cyber security: Trends in Africa*. Hague, Netherlands: Global Forum on Cyberspace Expertise.

Symantec (2012). Norton cybercrime report. Retrieved from http://now-static.norton.com/now/en/pu/images/Promotions/2012/cybercrimeReport/2012_Norton_Cybercrime_Report_Master_FINAL_050912.pdf. (accessed 20/05/2017).

United Nation Development Programme. (2017). *UNDP youth entrepreneurship portal final feasibility report*.

UN (United Nations). (2011). *ICT as an enabler for private sector development. Information Economy Report*, A United Nations Publication, New York and Geneva.

White House Office of the Press Secretary. (06/08/2014). FACT SHEET: partnering to counter terrorism in Africa. Retrieved from https://obamawhitehouse.archives.gov/the-press-office/2014/08/06/fact-sheet-partnering-counter-terrorism-africa (accessed 11/06/2017).

World Bank, (2015). African governments invest in skills in sciences, engineering, and technology. Retrieved from http://www.worldbank.org/en/news/feature/2015/07/01/african-governments-invest-in-skills-in-sciences-engineering-and-technology (accessed 20/06/2017).

World Economic Forum WEF. (2014). *Global agenda council on cybersecurity "White Paper"*. Retrieved from http://www3.weforum.org/docs/GAC16_Cybersecurity_WhitePaper_.pdf (accessed 27/06/2017).

Yonazi, E., Kelly, T., Halewood, N., & Blackman, C. (2014). *The transformational use of information and communication technologies in Africa*. Washington DC: World Bank Group. Retrieved from. http://documents.worldbank.org/curated/en/571361468192859438/Summary (accessed 26/06/2017).

Zahri, Y., & Syahrul, H. (2017). *Cyber terrorism and terrorist use of ICT and cyberspace. South-Eastern Asia Regional Centre for Counterterrorism*. Ministry of Foreign Affairs Malaysia. Retrieved from. http://www.searcct.gov.my/featured-articles/49-cyber-terrorism-and-terrorist-use-of-ict-and-cyberspace (accessed 21/07/2017).

# 11

# Participatory security in Africa

*Abdulmalik Auwal*

## Introduction

Participatory security has been a central concept in the framing and transformation of governance and development in Africa since its introduction in political development discourses and application on the continent between the late 1980s. This period witnessed a "frustrating transition to civil rule programmes; the limited scope of democratic space in its entire ramification; denial of civil and political rights; and unending economic deprivations as a direct consequence of the IMF/World Bank inspired Structural Adjustment Programme (SAP)" (Mohammed, 2010:2). Notwithstanding, these challenges spurred the proliferation of civil organisations and social movements in the African continent to act as whistle-blowers and vanguards against authoritarian regimes and agitation for the return to democracy. The existence of one-party system and prolonged military authorities in the region "consistently wages war against democratic forces and mass organisations" (Agbese, 1997:90); thus, throwing most of the civil groups into a state of confusion. With the return to democratic governance in most of Africa, the strategy of civil society changed from resistance and whistleblowing to that of creating awareness in enhancing citizen participation in the electoral process, increased demands for transparency and accountability, giving voices to most vulnerable and marginalised groups in society, engaging the state to ensure responsible leadership through promoting and consolidating democratic governance among others.

Later on, the *Al-Qaeda* and its extension namely Al-Qaeda in the Islamic Maghreb (AQIM), the mayhem orchestrated by the *Boko Haram* sect in the Lake Chad Basin, the Movement for Oneness and Jihad in West Africa (MUJAO), the National Movement for the Liberation of Azawad (MNLA), Ansar Eddine in Mali and Niger, Al-Shabaab, the conflict between National Resistance Army (NRA) and Lord's Resistance Army (LRA) in Uganda, the collapse of the Somali state, the Seleka and anti-balaka conflict in the Central African Republic (CAR) and the dastardly act of ISIL, etc. all impacted negatively in heightening security challenges, militia uprisings and violent attacks in the region. These violent terrorism and extremism act in Africa have compelled international and regional organisations, faith and community-based NGOs, women NGOs, and a host of other local organisations to partner with states in national and regional participatory security.

## Security crises in Africa: a review

The disintegration of the Soviet Union brought an end to the Cold War. The IMF/World Bank Structural Adjustment Programme (SAP) and the rise of the one-party system in some African states in the late 1980s and the early 1990s, resulted in waves of conflict and violence that have swept through the entire world in different places with Africa recording the highest casualties. Africa has been engulfed in convulsive fits of ethnic insecurity, violence, and genocide. However, it is imperative to note that wherever human beings exist, conflict is inevitable. There is considerable concern about the rise of insecurity in Africa. This is manifested in:

> Crisis of underdevelopment and political instability in the continent, resulting from mass poverty, stagflation, uneven development, alienation, mounting external debts and periodic outbreak of violence and military coup d'état. The multiple and unabated economic crisis in the African continent has been generally linked in recent times to the unsettled condition of widespread civil disorder and the accelerated syndrome of failed states in Africa. (Bassey, 2007:xv)

Lately, there is significant concern about the "mixture of natural and man-made disasters" (The Economist, 2000: 13–19) in Africa, manifested in floods, famine, and the rise of insurgency and terrorism. To illustrate, famine in Ethiopia; floods in Mozambique; civil war and genocide in Rwanda, Sierra Leone, Sudan, etc; xenophobia attacks in South Africa; terrorism and insurgent uprising in Nigeria, Cameroon, Mali, Chad, etc; and a string of other ethnoreligious conflicts, border conflicts, indigenes/settlers squabbles, political conflicts, farmers-cattle herders violent conflicts, etc, have been ravaging the corporate existence of Africa. These conflicts are so complex that a particular state in Africa experiences more than one conflict at a time. For instance, Nigeria has been battling with the dreadful problem of the violent Boko Haram conflict; in addition to the Fulani-Farmers conflicts; threats of the Niger Delta militants and that of secession from the Eastern region of the country orchestrated by the Independent People of Biafra (IPOB); identity conflicts and the spate of kidnappings and political uprising bedevilling the country internally.

These violent conflicts have displaced and killed more people in Africa than in any other part of the world in recent decades (the Commission for Africa in the House of Commons, 2006). It has been argued that "the International Human Suffering Index developed by the Population Crisis Committee in Washington DC, suggest that 90% of the countries with the highest level of human suffering were located in Africa" (cited in Bassey, 2007: xxiv). This disturbing condition is statistically analysed by Touray and Dunmoye (mentioned in Bassey, 2007) that some 26 armed conflicts erupted in Africa between 1963 and 1998, affecting 474 million people or 61% of the continent's population. At the sub-regional level, 79% of the population were affected in East Africa, 73% in Central Africa, 46% in West Africa, 51% in North Africa, and 29% in Southern Africa. These glaring statistics are suggestive of a continent in a paralysing crisis of underdevelopment, fuelled by accelerating economic stagnation. This systemic condition of hopelessness is causally linked to the various aspects of development failures in Africa as a continent.

The violent conflicts experienced by African countries can be attributed to pervasive ethnoreligious conflict; communal and trans-border dispute; prevalent poverty, excessive unemployment, and extreme level of corruption; political instability; poor governance and weak public institutions; and, porous borders that encourage the illegal influx and transfer of small arms across the region. Politicians have exploited these unfavourable conditions to serve their political or selfish interest further. The pervasive security challenges now call for a novel approach on how civil society can partner with those in authority to counter this rising security challenges bedevilling the region.

## The state and civil society in Africa: conceptual and theoretical framework

The concept of civil society has varying interpretations, and as such, it is not easy to discuss its evolution without clearly defining the idea behind its origin. A clear definition of civil society will help tremendously in discussing its development. In discussing the transition, the nature and substance of the relationship between the "individual" space and the "community" space are very vital. Ibeanu (2000) posits that the individual interstice is regarded as one of freedom, choice, and private material pursuits, while the community space is one of collective action, solidarity and public (state) power. As such, the community space is one that potentially or constrains individual space. The evolution of civil society in the west has been one in which the individual space progressively became "liberated" and separated from the community space. Civil society is considered an integral part of the development of the west, as is either market or state (Hyden, Court, & Mease, 2003 and Ibeanu, 2000). Ibeanu (2000) maintains that emergence of theories of civil society is traceable to the earlier western political thinkers of the Greek city-states like Socrates, Plato, Aristotle, etc., who wrote about how to overturn the moral and social disorder of their society into an ideal version to ensure a better livelihood for its people. For instance, Aristotle sees civil society as a "civilised and rational society" that was conterminous with the state. Aristotle's definition reflects the social transition from "rude" forms of life to a "polished" and or a "civilised" society, hence the "civilised society" or "civil society". Most (if not all) the earlier political thinkers (as demonstrated in their works) suggested a separation between the spheres of politics and economics and between the public and private spheres. The classical philosophical period witnessed "emphasis on individual rights; moral restraint on public power; the responsibility of rulers to the people they ruled; and the subordination of government to law. The only probable addition was the contention between the church and the state" (Ibeanu, 2000:6). The aftermath of the Greek city-states resulted in the medieval period, which also witnessed the crystallising of civil society within the context of a liberal paradigm.

The distinction between civil society and the state was traced to the late 18<sup>th</sup> century by John Keane, Adam Ferguson and Thomas Paine. They see civil society as "a precondition and an arena for the creation of a free and natural interaction among free individuals" (Ahrne, 1996:111). Both Locke and Hobbes concur in their argument that the state arises from society and is needed to restrain conflict between individuals. They argue that the government cannot have unlimited sovereignty since that would pose a threat to individual freedoms derived from natural law. Thus, there must be a social contract between rulers and ruled that guarantees these rights but also gives the state the authority to protect civil society from destructive conflict. There is a need for a constitutional arrangement that both state and civil society respect (Hyden et al., 2003).

Antonio Gramsci (1971), an Italian Philosopher, view civil society from a neo-Marxist angle. He argues that the potentially oppositional role of civil society is a "public room" or "public sphere" separate from state and market, in which ideological hegemony is contested. Gramsci (1971) further opines that civil society includes a wide range of organisations and ideologies, which both challenge and maintain the existing order. The political and cultural supremacy of the ruling classes and societal accord is formed within civil society. Gramsci's ideas influenced the resistance to totalitarian regimes in Eastern Europe and Latin America. Diamond (1994:5) captures this by noting that civil society is the:

> realm of organised social life that is voluntary, self-generating, largely self-supporting, autonomous from the state, and bound by a legal order or set of rules. It is distinct from society in general in that it involves citizens acting collectively in a public sphere to express their interests, passions and ideas, exchange information, achieve mutual goals, make demands, and hold state officials accountable.

The concept was applied to Africa in the mid-1980s and beyond and the point of discussion include the character of the state and economy (Ake, 1981), the African peasantry (Beckmam, 1988; Hyden, 1986; Williams, 1987), ethnicity (Nnoli, 1978), social movements (Mamdani & Wammba-dia-Wamba, 1995) and most recently democracy and participatory security. The focus of its applicability in Africa has been on characterising civil society in Africa which raised recent debate on democracy and democratisation in Africa.

## The nexus between state and civil society in security provisioning

There is no one way of defining civil society because of the numerous meanings attached to the concept and the attendant contradictions. While some scholars like Madunagu (1999) underscore the state-civil society relationship by declaring the two as antagonistic as each tries to defend its spheres of influence against encroachment by the other, other scholars like Diamond (1999), Rothchild and Lawson (1997), Mouzelis (1996), etc., stress the nexus between state and civil society. Diamond (1999) debunks the idea of conceiving civil society only as organisations independent of the state. He elaborates on the dysfunction between other groups and civil society organisations in society. To make clear this dysfunction, he listed elaborately five elements of civil society. These include the fact that civil society is pre-occupied with public ends, relates to the state, is pluralistic and diversified, does not represent the self-interests of an individual or community, and that civil society has a clear difference from the democracy-enhancing phenomenon of the civil community.

On the other hand, Rothchild and Lawson (1997) highlighted African political exigencies which explain the fragility of civil society against the backdrop of post-independence regime formation and management in Africa. They first capture the origin of the concept of civil society which they trace down to the early philosophers (such as Hobbes, Rousseau, Marx, and Gramsci) whose works engineered the evolution of the "social contract" from which civil society today derives its antecedent. Based on examples from the African continent (such as Nigeria, Somalia, Uganda, Sudan, Mozambique, Ghana, Burkina Faso, Zambia, etc.), Rothchild and Lawson (1997) claim the existing political environment in Africa provides a caricature basis for the principle of the "social contract". They particularly cite the instance of ethnic stupor in which African states conduct their politics on a divisive pedestal rather than an integrative platform:

> ethnic self-determination movements, large scale societal disengagement and ethnically based clientelism in numerous African countries indicate the absence of a social contract and these fundamentally divided societies are likely to produce civil societies significantly more sequenced than European philosophy would suggest, at least in the short run (Rothchild & Lawson, 1997:255).

The two writers delve deeper into the African context by examining the various categories of state-civil society relations in post-independent Africa. They distinguish four different regime types in Africa which have the capacity "for facilitating more constructive interactions between the state and civil society" (Rothchild & Lawson, 1997:256). These regime types include majoritarian democracy, pacted democracy (bargained settlements), state populism and state corporatism. The strength and autonomy of any civil society, they argue, is affected by these regime types, thus, regulating state-civil society relations in Africa. They conclude that a regime's ability to involve civil organisations in the realm of its political or public sphere tends to contribute more to state-civil society relations in domains of democracy and development. In his work, Mouzelis (1996) dwells solely on the linkage between the state and civil society during modernisation. This linkage, to him, occurs in three different modes through which the "political inclusion of the lower classes in the course of modernisation takes place" (1996:57) in society. The three spheres include Integrative, Incorporative-Clientelistic, and Incorporative-populistic. In the Integrative model, which he describes as dominant in North-west Europe, politics is portrayed as being inclusive and people-oriented. Under the second mode, Incorporative-Clientelism, there is an emphasis on the people but through personalistic, highly particularistic patron-client networks. Lastly, the Incorporative-Populist mode deviates from the political tendencies of the first two modes; this is because of the people (masses) involvement in political rallies around a charismatic leader whose political prowess becomes a source of political legitimation in the polity. The conclusion reached by Mouzelis is that culture and the nature of civil-society-state relations or linkages in the developing areas are not conclusive to development. Until this trend is reversed, Africa will scarcely experience growth.

Richard (2006), Joseph (2010), Mohammed (2010) and a host of other scholars concur with the above assertions by maintaining that civil society and the state are not totally detached from each other; they are mutually responsive. Government and civil society also relate in the provision of security in Africa in the following capacities: protecting the inhabitants living in the region; preventing violent conflicts from occurring, and empowering the powerless. Though, these organisations might lack the political will to carry out some policies effectively but "most civil society organisations depend on the military support of the member states" (Kotter, 2007:49) to foster security through participatory security. In African states', the conventional role of fighting terrorism and insurgencies such as the deployment of armed personnel to affected areas; use of traditional tactics and "scorched earth strategies" in counterinsurgency operations, declaration of a state of emergency; direct military action with its dire consequences on civilians etc., have all contributed to the de-legitimating of the state, leaving citizens' associations and other organisations to step in to fill the vacuum left by the state, which was increasingly incapable of maintaining public security, managing the economy and guaranteeing access to essential commodities and services at affordable prices. Civil society is increasingly playing an active and influential role as educators, advocates, intermediaries, observers, and pursuers of transnational justice. Jacob and Ayse (2009:176–177) are of the view that:

> Civil society [organisations] have an impact on changing behaviours, attitudes and negative stereotypes; educating the parties; healing trauma and injuries; disseminating ideas such as democracy and human rights; drafting committed people to do peace work; challenging traditional structures that perpetuate structural violence; mediating between conflicting parties; reaching out to governments to incorporate elements of peacebuilding in their policies; encouraging disarmament, reintegrating of soldiers and developing a sustained interfaith dialogue.

Kotter (2007:48) believes that a flourishing civil society typically depends on the security and predictability provided by an effective democratic state that is controlled by a government that ensures the rule of law and policies that respond to the needs of the population. As a result, we must emphasise that civil society and democratic states are highly complementary and even interdependent.

## Civil-military relations for security provisioning: volunteering for civilian joint task forces

In their work, *Civil-military relations and leadership crisis in 21$^{st}$century Africa*, Wogu and Ibietan (2014) are of the view that a civil-military relation (CMR) describes the relationship between civil societies as a whole and military organisation or organisations established to protect it. Specifically, it represents the relationship between the civil authority of a given state and its military authority. Studies on CMR often rest on the normative assumption that civilian control of the military is preferable to military control of the state. The principal problem is to empirically explain how civilian control over the military is established and maintained on a sustainable and efficient basis (Burk, 2002:7–9). As an area of study in political science, CMR involves the research and discussion of a diverse range of issues including but not limited to the civilian control of the military, military professionalism, war, civil-military co-operation (CIMIC), military institutional structures for managing civil challenges under the guises of Military Aid to Civil Authority (MACA) and Military Operations other than War (MOOTW) etc. The discussion in this area includes non-state actors or "voluntary sector" (Mandel, 2004:171–201), as well as more traditional state-centric analysis which dwells on the structure and elite behaviour in nation-states. Omoigui (2005, part 1) perceives CMR as the supremacy and guidance of the civil populace over the military. It requires full democratic control of the military as it plays its role as the ultimate guarantor of national security. In an ideal world, the military should be subservient to the society, and it has a monopoly over the means of violence in the interest of its citizens in response to popular will and consent.

Welch and Johanna (1998) view CMR as interactions between armed forces as institutions and the sectors of society in which they are embedded. Mainly, CMR focus on the relative distribution of power between the government and the armed forces of a country. As one specialist recently wrote, they involve a "process" in which civilian control is measured and evaluated by weighing "the relative influence of military officers and civilian officials in the decision of state concerning war, internal security, external defence, and military policy (that is, the shape, size, and operating procedures of the military establishment)" (Richard, 1997). CMR exist within the contexts of political systems. Though civilian control as an aspect of democracy has attracted the attention of policy-makers around the globe, it is difficult to achieve and maintain a state of equilibrium in CMR. In the conceptual framing of the role of the military in developed states, the CMR literature views armed forces as institutions exclusively geared towards defending the state against external threats. The military is cast as a professional outfit that is not only insulated from civilians, but it is also an autonomous institution designed to operate in both war and disaster management without civil support. This is without prejudice to the civil control of the armed forces in the political sphere where the control of the armed institutions is vested in the executive branch, a symbol of the contract between elected officials and electorates. Containing an institution whose primary business is its franchise on violence within the state is one of the essential components of a democratic state. Garba (2014), sees CMR as the totality of relations between the military and society within which it operates and is necessarily included. It entails all aspects of the role of the army (as a special professional institution) in the fundamental elements of national life. CMR also involves issues of the attitude of the military towards the society, the civilian society's perceptions of and attitudes to the military and the role of the armed forces concerning the state.

The earliest use of the conception of CMR according to Wogu and Ibietan (2014) can be traced to the writings of Sun Tzu (1870 [1971]) and Clausewitz (1832 [1989]). Both writers argued that military organisations were primarily the servants of the state. It is the responsibility of the state to tame this "master-servant" to secure both state and society, and civil society has a role to play in cooperating with the "guardian force" to advance collective security. The opinion of these writers is concerned with the growing militarism in societies all around the world. They, however, further stress a sharp rise in the number of cases that have been recorded so far. Studies which indicate direct contradictions to the presumed roles of the military in the society include Marshall (2005), Huntington (1957) and Janowitz (1960). They were some of the first thinkers who published their seminal books about CMR which effectively brought CMR into the academia, particularly in political science and sociology. The versatility and considerable force with which the Americans adopted Huntington's, and Janowitz's theoretical arguments have become the basis on which most studies of other nations' CMR have been conducted since security is a precondition of sustainable development.

Since the 1960s, the wave of political independence in African countries has been characterised by unstable governments, alarming frequency of military incursions, and authoritarian one-party regimes occasioned by a failure of leadership and non-existence of viable institutions of governance which have made the military forces of most African states less professional and more political. This therefore, has contributed towards the emergence of inadequate security sector governance framework and deteriorating CMR. After the Cold War in the 1990s, the restoration of democratic governments across Africa catapulted the need for an improvement in CMR and proper security sector governance as a precondition for the sustenance of democracy. However, the 1990s witnessed a mixture of democratic restoration and relapse to fascism or "democratic reversal" across Africa with implications for CMR. The democratic reversal in Africa was rooted in return of military rule (for instance, in Sierra Leone, Mali), civil war (Democratic Republic of Congo), sectarian violence (Central African Republic), insurgency (Ethiopia), state collapse (Somalia). In the 2000s, particularly after 9/11, African countries have witnessed a new wave of threats – militancy terrorism, insurgency, and sectarian skirmishes, which have impelled the state to reconsider its template of security provisioning. For instance, the Lake Chad Basin was ravaged with the dastardly Boko Haram violent attack. It threatened the very survival of the region because of the use of Improvised Explosive Devise (IED) bombs, hand used grenade bombs, AK47s, arson, and all sort of sophisticated weapons used by the insurgents in killing people. Further, their tactics involved kidnapping, rendering millions of people homeless, destroying properties worth billions, and causing serious economic and health hazard in the region. The ability of each country in this region to free itself from this menace was met with various challenges ranging from the politicisation of the conflict; high level of corruption; conventional military engagement consistently like deployment of security agents to the most affected areas, declaration of a state of emergency, call for internal assistance, relocation of military command centre; and the ill-preparedness of the security personnel logistically and operationally. The dire consequences of this violent clashes exerted pressure on African leaders. Hence, integration of civil society in complementing military action in combating insecurity in the region as was justifiable from the activities of the Civilian Joint Task Force (CJTF) assistance of the government's Joint Task Force (JTF) and the Joint Multinational Task Force (JMTF) (comprising troops from Nigeria, Niger Republic, Chad, and Cameroon) in launching military offensives against the insurgents.

The Civilian Joint Task Force (CJTF) – or *yangora* – is a youth vigilante organisation that functions as a community-based police force. It is a necessary creation that was born "in reaction to the failure of the Nigerian military to protect civilians against Boko Haram" (Daniel, 2015:14). Bamidele (2016) is of the view that the civilian JTF emerged and volunteered to assist the Special and Joint Task Force with the counterterrorism campaign. They are armed with mundane weapons such as bows and arrows, swords, clubs, and daggers and operate under the supervision of the civilian JTF sector commanders. With the aid of the CJTF, Borno state in Nigeria has experience normalcy to a certain high level and many Boko Haram members who feared the CJTF have run out of Maiduguri. The creation of civilian JTF as part of the mechanisms for combating the menace of Boko Haram terrorism in Nigeria represents a veritable example of a citizen-driven coordinated response to security challenge and an indication of how terrorism can be tackled and prevented. The civilian group exploits their knowledge of the communities to identify suspected Boko Haram members or other suspicious individuals. Civilian JTF members have been successful in stopping many attacks through swift identification of strange faces in their communities. They have also helped the security agencies to arrest Boko Haram members (Okereke, 2013, cited in Bamidele, 2016). The IASC (International Agency Standing Committee) (2008) posits that engaging military support for humanitarian operations is not a new endeavour. In today's security environment, however, the military is ever more involved in the "direct" provision of aid. At the same time, humanitarian actors are often faced with situations where there are no alternatives but to rely on the military, as a last resort, for safety and to access populations in need at the serious risk of compromising their neutrality, impartiality, independence, and thus their ability and/or credibility to operate. Combined with the tides toward "integration" and "whole-of-government" approaches, as well as the increased propensity of some governments to deploy mixed civilian-military teams to provide aid as a 'tool' to address security threats, the situation calls for enhanced understandings between the military and humanitarian professionals at all levels.

Insecurity story in Somalia is akin to what has been happening in other African countries. Bradbury and Healy (2010) maintain that for over two decades, the nature of the Somali crisis and the international context within which it is occurring has constantly been changing. It has mutated from a civil war in the 1980s, through state collapse, clan factionalism, and "warlordism" in the 1990s, to a globalised ideological conflict in the first decade of the new millennium. Between 2006 and 2008 the country further recorded violent insurgency, military occupation, rising *jihadism,* and massive population displacement has reversed the incremental political and economic progress achieved by the late 1990s in south-central Somali. The consequences of this dastardly act in the early 1990s include the "killing of an estimated 25,000 people, 1.5 million people fled the country, and at least 2 million were internally displaced"....by 2006–08, 1.3 million people were displaced, 3.6 million people required emergency food aid, and 60,000 Somalis a year fleeing the country" (Bradbury & Healy, 2010: 10–14). The role of international organisations, regional bodies and other NGOs such as the United Nations Mission in Somalia (UNOSOM), the Inter-Governmental Authority on Development (IGAD), the African Union Mission in Somalia (AMISOM) and a host of other women organisations like the Coalition for Grassroots Women Organisations (COGWO); the Peace and Human Right Network – *Iskuxirka Nabadaiyo Xuquuqal Adamiga* (INXA), the Network Women Pioneers for Peace and Life, known as HINNA (*Haweenka Horseedka Nabadda*), among others. These organisations have carried out a lot of activities in promoting peace-building in Somalia. For instance, the actions of UNOSOM in the early 1990s created awareness by turning world attention to the catastrophic happenings in Somalia and assisted in saving lives by securing food supplies. It facilitated some regional agreements that improved security, reopened Mogadishu airport and seaport, and supported the revival of critical services and the creation of local NGOs. It also provided employment and injected enormous resources into the economy. The Inter-Governmental Authority on Development (IGAD) has also been supporting past Somali reconciliation efforts to promote peace and security. For instance, the 2002 reconciliation between the Transitional National Government (TNG) and the Somali Restoration and Reconciliation Council (SRRC) was because of the IGAD initiative. Other women civil society organisations like Coalition for Grassroots Women Organisations (COGWO), HINNA, INXA, among others have also contributed immensely in participatory security in Somalia by uniting women voices and peace-building efforts; promote women's rights to support victims of violence; use of the poem as a strategy in promoting peace; initiatives to disarm and retain young militiamen; organising peace campaigns; promoting peace and political advocacy; and, stimulating the engagement of civil society organisations. Conclusively, the activities of civil society organisations have achieved much in the past two decades in Somalia by helping to "disempowered the warlords, reduced the significance of clan affiliation, ensured civil society representation is essential to any peace and reconciliation process and made progress on the participation of women in politics" (Faiza, 2010:65).

Uganda has experienced continual struggles for political control and violent conflicts since its independence. The conflict worsened between 1986 and 2006 because of successive insurgent groups who fought against the Ugandan government. The explosion of the conflict can be traced to the coming to power of Yoweri Museveni – the leader of the National Resistance Army (NRA) in 1986 after engaging the Uganda's government in a guerrilla war for five years. The formation of the national government by Museveni led to the rise of another leading rebel group named the Lord's Resistance Army (LRA) which further deteriorated the security situation in the country. The country has suffered escalated state violence, coercion, lawlessness, banditry, robberies, harassment, cold-blooded murders, and insecurity – "as security forces have been a dominant means of political control and retaining power" (Omach, 2016:82). The role of civil society in participatory security in Uganda according to Omach (2016) include championing the cause of human rights, provided leadership, engaged in advocacy for peaceful resolution of the conflict, facilitated contacts between rebel fighters and the government, promoted reconciliation between rebels and the community, organised workshops, issued statements, facilitated the formation of peace clubs to change community attitudes, carried out counselling and facilitated reintegration of abducted persons who escaped from rebel captivity, build a culture of peace, and foster reconciliation. The civil society organisations (CSOs) that took part in the Ugandan peace-building activities include the *Acholi* Religious Leaders Peace Initiative (ARLPI) – an interdenominational peace initiative comprising the Anglican Church of Uganda, Catholic Church, and Moslems, and Justice and Peace Commission of the Catholic Church; *Ker KalKwaro Acholi* – the cultural institution of traditional leaders and Human Rights Focus, a local NGO based in Gulu district; Gulu Save the Children Organisation (GUSCO); Kitgum Concerned Women's Association (KICWA); Civil Society Organisation for Peace in Northern Uganda (COSPNU), Human Rights Focus (HRF), and Gulu Hope for Peace (GHP).

The CAR has also suffered from heightened security challenges in the name of "persistent poor governance by a centralised state over many years before the Seleka rebellion in 2012, especially in the handling of the country's security and economy" (Thierry, 2015:7). In addition, Thierry (2015) further posits that fighting between the anti-balaka and ex-Seleka in the centre of the country has exacerbated and has been accompanied with fighting between the Muslim and non-Muslim communities in divided cities of the country; cattle herding and cattle theft; widespread banditry; border insecurity; constant insecurity that caused the formation of armed groups to defend oneself/group; and the government's chronic economic mismanagement also provoked deep resentment among the population while the absence of education or job opportunities made disenfranchised young people particularly vulnerable to recruitment by armed militia or manipulation by politicians. With state structures in disarray, efforts by local, regional, and international CSOs in promoting peaceful co-existence in CAR were strengthened as religious organisations organised ecumenical prayers and joint celebrations of Christian and Muslim festivals to symbolise religious tolerance in addition to their counter-narrative sermons. The Central African Brothers (CAB), Vitalite Plus (VP), the International Support Mission to the Central African Republic (MISCA) which was transformed in 2014 into a full-scale UN peace-keeping mission, the United Nations Multidimensional Integrated Stabilisation Mission in the Central African Republic (MINUSCA), Danish Refugee Council (DRC), Norwegian Refugee Council (NRC), Agency for Technical Cooperation and Development (ACTED), etc. also contributed in CAR peace-building activities by creating local peace committees and provide training for their members, raising public awareness of the need for peace and trying to mediate directly between communities in conflict, lobbying for re-construction initiatives, monitoring security and crime in the neighbourhood, developed training programmes for youth (considered primary perpetrators of violence).

## Challenges and prospects of functional partnership between the state and civil society

Attempts at providing security, entrenching and consolidating democracy in Africa by the CSOs had been a phenomenal task due to persistent military coup d' etats, one-party regimes, harsh economic conditions of the late 1980s and leadership crisis. Another problem experienced in Africa during this period was captured by Bereketeab (2013:61–74):

> statelessness factors, elitism and particularistic interests of most African leaders, and the factors of political legitimacy in governance among African states, as exemplified in the second Sudanese (North-South) civil war from 1983–2005 and the Darfur crisis; the 1998–2000 Ethiopia-Eritrea war; among others. Consequently, the rising wave of militarism and the attendant problems associated with it (leadership crisis) have in recent times, given writers and contemporary scholars on civil-military relations and political science, reasons to further ponder and extend their studies in the direction of identifying the root causes of these various acts of militarism and leadership crisis with a view to proffering solutions to the troubling cases of militarism within African states.

Also, CSOs faced either a litany of problems – such as insufficient funding which has threatened their existence, growth and functionality as most of them rely heavily on donor agencies and overseas countries (even then, donor support has now reduced drastically with the "wave of post-war reconstruction" projects in the world); lack of internal democracy due to the selfish interest of "NGO elites"; corruption and self-aggrandising tendencies; lack of transparency among many NGOs – on how donor funds are utilised or are out-rightly misappropriated, among others. "This tends to weaken the civil society organisation's moral right to engage the state. It also hinders people of integrity and value from associating with them. The impact of their advocacy for a change is also limited because it is stated that he who comes to equity must come with clean hands" (Omede & Bakare, 2014:17). Internal wrangling along political, social, identity and ideological factors also undermine the activities of some of this CSOs' ability to relate with each other. Due to the lucrative nature and profitability of working in the non-governmental area, "the emergent business, commercial and consultancy orientation is weakening the voluntary, selfless and sacrificial orientation and the focus on social assistance, welfare and support to the weak, vulnerable and less advantaged groups. There are now many self-interested, profit-making, exploitative, and un-altruistic NGOs that are operating and masquerading as civil society organisations" (Ikelegbe, 2013:47).

One of the most challenging problems those seeking to prevent conflicts must overcome is the lack of political will for action. CSOs in Africa lack the political will to execute policies which is crucial in preventing major humanitarian crisis or genocide at times; they possess a fragile capacity for mobilisation and cannot sustain a long period of protest; inability to access information; disconnection from rural organisations; lack of clear cut objectives and experience; and government patronage. These challenges are daunting and adversative to security provisioning, democratic consolidation, and good governance. CSOs can therefore be more effective in security provisioning, provision of humanitarian assistance, conflict prevention, peace-building, and democratisation process only when they form structures that correspond to the state's institutions and can therefore better respond to their challenges. However, despite the shortcomings of CSOs in Africa, they have been active in the struggle for good governance. Civil society organisations are an essential prerequisite for the entrenchment and promotion of good governance as their activities are crucial in the political, economic, and socio-cultural development of African countries. Omede and Bakare (2014) maintain that CSOs improve the quality of governance; they develop the capacity of governments to apply the principles of accountability, transparency and openness; and work towards gaining the commitment of all elected officials, public servants, and NGOs to good governance. Concisely, they have contributed enormously to democratic consolidation and sustainable development through a functional partnership with states in security provisioning in Africa. These organisations serve as the internal disciplinary mechanism to check and balance the activities of government to avoid wasteful spending, misappropriation and embezzlement of funds and help determine or prioritise the needs of the people.

According to the African Union (2006:v), some of the functional partnership between the state and civil society in security provisioning in Africa include the immediate humanitarian needs of affected populations, recovery and reconstruction efforts in post-conflict societies; demobilisation, disarmament, reintegration, and rehabilitation (DDRR) of former combatants; the return and reintegration of internally displaced persons (IDPs) and returnee refugees; grassroots level reconciliation; as well as the establishment of the foundations for good governance in both the political and socio-economic spheres. These tasks should also be undertaken in tandem with Africa's efforts toward regional integration and socio-economic regeneration. Despite the magnitude and complexity of the challenges at hand, however, the affected African countries, the Regional Economic Communities (RECs) and the AU Commission, with the support of a host of Africa's partners, continue to make a tremendous effort and register remarkable progress. Angola, Sierra Leone, Liberia, Cote d'Ivoire, Sudan, the Democratic Republic of Congo (DRC), Burundi, the Central African Republic (CAR) and Comoros have all made strides in their recovery and reconstruction efforts. Undoubtedly, the achievements made to date need to be consolidated further.

Other prospects of CSOs in security provisioning as outline by An International Directory of the European Platform for Conflict Prevention and Transformation (1998) include performing a preventive role through early warning function by alerting the international community of potential breakdowns in a distressed country's government or relations among the country's major domestic groups as was seen in many African countries; Human rights monitoring through the gathering of supplementary information in areas of tension, sending out a mission, etc.; Peace-building/strengthening civil society through small-scale local capacity building (training of local leaders, etc.); Supporting peace constituencies by establishing well-knit local infrastructures across the levels of society that empower the resources for re-conciliation; Conflict resolution activities through training of their employees and facilitating conflict resolution mechanisms; ensuring advocacy, lobby and education (International Directory, 1998). In the 21$^{st}$ century according to Cedric de Coning (2007), the focus of international conflict management is increasingly shifting from peace-keeping, which was about maintaining the status quo, to peace-building, which has to do with managing transitions. This development, from peace-keeping to peace-building has emerged as new, mostly civilian; dimensions were added to traditional military peace-keeping mandates. These new dimensions were aimed at assisting the host country to sustain the momentum of the peace process by supporting transitional arrangements; establishing new or reforming existing national institu-tions such as the defence force, police service, and the judiciary; assisting with the organising of elections; supporting constitution drafting processes; and, facilitating restorative justice initiatives.

## Conclusion

The capacity of a society to continue to exist despite prevailing violent conflicts depends on its ability to devise the means of curbing the negative impact of such disputes. The attempts made by civil society in partnership with the military across African region in security provisioning and promoting peaceful co-existence to some extent have recorded success since there is re-lative peace in most of the regions. At the same time, there still exists flash-light of conflicts in some part of Africa. The importance of a partnership between the civilians and the military in curbing the insecurity in Africa cannot be over-emphasised as many success stories were re-corded in Nigeria, Chad, Niger, Cameroon, Uganda, Somalia, CAR, among others, despite the negative impacts of human rights violations experienced by these informal security providers. CSOs are therefore an essential element in any peace-building process, without which it would be challenging to attain viable security and developmental programmes. Nevertheless, it is a matter of utmost urgency if state-society relations are to improve such that cycles of violence can be prevented and reversed.

## References

African Union. (2006). *Policy on post-conflict reconstruction and development (PCRD)*. Ethiopia: Addis Ababa.

Agbese, P. O. (1997). The military as an obstacle to the, enterprise, towards an agenda for permanent military disengagement from politics in Nigeria. In E. I. Udogu (Ed.), *Democracy and democratization in Africa, towards the 21st century*. Leiden: E. J. Brill.

Ahrne, G. (1996). Civil society and civil organisations. Organisation *Articles*, 3(1), 109–120.

Ake, C. (1981). *A political economy of Africa*. London: Longman Publishers.

An International Directory. (1998). *Prevention and management of violent conflicts*. Utrecht: European Platform for Conflict Prevention and Transformation Publication.

EPPCPT (European Platform for Conflict Prevention and Transformation). (1998). *Prevention and man-agement of violent conflicts: An international directory*. Utrecht, the Netherlands: European Platform for Conflict Prevention and Transformation.

Bamidele, O. (2016). Civilian Joint Task Force (CJTF) – A community security option: A comprehensive and proactive approach to counter-terrorism. *Journal for Deradicalization*, 7, 124–144, Ado-Ekiti, Nigeria: A Publication of Institute of Peace, Security and Governance.

Bassey, C. (2007). Introduction: The nexus of conflict and development crisis in Africa. In C. Bassey & O. Oshita (Eds.), *Conflict Resolution, Identity Crisis and Development in Africa*. Lagos, Nigeria: Malthouse Press Ltd.

Beckmam, B. (1988). Peasants and democratic struggles in Nigeria. *Review of African Political Economy (ROAPE), 15*(41), 30.

Bereketeab, R. (2013). State building, conflict and global war on terror in the Horn of Africa. In Sabelo, et al., (Eds.), *Bondage of boundaries and identity politics in post-colonial Africa: The northern problem and ethno futures*. South Africa: African Institute of South Africa.

Bradbury, M., & Healy, S. (2010). *Endless war: A brief history of the Somali conflict*. Accord: Conciliation Resources. www.c-r.org/accord-article/endless-war-brief-history-somali-conflict Accessed 30.09.2017.

Burk, J. (2002). Theories of democratic civil-military relations. *Armed Forces and Society, 29*(1), 7–29.

Clausewitz, C. (1832 [1989]). *On war*. Princeton: Princeton University Press.

de Coning, Cedric (2007). *Civil-military coordination in United Nations and African peace operations*. Mhlanga, South Africa: The African Centre for the Constructive Resolution of Disputes (ACCORD).

Commission for African, UK House of Commons. (2006). *Conflict and development: Peace building and post-conflict reconstruction, sixth report of session 2005-2006*, Vol. 1. London: International Development Committee.

Daniel, A. (2015). *Resistance to Boko Haram: Civilian Joint Task Forces (CJTF) in North-Eastern Nigeria. Conflict Studies*, Special Issue [Online], 3–22. Retrieved from csq.ro/wp-content/uploads/1-Daniel-AGBIBOA.pdf. Accessed 4 October, 2020.

Diamond, L. (1994). Rethinking civil society: Towards democratic consolidation. *Journal of Democracy, 5*(3), 4–17.

Diamond, L. (1999). *Developing democracy: Towards consolidation*. Baltimore: John Hopkins University Press.

Faiza, J. (2010). *Somali women and peace-building*. Accord: Conciliation Resources. www.cr.org/accord/somali-women-and-peacebuilding Accessed 30.09.2017.

Garba, M. K. (2014). *Civil-military relations in Nigeria: The case of parliamentary oversight of the defence sector: 1999-2004*, A PhD Thesis Submitted to the Department of Political Science. Zaria: Nigeria: Ahmadu Bello University.

Gramsci, A. (1971). *Prison notebooks: State and civil society*. New York: International Publishers.

Huntington, S. P. (1957). *The soldier and the state: The theory and politics of civil-military relations*. Cambridge: Harvard University Press.

Hyden, G., Court, J., & Mease, K. (2003). Civil society and governance in 16 developing countries, *World governance survey discussion paper 4*. London, UK: Overseas Development Institute (ODI).

Hyden, G. (1986). The anomaly of African peasantry. *Development and Change, 17*(4), 677–705. Leiden University. doi: 10.111/j.1467-7660.1986.tb00259.

IASC (International Agency Standing Committee). (2008). *Civil-military guidelines and references for complex emergencies*. New York: United Nations.

Jacob, B., & Ayse, S. K. (2009). Religion and meditation: The role of faith-based actors in international conflict resolution. *International Negotiation, 14*, 175–204.

Janowitz, M. (1960). *The professional soldier: A social and political portrait*. New York: Free Press of Glencoe.

Joseph, T. A. (2010). The hybridization of conflict resolution models and strategies in Nigeria: A case study of non-governmental organisations. In I. A. Olawale & I. O. Oloyede (Eds.), *Dynamics of peace processes*. Nigeria: Centre for Peace and Strategic Studies (SPSP), University of Ilorin.

Keane, J. (1988). Despotism and democracy: The origin and development of the distinction between civil society and the state 1750–1850. In J. Keane (Ed.), *Civil society and the state*. New York: Verso.

Ibeanu, O. (2000). History of Civil Society Theorization, A paper presented at the 2000 Research Training Workshop of the Centre for Research and Documentation, Kano, August 15, 2000.

Ikelegbe, A. O. (2013). State, civil society and sustainable development in Nigeria. *Monograph Series No. 7*. Benin City, Nigeria: Centre for Population and Environmental Development (CPED).

Kotter, T. (2007). Fostering human security through active engagement of civil society actors. *Human Security Journal, 4*, 44–55.

International Directory (1998). *Prevention and Management of Violent Conflicts*. Utrecht: European Platform for Conflict Prevention and Transformation Publication.

Madunagu, E. (1999). *Civil Society and the State. The Guardian (Lagos)*, November 11, 1999.

Mamdani, M. & Wammba-dia-Wamba, E. (Eds.). (1995). *African studies in social movements and democracy.* Dakar, Senegal: CODESRIA.

Mandel, R. (2004). The wartime utility of precision versus brute force in weaponry. *Armed Forces & Society, 30*(2), 171–201.

Marshall, M. G. (2005). *Conflict trends in Africa 1946-2004: A macro-comparative perspective. A report prepared for the African Conflict Prevention Pool (ACPP).* London, UK: Department for International Development (DFID), October 14.

Mohammed, H. (2010). *Civil society organisations and democratization in Nigeria: The politics of struggles for human rights.* Ibadan: Nigeria: Kraft Books Ltd.

Mouzelis, N. (1996). Modernity, late development and civil society. In L. Rudebeck & O. Tornquist (Eds.), Democratisation *in the third world.* Uppsala: Sweden: Uppsala University Press.

Nigerian Watch (2014, November 20). Borno state governor promises to arm civilian joint task force to fight Boko Haram. Retrieved from http://www.nigerianwatch.com/news/5832-borno-state-governor-promises-to-arm-civilian-joint-task-force-to-fight-boko-haram(Accessed 19.09.2017.

Nnoli, O. (1978). *Ethnic politics in Nigeria.* Enugu, Nigeria: Fourth Dimension.

Okereke, D. (2013 December 16). How Nigeria overcome terrorism, insurgency and instability. *Vigilance Magazine.* Retrieved from http://www.vigilance.securitymagazine.com/news/terrorism-watch/4542-how-nigeria-overcome-terrorism-insurgency-and-instability. Accessed October 5, 2020.

Omach, P. (2016). Civil society organisations and local level peace-building in Northern Uganda. *Journal of Asian and African Studies, 51*(1), 77–96.

Omede, A. J., & Bakare, A. R. (2014). The impact of civil society organisations on sustainable development in developing countries: The Nigerian experience. *African Research Review, An International Multidisciplinary Journal, Ethiopia, 8*(1), Serial No. 32, January, 205–227.

Omoigui N. (2005). History of civil-military relations in Nigeria: The second transition, parts 1 to 9. Available from http://www.dawodu.com/omoigui7.htm. Accessed 18.09.2017.

Richard, H. K. (1997). How democracies control the military. *Journal of Democracy, 8*(4), 140–153, October 8.

Richard, K. (2006). Responding to conflicts: The role of civil society in West Africa. In G. B. Shedrack (Ed.), *Introduction to peace and conflict studies in West Africa: A reader.* Ibadan, Nigeria: Spectrum Books Limited.

Rothchild, D., & Lawson, L. (1997). The interaction between state and civil society in Africa: From deadlock to new routines. In J. Harbeson, D. Rothchild, N. Chazan (Eds.), *Civil society and the state in Africa.* London: Lynne Reinner.

Sun Tzu (1870[1971]). *The art of war.* Oxford: Oxford University Press.

The Economist. (2000, May 13). *The Hopeless Continent.* London, UK: The Economist Newspaper Limited.

Thierry, V. (2015). Analysis of conflict and peace-building in the Central African Republic. *Conciliation Resources,* www.c-r.org/downloads/872, CR CAR report ENG FINAL, web.pdf Accessed on 30.09.2017.

Welch, C. E., & Johanna, M. (1998). *USAID programs in civil-military relations.* USA: USAID/Centre for Democracy and Governance.

Williams, G. (1987). Primitive accumulation: The way to progress. *Development and Change, 18*(4), 637–659. London: SAGE.

Wogu, I. A., & Ibietan, J. (2014). Civil-military relations and leadership crisis in 21st century Africa. *An Inquiry, International Journal of Innovative Social Sciences and Humanities Research, 2*(1), 48–61.

# Part II
# Transnational perspectives

# 12

# UN counterterrorism and counterinsurgency operations in Africa

## Paradigm shifts and emerging structures

*Lucky Imade*

## Introduction

Terrorism is not endemic to Africa; it is a global phenomenon that has inflicted a painful sting on the continent. It has been used by both states and non-state actors in the forms of tactics used by nationalist movements, coup d'état, political assassinations and groups insurgency to advance their goals and objectives during the continent's transition to independence and subsequent post-colonial period (Crenshaw, 1994). Undoubtedly, the violence perpetrated by major terrorist groups (such as Boko Haram in Nigeria and the environs, The Lord's Resistance Army in Uganda, al-Shabaab in Somalia and Al-Qaeda in the Islamic Maghreb in North Africa) has far-reaching national and international implications on the continent of Africa. Terrorism has halted Africa's development. It has alienated the continent from significant foreign direct investment (FDI), turning Africa into a pariah continent. More importantly, it has exacerbated the already tensed situation of ethnic strife and religious nationalism in many countries in Africa. For the most time, Africa doesn't appear to be high up on UN's security agenda as evident by the UN nonchalant attitude towards Rwanda Holocaust, Sudan's Darfur conflict and DRC crises until after 9/11. Counterterrorism and counterinsurgency play no significant role in the UN's peacekeeping operations. The UN has laid more emphasis on upholding one of the primary purposes of its charter: "to maintain international peace and security" (United Nations, 1945).

The events surrounding the terrorist attacks on the United States on 11 September 2001 provided a perfect backdrop for the UN to seek multilateral efforts in the fight against terrorism that resulted in the establishment of the UN Global Counterterrorism Strategy and Plan of Action, also referred to as the four pillars strategic framework:

1. Measures to address the conditions conducive to the spread of terrorism;
2. Measures to prevent and combat terrorism;
3. Measures to build the States' capacity to prevent and combat terrorism and to strengthen the role of the United Nations system in this regard; and

4. Measures to ensure respect for universal human rights and the rule of law as the foundation of the fight against terrorism.

This marked the first time in the history of the UN that the entire members of the General Assembly unanimously agreed upon a common strategy and a solidified plan of action, which underscores the steadfastness of the global community to fight terrorism. This study takes a holistic assessment of the UN's four pillars strategic framework in the areas of counterterrorism and counterinsurgency in Africa. With particular emphasis on three central bodies: Counterterrorism Committee (CTC) and Counterterrorism Committee Executive Directorate (CTED) that were established by Security Council's resolutions 1373 in 2001 and 1535 in 2004 respectively, including Counterterrorism Implementation Task Force (CTITF) set by the Secretary-General in 2005. It concludes with action-packed recommendations on counterterrorism and counterinsurgency operations in Africa.

## Conceptual issues

### What is counterterrorism (CT)?

Defining counterterrorism without first limiting terrorism is tantamount to "putting the cart before the horse"—to do first what ought to be done afterwards; to reverse the proper order of things. There are more than 1001 definitions of terrorism out there. It is difficult to define terrorism as a concept because of a vast range of different interpretations. The ambiguity surrounding the term is partly the result of the eagerness with which terrorism has been incorporated into the literature after 9/11.

Historically, terrorists in Africa have committed several atrocities under the guise of freedom fighters and revolutionaries in an attempt to liberate themselves from the hands of their oppressors and seeking an ultimate goal of self-determination. According to Gemson Freedman (2002:10), Terrorism has taken on three different characteristics—religion, geography and culture, which rendered it difficult to define. The definition of terrorism is in the eyes of the beholders. On one side, it can be seen as an act of revolution and struggle for freedom. In contrast, on the other side, it can be seen from the lenses of violence driven by ideological incompatibility. In this sense, terrorism is justifiable from both perspectives. Ahmed (1998:5) classified terrorism into five parts, namely:

1. State Terrorism
2. Religious Terrorism
3. Criminal Terrorism
4. Political Terrorism
5. Oppositional Terrorism

*State Terrorism*—is considered state-sponsored terrorism against foreign entities or their people. A perfect example of that was the 1998 Lockerbie bombing of Pan Am Flight 103, killing 270 people by the Libyan government. The normalisation of relations between Washington and Tripoli came after reparation payments deal for the families of the US victims was reached in 2008.

*Religious Terrorism*—is religiously motivated and influenced by moral sentiment. An egregious example will be Osama Bin Laden's terrorist attacks on 11 September 2001 in the United States.

*Criminal Terrorism*—refers to a violent act perpetrated on a civilian population to endanger the property, safety, health and welfare of the people.

*Political Terrorism*—involves a violent act that applies the same tactics of terrorism, but with different goals and objectives mainly aimed at making a political or ideological statement in protest of government policy or action.

*Oppositional Terrorism*—is politically, religiously, ideologically motivated and targeted at opponents in retaliation for wrongdoing.

Ahmed was instrumental in capitalising on these five parts in his definition of terrorism, which states as "The use of terrorising methods of governing or resisting a government" (ibid). He cited the example of Menachem Begin, former late Israeli Prime Minister, who was at one time or the other former Commander in Chief of the Irgun IsvalLeumi, a Zionist terrorist organisation. He was so notorious in his activities against the state that they placed a 1,000 pounds bounty on his head before becoming the Prime Minister of Israel. This is a testament to Ahmed's last statement that a "terrorist of yesterday is the hero of today and the hero of yesterday becomes the terrorist of today" (Ahmed, 1998:1).

Jessica Stein distinguishes two characteristics of terrorism that separate it from other forms of violence: first, its main targets are non-combatants and second, its primary intention is to stir up fear and hate-mongering with frenzy. These characteristics essentially influenced her definition of terrorism as "an act or threat of violence against non-combatants with the objective of exacting revenge, intimidating, or otherwise influencing an audience, all in the name of purifying the world" (Stein, 2003:20).

From the definitions of terrorism discussed above, it seems that there is no clear definition of terrorism. And this poses a significant challenge to the implementation of the Global Strategy at different stages. This ambiguity in defining the phenomenon of terrorism is, for all intents and purposes, a bad omen for the collective international efforts against terrorism. To reached a consensus definition that could break the stalemate, the UN Secretary-General in 2004 set up a high-level panel to look into the issue and make a recommendation, which appears below:

..., we believe there is particular value in achieving a consensus definition within the General Assembly, given its unique legitimacy in normative terms, and that it should rapidly complete negotiations on a comprehensive convention on terrorism.

That definition of terrorism should include the following elements:

a. Recognition, in the preamble, that State use of force against civilians is regulated by the Geneva Conventions and other instruments, and, if of sufficient scale, constitutes a war crime by the persons concerned or a crime against humanity;

b. Restatement that acts under the 12 preceding anti-terrorism conventions are terrorism, and a declaration that they are a crime under international law; and restatement that the Geneva Conventions and Protocols prohibit terrorism in time of armed conflict;

c. Reference to the definitions contained in the 1999 International Convention for the Suppression of the Financing of Terrorism and Security Council resolution 1566 (2004);

d. Description of terrorism as "any action, in addition to actions already specified by the existing conventions on aspects of terrorism, the Geneva Conventions and Security Council resolution 1566 (2004) that is intended to cause death or serious

*Table 12.1* Counterterrorism Models

| Model | Defensive | Reconciliatory | Criminal-Justice | War |
|---|---|---|---|---|
| **General Features** | Terrorism is a physical and psychological threat | Terrorism is a political problem | Terrorism is a crime | Terrorism is an act of war |
| **Goals and Methods of the State** | Protecting potential targets and victims | Addressing the root causes of terrorism | Arrest and punish terrorists according to the rule of law | Eliminate terrorism through military force |
| **Legal Aspects** | Corresponds in most cases to the elements of liberal democracy, with exceptions when practices undermine civil liberties | Corresponds with the law | Corresponds with the law and is subject to constant judicial oversight | Corresponds to laws of war, or may ignore the law entirely |
| **Agents** | Police, private security companies, firefighters and paramedics, other state and municipal agencies | Politicians, policymakers, brokers, diplomats | Police and the criminal justice system | Intelligence and military units |

Source: Ami Pedahzur, The Israeli Secret Services and the Struggle against Terrorism (New York: Columbia University Press, 2009), Table 1.1.

bodily harm to civilians or non-combatants, when the purpose of such act, by its nature or context, is to intimidate a population or to compel a Government or an international organisation to do or to abstain from doing any act" (United Nations, 2004:163–164).

In light of the above effort to define this critical phenomenon, still, there is no accepted definition of terrorism in the UN. In this chapter, I subscribed to the following description of terrorism by the FBI, which means "the unlawful use of force or violence against persons or property to intimidate or coerce a government, the civilian population, or any segment thereof, in furtherance of political or social objectives." (Federal Bureau of Investigation, 2006:16). Now that we have defined what terrorism is let us turn to what counterterrorism entails in dealing with this problem. The United States Counterterrorism Center (USCTC) defines counterterrorism as the "practices, tactics, techniques, and strategies that governments, militaries, police departments and corporations adopt in response to terrorist threats and/or acts, both real and imputed" (Kolodkin, 2016:7).

## What is counterinsurgency (COIN)?

The same argument about the definition of terrorism first before defining counterterrorism is applicable here, as we have to define insurgency first before delving into the true meaning of counterinsurgency. As H. Thomas Hayden, a retired Marine for over 35 years of experience in government and defence industry puts it: "insurgency is an organised movement aimed at the overthrown of a constituted government through the use of subversion, espionage, terrorism and armed conflict" (Hayden, 2007). And the manual further states that counterinsurgency may be defined as "comprehensive civilian and military efforts taken to defeat and contain insurgency and address its root causes simultaneously" (Hayden, 2007).

David J. Kilcullen described counterinsurgency as operating in a "conflict ecosystem" (Kilcullen, 2006). According to Kilcullen, it is a matter of survival of the fittest with many actors (both state and non-state) competing in a chaotic and unstable environment. He recommends the "three pillars" model—Security, Political and Economic as a basis for collaboration with robust and reliable information (Ibid).

## What is the difference between COIN and CT?

This section discusses the dichotomy between CT and COIN. CT and COIN will not be used interchangeably in this paper because they are different concepts with different meanings. However, sometimes some overlaps cut across violence as a means of ideological communication and social change, which suggest that the two are dichotomous, but distinct in their different principles. Essentially, the difference between CT and COIN is that while CT is more concerned with battling with the tactics and strategy adopted by terrorists, COIN focuses more exclusively on ways and manners political violence employed by minority groups, including terrorists can be suppressed. Some academics further categorised the strategy mostly used by terrorists into a three-stage process: disorientation, target response and gaining legitimacy (Neumann and Smith, 2008:32).

1. Disorientation seeks to sow within a general population a sense of insecurity and detract from the legitimacy of existing state structures, often through random acts of violence that prey upon the civilian population in general (Ibid, pp. 33–39)
2. Target response seeks to prompt a disproportionately harsh collective reprisal from a government, to radicalise the affected population and win international legitimacy, or to wrestle political concessions (Ibid, pp. 40–46)
3. Gaining legitimacy is where the terrorist group seeks to transfer legitimacy from the government to its cause through the skilful manipulation of the media, through grassroots social agitation, or alternative media such as the Internet. At this stage, ideology becomes crucial (Ibid, pp. 46–53)

As increasing attention is paid to repression, military and paramilitary action, and systematic human rights abuses, the critical role of CT and COIN can no longer be ignored. However, the strategy employed by both CT and COIN must not only focus on security concerns. Still, it must put on a human face by also focusing on the political, economic and social situations of the perpetrators (Santos, 2011). Let us now turn the background of the subject matter.

## Background: terrorism, insurgency and CT-COIN in comparative perspective

Terrorism and insurgency are not new to the continent of Africa. Still, the events surrounding 9/11 terrorists' attacks on the United States have brought terrorism and insurgency to the limelight of international discourse. Post 9/11 also brought the UN to the centre stage of the fight against Islamic extremism. Still, as Chandler and Gunaratna put it, "the opportunity has been missed, long-term visionary policies have been held hostage to short-term political expediency, and what should have been a watershed has become a trickle in the sand" (Chandler & Gunaratna, 2007). To fully understand the concepts of terrorism and insurgency in theoretical and practical terms, we must first and foremost view them from a historical perspective. It is only through an examination of history that one can fully understand the current environment within which terrorism and insurgency dwell and their implications for security and welfare of the people.

## 1973: invasion of Saudi Embassy in Khartoum, Republic of Sudan

On March 1, 1973, a terrorist group known as "Black September" invaded the Saudi Embassy in Khartoum, Sudan and kidnapped two top US diplomats—Ambassador Cleo Noel and his Deputy Chief of Mission, George Moore. They demanded among other things the release of Sirhan (a Palestinian convicted of assassinating US Senator, Robert F. Kennedy) and other Palestinians languishing in an Israeli jail. The top two U.S. diplomats were killed as Richard Nixon, who was the U.S. President at the time refused to negotiate with the terrorists. Former Chairman of the Palestinian Liberation Organization (PLO), Yasser Arafat was accused of aiding and abetting the terrorists, an accusation he denied up to his death on 11 November 2004 (Sibilla, 2013).

## 1988: Pan Am Flight 103 bombing in Lockerbie, United Kingdom

On 21 December 1988, the world stood still watching Pan Am flight 103 en route to New York's JFK airport from London's Heathrow airport exploded over Lockerbie, Scotland, killing all 243 passengers and 16 crew members on board, including 11 people on the ground. The investigation later traced the attack to be perpetrated by Libya, and the target was the 189 American victims on board in retaliation for the 1986 U.S. airstrikes against Libya that led to the death of Muammar al-Qaddafi's young daughter and several other people (Smith, 2014). Quaddafi denied any wrongdoing and refused bluntly to hand over the suspected Libyan intelligence agents Abdel Basset Ali al-Megrahi and Lamen Khalifa Fhimah to the US until 1999 when UN sanctions took its toll on Libyan economy. Finally, in 2003, Libya agreed to pay each victim's family approximately $8 million in exchange for the UN lifting the sanctions against Libya (CIA, 2012), (London Evening Standard, 2003).

## 1998: US Embassy bombings in Kenya and Tanzania

On 7 August 1998, terrorism entered a new phase in Africa as American interests in the horn of Africa were the targets. The al-Qaeda networks attacked U.S. Embassies in Nairobi, Kenya and Dar es Salaam, Tanzania simultaneously and with identical tactics in retaliation for the deployment of U.S. troops to Saudi Arabia. The U.S. government wasted no time in linking these attacks to Islamic Jihadists—al-Qaeda under the auspices of Osama Bin Laden. The dual terrorist attacks claimed the lives of 224 people, including 12 Americans, and more than 4,500 people sustained injuries of various kinds. On August 20, 1998, President Bill Clinton responded by ordering cruise missiles to be launched against Bin Laden's terrorist training camps and a pharmaceutical plant in Afghanistan and Sudan respectively in retaliation for the Embassy bombings. The State Department offers a bounty of $5 million for information leading to arrest or conviction of Osama Bin Laden. These events according to experts propelled Osama Bin Laden to the limelight of who's who in international terrorism (BBC News, 1998).

## 2002: Mombasa bombing, Kenya

In 2002, the Al-Qaeda network launched another attack in Africa, this time it was directed at the Israeli interests in Mombasa. There were plots masterminded by Al-Qaeda to attack an Israeli-owned Paradise Hotel in Mombasa, Kenya simultaneously and to lunch a surface-to-air missile towards an Israeli airliner en-route from Mombasa to Tel Avin with Israeli tourists on board. Although the two attempts were unsuccessful with few casualties the message was sound and clear, terrorism from Islamic fundamentalists is now a matter of concern and a clear and present danger for everyone in Africa. (Burgess, 2002:3).

Boko Haram phenomenon came to the limelight of political discourse in Nigeria in 2009. Still, its origin dates back to 2002 when Mohammed Yusuf (deceased) and some radical Islamic groups challenged the secular state status quo and called for its overthrown for the theocratic state as an alternative. At this time, Boko Haram was depicted in regional Hausa dialect, as "Western influence is a sin." Or "Western education is forbidden." Boko Haram officially refers to itself as "Jama'atuAhlis Sunna Lidda'awatiwal-Jihad", which means in Arabic as "People Committed to the Propagation of the Prophet's Teachings and Jihad". Boko Haram's initial goal focused exclusively on establishing an Islamic caliphate in Nigeria under the auspices of Sharia Law, while at the same time supporting Islamic education. Historically, Boko Haram has undergone three distinct transformations: (Aghedo & Eke, 2003:65–84).

*Phase One—2003–2005:* Kanama Hajra—this was characterised by the notion of "flight from the centre of infidels" to rural purity aimed at retreating from the decadence of society to a place that is holy and purified as evidenced by Mohammadu Ali (mentor of Muhammad Yusuf) who fled after criticising the government for corruption. Yusuf also travelled to Saudi Arabia to get away from this commotion that was going on at the time. When Yusuf returned to Nigeria, Boko Haram was coopted into the political arena by the former Governor of Borno State, Ali Modu Sheriff for political expediency during his electioneering campaigns for the gubernatorial elections in Borno state. This was short-lived as he dumped the group after he accomplished his mission, but reneged on the establishment of Sharia in the state.

*Phase Two—2006–2009:* Da'wah—this phase was characterised by "intensive proselytisation, recruitment, indoctrination, and radicalisation of its members." (Ibid) And this phase also leads to the death of Mohammad Yusuf.

*Phase Three—2009–Present:* Bloody Phase—Characterised by violent strategy—"drive-by shootings, kidnapping, beheadings, jailbreaks, sex slavery, use of child soldiers, and suicide bombings—more in line with global Salafist movements than its own past" (ibid).

If there is anything Boko Haram and the Maitatsine have in common, it is that they both usually view democracy and western influence with distaste. They also have a penchant for the establishment of a caliphate and to strengthen Islamic education in Nigeria. Boko Haram borrowed a leaf from Maitatsine, and most of their operational tactics, strategies and ideology are identical all shapes and forms. Boko Haram sees Nigeria's leaders (Muslims and non-Muslims) as infidels that are fixated with material possession to the detriment of the masses. The only solution is to replace the corrupt politicians and create an Islamic state.

The activities of Boko Haram in the North-eastern part of Nigeria underscored the importance of counterterrorism and counterinsurgency in Africa, particularly in Nigeria. According to the Internal Displacement Monitoring Center (IDMC) and the Norwegian Refugee Council (NRC), there are 3.3 million persons displaced by Boko Haram insurgency and other communal clashes in Nigeria. That figures put Nigeria in the third-place globally behind Syria and Colombia with 6.5 million and 5.7 million IDPs respectively. The changes these have brought to the North-Eastern part of Nigeria are unprecedented and impossible, which calls for urgent attention from the international community.

## 2005–2017: Al-Qaeda in the Islamic Maghreb (AQIM) terrorist activities in the Sahel

There is a direct link between Boko Haram and AQIM in the areas of training, intelligence sharing and logistics. AQIM is believed to be a subsidiary of Salafist Group for Preaching and Combat (GSPC) based in Algeria and also an affiliate of Islamic Salvation Army (FIS). AQIM's origin dates back to 1992 but came to be known internationally between 2005–2007 by kidnapping and assassination of UN aid workers and tourists from Western nations. (Onuoha, 2010:85). AQIM has been a nightmare to the United Nations Multidimensional Integrated Stabilization Mission in Mali (MINUSMA) by claiming responsibilities for more than 69 fatalities of its peacekeepers from July 2013 to August 2016 (United Nations, 2016:4a) United Nations (2016) (4a) Fatalities by Mission, Year and Incident Type." United Nations Peacekeeping. This peacekeeping mission in Mali is considered the deadliest on-going UN mission due to the activities of AQIM in the sub-region of West Africa.

## 1991–2017: Al-Shabaab violent extremisms in Somalia, Kenya and the sub-region of East Africa

Al Shabaab has its origin from the defunct Union of Islamic Courts that held helms of affairs in most of Mogadishu before being flushed out by Ethiopian armed forces in 2006. It has declared untold hardship on the people of Somalia and neighbouring countries such as Kenya (BBC News, 1998). Al-Shabaab has committed several atrocities on innocent citizens of Somalia and has gone as far as Kenya to lay attacks on innocent civilians on campuses and malls in retaliation for Kenya's support of the UN-backed Somali government and attacking Al-Shabaab militants. Although the group has been forced out of Somali's major cities from 2011 to 2012, their underground operations remain a threat for the fledgeling Somalia government to handle.

## 1989–2017: Lord's Resistance Army (LRA) insurgency in Northern Uganda, South Sudan, the Central African Republic and Democratic Republic of the Congo (DRC)

LRA originated as the Holy Spirit Movement under the auspices of Alice Lakwena and later morphed into a violent extremist group called LRA under the aegis of Joseph Konyi in Northern Uganda. Most of its logistical support came from Sudan but has subsided after the US intervened in protest. Ugandan People's Defence Forces (UPDF) staged a major offensive (Operation Iron Fist) against LRA but to no avail. They later backfired against UPDF as an unprecedented number of civilians lost their lives and the number of children abducted under 18 years old rose from approximately 12,000 in 2002 to 30,000 by 2004. This also increased the number of Internally Displaced Persons (IDPs) from an estimated 480,000 in 2001 to 1.8 million by 2005. LRA has since moved its operational activities to South Sudan, the Central African Republic and DRC. In 2015, a Washington-based Resolve LRA Crisis Initiative released a report saying the group membership has dwindled from 800 in 2009 to 200 by 2015 (Global Security.org, 2015). LRA committed numerous atrocities ranging from "abduction, rape, maiming, and killing of civilians, including children" (Global Security.org, 2015).

## UN counterterrorism and counterinsurgency operations: the case studies of CTC, CTED and CTITF

The General Assembly unanimously approved the Global Counterterrorism Strategy in its 2006 Summit orchestrated by then Secretary-General Kofi Annan. The events mark the genesis of the Four Pillars of the UN counterterrorism operations:

Pillar I—Measures to address the conditions conducive to the spread of terrorism;

Pillar II—Measures to prevent and combat terrorism;

Pillar III—Measures to build States' capacity to prevent and combat terrorism and to strengthen the role of the United Nations system in this regard; and

Pillar IV—Measures to ensure respect for human rights for all and the rule of law as the fundamental basis of the fight against terrorism (UN, 2001). This marked the first time that the entire members of the General Assembly unanimously agreed upon a common strategy and a solidified plan of action, which underscored the steadfastness of the global community to fight terrorism. This study takes a holistic assessment of these UN's four pillars strategic framework in the areas of CT and COIN in Africa with particular emphasis on CTC and CTED that were established by Security Council's resolutions 1373 in 2001 and 1535 in 2004 respectively. The study also looks at CTITF established by the Secretary-General in 2005 (UN's Security Council Resolution 1373, 2001).

The new transnational terrorism has increased violent extremism everywhere on the globe by leaps and bounds, and the UN has gone out of its comfort zone in countering violent extremism and terrorism by upholding one of its most foremost duties: "to maintain international peace and security" (United Nations, 1945). But previous assessments of the UN mission in fighting terrorism came short of expectation primarily due to the Cold War and decolonisation efforts in the colonial states by confining the fight against terrorism to the national levels. During this period, the UN lacked concerted efforts to fight terrorism because of varying definitions of the subject matter, which affected the 12 conventions passed in the past condemning terrorism as a transnational crime (Kramer & Yetiv, 2007). The call for concerted efforts fell on deaf ears as member states lack the capability and technical know-how to tackle the problems. It was not until the events of 9/11 that sparked the zeal and determination in every member to reach a consensus about the definitions and the fact that it affects everyone (Messmer and Yordan, 175). As former Secretary-General Ban Ki-moon puts it in his famous address to the General Assembly, "Terrorism hurts all nations—large and small, rich and poor. It takes its toll on human beings of every age and income, culture, and religion. It strikes against everything the United Nations stands for. The fight against terrorism is our common mission... Together, we must demonstrate that we are up to the task. Whether we like it or not, our generation will go down in history as one that was challenged to protect the world from terrorism" (Ban Ki-moon, 2007).

The events leading to 9/11 in the US were catalysts for change, which the UN Security Council seized as an opportunity to invoke Chapter VII of the UN Charter in which member states unanimously approved two counterterrorism resolutions as reprisals against the attacks: Resolutions 1373 and 1368 (SC Resolutions, 1373 and 1368). Resolution 1373 created a CTC, composed of all members of the Security Council and SC Resolution 1535 in 2004 divided CTC into three-tier body comprising of the following:

- The Plenary (composed of all members of the SC) and perform the following duties:

  o Set CTC's priorities for promotion and monitoring implementation of Resolution 1373 (2001);

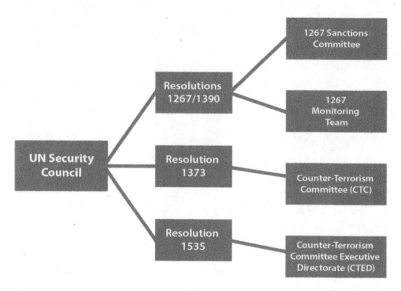

*Figure 12.1*   UN Framework for CT-COIN

- o  Refer to the Council difficulties in the implementation of the resolution provisions;
- o  Consider initiatives towards improving technical assistance;
- o  Strengthen contacts and coordination between CTC and other UN bodies
- o  Intensify interactions with international regional and sub-regional organisations to improve coordination;
- o  Approve the CTED's programme of work prepared by the Executive Director endorsed the proposals of the CTC Chairman on the subject. See Doc. S/2004/124, 19 February 2004 for the Chairman's proposals. (Doc. S/2004/124).

- • The Bureau (made up of the Chair and the three Vice-Chairs) their responsibilities include but not limited to:

- o  Act as first responder/screening agents to issues that are pertinent to the Plenary during the process of confirmation
- o  To coordinate and play second fiddle to the Sub-Committee on country reports by setting reachable guidelines (Doc. S/2004/124). Ibid,

- • The CTED—to complement the work of CTC, the SC adopted another resolution 1535 in 2004 that created the CTED. The CTED perform the following duties:

- o  Provides in-depth analysis of the implementation of Resolution 1373 (2001) by States;
- o  Engages states in a dialogue through letters, direct conversations and visits on a flexible and tailored basis;
- o  Facilitates capacity-building of the needy states in the area of technical assistance, compiles information on relevant best practices of international, regional organisations and entities;
- o  Cooperate with other relevant subsidiary bodies of the Council;
- o  Keeps in touch with international, regional, and sub-regional organisations (Counterterrorism Committee Executive Directorate, 2006).

In addition to CTC and CTED, the Secretary-General in 2005 created the CTITF charged with the responsibilities of harmonising the various entities in the UN system that are in any shapes or forms, directly or indirectly linked to counterterrorism mission of the UN. CTITF's initiatives are as follows:

- Factor counterterrorism into conflict prevention
- Provide a form for ending political and economic exclusion, especially among youths.
- Enhance technical assistance assessment, delivery and follow-up
- Improve UN coordination in planning the response to a terrorist attack that uses chemical, biological, radiological, or nuclear (CBRN) materials.
- Bring together stakeholders and partners to discuss and develop measures to counter the use of the Internet by terrorists for propaganda, incitement, and recruitment purposes.
- Find ways to meet international standards to block the financing of terrorism.
- Establish best practices to protect vulnerable targets—including UN field staff—and create a mechanism to share expertise.
- Assist countries in strengthening domestic legislation to protect human rights following international standards.
- Bring together victims from around the world to identify their needs and determine viable government responses to those needs (DPI/2439B/Rev.1).

Most of the UN CT operations in Africa were carried out by CTED and CTITF feeding information to CTC in carrying out its counterterrorism activity. In 2007, CTED shifted its focus in its counterterrorism approach in Africa from individual countries to more organised sub-regional demands for capacity building in technical related areas. In that direction, CTED has been very creative and productive in working with the African Center for the Study and Research on Terrorism (ACSRT) on a workshop to train West African law enforcement
officials in 2009. CTED has conducted numerous visits to West African states in collaboration with ACSRT, ECOWAS and other local NGOs to familiarise themselves with the expectations on the ground to design better and coherent strategies in linking the "donor" with the "recipient" states (Messmer & Yordan, 2011: 848). CTED main priorities are focusing on Resolution 1373 aspects of law enforcement and border control rather than being the jack-of-all-trades in its effort to fight terrorism in the West African region. For border security, CTED has acted as a surrogate for West African countries in several occasions in requesting cutting edge state-of-the-art equipment for border control from donors, but with minimal success. CTED also acted in other areas in West Africa in its counterterrorism operations. This includes activities such as improving travel-related documents issued by ECOWAS member states, organising training seminars on machine-readable travel-related documents, and creating computerised and reliable civil registries that can extend access to Interpol's 24/7 network.

## CTITF

191 UN Member states unanimously agreed to condemn violent extremism "in all its forms and manifestations" (Counterterrorism Committee Executive Directorate, 2006). Counterterrorism Committee Executive Directorate (2006) "The Role of the Counterterrorism Committee and its Executive Directorate in the International-Terrorism Effort". United Nations. During the 2005 world summit held in New York City. The

aftermath of this summit was the creation of the CTITF. CTITF has been very pervasive in engaging its more than 34 different entities, including CTC and CTED in counterterrorism operations in West Africa. One shining example is the work performed by UNDP in Integrated Assistance on Counterterrorism (I-ACT). This initiative is useful in no small measure in pooling all UN's traditional and non-traditional actors together to help countries in need of assistance in implementing the Global Counterterrorism Strategy. CTITF works in close contact with UNODC's Terrorism Prevention Branch (TPB) in conducting a needs assessment for CTITF members to sort out priority areas for assistance. CTITF then develops a platform for sharing critical information with all CTITF entities to fill the void. Nigeria and Burkina Faso are classic cases in point of countries that have taken advantage of these strategy-related capacity-building initiatives.

## Office of the high commissioner for human rights (OHCHR)

OHCHR has done a superb job in West Africa, especially in a country like Nigeria via I-ACT initiative about their draft counterterrorism bill. OHCHR is CTITF's leading partner in the West Africa region. It has conducted a series of activities in Protecting Human Rights While Countering Terrorism such as "working to convene regional meetings on human rights and counterterrorism, providing capacity-building assistance in the form of human rights training and legislative drafting assistance, and issuing and updating its Digest of Jurisprudence of the United Nations and Regional Organizations on the Protection of Human Rights While Countering Terrorism" (HR/PUB/03/1).

## UN counterterrorism strategies in Africa

Looking at the role of the UN in counterterrorism operations in Africa, former Secretary-General, Kofi Annan's name will feature prominently with his keynote address at the 2005 International Summit on Democracy, Terrorism and Security. Kofi Annan reiterated five elements that are critical to fighting terrorism in Africa that later form the basic building blocks for the UN Global Counterterrorism Strategy adopted in 2006. The five elements were dubbed the 5 D's as follows:

- Dissuade disaffected groups from choosing terrorism as a tactic to achieve their goals;
- Deny terrorists the ability to carry out their attacks;
- Deter them from supporting terrorists;
- Develop the capacity to prevent terrorism; and
- Defend human rights in the struggle against terrorism. (Kofi Annan, 2005).

Numerous entities within the UN system have done a lot of jobs trying to sensitise the importance of implementing UN counterterrorism strategy in Africa. The most pervasive are CTC, CTED and CTITF in the areas of enhancing national legislative framework, promoting border control and cooperation. Before CTC, CTED and CTITF, there were other matters relating to Security Council's mandate of maintaining peace and security that prompted the SC to adopt several resolutions germane to counterterrorism in Africa such as Resolutions 1044 of 1996 that calls upon the government of Sudan to expedite action in extraditing to Ethiopia for prosecution the three suspects from Sudan wanted in connection with an assassination attempt on the life of former President of Egypt, Hosni Mubarak. Resolution 1189 of 1998 relating to US Embassy bombing in Nairobi, Kenya and Dar-es-Salaam, Tanzania (Saul, 2005:151).

The last straw that sensitises the importance of counterterrorism operations in Africa came in 2011 when Boko Haram claimed responsibility for bombing the UN building in Abuja. The then UN secretary-general reiterated the need to strengthen international cooperation between states to combat international terrorism in all its forms and manifestations (Copeland, 2013:16).

There has been increasing attention to the on-going debates concerning whether UN Peacekeeping Operations should be expanded to include counterterrorism and counterinsurgency tasks. This is considered necessary due to the dire humanitarian situation attached to the crisis of violent extremism and terrorism worldwide, which have increased fatalities from 3329 in 2000 to 32,685 in 2004 (IEP, 2015) Opinion differs on the role of the UN when it comes to taking on the tasks of counterterrorism, especially in Africa. On the one hand are those who see the UN as an impartial arbiter in any disputes between member states and cannot take on the mandate of counterterrorism, mostly as the UN failed woefully to define the phenomenon of terrorism. On the other hand, some support expanding the UN mandate to include counterterrorism citing success stories of including enforcement brigades in United Nations Organization Stabilization Mission in the Democratic Republic of the Congo (MONUSCO) and United Nations Mission in the Republic of South Sudan (UNMISS). UN General Assembly, 2016)

The al-Qaeda threat in Mali presents the most fundamental challenge to the implementation of UN Global Counterterrorism Operations in Africa via the United Nations Peacekeeping Operation in Mali (MINUSMA). In 2016, UN's Security Council adopted Resolution 2295 authorising "more proactive and robust" mandate for MINUSMA, including using any "means necessary" to protect the civilian population against "asymmetric threats" (MINUSMA, 2016). Gowan described MINUSMA a dismal failure in peacekeeping operations due to the UN inability to understand entirely the threats posed by asymmetrical conflict (Gowan, 2013).

## The challenges facing the implementation of UN global counterterrorism strategy in Africa

The challenges confronting the implementation of the UN Global Counterterrorism Strategy and the stumbling blocks on the way of transforming the abstract concepts of the plan into the real-life situation in Africa are numerous and interwoven.

### Deconstructing the "Four Pillars"

Pillar I—Addressing Conditions that are Conducive to the Spread of Terrorism

Pillar I is also part of "including the roles that conflict, underdevelopment, education, culture, and the needs of victims can play in combating or inciting terrorism" (Stanley Foundation, 2007:22–23).

### Conflict and underdevelopment

The old saying that a hungry man is an angry man certainly applies to the fact that there is a direct link between conflict and development. Poverty, economic downturn and relative deprivation can trigger war and as a consequence, engender a breeding ground for terrorist recruitment. However, studies abound pointing to no direct evidence linking any single socioeconomic demographic to the development of terrorist groups. But in the final analysis, these factors can be an enabling environment for terrorist groups to thrive. So, the UN must address these issues on time.

## Education, religion and culture

Religious education is fundamental to weaken terrorist tendencies in youths. Religious education includes spiritual teachings and learnings that eschew extremist rhetoric, dispelling misconceptions about proselytising and religious interpretation. Adamawa Peace Initiative (API) has demonstrated to be a success story of inter-civilisation dialogue in Nigeria that can be replicated on a sub-regional basis. Participants from different religious background congregate on sharing best practices in peaceful coexistence with the principle of "live and let's live." The issue of semantics, perhaps also has a lot to do with the fight against radicalisation. Several instances have shown the government's use of language can go a long way in exacerbating the existing problem such as stereotyping terrorist fighters as "jihadists" and using hyperboles like "Great Satan," "Axis of Evil", and "Evil Empire" to describe adversaries.

One area where CTITF and UNESCO can make a huge difference is in producing educational materials and disseminating them via a variety of media sources in fighting against radicalisation and extremist ideology. Without any doubt, education plays a pivotal role in confronting religious intolerance, human rights monitoring, cross-cultural literacy and anti-corruption efforts, and all require some knowledge on the part of the citizenry.

## Victims of terrorism

According to the Internal Displacement Monitoring Center (IDMC) and the Norwegian Refugee Council (NRC), there are 3.3 million persons displaced by Boko Haram insurgency and other communal clashes in Nigeria. That figures put Nigeria in the third-place globally behind Syria and Colombia with 6.5 million and 5.7 million IDPs respectively. The changes this have brought to the North-Eastern part of Nigeria are unprecedented and impossible, which calls for the creation of an international system to protect and assist the world's 25–30 million IDPs. The world's refugee crisis is currently being taken care of by the OHCHR created in 1950 and the subsequent Refugee Convention adopted in 1951. But sadly enough, there is no provision for IDPs in that arrangement. The paper takes a holistic view of some impediments, such as the issues of sovereignty, institutional structures, and legal frameworks on the way of creating such an international system for IDPs.

## Pillar II—measures to prevent and combat terrorism

Of the 1566 UN entities, the CTITF and the CTED, including their numerous conventions, resolutions, and all other related documents, there is one thing that matters most when it comes to measures designed to prevent and combat terrorism — the success or failure of the strategy rests entirely on member states taking on their responsibility to execute the plan at their respective countries. These include but not limited to looking outside the box (to such areas as community policing, intelligence community and civil society), and not focusing on security's viewpoint alone.

## Community policing and intelligence initiatives

One of the significant challenges faced by UN counterterrorism and counterinsurgency operations in Africa is information sharing between the three-tier of society—the government, business and civil society. They must continuously work together for the betterment of society at large. The business sector, government and civil society are similar to a three-legged stool, without one of the legs, the stool will not be stable. It cannot provide the necessary support essentially needed in a society ravaged by security challenges. The Interpol dictates the pace as an integral part of the information and intelligence sharing among UN and non-UN entities. It must be integrated into this process by helping in capacity building in such areas as human intelligence, border patrol, cyber terrorism and prevent terrorists' access to WMD.

The media faces a terrible, painful and irreconcilable dilemma. On the one hand, "showing graphic details of crime scenes; beheadings; and injured victims creates powerful images, exposes emerging threats, and supports freedom of speech." On the other hand, "these media images can be exploited. For example, by traumatising victims' families, sensationalising violence, and repeatedly showing graphic images of destruction, the media can advertise the terrorists' cause, reinforce perceptions of the terrorists' "success" and exaggerate the importance and magnitude of the acts, ultimately creating precisely the climate of fear and insecurity that the terrorists are trying to create." (Stanley Foundation, 2007:30).

There is a blurred line between using the media for incitement and propaganda and using it for education and protecting freedom of speech. The Communications Decency Act of 1996 (CDA) was the closest form of censorship on the Internet and was struck down by the US Supreme Court. The act was orchestrated by Clinton's Administration to regulate pornographic materials on the Internet. (Communication Decency Act, 1996).

## Pillar III—building states' capacity to counter terrorism

There is no doubt that the link between counterterrorism and sustainable development underscored the significance of not focusing on counterterrorism alone at the detriment of alleviating poverty, unemployment, corruption and other social ills of the society at large. The primary responsibility of implementing the Global Counterterrorism strategy lies on the member states' capability to customise the directives received from the both UN and non-UN entities in consideration when they design their system, which of course will reflect on their customs, cultures, ways of life and their day-to-day activities (Ward, 2003). The member states will claim ownership when they become part of the process and strive for preserving its existence rather than a straightjacket approach or one-size-fits-all approach. Compliance, accountability, continuity of training and structured follow-up were among other challenges that threaten the foundation of Pillar III. One way of going around this stumbling block is by looking at it as a two-way street—participants and donors alike must work together to ensure their complementarity and reinforcement—as the old saying goes, it takes two to tangle (Bianchi, 2014). To avoid the issue of redundancy, comprehensive mapping of the division of labour will virtually eliminate overlapping functions capacity building both in CTED and CTITF initiatives. The way things are now, there is a disconnect between GA and SC in their mandates as evidenced in the lack of comprehensive architectural structure that spelt out completely the different ownerships of programs and initiatives. To overcome the challenges of lack of compliance oversight and accountability, some experts suggested, "regional peer mechanisms could be even more useful in generating both uniform compliance and long-term sustainability" (Stanley Foundation, 2007:34).

## Pillar IV—ensuring respect for human rights and advancing the rule of law

Some of the challenges facing the implementation of the UN Global Counterterrorism Operations in Africa stem from the problem of how to strike a balance between human rights protection for the victims of terrorism and insurgency versus protecting the rights of perpetrators of terrorism and insurgency within the due process of the law. The participants of the 42nd Conference on the United Nations of the Next Decade listed some rights that must be protected by the rule of law and summed it up thus:

- Right to Life. Protection from the controversial use of overwhelming military strikes against suspects, shoot-to-kill policies, and expansion of death penalties is necessary to ensure that counterterrorism actions are seen as legitimate and do not lead to more radicalisation.
- Right to Nondiscrimination. Protection from growing animosity against ostracised groups, both globally (regarding Muslims) and locally (for minority ethnic, religious, or cultural groups who may house some violent elements at the domestic level) is necessary to avoid indiscriminate policies.
- Right of Free Speech. Freedom of public expression against government actions (e.g., via the Internet and media) needs to be protected.
- Right to property. The United Nations and national governments should not freeze assets without due process.
- Right to a Fair Trial and protection from arbitrary detention without charge. Adjudicated courts should be used to vet suspects.
- Right to be Free of Torture and other ill-treatment. Freedom from abuse or torture to obtain intelligence is necessary, not only to protect the human rights of suspects but also to increase the effectiveness of counterterrorism efforts. Forced confessions may not always lead to better enforcement, and proper police procedures improve the reliability of intelligence obtained.
- Right of Return. Protection against torture or discrimination when refugees attempt to return to their homeland is a matter not only of refugee protection and the UNHCR mandate but will also strengthen counterterrorism efforts (Stanley Foundation, 2007:36).

When the Security Council via Resolution 1373 created CTC, there were several criticisms levied. The UN Charter forbids it from making international law, criminalising terrorism, and playing the role of a global legislator, which boils down to an infringement on the Universal Declaration of Human Rights (UDHR) adopted by the UN General Assembly at the 3rd session on 10 December 1948. In response to these criticisms, the Security Council passed Resolutions 1456 (2003) and 1624 (2005) calling on the Member States to "ensure that any measure is taken to combat terrorism comply … with international law, in particular international human rights, refugee, and humanitarian law" (UNHRC, 2005).

## Conclusion: towards an effective CT-COIN framework for the UN

The UN-CT and COIN operations in Africa are still in its nascent stages despite the euphoria that greeted the functions after 9/11 terrorists' attacks in the United States. The trio—CTC, CTED and CTITF were created to focus and monitor exclusively the commitment of various countries' implementation of Resolutions 1373, 1624 and the global strategy resting on four pillars—Pillar I—Measures to address the conditions conducive to the spread of terrorism; Pillar II—Measures to prevent and combat terrorism; Pillar III—Measures to build States' capacity to prevent and combat terrorism and to strengthen the role of the United Nations system in this regard; and Pillar IV—Measures to ensure respect for human rights for all and the rule of law as the fundamental basis of the fight against terrorism. Although the trio was successful and applauded by the global community initially, their performance in Africa is controversial due to numerous challenges serving as stumbling blocks to real progress such as the absence of a clear definition of terrorism, lack of funds and enforcement mechanism, human rights and decision-making capability. If there is any lesson to be learned from this dismal performance in Africa, it is that the UN CT and COIN operations in the region cannot succeed simply by military and security means alone, it must teach socioeconomic factors in countering terrorism. In the final analysis, all efforts to reinforce the dilapidating four pillars of the UN Global Counterterrorism Strategy in Africa must grabble with the following recommendations:

## Pillar I—CT and COIN with a human face

Formalise an established process with a human face taking into consideration the numerous conditions that are conducive to the spread of terrorism. This can be accomplished by using the capacities of the UN's CTC, CTED and CTITF in resolving, mediating and promoting peace-building efforts in prolonged violent conflict zones in Africa such as those in Mali, Somalia and DRC. In this regards, member states can tap on already established United Nations Alliance of Civilizations (UNAOC) and the United Nations Scientific, Educational and Cultural Organization (UNESCO). UNAOC is a brainchild of former UN Secretary-General, Kofi Annan, set up to bridge the gap between different cultures, communities around the world. Promote interfaith/intercultural dialogues among differing cultures in Africa via religious education and reeducation. This can clear up some misconceptions and underscore the importance of semantic development in counterterrorism lexicon by avoiding calling terrorist fighters as "jihadists" and using such hyperbole as "Axis of Evil" and "Great Satan", which fuels societal radicalisation and extremism. UNESCO, on the other hand, can be a resource in educating the masses about the problems mentioned above and helped in improving the material conditions of the people, especially youth's unemployment, marginalisation and political oppression. In most cases, these are avenues for terrorists to exploit for their recruitment and radicalisation exercises. Transitional justice program can also augment CT and COIN with a human face to address the needs of victims of terrorism and give them an international voice to embark on processes that will ensure justice, reparation, truth and reconciliation and institutional reform for the violence perpetrated on them and share their different stories to the world, especially Internally Displaced Persons (IDPs). The UN can open what some experts called "axis of communication" between victims to victims, victims to government and government to government.

## Pillar II—prevention is better than cure

Measures to prevent and combat terrorism should take into consideration how to dismantle the source of funding for terrorists, deny them haven by encouraging information sharing among all UN entities and member states. This will entails conducting and sharing periodic intelligence gathering to curtain terrorist-related transnational crime. Because most member states have porous borders, setting up programs to fight cyber terrorism, improve border patrol and travelling documents will go a long way to help prevent and combat terrorism in Africa. This is not enough to prevent terrorism since there is a direct correlation between poverty and terrorism. Therefore, any counter-terrorist measures embarked upon must take cognisance of the socioeconomic factors such as poverty, inequality and unemployment.

## Pillar III—state capacity-building

The UN can liaise with Northern donor states to match their interests with that of member states in Africa in the areas of training and assistance. Continuity of training sessions, as well as the constant follow-up, are the nuts and bolts of state capacity-building. Source of funding and resource scarcity, which have hindered state capacity building in Africa in the past should be addressed by Northern donor states. They can do this by voluntarily supplementing the scarce resources available to the UN, sharing best practices of capacity building across the board, and reconciling GA/SC mandates to avoid duplication of functions. This can be achieved by improving the structure of CTC, CTED, and CTITF to maximise their performance. Also, the UN can empower IAEA, OPWC, and WHO to put an end to the proliferation of Weapons of Mass Destruction (WMD) so as potential terrorists will not have access to them.

## Pillar IV—respect for human rights and the rule of law

The international community cannot afford to ignore human rights norms and conventions in countering terrorism because if they do, the ghost will come back and hunt them. Respects for fundamental freedoms and the rule of law are the basic building blocks for counterinsurgency and counterterrorism operations. They are intertwined to make sure human rights violators are brought to justice within the due process of the law, and there is reconciliation between human rights and counterterrorism operations.

National and international legal frameworks should be strengthened to make sure that citizens who are yawning for tight security are ready to make sacrifices about their privacy to preserve it. The case of the US Patriot Act is a shining example. To ensure the success of the implementation of UN Global Counterterrorism Strategy in Africa, its countries should do more to strengthen civil society. In the long run, this will champion government reforms, confront corruption, advocate respect for human rights, promote and defend democratic processes and institutions. The allegations of human rights abuses against the Nigerian army are the most egregious example of recent civil society conflict with the military over extrajudicial killings, torture and arbitrary arrest and detention of innocent civilians in the fight against Boko Haram. Some military personnel went to the extent of calling the offices of Amnesty International and Human Rights Watch to be shut down. Finally, the CT and COIN should work to integrate reports and recommendations from numerous existing mechanisms and formulate them into a holistic approach in addressing the problems of human rights and counterterrorism from such UN entities as Committee Against Torture, Human Rights Council, special rapporteurs in Human Rights and Counterterrorism. Others are human rights NGOs such as Amnesty International, Human Rights Watch, etc.

## References

Aghedo, Iro, & Eke, S. J. (2003). From alms to arms: The Almajiri phenomenon in Northern Nigeria. *Korea Journal of Policy Studies 28*(3), 3–4.

Ahmad, Egbal (1998). *Terrorism: Theirs & ours*. Seven Stories Press.

Annan, Kofi (2005). *Secretary-General Kofi Annan launches global strategy against terrorism in Madrid.un.org, PR SG/2095, March 10, 2005*.

Ban Ki-moon (2007). Statement to the General Assembly on the Follow-Up to the Adoption of the United Nations Global Counter-Terrorism Strategy.

Burgess, M. (2002). *Al-Qaeda Attempts to Widen War*. Center for Defense Information Terrorism Report.

BBC News (1998). US Embassies in Africa Bombed. News.bbc.co.uk.

Bianchi, Andrea (2014). *Assessing the effectiveness of the UN Security Council's anti-terrorism measures: The quest for legitimacy and cohesion. The European Journal of International Law, 17*(5), 5–7.

Chandler, Michael, & Gunaratna, Rohan (2007). *Countering terrorism: Can we meet the threat of global violence?*. London: Reaktion Books.

Crenshaw, Martha (Ed.). (1994). *Terrorism in Africa*. New York: G.K. Hall & Co.

London Evening Standard. (2003). *Libya sanctions to be lifted*, Friday, 12 September 2003.

CIA. (2012). Terrorist bombing of Pan Am Flight 103, CIA.gov.

Copeland, Foard (2013). *Boko Haram insurgency in Nigeria*. Civil Military Fusion Center.

Communication Decency Act. (1996). *Protection for Private Blocking and Screening of Offensive Materials 47 U.S.C. Sec 230*.

Counter-Terrorism Committee Executive Directorate. (2006). *The Role of the Counter-Terrorism Committee and its Executive Directorate in the International-Terrorism Effort*. New York: United Nations.

Federal Bureau of Investigation. (2006). Terror 2000, retrieved April 24th, 2013, from http://www.fbi.gov/publication/terror/terror2000_2001htm.

Freedman, Gemson (2002). *Superterrorism: Policy responses*. Blackwell Publishing.

Gowan, Richard (2013). *Diplomatic fallout: A summer of political storms looms for U.N. World Politics Review*, June 03, 2013.

Hayden, Thomas H. (2007). *Insurgency vs. terrorism*. U.S. Military Academy Training Manual Document.

IEP. (2015). *Global Terrorism Index*. Institute of Economics and Peace.

Kilcullen, David J. (2006). *Three Pillars of Counterinsurgency*. Remarks delivered at the *U.S. Government Counterinsurgency Conference*, Washington, D.C.

Kolodkin, Barry (2016). *What is Counter Terrorism?*. Seal, U.S.: National Counter Terrorism Center Foreign Policy (available at www.usforeignpolicy.about.com).

Kramer, Hilde Haaland, & Yetiv, Steve A. (2007). *The UN Security Council's response to terrorism: Before and after September 11, 2001. Political Science Quarterly, 122*(3), 1–24.

Messmer, Williams B., & Yordan, Carlos L. (2011). *A partnership to counter international terrorism: The UN Security Council and the UN Members States. Studies in Conflict and Terrorism 34*(11), 11–12.

Neumann, Peter, & Smith, M. L. R. (2008). *The strategy of terrorism: How it works, and why it fails*. Routledge Press.

Onuoha, F. C. (2010). *The Islamist challenge: Nigeria's Boko Haram crisis explained. African Security Review, 19*(2), 2–4.

United Nations. (2004). *A more secure world: Our shared responsibility, report of the high-level panel on threats, challenges and change*. New York: United Nations.

United Nations. (2016). United nations General Assembly. *Conclusions and Observations by the President of the Seventieth Session of the UN General Assembly*. New York: United Nations, 19 May.

United Nations. (2016). Lessons Learned Report, Sources Information Fusion Unit and the MINUSMA Intelligence Architecture: Lesions for the Mission and a UN Policy Framework. *Semi-Final Draft for USG Ladsous' Review*. New York: United Nations. 2016.

UNHRC. (2005). Report of the Office of the United Nations High Commissioner for Human Rights on the Human Rights Situation in Iraq in the Light of Abuses Committed by the So-Called Islamic State in Iraq and the Levant and Associated Group.

Action to Counter Terrorism. (2006). United Nations General Assembly Adopts Global-Terrorism Strategy. *UN News Center*. http://www.un.org/en/terrorism/strategy-counter-terrorism.

UN. (2001). Security Council Resolution 1373, S/RES/1373.

United Nations. (1945). Charter of the United Nations," 24 October 1945, 1 UNTS XVI (available at http://www.un.org/en/documents/charter/index.shtml).

Sodeman, William A. *Communication Decency Act of 1996*. Title V of the Telecommunications Act of 1996.

Security Council Resolution 1535. (2004). 26 March 2004.

Stein, Jessica (2003). *Terror in the name of god: Why religious militants kill*. HarperCollins.

Sibilla, Chris (2013). *A Moment in U.S. Diplomatic History*. Association for Diplomatic Studies and Training.

Santos, David (2011). *Counterterrorism vs. counterinsurgency: Lesons from Algeria and Afghanistan*, smallwarsjournal.com.

Smith, Mike (2014). *Combating Terrorism: The Pursuit of Justice Through Cooperation*. United Nations.

Stanley Foundation. (2007). Implementation of the UN Global Counterterrorism Strategy, 42nd Conference on the United nations of the Next Decade, June 8–13, 2007.

Ward, C. A. (2003). *Building capacity to combat international terrorism: The role of the United Nations Security Council. Journal of Conflict and Security Law, 8*(2), 2–3.

# 13

# European Union's counterterrorism and counterinsurgency strategy in Africa

*Gerald Ekenedirichukwu Ezirim*

## Introduction

The founding justification for the formation of the European Union was predicated on the burning necessity to coordinate member states' policies, harmonise national legislation, and support some operational works conducted by national authorities of member states. However, sequel to the 9/11 2001 attacks and, most importantly, the terrorist attacks in Madrid and London in 2004, which claimed hundreds of lives, the EU rededicated itself to combating terrorism by signing the EU Action Plan and adopting the EU Counterterrorism Strategy in November 2001 and December 2005, respectively. These, no doubt, have made the EU an increasing actor in global counterterrorism vanguard. Since November 2001, the EU has advanced counterterrorism legislation, initiatives, conventions, and treaties. These include the Lisbon treaty reforms that empowered the Union to sign agreements on terrorism with other third countries; develop internal institutional and legal capabilities such as Europol, Eurojust, the Counter-Terror Coordination, among others.

Global or transnational terrorism, whatever its causes or bases, seeks to intimidate people, societies, and governments across sovereign jurisdictions. It also threatens security and undermines both human rights and democratic processes. While some security analysts like Halliday (2002) and Funk and Said (2004) have attempted to portray the current wave of terrorism as a struggle between Islam and the West, it is misleading and counterproductive. Terrorists have threatened all types of societies and states, from the United States, India, Pakistan, and Saudi Arabia, to Spain, the United Kingdom and Kenya. For this reason, all societies and states, irrespective of ideological, religious or cultural orientation, face the threats of terrorism and must take appropriate measures to eliminate the root causes of terrorism and to prevent terrorists from achieving their political goals. However, it is acknowledged that an effective fight against transnational terrorism is beyond the capacity of a single state and, therefore, requires cooperation between various countries and organisations. It is mainly for this reason that the European Union's counterterrorism policies and strategies are predicated on collaboration within the EU as well as cooperation between the EU and other states. Accordingly, the EU anti-terrorism strategy is based on the belief that since these threats do not recognise borders, they must be confronted at both national and international levels. This further explains why the

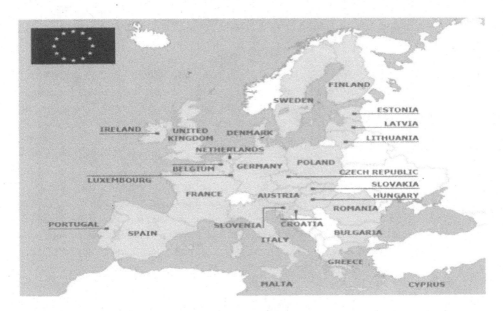

*Figure 13.1* The European Union in a Globalising World

European Union works with international organisations, including the UN and the Global Counterterrorism Forum, and regional organisations such as the Council of Europe, the Organization for Security and Cooperation in Europe (OSCE), the League of Arab States (Arab League), or the Organisation for Islamic Cooperation (OIC).

In recent times, the African continent has been embroiled in spates of insurgent and terrorist attacks of cataclysmic magnitude that verge on apparent intractability. Understanding the complex interdependence of States in the international system, particularly the fact that the destinies of states are inextricably tied together, the EU appeared to have presented itself as the global police on terrorism concerning continental insurgent operations in Africa. In a world of simmering domestic threats and growing global violence of multiple dimensions and expressions, the insurgency/terrorism distressed countries of Africa are increasingly welcoming and embracing external help from both the EU and NATO to the ultimate end of extricating themselves from the spectre of insurgency and terrorism. Since the revolutionary years of 2011 to 2013, often referred to as the *Arab Spring*, pockets and splinters of insurgency groups have sprung up in different African countries such as Tunisia, Egypt, Libya, Mali, Nigeria. Within this period, EU's intervention in Mali (2013) was experienced, just as NATO's light footing in Libya (2011) was observed.

The purpose of this chapter, therefore, is to explore the dynamics of the EU's counterterrorism and counterinsurgency strategy concerning continental insurgent operations in Africa. The chapter is structured into seven (7) sections. Section 1 (Introduction) has just introduced the study. Section 2 explores the European Union in a globalising world, giving a bird's eye view to the organogram of the EU. In contrast, Section 3 looks at the brief conceptualisations and conceptual framework for understanding the chapter. "Europe and the global war on terror" is the focus of Section 4. Section 5 examines the Africa-EU strategic partnership amidst Insurgencies. While Section 6 explores Countering transnational terrorism to ascertain whether Africa is genuinely immune, Section 7 undertakes the conclusion of the chapter.

The European Commission is headed by a President and is divided into departments that develop policies for specific areas, each headed by a Commissioner. The Commission is steered by a group of 28 Commissioners, known as "The College" who take critical decisions on the Commission's political and strategic direction. A new college of Commissioners is appointed every five years when the European Council, made up of EU heads of state and government – proposes a Commission presidential candidate to the European Parliament. The candidate for President is nominated based on the political makeup of the Parliament following European Parliament elections; typically, they will be chosen from the largest political family in the Parliament. The nominee is elected if an absolute majority of members of Parliament support him or her. The president-elect selects potential Vice-Presidents and Commissioners based on suggestions from EU countries. The list of nominees must be approved by all EU heads of state or government, meeting in the European Council. Each nominee must appear before the parliamentary committee with responsibility for his or her proposed portfolio. Committee members then vote on the nominee's suitability for the position. Once the 27 nominees have been endorsed, Parliament votes whether to approve the entire team. Following Parliament's vote, the Commissioners are appointed by the European Council. All Commissioners are equal in the decision-making process and held equally accountable for these decisions. The Commission collectively decides on its work through the written or oral procedure (EU Commission, 2018).

1..  The EU is an integration of twenty-seven (27) countries from the continent of Europe, viz: Austria, Belgium, Bulgaria, Cyprus, Czech Republic, Germany, Denmark, Estonia, Greece, Spain, Finland, France, Hungary, Ireland, Italy, Lithuania, Luxembourg, Latvia, Malta, Netherlands, Poland, Portugal, Romania, Sweden, Slovenia, Slovakia, and the United Kingdom.[1] It is a large-scale political community, embodying the elements of both a state and an international organisation and yet correspondingly squarely to none. McCormick (2011) provides some useful insights into the evolution of today's EU. According to him, what is today known as and referred to as the EU can be traced back to the signature of the 1951 Treaty of Paris, which created the European Coal and Steel Community (ECSC). Although a good start, the ECSC was limited in its aims and in 1957 the Treaty of Rome was signed, creating the European Economic Community, the core goal of which was the creation of a European single market. He noted further that only six states initially took part. Still, the first of the several waves of enlargement occurred in 1973, moving through stages to 2007 when the accession of Bulgaria and Romania took the membership to 27. Along the way, new treaties expanded the reach of integration into new areas of policy, a landmark change coming with the creation of the EU as a result of the 1992 treaty on the EU, and another coming in 1999 with the launch of the Euro. The EU is hardwired by some structures that perform specific functions. There are, for instance, (a) The European Commission, which is the administrative and executive arm of the EU, headquartered in Brussels, (b) The Council of Ministers, an intergovernmental body consisting of Ministers from each of the member states, (c) The European Parliament, and (d) The European Court of Justice.

Added to these is an increasing network of more specialised agencies dealing with specific aspects of EU policy. These include the European Central Bank, the European Aviation Safety Agency, the European Police (Europol), the European Space Agency, among others.

Since the eventual metamorphosis of the ECSC into the EU through the signing of the Treaty on European Union on 7 February 1992, expansion and enlargement have consistently topped the Union's agenda. Hence, in March 1994, referenda were held in Austria, Finland, Norway and Sweden, and the majority came down in favour in all except Norway. The entrance of these countries opened a floodgate of an influx of other countries.

Arising from its model of socio-economic and political organisation, which is founded on solidarity, the EU views itself as a social democracy. This being the case, it aspires to set a classic example for the rest of the world. Beyond the recognition of civic and political rights of its citizens, the member states of the EU view social and economic rights as obligatory norms for all the member nations as well as the Union as a whole. This expectation finds expression in one of the Union's foundational agreement – the Lisbon Treaty of 2007, which didn't come into effect until December 2009. As Meyer (2013: 1) rightly observed, "The EU has failed to move forward toward complete fulfilment of that promise in a way consistent with its self-imposed obligations and the need for European citizens."

Yet again, Europe's population growth is now entirely accounted for by net immigration, which presents a host of troubling political and social challenges. Polls suggest that only about 4% of Europeans consider themselves as such. In comparison, about 41% identify exclusively with the states of which they are citizens, and about 55% have some mixture of European and state identity. Only about half of EU residents feel a sense of attachment to the EU (McCormick, 2011).

There are now what McCormick (2011: 108) called "growing signs of a backlash" expressed in "Euroscepticism" and worries of democratic deficit. While the first suggests hostility and sceptical disposition to the much-vaunted merits of the integration, the second refers to the growing gap between the powers and authority of EU institutions and the ability of EU citizens to impact their functions. How these have undermined EU's effort at muscling up a commanding counterterrorism and counterinsurgency campaign across the globe in general and Africa, in particular, will become evident as the discussion develops and spirals down to its logical conclusion.

We must stress that the three fundamental pillars of the EU are social and economic factors; foreign and security policy; and justice and home affairs. Firstly, given that there is an apparent terrorist threat emanating from within Europe itself from vestiges of political terrorism, separatist-irredentism, Al-Qaeda, HAMAS, Hezbollah, etc., occasioned mainly by the migration trend, the EU had always treated these issues as internal to themselves. Thus they had always used internal mechanisms to deal with them. Therefore, there had been no robust engagement as a regional body. However, the EU's principal involvement with counterterrorism beyond its borders has always been diplomatic and economical. Secondly, the EU foreign policy is weak in the sense that it does not have any credible force projection capability or internal institutional access to specialist resources. There is no robust executive mandate, and EU member states get involved in security matters abroad without recourse to the EU platform.

The EU CT-COIN strategy encompasses an EU "anti-terrorism road map" of October 2001; a common/European Arrest Warrant (mutual extradition treaty); a Joint Investigative Teams (investigative collaboration); Eurojust (coordination of investigative endeavours); Europol (coordination of intelligence and investigative support); the Framework Decision on Combating Terrorism, and more recently (25/3/2004 & 10/5/2005), the European Council adopted the "Action Plan on Terrorism."

However, the EU lacks a democratically endorsed, obligatory and comprehensive, inter-Pillar EU counterterrorism policy that is readily enforceable and provides for a solid CT policy basis, but instead there is close coordination on EU intergovernmental policy levels and enhanced co-operation among member states. It also lacks a robust, integrated, and autonomous CT capability, as well as a useful intergovernmental CT tool to replace pre-Third Pillar capabilities, i.e. TREVI (Terrorisme, Radicalisme, Extremisme, Violence Internationale) (Zimmermann, 2006).

## Conceptual framework

Apart from the EU which we have familiarised ourselves with, the next most essential concepts in this Chapter are Counterterrorism and Counterinsurgency (CT-COIN). As the operational concepts, it is imperative to offer a modest clarification of these concepts. Part of the reason for this is the inherent, but abhorrent tendency to confuse the two and use them interchangeably as though they are the same thing. Although there is a fragile line between the two concepts, they have a slight difference that deserves some highlights for academic distinction and practical observation. As rightly noted by Boeke (2016: 12):

> It is important to distinguish between insurgents, terrorists and criminals, as the designated label channels a policy reaction that is anchored in the very different fields of counterterrorism and counterinsurgency (COIN) or law enforcement, each centred around its own principles, dogmas and common practices. The COIN approach as conducted in Afghanistan became very military-centric, and more sequential (shape, clear, hold and build) than for instance the comprehensive approach, which could see simultaneous efforts of diplomats, aid workers and the military.

### Counterterrorism

Counterterrorism focuses on eliminating the pull and push of radicalisation and violent extremism. Pratt (2010) observed that counterterrorism consists of actions or strategies aimed at preventing terrorism from escalating, controlling the damage from terrorist attacks that do occur, and ultimately seeking to eradicate terrorism in a given context. He went further to classify counterterrorism according to four theoretical models: *Defensive, Reconciliatory, Criminal-Justice,* and *War.* He noted that each model contains differences in threat perception, how to guard against that threat, how to frame terrorism in the law and constitution, and which agents effect counterterrorism. Therefore, a "counterterrorism approach that focuses on removing the drivers of radicalisation and violent extremism would ideally be civilian-led" (Boeke, 2016: 12).

### Counterinsurgency

According to the U.S. Government Counterinsurgency Guide (2009), counterinsurgency may be defined as "comprehensive civilian and military efforts taken to defeat and contain insurgency and address its root causes simultaneously." The *Guide* further clarifies that the term is: "The organised use of subversion and violence to seize, nullify or challenge political control of a region. As such, it is primarily a political struggle, in which both sides use armed force to create space for their political, economic and influence activities to be effective." As noted earlier, counterterrorism falls within four models: defensive, reconciliatory, criminal-justice, and war (Pratt, 2010), which invariably fit into the broader categories of COIN identified by Galula (1964). What seems to be the only difference between the two concepts is that while counterterrorism focuses more narrowly on combating the tactics and strategy of terrorism and those who employ it, counterinsurgency is a broader category of responses to political violence carried out by minority groups, both terroristic and otherwise (Pratt, 2010).

The differences notwithstanding, both Counterterrorism and Counterinsurgency are strategies and theories of combating abnormal anti-social forces and violent extremism. As a theoretical construction, they offer some theoretical and practical guides on how to approach, pursue and apprehend insurgency. There are two operational categories of terrorism and insurgency. In the first category, the insurgents/terrorists work in conjunction with, or a manner complementary to, conventional forces. Such was the case with the French resistance during World War II and the National Liberation Front during the Vietnam War. The strategy in these cases is for the irregular combatants to weaken and destabilise the enemy to such a degree that victory is comfortable or assured for the regular forces. The goal is to defeat the military strength of a state and take over the governance of the state in question out-rightly.

In the second category, the goal of the insurgents/terrorists is not to defeat the "occupying" military force or coercive machinery of the host state; that is almost always an impossible task given the disparity in resources. Instead, they seek, through ongoing campaigns of clandestine "sneak attacks", to inflict continuous casualties upon their superior enemy forces and thereby demoralise the occupying forces over time. It is a simple strategy of repeated pinpricks and bleedings that, though small in proportion to the total force strength, sap the will of the occupier or host sate to continue to fight. Thus, it is a synonym for Operation Weaken the Strong (OWS).

Without prejudice to the preceding, these two concepts (Counterterrorism and Counterinsurgency) are paired as CT-COIN in this chapter to reflect and capture events and/ or situations that embody or characterise the two concepts. This should not be mistaken for the confusion.

## Europe and the global war on terror

Most countries of Europe were sympathetic to the United State's 9/11 experience in the hands of terrorists. European public opinion was therefore initially incredibly supportive of U.S. military action against terrorism with the proviso that the response is targeted on the perpetrators of the 11 September attacks and their supporters. It should be noted that polls taken a few weeks after the attacks on the World Trade Centre and the Pentagon showed that 65% of German citizens supported their country's participation in US-led military action against the perpetrators of these heinous attacks. What is more, in France and Britain, public support was even more generous at that time (Golino, 2002). Although the initial thrust of the support later began to wane, the EU remained the United States' strongest supporter in the war on terrorism. The support was so strong that:

> The NATO and EU allies of the United States repeatedly pledged their total and unequivocal solidarity with the United States and offered the U.S. over-flight rights, access to their military bases, and logistical support. They are also providing critical assistance in the areas of diplomatic support and intelligence and police cooperation. The EU is developing a package of anti-terrorism measures that builds on work begun in 1997. The package includes proposals for a European arrest warrant, a common EU definition of terrorist acts, and expedited extradition procedures for suspected terrorists as well as other measures (Golino, 2002: 63).

With the policies enunciated, one wonders the extent to which these policies reinforce or undermine human rights and the principles on which democracy is based? Some of these policies, like the introduction of European Arrest Warrant, have been greeted with ambivalence on account of freedom of residence and movement. There have been hundreds of European arrest warrants issued since member states ratified the legal instrument and that includes extradition of suspected terrorists. In July 2005, for example, in Marseille, a suspect of Algerian descent was apprehended in a joint action by France and Italy at the request of Italy. The advantage of the instrument is speed. Extradition used to take up to a year, now that is down to two months (NATO Review, 2005). It is equally worthy of note that some EU member states, such as Germany, Ireland, Italy, Spain and the UK, passed counterterrorism laws and formulated strategies decades ago. Still, many of these were not conceived in a framework that would enhance human rights and promote democracy (Martin, 2006).

Ever since the administration of US President George W. Bush (2001 to 2009) which promoted counterterrorism measures that ignored or undermined human rights, international law and international norms, and the world was curious to see whether the EU would follow the US example or design its template. As it turned out, the EU template on counterterrorism was grounded in respect for human rights and democratic principles and processes. While it is plausible to associate the recent EU focus on counterterrorism with the events of 11 September 2001, and the subsequent UN Security Council Resolution 1373 of 28 September 2001, the EU strategy can also be explained by the terrorist attacks in Madrid in March 2004 and London in July 2005, and other threats that EU member states have faced or foiled in recent years. All the principal decision-making organs of the EU – the Council of the European Union, the European Parliament, and the European Commission – have been involved in shaping EU counterterrorism strategies.

The EU counterterrorism policy document claim that the EU is committed to combating terrorism locally and globally while respecting human rights and democratic principles. According to the policy documents, the EU is dedicated to jointly fighting against terrorism and to providing the best possible protection for its citizens. The EU Counterterrorism Strategy document (2005: 6) states that:

> The European Union is an area of increasing openness in which the internal and external aspects of security are intimately linked. It is an area of increasing interdependence, allowing for free movement of people, ideas, technology, and resources. This is an environment which terrorists abuse to pursue their objectives. In this context, concerted and collective European action, in the spirit of solidarity, is indispensable to combat terrorism.

While proclaiming its global ambition, the EU strategy is primarily continental. Its primary purpose is to "make Europe safer, allowing its citizens to live in an area of freedom, security and justice". The main document that guides EU counterterrorism strategy is the "Action Plan to Combat Terrorism", which was adopted by the Council in June 2004.

In December 2005, the EU announced that its efforts in the fight against terrorism would focus on four main goals: prevention, protection, pursuit, and response. To differentiate itself from the USA, and in the hope of providing alternative leadership worldwide, the EU proclaimed that it was committed to pursuing these goals "in a democratic and accountable way". The EU counterterrorism strategy, like its security policy, is subject to political oversight.

## Prevention

One of the EU priorities in the field of counterterrorism is to identify and tackle the factors which contribute to radicalisation and the processes by which individuals are recruited to commit acts of terror. The EU aims to address the root causes of terrorism or tackle the factors that lead to radicalisation and recruitment, not only in Europe but also globally. These factors include the lack of democracy, the flagrant abuse of human rights and rampant corruption. These underlying causes of terrorism are also prevalent outside Africa, but in some African states, the situation is deteriorating, and they are being exacerbated. The post-election violence in Kenya in 2008; the drastic deterioration in economic, political and social conditions in Zimbabwe in recent years; the military coup in Guinea in late 2008; and the continuing conflicts in the Democratic Republic of the Congo and Somalia are just the prominent examples. The prevention of terrorism in Africa requires strategies that aim to engender development and empower the people as well as to build and enhance democracy. The term development is used here to refer to self-sustained economic growth as well as the provision of basic needs, such as shelter, water, sanitation, health services and education. To this end, the Council adopted an EU strategy for combating radicalisation and recruitment to terrorism. Considering evolving trends, such as the phenomena of lone actors and foreign fighters or the growing potential of social media for mobilisation and communication, the Council adopted a revision of this strategy in June 2014. By December 2014, justice and home affairs ministers adopted a series of guidelines for the revised EU radicalisation and recruitment strategy. These guidelines set out a series of measures to be implemented by the EU and member states.

## Protection

This EU counterterrorism strategy is aimed at protecting citizens and infrastructure as well as reducing vulnerability to attack. Entailed in this include the protection of external borders, the improvement of transport security, the safety of strategic targets and the reduction of the vulnerability of critical infrastructure. This stems from the fact that in most of the recent attacks in Western countries, terrorists have targeted the necessary infrastructure, and especially the transport network. For example, the Madrid and London attacks of 2004 and 2005, respectively, targeted vital transport systems, and the then vulnerable air transport system in the USA was targeted in 2001. Unfortunately, public transport systems in most countries cannot be fully protected against every terrorist attack. In this area, the EU is currently working on legislation regulating the use of Passenger Name Record (PNR) data for law enforcement purposes.

## Pursuit

The EU aims to go after and investigate terrorists in Europe and globally, and to bring them to justice. It also plans to disrupt their networks, cut off their funding and impede their planning, travel and communications. Controlling the financing for terrorism requires considerable cooperation across boundaries, and between government and non-government entities. To achieve these goals, the EU has focused on strengthening national capabilities, improving practical cooperation and information exchange between police and judicial authorities (in particular through Europol and Eurojust), tackling terrorist financing and depriving terrorists of how they mount attacks and communicate. In this regard, the Council and the European Parliament adopted new rules in May 2015, to prevent money laundering and terrorist financing.

Given the porous nature of the borders of many African states and the inadequate capacity to control or monitor those who enter or leave these countries, the fight against terrorism will require the commitment of resources and capacity-building on a grand scale. For example, it would take many years and massive amounts of resources for countries such as Mozambique and Tanzania to be able to patrol their long and exposed Indian Ocean coastlines effectively.

## Response

The EU counterterrorism strategy focuses on providing timely *response* to terror threats. The EU aims to minimise the consequences of terrorist attacks by coordinating responses to such attacks within the EU and across the world, and by improving capabilities for dealing with the aftermath – including the needs of victims. Priorities in this area include the development of EU crisis coordination arrangements, the revision of the civil protection mechanism, the development of risk assessment or the sharing of best practices on assistance to victims of terrorism. An effective response to terrorist attacks calls for greater cooperation across borders and highly trained personnel in security agencies and the law enforcement sector within the EU. It also requires trained and competent personnel in the countries that are expected to cooperate with the EU.

In sum, the preceding reveals that the EU's war against terrorism which is an integral part of the global war on terrorism is no longer a makeshift war. Permanent institutions and far-reaching policies have been set in place towards giving the challenge frontal combat it deserves in a fast-changing international system. This has further necessitated the cooperation of the Union with many other bodies and countries outside continental Europe.

## The Africa-EU strategic partnership amidst insurgency

For whatever reasons, Africa is referred to as the black man's continent. This may have erroneously come from the description of the continentals[2] as black people, even when it has remained a severe matter of heated debate that nobody is black in the most real sense of the word. The reactionary shift from "black" to "dark" has, in many persons' opinion, not changed anything at all. Whether due to want of better description or sheer acceptance of imperialistic defeat, even Africans have come to accept and describe themselves as Black and/or Dark people.

This section interrogates the EU-African relationship in the face of insurgency and terrorism. A large chunk of what the EU does in Africa is undertaken within the framework of *The Africa-EU Strategic Partnership*. The Partnership establishes a Joint Africa-EU Strategy (JAES), which is founded on the shared vision and purpose of taking:

> ...the Africa-EU relationship to a new, strategic level with a strengthened political partnership and enhanced cooperation at all levels. The partnership will be based on a Euro-African consensus on values, common interests, and common strategic objectives. This partnership should strive to bridge the development divide between Africa and Europe through the strengthening of economic cooperation and the promotion of sustainable development in both continents, living side by side in peace, security, prosperity, solidarity and human dignity (European Commission/African Union Commission, 2007: 2).

Part of the second out of the four objectives of the strategic partnership is to strengthen and promote peace, security, democratic governance and human rights, fundamental freedoms, etc. Therefore, at the core of the partnership between Africa and the EU is the need for a strengthened dialogue and institutional cooperation that not only addresses issues of peace and stability in Africa but also challenges that Europe is facing (The Africa-EU Strategic Partnership, 2007). The Joint Africa-EU Strategy (JAES) and its Action Plan were formally adopted at the second Europe-Africa summit in Lisbon with the ambition to inaugurating a "new era" for Europe-Africa relations. Till the very eve of the third Africa-European Union summit held in

Tripoli between 29 and 30 November 2010, implementation remained constrained by institution-building without capacity-building and weak mobilisation on the part of both African Union and European Union member states (Bach, 2010).

Although the AU is patterned after the EU in both organ and structure, the AU is yet to emulate the success of the latter. Between 2006 and 2013, close to 600 terrorist attacks were recorded in the EU, and within this period, over 850 terrorist arrests were made (https://www. europol.europa.eu/latest_piblications/37). This is a feat that the AU has not been able to approximate its half, even in the face of rising terrorist attacks in many countries of Africa. There is, nevertheless, a possibility that sustained AU-EU engagement could, in the long-term, result in a convergence of operations. For instance, just recently, the EU agreed to hand over 50 million Euro to bolster counterterrorism in Africa. In a bid to combat active jihadist groups in the Sahel region, the EU pledged to fund a force made up of troops from Mauritania, Mali, Chad, Burkina Faso and Niger known as the Sahel G-5. Still, in the domain of security and counterinsurgency, the EU Political and Security Committee (EU-PSC) and the AU Peace and Security Council (AU-PSC) have held regular consultations on security matters, including the operationalisation of the African Peace and Security Architecture. These relate to the Continental Early Warning System and the African Standby Force. Much of the funding for African-led peacekeeping operations comes from the EU's African Peace Facility (APF), which has a budget of €900 million for the period 2014–2016. It should be borne in mind that the EU is the leading supporter of the African Peace and Security Architecture (APSA), whose activities are funded by the APF.

Still, on securitisation and counterterrorism, the EU had also funded the African Centre for the Study and Research on Terrorism (ACSRT), which was established in Algiers in 2004. The purpose of this centre is to centralise information on terrorism and terrorist organisations in Africa, initiate research and organise training programmes and symposia to raise awareness of the threat of terrorism on the continent. The main weakness of this initiative is that its activities are not located within the framework of building or promoting democracy. The EU has also funded a counterterrorism programme through the Intergovernmental Authority on Development (IGAD). The IGAD Capacity Building Programme Against Terrorism (ICPAT) was established in 2006 and is based in Addis Ababa. ICPAT is currently guided by a Steering Committee made up of local ministerial representatives of IGAD member states (Djibouti, Ethiopia, Kenya, Sudan and Uganda; Eritrea is not a participant). The six donor countries (Canada, Denmark, Italy, the Netherlands, Spain, and Sweden) sit on the steering committee as non-voting members. This is also a venue in which the fight against terrorism should be viewed in terms of development and democracy-building, but ICPAT is not sufficiently equipped to do so.

In the light of the foregoing, the JAES has continued to exude and reflect a partnership of unequal partners. It has continued to reflect the continually changing pattern of European relationship with other continents and countries of the world. In the 1990s, enlargement was described as the foreign policy thrust of Europe. However, since the mid-2000s, it is the securitisation of Europe's external frontiers and "near abroad" that federates converging and increasingly high-profile foreign policy initiatives of Europe. Arising from this:

> EU-Africa interactions reveal a sharp contrast between the elusive nature of the notion of "strategic partnership" as heralded by the JAES, and Europe's instrumentalisation of its security concerns during negotiations with North and sub-Saharan African states. This in turn undermines pledges to "treat Africa as one" since the securitization of Europe's

external boundaries tends towards the transformation of its North African neighbours into a buffer zone (Bach, 2010: 10).

The JAES is a legitimisation of long-time nursed European concerns to securitise its shores and borders from a people historically regarded as a threat to European civilisation, peace, and security. The coastal plain countries of Morocco, Algeria, Tunisia, Libya and others to have improved the chance of improved access to Europe and its market have become explicitly linked to their readiness to control their shores and land-borders, without which such prospect is but wishful thinking. In other words, whatever the terms of the partnership, adequate border and shore control on the part of Africans take pre-eminence to it. Currently, controls along the Sahel-Saharan borderlines and the intra-regional boundaries of Maghreb states have seen more significant extension. This extension of control mechanisms, according to Bach (2010: 9) "stems from the post 9/11 security overlay, stimulated by the terrorist attacks in Casablanca and Madrid and weariness that radical Islamists originating from Algeria and paying allegiance to Al-Qaida may transform the southern fringes of the Maghreb into a sanctuary."

The preceding gives a clear insight as to why the 5th EU-Africa Summit scheduled to take place in Abidjan, Ivory Coast, between 28 and 29 November 2017 has as its central theme: "Youth". There is fear amongst the European countries that migrant youths from Africa, apart from being a source of fresh pressure on the economy, could be susceptible and vulnerable to recruitment by fundamentalist cum terrorist groups. Hence, monitoring the African "youth" has become a key priority for Europe, in a context of African demographic trends creating significant challenges for young people in terms of migration, security and employment.

What is becoming increasingly apparent in the light of Afro-EU relations generally is that the full implications of the EU claiming to treat Africa as "one" and equal partner have not been objectively and adequately assessed. Bach (2010) describes the EU's strategic partnership with Africa as a mere "placebo", a term lucidly captured by Encarta (2009)[3] as "something prescribed for a patient that contains no medicine, but is given for the positive psychological effect it may have because the patient believes that he or she is receiving treatment". The real import of this picturesque description would become more evident when one replaces "patient" in the explanation with "Africa". A logical consequence of this becomes a "construction" of Africa that is bound to appeal to the European Council but remains oblivious of the diversity of interests and weak enforcement capacity – as reminded by the politics of overlapping membership within regional groupings and their poor performance as "building blocks" since the adoption of the Abuja Plan of Action in 1991. In the light of the preceding considerations, it seems apparent that the JAES, far from bringing relief to Africa, may end up further complicate her situation.

## Countering transnational terrorism: is Africa truly immune?

In the foregoing exploration, examination, and analysis of the dynamics of EU's counterterrorism/insurgency missions and operations in Africa, there is a fear that a "pathological success" in both regional and global counterterrorism may yield antithetical result. This may be in the form of the proliferation of Lone-wolfism, or Lone wolf-terrorism, which is another deadly variant of non-conventional terrorism. The usage of Lone Wolf may be strange in African literature on terrorism, but it is a transplantable existential reality in Europe and the US. Citing Artiga (2010: 1–2), Beam (1992) and Clemons (2010), Bakker and de Graaf (2010) made the following clarification:

The term "lone wolf" was popularised in the late 1990s by white supremacists Tom Metzger and Alex Curtis as part of an encouragement to fellow racists to act alone in committing violent crimes for tactical reasons. Other terms that have been used to describe similar or comparable forms of political violence include "leaderless resistance" and "freelance terrorism"… Infamous examples from the United States, Israel and Europe include Baruch Goldstein, an American-born Israeli citizen who was responsible for the death of 29 Muslims praying in the Cave of the Patriarchs in Hebron; the Austrian Franz Fuchs, who used letter bombs to kill 4 and injure 15 people; US army major Nidal Malik Hasan, who is accused of a mass shooting at Fort Hood in which 13 people died and 30 were wounded; and the American mathematician Theodore Kaczynsky, also known as the "Una Bomber", who engaged in a mail bombing spree that killed three and wounded 23. In addition, there have been several lone wolves who assassinated political leaders, such as Yigal Amir, the assassin of former Israeli Prime Minister Yitzhak Rabin; Volkert van der Graaf, who killed the Dutch politician Pim Fortuyn; and Mijailo Mijailovic, who is responsible for the death of the Swedish Minister for Foreign Affairs Anna Lindh.

By pathological success, we mean an apparent temporal defeat or surrender of a terrorist group which could come in the guise of destabilising its organisational and structural configuration without addressing critically the factors that incubated the act and obliterating them diametrically and concretely. Teich (2013) in his *Trends and developments in lone wolf terrorism in the western world: An analysis of terrorist attacks and attempted attacks by Islamic extremists* made five (5) remarkable findings of lone wolf phenomenon. He found that there is:

*   increased number of countries targeted by lone-wolf terrorists,
*   increased number of fatalities and injuries caused by lone wolves,
*   the increased success rate of United States law enforcement to apprehend lone wolves before they can carry out their attacks,
*   high prevalence and success rate of loners over Pantucci's other three types of lone-wolf terrorists, and
*   increased targeting of military personnel (Teich, 2013: 1).

Inferring from the above, therefore, lone wolf terrorism is admissibly an increasingly growing phenomenon. A lone wolf is first and foremost a terrorist or a terrorist-minded individual who generally prefers to indulge in his terrorist activities/attacks alone, unassisted by any group, but sometimes motivated by and sympathetic to a known/established terrorist outfit. Committed and dedicated members of a weakened terrorist group or ideological fans of such groups tend to transform into lone wolves, acting this time around, not as a member of any known terrorist group, but as a lone fighter who receives no orders or instructions from a standing terrorist organisation. Bakker and de Graaf's (2011) study shows that almost all lone wolves display a degree of commitment to, and identification with, extremist movements, adding that they are generally seen as individuals with established cases or traces of "psychopathology and social ineptitudes."

According to another study by the Dutch *Institute for Safety, Security and Crisis Management*, COT, a total of 72 lone-wolf terrorist incidents accounted for only 1.28% of the total number of terrorist incidents in the US, Germany, France, Spain, Italy, Canada and Australia (Bakker & de Graaf, 2011). Given the nature of the attacks and the atomistic character of the perpetrators, the 9/11 attacks in the US as well as some other attacks in the UK, Germany, France, Denmark, Sweden, Norway, Canada, and Spain between 2010 and 2013 have been seen and regarded as lone-wolf attacks (see Bakker & de Graaf, 2010). Since then, the total number of perceived lone wolf attacks/incidents in the United States – and in the Western world in general – has been on the increase. Second most-targeted countries are the United Kingdom and Germany. Over the past three decades, these three countries remained the most targeted; however, the number of countries targeted by Islamic lone wolves has equally increased (Teich, 2013).

Implicit in this trend, and in line with Teich's observation that "lone wolves are motivated by a combination of personal grievances and broader goals" (2013: 22), many more countries where large-scale personal and group grievances are still rife constitute probable candidates for lone-wolves attacks. Therefore, the truth that Africa has not officially recorded lone-wolf terrorism should not be taken as an automatic presupposition that Africa is immune to the phenomenon. In Mali, for instance, the clash of roles between the United Nations Multidimensional Integrated Stabilization Mission in Mali (MINUSMA) and international stabilisation force led to sporadic accusation of MINUSMA by different armed groups and citizens of not being impartial. This was exacerbated by incidents where Apache helicopters killed Tuareg rebels (that posed a threat to the force), and also when UN troops fired into a crowd, killing protestors (Center for Civilians in Conflict CIVIC, 2015).

In the same vein but another development, the EU and France got shocked when on 27 July 2013 the Movement for Unity and Jihad in West Africa (popularly referred to as MUJAO) threatened to hit polling stations and warned Malians not to vote. This came in the wake of the "*Operation Serval*" in Mali, which was a set of coordinated military actions by France/EU to quell the Salafi-Jihadist attack on Southern Mali. It was a shock because to the EU, the *Operation Serval* has been "successfully concluded" and it was time to transfer power to a new legitimate government. This, no doubt, was an indication that although the different terrorist groups may have been structurally disintegrated and vanquished as organic groups during *Operation Serval*, they have not entirely given up. As individuals and fragments, the same thrust of their mission coupled with a renewed zest to vent their pent-up frustration and grievances tend to remain evergreen and undying. Faced with the challenge of re-organisation, such individuals now constitute himself to a one-person squad, attacking alone in what has come to be popularly known as Lone-wolf terrorism.

## Conclusion

This chapter explores the dynamics of the EU's self-assumed global police on terrorism concerning continental insurgent operations in Africa. No doubt, Africa and Europe have had a long history of both satisfying and gory relationship until comparatively recently when the two continents, recognising the escalating propensity of terrorism and global insecurity, came up with a somewhat partnership deed or creed – The Joint Africa-EU Strategic Partnership. The partnership sought to strengthen the extant political relationship between the two continents and to further enhance their cooperation at all levels. It was to be based on a Euro-African consensus on values, shared interests, and common strategic objectives. Arising from one of the seminal goals of the strategic partnership, which is to strengthen and promote peace, security, democratic governance and human rights, fundamental freedoms, etc., African policymakers embraced the partnership with both hands. They had to because the continent of Africa since the turn of the 20th century has been deeply immersed in conflicts and insecurity of varying degrees of intensity. The common thought among African leaders and keen observers of African politics was that this partnership would go a long way in addressing arising insecurity in the continent. The AU came to be patterned after the EU, with occasional financial and logistical assistance from the latter.

However, existential realities on the ground, especially from the negotiations with North and sub-Saharan African states reveal that the EU-Africa interactions reflect a sharp contrast between the elusive nature of the notion of "strategic partnership" as heralded by the JAES and Europe's slanted dedication to its security concerns alone. One would be tempted to ask, wherein lies the pledges to "treat Africa as one" as contained in the partnership since the securitisation of "Europe's external boundaries tends towards the transformation of its North African neighbours into a buffer zone (Bach, 2010: 10)"?

Among others, the foregoing shows that this partnership in question is a partnership of unequal partners. The relationship, like Bach (2010) eloquently pointed out, is a "placebo". It is, indeed, something prescribed for Africa, which contains no strategic potential. It is given for the positive psychological effect it may have because Africa believes that she is receiving strategic assistance. While making some evidence-based reservations about the EU Missions in Africa, like the *Operation Serval* in Mali, the chapter expresses fears that a pathological success in both regional and global counterterrorism may yield antithetical result in the form of proliferation of Lone-wolf terrorism which is a variant of non-conventional terrorism. An antithetical result of this nature would inevitably question the rationale for the partnership in the first place. If this happens, Africa must not blame the EU, for every regional organisation is primarily a selfish or self-interest body that must seek its own good before those of others. This is the unspoken rule of all partnerships!

## Notes

1 The exit of Britain (Brexit) from the EU has affected the United Kingdom's membership of the EU.
2 The word/concept is used here in an operational sense to describe the people(s) of a continent, just the same way that indigenes of a nation are correspondingly referred to as "nationals".
3 Microsoft® Encarta ® 2009. https://www.googleadservices.com/pagead/aclk?sa=L&ai=DChcSEwi91 MupzYrcAhUPnO0KHZKADpAYABAAGgJkZw&ohost=www.google.com.ng&cid=CAASEuRoHB zpmngiGXA5Y_FipZnoOA&sig=AOD64_0sYJSBS5nHP6NQjTXkpLSlLZBI-g&q=&ved=0ahUKEw i8kMipzYrcAhVSTcAKHXTeA3gQ0QwIIw&adurl= A Accessed June 5th, 2017.

## References

Artiga, V. (2010). *Lone wolf terrorism: What we need to know and what we need to do.* Retrieved from: http://www.takresponse.com/index/homeland-security/lone-wolf_terrorism.html, on 2nd July, 2018.
Bach, D. (2010). The EU's 'strategic partnership' with Africa: Model or placebo. *Garnet Working Paper* No. 80/10, September.
Bakker, E., & de Graaf, B. (2010). *Lone wolves: How to prevent this phenomenon.* International Center for Counter terrorism, Expert Meeting Paper, November.
Bakker, E., & de Graaf, B. (2011). Preventing lone wolf terrorism: Some CT approaches addressed. *Perspectives on Terrorism, 5,* 5–6.
Beam, L. (1992). Leaderless resistance. *The Seditionist,* (12). Retrieved from: http://www.louisbeam.com/leaderless.htm (accessed 2nd July, 2018).
Boeke, S. (2016). *Transitioning from military interventions to long-term counter-terrorism policy: The case of Mali (2013-2016).* Leiden University – Institute of Security and Global Affairs.
Center for Civilians in Conflict (CIVIC). (2015). Fending for ourselves: The civilian impact of Mali's three-year conflict. Retrieved from: https://civiliansinconflict.org/wp-content/uploads/2017/08/Civilian_Impact_of_Mali_3-Year_Conflict_small.pdf (accessed 2nd July, 2018).
Clemons, S. (2010). *The real problem with "Lone Wolf" terrorism".* Retrieved from: http://www.thewashingtonnote.com/archives/2010/04/the_real_problem (accessed 2nd July, 2018).

EU Commission. (2018). How the Commission is organised. https://ec.europa.eu/info/about-european-commission/organisational-structure/how-commission-organised_en (accessed 11th July, 2018).

European Commission/African Union Commission. (2007). *The Africa-EU strategic partnership: A Joint Africa-EU Strategy.* http://www.africa-eu-partnership.org/sites/default/files/documents/eas2007_joint_strategy_en.pdf. (accessed 7th June, 2017).

European Council. (2003). *Presidency conclusions of the Brussels European Council (20 and 21 March 2003).* Available from: https://www.consilium.europa.eu/media/20858/75136.pdf. (accessed 7th June, 2017).

Funk, N. C., & Said, A. A. (2004). Islam and the west: Narratives of conflict and conflict transformation. *International Journal of Peace Studies, 9*(1), 1–28.

Galula, D. (1964). Counter-insurgency *warfare: Theory and practice* (pp. 54–56). Westport, Connecticut: Praeger Security International.

Golino, L. R. (2002). *Europe, the war on terrorism, and the EU's international role.* https://www.brown.edu/initiatives/journal-worldaffairs/sites/brown.edu.initiatives.journal-worldaffairs/files/private/articles/8.2_Golino.pdf (accessed 5th June, 2017).

Graaf, B., & Bakker, E. (2011). Preventing lone wolf terrorism: Some CT approaches addressed. *Perspectives on Terrorism, 5*(5–6), 43–50.

Halliday, F. (2002). *Two hours that shook the world: September 11, 2001: Causes and consequences.* London: Saqi Books.

Martin, G. (2006). *Understanding terrorism: Challenges, perspectives and issues* (2nd ed.). London: Sage Publications.

McCormick, J. (2011). *European Union politics.* UK: Palgrave foundation.

Meyer, T. (2013). Editorial. *Journal of Social Democracy, International Quarterly Edition, 2,* 1.

NATO Review. (2005). *Combating terrorism.* Retrieved from: https://www.nato.int/docu/review/2005/combating-terrorism/Gijs-de-Vries-counter-terrorism/EN/index.htm, on 2nd July, 2018.

Pratt, S. (2010). What is the difference between counter-insurgency and counter-terrorism? http://www.e-ir.info/2010/12/21/what-is-the-difference-between-counter-insurgency-andcounter-terrorism/ (assessed 8th June, 2017).

Teich, S. (2013). *Trends and developments in lone wolf terrorism in the western world: An analysis of terrorist attacks and attempted attacks by Islamic extremists. International Institute for counterterrorism.* International Institute for Counter-Terrorism (ICT).

U.S. Government Counter-insurgency Guide. (2009). Bureau of political-military affairs, department of state (accessed 5th June, 2017).

UN News Centre. (2015, January 21). Mali: UN mission wards off rebel attack; urges armed groups to respect ceasefire. https://reliefweb.int/report/mali/mali-un-mission-wards-off-rebel-attack-urges-armed-groups-respect-ceasefire (accessed 10th July, 2018).

UN News Centre. (2015, January 28). Mali: UN Mission to investigate deadly protests against compound. https://news.un.org/en/story/2015/01/489582 (accessed 10th July, 2018).

Zimmermann, D. (2006). Terrorist Threats, the European Union and Counter-Terrorism 25 May. https://www.slideserve.com/molimo/terrorist-threats-the-european-union-and-counter-terrorism.

# 14

# NATO's counterterrorism and counterinsurgency strategy in Africa

*Celestine Uchechukwu Udeogu*

## Introduction

The end of World War II in 1945 saw the emergence of the United States of America (USA) and the defunct Union of Soviet Socialist Republic (USSR) as the two most powerful countries of the world. These were the two countries which, as part of the allied powers, successfully defeated the axis powers spearheaded by Nazi Germany. However, sooner than later, the relationship between the two emergent superpowers was to plunge the already heavily battered international system into an unhealthy bipolarity. With each of these two countries championing one pole, other independent and sovereign countries were cajoled into pitching their tents with one of these two parallel ideological blocs — Capitalism for US and Socialism/communism for USSR. With all countries of the West (Europe, Australia, and the Americas) aligning with the US under the umbrella of the North Atlantic Treaty Organisation (NATO). This organisation was formed by the United States, Canada, and several Western European nations in the year 1949 to provide collective security against the communist Soviet Union. For about ten years, countries of the East (Asia mostly) observed the activities, programmes, and relational dynamics of NATO. They decided to group under the pavilion of Warsaw Treaty Organisation (WTO) or Warsaw Pact, formed in 1955 by the Soviet Union and seven other Eastern European states, to counterbalance NATO's incursive tendencies towards the east. Between 1949 and 1955, the years the NATO and WARSAW Pact were respectively formed, the international system was already ripe for deep-rooted ideological warfare (Cold War) and nuclear Armageddon with potentials of Mutually Assured Destruction (MAD) between the two blocs of the global community. Hence, all through the period of the Cold War, two out of the three Cs of international relations (Cooperation, Competition and Conflict) became very pronounced. These, of course, were "Competition" and "Conflict". Although at the precipice of conventional warfare, no bullet was fired in combat from any of the poles all through the unholy Cold War era until its culmination in early 1990, which Hassner (1973:43) had argued ushered in "hot peace" in place of the "Cold War" in the international arena.

The Cold War period did not witness any significant warfare or exchange of fire because of the distinctive doctrines of "deterrence" and "détente". Recognising the existence of MAD, the two blocs were mindful of the consequences of conventional warfare. Hence, from the late

1960s until the start of the 1980s, the doctrine of mutual nuclear deterrence (restraining each other from taking deadly action by instilling fears and anxiety) characterised relations between the United States and the Soviet Union. Periods when the Cold War hanged at the precarious precipice of getting "hot", were often doused by moments of relaxed tensions and peaceful co-existence (détente) between the US and the USSR. This was expressed on one occasion through the visit of President Richard M. Nixon of US to the Secretary-General of the Soviet Communist Party, Leonid I. Brezhnev, in Moscow, in May 1972. During this historic visit, the two leaders signed seven agreements covering the prevention of accidental military clashes; arms control, as recommended by the then-recent Strategic Arms Limitation Talks (*SALT*); co-operative research in a variety of areas, including space exploration; and expanded commerce. This situation needless to say, intensively rolled the imminence of lethal warfare back.

It is worthy of note that NATO, *ab initio*, was never an outfit formed on the principles, logic, and mission of countering terrorism—neither in Europe nor elsewhere. Like its counterpart (Warsaw Pact), NATO was a child of historical necessity, the ovum of which was fertilised by the need for cooperation, delivered through the orifice of fear of consuming *conflicts* and natured into maturity by capitalist *competition* in the face of fast-rising socialist threat. To legitimise its existence after the disintegration of the USSR, which is assumed to be coincident with the end of the Cold War, since 1990 NATO has embarked upon gradual role differentiation, thereby integrating into its mission and vision nuanced attributes and roles that were initially not part of the establishing principles and treaty. Outstanding among these has been "Counterterrorism", defined as "all offensive measures taken to neutralise terrorism before and after hostile acts are carried out….such measures include those counterforce activities justified for the defence of individuals as well as containment measures implemented by military forces or civilian organisations" (Kuhar, 2014: Viii–ix). What could be described as NATO's inaugural counterterrorism move was the invocation of its Collective Defence response under Article 5 of the Washington Treaty as a reaction to the 9/11 (2001) terrorist attacks against the United States in 2001. The action was couched on the doctrine of "an attack against one is an attack against all", since the US is not just a member, but a leading one.

In keeping with this renewed role and goal, NATO subsequently published at least five (5) policy documents on counterterrorism (Military Concept for Defence Against Terrorism, 2002; Partnership Action Plan Against Terrorism, 2002; Defence Against Terrorism Program of Work, 2004; NATO-Russia Joint Review of the 21st Century Common Security Challenges, 2010; and NATO Policy Guidelines on Countering Terrorism, 2012). It has equally carried out and is still resolved to carry out several counterterrorism campaigns in Europe, the Middle East, and Africa. The conviction is that recent developments in the broader Middle East and North Africa underline, once again, the importance of collective defence posture against terrorism for NATO (Kuhar, 2014).

With the spate and rapidity at which insurgency now haunts many states in Africa, from Egypt to Libya to Nigeria to Togo to Mali to Somalia, the continent, more than ever before, appears incapable of violent wrestling extremism and therefore more than willing to accept helping hands from any quarter of the globe to the end of combating insurgency. In addition to this, the inclusion of any reference to "recent developments in wider Middle East (to which some African countries like Egypt is a part), and North Africa" as underlining "the importance of defence against terrorism for NATO" by the above report provides the enquiring impetus to explore *NATO's Counterterrorism and CounterInsurgency Strategy in Africa.*

The chapter argues that the transformation of NATO into a global counterterrorism/counterinsurgency outfit reflects the alliance's dynamic response and poise to the dynamics of international politics. Although the organisation aspires to fight violent extremism across the globe, its immediate concern is its members. This being the case, NATO's war against terrorism/insurgency in Africa, apart from being subsidiary, is inherently laden with opportunistic calculus. The chapter is divided into seven sections. Following this *introduction* is an overview of the *evolution and transformation of NATO*, which in turn is accompanied by an exploration of *theoretical framings of NATO's path to counterterrorism*. The next section addresses *NATO's Counterterrorism Policy Guidelines versus global practical realities*.

*In contrast,* the section following this interrogates *NATO and violent extremism in Africa,* raising questions on whether the alliance can *fight justly for strangers (Africa).* The penultimate section sets out to explore the possibility of contriving a pragmatic counterinsurgency mission in Africa through *NATO-EU cooperation.* The last section *concludes* the chapter.

## The North Atlantic Treaty Organisation (NATO): evolution and transformation

With the admission of Montenegro as the 29th member on the 5th of June 2017, NATO is now an alliance of twenty-nine (29) independent countries from Europe and North America. It provides a unique link between these two continents for consultation and cooperation in the field of collective defence and security and the conduct of multinational crisis-management operations. Table 14.1 shows the necessary information about NATO-member countries.

Outside these member nations, NATO maintains close cooperation with several international organisations and countries in different structures. A brief exploration of these partners and their composition, it is believed, would offer a nuanced and balanced appreciation of the issue which the chapter undertakes, especially given the fact that the study focuses on Africa. Given this, efforts should be made at understanding the role of Africa in these groups.

One of these partnership outfits is the *Euro-Atlantic Partnership Council (EAPC)* which consists of all NATO member countries and many other partner countries across Europe and America. It is striking to remark that no African country is a member of the EAPC. There is however the *NATO's Mediterranean Dialogue*, which includes seven countries, five of which are African states: Algeria, Egypt, Israel, Jordan Mauritania, Morocco, and Tunisia.

The *Istanbul Cooperation Initiative* (ICI) appears to be designed for Asian Muslim countries. To date, the following four countries of the Gulf Cooperation Council have joined: Bahrain, Qatar, Kuwait, and United Arab Emirate (http://www.nato.int/cps/en/natohq/nato_countries.htm). It aims to contribute to long-term global and regional security by offering countries of the broader Middle East region practical bilateral security cooperation with NATO.

Apart from the preceding, NATO also maintains some official partners across the globe. The organisation cooperates with a range of countries which are not part of these structures. *Partners Across the Globe,* a vocabulary for these countries, develop cooperation with NATO in areas of mutual interest, including emerging security challenges, and some contribute actively to NATO operations either militarily or in some other way. As usual, no African country is among these "Partners Across the Globe". African countries are not in NATO's global strategic schemes because NATO is primarily interested in the security of its members. Africa, at present, has not proven to be capable of actively contributing to NATO's operation like other partner countries. Still, in terms of cooperation, NATO relates and partners with some international organisations, outstanding among which are the United Nations (UN), the European Union (EU) and Organisation for Security and Co-operation in Europe.

A stream of argument started flowing from the initial overview of the constitution and partnering nature of NATO. For all intent and purposes, NATO has proved its mettle as an organisation of, and for, Europe and North America. Far from being a global organisation cutting across continents of the globe, it is a bi-regional organisation. Indeed, a white man's

Table 14.1 Basic Information about NATO-Member Countries

| S/N | Country | Population | Landmass | GDP | Military Strength |
|---|---|---|---|---|---|
| 1. | Albania | 2,876 million | 28,748 km² | 11.93 billion USD | 64,000 |
| 2. | Belgium | 11.35 million | 30,528 km² | 466.4 billion USD | 38,800 |
| 3. | Bulgaria | 7.128 million | 110,994 km² | 52.4 billion USD | 52,650 |
| 4. | Canada | 36.29 million | 9.985 million km² | 1.53 trillion USD | 111,250 |
| 5. | Croatia | 4.171 million | 56,594 km² | 12,090.67 USD | 21,525 |
| 6. | Czech Republic | 10.56 million | 78,866 km² | 192.9 billion USD | 29,050 |
| 7. | Denmark | 5.731 million | 42,931 km² | 53,417.66 USD | 75,150 |
| 8. | Estonia | 1.316 million | 45,336 km² | 17,574.69 USD | 35,000 |
| 9. | France | 66.9 million | 643,801 km² | 2.465 trillion USD | 387,635 |
| 10. | Germany | 82.67 million | 357,376 km² | 3.467 trillion USD | 210,000 |
| 11. | Greece | 10.75 million | 131,957 km² | 194.6 billion USD | 413,750 |
| 12. | Hungary | 9.818 million | 93,030 km² | 124.3 billion USD | 77,250 |
| 13. | Iceland | 334,252 | 103,000 km² | 20.05 billion USD | 43,000 |
| 14. | Italy | 60.6 million | 301,338 km² | 1.85 trillion USD | 267,500 |
| 15. | Latvia | 1.96 million | 64,589 km² | 27.68 billion USD | 17,155 |
| 16. | Lithuania | 2.872 million | 65,300 km² | 14,879.68 USD | 23,015 |
| 17. | Luxemburg | 582,972 | 2,586 km² | 59.95 billion USD | 45,500 |
| 18 | Montenegro | 622,781 | 13,812 km² | 6,701.00 USD | 1,950 |
| 19. | Netherlands | 17.02 million | 41,543 km² | 770.8 billion USD | 53,205 |
| 20. | Norway | 5.233 million | 385,203 km² | 370.6 billion USD | 72,500 |
| 21. | Poland | 37.95 million | 312,679 km² | 469.5 billion USD | 184,650 |
| 22. | Portugal | 10.32 million | 92,212 km² | 204.6 billion USD | 268,500 |
| 23. | Romania | 19.71 million | 238,397 km² | 186.7 billion USD | 177,750 |
| 24. | Slovakia | 5.429 million | 49,035 km² | 89.55 billion USD | 14,675 |
| 25. | Slovenia | 2.065 million | 20,273 km² | 21,304.57 USD | 15,500 |
| 26. | Spain | 46.56 million | 505,990 km² | 1.232 trillion USD | 174,700 |
| 27. | Turkey | 79.51 million | 783,562 km² | 857.7 billion USD | 743,415 |
| 28. | United Kingdom | 65.64 million | 242,495 km² | 2.619 trillion USD | 232,675 |
| 29. | United States | 323.1 million | 9.834 million km² | 18.57 trillion USD | 2,363,675 |

**Source:** Author's compilation

club for the deliberation of the affairs of the white man, the only exception, perhaps, is Turkey's membership of NATO which seems to have given the organisation a global and trans-Mediterranean outlook. Granted that at the formation of NATO, most African countries were still colonies. It is paradoxical that at a time when the gospels of liberal internationalism, complex interdependency and globalisation of complementarities, are being ironically preached by the "super countries" of NATO, exclusion rather than the inclusion of African countries have remained conspicuous. Not even arguments bordering on geographical peculiarities (North Atlantic) would be potent enough to justify this exclusionism, for the concept of north and south are mere accident of cartographical convention (Mazrui, 1979). The dynamic and complex nature of the international system and the issues it constantly throws up have not only brought to fore the apparent meaninglessness of geographical particularisation, but it has also further vitiated the sublimity of the polemics of geo-spatial determinism.

The ongoing argument could be stretched further to interrogate why and how an organisation with little or no affiliation could objectively and disinterestedly pursue a costly course of

*Table 14.2* NATO's Mediterranean Dialogue Members

| S/N | Country | Population | Landmass | GDP | Military Strength |
|-----|---------|-----------|----------|-----|-------------------|
| 1. | Algeria | 40.61 million | 2.382 million km² | 156.1 billion USD | 792,350 |
| 2. | Egypt | 95.69 million | 1.01 million km² | 336.3 billion USD | 1,329,250 |
| 3. | Israel | 8.547 million | 20,770 km² | 318.7 billion USD | 718,250 |
| 4. | Jordan | 9.456 million | 89,342 km² | 38.65 billion USD | 170,600 |
| 5. | Mauritania | 4.301 million | 1.03 million km² | 4.635 billion USD | 20,870 |
| 6. | Morocco | 35.28 million | 446,550 km² | 101.4 billion USD | 373,000 |
| 7. | Tunisia | 11.4 million | 163,610 km² | 3,688.65 USD | 50,150 |

**Source:** Author's compilation

action, both in terms of military and finance, for a continent in peril. We shall revisit this argument in subsequent sections.

## Theoretical framing of NATO's path to counterterrorism

In an academic enterprise, a theory is meant to guide practice, just as practice is expected to conform to theoretical postulations. A positive synthetic level of knowledge often referred to as praxis is attained when the practice meets, or is patterned, after theory. For an indebt and worthwhile analysis and projection of NATO's path to counterterrorism, it is imperative to explore some key theoretical framings of counterterrorism and counterinsurgency (CT-COIN).

Kilcullen's (2006) *Three Pillars Counterinsurgency*, in our opinion, remains one of the finest and most ingeniously articulated Counterinsurgency Theory (Coin-T). In his "Three Pillars of Counterinsurgency", Kilcullen (2006) recognised and described a framework for interagency cooperation in counterinsurgency operations. The three constituent pillars, namely: *Security, Political and Economic*, stand as a buffer and supporting beam upon which the all-important and overarching goal of *Control* is built or anchored. The effectiveness of both the three pillars and the Control as the roof is however heavily contingent upon yet another elemental variable, which is *Information*. He explained further in the following lines:

This is because perception is crucial in developing control and influence over population groups. Substantive security, political and economic measures are critical, but to be effective, they must rest upon and integrate with a broader information strategy. Every action in counterinsurgency sends a message; the purpose of the information campaign is to consolidate and unify this message. Importantly, the information campaign has to be conducted at a global, regional and local level—because modern insurgents draw upon global networks of sympathy, support, funding and recruitment (Kilcullen, 2006).

In Kilcullen's estimation, the three pillars are of equal importance, because unless they are developed in parallel, the campaign becomes unbalanced. He elucidated this by remarking that too much economic assistance with inadequate security, for example, simply creates an array of soft targets for the insurgents. Similarly, too much security assistance without political consensus or good governance simply creates more capable armed groups. In developing each pillar, we measure progress by determining effectiveness (capability and capacity) and legitimacy (the degree to which the population accepts that government actions are in its interest) (Kilcullen, 2006). The overall goal, according to this model, "is not to reduce violence to zero or to kill every insurgent, but rather to return the overall system to normality — noting that 'normality' in one society may look different from normality in another. In each case, we seek not only to

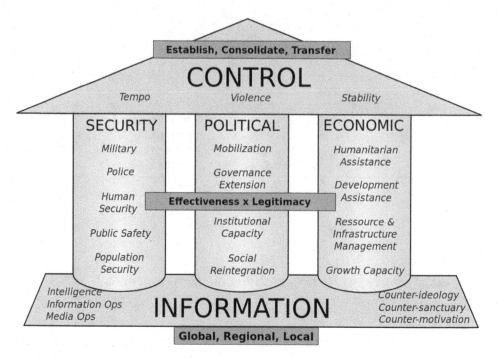

*Figure 14.1* Kilcullen's Three Pillars of Counterinsurgency

establish control but also to consolidate that control and then transfer it to permanent, effective, and legitimate institutions" (Kilcullen, 2006).

However, a thesis on counterinsurgency or counterterrorism theory would fall short of the plenary just as analysis on the issue is shabby unless it devotes to the classical contribution of Van-Creveld on counterinsurgency. In his analysis of why so many counterinsurgencies by powerful militaries fail against weaker enemies, Van-Creveld (2008) identifies a key dynamic element illustrated by the metaphor of killing a child. He observed that regardless of whether the child started the fight or how well armed the child is, an adult in a fight with a child will feel guilty if he harms the child, and foolish if the child harms him; therefore, he will wonder if the fight is necessary. Van-Creveld argues that "by definition, a strong counterinsurgency organisation which uses its strength to kill the members of a small, weak organisation of insurgents — let alone the civilian population by which it is surrounded, and which may lend it support—will commit crimes in an unjust cause," while "a child who is in a serious fight with an adult is justified in using every and any means available—not because he or she is right, but because he or she has no choice" (Van-Creveld, 2008:226). So every act of insurgency becomes, from the perspective of the counterinsurgent, a reason to end the conflict, while also being a reason for the insurgents to continue until victory. In this connection, Trường Chinh, second in command to Ho Chi Minh of Vietnam, wrote:

The guiding principle of the strategy for our whole resistance must be to prolong the war. To protract the war is the key to victory. Why must the war be protracted? If we throw the whole of our forces into a few battles to try to decide the outcome, we shall certainly be defeated, and the enemy will win. On the other hand, if while fighting we maintain our forces, expand them, train our army and people, learn military tactics… and at the same time wear down the enemy forces, we shall weary and discourage them in such a way that, strong as they are, they will become weak and will meet defeat instead of victory (in Van-Creveld, 2008:229-230).

Following from the foregoing, Trường Chinh Chinh identified "superb or superior intelligence" and utter "massacre" as two great methods of executing a successful counterinsurgency/terrorism. Accordingly, the first method relies on superb intelligence, provided by those who know the natural and artificial environment of the conflict as well as the insurgents. The second method as exemplified by the regime of the former Syrian president, Hafez al-Assad, in 1982 involves overwhelming massacre by means of which the insurgency of the Muslim Brotherhood in Syria was successfully quelled (the Hama massacre). While noting that Niccolò Machiavelli might have written them, Van-Creveld summarised al-Assad's strategy into five rules, viz:

1. There are situations in which cruelty is necessary and refusing to apply necessary cruelty is a betrayal of the people who put you into power. When pressed to cruelty, never threaten your opponent but disguise your intention and feign weakness until you strike.
2. Once you decide to strike, it is better to kill too many than not enough. If another strike is needed, it reduces the impact of the first strike. Repeated strikes will also endanger the morale of the counterinsurgent troops; soldiers forced to commit repeated atrocities will likely begin to resort to alcohol or drugs to force themselves to carry out orders and will inevitably lose their military edge, eventually turning into a danger to their commanders.
3. Act as soon as possible. More lives will be saved by decisive action early, than by prolonging the insurgency. The longer you wait, the more inured the population will be to bloodshed, and the more barbaric your action will have to be to make an impression.
4. Strike openly. Do not apologise, make excuses about "collateral damage", express regret, or promise investigations. Afterwards, make sure that as many people as possible know of your strike; media is useful for this purpose, but be careful not to let them interview survivors and arouse sympathy.
5. Do not command the strike yourself in case it does not work for some reason and you need to disown your commander and try another strategy. If it does work, present your commander to the world, explain what you have done and make certain that everyone understands that you are ready to strike again (Van-Creveld, 2008:241–245).

In the light of the foregoing exploration of some theoretical postulations, some of which were informed by practical war/insurgency/counterinsurgency experiences, it is decent enough to now examine NATO's path to counterterrorism/insurgency so far across the globe, before situating it to Africa. It can be substantively argued based on evidential historical realities from Afghanistan, Ukraine, Syria, Iraq, Yemen, Libya, Egypt, ETC, where NATO had had some military presence, that NATO's path to counterinsurgency/terrorism is ostensibly concerned with the protection of areas/spheres of influence and regime change so as to reduce the degree of real and potential threat/enemy. Therefore, regardless of the severity of human rights abuse and anti-democratic policies and agenda of friendly/loyal countries, member countries of NATO have always tended to close their eyes to the untoward happenings of such countries. Their 'sins' would always be forgiven (if at all seen as sins). By contradistinction, however, events of the past have shown that the full wrath of NATO's might and cantankerous dealings have always tended to be visited on countries that had, in the immediate or remote past, given US/NATO countries tough time, or embody potentials of constituting a future threat to the strategic positions of the super member nations of the alliance. It is on record that from the

1980s through the 1990s, and into the early 21$^{st}$ century, Gaddafi had been the *bête noir* of the United States and European governments (Mueller, 2015:12).

The foregoing being the case, NATO hardly intervenes in any global, regional, or national fracas with dispassionate objectivity, diametrically devoid of opportunistic tendencies. Because of this predilection, NATO's counterinsurgency/terrorism strategies have hardly integrated the essentials of time-honoured theories and principles of counterinsurgency, some of which have been examined above. In Libya, for instance, the defeat of Colonel Muammar Gaddafi and his men by NATO, and subsequent institution of a quasi-democratic regime between March and October 2011 were soon seen to be the end of the crisis. As such, no determined effort was made at addressing the humanitarian crisis that soon took the central stage. Even in the hit of the fight between the rebel side and the NATO forces, the population had already begun expressing dissatisfaction with the latter on account of its apparent insensitivity to the plight of the Libyan population. As a result, the much anticipated and useful help and support which NATO would have ordinarily enjoyed from the populace became conspicuous by its absence.

This, regrettably, stands in sharp contrast to what David Galula who gained his practical experience in counterinsurgency as a French officer in the Algerian War had advised. Galula (1964), whose theory of counterinsurgency emphasises a combination of military, political and social actions under the strong control of a single authority, proposed four "laws" for counterinsurgency, which are:

1. The aim of the war is to gain the support of the population rather than control of territory.
2. Most of the population will be neutral in the conflict; support of the masses can be obtained with the help of an active friendly minority.
3. Support of the population may be lost. The population must be efficiently protected to allow it to cooperate without fear of retribution by the opposite party.
4. Order enforcement should be done progressively by removing or driving away armed opponents, then gaining the support of the population, and eventually strengthening positions by building infrastructure and setting long-term relationships with the population. This must be done area by area, using a pacified territory as a basis of operation to conquer a neighbouring area.

He emphatically contends that:

A victory [in a counterinsurgency] is not the destruction in each area of the insurgent's forces and his political organisation. A victory is that plus the permanent isolation of the insurgent from the population, isolation not enforced upon the population, but maintained by and with the population.... In conventional warfare, strength is assessed according to military or other tangible criteria, such as the number of divisions, the position they hold, the industrial resources, etc. In revolutionary warfare, strength must be assessed by the extent of support from the population as measured in terms of political organisation at the grassroots. The counterinsurgent reaches a position of strength when his power is embedded in a political organisation issuing from, and adamantly supported by, the population (Galula, 1964:54–55)

The wars in Iraq and Afghanistan have resulted in increased interest in counterinsurgency within the United States American military, as exemplified by the 2006 publication of a new joint Army Field Manual 3–24/Marine Corps War-fighting Publication No. 3–33.5, *Counterinsurgency*, which replaced the documents separately published by the Army and Marine Corps 20–25 years before. According to Hodge (2009), views of the doctrine contained in the manual have been mixed. He contended that the 2014 version of FM 3–24/MCWP 3–33.5 acquired a new title, *Insurgencies and Countering Insurgencies*, and consists of three main parts. Part one provides strategic and operational context, part two provides the doctrine for understanding insurgencies, and part three provides doctrine for defeating an insurgency. In short, FM 3–24/MCWP 3–33.5 is organised to provide the context of a problem, the problem, and viable solutions (FM 3–24/MCWP 3–33.5 Insurgencies and Countering Insurgencies). Meanwhile, in the recent conflicts, the 101st Airborne Division (Air Assault) has been increasingly involved in conducting special operations, especially the training and development of other states' military and security forces (Bryant & Bryant, 2007).

## NATO's counterterrorism policy guidelines versus global practical realities

Following the reaffirmation of the member nations that the Alliance must "deter and defend against emerging security challenges where they threaten the fundamental security of individual Allies or the Alliance as a whole" (NATO, 2012), the NATO Policy Guidelines on Countering Terrorism were agreed upon in April 2012 and endorsed by NATO Heads of State and Government at the Chicago Summit on May 20, 2012. The guidelines provide a new framework to NATO's role and activities in countering terrorism, based essentially on three principles (Compliance with International Law, NATO's Support to Allies, and Non-Duplication and Complementarity) as well as three areas of focus (Awareness, Capabilities, and Engagement). A little exploration of these principles would suffice. On *Compliance with International Law,* NATO plans to continue to act in accordance with international law, the principles of the UN Charter and the Universal Declaration of Human Rights. The UN Global Counterterrorism Strategy, International Conventions and Protocols against terrorism and relevant UN Resolutions provide the framework for all national and multilateral efforts to combat terrorism, including those conducted by the Alliance. On the other hand, *NATO's Support to Allies* reaffirms that individual NATO members have primary responsibility for the protection of their populations and territories against terrorism. Cooperation through NATO can enhance Allies' efforts to prevent, mitigate, respond to, and recover from acts of terrorism. NATO, upon request, may support these efforts. Under the *Non-Duplication and Complementarity* principle, NATO seeks to promote complementarity with and avoid unnecessary duplication of existing efforts by individual nations or other International Organisations. NATO plans to coordinate and leverage its expertise and resources and will focus on targeted programmes where it can contribute to and/or reinforce the actions of Allied nations and other international actors, as appropriate (Santamato, 2013).

Key areas in which the Alliance seeks to undertake initiatives to enhance the prevention of, and resilience to, acts of terrorism constitute the major focus of the Guidelines. In the following paragraphs, we summarise Santamato's (2013) elaboration of these foci.

The focus on *Awareness* represents NATO's determination to ensure shared awareness of the terrorist threat and vulnerabilities among Allies through consultations, enhanced sharing of intelligence, continuous strategic analysis, and assessments in support of national authorities. The essence is to enable both allies and the Alliance at large to prepare effectively and to take possible mitigating action in the prevention of, and response to, terrorist attacks. Added to this is the promotion of a mutual understanding of its counterterrorism role as part of a broader international effort through engagement and strategic communications and information sharing.

On *Capabilities,* NATO strives to ensure that it commands enough capabilities to prevent, protect against and respond to terrorist threats, based on the level of ambition as defined in the Political Guidance. As outlined by Santamato (2013), NATO will do so by considering capability developments, innovative technologies and methods that address asymmetric threats in a more comprehensive and informed way, including through the Defence Against Terrorism

Programme of Work. NATO strives to maintain its operational capacity and capitalise on the lessons learned in operations, including experience gained through Special Operations Forces.

The focus on *Engagement* is based on the belief that the challenge of terrorism requires a comprehensive approach by the international community, involving a wide range of instruments. It represents NATO's express willingness to tackle insurgency and terrorism by cooperating with partner countries and other international actors and regional organisations. NATO seeks to "enhance consultations and ensure a more systematic approach to practical cooperation with partner countries using existing mechanisms, including scientific cooperation on technological innovation for improved security. NATO places particular emphasis on raising awareness, capacity building, civil-emergency planning, and crisis management to respond to the specific needs of partner countries and Allied interests" (Santamato, 2013:30).

In sum, the foregoing principles and areas of focus, no doubt, were informed by NATO's and the Allied nations' chequered experiences in wars and counterterrorism operations in different climes and times. Yet, the Alliance's experience in Libya was to pose a big question to the effectiveness of these principles and areas of focus, as will be illuminated later in this chapter.

## NATO and violent extremism in Africa: fighting justly for strangers or "responsibility to protect"?

Never in the history of the African continent has the continent experienced violent extremism expressed in the form of militancy, insurgencies, and full-blown terrorism than in the aftermaths of the end of the Cold War in 1990. In the decades after the Cold War, Africa witnessed the bushfire of civil wars, resource conflicts, terrorism and insurgency which plunged the continent into the abyss of violent instability. With insurrection in Libya, Boko Haram Insurgency in Northeast Nigeria, the bloody civil war raging in Algeria until the end of the 1990s, Libya's autocratic Gaddafi and frequent coups in Niger and Mauritania (Boeke, 2016), ETC, Africa is arguably the world's most violent extremism-prone continent.

Since the end of the Cold War in the early 1990s, NATO has transformed into a global stabilising outfit. Like the proverbial whirlwind, the force of which causes every tree it comes in contact with to bend or get broken, NATO tends to deploy naked power and brute force against any apparent stubborn state or individual that refuses to bend in the direction of its pervasive wind of stabilisation. With this premise set, NATO's counterinsurgency missions in Africa, like that of France and the EU, have invariably taken an interventionist character. Sometimes, eclecticism rather than the specificity of plans and objectives tend to define these interventions. In Mali, for instance, the French "Operation Serval" named after a desert cat served as an example of a clear objective and mission. In response to the Malian government's cry for help, the French military intervened to stop the Salafi-Jihadist attack on the South. The intervention had three phases: stopping the jihadist attack, reclaiming the north from terrorist control, and clearing their hideout in the Adrar des Ifoghas.

There were two broad objectives of Operation Serval which could be described as follow:

(a) Manifest Official Objectives and
(b) Latent Strategic Objectives

On 12 January 2013, the French Ministry of Defence shared the Manifest official objectives of Operation Serval, and these were (1) to stop the jihadist advance; (2) to prevent jihadist groups from endangering stability in Mali; and (3) to protect European and particularly French nationals in Mali.[1] And as added a day later by the French Minister of Foreign Affairs (4) the restoration of Malian territorial integrity, was the final objective of Operation Serval.[2] As unrivalled as oracular truth is that the objective of safeguarding 6 000 French nationals in Bamako provided a clearly defined national interest (Boeke, 2016:40). Herein lies the latent strategic opportunistic objectives of French counterinsurgency mission in Mali. There could be no doubting the fact that the intervention was launched in response to an urgent problem—resurgent jihadism threatening local and international interests—but once the initial military victory was achieved, the complexities of transition raised their ugly head, and the interventionist forces were nowhere to be found, having disengaged without consolidating the precarious "gain" made. What could be more important to a battered population than the provision of basic infrastructure? Shockingly, the French interventionists did not give a thought to the fact that:

A population in a conflict area does not judge the government on its counterterrorism strategy but on the provision of basic state services such as electricity, drinking water, health care and education. If these are non-existent or seriously lacking, government legitimacy will suffer. In the north of Mali, two years after the French intervention, the state is still struggling to deliver these basic services. As a result, certain elements of the population are developing some nostalgia for the time that the jihadists were in control and actually managed to ensure more consistent electricity provision than the state (Boeke & de Roy van Zuijdewijn, 2016:13).

France, it must be noted, had had an elaborate and permanent military presence in Africa, with military bases dotting the continent even before the Malian crisis. The Sahel is effectively flanked by a military base in Senegal in the West, and Djibouti in the East. In the middle of Africa, in Chad, France has stationed a dozen warplanes and helicopters that are able to operate within a broad radius of Ndjamena. The prepositioned troops are well trained, equipped and acclimatised to their environment, and can thus be deployed at a moment's notice in crises across the continent. Given this fact, it was therefore not surprising that in 2013, that Operation Serval and the intervention in the Central African Republic had to activate this extended network of military locations throughout Africa to their strategic advantage. At the termination of Operation Serval in 2014, a new regional counterterrorism mission christened Operation Barkhane was launched, this time around, covering five West African countries of Chad, Burkina Faso, Niger, Mali, and Mauritania. An impressive tone of 3,000 troops already predominantly deployed in the West African region was designated to this mission. Barkhane established a unified headquarters and new Counterterrorism operational tasking of units present, adding specific intelligence and strike capacity. France received help and assistance from many other European countries, but as Boeke (2016:39) rightly noted: "all the Western and NATO assistance was, however, of a non-combat nature".

Contrary to the situation in Mali, NATO's intervention in Libya was vaguely defined. It was mandated to impose a no-fly zone to protect Libyan civilians— "Responsibility to Protect" (R2P). NATO's mission was to confront "state terrorism" by applying over-bearing military power on an erratic state and its eclipsing regime. However, as has been elsewhere stated in this chapter, NATO's path to counterinsurgency/terrorism is ostensibly concerned with the protection of areas/spheres of influence and regime change so as to reduce the degree of real and potential threat/enemy. According to Boeke (2016:9), "The US, France and the UK were at pains to deny that 'regime change' was the objective, but emphasised that there could be no solution with Gaddafi remaining in power. This considerably complicated the military operation and the strategic narrative". Thus, the stated NATO objective of protecting civilians effectively ceased once Gaddafi was killed, and while both the intervening powers and the host-nation state were adamant in not wanting "foreign" boots on the ground, the security situation nosedived as a result (Boeke, 2016).

Because countering terrorism/insurgency was never NATO's mission in Libya (Boeke & de Roy van Zuijdewijn, 2016:13), necessary effort and requisite actions were not taken by the organisation to pre-empt and forestall possible factors that could possibly throw up, nurture and sustain terrorist feelings and manifestations in the near future. First was the "light-footprint strategy", which implied that NATO's heavy presence that could have crushed vestiges of insurrection was lacking. "What had been a light footprint intervention would only become lighter, as both the Libyan NTC and NATO were not keen on troops on Libyan soil" (Boeke & de Roy van Zuijdewijn, 2016:53). It did not occur to the allied countries of NATO that it is better to go too far than never far enough. Hence, with the death of Gaddafi in October 2011, and the immediate disengagement of NATO, the intervening powers only provided a minimum of post-conflict aid and assistance, remaining on the sidelines as Libya descended into chaos and internal conflict (Boeke & de Roy van Zuijdewijn, 2016:15). The authors further noted that:

The security situation continues to deteriorate and has already led to the death of more than 4,500 people. Institutions are deadlocked with two separate governments, one in Tobruk in the east of Libya and another in Tripoli in the west, both claiming to be the legitimate authority. Adding to this volatile situation is the fact that the Islamic State (IS) has consolidated its presence in Libya over the past year. This worsening security situation has led to speculation that another military intervention is being considered, this time led by the US and France, and supported by Italy and the UK. It has been reported that, amongst others, French Special Forces have already been involved in covert operations against the group Islamic State in Libya (Boeke & de Roy van Zuijdewijn, 2016:15).

While it can be sustainably argued that the involvement of NATO in counterinsurgency operations in Libya (*Operation Odyssey Dawn and NATO Operation Unified Protector*) in particular and Africa, in general, could take benign forms, it could also fuel local conflicts when, as the case was in Libya, foreign powers actively support their own proxies or allies. Still, in Libya, both Qatar and Turkey supported, albeit clandestinely, Islamist factions that oppose the elected government in Tobruk, thus emboldening these terrorist groups to survive and perpetuate their acts of terror. Elsewhere in Afghanistan, Pakistan has played a nefarious role in consistently providing a haven to the strategic leadership of the Taliban. While in the latter case, the US and NATO have deliberately chosen not to confront their ally (Boeke, 2016:14), in Libya, the NATO chose to ignore the sabotaging efforts of Turkey and Qatar. It is shocking that since NATO's 1999 *Operation Allied Force* (Kosovo), several critical shortfalls in capacity, specifically on the European side, have been identified. These include Intelligence, Surveillance, Target Acquisition and Reconnaissance (ISTAR) platforms and capacity, aerial refuelling, precision munitions and strategic transport. These shortages have still not been alleviated (Boeke 2016). These coupled with veiled strategic national interest primacy and poor attitude towards post-crisis humanitarian crisis have all combined to undermine the effectiveness of NATO to constitute a formidable bulwark for countering terrorism/insurgency, especially in Africa.

## NATO-EU co-operation: in search of pragmatic counterinsurgency mission in Africa

Both NATO and the EU have reacted to terrorist threats in characteristically different ways —"hard power" for NATO and "soft power" for the EU. They have also coalesced both soft and hard powers as a unifying strategy for fighting terrorism. While this distinction is not watertight, it goes to show variation in policy preferences towards terrorism between the two organisations. Although the EU has had to come down hard militarily on the situations in Mali and Tunisia, it is an organisation that tends to see "military force as of limited value and has characteristically argued for a more integrated policy response, both within the EU and without" (Cornish, 2006:20), as opposed to NATO that tends to glorify the show of naked (military) power. Thus, both sides have acknowledged the need for policy co-ordination, at the very least, and the two organisations have exchanged information and data on relevant inventories. High-level meetings have also been held regularly between NATO's North Atlantic Council and the EU's Political and Security Committee, addressing such issues as counterterrorism policy and CBRN proliferation (Cornish, 2006).

While advocating that NATO-EU cooperation is both necessary and possible, such co-operation may not be without some internal unexpressed distrusts and fear. History is replete with instances of where friendly alliances formed at war or desperate times for the purposes of defeating a common enemy ended up breeding and encouraging yet another animosity from within at the eventual defeat of the common enemy. The Cold War that gave birth to NATO, for instance, has its origin in this. With the defeat/death of Hitler (the common enemy) by the allied forces, ably led by the US and USSR, the two world Superpowers turned against each other and embarked upon protracted ideological warfare (the Cold War). In the same vein, with the end of the Cold War, fear of a US-dominated NATO began to be expressed by other European countries. The resulting declaration of the EU December 1998 meeting in St. Malo, France between Tony Blair (the then British Prime-Minister) and Jacques Chirac (former President of France) expressed EU's position to play "its full role on the international stage, [EU] should have the capacity for autonomous action, backed up by credible military forces, the means to decide to use them, and the readiness to do so (an idea that might be read as code for independence from the United States)" (McCormick, 2011:417). Two years earlier, agitations from EU members of NATO prevailed on NATO ministerial meeting to adopt that the Western European Union (WEU) would be responsible for the development of a European Security and Defence Identity (ESDI). This would allow European NATO members to act independently where NATO did not wish to and would be run politically by WEU (McCormick, 2011).

## Conclusion

This chapter critically examined NATO's Counterterrorism and Counterinsurgency drive in Africa. The aphorism that necessity is the mother of invention seemed to have found firm justification in NATO's sudden role differentiation. *Ab initio*, countering terrorism was not part of NATO's primary concerns. Hence, in its periodic in-depth review of 1991, allied members of NATO noted "terrorism" as a threat but casually dropped it at the bottom of NATO's "things-to-do" list. However, in keeping with its doctrine of "an attack against one is an attack against all", NATO invoked its Collective Defence response under Article 5 of the Washington Treaty as a reaction to the 9/11 terrorist attacks against the United States in 2001. In furtherance of this new role in the war against terrorism, NATO, in its summit held in Prague in 2002, officially drew up a document on counterterrorism—the "Military Concept for Defence against Terrorism". By early 2012 agreement had been reached and endorsed on NATO's Counterterrorism Policy Guidelines. With reference to these "Guidelines", especially its three pillars of "Awareness, Capabilities and Engagement" as the most summary approach to counterterrorism across the globe, the capacity of NATO in mounting a successful counterinsurgency campaign in Africa was critically explored. Viewed from the theoretical insights of Kilcullen's *Three Pillars of Counterinsurgency Model*, the inherent weaknesses of NATO in countering insurgency in Africa were brought to fore.

At best, NATO's current global effort at counterterrorism could be described as "Members self-interest" disguised as "global charity". In particular, NATO's seemingly generosity towards the African States and people is not entirely charitable: peace and economic reconstruction suited NATO/American interests, re-enforcing the Alliance's ability to resist and offset Russia's influence, building an important market for US/EU exports, and establishing Western Europe as a critical political and economic partner of the United States (McCormick, 2011). The eloquent position is that by "neglecting to follow-up on the military intervention and invest in a transition, the NATO has contributed to making the complex and dangerous situation in Libya that more intractable" (Boeke & de Roy van Zuijdewijn, 2016:54).

Although at the end of the Cold War, NATO and Russia had an agreement that the former was not going to come to the doorpost of Russia, what could be seen and regarded as NATO's, greatest tactical and strategic mistake as far as the corporate interest of NATO's allied members is concerned was allowing China to rise and aligning with Russia. In view of this ugly trend, both for the purposes of its own benefits and for a level of pragmatic war against violent extremism in Africa and elsewhere, a recommendation for a functional NATO-EU Co-operation (its challenges notwithstanding) is hereby proffered.

## Notes

1   Ministère de la Défense, "Conference De Presse Du Ministre De La Défense, Jean-Yves Le Drian," 12 January 2013.
2   France Diplomatie, "Mali - Somalie - Russie - Entretien Du Ministre Des Affaires Étrangères, M. Laurent Fabius, 13 January 2013, accessed 23 May 2017, http://basedoc.diplomatie.gouv.fr/vues/Kiosque/FranceDiplomatie/kiosque.php?fichier=bafr2013-01-14.html#Chapitre 5.

## References

Boeke, S. (2016). *Transitioning from military interventions to long-term counter-terrorism policy: The case of Mali (2013-2016)*. Leiden University – Institute of Security and Global Affairs (2016).
Boeke, S., & de Roy van Zuijdewijn, J. (2016). *Transitioning from military interventions to long-term counter-terrorism policy: The case of Libya (2011–2016)*. Leiden University – Institute of Security and Global Affairs.
Bryant, Russ, & Bryant, Susan (2007). *Screaming Eagles: 101st Airborne Division*. MBI Publishing Company.
Cornish, P. (2006). *EU and NATO: Co-operation or competition?* Briefing Paper. European Parliament; Policy Department External Policies.
Eizenstat, S., Porter, J. E., & Weinstein, J. (2005). Rebuilding failed states. *Foreign Affairs, 85*(1), 134–146.
Galula, D. (1964). *Counterinsurgency warfare: Theory and practice* (pp. 54–56). Westport, Connecticut: Praeger Security International.
Hassner, P. (1973). *Cold war to hot peace. The New York Times, October 16.*
Kilcullen, D. J. (2006). *Three pillars of counter-insurgency*. Remarks delivered at the *U.S. Government Counterinsurgency Conference*, Washington D.C., 28 September available online at: http://www.au.af.mil/au/awc/awcgate/uscoin/3pillars_of_counter-insurgency.pdf (accessed on 23rd May, 2017).
Kuhar, K. S. (2014). *NATO's counterterrorism & counterinsurgency experience in Afghanistan: Lessons learned workshop report. NATO Centre of Excellence Defence Against Terrorism/ANKARA.* Online: https://www.tmmm.tsk.tr/publication/workshop_reports/05-CounterterrorismCounterinsurgencyExperience.pdf. Accessed on 4 October 2019.
Mazrui, A. (1979). *The African condition. Reith Lectures.* Transmission: Radio 4, 7 November. Online: http://downloads.bbc.co.uk/rmhttp/radio4/transcripts/1979_reith1.pdf. Accessed 1 November 2019.
McCormick John, (2011). *European Union Politics.* London: Macmillan.
McClintock, M. (1992). *Instruments of statecraft: U.S. guerrilla warfare, counter-insurgency, and counter-terrorism, 1940–1990.* New York: Pantheon.
Mueller, K. P. (2015). *Precision and purpose: Airpower in the Libyan civil war.* Santa Monica, Calif: RAND Corporation.

NATO. (2012). NATO's policy guidelines on counter-terrorism: Aware, Capable and Engaged for a Safer Future. Available online @ http://www.nato.int/cps/en/natohq/official_texts_87905.htm.

Porch, D. (1986). Bugeaud, Galliéni, Lyautey: The development of French colonial warfare. In P. Paret, G. A. Craig & F. Gilbert (Eds.), *Makers of modern strategy: From Machiavelli to the nuclear Age* (pp. 376–407). Oxford: Oxford University Press.

Santamato, S. (2013). *The new NATO policy guidelines on counterterrorism: Analysis, assessments, and actions.* Center for Strategic Research Institute for National Strategic Studies National Defense University.

Trinquier, R. (1961). *Modern warfare: A French view of counter-insurgency.* New York: Ballantine.

U.S. Government Counter-insurgency Guide. (2009). *Bureau of Political-Military Affairs.* Department of State. Retrieved May 30th, 2017.

Van-Creveld, M. (2008). *The changing face of war: Combat from the Marne to Iraq.* New York: Ballantine.

Zambernardi, L. (2010). Counterinsurgency's impossible trilemma. *The Washington Quarterly, 33*(3), 21–34.

# 15

# Afro-European partnership for counterterrorism and counterinsurgency in Africa

*Felix Oludare Ajiola and Olawale Taofeeq Lawal*

## Introduction

Terrorism and insurgency in Africa have assumed a new dimension in scope and operation and pose serious security challenges for Africa and the world at large. The quantum destruction of lives and properties witnessed in recent times in countries such as Nigeria, Somalia, Libya, Egypt, Kenya, Mali, Sudan, and South-Sudan to mention. Still, a few called for more international and regional cooperation and collaboration in countering terrorism and insurgency for the attainment of regional and global peace and security. The three terrorist groups in Africa; Alshabaab, Boko-Haram and the Islamic brotherhood in North Africa, which is linked to Al-Quaeda terrorist organisation have undergone a significant transformation by extending their ideological scope and territorial base. They have become global terrorist organisations by their allegiance with the international terrorist groups such as *Al-Quaeda* and Islamic State in Syria (ISIS). Their scope now spanned beyond the continent of Africa; they are now globally based. The chapter examines the partnership and other efforts of the European Union in countering terrorism and insurgency in Africa.[1] It discusses terrorism and insurgency and identifies the driving force behind its spread. Terrorism and insurgency constitute an enormous threat to national, regional, and global peace and security. These crises in many African countries are caused by globalisation, the rise of Islamic radicalism and militancy, ethnic-religious animosities, and principally failed governance and economic structures. There is a need for a more concentrated EU as well as other international and regional cooperation and commitment in countering and flattening the tone and tenor of terrorism in Africa.

The 21st century has witnessed the proliferation of Islamic terrorism across the world. The terrorist organisations such as the ISIS, Al-Qaeda, Al-Shabaab, Boko-Haram and other emerging Islamic fundamentalists across the globe are a threat to world peace and security. The spread of these terrorist groups' ideology across the world points to the fact that the world is no longer a safe place. This hitherto constitutes a significant threat to the security of lives and properties.[2] These terrorist groups continue to wreak havoc in their host countries and beyond, killing thousands of people through suicide bombing, indiscriminate shooting on vulnerable citizens irrespective of age, gender and religion, vis-à-vis destructive attacks on government properties and security personnel. Terrorism and insurgency indeed have become significant challenges not only in Africa but in the world at large. This, however, explains why it has become necessary for the European Union, as well as other international and regional bodies to partner with African countries and counterterrorism and insurgency in Africa.[3]

The EU's response to terrorism and insurgency in Africa has been firm and resolute following various attacks on innocent citizens across the world, especially after the 11 September 2001 attack on the American World Trade Centre. The EU has made terrorism one of the cardinal elements of its political dialogue with states and regional bodies in Africa given the fact of the international terrorist organisations are using Africa states such as Somalia, Sudan, South Sudan, Mali, Nigeria, Congo and Libya as their bases of finance and training. The EU's counterterrorism and counterinsurgency (CT-COIN) strategy in Africa is aimed at checking the spread of terrorism across the globe and strengthening regional and global peace and security architecture for the protection of its strategic and economic interests in Africa. This chapter, therefore, examines the Euro-African partnership for CT-COIN in Africa.

## Conceptualising terrorism and insurgency

Terrorism as a concept is overly complicated because individuals or groups conventionally perceived as terrorists did not see themselves as such. Therefore, it is challenging to find a universally acceptable definition of terrorism. However, several interpretations have been given to terrorism by scholars and international and regional organisations. Terrorism could manifest through a threat or use of physical coercion primarily against non-combatants, especially civilians, to create fear to achieve various political objectives. At the same time, Joes sees terrorism as the deliberate targeting of civilians for death or injury.

The League of Nations in its convention in 1937 defined terrorism as all criminal acts directed against a State and intended or calculated to create a state of terror in the minds of particular persons or group of persons, or the general public. The convention further sees terrorism as an act of terror that cause death or bodily harm to institutions, state, or government (Shultz & Dew, 2015). Terrorism is an act carried out to achieve the inhuman and pernicious objective and involving a threat to the security of any kind and violation of rights acknowledged by religion and mankind (Taskhri, 1987),[4] The United Nations General Assembly sees terrorism as a criminal act intended or calculated to provoke a state of terror in the general public, a group of persons for political purposes are in any circumstance unjustifiable, whatever the considerations of a political, philosophical, ideological, ethical, religious, or any other nature (Paul, 2005).

Terrorism in the English translation was first used during the French Revolution "the Reign of Terror" when the revolutionary group, the Jacobins who ruled the Revolutionary state, employed violence, including mass executions by a guillotine to compel obedience to the state and intimidate the perceived enemies of the regime: about 40,000 people were executed by guillotine during the French Revolution (Hoffman, 1998). The revolutionary group began to associate with the non-governmental groups.[5] Its ideology metamorphosed from anarchism to nationalism and later anti-monarchism which led to the elimination of Louis XIV of France and the concomitant revolution that spread to other European countries, for instance, Russia with the assassination of Tsar Alexander II on March 1, 1881, by a Russian populist group known as Narodinaya (Alan, 1993:21).[6] It took the joint military effort of other European countries such as Britain, Russia, and Germany to prevent the escalation of the Revolution across Europe.

The defeat of the leader of the revolution, Napoleon Bonaparte at the Battle of Waterloo was a turning point in the eventual collapse of the revolutionaries. The revolutionaries were motivated by the Marxist ideology which created a fertile sense of unrest and offering a means from a radical change from the old order to a new order which was met with severe resistance across Europe. Still, it had a positive impact as it created a reform on governance and accountability not only in France but across Europe (CIPRA Centre for Indian Political Research and Analysis, 2007).

Since the last decade of the 20th century, however, the modus vivendi of terrorists and insurgents in the international system has changed from the nationalists and Marxists ideological struggle for the social and economic transformation of the society to a religious, cultural and anarchist undertone. Consequently, the innocent citizens of the world are at the receiving end, instead of the government. The rate at which religious terrorism and insurgency are spreading across the world is alarming, and the threat they pose to the national, regional and global peace and security require international and regional corporation and collaboration in countering the phenomenon not only in Africa but also at the worldwide stage.[7]

## Terrorism and insurgency in Africa: a threat to peace, security and regional development

Terrorism and insurgency can hardly be separated from one another because they both represent violent struggles; however, the central area of departure is that the insurgent groups are usually open to dialogue and are not faceless like the terrorist groups. Insurgency according to Imobighe and Eguavon (2016) can be viewed as a struggle or agitation for socio-economic and political inclusion and development, resource control, religious tolerance or self-determination by a group employing violence against constituted authority to put forward their grievances. Terrorism, on the other hand, is a religiously or politically motivated violence unleashed on a targeted population, government properties or infrastructures to destroy lives and properties.[8] The objective of this violence is to create far-reaching psychological effects beyond the immediate victims or object of attack, leaving its fearful trails and indelible marks (Abubakar & Ogbeidi, 2014:26).

Insurgencies in post-independence Africa are mostly consequences of the socio-economic exclusion of some ethnic groups or region, poverty, lack of political participation, and underdevelopment.[9] Political events in Africa have also contributed to the multi-faceted insurgencies across the continent. Some of the Insurgent groups in Post independent Africa includes; Movement for the Emancipation of Niger Delta (MEND), Liberation for the Emancipation of Niger-Delta (LEND), and the Niger-Delta Avengers (NDA), all in Delta region of Nigeria, Mai Mai in the Democratic Republic of Congo, the National Movement for the Liberation of Azawad (NMLA) in Mali known as Northern Mali conflict, Sudan People Liberation Movement (SPLM) in South Sudan, Sudan Revolutionary Front (SRF) in Sudan, Lord's Resistance Army (LRA), an insurgent group in Seleka, Central African Republic, others include the Al-Qaeda affiliated Salafi Jihadist in the Maghrebian centres of Morocco, Mauritania, Niger and Mali, Front for the Liberation of the Enclave of Cabinda(FLEC) in Angola, the Revolutionary insurgent groups in Libya and Movement for the Democratic Forces (MDF) of Casamance in Senegal (Faliu, 2009:226).

The 21st-century Islamic terrorism defies boundary, unlike insurgency that is usually restricted to a locality, region, or territorial boundary in pursuance of the group objectives. In Africa, Nigeria has had its share of insurgency and terrorism.[10] The insurgency in the Niger Delta region by the Movement for the Emancipation of Niger Delta (MEND) which later metamorphosed into Niger Delta Avengers (NDA) arising from socio-economic exclusion, poverty and underdevelopment of the region indulged in activities such as the bombing of oil pipelines, kidnapping and killing of oil expatriates and other facilities, oil bunkering, and creating a hostile environment to halt production of crude oil by the major oil companies in the region, an act which recently harmed the Nigeria economy as production dropped significantly. It is worthy of note that the 2009 amnesty program failed to maintain peace in the region due to poor implementation of the program. The major stakeholders in the struggle were not carried along, and more importantly, the root causes of the crisis such as poverty and high rate of youth unemployment, underdevelopment, environmental degradation as a result of an oil spill, soil and water pollution thereby making agricultural practices which are the major occupation of the region difficult were not addressed.

The greatest security challenge in Nigeria comes from *Ahli-Sunna Lidda'awati wal-jihad* (People Committed to the Propagation of the Prophet's Teaching and Jihad) Islamic sect known as Boko-Haram. The Boko Haram is an Islamic terrorist organisation that has its operational base in the north-eastern states of Borno, Yobe and Adamawa states of Nigeria. Boko Haram is driven by an ideology of total rejection of western education, values and civilization which characterised its name Boko Haram meaning "western education is forbidden" in the local Hausa language. The terrorist group since 2009 has killed thousands of people by arm attacks and suicide bombing targeting vulnerable people, churches, mosques, marketplaces, and a large gathering of people. The terrorist' main operational base was the Sambisa Forest in the Northeast. Between 2013 and 2015, the group had seized fifteen of the twenty-seven Local Government Areas in Borno State. With the strong effort of the administration of President Muhammadu Buhari in combating terrorism, the government declared in 2017 that Boko Haram had been technically defeated. However, several debilitating attacks against the Nigerian military by the terrorists in the Northeast of the country, further indicated that Boko Haram terrorism constitutes a formidable force which requires external interventions and supports to defeat.

Since 2011, Boko Haram is estimated to have killed over 20,000 people, and in 2014 alone, it was responsible for around a third of all civilians killed in the conflict in Africa's (Lonel, 2016). Though some of the kidnapped schoolgirls in Chibok town, Borno state in April 2014, have been released by the terrorist group, a number of them are still held captive, despite reactions, sympathy and solidarity by International organisations, regional bodies, religious groups, and individuals across the globe. It should be noted, that the release of some of the kidnapped girls by the insurgents in 2017 and 2018 were the result of the diplomatic effort of the Federal government of Nigeria in ensuring the safe return of the girls to their original homes. This exemplifies the importance of diplomacy in the resolution of a conflict of this magnitude.

As a result of the threats of BH, a regional security arrangement under the aegis of Multinational Joint Task Force (MNJIF) was established in 2014 by member-state of the Lake Chad Basin Commission (LCBC) to counter the operations of the terrorist group. The threat of transnational terrorism in Africa is evidence with the spread of terrorism across Africa countries. Like the Boko-Haram sect, Al-Shabaab is another dreaded terrorist organisation with an operational base in Somalia. The prolonged civil unrest in Somalia and the apparent weak government made Somalia a fertile ground for terrorist activities. Like Boko-Haram, Al-Shabaab has a link with the international terrorist group Al-Qaeda which provides support to the rebels who fought with the United Nations operation in Somalia (UNISOM).[11] The UNISOM II leader's failure to quickly recognise the importance of international and transnational linkage and the role of external agents such as Al-Qaeda was a tactical mistake. Al-Qaeda terrorist organisation has been aiding insurgent group with finance, arms procurement and material need to fight both the peacemaker UNISOM II and the government in power. Due to the protracted civil war, the international terrorist groups identifies Somalia as a suffering and training ground for their combatants since the early 1990s in a fragile state of Somalia in which life has been miserable for people as a result of economic stagnation, brutality, abject poverty and hostile political climate.[12]

On August 7, 1998, the Al-Shabaab terrorist group detonated two bombs which exploded simultaneously at the US embassies in Nairobi, Kenya, and Dares Salam in Tanzania. Not less than 213 people were killed in the attacks including 12 United States citizens. They left more than 5000 injured (Imobighe & Eguavon, 2016). This terrorist act drew the world to terrorism risk in Africa. Al-Shabaab has been waxing stronger in Somalia, and the neighbouring countries of Ethiopia, Kenya, Eritrea, and Uganda with several deadly attacks have claimed many lives. Notable among them was the attacks on Garissa University College, killing more than 145 people in Kenya. This has undermined the regional peace and stability because terrorism in a particular country can readily become a threat to regional peace and security. The new elected President Mohammed Abdullahi Mohammed during his campaign, promised to be open to negotiation warring parties to embrace peace and help build a virile Somalia nation.[13]

In the Maghrebian region, terrorism has become a tool for political struggle following deteriorating socio-economic conditions in the region, poverty, corruption, and colossal disparity between the rich and the poor gave a platform for terrorist activities in Algeria.[14] The leadership highhandedness and lack of democratic principles coupled with the cancellation of election in which Islamic fundamentalist was poised to win in 1992, denying the people their fundamental rights to determine the type of government they want gave rise to hostility and terrorist act by the Islamic fundamentalists.

In Egypt, the constant terrorist activities have become a norm in the country. The recent attack on a Coptic church in Alexandria on Palm Sunday 9th, April 2017, killing not less than 45 worshippers and injuring many was an evidence of the threat terrorism pose to the country, region and the world peace and security. The IS claimed responsibility for the attack which testifies to the linkage between the national and international terrorism. Before this attack, several attacks had been carried out in places of worship, public areas, and on government infrastructures. The Islamic Brotherhood in Egypt, many of whom were arrested for the various terrorist act after the impeachment of the former president of Egypt Mohammed Morsi following mass protests against his rule in 2013 heightened tension and fear of many terrorist activities in Egypt. Since the ouster of Morsi, terrorist activities have increased in Egypt.[15] The French intervention in Mali in early 2013 due to the establishment of the radical Islamic regime in Northern Mali and the Libya conflict exemplifies insurgent activities with terrorism tendency due to the act of terror employed to achieve political activities coupled with the influx of foreign fighters in Libya to aid their foreign fundamentalists to pose a severe threat to the world peace and security.[16]

In Morocco, following the May 16, 2013 bombing, investigated by the Moroccan authority in which the investigation uncovered extremist sect, Salfiya Silidiya across the country planning and organising terrorist acts against the state. The civil unrests in Sudan and South-Sudan also pose security challenges to regional peace and stability. The act of terror employed by the incumbent president, Al-Bashir to suppress opposition in Sudan raises the alarm of infiltration of terrorism into the country.[17] Thousands of people were killed at the peak of the civil war by the government forces which made the International Court of Justice call for the arrest of President Al-Bashir, who was alleged of genocide. It was reported that Osama-Bin-Ladin lived in Sudan for about six months after the 2001 September 11 attack on the World Trade Centre, recruiting and training forces for the terrorist engagements across the globe.[18]

The South Sudan civil unrest which started in 2013 between the forces loyal to the president Kiir Salva and his former deputy Rick Macher after the former and ten other were accused of coup-de-tat against the latter (Stephen, 2001: 57), resulted in a violent conflict between the Sudanese People's Liberation Movement (SPLM) and the SPLM in opposition.[19] In this conflict, thousands of people lost their lives and rendering more than a million people homeless as refugees in neighbouring states of Uganda, Ethiopia, Kenya, and Congo DR (Regional Impact Situation Report, 2016). The act of terror exhibited by the government forces, about 300,000 people were killed, including notable atrocities such as the 2014 Bentiu Massacre (News 24, 2016).[20] From the above it is apparent that terrorist organisations usually take advantage of internal political crisis, weak government and a failing state to attempt to impose their ideology on the captured territories through the act of terror to create psychological imbalance, fear and confusion to consolidate on their gains.[21] This, however, reveals how terrorist groups can exploit a state where democratic principles are lacking, poverty, corruption, lack of political participation, socio-economic exclusion and underdevelopment to intervene by directly or indirectly supporting the rebels as seen above in order to attract sympathy and membership across the world.[22]

## Afro-European partnership for counterterrorism and counterinsurgency in Africa

The European Union has played a decisive role in the throes and fights against terrorism and insurgency in Africa, the rationale behind the EU engagement with Africa in counterterrorism and counterinsurgency can be viewed from its commitment to global peace and security and its strategic economic interest. This is so because Africa is seen as incapable of protecting their huge investments in Africa. More so, Africa also needs Foreign Direct Investment (FDI) from industrialist Europe and across the globe to foster the much-desired economic growth and development. The EU intervention is thus predicated on the recognition that without peace and security, the African economic environment would discourage requisite foreign capital and investments from engendering economic growth and sustainable development.

Counterterrorism requires enormous reliance on intelligence and counterintelligence measures, technical training to the military forces, military equipment such as fighter jets, amour tanks, anti-bomb devices and surveillance and the likes.[23] The central goals of counterterrorism are prevention, disruption and pre-emption of terrorist activities and network. (Imobighe & Eguavon, 2016). The EU's commitment to combating terrorism in Africa was an offshoot of the 2000 Cotonou Agreement with Africa, Caribbean, and Pacific Countries (ACP) which grew out of the 1975 Lome Convention. Africa-EU relations are framed by the Joint Africa-EU Strategy (JAES) adopted by 80 African and European Heads of States and Government of the Lisbon Summit in 2007. This strategy revolves around Africa-EU partnership, with a political framework which defines bilateral relations. Its cardinal goal is a partnership between equals that will jointly tackle issues of mutual concerns (European External Action, 2016). This commitment was reaffirmed at the 4th EU-Africa summit held in April 2014 in Brussels which focused on counterterrorism and the attainment of national, regional, and global peace and security. In adopting its 2014–2017 road map, the Brussels summit focused on cooperation in 'strategic fire areas'; peace and security, democracy, good governance and human rights, human development, sustainable growth and development and continental integration, and emerging global issues.

The EU contributed tremendously to countering terrorism and insurgency effort in Africa. Consequent upon the massive terrorist attacks in Europe, the United States and Africa, by Islamic fundamentalist, the European Union produced counterterrorism strategy underlined the need for intensified regional cooperation in the fight against terrorism globally. European

Union made counterterrorism an essential element of its political dialogue with the regional organisation and states Africa. The European Union (EU) counterterrorism strategy adopted in 2005 was based on four main stands: prevention, protection, tracking and response (European Parliamentary Research Services, 2016). These were the pillars in which counterterrorism effort in Africa and other parts of the world were built.

The EU in its commitment to counterterrorism and counterinsurgency in Africa budgeted 750 million pounds between 2014 and 2016 for African Peace Facility which served to provide much of the funding for African led peacekeeping operations as well for operationalising the African Peace and Security Architecture (APSA) (European External Action, 2016).[24] This initiative helped profoundly to improve Africa's capacities and mechanism to prevent and manage conflicts and crisis within the African region. The beneficiaries of this fund were the African Union Mission in Somalia (AMISOM), and the African led International support mission to the Central African Republic (MISCA). The European Union's strong commitment to counterterrorism in Africa was noticeable in its financial and technical assistance to Nigeria in the Fight against the Boko-Haram sect in the Northeast of Nigeria. Other areas of service include, but not limited to, intelligence gathering and coordination.[25] The E.U in February 2016 pledged 50 million dollars as support Nigeria and the African Union against the Boko-Haram as well as continuous support for the Internally Displaced Persons (IDPs) in Nigeria (Achibong, 2016).

This support came at a time of renewed efforts by the member countries of the Lake Chad Basin Commission (LCBC) and Benin to neutralise the threat posed by the Boko-Haram terrorist sect for the rehabilitation of the affected areas by the activities of the terrorist group as well as the construction of Multinational Joint Task Force (MNJTF) headquarters in Ndjamnewa, the Chadian capital. Boko- Haram attacks on the civilian population have led to the destruction of lives and properties. Indeed, over 20,000 people have been killed, while over 2.5 million people are homeless. During the 6th Nigeria-EU ministerial dialogue, the EU Vice President, Federica Mogherini pledged a continuous EU support on the fight against Boko-Haram, humanitarian and economic development and reconstruction of the destroyed infrastructure in the North-East (Udo, 2017).

The EU's strategy for security and development in the Sahel formulated in 2012 is based on securitisation and socio-economic development of the countries in the Sahel region. The link between security and development agendas has been fundamental to the various EU policies, for example, the Joint African-EU Strategy of 2007,[26] which has been revised strongly than the EU-ACP Cotonou Partnership Agreement since 2000. The EU has been at the forefront of ensuring peace and security in Africa partly because of its strategic economic interest of its member states in the continent and coupled with the general commitment to world peace and security. The EU envisaged the need for good governance through democratic principles and socio-economic development in Africa in ensuring peace and stability. This is because many violent conflicts in Africa emanated from bad governance, lack of political participation, abuse of power, absence of democratic principles and socio-economic exclusion of groups that constitutes minority in their country. EU member countries have investments across African states, ranging from engineering, communication, banking, agrochemical, transportation, to mention a few.[27]

The European Union recently proposed and approved 44 billion Euro investments for Africa and the Mediterranean as part of the European Investment Plan aimed at helping to fight illegal migration. The plan is an innovative new youth investment plan for Africa, considering the illegal migration and the growing radicalisation of able youths in the continent (Mogherini, 2016). The fund was partly to help private sector players to invest in fragile states and contribute to the fight against poverty by creating opportunities for young people especially in the African continent for the promotion of peace, economic growth and development.[28] The EU has also contributed immensely in the area of women empowerment, reduce girls and gender-based violence under the European Investment for Democracy and Human Rights and its contribution to the Global Partnership on Education (GPE) that supports increased access to education in the region (Andrew, 2016). This is aimed at preventing terrorism and insurgency while simultaneously strengthening capacities in the strategic countries in Africa.

The EU offered counterterrorism training to help East African security agencies to improve cross-border investigations and prosecution in areas vulnerable to Al-Shabaab terrorist sect.[29] The training benefits countries like Kenya, Ethiopia, Eritrea, Uganda, DjiBouti, South Sudan and Yemen, which cost about 12 million dollars. The training also straddles the local law enforcement agencies and judiciaries on how to carry out cross-border investigations and construct criminal prosecution (Reuters, 2015). EU Trans-Saharan Counterterrorism Partnership established in 2008 funded and implemented a multi-layered effort to build capacity and cooperation, using the military, law enforcement and civil rule across North and West Africa to counterterrorism.[30] Nigeria and other ECOWAS countries belong to the Inter-Governmental Action Group against money laundering in West Africa, a Financial Action Task Force body.[31] This integrated body of ECOWAS was designed to track the financial of crimes and funds linked to terrorist groups. Other Regional bodies of this task force the Middle East North Africa Financial Action (MENAFATF), Groupe d'Action Countre La Afrique Countrale (GABAC) and East and Southern Africa Anti-money laundering Group.

The EU provided intelligence support to track any suspected money laundering act by individuals alleged to have a link with any terrorist group in the world. The EU also supports African countries in strengthening their judicial system.[32] The EU factually financed three projects in Nigeria in the value of 98 million Euros to support justice, anti-corruption and drug abuse through the United Nations Office on Drugs and Crime (UNODC). The EU also signed 35 million Euros Financial Agreement with Nigeria to consolidate the government's effort in preventing and fighting corruption.[33] The Beneficiaries of the above projects include Bureau of Public Procurement, Code of Conduct Bureau/ code of conduct Tribunal, Public Complaints Commission, EFCC, National Financial Intelligence Unit, Special Control Unit against Money laundering and technical unit on governance and anti-corruption reforms. (United Nations Office on Drugs and Crime, 2017).[34]

The study has thus far explained terrorism and insurgency in Africa and the role the EU has played in countering the phenomenon in Africa. The study also describes the root causes of terrorism and the rationale behind its spread and inter-governmental effort in combating terrorism in the case of Multinational Joint Task Force (MNJTF) against Boko- Haram in the North-Eastern part of Nigeria and the African Union Mission in Somalia (AMISOM). The EU underlined the need for good governance, the rule of law and promotion of sustainable development policies, political participation, education and socio-economic inclusion of minority groups that make up a nation in the prevention of terrorism and insurgency in Africa and indeed, the world at large.

It has been established in this paper that insurgency and violent crimes in Africa are products of social and economic deprivations, poverty, oppression, underdevelopment, and the growing wings of religious crises. Insurgency and violent conflict historically emanated from the above factors and metamorphosed into terrorism as seen in Somalia, Algeria, Mali and Egypt which saw Islamic Brotherhood and the insurgent groups employed act of terror to achieve a political objective. Military operation alone cannot solve the problem. Eliminating the head of a terrorist group without destroying their ideology would always end in fiasco. There is need for a more holistic international and regional cooperation as well as the promotion of good governance, the rule of law, transparency and accountability as well as socio-economic growth and development to reduce poverty in the region and across the globe for the realisation of sustainable peace and enduring stability.

Considering the above, we propose the following recommendations. African governments must, as a matter of urgency, address socio-economic challenges bedevilling all African states virtually. The creation of economic opportunities and wealth are the cardinal responsibilities of nations. Policies that will aid economic growth and development must be encouraged to create job opportunities for the teeming youths that can be easily brain-washed by terrorists and insurgent warlords to perpetrate a crime against their states and beyond with mundane inducement. Good governance is sin-qua-non to development. Poor leadership in Africa has contributed immensely to the continent's underdevelopment. There is a need for quality governance with adequate knowledge and a good sense of service to their people. Corruption has become a norm in many African states, and this has undermined the much-desired growth and development. Finally countering terrorism requires decisive and formidable leaders at EU, UN, ECOWAS, and states' platform.

There is also an urgent need for African states to embrace democratic principles and the rule of law, it will go a long way in addressing social injustice, lack of political participation and abuse of power, given that socio-economic and political exclusion of groups has led to an uprising in many African countries since independence. Religious tolerance, respect for people's culture and beliefs will help in addressing the issues of terrorism globally. The idea of imposing a particular religion, ethics, or culture on a group or nation should be de-emphasised and de-programmed from the psyche of Muslim political elites across Africa. This will promote peaceful co-existence among people irrespective of their race, religion, and cultural affiliation. There is need to demilitarise the counterterrorism approach to be able to appeal to the conscience of the insurgents. Emphasis should fundamentally be on good governance, social justice, and religious tolerance, promotion of democratic principle, dialogue, and the rule of law.

## Notes

1 The contemporary battle before the world body and state actors are terrorism and militia groups across the world which have become a global threat to peace and security after the September 11, 2001 attack on the World Trade Centre (WTC) in the United States of America.

2 The threat to global peace and security carried out by the insurgent and terrorist groups is a violation of people's rights as enshrined in Chapter VII of the United Nations Charter and acknowledged by religion and mankind.

3 Terrorism is a criminal act, and its purposes are in any circumstances unjustifiable.

4 Traditional terrorism was primarily used to achieve political objectives. The Zealots of Judea were opposed to the Roman rule. They resulted in the assassination of the Romans and Jews collaborators when they could not contend with the supremacy of the Roman Army. The group's objective was to end the political dominance by the Church.

5 The term terrorism was first used in English translation during the French Revolution known as (the reign of terror) when the Jacobins, a socio-political group who ruled the revolutionary state-employed violence and execution in pursuit of its socio-political objectives.

6 The French Revolutionary group during its struggle transformed itself with governmental groups and elites in its bid to put an end to the monarchical system of government in France and across Europe. This, however, led to the execution of Louis XVI by guillotine on 21 January 1793.

7 It took the collaborative efforts of several European countries to halt the spread of the revolution across European countries. The defeat of the revolutionary leader, Napoleon Bonaparte at the Battle of Waterloo was a turning point in the eventual collapse of the revolutionaries.

8 The Thugee was a religiously-motivated terrorist group in India who killed people as a sacrifice for its

Hindu goddess. The group adopted guerrilla warfare tactics in attacking its victims. More than a million people were killed between the 17<sup>th</sup> and mid-19<sup>th</sup> century.

9  The 20th-century terrorism is characterised as anarchist, socialist, fascist, and nationalist groups, many who engaged in the anti-colonial struggle in Africa and the Middle East. These groups employed violence means such as suicide bombing, arms attacks, hostage keeping and plane hijacking in pursuance of their political objectives.

10  In the 20<sup>th</sup> century, especially in Africa during colonial rule, many nationalist groups who engaged in anti-colonial struggle deployed act of terror in achieving their political objectives.

11  The September 11, 2001 attack on the World Trade Centre (WTC) was a turning point in the global spread of Islamic terrorism carried out by Osama Bin Ladin led Al Qaeda terrorist organisation. Since September 11, 2001 attack, various terrorist organisations have come to the limelight.

12  The Al Qaeda terrorist organisation claimed responsibility for the attack on the World Trade Centre (WTC) in 2001, which led to the loss of many lives and left many wounded.

13  Insurgency in Africa is primarily caused by socioeconomic deprivation and political exclusion of groups who felt marginalised or oppressed. Insurgency and terrorism can hardly be separated because they both employed violence means. Still, the main area of departure is that terrorism is religiously and politically motivated and thrive in failing or failed states.

14  The political events in Africa especially in Congo, Mali, Nigeria, Sudan, Central African Republic, Somalia, Burundi, Angola, South Sudan, to mention but a few contributed to the multifaceted insurgencies across the continent.

15  Boko Haram terrorist group activities in the North-Eastern part of Nigeria have killed more than 20,000 civilians since 2011 and rendered more than 3 million people homeless.

16  The activities of Al Shabab terrorist group in East Africa have claimed many lives and quantum destruction of properties with several bombings of government buildings, embassies, hotels, and marketplaces.

17  In the Maghrebian, the activities of Islamic fundamentalists such as the Islamic Brotherhood are politically and religiously motivated. The perceived lack of fairness, oppressive rule, and highhandedness by their leaders, coupled with the deteriorating socio-economic conditions have led to a series of attacks and unrest in the region.

18  The extremist sect, the Salfiya Salidiya poses a significant threat to peace and security of Moroccan people. The sect was against the oppressive rule and perceived injustice and lack of openness by the Moroccan authority.

19  In Sudan, Al Bashir was accused of state terrorism again opposition. Several people have been killed in a confrontation between the Sudanese forces and the rebel group.

20  The South Sudanese civil unrest which started in 2013 was fuelled by mutual distrust, suspicion, and rivalry between the President, Kiir Salva and his former vice, Rick Mac Macher.

21  The Sudanese civil unrest led to the death of thousands of people and caused a severe refugee crisis in the neighbouring countries of Uganda, Ethiopia, Kenya, and the Congo Democratic Republic.

22  The Sudanese forces have killed thousands of people perceived to be opposition, including notable Bantu massacre in 2014.

23  In counterterrorism and counterinsurgency efforts, intelligence gathering, weaponry, deployment of technology and trained personnel are the ingredients needed in combating terrorism in Africa and beyond. Good governance and life-changing economic policies that will aid Foreign Direct Investment (FDIs) in solving the massive rate of youth unemployment are also required.

24  Africa-EU partnership in the areas of economic, political and security have helped reduce the threat posed by various terrorist groups across Africa. This is done through investments, provision of financial aid and technical assistance to countries affected by insurgency and terrorism.

25  EU counterterrorism strategy adopted in 2005 was based on four major pillars; Prevention, Protection, tracking of terrorist finance and movement and respond to threat to peace and security.

26  EU financial aid to Africa n counterterrorism and counterinsurgency have aided African peacekeeping operations in countries such as Sudan, and Somalia as well as for the operationalising the African and Security Architecture with the objective of an effective response to conflict within African region.

27  In 2016, EU pledged 50 million dollars to support the Internally Displaced Persons (IDPs) in the North-Eastern part of Nigeria as more than 2 million people were rendered homeless by the activities of Boko Haram terrorist group.

28  Boko Haram attacks on the civilian population in the North-Eastern part of Nigeria have led to the

loss of lives and destruction of properties and major infrastructure in the affected areas, which require a considerable sum to rebuild. Boko Haram activities include indiscriminate arms attack on civilians, suicide bombings, kidnapping, arson, raiding markets to cart away foodstuff and other materials needed.

29  During the 6th Nigeria-EU ministerial dialogue on September 19th 2016, EU Vice President, Federica Mogherini pledged EU continuous support on the fight against Boko Haram, humanitarian and economic development and reconstruction of the destroyed infrastructure in the areas affected by the activities of Boko Haram terrorist group. Some Internally Displaced Persons have been safely returned to their original homes after reconstruction of their homes.

30  In a bid toward solving the menace of illegal migration from Africa to Europe, the EU proposed and approved 40 billion Euro investments for Africa and the Mediterranean to help fight illegal migration and the growing radicalisation of youth caused by lack of economic opportunities.

31  Under the European Investment for Democracy and Human Rights, EU have given priority to women empowerment, girls and gender-based violence and increased access to education in Africa in a bid to promote equal opportunities, eliminate gender-based violence and youth empowerment for self-reliant.

32  The EU offered technical assistance to help the East African states and Yemen security agencies fight terrorism and insurgency, check cross border movement, and conduct investigations. The countries that benefited from the training are Kenya, Ethiopia, Uganda, Djibouti, South Sudan, and Yemen.

33  The collaboration between Nigeria and other Economic Community of West African States (ECOWAS) is aimed at checking money laundering, Financial Action Task Force to track financial crimes and funds linked to the terrorist groups within the region.

34  The EU provided intelligence support to track money laundering and terrorist financing and provided support to the strengthening of Africa's judicial system in delivering justice, tackle corruption and drug abuse. The EU financed three projects through the United Nations Office on Drugs and Crime (UNODC) worth 98 million Euros in Nigeria as part of its commitment to institutional strengthening.

# Bibliography

Abubakar, M. D., & Ogbeidi, M. M. (2014). *Beyond the guns: Policing terrorism in a democratic system* (p. 26). Ilishan -Remo: Babcock University Press.

Achibong, E. (2016). EU donate 50 million dollars to fight against Boko Haram in Nigeria. *Business Day*, February 11, 2016, https://www.businessday.com. Retrieved 7 November 2017.

Alan, W. (1993). *The origin of the Russian Revolution 1861–1917*. London: Routledge.

Andrew, S. (2016). EU strategy for security and development in the Sahel: An indicator for the future of EU. https://wikepedia.andrewsweiss.CarnegieEndowment.org. Retrieved 20 May 2017.

Taskhri A. (1987). Definition of terrorism. https://www.justresponse.net. Retrieved 27 November 2017.

Bassey, U. (2017 April 12). Nigeria-EU to deepen partnership in fight against Boko Haram. *Premium Times*, https://www.premiumtimesng.com. Retrieved 27 November 2017.

Bin Ladin Claims Responsibility for 9/11: BBC News, (October 29, 2004), https://www.news.bbc.co.uk. Retrieved 11 January 2018.

Bureau of Counter Terrorism and Counter Violence Extremism. (2015). *Country reports on Terrorism*. U.S. Department of State, 2015. https://en.Wikipedia.org. Retrieved 11 January 2016.

CIPRA (Centre for Indian Political Research and Analysis). *Merchants of Terror*, Vol. 1, (2007).

Duncan, B. C. Capturing a Desert Fortress: Flavius Silva and the Siege of Masada Ancient Warfare. In M. D. Abubakar & M. M. Ogbeidi (Eds.), *Beyond the guns: Policing terrorism in a democratic system*. Ilishan -Remo: Babcock University Press.

European Parliamentary Research Services, 22 March, BBC News, 11 January 2016.

European External Action, *Africa and the EU Brussels* (2016).

EU (European Union). (2016). *Africa and the EU: European External Action*. Brussels: European Union.

EU (European Union). (2016). *Brussels, External Parliamentary Research Services, 22 March 2016*. Brussels: European Union.

EU (European Union) to Launch Counter Terrorism Training Across East Africa, Reuters, June 24, 2015, https://www.reuters.com. Retrieved 27 November 2016.

Faliu, J. (2009). *Local and global jihad: Al Qaeda in the Islamic Maghreb, Middle East (Spring)*, 21–26.

Hoffman, B. (1998). *Inside Terrorism*. New York: Columbia University Press.

Imobighe, T. A. & Eguavon, A. N. T. (2016). *Terrorism and Counter Terrorism: An African Perspective.* Ibadan, Nigeria: Heinemann Educational Book.

Lia, B. (2006). *The Society of the Muslim brotherhood in Egypt: The rise of an Islamic mass movement.* Ithaca. https://www.radicalisationresearch.org. Retrieved 20 January 2017.

Lonel, Z. (2016). *African led counter terrorism measures against Boko Haram.* The European Parliamentary Research Service. https://www.europa.europa.eu/thinktank/en/document.html. Retrieved 10 October 2017.

Michael, G. (2001, September 12). Terrorism hijack 4 airlines destroy world trade centre hit Pentagon, https://www.washingtonpost.com. Retrieved 27 November 2018.

Mogherini, F. The EU Foreign Affairs Minister, 19 September, 2016 https://wikipedia.etty.images.ca. Retrieved November 2017.

Paul, R. (2005, September 14). UN stagers on road to reform. https://news.bbc.co.uk. Retrieved 11 January 2018.

News 24 "WTC South Sudan is Dying and No Body is Counting", News 24, (11 March 2016), https://m.news24.com. Retrieved 4 April 2016.

Reuters (2015). *EU to launch counter terrorism training program across East Africa.* Reuters June 24.

Regional Impact Situation Report. (2016). *World food program. South Sudan Crisis,* 5.

Shultz, R. H., & Dew, A. J. (2015). *Insurgents, terrorists and militias: The warriors of contemporary combat* (p. 12). New York: Columbia University Press.

Stephen, E. (2001). *The mask of anarchy* (p. 57). London: Hurst and Company.

United Nations Holocaust Museum. Nazi Terror Begins, June 20, 2014, https://wn.wikipedia./encyclopedia.ushmm.org. Retrieved 20 November 2018.

Udo, U. (2017). Economic sabotage by Boko Haram insurgents in recent weeks. *ThisDay Newspapers (Nigeria),* 15 May 2017.

United Nations Office on Drugs and Crime (2017). https://w/en.m.wikipedia._org. Retrieved 5 March 2018.

World Food Program (2016). *Regional impact situation report,* New York.

World Food Program. 5 April, https://en.m.Wikipedia.org/wiki/world_food_program. Retrieved 20 October, (2017).

# 16

# United States' counterterrorism and counterinsurgency strategy in Africa

*Yusuf Abdullahi Manu*

## Introduction

The September 11, 2011 terror attack on the United States of America by *Al-Qaeda* terrorist group provided a trigger for the Global War on Terror. The attacks have added momentum among states to collaborate, fight and defeat terrorism and insurgency worldwide collectively. Virtually all parts of the world are battling to contain terrorist and insurgence related activities. Africa is not left in the war against terrorist groups like *Al Shabab* of Somalia, *Janjaweed* of Darfur, Al-Qaeda in the Maghreb (AQIM) of Mali, the Movement for Unity and Jihad in West Africa (MUJAO) operating in West Africa and *Boko Haram* of Nigeria among others. The globalisation of the fight against terrorism as exemplified by the Global War on Terror and the transnational nature of terrorist groups compelled the United States of America to embark on global-scale counterterrorism measures to eradicate terrorist networks across the world. It is in this regard that the US becomes the arrowhead in counterterrorism and counterinsurgency operations in many parts of the world. The chapter argues that the US is involved in numerous counterterrorism and counterinsurgency operations in Africa by putting in place a robust architecture involving the US Africa Command (AFRICOM), Trans-Sahara Counterterrorism Partnership (TSCTP), the East Africa Counterterrorism Initiative (EACTI) and the Joint Task Force-Horn of Africa (JTF-HOA). The US interventions had provided the continent with a collaborative framework for joint training of troops in asymmetric warfare and special operations, provision of armaments and intelligence through bilateral and multilateral cooperation. This has reduced the spread and coordination of terrorist cells in the continent. However, the US CT-COIN is marred by challenges of weak legislation and poor capacity of law enforcement and failure to acquire credible actionable information as a result of Africa's rough terrain and uncooperative local population thus rendering US CT-COIN strategy in Africa less effective. The chapter recommends that there should be enhanced synergy in intelligence gathering, training and retraining of troupes, the supply of armament and technology (especially ICT), and funding joint operations between the US and military forces in the states infested by terrorist activities.

The coordinated attacks by Al-Qaeda terrorist group on the Pentagon and the World Trade Centre in Washington DC and New York respectively on 11 September 2001 have signalled to states in the international system that they are susceptible to attacks by terrorists. The attacks on the United States (US) provided the trigger for the emergence of the "Global War on Terror" through enhanced cooperation among states to fight and defeat terrorist groups globally with the US at the forefront. Since 2001 the US has been interestingly involved in numerous counterterrorism and counterinsurgency operations across the world.

Global terrorism is a new form of threat to humanity. Terrorist activities in the middle and late 20th century have been on a steady rise, most especially in fragile regions like Africa and the Middle East. These illegal groups have multiple goals that range from secession to religious factionalism and the toppling of the constituted authorities of their local "host" states (Pitchette, 2015). The proliferation of terrorist organisations across the globe is unprecedented and requires a concerted effort from all and sundry through enhanced collaboration among states and allies to ensure collective security and the protection of their national interest. It is in this regard, that the US is actively prosecuting the war on terror in Iraq and Afghanistan for over a decade; and in Pakistan, the Philippines, Trans Sahara (Northern Africa), Horn of Africa, West Africa and the Red Sea.

The US gave much concern to Africa because it's regarded as the hub and breeding space for terrorist organisations. This is due to the internal contradictions embedded in African states. The continent is characterised by numerous socioeconomic debacles that have served as a catalyst for the proliferation of terrorist organisations across the continent and beyond. Post-independent African states are engulfed in a crisis of development and human insecurity due to the adverse effects of bad governance, poverty and economic retardation, electoral violence, resource wars, environmental degradation, poor healthcare and livelihood conditions, declining relevance of treasured indigenous values due to modernisation. These changes resulted in political instability primarily because of coup d'états engrained by the culture of poor governance characterised by general corruption and weak leadership (Attuquayefio, 2014; Oche, 2014). The repercussion of all these results in deprivation and dispossession of the people, resentment and violent armed conflicts that challenge the legitimacy and survival of the state.

Since most trans-national terrorist organisations lack the capacity to hit the US directly, they often resort to targeting the US interests in other countries in Africa. The coordinated bombings of the US embassies in Kenya and Tanzania on 7 August 1998 that resulted in the death of over 224 persons and injuring thousands (Pickert, 1998) and the abduction of two Us citizens from an oil supply vessel off the coast of Nigeria in 2013 (Unger, 2013) are good examples. However, the fight against terrorism did not commence in Africa or on 11 September 2001. The war on terror could be traced back to 1990s when the Republic of Sudan was indicted for harbouring Osama bin Laden, a fugitive who attacked US interest in Africa and Asia. Bin Laden challenged Egyptian President Hosni Mubarak in 1995. He challenged Mubarak because of the relationship and support that he was giving to the US and Israeli government in the Middle East. In 1998, Al Qaeda attacked US Embassies in Nairobi and Dar es Salaam in East Africa. The dual bombing of US Embassies was carried out utilising vehicle-borne explosives made the US government shift its focus to Africa in a bid to stem terrorist's networks on the continent.

The 9/11, terror attacks on the US has further accelerated the tempo of the fight against terrorism in Africa. Lyman (undated, 1) states that:

> After 9/11, U.S. focus on terrorism in Africa became much more pronounced. For the first time since 1993, the United States deployed a sizeable contingent of American troops on the continent, with the establishment in late 2002 of the Combined Joint Task Force–Horn of Africa (CJTF-HOA) in Djibouti. In addition, President Bush announced a

$100 million counterterrorism initiative for East Africa and the Horn in 2003. At the same time, the U.S. European Command (EUCOM) spearheaded a series of training and military support operations in the Sahel, aimed at the Algeria-based GLPF; the program later blossomed into the much larger Trans-Sahara Counter terrorism Initiative that now involves both North African and Sahelian states.

These efforts are not only aimed at reducing terrorist acts in Africa but pre-empting the threats it poses to American citizens and safeguarding her national interest. To this end, the US provided numerous supports to the African Union's (AU) peace operations in Somalia and other conflict spots on the continent. This is because of the lack of capacity and resources on the part of local African states, regional economic cooperation (RECs) and the African Union. This is because most African states are challenged by internal contradictions that have had negative repercussion on sustainable growth and development. States such as Somalia, Nigeria and Rwanda among others are faced with internal security challenges.

It is against this backdrop, that this chapter examines the US CT-COIN operations against terrorist's organisations like *Al-Shabab*, *Al-Qaeda* in the Islamic Maghreb (AQIM), *Boko Haram* insurgency in the Lake Chad Basin, Movement for the Independence of Azawad in the Sahelian region and Lord Resistant Army in the Horn of Africa. The chapter examines both bilateral and multilateral cooperation between the US and African states under different initiatives such as US Africa Command, Trans-Sahara Counterterrorism Partnership (TSCTP), the East Africa Counterterrorism Initiative (EACTI) and the Joint Task Force-Horn of Africa (JTF-HOA) among others. The chapter is structured into five sections. Section 1 contains this introduction. Section 2 operationalises the concepts of terrorism, insurgency and counterterrorism and counterinsurgency. Section 3 explores the US counterterrorism and counterinsurgency response in Africa. Section 4 focuses on the challenges of US CT-COIN in Africa. The last Section concludes the chapter and offers some recommendations.

## Conceptualizing terrorism, insurgency, counterterrorism and counterinsurgency

The concept of terrorism is a highly contested concept, most especially after the 11 September 2001 terror attacks on the US. The inference that "One man's terrorist is another man's freedom fighter" describes the complexities that surround the concept. The term is originally derived from a Latin and French word: *terrorem* and *terrorisme*, meaning "to frighten," and "state of being ruled by terror". According to Hoffman (2006:41) terrorism is the planned creation and utilisation of instruments of mass violence to achieve a political change. Gupta (2008:10) view terrorism as a "politically motivated violent attacks by non-state actors". The foregoing definitions are too simplistic and shallow by limiting terrorism to activities of violent non-state actors. State-sponsored terrorism appears to be missing in these conceptualisations. They do not take into cognizance the roles played by states like Cuba, Sudan, Syria, and Libya, among others, in sponsoring terror.

The African Union (AU) (1999) *Convention on the Prevention and Combating Terrorism* Article 3 provides a more comprehensive definition of terrorism and its it is worth quoting in extent:

> [Terrorism is]...any act which is a violation of the criminal laws of a state party and which may endanger the life, physical integrity or freedom of, or cause serious injury or death to any person, any number of group of persons or causes or may cause damage to public or

private property, natural resources, environmental or cultural heritage and is calculated or intended to:

i. Intimidate, put in fear, coerce or induce any government, body, institution, the general public or any segment thereof, to do or abstain from doing any act, or to adopt or abandon a particular standpoint or to act according to certain principles; or
ii. Disrupt any public service, the delivery of any essential service to the public or to create a public emergency; or
iii. Create general insurrection in a state.

In other words, terrorism can be defined as the calculated use of instruments of mass violence, either by state or non-state actors to instil fear among the population through a sustained attack on both soft and hard targets for the purpose of bringing about political or economic change.

On the other hand, an insurgency is a contested terminology. The concept is usually associated with terms such as asymmetric warfare, guerrilla warfare, small wars, hybrid wars, civil war and so forth. According to David (2013:26) insurgency is a planned resistant movement targeting at subversion, destruction through acts of violence to achieve stated objectives. Anold (2012; 126) view insurgents as people who forcefully rejects constituted authorities most especially when they resort to armed violence against the government or laws governing the state. Similarly, Saud Al Otaibi (2004:15) sees insurgency as a grass-root rebellion movement that is aimed at removing a legitimate government and existing social structures through the use of instruments of the weak (subversion, guerrilla tactics, and terrorism) against a legal government or its conventional military forces.

Adamu, Glenn, and Umar, (2016:13) are of the view that insurgency:

> ...is a religious or political battle launched among an organised, sponsored, and aggrieved set of people in order to change the order of government in an attempt to enforce or instil a certain principle or ideology that is contrary to the will of government and the people usually using high calibre ammunitions to lunch attacks and defend themselves mostly using the guerrilla warfare approach of hide and seek (attack and retreat).One of the basic feature of such group is that, it take time and space to actually understand their modus operandi and what they actually trying to achieve by causing public disorder where every opportunity avail itself.

One common consensus among definitions from these scholars' above is the belief that the goal of insurgents is to remove and replace an existing government. However, not all insurgent groups aim at toppling the existing government. The overall goal of reformist insurgents is to compel the ruling and governing elite to introduce new radical reforms aimed at changing the status quo and not changing the government. In line with the foregoing definitions, insurgency can be defined as a subversive movement by disgruntled people having the feeling of being marginalised and alienated by the state or the ruling class and thus deploying the use of militancy and other subversive means to achieve overt or covert motives.

The concepts: counterterrorism and counterinsurgency (CT-COIN) is a bandwagon concept that together, refers to coordinated effort to address both the root causes and manifest repercussion of violent tendencies perpetrated by groups and/or individuals to achieve their destructive objectives. There are attempts to disentangle the two terms- "counterterrorism" and "counterinsurgency". Shor (2011) sees counterterrorism as state legislated policies, put in place as a response to terrorist threats aimed at reducing or eliminating real or perceived acts of terrorism. Similarly, Bamidele (2016:111) sees counterterrorism as primarily concerned about safeguarding "homeland security" in particular the protection of unarmed civilians with extreme alertness through the application of safety measures, intelligence, law enforcement, interagency synergy, and the utilisation of force, if required. This definition suggests that the use of force is the option last resort.

On the other hand, counterinsurgency deals more with proactive measures that are aimed at thwarting anti-establishment and anti-statist threats through collaborative efforts of security and strategic agencies, both domestically and internationally, in order to protect citizens and non-combatant civilians. Scotts (2007) is of the view that counterinsurgency is a comprehensive set of political, economic, social and security steps aimed at eliminating or preventing the occurrence of armed violence through the creation and maintenance of a stable political, economic and social structure, by addressing its root causes and promoting conditions that will engender and guarantee lasting peace and stability. According to Thomas (2016), counterinsurgency has a soft underbelly aimed at fortifying local social, economic and political structures so as to create the underlying conditions for peace and stability, and to "win hearts and minds," of locals to discourage them from joining or supporting for armed militancy. Counterinsurgency is not restricted to combat or police actions on terrorists or insurgents but it involves actions aimed at protecting and building a self-sustaining local community. The ultimate goal is the construction of stable state with fewer tendencies of degenerating into terrorism, normally through deepening of democratic structures such as civil liberties, equal franchise, economic opportunities and infrastructural development that will enhance the living standard of the citizenry.

## United States' counterterrorism and counterinsurgency strategy in Africa

Since 2001, the US has put in place numerous counterterrorism and counterinsurgency response across the African continent. The US has put in place a robust security architecture in Africa that are aimed at identifying and thwarting terrorist groups through the establishment and funding of different partnerships that are both bilateral and multilateral. These bilateral and multilateral initiatives are the Multinational Joint Task Force in the Chad Basin, the USA Africa Command (AFRICOM), Trans-Sahara Counterterrorism Partnership (TSCTP), the East Africa Counterterrorism Initiative (EACTI) and the Joint Task Force-Horn of Africa (JTF-HOA), African Union and Intergovernmental Authority on Development (IGAD) among others.

### Combined Joint Task Force-Horn of Africa (CJTF-HOA)

The US has regarded East Africa and the Horn of Africa as the most volatile and threatened region in Sub-Saharan Africa. These threats emanate from both indigenous and transnational terrorist groups. The region has become the podium for incessant internal strife and conflicts in recent decades (Shinn, 2003). At the heart of the regions, an apparent crisis of security that is the efflorescence of terrorism and intermittent conflicts are poor governance structures; decay in state institutions; porous borders that allow unhindered movement of people, criminal activity and proliferation of illicit arms; increased propensity for violent extremism, religious fanaticism and radicalisation among vulnerable and unsuspecting citizens. All these factors were compounded by poor socio-economic conditions that created a fertile ground for the incubation of terrorist groups (Kimunguyi, 2011).

The region is composed of volatile countries such as Somalia, Eritrea, Sudan, and Uganda who have experienced turbulent histories of violent civil wars, rebellion and sectarian upheavals; however, other countries in the region such as Ethiopia, Kenya, Tanzania and Djibouti have been struggling to build a fragile peace and development both at home and in the immediate neighbourhood. *Al-Qaeda* and its other affiliates operated in the East African region for over 20 years, even though their activities varied over time. The long year of civil war in Somalia since 1991 has rendered the country divided and without a national (despite external efforts to bring about national political reconciliation) has served as a conduit pipe for the proliferation of Islamic militancy in the Eastern region (Kimunguyi, 2011).

The East African region's unmanned porous borders, its geographical contiguity to the Arabian Peninsula, weak laws and inability to enforce the laws and weak judicial institutions, corruption, and, in some instances, state conspiracy in terrorist activities, coupled with nearly 20-years absence of central government in Somalia, paved way for the creation of a conducive environment for the flourishing of *Al-Qaeda* and other violent extremism in the region. Many states in the region became terrorist's safe havens, stagecoaches areas, or navigating points, targeting the interests of the U.S. and her allies', this compelled the US to heighten security steps in the region and engaged regional allies to fortify their counterterrorism potentialities (Ploch, 2010).

The U.S. military campaign in the Horn of Africa (HOA) is based in Djibouti and it was established on 12 December 2002. The CJTF-HOA headquarters came on board to spearhead and support the global war on terrorism in the Horn of Africa region as part of Operation Enduring Freedom-Horn of Africa with Camp Lemonnier as its only military operational facility in Africa. It is Combined Joint Task Force-Horn of Africa (CJTF-HOA). The CJTF-HOA is a broader component of the U.S. Africa Command (AFRICOM) that was established in October 2008, less than a decade after 9/11 to provide a standing force for dealing with terrorism in Africa. The sphere of operation of CJTF-HOA covers Kenya, Ethiopia, Eritrea, Sudan, Somalia, Djibouti, Yemen, and Seychelles; it also operates in Uganda and Tanzania. The primary objectives of CJTF-HOA are to (i) to foster a regional perspective on security problems (ii) build littoral capabilities, and (iii) support the AU and UN peacekeeping operations. For example, the CJTF-HOA took part in the logistical organisation of transportation and supported Ugandan troops in the AU peacekeeping force, which were deployed to Mogadishu after the collapse of the Islamic Courts Union (Kimunguyi, 2011).

To boost local capacity for CT-COIN, CJTF-HOA personnel are also saddled with the responsibility of training the region's security forces in CT-COIN, especially in areas of aerial reconnaissance, joint training, intelligence, civil-military relations, providing support for humanitarian intervention, and playing an advisory role to multilateral peace support operations. Furthermore, it provides technical support to African militaries through the US State Department's African Contingency Operations Training Assistance (ACOTA) program, which has enhanced the building of African troop's peacekeeping capacity. Moreover, CJTF-HOA further gave military assistance and trained military contingents send in support of the African Union Mission in Somalia (AMISOM) in collaboration with ACOTA. While most of these initiatives might not have an explicit counterterrorism mandate, the Department of Defence (DOD) indicates that they prioritise increasing partnership capability of African states to respond to terrorist threats by protecting their own territories themselves, thus minimising the scope of terrorist's likely activities (Ploch, 2010).

The CJTF-HOA has partnered with other foreign powers specifically the United Kingdom (UK) in the provision of CT-COIN training in Yemen and the building of its Coast Guard. US military support is aimed at strengthening Yemen's resilience for fighting terrorism and piracy in the Gulf of Aden-it should be noted that the Gulf of Aden constitutes a major security challenge not only to Yemen but the littoral states of Somalia and Kenya. The US adopt coordinated support on all countries sharing coastal front with the Gulf of Aden. Similarly, the CJTF-HOA provides training to the army in Ethiopia, Uganda, and Djibouti. It also trains the navies of Kenya and Djibouti to boost coastal security by continued patrol through the provision of equipment and combined military exercise with the US army. The CJTF-HOA is known for its involvement in humanitarian and developmental missions in the region. By 2007, it has built over fifty schools and thirty clinics, immunised several people in the region against diseases, dug several wells for drinking water and irrigational purposes, and immunised thousands of livestock's against diseases in the Horn of Africa (Robert, 2007: 44).

Even though intelligence is gathered through reliance on Human Intelligence (HUMINT) and other US intelligence assets such as satellite, drones etc. the partner countries and the CJTF-HOA share intelligence. Though in most instances the US unilaterally carry out airstrikes and raids on perceived terrorist targets. On the intelligence front, the commanders of the CJTF-HOA claimed that it arrested several dozens of terrorists and thwarted not less than five terrorist attacks (Shanin cited in Kagwanja, 2016). There are claims that the Horn has being militarised with the largest concentration of US military presence in Africa. As at 2002, the US has positioned around 1,200 to 18,000 soldiers in Djibouti under the auspices of CJTF-HOA. The CJTF-HOA partook in joint allied surveillance of the Red Sea coastal area and carried out several civil and military training operations in the greater Horn of Africa; it also collected and shared with African countries intelligence on imminent terrorist infiltration in the region. In 2003, President Bush declared a $100 million program to improve intelligence, border control, improved capacity of states police in the region, with the ultimate objective of building a system of regional coordination that can intercept, undermine and interdict the movement of terrorists, arms, money, and other related assistance emanating from the Middle East to the Horn and the coastal areas within the region (Lyman, undated). In 2006, the US gave implicit assistance on intelligence and technical support to the Armed Forces of Ethiopia in its CT-COIN mission in Somalia. This led to the forceful removal of the radical Islamic government that was then in control of Mogadishu. This has led to the dislodgment and fleeing of the followers of the regime to the south and the subsequent bombing of perceived terrorist leaders by the US (Lyman, undated).

An important dimension of the US CT-COIN strategy in the Horn is the use of aerial surveillance technology-particularly Unmanned Aerial Vehicles (UAVs) or drones fitted with state-of-the-art devices to detect and liquidate terrorists in their hideouts. In its response to counter terrorist threats, the US found the utilisation of drones to be highly effective in the war against terror in the Horn of Africa. For instance, in 2001, the US received and refurbished Camp Lemonnier from the armed forces of Djibouti and in May 2003 used the facility as its base for the Combined Joint Task Force-Horn of Africa (CJTF-HOA). Camp Lemonnier eventually earned the reputation as a vital launching pad base for drone surveillance and interdiction mission across the Horn of Africa and Yemen (Attuquayefio, 2014).

## The US Africa command

In February 2007, President Bush declared the establishment of a unified military command for Africa (USAFRICOM) to coordinate US CT-COIN strategy in Africa. This establishment puts the continent on the same page, in the Pentagon's radar with other commands such as the Pacific Rim (Pacific Command), Europe (European Command), Latin America (Southern Command), the Middle East (Central Command), and North America (Northern Command) (Hanson, 2007). The creation and enlargement of USAFRICOM stressed a new direction in

US investment for security in Africa, decapitate, degrade, and defeat emerging terrorist networks on the continent.

The command is involved in a wide range of activities on the continent. These include; the coordination of war against *Al-Shabab*, Al-Qaeda in the Maghreb (AQIM), Lord Resistant Army (LRA) and other terrorist groups in the continent and the provision of a forward operating base for NATO mission to ouster Muammar Qaddafi of Libya in 2001. The USAFRICOM put a strain on the US defence budget; in 2016 alone, the operational cost of the command had exceeded $156 million to provide support to US regional proxies; provide technical and financial support for anti-piracy strategy in the Gulf of Guinea and supporting clandestine mission in liaison with the Ugandan Armed Forces to scout for and possibly exterminate Joseph Kony, leader of the Lord's Resistance Army (LRA), and his men who were scattered across in Central Africa (Turse, 2017).

To ensure that it reduces security threats against US interests, the USAFRICOM introduced numerous initiatives to bolster the armed forces of African states:

i. *Bilateral and Multilateral Joint Training Programs and Military Exercises*
This involved the provision of military training for African military forces, both through joint training and provision of support for African defence academies, command and staff colleges in the area of professional military education which involves all-round and co-ordinated packages of education/training at the tactical, operational and strategic levels. More so, it conducted several military drills in African diverse operational terrains-tropical rain forests, deserts, deltas etc-jointly with the African troops and in collaboration with the troops of its European allies. They provided training for others and trained its own army for immediate deployment to Africa in an event of any future need. One of the exercises under this program is the 2005 and 2007 Flintlock exercise conducted as part of Operation Enduring Freedom- Tran-Saharan Counterterrorism Partnership TSCTP. The 2005 Flintlock exercise was conducted in June 2005, were more than 1000 US and more than 3000 African soldiers from Algeria, Senegal, Mauritania, Mali, Niger and Chad were deployed to North and West Africa for counterterrorism operations. By April 2007, US Army Special Forces were for the first time deployed to Niger and by August 2007 about 350 American soldiers were deployed to Mali for three weeks Flintlock 2007 operations exercise in collaboration with troops from Algeria, Chad, Mali, Mauritania, Morocco, Niger, Nigeria, Senegal, Tunisia, Burkina Faso, France, Holland, and the United Kingdom (Volman, undated).

ii. *Africa Contingency Operations Training and Assistance Program (ACOTA)*
This programme commenced in 2002 and replaced the African Crisis Response Initiative (ACRI) that was inaugurated in 1997 by the Clinton administration. By 2004, it became part of the Global Peace Operations Initiative (GPOI). GPOI is a five-year multilateral program; the US in funding and supporting the initiative contributed $660 million from 2005 to 2009. The main objective of the initiative is to train and equip 75,000 African soldiers, for peacekeeping operations in 2010. The GPOI further provided support for the Centre of Excellence for Stability Police Units (CoESPU). It is an Italian training centre purposely meant for training of gendarmes (constabulary police) forces in Vicenza, Italy. More so, GPOI is aimed at promoting the development of an international transportation and logistics support system for peacekeepers and is encouraging an information exchange to improve international coordination of peace operations training and exercises in Africa (Serafino, 2009).

237

ACOTA was officially established to give training to African military forces to enhance their operational and combat readiness in executing peacekeeping operations and special missions, in complex emergencies and "ungoverned spaces" which local African states seek to recapture from terrorist groups. These trainings involve both defensive and offensive military campaigns; aided the capacity of troupes to engage in police operations against unarmed civilians, counterinsurgency operations, and indeed symmetrical military campaigns against the soldiers of other countries. By 2007, 19 African countries had participated and benefitted from the program. Benin, Botswana, Burkina Faso Ethiopia, Gabon, Ghana, Kenya, Malawi, Mali, Mozambique, Namibia, Niger, Nigeria, Rwanda, Senegal, South Africa, Tanzania, Uganda, and Zambia had benefitted from the training of their soldiers in CT-COIN strategies. Ten African countries soldiers totalling 16,000 received training from the onset of ACRI/ACOTA programs. $33 million in 1998 was provided between 1998 and 2005 to finance and support the classroom training of 31 foreign soldiers through the Foreign Military Financing Account's Enhanced International Peacekeeping Capabilities program (EIPC) (Serafino, 2009).

iii. *International Military Education and Training Program (IMET)*

This program came into effect in 1976. As it currently stands, it is designed to be a low-cost policy program aimed at providing training in US Defence Department schools to primarily train military students that are friendly to the US base on grants (Grimmett, 2004). The program gave African military officers the opportunity to attend military academies and other military educational institutions in the US with professional training. Most African states have so far participated in this program, including Libya for the first time in 2008. 14,731 African military students received training except for Egypt at the cost of $14.7 million. The program is viewed by many African countries as a ploy by the US to advance its foreign policy goals in the aftermath of the Cold War. There is also the notion among many participants that the training related to human rights concerns and exposure to American democratic institutions is conducted in a pro forma fashion, this, in essence, made many participants be unserious with the program (Grimmett, 2004).

iv. *Foreign Military Sales Program (FMS)*

This program was purposely designed for the selling of military armament to African states; these transactions are carried out by the Defence Security Cooperation Agency of the Defence Department. Under this facility, the US government gave loan facilities to African states to finance the purchase of relevant military equipment through the Foreign Military Financing Program (FMF). However, the refund of such grants by the government in Africa was virtually waived, it is a free grant. Sub-Saharan African states in 2006 got almost $14 million in FMF funding, while the Maghreb states of Morocco and Tunisia got nearly $21 million; in 2007, the Bush administration voted almost $15 million for sub-Saharan Africa states while $21 million was voted for Morocco and Tunisia; in 2008, the administration sought for almost $8 million for sub-Saharan Africa and almost $6 million for the Maghreb (Volman, 2007). This indicates that countries in the Maghreb received the highest contributions from the program. This may not be unconnected with the fact the Maghreb is considered as the hub of terrorism in the continent. The granting of waiver can also be viewed as a strategy deployed by the US government to outsource the maintenance of security to weak states in Africa and as a move to seek for concessions in the areas of establishing military facilities on the continent.

v. *African Coastal and Border Security Program (ACBS Program)*

This is a specialised program that was established in 2005 to provide equipment such as patrol vessels and vehicles, communications equipment, night-vision goggles, and electronic monitors and sensors to African states for capacity enhancement to man and protect Africa's coastal waters and borders from terrorist activities, smuggling, and other illegal acts. In some instances, airborne surveillance equipment's and technical training were provided. In 2006, the ACBS Program attracted $4 million in Foreign Military Financing (FMF) funding. In 2007 the Bush administration voted $4 million in FMF funding for the program. Nigeria is one of the beneficiaries of the program, for example, Nigeria participated in the National Guard State Partnership Program in collaboration with the California National Guard. This development earned the Nigerian Army $2.2 million from the Department of Defence for the improvement of its counterterrorism infantry unit. Nigeria further received $6.2 million meant for enhancement of its tactical communications and interoperability within its counterterrorism unit (Ploch, 2011).

vi. *Naval Operations in the Gulf of Guinea*

The Gulf of Guinea (GoG) serves as a strategic maritime corridor in the Atlantic Ocean linking six coastal capital cities, eight coastal economic centres, and ten deepwater ports to the rest of the world; the US placed a heavy premium on the GoG by deploying a naval ship to monitor and secure the region in partnership with states of the region. West African states bordering the GoG are endowed with both human and natural resources which, if diligently managed; have the potentials of making the region a powerful economic bloc and an engine room for growth and development, as well as a key player in global affairs. Paradoxically, these same endowments have served as a source of war and resource flight in the region as a result of poor governance structure, civil war and complex political emergencies; examples include Liberia and Sierra Leon which were brought their knees by ravaging civil wars and domestic strife. It became sources of instability and conflict, smuggling, trafficking, with violent extremist groups competing with local and foreign commercial interests for hegemony (United States Africa Command, 2014). The perpetuation of local conflicts has often attracted foreign intervention in the name of bilateral or multilateral military support to restore the collapsing state.

It was due to the strategic importance of the GoG that the US established the US AFRICOM's permanent presence in the region. Since 2010, the USAFRICOM has been hosting Exercise Obangame Express, which has become a routine annual naval exercise. By 2015, 23 states from both the region and beyond partook in the exercise. In a landmark achievement of its Navy operations in Africa, the US stationed in November 2007, the U.S.S. Fort McHenry amphibious assault ship in the GoG. The ship contained between 200–300 sailors and US Coast Guard personnel to provide support across eleven states in the region. Angola, Benin, Cameroon, and the Republic of the Congo, the Democratic Republic of the Congo, Equatorial Guinea, Gabon, Ghana, Nigeria, Sao Tome and Principe, and Togo. The mission served as a "floating schoolhouse" for the training of local security forces in ports and oil-platform security, search-and-rescue missions, medical and humanitarian assistance (Volman, 2007). The Gulf of Guinea is one of US AFRICOM utmost importance hence, the US desire to enhance security in the gulf by protecting its interest within the African continent. About 33% of oil consumed in the US is exported from Nigeria amounting to nearly 10% of its oil imports. Piracy links in Western Africa may have wider consequences for global security. Unlike the Somalian pirates, the Nigerian pirates are more linked with transnational terrorist's networks. Oil bunkering through the hijacking of oil vessels serves as a supply route to Lebanese and Eastern European criminal interests, as they utilise the black market for buying of stolen crude oil and refined products (Captain, 2013).

Despite the interventions and supply of maritime equipment's to ensure security in the GoG, the prevalence of attacks became on the increase. 2016 saw a monumental upsurge in the number of maritime attacks over the past years. For example, Denmark-based Risk Intelligence reported that there were 119 attacks by criminal gangs on different kinds of vessels in West Africa (Senegal to Angola) as against 82 in 2015. Most of the attacks were carried out by Nigerian criminal gangs (Steffen, 2017). The increase in attacks over the year may not be detached with the fact that the US interest in Nigerian oil declined over the years.

## Trans-Sahara counterterrorism partnership

This is the main U.S counterterrorism policy in North Africa. It was created in 2005; as a multiyear, multiagency initiative to reinforce diplomacy, development, and military support to curtail the proliferation of violent extremism in nine states in the region. Algeria, Chad, Mali, Mauritania, Morocco, Niger, Senegal, Nigeria, and Tunisia. Its present membership has grown to eleven African states including two additional states: Burkina Faso and Libya. The partnership is spearheaded by the Africa Bureau of the US Department of State in partnership with other agencies: Department of State (DOS), the U.S. Agency for International Development (USAID), and the Department of Defense (DoD) (Bray, 2011).

The partnership has the following goals:

i. *Military Capacity-Building*: This involves the provision of training and material support to partner states counterterrorism forces to ensure effective monitoring and control of their borders, and deal with terrorist elements in partner states.

ii. *Anti-Terrorism Capacity-Building*: This is aimed at improving the investigative capabilities of partner states' law enforcement establishment and to bolster the capability of law enforcement personnel's in safeguarding vital infrastructure and curb illegal trafficking of contrabands and small arms along their borders.

iii. *Justice Sector Counterterrorism Capacity-Building:* This is aimed at enhancing partner states judicial capability to prosecute and jail terrorists, better prison administration to combat prison radicalisation, and combating transnational coordinated crime.

iv. *Public Diplomacy and Information Operations:* This involves working in partnership with partner states to enhance moderation and tolerance, combat extremist ideology, and to spur the populations to report security challenges to partner states security forces.

v. *Community Engagement*: This Involves fostering a productive partnership between civil society groups in partner states to reduce conflict and combat violent extremism, providing humanitarian relief to displaced and deprived vulnerable populations that are likely to be susceptible to terrorist recruitment.

vi. *Vocational Training*: This involves the provision of skills and entrepreneurship training and support to vulnerable populations in partner states and expanding opportunities for social and economic to reduce the recruitment of the deprived population into terrorist organisations.

In essence, TSCTP adopts a multidimensional approach that deals with an initiative that privileges both military-oriented and non-military measures that targets the deprived and vulnerable populations by providing them livelihood strategies that will discourage them volunteering for terrorist causes, and strengthening of the capacity of law enforcement agencies in partner nations to mitigate the spread of fundamentalism and reduce the recruitment and subsequent radicalisation of terrorists. Despite some major setbacks such as unstable political systems, ethnic crisis and extra-legal actions that disrupted the partnership in member countries. TSCTP has achieved a lot in enhancing the capabilities of both state and civil society among partner states. The goal of the US is to foster regional cooperation through enhanced assistance programs for member states. An example is the formation of the Multinational Joint Task Force (MJTF) against *Boko Haram* insurgents in the Lake Chad Basin. The MJNTF is a partnership for collective security between Nigeria and her neighbours which has recorded modest success in degrading *Boko Haram* in the region.

## Challenges of US CT-COIN in Africa

The US-COIN strategy in Africa is driven by developmental and security crises on the continent. Africa is home to some poorest populations in the world despite the abundant natural and mineral resources on the continent. Africa is home to 34 countries out of the fifty Least Developed Countries (LDC) in the World (Gambari, 2004). Corruption and abuse of public resources by state personnel and politicians have conspired to undermine development and security in the continent. The deprivation and social exclusion of most of the populations serve as a catalyst for the easy recruitment and radicalisation of terrorists. It is estimated that 46.4% of Africa's population are poor and live on less than $1 per day (World Bank, 2005). Poverty and widespread unemployment in Africa is one of the major causes of insurgency or terrorism on the continent. The underdevelopment of the continent paves way for easy incubation of terrorist's cells. Similarly, there is the challenge of sustaining partner states capability to counter the threats of terrorism. This is because most countries in the continent are poor and have little capacity to sustain the equipment's provided by the US. For example, countries in the East African region are challenged by inadequate funds to manage equipment's and sustain the training they gained through U.S. intervention programs. (Ploch, 2010).

Another challenge to US CT-COIN in Africa is the incipient misreading and suspicion by state officials and civil society groups against the real motives of the US in the continent and beyond. The predominance of the US counterterrorism operations across the globe has elicited opposition among several international actors due to its posture as an "imposed regime", thereby having implications on compliance by many states thus rendering the US CT-COIN regime ineffective at large (Elise, 2010). For example, the establishment of the Africa command by the Bush administration in 2007 was criticised by many critics in the US and several African leaders as an attempt to oversee military activities in Africa. This, in essence, fuelled fears and anti-American sentiments among Africans and thus reinforcing the perception that the US was "occupying force" bent on militarising its foreign policy through the establishment of new military camps on the shores of the continent. It was perhaps as a result of these mounting criticisms; the Pentagon had to put off its plan to establish the headquarters of Africa command in the continent and instead retained it in Germany (Whitlock, 2013). Public opinion in most African countries is not predisposed to the idea of the US establishing bases in their country. Nigeria, South Africa, and many other countries resisted the attempt by the US to establish such bases in their countries. They saw it as a reincarnation of colonialism on the African continent.

Thirdly, intelligence failure, particularly the failure to acquire credible actionable information because of Africa's rough terrain and uncooperative local population, has adversely hampered US C-T COIN operations in Africa. Military campaigns against terrorist groups depend on reliable, accurate and timely intelligence about terrorist's movements and operations. Reliable, accurate and timely intelligence is not readily available in most African states that are failed states with an unpredictable environment. U.S. technical intelligence capacities are ineffective in areas where there is poor communication infrastructure; in large swathes in Africa, communication is usually face-to-face or by messenger. The U.S. intelligence agencies are constrained in intelligence gathering in failed states as they are not on the ground, and even in countries, they establish their presence, the ability of local informants to effectively operate and supply reliable information on local terrain is constrained by inadequate security, suspicion, anti-American sentiments, language barrier and hostile local customs, poor communications, transportation, infrastructure and weak social service delivery (Dempsey, 2006).

The fourth challenge against US C-T COIN strategy in Africa is the inadequacy of local military and security personnel to meet the growing expectation of US involvement in COIN operations in CT-COIN operations in the continent. For instance, the CJTF-HOA witnessed inadequate military contingents to the region. About 2000 troops were deployed to the region to provide CT-COIN operations in partner states. The military contingents lasted for some few months and at maximum one year, giving the operatives little time to acclimatise with the host, get grips with an operational plan or interagency procedures (Government Accounting Office, 2010).

Finally, US C-T-COIN strategy in Africa is marred by weak legislation and poor capacity of law enforcement. After the September 11, African countries have sought to strengthen their anti-terror laws where it exists and the enactment of new ones where it does not exist. However, there exists a huge gap between legislation and enforcement of anti-terror law

## Conclusion

The chapter examined the US CT-COIN operations in Africa particularly after 9/11, terror attack on the US by *Al Qaeda* terrorist group. It is argued that the terror attacks on the US, added vigour in the global war on terror as spearheaded by the US and its allies to contain the rise of terrorism and insurgency globally. In Africa, the US anti-terror strategy has led to increased support for African militaries to enhance their capacity for CT-COIN. It is further argued that the continent is the hub of global terrorism and insurgency. The threats posed by terrorist groups in Africa to the interest of Americans and her allies compelled it to introduce numerous CT-COIN operations in different regions in Africa contain the activities of terrorist groups like *Al Shabab* of Somalia, *Janjaweed* of Darfur, *Al Qaeda* in the Maghreb (AQIM) of Mali, the Movement for Unity and Jihad in West Africa (MUJAO) *Boko Haram* in Nigeria and so forth. The US CT-COIN operations in Africa were executed under the auspices of US Africa Command, Trans-Sahara Counterterrorism Partnership (TSCTP), the East Africa Counterterrorism Initiative (EACTI) and the Joint Task Force-Horn of Africa (JTF-HOA). The chapter also argued that intervention of the US CT-COIN operations in Africa has benefitted the continent in diverse ways such as training of its troops, a supply of armaments, and intelligence sharing and so on which has drastically reduced the spread and coordination among terrorist cells in the continent. However, the US CT-COIN operations in Africa is marred by challenges of widespread poverty and crises of underdevelopment, the incipient misreading and suspicion by state officials and civil society groups against the real motives of the US, intelligence failure, particularly the failure to acquire credible actionable information as a result of Africa's rough terrain and uncooperative local population, weak legislation and poor capacity of law enforcement among others to a large extent, rendered the US CT-COIN strategy less effective.

To enhance US CT-COIN strategy in Africa, it is imperative to maintain synergy in intelligence gathering, training and retraining of troops, armament, technology (especially ICT), and funding joint operation between the US and military forces in the states infested by terrorist activities. The US should share credible intelligence intercepted using drones with local forces and allow local forces to be at the forefront of military campaigns. This to a considerable extent will boost the confidence of sceptic African leaders and other critics of the US foreign policy in Africa.

Secondly, the US CT-COIN strategy should focus more on the improvement of the socio-economic condition of Africans through increased spending on the provision of welfare to the people so as to improve their living conditions and reduce the drivers or root causes of terrorist recruitments and subsequent radicalisation. Thirdly, African leaders should improve on intelligence gathering and improvement on communication infrastructure to monitor the movements of goods and services and intercept communications from terrorist groups across the shores of African states and beyond. This will avail governments with adequate information on terrorist and avert attacks on time.

Fourthly, African states should ensure that they enforce relevant laws and conventions that deal with terrorism and anti-money laundering laws. The implementation of such laws will reduce the spate of terrorist activities and serve as deterrence to others who would indulge in terrorist-related act.

# References

Adamu, T. V., Glenn, M. K., & Umar, K. (2016). The Effects of Boko Haram insurgency on food security status of some selected local government areas in Adamawa State, Nigeria. *Sky Journal of Food Science*, *5*(3), 12–18.

Anold, D. O. (2012). *The implications of insurgency in the world global system*. London: Oxford University Press.

Attuquayefio, P. (2014). Drones, the US and the new wars in Africa. *Journal of Terrorism Research*, *5*(3), 1–13.

Bamidele, O. (2016). Combating terrorism: Socioeconomic issues, *Boko Haram*, and insecurity in the north-east region of Nigeria. *Military and Strategic Affairs*, *8*(1), 109–131.

Bray, F. J. (2011). *The Trans-Sahara counterterrorism partnership: Strategy and institutional friction*. Retrieved on July 27, 2017 from http://www.dtic.mil/dtic/tr/fulltext/u2/a553056.pdf.

Barnes, C., & Hassan, H. (2007). The rise and fall of Mogadishu's Islamic courts. *Journal of Eastern African Studies*, *1*(2), 151–160. doi:10.1080/17531050701452382.

Captain, G. (2013). *West African piracy and its growing effect on U.S. interests*. Retrieved on November 20, 2017 from http://gcaptain.com/u-s-strategic-interests-west-africa/.

Country Reports on Terrorism (2016). *Bureau of counterterrorism and countering violent extremism*. Retrieved on September 6, 2017 from https://www.state.gov/j/ct/rls/crt/2016/272229.htm.

David, A. (2013). *The upsurge of insurgency and the quest for national development*. London: Oxford University press.

Dempsey, T. (2006). *Counterterrorism in African failed states: Challenges and potential solutions*. Retrieved on July 22, 2017 from https://ssi.armywarcollege.edu/pdffiles/PUB649.pdf.

Elise, B. W. (2010). Compliance among weak States: Africa and the counter-terrorism regime. *Review of International Studies*, *36*, 639–662.

Eneanya, A. N. (2015). Terrorism and global domestic insurgency nexus: A case of *Boko Haram* insurgency in Nigeria. *Journal of Public Management & Social Policy*, *21*(1), Article 6. Available at. http://digitalscholarship.tsu.edu/jpmsp/vol21/iss1/6.

Gambari, I. A. (2004). Has Africa Any Role in the Current Efforts Against World Terror?. "The African Leaders' Lecture Series" at the Africa Group And Wats on Institute for International Relations, Brown University, Friday, 5 November 2004.

Government Accounting Office (2010). Report to the Subcommittee on National Security and Foreign Affairs Committee on Oversight and Government Reform: DOD Needs to Determine the Future of Its Horn of Africa Task Force, GAO-10-504, April, 2010.

Grimmett, R. F. (2004). *International military education and training program*. Retrieved on November 12, 2017 from https://www.hsdl.org/?view&did=717523.

Gupta, D. K. (2008). *Understanding terrorism and political violence: The life cycle of birth, growth, transformation and demise.* Abingdon, Oxon: Routledge.

Hanson, S. (2007). *U.S. Africa Command (AFRICOM).* Retrieved on June 27, 2017 from https://www.cfr.org/backgrounder/us-africa-command-africom.

Hoffman, B. (2006). *Inside terrorism* (Revised Edition.). New York: Columbia University Press.

James, D. (2014). Command signals Africa's increasing strategic importance. *Co rnel l International Affairs Review, 8*(1), 1/1.

Kagwanja, P. (2016). *Counter-terrorism in the Horn of Africa: New security frontiers, old strategies.* Arica Policy Brief, Issue No.7. Retrieved on September 8, 2017 from http://tafiticenter.africapi.org/wp-content/uploads/2016/02/Counter-Terrorism-in-the-Horn-of-Africa.pdf.

Kimunguyi, K. (2011). *Terrorism and counter terrorism in East Africa.* Retrieved on July 22, 2017 from http://artsonline.monash.edu.au/radicalisation/files/2013/03/conference-2010-terrorism-counter-terrorism-eafrica-pk.pdf.

Julius, U. O., & Felix, O. E. (2016). Democracy, development and insurgency: The Nigerian experience in the fourth republic. *African Research Review, 10*(2), S/NO 41, 31–46.

Lyman, P. N. (undated) .*The war on terrorism in Africa.* Retrieved on May 1, 2017 from http://www.cfr.org/content/thinktank/Lyman_chapter_Terrorism.pdf.

Miller, S. (2009). *Terrorism and counter terrorism: Ethics and liberal democracy.* London: Blackwell Publishing.

Nzau, M. O. (2010). Counter-terrorism in the Greater Horn of Africam2004–2010: revisiting the Somalia question. *Journal of Language, Technology & Entrepreneurship in Africa, 2*(2), 163–177.

Oche, I. A. (2014). Africa and the resurgence of terrorism-revisiting the fundamentals. *Global Journal of Arts Humanities and Social Sciences, 2*(2), 1–13.

Pickert, K. (1998). *Diplomacy under Fire U.S. Embassies in Tanzania and Kenya.* Retrieved October 30, 2017 from http://content.time.com/time/specials/packages/article/0,28804,1842608_1842698_1842652,00.html.

Pitchette, A. (2015). The Rise of *Boko Haram:* An Analysis of Failed Governance. *Outstanding Gateway Papers.* Paper 9. http://digitalcommons.iwu.edu/gateway/9.

Ploch, N. (2010). *Countering terrorism in East Africa: The U.S. response.* CRS Report for Congress. Retrieved on April 23, 2017 from https://fas.org/sgp/crs/terror/R41473.pdf Scott, R. M., 2007. 'The Basics of Counterinsurgency'. Retrieved on May 2, 2017 from http://www.smallwarsjournal.com/documents/moorecoin.

Ploch, L. (2011). *Nigeria: Elections and Issues for Congress.* Congressional Research Service, Retrieved on November 20, 2017, http://assets.opencrs.com/rpts/RL33964_20110401.pdf.

Robert, B. G. (2007). *Africom's dilemma: The global war on terrorism, capacity building, humanitarianism and the future of U.S. Security Policy in Africa.* Pennsylvania: U.S. Army War College, Strategic Studies Institute. Retrieved on July 27, 2017 from http://www.strategicstudiesinstitute.army.mil/pdffiles/PUB827.pdf.

Saud Al Otaibi, S. (2004). *Global Islamist insurgency.* Retrieved on November 2, 2017 from File:///C:/Users/Yusufm~1/Appdata/Local/Temp/Kilcullen-1.Pdf.

Scotts, R. M. (2007). *The basics of counterinsurgency.* Retrieved on October 15, 2020 from http://smallwarsjournal.cccom/documents/moorecoinpaper.pdf.

Serafino, N. M. (2009). *The global peace operations initiative: Background and issues for congress.* Retrieved on November 12, 2017 from https://fas.org/sgp/crs/misc/RL32773.pdf.

Shinn, D. H. (2003). *Terrorism in East Africa and the Horn: An overview. The Journal of Conflict Studies, 23*(2), 43–57.

Shor, E. (2011). Constructing a global counterterrorist legislation database: dilemmas, procedures, and preliminary analyses. *Journal of Terrorism Research, 2*(3), 49–77.

Steffen, D. (2017). Maritime security in the Gulf of Guinea in 2016. Retrieved on November 20, 2017 from https://maritime-executive.com/editorials/maritime-security-in-the-gulf-of-guinea-in-2016.

Thomas, C.G. (2016). *The U.S. can't fight terrorists in Africa. So guess what it does instead.* Retrieved on May 5, 2017 from https://www.washingtonpost.com/news/monkey-cage/wp/2016/02/01/the-u-s-cant-fight-terrorists-in-africa-so-guess-what-it-does-instead/.

Turse, N. (2017). *The U.S. military moves deeper into Africa.* Retrieved on September 9, 2017 from https://www.commondreams.org/views/2017/04/27/us-military-moves-deeper-africa.

Unger, D. J. (2013). *Americans taken from oil ship near Nigeria. Why pirates are moving west.* Retrieved on October 30, 2017 from https://m.csmonitor.com/Environment/Energy-Voices/2013/1024/Americans-taken-from-oil-ship-near-Nigeria.-Why-pirates-are-moving-west.

United States Africa Command (2014). *Maritime Security Symposium held to build capacity in the Gulf of*

*Guinea*. Retrieved on September 9, 2017 from http://www.africom.mil/media-room/article/23605/maritime-security-symposium-held-to-build-capacity-in-the-gulf-of-guinea.

Volman, D. (2007). *Africom: The New US Military Command for Africa*. Retrieved on September 9, 2017 from https://www.pambazuka.org/governance/africom-new-us-military-command-africa.

Volman, D. (undated). *China, India, Russia and the United States: The Scramble for African Oil and The Militarization of the Continent*. retrieved on November 19, 2017 from https://books.google.com.ng/books?id=SwdhCwAAQBAJ&pg=PA314&lpg=PA314&dq=i.%09Bilateral+and+Multilateral+Joint+Training+Programs+and+Military+Exercises+for+troops&source=bl&ots=CHKGKFEoVq&sig=NEHCSJUMvFlVWy8cC598Fb9SgWA&hl=en&sa=X&ved=0ahUKEwjh5O0i8rXAhWHQBoKHZueAhYQ6AEILTAB#v=onepage&q=i.%09Bilateral%20and%20Multilateral%20Joint%20Training%20Programs%20and%20Military%20Exercises%20for%20troops&f=false.

Warner, L. A. (2014). *The Trans Sahara Counter Terrorism Partnership: Building Partner Capacity to Counter Terrorism and Violent Extremism*. Retrieved on August 10, 2017 from https://www.cna.org/CNA_files/PDF/CRM-2014-U-007203-Final.pdf.

Whitlock, C. (2013). *U.S. counterterrorism effort in North Africa defined by decade of missteps*. Retrieved on September 6, 2017 from https://www.washingtonpost.com/world/national-security/us-missteps-defined-anti-terror-effort-in-n-africa/2013/02/04/b98640ba-6cab-11e2-a396-ef12a93b4200_story.html?utm_term=.9d0d50ffb7f2.

World Bank. (2005). *World Development Indicators 2005*. New York: Oxford University Press.

# 17

# United Kingdom's counterterrorism and counterinsurgency policy in Africa

*Idamwenhor Napoleon Enayaba*

## Introduction

This chapter examines the efforts of the United Kingdom (UK) countering terrorism and in-surgency in Africa. It provides an overview of the apparent vulnerability of the region to increasing terrorist-related activities. It describes the UK's long-term effort to deny terrorist groups the space to operate, to help vulnerable African countries develop their law enforcement capabilities, to address the injustice and conflicts which terrorists exploit, and to combat their ideologies. Highlighting the responses to terrorism by continental organisations and the UK, the Chapter examines the UK support to Africa countries and organisations in the region to enhance their capacities to counter terrorism. Further, it equally elaborates considerable progress being made to develop coherent and effective counterterrorism and counterinsurgency approaches in Africa and the many challenges of the UK government support to Africa. They include extreme mutual suspicion, institutional rivalry, increasing Islamic radicalisation, lack of state capacity, corruption, competing national priorities, poor sustainability planning, lack of local ownership, political sensitivity surrounding the very notion of counterterrorism among others. Most counterterrorism and counterinsurgency efforts have focused on short-term security, and law enforcement efforts but inconsistent policies, and lack of political will negatively affect longer-term measures to tackle the primary conditions that encourage the spread of terrorism.

According to the British Army Field Manual (BAFM) Volume 1 Part 10, Countering Insurgency is fast emerging as a buzzword in global security studies and practice:

> Until recently, the word counterinsurgency was synonymous with low-intensity opera-tions, or operations other than war. It conjured up images of British soldiers in the Malayan jungle, or on the streets of Northern Ireland. The U.S. military's experience in Iraq 2003–2008, and the British campaign in Helmand Province in Afghanistan since 2006 have demonstrated that military operations against irregular insurgents can be as intense as combat in conventional warfare (British Army Field Manual, 2010: 1)

The BAFM describes "counterinsurgency as warfare". Too often, scholars and practitioners have struggled with delineating the difference between counterinsurgency and counterterrorism.

Scholars agree that terrorism is a disputed term, and very few of those labelled terrorists describe themselves as such. It is common for opponents in a violent conflict to call the other side terrorists or as practising terrorism (Reynolds, 2005). Counterterrorism and counterinsurgency debates are short-sighted (Rineheart, 2010). There is excess attention on the strengths and weaknesses of the extent of commitments against violence extremism. This neglects pivotal conversation around sustained counterterrorism strategy. Likewise, some endeavours in the past have framed counterterrorism within the context of counterinsurgency warfare, leading to the misleading conclusion that both strategies were mutually reinforcing (Rineheart, 2010). Gary Anderson has argued regarding the heated debate in the US military about dealing with militants in Afghanistan that the discussion is less about tactics than it is about the future philosophical orientation of the Army beyond Afghanistan. Globally, in the event of violent extremism, there are typically two sides that often emerge by nature: those that think that the best way to deal violent extremists is by winning over the populace (heart and mind), population-centric counterinsurgency. On the flip side of the coin, there is another that believes in the utilisation of extreme military force (Angstrom, J. & Duyvesetyn, I., 2010), kill the insurgents and destroy their cadres; this is known as counterterrorism (CT) (Anderson, 2010). In sum, the debate about CT and COIN is more about strategy and campaign planning and applying judicious utilisation of available resources to achieve an end goal.

Michael Boyle once asked the question of whether counterterrorism and counterinsurgency go together. He concluded that there is no reason to think that both strategies are fully compatible or mutually reinforcing. Despite the recent conflation of the two doctrines, a counterinsurgency strategy should not be a counterterrorism strategy and vice-versa (Boyle 2008: 191).

For the avoidance of doubt, insurgency and counterinsurgency are two sides of a very complex form of warfare, and it is essential to understand the strengths and weaknesses of each to appreciate the offsetting effects they might have fully. Counterinsurgency strategy can provide a clear framework for success if the situation is right for this type of warfare. On the one hand, we have insurgency where a group or groups have resort to violence and have taken up arms to replace an existing government or are securing the status quo and challenging a young or emerging state. On the other hand, counterinsurgency seeks to prevent these people from archiving their political aim and doing harm to the public and public property. However, a modern insurgency is quite asymmetric, exploit the vulnerabilities of regular forces and utilise terrorism and subversion. More so, the measure for counterinsurgency is quite distinctly political, not primarily military but equally involves the people. Counterinsurgency has been defined as "those military, paramilitary, political, economic, psychological and civic actions taken by a government to defeat an insurgency while addressing the root causes" (British Army Field Manual, 2010:6). AFM describes how the British Army plans and conducts counterinsurgency operations at the tactical level. The AFM further describe insurgency as "... an organised, violent subversion used to effect or prevent political control, as a challenge to established authority." (British Army Field Manual, 2010:5). The AFM explains that efforts must be focused on securing the local population and gaining and maintaining popular support. However, how much is achieved with counterinsurgency is dependent on the commonality of different stakeholders in a state.

The UK's ten principles for counterinsurgency, as explained in British Army Field Manual are:

1. Primacy of political purpose.
2. Unity of effort.
3. Understand the human terrain.

4. Secure the population.
5. Neutralise the insurgent.
6. Gain and maintain popular support.
7. Operate in accordance with the law.
8. Integrate intelligence.
9. Prepare for the long term.
10. Learn and adapt.

It is on the bases of these principles that the UK counterinsurgency support in Africa and overseas are built.

What threats are we talking about? Since the attack on the World Trade Centre in the United States on 11 September 2001, the UK counterterrorism policy has changed immeasurably (House of Commons Home Affairs Committee, 2014). More so, several other events where many more UK citizens have been victims in other parts of the globe have continued to shape its relations and interest abroad. Between 2000 and 2015, 90 people have been killed in the UK in terrorist attacks, according to figures from the Global Terrorism Database (Global terrorism Database, 2017). Although not on British soil, a further 30 British people were killed in Tunisia when a gunman attacked a hotel popular among Western tourists.

Among others, the Arab Spring has widened the landscape of threats to the UK and the west creating states in anarchy that enables terrorism to flourish. Despite the massive military blow on Al Qaeda and Islamic State in Syria and its affiliates, grave threats abound, taking advantage of state fragility and failure. As military onslaught continues to degrade Al Qaeda, experience has shown that the group has evolved less of an organisation into more of a movement. The UK understands that threats too enormous both home and abroad and guards are not being led down. Many indoctrinated foreign fighters from Africa might be currently in the UK ready to attack the British mainland. This is not news to the UK. In recent times, some lone-wolves and returnees have attempted a brutal attack in the absence of weapons that can be used to create mass casualty. The most disturbing of these attacks was the attack in Manchester, where 22 people died including a few children after an explosion tore through a pop concert at Manchester Arena (*Manchester Evening News*, 2017). Around 120 other people were injured in the blast at an Ariana Grande concert on 22 May 2017.

Similarly, the Lorry attack in Westminster, signalling that people without weapons could opt for any other crude means to carry out an attack. The UK counterterrorism strategy has well-articulated plans to deal with marauding attackers inflicting mass casualties as was first seen in the Mumbai hotel attack in 2008. The system also incorporates measures to deal with vehicle ramming in crowded places, which has led to the proliferation of concrete bollards and other defences in most British city centres.

The threat to the UK has dramatically become more diverse than ever, geographically more diverse even against its interest overseas. The threat from terrorism has significantly changed since 2001. The fact that the UK features, unfortunately, as one of the primary targets of terrorist operations, requires the UK to device broader measures beyond its geographical representation to tackle these fears.

## The global nature of terrorist threat

In recent times, terror attacks on the UK, other European countries, and its spread to other countries where they never existed have formed reminders of the global nature of the terrorist threat and its ability to impact upon UK security and interests. For instance, the 2013 attack in Amenas in Algeria, included six British citizens amongst the 40 dead.

Following the attack on the Westgate shopping Mall in Nairobi, Kenya (in which six British citizens also died), *Al-Shabaab*, a terrorist group based in Somalia, has proved its capability to mount coordinated attacks throughout the Horn of Africa. The bomb blast in Addis Ababa, which killed two people in late 2013, was once interpreted as a sign of *Al-Shabaab* targeting Ethiopia (House of Commons Home Affairs Committee, 2014). The Tunis beach shooting in 2015 was the most significant attack against British citizens since the London transport bombings 13 years ago has equally got the UK thinking about how best to secure its citizens abroad (Cable News Network, 2005). This attack triggered, even more, the need for the UK to look beyond its borders and other places like the Middle East into Africa to protect its citizens and interest.

Unfortunately, many states affected by terrorism do not have the requisite capacity and political will, resources, and expertise to deal with the problem. With UK wealth of experience dealing with terrorism and insurgency and its technical ability have brought more value to these states in terms of dealing with these threats. Beyond human resource, more other things have been lost to terrorist activities. In many cases ransoms have been paid, and the British Government conservatively estimates that AQ affiliates and other extremist groups have collected at least $60 million in foreign national ransom payments since 2008 (The Telegraph, 2013).

The involvement of Africans in terrorist activities in the UK has tremendously increased. According to Home Office figures, of the 2,419 persons arrested for terrorism-related offences since 11 September 2001 till 2013, 1,198 (50%) self-declared their nationality as from Great Britain or of British dual nationality. Of the remaining persons arrested the most frequent self-declared nationalities were: Algeria (152 persons), Pakistan (125 persons), Iraq (115 persons), Afghanistan (74 persons), Iran (63 persons), India (56 persons), Turkey (45 persons) and Somalia (44 persons). Unlike the past, Sub-Saharan Africa has gained the increased interest of the UK overseas technical and aid support to enable the government to deal with injustice and the root cause of terrorism (Home Affairs Committee, 2014).

Africa currently suffers from a myriad of wars against insurgency. Violent extremists pose a serious threat to international peace, security and stability and constitute a criminal act that undermines efforts aimed at achieving democracy, good governance and development, as well as the full enjoyment of the human and peoples' rights. These groups also pose threat to western interest in Africa, global peace, security in Europe and America and triggers global migration. The spectrum of democratic and development gains of past decades (Bandfield J. Tell, 2015) are shrinking owing to the chaos caused by these elements. Islamist extremists' activities in recent years within Africa have demonstrated the gravity of the threat they pose and the need for greater enforcement of existing countermeasures to prevent, respond and confront various acts, such as abductions and hostages-taking, hijacking, bomb attacks, etc, that member states of Africa are currently experiencing.

Learning from the experience in Iraq (Alderson 2008), the UK believes more in foreign policy that addresses the circumstances in which terrorism thrives overseas rather than a military solution. In the words of William Hague, "but there is rarely, if ever, a purely military solution to terrorism" (William, 2013). The government of the UK as part of its counterinsurgency and counterterrorism strategy supports a long, generational effort that denies extremist groups the space to operate. Likewise, it helps vulnerable countries develop their law enforcement capabilities, to address the injustice and conflict which terrorists exploit, and to combat their ideology. This, in the simplest term, describes the United Kingdom's counterterrorism and counterinsurgency assistance in Africa.

## A brief overview of security and insurgency in Africa

Except for Syria and Yemen, African countries currently get the worst media mention when it comes to violence and conflict. From political violence to ethnic violence, intergroup clashes, cut clashes, religious violence, violent protest, insurgency and terrorism, the list goes on and on. Africa is immersed in a cycle of simultaneous violence that has undermined peaceful co-existence, development, political stability, peace, and democratisation. A sizeable proportion of countries in West, East and North Africa are currently plagued by terrorist violence while ethnic conflict and insurgency remain pervasive in Central Africa and parts of southern Africa. All the 39 countries which have suffered civil wars since 2000 also had one in the previous three decades, something that was true of far fewer in the 1960s. Moreover, "lesser" forms of violence are worsening to a point where they can be more deadly than civil war itself. In 2012, Tuareg ethnic group in Mali with support from Al-Qaeda in the Islamic Maghreb's (AQIM) over-ran Bamako. Seven of the world's top 10 "failed states" are in Africa, according to a study published in the United States (Kemp, E., 2016). Failed states in African barely perform basic functions of government such as education, security, or governance, due to fractious violence or extreme poverty (Global Policy Forum, Failed States, 2016).

An estimated 12.4 million people were displaced in Africa as a result of conflict and violence, this figure is 30% of the total number of people internally displaced by conflict globally (40.8 million people) and twice the total number of African refugees (5.4 million).

However, there is an increasing military onslaught against extremist elements in the Middle East and North, West, and East Africa but the threat they pose to political stability and peace are not decreasing. The major factors that have largely influenced Africa vulnerability include: Presence of local radical Islamic groups and extremist cells; Conflicts, political instability, collapsed states and presence of rapacious rebel groups; The vast Sahel region weakness to check extremists and traffickers; Black markets for natural resources such as oil and diamonds; Lack of rule of law and regulatory policies; Weak law enforcement and criminal justice institutions that are prone to chronic corruption; Poverty, inequalities and lack of dynamic government policies for disadvantaged communities; Prevalence of drugs, arms and human trafficking, piracy, organised crime and money laundering, which help to sustain funding for extremist activities and climate change (the lake chad basin). Within West Africa alone, extremist activities have cost a major humanitarian crisis and set lots of countries back by years. In Nigeria, the governor of Borno State (one of the States worse hit by Boko Haram), Kashim Shettima said Boko Haram now known as (Islamic State's West Africa Province – ISWAP) has destroyed infrastructure that may cost more than $1 billion to rebuild in Northeastern State of Borno alone (Chicago Tribune, 2015).

Extremist activities and groups are on the rise across Africa as renowned global terror groups, including ISIS and al-Qaeda affiliates, continue to overtake local insurgent organisations and transform them into regional and international threats. In West Africa, there is a silent scramble by Terror groups for control of local extremist groups. In an effort to expand their terror acts, some sophisticated extremist elements that have evolved, have either joined forces with foreign groups, absorbed smaller ones or become an arm of a foreign group to perpetrate violence within the region. In 2012 at the peak of the Malian crisis, began as a local movement in Northern Mali, but was successfully overtaken by the National Movement for Unity and Jihad in West Africa and al-Qaeda in the Islamic Maghreb absorbed several local groups, threatening countries and even entire regions.

There is a similarity between what Boko Haram is doing now and what the Salafist Group for Preaching and Combat (GSPC) and now Al-Qaeda in the Lands of the Islamic Maghreb

(ALQIM) did in 2006. Pledging their allegiance to ISIS in April 2015 and renaming itself as Islamic State's West Africa Province (ISWAP); a famous name can enhance ISWAP's legitimacy among extremists and facilitate recruitment, while enabling ISIS to burnish its international credentials and, potentially, spread to other African countries. Since the expulsion of ALQIM from its' operational base near the Mediterranean by an Algerian counterterrorism campaign force, the group currently operates in the Sahel region that includes Niger, Mauritania, and Mali as its' established footholds. Similarly, Boko Haram is also consistently ensuring interval attacks on Cameroon, Niger, and Chad as a way of bolstering regional relevance. However, the danger in the scramble is the risk of an eventual merger of the entire group. Africa has seen an uptick as of late in terrorist funding and activity. Some experts look at the power vacuums in states such as Somalia and see them ripe for terrorist influence. To see how and why these influences can spread so easily, it's important to look back at events in history.

## History of insurgency in Africa

Counterinsurgency in Africa dates back beyond Al Qaeda attack at on the World Trade Centre on September 11, 2001. Many scholars have traced the history of insurgency to colonial Africa (Miraftab & Wills, 2005) just as many agree that insurgency in Africa date back into the colonial era and beyond. Some cases to remember during British reign in Africa are Mau Mau uprising (French, 2011) in Kenya, first (Knightley, P., 1976) and second (Pakenham, 2015) Boer war, among others. On 1 March 1973, 8 members of a group known as "Black September" invaded the US Embassy in Khartoum, Sudan and captured 10 hostages to demand the release of numerous Palestinians held in Israeli jails. The US ambassador to Sudan, Cleo Noel, and his deputy chief of mission, George Moore were among hostage and he was later killed. On December 21, 1988, two Libyan agents masterminded the explosion of a Pan Am flight 103 over the small town of Lockerbie in southern Scotland en route from London's Heathrow airport to New York's JFK airport. A total of 270 people were killed, including all passengers and crew members on board and an additional 11 people on the ground. Al-Qaeda members have begun recruitment and operations in Africa. Following the expelling of Osama Bin Laden from Saudi Arabia, he moved into Sudan (CNN, 2011) where he operated and carried attack against Egyptian president Hosni Mubarak. In 1998, al-Qaeda, one of Al Qaeda cells blew up the American embassies in Nairobi and Dar es Salaam. He was instrumental to several attacks and bombings in North Africa and supporting parties in civil wars in Eritrea and Somalia. A series of coordinated bomb blasts that tore through four Spanish commuter trains, killing at least 198 people (Vitzthum, Johnson, & Champion, 2004) was linked to cells in Morocco and Algeria, which interact with North African residents in Europe, and both countries themselves have been victims of recent terrorist bombing attacks.

There are many other wars, violence in Africa that are often not referred to as terrorist groups but as ethnonationalist groups that have sprung up in Africa creating civil wars and power vacuums in already vulnerable areas. These have had an impact on the insurgency in Africa. The Eastern African region of Ethiopia, Eritrea, self-proclaimed Somaliland, and Somalia has especially been victim to civil wars and guerrilla warfare in the last thirty years (Spies, 2013). In the last decade of the 1990s, disturbing levels of ethnic violence and genocide emerged in countries like Rwanda and Burundi. Studies have revealed that the exploitation of economic difference to instigate violence in dates to the colonial era — a major tool used by colonial powers to sustain conflict for Africa economic resource exploitation. Unfortunately, the consequential effect of chronic marginalisation of the poor has provided fertile ground for those promoting ethnic conflict as a means of sustaining their control. Over time, ethnic violence has, unfortunately, emerged as part of the culture of war in Africa. According to the International Crisis Group:

The Islamic State (IS), al-Qaeda-linked groups, Boko Haram and other extremist movements are protagonists in today's deadliest crises, complicating efforts to end them. They have exploited wars, state collapse and geopolitical upheaval in the Middle East, gained new footholds in Africa and pose an evolving threat elsewhere (International Crisis Group Special Report, 2016).

More so, several facts have aggravated conflict in Africa beyond the exploitation of ethnic differences. These factors even became pronounced by the end of the Cold War, such that conflict became more widespread through the 1990s (Gurr, 1994). By the end of the Cold War, many states in Africa failed to manage their economy properly, building highly centralised but weak states. Many countries were unable to provide basic policing, guarantee public safety and security. Coupled with inadequate social services helped to lead to the weakening of state authority.

A fundamental problem for developers is that most developing countries have weak States which are incapable or unwilling to provide basic public goods such as law enforcement, order, education, and infrastructure. Like many developing countries across the globe, African states are weak, unable to enforce law and order (Daron, Isaìas, et al.). The weakness or lack of capacity of states in impoverished countries is a fundamental barrier to their development prospects. These many problems have a global implication on migration and security. Among many other factors, the understanding of the threat that underdeveloped economies pose to tranquillity and sanity has triggered western interest in Africa and other third world countries. From economic to governance, justice, security, defence, peacebuilding and recently, counterterrorism and counterinsurgency, the list goes on and on.

The weakness of modern Africa State, informed by the shortcomings, triggered internal (Jackson & Rosberg, 1982) grumbling, then conflict that dramatically began to transform and manifest in different forms throughout the 1990s. In many recorded cases, division fostered the emergence and proliferation of splinter groups, which in turn divided into warring factions. For instance, in Sudan, the South never felt a sense of belonging as the political structure did not reflect their uniqueness. The very nature of conflict changed. The civilian population increasingly became the target of fighting in factional wars and subjected to significantly elevated levels of violence and abuse. This resulted in massive displacement as well as social and economic distress (DFID, 2001).

As the factors of ethnic division exploit the weak state, there were equally vulnerable leaders, many of whom were autocratic leaders, who emerged at the end of the colonial rule and cold war. As many of these ailing, authoritarian leaders in Africa lost control and external support, several states began to collapse. Examples of these states are Liberia, Somalia, Sierra Leone, and Zaire. These states soon became centres of African insecurity. Many other powers who felt threatened by the insecurity of these states intervened. For instance, Nigeria intervened in the Liberian civil war, and it struck a deal that culminated in the resignation of Charles Tailor and made similar attempts in Sudan.

## Impact of history of conflict on Africa

Over time, these conflicts have escalated, triggered similar clashes in states that were hitherto relatively peaceful. Similarly, these conflicts have continued to respond to global conflict dynamics. Presently, parts of Africa have become battlefronts in the fight against terrorism by jihadists and other extremists. Consequently, Africa has seen an upsurge in terrorist funding and activity. Nigeria's Boko Haram emerged as the deadliest extremist group in 2015 and Somalia's Al-Shabab in 2016 (Global Terrorism Index, 2015). Currently, Boko Haram violence has spilt into neighbouring Chad, Cameroon, and Niger. In Somalia, al-Shabab has come under pressure from regional African forces but has responded by striking beyond its borders. Kenya has been particularly hard hit. Since the siege on Westgate Mall in Nairobi, the capital, in 2015, a series of coastal attacks has cost hundreds of lives and hammered the tourism industry.

In North Africa, terrorism and insurgency have brought some states to a halt. Libya is currently without a central government while Egypt and Tunisia have suffered from several suicide bomb attacks; a fallout of the 2011 protests, which left behind a dangerous combination of weak governments and available weapons. The hoister of Muammar Qaddafi from Libya has created a stateless Libya. Britain and America have since 2013 and 2014, respectively evacuated its staff from Tripoli, capital of Libya. The breakdown of law and order in Libya has allowed the Islamic State (ISIS) terrorist organisation to capture pockets of territory and gain a foothold on the continent. Some jihadi groups want to impose strict Islamic law, which calls for floggings, stoning, and executions of nonbelievers. This situation which currently threatens stability in Africa, also threatens global peace and security as many of these elements are presently utilising transition routes into saner countries of the world.

## The United Kingdom's development and security objectives in Africa

The recent history of the United Kingdom's engagement with regards to Africa offers some useful insights as to the changing nature of UK priority towards Africa. In 2001, a census in Britain found that Sub-Saharan Africa constitutes Britain's fastest-growing minority group during the 1990s with 486,000 respondents recording their ethnicity as Black African, outnumbering Britain's Caribbean population. More so, illegal migration and related underreporting suggest this figure is an incredibly significant underestimate. Many new British citizens are moreover of African origin currently. In a similar order, United Nations Conference on Trade and Development (UNCTAD) figures found that British export to Sub-Saharan Africa had risen by $11.6bn in 2008 ($9.7bn in 2007) and import from the UK to Sub-Saharan Africa $15.07bn in 2008 (13.7bn in 2007) (World Investment Report, 2009). Despite these figures, South Africa is a UK top priority country in Africa (the UK, owing to a considerable proportion of foreign investment in the country) played a significant role. The UK interest in Nigeria has grown over time. It emerged second-largest trade partner in Sub-Saharan Africa and 33rd largest overseas in 2007-9. It is important to note that Aid rather than the trade was the key driver of UK interest under the then leadership of the Labour Party. It is instructive to note that it was under the Labour Party that the Department for International Development (DFID) was set up. At this time, the department played a significant role in UK interest over the Foreign and Commonwealth Office (FCO), focusing more on development, poverty reduction and later, Security and Justice Governance, Access to Justice among others. Before the end of this dispensation, the UK made more attempt to make its overseas interest more explicit. Critical to this was the UK Public Service Agreements (PSAs) and the FCO Strategic Priorities and Strategic Framework. In a bold step, in 2006, the UK set out its International Strategic Priorities in FCO 2006 White Paper, *Active Diplomacy for a Changing World*. This also came with lots of restructuring of the Foreign Office. Being a focus of the UN Security Council, Africa featured prominently in one of the eight Department Strategic Objectives that were created in 2008 owing to counterinsurgency and counterterrorism in the continent. This, however, does not understate the level of influence of relative power and strategic interest without any specific mention. However, African states will need some measure of stability for these to manifest.

The UK interest in Africa under Tony Blair saw the beginning of an integrated and up-graded engagement since the end of colonial rule. Labour politicians and government officials underscored the symbolic role Africa policy have come to fill in UK perception as a "morale" willing to do good, and they were able to do that since they were operating in an arena where there were limited party political or media decent (Gallagher, Matthew, et al.). Remarkably, the Labour Party set the tone for a more robust international role for the UK and indoctrinated it as the primary yardstick of negotiating with the electorate for power. By 2010, all parties in the election support 0.7% of national income for international development by 2013. Many have come to accept it that it will be a massive waste of taxpayer money for the UK to cut its support to Africa. At this time, in point as other countries will benefit from the stability that the UK worked for. Subsequently, succeeding democratic liberal government ever since has remained committed to this course, stretching to other aspects including security, democratisation, peacebuilding, among others.

True be told, the much of the 1990s for the UK in Africa was more of managing colonial legacy disputes and providing aid. It is worthy of note to unequivocally state that the UK relationship with Africa before Tony Blair only just over 3% of British exports came to Africa compared to six or seven years after. Likewise, before this time, less than 2% of the total import from overseas came from Africa. Christopher Clapham argued that only meagre aid support came to Africa, equating with those of Sweden and Canada, and stood at merely one-third of Italy's, and one-sixth of France's, aid to the continent. Further, he held that:

> From an African viewpoint, likewise, the British simply did not provide the peculiar mix of support and subordination that the Francophones received from France, while the fact that the key formerly British countries were so much bigger that the formerly French ones meant that they were not, and did not see themselves as being, in the same kind of dependent relationship. No way was an African superstate like Nigeria going to see itself as a British client, while a relatively high proportion of the more radical African leaders at independence, including Nkrumah, Nyerere, Obote and Kaunda, governed Commonwealth African states. These, rather than British-oriented rulers like Banda or Seretse Khama – or even the leaders of more substantial states like Kenyatta or Balewa – made the running in the African fora, notably the Organisation of African Unity, within which continental attitudes to the outside world were increasingly defined. (Clapham, 2014).

More so, countries like Nigeria, who currently constitutes a big priority for the UK were in forceful military rule characterised by the flagrant violation of human rights and citizens inability to determine who govern them. The appetite to provide support for the oppressive government has always been low in the face of flagrant human rights violations. However, with the stability of democratic rule-setting into Africa at the onset of the 21st century, it was easy for the progressive and apparent reality of the Labour Party to be integrated into Africa. Blair's Africa's legacy is classic and remarkable in many ways. In 2000, Blair authorised the deployment of 800 British para-troopers on the ground to Sierra Leone to support UN and regional peacekeeping operation in the country. This decision of Tony Blair on Sierra Leone reflects UK interest to restore democracy where it has been and to uphold it where it exists. They backed the democratically elected government, whose army had fallen into decay and disarray, against a rebel army and insurgent with a record of recruiting child soldiers, disembowelling pregnant women, want to topple the government in power, terrorising civilians and chopping off limbs. The contribution of British troop transformed the Sierra Leone Army and upturned the tide. From a losing army, Britain helped to rebuild the government armed forces, bringing discipline (British Broadcasting Service, 2007), hardware, and expertise that result in restoration of peace in Sierra Leone. There were similar interventions reign in Darfur, Rwanda Genocide, among others. The UK played a crucial role in ensuring that other countries in the world demonstrate an interest in the humanitarian situation in Africa. Blair took advantage of the G8 summit in 2001 to make the big win. Through the article, he wrote entitled "The World Must Judge us on Africa", Blair emerged as the world's leading apostle of security and humanitarian intervention. Furthermore, Tony Blair established the Commission for Africa, also known as the Blair Commission for Africa. The Initiative was put in place by the British government to examine and provide motivation for development in Africa. The objective seeks to generate innovative ideas for development. Likewise, it sought to provide an implementation of the then international commitments towards Africa while working closely with Africans. Pertinent to note that the UK has since rolled many approaches to Africa, responding to dynamic security and developmental needs.

The modern UK promotes its overseas policy through the Foreign and Commonwealth Office. The FCO has a worldwide network of embassies and consulates, employing over 14,000 people in nearly 270 diplomatic offices with Africa having over 45 embassies and consulates. The primary focus of the Foreign and Commonwealth Office (FCO) is the promotion of the United Kingdom's interests overseas, supporting its citizens and businesses around the globe. These interests are mutually benefiting to the UK and overseas countries. Through the work of the FCO, the UK can create a platform and channels to safeguard its national security by countering terrorism and weapons proliferation and working to reduce conflict. In partnership with international organisations, the UN Security Council and the Commonwealth, the UK has immensely contributed to political stability, security and development in Africa and the world at large. Development is a key objective of the British Government policy in Africa and other countries of the world, UK effort in Africa helped in poverty reduction, fostered peace and stability. The FCO also assist the UK government to build prosperity by increasing exports and investment opportunities, opening markets, ensuring access to resources, and promoting sustainable global growth. As has already been alluded to early in this chapter, the counterinsurgency approach is quite holistic, amongst is the link to development and potency of governance and institutions of government.

## Why Africa?

The UK is a stronger believer in the premise that "insecurity in one place is a threat to security in all other places". Among the many responsibilities (FCO, 2017), the Foreign Secretary and the FCO Board of Management have set the projection of global influence and promotion of UK's prosperity as its priority Outcomes for 2017 to 2018; a pivotal aspect of its foreign policy priorities of protecting its people. "Her Majesty Government Conflict Funding is managed jointly by FCO, the Department for International Development and the Ministry of Defence and is worth £644 million for 2012 to 2013. It covers conflict prevention work and the UK's contribution to international peacekeeping missions." (HMG, 2017)

According to the information contained on the UK government official website (https://www.gov.uk), the Foreign & Commonwealth Office (FCO) uses its Official Development Assistance (ODA), also known as its overseas aid budget to support and deliver the 4 strategic objectives of the government's 2015 Aid Strategy which aligns the government's global efforts to defeat poverty, tackle instability and create prosperity in developing countries (factors which underpins UK counterinsurgency). Presently, UK support in Africa is geared towards strengthening peace, security, and governance; resilience and response to crises; economic prosperity and development and tackling extreme poverty bedevilling vulnerable people. Over time, these supports have evolved from DFID to include other programmes at the FCO.

In July 2000, the Government announced that the Foreign and Commonwealth Office, the Department for International Development and the Ministry of Defence, in association with the Cabinet Office and HM Treasury, would work more closely together to improve the effectiveness of Britain's contribution to peacekeeping, conflict prevention and conflict management in Sub-Saharan Africa and elsewhere in the world (DFID, 2001). A spokesperson for DFID said: "Our international development budget only increases when the UK economy grows, a sign of our economic success" [DFID, 2001]. This money is an investment in Britain's own security – ensuring the world is more prosperous, developed, and stable. "Whether it's stepping up our support for desperate Syrian refugees, tackling the lethal legacy of landmines or giving life-saving aid to stop people dying of hunger in East Africa, UK aid is keeping Britain safe while helping the world's poorest stand on their own two feet" [Anthony Mangnall].

To wrap up here, presently, of the six major terror groups namely: ALQIM, Boko Haram Al-Shabaab, ISIS, AQ-AP, Al-Qaeda Core (AQ Core) group, three of them are in Africa. However, the issues for which the UK is concerned and informs its security interest and investment are on the bases of:

11. The threat to the UK and interests from international terrorism is SEVERE.
12. The terrorist threats the UK face now are more diverse than before, dispersed across a wider geographical area, and often in countries without effective governance.
13. Terrorism is increasingly transnational in nature, operating across national borders and has a global reach for recruitment, influence, and radicalisation.

As the former Home Secretary made clear in her Washington speech in February 2016, and as we have seen in more recent events, we must continue to look beyond solely domestic solutions to deal with the terrorist threats we face. Over the course of 2015, we worked with our international partners to ensure that collaboration on counterterrorism is matched with coordinated action which has a lasting impact (UK CONTEST, 2015). The UK has a long history and wealth of experience tackling insurgency. In many ways, Britain has a good record in preventing radicalisation and terrorism. Despite an infamous statistic that more British Muslims have joined the Islamic State in Syria than have joined the British Army, the per capita count of those defecting to Syria is lower than in countries like Belgium and France, experts say (New York Times, 2017).

Historically, the British counterterrorism and counterinsurgency approach is premised on the British colonial policy of association. There was less resistance against British colonial domination than in other parts of Africa where the French attempted the policy of assimilation. The British colonial rule was paternalistic. Where the British encountered "native African" resistance or rebellion, they responded with restraint in many cases. While other colonial powers were excessively utilising disproportionate force, the British had developed a methodology for conducting counterinsurgency that managed and minimised resistance. Despite some difficulties like the Mau Mau rebellion in Kenya, these methods had, in the end, prevailed in South Africa, Nigeria, the Gold Coast (now Ghana) and other places. According to John Newsinger, two of the key elements of the methodology were "minimum force" and "hearts and minds" (Newsinger, 2015). Again, at the centre of the UK counterinsurgency is the heart and the mind. In fact, the British approach to counterinsurgency since the "Malayan

Emergency" of 1948–60 has been described by Field Marshal Sir Gerald Templer as "hearts and minds". This approach emphasises "winning the hearts and minds" of the people by using less coercive tactics against insurgents and thereby securing the support of the people. Unfortunately, this approach contrasts African's less effective method of using more violent, conventional warfare tactics with an overwhelming force. According to Paul 2009, the British counterinsurgency model has been analysed for its lessons for counterinsurgency in Afghanistan and Iraq. It has also been argued that the "Global War on Terrorism" is an insurgency and could be fought more effectively as a counterinsurgency campaign. The British approach remains a major influencer of the United States counterinsurgency framework but remain different in many ways.

Even though the British paternalistic measure saved the day in some cases, African colonies resisted British rule passively and actively. In recent instances, Africans persistently utilised pure violence to agitate for freedom from colonial rule and to take over the authorities. However, nature and how the British feel affected by insurgency in Africa changed following decolonisation of Africa. With Britain no longer directly in charge of Africa, insurgents that emerged were groups attempting to topple powers like in Uganda, Congo, and the rest of them. More so, in recent time, terrorism has incrementally assumed the major conflicts in the continent.

Unfortunately, affected African countries have resorted over-utilisation of armed forces. These approaches are often highhanded. Many a time, citizens of terrorism infested States in Africa trapped in conflict, struggle to reconcile which the greater evil is between government and militia groups utilising extreme violence for their course. Consequently, there is an apparent sheer resilience of terrorist groups to increasing large-scale application of force by government forces. Up till recently, many African countries battling terrorism are without counterterrorism strategy. More so, these countries have struggled with articulating the best strategy for dealing with the menace. Where these strategies exist, they are often characterised by sheer impracticability of the pre-sets and principles, or unwillingness and impatience of these state actors to follow the logic in the strategy. Other challenges are under-funding, lack of political will, poor human rights record, corruption, poor capacity, excessive political interferences among others. The greatest misadventure dwells more on the appetite for utilisation of force a mix of military and other tactics where good strategy exist.

At the continental level, the African Union has led policies and frameworks development for both COIN and CT. They have also provided platforms for inter-state coordination and more importantly, coordination of Africa forces for the restoration of peace and stability in vulnerable countries. Instances are the African Union Mission to Somalia (AMISOM), the African Union Mission in Sudan (AMIS), African-led International Support Mission to Mali etc. Africa's counterterrorism and counterinsurgency (CT-COIN) architecture is based on the legal and institutional foundation of the African Unity (AU). Many African countries have also domesticated or adapted these legal frameworks to conform to their peculiarities. However, the AU is equally challenged like other countries in these conflicts on the continent; poor funding, bad management of funding, non-progressive bureaucracies, politics, absence of capacity and innovation, poor research and tactics, lack of political will, shifting priorities of the union but few to mention. The AU has focused more on creating apparatus that addresses insecurity rather than those that ensures that insecurity does not arise in the first place. Unfortunately, these apparatuses have on their own accord failed. An instance, the Africa Standby Force was rejected by Burundi in December 2015. Presently, there is an increasing emergence of the military across blocs. From the Economic State of West African State Standby Force to the Multinational Joint Task Forces in the Lake Chad tackling Boko Haram and to the Sahel G5 Force tackling ALQIM but the list goes on.

There has also been substantial bilateral and multilateral support for counterterrorism efforts in Sub-Saharan Africa by the wider international community and the UK. These supports are often complex, like the counter-violence extremism which is addressed through multifaceted support. Notwithstanding, it suffices to say that general United Kingdom Counterterrorism (UK-CT) are often guided by the CT pillars namely:

14. PURSUE terrorists wherever they are and stop terrorist attacks.
15. PREVENT people from becoming terrorists or supporting violent extremism.
16. PROTECT the UK by strengthening defences against terrorism.
17. PREPARE to respond to an attack to lessen its impact.

United Kingdom Counterterrorism Strategy (UK CONTEST) Pursue Pillar currently provides support in a range of countries across Africa around justice and human rights pathway. These supports cover training, advice and mentoring to build counterterrorism capabilities, thereby increasing their ability to conduct effective evidence-based counterterrorism investigations and to disrupt attack planning inline within the rule of law. In Nigeria, for example, there are well-established programmes to strengthen investigatory and judicial frameworks for dealing with terrorism. This is underpinned by clear human rights principles (UK CONTEST 2015). On Protect and Prepare (crisis response) pillars, the UK reported in 2015, that it's Home Office and Foreign and Commonwealth Office team were facilitating efforts across government and the private sector to strengthen security in key locations overseas, including Africa. According to the CONTEST, these endeavours included an understanding of existing local capability to protect key sites and respond rapidly and effectively to attacks; and working collaboratively with host countries to reduce the risk. Depending on the benefiting Africa country, this may include the provision of training, mentoring or equipment. Some of this work is progressing in partnership with the US, UN, and European countries. These efforts are often done either through a Government to Government programme or in partnership with our security institutions of government.

It will interest the world to know that the UK is not directly involved in field battle against insurgents in Africa. The aftermath of the controversial military operation in Afghanistan has driven the UK into focusing less on boot on the ground. In as much as the UK has soldiers on the ground in parts of Africa, these soldiers are peacekeeping forces like in Darfur or providing technical support like in Nigeria, Mali etc. There is therefore little appetite for foreign adventures. More so, the UK does not think force can win the war against insurgency and terrorism. The main tenet of counterinsurgency recognises that a military-only solution is not feasible, it, however, accommodates dual military-political solution that adopts a population-centric approach. In a more generic approach, counterinsurgency doctrine is nurtured on the pillars of protecting the public population, the advancement of good governance, removing space that enables the enemy to function, and building public resilience against insurgents and acts of terror. Classical counterinsurgency seeks to combat an insurgency confined within the borders of a nation-state, while modern counterinsurgency theory takes these classical principles and applies them at the international level, or what Bruce Hoffman calls Global Counterinsurgency (GCOIN), which ultimately seeks to combat international terrorism while addressing the underlying socio-economic conditions that supposedly allow terrorism to thrive (Rineheart, 2010).

Thus, the UK foreign policy in Africa tries to address the circumstances in which terrorism thrives. However, the UK is supporting Africa's long generational effort to deny terrorist groups the space to operate, by helping vulnerable countries like Somalia, Nigeria, Sudan, Kenya, Mali, Uganda among others to develop their law enforcement capabilities, to address the injustice and conflict which terrorists exploit, and to combat their ideology. In 2015, former

Foreign Secretary William Hague announced major up light of the UK training and capacity-building support to the Nigerian military to help it counter the violent extremist organisation known as Boko Haram (Michael Fallon, 2015). In Nigeria, there is a UK resident British Military Advisory and Training Team (BMATT). Dating back to as far as 2014, the UK Government has had three teams of advisors in Nigeria, including experts in counterterrorism, hostage negotiation and victim support, assisted by an RAF surveillance aircraft that is based in Ghana. The UK equally has a team that is helping to provide further assistance to regional security and intelligence cooperation. Likewise, in 2002, the UK established the International Military Advisory & Training in Sierra Leone to help develop the Sierra Leone Armed forces into a democratically accountable, effective and sustainable force, capable of fulfilling security tasks required by the Government of Sierra Leone. In East Africa, there is the British Peace Support Team (BPST) responsible for the coordination of UK military assistance to armed forces in Eastern Africa to contribute to Security Sector Reform and to increase peacekeeping capacity. The BPST is made up of three organs namely:

1. International Mine Action Training Centre (IMATC)
2. Peace Support Training Centre (PSTC)
3. A presence in the Kenyan Defence and Staff College (DSC)

Information contained on the British Army website says the IMATC is a joint British and Kenyan venture, humanitarian in nature, aimed at alleviating the suffering caused by landmines and Explosive Remnants of War by providing high-quality Mine Action Training. More so in Kenya, British Army Training Unit Kenya (BATUK) is a permanent training unit that provides demanding training to exercising units preparing to deploy on operations or assume high readiness tasks (Live Fire and Tactical Effects Simulation (TESEX). There are also Royal Engineer exercises which carry out civil engineering projects and medical deployments which provide primary health care assistance to the civilian community. The present figure of BATUK consists of around 100 permanent staff and reinforcing short tour cohort of another 280 personnel.

Also, increasing numbers of UK military personnel are joining short-term missions to Uganda where they are helping to prepare the nation's army, the Uganda People's Defence Force (UPDF), for a difficult deployment to nearby Somalia (Kean, 2011). Through the training provided to Uganda People's Defence Force (UPDF) in areas such as medical care, operational law, combat logistics, and media operations, British personnel are making a key contribution to the fight for peace and stability. Being the leading country in the African Union Mission in Somalia (AMISOM)'s counterterrorism against Al-Shabaab, sharing British military expertise with UPDF has helped to engender the capacity of the army in both counterinsurgency and counterterrorism.

Similarly, there is the British Peace Support Team (BPST) based in Pretoria at the Peace Mission Training Centre, in South Africa. This team currently advise the South African Department of Defence (SADD) on aspects of democratic defence management and peace support operations. The BPST (SA) is composed of nine military officers and one civilian support staff.

Similarly, the UK is collaborating with the US to provide educational support intended for millions young girls and boys affected by Boko Haram crisis in northern Nigeria Particularly, there is increased support for girl's education to help better protect those who are most vulnerable. Through Department for International Development (DFID) there is a deliberate UK aid support to Africa that focuses on humanitarian, developmental and prosperity issues, ensuring that basic services and infrastructure is provided to those communities most at risk. Likewise, through other instruments of support, the UK is supporting civil society organisation capacity to engage government and government capacity to respond lawfully to demand from the public. More broadly, UK support across defence, security, justice administration, governance and elections, tourism, economic prosperity has engendered Africa's capacity to addressing underlying causes of terrorism, addressed existing political grievances, development, peace and stability in the continent.

## Challenges of United Kingdom counterterrorism and counterinsurgency assistance to Africa

There are quite hands full of challenges experience by the UK with regards to proving CT and COIN assistance to Africa and countries of Africa. Some of these challenges:

*Mutual suspicion and colonial legacies:* some Africa countries don't trust that the UK will offer support without the intention of planning to gain something in return. Besides the government, many government institutions treat HMG representatives with mutual suspicion. Many times, there are instances where the military and other government institutions deliberately frustrate foreign supports.

*Bureaucracies in Africa:* The Foreign Secretary, Philip Hammond MP, announced £5m UK support for a regional Task Force to tackle Boko Haram in northern Nigeria and the Lake Chad Basin area. However, getting the money from the AU to the MNJTF involved several bureaucracies that in some ways have affected prompt utilisation of the fund. It was impossible for the UK to provide funding to the MNJTF directly. These are like the bureaucracies of working with institutions of government in Africa which often frustrate appetite for support.

*Poor Human Rights and corruption record:* assistance to African countries including the sale of defence equipment are often hampered by the extremely poor human rights record of the military in Africa. Local and international reports of these violations backed with evidence abounds. For instance, in one its reports, Amnesty reported alleges some 600 people were killed by the military after a Boko Haram attack on Maiduguri's Giwa barracks on the 31 March 2014 (Amnesty International, 2014). In the same vein, maiming is prevalence in Africa, most times involving government institutions and individuals who are supposed to be the primary beneficiaries of foreign government assistance. Owing to the principle of aid support in such countries, these supports became a challenge on this basis.

*Poor Capacity to deliver:* in many instances, HMG representatives were alarmed by the general absence of capacity by government institutions to absorb the capacity support that is intended for the personnel of benefiting government institutions. Many times, the foreign government are compelled into improvising to be able to deliver on intended support.

*Sustainability:* many supports often offered by foreign government ceases to be practiced as soon the project through which the support is provided ends. This is like the provision of equipment. Owing to poor maintenance culture, the equipment is soon faulty and left to languish. In some other cases, the equipment could even be vandalised by government officials. This is also like corruption in the selection of beneficiaries of foreign government capacity support. Many people who are not in the place where the capacity will be utilised are selected on the basis of favouritism to attend training for which they will not be on the ground to use the capacity.

## Conclusion

The UK operates a comprehensive counterinsurgency strategy, simultaneously utilising a blend of civilian and military efforts to deal with insurgencies. This is an age-long strategy that is rooted in the British style of engagement. Besides utilising this strategy to manage and deal with rebellion in its colonial empires before decolonisation, the UK has used this pattern to address the root causes of insurgency, contain and defeat it both home and abroad.

However, it is instructive to note that the British style of counterinsurgency has evolved over time to become more adaptive to the modern sovereign state system and multi-polar international order. With respect to Africa, UK counterinsurgency campaigns support to African states focuses on integration and harmonisation of political, security, economic, and informational components that reinforce governmental legitimacy and effectiveness while reducing insurgent influence over the population.

The pivotal aspect of the UK counterinsurgency (COIN) campaign lies the population. In contrast with Africa, the UK places a premium on building public confidence and trust that the government offers a better deal than the insurgents. As elements, the UK ensures that security of the person and property, and the establishment of the rule of law, are paramount considerations. The UK is supporting in many ways to ensure that Africans countries have the requisite capacity to meet these standards.

Put the British counterinsurgency (heart and mind) against the African pattern, a sharp overlap; an excessive application force over other ingredients of counterinsurgency will emerge. From a holistic British strategy to a skewed reliance on force alone, it is apparent that African will no doubt miss on this journey to restoring lasting peace in the continent. This sharp divide is not the only place where the divergence arises but also the conflict. While many African countries would wish they have weapons that equate UK's to wipe away every dissenting voice in the continent, the millions that have died have never reduced the growing millions as picking up weapons against the modern government in the continent except there is a rethink of approach. It is no doubt why Africa is not only increasingly having more and more spaces governed by insurgents but it also loosing trained soldiers, equipment and expending more weapons at the detriment of infrastructure and social amenities that can help people lead a good life.

Similarly, considering the risk that of terrorism to public safety in the UK, supporting Africa to ensure the elimination of safe space for terrorists to recruit or act sounds mutually beneficial. It allows the UK to watch against any effort capable of harming its public both home and abroad while Africa also has the requisite peace for political stability, security, and development. The CONTEST has played a vital role in this regard, serving as that framework that enables the UK to organise effort and counter all forms of terrorism.

In concluding this chapter, the classical brand of the UK assistance to counterterrorism and counterinsurgency in Africa is holistic as against African's militaristic approach. The interaction between UK's expertise drawn from years of experience in counterterrorism and counterinsurgency has brought value to Africa novel experience with the scourge of violent extremism in Africa. Consequently, these exchanges of expertise have further inculcated effective practices that can help deter more people from going into violent extremism, address the root causes and find inclusive but sustainable solutions to existing threats against development, political stability and peace across the continent of Africa.

# References

Acemoglu, D., Chaves, I. N., Osafo-Kwaako, P., & Robinson, J. A. (2014). *Indirect Rule and State Weakness in Africa: Sierra Leone in Comparative Perspective* https://scholar.harvard.edu/files/jrobinson/files/indirect_rule_nber_4_0.pdf (accessed 27 July 2018).

Alderson, A. (2008). Iraq and borders: The role of barriers in counter-insurgency. *RUSI Journal, 153*(2), 18–22.

Amnesty International (2014). *Nigeria: No Justice for the 640 Men and Boys Slain by Military Following Giwa Barracks Attack Two Years Ago* https://www.amnesty.org/en/press-releases/2016/03/nigeria-no-justice-for-the-640-men-and-boys-slain-by-military-following-giwa-barracks-attack-two-years-ago/ (accessed 22 July 2018).

Anderson, G. (2010). Counter-insurgency vs. Counter-terrorism: A Civilian's View, small war journal, https://smallwarsjournal.com/blog/journal/docs-temp/375-anderson.pdf (accessed 20 July 2018).

Angstrom, J., & Duyvesetyn, I. (Eds.). (2010). *Modern war and the utility of force: challenges, methods, strategy* (pp. 286 Class: 355.01 ANG). London: Routledge.

BBC News 2007. What is Blair's African legacy? http://news.bbc.co.uk/1/hi/world/africa/6693055.stm.

Bennhold, K. (2017). *At least One London assailant was on police radar, exposing gaps.* New York Times (5 June 2017), https://www.nytimes.com/2017/06/05/world/europe/uk-terrorism-target.html?mcubz=0 (Accessed 26 August 2018).

Boyle, M. (2008). The War on terror in American Grand Strategy. *International Affairs, 84*(2), 191–209.

British Army Field Manual (2010). Vol 1 Part 10: Countering Insurgency. MoD, Warminster. https://urgencedigitaleafrique.org/wp-content/uploads/grid-ebook/preview/ARMEE/ARMY%20Field%20Manual%20countering%20insurgency-uda.pdf (accessed 2 July 2018).

British Army Field Manual (2009). Vol 1 Part 10: Countering Insurgency. MoD, Warminster. http://news.bbc.co.uk/1/shared/bsp/hi/pdfs/16_11_09_army_manual.pdf.

British Broadcasting Service (2007). *What is Blair's African legacy?* http://news.bbc.co.uk/1/hi/world/africa/6693055.stm (accessed 12 July 2018).

Cable News Network (2005). *London Bombings Fast Facts* http://edition.cnn.com/2013/11/06/world/europe/july-7-2005-london-bombings-fast-facts/ (accessed 3 July 2018).

Chicago Tribune (2015). *Boko Haram's cost to Nigeria's Borno: $1 billion and rising*, http://www.chicagotribune.com/news/sns-wp-blm-news-bc-nigeria-bokoharam09-20150909-story.html (accessed 17 August 2018).

Clapham, C. (2014). *UK-African relations: The background to Labour's Africa policy, Workshop on UK-Africa relations: Labour and after's Policy* (p. 16.2 (2014)). Alison Richard Building, 7 West Road, Cambridge CB3 9DP, UK: January 2014 Centre of African Studies, University of Cambridge. https://www.open.ac.uk/socialsciences/bisa-africa/files/uk-africa-policy/Clapham%20speaking%20notes.pdf (accessed 23 July 2018).

Cloake, J., & Templer (1985). *Tiger of Malaya: The life of Field Marshal Sir Gerald Templer.* London: Harrap.

CNN (2011). Timeline: Osama bin Laden, over the years. http://edition.cnn.com/2011/WORLD/asiapcf/05/02/bin.laden.timeline/index.html.

2014 *DailySignal,* (2014). *Al-Qaeda and Other Extremist Groups Increasing in Africa,* http://dailysignal.com/2014/05/06/al-qaeda-extremist-groups-increasing-africa/ (17 August 2018).

Department for International Development 2001. draft paper to examines the causes and consequences of conflict in Africa: the causes of conflict in Africa. Viewed August 1st 2017 via http://webarchive.nationalarchives.gov.uk/+/http:/www.dfid.gov.uk/pubs/files/conflict-africa.pdf.

Foreign and Commonwealth Office 2018. *Our Funding Programmes.* Accessed 28th August via https://www.gov.uk/government/organisations/foreign-commonwealth-office/about.

Foreign and Commonwealth Office 2017. About us viewed 28th August 2017 via https://www.gov.uk/government/organisations/foreign-commonwealth-office/about.

French, D. (2011). *The British Way in Counterinsurgency 1945–1957* (pp. 11–41). Oxford OX2, 6DP: Oxford University Press.

Gallagher, M. W., Lopez, S. J., & Preacher, K. J. (2009). The hierarchical structure of well-being. *Journal of Personality, 77*(4), 1025–1050.

Global Policy Forum, Failed States, (2016). *Africa Report on Internal Displacement* https://www.globalpolicy.org/nations-a-states/failed-states.html (accessed 23 July 2018).

Global Policy Forum (GPF) Report Building (2016). *The Pillars of Sustainable Inclusion.* Alliance for Financial Inclusion https://www.afi-global.org/sites/default/files/publications/2017-02/AFI2016_GPF%20report_digital.pdf (Accessed 27 July 2018).

Global terrorism Database https://www.start.umd.edu/gtd/ (accessed 11 September 2017).

Global Terrorism Index (2015). https://www.files.ethz.ch/isn/194968/Global-Terrorism-Index-2015.pdf, The Institute for Economics and Peace (IEP) York (accessed 2 August 2018).

Gurr, R. T. (1994). Peoples against states: Ethnopolitical conflict and the changing world system: 1994 presidential address. *International Studies Quarterly*, *38*(3), 347–377.

Hannay, D. (2004). High Level Panel on Threats, Challenges and Change, Reynolds P. UN Staggers on road to reform BBC News http://news.bbc.co.uk/2/hi/americas/4244842.stm (accessed 28 August 2018).

HannahRitchie, Joe, Hasell, Cameron, Appel and Max, Roser(2013).*Terrorism. Global terrorism Database*https://ourworldindata.org/terrorism.

House of Commons Home Affairs Committee (2014). Counter-Terrorism–Seventeenth Report of Session 2013–14.

International Alert (2015). Tell it like it is: The role of civil society in responding to serious and organised crime in West Africa. https://www.international-alert.org/sites/default/files/CVI_CivilSocietyWestAfrica_EN_2015.pdf (accessed 20 July 2018).

International Crisis Group Special Report (14 March 2016). Exploiting Disorder: al-Qaeda and the Islamic State, https://www.crisisgroup.org/global/exploiting-disorder-al-qaeda-and-islamic-state (accessed 27th August 2018).

Jackson, R. H., & Rosberg, C. G. (1982). Why Africa's weak states persist: the empirical and the juridical in statehood. *World Politics*, *35*(1), 1–24.

Kean, S. (2011). *Spreading the British Army's influence in Africa*, UK Ministry of Defence. 17 February. https://www.gov.uk/government/news/spreading-the-british-armys-influence-in-africa.

Kemp, E. (2016). *Africa Report on Internal Displacement*, http://www.internal-displacement.org/library/publications/2016/africa-report-2016/ (accessed 7 August 2018).

Knightley, P. (1976). *The first casualty: from the Crimea to Vietnam: the war correspondent as hero, propagandist, and myth maker* (pp. 465.12.95). New York: Harcourt Brace Jovanovich.

LaFree, G., & Dugan, L. (2007). Introducing the global terrorism database. *Terrorism and Political Violence 19*(2) https://www.start.umd.edu/gtd/ (accessed 24 July 2018).

Manchester Evening News (2017). *Manchester Terror Attack.* http://www.manchestereveningnews.co.uk/all-about/manchester-terror-attack (accessed 28 August 2018).

Michael Fallon MP (2015). UK bolster training in Nigeria to help combat Boko Haram. https://www.gov.uk/government/news/uk-bolster-training-in-nigeria-to-help-combat-boko-haram (accessed 11 August 2018).

Miraftab, F., & Wills, S. (2005). Insurgency and spaces of active citizenship: The story of Western Cape anti-eviction campaign in South Africa. *Journal of Planning Education and Research*, *25*(2), 200–217.

Newsinger, J. (2015). Hearts and minds: The myth and reality of British counter-insurgency. *International Socialism* 148, http://isj.org.uk/hearts-and-minds/ (accessed 11 August 2018).

Norwegian Refugee Council (2016). *Global Report on International Displacement.* http://www.internal-displacement.org/globalreport2016/pdf/2016-global-report-internal-displacement-IDMC.pdf (accessed July 2018).

Pakenham, T. (1993). *The Boer War.* UK: Hachette.

Pakenham T. (2015). *The Boer War.*

Paul, D. (2009). 'Hearts and Minds'? British Counter-Insurgency from Malaya to Iraq. *Journal of Strategic Studies*, https://doi.org/10.1080/01402390902928172 (accessed January 2019).

Reynolds, P. (2005 ). *UN staggers on road to reform.* BBC News, September 14. http://news.bbc.co.uk/1/hi/world/americas/4244842.stm.

Rineheart, J. (2010). Counter-terrorism *and Counterinsurgency*, 4(5). Perspectives on Terrorism, http://www.terrorismanalysts.com/pt/index.php/pot/article/view/122/html (accessed January 2019).

Spies, R. (Apr 24th, 2013). *History of Terrorism in Africa* http://sites.stedwards.edu/apsmg434701-group1/history-of-terrorism-in-africa/ (accessed 24 August 2017).

Tell, B. J. (2015). Like It Is the role of civil society in responding to serious and organised crime in west Africa, International Alert, September 2015.

The Government of the United Kingdom (2001). British Army Field Manual. *1*(10), *Countering Insurgency* http://www.freeinfosociety.com/media/pdf/4868.pdf Pp 1, 5, 6 (accessed January 2019).

The Government of the United Kingdom (2004). −*Seventeenth Report, House of Commons Home Affairs Committee,* https://publications.parliament.uk/pa/cm201314/cmselect/cmhaff/231/231.pdf (accessed 18 August 2018).

The Government of the United Kingdom (2015). *Foreign and Commonwealth Office: "About us",* https://www.gov.uk/government/organisations/foreign-commonwealth-office/about (accessed 28th August 2018).

The Government of the United Kingdom (2000). *The causes of conflict in Africa: the causes of conflict in Africa. Cabinet Sub-Committee on Conflict Prevention in Africa*http://webarchive.nationalarchives.gov.uk/+/http://www.dfid.gov.uk/pubs/files/conflict-africa.pdf (accessed 1 August 2018).

The New York Times 2017.At Least One London Assailant Was on Police Radar, Exposing Gaps 5 June https://www.nytimes.com/2017/06/05/world/europe/uk-terrorism-target.html.

The Telegraph (2013). *David Cameron tells .G8 nations to stop paying ransoms to terrorists* http://www.telegraph.co.uk/news/politics/conservative/10104374/David-Cameron-tells-G8-nations-to-stop-paying-ransoms-to-terrorists.html, (accessed 9 August 2017).

UK Aid, Anthony Mangnall https://www.anthonymangnall.co.uk/campaigns/uk-aid

UK CONTEST 2015. *The United Kingdom's Strategy for Countering Terrorism: Annual Report for 2015* https://assets.publishing.service.gov.uk/government/uploads/system/uploads/attachment_data/file/539683/55469_Cm_9310_Web_Accessible_v0.11.pdf.

Vitzthum, C., Johnson, K. and Champion, M. (March 12, 2004). Train Bombings Kill At Least 198 in Spain: Basque Group or al Qaeda Is Suspected in Attack On a Staunch U.S. Ally, *Wall Street Journal,* https://www.wsj.com/articles/SB107899319607552435 (accessed 22 February 2019).

Wesseling, H. L. (1996). *Divide and rule: The partition of Africa, 1880–1914.* No. 275-95133. Westport, CT 06881: Praeger Publishers.

William, H. (2013). *Countering terrorism overseas,* https://www.gov.uk/government/speeches/countering-terrorism-overseas (accessed 10 August 2018).

Wire Staff (May 2, 2011). *Timeline: Osama bin Laden, over the years,* http://edition.cnn.com/2011/WORLD/asiapcf/05/02/bin.laden.timeline/index.html.

World Investment Report (2009). *United Nations Conference on Trade and Development (2009),* http://unctad.org/en/docs/wir2009_en.pdf Transnational Corporations, *Agricultural Production and Development* (accessed 18 June 2017).

# 18

# France's counterterrorism and counterinsurgency strategy in Africa

*Gani Joses Yoroms*

## Introduction

The date 9/11 has become an episodic dark spot in the history of contemporary Western civilisation as scholars continue to reflect on the attacks perpetrated by Osama Bin Ladin's Al Qaeda on the World Trade Centre and the Pentagon in the US. The attacks changed the landscape and the narratives of liberal capitalist dominance in the envisaged uni-polar world system. This development led to a shift from post-Cold War euphoria, defined as the New World Order, following the collapsed of the Berlin Walls (being the landmark of the cold war) to the era of a new world infested with Non State Violent-Actors (NSVAs). Countries like US, Britain and France among others that are learned on the application of weapons of warfare were not only caught hands down but found themselves at risk grappling with difficulty; on how to confront the fluid power of the NSVAs. As a result, since 9/11 Al-Qaeda multiplied its tentacles in Africa, Asia, and the Middle East. The threats from VNSAs include terrorist and insurgent manifests from Al-Qaeda, Al-Qaeda in the Islamic Maghreb (AQIM), Ansa Dine, Taliban, Al Shabaab, Boko Haram, and Al-Mouraboun among others. They may not have a direct link to or with Al Qaeda but are inseparably bound by ideological soul- tie defined in terms of distorted Islamic principles in the context of political Islam (Yoroms, 2013). Today global governance around the world is faced with diverse challenges from these terrorist and insurgent groups (Makinda 2003, Abiodun: 43–57); that are determined to:

i. Undermining the values and core interests of western civilisation,
ii. Challenging the structures of the global governance envisaged with a high stake in the UN (as an international regulatory mechanism against threats to international peace and security),
iii. Jeopardising the integration of the global economy and its investment in the peripheral societies, and
iv. Deconstructing the essence of human rights and the drive of western civilisation towards global secularism, postmodernism, and anthropogenic world (a logical measure to liberate and disconnect pristine societies from their backward world-views).

Therefore, like the biblical Samson who had the seven locks (source of his power) of his head shaved off by his enemies, the capitalist world is being incapacitated by NSVAs challenging the philosophy of secular liberalism, and in effect the security of the western civilisation in the global context. It is within this context that this chapter will be focusing on France, one of the five (5) permanent member states of the United Nations, foremost in the pursuit of global secularism and a noted empire builder. France does not take lightly threats of terrorism and insurgency, not only in France or Europe but in the global context. This chapter, therefore, attempts to interrogate the narrative of France counterterrorism and counterinsurgency policy and efforts in Africa.

In this case, the chapter looks at the concepts of terrorism/counterterrorism, insurgency/counterinsurgency from the perspective of France, and linking them to the critical question of how to maintain international peace and security. As a follow-up, the second section of the chapter tries to establish how France has been involved in conflict management in Africa especially being a dominant former colonial authority. It is based on this that the section specifically identifies France's policy on terrorism/insurgency as a means of protecting its interest in Africa. The third section sets out to define and present an overview of France counter operations in Africa against terrorism and insurgency. It focuses on operations that are related to terrorism and insurgency and less on generic peacekeeping operation like the case in Cote d'Ivoire which had little to do with terrorism. The chapter further assesses the challenge generated from France's involvement in conducting counterterrorism and counterinsurgency operations in Africa.

## France perception and approach to counter terrorism and counter insurgency

In Chapter 2 of this seminal work, Kenneth Omeje has quintessentially provided a conceptual clarification of the components of counterterrorism and counterinsurgency in the African context. This effort has also given us a general template on which this chapter intends to build or construct an empirical justification for carrying out this research. Similarly, in Chapter 16, Napoleon Enayaba examined the UK's counterterrorism policy in Africa. The chapter reveals the behaviour of a former colonial master in the defence and security of her erstwhile colonies. This chapter focuses on France's perception and its approach to counterterrorism and counterinsurgency. Arriving at a common doctrine of Counterinsurgency (COIN) by countries remains complications but what matters much is how countries should collaborate to address the menace of terrorism/insurgency (Kilcullen, 2006).

Terrorism takes its root from the French word *terre*, originally depicting fear as expressed in 1879 French revolution when its monarchical authorities exercised an extreme massacre of the citizens. Terrorism is a fluid concept and very flexible and has grown in dimension with its manifestative attributes in revolutionary warfare, anarchism, fascism, and religious extremism. Each phase of the manifestation is informed by political and/or ideological underpinnings. France had had the experiences of all of these in history (Shafer, 1988). France/French interests have suffered over the centuries, and they continued to face a series of terrorist attacks up to the present time. They have been the target, by both national and international terrorism, from homegrown terrorist networks and from terrorist operations in the Middle East, Asia, and Africa, respectively. Thus, France often sees itself as being at risk both at home and abroad (France Diplomatic, 2017). Therefore, France's perception of terrorism and terrorist activities are defined within the context of the perception of one of a limited list of criminal offences in connection with an individual or a collective undertaking, with serious intention to disturb

public order through intimidation or terror (France Diplomatic, 2017) in order to score political and ideological goals.

On this, France maintains a perception that terrorism can metamorphose into an insurgency.
This can happen in phases. As shown in Table 1 below, the first phase begins with a legitimate
protest as legally guaranteed. But where the protest to achieve a purpose is mismanaged by both
aggrieved and political authority; in terms of negotiation, it may degenerate to resistance and
subsequently into insurrection; interfacing with terrorism and guerrilla warfare; both of which
are not mutually exclusive. The end state of the process will be an insurgency. Accordingly, an
insurgency is organised and structured in a way to gain the support of the population through its
Cell operations in relation to its environment, and, in particular, in relation to the population
which represents the major stake. This point is fundamental because insurgents will seek to
control the population from which it galvanises supports morally or otherwise.

As stated in the French doctrine on Counterinsurgency (COIN), an insurgency is based on
the principle that when there is *"terrorism in the town, a guerrilla in the countryside, war has begun"*
(Forces Employment Doctrine Centre, 2010:11). In this respect insurgents avoid a decisive
battle confrontation with a force (France) which has technological superiority; therefore, by
preventing the French Forces from concentrating their efforts and being everywhere at the
same time, and ensuring the availability of a fallback area that is secure and difficult to access by
the regular French Forces. (Forces Employment Doctrine Centre: 2010:11) remains their goal.
Thus, guerrilla warfare insurgents do not seek direct confrontation with the regular forces but
simultaneously strive decisively to win the support of all or part of the population in order to
use it for propaganda.

Prior to 2001, France put some countermeasures in place to dismantle several terrorist cells
from attacking France since 1986 through article 421 of its penal code. In 2012, the parliament
adopted Act 2012-1432 on security and action against terrorism, sanctioning incitement on the

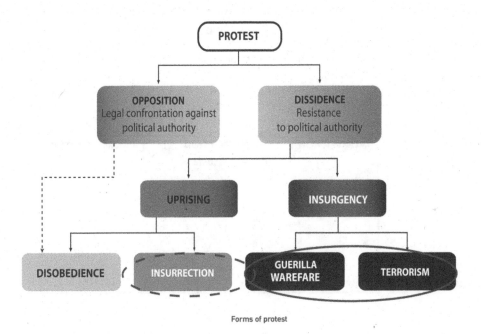

Forms of protest

*Figure 18.1* Types of Armed Protest and their Organisation

internet and prosecution of French nationals including those abroad. In 2014 a further draconian law against terrorism was enacted and assented in 2015. It is the 14th of the laws against
terrorism since 1986, targeting lone wolves or individuals planning attacks on France. Human
rightists have kicked against the laws as too draconian. France has defended them taking the
hard position that it has been the largest breeding ground for terrorists striving in the western
world whereas at today 1,089 French or foreign nationals living in France are involved in
jihadist networks in Syria or Iraq. As at today 368 are currently waging war in Syria, 212 have
returned; 256 are actively planning to leave to theatres of terrorism around the world, 205 are in
transit and46 have died in Syria and in Iraq. (Dall'Armellina, 2014).

Therefore, the purpose of the law is first, based on a mission designed to expose, dismantle,
and eliminate the rebel nerves that have entrapped the population. Second, countering insurgency to ensure a lasting victory in captured places; the destruction of the insurgent organisation must be followed by "construction of peace and establishment of a new order" (Shafer,
1988:155). Without this insurgency tend to flourish when there is insufficient government
control over the population (Shafer, 1988:155), giving them the opportunity to propagate and
reproduce their ideology of terror.

Thus, contrarily under the English legal system, it is easier for a criminal to get away with a
crime committed than in the French legal system. It is this loophole in the English legal system
that terrorists including Boko Haram Terrorists (BHT) in Nigeria exploit to get away with their
heinous criminalities. This has led to the breeding ground for the sustainability of terrorism/
insurgency in such a system.

As for France the stability of the state can only be maintained or restored by enforcing
security and engaging the insurgents in continuum phases (Figure17.2): the intervention phase,
stabilisation phase and normalisation phase. In each phase military intervention is inevitably
interfaced with the non-kinetic approach, taking into account types of actions and desired
effects on the primary target of the insurgents such as the population, institutional symbols and
the allied forces. Therefore, the course of action the French doctrine envisage to pursue
"depend upon the degree of violence desired, i.e. protection, expanded security, and domination. Thus, they are described in relations to their end state: evacuation of the threatened
population (protection), area control, and interposition (expanded security) and COIN
(domination) (Kilcullen, 2007:10).

France, given its previous experience and disposition in the Algeria and Indochina wars of
independence, knows the tactics of insurgents. Except there are other motives, its preference for

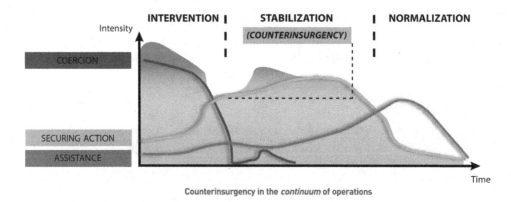

Counterinsurgency in the *continuum* of operations

*Figure 18.2* The Phases of Counterinsurgency Operations

enemy-centric approach runs contrary to the philosophy behind the creation of the United Nations and liberty of freedom which France previously stands for. While the enemy-centric approach is a template for peace enforcement, the population-centric approach sets the standard and yardsticks for arbitration and reconciliation. Therefore, the critical question that both France and the UN may find difficult to answer is, how can peacekeeping approach cope in a contemporary asymmetric warfare where the rules of engagement are constantly challenged by the insurgents with reckless abandon? This dilemma falls within the French Defence policy, as the then French Minister of State for Defence, François Leotard, noted, while endorsing the new post-cold France Defence Policy, that "France's presence oversea, the influence we exercise in Africa, our *direct and indirect* interests in a great many regions forbid us to limit our strategy to a purely continental dimension (in Europe). I, therefore, wanted to...clearly consider the demands proceeding from the global dimension" (Republic of France MInistry of Defence, 1994: 1).

## France: conflicts, terrorism and insurgency in Africa

The post-colonial African state went through a series of conflicts that define and shape its relations with the world. The extended period of the cold war (1945–1989) frustrated Africa from reaping the benefits of the struggle for independence. The independent African countries were ferried into the camps of the two superpowers, either with the capitalist world led by the US or the socialist world by the defunct Union of the Socialist Soviet Republics (USSR). This exacerbated inter-state conflict on the continent as Africa was torn and turned into a sphere of influence for both superpowers. Africa became a battleground where both ideological contenders drew on economic, political, and strategic interests that populated conflicts on the continent; and thereby rendering democracy and development on the continent impossible. One of the enduring legacies of the cold war was the testing of France's atomic bomb in the Sahara Desert against all protest by the Organisation of African Unity (OAU). Today, the same Sahel Sahara has become a strategic zone for terrorism where France is made to defend.

Like all the Europeans, France believes Europe is affected by terrorist threats from Africa not only in terms of its geographical proximity to continent but the shared interest in sustaining France's global governance threatened by terrorism (Gowan, 2017). Being one of the growing hubs of terrorism in Europe in the 1980s, France gradually improved its tactical and operational intelligence, especially following the attacks on the Rue Copernic in Paris. Thus, despite some recent attacks in France, it has by contrast been successful in preventing notable attacks in Europe. By 1990s France was able to assist the US and Canada to track down a French national with Algerian roots, Ahmed Ressam, the attacker of Los Angeles International Airport. Though based in Canada, Ressam was monitored and tracked for a period of three years. Another instance was the arrest and "provisional detention" of Adlene Hicheur, a nuclear physicist of Algerian origin, following a conversation and discovery of email on the planned attacks; in collaboration with AQIM. A typical example of France's control mechanism in Africa can be traced to an interesting conflict in Chad. This has been duplicated in other francophone enclaves such as Cote D'Ivoire, Central African Republic, Congo Brazzaville and Djibouti among others. Prior to Operation Epervier in 1986, France had carried out *Operation Manta* between 1983–1984 in Chad in defence of President Hissene Habre who was threatened by Ghadafi of Libya who supported Goukoni Oueddai and his rebel group. Though each country has its unique *histropolitical* relations with France, the general pattern of France control predominates.

## Overview of France counterterrorism operations in Africa

Our previous interrogations have shown that France interventions are peace enforcement as a measure of achieving its economic interest in Africa. When France deploys for either peace-keeping or counter terrorism/counter insurgency (peace enforcement) it ensures that its operation maintains the superiority of control in the mission field. This gives her the latitude to define the mandate of its operation beyond what the UN envisages. Being the only country of western civilisation able to deploy large combat troops on the ground beyond European shores gave her the latitude to exercise a privilege which the UNSC has acquiesced. France's counter operations in Africa therefore can be categorised into four parts. These are the Maghreb Operation, Operation Serval in Mali, the Barkhane Counter Operations with the focus on and the creation of G 5 Sahel, and the Lake Chad Counter Operation.

### The Maghreb counterterrorism operation

The Maghreb countries are made up exclusively of Arab and some indigenous minority Africa ethnic groups such as the Barbers, the Tuaregs, other black population and the Coptics; among other variance within the axis of North Africa: Algeria, Egypt, Mauritania, Morocco, Libya and Tunisia. Most of these countries have experienced French colonial impacts. This indeed has strengthened the resolve of the French military and intelligence system to step up their presence in Africa.

Furthermore, moved by their interests to remove Ghadafi, without learning the lessons in Iraq the western powers influenced the passage of UNSC Resolutions1970 which granted Libya a warning against coming war crimes, and later UNSC Resolution 1973, providing a coalition of the willing (or invaders) against Libya in 2011. The US, United Kingdom and France led the air cover to back anti-Ghadafi forces. In addition, France and the UK deployed troops and fighter planes in support of anti-Ghadafi militants. This culminated in the death of Muamar Ghadafi and the collapse of the state of Libya. The death of Ghadafi however, ignited the emergence and break up of factional groups gaining access to government armoury and disposing of them abroad. This has led to the proliferation of small arms and light weapons which has exacerbated the menace of conflicts in Africa. (Conor, 2016).

### AFISMA and "Operation Serval": between peacekeeping and French counter operations

Mali has been in crisis since independence when the Tuaregs have been fighting for greater autonomy from Bamako. Several political agreements were concluded but no concrete political settlement was accepted. The northern axis has become "ungovernable" as the presence of the government in Bamako remains absent. The concept "ungovernable" is used here to distinguish it from the common usage of the concept of ungoverned territory. "Ungovernable" space/territories have to do with the failed state and its insufficient ability to either take control of a terrain/territory it owned. But where a place is "ungoverned" it is an indication of failed governance. There is the need to distinguish between failed states from failed governance, which has to do with weak institutions of governance.

The threat to political stability in the country especially from the north continued to create instability as Bamako was equally unable to provide logistics for the Malian Defence and Security Forces to tackle the threats from the North. This necessitated the military to takeover power on the pretext of government neglect amidst the threats from the rebels. Meanwhile, the threats from the North became real as the rebels continue to arm themselves more than Malian military. Further to this was the integration of the well-trained Libyan Tuaregs arriving northern Mali after the death of Ghadafi, and the collapse of the state of Libya. This exacerbated the rebellion in northern Mali. Thus, the rebel groups including the National Movement for the Liberation of Azaward (NMLA) fought the government of Mali and in the process declared the independent state of Azaward from Mali with full implementation of Sharia legal system. However, NMLA runs into conflict with another group *Ansar Dine,* and the Movement for Oneness and Jihad in West Africa (MOJWA). This became a major concern for both ECOWAS and the AU. This necessitates the drive for the deployment of peacekeeping forces which ECOWAS/AU backed by the UNSC Resolution 2085 of 2012 to deploy AFISMA by January 2013 to Mali. Ahead of the conclusion of the development of the Concept of Operation (CONOPS) the Force Commander of AFISMA, Major General Shehu Abdulkadir, a Nigerian military officer, was appointed by ECOWAS.

However, with NMLA taking over Northern Mali, the government of Mali no longer has confidence in AFISMA, preferring France's intervention. Indeed, France responded quickly by launching Operation Serval, deploying 3,000 troops immediately to Mali. Unfortunately, when the West African troops from Burkina Faso, Guinea, Ghana, Niger, Senegal, and Togo arrived in February 2013 Operation Serval had already taken firm control of the theatre of operation across Mali. Before AFISMA could settle for any action Chad and Malian troops, led by France had begun to repel the insurgents from entry into Bamako.

France reinforced troop deployment with a dispatch of two mirage F1CR Reconnaissance and six 2000D fighter jets from its operational base in Chad. Additional supply included KC -135 strato-tanker planes, one C-130 Hercules and one Transsall C-160 transport planes. By 13 Jan 2013, four mine fighter squadron jets flew from Saint Dizier Airbase, France, to Ndjamena from where they took off to the operational base in Gao, Northern Mali. Further, Airbus A310 and A30 Transport squadron further conveyed troops to Bamako, with a detachment of Fusiliers Commandos also was deployed to Bamako to enhance the security of French Air Force assets as well as conducting search and rescue operation. With support from USAFRICOM, EU, Canada; providing lift capability and other coordination, France was able to stabilise Mali between February and August 2013.

## MINUSMA: UN counter terrorism/insurgency operation

As the threats continue the UNSC created the UN Multinational Mission for the stabilisation in Mali (MINUSMA) by Resolution 2100 of April 2013 to reinforce Operation Serval, with the authorisation to operate a robust mandate; using all necessary means to address threats to its mandate, protect civilians under imminent threats of physical violence as well as protecting UN personnel from residual threats within its capabilities and its areas of deployment. This runs contrary to normative UN doctrine and policy on peacekeeping which has for decades avoided the use of force. However, with subsequent development in peacekeeping, the use of force has been selectively authorised by the UN. The example set by France's Operation Serval in Mali was uniquely conducted to avoid an invitation of anarchy as the terrorists were poised to overrun Mali. Though MINUSMA conduct edits for its own operation in cooperation with Malian Defence and Security Forces the *Operation Servility* turned out that Operation Serval was the one offering support to MINUSMA when faced with imminent and serious threats. As at 2016 MINUSMA had suffered 279 IED attacks with 119 fatal deaths and 453 casualties, becoming the deadliest UN PKO in most recent time (John, 2017).

Thus, despite the entire logistical infrastructure at its disposal MINUSMA was not able to cope with the robust mandate. The MINUSMA's Force Commander, Major General Michael Lollesgard regretted this and lamented the number of deaths recorded. He said "I am very sad about the fact. It is my responsibility; it is my task to set up the troops in the best conceivable way, to make sure that the soldiers are safe as possible" (Conor, 2016). The UNSG, Ban Ki-Moon was compelled to recommend to the UNSC the scaling up of the number troops from 12,500 from 11,500 and the busting of the capacity of the mission in key areas such as improvised explosive devices, which the insurgents have increasingly used against the mission and the population. Nevertheless, as noted by General Lollesgard, putting troops is not the only means of guaranteeing mission success. He believes the situation can only be improved in the long term only through the political process, and not by increasing the number of peacekeepers in the mission field. (Conor, 2016).

## "Operation Barkhane": a counterinsurgency in G5 Sahel

The initial success recorded with Operation Serval made France draw down its troops with replacement from MINUSMA. Effectively, MINUSMA should carry on with the stabilisation process. Unfortunately, MINUSMA despite its itself weakness took over from Operation Serval and re-launched the peacekeeping process into the deadliest battlefield where it suffered most of the alarming death casualties. This prompted France to refocus its counterterrorism and counterinsurgency operation in Africa by strategically creating the Sahel G 5countries with the surfacing of the Operation Barkhane to operate alongside MINUSMA, with unhindered latitude. While announcing the new phase of counterterrorism and counterinsurgency with the creation of Operation Barkhane at a military base in Niamey, on 19 July 2014, President Francois Hollande said the challenge of security in Africa has not only become a dilemma for Europe and America but a burden of responsibility for France. For France to conduct this responsibility effectively it needs direct use of hard power to tackle the security crisis caused by a regional power vacuum in the 5 Sahel countries. These countries are Burkina Faso, Chad, Mali, Mauritania and Niger which have become a thriving zone for terrorist and militants from the Al-Qaida in the Islamic Maghreb (AIM), Al-Mourabitoun, and a splinter of AQIM headed by an Algerian militant known by name Belmokhtar. It is believed the ungovernable spaces spanning the five (5) countries guarantee a haven for terrorists and insurgents in their criminal activities including transnational crimes. In 2007, AQIM had moved to ungovernable space in Northern Mali. It aligned with groups of militants such as *Ansar Dine,* Movement for Oneness and Jihad in West Africa. Thus, Operation Barkhane was launched with the deployment of the anti-terrorist unit, the National Gendarmerie International Group (GIGN) totalling 3,500 troops. They constitute France Counterterrorism Operation. The strategy was based on "leading from the side" or leading from the back to stabilise the region from terrorism and insurgency.

## MISCA and "Operation Sangaris" in the Central African Republic

Operation Sangaris was embarked upon by France in November 2013 with the initial deployment of 600 troops prior to the UNSC resolution 2127 of 5 December 2013. The aftermath of the UNSC Resolution 2127 was the authorisation for the deployment of the African-Led International Support Mission to the Central African Republic (MISCA). When MISCA was eventually deployed it was left to play a nominal role behind Operation Sangaris. This was like the case of AFISMA in Mali. Expected to be as harmless as butterflies, Operation Sangaris was set up to tackle contentious struggle for power between the Seleka, a Moslem militia and the anti–Baleka militias, also predominantly Christians. At the beginning of the crisis, President Francois Bozize requested France and the US to intervene to stop the impending onslaught by the Seleka militias against his government.

However, the delay from France and the USA to intervene on time led to the overthrow of President Bozize in March 2013. Michel Djotoko perceived to be representing the interest of the Seleka Rebels, fortuitously took over as the situation worsened. Amnesty International report confirmed initial causalities of 1000 and 60 deaths from both sides of the Anti-Baleka and Seleka, respectively. France later intervened as the situation was deteriorating to genocide by scaling up the deployment of troops to 1, 200. Later the number increased to 1,600 after the AU Peace and Security meeting in Paris. Both Operation Sangaris and MISCA were able to secure Bouas and Bossangoa towns though without resistance from the Seleka rebels who doubted the neutrality of France while the Anti-Baleka also doubting the disarmament process involving the Chadian forces that were operating alongside French military. The scenarios in the crisis became so bizarre that the new president, Michel Djotidia could not cope, but had to resign from office together with his Prime Minister, Nicolas Tanganye.

Like the French Operations in Mali, Operation Sangaris in CAR received support from Britain which provided C-17 travels and Germany (medical transport plane), Belgium gave out Airbus A-330 and Hercules C-130 transport plane. EU provided EUFORCA, an operational force led by the EU in April 2014 with a total of 350 personnel as a framework operation for EUROCORPS. Morocco sent in 250 soldiers under UN Integrated Pearce building Office in CAR (BINUCA). To sustain the tempo of operation, on 10 April 2014, the UNSC in a resolution set up of MINUSCA replaced MISCA. MINUSCA began operation on 15 September 2014 with troops contributed from among African countries which operated parallel with Operation Sangaris.

## Lake Chad Region: France's CT-COIN Operation in "Zone of (In) Stability"

Another area that drew France's interest was the Lake Chad region where Boko Haram insurgency in the North-eastern part of Nigeria has held sway. Except for Nigeria, countries in this axis are mostly former French colonies. They include Chad, Cameroun, and Niger. Prior to this time, the Lake Chad region has been a zone of conflict since the pre-colonial period between the Kanem-Bornu and Barguirmi empires. Exacerbated by competition for the control of the economic hub of the region because of the surging environmental migrants' insurrections began to develop (Africa Report, 2017:3). It was indeed a fortress for successive armed opposition groups during the Chadian civil wars in the late 1970s and 1980s. The Third Army ( a strand of FROLINAT) later named Popular Movement for the Liberation of Chad (MPLT) and Habre's Movement for the Defence of Democracy (MDD), established a base here and recruited some Nigerians and other from neighbouring countries into their armed groups. At the end of the Chadian crisis, some of the rebel forces fled to Nigeria and the neighbouring countries and hibernate there. In Nigeria, under its weak legal and security system they constituted themselves into armed bandits. When Boko Haram surfaced, they congregated from Cameroun, Chad, and the Central African Republic to become a reckoning force.

The Sambisa forest and the Lake Chad region became fertile grounds for ease recruits into the Boko Haram insurgency. Already Chad and Cameroun axis had the concentration of the adherents of Yusuf Mohammed, the founder who became a martyr in 2009; through listening and reading his cassettes and pamphlets in their dialects, respectively. As at the time Boko Haram turned to insurgency Chad and Cameroun had become the sect's fortresses. Both countries became affected by the attacks from Boko Haram. It became necessary for them to reinforce the efforts of Nigeria to counter the insurgents. The AU-led Multinational Joint Task Force (MNJTF) was eventually set up with the Headquarters in Ndjamena for this purpose. Each member countries within the Lake Chad region was made to contribute troops totalling 8,700. Given that most of the member states of Lake Chad Basin are Francophone, France has the latitude to extent Operation Barkhane to such countries except Nigeria. However, France has Boko Haram coordination cells in this axis with 10 dedicated French staff and their partners from Chad, Niger, and Cameroun. (Miter, 2015) One of the cells in Difa in Niger congregates other western countries like the US, Canada, France and forces the member state of the Lake Chad Basin.

## Challenges and implications of France CT-COIN operations for Africa

The challenges and implications brought about by France CT-COIN operations are like the double-edge sword piercing not only France and the western civilisation but, perhaps more importantly, affecting Africa in terms of economic deprivation, human rights abuses, and deaths, among others.

### UN, France and the dilemma of CT-COIN operations in Africa

Since the end of the post-Cold War, and in particular, after 9/11, the drive towards asymmetry warfare became a big challenge to the UN; on how to maintain its tradition of peacekeeping amidst the preponderance ravage of terrorists and insurgents. This was a big challenge when AFISMA was re-hated to become MINUSMA (using its French acronym). AFISMA was deployed to play traditional peacekeeping role in Mali but because the situation on the ground could not condone this, Mali and France moved in with Operation Serval providing counterterrorism and insurgency. This puts the United Nations in a clearly defined dilemma, on how to replace traditional peacekeeping with counterterrorism and counterinsurgency. Though being aware of this, UN Secretary-General Ban Ki-Moon was critical of AFISMA for its inability of living up to expectation. The formal accusation by Ban Ki-Moon could be a deliberate design to frustrate the efforts of ECOWAS/AU (by AFISMA) to enable France to continue to maintain its dominant interest in Africa. The failure of AFISMA was a *fait accompli* as it winded-up its parallel operation with French Operation Serval with the latter left to hold.

Unlike AFISMA that suffered logistical support, Operation Serval received all the required assistance and support from the US, Canada, the UK, and EU in terms of logistics, training, and funding. The European Union Training Mission (EUTM) offered training assistance for 5,500 troops under General Pradal, a French Commanding Officer, in Koulikoro, Mali. These were opportunities that AFISMA was not privileged. The UN Trust Fund proposed for AFISMA to address the lapses confronting it, merely raised the sum of USD 26.7 million out of USD 368 million advanced to it (*The Economist*, 2013). It was clear that AFISMA was dead on arrival in Mali. Rather than addressing the challenges of funding and logistics, the UN Secretary-General, Ban Ki-Moon was instead very apprehensive of AFISMA's performance, in terms of abuses of human rights in its operation. The lacklustre way the UN received AFISMA despite the initial approval was appalling. And yet Operation Serval which was not operating with the ambience of UN Keeping principles could conduct its operations alongside MNUSMA with robust mandate to deal decisively with the terrorists. Unfortunately, Ban Ki-Moon continued to warn of the ill-conceived and ill-equipped intervention by AFISMA which has put the operation in jeopardy. He went as far as calling on the UN Human rights monitoring team to be deployed alongside AFISMA to effectively police it (Abiodun, 2013).

AFISMA should not be blamed because the UN failed to buffer it with a robust mandate which the previous panel had recommended for future peacekeeping especially the Brahimi report. and the recent High-Level Independent Panel on United Nations Peace Operations (HIPPO) which also called for a robust mandate as a necessity suited to engage in military counterterrorism operations (HIPPO: 2015). Though in his review of HIPPO report the relent on this on the ground that though "political efforts must be backed by firm resolve, including where required, the use of force ... However, a UN Peace operation is not designed or equipped to impose political solutions through sustained use of force" (UNSG implementation Report:2015: Para 15, p.4). Yet this was not followed through in the case of the mandate giving to MNUSMA thereby creating contradictions between the legal status of the UN Charter and the reality in the mission fields. The challenge is how to integrate the prevention of violent extremism using force into the activities of the UN peace operations. (Gienanth, Hassen, & Kugel, 2015:5). This gap notwithstanding, France was left with the latitude to operate on the use of force in both Mali and CAR operations. It had a choice of deciding countries to join her in the operation. In Mali, it preferred *Chad's Forces armees tchadiennes d' intervention au Mali* (FATIM) in the fight against the terrorists. While in CAR, it co-opted Burundi contingents and others into her operational capability. The French commanders acted alone and hardly consulted AFISMA or MINUSCA Force Commanders.

## France counter operations and the context of Francafrique policy

The inability of the international community to find an acceptable resolution mechanism to African conflicts has made it possible to assume that only France has the solution. This assumption has strengthened France's Francafrique policy, hitherto becoming weak. Member states of the European Union and the United Nations Security Council now rely on France for a second opinion after the African Union, when addressing the challenges of conflicts in Africa. Nigeria no longer matters. Therefore, the operations conducted by France in Africa were seen in the light of perpetuating *Francafrique policy,* a basis for re-laundering France power and image in Africa. *Francafrique* is a neo-colonialism policy, the imperialism of a kind but coloured with an assumption of a benign effort not to neglect its former colonies; a policy that has generated tension in EU (between Italy and France) over African immigrants in Europe.

Meanwhile, in the light of this colonial policy General Francisco Soriano, the Force Commander of Sangaris Operation has said that the sacrifices of French deployment to CAR among others were a real performance that no country could match, as it has prevented the outburst of violence: "It is clear that we prevented a number of massacres" (Centrafrique 1 express, 2014). Similarly, Dominique Trianuand, former UN Chief of the Military Affairs commended France, noting that rather than criticising France "the best is to criticise those doing nothing than those acting. Equally too, the former French Prime minister Dominique de Villapoin, sees French intervention as "benevolent re-colonisation policy", as France has a duty to act, but the interdiction to act alone. How can we break the dilemma? "... if France does not intervene nobody will do anything" (*Radio France International*, 12 Feb 2014:17:12). Indeed, France might have come at the right time to assist at a critical moment, it also failed to build an African interest into the process. It dictated the operations by defining the rules of engagement, acting out a typical colonial lordship in the context of its "civilising mission" in Africa (Eads: 2014). It pursues a quick fix operation without sustaining cooperation with the local forces.

## Human rights abuses under French operations

France assumes and rightly too that her intervention in Africa to counter terrorism and insurgency was a humanitarian operation to protect civilians. As vague as the concept of humanitarian operation or protection of civilians; or even the right to protect means, their relevance can only be explained within the context of the rule of law and/or the law of armed conflict. This is important for France because France is seen in the eyes of the world as the custodian of the enlightenment age. It is expected to stand for and guarantee the liberty of its citizens and humanity in general. However, its operations in Africa have placed her on a scale that runs contrary to its ideal of liberty and freedom. There is a gulf between balancing her human rights principles (spirit of enlightenment) with how to conduct the counterinsurgency operations, especially in Africa (Staunton, 2015).

As Peter Bouckaert of Human Rights Watch noted, France underestimated the CAR crisis as it hoped that the operation would be quick in disarming the militias. It indeed had some quick fix operations in Mali and in some places in CAR. However, Operation Sangaris failed to intervene in PK 13 Bangui where there was massive human rights abuse, contradicting its position and responsibility not to intervene in any conflict but to prevent massacre without taking sides. The PK13 massacre was not prevented. The curiosity here is how is it possible to prevent a massacre without intervening in a conflict? Intervening in a conflict is not synonymous with taking a side. Obviously one can intervene by taking side if it chooses to do so. If it fails to intervene for the purpose of not taking sides, it has in principle taken a side. The docility of the French troops was noticed in most cases when they never left their armoured vehicles and only did so in a safe populated neighbourhood to conduct reports and not to counter the operations by both sides of the militias (Liberation, 2014:105). There were instances that troops and contingents from CAR, Rwanda, Burundi, Congo, and Chad (not France forces) were the ones that save people faced with imminent threats. Thus, as Laurent Correau and Olivier Fourt from the Radio France International (RFI) noted, the outcome of Operation Sangaris was "a bitter-sweet". Accordingly, France provided stabilisation in Bangui and Bouar, secured the supply routes between Cameroun and Nagui but failed to manage to really disarm the Seleka and the anti-Baleka groups. The initial disarmament operation targeted mostly at Selake led to a wave of popular violence against the defenceless Muslims.

Meanwhile, Operation Sangaris received the most damaging UN Report on the allegation of sexual abuses of young children perpetrated by French forces in the CAR's IDP. Accordingly, in April 2015 French troops in the IDP abused and exploited children by raping them and getting them involved in sodomy in exchange for food. Further allegations were reported of 100 cases against the French commander in March 2016. He was accused of tying up 4 undressed girls in a camp and forced them to have sex with dogs in 2014 before they were given 5,000 CA France (the equivalent of the sum British 6 pounds) (South, 2016). Though the evidence was overwhelming enough neither the French authority nor the UN brought the accused to stand trial. In an interview with a senior military Staff Officer in the CAR Armed Forces who was in Nigeria for special assignments, he said "France ambushed the report from the UN, promising to take it up under French law in Paris. Yet nothing has been heard since then" (Interview in Abuja, July 2017). Curiously, the issue actually seems to have been buried as "the sources have passed the details".

## The "war economy" and economic exploitation

The war against terrorism/insurgency in Africa has been of economic benefits to France. France economy has been in doldrums found leeway in counterterrorism and counterinsurgency to tighten its grips on the continent. This is important to avoid the penetration of China, India, and Brazil into Africa to displace her economic interests. In most of the areas, France was involved with CT-COIN in Africa has revitalised its economic growth and development at home. For instance, France had wanted the independence of the state of Azaward where the insurgents had taken control, with the hope that it could control the resources once the area breaks away from greater Mali. The official France 24 television made several reports to the effect that France had a grip- hand on the rebels in the northern Azaward region. However, in "…a volte-face France turned its support to the government in Bamako. The [former] French President Francois Hollandes sold the story of how France's interest was about stopping the rebels in West Africa before they become a threat to Europe (Richard, 2017:44). It is not clear what brought about this *volte face* other than the fact that either way her economic and political interests could still play out favourably. Similarly, the Sahel G5 countries comprising Chad, Mauritania, Niger, and Burkina Faso have continued to maintain strong political and economic ties with France. In its new Defence Strategy France stressed the importance of the new European neighbourhood ranging from Mauritania to the Horn of Africa. This ungovernable zone can only be managed by France if Africans lack the capacity to control their territories and resources. Therefore, France's interest has never been exclusively about countering terrorism as it has reopened 'African Cell in the Elysee Palace, Paris, where *Francafrique* policy is initiated'. This has come up despite an earlier decision by both Presidents Sarkozy and Holland to end the *Francafrique* policy. Most importantly the removal of Ghadafi was linked to the drive for oil resources in the North African region by the West, especially France, US, and the UK. In the Niger Republic, Areva, a French mining company has invested in the mining of uranium, investing the sum of 136 million dollars (100 pounds sterling). In the Lake Chad regional conflict, France initially propelled support for Boko Haram when some supplies were allegedly dropped from the air to the insurgents across Nigeria borders with Cameroun. In 2015, five French nationals were apprehended in Cameroun for fighting for Boko Haram. They were handed over to France. Since then no further information has been heard about their trials. France has not only launched the Sahel Force it has equally planned to invest 42 million euro (47 million dollars between 2017 and 2022 for the Sahel countries (Chad, Niger, Burkina Faso, Mali, and Mauritania) in order to tackle the vulnerability of the area to an insurgency, and possibly sustain its economic interest. In 2013, it launched its new policy on Africa "A Partnership for the Future" which it intends to develop African resources and engage in keen competitions with other rivals like China (Eads, 2014). It hopes to use the partnership to generate 200 000 jobs in France within the five years it was launched but no clear indication of how Africa will also benefit from this. This has become too important to France because it feared, Gabon for instance (under President Bongo) may still nurse the ambition to take over Elf the drilling of its oil fields and to replace it with America oil companies. Similarly, Niger under Mamadou Tandhja had also threatened to hand over the uranium mining fields to the Chinese (Aljazeera, 2014, Associate Press, 2017).

## Conclusion

This Chapter presents France as fitting the designation of the "gendarme of Africa". Its new Defence Policy released in 2013, at the peak of its counter operations in Africa, arrogates to itself the obligation of securing Africa. It is the only country with the political and military will to pay the sacrifice of protecting the interest of western civilisation on the African continent. Hence, a "coalition of unwilling" countries like the US, Canada, and the UK are no longer ready to put their boots on the ground in Africa. However, this is also deliberate as it helps

France to lubricate its *Francafrique policy*, from which it derives its economic interest in Africa. This caveat presumably helps the appeal that France is also defending western civilisation in taking the fights against terrorists and insurgents to their base in Africa. By implications, therefore, France has gained authorisation from the UNSC to conduct self-glorifying counter operations in Africa, as well as racking in funds and logistic supports from the coalition of unwilling countries. Thus, France further gained the leverage to conduct a solo operation in Africa at will, and with reckless abandon. This is unfortunately detrimental to African peace-keeping forces that have been denied the collaborative role they should have played in joint counter operations.

The cherished excuse in the western world that African troops lack capacity in terms of equipment, logistics, intelligence, and interoperability is indeed untenable. The same African troops facing these accusations were trained by France and other western powers; for the purpose of conducting both asymmetry and symmetry warfare. Then how could it have been impossible for them not having the prerequisite capacity to use their training? Could it not have been possible to provide African troops with similar equipment and capacity just as France was supported? Therefore, with the continuing neglect of African troops in various counter operations in Africa, France may end up with armada Africa. There might be a likelihood of backlash of insecurity in Africa that it may no longer sustain in some future counter operations. If this happens, her image would have been soiled alongside the United Nations that tacitly kept mute over France's over-killed operations and condoning the allegations of sexual and human rights abuses by her troops in African missions. Indeed, the success of France's operations in Mali, CAR and Lake Chad/Sahel region including the Maghreb remain a pyrrhic victory until they are followed-up with massive "marshal plan" of stabilisation and development.

## References

Abiodun, J. O. (2013). The African Union and the Conflict in Mali: Extra Influence and the limitation of a Regional Actor. Online: www.lidenwood.edu/file/reserves/106–120pdf, accessed 3 June 2017.

Africa Report. (2013). Fighting Boko Haram in Chad. *Beyond Military Measures International Crisis Group*, *246*(3), 1–37, 8 March 2017.

Africa Report. (2017). Fighting Boko Haram in Chad. *Beyond Military Measures International Crisis Group*, *246*(3), 1–37, 8 March.

Aljazeera. (2014). *The French African Connection*, 7 April.

Associate Press. (2017). *Macron in Mali: France will be 'uncompromising' in fight against terrorists*, 19 May.

Associate Press. (2017). *France's Macron: Fighting Terrorism abroad is top Priority* August 29.

Centrafrique: Une Performance don'tpeud'armees Seraint Capables l express 5 Feb (2014).

Conor, G. (2016). How is France fighting militant Islamism in Africa *Newsweek*, Oct 20 www.newsweek.com, accessed 15 June 2017.

Conor, G. (2016) Peace keeping in Mali: the UN most dangerous mission *Newsweek*.

Chergui, S. (2015). Counterterrorism requires multidimensional approach. *African Defence Forum*, 8, Quarter 2.

Dall'Armellina, V. (2014). France Enacts Controversial New Anti Jihadist Law, Online www.news.vice.com/article/france-enact-controversial-new–anti- jihadist -law, accessed 29 Sept 2017.

Eads, B. (2014). France is slowly reclaiming its old African Empire *Newsweek*, 30 October. www.newsweeek.com.

The Economist. (2013). A hopeful continent. Available https://www.economist.com/special-report/2013/03/02/a-hopeful-continent, accessed on 16 June 2019.

France Diplomatic. (2017). Terrorism. Available www.diplomatie.gouv.fr/en/french, accessed 29 September 2017 at 03.01hours.

Gienanth, T. V., Hassen, W., & Kugel, A. (2015). *Making Reform Reality-Enabling Change for the United Nations Peace Operations* ZIF Background Paper.

Griffin. (2015). Operation Barkhane and Boko Haram: French Counterterrorism and military cooperation in the Sahel Trends Research and Advisory, Abu Dhabi, UAE. www.tandfonline.com>doi>abs.

Gowan, R. (2017). Bordering on Crisis: Europe Africa and New Approaches to Crisis Management European Council on Foreign Relations, *Policy Brief.* European Council on Foreign Relations. www.ecfr.cu.

*Interview with a senior officer of the CAR Armed Forces in Abuja*, 20, July 2017.

John, K. (2017). Towards UN counter terrorism operations. *Third World Quarterly, 38*(6), 1215. http://dx.doi.org/10/.1080 p.1219.

Karlsrude, J. (2017). Towards UN counterterrorism operations? *Third World Quarterly, 28*(6), 1215–1231.

Kilcullen, D. J. (2006). *Three Pillars of Counterinsurgency, US Government Conference*, Washington DC, 28 September 2006:2.

Kilcullen, D. J. (2007). *Two Schools of Classical counterinsurgency*. SWBlog, 27 January 2007.

Lacey, M. (2010). *After Battle in Capital, Chad Threatens to expel Sudanese. The New York Times.* nytimes.com/2006/04.

Liberation. (2014). Centrafrique; *Less Francaisnequitlantpass Solventleersblindes*. 20 Jan.

Lohmann, A. (2011). *Who Owns the Sahara*, Friedrich Ebert Stiftung, and Abuja.

Makinda, S. M. (2003). Global governance and terrorism. *Global Change, 15*(1), 43–57, Feb 2003.

Miter, S. (2015). The Widening War Against Boko Haram. *Daily Beast.* thedailybeast.com/the-widening-war-against-boko-haram/. accessed 11 August 2017.

Republic of France MInistry of Defence. (1994). France Defence Policy, Paris, Ministry of Defence.

Richard, Murphy. (2017). Is oil the true ideology of Boko Haram. *Daily Trust, Abuja, 44*, August, 8.

Shafer, M. (1988). *Deadly paradigm: The failure of US counterinsurgency policy* p. 154. Princeton Univ. Press.

South, F. (2016). French Anti-Terror Efforts in Africa's Sahel Region. *Global Research.ca/French*, April 1.

Staunton. (2015). *France, Cradle of Liberty, struggle to balance anti-terrorism laws and rights*. Australia: The University of Queensland, May 7.

Jacques, A. (1958). Vérités sur 'l' Affaire Algeriene RDN, 26 Jan: 10.

Yoroms, G. (2013). *Terrorism and Regional security in West Africa: The menace of Boko Haram and Challenges for Political Stability in Geo- Strategic Zone of Sahel –West Africa*. Being a paper presented at the *West African Network on Democratic Governance (WANSED)*, Niamey, Niger, 23–24 April.

Yoroms, G. J. (2015). France Counter terrorism/insurgency against Boko Haram in Nigeria: From Cautious Diplomacy to Proactive Foreign and Defence Policy. Paper presented at the *Department of Political Science Seminar*, Bingham University, Karu, Nigeria, May.

# 19

# China's counterterrorism and counterinsurgency strategy in Africa

*Usman A. Tar and Sulaiman Saidu Abubakar*

## Introduction

This chapter examines the nature and scope of China's strategic interest in Africa, regarding China's Counterterrorism and Counterinsurgency (CT-COIN) initiatives in the continent. CT-COIN is a novel item on Sino-African relations. The issues of security and counterterrorism were not given so much prominence in Sino-African relations until recently; trade and investment, exports and imports, mining, agriculture, political cooperation, cultural exchanges, cooperation in other areas among others were always given more priority.

The chapter argues that security issues, counterinsurgency and counterterrorism are new items on the Sino-African relations; that in trying to achieve its CT-COIN in Africa, China does not intend to unilaterally send boots on the ground instead Beijing wants to use the UN Security Council as the primary vehicle to achieve its CT-COIN initiatives in Africa. Thus, this informs China's recent growing participation in UN peace support operations in the continent. The chapter further highlights the challenges of China's CT-COIN initiatives in Africa. The chapter concludes that China was caught up in the recent spate of terrorism, insurgency, piracy and other crimes in the continent hence left without many choices but to increase its support to the continent's stability, peace and security and that China is not mainly in Africa to secure the continent or engage in counterterrorism or counterinsurgency initiatives but rather to pursue its national interest and explore the continent's natural resources.

The Chapter is divided into seven parts. After the introduction, Section 2 deals with China's Counterterrorism and Counterinsurgency Initiatives in Africa. Section 3 deals with China's Grand Strategy for Africa: the Forum on China-Africa Cooperation (FOCAC). Section 4 deals with China's Military Co-operation with the African States, the African Union (AU), and Regional Economic Co-operations (RECs). Section 5 deals with Countering Violent Extremism through Peacekeeping: China's Participation in Peace Support Operations in Africa. Section 6 treats Challenges to China's CT-COIN Drive in Africa, and Section 7 gives the conclusion.

## Background to Sino-African Relations in the 21st century

Sino-African relations can be traced as far back as 15th century, when a Chinese admiral, Zheng He led some 300 ships across the world. "Although He's celebrated expeditions between 1405 and 1423 took him as far as the eastern coast of Africa, China had little to do with Africa for the next 500 years" (Foerstel, 2008:10–11). Chibundu (2000:1–8) has stated that a brief contact took place between China and Africa hundreds of years ago in past centuries. He noted that both countries fought feudalism, imperialism, and colonialism before independence. In the same vein, Anshan (2005:59), (a Chinese professor at the School of International Studies, Peking University) argued that "China had a long contact of history with Africa. There was a cultural exchange between China and Egypt as early as the Han Dynasty (206BCE-220CE)". He further noted that:

> Du Han, a Chinese in the Tang Dynasty (C.E 618–907) visited Africa in the eighth century and is probably the first Chinese to have left a written record about Africa. The great African traveller of Yuan Dynasty (C.E 1271–1368), Ibn Batutta, visited China in the fourteenth century and left a vivid description of a metropolitan life. A Chinese fleet led by Zhen He visited East African coast several times during the fifteenth century. Interestingly enough, African animals, the zebra, and the giraffe, appeared in Chinese classics of the Ming Dynasty (1368–1644), and archaeological discoveries have also suggested early contact between China and Africa. Chinese archaeologists found a terra-cotta black figure in the tomb of "Madame Pie" of the Tang Dynasty. Chinese porcelains produced from the Tang to the Ming Dynasties have been found in many parts of East Africa, and five pieces of Tang currencies were discovered in Africa as well. From the eighteenth century on, more and more contacts existed between China and Africa (Anshan, 2005:59).

During the epoch of 1960s, 70s and even 80s, many African countries got their political independence, a successful period for African nationalists. Within a short span of the 1960s, 19 African countries joined the UN General Assembly providing Africans with the opportunity to establish a diplomatic presence in the UN (and other countries), as well as the leverage to decide on global affairs. The Chinese realised the potentials of Africa incredibly early in the new dawn of political independence in the continent. This was at a time when European interest was regressing as European colonial powers were forced to return power to indigenous African nationalists. While the Europeans were packing out of Africa, the then Chinese Premier-Zhou Enlai- visited Africa from December 1963 to June 1965, three times including eleven African countries. No doubt the foundation of modern-day Sino-African Relations was laid during this period. It is worth noting that the end of World War II fast-tracked the political independence of many countries under colonial domination in Asia and Africa. Also, the struggle for political autonomy in India led by Mahatma Gandhi motivated many nationalists across Africa to struggle harder for independence, and to forge South-South relations (Tar & Abubakar, 2016).

In 1955, a conference of newly independent countries of Asia and Africa was organised in Bandung-Indonesia, to foster Afro-Asia economic and cultural cooperation and to bring about political independence from the colonialists. Furthermore, countries in attendance agreed on the Non-Aligned policy, not to support either the West or the East in the Cold War struggle. China was instrumental to some of the far-reaching decisions taken at the Conference and after that: "Chinese Premier Zhou Enlai played a particularly strong role in the conference and launched China's first foray into international politics. The first modern-day Sino-African diplomatic ties were established with Egypt in 1956; within ten years, China had solidified relations with more than a dozen African countries" (Foerstel, 2008:11).

The 1960s and 70s was the era Africa had international recognition and the establishment of the Organisation of African Unity (OAU) now the African Union (AU). Some few years after the colonisers departed Africa, the continent was confronted with many challenges; ethnic violence erupted in most parts of the continent. There were also coups and counter military coups across Africa. From Congo Kinshasa (1965), Algeria (1965), Nigeria (1966), Ghana (1966), Togo (1967), Mali (1968), and Libya (1969), the military took over political power, (Ngwane, 2006). This trend continued into the 70s and 80s, for instance, there was a military coup in Uganda (1971) by Idi Amin, Ethiopia (1974) by Colonel Mengistu Haile Mariam, Nigeria (1975) by General Murtala Muhammad, and in Ghana in 1979 by Flight-Lieutenant Jerry Rawlings. In the 1980s, a plethora of military coups was staged in Liberia in 1980 by Master-Sargent K. Doe; Ghana in 1981; Nigeria in 1983 and 1986 by Major-General Muhammadu Buhari; and General Ibrahim Babangida respectively; Burkina Faso in 1983 by Captain Thomas Sankara; Guinea in 1984 by Colonel Lansana Conte; and Uganda in 1986 by Yoweri Museveni. Some of the coups were supported either by the West or the East to promote the ideology of Capitalism or Socialism in the height of the Cold War era.

Ethnic violence, corruption and mismanagement of state resources pervaded most states in Africa. By 1986 Africa's foreign debt from the West had reached $162 billion, and interest payments alone were eating up two-thirds of all the money the continent received in foreign aid (Foerstel, 2008:14–15). By the end of the 1980s, African states got disenchanted with the Western financial aid and the strings attached to them. African leaders turned to China for financial aid, "many African leaders felt China could offer an alternative model in which bread comes before the freedom to vote" (Obiorah, 2007:44).

During the 1970s and 1980s, China was busy consolidating her economic diplomacy and political adventure in Africa. For instance, China established diplomatic relations with Nigeria in 1971; she completed the construction of Tazara Railway in 1975; in 1983 the Sino-Moroccan Cooperation was established; in 1995 China National Petroleum Cooperation (CNCP) obtained oil exploration and production rights, to mention but just a few (Ekenedirichukwu, 2007). Those deals formed the fulcrum for China's eventual inroad into other parts of the continent. In 1989, the Soviet Union collapsed, unceremoniously. This created a substantial ideological gap in Africa as many Afro-Marxist Regimes (such as Benin Republic, Angola, Mozambique, Tanzania, etc.) were suddenly "orphaned" by the untimely demise of the Socialist Bloc and its exit from the global power equation. However, China had no interest in exporting its Communist ideology to Africa. China was only interested in economic gains in Africa. The only major ideology China promoted in Africa was the fight against colonialism and imperialism.

The 21st century brought with it so many events and issues that altered the global political configuration. For instance, China emerged as a superpower, Russia re-emerged in international politics, and newly industrialised countries of Asia such as Malaysia, Indonesia, and South Korea emerged as emerging economic powers. The 21st Century provided both "opportunities" and "challenges" for China's emergence as a global power. One of these opportunities is that China's emergence as a global superpower has altered the supremacy of the Euro-Americans on the worldwide scene and one of the challenges could be the ability of China to maintain its new status in world politics.

The 21st century downed when China was under the dynamic leadership of former President Jiang Zemin who ruled from 1993–2003. President Zemin not only spearheaded a new vista of China's expansion across the world but perhaps more importantly committed sufficient Chinese investment in Africa; this was taking place at a time when Europe and America had beat a strategic retreat from the continent. President Zemin organised a conference in Beijing to foster economic, social, cultural, and political ties between Beijing and Africa. This conference was held from 10 to 12 October 2000. It attracted some 80 ministers from China and 44 African states and representatives of 17 regional and international organisations and leaders from the business community of China and Africa. This was the first ministerial conference of the Forum on China-Africa Cooperation (FOCAC); it was at this conference that China announced debt cancellation to heavily indebted developing African countries and her long term plan in her engagement with Africa. In other words, the foundation for the 21st Century Sino-African Relations was laid down with the establishment of FOCAC as a long-term strategic forum for the engagement between China and Africa. The FOCAC meeting was to be held after every three years since 2000. This is a clear indication of China's willingness to enter a medium and long term diplomatic and economic relations with Africa.

Since 2000, China has consistently been spreading its influence across Africa. China has spent so hugely on infrastructures in the continent—such as roads, railways, airports, stadiums, housing, electricity, dams, and schools, and imported from the continent natural commodities such as crude oil, diamond, timber, and cotton among others.

China's growing presence in Africa is greeted with mixed reactions, from ordinary people, bureaucrats, politicians, civil society to academics. Some scholars favour the extreme view by the Euro-America of China as a rival and newest coloniser in the continent; others see China as a legitimate competitor against Europe and America; while to others, China gives the continent a second chance and a new model for development and some even talk of China as a soft colonial power in the continent. African leaders are attracted by China's "no-strings-attached approach" and "non-interference" policies in its relations with African countries. This is a fundamental deviation from the Western-style in which Africans were treated as inferior partners and clueless community that receives coaching in economic finesse and political gerrymandering from civilised Western countries and bilateral agencies.

African leaders have clearly expressed complacent posture and a deep sense of enthusiasm in "doing business" with China and provided sufficient reasons for their acquiescence. For example, the former President of Senegal, Mr Abdoulaye Wade noted that:

China's approach to our [Africa's] needs is simply better adapted than the slow and sometimes patronising post-colonial approach of European investors, donor organisation and non-governmental organisations. In fact, the Chinese model for stimulating rapid economic development has much to teach Africa (*Financial Times*, 2008: 6).

Mr Wade supported the "efficiency" of the Chinese compared to the "red-tapism" and "bureaucratic delays" of Western technocrats and lending agencies: "I have found that a contract that would take five years to discuss, negotiate and sign with the World Bank takes three months when we have dealt with Chinese authorities". Similarly, Sahr Johnny, former Sierra Leone's Ambassador to Beijing observed thus: "The Chinese are doing more than the G-8 to make poverty history, if a G-8 country had wanted to rebuild the stadium, we would still be holding meetings. The Chinese just come and do it; they do not hold meetings about environmental impact assessment, human rights, bad governance and good governance" (Beeston, 2006:42).

Even African leaders considered by European as heads of "rogue states" were not left out in trooping to China for new friendship, a testimony of Chinese capacity to deal with every African leader with no string attached. An example of Africa's rogue leader doing business with the Chinese is President Robert Mugabe of Zimbabwe who had experienced (and remarkably withstood) decades of debilitating bashing from Western powers for his shoddy democratic credentials and destructive land policy in his country. President Mugabe had complementary and patronising words about the Chinese: "China is opening itself up to Africa, coming with assistance; we have nothing to lose but our imperialist chains" (Watts, 2006: 24).

## China's counterterrorism and counterinsurgency initiatives in Africa

Speaking at the United Nations in January 2013, the then Chinese Vice Foreign Minister, Cui Tiankai, clearly articulated China's international counterterrorism cooperation:

> China fully respects the sovereignty and territorial integrity of the countries that are combatting terrorism, China seeks to leverage the UN and the Security Council as the main channel of cooperation and welcomes the establishment of the UN Counterterrorism Centre, China believes in a comprehensive approach that addresses the root causes as well as the symptoms of terrorism, and that there should be no double standard; all terrorist organizations including the East Turkistan Islamic Movement (ETIM), a terrorist group linked to Xinjiang must be condemned and defeated (Shinn, 2013).

As a rising global power, China is continuously challenged by the increase in global terrorism, both at home and abroad. Chinese are now facing increasing risk to personal security similar to those faced by Europeans and Americans: for instance, in 2015 Fan Jinghui—a Chinese—was kidnapped and killed by ISIS in Syria (Wu, 2015); a Chinese was also among the victims of the Paris-November-13, 2015 attacks. These incidents sent shivers amongst Chinese expatriates and diplomats across the world. Threats from terrorism and insurgency against China's interests and citizens abroad have forced China to do a re-think on its legendary "non-interference" policy. Thus, in December 2015, China's top legislature passed counterterrorism legislation which allows Beijing to "send personnel outside the border to carry out anti-terror activities" when the "relevant country" agrees, (Xinhua News, 2015). Of course, this is a major shift from China's policy of not "sending boots on the ground". China intends to use the UN and its permanent seat in the UN Security Council as the primary vehicle to achieve its counterterrorism initiatives abroad. It is evident that this new shift in China's policy informed her increased roles in the UN Peace Support Operations (PSOs), especially in Africa where she has over 2,500 troops serving under the UN PSOs in Mali and South Sudan. In addition, China's warships are engaged in anti-piracy operations in the Gulf of Aden, and off the coast of Somalia, China is also building a naval base in Djibouti.

The recent rise in terrorism and insurgency in Africa has threatened not only the continent but also the international community. From *Al-Shabab* in Somalia to ISIS in Libya, from al-Qaeda in the Islamic Maghreb to Boko Haram in West Africa – mainly, North Eastern Nigeria, Cameroon, Chad and Niger – it is apparent that the entire continent is enmeshed in insecurity. As one of the countries with the most extensive economic interests and investments in the continent, China has expressed its worries on the prevalent insecurity in the continent. China is beginning to endure most of terrorism in Africa. For instance, in 2015, three Chinese executives from the state-owned China Railway Construction Corporation were among the dead after the attack by the terrorist group – *Al–Murabitoun* – on the Radisson Blu Hotel in Mali's capital of Bamako, (Jackson, 2015), In 2014, ten Chinese workers were among 27 people held captive by Boko Haram in Northern Cameroon (Nzouankeu, 2014), and in 2012, 25 Chinese were kidnapped in Egypt, and within the same period another 29 Chinese were seized by rebels in Sudan (Wee, 2012). As a result, China has stepped up its CT-COIN drive on the continent, but China's CT-COIN intervention is characteristic of China's cautious foreign policy on the continent. In addition, China trades with care in terms of intervening in the internal affairs of African countries, even on matters relating to violent terrorisms.

China's Counterterrorism and Counterinsurgency initiatives in Africa shall be discussed under the following themes: China's Grand Strategy for Africa: the Forum on China-Africa Cooperation (FOCAC), the AU and RECs in the continent; and Countering Violent Extremism through Peacekeeping: China's Participation in Peace Support Operations in Africa.

## China's grand strategy for Africa: the Forum on China-Africa Cooperation (FOCAC)

FOCAC was established in 2000 to foster cooperation between China and Africa. Its meetings were to be held after every three years. China's policy on the continent is always declared and reviewed in this forum. As early as the 1st ministerial conference of FOCAC, China and Africa agreed to "work together to improve co-operation in the fight against terrorism to eliminate this phenomenon in all its forms and manifestations" (FOCAC Archives, 2009); however, China's counterterrorism initiatives in the continent at as then did not go beyond this declaration.

The 2nd ministerial conference was held in Addis Ababa, the capital of Ethiopia in2003. Here, China pledged to "support Africa's efforts to prevent and combat terrorism, including its adoption of a counterterrorism convention and the establishment of a centre of studies and research on terrorism in Algiers", China also agreed to strengthen further its cooperation with Africa "in combating terrorism under the auspices of the United Nations and at other international fora", (FOCAC Archives, 2009). China and Africa observed that terrorism threatens the peace and security of all countries and, therefore, must be fought through close and practical cooperation.

The 3rd ministerial conference was held in Beijing in 2006. At this conference, China stated that it supports "the United Nations and UN Security Council in playing a leading role in the international campaign against terrorism and in helping African countries improve their counterterrorism capability". Also, China noted with pleasure "the entry into force of the AU Convention on the Prevention and Combating of Terrorism and the establishment of the African Centre for the Study and Research on Terrorism, and will explore ways of counterterrorism cooperation with African countries" (FOCAC Archives, 2009).

The 4th ministerial conference was held in Sharm El Sheikh, Egypt, in 2009. In this conference, China's counterterrorism commitment to Africa was not too far from that of the 2006 conference. It was more of a reaffirmation of the promise in the previous discussion. It states that:

> The international community should make every effort to combat terrorism in accordance with the Charter of the United Nations and other universally recognized international law and norms governing international relations. The two sides [referring to China and Africa] will strengthen counterterrorism cooperation in order to safeguard their own national security and promote new progress in international counterterrorism cooperation (FOCAC Archives, 2009).

The 5th ministerial conference was held in Beijing, 2012. Here, apart from the usual commitment of strengthening communication and cooperation on fighting all forms of terrorism and the support of the United Nations and its Security Council in playing a leading role in international counterterrorism cooperation, China and Africa pledged to take "a holistic approach [in] addressing both the symptoms and root causes of terrorism, and will strive for new progress in international cooperation against terrorism" (FOCAC Archives, 2012).

The 6th ministerial conference was held in Johannesburg, South Africa, 2015. In this conference, China elaborately stated its support to Africa, the AU and the Regional Economic Co-operations (RECs) in their roles in solving peace and security challenges in the continent and its continuous support for African solutions to African challenges without external interference. Thus, "[t]he Chinese side [will] continue to support the African Union, its Regional Economic Communities and other African sub-regional institutions that play a leading role in coordinating and solving issues of peace and security in Africa and further continues to support and advocate for African solutions to African challenges without interference from outside the continent" (FOCAC Archives, 2015).

China has offered to provide "the AU with US$60 million of free military assistance over the next three years, support the operationalisation of the African Peace and Security Architecture, including the operationalisation of the African Capacity for the Immediate Response to Crisis and the African Standby Force" (FOCAC Archives, 2015). China and Africa pledged to "maintain the momentum of mutual visits by the defence and military leaders, continue to deepen exchanges on technologies and expand personnel training and joint training and exercises" (FOCAC Archives, 2015). China and Africa are to:

> strengthen information and intelligence exchanges and experience sharing on security, and will share this information timeously to support mutual efforts in the prevention and fight against terrorism, in particular its symptoms and underlying causes... enhance cooperation in preventing and combatting the illegal trafficking of humans, fauna and flora products, marine products, narcotics, psychotropic substances and precursor chemicals (FOCAC Archives, 2015).

China and Africa resolved to "continue to support the United Nations (UN) in its efforts to play a constructive role in helping resolve regional conflicts in Africa and will intensify communication and coordination with the UN Security Council" (FOCAC Archives, 2015). China reaffirmed that it would "continue to take an active part in UN peacekeeping missions in Africa, offer the African side support on peacekeeping training and intensify communication and coordination with Africa in the UN Security Council, in adherence to UN Security Council Resolution 2033 that recognises the importance of an enhanced relationship between the United Nations and the African Union, as well as a strengthened capacity of regional and sub-regional organisations, in particular the African Union, in conflict prevention and crisis management, and post-conflict stabilisation" (FOCAC Archives, 2015).

Furthermore, China and Africa pledged to:

> Strengthen cooperation on safeguarding the security of shipping routes in the waters concerned and peace and stability in the region [that is, the Gulf of Aden, the Gulf of Guinea and waters off the coast of Somalia]. In this regard, the two sides agree that emphasis should also be placed by the international community on addressing the root causes of piracy, namely poverty, underdevelopment, and illegal fishing (FOCAC Archives, 2015).

The 7th ministerial conference was held in Beijing. It was the last FOCAC ministerial conference. In comparison to all the previous conferences held, counterterrorism and security got more attention at this conference. The 2018 Beijing FOCAC conference lasted between 3–4 September, with the theme: "China and Africa: toward an even stronger community with a shared future through win-win cooperation" it had 53 out of the 54 African countries in attendance. Xi made a unique point of welcoming three new members to the 2018 FOCAC summit: the Gambia, Sao Tome and Principe, and Burkina Faso. All three had severed ties with Taiwan and established diplomatic relations with China since the 2015 summit – leaving eSwatini (formerly Swaziland) as the only African country still recognising Taiwan (Tiezzi, 2018).

President Xi Jinping hailed the conference as a success as Beijing partnered with Africa to build up "a community of shared destiny." He committed $60 billion to assist Africa or to support the implementation of his flagship Belt and Road Initiative on the continent. Among the commitments for the $60 billion China has earmarked are $15 billion for grants and no-cost or low-cost loans; $10 billion for a special Sino-African fund; and $5 billion for supporting African exports to China. But there is one notable change, with the allocation of $5 billion to support African exports to China. True, it is only 8% of the total. That ratio reflects Beijing's priorities as regards assistance to African countries to build sustainable economic capacities, such as has often been the focus of Western and Japanese development funding (Tsang, 2018).

On Sino-Africa security relations, President Xi stated that "let us build a China-Africa community with a shared future that enjoys common security... China champions a new vision of security featuring common, comprehensive, cooperative and sustainable security. We firmly support African countries and the African Union as well as other regional organisations in Africa in solving African issues in the African way, and we support the African initiative of 'Silence the Guns in Africa'. China is ready to play a constructive role in promoting peace and stability in Africa and will support African countries to strengthen their independent capacity for safeguarding stability and peace" (Xinhuanet, 2018).

Furthermore, he added "we will launch a peace and security initiative. China decided to set up a China-Africa peace and security fund to boost our cooperation on peace, security, peacekeeping, and law and order. China will continue to provide military aid to the AU and will support countries in the Sahel region and those bordering the Gulf of Aden and the Gulf of Guinea in upholding security and combating terrorism in their regions. A China-Africa peace and security forum will be established as a platform for conducting more exchanges in this area. Fifty security assistance programs will be launched to advance China-Africa cooperation under the Belt and Road Initiative, and in areas of law and order, UN peacekeeping missions, fighting piracy and combating terrorism" (Xinhuanet, 2018).

The issues of security and counterterrorism were not given so much prominence in Sino-African relations until recently; trade and investment, exports and imports, mining, agriculture, political cooperation, cultural exchanges, cooperation in other areas among others are always given more priority, "compared to sections on economic relations, these commitments [referring to China's commitments to Africa's peace and security] are brief, ambiguous in detail and appear to be somewhat rhetorical" (Alden, 2011:140). This is evident in the previous FOCAC conferences, for instance, from the 1st ministerial conference of FOCAC to the 5th conference, China's counterterrorism initiatives in Africa were not clearly stated. However, as seen in the 6th and 7th FOCAC conferences, China is beginning to take proactive measures in its counterterrorism initiatives in Africa. Subsequent conferences may articulate, in clearer terms, the scope, direction and strategies for China's CT-COIN policy in Africa. It is worthy of note, however, that China's nascent strategic posture in Africa may not deviate from China's legendary approach of "cautious diplomacy": it would not be surprising if China invests more in "soft military cooperation" – for instance, intelligence, training, capacity-building, and

*Table 19.1* Forum on China-Africa Cooperation Ministerial Conferences

| Year | Venue | Conference Outcome |
|------|-------|--------------------|
| 2000 | Beijing, China | Beijing Declaration of FOCAC Programme for China-Africa Cooperation in Economic and Social development |
| 2003 | Addis Ababa, Ethiopia | Addis Ababa Action Plan (2004–2006) |
| 2006 | Beijing, China | Beijing Declaration Beijing Action Plan (2006–2008) |
| 2009 | Sharm El Sheikh, Egypt | Declaration of Sharm El Sheik Sharm El Sheik Action Plan (2010–2012) |
| 2012 | Beijing, China | Beijing Declaration Beijing Action Plan (2013–2015) |
| 2015 | Johannesburg, South Africa | Johannesburg Action Plan (2016–2018) |
| 2018 | Beijing, China | China and Africa: Toward An Even Stronger Community with a Shared Future through Win-win Cooperation |

*Source:* Developed by the Authors, 2018

information and communication technology (ICT) – as opposed to hard-line military action or "putting boots on the ground". In the short and medium terms, China is poised to "speak with Africans" before taking any action on CT-COIN. The following section discusses the nature and scope of Sino-African defence cooperation, particularly China bilateral relations with specific states, and its multilateral relations with the AU and RECs.

## China's military co-operation with African States, the AU and RECs

As part of its counterterrorism and counterinsurgency initiatives in Africa, China is providing military aid, training, equipment donations, education programmes, grants and in many occasions has established bilateral military ties with most African countries that it has diplomatic relations. In 2015, China was the second-largest supplier of military weapons to sub-Saharan Africa after Russia, accounting for about 22% of arms transfers to the continent (Fleurant et al., 2015). Thus, in 2001 China granted Nigeria 1 million US Dollar to upgrade its military facilities (Shinn, 2008:167), in 2005 after the Liberian defence minister visited China, it was announced that the Chinese government would pledge 600,000 US Dollar for the capacity building of the Liberian military (FOCAC website, 2005), Ghana's government got a loan of 30 million US Dollar from China's Export Import Bank to "acquire military equipment and build a dedicated communications system for the police, armed forces, prison services and other security agencies" (Shinn, 2008:167), in 2006 Angola "announced the creation of an elite tactical and operational support unit, with 6 million US Dollar in financing from China for the unit's training centre" (Shinn, 2008: 165), in 2010 China agreed to donate 1.5 million US Dollar to Mauritania to buy military engineering equipment (Voice of America, 2010), in 2012, China pledged $2.4 million for training and equipping the Ugandan People's Defence Forces, in 2013, China donated $2.6 million worth of security communications equipment to Kenya (Shinn, 2013), and a Chinese company—Xing, Xing Corporation, in collaboration with the Chinese Ministry of National Defence—constructed a barracks at the cost of 5.5 million US Dollar by China to the Liberian army (The Informer, 2009). Cameroon, Ethiopia, Namibia, Nigeria, Zimbabwe, Sudan, Zambia, Algeria, Ghana, Tanzania, Egypt, Angola, South Africa, and Uganda are among top customers of the Chinese arms industry (SIPRI Arms Transfers Database, 2016).

China's 2006 Africa Policy states that "China will promote high-level military exchanges between the two sides and actively carry out military-related technological exchanges and co-operation. It will continue to help train African military personnel and support defence and army building of African countries for their security" (China's Africa Policy, 2006:4). China's military co-operation with African countries is mostly shrouded in secrecy and "cautious diplomacy". China does not treat its African partners with contempt, or heavy political conditionalities for bilateral defence deals, as has been done by countries of the Western hemisphere. The military assistance comes under China's pledge of "capacity building" with "no strings attached" to African nations, AU and RECs. "China offers at least modest quantities of military assistance or training to nearly every African country with which it has diplomatic relations" (Shinn, 2008:161).

In pursuit of its capacity-building drive for African military personnel to boost their capabilities for CT-COIN operations, China has trained military officers from different African countries: for instance, 15 senior military officers from 15 African countries took part in a 12-day course organised by the Chinese College for Defence Studies, China's People's Liberation Army (PLA) and National Defence University in May 2010 (PLA Daily, 2010); about 30 Angolan military personnel received training in China every year (Shinn, 2008:165); and, in 2008, the People's Liberation Army (PLA) sent 16 trainers to DRC as part of a training programme that continued throughout 2009, (United Nations Security Council, 2009). In Guinea, China trained elite commando units between 2004 and 2008, and PLA army instructors have been seconded to the Zimbabwe Staff College to provide specialist training in special operations (International Crisis Group, 2010; Shinn, 2008).

Another aspect of China's counterterrorism initiative in Africa is that China has contributed immensely to de-mining programmes on the continent. Thus, "in 2007, China launched a de-mining assistance programme for Africa, providing training for de-mining personnel and landmine removal devices", (Alden 2011:39). China has also conducted training courses "for personnel from Angola, Mozambique, Chad, Burundi, Guinea-Bissau and Sudan with equipment and funds being supplied to those countries, in addition to Ethiopia and Egypt" (Alden 2011:39). In 2010, the Engineer Command College of the PLA gave a six-week training course to 21 Sudanese de-miners in China (PLA Daily, 2010).

To boost its anti-piracy patrol, peacekeeping and humanitarian missions in Africa, China recently built a naval base in Djibouti. "Ships carrying personnel for China's first overseas military base have set sail to begin setting up the facility in Djibouti" (Aljazeera, 2017). China's agreement with Djibouti ensures its military presence in the country up until 2026, with a contingent of up to 10,000 soldiers. The base will be used to resupply navy ships taking part in peacekeeping and humanitarian missions off the coasts of Yemen and Somalia, in particular. It will be China's first overseas naval base, though Beijing officially describes it as a planning facility. The base will ensure China's performance of missions, such as escorting, peacekeeping, and humanitarian aid in Africa and west Asia (Aljazeera, 2017). China's new military base in Djibouti is seen as a rival (counterweight) to the US existing military base in the country. This development is likely to trigger a review of US military strategy in Africa. Still, it is reasonable to argue that both China and the USA will likely adopt a condominium posture to enable them to co-exist and pursue their national interest in Africa. African countries, too, may take advantage of this tenuous military co-habitation of China and USA in Djibouti. For obvious reasons, both countries will likely be disposed to strengthening their defence cooperation on the continent; also, whilst operating under the banner of defence cooperation, both China and USA may probably use their African bases to conduct other covert operations that will promote their national interest across Africa.

China has given a lot of financial donations to the AU's counterterrorism and stabilisation mission in Somalia (African-Defense.com, 2015): for instance, in September 2015, President Xi offered military aid of up to 100 million US Dollar to the AU's rapid response mechanisms – the African Standby Force (ASF) and its blueprint, the African Capacity for Immediate Response to Crises (ACIRC) – representing a major increase in China's investment in the organisation. As part of this effort to strengthen the AU-led African Peace and Security Architecture (APSA), China also directs a significant part of its military assistance – funds, transfer of equipment, training missions – towards sub-regional organisations, such as the Economic Community of West African States (ECOWAS) or the Intergovernmental Authority on Development (IGAD) in the Horn of Africa (Sonnad, 2015).

## Countering violent extremism through peacekeeping: China's participation in peace support operations in Africa

One of the most important aspects of China's counterterrorism and counterinsurgency initiatives in Africa is its growing participation in UN peace support operations in the continent. Recently, China's commitment to UN PSOs has increased tremendously. China is now the eighth-largest troop contributor to UN peacekeeping, and since 2007 has been the top among the five permanent members of the Security Council (UN Peacekeeping Statistics, 2016). China is the only country that plays a significant role as a contributor of both troops and finance—for the 2017–2018 UN Peacekeeping budget—China is the second-largest financial contributor (10.25%) after the United States (28.47%), (Financing peacekeeping, 2017). It is also the largest contributor of medical staff, engineers, and transportation units (Lei, 2014). China's first deployment of civilian observers on UN peace operations was in 1989 to Namibia. In April 1990, China deployed military observers to the Middle East, marking the PLA's first participation in a UN peacekeeping operation (Ping, 2007).

In his first address to the UN General Assembly in 2015, president Xi announced China's decision to "establish a 10-year 1 billion US Dollar China-UN peace and development fund to support UN work, advance multilateral cooperation and contribute more to world peace and development" (Sonnad, 2015:6). He further noted that "China will join the new UN Peacekeeping Capability Readiness System and has thus decided to take the lead in settling up a permanent peacekeeping police squad and build peacekeeping standby force of 8,000 troops (Sonnad, 2015: 16). He further added that China "will contribute to the training of 2,000 third-country peacekeepers and delivery of 10 de-mining assistance programmes (including training and equipment) by 2020 and contribution of a helicopter squad to a UN peacekeeping operation".

In Africa, China has sent its personnel to peacekeeping operations in Mozambique, Sierra Leone, Liberia, the DRC, Côte d'Ivoire, Burundi, Sudan, Western Sahara, Ethiopia, and Eritrea (Xinhua News, 2010). China's first combat troops were deployed to South Sudan in 2012. At the moment, there are over 2,500 Chinese troops and police officers deployed in blue-helmet missions across Africa with the largest deployments in South Sudan (1,051), Liberia (666), and Mali (402) (UN Peacekeeping Statistics, 2016). Before 2012, China had only sent non-combat troops, such as medics, logistical troops, and engineers (Gill and Huang, 2009). Under the UN-sanctioned anti-piracy mission, the Chinese navy is engaged in anti-piracy patrol off the Somali coast in the Gulf of Aden since December 2008 (Zhou and Seibel, 2015).

Before 2012—that is before China sent its combatant troops to UN peacekeeping missions in Africa—the Chinese peacekeepers in the continent consisted of an engineering company and medical personnel. As of July 2010, China's peacekeeping personnel under the United Nations Mission in Liberia (UNMIL) were 585, the fifth largest contingent after Pakistan (2,978), Nigeria (1710), Bangladesh (1470) and Ghana (740). It was reported that UNMIL depended entirely on "Chinese transport company to transport personnel, fuel, water and other essential goods around Liberia" (Gill and Huang, 2009:30). UNMIL Chinese engineers have been engaged in the rehabilitation of various roads in the country, as well as the maintenance of supply routes, construction and maintenance of bridges, and maintenance of runways at Liberia's international airport and various airfields. The Chinese hospital provided basic health care to local communities, and Chinese medics also worked on building local capacity. Chinese police officers mentor and advise their Liberian counterparts and have trained the police force in anti-armed robbery operations and conducted training in weapons handling and riot control (UNMIL, 2010).

In November 2007, the advance force of Chinese engineers in Darfur took the lead in building a large-scale and fully equipped camp that would be used by peacekeepers following behind them (Jiang, 2010). By "providing engineers, transport battalions and field hospitals, China contributes critically needed capabilities – as well as a degree of legitimacy – at a time when UN peacekeeping is severely overstretched" (Gill and Huang, 2009:12). Since their first deployment under the UN mandate, it is estimated that Chinese peacekeepers have altogether built or repaired more than 8,000 km of roads and more than 200 bridges, dismantled 8,700 mines and explosives, transported 4,300,000 tonnes of goods and provided medical treatment for 60,000 patients (Jiang, 2010:3). In March 2010, the Liberian President Ellen Johnson-Sirleaf praised Chinese peacekeepers for contributing not only to the security and peace of Liberia but also to the country's post-war reconstruction and development by helping build infrastructure and providing medical treatment to local communities (Ministry of Foreign Affairs of the People's Republic of China, 2010). During the recent Ebola outbreak in Sierra Leone, the PLA sent three military medical teams, including doctors and staff from a military hospital in Beijing, to set up an Ebola treatment centre (Lu Yingying et al., 2016). This gesture was applauded across Africa as a benevolent act that would endear the Chinese to Africans. In contrast, others view it as 'a masked medical diplomacy to promote China's material interest in Africa'.

At present, China has combatant troops in Mali and South Sudan under UN peacekeeping missions. These Chinese troops are engaged in counterterrorism and counterinsurgency operations under the Multidimensional Integrated Stabilization Mission in Mali (MINUSMA) and the United Nations Mission in the Republic of South Sudan (UNMISS). The UN Security Council gave MINUSMA the mandate to use "all necessary means, within the limits of its capacities and areas of deployment" to "stabilise" population centres in northern Mali and to "deter threats and to take active steps to prevent the return of armed elements in those areas" (UNSC resolution 2100, paragraphs 16 (a)(i) and 17). Also, as part of China's involvement in this peacekeeping mission, Chinese troops are protecting the United Nations (UN) personnel of other nationalities. By dispatching a protection unit in Mali, the Chinese troops are exposed to dealing with frequent attacks by extremist organisations on UN personnel. The UN Security Council Resolution 2155 states that the mandate of UNMISS includes: "To deter violence against civilians, including foreign nationals, especially through proactive deployment…and identification of threats and attacks against the civilian population…in areas at high risk of conflict including … oil installations" (Security Council resolution 2155, 4 [a] [ii]). Also, like in Mali, the Chinese troops are providing security to the UN personnel in South Sudan.

## Challenges to China's CT-COIN Drive in Africa

China's CT-COIN initiatives in Africa are confronted with many challenges. First, is the abuse and diversion of CT-COIN to support regime security rather than national security. On many occasions, the training and arms given to African militaries end up being used to quell protest and suppress opposition against the incumbent government. Instead of ensuring national security and human security, it appears Chinese military support and technical assistance are used to bolster "regime security". For instance, in Guinea, Chinese-trained elite Commandos were one of the units involved in the killing of 150 people in response to a political protest in September 2009 (Amnesty International, 2010:32). The troops of the Armed Forces of the Democratic Republic of Congo (FARDC) who were trained in the eastern part of Democratic Republic of Congo (DRC) by the Chinese were also accused of violations of international humanitarian law, the displacement of communities and failure to protect citizens in the east (United Nations Security Council and, 2009:4).

Another challenge to China's counterterrorism and counterinsurgency in Africa is that the Chinese troops deployed for operations across the continent are faced with language barriers, healthcare crisis (especially heat rash and fever), and frequent attacks by extremist organisations on UN peacekeeping personnel in countries like Mali and South Sudan. There is also rising resentment against UN peacekeeping personnel by residents. For instance, on 27 January 2015, there was a demonstration by residents in front of the MINUSMA headquarters—United Nations Multidimensional Integrated Stabilization Mission in Mali—in Gao which turned violent and resulted in UN police officers shooting and killing three civilians (un.org/press/en). Furthermore, Chinese troops find it difficult to interact with troops from other countries, particularly troops from developed nations.

It could be argued that the greatest challenge to China's CT-COIN initiatives in Africa is its "non-interference" policy under which China maintains a silent non-interventionist posture even where states engage in human right violations that can warrant "responsibility to protect" measures. For instance, in South Sudan – where China has investments in oil – Beijing had to hide under the UN peacekeeping operations to protect its interest and that of its citizens in the country. America or any EU-member nation would have unilaterally deployed troops into any country to defend its interest.

## Conclusion

Trade and investment, exports and imports, mining, agriculture, political cooperation, cultural exchanges, cooperation in other areas among others were always given more priority in the Sino-African relations. However, recently, counterterrorism and counterinsurgency, defence and security issues are gradually making their way into the Sino-African relations. Of course, China is not in Africa to secure the continent or engage in counterterrorism or counterinsurgency initiatives but to pursue its national interest and explore the continent's natural resources. It is estimated that there are over 2,000 Chinese companies and about one to two million Chinese nationals across Africa. China was caught up in a recent spate of terrorism, insurgency, piracy, and other crimes in the continent hence left without many choices but to increase its support to the continent's stability, peace, and security. Therefore, recently, Beijing reluctantly had to increase its commitment to providing peace and security in Africa.

Beijing's CT-COIN initiatives in Africa involves, on the one hand, bilateral military cooperation with individual African countries and, on the other hand, multilateral support to AU and RECs on their peace and security programmes and most recently its increased participation in UN peace keeping operations in Africa, particularly the deployment of combatant troops. Beijing also believes in a comprehensive approach that addresses the root causes as well as the symptoms of terrorism and the capacity building of African countries, AU, and sub-regional organisations.

# References

African-Defense.com. (2015). China Donates to AMISOM Mission. African Defense, 9 September 2015, available at http://www.african-defense.com/defense-news/china-donates-to-amisom-mission/ (accessed on 7th April 2017).

Alden, C. (2011). *China's growing role in African peace and security*. Saferworld Report. London: Saferworld.

Aljazeera. (2017). China to open first overseas military base in Djibouti, *Aljazeera* at http://www.aljazeera.com/news/2017/07/china-open-overseas-military-base-djibouti170712135241977.html?xif=http:/www.aljazeera.com/news/2017/07/china-open-overseas-military-base-djibouti-170712135241977.html (accessed on 3rd September 2017).

Amnesty International. (2010). *Guinea: You Did Not Want The Military, So Now We Are Going To Teach You A Lesson – The Events Of September 28 2009 And Their Aftermath*. London: Amnesty International.

Anshan, L. (2005). African studies in China in the Twentieth Century: A Historiographical survey. *African Studies Review, 48*(1), 59–87.

Beeston, R. (2006). West could learn from straightforward approach. *The Times (London), 42*.

Chibundu, V. N. (2000). *Nigerian-China Foreign Relations, 1960-1999*. Ibadan: Spectrum Books Limited.

China's Africa Policy. (2006). 4. (1). Ministry of Foreign Affairs of the People's Republic of China. Available at https://www.fmprc.gov.cn/zflt/eng/zgdfzzc/. Accessed on 29 August 2017.

China's Ministry of Commerce (MOFCOM) country reports. (2014) and 2015, available at http://fec.mofcom.gov.cn/article/gbdqzn.

Ekenedirichukwu, E. G. (2007). Reflections on the China-in-Africa Debate: Mercantilism, Partnership or Resurgence of Hegemony? *African Journal of Peace and Development Studies?, 3*(1), 50–82.

Financial Times. (2008). Africa-China Trade: Time for the West to practice what it preaches. *Financial Times Special Report*. January, 24, p. 6.

Fleurant A., Sam P.-F., Pieter D. W., & Siemon T. W. (2015). Trends in International Arms Transfers, 2015. *SIPRI Fact Sheet*, February 2016, available at http://books.sipri.org/files/FS/SIPRIFS1602.pdf.

FOCAC Archives. (2009). FOCAC Archives. Available at: https://www.fmprc.gov.cn/zflt/eng/ltda/dyjbzjhy/. Accessed on 26 August 2017.

FOCAC Archives. (2012). Available at: https://www.fmprc.gov.cn/zflt/eng/ltda/dwjbzjjhys/. Accessed on 26 August 2017.

FOCAC (Forum on China and Africa). (2015). *FOCAC website* at http://www.focac.org/eng/ltda/ltjj/.

Foerstel, K. (2008). China in Africa. *CQ Global Researcher, 2*(1), 1–26.

Gill, B., & Huang, C. (2009). *China's Expanding Role in Peacebuilding: Prospects and Policy Implications*, SIPRI Policy Paper, number 25, November 2009, available at http://books.sipri.org/files/PP/SIPRIPP25.pdf.

International Crisis Group. (2010). *Guinea: Reforming the Army Africa*, Report no. 164. London: ICG.

Jackson, D. (2015). 3 Chinese nationals killed in Mali hostage crisis, 4 rescued after special forces storm building, at http://shanghaiist.com/2015/11/21/3_chinese_nationals_killed_in_mali_hostage_crisis.php). Accessed on 15 September 2017.

Jiang, Z. (2010). China's Participation in UN Peacekeeping Operations in Africa, paper presented at the *China-Africa Civil Society Forum on Peace and Development*, Beijing, 2–4 June 2010.

Lei, X. (2014). *China as a Permanent Member of the United Nations Security Council*, FES Publication Series (p. 10, available as a pdf at). Berlin: Friedrich-Ebert-Stiftung, Global Policy and Development, April 2014), http://www.fes.de/gpol/inhalt/publikationen_unsc.php.Accessed1st September 2017.

Lu Yingying et al., (2016). Chinese military medical teams in the Ebola outbreak in Sierra Leone. *Journal of the Royal Army Medical Corps*, 7 January 2016, available at http://jramc.bmj.com/content/early/2016/01/07/jramc-2015-000562.full.

Ministry of Foreign Affairs of the People's Republic of China. (2010). 'Liberian President Paid Tribute to Chinese Peacekeepers', 3 March 2010. Available at: http://lr.china-embassy.org/eng/sghdhzxxx/t662261.htm. Accessed on 26 August 2017.

Ngwane, M. G. (2006). The Military and African Politics". Retrieved from http://www.gngwane.com/2006/10/the_military_an.html accessed on 19 February 2016.

Nzouankeu, A. M. (2014). Ten Chinese workers among 27 hostages freed in Cameroon; *Reuters*, at http://www.reuters.com/article/us-cameroon-hostages-idUSKCN0I006J20141011). Accessed on 18 August 2017.

Obiorah, N. (2007). Who's Afraid of China in Africa? In F. Manji & S Marks edited by, *African Perspectives on China in Africa* (pp. 35–56). Oxford: Fahamu Publishers.

Ping, Z. (2007). Remarks on the Chinese People's Liberation Army's Participation in UN Peacekeeping Operations at conference on 'Multidimensional and Integrated Peace Operations: Trends and Challenges', Beijing. 26–27 March 2007. Retrieved from http://www.regjeringen.no/upload/UD/Vedlegg/FN/Multidimensional%20and%20Integrated/Chinese%20Ministry%20of%20Defence%20%20PLA%20Participation%20in%20UNPO.doc. Accessed 30 August 2017.

PLA Daily. (2010). Ma Xiaotian meets commanders from English speaking African countries, 27 May 2010. Available at https://idsa.in/TWIR/11_3_2010_China. Accessed on 28 August 2017.

Shinn, D. (2008). Chapter 8: Military and Security Relations: China, Africa and the Rest of the World. In Robert Rotberg (Ed.), *China into Africa: Trade, Aid, and Influence*. Cambridge: Brookings.

Shinn, D. (2013). China Confronts Terrorism in Africa – *China US Focus*, at http://www.chinausfocus.com/peace-security/china-confronts-terrorism-in africa/ Accessed on 16 August 2017.

SIPRI (Stockholm International Peace Research Institute). (2016). *The SIPRI Arms Transfers Database*, available at https://www.sipri.org/databases/armstransfers. Accessed on 21 August 2017.

Sonnad, N. (2015). Xi Jinping's first UN Address, https://qz.com/512886/read-the-full-text-of-xi-jinpings-first-un-address/.

Tar, U. A., & Abubakar, S. S. (2016). 'Globalisation of Dragon: Sino-African relations in the 21st century'. In Tar,U. A., Tedheke, M. E. U., & Mijah (Eds.), B. E.*Readings on globalisation and development in Africa*. Kaduna: Nigerian Defence Academy Press.

The Informer. (2009). China Again! – Turns over US$5.5 million Barracks. 30 April 2009. Retrieved from http://www.rscsl.org/Clippings/2009/2009-04/pc2009-4-30.pdf. Accessed on 29 August 2017.

Tiezzi, S. (2018). FOCAC 2018: Rebranding China in Africa, the Diplomat, https://thediplomat.com/2018/09/focac-2018-rebranding-china-in-africa/ (September 05, 2018). Accessed on 20 September 2018.

Tsang, S. (2018) *Is China's Africa investment more than a 'new version of colonialism?'* Arab News. http://www.arabnews.com/node/1373416#.W5_2NI6e1EE. Accessed on 20 September 2018.

UN. (2016). *Peacekeeping statistics*. http://www.un.org/en/peacekeeping/resources/statistics/. Accessed on 10 September 2018.

UN DPK (United Nations Department of Peacekeeping) Financing peacekeeping. (2017). available at http://www.un.org/en/peacekeeping/operations/financing.shtml accessed on 10th September 2017.

UN Peace Keeping Statistics. (2016). Available at: https://peaceoperationsreview.org/strategic-summary-2016-un-peace-operations-by-the-numbers/. Accessed on 23 August 2017.

UN Security Council resolution 2155 4 (a) (ii). New York: United Nations. Available at https://www.un.org/press/en/2014/sc11414.doc.htm. Accessed on 2 September 2017.

United Nations Department of Peacekeeping Operations (DPKO). (2010). *UN Missions Summary by country*. Available at https://peacekeeping.un.org/en/troop-and-police-contributors. Accessed on 23 August 2017.

United Nations Security Council. (2009). *Final Report of the Group of Experts on the Democratic Republic of Congo S/2009/603* (p. 63). New York: United Nations.

UNMIL (United Nations Mission in Liberia). (2010). UN Envoy extols Chinese police peacekeepers for strengthening Liberian police capacity. 6 January 2010. Available at https://peacekeeping.un.org/en/mission/unmil. Accessed on 25 August 2017.

UNSC Resolution. (2003). *Resolution 1509 (2003) Adopted by the Security Council at its 4830th meeting*. New York: United Nations.

Voice of America. (2010). China Donates $1.5 million to Boost Mauritania's Defence. 20 April 2010. Available at http://www1.voanews.com/english/news/africa/China-Donates-15-Billion-to-Boost-Mauritanias-Defense-91607329.html. Accessed on 8 December 2017.

Watts, J. (2006). The savannah comes to Beijing as China hosts its new empire. *The Guardian*. Retrieved from http://www.theguardian.com/world/2006/nov/04/china.jonathanwatts.on 27 July 2015.

Wee, S.-L. (2012). Chinese workers kidnapped in Egypt freed: *Reuters*, at http://www.reuters.com/article/us-china-workers-egypt-idUSTRE81011520120201).

Wu, Y. (2015). IS killing of Chinese hostage: A game changer? *BBC Chinese*, at http://www.bbc.com/news/blogs-china-blog-34865696.

www.un.org/press/en/2015/db150402.doc.htm.

Xinhua News. (2010). UN official lauds China's contribution to peacekeeping efforts. 31 July 2010. Available at http://www.xinhuanet.com/english/. Accessed on 15 December 2017.

Xinhua News. (2015). *Highlights of China's newly adopted counter-terrorism law*, Xinhua news, at http://www.icrosschina.com/news/2015/1228/22786.shtml.

Xinhuanet. (2018). Full text of Chinese President Xi Jinping's speech at opening ceremony of 2018 FOCAC Beijing Summit. Available at http://www.xinhuanet.com/english/2018-09/03/c_129946189.htm. Accessed on 20 September 2018

Zhou, H., & Seibel, K. (2015). Maritime Insecurity in the Gulf of Guinea: A Greater Role for China? *China Brief, 5*(1), 9 January 2015, available at http://www.jamestown.org/regions/africa/single/?tx_ttnews%5Btt_news%5D=43373&tx_ttnews%5BbackPid%5D=55&cHash=483fbf16901b97355cef6d1dcc362e91#. V1xDi-Z95QM.

# Part III
# Regional perspectives

# 20

# African Union

## Emerging architecture for regional counterterrorism and counterinsurgency in Africa

*Usman A. Tar and Anne Uchenna Ibobo-Eze*

## Introduction

The Continent of Africa finds itself on the front-line of the global fight against terrorism. As illuminated by Omeje in this volume, Africa constitutes a peculiar front of the "Global War on Terror" (GWOT) with all its attendant challenges. Africa's counterterrorism and counterinsurgency (CT-COIN) architecture is based on the legal and institutional foundation of the African Union (AU) which was transformed from the Organisation of the African Unity (OAU) at a period when Africa was faced with the threat of transnational terrorism. Today, the scope of terrorism in Africa has intensified, while the AU's CT-COIN strategy is becoming difficult to accomplish due to some challenges. Against the background of the progressive evolution of terrorist groups on the continent (such as Boko Haram, AQIM, Al-Shabab and LRA), this chapter evaluates the AU's emerging architecture for CT-COIN through the AU's legal and institutional framework, identifies the AU's challenges in preventing and combating terrorism in Africa and articulates a realistic blueprint for action.

The OAU was transformed to AU on 26 May 2000 during the 36th Ordinary Summit of the OAU Assembly of the Heads of State and Government in Lomé, Togo, with the objective of articulating in the Article 3 of the Constitutive Act (Eyinla, 2013:124). The AU arose as the new continental organisation for actualising the goal of Africa's political emancipation, securing Africa's democracy, human rights, sustainable economy, bringing to an end the intro-African conflict that has plagued the continent and deepening integration among African Countries. Consequently, the advent of AU was for countries in Africa a much-awaited instrument to collectively address multifaceted security, social, economic, and political challenges facing the continent. The AU's CT-COIN drive is determined by the amount of sovereignty and in-dependence which member states are willing to exert taking into consideration the geopolitical and economic situations of the continent. The AU consists 54 member States except for Morocco which opted out due to the adversarial position of the AU on the vexed issue of Western Sahara, a former Spanish colony conquered by Morocco since 1970s after the de-parture of the Spanish colonialists.

The grand norm of the AU's CT-COIN strategy is contained in Article 3 (f) of the AU Constitutive Act which seeks to promote peace, security, and stability on the continent and the attainment of the objectives of the union (African Commission on Human and Peoples' Rights, 2006:11). This is against the backdrop of the fact that after the US 9/11 attack, Al-Qaeda has increased its presence on the African continent: in the Horn by terrorist groups like *Al-Shabaab*; in the Arab Maghreb through it local franchise, Al-Qaeda in the Islamic Maghreb (AQIM); in the West through local structures like Boko Haram in Nigeria; and now increasingly South Africa. Consequently, Islamist terror attacks across the continent have escalated (ICSR, 2011), making CT-COIN a key part of the African Union Peace and Security architecture, as the 1999 OAU Convention on Prevention and Combating of Terrorism in Algiers, Algeria was entered into force since December 2002, with the ratification of 40 Member States (AU Peace and Security, 2015). Other AU Legal and Institutional CT-COIN frameworks include the 2004 additional protocol to the 1999 convention and the 2011 African Law on CT-COIN. In addition, the AU has, over the years, developed a robust institutional architecture for CT-COIN: the Africa Peace and Security Council (AU/PSC); the Continental Early Warning System (CEWS); African Peace and Security Architecture (APSA); the African Standby Force (ASF) and the African Centre for the Study and Research on Terrorism (ACSRT). Together, these agencies have provided the launching pad for CT-COIN in Africa.

Despite what appears to be a fast-evolving CT-COIN framework, AU is (and its member states are) still faced with challenges in preventing and combating terrorism in Africa: lack of adequate resources, the reluctance of member states' to embrace the AU's CT-COIN policy at the National level and Non-compliance of Ratification as a component of Terrorism prevention by nations. There are several key questions in this regard: what are the nature and dynamism of terrorism and insurgency in Africa? How fast is the AU in developing an efficient CT-COIN framework to overcome the challenges of terrorism and insurgency in the continent? Why are the AU CT-COIN frameworks adjudged to be failing? What can be done to solve the AU CT-COIN challenges? This Chapter is divided into six sections: (1) introduction (2) conceptual clarification (3) overview of terrorism in Africa with particular reference to BH, AQIM, *Al-Shabaab* and LRA (4) the AU's emerging architecture for CT-COIN (5) the challenges confronting AU's CT-COIN drive, and (6) conclusion.

## Conceptualisation: terrorism, insurgency, counterterrorism and counterinsurgency

The key terminologies that scaffold this chapter are terrorism, insurgency, Counterterrorism and Counterinsurgency (CT-COIN). *Terrorism* is defined from three different perspectives: institutional, practitioners and organisational. From the institutional point of view, terrorism is the deliberate act of violence aimed at the state and its infrastructure (hard target) and civilians, unarmed persons, and civil infrastructure (soft target), to achieve political ends. From the practitioners' perspectives, it is the premeditated, deliberate, systematic murder, mayhem, and threatening of the innocent to create fear and intimidation to gain a political or tactical advantage, usually to influence the audience. While, from the organisational point; it is the unlawful use of force or violence against persons or property to intimidate or coerce a government, the civilian population, or any segment thereof, in furtherance of political or social objectives (Obene, 2015:4). Terrorism is equally a tactics of using violence or the threat of violence as a coercive strategy to cause fear and political intimidation. It is featured within resistance movements, military coups, political assassinations, and various intra- and inter-state wars that have affected most African states at some point during the continent's transition to independence and subsequent post-colonial period. (James et al., 2011). There are many definitions of terrorism, but for in this chapter, we view terrorism as the deliberate use of threat, violence, and brutality by terrorist groups to achieve a religious, ideological or political aim through intimidation, killing and destruction of both government structures and citizen's property in a giving environment of a nation, sub-region, region and continent. According to Gallup (2004:46) "Terrorism is an effect rather than a cause of societal unrest". This means that there are two dimensions of terrorism: on the one hand, it is caused by violent human agents to achieve sundry objectives aimed at destroying an established norm and status quo. On the other hand, terrorism is the destructive effect of the act of violence committed by terrorist organisations and individuals.

*Insurgency* refers to the act of violence by groups or individuals aimed at dismantling the existing state to replace it with an alternative political system. Insurgents are often utterly dissatisfied with, or disloyal to, the state and seek violent means to destabilise, discredit, destroy and replace it with their own – often divisive and narrow – mould of the state. An insurgency can take the form of cause and consequence. As a cause, it is the act of violence that challenges the legitimacy of the state. As consequence, it refers to the aftermath of an act of violence aimed at destroying the state. This can be *short term* destabilisation of the state as in Liberia during the rebellion against President Samuel Doe, or *long term* "state collapse" as in Somalia after General Siad Barre. Finally, *Counterterrorism and counterinsurgency* (CT-COIN) is a bandwagon concept that conjures the practices, tactics, techniques, and strategies that governments, militaries, police departments and corporations adopt in response to terrorist threats or acts, both real and imputed (Kolodkin, 2016). It also refers to the domestic military and legal measure put in place by the government of any state to prevent and counter terrorism in collaboration with sub-regional, regional, and continental organisational instruments. This is achieved by intercepting communications, monitoring internet and social media habits, and blocking access to terrorist training materials, funding and building of genetic capacity of the national criminal justice system.

## Background: the anatomy of terrorism and insurgency in Africa

What sort of terrorist organisations and associated threats are African countries facing? A plethora of terrorist and insurgent movements bedevil African countries with far-reaching implications for national, regional, and global securities. The recurring news coverage of *Ansar Deen, Boko Haram, Al-Shabaab,* and countless other terrorist groups point to Africa's vulnerability to dangerously armed and globally connected Violent Non-State Actors (VNSAs). VNSAs pose a threat to peace, security, and the existence of a host of African countries (Ewi and A, 2006). More often than not, their method of operation (MO) is aimed at the so-called "soft targets", that is, innocent civilians (non-military citizens) and civil infrastructure that sustain life and communal life are the primary targets of terrorist and insurgents depriving them of their most fundamental human right to life; this is in addition to threatening the territorial integrity of the host state. In the last few decades, African countries have been struggling with domestic terrorism and the challenge of the emergence of transnational terrorist groups that have turned African continent to a centre to transmit attacks against both domestic and international targets and also to progress and sustain operations as Terrorism has always been a threat to security in Africa, but the serious involvement of intergovernmental organisations in efforts to address the threat is a recent development (Ewi and Aning, 2006). Terrorists and insurgents have succeeded in curbing "ungoverned spaces" in their host states as exemplified by the Boko Haram Insurgency in Nigeria. Through acts of violence, the Boko Haram had effectively challenged and usurped the legitimacy and authority of the state in their domain of influence – that is, the contingent territories of the Sambisa Forest in north-eastern Nigeria comprising large swathes of local government areas in Adamawa, Borno, and Yobe States.

Terrorist groups such as the *Al-Shabab* in Somalia and Kenya benefit from illicit trade, take advantage of corrupt systems in the state structure, and use clandestine channels to engage in money laundering, while also investing in weapons acquisition and training. These violent groups challenge the state and even curve out "ungoverned spaces" out of their host state and secure effective control of the acquired territory under their control (Tar & Mustapha, 2017; Tar & Mustapha, 2016). Some of the major activities/attacks by terrorists in Africa include the 1998 bombing of US embassy in Kenya and Tanzania; the 2002 bombing of an Israeli-owned hotel and aeroplane; the 2005 Bombing attacks by the Abdullah Assam Brigades at Sharm el-Sheikh, an Egyptian resort city; the 2006 Dahab bombing in Egypt; the 2011 Christmas Day bombings in Nigeria resulting in coordinated, spontaneous bomb blasts and shootings at churches in Madalla, Jos, Gadaka, and Damaturu; the 2014 *Al-Shabaab* attack in Mogadishu, Somalia; the 2014 *Boko Haram* attack of a borderline village in Cameroon, the kidnapping of over 200 schoolgirls on the night of 14–15 April 2014 at Chibok in Borno State; and attacks against UN buildings in Algeria and Nigeria (James et al., 2011). Others are the attack by *Al-Shabaab* at the Westgate Mall in Nairobi on 21 September 2013; the bombings on 3 and 4 April 2014 in Mombasa and Nairobi on the abuses committed by the Al-Qaeda in the Islamic Maghreb against innocent civilian populations; the bombing of a bus station in Abuja leading to the death of 71 people and 124 wounded persons on 14 April 2014, and the killing of 150 people in a village in Borno State in northern Nigeria on 7 May 2014 (African Commission on Human and Peoples' Rights, 2014). These attacks clearly point to the boldness, lethality, and sophistication of VNSAs in Africa. They also show the vulnerability of the state in the face of terror. Finally, they show the inter-connected nature of terrorist organisations across Africa and the world.

African countries and regional organisations have come to the realisation of the seriousness of terrorism. The 2011 Communiqué of AU Peace and Security Council (PSC) mentioned that the growing links between the terrorist groups as well as their involvement in other forms of crime are quite alarming. The Communiqué pointed out *Boko Haram* (BH) in Nigeria, *Al-Qaida in the Islamic Maghreb* (AQIM), *Al-Shabaab in Somalia* and the *Lord's Resistance Army* (LRA) in Uganda as the major terrorist groups in Africa (Vanguard, 2011). African countries have taken the necessary steps to stem the tides of terrorism on the continent. For instance, at the Summit of the Regional Cooperation Initiative for the Elimination of the Lord's Resistance Army (RCI-LRA), held on the margins of the 28th Ordinary Session of the Assembly of Heads of State and Government of the African Union held in Addis Ababa, Ethiopia on 29 January 2017, the AU's Commissioner for Peace and Security, Ambassador Ismail Chergui (2017) made a passionate presentation on the status of the implementation of the mandate of the RCI-LRA. It noted in particular, the progress made by the RCI-LRA in combatting and degrading the Lord's Resistance Army terrorist group. The meeting acknowledged that the LRA remains a threat to civilians, peace and security in the Central African Republic (CAR), the Democratic Republic of Congo (DRC), South Sudan and the region as a whole, and called for a renewed momentum in the fight against the LRA to ensure its final elimination. Ambassador Chergui also stressed the urgency of providing an immediate and adequate response for the humanitarian crisis triggered by the atrocious activities of the LRA. As a way forward, the meeting mandated the AU Commission to urgently convene a planning meeting of the members of the RCI-LRA to develop a comprehensive roadmap for the full accomplishment of the RCI-LRA mandate.

The *Boko Haram* is a terrorist-insurgent group that emerged in Nigeria in 2009 but with antecedent dating back to 2002 when a Wahabist strain of the Group emerged to preach against the secular state and called for a return to theocratic state. The name "Boko Haram" is usually translated as "Western education is forbidden." It is also translated as "Western influence is a sin" or "Westernisation is sacrilege". The origin is traced to the meeting between two young Nigerian Islamic scholars (Mohammed Ali from Borno State and Abu Umar from Kano) met a Syrian preacher, Abu Albasir al-Dardus while on pilgrimage in Saudi Arabia. Al-Dardus indoctrinated the fledgeling Nigerian preachers in the line of rejecting western education and all symbols of modern governance, based on corrupt interpretation of some *Hadith* (tradition) of the Prophet Muhammad. After the indoctrination, Muhammed Ali and Abu Umar came back to Nigeria. They started converting "opinion moulders" especially marginal Sunni preachers who have already demonstrated a penchant for extreme interpretation of Islam. Bello Dama and Muhammad Yusuf happen to be one of the first converts. Muhammad Yusuf emerged as the leader of the group called Boko Haram in 2002. He built an Islamic centre called *Markas Ibn Taimiyya* named after a Salafist philosopher and founder of Wahabism in Saudi Arabia (Omotoso, 2016:56).

The group got into politics in Borno during the 2003 and 2007 governorship elections to support the then Governor of Borno State, Senator Ali Modu Sheriff (SAS). They converted many emotionally vulnerable youngsters: many graduates burned their certificates, as a mark of abdication of western values, science, and knowledge system, and joined ranks with the group. Worse still, some students at universities and colleges also absconded school to join the group. *Boko Haram* eventually became an armed insurgency when in 2009, a funeral procession of the members of *Markas Ibn Taimiyya* was accosted by security agents for a traffic violation. The group spread its tentacles beyond Bono State to other northeastern states of Nigeria intending to establish an Islamic state in Nigeria termed as the Jihad "Holy War". The group destroyed the lives and properties of people and government of Nigeria. All efforts put in place by the state proved abortive as the group collaborated with the global Islamist fraternity, especially Al-Qaeda of the Islamic Maghreb and ISIS for funding and technical support. Presently, the group activities have been drastically tamed through the effort of Multinational Joint Task Force (MJTF) of the four Nigeria's neighbouring countries and the resilient and untiring efforts of President Muhammadu Buhari JCFR. Boko Haram operation/activities to a reasonable point, have been defeated by the sub-regional MJTF.

Meanwhile, the Al-Qaeda in the Islamic Maghreb (AQIM) is a Salafi-jihadist militant group designated by the US Government as a Foreign Terrorist Organisation (FTO) operating in the Sahara and Sahel. The group traces its antecedent to Algeria's civil war of the 1990s and has in the past decade become an al-Qaeda affiliate with regional ambitions. AQIM and its offshoots pose the primary transnational terror threat in North and West Africa but are unlikely to strike in the United States and Europe, according to US officials. Much of AQIM's leadership is believed to have trained with other Arab volunteers (among them Osama bin Laden) in Afghanistan during the 1979–1989 war against the Soviet occupation. Many returned to the Middle East and North Africa as radicalised fire eaters (Laub, 2015). Referring to the West Point's Combating Terrorism Centre, Laub (2015) notes that AQIM's objectives include "ridding North Africa of Western influence; overthrowing governments deemed apostate, including those of Algeria, Libya, Mali, Mauritania, Morocco, and Tunisia; and installing fundamentalist regimes based on sharia." Pundits have observed that "AQIM's ideology blends global Salafi-jihadist dogma with regionally resonant elements, including references to the early Islamic conquest of the Maghreb and the Iberian Peninsula." According to the US State Department (in Laub, 2015), the group has about one thousand members in Algeria, and smaller numbers in the Sahel region, which includes areas in Chad, Mali, and Mauritania. It also has cells in Libya, Nigeria, and Tunisia. The UN Security Council's Al-Qaeda Sanctions Committee observes that European cells are a source of the group's funding. As the US States Department (2012) notes further, AQIM had coordinated with other terrorist groups in the region, including Nigeria's Boko Haram, Somalia's, Al-Shabaab, and Yemen's Al-Qaeda in the Arabian Peninsula (AQAP), with arms and funds flowing among them. In preventing and combating the AQIM activities, the UNSC in 2012 authorised a military peacekeeping mission in Mali, while the Economic Community of West African States, pledged thousands of troops. Meanwhile, French forces were deployed together with the African-Led peacekeeping mission were also deployed to Mali in 2015. The US State Department (2012) believes that the best strategy for dealing with AQIM remains by working with the regional government to increase their capacity, foster regional cooperation, and counter violent extremism.

The *Al-Shabaab*, the violent terrorist organisation with Wahabi-Salafist roots, was born in Somalia in the aftermaths of the collapse of the country after 1991. Still, its tentacles had since spread to most of Somalia's neighbouring countries. Al-Shabaab means "The Youth" in Arabic. It emerged as the radical youth wing of Somalia's now-defunct Union of Islamic Courts, which controlled Mogadishu in 2006, before being forced out by Ethiopian forces. There are numerous reports of foreign jihadists going to Somalia to help al-Shabab, from neighbouring countries. It is banned as a terrorist group by both the US and the UK and is believed to have between 7,000 and 9,000 fighters. Al-Shabab advocates the Saudi-inspired Wahhabi version of Islam, while most Somalis are Sufis. It has imposed a strict version of Sharia in areas under its control, including stoning to death women accused of adultery and amputating the hands of thieves. The group is currently lead by Ahmed Umar (known as Abu Ubaidah), who the US issued a $6 million reward for information leading to his capture (BBC News, 2016). The Al-Shabaab have recently penetrated Kenya because it share common border with Somalia and launched attacks in Garissa University, the Westgate Shopping Centre in Nairobi, and the border areas. The group equally started a network in Kenya and carried out attacks, even as the military operation is weakening their activities. Al-Shabaab pledges obedience to al-Qaeda head Ayman Al-Zawahiri as there have been rumours that it formed links with the Islamic Maghreb and Boko Haram, based on the Sahara Desert. The AU-Led ground offensive forced the group out of Somalia's capital Mogadishu in 2011 and the vital port of Kismoya in 2012. These hindered the group's financial inflow through Charcoal trade.

The *Lord's Resistance Army* (LRA) began life in 1988 in northern Uganda. It emerged from the remnants of the Holy Spirit Movement army founded by Alice Auma Lakwena, a priestess and distant relative of Joseph Kony, the LRA leader. Kony, a former catechist, capitalised on a power vacuum created by the defeat of resistance movements in the north – some of which abandoned their military campaigns and made peace with the government in the1990s – to start the LRA. The group first operated as the United Holy Salvation Army before it was named the Uganda Christian Army/Movement and eventually the LRA. It adopted this name sometime in 1992. The LRA gained a reputation for brutality as it waged an armed rebellion seeking to remove the government of Yoweri Museveni, the Ugandan president, and rule the country on the Biblical Ten Commandments. The vast majority of the LRA fighters came from the northern districts of Gulu, Kitgum and Pader (Al-Jazeera, 2011). According to the US States Department (2012), the LRA has killed more than 2,400 people and abducted more than 3,400 persons since 2008. The United Nations in 2011, also estimated over 380,000 people displaced across CAR, DRC, and South Sudan because of LRA activity. The LRA recruited most of their fighters forcefully and killed those reluctant to join after series of defeat from the Ugandan military. The group spread to the neighbouring countries of DRC, Sudan, and CAR.

They receive financial support mostly from Sudanese People. In preventing and combating the operations of the LRA, former US President Barack Obama signed into law the LRA Disarmament and Northern Uganda Recovery Act, which lead to the capture of 19 LRA rebels in CAR by Uganda troops in December 2013.

Other terrorist/insurgent groups in Africa, which share a lot in common with the preceding examples, include the *Al-Qaeda in the Arabian Peninsula* (AQAP), the *Jama'a al-Islamiyya in Egypt*, *Ansar Dine* in Mali, *Ansar al-Sharia* in Benghazi in Libya, *Ansar al-Sharia* in Tunisia, *Ansar Bayt al-Maqdis* in Egypt, the Libyan *Islamic Fighting Group* (LIFG), the *Egyptian Islamic Jihad*, *Muslim Brotherhood, Jamaatul Islamiya, Allied Democratic Forces, Armed Islamic Combatant Group, Al-Mourabitoun, Al-Barakat*, the *Ras Kamboni Brigades Soldiers* of Egypt, *Al-Jama'a al-Islamiya*, the *Tunisian Combatant Group*, and so on. These groups share common appeal to dismantling the modern post-colonial state in Africa and replacing it with a theocratic variant.

## AU's legal and institutional frameworks for CT-COIN

The AU efforts in CT-COIN can be traced to the 1999 *OAU Counterterrorism Convention* which was entered into force in December 2002 and ratified by 40 members to date. A High-Level Inter-Governmental Meeting on the Prevention and Combating of Terrorism was also held in Algiers in 2002, giving concrete expression to the commitment and obligations of member States to fight Terrorism. The AU Plan of Action on the Prevention and Combating of Terrorism was also adopted. Article 10(d) identifies the intimate relationship between terrorism, corruption, and money laundering (Fagbohun, 2013). A bold measure taken by the AU to overcome terrorism and insurgency was the establishment of the African Centre for the Study and Research on Terrorism (ACSRT) in 2004, as part of the implementation of the *AU Plan of Action on the Prevention and Combatting of Terrorism in Africa* (AU, 2002). In addition, the AU Peace and Security Council (PSC) has initiated bold steps to implement the Algiers Convention and other relevant international regional and sub-regional instruments to fight terrorism.

Under Article 4(a-g) of the African Union Constitutive Act, African leaders sought to, among other objectives, (a) establish a common defence and security; (b) pursue peaceful resolution of conflicts among the Member States through such appropriate means as may be decided by the Assembly; (c) prohibit the use of force/threat among member states of the Union; (d) pursue the principle of non-interference by any member state in the internal affairs of others; (e) promote the right of the Union to intervene in a member state according to a decision of the assembly in respect of grave circumstances, namely: war crimes, genocide and crimes against humanity (f) encourage peaceful co-existence amongst member states and establish their right to live in peace and security and (g) pursue the right of member states to request intervention from the Union in order to restore peace and security (Ogwu, 2002:186).

### The legal infrastructure of CT-COIN in Africa

On the legal front, the AU's architecture for CT-COIN comprises the following:

1. The OAU/AU Constitutive Act: This instrument sets out the organisational framework for the new AU signed in 2000 at Lome, Togo under which the African Union was transformed and shouldered with the responsibility for ensuring peace, security and development in Africa. The Act empowered the AU to conduct regional affairs and intervene in the internal affairs of African states if there are compelling reasons to do so. The Act was

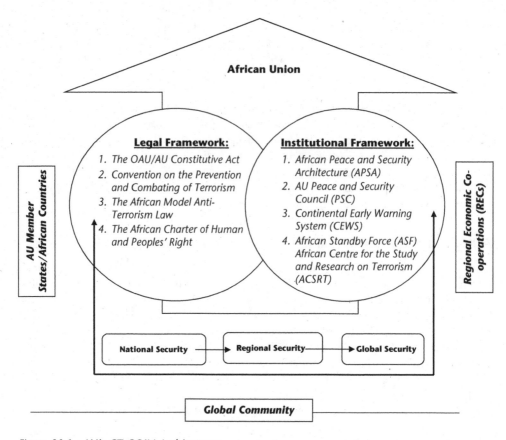

*Figure 20.1*   AU's CT-COIN Architecture

entered into force after convention ratification of 53 signatory nations of Africa. The Constitutive Act serves as the first Legally binding instrument empowering the AU in its counterterrorism efforts as Article 3(f) of the Act states that the objective of the Union shall be to promote peace, security, and stability on the continent (AU, 2000: 5). Hence, by virtue of its Constitutive Act, the AU was tasked to play a prominent and leading role in the fight against terrorism on the continent.

2.  The OAU Convention on the Prevention and Combating of Terrorism: The Convention was adopted on 1 July 1999, at a summit in Algiers, Algeria, entered into force on 6 December 2002, and last signed on 27 July 2015. The 1999 Convention required that states parties criminalise Terrorist act under national laws as defined in the Convention by building cooperation among state, establishes state Jurisdiction over Terrorist acts, and provides a legal framework for extradition as well as extra-territorial investigations and mutual legal assistance. The 2004 additional protocol the 1999 Convention recognises the growing threat of terrorism and its linkages between drug trafficking, transnational orga-nised crime, money laundering and illicit proliferation of arms and light weapons (AU Peace and Security, 2015). The 2002 protocol was adopted on 9 July 2002, entered into force on 26 December 2003 and last signed on 24 December 2013. The protocol aims to give effect to Article 3(d) of the Protocol relating to the establishment of the Peace and

Security Council with the responsibility to co-ordinate and harmonise continental efforts in the prevention and combating of international terrorism in all its aspects (AU, 2016).

3. The African Model Anti-Terrorism Law: This was adopted by the 17th Summit, held in Malabo, Equatorial Guinea in July 2011. The Law is ready-made technical assistance/aids to African states to bring their CT legislation up to date and provide guidance in the effective implementation of international and regional CT instrument (Larissa, Larissa, & Nico, 2013:163). The law enables member nations of the AU to pursue or extradite terrorists active on their territory and calls for drawing up a list of known terrorist and terrorist entities. The proposed model law features all the necessary legal procedures to prevent and combat terrorist acts, including the criminalisation of terrorist acts, the establishment of channels of cooperation, enhancement of surveillance on the border, exchange of intelligence, judicial cooperation and combating terrorist financing (Lebovich, 2010). In the African Model Law, Chapter 1 deals with the offences associated with terrorism: violent acts of mass destruction, financing of terrorism, money laundering by individuals, financing terrorism and money laundering by legal persons etc. Chapter 2 covers higher terror offences such as the hijacking of aircraft; destroying, damaging or endangering the safety of aircraft; other acts endangering or likely to endanger the safety of aircraft; acts of violence at airports serving international civil aviation. Chapter 3 deals with highest level capital offences such as endangering the safety of maritime navigation and fixed platforms located on the continental shelf; offences against internationally protected persons; hostage-taking; offences relating to nuclear material and nuclear facilities; terrorist bombings; offences relating to unmarked plastic explosives and Offences associated or connected with financing specified offences (The African Model Anti-Terrorism Law, 2011).

4. The African Charter of Human and Peoples' Right: The Charter was adopted on 1 June 1981, entered into force on 19 May 1986, and signed last on 19 May 2016 (AU, 2016). The African Charter on Human and Peoples' Rights is an international human right instrument that protects civil and political rights as well as economic, social, and cultural rights. The instrument is meant to promote and protect human rights and basic freedom in Africa. Article 23 (1 and 2) of the African Charter provides for "the Right to National and International Security and Peace" and states thus: "1. All peoples shall have the right to national and international peace and security. The principles of solidarity and friendly relations implicitly affirmed by the Charter of the United Nations and reaffirmed by that of the Organisation of African Unity shall govern relations between States. 2. For the purpose of strengthening peace, solidarity and friendly relations, State Parties to the present Charter shall ensure that: a. any individual enjoying the right of asylum under Article 12 of the present Charter shall not engage in subversive activities against his country of origin or any other State Party to the present Charter; b. their territories shall not be used as bases for subversive or terrorist activities against the people of any other State Party to the present Charter" (African Commission on Human and Peoples' Rights, 2005).

## Institutional framework of CT-COIN in Africa

The institutional framework of the AU CT-COIN Infrastructure has the following components:

1. African Peace and Security Architecture (APSA): This refers to the broad continental framework for maintaining peace and security in Africa, of which CT-COIN is a crucial component.

APSA is rooted in the 1990s when a substantial number of African countries were engulfed in monumental civil wars. This was against the backdrop of the failure of the United Nations to come to the rescue of African countries after the Cold War. In particular, the collapse of Somalia in 1991, the Rwandan Genocide of 1994 and violent civil wars in Angola, DRC, Liberia and Sierra Leone exposed the vulnerability of Africa states. It compelled them to re-calibrate the African Union and RECs to devise local means of dispute resolution and crisis management. However, in the 1990s, the Charters of the Organisation of African Unity (OAU) and RECs did not allow for interference in the internal affairs of member states. If anything, they affirmed the inviolability of the territorial integrity and sovereignty of African states. The transformation of the OAU to AU in 2002 was followed, two years late, by the establishment of APSA. The constitutive instrument of the AU contained the essence of continental mechanism not only for conflict management and resolution but also for inter-African cooperation to address the roots of terrorism and confront the scourges of terrorism. Article 4 (h) and (j) of the constitutive act allows AU member states to intervene in a third state even against the will of the respective government in case of genocide, war crimes and a crime against humanity. This is a total deviation from the "non-interventionist norm" that bedevilled the defunct OAU for over 50 years. APSA's three central instruments are conflict prevention, conflict management and peacebuilding of the African Union (AU), the Regional Economic Communities (RECs) as well as the Regional Mechanism (RMs). At the continental level, the new AU Charter of 2002 provides the broad platform for a collective decision relating to conflict intervention and African peer support in cases of terrorism and insurgency. This is provided in Article 2 of the AU which provides for five pillars of the APSA: (1) the Peace and Security Council (PSC), which is the central organ of the AU; (ii) the Panel of the Wise (PoW); (iii) the Continental Early Warning System (CEWS); (iv) the African Standby Force (ASF) (v) the Peace Fund. Together, this five-pronged mechanism provides a robust frame-work for African countries to overcome the problems of terrorism and insurgency. At the regional levels, the RECs have developed their own regional mechanism for CT-COIN. For example, in West Africa, the ECOWAS provides for specific legal, institutional, and coercive instruments for addressing the root causes and manifestations of terrorism within the region.

2. AU Peace and Security Council (AU/PSC); The AU/PSC is composed of 15 member states elected on a regional basis by the Assembly. It was established in December 2003 and en-visioned as collective security and early-warning arrangement to facilitate a timely and ef-fective response to crisis and conflict situation in Africa (Eyinla, 2013:130). The AU/PSC's authority derives from Article 20 of the Constitutive Act (as inserted by article 9 of the Protocol on Amendments to the Constitutive Act 2003) (AU, 2003) together with article 2 of the 2002 Protocol Relating to the Establishment of the Peace and Security Council of the African Union. Under article 7 of the Protocol, the AU/PSC's key powers include to: (i) Anticipate and prevent disputes and conflicts, as well as policies, which may lead to genocide and crimes against humanity; (ii) Undertake peace-making, peace-building and peace-support missions; (iii) Recommend intervention in a Member State in respect of grave circumstances, namely war crimes, genocide and crimes against humanity; (iv) Institute sanctions; (v) Implement the AU's common defence policy; (vi) Ensure implementation of key conventions and instruments to combat international terrorism; (vii) Promote co-ordination between regional mechanisms and the AU regarding peace, security and stability in Africa; (viii) Follow-up promotion of democratic practices, good governance, the rule of law, protection of human rights and fundamental freedoms, respect for the sanctity of human life and international humanitarian law; (ix) Promote and encourage the implementation of

conventions and treaties on arms control and disarmament; (x) Examine and take action in situations where the national independence and sovereignty of a Member State is threatened by acts of aggression, including by mercenaries; (xi) Support and facilitate humanitarian action in situations of armed conflicts or major natural disasters.

3. Continental Early Warning System (CEWS): this is an African regional mechanism for detecting the root causes of conflict, including terrorism and insurgency, within member states. Supported by UN Security Council Resolution 1809 (UN, 2008), CEWS seeks to provide African states with a continental platform for intelligence gathering on the root causes, risks and prevalence violent conflict and acts of terrorism. CEWS provides for conflict data station to be based in the headquarters and regional offices of the AU. Such data stations will provide a baseline and complex data for intelligent estimation and prognosis of the vulnerabilities to, and spread of conflict and violent activities, including acts of terrorism, militancy and insurgency that may threaten the existence and integrity of African states. As a continental platform, CEWS is expected to provide strategic information to CT-COIN infrastructure of the AU – especially PSC and ASF – and defence establishments of member-states. In addition, it is expected to provide vital data to external stakeholders and sister early warning stations in other parts of the world; in addition, it is well-positioned to tap into rich data from external stakeholders be they state-owned, multilateral or non-governmental. AU's CEWS serves as the intelligence arm of the AU's emerging CT-COIN infrastructure. Nonetheless, the challenge is that presently CEWS is not well-resourced.

4. African Standby Force (ASF): This is a multinational task force established by the AU to provide for quick response to situations of crisis and complex political emergencies, including acts of terrorism and insurgency that may overwhelm and/or threaten the survival and territorial integrity of member-states. ASF is designed as a hybrid force with military, police, and civilian components with an initial military strength of about 15,000 armed personnel continent-wide as contained in Article 13 of the Protocol Relating to the Establishment of PSC. The Article also provided that the multidisciplinary standby contingents would include civilian and military components in their countries of origin, ready for rapid deployment at appropriate notice. For that purpose, the Protocol urged the member states to take steps to establish standby contingents for participation in conflict intervention missions decided on by the PSC or authorised by the AU Assembly. Further, the Standard Operating Procedures (SOPs) for CT-COIN provides for the nature and strength of contingents, their level of readiness and general location; this is subject to periodic reviews depending on prevailing crisis and conflict situations. According to the PSC Protocol, signed in 2002, the ASF should enable the PSC to perform its responsibilities. Article 13 of the Protocol specifically directs several functions to the ASF. One of these functions have to bear with CT-COIN: "intervention in a Member State in respect of *grave circumstances* or at the request of a Member State in order to *restore peace and security*, in accordance with Article 4(h) and (j) of the Constitutive Act." Reference to "grave circumstances" and "restoration of peace and security" presupposes any collaborative action by African states to join forces to confront or fight terrorism and restore law and order. The Protocol Relating to the Establishment of the Peace and Security Council of the African Union, signed in July 2002, and into force in December 2003, provided for the establishment of the ASF. The command and control of the ASF, as presented in the Maputo Report of July 2003, provided for five regional Standby Brigade forces: A North Africa Regional Standby Brigade (NASBRIG), an East Africa Standby Brigade (EASBRIG); a Force Multinationale de l'Afrique Centrale (FOMAC); a Southern Africa Standby Brigade (SADCBRIG); and an ECOWAS Standby Brigade (ECOBRIG). The ASF Policy

Framework Document from May 2003 aimed the development of the ASF in two phases. The first phase (up to 30 June 2005) envisaged the establishment of a strategic level management capacity for the management of missions, while Regional Economic Communities (RECs)/Regions would complement the African Union (AU) by establishing regional standby forces up to a brigade-size to scale up the operational capacity of the brigades. The second phase 1 July 2005 to 30 June 2010. By the year 2010, the AU planned to have developed the capacity to manage complex peacekeeping operations, while the RECs/ Regions will continue to develop the capacity to deploy a Mission Headquarters (HQs) for joint field deployment involving AU/Regional peacekeeping forces.

5. The African Centre for the Study and Research on Terrorism (ACSRT): The African Centre for Study and Research on Terrorism (ACSRT) was inaugurated on 13 October 2004 with Headquarters in Algiers, Algeria, as a structure of the African Union Commission, in conformity with the Protocol to the 1999 OAU Convention on the Prevention and Combating of Terrorism. The establishment of ACSRT is as constituted under Section H, Paragraphs 19 to 21 of the AU Plan of Action on the Prevention and Combating of Terrorism and pursuant to the relevant decisions adopted by the policy Organs of the Union with the purpose of functioning as a research Centre of excellence in matters concerning the prevention and combating of terrorism in Africa. The ultimate objective of ACSRT is to eliminate the threat posed by terrorism to peace, security, stability, and development in Africa. To this end, the Centre conducts research and study into Terrorism. The Centre also maintains a database, collects, and centralises information, studies and analyses on terrorism and terrorist groups. The Centre also seeks to build counterterrorism capacity in the Member States and therefore develops training programs and packages and runs training sessions, workshops, meetings and symposia with the assistance of a myriad of stakeholder partners (ACSRT African Centre for the Study and Research on Terrorism, 2016). The ACSRT interacts with the Member States through the National Focal Points (FP). The FP is a governmental body that coordinates the activities of all actors involved in the prevention and combating of terrorism at the national level. Functions and interactions between the ACSRT and the FP are established in accordance with the Code of Conduct adopted during the Second Annual Meeting of FP, held in Algiers from 18 to 20 May 2006. The ACRST also collaborates closely with several regional and international partners. These include the European Union (EU); the UN Counterterrorism Committee (CTC) and its Counterterrorism Executive Directorate (CTED); the UN Counterterrorism Implementation Task Force (CTITF); the United Nations Office on Drugs and Crime (UNODC); the relevant committees established pursuant to UN Security Council resolutions; the International Civil Aviation Organisation (ICAO) and the Global Counterterrorism Forum (GCTF) (AU Peace and Security, 2015).

## The challenges of AU's counterterrorism and counterinsurgency framework

There are several challenges confronting the AU's CT–COIN architecture. First, there is a lack of adequate resources. The quest for adequate funding for the successful functioning of the AU has been a source of worry. The International concern about Africa has more to do with the weak states providing a haven for terrorists, from which to finance and launch terrorist attacks or hide from international retribution (Fagbohun, 2013:599). To buttress the above point, the African Union is solemnly dependent on its external partners for funding (EU, Germany, China, World Bank and Turkey). The partners assume a dubious role of supervising and imposing an external governance agenda and different peace and security architecture, thereby, making the AU accountable to their financial donors. Eyinla (2013: 136–140) explains that the European Union (EU), is the single largest contributor to the AU, allocating 1b to the African peace facility and 95m to the African Union capacity building programme under the 9th and 10th EU development fund. Beyond the contribution from various states of the EU to the AU, 30 million was provided by Germany in 2012 to support AU various programmes, 42m provided by Germany to AU for operationalisation of the African Peace and Security Architecture(APSA) in 2019, US$200m estimated AU conference and office building in Addis Ababa, donated by the government and people of China, US$95m by China over three years (2012–2015) period, and over US$100m US annual support. Consequently, the World Bank provides close to three-quarter of funding for AU's programmes. This calls to question the autonomy and sustainability of AU's CT-COIN architecture.

Secondly, member states of the AU have often demonstrated ominous reluctance to embrace AU's CT-COIN framework. AU member states tend to pay more attention to the existential and livelihood challenges of their citizens, of which terrorism is a manifestation. Rather, many nations devote concentration on issues they find as priorities like poverty alleviation, corruption, economic growth, development, disease prevention and so on. This is based on the common belief that investing in the welfare and survival of citizens reduces the risk of terrorism by a significant margin. Nevertheless, there is a need to strike the balance between public welfare (soft security) and anti-terrorism (hard security). In addition, a terrorist attack can come externally, and there is a need for joint efforts to prevent and counter terrorism through sub-regional, regional, and continental legal frameworks and architecture. A speech given by former US President Bill Clinton, (2004:72), following a terrorist attack in the US, is apt even for the African scenario: "when we are attacked … we come together. We need to get the very best Ideas we can and we need to move as quickly as we can, do everything we can to try to strengthen this country's hand against terrorism. This has got to be a long, discipline, concerted and united effort."

The third challenge is the non-compliance of anti-terror legislation and protocols by African states: African states are identified by poor rates of compliance and/or ratification of peer national anti-terror legislation and national anti-terror strategies. Ratification provides a legal foundation for institutionalising and domesticating terrorism prevention by creating access to a cross-national mechanism for anti-terror legislation and application. At the continental level, implementation of ratified AU instruments remains as important as ratification itself; unfortunately, many African nations hardly build the genetic capacity of the national criminal justice system to efficiently protect its people of their rights and prevent and counter terrorism. Majority of the African leaders who finds it difficult to comply with constitutional and AU CT-COIN instrument are influenced by foreign powers, thereby, weakening the resolve of African countries for countering terrorism and insurgency. Nwolise, (2013) confirms that most African leaders have been too self-centred, visionless, anti-people, corrupt, and readily manipulated by foreign powers. According to Emmanuel Tanay (2004:47): "when people are caught in a system that does not represent them and does not consider their mental, physical, and emotional needs, they may lash out against that system."

## Conclusion

In the context of Africa, an effective continental CT-COIN framework exists in principle. Still, this framework is not without its challenges – such as lack of fund, the reluctance of member state to key into the framework. The AU's CT-COIN framework requires the commitment of member states, and the AU itself to be implemented. However, due to the AU's inability to fund itself and its dependence on external partners, AU's CT-COIN framework is at the mercy of resource and external stakeholders. In addition, the reluctance of member states to embrace AU's CT-COIN architecture, and the noncompliance to ratified instruments, especially at the national level, have made it extremely difficult to counterterrorism and insurgency on the continent.

What are the solutions to the challenges confronting AU's CT-COIN drive? First, the AU should examine the issue of funding to bring relief on the affordability and functionality of the AU, even as it struggles to meet its organisational problems. In line with the AU's strategic plans of financing its inclusive growth and sustainable development, the Union should lay down concrete measure/plans to generate sufficient funds within and outside Africa to empower the AU's operational budget and have enough as a reserve. An international donor summit would not be a bad idea. Also, AU should consider securing a substantial financial commitment from the part of member-state. Secondly, at the national front, AU member states should embrace AU CT-COIN legal framework and make it relevant apparatus to beef up national security. Law is a strategic asset in countering terrorism, and the global CT effort is premised upon national level. For African nations to effectively ratify and embrace AU legal instrument, the following needs to be strengthened: first, AU frameworks must provide a basis for criminalisation provisions in national law and allow states to adopt the offences described in the instrument. Second, sub-regional, regional and continental architecture of African security needs to be strengthened and finally, Peace and Security Council (PSC) needs to be greatly strengthened at the regional and continental level, to create institutional ties between PSC and sub-regional entities as well as between it and national governments and the broader international community.

Finally, the AU needs to improve its enforcement framework by ensuring that member states comply with AU's CT-COIN Policy and ensure its effective implementation. The AU should make a resolution on the ratification of relevant CT-COIN instruments by creating binding thresholds on national CT-COIN performance. The AU leadership should put in place a CT-COIN benchmark that will hold member-states accountable to their performance at the national and sub-regional theatres of operation.

# References

African Commission on Human and Peoples' Rights. (2005). *African commission on human and peoples' right, legal instrument.* Online: http://www.achpr.org/cgi-bin/dada/mail.cgi Accessed 24.01.17 at 11.50 hours.

African Commission on Human and Peoples' Rights. (2006). *Legal instruments, constitutive act of the African Union.* Addis Ababa: African Union.

African Commission on Human and Peoples' Rights. (2014). 276: Resolution on Terrorist Acts in Africa, the 55th Ordinary Session of the African Commission on Human and Peoples' Rights, Luanda, Angola, from 28 April to 12 May 2014. Available: https://www.achpr.org/sessions/re-solutions?id=323. Accessed on 2 February 2019.

ACSRT (African Centre for the Study and Research on Terrorism). (2016). *Institutional profile.* Online: www.caert.org.dz Accessed 25.01.17 at 10.42 hrs.

AU (African Union) (2000). Constitutive Act of the African Union. Addis Ababa: African Union. Available: https://au.int/sites/default/files/pages/34873-file-constitutiveact_en.pdf. Accessed on 12 January 2019.

AU (African Union) (2002). AU Plan of Action on the Prevention and Combatting of Terrorism in Africa. Addis Ababa: African Union. Available: https://www.peaceau.org/uploads/au-anti-terrorism-plan-of-action.pdf. Accessed on 2 January 2019.

AU (African Union) (2003). Protocol on Amendments to the Constitute Act of the African Union. Addis Ababa: African Union. Available: https://au.int/sites/default/files/treaties/35423-treaty-0025_-_protocol_on_the_amendments_to_the_constitutive_act_of_the_african_union_e.pdf. Accessed on 2 February 2019.

African Union. (2011). *African model anti-terrorism law*. Addis Ababa: African Union.

Aguilar, M. Watson, T., & Verge D. (2008). *African Union: The 2008 National Model United Nations Guide (NMUN)*. Online: http://www.nmun.org/ny_archives/08%20Guides/AU_08.pdf Accessed 03.07.2017 at 12.09hrs.

Al-Jazeera. (2011). *Profile: The Lord's Resistance Army*. Online: http://www.aljazeera.com/news/africa/2011/10/2011101418364196576.html Accessed 03.07.17 at 12.09hrs.

AU Peace and Security. (2015). *Countering terrorism and violent extremism*. Addis Ababa, Ethiopia: African Union Commission.

AU (African Union). (2016). *African Charter on Human and Peoples' Right*. https://www.au.int/web/en/treaties/african-charter-human-and-peoplesrights Accessed 23.01.17 at 12.45hrs.

AU (African Union). (2016). *Protocolrelating to the establishment of the Peace and Security Council of the African Union*. African Union Headquarters. Online: https://www.au.int/en/treaties/protocol-relating-establishment-peace-and-security-council-african-union Accessed 23.01.17 at 04.08hrs.

AU, Peace and Security Council (PSC). (2017). *Profile*. Online: https://www.au.int/en/organs/psc. Accessed 23/1/2017 at 03.20hrs.

AU/PSC. (2015). About the African Centre for the Study and Research on Terrorism (ACSRT), African Union Peace and Security. Online: http://www.peaceau.org/en/page/2–3591-static-about-african-centre-for-study-and-research-on-terrorism-ACSRT Accessed 25.01.17 at 11.15hrs.

BBC News. (2016). Who are Somalia's al-Shabab? Online: www.bbc.com/news/world-africa-1536689 Accessed 02.02.2017 at 15.55hrs.

Chergui, Smail. (2017). *The Summit of the Regional Cooperation Initiative for the Elimination of the Lord's Resistance Army*, 29 January 2017. African Union Peace and Security. Online: http://www.peaceau.org/en/article/the-summit-of-the-regional-cooperation-initiative-for-the-elimination-of-the-lord-s-resistance-army-29-january Accessed 02.02.17 at 14.45 hrs.

Clinton, B. (2004). Combating terrorism. In H. Kawilarang (Ed.), *Quotations on terrorism*. Victoria, B.C. Canada: Trafford Publishing.

Ewi, M., & Aning, K. (2006). "Assessing the Role of the African Union in Preventing and Combating Terrorism in Africa". *African Security Review*, 15(3), 32–46.

Eyinla, B. M. (2013). The role of external partnership in supporting African Union's institutional architecture. In Akinterinwa B. A. (Ed.), *OAU/AU at 50: Challenges and prospects of self-reliance in Africa*. Lagos: Nigerian Institute of International Affairs.

Fagbohun, D. (2013). AU and the Future of Terrorism in Africa. In Akinterinwa B. A.(Ed.), *OAU/AU at 50: Challenges and Prospects of Self-Reliance in Africa*. Lagos: Nigerian Institute of International Affairs.

Gallup, D. (2004). Terrorism. In H. Kawilarang (Ed.), *Quotations on terrorism*. Victoria. B.C. Canada: Trafford Publishing.

ICSR. (2011). *The challenge of counter-terrorism in Africa*. London: Department of War Studies, Kings College.

James, J. F. Forest, & Giroux, J. (2011). *Terrorism and political violence in Africa: Contemporary trends in a shifting terrain. Perspectives on Terrorism*. Online: http://www.terrorismanalysts.com/pt/index.php/pot/article/view/152/html Accessed 03.07.2017 at 12.45 hrs.

Jolyon, F. (2011). *African counter-terrorism legal frameworks a decade after 2001*. Pretoria, South Africa: Institute for Security Studies (ISS).

Kolodkin, B. (2016). *What is counterterrorism?*. National Counterterrorism Center (NCTC). Online: http://usforeignpolicy.about.com/od/defense/a/what-is-counterterrorism.htm Accessed 03.07.17 at 12.35 hrs.

Larissa, J. H., Larissa, V. D. H., & Nico, S. (2013). *Counter-terrorism strategies in a fragmented international legal order: Meeting the challenges*. Cambridge: Cambridge University Press.

Laub, Z. (2015). *Al-Qaeda in the Islamic Maghreb (AQIM).Council on Foreign Relations*. Online: http://www.cfr.org/terrorist-organizations-and-networks/al-qaeda-islamic-maghreb-aqim/p12717 Accessed 02.02.17 at 16.30 hrs.

Lebovich, A. (2010). *Guest post from Xavier Rauscher: How the African Union defines terrorism*. Online: https://thewasat.wordpress.com/2010/12/21/how-the-african-union-defines-terrorism/ Accessed 23.01.17 at 03.05 hrs.

Nwolise, O. B. C. (2013). "Political will and the African Union's Capacity for Peace and Security in Africa: Past, Present and Future", *OAU/AU at 50: Challenges and Prospects of Self-Reliance in Africa*. Lagos: Nigerian Institute of International Affairs.

OAU/AU Constitutive Acts of the African Union. 2000. Online: http://www.peaceau.org/uploads/au-act-en.pdf Accessed 03.07.17 at 16.30 hrs.

Obene, W. R. (2015). "Combating Terrorism and Insurgency in Nigeria: An Appraisal of the Current Approach". *Constructive Engagement (Journal of Alumni Association of National Defence College, Nigeria)*, *1*(7), 15–32.

Ogwu, J. U. (2002). *The African Union and the problems of collective defence and security, the African Union and the challenges of cooperation and integration*. Ibadan, Nigeria: The Ministry of Cooperation and Integration in Africa, The Presidency, Abuja, Nigeria & Spectrum Books Limited.

Omotoso, F. (2016). *Origin of Islamic radicalism in Nigeria, terrorism in Nigeria: The war against Boko Haram*. Ibadan, Nigeria: Net View Books.

Tanay, E. (2004). *Terrorism*. In H. Kawilarang (Ed.), *Quotations on terrorism*. Victoria, B.C. Canada: Trafford Publishing.

Tar UA , & Mustapha M. (2017). '*The Emerging Architecture of a Regional Security Complex in the Lake Chad Basin' Africa Development*, Vol. *XLII*, 99–118.

Tar, U. A., & Mustapha, M. (2016) Emerging Architecture of Regional Security Complex in the Lake Chad Basin. Being a Paper Presented at the *International Conference on Security Regimens in Africa Organised by CODESERIA*, Held at Azalai Grand Hotel, Bamako, Mali, 28–29 September 2016.

The African Model Anti-Terrorism Law. (2011). *Final Draft as endorsed by the 17th Ordinary Session of the Assembly of the Union, Malabo*. Online: www.caert.org.dz/official-documents/african-model-law-en.pdf Accessed 23.01.17 at 03.42 hrs.

The US States Department. (2012). *Profile: The Lord's Resistance Army. Al-Jazeera*. Online: http://www.aljazeera.com/news/africa/2011/10/2011101418364196576.html Accessed 03.07.17 at 12.09hrs.

UN (United Nations). (2008). UN Security Council Resolution 1809 Adopted by the Security Council at its 5868th meeting on 16 April 2008. New York: United Nations. Available: http://unscr.com/en/resolutions/doc/1809. Accessed on 2 January 2019.

Vanguard. (2011). AU Lists Boko Haram, Al-Shabaab, others terrorist groups. Online: http://www.vanguardngr.com/2011/12/au-lists-boko-haram-al-shabaab-others-terrorist-groups/Accessed 03.07.17 at 12.15 hrs.

# 21

# ECOWAS

## Emerging regional architecture for counterterrorism and counterinsurgency in West Africa

*Sharkdam Wapmuk*

## Introduction

The chapter undertakes an assessment of the Economic Community of West African Countries (ECOWAS) Counterterrorism and Counterinsurgency (CT-COIN) initiatives. It argues that terrorism is not new in West Africa. However, its intensification in the region culminated in the adoption of regional initiatives towards CT-COIN in the region (Maiangwa, 2017; Ewi, 2013). Following the terrorist attacks in the United States on 11 September 2001, international attention on terrorism did not only increase globally with the "Global War on Terror" (GWOT), but the searchlight beamed on the called "un-governed territories in Africa" (Rabasa et al., 2007). The ungoverned territories are defined with respect to physical spaces and the level of governmental control, particularly due to state failure or collapse. According to Rabasa et al. (2007), the area where central government authority does not penetrate in Africa provides fertile ground for radicalisation and violent extremism. Thus, the vacuum left by limited or total lack of governmental presence is filled by criminal gangs, terrorists, and other violent non-state actors. Since the 9/11 attacks, many violent non-state actors have emerged to challenge state authority and established terror networks beyond state control.

In West Africa, the increased activities terrorist groups created serious concerns. These include the Al-Qaeda in the Islamic Maghreb (AQIM), the Movement for Unity and Jihad in West Africa (MUJAO), Ansar Dine, Jamaatu Ah lis Sunna Lidda a Waati Wal Jihad (Boko Haram) and Jama'atu Ansarul Musilimina Fi Bi ladis Sudan (Ansaru), amongst others (Onuoha & Ezirim, 2013). These challenges required collective response at various levels and called for stronger cooperation to counter acts of terrorism and insurgency. While national and bilateral efforts are critical to CT-COIN, coherent and coordinated regional responses needed to be developed and maintained. This especially holds for West Africa as most countries do not have the individual capacity, experiences, resources, and technology to counter the scourge of terrorism and insurgency on their own.

Many factors highlighted the need for a regional response to terrorism in West Africa. These include, but not limited to, poorly governed and porous borders area, the increasing networks of criminal networks across borders, the proliferation of small arms and light weapons, the free movement of people and goods, and lack of security and safety nets in the border areas. The West African region has become a fertile ground for arms, drugs, human trafficking, and organised crime (Fulgence, 2015). At the national level, diverse security threats have emerged due to failures in the areas of political, economic, developmental, and social provisioning in many West African countries. Economic marginalisation and poverty, weak governance structures, high prevalence of crime and banditry, and inefficient security structures, have contributed to an impoverished populace. Criminal groups ranging from bandits to armed groups and militia have evolved on this basis. More worrying is that these criminal groups are ready and willing to work together with and support terrorists to further weaken security on the region. In the West African region, discontentment provides the space for the easy recruitment of locals for terrorist groups. Many of the recruited are impoverished and comprise frustrated youth that is poorly educated or uneducated, and unemployed. Terrorism in West Africa and the links amongst terrorist networks continue to increase in countries such as Mauritania, Mali, Niger, Chad, and Nigeria, amongst others.

Terrorism has implications for the security, political and economic development dimensions of member states and the whole region. This has therefore become of increased concern for the ECOWAS, leading to the adoption of several initiatives aimed at countering terrorism within the region. In realisation of the increasingly negative impact of terrorism on the region, West African leaders' commitment themselves to work together to address this scourge. On 27 and 28 February 2013, this commitment was embodied in the Political Declaration on a Common Position against Terrorism, which included a Counterterrorism Strategy and Implementation Plan, adopted by the Authority of Heads of State and Government of the Economic Community of West African States (ECOWAS) at its 42$^{nd}$ ordinary session in Yamoussoukro, Cote d'Ivoire. The Strategy is the result of an inclusive process that began in 2009 and has involved national, regional, and international experts, civil society, and media organisations (ECOWAS, 2013). The ECOWAS counterterrorism strategy is not a stand-alone initiative but associate with other global, continental, and regional CT-COIN initiatives as well as National Laws of member states.

The primary purpose of the Declaration and Strategy is to prevent and eradicate terrorism and related criminal acts in West Africa, to create conditions conducive to sound economic development and ensure the wellbeing of all ECOWAS citizens. The initiative also seeks to give effect to regional, continental, and international counterterrorism instruments and to provide a common operational framework for action. At a time of rising transnational criminal activities and terrorism in West Africa, the Declaration was hailed as a historic achievement in ECOWAS's efforts to combat terrorism (Maiangwa, 2017). Military coups, internecine conflicts, mercenary activities, and authoritarian regimes have exposed West Africans to different incarnations of terrorism. The recent intensification of terrorist attacks in the region, particularly following the escalation of the Niger-Delta conflict in 2006 and the resurgence of Boko Haram in 2009, as well as the occupation of northern Mali by terrorist groups in 2012, have alarmed not only West African countries but also the broader international community. These developments have exposed the fragility of West African states and the profound threat that terrorism poses to peace, stability, development, and territorial integrity (Ettang, 2011).

The key questions, therefore, are: what are the major tenets of the Declaration and Strategy and can it solve the complicated problem of terrorism in West Africa? What are the other major ECOWAS CT-COIN initiatives? What are the prospects and challenges in implementing the ECOWAS CT-COIN? This chapter seeks answers to these questions and examines the regional CT-COIN drives in ECOWAS. The chapter, which is divided into six sections, begins with the introduction and follows by the examination of the Complex Region of West Africa and Security Challenges. While the third section focuses on trends and Regional Dynamics of Terrorism in West Africa, the fourth assesses the ECOWAS CT-COIN Initiatives. The fifth section is titled Prospects and Challenges of Implementing the ECOWAS CT-COIN, and the sixth section is the Conclusion.

## The complex region of West Africa and security challenges

The West African region is made up of 16 states namely Benin, Burkina Faso, Cape Verde, Cote d'Ivoire, Gambia, Ghana, Guinea, Guinea-Bissau, Liberia, Mali, Mauritania, Niger, Nigeria, Senegal, Sierra Leone, and Togo. While 11 countries lie on the coast of the Atlantic Ocean, five countries form part of the Sahel. These countries, except for Mauritania, which opted out are members of the regional Economic Community of West African States (ECOWAS) that was established on 28 May 28 1975. The complexity of the region of West Africa is typified by its "affluence and affliction" (Onuoha & Ezirim, 2013). Several factors shaped the tendency towards regional cooperation and integration in West Africa. This is underscored by the pervasive presence of partitioned ethnic nationalities during the colonial venture into African territories. These trans-border peoples have continued to maintain a wide range of socioeconomic, cultural, and even political links with each other, notwithstanding imposed boundaries and other barriers imposed by colonial heritage — the factors facilitating contacts and interactions and therefore integration in West Africa, even in the post-colonial era, including cross-border trade, trans-border natural resources, historical and cultural links (Okpeh, 2013). On a broad scale, EOWAS states are diverse in terms of sizes of territories they occupy, population, and resource endowments. At the same time, ECOWAS states are not at the same level of growth and development. However, they are confronted with a multitude of governance and security challenges, some of which require collective efforts to address.

In terms of territorial size, the West Africa region, 4.7 million square kilometres in area, is more than twice the size of Western Europe (Musah, 2009). Its 6,000-kilometre coastal arc, stretching from the upper reaches of Angola in South-West Africa to the lower reaches of Western Sahara to the north and washed by the Atlantic Ocean. Its population is estimated at about 362 million people as of 2016 accounts for 30% of the African continent's population (African Union, 2017: 4). ECOWAS countries are well endowed with huge reserves of natural resources. West Africa is endowed with oil and gas, precious and strategic natural minerals, including gold, uranium, diamonds, and titanium and fertile land for agriculture. Despite its resource endowment, most West African countries are poor and confronted with different levels of security, governance, and development challenges.

The political and economic malaise in West Africa have been linked to the so-called "resource curse", a thesis whose explanations are not farfetched (Badeeb et al., 2017). Although West Africa is among Africa's most resource-endowed regions, most countries, if not all, within the region are among the poorest and least-developed on the continent and in the world. Their resource endowments, rather than being blessings - bringing prosperity, development, stability, and peace, have been sources of contestations, conflicts, and general state of insecurity – a curse (Badeeb et al., 2017). Member states of ECOWAS are well endowed with abundant natural resources and arable land suitable for agriculture. However, poor management of national wealth and its distribution has left almost two-thirds of the population impoverished, living on less than US$1.25 a day. Poverty in West Africa stems from inefficient use of available resources, the mismanagement of public funds and the frequent outbreak of conflicts that leave many internally displaced and creating deep humanitarian situations (Musah, 2009).

Insecurity in West Africa often takes the form of conflicts between different ethnic, religious, and communal groups for control of the state power, resources, and influence. The expectations of the people that in the post-colonial era, the leadership in West Africa states will promote the good life remain a dashed hope. Many leaders have failed to strengthen national unity and would rather promote ethnic and religious division to further their selfish interests. These are complicated by the porosity of national borders, the uncontrolled movement of violent non-state actors (VNSAs) and the proliferation of illegal arms and weapons (SALWs) that increase the risk of spill-over from conflicts in neighbouring states. For example, in West Africa, the emergence of the Boko Haram insurgent group has led to the escalation of violence in the North-eastern part of the country, spreading to neighbouring countries, and leading to the destruction of lives and properties including the kidnap school children for ransom. Similarly, cross-border crime is an enduring threat to the security and livelihoods of civilians. In the border areas of the Sahel, criminal gangs continue to endanger the lives of civilians.

West Africa experienced multiple wars and a succession of conflicts in Côte d'Ivoire, Guinea, Gulf of Guinea, Liberia, Mali, Niger, Nigeria, and Sierra Leone. These conflicts have not been restricted by state borders. The nature of violence in West Africa has changed significantly over the last decade. Conventional and large-scale conflict events, and civil wars, have receded in scale and intensity, replaced by more complex increasing threats. These include, but not limited to, election-related violence, extremism and terror attacks, drug trafficking, maritime piracy, and criminality. In addition, wars are increasingly being fought on the periphery of the state by armed insurgents who are both factionalised and in some cases militarily weak, as evidenced by the campaign carried out by Boko Haram in Nigeria and the Tuareg and Arab uprisings in Mali (Vanguard News, 2018). Though ECOWAS had made efforts in the past to address increasing security challenges in the region, the surge in terrorism has necessitated the rethink of the security architecture of the region. Against the backdrop of these increasing terrorist activities in the West African region, the leaders had to confront the realities of building synergy and cooperation in addressing the scourge of terrorism.

## Developments and regional dynamics of terrorism in West Africa

The ECOWAS as the largest regional integration organisation on the African continent has moved from a mere economic to political union. Since its establishment in 1975, it has undergone internal reorganisation and transformation to confront the security challenges confronting its member states (Ewi, 2012). During the civil wars in Liberia and Sierra Leone in the 1990s, the organisation created the ECOWAS Monitoring Group (ECOMOG) as a peace-keeping force to resolve the conflict, restore order and establish a democratically elected government. The establishment of the ECOMOG was in response to both regional instability and heavy refugee flow.

Over the years, the ECOWAS region has been confronted with armed conflicts, growing insecurity, civil wars, and terrorism. Among these security challenges, terrorism has emerged as an arduous threat to regional security in West Africa. According to Ewi (2012), though terrorism is considered a recent development in West Africa, the use of terror as a strategy is not new. Among the several acts of terror in West Africa in the past was the bomb that exploded in Accra in 1964 predating the assassination of President Kwame Nkrumah; Kidnapping in the post-independence period occurred in Kaduna, Nigeria when ZANU-PF kidnapped ten people in the British Consulate; use of letter bomb to kill a renowned journalist, Dele Giwa on 19 October 1986; Bilma bombing,

19 September 1989; bomb exploded at Ilorin Stadium, Nigeria on 30 May 1995 (Ewi, 2012: 8). The terror acts at that time in West Africa were largely characterised by kidnapping, hijacking, hostage-taking, bombing, suicide attacks, and murder, amongst others. However, the years from 2000 to 2010 have been described as the deadliest terrorist decade in West Africa (Ewi, 2012: 8).

The stack reality that terrorism posed to the region was underscored by the Africa Report of 12 April 2016 noting an increase of attacks in Mali, Burkina Faso, Cote d'Ivoire and Nigeria. The Africa Report also stated that intelligence agencies have warned that of "credible terrorist's threat" faced in all the 16 member countries in the West African region (Laary, 2016). The terrorist attacks have been carried out by groups alleged to have links with Al-Qaeda in the Islamic Maghreb (AQIM). Nigeria has emerged as the country with the highest instance of terrorist activity within the ECOWAS region. Several terrorist groups have emerged in West Africa. According to the Global Terrorism Index 2018, compiled by the Institute for Economics and Peace (IEP) these include Ansar Dine, le Mouvement pour la Liberation de l'Azawad (MNLA), Mouvement pour l'Unicité et le Jihad dans l'Afrique de L"Ouest (MUJAO), Boko Haram, Fulani Militants and Al-Shabab (Institute for Economics and Peace, 2018; Kwaga, 2016). Nigeria was ranked as the third after war-torn countries like Iraq, Afghanistan and ahead of Syria and Pakistan as the most terrorised nation worldwide, with the Boko Haram being responsible for 1,254 deaths in 2017 (The Punch, 2018). Current trends of terrorism in West Africa manifest in various forms. Terrorism in northern parts of Nigeria and Mali take forms of insurgency of armed fighters seeking to create independent territory (Boko Haram), armed factionist (Delta Niger), separatists (Tuareg in Mali and Niger) and other forms of terrorism. These terrorist groups engage in robberies, suicide bombings, kidnappings, hostage-taking of children and girls. According to (Ewi, 2012), while about 50 major attacks between 2000 and 2009, more than 300 attacks took place between 2010 and 2012 within the region and 90% of attacks occurred in Nigeria. He argued that West Africa's vulnerabilities to terrorism are the result of bad governance, coups and ethnic tensions, porous borders, the proliferation of arms and light weapons, poverty and mass youth unemployment, corrupt leadership, weak institutions, conflicts between Muslim-Christian, farmers-grazers land conflicts, and failed states (Ewi, 2012: 5). Terrorism has implications for the security, political and economic development dimensions of member states and the whole region. This has therefore become of increased concern for ECOWAS. Terrorism has had a colossal impact in the region by creating insecurity and political instability. On the economic front, "attacks or even the threats of attacks have far-reaching ramifications on trade, investment, tourism and the free movement of people, goods and services," and leads to diversion of scarce resources and funds that could have been channelled for developmental purposes (ECOWAS, 2013:4).

## Assessment of ECOWAS CT-COIN initiatives

ECOWAS has been involved in preventing and combating terrorism. In this section, we examined various initiatives introduced with the aim of preventing and combating terrorism in the West African region. In examining the ECOWAS CT-COIN, the chapter focused on the major ECOWAS anti-terrorism related Conventions/ Treaties and Institutional Mechanisms, the ECOWAS Counterterrorism Strategy and Implementation Plan adopted in 2013, ECOWAS Counterterrorism Financing Initiative under GIABA, Capacity Building Initiatives, Counterterrorism Strategy Tracker managed by Centre for Democracy and Development (CDD), and Extra-Regional Initiatives and partnerships in the Fight Against Terrorism in West Africa.

## Anti-terrorism related conventions/treaties and institutional mechanisms

ECOWAS has initiated several joint and common policies in the areas of defence and security, and several conventions and protocols that are applicable to the fight against terrorism. These instruments are not only relevant in coordinating ECOWAS member states in their efforts in CT-COIN, but also their implementation by member states are relevant to the assessment of West Africa's CT-COIN. These include:

- 2008 ECOWAS Conflict Prevention Framework;
- 2006 ECOWAS Convention on Small Arms and Light Weapons, Their Ammunition and Other Related Materials;
- 2006 Protocol A/P1/01/06 Relating to the Establishment of an ECOWAS Bureau of Intelligence and Investigation on Criminal Matters;
- 2001 ECOWAS Protocol A/P3/12/01 on the Fight against Corruption;
- 2001 Protocol on Democracy and Good Governance Supplementary to the Protocol Relating to the Mechanism for Conflict Prevention, Management, Resolution, Peacekeeping and Security;
- 2001 Protocol A/SP1/12/01 on Democracy and Good Governance Supplementary to the Protocol Relating to the Mechanism for Conflict Prevention, Management, Resolution, Peacekeeping and Security;
- 1999 Protocol A/AP1/12/99 Relating to the Mechanism for Conflict Prevention, Management, Resolution, Peacekeeping and Security;
- 1994 ECOWAS Convention A/P1/8/94 on Extradition;
- 1992 ECOWAS Convention A/P1/7/92 on Mutual Judicial Assistance in Criminal Matters;
- 1982 Convention A/P5/5/82 on Mutual Administrative Assistance in Customs Matters;
- 1981 Protocol A/SP3/5/81 on Mutual Assistance on Defence Matters;
- 1978 Protocol on Non-Aggression; and the
- 1977 Framework Agreement of the Protocol on Non-Aggression and Assistance in Defence (ECOWAS, 2013).

Apart from these protocols that ECOWAS has already adopted in relation to conflict resolution in the region, the organisation has also established a Warning and Response Network known as the ECOWAS Warning and Response Network (ECOWARN). ECOWARN provides the sub-region with the capacity to evaluate, inform and guide responses to potential transnational crime and threats, including terrorism (Maiangwa, 2017). ECOWAS member states are members of the West African Police Chiefs Committee (WAPCCO), which facilitates the exchange of information among its members on potential terrorist and other international criminal activity (Ipe, Cockayne, & Millar, 2010: 13). On a broad scale, the composition of instruments outlined above affirms the resolve of ECOWAS member states to address the evolving security challenges in the region, including terrorism. However, these initiatives have not been able to curb terrorism in the West African region. After 9/11, the focus of the US on West Africa as one of the global sites for its war on terror became an issue of concern. This led some scholars to question whether terrorism in West Africa was real, emerging or imagined threats (Obi, 2006: 87; Ipe et al., 2010). It wasn't long after stakeholders recognised that terrorism is real and the imperative of action to counter the same in West Africa. According to Yoroms (2007:27)

> There is therefore, no doubt that international terrorist organizations have a presence in West Africa and have used the sub region as an operational base without carrying out any major

terrorist attacks of international significance…..The absence of a major attack on any international terrorist target situated in West Africa may, therefore, deliberate tactic to insulate their
hiding place from prying eyes of the international community in order to sustain their activities.

In recognition of the threat posed by terrorist acts to their countries, some individual member
states of ECOWAS had initiated national measures to prevent and combat terrorism. In contrast, others had adopted and strengthened aspects of their national laws criminalising terrorism.
ECOWAS member states had signed, ratified and/or acceding to regional, continental, and
international counterterrorism legal instruments. These include the OAU Convention on the
Prevention and Combating of Terrorism, and submission of reports to the UN Security
Council Counterterrorism Committee (CTC) pursuant to the Security Council resolution
1373 adopted in 2001 (ECOWAS, 2013). Some member states had also established national
mechanisms such as counterterrorism units to coordinate national counterterrorism measures;
and, financial institutions to strengthen regulations on financial and economic activities to
suppress or prevent the abuse of financial systems by terrorists (Kwaga, 2016). Despite these
efforts, West Africa continued to face growing threats of terrorism and insurgency. Terrorist
and insurgent groups such as Boko Haram, Movement for the Emancipation of the Niger Delta
(MEND), Al Qaeda in the Islamic Maghreb (AQIM), Hizbollah, amongst others, intensified
their activities within the region (Yoroms, 2007). Thus, terrorist activities in West Africa during
the past decade have demonstrated the seriousness of the threat posed to member states and the
need for a stronger regional initiative aimed at CT-COIN.

This served as the impetus for harmonisation of efforts of ECOWAS member states and to
provide a regional framework within the ECOWAS for the prevention and combating of
terrorism. A harmonised framework is to serve as an operational policy framework for
ECOWAS counterterrorism actions and for promoting a common regional approach to the
prevention and combating of terrorism within the region. Accordingly, ECOWAS then took a
step further in 2013 to adopt a Political Declaration and Common Position against Terrorism
which resulted in the ECOWAS Counterterrorism Strategy and Implementation Plan
(ECOWAS, 2013). Following a series of negotiation and consultations, the ECOWAS member
state at its 42nd ordinary session in Yamoussoukro, Côte d'Ivoire, on 27 and 28 February 2013
adopted the ECOWAS Counterterrorism Strategy and Implementation Plan. The ECOWAS
strategy built on regional, continental and international counterterrorism instruments, such as
the Organization of African Unity (OAU) Convention on the Prevention and Combating of
Terrorism and its Protocol; the African Union (AU) Plan of Action on the Prevention and
Combating of Terrorism in Africa, Comprehensive African Anti-Terrorism Model Law, and all
other decisions and measures taken by the AU (ECOWAS, 2013).

The strategy outlined measures to be undertaken by various agencies in the Member States
and provides a strategic policy direction towards the containment and elimination of the threat
posed by terrorism to the region. As contained in the ECOWAS strategy, the Authority approved the establishment of an ECOWAS Counterterrorism Coordination Unit; an ECOWAS
Arrest Warrant; an ECOWAS Black List of Terrorist and Criminal Networks, in order to
facilitate coordination and information-sharing among the Member States and, sub-regional
Counterterrorism Training Centre (ECOWAS, 2013). The ECOWAS counterterrorism
strategy, which built on the foundation of existing international, continental, and other regional CT-COIN initiatives outlined the following as objectives of the strategy:

Enhance coordination among the Member States, particularly in the fields of intelligence,
law enforcement, investigation, and the prosecution of terrorist crimes;

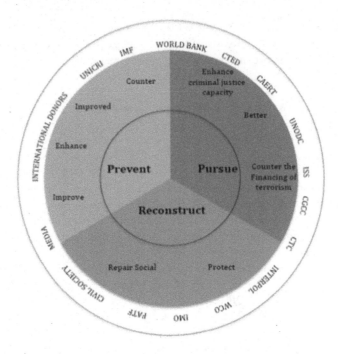

*Figure 21.1*   ECOWAS Counterterrorism Strategy
*Source:* ECOWAS (2013). *ECOWAS Political Declaration and Common Position against Terrorism*, pp.45.

Strengthen national and regional capacities to detect, deter, intercept, and prevent terrorist crimes;

Promote a criminal justice approach that emphasises the rule of law, due process, respect for human rights and the protection of civilians in counterterrorism activities

Prevent and combat violent religious radicalism/extremism;

Harmonise responses to terrorism, including counterterrorism legislation; and

Promote regional and international cooperation on terrorism-related matters, including extradition and mutual legal assistance (ECOWAS, 2013).

The document also clearly outlined the core principles of the strategy as follows:

Terrorism has emerged as a serious threat to peace, security, stability, development, and social cohesion in West Africa;

The primacy of prevention and respect for human rights;

Good governance and democratic culture are prerequisites for effective counterterrorism;

Counterterrorism requires both military and non-military strategies and tools; and

Cooperation among states and technical assistance in all fields constitute the cornerstone for the successful implementation of this Strategy (ECOWAS, 2013).

Towards achieving the objectives of, the ECOWAS counterterrorism Strategy, three key pillars for actions against terrorism was adopted, namely, "Prevent, Pursue and Repair" (PPR) (ECOWAS, 2013: 25). A summary of the ECOWAS strategy is presented in Figure 21.1.

The first pillar, "Prevent" pillar seeks to address and eliminate conditions conducive to terrorism as contained in the UN General Assembly' 2006 Global Counterterrorism Strategy. Under this pillar, member countries are expected to promote policies that address root causes of terrorism, such as poverty and widespread unemployment, economic and political marginalisation of some groups, human rights abuses, corruption, weak security institutions and illicit trans-border activities. ECOWAS states are also expected to develop to counter terrorist propaganda, deny terrorist access to funds, materials, and space with which to plan and launch their attacks. Under the second pillar, which is "Pursue" ECOWAS states are expected to undertake urgent, timely and effective responses to terrorism when it occurs. Equally important is the third pillar termed "Reconstruct," which directs ECOWAS states to rebuild the society and enable the state to heal social wounds caused by terrorism and counterterrorism. Importantly, the strategy underscored the important roles of ECOWAS CT-COIN Mechanisms including ECOWAS Authority, which is the supreme policy-making body; the Executive Council, which is the main policy-making organ; Community Court of Justice, which deals with legal matters and human rights; the ECOWAS Commission that monitors and ensures policy implementation, that deals with coordination of policies; WAPCCO that deals with police coordination on criminal matters; and, CCSS, which deals with coordination of security agencies (Ewi, 2013). The ECOWAS strategy also recognised the key role of financing as a live wire of terrorism in the region.

## Counterterrorism financing initiative in West Africa

The Inter-Governmental Action Group Against Money Laundering in Africa (GIABA) was established in 2000 by the ECOWAS Heads of State and Government and charged with the responsibility for facilitating the adoption and implementation of Anti-Money Laundering (AML) and Counter-Financing of Terrorism (CFT) in West Africa. GIABA, therefore, co-ordinates actions against money laundering and assists governments to enact legislation to counter terrorism funding. GIABA member states include Benin, Burkina Faso, Cape Verde, The Gambia, Guinea-Bissau, Liberia, Niger, São Tomé and Príncipe, Sierra Leone, Côte d'Ivoire, Ghana, Guinea, Mali, Nigeria, and Senegal. The extension of GIABA's mandate to include counterterrorism funding derived from the evidence that terrorist groups are also engaged in many businesses and generating funds to buy arms, pay their fighters and equip their activities. According to GIABA, non-governmental organisations (NGOs), charitable organisations, trading, taking hostages and kidnapping, bank robberies and banditry, are some of the ways of either delivering materials or financing terrorist activities. Drug trafficking is also one of the major ways terrorist groups enrich themselves and this has been made possible by the protocol on free movements on people and goods where illicit products, malefic and harmful objects can easily pass through porous borders. The weakness of surveillance on small border entry between ECOWAS member countries makes it easy to infiltrate illegal goods that may contain packages destined to terrorist groups. Accordingly, the 29th ordinary Summit of Heads of State and Government, of ECOWAS held on 12 January 2006 in Niamey approved the revised Regulation of GIABA, which expanded the mandate of the institution to include responsibility for leading the regional effort to combat terrorism in addition to its other functions of combating drug trafficking and money laundering (Orioha, 2015).

Since its establishment, GIABA has implemented three major strategic plans from 2007–2014 and is in the process of implementing its fourth strategic plan (2016–2020) (Orioha, 2015). The outcomes of these strategies are that all its member states have a body of Anti-Money Laundering and Combating the Financing of Terrorism (AML/CFT) legislative and regulatory laws that in varying degrees are in compliance with the 40 Financial Action Task Force (on Money Laundering) (FATF) recommendations; sixteen (16) GIABA member states have Financial Intelligence Units (FIUs) that are operational in the domain within each member state. GIABA works with not only governments and state institutions, but also with non-state actors such as civil society groups and think tanks (Fulgence, 2015). GIABA constructs typologies to determine the trends, methods and intermediaries of money laundering and terrorist financing. It also organises discussions, plenary meetings, and enlightenment workshops on a broad range of issues concerning AML/CFT regimes in West Africa, as well as the role of GIABA as a regional initiative, trends of Laundering and Terrorism Financing (ML/TF) in the region, threats of ML/TF to peace and security in the region, threats of ML/TF to sustainable development and impact on youth employment (GIABA, 2019).

## Capacity building initiatives

The implementation of the ECOWAS CT-COIN strategy aims at harnessing the roles of the National Taskforce on counterterrorism and calls for the establishment of the ECOWAS Counterterrorism Coordination Unit or Centre with features like the ECOWAS Arrest Warrant and Black List of Terrorist and Criminal Networks. This required the adoption of an ECOWAS Counterterrorism Training Manual and establishment of a training centre for counterterrorism capacity building (Maiangwa, 2013). Member states are saddled with the major responsibility for the implementation of this strategy which entails periodic evaluation and reporting on its implementation (ECOWAS, 2013). The strategy underscores the importance of mutual legal assistance in intelligence, investigation, prosecution, and counterterrorism operation as an absolute necessity to meet the shortfall and disparities in capabilities of member states. To ensure regular follow-ups for accountability and effective monitoring of the process, ECOWAS includes a role for international organisations and civil society organisations (Shuaibu et al., 2015).

## ECOWAS Counterterrorism Strategy Tracker (ECTS-Tracker)

Towards providing information and monitoring the implementation of the ECOWAS Counterterrorism Strategy, the ECOWAS Counterterrorism Strategy Tracker (ECTS-Tracker) has been established and managed by the Centre for Democracy and Development (CDD) in Abuja. It serves as an open data platform that provides a practical analysis of operational policy framework for ECOWAS counterterrorism, actions, supports and serves as a knowledge base that promotes a common regional approach for counterterrorism by both state and non-state actors through the documentation and analysis of cases, activities, and incidences of extremist violence across the West African region. This is done specifically by looking at the location, trends, and patterns of incidences of violent extremism within the West Africa region. The ECTS-tracker also serves as a tool in monitoring the efforts of states in implementing the ECOWAS Counterterrorism Strategy (CTS).

## Extra-regional initiatives in the fight against terrorists

There are several joint initiatives between the ECOWAS member states and international partners with the aim of effective CT-COIN in West Africa. An example in this regard is the Trans-Sahara Counterterrorism Initiative (TSCTI) that was created by the US to counter terrorism in African countries such as Algeria, Tunisia, Morocco, Senegal, Ghana, and Nigeria.

The inclusion of ECOWAS and the Sahelian and Saharan belts of West Africa as part of this counterterrorism partnership with the US and its G-8 allies is as a result of the focus on the African region as one of the global sites for the US' war on terror. Collectively, partners with ECOWAS in CT-COIN in West Africa include the Security Council's Counterterrorism Executive Directorate (CTED), United Nations Office on Drugs and Crime (UNODC), the African Union (AU), the European Union (EU), and the US. These partners have provided technical and other counterterrorism capacity-building assistance to several countries in the sub-region. It is critical that ECOWAS explore these partnerships at the regional level and find opportunities for engagement and collaboration on a wide range of counterterrorism initiatives, such as harmonisation of policies, capacity-building, technical assistance and information sharing (Maiangwa, 2017).

## Prospects and challenges of implementing the ECOWAS CT-COIN

Although a number of joint and common policies, conventions and protocols exist in the ECOWAS region that are applicable to the fight against terrorism, the ECOWAS Declaration and the Strategy could be regarded as a more region-wide comprehensive initiative that was framed specifically to address contemporary challenges posed by terrorism and insurgency. There are prospects for the implementation of the ECOWAS CT-COIN. The ECOWAS counterterrorism strategy is not a stand-alone initiative but connected with global, continental, regional CT-COIN initiatives as well as national laws of member states. Already, some member states have put in place national legislation and laws relating to CT-COIN. Amongst these are Sierra Leone 1861 Malicious Damage Act; Niger Titre VI du Terrorisme du Financement de Terrorism (2003); Ghana Anti-Terrorism Bill (2005) and the Anti-Money laundering Bill (2007); Senegal Loi Modificantle Code de procedure Penaleet Relative a lalutte Contre les Actes de Terrorisme (2007); Gambia Anti-Terrorism Act (amended) 2008 and the Money Laundering Act (2003); and Nigeria Counterterrorism Bill 2010 and the Anti-Money Laundering Bill (amended in 2013) (Ewi, 2013). Several ECOWAS member states have signed and ratified various counterterrorism conventions of the AU and the UN. Even so, not all of them have domesticated or incorporated them as part of national legislation. As noted by Haacke and Williams (2008: 8) they are yet to 'close the wide gap between rhetoric and practical implementation at the national level'. Furthermore, some states in West Africa have anti-money laundering laws in place, although not all the laws are applicable in terrorist financing scenarios.

That notwithstanding, ECOWAS faces several challenges in the implementation of its CT-COIN. The first major challenge is a lack of institutional and operational capacity for implementation. According to Ford (2011: 37), 'there is a general lack of institutional and operational capacity to effectively implement the instruments' because most states have yet to take legislative and practical CT-COIN measures that conform to international standards. He argues further that legal cooperation in West Africa region is made more challenging due to divergence of Anglophone and Francophone systems and suspicion between these ECOWAS member states. Where trust is lacking, it can affect intelligence sharing. Field (2009: 997) opines that the creation of an effective counterterrorism network requires that institutional boundaries be broken down to enable free flow of information through the intelligence community. Terrorist activities often involve more than one state. Terrorist groups can plan and carry out activities in another state while hiding in one, hence intelligence sharing among regional security agencies is key to fighting terrorism within the West African region. The inadequacy of response by ECOWAS in the Malian crisis revealed how differences among member states as well as rivalries, lack of intelligence sharing, lack of planning and military capacity can hamper counterterrorism efforts (Ariel, 2013: 7).

The second challenge for the ECOWAS in the implementation of the CT-COIN is the sensitivity that characterises discourse on terrorism within and among member states in West Africa. According to Shuaibu et al. (2015) the political discourse on CT-COIN in West Africa is often framed in the 'context of sensitivity', particularly in relation to religion, ethnicity, region, politics, and even gender. Similarly, debates on terrorism in West Africa tend to be framed as a Western problem, and counterterrorism as a Western-imposed priority (Maiangwa, 2017). For example, the given the socio-political make-up of the Nigerian state, any discussion on external intervention in the country is often very problematic. According to Hutchful (2007) counterterrorism is often perceived in 'ethnically and religiously diverse societies as a form of racial, ethnic and religious profiling'.

The third challenge hinges on the current obsession with pro-military approaches to CT-COIN in most ECOWAS countries. As a result of the escalation of terrorism in West Africa, some scholars, analysts and observers have proposed various CT-COIN roadmaps that centre largely on military deployment and long-term peace operations are most needed to eliminate terrorists in West Africa (Vines, 2013; Sidibé, 2012). Blyth (2013) argues that the disadvantages of responding militarily may limit the efficacy of counterterrorism initiatives. Where military solutions become the prime response, the local populations may "feel alienated, invaded and colonised" (Maiangwa, 2013: 11). The case of Mali, where Malian and French military might have been deployed against the Tuareg rebellion, and to some extent the military onslaught against the Boko Haram by the Multinational Joint Task Force (MNJTF) of the Lake Chad Basin Commission (LCBC) does not suggest that the military approach or solutions are adequate in CT-COIN. An alternative approach to CT-COIN in ECOWAS should seek to identify the root causes of terrorism and insurgency. This approach involves "the task of reducing conditions that can be exploited by terrorists as a goal" (Dempsey, 2006:19) and dealing with fundamental problems such as economic distress, ethnic and religious fissures, fragile governance, weak democracy, and rampant human rights abuses that create an environment in which terrorists thrive.

Another equally important challenge to the implementation of ECOWAS CT-COIN is funding. It has been argued that "funding plays a crucial role in counterterrorism at the national, regional or global level particularly in relation to police training, gathering intelligence, research, joint military operations, peacekeeping, peace-building, tracking terrorist finance or passing legislation on terrorism" (Williams, 2017:11). Where cooperation does not manifest in financial commitments, the ECOWAS will lack the wherewithal to implement its counterterrorism framework. Maiangwa (2013: 12) and Hutchful (2007: 117) have argued that ECOWAS Member states have been slow in responding to financial requests from the ECOWAS Secretariat. Added this is the fact that member states still find it difficult to urgently mobilise sufficient military, police, or financial resources to address pressing security challenges as demonstrated in the cases of terrorism and insurgency in Nigeria, Mali, Algeria, Niger, Mauritania and Chad (Laremont, 2011: 58). It is inconceivable for ECOWAS, as currently constituted, to make progress without some form of external assistance. Institutions like the International Police Organization (INTERPOL) which has established a programme called OASIS Africa, is being funded by Germany (Cockayne & Williams, 2009: 20). The EU support has been pivotal in rebuilding the Malian army. While such supports are significant in building capacity of the military in CT-COIN, for optimal results, such external support should be coordinated by ECOWAS. Fighting terrorism requires huge financial resources, given the nature of the threats of terrorism and insurgency in the region. If states are not financially committed to this course the ECOWAS will continue to struggle and no matter how comprehensive and well-crafted the ECOWAS CT-COIN, effective and timely implementation will be far from being achieved.

## Concluding remarks

The chapter examined the ECOWAS CT-COIN initiatives. It notes the increase of various security challenges, of which terrorism has emerged as the most devastating in recent times. West Africa plays host to and serves as a theatre for, extremist groups and terrorist cells; conflicts, political instability, collapsed states and presence of rebel groups; and the vast Sahel region, with little or no law enforcement, which has become a conduit for terrorists and traffickers. Despite the signing and ratification of a few joint and common policies in the areas of defence and security- some of which are also applicable to the fight against terrorism, insecurity in the region has not abated. Terrorism has emerged in recent years as a major threat to regional peace and security in West Africa. The increase in terrorist activities as exemplified by the Boko haram in North-eastern Nigeria and other groups in West Africa affiliated with AQIM propelled the ECOWAS member states to a comprehensive CT-COIN. A detailed assessment of the ECOWAS CT-COIN peruses various ECOWAS Conventions/Treaties and Institutional Mechanisms related to terrorism, the ECOWAS Counterterrorism Strategy and Implementation Plan (including the objectives, core principles and the three key pillars -prevent, pursue and repair). The chapter also examined the ECOWAS counterterrorism financing initiative under GIABA, Capacity Building Initiatives, Counterterrorism Strategy Tracker and Extra-Regional Initiatives in the Fight against Terrorists. The chapter revealed that while prospects for implementation of the ECOWAS CT-COIN abound, it equally faces several challenges, which surmountable.

Overall, ECOWAS CT-COIN initiatives, though diverse, fundamentally aim at denying terrorists of havens, eradicating sources of terrorist financing, reducing state vulnerability, and enhancing emergency preparedness and response capabilities with the ultimate goal of preserving the territorial integrity and sovereignty of the state, thus ensuring the safety of citizens. In this pursuit, counterterrorism initiatives in West Africa are "guided by the idea of collective security where threats confronting nation-states cannot be solved by states alone but requires a synergy of capacity and strategy" (ECOWAS, 2013). The implementation of counterterrorism initiatives inadvertently provides responses to other forms of criminality such as money laundering, human trafficking, resource exploitation and drug trafficking and also prevents any form of mutual and/or symbiotically reinforcing relationship between terrorism and any other criminality. Regional responses will require a commitment by the leadership of member states to harmonise policies and work together despite their varied interests and resources. Effective collaboration will therefore require individual member states to give up some aspects of their national independence to contribute to the wider goals and the group collective. Furthermore, countries in the ECOWAS region yet to put into place legislation to combat terrorism should as a matter of urgency do so. ECOWAS' role is thus critical in creating awareness and engaging with member states to put stronger legislations into place and to ensure that compliance is achieved. The emerging trends of terrorism call for enhanced cooperation, financing, intelligence sharing and political will on the part of member states. The role of ECOWAS secretariat in addressing and combating these contemporary trends is critical. In conclusion, the ECOWAS is viewed as one of the strongest regional bodies on the African continent and has the potential to play a leading role in advancing CT-COIN in West Africa.

# References

African Union. (2017). *Second session of the Specialised Technical Committee on Health, Population and Drug Control (STC-HPDC-2)*. Addis Ababa, Ethiopia 20–24 March 2017. Retrieved from https://au.int/sites/default/files/newsevents/ workingdocuments/32187-wd-state_of_africas_population_-_sa19093_-e.pdf.

Ariel, A. (2013). *CRS report for Congress prepared for members and committees of Congress* (pp. 1–18). Crisis in Mali: Congressional Research Service.

Badeeb, R., Abubakr, L., Hooi, H., & Jeremy, C. (2017). The evolution of the natural resource curse thesis: A critical literature survey. *Resources Policy, 51*, 123–134.

Blyth, F. (2013). *Is the French military the best counterterrorism response in Mali?* Retrieved from http://www.theglobalobservatory.org/analysis/498-is-the-french-military-the best counterterrorism- response-in-mali.html.

Bolaji, K. A. (2010). Preventing terrorism in West Africa: Good governance or collective security? *Journal of Sustainable Development in Africa, 12*(1), 207–222.

Cockayne, J., & Williams, P. (2009). *The invisible tide: Towards an international strategy to deal with drug trafficking through West Africa*. New York: International Peace Institute, October.

Dempsey, T. (2006). *Counterterrorism in African failed states: Challenges and potential solutions*. Retrieved from http://www.StrategicStudiesInstitute.army.mil/.

ECOWAS. (2013). *ECOWAS Political Declaration and Common Position against Terrorism*, 28 February, Yamoussoukro. Retrieved from http://www.edup.ecowas.int/wp-content/uploads/2016/11/Ecowas-CT-strategy_ENGLISH-Published.pdf.

Ettang, D. (2011, January 24). *Regional responses to terrorism: The case of ECOWAS*. Retrieved from http://www.polity.org.za/login.php?url=/article/regional-responses-to-terrorism-the-case-of-ecowas-2011-01-24&functionality=1.

Ewi, M. A. (2013, March 13). *West Africa: The new ECOWAS Counter-Terrorism Strategy and Its Implications*. ISS Today. Retrieved from http://www.issafrica.org/iss-today.

Ewi, M. A. (2012). *The complex dimension of terrorism in West Africa vulnerabilities, trends and notorious terrorist networks*. Presentation prepared for SWAC/OECD. Pretoria: ISS, June 12.

Field, A. (2009). Tracking terrorist networks: Problems of intelligence sharing within the UK intelligence community. *Review of International Studies, 35*(1), 997–1009.

Ford, J. (2011). *African counter-terrorism legal frameworks a decade after 2001*. Monograph 177. Pretoria: Institute for Security Studies.

Fulgence, N. (2015). War on terrorism in Africa: A challenge for regional integration and cooperation organisations in Eastern and Western Africa. *Journal of Political Sciences & Public Affairs, 1*(7), 1–7.

GIABA. (2019). *About GIABA*. Retrieved from https://www.giaba.org/about-giaba/index_656.html.

Haacke, J., & Williams, P. D. (2008). *Transnational challenges', security, cultures and regional organisations*. End of Award Report, RES 223-25-0072. Swindon: ESRC.

Hutchful, E. (2007). ECOWAS counter-terrorism efforts. In L. Sage (Ed.), *African counter-terrorism co-operation* (pp. 113–126). Washington, DC: Africa Center for Strategic Studies.

Institute for Economics and Peace. (2018). *Global Terrorism Index 2018: Measuring the Impact of Terrorism*. Sydney: IEP. Retrieved from https://www.economicsandpeace.org/wp-content/uploads/2020/08/Global-Terrorism-Index-2018.pdf.

Ipe, J., Cockayne, J., & Millar, A. (2010). *Implementing the UN Global Counter-Terrorism Strategy in West Africa*. New York: Center on Global Counterterrorism Cooperation.

Kwaga, V. (2016). *Terrorism, collective security and regional Co-operation: Impact and assessment*. The Center for Public Policy Alternatives.

Laary, D. (2016, April 12). *ECOWAS frets over growing terrorist attacks amid dwindling funds*. The Africa Report (Online Magazine). Retrieved from http://www.theafricareport.com/West-Africa/ecowas-frets-over-growing-terrorist-attacks-amid-dwindling-funds.html. Accessed 17.06.16.

Laremont, R. R. (2011). *Islamic law and politics in Northern Nigeria*. Trenton (NJ): Africa World Press.

Maiangwa, B. (2013). West Africa's terrorist challenge and the dynamics of regional response. *Insight on Africa, 5*(1), 1–18.

Maiangwa, B. (2017). Assessing the responses of the Economic Community of West African States to the recurring and emerging security threats in West Africa. *Journal of Asian & African Studies, 52*(1), 103–120.

MC Modern Ghana. (2013, February). Regional counter terrorism strategy for consideration at extra-ordinary mediation and security meeting in Abidjan. Retrieved from https://www.modernghana.com/news/447714/regional-counter-terrorism-strategy-for-considerat.html.

Musah, A. F. (2009). West Africa: Governance and security in a changing region, *Africa Program Working Paper Series*. New York: International Peace Institute, February.

Nkwi, W. G. (2015). Terrorism in West African History: A 21st Century Appraisal. *Austral: Brazilian Journal of Strategy & International Relations*, 4(8), 78–99.

Obi, C. I. (2006). Terrorism in West Africa: Real, emerging or imagined threats? *AfricanReview Security*, 15(3), 87–101.

Okpeh, O. O. (2013). Globalisation and regional impulses from the Global South: A comparative study of ECOWAS and ASEAN. In Toyin Falola & Jessica Achberger (Eds.), *The Political Economy of Development and Underdevelopment in Africa* (pp. 147–175). New York: Taylor & Francis.

Onuoha, F. C., & Ezirim, G. E. (2013). *"Terrorism" and transnational organised crime in West Africa*. Al Jazeera Centre for Studies.

Orioha, L. (2015, August 27). GIABA to unveil new strategic plan against financial crimes, money laundering. *The Guardian*. Retrieved from https://guardian.ng/business-services/business/giaba-to-unveil-new-strategic-plan-against-financial-crimes-money-laundering/.

Rabasa, A., Boraz, S., Chalk, P., Cragin, K., Karasik, T. W., Moroney, J. D. P., Kevin, A., & O'Brien, J. E. P. (2007). *Ungoverned territories understanding and reducing terrorism risks*. Rand Corporation.

The Punch. (2018, December 6). *Nigeria third most terrorised nation, says Global Terrorism Index 2018*. https://punchng.com/nigeria-third-most-terrorised-nation-says-global-terrorism-index-2018/.

Shuaibu, S.S., Salleh, A.F., & Shehu, A. (2015). The impact of Boko Haram insurgency on Nigerian National Security. *International Journal of Academic Research in Business and Social Sciences*, 7(1), 254–266.

Sidibé, K. (2012). Security management in Northern Mali: Criminal networks and conflict resolution. IDS Research Report 77. Institute of Development Studies.

Souaré, I. K. (2010). AA *critical assessment of security challenges in West Africa*. Institute for Security Studies Situation Report. Retrieved from http://www.humansecuritygateway.com/documents/ISS_ACritical AssessmentOf SecurityChallengesInWestAfrica.pdf.

Vanguard News. (2018, August 1). *ECOWAS, ECCAS vow to check insecurity in sub-region*. Retrieved from https://www.vanguardngr.com/2018/08/ecowas-eccas-vow-to-check-insecurity-in-sub-region/.

Vines, A. (2013). Renamo's rise and decline: The politics of reintegration in Mozambique. *International Peacekeeping*, 20(3), 375–393.

Williams, D. U. (2017). The African Union (AU) Counterterrorism Framework and the rhetoric of regional cooperation. *International Journal of Peace and Conflict Studies (IJPCS)*, 4(2), 1–19.

Yoroms, G. J. (2007). Counter-terrorism measures in West Africa. In Wafula Okumu & Annedi Botha (Eds.), *Understanding terrorism in Africa: Building bridges and overcoming the gaps*. Pretoria: Institute of Security Studies.

# 22

# IGAD

## Emerging regional architecture for counterterrorism and counterinsurgency in the Horn of Africa

*Mesfin Gebremichael*

---

## Introduction

Terrorism and insurgency are some of the major peace and security threats in the Horn of Africa (HoA). In this region and indeed the whole of Africa, terrorism became a main threat in the mid-1990 when some jihadist group led by Osama Bin Laden operated from Sudan to expand terrorist activities in the countries of the Horn of Africa. They influenced some factions in Somalia to kill American forces who were engaged in a peacekeeping mission. Since 2006, Al-Shabaab in Somalia, which is connected to the global terror fraternity has become a collective security threat to the whole member states of the region.

The Horn of Africa is well known for protracted civil wars that marked the struggles for independence and regime change. For example, in the 20th century, the Eritrean and South Sudanese insurgent groups have fought for independence from Ethiopia and Sudan, respectively. Other insurgent groups in Ethiopia and Uganda have also fought for regime change during the 1970s and 1980s. Currently, in Sudan's Darfur and Nuba enclaves, there are insurgent groups who seek some level of accommodation at the centre and a decentralised form of governance in the regional administrations. In South Sudan, a civil war, which has caused hundreds of thousands of deaths and mass displacements, has been fought by insurgent groups against the incumbent government. Several international and regional institutions such as United Nations (UN), African Union (AU) and Intergovernmental Authority for Development (IGAD) have made a lot of efforts including the deployment of peacekeeping forces with more than 50,000 UN and AU troops in Darfur (Sudan), Abyei, Somalia and South Sudan to counter terrorism and insurgency in the region (IGAD Strategy, 2016).

This chapter investigates the extent to which IGAD emerged as an institution to counter terrorism and insurgency in the Horn of Africa. It examines the dynamics of terrorism, insurgency, and the institutional capacities of IGAD and its engagement in Somalia and South Sudan. Finally, the chapter outlines the challenges that face IGAD in countering terrorism and insurgency and the way forward to address them.

## IGAD in a historical perspective

The IGAD region is one of the eight blocks of the Regional Economic Communities (RECs) of the African Union (AU). It includes Ethiopia, Eritrea, Sudan, Somalia, South Sudan, Kenya, Uganda, and Djibouti. The region is known by internal and external political, economic and social problems that cause extreme poverty, income inequality and governance problems. It is exposed to several peace and security threats including socio-economic issues, demographic pressures, climate change and environmental strains, a discrepancy in governance, border disputes and weak cross border governance, transnational threats and organised criminal activities, and spillover effects of an unstable neighbourhood (IGAD report, 2016). The governments of the member states exacerbated these problems because either they are very weak to provide public goods such as security, employment opportunities, and justice to their citizens; or are predatory and take advantage of their citizens and display preference to members of the elite group who control the state.

IGAD is one of Africa's youngest sub-regional organisations founded in 1996. It succeeds the Inter-Governmental Authority on Drought and Development (IGADD) founded in 1986 by the then drought-afflicted Eastern African countries of Djibouti, Ethiopia, Kenya, Somalia, Sudan, and Uganda. Its objective was limited to coordinating approaches to environmental protection, food security and the management of natural resources. During the fifth IGADD Summit held in Djibouti on 25–26 November 1996, an agreement was made to change IGADD into IGAD, a premier Regional Economic Community (REC), to achieve sustainable peace and development in the region. As stipulated in Article 7 of the Agreement in 1996, IGAD's mission is to promote regional cooperation and integration through joint development activities including coordinating macroeconomic policies, trade rules and regulations; developing and improving complementary infrastructures, and promoting peace and stability in the region. To implement these objectives, IGAD mobilises resources, provides capacity development activities at regional and national levels. It supports researches that generate and disseminate information for the development of the region.

IGAD focuses on three programme priority areas including food security and environmental protection; economic cooperation, regional integration and social development; and peace, security and humanitarian intervention (IGAD strategy, 2016). To implement the programme priority areas, the IGAD Secretariat, situated in Djibouti, serves as the executive body of the authority. The Secretariat is headed by an Executive Secretary and is assisted by four Directors responsible for: agriculture and environment, economic cooperation and social development, peace and security; and administration and finance.

In addition to the Secretariat, IGAD has specialised institutions and programmes hosted by the member states. These include the IGAD Conflict Early Warning and Response Mechanism (CEWARN), the IGAD Security Sector Programme (ISSP), the IGAD Centre for Pastoral Area and Livestock Development (ICPLD), and IGAD's Climate Prediction, and Application Centre (ICPAC). The IGAD Office of Special Envoys for South Sudan (OSESS) and Monitoring and Evaluation Mechanism are also established to facilitate the peace process in South Sudan (IGAD report, 2016). The peace and security work of IGAD is guided by the Peace and Security Strategy formulated in 2010 and revised in 2016.

## Background: terrorism and insurgency in the Horn of Africa

### Al-Shabaab: a transnational terrorist group

The Cambridge dictionary (2003) defines terrorism "as violent action for political purposes." The conceptualisation of terrorism involves "premeditated politically-motivated extreme violence perpetrated against civilian or symbolic targets by some organisation that seeks to influence some states by means of intimidation of an audience" (Schinkel, 2009:181). Terrorism can be caused due to political, economic, environmental factors including rapid modernisation and urbanisation, lack of democracy, the rule of law and historical forces. The manifestations could be in ethnic or religious forms. They may be triggered by different factors such as lack of opportunity for political participation and real grievances of communities and perceived feelings of discrimination based on ethnic or religious origins, etc. These factors could call for retaliation or action that can be manifested in terrorism and other types of violence (European Commission (EU) Report on Transnational Terrorism 2008).

Terrorism has evolved through three generations in the IGAD region. The first generation is when Osama Bin Laden and his team operated from Sudan to support Jihadist activities around the world and in the Horn of Africa. For instance, in 1995 a Jihadist group who were believed to be trained in Sudan under the tutelage of Bin Laden attempted to kill Hosni Mubarak, the former Egyptian President, during his arrival to attend AU Summit in Addis Ababa. During this period, the Islamist extremists played a dominant role in Sudan as the state officially changed to an Islamic state. It is believed that the Somali factions of the terror cell, who killed 18 US soldiers in Mogadishu in October 1993, were also trained by the Group led by Osama Bin Laden.

The second wave of terrorism emerged from 1996–2002. In this period, Jihadist cells increased in many countries of the HoA, and they primarily focused on attacking American interests in the region. American Embassies in Dare-es Salaam and Nairobi were bombed by simultaneous truck bomb explosions on 7 August 1998 and killed more than 200 people (Keller, 2005). Following the bombings of the embassies, the United States acknowledged the danger of the terrorist group in the region: the Clinton Administration launched cruise missile attacks on chemical plants that were thought to be producing elements of chemical weapons for Al-Qaeda in Sudan.

The third wave of terrorism in the HoA emerged from 2002-present. This generation is led by Al-Shabaab, a Somalian terrorist group, primarily operating in the territories of Somalia. However, its reign of terror has been felt in countries through the HoA. Before the establishment of Al-Shabaab a radical Islamic group called Al-Ittihad al-Islamic (AIAI), operated in Somalia to overthrow Mohamed Siad Barre, the late former Somalian President, established an Islamic state and intended to expand it to the neighbouring countries. The group launched cross-border attacks in Ethiopia to gain control of the Ogden region, which was considered as part of Somalia by the Somalia nationalists, to establish a greater Somalia. The group also organised attacks in the mid-1990s in the capital of Ethiopia to kill some prominent Ethiopian Somalis who were perceived to be loyal to the government of Ethiopia. AIAI was weakened due to the frictions between the rival militias, and attacks by Ethiopian military forces at the end of 1990s (West, 2006).

Following the demise of AIAI, several Islamic courts were established by Islamic clerics of clans in different parts of Somalia, and they formed a Union of Islamic Courts (UIC) in 2000 (Barnes & Hassan, 2007). UIC promoted religious extremism and Somali nationalism. Many of the UIC leaders inspired by Somali Islamic scholars trained in Saudi Arabia as staunch followers and protagonists of Wahhabi ideology. The nationalist and religious affiliation of UIC attracted young Somalis. It helped the organisation to get control of most parts of Somalia, including Mogadishu, until it was pushed back to the surroundings of the capital due to the intervention of the Ethiopian National Defense Force in 2006.

Al-Shabaab is a successor of both AIAI and UIC. It is descendant of AIAI because most of its organs are much associated with AIAI and inherited its extremist thoughts from AIAI. For example, Al-Shabaab maintains hostility against followers of Sufi traditions because it is highly

influenced by the Wahhabi ideology that has been promoted by Saudi affiliated religious or-
ganisations in the region. It is also a successor of the UIC because the extremist elements of the
Union joined the Al-Shabaab when the Union disintegrated due to the military intervention of
Ethiopia in 2006. For instance, Aden Hashi "Ayro" who established Al-Shabaab was a military
Chief of the UIC who trained with Al Qaeda and the Taliban in Afghanistan.

Since its establishment, Al-Shabaab has been organised as a fighting force with thousands of
members. The fighting force is primarily composed of Somalis and other members of Saudi, Egyptian,
Pakistani and Yemeni origins. Al-Shabaab is guided by a Sharia Council which issues policies and
directives to guide the fighting force and local administrations. Also, though Al-Shabaab has a central
leadership, it follows the clan structure of Somali society to get support from the local population to
execute its operations. The fighting force does not have a strict centralised command system and
operates in decentralised structure following the clan structure. Thus, Al-Shabaab organises multiple
structures such as cells, units, and divisions along with the complex social structures of Somali society.
This has helped the organisation to sustain itself using autonomous units which have rights to manage
operations in the context of the different regions of the country (Hansen, 2013; Dobos, 2016).

Beyond Somalia, Al-Shabaab has spread its reign of terror to the HoA, and therefore,
constitutes a regional security threat. It has organised several deadly attacks in neighbouring
states. For instance, it carried out a fatal attack on the Westgate shopping mall in Nairobi, Kenya
in September 2013, which resulted in at least 72 deaths. It also killed more than 147 college
students at Garissa University on 2 April 2015 in the same country. Before the Attacks in
Kenya, it launched several attacks against crowds watching a football match in Kampala in July
2010, killing more than 74 people (Telegraph, 2015).

The expansion of religious radicalisation has created significant popular support to Al-
Shabaab to expand its operations in East Africa. The extremist Islamic Sect, with its main Salafi
base, has got ground in many East African countries due to the financial support from extremist
elements in Gulf countries, including Saudi Arabia, Qatar, and Kuwait. There is the infiltration
of the Islamic State of Iraq and the Levant (ISIS) in Puntland and Ethiopia. Research indicated
that the Salafi sect had got enough ground in Jima areas of Oromia regional state in Ethiopia
(Abiy, 2017). The Ethiopian Supreme Court also persecuted recently extremist Jihadist cells
who wanted to establish an Islamic state in Jima area.

Al-Shabaab gets significant financial support from internal sources such as taxation, zakat, port
rents, and protection money from business, aid community, pirate connections, Charcoal trade and
other illegal trades. It collects more than 150 million USD annually from these sources (AOAV,
2017). Moreover, it gets financial support from diaspora remittance, Islamic charity organisations,
and affiliated persons from the Middle East. A parallel economy that runs through Yemen – due to
the existence of more than 1 million Somalis in Yemen – and money laundering that is masterminded in Dubai and Nairobi, provide financial support to Al-Shabaab (Fanusie & Entz, 2017).

In sum, Al-Shabaab is a threat to the peace and security of the Horn of Africa. Though its
territory capacity has been decimated, Al-Shabaab still controls some of the rural fringes of
Somalia, and this is primarily because of its ability to sustain the loyalty and sympathy of the
local population. It advances terrorist activities using deadly attacks in the region. It is well
funded through foreign support and local means.

## Insurgent Groups

Metz and Millen define insurgency as a strategy "adopted by groups which cannot attain their
political objectives through conventional means or by a quick seizure of power" (2004:2).
Insurgency is characterised by the sustained deployment of violence against both hard and soft

targets to a view to acquiring and controlling territory from the host state. Insurgent groups use different mechanisms, including physical and psychological warfare, and political manipulation, to undermine the legitimacy of the ruling party/government and change the balance of power to their benefit. Insurgencies can be caused by different factors, including:

> Discontent arising from globalization; the failure of economic development to keep pace with expectations; the collapse of traditional political, economic and social orders; widespread anger and resentment; environmental decay; population pressure; The presence of weak regimes; the growth of transnational organized crime; and the widespread availability of arms (Metz & Millen, 2004:1).

The objectives of the insurgent groups may be separation, autonomy, or alteration of a particular policy. Accordingly, there are two types of insurgent groups: national insurgencies and liberation fronts. National insurgencies are those who aim to change power and economic relationships between the ruling elites and marginalised groups. The "bone of contention" between the insurgent groups and ruling elites is often underpinned by disparities in class, ideology or some other political factors. On the other hand, liberation insurgency groups fight against colonial power and their benefactors and allies. The goal of the liberation insurgency groups is stiff, which is to liberate their nation from foreign occupation. However, the distinction between the two types of insurgency can be changed from one to the other, due to changes of circumstances including regional and international political and economic factors (Metz & Millen, 2004)

The IGAD region is historically well known as a hub of liberation struggles that fought for the independence of some regions/provinces of the member countries. The Eritrean armed groups and, in particular, the Eritrean Peoples' Liberation Front (EPLF) fought for the independence of Eritrea from 1962–1991, which concluded by the independence of the country after the referendum in 1993 (Henz 2001). The South Sudanese liberation forces and notably, the Sudan People's Liberation Army (SPLA) also fought for independence. This led to the independence of the country after the referendum monitored by the international community in 2011.

The Oromo Liberation Front (OLF) is one of the insurgent groups which fight for the independence of the Oromia regional state in Ethiopia. With this objective, it fought against the Ethiopian military regime from 1975–1991 and participated in the transitional government established after the downfall of the military regime. However, after it stayed in the transitional government for about a year, it resumed the insurgency due to disagreements with the main ruling party, the Ethiopian People's Revolutionary Democratic Front (EPRDF). OLF attempted to conduct a guerrilla fighting and lost its armed wing due to attacks from the government forces (Clapham, 2017). The group was one of the insurgent groups that had been categorised as terrorist by the parliament of the country until the change of government in 2018 that caused removing OLF from the list of terrorist groups in the country.

The Ogaden National Liberation Front (ONLF) is also another group that claims to fight for the independence of the Somali region of Ethiopia. It started the insurgency during the military regime in 1984. After the downfall of the military regime, ONLF participated in the transnational government and initially controlled the regional government. However, it left the transnational government due to disagreements with Ethiopian Somali Democratic League (ESDL) the partner of EPRDF in the region (Clapham, 2017). Since then it resorted to its guerrilla insurgency against the EPRDF led government by the support of the Eritrean government taking Somalia as a haven. Nevertheless, it has become fragile to attack the Ethiopian National Defense Forces after the Ethiopian military crossed the borders of Somalia to attack the UIC in 2006. ONLF was also one of the groups that had been categorised as terrorist by the Parliament of Ethiopia until it was erased from the list of terrorist groups after the change of government top leadership in 2018.

Other nationalist insurgent groups have been fighting to gain either self-autonomy or better accommodation or resource distribution from the centre. The insurgent groups that operate in South Sudan are a typical example of national insurgents. South Sudan got its independence from Sudan in 2011. As a young state, South Sudan established a government composed from the SPLA—a front fought against Sudan during the armed insurgency for independence. After three years of independence, a conflict between President Kiir and the Vice President, Dr Machar, occurred. President Kiir reshuffled his ministerial cabinet and sacked most of the supporters of Dr Machar, who are of Nuer ethnic identity (Mutanda, 2015). The Dr Machar group claimed of being marginalised from power and resource distribution from the centre. However, several structural factors caused the conflict. Historically, there appears to be a hangover of marginalisation in South Sudan, which has been one of the marginalised regions in the former Republic of Sudan. Thus, public goods were unevenly distributed and were out of reach to most communities of South Sudan. This has not been redressed after independent because the newly established South Sudan government has been weak to provide public services to the broad spectrum of its population outside of the central city, Juba. This has been aggravated by the predatory nature of the state and the military generals who controlled both the military structure and the civil administrations throughout the country. As a result, loyalty to the higher authority became the main factor in getting more resources to be trickled down to ethnic consistency. This has become a cause for widespread frustration mainly within the non-Dinka ethnic groups in the country. Such type of relationship between the Dinka ethnic group and the others created perceived inequalities which in turn allowed the political elites to manipulate mass grievances for their political benefits.

Following the conflict in 2013, ethnic violence erupted as many members of the Nuer group were targeted and killed in Juba and other places. Regardless of the effort by IGAD to bring the conflicting parties into peaceful conflict resolution, the violence escalated into a civil war with devastating repercussions. Approximately 1.9 million people displaced from their homes; about 4.9 million people became food insecure, and more than 1.7 million people have sought refugee status in the neighbouring countries (WFP, 29 April 2017). Moreover, since the development of the conflict into a civil war, other leaders of ethnic groups have also started insurgent activities mainly in the areas where they can get better support. The South Sudan President signed a peace deal with the prominent rebel leader Riek Machar in September 2018, formally ending the five-year war that has killed thousands of people. However, the peace deal requires further reconciliation between the opposing parties to revitalise it and prevent the escalation of conflicts.

In Sudan, the political, economic, and cultural marginalisation of the periphery areas has become the main factor for the proliferation of insurgent groups. Accordingly, different rebel groups such as Sudan People Liberation Army North (SPLA) and others (Darfur based armed movements) have been fighting against the centre in different forms such as ethnic and religious. Almost all the rebel groups fight for regime change to get better accommodation in the centre and for decentralised regional and local governance.

## IGAD's legal and institutional framework for counter terrorism and counter insurgency (CT-COIN)

### The legal Infrastructure of CT-COIN in the IGAD region

The IGAD protocol is the main legal framework for countering terrorism and insurgency in the Horn of Africa. In Article 7 of its founding Charter, IGAD has clearly stated that it aims to promote peace and security in the region by preventing, managing and resolving interstate and intrastate conflicts through dialogue. This aim indicates that IGAD during its establishment primarily focused on addressing insurgence's that caused intrastate and interstate conflicts in the region (IGAD protocol, 21 March 1996).

After terrorism became a major threat to the member states, IGAD adopted laws and conventions which directly or indirectly address terrorism in the region. These include IGAD mutual legal assistance and extradition of criminals who are wanted by the member states. The former convention enables each country to cooperate to prevent, suppress and trace crime and confiscate the proceeds of crime more effectively. The latter convention helps each state to extradite a criminal suspect upon request, in accordance with the provisions of the convention and the respective domestic law. The conventions have been approved by the Council of Ministers of each country. These multilateral legal instruments help IGAD and its member countries to collaborate in combating transnational crime and maintaining the peace and security of the region.

Moreover, some IGAD member states have ratified laws to counter the financing of terrorist activities in the region. For example, countries such as Ethiopia and Kenya have enacted anti-money laundering laws. They have also created anti-money laundering institutions to counter financing of terrorism in the respected territories. Ethiopia has also passed the anti-terrorism law.

## Strategies and programme priority areas

IGAD has developed its core peace and strategic security objectives for the period 2016–2020 to enhance regional capacity in preventing insurgency and terrorism in the region. To implement the strategic goals, it has developed six priority areas. These include conflict early warning and early response; preventive diplomacy and mediation; collaboration against transnational security threats; governance; democracy, the rule of law, and human rights; humanitarian affairs and post-conflict reconstruction; development and gender equality; and women's empowerment for peace (IGAD strategy, 2016). In this chapter, a focus is given to the three priority areas which include conflict early warning and early response, transnational security threats and preventive diplomacy and mediation which play a direct role in countering terrorism and insurgency in the region.

## Early warning and early response

Conflict Early Warning and Early Response (CEWARN) was established by IGAD's "Khartoum Declaration" issued by IGAD's heads of state in 2000. Following the declaration, a protocol was ratified by IGAD member states in January 2002. The Protocol seeks to collect and analyse information and establish networks of cooperation in the region. The CEWARN programme focuses on building the analytical capability and response to conflicts of IGAD member states. CEWARN analyses information and disseminates it to all decision making organs of the IGAD Secretariat, and the Conflict Early Warning and Response Units (CEWARUs) of the member states. It also sets standards and monitors information collection and reporting within the region. It networks among information-gathering organisations in the region. Concerning the decision-making process, while CEWARN primarily plays a co-ordinative role, the member states take the responsibility of decision for implementation. The role of the CEWARN at the secretariat is also facilitated by regular consultations of the permanent secretaries organised from the member states.

CEWARN has conducted different activities including producing analytical reports and terror alert news on pastoral and other conflicts in the region. CEWARN has also been able to build and strengthen its relationship and linkages with government and non-governmental institutions. CEWARN has used Information and Communication Technology (ICT) to expand its operations across the region. It involves civil societies to gather information and national research institutions to carry out trend analysis. This has created a sense of transparency and local ownership of its operations in the region. By doing this, it has contributed significantly to managing and preventing pastoralist related conflicts. Recently, it has included terrorism and other violent conflicts to its thematic focus areas, and this has been effected at pilot levels in Kenya, Somalia and Sudan; to be implemented at the regional level after an evaluation of the programme.

However, it is notable that CEWARN faces several challenges. These include poor infra-structural access in the pastoral areas due to inaccessibility of areas and limitations in member states capability to ensure physical security throughout their territories. Moreover, CEWARN's capacity to implement the programme priority areas depends on the collaboration among member states.

## Preventive diplomacy and mediation

IGAD established a team of mediators composed from 21 eminent persons nominated by re-spective member states who will be deployed upon approval by the IGAD's Council of Ministers of Foreign Affairs. In August 2014, IGAD conducted a capacity building programme to enhance the skills of the potential mediators and experts in Kampala. The objective of the training was to strengthen IGAD's normative capacity on preventive diplomacy, mediation and develop skills that help manage and resolve conflicts by utilising homegrown solutions to home problems. IGAD also established different desks in its Secretariat office (such as South Sudan and Somalia Desks) to facilitate the activities for preventive diplomacy and mediation. Moreover, IGAD appointed various envoys for South Sudan after the eruption of the violence in December 2013. The envoys assisted the conflicting parties to agree on parameters for the establishment of a transitional unity government in 2015.

## Dealing with transnational threats

Another priority of IGAD focuses on transnational security threats. This is a programme which enhances IGAD's member states capabilities to respond to transnational threats and international crime in the region. It includes counterterrorism, countering violent extremism, countering organised crime, cross-border security governance, maritime security, extradition of criminals, and border control for small arms trade, among others. Dealing with these security threats necessitates the development and implementation of processes and mechanisms focused on regional issues (IGAD strategy, 2016). For this purpose, IGAD has launched a security sector programme. This includes cooperation and coordination of member states against existing, evolving and emerging transnational security threats, enhancing of member states capacities' and encouraging the development of regional and international policies, frameworks and pro-grammes to deal with the trans-national security threats.

For the implementation of the above programmes, the IGAD Capacity Building Programme Against Terrorism (ICPAT) was launched in 2006. ICPAT engaged in a lot of activities such as border security and piracy. Following the security dynamics, ICPAT was replaced by IGAD Security Sector Programme (ISSP) in 2011 with a mandate of dealing with terrorism, transnational organised crime (TOC), maritime security, and security institutions capacity building. ISSP gives focus on capacities development for interdepartmental cooperation and border control of the member states. A research centre has been established in Djibouti that provides assessments and research outputs on countering terrorism to IGAD. It helps strengthen the engagement of IGAD and its member states on countering terrorism in the region.

Since its establishment, ISSP has done several activities. It conducts continuous threats assessments and analysis, which is shared with the member states. For example, in collaboration with the Global Centre on Cooperative Security (GCCS), a baseline survey on money laundering was conducted and shared with member states in 2012 (Tu'emay & Cockayne, 2012). In 2016, ISSP also organised a study on human trafficking routes and how terrorist groups benefit from the process. A survey of migration is being carried out by ISSP to see the extent to which terrorist groups are using forced migration to facilitate their activities in the region. It has provided many capacity development training to the security institutions of the member states. It drafted different conventions such as the Mutual Legal Assistance (MLA) in criminal matters and another convention for the extradition of criminal suspects from one member state to another. It also produced reports that contributed to the establishment of the centre of countering terrorism in Djibouti.

However, ISSP is confronted by financial constraints to facilitate the implementation of the programmes and priority areas in the region: IGAD member states have not lived up to their financial obligations of funding ISSP and other agencies within IGAD. Moreover, regardless of the capacity development training provided by ISSP, the countries have varying levels of capacities to implement the programmes in their territories. Hence, issues of border control, money laundering and human trafficking will continue as serious security challenges for the foreseeable future in the region.

## IGAD's approach to countering terrorism and insurgency in the Horn of Africa

### IGAD's role in Somalia

IGAD's role in Somalia is primarily associated with countering terrorism. In this regard, IGAD member states have been engaged collectively, and specifically through, for instance, a Somali Desk established in the IGAD Secretariat in 2008. Furthermore, IGAD prepared a platform that helped facilitate the establishment of a constitutional government with decentralised administration at the regional and local level in Somalia. Accordingly, regional governments were established in Puntland, Jubaland, Southwest and Wabishebele regions. A constitutional consensus has been reached to establish a federal type of government that decentralises power and resources to the regional governments. Continuous capacity building has been given to strengthen the capacity of the deep state institutions, including the army and the police (Elowson and Lins de Albuquerque, 2016). Overall, IGAD has played a significant role in supporting the state-building process in Somalia; this has created a Parliament with the upper house, lower house, and Executive Committees shared between the clans in the country.

Another initiative of IGAD in Somalia is strengthening the peace process using mediation efforts to reconcile warring clans and sub-clans. Since the collapse of the Somali state in 1991, the Somali clans and sub-clans have had several conflicts encouraged by warlords. After the establishment of the transitional government in Mogadishu, the government secured control of many parts of Somalia through the support of the African Union Mission to Somalia (AMISOM) and IGAD countries military forces. IGAD encouraged reconciliation between clans and sub-clans. All regional states, including Jubaland, Puntland and others, have made reconciliation activities between clans and sub-clans. This has contributed to the recent developments of the peaceful relationship between the clans and sub-clans in the regions. Such types of reconciliation activities in Somaliland between 1992 and 1995 created a ground for the peace and stability of the country that has been sustained until now.

IGAD member states have also made substantial progress in fighting Al-Shabaab in Somalia. This has been done by joint engagements of the AMISOM forces and the merging Somali National Armed Forces (SNAF). As a result, government forces have regained control of seaports and airports which have been previously controlled by Al-Shabaab. For example, before the AMISOM forces started operation in 2007, 85% of North-South Somalia, which is now under the control of the transitional government and AMISOM, was under the control of Al-Shabaab. As a result of sustained CT-COIN operations, Al-Shabaab has lost not only territory but also significant public support and its fighting forces have reduced significantly. It has lost command and control due to the coordinated attacks of the AMISOM, United States of America (USA) and neighbouring countries armed forces. Nevertheless, it has continued to take advantage of the weak relationship between the federal and regional governments and the clan social grouping of the people in the country (Anzalone, 2018).

## IGAD's role in South Sudan: preventive diplomacy and mediation

In facilitating the mediation process in South Sudan, IGAD convened a Summit in Nairobi on 27 December 2013 and afterwards, appointed three special envoys from Kenya, Ethiopia and Sudan. The main objective was to support the warring parties to resolve their differences through peaceful means and establish an all-inclusive Transitional Unity Government (TUG). IGAD also established a Special Office in its Secretariat to support the process. The mediation process was endorsed by IGAD-Plus, which included other regional and international actors. The IGAD Plus played a vital role in providing political, technical and financial support to the peace process.

After several peace deal attempts, IGAD supported the conflicting parties to sign a peace agreement that caused an establishment of a transitional unity government in 2015 (Muhabie, 2018). The mediation process included all the concerned parties such as delegates of the government, delegates of the opposition, members of the former detainees, representatives of other political parties, representatives of the Civil Society Organizations (CSOs), and representatives of women and eminent personalities. Regardless of halting many times because the parties had differing views on certain critical matters during the peace talks, the peace agreement put a ceasefire as a precondition and gave 18 months for the conflicting parties to sort out the causes of conflicts and organise an election to bring a sustainable solution for the causes of conflicts

However, the peace agreement has not been implemented according to the agreed modalities. In the first place, President Kiir signed the peace accord with some reservations. Moreover, the two key opponents President Kiir and Machar were not prepared to work together. This is because a real reconciliation has not been reached between the opposition parties after the eruption of the conflicts in 2013. Thus, after three months of fragile peace, another round of violence erupted that caused Dr Machar to leave Juba for the second time to lead the insurgency from outside of the country.

Nevertheless, some of the factions of Machar and the civil societies who participated in the peace agreement decided to continue working with President Kiir. Following this, President Kiir appointed a Nuer general from the Machar faction, and this created an excellent opportunity for the president to declare the continuity of the TUG. IGAD decided to continue its support for the TUG, and subsequently, all the member states declined their support to Machar. Nevertheless, there was a suspicion that the Republic of Sudan supported Machar. President Kiir also suspects Ethiopia for supporting Machar. Uganda and Kenya have also shown great sympathy to support the president from the beginning.

Thus, the fragile peace process in South Sudan revealed three factors. First, for organisations like IGAD dealing with insurgency does not mean that supporting the government in power will weaken the insurgent groups who claim being marginalised from the benefits of the centre. In other words, an insurgency in the post-Cold War era can be dealt with by bringing the conflicting parties to a round table to resolve their differences, and assist the government in power to make some reforms to redress the concerns of the insurgent groups. Accordingly, the efforts of IGAD in South Sudan are one step forward to deal with the causes of insurgency through peaceful mechanisms. Second, regardless of the collective action of the IGAD countries, still, the peace process could not provide the required fruits because a real reconciliation has not been reached between the conflicting parties to resolve their differences sustainably. Finally, the absence of commitment of the member states to implement the collective decisions on peaceful resolutions and facilitate the reconciliation process between the conflicting parties has contributed to the continuation of the civil war.

## The challenges of IGAD's counterterrorism and counterinsurgency framework

Terrorism has been internationalised in the Horn Africa. This is due to geopolitical factors and the internal situation in Somalia. Al-Shabaab has become a ruthless terrorist organisation that is publicly affiliated to Al-Qaida, and well-networked with terrorist groups in the Gulf countries, including Yemen. The Somalian government was not strong enough to provide the necessary security as a public good to its citizens. Tendencies of radicalisation among the youth in Somalia and the region have also created a fertile ground for the expansion of terrorism in the region. Thus, regardless of the attempts of Somalia's federal government forces, AMISOM and the neighbouring countries to defeat terrorism, Al-Shabaab has posed a security threat not only to Somalia but also to the region. A recent survey conducted by the UN showed that marginalisation of the youth from economic benefits, political participation, and perceived power abuse have significantly contributed to the expansion of radicalisation and recruitment of the African youth by terrorist groups (United Nations Development Programme (UNDP) 2017). Forced migration is another key challenge in the region. South Sudan, as a new centre of conflict, has created immense pressure on the region in terms of internal displacements and refugees. This has been aggravated by food insecurity caused by climate change and environmental degradation, which in turn has created a favourable condition for terrorist groups to recruit their personnel's in the region.

There is weak cross-cultural communication between the countries. This is primarily caused by a poor relationship and mistrust between the member states. This is manifested by suspicion member states in supporting insurgent groups. For example, South Sudan and Sudan governments suspect each other for supporting insurgent groups of both countries. The Eritrean government has been accused of supporting the insurgent/ terrorist groups in Ethiopia and Somalia. Such a relationship between the countries in the region undermines the cross-border cooperation to counter terrorism and insurgency in the region.

IGAD member states lack adequate institutional capacities to play their role in the security of the region. IGAD professes pan-regional cooperation and, in particular, regionalisation of security.

Over the last decades, this has led to a multitude of agreements and collaborations at regional levels. However, the commitments and agreements have not created significant cross-border mobility of people, regional trade of goods, the delivery of financial services and coordinated approaches to natural resource management, and peace and security. Such weak economic relationship between countries in the region has contributed to the marginalisation of the people in the border areas, which in turn has encouraged cross-border armed trade, money laundering and other security threats in the region.

There is an absence of coordination among stakeholders in fighting terrorism in the region in general, and Somalia in particular. Though there were several attempts to establish coherent law enforcement agencies in Somalia, it has been hindered by different internal, external and factors. For example, there is weak coordination among the police of the Somalian government and the army in fighting Al-Shabaab due to the clan politics in the country. AMISOM forces also do not have strong command system that enables them to be answerable to one central system. This has obstructed them not to use their resources in fighting terrorism effectively.

There is weak cross-border governance between countries. This is affected by two factors. First, IGAD member states do not adequately control their borders. Hence, an insurgent group of one country could easily move across borders or hide in the territory of the other country. For example, the OLF and ONLF activists are known to have found clandestine shelter in the territory of neighbouring countries before they formally signed a peace deal with the Ethiopian government in 2018. The second factor is the proliferation of small arms across the borders. Several studies have indicated that weak cross-border governance has created an enabling environment to move small arms from Uganda through South Sudan to Ethiopia (e.g. Aemro, 2016; Gerensea, 2017).

There is limited research engagement to explore the *Modus Operandi* of the terrorist groups, their strategy and tactics in destabilising the countries of the Horn of Africa and their affiliation to other international theorist groups. IGAD has created a research institution in Djibouti for this purpose. ISSP has also carried out a lot of assessments in this regard. However, ground-breaking research has to be done to bring a real influence on the policy-making processes in the member countries. Finally, there is a lack of resources to implement the programmes on countering terrorism and the insurgency in the region. External allies have primarily funded financing of the programmes. However, the sources are not only insufficient to finance the activities of the programmes, but they are also not well coordinated to implement the programmes effectively.

## Conclusion

Terrorism and insurgency are regional security threats in the Horn of Africa. The causes are related primarily to domestic political, economic and environmental factors of the member states. Therefore, creating an inclusive government in the conflict-prone countries is a pre-condition to creating a political environment to countering insurgency and terrorism in the region. Accordingly, a real reconciliation is required to create an inclusive government owned by the South Sudanese to end the civil war. In doing this, the IGAD institution should support the peace process backed by a strong commitment from the member states.

Working on de-radicalisation is also a precondition to fighting terrorism in the region. IGAD has to work on de-radicalisation among the population of the member countries, in general, and the youth, in particular. This can be done by creating an enabling environment to religious institutions to give focus on common aspects of all religions such as tolerance as common values of both Christian and Islam religions. Moreover, working on the structural causes of radicalisation of the youth, including unemployment, injustice and marginalisation from economic benefits are prerequisites to address radicalisation. For this, regional economic integration should be encouraged for the interdependency between countries regarding infrastructural development, including trade, free movement of people and equal distribution of resources to the people in the peripheries.

Border-related conflicts between the countries should be resolved. There is a long-standing border-related conflict between Eritrea and Ethiopia; and between Eritrea and Djibouti. In collaboration with other continental and international organisations, IGAD member states should take the initiative to resolve such conflicts. Doing this, would not only encourage trust between each member states but also facilitate the regional integration programme of IGAD, which will contribute to the sustainable solution in countering insurgency and terrorism in the region significantly.

Lastly, there is a need to create consensus among member states on regional peace and security threats and how they can be managed. For this purpose, the relevant departments in the IGAD Secretariat should focus on sensitisation programmes to be supported by research outputs to create better awareness on the dynamics of security threats and implementation of decisions by the member states.

# References

Abiy, M. (2017). *Social capital and its role in traditional conflict resolution in Ethiopia: The case of inter-religious conflict in Jima Zone*. PhD thesis. Institute for Peace and Security Studies, Addis Ababa University.

Aemro, T. (2016). *Regulating proliferation and misuse of small arms in Eastern Gojjam Zone of Amhara regional state*. Master's Thesis. Institute for peace and security Studies, Addis Ababa University. Online. http://etd.aau.edu.et/handle/123456789/11390 Accessed 28.09.17 at 1:35 PM.

Anzalone, C. (2018). Black banners in Somalia: The state of al-shabaab's territorial insurgency and the Specter of the Islamic state, vol. ll, Issue. 3. Online. https://ctc.usma.edu/black-banners-somalia-state-al-shabaabs-territorial-insurgency-specter-islamic-state/.

AOAV (2017). *Sources of funding(including self-funding) for the major groupings that perpetrate IED incidents al-shabaab, online*: https://aoav.org.uk/2017/sources-funding-including-self-funding-major-groupings-perpetrate-ied-incidents-al-shabaab.

Barnes, C., & Hassan, H. (2007). The rise and fall of Mogadishu's Islamic cohorts. *Journal of Eastern African Studies*, 1(2), 151–160. http://www.tandfonline.com/doi/abs/10.1080/17531050701452382 Accessed 17.07.17 at 1:50 PM.

Clapham, C. (2017). *State formation and decay*. London: Hurst & Company.

European Commission (EU) Report on Transnational Terrorism. 2008. *Concepts of terrorism: Analysis of the rise, decline, trends and risk*. Online. www.transnationalism.eu Accessed on 27.9.17at 11:16 AM.

Dobos, B. (2016). Shape shifter of Somalia: Evolution of the political territoriality of Al-Shabaab. *Journal of Small Wars & Insurgencies*, 27(15), 937–957. Online. http://www.tandfonline.com/doi/abs/10.1080/09592318.2016.1208282 Accessed 27.09.17 at 10:35 AM.

Elowson, C., & de Lins de Albuquerque (2016). *Challenges to peace and security in Eastern Africa: The role of IGAD, EAC and EASF*. Studies in African Security. Online. https://www.foi.se/download/18.2bc30cfb157f5e989c31188/1477416021009/FOI+Memo+5634.pdf Accessed 28.04.17 at 10:39 AM.

Fanusie, Y. J., & Entz, A. (2017). *Al-shabaab financial assessment*. Centre on Sanctions & Illicit Finance. Online. http://www.defenddemocracy.org/content/uploads/documents/CSIF_TFBB_Al-Shabaab_v05_web.pdf Accessed 27.09.17 at 10:52 AM.

Gerensea, R. (2017). *Challenges of international cross border ethnic based conflict to Ethiopian security: The case of Murle of South Sudan Vs Nuer of Ethiopia*. Master's thesis. Institute for Peace and Security Studies, Addis Ababa University.

Hansen, S. J. (2013). *Al-shabaab in Somalia: The history and ideology of a militant Islamist group* (pp. 2005–2012). Oxford University Press.

Henz, P. (2001). *Eritrea's war: Confrontation, International response, outcome, prospects*. Addis Ababa: Shama Books.

Intergovernmental Authority on Development (IGAD) Report. (2016). *IGAD State of the region: A popular version*. Online. https://igad.int/featured-magazine/1542-state-of-the-regionAccessed 26.04.17 at 12:19 PM.

Intergovernmental Authority on Development (IGAD). (2016). *IGAD regional strategy* (Vol. 1). The Framework. Online. https://igad.int/featured-magazine/1541-igad-strategy-the-framework-volume-one Accessed 28.04.17 at 11:07 AM.

Intergovernmental Authority on Development (IGAD). (2009). *Convention on Extradition*. Online. www.igadssp.org/index.php/documentation/ploicies/igad-convention-on-extradition Accessed 15.09.17 at 11:58 AM.

Intergovernmental Authority on Development (IGAD). (2009). *Convention on mutual legal assistance in criminal matters*. Online. www.igadssp.org/…/igad-convention-on-mutual-legal-assistance-in-criminal-matters/d Accessed 15.09.17 at 12:00 PM.

Intergovernmental Authority on Development (IGAD). (2016). *Al-shabaab as a transnational security threat*. IGAD Security Sector Program and Sahan Foundation.

Intergovernmental Authority on Development (IGAD) Protocol. (21 March 1996). *Agreement establishing the Inter-Governmental Authority on Development*. Online: www.chr.up.ac.za/undp/subregional/docs/igad1.pdf Accessed 27.09.17 at 12:18 PM.

Intergovernmental Authority on Development (IGAD) Protocol. (1996). *On the Establishment of a Conflict Early Warning and Response Mechanism for IGAD member states*. Online. http://www.operationspaix.net/DATA/DOCUMENT/3860~v~Protocol_on_the_establishment_of_a_Conflict_Early_Warning_and_Response_Mechanism_for_IGAD_Member_States.pdf Accessed 29.09.17 at 11:29 AM.

Keller, W. W. (2005). *Anatomy of terror attack: An in-depth Investigation into the 1998 bombings of the U.S. Embassies in Kenya and Tanzania*. Online.https://www.files.ethz.ch/isn/26356/05_anatomy_terr_attack.pdf Accessed 29.09.17 at 3:41 PM.

Metz, S., & Millen, R. (2004). Insurgency and counterinsurgency in the 21st Century: Reconceptualising threat and response. Online. http://ssi.armywarcollege.edu/pdf files/pub586.pdf Accessed 28.04.17 at 11:15 AM.

Muhabie, M. M. (2018). The role of regional economic communities in conflict resolution in Africa: The case of IGAD's peace process in South Sudan. *Global Journal of Political Science and Administration, 6*(1), 199–229.

Muhabie, M. M. (2015). The root causes of conflicts in the Horn of Africa. *American Journal of Applied Psychology, 4*(2), 28–34. Online. http://article.sciencepublishinggroup.com/pdf/10.11648.j.ajap.20150402.12.pdf Accessed 29.09.17 at 1:20 PM.

Mutanda, D. (2015). The genesis, dynamics and effects of the civil war in South Sudan. *International Journal of African Society, cultures and traditions, 3*(1), 18–31. Online. www.eajournals.org Accessed 27.09.17 at 11:56 AM.

Schinkel, W. (2009). On the concept of terrorism. *Contemporary Political Theory, 8*(2), 176–198. Online. www.palgrave-journals.com/cpt/ Accessed 27.09.17 at 9:47 AM.

Pflanz, M. (2015). Al-Shabaab profile: A history of Somalia's insurgent movement. *Telegraph*. 03 April 2015. Online.http://www.telegraph.co.uk/news/worldnews/africaandindianocean/somalia/11513886/Al-Shabaab-profile-A-history-of-Somalias-insurgent-movement.html Accessed 27.09.17 at 10:22 AM.

Tu'emay, A., & Cockayne, J. (2012). *ISSP_CGCC joint baseline study in anti-money laundering and countering the financing of terrorism in the IGAD region*. Online. http://globalcenter.org/wp-content/uploads/2012/11/AML_Report.pdf Accessed 29.09.17 at 11:17 PM.

United Nations Development Programme (UNDP). (2017). Journey to extremism in Africa: Drivers, incentives and the tapping point for recruitment. Online. http://journey-to-extremism.undp.org/en/reports Accessed 29.09.17 at 4:43 PM.

West, S. (2006). Somalia's ICU and its Roots in al-Ittihad al-Islamic . *Terrorism Monitor, 4*(15). Online.https://jamestown.org/program/somalias-icu-and-its-roots-in-al-ittihad-al-islami/ Accessed 17.07.17 at 2:10 PM.

World Food Program (WFP). (2017). *South Sudan situation report #174*.29 April. Online. https://reliefweb.int/sites/reliefweb.int/files/resources/WFP%20South%20Sudan%20Situation%20Report%20%23174%2C%2029%20April%202017.pdf Accessed 28.09.17at 12:14 PM.

# 23

# Southern Africa

## Regional architecture for counterterrorism and counterinsurgency

*Pamela Machakanja and Chupicai Shollah Manuel*

## Introduction

Africa became the new breeding ground and incubator for terrorism, insurgency, and extremism in the last ten years, although terrorism dates to colonial times in southern Africa. The Al-Shabaab attack on the hotel in Kenya on the 15 January 2019 is testimony to the vulnerability of Africa in general to terrorist attacks and insurgencies. On the other hand, intractable wars in East African countries such as Somalia and South Sudan have created fault lines through which extreme Islamic groups attack critical infrastructures, and author several casualties in Africa. Several scholars concur that Africa has been increasingly recognised as a region warranting special counterterrorism attention (Thurston, 2017; Abrahamsen, 2004; Cilliers, 2003). The motivation the above position is the glaring facts that since the late 1980s, sub-state terrorist activity in countries such as Rwanda, Kenya, Burundi, the Democratic Republic of the Congo, Liberia, and Sudan has resulted in the loss of almost a million lives and significant destruction of physical property (Cilliers, 2003. Some statistics show that between 1974 and 2008, a total of 4,993 terrorism incidents took place in sub-Saharan Africa, of which 261 groups claimed responsibility (Elu & Price, 2012). An ever-growing concern is that terrorism is a binary factor of apocalyptic and radical religious beliefs, while others contend to it as a glaring backlash of global inequalities (Abrahamsen, 2004). Of grave concern again in Africa is the increasing advent of Boko Haram in North of Africa, specifically in Nigeria, which had a record of abducting the Chibok girls. In line with this view is the British counterterrorism objectives in Africa recognise that there are more Muslims in Africa than there are in the Middle East which may further increase the likelihood of radical Islamist terrorism (Elu, 2012). The equation is at disequilibrium where on one hand terrorism in Africa is expanding counterterrorism measures, policies and counterinsurgency responses in Southern Africa remain disproportionate or non-existent. It is against this background that this chapter examines the regional architecture for counterterrorism and counterinsurgency in Southern Africa in the context of the evolving discourses and increasingly continental concern on security and safety.

This chapter examines the regional architecture for counterterrorism and counterinsurgency in Southern Africa in the context of the evolving discourses. The chapter examines the level of vulnerability of the southern African region to terrorism and insurgency attacks and efforts by both the African Union and regional bodies in trying to counter terrorism and insurgency. The chapter starts by problematising the key concepts of terrorism and insurgency, the nature and causes of terrorism and insurgent activities, the possible reasons for an upsurge in terrorist, the regional and external factors involved in ensuring that Southern Africa is not vulnerable to the increasing terrorism scourge. The chapter argues that while Southern Africa remains relatively secure regarding the high intensive and the number of terrorist activities, it cannot remain complacent to this phenomenon given the complexities involved, the developmental challenges regarding youth unemployment, the rise in Islamic radicalisation and high levels of political polarisation which give rise to sporadic intra-state conflicts. As such the chapter argues that the more traditional frameworks for countering terrorism and insurgency, which structure terrorism debates using state-centric, military/war or criminal justice models, are inadequate given the evolving complexities that characterise emerging terrorism and insurgent phenomena. The chapter argues for a holistic, comprehensive systems regional integrated approaches to countering terrorism and insurgency; responses which are inclusive of both dialogical, human intelligence, structural and technological advancement if the region is to remain secure and achieve the desired human and development agenda in line with the African Union's Agenda 2063 and the region's industrialisation and modernisation agenda. The proposed framework, structures the terrorism and insurgency discourses around hard and soft power tactics and thinking systems, thereby shifting this debate from the open battlefields of counterterrorism to sophisticated intelligence, dialogical and technological spaces and narratives of counterterrorism and counterinsurgency.

## Conceptualizing terrorism and insurgency

The term terrorism has been variably defined depending on the conceptual lens one uses the contextual situation and who is defining it. Because of these variances, scholars have struggled to define these terms, thereby reaching no conclusive consensus as some definitions are aligned more to politics, crime, war, or the religious realm. Despite these definitional variances, many scholars view terrorism as a politically motivated tactic involving the intentional use of threat, force, or violence in which the pursuit of publicity plays an influential role. These concepts denote illegal or unlawful activities perpetrated by actors who are dissatisfied with the legitimacy of government or operations of a system. However, these classical conceptualisations are proving to be inadequate on how to counter the complexities that characterise modern-day pervasive terrorism and insurgency activities. This is because of the aim of committing terrorist or insurgent activities wide-ranging from creating fear or intimidation to causing serious bodily harm which leads to the death of innocent people, destruction of property and infrastructure as a way of expressing anger and dissatisfaction or making a statement about the hidden powers of the perpetrators. These concepts are now framed in intricate multi-faceted ideological veils of understanding requiring similar response approaches. A nuanced examination of what terrorism and insurgency mean reveal a close but blurred analytical relationship. The terrorist strategies from Al-Qaeda to Al-Shabaab and Boko Haram have become more pervasive and convoluted than the classical responsive goal of dismantling and defeating them. Duffy points out that terrorism encompasses criminal acts directed against a state and intended to create a state of terror in the minds of a particular group of people or the whole nation. As such, this chapter adopts the definition by the UN Security Council Resolution 1566 (2004 which takes a comprehensive and human rights-compatible offence and crime perspective encompassing three cumulative characteristics of terrorism as any unlawful act committed by a person with the sole intention of causing a) death or serious bodily injury; b) serious damage to public or private property, including places of public use, state or government facilities, public transportation, infrastructure or the environment aimed at causing economic loss; c) provoking a state of terror when the purpose and the conduct, by its nature or context, is to intimidate a population or to compel a government or an international organisation to do or abstain from doing any act. Hence the lines between counterterrorism and counterinsurgency strategy have become increasingly blurred, thereby requiring equally adaptive and sophisticated strategies inclusive of strategic, psychological, and emotional intelligence.

Analytically, terrorism follows a three-stage process involving disorientation, target response and gaining legitimacy (Neuman & Smith, 2008:32; Ganor, 2005). First, disorientation aims at implanting a general sense of insecurity by perpetrating random acts of violence among the population, as a way of putting pressure upon an entity to diverting attention from the legitimate state system. Second, target response prompts swift and excessive collective retaliation from a government, to manipulate or radicalise the affected population as a way gaining international legitimacy, which may force political concessions (ibid,40–46). Third, gaining legitimacy is where the terrorist group seeks to transfer legitimacy from government to its cause through the skilful manipulation of the media or internet as a way agitating the grassroots constituency (ibid, 46–53). All these acts could be driven by a combination of ideological, political, religious, or personal motivations. Despite lack of a concise, comprehensive and universal legal definition of these terms the presented definitional approach draws from existing conventions and resolutions where terrorism or insurgency conduct is unjustifiable whatever the considerations that may be invoked to justify them.

Likewise, counterterrorism consists of actions or strategies aimed at preventing terrorism from escalating, preventing the damage from terrorist attacks, intending to eradicate terrorism in a particular contextual situation. By using a four theoretical model, Pedahzur (2009) classified counterterrorism as encompassing defensive, reconciliatory, criminal-justice and war processes, with each model varying in threat perceptions, how to guard against the threats, how the concept of terrorism is legally and constitutionally framed, and the agents that affect counterterrorism. Using Pedahzur's (2009) counterterrorism defensive model terrorism is viewed as a physical and psychological threat, whose goal is the protection of potential targets and victims by the state machinery such as the police and intelligence units with legal and constitutional obligations. From a reconciliatory model, counterterrorism is a political problem, which should be addressed by state and non-state actors through its political agents such as politicians, the military, the police, religious actors, policymakers and dialogical diplomatic means per domestic and international laws. By using the criminal-justice model, terrorism is a crime, and those who perpetrate terrorism must be arrested by the police and punished by the criminal justice system with judicial oversight as part of the rule of law. Finally, the war counterterrorism model views terrorism as an act of war, which should be eliminated through military force and the use of intelligence. Waging such war is at most framed within the 'just war theory' if peace and stability are to be maintained. According to Pedahzur (2009), any country's comprehensive counterterrorism strategy should combine the use of all these models for effective outcomes.

## Counterterrorism and counterinsurgency: a comparative analysis

The distinction between counterinsurgency and counterterrorism, though interpreted as being dichotomous, is inextricably linked as both employ violent action communicated as at most ideological strategy of psychological warfare against vulnerable populations as targets to gain legitimacy over perceived grievances (Pratt, 2010). As Pratt argues the difference between insurgency and terrorism is that insurgency is a situation of political resentment that escalates to violence. In contrast, terrorism is a violent strategy that those with either political, religious or social grievances may employ to gain attention and legitimacy. Thus, terrorism, according to Pratt is best understood as a strategy used by those involved in the insurgency. But whether terrorism is possible outside a situation of insurgency, depends on whether there is a thresh-hold beyond which a minority group engaging in violent activism is sufficiently large enough to be called insurgent.

It can be argued that since terrorism is best understood as a strategy of insurgency, counterterrorism can thus be understood as a component of counterinsurgency. Thus, following Pratt's argument, counterterrorism focuses on combating the tactics and strategy of terrorism and those who employ it, counterinsurgency is a broader category of responses to political violence carried out by minority groups.

## The global counterterrorism and counterinsurgency master plan

The United Nations Global Counterterrorism Strategy was adopted by the General Assembly (GA) on September 8, 2006 (General Assembly Resolution 60/288) marked a watershed where member states agreed to a comprehensive, global, strategic framework on counterterrorism since the issue came before the League of Nations in 1934. The strategy aims to bring all the counterterrorism activities of the United Nations system into a common framework, putting particular emphasis on the Security Council's Counterterrorism Executive Directorate (CTED) and the Secretariat's Counterterrorism Implementation Task Force (CTITF) (General Assembly Resolution 60/288).

Thus, based on extant resolutions including 1267 (1999), 1333 (2000), 1363 (2001), 1373 (2001), 1390 (2002), 1452 (2002), 1455 (2003), 1526 (2004), 1566 (2004), 1617 (2005), 1624 (2005), 1699 (2006), 1730 (2006), 1735 (2006), 1822 (2008), 1904 (2009), 1988 (2011), 1989 (2011), 2083 (2012), 2133 (2014), 2161 (2014), 2170 (2014), 2178 (2014), 2195 (2014), 2199 (2015), 2214 (2015), 2249 (2015), 2253 (2015), 2309 (2016), 2322 (2016), 2331 (2016), 2341 (2017), 2347 (2017), 2354 (2017), the UN Security Council reaffirmed that terrorism in all forms and manifestations constitutes one of the most serious threats to peace and security and that any acts of terrorism are criminal and unjustifiable regardless of their motivations, whenever, wherever, and by whomsoever committed, and reiterating its unequivocal condemnation of all terrorist groups, associated individuals, undertakings, and entities for ongoing and multiple criminal terrorist acts aimed at causing the deaths of innocent civilians and other victims, destruction of property, and the undermining of peace and stability (UN,SRES/2368 (2017, S/RES/2331 (2016), S/RES/2199 (2015), S/RES/2129 (2013).

Since then the United Nations through the UN Charter gives the Security Council primary responsibility for the maintenance of international peace and security and the recognition that terrorism poses a threat to international peace and security and that countering this threat requires collective efforts at national, regional and international levels on the basis of respect for international law and the Charter of the United Nations. The UN further reaffirmed that terrorism cannot and should not be associated with any religion, nationality, or civilisation (Masabo et al., 2014).

All these resolutions mandate states to pursue counterterrorism measures, but of significance, they are meant to create binding obligations upon member states to:

- Reform their national laws, law enforcement and border control systems, and financial systems;
- Criminalise the commission, funding, incitement to, or preparation of, terrorist attacks;
- Detect and freeze assets of terrorists and their supporters;

- Deny safe havens and free movement to terrorists;
- Deny terrorist access to weapons and explosives and other means;
- Cooperate with other justice systems, including through extradition and other forms of exchange of suspects or information by legal means;
- ensure respect for human rights for all and the rule of law as the fundamental basis of the fight against terrorism, and
- Ratify and align the implementation the universal legal instruments, among others (S/RES/2368 (2017), S/RES/2354 (2017).

Central to this was for all counterterrorism and counterinsurgency efforts to be aligned with human rights in ways that recognise and promote the inherent synergies between these frameworks. There is now the realisation that the global community will not succeed in implementing the Global Strategy simply by military or security means, but the need for comprehensive and robust holistic efforts which reconcile the dichotomy between counterterrorism and human rights paradigms thereby seeking to promote common ground.

## African Union's counterterrorism and counterinsurgency drive

The African Union's broad-based continental normative framework to combat terrorism has a number of anti-terrorism treaty instruments, notably the OAU Convention on the Prevention and Combating of Terrorism 1999 and its Protocol, which was adopted in 2004; and the AU Protocol Relating to the Establishment of the Peace and Security Council of the African Union 2002 (Solomon, 2015). The Convention on the Prevention and Combating of Terrorism popularly known as the Algiers Convention was the African legal instrument to define the term terrorism with a focus on preventing and combating terrorism. The definitional understanding as stipulated in the Convention enabled African states to classify criminal offences in domestic law based on a shared, internationally negotiated conceptualisation, in line and complementarity to other legal instruments and conventions. Of significance to note is that the Protocol to the 1999 Algiers Convention stresses in its preamble "the imperative for all member states…to implement all relevant continental and international humanitarian and human rights instruments" alongside the effective implementation of UN and AU instruments, resolutions and schemes. Article 3 (1) (j) contains the undertaking of signatories to the protocol to become parties to all continental and international instruments on terrorism. Under Article 1 (3), a terrorist act is any act or threat which among others, is in violation of the criminal law of the member state, thus emphasising the need for criminalisation under domestic law. Its 2004 Protocol gives responsibility to the AU Peace and Security Council (PSC) to coordinate and harmonise continental efforts in preventing and combating all forms of international terrorism. Thus, the highlight of the Convention was its attempt to address terrorism holistically focusing on a) addressing the structural conditions contributing to the spread of terrorism and insurgency, b) capacity-building of member states with the view to increase resilience, c) instituting preventive measures and d) promoting human rights and the rule of law. (Solomon, 2015; Ford, 2011).

Several scholars including (Solomon, 2015; Ford, 2011) appreciate that AU's establishment of the African Centre for the Study and Research on Terrorism (ACSR) in 1999, in Algiers was a strategic way to create a centralised hub for information and research on terrorism as well as developing a counterterrorism capacity-building framework providing a forum for interaction and cooperation among the Member States and Regional Mechanisms. The creation of a Special Representative for Counterterrorism in October 2010 further strengthened AU counterterrorism efforts and political will. This was followed by the adoption by the AU Assembly, of the African Model Law on Counterterrorism, a legislative framework aimed at harmonising all counterterrorism and counterinsurgency efforts. As such, the Southern African region has always emphasised the need to strengthen its legal framework as the first step to any sustainable counterterrorism and counterinsurgency measures (Ford, 2011).

As part of showing sustained commitment to earlier efforts, on 2 September 2014, the AU convened a Heads of State-Level Peace and Security Council (PSC), meeting in Nairobi, Kenya where the PSC set up a series of objectives for both the AU Member States and the AU Commission. It is at that meeting that the AU Commission was mandated to set-up a Counter-Terrorist Fund and convene an annual Coordination Forum to coordinate all efforts and initiatives on Counterterrorism. In line with the AU Non-Aggression and Common Defence Pact, the PSC resolved to establish specialised joint counterterrorism units at the sub-regional level within the framework of the envisioned African Standby Force (ASF) and the African Capacity for Immediate Response to Crises (ACIRC). The PSC also encourages efforts towards strengthening legislative mechanisms, information sharing, operational capability and co-ordination through various AU-led initiatives including the Sahel Fusion Liaison Unit, (UFL), the Nouakchott Process, the Committee on Intelligence and Security Services of Africa (CISSA), and the African Centre for the Study and Research on Terrorism (ACSRT) and the African Mechanism for Police Cooperation (AFRIPOL) with its mandated focus on inter-state police cooperation and combatting international crime. The Council's determination to strengthen the operationalisation of the PSC Sub-Committee on Counterterrorism with the investigative capacity to monitor the financing of terrorist groups can be viewed as a way of strengthening AU's sanctioning regime (Solomon, 2015; Ford, 2011).

## Nature and causes of terrorism and insurgency in Southern Africa

The source of insecurity in most countries in Africa has to do with unsolvable or unsolved internal ethnic conflicts, power-sharing disputes, a greater deal of injustice, lack of rule of law, undemocratic and weak institutions, border disputes between countries, religious and cultural differences, poor agricultural reforms. Elevated levels of unemployment have made the youth easy prey for terrorist groups (Solomon, 2015). Most terrorist groups that immerged in Africa are based on revolutionary agenda, religious antagonism leading to extremism, appeal to institutional change, claiming recognition from an oppressed minority. The fragility of institutions, ephemeral or overstaying governments based on the ethnic basis for either election or resources and power-sharing. Failure of social inclusion policies to allow participation, macroeconomic disequilibrium, lack of effective border control, inefficient crime prevention and unequipped counterterrorism organisations, climatic conditions, uncontrolled or uncontrollable migration through porous borders, complicity and complexity in criminal activities by even the government officials who are expected to protect citizens. A response to these causal factors requires building effective law-based domesticated counterterrorism preventive strategies founded on democratic principles of inclusion, the participation of all key stakeholders, as well as political will and dedication that goes beyond the ratification of conventions or protocols or rudimentary implementation of counterterrorism legislation (Ford, 2011).

### Failed state and state fragility in Southern Africa

The governance architecture of most countries in Africa can be characterised as being fragile, weak, or failing, a situation which does not render itself for good governance and effectively combatting terrorism. Underpinned by severe poverty this poses a significant threat to international security as such states offer a haven for illicit trade, drugs-production, and weapons-smuggling. Corruption presents an endemic problem, and the global result is likely to be a regional spill-over of the effects of conflict, terrorism, and a failure to manage epidemic diseases.

While there may be no simple answer to this fundamental problem, scholars argue that good governance is central to the effective administration of a state's resources, instituting the rule of law, the creation of a functioning public and private sector and the development of a strong civil society. The lack of a functional civil service, armed forces and security services also mean that crisis mitigation following an attack is uncoordinated and ineffective. This can lead to the response to an attack being more damaging than the attack itself. While, early warning of terrorist attacks is a challenge for all security services, weak governance inefficient ministries and lack of effective coordination between government agencies and ministries in some African countries compounds the problems of implementing effective counterterrorism and counterinsurgency strategies. Therefore, good governance is a prerequisite for effective counter-terrorist measures because, without strong governance institutions, it will be exceedingly difficult to counter terrorism effectively.

## Southern Africa's vulnerability to terrorism and insurgency

Revealing evidence show that Southern Africa is not immune to terrorism than any other continent because of the growing phenomenon of Islamic inspired fundamentalism and extremism (Solomon, 2015; Ford, 2011). It is also generally agreed that Africa as a continent remains a conducive environment for breeding terrorism as it accommodates the largest Muslim population which today is significantly associated with a radical interpretation of doctrine and philosophy of Islam. Botha and Solomon (2014:3) argue that the continent of Africa harbours the largest Muslim population, which makes it a conducive breeding ground for youth who can be easily manipulated towards fundamentalist and extremist violent behaviours. This situation is compounded by the high rate youth unemployment on the continent and lack of political will on the many African governments to respond positively to fundamental issues of seriously empowering youth as future leaders of the continent. Unless African leaders realise that creating employment opportunities would be a potentially effective tool to prevent conflict and deter radicalisation, youth unemployment in Africa remains a ticking time bomb for the region's security. While we might not know exactly what prompts an individual to support violent extremist ideas, and the knowledge that the drivers of radicalisation are complex and multi-faceted psychology and sociological theories inform us that unemployment, marginalisation and impoverished youth can be easily manipulated and recruited into armed conflict and radicalised into violent extremism (ibid). Both these "push and pull factors" can drive youth into extremism. For example, the push factors which resonate well with most governments in Southern Africa include "inequality, lack of access to justice and civil rights, repressive regimes, unresolved conflicts, and marginalisation"; and pull factors include "the appeal of ideology," a charismatic leader such as Osama Bin Laden who might be admired by these idle youth, peer pressure, and appealing social networks. These interrelated social conditions create what can be called a demand-side and supply and context that breeds extremists. In the context of Southern Africa, the demand side consists of youth who are looking for a 'meaning of life' through exploring faith as they try to make sense of what is happening in the world in terms of international relations, and searching for a place in society. The 'supply' factor consists of rebel groups known to youth such as al-Qaeda, Boko Haram, Janjaweed and other similar radical movements which can easily offer answers to the youth's searching questions through a mix of engaging and appealing social, political, religious and ideological narratives. While everyone might have a certain resilience to these extremist discourses, the current social and economic context in Southern Africa is a breeding ground for exploitable frustrations (ibid, Ford, 2011).

As such, the threat of terrorism to Africa, mainly the Islamic inspired ones has been recorded in the regions of Maghreb, particularly Egypt, Algeria, Morocco, Libya, Tunisia, Chad; West African region – Nigeria and Mali; The Horn of Africa – Ethiopia, Somalia, Kenya and Tanzania; and the Southern African Development Community (SADC) – South Africa. For example, Botha & Solomon (2014:3) argue that since 1995, Africa has been subjected to an increase in the number of terrorist and insurgent attacks against foreigners or foreign interests. The jihadist group attack on Bamako's Radisson Blue Hotel collaborated with the Saharan Emirate of Al-Qaeda of Islamic Maghreb. In 2015, the Al-Mourabitoun, a jihadist group carried out an attack with Al Qaeda's affiliated group, the Al Qaeda in the Islamic Maghreb (AQIM) on the Radisson Blue Hotel in Bamako. Princeton (2008) concur with Thurston (2017) that in the 1990s Osama bin Laden operated in the Horn of Africa where it is alleged that he organised an attack on the Egyptian President, Hosni Mubarak. Three years later in 1998, Al-Qaeda inspired terrorists blew up the United States Embassies in Nairobi, Kenya, and Dar-es-Salaam, Tanzania. The consequence of these attacks has led to many migrating to more relatively peaceful states South of the Sahara, triggering possibilities of spreading the phenomenon of radicalisation manifesting into terrorist-inspired violence.

Scholars such as (Solomon, 2015; Elu, 2012; Thurston, 2017) attribute this phenomenon to the main factors firstly that Africa sluggish response to this emerging phenomenon provides the nurturing of terrorism and insurgent tendencies. The second factor relates to the lack of interest and definitive commitment by both the African governments and the developed world to pro-actively counter these threats. Third, African governments need to realise that ratification of universally greed anti-terrorist conventions is an important way which provides a legal framework for institutionalising and domestication of terrorism prevention as stated in paragraph 3 (d) of (Security Council Resolution 1373 of 2001). As Ford (2011:13) points out, the overall objective of ratification is to harmonise all national laws in ways that create a seamless web of preventive, punitive and international cooperative legally informed counterterrorism measures. Botha and Solomon for example, associate the escalation of transnational terrorism with the 1998 Kenyan and Tanzanian bombings against the US embassies to the failure of both African governments to pay attention to the proliferation of Muslim jihadists, despite the fact that earlier in 2013 the 10th Conference of Committee for Intelligence and Security Services for Africa (CISSA), in its Southern Region Report revealed the escalation of terrorism and extremism on the continent. The report showed all indications of how Africa was becoming a fertile ground for the growth of jihadist-terrorism. Such evidence was corroborated by Osama bin Laden in a statement in July 2006 when he clearly singled out Somalia as an important jihadist front of the future, a reality which continues to haunt Africa today. Despite Ethiopia's intervention, the country remains in the grip of Islamic fundamentalists and there is much reason for pessimism.

Further studies on terrorism-insurgency in East Africa track how Kenyan cell operatives, having been radicalised, struck an Israeli-owned Paradise Hotel in Mombasa. According to Botha & Solomon (2014:4) the suspects, Fumo Mohamed Fumo and Haruni Barusa, both Kenyan nationals had been radicalised and inspired by Al-Qaeda. However, Kenya's response to both the 1998 and 2002 attacks was that these were orchestrated from abroad. As a result, this denial attitude is viewed as negatively impacting on the proficiency to pro-actively respond to these attacks and taking preventive counter-terrorist measures and radicalisation from within. Prior to this, Boko Haram had just leapt on the region's agenda in August 2011, when it bombed the United Nations compound in Abuja, killing 23 innocent people (Walker, 2012:2).

Botha & Solomon (2014:3) further present quantitative figures to justify an upsurge in terror attacks on the continent as follows:

However, despite earlier denials and lukewarm approaches to counterterrorism and counterinsurgency, there is a general feeling that terrorism and radicalisation are on the rise. While national actions may take shape from globally applicable agreements, the success or failure of the global strategy against terrorism will depend on African governments' political will individually and collectively to build both human and institutional capacities including national justice systems to implement global frameworks. Central to these processes would be the capacity of both justice and security systems to detect, investigate, prevent and prosecute those

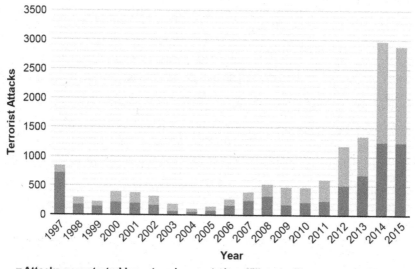

■ Attacks perpetrated by actors known to be affiliated with an organization
■ Attacks perpetrated by actors not known to be affiliated with an organization

*Figure 23.1*  African countries attacked by Islamic groups between 1997 and 2015

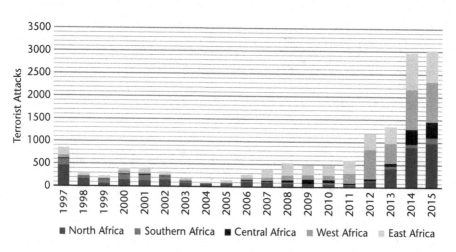

■ North Africa   ■ Southern Africa   ■ Central Africa   ■ West Africa   ▨ East Africa

*Figure 23.2*  Terrorist attacks in Africa 1997–2015, by region

who engage in terrorist and insurgent activities while maintaining the rule of law and respect of human rights.

## Southern Africa's regional strategies to combating terrorism and insurgency

Southern Africa's counterterrorism and counterinsurgency approach derive its base and legitimacy from a host of counterterrorism legal frameworks ranging from the 13 major UN Conventions and Protocols which the African Union states have either ratified or are still to do so (Fink, 2012). Out of the 13 major UN Conventions and Protocols, the African Union has crafted its own, the 1999 Algiers Convention on the Prevention and Combating of Terrorism. In addition, to effect counterterrorism monitoring, SADC countries, for example, complement their efforts through their own inter-state Defense and Security Committees that closely cooperate with other international and non-governmental agencies like the "Committee for Intelligence and Security Services for Africa" (CISSA) Southern Africa Region. At the CISSA, 10th conference held in Harare, Zimbabwe and a follow-up meeting held in Windhoek, Namibia on the 19–20 August 2013 whose focus was "Anti-Money Laundering and Combatting the Financing of Terrorism," counter-intelligence and security chiefs agreed that the treatment of international terrorism remained a source of concern for the Southern African region. These meetings committed to enacting Anti-Terrorism legislation, Anti-Money Laundering legislation and the establishment of Financial Intelligence Agencies and the enhancement of cooperation between member states.

The Financial Action Task Force (FATF), as the international standard-setting body to address threats of money laundering, terrorist financing, and other related crimes, has established a network of countries around the world. These FATF-Style Regional Bodies (FSRBs) have the potential to serve both as a disciplinarian and as a resource. In sub-Saharan Africa, there are two such bodies recognised by the FATF: the Eastern and Southern Africa Anti-Money Laundering Group (ESAAMLG) and the Intergovernmental Action Group against Money Laundering and Terrorist Financing (GIABA). Like FATF and the other FSRBs, they conducted mutual evaluations, worked on various framework and implementation issues, and provided training for their members. Despite the existence and activities of these groups, Africa remains the single region in the world without FSRB coverage over a wide band of its countries. FATF has attempted to organise an RSRB in Central Africa, where most unsubscribed countries are located.

### The Trans-Sahara Counterterrorism Partnership (TSCTP)

The Trans-Sahara Counterterrorism Partnership (TSCTP) is a multi-faceted, multi-year strategy designed to combat violent extremism, and contain and marginalise terrorist organisations by strengthening individual-country and regional counterterrorism capabilities, enhancing and institutionalising cooperation among the region's security and intelligence organisations, promoting democratic governance, and discrediting terrorist ideology. The overall goals are to enhance the indigenous capacities of governments in the pan-Sahel (Mauritania, Mali, Chad, and Niger, as well as Nigeria, Senegal, and Burkina Faso); to confront the challenge posed by terrorist organisations in the trans-Sahara; and to facilitate cooperation between those countries and US partners in the Maghreb (Morocco, Algeria, and Tunisia).

The TSCTP was developed as a follow-on to the Pan-Sahel Initiative, which focused solely on the Sahel. Ongoing concern that extremists continued to seek safe havens and support networks in the Maghreb and Sahel – as well as recognition that al-Qaeda and others were seeking to impose radical ideologies on traditionally moderate Muslim populations in the region – highlighted the urgency of creating an integrated approach to addressing current threats and preventing conditions that could foster persistent threats in the future.

## Strategies designed to decapitate terror networks

Southern Africa has come to realise that the fight against terrorism is not a job which can be undertaken by one single agency, it requires teamwork and input from a wide range of national and international organisations including law enforcement agencies, the military, the intelligence services, the financial sector, the diplomatic service and health organisations. The key to success is Organisation, Cooperation and Coordination hence the need for an integrated regional counterterrorism and counterinsurgency architecture. However, the sheer size of Southern Africa, the mosaic of cultural and societal differences creates daunting problems for intelligence gathering to penetrate some of the volatile terrains and decapitate multiple alliances of terrorist networks and organisations. This requires an integrated intelligence community that understands the dynamics of the culturally embedded sub-clan structures that are used to motivate, harbour terror groups, as the case of Somalia has shown.

## Southern African Development Community: counter terrorism strategies

Although SADC has a small Muslim community when compared to the other regions, the period beyond 2001, has shown a steady growth of terror threat emanating from Islamic fundamentalism. As such, the Southern African Development Community (SADC) as a regional body has identified the international dimensions of terrorist which range from terrorist recruitment and training, financing, and operations that include sleeper cells operatives and human traffickers. As a result, the region's combat posture necessitated the formation of regional statutory bodies like; Migration Dialogue for Southern Africa (MIDSA), Inter-state Defence and Security Committee (ISDSC), Inter-state Politics and Diplomacy Committee (ISPDC), Ministerial Committee Organisation (MCO) and the Committee of Intelligence and Security Services for Africa (CISSA) Southern Region among a host of other counter-terrorist and counterinsurgency initiatives.

The concept of security in the Southern African Development Community (SADC) is an elusive one as it encapsulates the critical aspects of human, economic, social, and environmental security. Security is an elusive concept in the sense that in SADC it mainly concerns with state security in Africa while other forms of security such as human security (economic, social, cultural, community, personal) are relegated to the terraces. This has been evidenced by the operations and guidelines of the Organ for Peace and Security in Southern Africa that do not articulate on security in its holistic sense by in terms of state security. This inclusive concept of security provides for a holistic governance paradigm for the Southern African States in fulfilling their responsibilities to protect the lives and property of their citizens, as identified in the regional policy frameworks of the Strategic Indicative Plan for the Organ (SIPO) and the Regional Indicative Strategic Development Plan (RISDP). Given this sort of regional predisposition, the importance of regional States to steer clear of what one participant called "a blanket security approach," which would ignore the dynamics through which security and development affect each other and make it easier for peoples' rights to be violated.

To buttress the argument that Southern African is on high alert regarding terrorist threats, the Southern African Development Community (SADC) developed a Regional Counterterrorism Strategy which was adopted at the SADC Heads of State Summit on 18 August 2015. The new strategy is a response to confronting a number of threats and violent terrorist acts experienced on the continent also came at the request of the SADC Secretariat and the African Union's Centre for Studies and Research on Terrorism (CAERT). This strategy which is modelled on the UN Counterterrorism Strategy (UNCCT) and the Bogota Guiding Principles for Counterterrorism Strategies focuses on the comprehensive prevention of terrorist activities that threaten to spill over from other regions. Since its adoption, UNCCT has helped to organise several expert workshops which bring together practitioners and Counterterrorism focal points from every SADC country. The workshops address measures to prevent and combat terrorism, conditions conducive to the spread of terrorism, and the capacity-building needs of the Southern Africa region. For example, between November 2014 and October 2015, six such workshops have been organised thereby revealing evidence of the region's vulnerability. Such workshops include the Southern African Development Community (SADC) Regional Counterterrorism Strategy drafting workshop on measures to prevent and combat terrorism. Held in Harare, Zimbabwe on 5–7 November 2014. Another initiative is that of The Integrated Counterterrorism and Non-proliferation of Arms Strategy for Central Africa drafting workshop on conditions conducive to the growth of terrorism and human rights and the rule of law that was brought about through a workshop held in Luanda, Angola, on 24–26 February 2015. The Southern African Development Community (SADC) Regional Counterterrorism Strategy drafting workshop which addressed the conditions conducive to the spread of terrorism and upholding the rule of law, held in Livingstone, Zambia, on 24–26 March 2015. The Integrated Counterterrorism and Non-proliferation of Arms Strategy for Central Africa drafting workshop on terrorist financing and money laundering held in Libreville, Gabon, from 19–21 May 2015. The Southern African Development Community (SADC) Regional Counterterrorism Strategy drafting workshop on counterterrorism capacity building needs in the Southern Africa region, held in Gaborone, Botswana, on 10–11 June 2015, which also reviewed the draft strategy and associated Plan of Action that had been prepared by the SADC Secretariat, with extensive input from UNCCT, CAERT and the SADC Troika and the Integrated Counterterrorism and Non-proliferation of Arms Strategy for Central Africa drafting workshop on criminal justice responses to terrorism, held in Libreville, Gabon, from 29 September–1 October 2015. The thematic areas covered in all these workshops include police, security and intelligence matters; customs, immigration, border control and small arms trafficking; conditions conducive to the growth of terrorism and human rights and the rule of law; terrorist financing and money laundering; and criminal justice responses to terrorism. Despite these efforts, Menkhaus in Zimmerman and Rosenau (2009:98) makes some inference on SADC in that is offers a conducive terrorist-prone environment in that "Sub-Saharan-Africa's weak security sector and failed states continue to provide some non-African diasporas with safe heaven beyond the easy reach of counterterrorism operations." He thus, cites Haroon Rashid Aswat, an Indian-born citizen of the UK, a suspect in the 2005 London bombings, who sought safe haven in Zambia, as a vindication of his argument (Menkhaus in Zimmermann and William, ibid).

## Challenges of CT-COIN in Southern Africa: regional policy options

The fight against terrorism is a real problem because of the difficulties of identifying the enemy, especially due to the fact that there are no common signals between terrorists as they are recruited from different countries, ethnicities, and age groups; this makes tracking this enemy and defeating it difficult with traditional means. It can be argued that one of the most marked changes in the world of terrorism and counterterrorism during recent years is the increasingly sophisticated use of the internet and media by various terrorist groups to spread their propaganda and recruit supporters. The technology has improved, especially the use of the production videos designed to appeal to young men dissatisfied with their current lives or looking for a cause. The use of the internet has stimulated the emergence of what is called "lone wolves" as well as foreign fighters who may have unknown or undetectable direct contacts with terrorist groups but are inspired by what they see and hear on their computers.

Another major challenge in the arena of emerging technology is the threat of cyber-terrorism. Hacking of government and private sector websites, some of it perpetrated by hackers for economic or espionage motives is also taking place. But cyber-terrorism aimed at disrupting a country's electric power supplies, communications and other vital systems is the most dangerous threat to a country's infrastructure and ability to function. Thus, the internet and its various uses or misuses are likely to increase challenges to the counterterrorism and counterinsurgency efforts in Southern Africa and the entire world.

It needs to be reasserted that the Southern Africa's counterterrorism and counterinsurgency strategy on preventing attacks should rest on three axes informed by the UN Global Counterterrorism Strategy of 2006 and the African Union 1999 Convention on the Prevention and Combatting of Terrorism and Insurgency. First, efforts should be on prevention and protection of populations, infrastructures, and transports via the support to security infrastructure. One strategy is to make it mandatory that all public and crucial infrastructures such as airports and private hotels be installed with detectors and surveillance appliances to help counter terrorist actors. Second, tracking down terrorists through intelligence and security mechanisms should scale up. Such a strategy could be achieved by way of setting a desk with the Africa Union that will provide early warning systems as well and coordinate with existing arms of with the regional groupings in Africa such as SADC, ECOWAS and COMESA and this will increase deterrence. Third, preventing radicalisation and enrolment of young people should be curtailed. This could be achieved by way of introducing out of school youth entrepreneurship training and provide youth grants that will deter the youth from being lured into radicalism as a means to deal with their economic frustrations.

Secondly, workshops and training on the consequences of terrorism and radicalism could be taught at community level and schools with the help of Non-Governmental Organisations and schools.

Fourth, the Global Strategy demonstrates the international community's determination to fight terrorism through the following strategies:

•poverty alleviation
•employment opportunities
•conflict resolution
•inter-cultural dialogue
•improving good governance and the protection of human rights, including the rights of victims of terrorism

Another sound commitment from the Global Strategy states that all States and international organisations should provide the moral high ground in counterterrorism and counterinsurgency activities and expose the poverty of the terrorists' narratives on youth.

This is because terrorism is complex and requires a multi-faceted response. Countering terrorism and insurgency through law enforcement or hard security measures is no longer sufficient; instead, this chapter argues for multi-faceted, multi-sectoral and multi-level strategies.

While this requires strong cooperation between national and regional law enforcement agencies, the inclusion of other stakeholders in counterterrorism strategy-making delivers a more holistic and preventative response. This chapter, therefore, argues for the Southern African States to adopt a "new mindset" at the regional level to combat terrorism and insurgency.

This integrated effort it is hoped will stop the conditions that favour extremism, radicalisation and the exploitation of young people, using cooperation between member countries and institutions of the regional blocks but also with external partners and international organisations. As such, the Southern African regional integrated security framework and regional early warning systems should be strengthened to ensure that they provide effective and efficient intelligence alerts to potential insecurity and instability. The Southern African States must not grow complacent against the threat and must prevent the region from potentially becoming a haven or a soft target for terrorists and insurgents. Finally, understanding today deeper complexities involving terrorism and insurgent activities requires a paradigm shift from traditional counterterrorism approaches to providing more holistic approaches to counterterrorism which do not rely on the state system the primary instrument to combat terrorism but aim at addressing the root causes driving the problem using a multi-dimensional lens that promote sustainable regional peacebuilding and military and civilian cooperation strategies for counterinsurgency and counterterrorism.

## Conclusion

In contrast to other regions in Africa, the threat posed by domestic or international terrorism within Southern Africa, historically speaking, has been low. Consequently, despite notable exceptions, the development and implementation of national and regional counterterrorism and counterinsurgency legislative instruments and practical measures aimed at strengthening interagency and inter-State cooperation have understandably not been a top priority for all regional States. While the African Union (AU) has a well-established normative legal framework to counterterrorism and insurgency informed by the 1999 African Union Convention on the Prevention and Combatting of Terrorism and Insurgency and UN Global Strategy on Counterterrorism, this chapter argues for more practical implementation strategies that transcend ratification of counterterrorism conventions, protocols, policies to practical strategies responsive to complex and pervasive nature of today's terror activities.

This chapter underscores the need for a "systems integration" approach, which entails a grounded and institutionalised government-supported mechanism that allows for a functional and practical exchange of priorities and methodologies between all relevant stakeholders in order to counter terrorism and insurgency through a comprehensive approach which goes beyond traditional state-militaristic approaches. Systems integration is broader and more inclusive intersecting with human rights, development and governance than unilateral-state centric approaches to counterterrorism and counterinsurgency. The role of the United Nations, the African Union and the Southern African Development Community (SADC) should be supported, and specific focus is placed in strengthening the United Nations Counterterrorism Implementation Task Force Office CTITF's role in facilitating the development of sub-regional and national counterterrorism and counterinsurgency implementation plans and strategies. Adoption of the United Nations Global Counterterrorism Strategy offers a major opportunity to strengthen principled multilateralism in world affairs. The strategy properly asks member states; the United Nations; and other appropriate international, regional, and sub-regional organisations to support its implementation.

# References

Abrahamsen, R. (2004). A breeding ground for terrorists? Africa and Britain's war on terrorism. *Review of African Political Economy, 31*, 677–684.

Alison, S (2016). *African Union and the scourge of terrorism*. The Herald [Zimbabwe]. 1 February 2016.

Botha, A. (2014). *Political dissent and terrorism in Southern Africa*. ISS Paper 265. http://www.issafrica.com Accessed 7.07.17.

Botha, A., & Solomon, H. (2014). *Terrorism in Africa*. Pretoria: Center for International Political Studies (CiPS). http://www.issafrica.com. Accessed 7.07.17.

Botha A. (2014). Radicalisation in Kenya recruitment to al-Shabaab and the Mombasa Republican Council, ISS Paper 265, September, 2014. Available from: www.issafrica.com Accessed 20.07. 17.

Broomhall, B. (2004). State Actors in an international definition of terrorism from a human rights perspective. *Case Western Reserve Journal of International Law, 36*(2), 421–441.

Cilliers, J. (2003). Terrorism and Africa. *African Security Review, 12*(4), 91–103.

Cartalucci, T. (2016). *US-NATO Invade Libya to fight terrorists of its own creation* (p. 11). Zimbabwe: The Herald. 28 January 2016.

De Albuquerque, A. L. (2017). *Terrorism in Africa: A quantitative analysis*. Sweden: Swedish Defence Research Agency, FOI.

Docking, T. (2004). *Terrorism in the Horn of Africa*. Washington, DC: United States Institute of Peace, Special Report 113, January 2004.

Elu, J., (2012). Terrorism in Africa and South Asia: Economic or Existential Good? *Journal of Developing Areas, 46*(1), 345–358. doi: 10.1353/jda.2012.0008.

Elu, J. U., & Price, G. N. (2012). Remittances and the financing of terrorism in sub-Saharan Africa: 1974–2006. *Peace Economics, Peace Science, and Public Policy, 18*(1), 5.

Elu, J. U., & Price, G. N. (2013). *Terrorism and regional integration in sub-Saharan Africa: The case of the CFA Franc Zone in advances in African economic, social and political development*. New York: Springer Publishers.

Fink, N.C. (2012). *Meeting the Challenge: A Guide to United Nations Counterterrorism Activities*. New York: International Peace Institute.

Ford, J. (2011). *African counter-terrorism legal frameworks: A decade after 2001*. Tshwane, (Pretoria), South Africa: Institute of Security Studies.

Duffy, H. (2005). *The 'War on Terror' and the framework of international law*. Cambridge: Cambridge University Press.

Galula, D. (1964). *Counterinsurgency warfare: Theory and practice* (pp. 3–6). Westport, Connecticut: Praeger Security International.

Ganor, B. (2005). *The counter-terrorism puzzle: a guide for decision makers*. New Brunswick, NJ: Transaction Publishers.

Hubschle, A. (2007). *Terrorist financing in Southern Africa: Are we making a mountain out of molehill?*, Institute for Security Studies Paper 132. Pretoria, SA: Institute for Security Studies. Available: https://www.files.ethz.ch/isn/98922/PAPER132.pdf. (accessed June 7, 2017).

Lando, B. (2015). *From Paris to Mali: Nightmare continues*. Zimbabwe: The Herald. 24 November 2015.

Masabo, C. J., Wama, M, & Mlyansi, T. P. (2014). The role of regional integration in fighting crime and terrorism: the case of the African Union's (AU's) initiatives, 1999–2014. *Peace and Conflict Monitor*. Addis Ababa: University for Peace. Available: http://www.monitor.upeace.org/innerpg.cfm?id_article=1066. (accessed June 7, 2017).

da Silva, Marina (2014). The challenges of African engagement with the United Nations Security Council. *Regional colloquium of the South African Association of Political Studies*. Vaal Triangle Campus of the North West University, September 18, 1 October 2015.

Neuman, P. R., & Smith, M. L. R. (2008). *The strategy of terrorism: How it works, and why it fails*. London: Routledge.

Mack, A. (1975). Why big nations lose small wars: The politics of asymmetric conflict. *World Politics, 27*(2), 177.

Pedahzur, A. (2009). *The Israeli secret services and the struggle against terrorism*. New York: Columbia University Press.

Pratt, S. (2010). What is the difference between counter-insurgency and counter-terrorism? http://www.e-ir.info/2010/12/21/what-is-the-difference-bettween-counter-insurgency-and-and-counter-terrorism? Accessed 06.07. 17 at 18.35hrs.

Princeton, L. N. (2008). The war on terrorism in Africa. In Harbeson, J. (Ed.), *Africa in world politics*. Westview Press, Perseus Books Group.

Solomon, H. (2015). *Terrorism and counter-terrorism in Africa: Fighting insurgency from Al Shabaab, Ansar Dine and Boko Haram*. London: Palgrave, Macmillan.

Solomon, H. (2015). *African solutions to Africa's problems? African approaches to peace, security and stability*. *Scientia Militaria: South African Journal of Military Science*, 43(1), 45–76.

Solomon, H. (2015). *Islam in Africa: From Sufi moderation to Islamist radicalization*. *Journal of Contemporary History*, 40(2), 176–196.

Solomon, H. (2015). *The African Union and counter-terrorism*. Workshop of the Southern African Centre for Collaboration on Peace and Security: Perspectives on African peace and security. Bloemfontein: University of the Free State, 12 February.

Solomon, H. (2015). *The human rights challenges that governments face responding to terrorist threats*. Workshop on Conditions Conducive to the Spread of Terrorism and Respect for Human Rights and the Rule of Law in the Fight Against Terrorism. Livingstone, Zambia: UN Counter Terrorism Centre and the Southern African Development Community, 24 March.

Thurston, A. (2017). *Boko Haram: The history of an African Jihadist Movement, Princeton Muslim Politics Series*. Princeton: Princeton University Press.

UN (United Nations). (2004). UNSC Resolution 1566. New York: United Nations. Available: https://www.un.org/ruleoflaw/files/n0454282.pdf. Accessed 2 October 2020.

United Nations Security Council Resolution S/RES/2368 (2017), *Threats to international peace and security caused by terrorist acts*. Available: http://undocs.org/S/RES/2368(2017). Accessed 06.07.17 at 19.35hrs.

United Nations Security Council Counter-Terrorism Committee, S/RES/2354.(2017). *Countering terrorist narratives*. Available: https://www.un.org/press/en/2017/sc12839.doc.htm. Accessed 06.07.17 at 19.55hrs.

United Nations Security Council Counter-Terrorism Committee, S/RES/2331.(2016), *Maintenance of international peace and security*. Available: https://www.un.org/en/ga/search/view_doc.asp?symbol=S/RES/2331%20(2016). Accessed 07.07.17 at 19.55hrs.

United Nations Security Council Counter-Terrorism Committee, S/RES/2250.(2015). *Maintenance of international peace and security*. Available: https://www.un.org/press/en/2015/sc12149.doc.htm. Accessed 07.07.17 at 20.55hrs.

United Nations Security Council Counter-Terrorism Committee, S/RES/2129. (2013). *Mandate of the Counter-Terrorism Committee Executive Directorate (CTED) until 31 December 2017*. Available: https://www.un.org/press/en/2013/sc11219.doc.htm. Accessed 07.07.17 at 21.55hrs.

Walker, A. (2012). *What is Boko Haram?* Washington DC: United States Institute of Peace. http://www.usip.org Accessed 7.09.17 at 14.44hrs.

Weinberg, L., Pedahzur, A., & Hirsh-Hoefler, S. (2010). The challenges of conceptualising terrorism. *Terrorism and Political Violence*, 16(4), 782, 2010.

Wilkinson, P. (1977). *Terrorism and liberal state*. London: Macmillan.

Worcester, M. (2015). *Combatting Terrorism in Africa*. Berlin: Institut fur Strategic-Politik-Sicherheits-und Wirtschaftsberatung. http://www.files.ethz.ch/isn/50103Combatting_Terrorism_in_Africa Accessed 26.08.17.

Zimmerman, D., & Rosenau, W (2009). *The Radicalisation of Diasporas and Terrorism, Center for Security Studies*. ETH Zentrum SEI Publications. Available from: http://www.css.eth.ch/publications Accessed July 2017.

# 24

# Gulf of Guinea

## Regional architecture for anti-piracy and maritime security

### C. Nna-Emeka Okereke

## Introduction

The geo-strategic importance of the maritime domain across the world remains enormous. This relates to the massive haulage of goods and services by sea as well as the vast deposits of natural resources and animal life useful to human existence. Yet, the security of the maritime domain has over the centuries been fraught with changing dimensions of threat requiring robust maritime security architecture to safeguard the seaways.

In Southeast Asia, piracy emerged a significant security concern in the aftermath of the Cold War. The International Maritime Bureau's Piracy Reporting Centre (IMB-PRC) based in Kuala Lumpur recorded a sustained increase in reported incidents of piracy in the 1990s accompanied by a sudden rise from 94 incidents in 1998 to 257 in the year 2000 (Storey 2016, United Nations, (UN) 1982).[1] As a response to this problem of piracy and sea robbery, regional states enacted measures to improve maritime security in areas under their jurisdiction. For instance, Indonesia, Malaysia, and the Philippines agreed to engage in coordinated naval patrols in the Sulu Sea. Similarly, littoral states in the Straits of Malacca and Singapore (SOMS) notably Indonesia, Malaysia and Singapore, embarked on measures to strengthen the security of their ports, territorial waters and Exclusive Economic Zone (EEZ).[2] In July 2004, these countries launched a trilateral naval patrol in their vital waterways known as the Malacca Straits Patrols (MSP). It consists of three elements, namely the coordinated naval patrols, combined aerial patrols and institutionalisation of information and intelligence exchange. Thailand joined the MSP in 2008. Subsequently, 14 Asian countries motivated by Japan's initiative signed the Regional Cooperation Agreement on Combating Piracy and Armed Robbery against Ships in Asia (ReCAAP) in November 2004.

The ReCAAP Agreement outlined the obligations undertaken by member countries to effect measures to prevent and suppress piracy and armed robbery against ships. In addition, it outlined the framework for cooperation among member countries based on three pillars, notably information sharing, capacity building, and operational collaboration. (National Archives of Singapore, 2006).[3] A depository for the ReCAAP agreement was opened in Singapore on 28 February 2005 while the agreement came into force on 4 September 2006. The 14 countries that have signed and ratified the ReCAAP Agreement are Bangladesh, Brunei,

Cambodia, China, India, Japan, Republic of South Korea, Laos, Myanmar, the Philippines, Singapore, Sri Lanka, Thailand and Vietnam.[4] However, Malaysia and Indonesia, which are two significant Southeast Asian countries, declined to sign the ReCAAP Agreement siting issues of state sovereignty. Both countries have demonstrated interest to cooperate with the ReCAAP Information Sharing Centre (ISC).

Since the dawn of the 21st Century, the incidence of piracy in the Gulf of Aden has become a global concern. This relates to the fact that an estimated 21,000 commercial ships pass through the Gulf of Aden annually, of which over 10% of international oil transportation is included. In addition, 7% of international commerce transit across the Suez Canal, which links Asia, East Africa, and Europe through the Gulf of Aden to the Mediterranean through the Red Sea. The economic viability of the Gulf of Aden has been exploited by criminal enterprises engaged in piracy since the first decade of the 21st Century (Carafano, Richard, & Martin, 2009).[5]

The core objective of the pirates in the region is money-making, and the systematic methodology is taking over a ship, seizing hostages and cargo and compelling the shipping company to pay ransom estimated at $1 million to $2 million per ship.[6] In addition to threats to sea routes and global seaway transportation, piracy in the Gulf of Aden has been linked to the persistent insecurity in the Horn of Africa as it is one of the core sources of funds for the Al Shabaab al-Mujahideen which engages in violent extremism and transnational terrorism. As a key facilitator of piracy in the Gulf of Aden the Al Shabaab emerged following prolonged period characterised by the absence of state control in Somalia. It, therefore, became imperative for multinational action to combat the scourge of piracy in the Gulf of Aden.

The United Nations, North Atlantic Treaty Organisation and European Union as well as various national governments, organised distinct maritime security operations in the Gulf of Aden and the Red Sea area. While the United States activated the multinational Combined Task Force 150 (CTF-150), which is an aspect of the Combined Force Maritime Command of the United States-led Operation Enduring Freedom (OEF) integrated counter-piracy to its counterterrorism mandate. Subsequently, 24 member states of the United Nations joined a Contact Group on Piracy Off the Coast of Somalia (CGPSC) established on 14 January 2009. These operations were in line with the United Nations Security Council resolutions calling for international action against pirates.

As the Gulf of Aden, the maritime domain in the Gulf of Guinea is strategic to the global and regional economy as it offers enormous potentials for sea transportation, fishing, aquaculture, mining and other economic activities needed for development in the continent. However, as the geo-strategic importance of the Gulf of Guinea to global sea trade increases, the area remains inundated with maritime threats that continually exposes the limited capabilities of member states to secure their maritime domains individually. This relates to the recurrence of sea robbery, piracy, and the hijacking of ships. Illegal unreported and unregulated fishing, illicit transnational trafficking in arms and drugs, irregular migration, and human trafficking have continuously constituted threats to local economies, the international energy, and global shipping thereby raising the stakes for continued maritime domain awareness in the Gulf of Guinea (Global Sentinel, 2017).[7]

The Gulf of Guinea has assumed a significant status as the world's leading space for piracy, in terms of the number and gravity of attacks. The fragile maritime security structures and weak navies of several member states have proved unable to contain these threats. These have raised the importance of regional security architecture to strengthen the capabilities of member states to meet the emerging and imagined maritime threats in the Gulf of Guinea. This paper, therefore, examines the regional architecture for maritime security in the Gulf of Guinea with emphasis on the Yaoundé Code of Conduct 2013 and other relevant instruments on integrated maritime security for Africa. The paper will examine the nature of the threat.

## Geo-strategic importance of the Gulf of Guinea

The Gulf of Guinea, also referred to as the Bight of Benin, is presumably located at the intersection of the Equator and the Prime Meridian (0⁰0'0",0⁰0'0") or the region from Guinea to Angola (-15⁰0'0", -15⁰0'0") (Chatham House, 2013).[8] It is estimated to cover over 6,000 km of unbroken coastline and an area of 5,629,471 km² possessing an estimated population of about 260 million people (Gulf of Guinea Commission, 2011).[9] The countries within this space include Angola, Benin, Cameroon, Central Africa Republic, Cote d'Ivoire, Democratic Republic of Congo (DRC), Equatorial Guinea and Gabon. Others include Ghana, Liberia, Nigeria, Republic of Congo, Sao Tome and Principe, Senegal, Sierra Leone, and Togo.

The maritime domain in the Gulf of Guinea remains of strategic importance to global energy trade in terms of shipment from Africa and supply to target locations. Oil exports from the Gulf of Guinea account for about 5.4 million barrels per day (mbd) of mostly low-sulphur crude which is crucial to the oil needs of Japan, China, United States of America and parts of Europe (Chatham House, 2013).[10] The prosperous existence of hydrocarbon resources has attracted major oil companies from across the globe for business engagements in the region. Beyond the vast crude oil deposits, the Gulf of Guinea is also rich in terms of fishing and forestry resources.

The Gulf of Guinea is also vital for sea-route imports and exports between Europe and America with the countries of West, Central and parts of Southern Africa. This is especially important as over 90% of imports and exports of countries in the region are done by sea. In addition to its relevance as a sea route to its coastal countries, the Gulf of Guinea is critical to major imports and exports of landlocked countries like Burkina Faso, Central Africa Republic, Chad, and Mali. It is, therefore, a key facilitator of economic growth in the region. This Gulf region has proved a safer though longer route for global navigation between Europe and the Far East, especially during the zenith of piracy in the Gulf of Aden. The region is of strategic significance to the global economy as well as the economies of countries in West and Central Africa.

As measures to facilitate inter-state cooperation among countries that share littoral access to the Gulf of Guinea, the Gulf of Guinea Commission (GGC) was established on 3 July 2001 by Angola, Congo, Gabon, Nigeria and Sao Tome and Principe. In 2008, Cameroon and the Democratic Republic of Congo (DRC) joined the GGC. The GGC was tasked among others to defend the common interests of member states while promoting peace and socio-economic development based on dialogue, consensus, ties of friendship, solidarity and fraternity.[11] The GGC operates as a framework for consultation in the pursuit of cooperation and development among countries of the Gulf of Guinea. Also, the GGC also coordinates engagements targeted at the prevention, management and resolution of conflicts that may arise from the delimitation of borders and the economic and commercial exploitation of natural resources within the boundaries. It is, however, essential to note that the existence of the GGC has not eradicated the recurrence of acts of criminality in the maritime domain. Consequently, the sub-region is characterised by the surge of illegal activities of piracy, illicit drugs, human trafficking, and illegal immigration amidst environmental degradation. The subsequent section focuses on piracy in the Gulf of Guinea.

## Dynamics of piracy and maritime security in the Gulf of Guinea

The International Crisis Group (ICG) identified the Gulf of Guinea as a New Danger Zone for maritime threats (International Crisis Group, 2012).[12] This is not unconnected with the scourge of illicit maritime activities perpetrated by several non-state actors either acting alone or sometimes acting in collaboration with certain security personnel in coastal states within the region.

The question of piracy and maritime security in the Gulf of Guinea will be critically reviewed based on theoretical and empirical narratives. First, it is essential to note that piracy, drug trafficking, trafficking in persons, pharmaceutics, waste dumping and pollution remain the major security challenges in the Gulf of Guinea. Other forms of illicit transnational activities taking place in the Gulf of Guinea include arms trafficking, attacks on critical infrastructure, crude oil theft, illegal trade in wildlife, as well as Illegal, Unreported and Unregulated (IUU) Fishing (IMO, 2017).[1] Also, the region further experiences environmental damage caused by the dumping of toxic waste and discharge of oil and other pollutants, which leads to general threats to maritime safety. These maritime threats were unequivocally articulated in resolution 67/68 of the Oceans and Law of the Sea adopted at the 67th Session of the United Nations General Assembly on 5 December 2012 which:

> Notes with concern the continuing problem of transnational organised crime committed at sea, including illicit traffic in narcotic drugs and psychotropic substances, the smuggling of migrants and trafficking in persons, and threats to maritime safety and security, including piracy, armed robbery at sea, smuggling and terrorist acts against shipping, offshore installations and other maritime interests, and deploring the loss of life and adverse impact on international trade, energy security, and the global economy resulting from such activities (UN, 2012).[14]

Of the above dimensions of maritime threats in the Gulf of Guinea, sea piracy remains the most disturbing trend to international navigation in the region. Sea piracy and sea robbery in the Gulf of Guinea accounted for about 30% of reported attacks in African water. At this stage, it is imperative to provide a detailed explanation of piracy and armed robbery on ships at this stage of the paper to neutralise any ambiguity of concepts. The provisions of the United Nations Conventions on the Law of the Sea (UNCLOS) and the International Maritime Organisation's Code of Practice A.1025 will be followed. The operational definitions for this study are further justified by the fact that the Yaoundé Process also subscribes to both purposes. Article 100 of the 1982 UNCLOS described piracy as:

a.  any illegal acts of violence or detention, or any act of depredation, committed for private ends by the crew or the passengers of a private ship or a private aircraft, and directed:

  i.  on the high seas, against another ship or aircraft, or persons or property on board such ship or aircraft;
  ii.  against a ship, aircraft, persons, or property in a place outside the jurisdiction of any State;

b.  any act of voluntary participation in the operation of a ship or of an aircraft with knowledge of facts making it a pirate ship or aircraft;
c.  any act inciting or of intentionally facilitating an act described in subparagraph (a) or (b) (UN, 1982).[15]

Closely related to sea piracy is the incidence of armed robbery against ships. The Code of Practice for the Investigation of the Crimes of Piracy and Armed Robbery Against Ships (Resolution A.1025 [26], Annex, Paragraph 2.2) describes armed robbery at sea as:

a. any illegal act of violence or detention or any act of depredation, or threat thereof, other than an act of piracy, committed for private ends and directed against a ship or persons or property on board such a ship, within a State's internal waters, archipelagic waters and territorial sea;

b. any act of inciting or of intentionally facilitating an act described above (IMO, 2010).[16]

Scholars have made various attempts at explaining the nature and dynamics of piracy and maritime security in the Gulf of Guinea. Freedom Onuoha notes that piracy attacks in the Gulf of Guinea constitute a fair share of the incidents of piracy in Africa. He notes that pirates in the region have expanded their nefarious activities beyond hijacking of fishing vessels to attacks on oil vessels with the aid of transnational mafia that includes the people with a vast knowledge of the oil sector. He locates the explanation for incidence of piracy in the region to bad governance, youth grievances, arms proliferation and the excessive supports given to national armies without adequate fairness to the navy (Onuoha, 2012).[17]

As Charles Ukeje and Wullson Mvomo noted, since the 1990s, there exists growing curiosity about maritime safety and security in the Gulf of Guinea due to the numerous insecurities in region. They likened the region to the Straits of Malacca and the Gulf of Aden. They argued that the insecurities on the seas increasingly portend grave danger to stability and prosperity for countries in the region. It is their view that given the degree of maritime insecurity, the countries of the region have been unable to develop a clear and coherent maritime security policy, strategy and framework to effectively tackle the threats (Ukeje and Ela, 2013).[18] This requires the establishment and implementation of effective and sustainable maritime governance regimes in the medium and long term.

Similarly, James Bridger cautioned against the Somalization of the Gulf of Guinea, noting that the problem of piracy in the Gulf of Guinea spreads from Senegal to Angola, thereby encompassing about 12 countries. He identified Nigeria as the historical epicentre where pirates and sea robbers began from ransacking docked ships, stealing crude oil from anchored and refuelling ships for resale in the black market to attempting and sometimes actually boarding and robbing slow-moving vessels (Bridger, 2012).[19] For him, beyond this economic dimension to piracy and sea robbery in Nigeria is the political dimension which involved the fusion of historical grievances of the Niger Delta people against the Federal Government revolving around oil politics. It was this fusion that led to the emergence of armed militancy with groups like the Niger Delta Peoples Volunteer Force (NDPVF) and the Movement for the Emancipation of the Niger Delta (MEND) taking the significant stage by heightening insecurity in the maritime domain of Nigeria and larger Gulf of Guinea. In another publication, James Bridger notes that the global piracy in the Gulf of Guinea sometimes exceeded that of the Gulf of Aden where the Somali pirates operated with the expansion of the criminal enterprise beyond Nigerian waters to the Republic of Benin, Cote d'Ivoire, and Togo have also become vulnerable (Bridger, 2013).[20] He, however, notes that the leadership of West African states are increasingly engaging to address the maritime threats in the region.

Patrick T. Paterson identifies the Gulf of Guinea as one of the most critical energy regions in the world, noting that the United States declared it as an area of strategic national interest that could require military intervention to protect its resources. While Paterson recognises that the US could intervene in the region, he adds that the challenge of operating in the region could prove dangerous for the US military (Paterson, 2007).[21] Paterson identifies Nigeria as the linchpin in the region and a regional hegemon in terms of economy and military might but notes that the country has a record of armed militancy which heightens insecurity in the Gulf of Guinea. He further states that the region is layover point for narcotic smugglers trying to access the lucrative markets of Europe. These realities make the Gulf of Guinea a region of strategic national interest to the United States such that the protection of the region's maritime domain has become a critical engagement of the US Navy.

The incidence of sea piracy in the Gulf of Guinea extends from Senegal in the West end to Angola in southern Africa with Nigerian waters as one of the most vulnerable for pirate attacks. Between 2008 and 2013, the maritime domains of Benin, Nigeria and Togo have variously taken the lead in the incidences of piracy in the region. Others include Cote d'Ivoire and Ghana. It is estimated that out of the 1,434 incidences of sea piracy and robbery on ships in African waters before 2013, a total of 427 were reported in the Gulf of Guinea (Ukeje and Ela, 2013).[22] In 2010, the International Maritime Organisation (IMO) recorded 47 incidents of piracy while in 2011, it increased to 61 incidents. By 2013, out of the 47 cases of sea piracy that occurred along the Gulf of Guinea, 29 incidents took place along the coast of Nigeria. A total of 1,871 seafarers were victims of piracy attacks in 2013, with 279 taken hostage (Osinowo, 2015).[23] The United Nations Office for West Africa (UNOWA) alert on the emergence of United Nations Office for West Africa and the Sahel (UNOWAS) reports that 610 incidents of piracy have been recorded in the Gulf of Guinea since 2002 by the IMO.

It is estimated that between 2007 and 2016, an average of 122 maritime security incidents occurred in the Gulf of Guinea per annum. This ranged between 80 and 140 incidents annually, with Nigeria accounting for about 87 of the attacks yearly (Steffen, 2017).[24] The International Maritime Organisation (IMO) ranked the Gulf of Guinea second with 62 piracy-related attacks on the incidence of global piracy in 2016. This represented a 77% increase from the 35 incidents reported in 2015 (IMO, 2017).[25] The South China Sea which had 68 incidents in topped the list. A total of the 33 out of the 62 reported incidents (some attempted and some successful) piracy in the Gulf of Guinea occurred in international waters as against 10 incidents in 2015 representing an increase in 89% (IMO, 2017).[26] These data are from incidents reported to the IMO. The however exists varying statistics on the actual number of incidents.

Data from the Risk Intelligence, a Danish think tank indicated that in 2016, there were 119 verified attacks by criminals on vessels in the Gulf of Guinea as against 82 reported incidences in 2015 and 84 of the confirmed attacks occurred in Nigeria's maritime space (IMO, 2017).[27] It is reasoned that the resurgence of armed militancy in the Niger Delta escalated the incidents of maritime threats in the Gulf of Guinea. Furthermore, a critical diagnosis of IMO reports on incidents of piracy in the Gulf of Guinea indicates that most of the attacks usually occur in the international waters while the ships are steaming using motherships converted to shipping trawlers and also at ports areas in the territorial waters. Some attacks have occurred while ships are at anchor. Pirate attacks in the Gulf of Guinea could be a clear case of hijack or stealing, and the attackers which range between 1 and 10 pirates are usually armed with guns and knives. A UN assessment mission in 2011 concluded that pirates in the Gulf of Guinea were resorting to sophisticated modes of operation and utilisingsing heavy weapons (Bridger, 2013).[28] Parts of the ship where pirates raid during operations include the main deck, master and crew accommodation, cargo areas and storerooms. So far, although there has been actual violence to members of the crew, scarcely are lives lost.

In a study of three acts of piracy in the Gulf of Guinea, Bridger (2013) noted that the hijack of *Abu Dhabi Star* off the coast of Lagos in September 2012 demonstrated the combat preparedness of the pirates who swarmed the ship with four high-powered speedboats as well-armed pirates in full-combat gear boarded the vessel disabling its communication equipment.[29] Similarly, the pirates that hijacked *MT Orfeas* from the anchorage off the Coast of Cote d'Ivoire sailed 600 nm to Nigerian waters while pilfering 3,000 tons of gasoline. Also, the kidnapping of seven European crew members from the *Bourbon Liberty*, (a tug owned by French business interests) off the coast of Nigeria in October 2012 immediately its escort vessel returned to the shore reveals the utility of quality operational intelligence by the pirates (Bridger, 2013).[30] *MT Kerala*, a tanker seized around Luanda coast, Angola, was found around Tema port, Ghana in January 2014 with its oil cargo was siphoned. The hijack of *Maximus*, an oil tanker in February 2016 (later rescued by Nigerian Navy) and the attack on Saronic Breeze, a Panama flagged vessel at 80 nm off Cotonou in November 2016, suggests that the challenge of piracy in the region persists with growing sophistication in the Gulf of Guinea.

Records suggest that the nationality of many of the pirates operating in the Gulf of Guinea is Nigerian. However, other Africans and non-Africans from Eastern Europe, Philippines and Britons have also been arrested for maritime violations associated with piracy and oil theft in the region.

## Anti-piracy initiatives for the Gulf of Guinea

Before the adoption of the Yaoundé Process, countries in the Gulf of Guinea had established various anti-piracy measures to protect their respective maritime domains. For instance, the ECCAS launched the Integrated Strategy for Maritime Security (ISMS) since 2008, which stresses the imperative for a common regional framework for regulating maritime security in Central Africa. In West Africa, the ECOWAS is committed to evolving an Integrated Maritime Strategy to strengthen security in the maritime domain at the regional level. There are however national and bilateral measures taken by member states of ECOWAS and ECCAS towards securing their respective maritime domains. For instance, Nigeria strengthened collaborations between the Nigerian Navy and Nigeria Maritime Administration and Safety Agency (NIMASA) which led to a reduction in maritime violations around the Lagos Harbour. The direct consequence of this was the escalation of piracy around the waters of neighbouring Benin Republic and Togo.

The Republic of Benin which recorded no incident of piracy in 2009 had one incident in 2010 and 20 incidents in 2011 leading to over 15% drop in cargo tonnage at Cotonou port and a corresponding loss of $81 million in customs revenue. As a response, President Boni Yayi of Benin sought assistance from Nigeria in the form of collaborations between the Beninese Navy and the Nigerian Navy-NIMASA collaborative platform. This collaboration led to a drop in the incidents of attempted and actual piracy attacks from 20 in 2011 to 2 in 2012 and zero in 2013.[31] With the intensification of joint patrols between Nigeria and Republic of Benin. there was a noticeable increase in piracy attacks in Togo maritime space which recorded about 15 known such attacks in 2012 in which 79 hostages were seized (Osinowo, 2015).

The efforts to establish a dedicated focal point for receiving up-to-date maritime guidance, information sharing and incident reporting, core actors in the shipping industry established the Maritime Trade Information Sharing Centre for the Gulf of Guinea (MTISC-GOG) at the Regional Maritime University in Accra, Ghana. The MTISC-GOG releases 24-hours daily security reporting to participating vessels, national maritime operational centres in the region and the International Police (INTERPOL).

Against the backdrop of the recurrent incidents of piracy in the Gulf of Guinea, the United Nations Security Council (UNSC) adopted Resolution 2018 of 31 October 2011. This resolution calls for cooperation between shipping industry, the insurance industry and

*Table 24.1* Incidents of Piracy in the Gulf of Guinea between 2009 and 2017

| Date | Incident | Remark |
|---|---|---|
| 1. 4 January 2009 | Hijack of a France registered vessel, *Bourbon Leda*. It has five Nigerians, two Ghanaians, one Cameroonian and one Indonesian on board. | The ship was released on 9 September 2009. Not certain of the amount paid as ransom. |
| 2. 21 January 2009 | Hijack of *MT Meredith* a Malaysia flagged oil tanker with a Romanian abducted. | The ship was released a day later but no known detail if any ransom was paid. |
| 3. 23 January 2009 | Attack on *MV Ngoni*, a Nigeria/US flagged crude oil tanker belonging to Exxon. | The ship was released the same day but several items were stolen from it. |
| 4. 21 April 2009 | A Turkish flagged ship, *Ilena Mercan*, carrying crude oil was attacked. | The ship was released about a fortnight later 5 May 2009. |
| 5. 23 November 2009 | A Nigerian owned crude oil vessel, *African Prince*, was attacked. | The vessel was released on 1 December 2009. |
| 6. 24 November 2009 | Pirates stormed a Liberia/Ukraine flagged ship, *Canacle Star* carrying crude oil off the coast of Benin killing one Ukrainian on board. | The vessel was released the same day. |
| 7. 14 September 2011 | A Cyprus/Spain flagged ship, *MT Mattheos 1*, was hijacked by pirates some 62 nautical miles off the coast of Cotonou in the Republic of Benin. | The twenty-three (23) members of a crew comprising of Filipino, Spanish, Peruvian, and Ukrainian nationals were abducted, but the vessel was released on 26 September 2011. |
| 8. 13 October 2011 | Pirate attack on *MT Cape Bird*, a vessel registered in Marshal Islands, off the coast of Nigeria some 90 nautical miles South of Lagos. | The vessel and kidnapped crew members were released a day later. |
| 9. 19 October 2011 | Attack on AHST Wilbert Tide, a Bangladesh flagged oil tanker chartered by ExxonMobil as offshore support vessel between Bonny and Calabar River. | The Bangladeshi Master was abducted leaving the 19 other crew members. |
| 10. 1 November 2011 | Pirate hijack *MT Halifax*, a Malta-flagged but Greek owner oil tanker off the coast of Port Harcourt in the Niger Delta region. | Its twenty-five (25) member crew comprising of one Bulgarian and 24 Filipino were abducted along with the ship but later freed on 1 December 2011. |
| 11. 29 February 2012 | Eight Pirates attack *MV Bleiz* Klipper, a Curacao flagged but Dutch-owned refrigerated cargo ship off the coast of Lagos. | They stole personal effects of crew members, kidnapped the Master and Chief Engineer but later released. |
| 12. 7 May 2012 | Hijack of a Singapore offshore Supply Vessel, *Ark Charly* at Latitude 04.26:19 North and Longitude 004:58:44 East of Nigeria. | The attack occurred by 0640 UTC but they released all 17 crew members safely by 1755 UTC on the same day. |

*(Continued)*

C. Nna-Emeka Okereke

TABLE 24.1 (Continued)

| Date | Incident | Remark |
| --- | --- | --- |
| 13. 17 May 2012 | A Curacao flagged landing craft *UAL Transporter* was attacked at 45 nm offshore Escravos by 15 armed pirates. Four out of the eight members of its crew were unable to enter the citadel and were beaten by the pirates. | This vessel was also attacked later same day by another set of pirates. All the crew members entered the citadel safely during the second attack. |
| 14. 25 June 2012 | 12 pirates attacked a Liberian flagged Chemical tanker at 50 nm south of Lagos. The boat was forced to sail towards Togo and back. | The pirates were on board for 45 hours and after stealing from the crew disembarked off Escravos terminal. The crew were safe. |
| 15. 3 August 2012 | St Vincent and Grenadines Barge *Jason 33* was attacked at anchor around 45 nm Southwest of Bonny Island Nigeria at 2220 hours Local Time | The pirates killed two naval officers on board and injured another two. They also stole and kidnapped four crew members before escaping with the hostages who were later released on 23 August 2012. |
| 16. 28 August 2012 | Hijack of a United Kingdom flagged ship, *Energy Centurion* at anchor in Lome, Togo. | Togolese Navy tried unsuccessfully to stop the hijack but the ship was moved towards the Benin waters. |
| 17. 5 September 2012 | A Singapore flagged chemical tanker, *MT Abu Dhabi*, was hijacked East of Lagos anchorage area. | The crew contacted their owners and the International Maritime Bureau Piracy Reporting Centre was notified the Nigerian authorities who sent out a rescue team. |
| 18. 13 December 2012 | Pirates boarded a Honduras flagged vessel *PM Salem* at 25 nm off the Bayelsa coastline. | The security team and crew retreated to the citadel and after about 20-minute gun duel, one security guard was killed and the pirates retreated |
| 19. 17 December 2012 | Hijack of a Marshal Island oil tanker *MT Brussels* at 40 nm off the Nigerian coast. | The pirates robbed the ship and took five crew members hostage for 40 days before they were released. |
| 20. 23 December 2012 | Seven pirates using two tugboats hijacked an Italian oil vessel *Asso Ventuno* at 40 nm off the coast of Bayelsa | Pirates stole oil from the vessel and took four crew members hostage but released them after 17 days. |
| 21. 16 January 2013 | Pirates attack a Panama flagged oil tanker *Koda Maritime* | The vessel was released on 24 January 2013 |
| 22. 16 January 2013 | Pirates invade a Panama flagged oil tanker *MV Itri* while preparing to deposit oil cargo at Abidjan anchorage in Cote d'Ivoire | The vessel and its 16 Nigerian crew members were held hostage while the oil cargo was stolen. It anchored at Lagos on 22 January with crew safe. |
| 23. 15 August 2013 | Hijack of a Greek-owned oil career by 7 pirates off the coast of Calabar | The Pirates open fire on a detachment of the Nigerian Navy |

368

| Date | Incident | Remark |
|------|----------|--------|
|  |  | on Routine patrol along Nigeria-Cameroon border. Six pirates killed in the ensuing gunfight while one surrendered. |
| 24. 15 August 2013 | Pirate attack on Saint Kitts and Nevis-flagged gasoline tanker *MT Notre* by a group of 16 heavily armed pirates. | Nigerian Navy spotted the vessel after four days and 12 of the 16 pirates were killed in gun combat. |
| 25. 20 January 2014 | Pirates around Luanda port stole MT Kerala in Angola. | The vessel was found around Tema port in Ghana eight days later with its oil cargo stolen. |
| 26. 16 February 2016 | Six heavily armed pirates boarded *Bourbon Liberty* 25,155 nautical miles off the coast of Nigeria. | This vessel had previously been hijacked in October 2012. |

*Source:* Author's Research Data, September 2017.

the International Maritime Organisation (IMO) to issue to ships entitled to fly their flag, appropriate advice and guidance within the context of the Gulf of Guinea, on avoidance, evasion and defensive techniques and measures to take, if under the threat of attack, or attack when sailing in the waters of the Gulf of Guinea (UNSC, 2018).[32] It further calls on the member states of the ECOWAS, ECCAS and Gulf of Guinea Commission to work in conjunction with flag States and States of the nationality of victims or of perpetrators of acts of piracy or armed robbery at sea, to cooperate in the prosecution of alleged perpetrators, including facilitators and financiers of acts of piracy and armed robbery at sea committed off the coast of the Gulf of Guinea, following applicable international law, including human rights law (UNSC).[33]

In February 2012, the UNSC further adopted Resolution 2039 which supported the initiatives taken by the ECCAS, ECOWAS, GGC and Maritime Organisation for West and Central Africa (MOWCA) to enhance maritime safety and security in the Gulf of Guinea. Resolution 2039 recognises the utility of the ECCAS comprehensive joint maritime security architecture explicitly to counter piracy in the Central African region, including the strategy adopted by the ECCAS Peace and Security Council in February 2008, the establishment of the Regional Centre for Maritime Security in Central Africa (CRESMAC) in Pointe-Noire, Congo, as well as the multinational coordination centres in the region.

The UNSC Resolution 2039 also stressed the primary responsibility of the member states of the Gulf of Guinea to counter piracy and armed robbery at sea urging the states through the ECOWAS, ECCAS and GGC to convene a joint Summit to develop a regional anti-piracy strategy in cooperation with the African Union (UNSC, 2012).[34] It subsequently urged the United Nations Office for West Africa (UNOWA) and the United Nations Office for Central Africa (UNOCA) to support these regional organisations in convening the joint Summit. The Economic Community of Central African States (ECCAS), Economic Community of West African States (ECOWAS) and the Gulf of Guinea Commission (GGC) were further encouraged to develop and implement transnational and trans-regional maritime security coordination centres covering the whole of the Gulf of Guinea while building on existing initiatives of the International Maritime Organisations.

Sequel to the drive expressed in UNSC Resolutions 2018 (2011) and 2039 (2012), the ECCAS, ECOWAS and GGC collaborated to develop a comprehensive strategy for a trans-regional framework to counter piracy while strengthening related domestic laws and regulations. The consequence was the adoption of the Code of Conduct Concerning the Repression of Piracy, Armed Robbery against Ships and Illicit Maritime Activity in West and Central Africa at Yaoundé in 2013. Signatories to this instrument which is now generally referred as the "Yaoundé Code or Yaoundé Process" pledged commitments to cooperate to the fullest possible extent in the repression of transnational organised crimes in the maritime domain, maritime terrorism, Irregular Unreported and Unregulated (IUU) fishing including other illegal activities at sea. Following a Memorandum of Understanding (MoU), the ECCAS, ECOWAS and GGC agreed to hold annual meetings to provide guidance, monitoring and evaluation of regional cooperation while also creating an Inter-regional Coordination Centre (ICC) for the implementation of the Yaoundé Code in June 2013.

## Yaoundé Code of Conduct as a regional security instrument

The Yaoundé Code of Conduct concerning the Repression of Piracy, Armed Robbery against Ships, and Illicit Maritime Activity in West and Central Africa also referred as the Yaoundé Process, was adopted at Yaoundé, Cameroon on 25 June 2013 by 25 countries of West and Central Africa referred as signatories. The instrument which contains twenty-one distinct but related Articles were adopted to foster collective efforts of the Gulf of Guinea states at interdiction of vessels suspected to be engaged in illegal activities, apprehension and prosecution of arrested persons and vessels while reporting and sharing relevant information. It also supports victims while facilitating the care and repatriation of seafarers' subject to illegal activities. Also, the Yaoundé Code of Conduct also outlines measures to be adopted by signatories at combating threats to their shared maritime domain.

In his opening speech during the Summit, President Paul Biya of Cameroon noted that although the countries in the Gulf of Guinea were witnessing a boom, with strong economic growth the incidence of piracy remained a potent threat requiring holistic efforts by states in the region. He, therefore, stated *inter ,alia:*

> ...Our determination, our national and regional capacities, as well as our efforts to eradicate piracy seem inadequate to prevent or effectively stamp out the threat. Therefore, collective effort is a must, for us to avoid a situation where once eliminated in one country or area of the Gulf of Guinea, this scourge would rear the head in another (Biya, 2013).[35]

The objectives of the Yaoundé Process, as outlined in the Purpose and Scope, focuses on the following:

a. Sharing and reporting relevant information
b. Interdicting ships and aircraft suspected of engaging in transnational organised crime in the maritime domain, maritime terrorism, IUU fishing and other illegal activities at sea;
c. Ensuring that persons committing or attempting to commit any transnational organised crime in the maritime domain, maritime terrorism, IUU fishing and other illegal activities at sea are apprehended and prosecuted; and
d. Facilitating proper care, treatment and repatriation of seafarers, fishermen, other shipboard personnel and passengers subjected to transnational organised crimes in the maritime

domain, maritime terrorism, IUU fishing and other illegal activities at sea, particularly those who have been subjected to violence.[36]

In pursuit of the above objectives, Article 6 (1) of the Yaoundé Process charges all the signatories to cooperate in the following areas fully:

a. Arresting, investigating, and prosecuting persons who have committed piracy or are reasonably suspected of committing piracy;
b. Seizing pirate ships or aircraft and the property on board such ships or aircraft; and
c. Rescuing ships, persons, and property subject to piracy.[37]

Article 6 (3) stresses that any pursuit of a ship, where there are reasonable grounds to suspect that the ship is engaged in piracy, extending in and over the territorial sea of a Signatory is subject to the authority of that Signatory. No Signatory should pursue such a ship in or over the territory or territorial sea of any coastal state without the permission of that state.[38] Article 4 (1) of the instrument focuses on the measures to be adopted at the various national levels to include:

a. Appropriate national maritime security policies to safeguard maritime trade from all forms of unlawful acts;
b. National legislation, practices, and procedures, which together provide the security necessary for the safe and secure operation of port facilities and ships at all security levels; and
c. National legislation which ensures adequate protection of the marine environment.

Article 10 of the Yaoundé Process further stipulates that national laws of the territory where an asset was seized should be the basis for disposing of such confiscated assets. The emphasis on information sharing and coordination is outlined in Article 11. In line with this, each State Signatories are to establish piracy information sharing centres and focal points capable of receiving and responding to alerts and requests for information and assistance. With regards to incident reporting, the Signatories intend to undertake the development of uniform reporting criteria to ensure accurate assessment of the threat of piracy in West and Central Africa in line with the recommendations of the IMO. This is tacitly captured in Article 12 of the Yaoundé Process.

Generally, the scope of Articles in the Yaoundé Process covers relevant Definitions, Purpose and Scope, Guiding Principles, Measures at the National Level, Protection Measures for Ships, Measures to Repress Piracy and Measures to Repress Armed Robbery against Ships. Others include Measures to Repress Illegal, Unregulated and Unreported Fishing, Embarked Officers, Asset Seizure and Forfeiture as well as Coordination and Information Sharing including Incident Reporting. Also, the instrument also covers Assistance among Signatories, Training and Education, Indictment, Prosecution and Conviction, Settlement of Disputes, Consultations, Claims and Miscellaneous Provisions. It ends with the articles on Signature and Entry into Force as well as Languages.

Under the Yaoundé Process, regional organisations such as the ECCAS and ECOWAS are responsible for strategy while the respective member states are responsible for operations. In furtherance of the ISMS, the ECCAS further established the Regional Coordination Centre for Maritime Security in Central Africa (CRESMAC) at Pointe-Noire in the Republic of Congo. Also, an Inter-Regional Coordination Centre (ICC) to implement a regional strategy for maritime safety and security was established at Yaoundé, Cameroon.

The Yaoundé Process is receptive to strategic partnerships and initiatives targeted at providing technical assistance, training and other forms of capacity building for states in the Gulf of Guinea especially their respective Navies, upon request to enhance their capabilities to strengthen maritime security in the region. In furtherance of this, the 28th Session of the Assembly of IMO unanimously adopted Resolution A.1069(28) in December 2013 focusing on the Prevention and Repression of Piracy, Armed Robbery against Ships and Illicit Maritime Activity in the Gulf of Guinea. This Resolution calls upon various Governments, in co-operation with the IMO to assist the Gulf of Guinea states through contributing to the IMO Central and West Africa Maritime Security Trust Fund.

Presently, littoral states of the Gulf of Guinea also engaged in Exercise Obangame Express which is a United States Naval Forces Africa (NAVAF) at-sea maritime exercise designated to improve cooperation among participating nations to boost maritime safety and security in the Gulf of Guinea. The Exercise involves drills on maritime interdiction operations, visits, board, search, and seizure techniques for African partner navies on routine operations in the Gulf of Guinea. Exercise Obangame Express 2017 was geared at improving the law enforcement capacity of Gulf of Guinea navies, promote regional security, inform African Maritime Law Enforcement Partnership (AMLEP) planning and operations while shaping Security Force Assistance (SFA) efforts (AFRICOM, 2017).[39] The AMLEP is maritime security capacity building program implemented under the African Partnership Station by the US Naval Forces Africa. The AMLEP is designed to help combat maritime violations such as piracy, IUU fishing, including illicit transnational trafficking in drugs, arms and human cargo (Heyl, 2013).[40] So far, the AMLEP has assisted African countries in seizure and prosecution of perpetrators of maritime violations in the Gulf of Guinea.

The Nigerian phase of Exercise Obangame Express 2017 took place in Nigeria's waters from 24 to 28 March with the participation of *Nigerian Navy Ship (NNS) Okpabana, NNS Centenary, NNS Sagbama* and one helicopter with a French Navy ship, *Jacoubet*, which sailed into the Nigerian waters from Cameroon. The purpose was to practice the naval forces in realistic scenarios that reflect past piracy incidents whereby a hijacked vessel will transit from one territory to another (Dahun, 2017).[41] As part of the Exercise, Maritime Operations Centres (MOCs) were challenged to recognisese these illicit acts appropriately and share with other MOCs. It was also designed to assess the capability of the Navy to patrol the Exclusive Economic Zones (EEZ) and detect and prosecute illegal activity accordingly.

As part of measures geared at the implementation of the Yaoundé Process, the Nigerian Navy and NIMASA maintained the use of Secure Anchorage Area (SAA) which is an initiative adopted since May 2013 in collaboration with two Private Maritime Security Companies (PMSCs) to secure vessels in designated areas off Lagos port. Under the Secure Anchorage, vessels intending to either anchor or conduct ship-to-ship transfer operations are provided armed protection. In 2016, about 16 companies entered agreements with the Nigerian Navy to provide offshore security in the oil field while also enhancing the safety of merchant vessels in Nigerian waters. It is estimated that there are about 100 privately contracted security vessels operating in Nigeria's waters (Steffen, 2017).[42]

Under the Nigerian Navy-PMSC arrangement, private companies are to supply and maintain patrol boats. Still, the gun crew will be drawn from personnel of the Nigerian Navy who mounts weapons and ammunitions utilised in the protection of vessels in the maritime domain. There is however a political angle to the PMSC engagements in Nigeria as former leaders of militant groups such as Boyloaf and Government Ekpemopulo known as Tompolo were given a contract to provide pipeline security. Others like Asari Dokubo and Ateke Tom also had related agreements. This measure contributed significantly to reducing maritime violations in the region.

Surveillance of Nigeria's maritime domain was enhanced in 2014 through the Satellite Surveillance Centre (SSC). This is a collaboration between the Nigerian Air Force, Nigerian Navy and NIMASA and was introduced to facilitate the tracking of all vessels within Nigeria's territorial water. The SSC tracks the vessels by identifying the IMO numbers.

In April 2017, the Association of African Maritime Administration (AAMA) held its 3rd Conference on maritime safety in Africa at Abuja Nigeria under the theme "Sustainable Use of Africa's Oceans and Seas". Nigeria's Vice President, Professor Yemi Osibanjo, who represented President Buhari affirmed that Nigeria had approved a new maritime architectural framework that would effectively make waters of Nigeria free from pirates and improve international trade. One such initiative is *Operation Tsare Teku*, which accompanied the successful rescue operation of the oil vessel, *Maximus* in February 2016. He further affirmed that the Nigerian government will also strengthen defence to protect and safeguard business (cited in Oscar Onwuemenyi, 2017).[43] These measures can rightly be considered a bold acknowledgement by the Nigerian government of the challenge of piracy in its territorial waters. In a Joint Communiqué issued at the end of the conference, the IMO affirmed its readiness to support Maritime Administration in Africa to combat security challenges and in building human capacity equipped to implement, monitor and enforce international instruments in the continent (NIMASA, 2017).[44]

While it is evident that the Gulf of Guinea states has undertaken several bold initiatives at combating threats to maritime security in the region, the incidents of piracy still persist. This is connected with inherent weaknesses in the respective national security architectures of coastal states in the region which renders them incapable of effectively implementing the provisions of the Yaoundé Process. Some of these lapses are identified below.

## Obstacles to the implementation of the Yaoundé Code

The deficit of requisite capacity to implement maritime security infrastructure in the region constitutes a major obstacle. For instance, virtually all the navies littoral states in the Gulf of Guinea lack adequate capacities for maritime surveillance and intervention. Some do not have basic capacities. The existing variations in the capacities for information sharing, maritime domain awareness and law enforcement constitutes major inhibition.

Under the Yaoundé Process, there is no role for the utility of Private Maritime Security Companies (PMSCs) as littoral states remain cautious of such security outfits. Also, foreign armed guards are prohibited in territorial waters of local states. The consequence is that transiting vessels are left with the option of hiring navies of the states as they embark and disembark along the route. There exist various dimensions of reliance on the PMSCs in the region. For instance, the navies of Benin and Togo operate secure anchorage alongside providing navy troops through agents and local security companies. So far, the only Secure Anchorage promulgated on the Admiralty Chart in the Gulf of Guinea is off Lagos. The imperative of PMSCs in maritime domain surveillance and intervention is, therefore, necessary since several navies in the region lack adequate platforms to perform their mandates.

One core contraction to the implementation of the Yaoundé Process is the deviation from the African Union's Integrated Maritime Strategy (AUIMS) 2050. It is instructive to note that the African Union envisions a common African maritime space without barriers. Consequently, the AUIMS stresses the establishment of a Combined Exclusive Maritime Zone of Africa. On the other hand, the Code of Conduct at Yaoundé in June 2013 urges states to declare their EEZ, enforce their respective local laws within their domain. This runs contrary to the expectation that littoral states in Africa as well as regional organisations, would initiate measures that are consistent with the AUIMS.

The challenge of sharing the financial burden of maritime security in the Gulf of Guinea is another obstacle for the region. This is because implementing the regional maritime security architecture entails enormous cost in terms of human and material resources. For instance, the establishment and sustenance of regional institutions come with additional cost for the partner states. In the Gulf of Guinea, the task of securing the maritime domain elicits active engagement of, and coordination of efforts by regional organisations like the ECCAS, ECOWAS and the GGC. So far, there is not yet any clear agreement on funding the partnership. The challenge of financing the Yaoundé Process is more glaring bearing in mind that ships plying the routes are from beyond Africa. IMO has however established a Maritime Security Trust Fund for West and Central Africa to which interested strategic partners could contribute.

Beyond the challenge of financing the arrangement and weak institutional capabilities of coastal states in the region is the reality of general concern on the intents of regional hegemon like Nigeria and the persistence of disputed maritime borders among states in the Gulf of Guinea. Nigeria and Cameroon have through the Cameroon-Nigeria Mixed Commission been managing the delicate balance that accompanied the 10 October 2002 International Court of Justice (ICJ) verdict on land and maritime boundaries between both countries and subsequent implementation of the Green Tree Agreement of 12 June 2006. However, territorial uncertainties still exist as vessels of the Nigerian Navy in the Eastern Naval Command, Calabar cannot effectively navigate out without entering Cameroon maritime space. Countries like Angola/Democratic Republic of Congo, Ghana/Cote d'Ivoire and Gabon/Equatorial Guinea are still yet to work out sustainable arrangements on border demarcations in their shared maritime domains.

It is important to note that several states in the Gulf of Guinea lack requisite extant legislation to strengthen anti-piracy operations of respective navies in the region. This has tended to hinder the effective implementation of the Yaoundé Process. For instance, it was only on 24th May 2019 that Nigeria's Eight National Assembly passed the country's Suppression of Piracy and other Maritime Offences Act which President Muhammadu Buhari assented on 24th June 2019 thereby bring the Act into existence to strengthen the counter-piracy operations of the country. Meanwhile, the question of sovereignty of states and limits to collective actions also contributes to causing constraints to the implementation of the instrument as naval forces of the individual state are constrained from chasing pirates into another country's maritime domain regardless of the interdiction capacities of the nations involved.

## Strengthening the implementation of the Yaoundé Code of Conduct

Bearing in mind the objectives of the Yaoundé Process especially its utility towards the pursuit of sustainable maritime safety and security in the Gulf of Guinea, it is necessary to bring to reality the planned ECOWAS Integrated Maritime Strategy (EIMS) adopted at Yamoussoukro, Cote d'Ivoire on 25 March 2014. The EIMS is designed to strengthen maritime cooperation in Pilot Zone 'E' involving Benin, Nigeria, and Togo, including the F and G zones. It further approves the establishment of the planned Regional Coordination Centre for Maritime Security in West Africa (CRESMAO) which is like the CRESMAC in Pointe-Noire.

Secondly, proceeds from the levies and fines obtained from seizures and prosecution of maritime offenders in African waters should be utilised to underwrite the maintenance and operating costs for maritime forces engaged in anti-piracy operations in the Gulf of Guinea. So far, the African Maritime Law Enforcement Programme (AMLEP) which is a partnership between the United States Navy and international militaries targeted at combating illicit trafficking in human cargo, drug trafficking and arms trafficking has led to several successful seizures from maritime offenders in the Gulf of Guinea. Such operations should therefore be sustained while anti-piracy activities are commercialised either fully or partially.

The importance of building economic and security governance of states in the region is also vital to implementing the Yaoundé Process. This is because economic deprivations stimulate insecurities that propel youths to maritime criminalities in the Gulf of Guinea. The contradictions of wealth, human misery and crime in the Niger Delta constitute clear explanations for this prescription. In addition to the above, there should be strengthened inter-navy cooperation to enhance anti-piracy operations in the region. The utility of Exercise Obangame Express towards actualising this objective is very vital.

Countries of the ECCAS, ECOWAS and the GGC should also embark on enforcement harmonisation. This is considered vital to prevent pirates from fleeing from countries of strict penalties and enforcement to countries of porous penalties and enforcement. This measure requires the review of each country's legal regimes and judicial system to ensure that they are adequate to serve as a deterrent.

Also, member states of the Gulf of Guinea should embark on the acquisition of relevant platforms and requisite training to meet the demands of anti-piracy operations in the region. Such platforms include Coastal Patrol Boats (CPBs) and Offshore Patrol Vessels (OPVs) and requisite radar and surveillance equipment. This requires sustained partnerships with critical actors in maritime security within and beyond the region.

## Conclusion

The Gulf of Guinea will continue to remain of strategic importance to the global economy because of the volume of world trade, massive energy deposits and a wide variety of fish and aquatic splendour inherent in the sub-region. While the Gulf of Guinea states in West and Central Africa have adopted the Yaounde process to strengthen maritime domain awareness and governance, it is, however, essential to note that the persistence of fragile state syndrome and weak navies of coastal states in the Gulf of Guinea as well as the realities of youth bulge and high unemployment rates will continue exposing the entire area to piracy and other insecurities in the maritime domain.

Consequently, it is therefore crucial that national government strengthen domestic regulations and relevant institutions of the state to give strength to countering piracy within the sub-region. In addition, policies and programmes targeted at youth empowerment and inclusiveness in national productivity will remain core to combating the piracy challenge in the Gulf of Guinea.

## Notes

1 Storey, I. (2016), Addressing the persistent problem of piracy and sea robbery in Southeast Asia. Perspective, Issue No. 30, p. 2.
2 Ibid.
3 National Archives of Singapore. (2006). *Factsheet on the Regional Cooperation Agreement on Combating Piracy and Armed Robbery Against Ships in Asia (ReCAAP)*, http://www.nas.gov.sg/archivesonline/data/pdfdoc/20061129970.pdf Accessed 24.01.19.
4 Ibid.
5 Carafano,J.J., Weitz, R. & Andersen, E.M. (2009). Maritime security: Fighting piracy in the Gulf of Aden and beyond. *Heritage Special Report*, SR 59, p. 8.
6 Ibid.
7 Global Sentinel. *Buhari Emerges Chairman of Gulf of Guinea Commission*.https://globalsentinelng.com/2017/11/23/buhari-emerges-chairman-gulf-guinea-commission/ Accessed 20.1.19.

8 Chatham House. Maritime security in the Gulf of Guinea. *Report of the Conference held at Chatham House, London, 6 December 2012*, (London, Chatham House, March 2013).

9 Gulf of Guinea Commission, http://cggrps.org/en/ Accessed 9.06.11.

10 Chatham House. Maritime security in the Gulf of Guinea. *Report of the Conference held at Chatham House, London, 6 December 2012*, (London, Chatham House, March 2013).

11 Gulf of Guinea Commission. The Gulf of Guinea Commission, https://cggrps.com/en/the-gulf-of-guinea-commission/ Accessed 20.01.19.

12 International Crisis Group. The Gulf of Guinea: The new danger zone. *Africa Report*, No. 195, 12 December 2012.

13 International Maritime Organisation (IMO). Implementing sustainable maritime security measures in West and Central Africa, April 2017.

14 United Nations (UN). Text of Resolution 67/68 on Ocean and Law of the Sea adopted by the United Nations General Assembly on 5 December 2012.

15 United Nations (UN), Article 100 of United Nations Convention on Laws of the Sea (UNCLOS) 1982.

16 International Maritime Organisation (IMO), Code of Practice for the Investigation of the Crimes of Piracy and Armed Robbery Against Ships (Resolution A.1025) adopted on 2 December 2009, Assembly/26/Res/1025, 18 January 2010, http://www.imo.org/en/OurWork/Security/PiracyArmedRobbery/Guidance/Documents/A.1025.pdf Accessed 11.09.17.

17 Freedom Onuoha. Piracy and maritime security in the Gulf of Guinea: Nigeria as a microcosm in *Report of Al Jazeera Centre for Studies*, 12 June 2012.

18 Ukeje, C. & Mvomo, E.W. (2013). African approaches to maritime security: The Gulf of Guinea. (Abuja: Friedrich Ebert Foundation.

19 Bridger, J. Piracy in West Africa: Preventing a Somalization of the Gulf of Guinea. PT,1. *Africa Strategic Outlook*, Centre for International Maritime Security, 12 December 2012.

20 Bridger, J. Crafting a counter-piracy regime in the Gulf of Guinea. *Capability Analysis Strategic Outlook*, (Centre for International Maritime Security, July 2013), http://cimsec.org/crafting-a-piracy-regime-in-the-gulf-of-guinea/6232 Accessed 8.09.17.

21 Paterson, J.P. Maritime security in the Gulf of Guinea in *JFQ Forum*, Issue 45, 2nd Quarter 2007.

22 Ukeje and Mvomo, Op. Cit.

23 Osinowo, A.A. Piracy in the Gulf of Guinea. *Africa Security Brief*, No. 30, February 2015.

24 Steffen, D. Gulf of Guinea maritime security in 2016. Report of the Centre for International Maritime Security, 11 April 2017.

25 International Maritime Organisation (IMO), *Report on Acts of Piracy and Armed Robbery against Ships*, MSC. 4/Circ. 245 of 30 March 2017.

26 Ibid.

27 Ibid.

28 Bridger, J. Pirate horizons in the Gulf of Guinea. *Centre for International Maritime Security*, 10 January 2013.

29 Ibid.

30 Ibid.

31 Ibid.

32 United Nations Security Council (UNSC) (2011). UNSC Resolution 2018. http://unscr.com/en/resolutions/doc/2018 Accessed 28.08.17.

33 Ibid.

34 United Nations Security Council (UNSC). UNSC Resolution 2039 of 29 February 2012 (S/RES/2039). http://www.securitycouncilreport.org/atf/cf/%7B65BFCF9B-6D27-4E9C-8CD3-CF6E4FF96FF9%7D/UNOCA%20SRES%202039.pdf Accessed 09.09.17.

35 Biya, P. Opening remarks at the Summit of Heads of State of ECCAS, ECOWAS and Gulf of Guinea Commission on Maritime Security in the Gulf of Guinea held at Yaoundé in June 2013.

36 Code of Conduct Concerning the Repression of Piracy, Armed Robbery against Ships and Illicit Maritime Activity in West and Central Africa, Yaounde, June 2013.

37 Ibid.

38 Ibid.

39 United States Africa Command (AFRICOM). *Obangame express*. http://www.africom.mil/what-we-do/exercises/obangame-express Accessed Monday, 25.09.17.

40 Heyl, J.P. West and Central African Leaders Unite against Piracy in the Gulf of Guinea. Paper presented at the 3rd United Arab Emirates International Counter Piracy Conference, Dubai, 11–12 September 2013.
41 Dahun, S. *Nigerian navy deploys ships, helicopter for Obangame express.* March 22, 2017, https://prnigeria.com/security/nigerian-navy-obangame-express/ Accessed Monday, 25.09.17.
42 Steffen, D. Gulf of Guinea maritime security in 2016. *Centre for International Maritime Security; Current Operations,* 11 April 2017.
43 Onwuemenyi, O. AAMA Confab: IMO to address maritime security challenges in Africa. *Sweet Crude Reports,* 25 April 2017.
44 Nigerian Maritime Administration and Safety Agency (NIMASA), Association of African Maritime Administration (AAMA) Communique, Abuja, 2017 Record of Decisions, Recommendations and Resolutions.

## References

Biya, P. (2013) Opening remarks at the summit of Heads of State of ECCAS, ECOWAS and Gulf of Guinea Commission on maritime security in the Gulf of Guinea held at Yaoundé in June 24-25; https://au.int/ar/node/27463 Accessed 10 October 2020.
Bridger, J. (2012). Piracy in West Africa: Preventing a Somalization of the Gulf of Guinea, PT,1. *Africa Strategic Outlook.* Centre for International Maritime Security, 12 December.
Bridger, J. M. (2013). *"Pirate Horizons in the Gulf of Guinea" OceanusLive.org,* 9 January, http://www.oceanuslive.org/main/viewnews.aspx?uid=00000599 (accessed 10 October 2020).
Bridger, J. (2013). Crafting a counter-piracy regime in the Gulf of Guinea.*Capability analysis strategic outlook.* Centre for International Maritime Security, July, http://cimsec.org/crafting-a-piracy-regime-in-the-gulf-of-guinea/6232 Accessed 8.09.17.
Carafano, J., Andersen, M, & Weitz, R. (2009). *Maritime security: fighting piracy in the Gulf of Aden and Beyond" Heritage Special Report, SR 59, June 24,* https://www.heritage.org/defense/report/maritime-security-fighting-piracy-the-gulf-aden-and-beyond. Accessed 10.10.20.
Chatham House. (2013). Maritime Security in the Gulf of Guinea. *Report of the conference held at Chatham House, London, 6 December 2012.* London: Chatham House, March.
Dahun, S. (2017). *Nigerian navy deploys ships, helicopter for Obangame express.* March 22, https://prnigeria.com/security/nigerian-navy-obangame-express/ Accessed Monday, 25.09.17.
Global Sentinel. (2017). *Buhari emerges chairman of Gulf of Guinea Commission.* https://globalsentinelng.com/2017/11/23/buhari-emerges-chairman-gulf-guinea-commission/ Accessed 20.01.19.
Gulf of Guinea Commission. http://cggrps.org/en/ Accessed 09.06.11.
Gulf of Guinea Commission. The Gulf of Guinea Commission. https://cggrps.com/en/the-gulf-of-guinea-commission/ Accessed 20.01.19.
Heyl, P. J. (2013). West and Central African Leaders Unite against Piracy in the Gulf of Guinea. Paper presented at *the 3rd United Arab Emirates International Counter Piracy Conference,* Dubai, 11–12 September.
International Maritime Organisation (IMO) (2017). *Report on Acts of Piracy and Armed Robbery against Ships, Annual Report -2016, MSC.4/Circ.245.* http://www.imo.org/en/OurWork/Security/PiracyArmedRobbery/Reports/Documents/245%20Annual%202016.pdf (accessed 10 October 2020).
International Crisis Group (ICG). (2012). *The Gulf of Guinea: the new danger zone" Africa Report, No. 195, 12 December,* https://www.crisisgroup.org/africa/west-africa/guinea/gulf-guinea-new-danger-zone. Accessed 10.10.20.
International Maritime Organisation. (2017). *Implementing sustainable maritime security measures in West and Central Africa, April,* http://www.imo.org/en/OurWork/Security/WestAfrica/Documents/WCA%20Strategy_English_April%202017.pdf. Accessed 10.10.20.
International Maritime Organisation, (IMO) (2010). *Code of Practice for the Investigation of the Crimes of Piracy and Armed Robbery Against Ships (Resolution A.1025)* adopted on 2 December 2009, Assembly/26/Res/1025, 18 January 2010, http://www.imo.org/en/OurWork/Security/PiracyArmedRobbery/Guidance/Documents/A.1025.pdf. Accessed 11.09.17.
National Archives of Singapore (2006). *Factsheet on the Regional Cooperation Agreement on Combating Piracy and Armed Robbery Against Ships in Asia (ReCAAP).* http://www.nas.gov.sg/archivesonline/data/pdfdoc/20061129970.pdf. Accessed 24.01.19.

Nigerian Maritime Administration and Safety Agency. (2017). *Association of African Maritime Administration (AAMA) communique, Abuja, record of decisions, recommendations and resolutions*, https://nimasa.gov.ng/wp-content/uploads/2019/08/VOYAGE2017-Q2.pdf. Accessed 10.10.20.

Onuoha, F. (2012). Piracy and Maritime Security in the Gulf of Guinea Nigeria as a Microcosm, https://www.academia.edu/834084/. Accessed 10.10.20.

Onwuemenyi, O. (2017). *"AAMA Confab: IMO to address maritime security challenges in Africa". Sweet Crude Reports, 25 April*, https://sweetcrudereports.com/aama-confab-imo-to-address-maritime-security-challenges-in-africa/. Accessed 10.10.20.

Osinowo, A. A. (2015). *"Piracy in the Gulf of Guinea" Africa Security Brief No. 30*, February 25, https://africacenter.org/publication/combating-piracy-in-the-gulf-of-guinea/. Accessed 10.10.20.

Paterson, P. J. (2007). *"Maritime Security in the Gulf of Guinea" in JFQ Forum*, Issue 45, 2nd Quarter.

Steffen, D. (2017). *"Gulf of Guinea Maritime Security in 2016" Report of the Centre for International Maritime Security, 11 April*, http://cimsec.org/gulf-guinea-maritime-security-2016/31716. Accessed 10.10.20.

Storey, I. (2016). Addressing the Persistent Problem of Piracy and Sea Robbery in Southeast Asia, *Perspective*, 30, June 7, https://www.iseas.edu.sg/images/pdf/ISEAS_Perspective_2016_30.pdf Accessed 10.10.20.

Ukeje, Charles, & Mvomo, E. W. (2013). *African approaches to maritime security: The Gulf of Guinea*. Abuja: Friedrich Ebert Foundation.

United Nations, (UN). (1982). *Article 100 of United Nations Convention on Laws of the Sea (UNCLOS) 1982*, https://www.un.org/Depts/los/convention_agreements/texts/unclos/unclos_e.pdf. Accessed 10.10.20.

United Nations Security Council (UNSC) (2011). UNSC Resolution 2018. http://unscr.com/en/resolutions/doc/2018. Accessed 28.08.17.

United Nations Security Council (UNSC) (2012). UNSC Resolution 2039 of 29 February 2012 (S/RES/2039).http://www.securitycouncilreport.org/atf/cf/%7B65BFCF9B-6D27-4E9C-8CD3-CF6E4FF96FF9%7D/UNOCA%20SRES%202039.pdf. Accessed 09.09.17.

United Nations, (UN). (2012). *Text of resolution 67/68 on Ocean and Law of the Sea (A/RES/67/78) adopted by the United Nations General Assembly on 5 December*, https://documents-dds-ny.un.org/doc/UNDOC/GEN/N12/483/28/PDF/N1248328.pdf?OpenElement. Accessed 10.10.20.

United States Africa Command, (AFRICOM), *Obangame Express*. http://www.africom.mil/what-we-do/exercises/obangame-express. Accessed Monday, 25.09.17.

International Maritime Organisation. (2013). *"Code of conduct concerning the repression of piracy, armed robbery against ships and illicit maritime activity in West and Central Africa""*, Yaounde, June, http://www.imo.org/en/OurWork/Security/WestAfrica/Documents/code_of_conduct%20signed%20from%20ECOWAS%20site.pdf. Accessed 10.10.20.

# 25

# Lake Chad Basin

## Emerging regional architecture for counterterrorism and counterinsurgency

*Usman A. Tar and Bashir Bala*

## Introduction

With the breeding level of conflicts in Africa, the continent has experienced two waves of regionalisation – particularly regional and sub-regional securitisation. The first is attributed to colonisation, de-colonisation, and Pan-Africanism, while the second is associated with the loosened shackles of the Cold War in the late 1980s (Franke, 2007: 32). In spite of the political and ideological orientations of the regionalisation, the second wave dealing with the devastating consequences of the end of Cold War has resulted in a milestone change in Africa's cooperation and integration especially with regards to security. The collapse and withdrawal of the Soviet Union and its successor, Russia, and the instant non-interventionist disposition in Africa's conflicts by the US and France caused for the resort to internal-sourcing of mechanisms; for security and peace. In this regard, African began to develop regional international relations as a panacea to what Ochiai (2006: 2) referred to "changes in the international scene".

In Africa's Lake Chad Basin, the last four decades were characterised by many violent conflicts. They include warlordism, clashes of civil militias, guerrilla wars, insurgencies, and insurrectional movements emanating largely from the Chadian civil war of the 1980s, in addition to armed rebellion and the factional militias in both Niger and the Central African Republic that had attempted to, and in some cases succeeded in taking over the ungoverned spaces created by "lack of political legitimacy, leadership squabbles, and political fragmentation that bedevilled states across the region" (Tar and Bala, 2018a: 162). However, the evolving nature of the dreaded Islamist terrorist group *Boko Haram* in the region has hugely changed the trend and dynamics of stability with huge implications on the security and development of the region. In spite of the concomitant attempts to crack down on the activities of violent groups in the region, there are still widening networks of operational relationships among insurgent groups in the LCB that involve the exchange of wide-range of items detrimental to sub-regional peace and security.

The compelling need to curb the terrorism and insurgency coupled with operational imperatives for collective security cooperation necessitated the need for urgent intervention in the region. This saw to the creation and re-mandating of several platforms with the operational mandate of representing the regional security architecture in the Lake Chad Basin. Overall, such outfits are meant to create the institutionalisation of regional security mechanisms technically essential for dealing with the menace of threats to the region. Against this backdrop, this chapter seeks to carefully engage the trends, dynamics, grouping system and institutional actors defining and reshaping the emergent regional security architecture in the region. To achieve this, a topographical analysis of the region can aid in the grasp of the broad description of the terrain.

## Background: The Lake Chad Basin

The Lake Chad Basin is situated between Latitude 12°00'N and 14°30'N and Longitudes 13° E and 15°30'E as the 4th largest lake in Africa, providing means of sustenance for 37 million people. At the same time, it delineates the boundary of four littoral states. The Member States in the basin have a combined total population of 237 million people estimated to reach 390 by 2025. Urbanisation in the basin is about 50%; however, it is projected to 70% in 2030 (Ifabiyi, 2013: 199). The population consists of groups with several linguistic affiliations like the Kanuri, Kanembu, Buduma, Hausas, Godogodo, Mabas, Saras, Tubuos and Fulanis (Maianguwa & Audu, 2017: 328). Though the Lake has shrunk by about 90% couple with the altered focus by anthropogenic activities caused by the problem of climate change, it is still home to 120 species of fishes and 372 birds. The area encompasses the Saharan, Sahelo-Saharan, Sahelo-Sudanian, Sudano-Sahelian and Sudano-Guinea ecological zones as the five bioclimatic zones (Ifabiyi, 2013: 199). The currents of South-west humid Atlantic and the north-east Egyptian hot and dry (harmattan) influence the climate and "consequently the ecological zonation of the basin". And the "cool, dry, dust-laden ——harmattan" coming from the Saharan in the north during the winter months is accompanied by low humidity, cool nights, and warm days. In contrast, the moisture-laden winds blow from the Gulf of Guinea in the south during summer "bringing high humidity, rains, and more uniform diurnal temperature. The monsoon advances from the south, so that rains start earlier, are heavier and last longer in the southwards. However, there is high spatial and temporal variability over the entire area" (Ifabiyi, 2013: 199-100).

In terms of trans-boundary waters, the LCB is partitioned into six (6) 6 hydrological units. The first unit, according to Ifabiyi (2013: 200), in the Lake Chad with an elevation of 279 m covering approximately 25,000km$^2$ and currently passing through a demeaning shrinkage. The second is the Lower Chari which has the largest rivers and serves as an integral aspect of the basin as it collects water that feeds the lakes. The third is the Flood Plain of the Logona which is a major source of fisheries and livestock and has a landmass of about 25,000km$^2$. The Grand Yaeres and the Waga national parks are all inhabited within this hydrological unit. The third is the Komadogu-Yobe which infiltration and evapotranspiration drain its water, and it has the highest number of dams. The basin is the powerhouse of food production in Nigeria and neighbourhoods. The fourth unit is the Borno drainage which contains the Yedseram, Ngadda and Gobio Rivers. The Sambisa game reserve that is ravaged by the Boko Haram insurgency and serving as a current hideout area for terrorists and other armed groups and Chad Basin National Park are in this unit. The fifth unit is the Bornu Diagnostic Basin which is "an arid basin, and it is a zone of dune mobilisation by trampling livestock and deforestation". And the sixth hydrological unit is the Lake Filtri which is pasture. "This zone is under intensive competition from indigenous people overgrazing. It is home to conflict over resource use."

Despite the vast expanse of land it covers, and the deteriorating effects of climate change it suffers, the general area of the LCB is still identified with varying environmental problems. These include the variability in river regime and water availability. The negative impact of this is that it resulted in insufficient access to water, low availability of livestock, unfruitful crops cultivation, reduced fishing rate, skyrocketing unemployment and a heightened level of poverty in the area with high consequences on Cameroon, Chad, Nigeria and Niger. Second is the "decreased viability of biological resources" this reduced the productivity of the ecosystem, accentuated poverty, and loss of biodiversity. The third impact is that of pollution caused by the lack of compliance in the implementation of environmental standards to control pollution and other environmental hazards. While the third is the "loss and modification of ecosystem" caused by the heightening desiccation due to population explosion and massive urbanisation has destroyed the area by about 50%, and "endangered wetlands of the LCB" (Ifabiyi, 2013: 201–202). Despite these problems, the area constitutes a strategic pot for sub-regional food security for countries bordered by the Lake Chad (Umara, 2014a :93) and has continued to provide means of economic livelihood for millions of people cohabiting within the areas in the four riparian states of Cameroon, Chad, Nigeria and Nigeria (Onuoha, 2009). Important to differentiate that, the critical area of study in this Chapter is the northern Cameroon which spanned across Fotokol with proximity to Abadam in north Borno state in Nigeria, southwest of Chad and Diffa area which is southeast of Niger as the area circumference is worst hit by the dreaded activities of insurgent groups and other transnational armed elements. Having analysed the terrain configuration of the region to aid the understanding of the region's dynamic peculiarities, the next section will unpack the VNSAs in the LCB region.

## Mapping violent non-state actors in the Lake Chad Basin

In the LCB region, Nigeria constitutes the vortex of violent extremism and other forms of conflict. The country is managing violent conflicts at different zones: environmental militancy in the Niger Delta; Boko Haram insurgency in the North-East; communal conflict in the North Central; and farmer-herder conflict across the whole federation. The oil-rich Niger Delta region is the scene of a sustained armed rebellion having suffered from considerable environmental challenges and socioeconomic hurdles. The region became fused with several ethnic militias engaging in agitations and some even extending the line to secessionist movements. In 2004, groups like Movement for the Emancipation of the Niger Delta (MEND), Niger Delta People's Volunteer Force (NDPVF), Joint Revolutionary Council (JRC) and Niger Delta Vigilante (NDV) emerged while the continued escalation of the violence saw the emergence of the recently-tagged Niger Delta Avengers. Among these groups, the NDPVF which Asari Dokubo heads and the Ateke Tom-led NDV are more violent and involved in pyro-terrorism before the actual unveiling of the Niger Delta Avengers. MEND and Niger Delta Avengers are to be considered in this chapter due to the intensity of their attacks and high-profile sabotage against the Nigerian state which invariably affected the economic output of the country and have maintained the status of being the two major factions dominating the conflict landscape of the Niger Delta.

This is not to disregard the argument of Mohammed (2017: 50) that though other splinter militant groups enjoy relative autonomy, they still key into the mutual alliances with either the NDPVF or NDV and thus receive a moderate level of combat training on weapons handling and manoeuvre tactics as well as the stocked inventory of arms of different calibres. The NDA emerged recently and aimed to carve out a sovereign political entity for the Niger Delta region and thus threaten the corporate unity of Nigeria. It evolved around January 2016 but came into national prominence in March 2016 after a series of violent activities they carried out clandestinely. The militant group has established links with Niger Delta Red Square, Niger Delta Greenland Justice Mandate, Joint Niger Delta Liberation Force, Red Egbesu and Water Lions among others (Mohammed, 2017: 51). The composition of the group and the sophistication of its attacks on oil installations vouched for its claim that it has members drawn from the most intelligent palate in the region. Suffice it to say, the group has reduced its frequent attacks as a result of the quick intervention of the federal government and the involvement of regional elders where negotiating terms were reached and complied upon by both parties. The clear indicator is that this group has a potency to scale down oil production in the area which would have a direct bearing on the fiscal impact of Nigeria on the LCB.

Another group that surfaced in the South East of Nigeria is the Movement for the Actualisation of the Sovereign State of Biafra (MASSOB) as a first non-violent social movement that came to limelight after formed by Ralph Uwazuruike. At several times, the activities of the MASSOB led to violent encounters with the security forces at the formative stage of the group, it received less attention from the "international media and community." Over time, Nnamdi Kanu, a Nigerian-British based in London, rekindled the dream for the independence of Biafra as he realised that it could not be realised through MASSOB. Kanu employed the modern tools of communication and mainly established a radio station - Radio Biafra to broadcast propaganda against the Nigerian. Through hate speech in radio and social media, Kanu drew millions of pro-Biafra independence activists into his fold and subsequently turned violent against the state (Ugorji, 2017). The violence that erupted after the bail of the Nmandi Kanu from custody coupled with the use of misguided and obscene expressions against the unity of Nigeria, which are considered to be "hate speech and incitement to violence and war," the Nigeria Army proscribed the IPOB as a terrorist group whose activities undermine the existence and stability of Nigeria. Thus, the IPOB is today seen as one violent group that threatens national security and capable of instigating other separatist movements in the LCB region.

An interlink between MASSOB and IPOB remains a crucial step in understanding the intrigues and operational activities of the two groups. MASSOB claimed to be more involved in visitations, consultations and bringing all pro-Biafra groups under one umbrella for the revival of brotherhood consciousness among various ethnic groups. The group particularly embarked on prayers, supplications, and sober reflections on the actualisation of the Republic of Biafra as part of the anniversary celebration of our 19 years of establishment. MASSOB is determined to ensure the actualisation and restoration of Biafra through initiating enhanced diplomatic and international engagements (Uzodinma, 2018). Both MASSOB and IPOB are yet to deviate from the rays of demanding for Biafra State even though they have all failed to clearly articulate the convincing justification for such demand, the modalities of establishing the state and the various ethnic nationalities that would constitute the state. Both MASSOB and IPOB are busy drawing and redrawing maps without consideration of other ethnic groups who are at variance with their restoration campaign (Fasan, 2017). IPOB has gone a step further in this direction by issuing counterfeit visas, producing fake monetary currencies, establishing a phantom link between the Igbo and the Jews and professing faith in a Jewish faith (Fasan, Ibid). This has particularly exposed the separatists' lack of clear and realistic agenda to actualise their dream of a Republic of Biafra. There is a further claim of splinter groups among IPOB, which is clearly evidenced by the emergence of the Re-branded Indigenous People of " Biafra" (TRIOPOB). The group broke away from the Kanu-led IPOB due to what they perceived as the "defeatist position" of IPOB. The splinter group has a distinct agenda trajectory with IPOB as they denunciated a secessionist Biafra and intend to pursue the spirit and intent of Biafra within Nigeria (IRB, 2016). Across the LCB, the Al-Qaeda in the Islamic Maghreb (AQIM) is a Violent Non-State Actor (VNSA) which has projected itself as a Salafi-jihadist militant group and "U.S.-designated foreign terrorist organisation (FTO)." The group exploits its origin to Algeria's civil war in the 1990s and has, over time, become an al-Qaeda affiliate with the quest for regional expansionism (Laub & Masters, 2014: 1). AQIM, is the only organised, violent Islamist group that is conducting operations in the four Sahelian countries of Chad, Mali, Mauritania and Niger while initially known as the Salafist Group for Preaching and Combat (Cocodia, 2017: 56). Its objectives include "ridding North Africa of Western influence; overthrowing governments deemed apostate, including those of Algeria, Libya, Mali, Mauritania, Morocco, and Tunisia; and installing fundamentalist regimes based on sharia" in spite of the incendiary transnational terror threat its continue to posed in North and West Africa in conjunction with its affiliates (Laub & Masters, 2014: 3). AQIM was uprooted off its base of operations along the Mediterranean coast south to the Sahel region by a robust Algerian counterterrorism campaign and thus transcended to the Sahel region with a regional ambition of establishing its strongholds. AQIM has affiliations with other terrorist groups such as Nigeria's Boko Haram, Somalia's al-Shabab, and Yemen's AQAP, "with arms and funds flowing among them. AQIM's tactics include guerrilla-style raids, assassinations, and suicide bombings of military, government, and civilian targets. Its members have frequently kidnapped, and sometimes executed, aid workers, tourists, diplomats, and employees of multinational corporations" (Laub & Masters, 2014: 4). Going by the massive wealth acquired by the group, and the speed and momentum of its mobility, its sources of funds are worth noting as it engaged in large-scale farming in the Lake Chad, kidnapping for ransom and smuggling arms and vehicles; and smuggling into its operational area of the remnants of the NATO-grade Libya air campaign in 2011. The most violent insurgent group among all the AQIM's alleged subsidiaries is the Boko Haram.

*Boko Haram* has unleashed mayhem on the LCB region as it fights to enforce strict Shariah law and propagate itself as *Jama'aAhl as-Sunna Li-da'wa'atil Jihad* (People Committed to the Propagation of the Prophet's Teachings and Jihad) (Bala, 2017: 4). At the onset, the group carried out armed insurrection in 2009 within the Maiduguri metropolis targeting state's security infrastructure such as police stations, home of police officers, checkpoints operated by JTF personnel and other security agencies (Abubakar, 2017: 37). *Boko Haram* is ranked as one of the world's most brutal terrorist groups, killing more people than the dreaded Islamic State in Iraq and Syria (ISIS). The group has killed over 30,000 civilians since 2009 and caused the internal displacement of over 2,152,000 people in Nigeria, Chad, and neighbouring Cameroon. In August 2014, the violent group escalated its campaign of territorial conquest by dislodging civilians and taking hold of their towns, villages and important facilities around Gwoza – Nigerian border with Cameroon and subsequently declared itself a caliphate (Bala, 2017: 4). After series of violent confrontations with the Nigerian-constituted Military Joint Task Force (MJTF), Muhammed (2014: 9) opined that the group went underground, reorganised with a more disastrous resurgence on the public limelight and a remarkable prison break at Bauchi in October 2010. The group employ the hit-and-run tactics couple with targeted "assassinations, drive-by shootings, suicide bombings, and massive deployment of improvised explosive devices (IEDs), vehicle-borne IEDs, and, lately, kidnapping and hostage taking." With sustained counterinsurgency operations in the LCB, the group's structure and networks were penetrated, and this resulted in factionalising the group into some violent splinter sects.

The sustained propaganda on the part of the counterinsurgents in the LCB with what Oftedal (2013: 14) referred to as the "internal disagreements and fragmentation" of the Boko Haram group, a group known as Ansaru announced its formation as a breakaway faction from Boko Haram. Ansaru split because of Boko Haram's indiscriminate killing of Muslims which the group detest and pronounced as "inhumane" and "inexcusable." The coming of the Ansaru into the regional landscape of VNSAs in the LCB was further recognised by the six major incidents involving the group that Atimbobi (2016: 32–33) articulated in his work on the transnationalisation of the Boko Haram terrorism. These include kidnappings of foreign expatriates at four consecutive times, an attack on a detention facility in Abuja and an ambush on Nigerian soldiers earmarked for a peace support operation in Mali heading for their pre-deployment training in Jaji. A point of note here, Ansaru seems to be more against Western values and in a bit more internationally oriented than the Shekau's faction of Boko Haram. It has also had a spell of attacks on foreign convoys and personnel going by its raid on a French engineer in Katsina and it attacks French troops while on a mission to Mali. These instances and several others were supported by Atimbobi (2016) to depict the regionalisation of terrorism within the LCB region. The concentration of insecurity in the region caused by the activities of these VNSAs calls for regional securitisation and thus, the next section will examine the emergent regional infrastructure of security in the LCB.

In the republic of Chad, sustained rebellion and insurgency have marked the country's post-colonial history. This rebellion has often crossed to neighbouring countries in search of op-erational space and resources. Chadian rebels are by formation like paramilitary groups with alliances mostly from the Arabs, Toubou and Zaghawa as the strength-sourcing ethnic groups of the rebellion. The rebel group recruits members from the disbanded Chad's armed and security groups. With the considerable richness in oil deposits in the country and the desire to accomplish unfettered access to resources, the rebel leaders struggle to take over the political power in N'Djamena (Pamminger, 2009: 68) a maximum number of 10,000 fighters The ground forces of the group are equipped with "cheap, easily available Small Arms and Light Weapons (SALW) and use all-terrain "technology," under the form of Toyota Land Cruisers to move around. Their SALW inventory includes AKM assault rifles, also known as AK-47 "Kalashnikov" rifles, RPG-7s, i.e. Russian rocket-propelled anti-tank grenades, French (MILAN) anti-tank guided missiles" (Pamminger, 2009: 69). With the rebel possession of ground to air missiles and vast network of communication and information technology coupled with accessibility to weapons through illegal arms markets in the Chad-Sudan area, the mobility and manoeuvrability of the group remain both surprising and threatening. Thus, compounding sub-regional security issues in the LCB.

## Emerging regional security architecture in the Lake Chad Basin

In the LCB, the geostrategic implications of Boko Haram insurgency have altered the power configuration (Tar & Mustapha, 2016). This has called for the necessary deployment of a se-curity regimen. As a result of the frequency of security threats posed by BH, the LCB is undergoing the emergence of a new security order and regional configuration. As a regional power, Nigeria and its neighbours in the region realized the tremendous negative geostrategic consequences of Boko Haram transnational border attacks. They demanded the supply of collective regional security arrangement to decimate the insurgency and other criminalities (Tar & Bala, 2019b).

The LBC is a contagious region of West Africa. Here, a formidable regional integration and security regionalisation have emerged to foster security and development in the region. The ECOWAS was established in 1975 to promote regional cooperation and economic develop-ment in West Africa. In 1990, it inaugurated and inducted its military branch designated ECOWAS Cease-fire Monitoring Group (ECOMOG). Though ECOWAS was initially conceived as an economic community, with the implementation of its military arm, its regional security initiatives were saddled with the Mediation and Security Council (MSC). The explicit authority rests with the governing body of the regional establishment. Still, the MSC is also empowered to make certain decisions in connection with peace and security at national and regional levels in West Africa (Ochiai, 2006: 6). In light of this, the ECOWAS recognised the

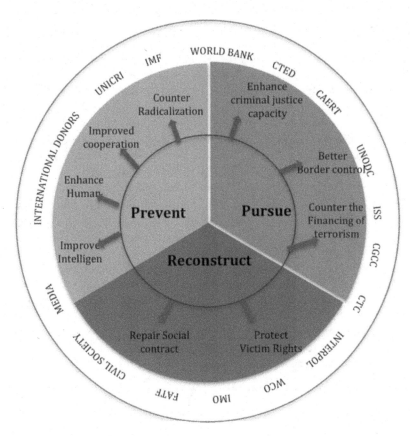

*Figure 25.1* The Three Pillars of CT-COIN Strategy in ECOWAS and LCB Source: Barakafintiye, (2013)

consequences of the emerging threats to security within its member states of the LCB and launched a counterterrorism and counterinsurgency campaign while deploying resources.

The objectives of the ECOWAS CT-COIN strategy include the dispensing of impact to regional, continental, and international counterterrorism instruments and to further avail a common operational framework for the pre-emption and countering of terrorism and related criminalities in West Africa; operationalise regional and international counterterrorism instruments in West Africa; augment and "consolidate cooperation, coordination, harmonisation, and synergies in national counterterrorism actions; ensure adequate protection of fundamental human rights in states counterterrorism activities; strengthen ECOWAS role including that of states, civil society organisations and media networks in the prevention and combating of terrorism" (ECOWAS, 2013: 16). In achieving these objectives, the ECOWAS framework for CT-COIN phases the pillars as shown on the chart below:

From the foregoing chart, it can be deduced that the three pillars are what guide and orientate the ECOWAS projection for combating terrorism and insurgency in West Africa and this has a direct impact on the LCB region. The first pillar, as better captured by ECOWAS (2013: 27–34) in its work on "ECOWAS CT Strategy and Implementation Plan," defined it as it encompasses the central pillar of the Strategy and is based on the concept of detect, intercept, and deter. It also attempts to contain terrorism in economic, political, and cultural activities with the purpose of eliminating grounds conducive for terrorist activities. It also seeks to emphasise the need to identify and tackle the risks of terrorism using legislative, financial, political, security and defence tools. The second pillar seeks to establish conditions for timely and effective responses to terrorist acts and it is the scaffold on a "criminal justice approach which provides for both military and non-military responses to terrorism." While the third pillar emphasises the need to rebuild society and reassert the authority of the state after a terrorist attack and "deals with the social consequences of an attack." This pillar also demands collaboration with and engagement of social and media groups in combating terrorism. It is germane to note that, the ECOWAS, in its effort to ensure the regional security of the LCB region, initiated and opened a trust fund for member states to contribute financial resources to the reinvigorated sub-regional security outfit in the LCB called the MNJTF.

Aside from the ECOWAS intervention, also it is observed that with the primary authority of the United Nations Security Council (UNSC) added to the regional effort by some member states of the LCBC, the AU to the remodelling of regional security architecture under the umbrella of the Multinational Joint Task Force (MNJTF) to contain the increasing wave of Boko Haram insurgency and other trans-border crimes in the region (Bala and Tar, 2020). After the 2015 Paris Conference, the counterinsurgency alliance of Cameroon, Chad, Niger, and Nigeria finally kicked up. The platform's commencement of operation helped in reducing the mistrust among the countries in the LCB particularly between Nigeria and Chad (Aning & Amedzrator, 2016: 83). The Lake Chad Basin Commission decided to remodel the structure and doctrinal posture of the force and extend its mandate and operational scope to engage in containing the increasing regional threats of Boko Haram. This was achieved at the LCBC 14th summit of heads of states and governments, held in Chad in April 2012 (Bala and Tar, Ibid). It is in this regards that the operational mandate of the MNJTF was established:

i.. To create a safe and secure environment in the areas affected by the activities of Boko Haram and other terrorist groups, in order to significantly reduce violence against civilians and other abuses, including sexual- and gender-based violence, in full compliance with international law, including international humanitarian law and the UN HRDDP;
ii.. To facilitate the implementation of overall stabilisation programmes by the LCBC Member States and Benin in the affected areas, including the full restoration of state authority and the return of IDPs and refugees; and
iii.. To facilitate within the limit of its capabilities, humanitarian operations, and the delivery of assistance to the affected populations (AU PSC, 2015: 6).

Despite the successes recorded by the MNJTF in its operations against insurgency within its Ares of Responsibility, it is still been impeded by certain challenges. These range from the lack of adequate equipment to prosecute its operations, to the inadequate financial base and to lack of complete willingness of the formally agreed Troops Contributing Member States to insert full complement of manpower as they pledged. These and several other factors stand on the way to a more robust defence and security mechanism for the LCB region.

Another element of the emergent security architecture in the LCB is the establishment of the Civilian Joint Task Force (CJTF) in Northeast Nigeria which partly plays roles in CT-COIN operations along the LCB borders. The CJTF emerged in June 2013 to complement and aid military activities against Boko Haram insurgency. Osakwe and Audu (2017: 5) even attempt to argue that, the non-state group came into being to end the brutal harassment of the BH. Though this chapter disagrees with this stand as there are other factors responsible for the resilience which may include poverty, unemployment, patriotism and what we called "high sense of attachment with ancestral lineage" which psychologically people can give their last ounce not to be detached from. Umara (2014a) identified more valid argument that the critical factor that led to the formation of the CJTF was the apparent struggle by the national security forces to contain the threats posed by the insurgent group and the extreme lethality of the group's attacks on critical state infrastructure. Innocent civilians were also maimed and waylaid by the group, and this showcases and highlights inadequacies to personal and national security within the region. Compounding issues on the part of the national forces is the inability to identify the insurgents, distinguish them amongst innocent civilians and even put on with their "ubiquitous guerilla warfare tactics". In the apparent lack of terrain knowledge by the military, the insurgents unleashed terror on the civilian populace in broad daylights and sneaked their way out of the scene unnoticed and not apprehended.

It was under this condition that the people of Northeast Nigeria continued to wallow in panic and intimidation exacerbated by the group's lethal attacks. The level of the group's destruction of lives and property witnessed a horrendous marked intensification as once a person is perceived as a threat to the group's agenda and ideology; the group's order the member of the family from the followership of either stabbing to death or gunning down the perceived enemy. Parents were forced to allow their children to embrace the ideology of the group and even conceal weapons and other incriminating materials for their children that are already in the group. Women were kidnapped, raped, and compelled to provide information on the movements of security forces. In some instances, they were also used as couriers and runners (Umara, 2014b).

With such frustration on the part of the civil populace and the level of eroding state security in Borno State then that, the youth realised the need to come out and complement the effort of the Nigerian military in confronting the threat posed by Boko Haram. This they do by engaging in small arms confrontation with the insurgents and helping in identifying, arresting and handing over the insurgents to the military. This is not to regards the fact that, there were instances where the youths of the CJTF took laws into their hands as there are many cases of alleged gross violations of human rights committed by the CJTF. However, contrary to the numerous challenges confronting its operations, the CJTF as articulated by Dauda (2017:), that is today reckoned with availing the Nigeria military with actionable intelligence in addition to assisting in fishing out their peers belonging to BH group or their accomplices. It was through this traditional method that intelligence was gathered on the group's activities, and BH was routed out of Maiduguri and had to relocate in the Sambisa Forest.

## Geo-strategic politics of counterterrorism and counterinsurgency in the Lake Chad Basin

The geopolitical realities in the Lake Chad Basin region have undermined a robust multi-national effort at combating the threats of transnational organised crimes within the region. These geopolitical realities go beyond the traditional discourse of security regionalisation and involved factors that are beyond personal and national efforts. These efforts can only be achieved through a reliable platform for addressing the overwhelming implications of the practical issues that tend to stall the progress and coherence of strong regional security co-operation among the riparian states.

The first reality is that of political mistrust among the leadership of the LCB Member States. This problem manifested even in the regional fight against Boko Haram. In containing the insurgency, the defence and security community have suffered significant loses because the two countries of Cameroon and Chad have demonstrated an appearance of political rivalry and mutual recriminations in cooperating with Nigeria. Though the countries tend to pretend of normalcy in a relationship at the global stage, they still do not have sound relation with Nigeria. Consequently, the so-called mutual security agenda was momentarily threatened by mutual suspicion. Albert (2016:9) submitted that this particularly beckoned the foreign intervention of Britain and the US to assist in countering this problem as they provided intelligence to Nigeria on the locations, dispositions, capability and likely intent of the terrorists to and from the neighbouring countries. They also provide Nigeria with capacity building in the form of training and tactical supports for dealing with the insurgents. On the other hand, the posture of France gave Nigeria's neighbouring Francophone countries a supporting base to their share of the countering the insurgency. The problem started with the perceived attitude of the two countries to the plight of Nigeria when the crisis started as been a purely Nigerian problem. This geostrategic issue is further aggravated by the longstanding conflicts of diplomacy and boundaries between the three countries.

Historically, Nigeria has always been in a challenging diplomatic relationship with Chad among all its neighbours. The historical animosity around boundary and resource disputes between Nigeria and Chad has compounded the intensity of other forms of crisis, including the Boko Haram insurgency. The ownership of the Trans-boundary water of the Lake Chad constitutes a cause of disagreement Nigeria and Chad. However, both countries have always had border disputes around the Lake because of the unclear demarcation of the boundary between the two nations by the European colonial powers. The boundaries, consisting of a straight line running for about 76 km joining the Niger tri-point at Latitude 13.05 degree north and longitude 14.05 degree East are bereft of necessary beacons or buoys. In the quest for resource control and accessibility, subjects within the border villages resort to different forms of self-help strategies to acquirer and maximise scarce environmental resource within the Lake region. Some of the disputed villages have fishery and invaluable mineral resources. The borderland disputes have assumed new dimensions up to the present (Bala & Tar, 2019b). This has had a huge impact on the success of the counterinsurgency in the region particularly when the subjects are not ready to cooperate with the national forces of another neighbouring country and inter-defence forces' synergistic relationship was hampered at the beginning of the campaign in the LCB region.

The key segment of resource-control in the regional power politics is the infusion of "oil geopolitics into an already volatile mix of ecological factors pushing socio-economic devastation of the region" (Tar & Mustapha, 2016: 11). The "regionalisation of neo-patrimonialism" caused by the discovery and exploration of oil in Chad resulted in competition among divergent regional orders and comprador bourgeoisie so injuries to CT-COIN in the region. This was further projected by the investment interest of powerful politicians in Chad's oil market and their selfish aspiration of having undistracted and exclusive access to oil deposits at the expense of sub-regional security cooperation to tame Boko Haram insurgency. In the light of this reality, Tar and Mustapha (2016: 12) advance that, "the oil wealth beneath the Chad Basin in which some Nigerians and Chadians have made investments is fanning the embers of insurgency in Nigeria. Vested economic interests in the crude oil exploration in the Chad Basin are fuelling the machinery of Boko Haram and its attacks on Nigeria…Thus, both Nigeria and Chad consider the instability of the region as vital to their geopolitical interests leading to the securitisation of territorial-based geopolitics."

## Conclusion

The phenomenal growth of terrorist and insurgent groups, the frequency as well as sophistication in the methods they employ in carrying out attacks remain sources of regional concern not only to the Lake Chad Basin Member States but Africa and world at large. In the LCB region, attacks by

BH on soft and hard targets have resulted in causing dire humanitarian crises that require huge reconstructive and peacebuilding commitments at all levels to contain. Considering this, as discussed in this chapter, the region has recently witnessed the proliferation of secessionist movements and other forms of insurrections threatening the survivability and viability of its defence infrastructure. Though the security architecture in the region is operationalised by the mandate of the African Union and explicit authorisation of the UN Security Council, certain structural problems, ideological fractions and mutual recriminations among the riparian states constitute an obstacle to the progress of such platforms. In light of this, the chapter illuminates the future trajectories of the regional security architecture in the Lake Chad Basin into four bearings. The first is that the growing scale and ubiquity of the Violent Non-States Actors in the region would continue to wallow and pocket the collaborative efforts of the sub-regional outfit provided some fundamental socio-economic and political grievances have not been addressed. The implication of this is the level of poverty and internal displacement that ravage the states in the region and thus subject the populace to untold hardship of struggling with insurgents and look-out for means of livelihood. The second trajectory is the caveat that, without the needed political will and commitment on the part of the leadership of the member states of the LCBC to counter insurgent activities within their region, the counterinsurgency operations would not create the desired impact. This is particularly paramount considering how BH was emboldened in taking territories and carrying out large scale attacks in Nigeria and later Cameroon, Chad, and Niger at the onset of the insurgency. This was attributed to the lack of cooperation among the riparian states then. However, the renewed vigour and commitment of the political leadership in those countries resulted in a modest sub-regional counterinsurgency campaign that weakens BH capacity to sustain its large-scale attacks. The third is that the financing of the regional security architecture and the provisioning of the needed equipment for the defence force to counter security threats in the LCB would become the major preoccupation of the international system going by the ongoing humanitarian crises in the region. Considering the thousands of internally displaced persons, refugees, and other affected population in the LCB, the attention of the international community has been directed to finding a lasting security solution. The solution must also be multi-dimensional considering both military and non-military approaches to peace restoration and building. The solution would further avail the needed financial resources and military equipment for the MNJTF to execute its operational mandate. The fourth trajectory is that the devastating consequences of BH terrorism and insurgency would force a sub-regional security alliance that would result in the emergence of a more viable and stable Lake Chad Basin region with formidable leadership aiming to commit theirs all towards the improvement of the material conditions of the region. This would contribute to the attainment of a sound counterinsurgency strategy.

## References

Abubakar, D. (2017). From sectarianism to terrorism in Northern Nigeria: A closer look at Boko Haram. In C. Varin & D. Abubakar (Eds.), *Violent Non-State Actors in Africa*. New York: Palgrave Macmillan.

Albert, I. O. (2016). Rethinking the Functionality of a Security Community for Managing Boko Haram Crisis in the Lake Chad Basin. Being a paper presented at *the International Conference on Security Regimens in Africa organised by CODESERIA*, held at Azala Grand Hotel Bamako, Mali, 28 – 29 September.

Aning, K., & Amedzrator, L. (2016). Critical perspectives on transnational criminality in West Africa. *Journal of Military and Strategic Studies*, 17( 2), 70–85.

Atimbobi, F. Z. (2016). *Transnationalisation of Boko Haram in the Lake Chad: The case of Boko Haram*. A thesis submitted to the Department of Development Studies for the award of Master of Science (MSc.) in peace, conflict and international relations. West Africa: Pan-African Institute for Development.

Atimbom, F. Z. (2016). *Transnationalisation of terrorism in the Lake Chad Basin: The case of Boko Haram*. An unpublished MSc. thesis in peace, conflicts and international relations. West Africa: Pan African Institute for Development .

AU PSC(African Union Peace and Security Council (2015). *Communiqué Adopted by the Peace and Security Council (PSC) of the African Union (AU), at its 898th meeting held on 28 November 2019, on the renewal of the mandate of the Multinational Joint Task Force (MNJTF) against the Boko Haram terrorist group*. Available: https://reliefweb.int/sites/reliefweb.int/files/resources/psc898commrenewal-mnjtf-mandate-28-11-2019.pdf. Accessed on 4.5. 2019.

Bala, B. (2017). *The challenges of counter-insurgency and national security: A study of the Nigerian Army operation against Boko Haram*. An unpublished MSc. thesis submitted to the Department of Political Science and Defence Studies. Kaduna-Nigeria: Nigerian Defence.

Bala, B., & Tar, U. A. (2019b). Multi-national joint task force: Emerging regional security architecture in the Lake Chad Basin. In U.A. Tar & B. Bala (Eds.), *New architecture for regional security in Africa: Perspectives on counter-terrorism and counter-insurgency in the Lake Chad Basin*. Lanham, MD: Lexington Books.

Bala, B. & Tar, U. A.(2020). *Insurgency and Counter-Insurgency in Nigeria: Perspectives on Nigerian Army Operations against Boko Haram*. Kaduna: NDA Press.

Barakamfitiye, D. (2013). *ECOWAS counter-terrorism strategy and implementation plan*. Institute of Strategic Studies Regional Office for West Africa. Draft Director. A draft publication for Workshop Accessed on the15 August 2018 from www.cafrad.org/Workshops/Ouagadougo25–27_03_13/ECOWAS.pdf (Accessed on 15.08.18)

Cocodia, J. (2017). Nationalist sentiment, terrorist incursions and the survival of the Malian state. In C. Varin & D. Abubakar (Eds.), *Violent non-state actors in Africa*. USA: Palgrave Macmillan.

Dauda, A. (2017). From sectarianism to terrorism in Northern Nigeria: A closer look at Boko Haram. In C. Varin & A. Dauda (Eds.), *Violent non-state actors in Africa: Terrorists, rebels and warlords*. Palgrave Macmillan.

ECOWAS (2013). *ECOWAS counter-terrorism strategy and implementation plan*. Available: https://www.ecowas.int/wp-content/uploads/2019/05/IMPLEMENTATION-PLAN-CT.pdf. Accessed on 15.01.19.

Fasan, R. (2017). IPOB/MASSOB: Beyond the symbolism of a struggle. *Vanguard Newspaper*.https://www.vanguardngr.com/2017/06/ipobmassob-beyond-symbolism-struggle/ Accessed on 12.02.19.

Franke, B. F. (2007). Competing regionalisms in Africa and the continent's emerging security architecture. *African Studies Quarterly, 9*(3), 31–60.

Ifabiyi, I. P. (2013). Recharging the Lake Chad: the hydro-politics of national security and regional integration in Africa. *African Research Review, 7*(30), 196–216.

Immigration and Refugee Board of Canada (IRB). (2016). *Nigeria: The Indigenous People of Biafra (IPOB), including objectives, structure, activities, relations with other Biafran independence groups, and treatment by authorities*. A report prepared by the Research Directorate, Immigration and Refugee Board of Canada, Ottawa. https://www.ecoi.net/en/document/1256720.html Accessed on 14.01.19.

Laub, Z, & Masters, J. (2014). *Al-Qaeda in the Islamic Maghreb (AQIM)*. Council on Foreign Affairs.

Luab, Z., & Masters, J. (2015). *Al-Qaeda in the Islamic Maghreb*. A Publication of the United States Council for Foreign Relations.

Maianguwa, J. S., & Audu, A. R. (2017). Civilians in frontlines: Evolving grassroots force for counter-insurgency operations in the Lake Chad Basin region. In U. A. Tar (Ed.), *Defence transformation and the consolidation of democracy in Nigeria*. Kaduna-Nigeria: Nigerian Defence Academy Press.

Mohammed, N. S. (2017). The Niger Delta avengers, autonomous ethnic clans and common claim over oil wells: The paradox of resource control. *African Research Review, 11*(12), 42–55. http://dx.doi.org/10.4314/afrrev.v11i2.4.

Muhammed, K. (2014). The message and methods of Boko Haram. In M.A. Pérouse de Montclos (Ed.), *Boko Haram: Islamism, politics, security and the state in Nigeria*. Netherlands: Published by African Study Centre.

Ochiai, T. (2006). *Regional security in Africa*. Afrasian Centre for Peace and Development Studies, Ryukoku University. Working Paper Series No. 14.

Oftedal, E. (2013). *Boko Haram: A transnational phenomenon*. University of Oslo. Master's thesis submitted to the Department of Political Science.

Onuoha, F. C. (2009). Environmental degradation, livelihood and conflict: A focus on the implications of the diminishing water resources of the Lake Chad for north-eastern Nigeria African. *Journal on Conflict Resolution, 8*(2), 35–61.

Osakwe, C. C. C., & Audu, B. J. (2017). Nigeria's military operations in the Lake Chad Basin. *Journal of Defence Management*, 7(1), 1–5. 10.4172/2167-0374.1000162.

Pamminger, G. C. (2009). State-internal actors in the armed conflict in Chad. In G. Hainzl & W.C. Feichtinger (Ed.), *EUFOR T Chad/RCA revisited*. Vienna: Institute for Peace Support and Conflict Management at the Austrian National Defence Academy.

Peace and Security Council 484th Meeting at the Level of Heads of States and Governments. (2015). *Report of the Chairperson of the Commission on Regional and International Efforts to Combat the Boko Haram Terrorist Group and the Way Forward*. Addis Ababa, Ethiopia. 29 January.

Tar, U. A., & Bala, B. (2018a). Boko Haram insurgency, terrorism and the challenges of peacebuilding in the Lake Chad Basin. In K.C. Omeje (Ed.), *Peacebuilding in contemporary Africa: In search of alternative strategies*. London: Routledge.

Tar, U. A., & Bala, B. (2019b). Terrorism, insurgency and the challenges of counter-terrorism and counter-insurgency. In U. A. Tar & B. Bala (Eds.), *New architecture for regional security in Africa: Perspectives on counter-terrorism and counter-insurgency in the Lake Chad Basin*. Lanham, MD: Lexington Books.

Tar, U. A., & Mustapha, M. (2016). Emerging architecture of regional security complex in the Lake Chad Basin. Being a paper presented at *the International Conference on Security Regimens in Africa organised by CODESERIA*, held at Azalai Grand Hotel, Bamako, Mali, 28 – 29 September.

Ugorji, B. (2017). *Indigenous People of Biafra (IPOB): A revitalized social movement in Nigeria*. International Center for Ethno-Religious, New York Mediation. Retrieved 2 November 2017 fromhttps://www.icermediation.org/publications/indigenous-people-of-biafra-ipob-a-revitalized-social-movement-in-nigeria/.

Umara, I. (2014a). *National interest and foreign policy options for Nigeria in the Central African Sub-region*. Kaduna: Joyce Publishers.

Umara, I. (2014b). *Study of the activities of civilian joint task force in Maiduguri Metropolitan Council and Jere Local Government Areas, Borno state*. NSRP. British Council, Abuja-Nigeria in collaboration with the CPDDS. Nigeria: University of Maiduguri.

Uzodinma, E. (13 September 2018). MASSOB reacts to IPOB's sit-at-home order, speaks on relationship with group. *Dailypost Newspaper*.http://dailypost.ng/2018/09/13/massob-reacts-ipobs-sit-home-order-speaks-relationship-group/. Accessed on 13.01.19.

# Part IV

# National perspectives

# 26

# The state and the fight against Boko Haram insurgency in Nigeria

*Kyari Mohammed*

## Introduction

Nigeria is Africa's most populous country with an estimated 190 million people of diverse ethnic, religious, cultural, and regional groupings. These fault lines have shaped its politics and inhibited national cohesion. The management of this diversity has been a cardinal policy of successive governments since independence from British colonial rule in 1960. This was pursued through affirmative action legislation such as federal character and quota system to engineer inclusiveness and balanced development. This policy has ensured that the country remained one undivided entity, with stresses and strains often leading to violent conflicts between and among its diverse groups. Nigeria has been gripped by a debilitating conflict which has questioned the state's capacity since 2009. A group of religious zealots known to history as Boko Haram (Hausa: Western education is forbidden) but which prefers to go by the name of Jama'atu Ahlis Sunna Liddawa'ati wal Jihad (People committed to the Prophet's teaching and Jihad) have been primarily responsible for the conflagration that engulfed the north-eastern corner of Nigeria and gradually spread to other parts and its near neighbours of Niger, Chad and Cameroon by 2014.

The insurgency attributed to Boko Haram and the counterinsurgency operations adopted by Nigerian security agencies has led to thousands of deaths, about two million people internally displaced, about 200, 000 refugees and the economic devastation of an otherwise food-rich region of the country, which is now facing massive humanitarian disaster (Reliefweb, 2017). An estimated 7.7 million people need humanitarian assistance in the three severely affected states of Adamawa, Borno and Yobe. Of these, 3.9 million people were very vulnerable to food insecurity (Reliefweb, 2018; Care, 2018). The Boko Haram insurgency is reckoned to be one of Nigeria's most deadly and brutal conflicts often compared to the fratricidal civil war of 1967–1970, but even more challenging to manage. Boko Haram adherents are fanatically committed to their beliefs, and the group has continuously changed its strategies and tactics, including a resort to asymmetrical warfare as its modus operandi. Relations between the state and Boko Haram has been characterised by conflict from the beginning, driven and sustained by violence, and had escalated primarily due to reciprocal state violence. This ensured that Boko Haram became one of the most violent insurgencies in the world in 2014.

The Boko Haram insurgency is one in a series of state threatening conflicts which are eroding the legitimacy and authority of the Nigerian state. The primary responsibility of the state, according to Nigeria's current constitution, is the protection of lives and property (FGN, 1999); and the insurgents ensured that the state was unable to do either in some parts of its territory for several months between 2013 and 2014. By mid-2014 Boko Haram had laid claims to large swathes of territory in parts of Borno, Yobe, and Adamawa states declared itself a "caliphate". They offered allegiance to the Islamic State of Syria and Levant (ISIS/ISIL). These symbolic acts and the abduction of 276 female students in their school in Chibok in April 2014, the cold-blooded killing of 42 school children at Mamudo and 59 at Buni Yadi in 2013 and 2014 respectively, the escalating violence on combatants and non-combatants alike, and the wholesale ravaging of communities, had seriously called to question the capacity of the Nigerian state. The state had responded to the insurgent's violence with excessive force thus eliciting accusations of human rights abuse, extra-judicial-judicial killings, dragnet arrests, and detention without trial, further fuelling the insurgency and alienating the military from the populace in the theatre of operations (Amnesty International, 2012, 2015, Human Rights Watch, 2012).

The Nigerian state is a behemoth affecting all aspects of the lives of the people. Yet, it has failed woefully to meet their expectations and be a neutral arbiter in disputes between different sections and classes in society. It has dominated all facets of life at all tiers of government in the country, from production to distribution, from education to health and social services, from governance to religion. Central to the relationship between the state and the people is the character of the state. The Nigerian state has been characterised as neo-colonial, prebendal, and sometimes even predatory (Joseph, 1983, 2013; Osaghae 2015, Abdullahi 2018, Abubakar 2016, Adeniyi 2011). The defining element of this prebendalism is the parasitism of the ruling class who plunder the commonwealth. Several decades of military rule, endemic corruption, and since 1999, a civilian crop of politicians who act like military despots has blurred the relationship between the public and private, undermined the legitimacy of the state and led to the personalisation of the public domain for private interests. The citizenry was for long alienated from the state forcing some sections of it to either completely avoids the state or engage it in antipathy. This de-link between the post-colonial state and the people had generated conflicts, excavated existing ones, and re-ignited dormant ones with horrendous consequences for development, national cohesion and stunted the country's march to greatness. The Boko Haram insurgency, militancy in the Niger Delta, rural banditry and farmer-herder clashes across central and north-western Nigeria, increasing cases of armed conflicts, kidnappings for ransom, cattle rustling, are some of the conflicts chipping away at the capacity and legitimacy of the state. Boko Haram is morbidly anti-state, anti-secularism, anti-democracy, anti-modernity and anti-education, and the modern Nigerian state symbolises everything they despise. This antipathy towards the state and professed desire to overthrow it and enthrone an Islamic system based on the Shari'a has pitched the Boko Haram in perpetual conflict against the state. The rejection of secularism and a commitment to Shari'a, indicates what one scholar describes as the group's "will to power" (Anon, 2012) or adherence to politics (Perouse de Montclos, 2014b). The Nigerian state, on the other hand, was not willing to concede its authority to any non-state armed group much less one who aspires to overthrow it and enthrone an Islamic theocratic state at variance with its professed claims of secularism, liberal democracy, and unified management of its ethnic, religious and cultural diversity to build a modern nation-state. These irreconcilable differences between the two conflicting groups did not leave much room for peaceful resolution of the conflict.

This chapter aims to account for the state's response to the challenge posed by Boko Haram. How did the state view and respond to the Boko Haram insurgency? What are the successes and failures of this response? What lessons can be learnt from the insurgency? These are some of the issues this chapter intends to address. The chapter is divided into three parts. The first part briefly introduces Boko Haram to set the tone for our discussion. The second part outlines the various methods adopted by the Nigerian state to apprehend the insurgency. The third part concludes by outlining the lessons to be learnt from the insurgency and the state's counter efforts by way of a conclusion.

## The Boko Haram insurgency

Boko Haram is one of the most misunderstood groups in the recent history of Nigeria. This has led to its multiple characterisations in religious, ideological, and political terms as "sect," "ji-hadi," "Islamist," "movement," "insurgency," "terrorist," etc. This inability to clearly define the sectsect, much less understand it, has equally affected the state's response, which comes out as uncoordinated, conflicting, and often counterproductive.

Boko Haram began as a tiny fringe group within Islam in north-eastern Nigeria in 2003 whose adherents emigrated out of urban centres to found a commune in rural Kanamma where they attempted to practice their faith without being corrupted by what they see as the sleaze and filth of the wider society. Emigration out of hostile territory in defence of one's faith is an accepted prophetic tradition in Islam, and it has been standard practice in pre-colonial northern Nigeria (Last, 2014). The Kanamma years turned out to be a dress rehearsal for the events of July 2009, as the group metamorphosed from a tiny band of rancorous preachers to a violent jihadi movement capable of holding territory and engaging the Nigerian military in open battles. The recent history of the group has been rendered fairly accurately in Higazi (2013), Mohammed (2014, 9–32; forthcoming), Perouse de Montclos (2014a), Mustapha (2014, 147–198), and Thurston (2018), and therefore need not detain us here. Under intense crackdown from the security agencies, Boko Haram evolved, adapted, and remodelled itself into a notorious jihadi movement driven. By local grievances but with aspirations to global fame. The group gained this notoriety following the bombing of United Nations offices and police headquarters in Abuja in 2012, and the abduction of Chibok schoolgirls in 2014.

Boko Haram initially began as a tendency within Salafi Islam. It worked closely with the *Jama'atu Izalatul Bidia wa Ikamatis Sunnah* (Society for the Removal of Heretical Innovation and the Establishment of the Prophet's Model) before their differences became irreconcilable and the two became arch enemies by 2008. This dispute took on a very violent character in Borno state where each group accused the other of apostasy and justified their extermination (Mohammed 2014, 18–19). This animosity was less pronounced in other parts of the country where Boko Haram presence was not large. Having failed to gain firm footing within local communities and under sustained pressure from the military Boko Haram looked outwards to international jihadi networks for support. This led to a declaration of "caliphate" around Gwoza and allegiance to ISIS/ISIL in 2014. This, however, did not markedly improve their fortunes as they continued to lose territory earlier held and suffer defeat in the hands of Nigerian and regional security forces. By December 2016, the Nigerian state had declared the group defeated, but it still can attack soft targets and render several parts of the northeast ungovernable. Many citizens remained displaced, most of them moving into urban centres where there was some semblance of security, and thereby putting pressure on limited urban infrastructure and leaving farmlands fallow. This undoubtedly contributed to the food insecurity that characterised liberated areas.

Boko Haram has been responsible for killing thousands of unarmed civilians, security personnel, kidnappings, and abductions, forced enslavement, forcible conscription of young boys, and mass displacement of peoples in their areas of operation. The group's cruelty and human rights abuses had elicited international opprobrium and condemnation leading to their activities been termed as war crimes (Dakas, 2014:23). Boko Haram atrocities and the military reaction have created a cycle of violence which had escalated and sustained the conflict with grievous consequences. The insurgency attracted state counterinsurgency violence, both of which increased the scale, scope, gravity, and intensity of the war. The conflict took a life of its own, thereby making non-military conclusion challenging to achieve.

## Counter insurgency operations

The Nigerian state is not new to dealing with violent conflicts laying claim to religion, especially Islam. The Maitatsine uprising affected several communities between 1980 and 1985 before it was finally crushed (Lubeck, 1985). Though Boko Haram and Maitatsine are similar in many respects, the latter differs on account of its ability to adapt and change its strategy and tactics when confronted by the state's coercive force. The counterinsurgency strategy adopted by the Nigerian state has been the use of military force to overwhelm and suppress the opponent and contain the insurgency. This had worked against the Maitatsine but was not remarkably successful against Boko Haram. Maximum use of force escalated the conflict, radicalised, and mobilised passive members of the group and threw up new grievances that sustained the conflict. At onset in July 2009, President Umaru Musa Yar'Adua (2007–2010) had directed the military to "deal squarely and promptly" with Boko Haram (Adewumi, 2014:7). This presidential directive was interpreted to dismantle the group's command and control structure at the sect's headquarters, Markaz Ibn Taymiyyah (Ibn Taymiyyah Centre), extra-judicially kill its leadership even while in captivity and disperse its members.

To strengthen this strategy of containment President Goodluck Jonathan declared a state of emergency on some 15 local government areas of Borno, Yobe and Plateau states in December 2011, renewed same and extended its coverage in May 2013. This second round of state of emergency was because the insurgents had waxed stronger, laid claims to some portions of Nigeria's territory, and questioned the country's sovereignty. In his address to the nation declaring the emergency, President Jonathan said (As cited by Adewumi, 2014:7):

> Already, some northern parts of Borno have been taken over by groups whose allegiance is to different flags and ideologies... In many parts they have destroyed the Nigerian flag and other symbols of state authority and in their place hoisted strange flags suggesting the exercise of alternative sovereignty ... These actions amount to a declaration of war and a deliberate attempt to undermine the authority of the Nigerian state and threaten her territorial integrity. As a responsible government, we will not tolerate this.

The state of emergency led to a change in strategy: the Joint Task Force, comprising of different services of the military, police, secret service, customs and immigration and a plethora of other security agencies, was disbanded and in its place, the Seventh Division of the Nigerian Army was established at Maiduguri. More troops were deployed into combat operations, and legal encumbrances against arbitrary arrests, detentions, and invasion of homes were relaxed. The emergency led to increased human rights abuses and further loss of hearts and mind by the military with insidious consequences for the counterinsurgency operations. President Jonathan's nonchalance or tacit approval of the military's excesses emboldened the military but estranged the local populace.

Two Nigerian Presidents, Umaru Yar'Adua in whose tenure the current phase of violence began, and his successor Goodluck Jonathan under whose watch Boko Haram became a real threat to the Nigerian state, both ordered military crackdown on Boko Haram. This was both an underestimation of the insurgents' capacity and an overestimation of the capacity of the Nigerian military which basked in its glorious past but was clearly unprepared for the new kind of war thrust upon it by the insurgents. The military was plagued by several self-inflicted ills arising from long years of incursion into politics which had affected its professionalism, debilitating corruption resulting in poor troop morale and obsolete equipment, and inadequate training for asymmetric warfare. These ensured that the military struggled in the war with Boko Haram. The insurgency was, therefore, a first both at the legal and military levels. The state responded expectedly with massive force, in the process wreaking untold hardships on the local communities by its inability to distinguish Boko Haram from civilians. Faced with incessant attacks by Boko Haram who had taken refuge among civilians in populated areas, the military responded by the collective punishment of such communities, thereby alienating the local populace, and hampering the counterinsurgency operations. This led to the relentless calls for troop withdrawal by local community-based organisations and stakeholders such as the Borno Elders and Leaders of Thought, the local Borno branch of the Nigerian Bar Association, and the numerous documented works of Amnesty International and Human Rights Watch, among others (Mohammed, 2014, 25–28; AI 2012, 2015; HRW 2012).

The fight against Boko Haram was securitised by the state. There was no coordinated response other than deployment of brute force. The operation was led and dictated by the military, with the support of other security services such as the police and state security services. Even this was uncoordinated as it led to difficulty in coordination, inter-service rivalry, and haphazard response with poor results. As it was military-led, it took on the form of military "operations" starting with "Operation Restore Order I and II," "Operation Boyona," "Operation Zaman Lafiya," "Operation Lafiya Dole," "Operation Deep Punch I and II," etc. All counterinsurgency operations involved military force which is a necessary and vital component, but not a sufficient condition for defeating the insurgency. Successful counterinsurgency measures must include identifying and dealing with the root causes of the conflict and addressing these comprehensively. The military component is both the strength as well as weakness of the counterinsurgency operations. These security measures, according to Mustapha (2014:152), forced a change of tactics by Boko Haram but "hardly made a dent on the level of violence."

As mentioned earlier, the military had struggled against Boko Haram between 2009 and 2014; however, by the beginning of 2015, a reinvigorated military under new command had started to reverse the gains made by the insurgents. By December 2016, the military had declared a premature victory against Boko Haram. Undoubtedly, the capacity of Boko Haram as an organised fighting force has been degraded but it still has enough capacity to attack vulnerable soft targets, deploy suicide bombers, kidnap a large number of schoolgirls as happened in Dapchi in February 2018.

The Nigerian military suffered casualties in the hands of Boko Haram, but their heavy-handed response had attracted local and global condemnation. The state's human rights abuses dogged the fight against insurgency from the onset, and these continued unabated. First, there was the celebrated extra-judicial killing of Boko Haram leaders, Mohammed Yusuf, Buji Fwoi and Mohammed Yusuf's father-in-law, Baba Fugu Mohammed, and several suspected members of the sect in police captivity in July and August 2009. These killings became one of the major grievances as well as a rallying point for the group, as it used it to mobilise dormant members and seek local support. Other grievances include the destruction of their headquarters and mosque, the *Markaz Ibn Taymiyyah* in Maiduguri, illegal detention of their members including women and children, who were held in place of their fugitive husbands and parents, freedom to practice their faith as they deem fit, etc.

Second, even though the rights abuses mentioned above had continued unabated, it progressively got worse as Boko Haram became more violent following the Bauchi prison break of 7 September 2010. The state responded by massive troop build-up and declaration of a state of emergency in 2012. This state of emergency removed some of the legal impediments that constrained the security agencies, but this had the effect of increasing human rights abuses. The main concerns raised by local and foreign observers regarding human rights abuses include extra-judicial killings, collective punishment of communities for the infractions of a few, dragnet arrests, illegal detention without trial, inhumane treatment of prisoners, and starvation of detainees, etc. (Mohammed, 2014, 25–28; AI 2012, 2015; HRW 2012). The state continuously denied these accusations even where it had said it was investigating some officers and men over these allegations. Following incessant criticisms, the military has established Human Rights Desk to investigate allegations of rights abuses against its forces, strengthen the army's capacity to protect human rights, and report annually on progress (NA 2016).

Third, the allegations and counter-allegations of rights abuses created a severe diplomatic problem for Nigeria as several European governments and the United States used that as a pretext to deny them access to direly needed military equipment and supplies thus blunting its capacity to fight the insurgency effectively. The USA for example not only invoked the Leahy Law to deny Nigeria access to its arms market but blocked Israel and Brazil from selling military attack helicopters in 2015 (Pileggi, 2015; Soriwei, 2016). The Leahy Law prevents the US defence sector from aiding countries adjudged to be engaged in rights abuses. This US blockade compelled the state to seek to acquire military equipment in the black market in Ukraine and South Africa. This caused the country some diplomatic blunders following the detention of a Nigerian registered plane that smuggled fifteen million US dollars into South Africa. The Nigerian government later laid claim to the money (Tukur, 2015). The issue of human rights abuse continues unabated, and it still dogs the fight against insurgency. For all the efforts of a new Chief of Army Staff, Lieutenant General Tukur Yusuf Buratai, who has taken it upon himself to professionalise the army, this aspect continues to be a blight in the performance of the armed forces.

By 2014, insecurity in general and the Boko Haram insurgency, in particular, had become a major campaign agenda of the main opposition candidate, Muhammadu Buhari of the All Progressive Congress (APC), in the upcoming presidential election. This had portrayed serving President Jonathan of the ruling People's Democratic Party (PDP), who was also on the ballot, as a weakling who was unwilling or incapable of defeating the insurgents – this stereotype of the sitting president contrasts sharply with that of Muhammadu Buhari, a retired army general with a reputation for commanding daring military campaigns when he was in service. A coalition of civil society activists organised under the hashtag "#Bring Back Our Girls" was also putting massive pressure on the state to rescue the Chibok girls, and the government was clearly struggling in the counterinsurgency operations. These factors and the refusal of some foreign countries to sell arms to the country, following its poor human rights record in counterinsurgency operations and President Jonathan's desperate attempts to end the insurgency in the run-up to 2015 elections led the state to seek the services of a firm of mercenaries with the name, Specialised Tasks, Training, Equipment, and Protection (STTEP). Made up of former apartheid South African soldiers, they helped the military in degrading Boko Haram but not crushing it (Murphy, 2015). The Buhari administration did not continue with the services of the mercenaries.

Fourth, by March 2013 the state had reached the conclusion that it required more than brute force alone to defeat the Boko Haram insurgency and restore normalcy. Thus, the Office of the National Security Adviser rolled out what it termed the soft options in countering violent extremism leading to terrorism. Aimed at Boko Haram detainees in prison and breaching the divide between government and communities, this programme included de-radicalisation, counter-radicalisation, and strategic communication (Dasuki, 2014). This programme, though promising, was discontinued following the defeat of Goodluck Jonathan in 2015. This is because the coordinating agency, Office of the National Security Adviser, was embroiled in allegations of theft and grand larceny as funds meant for prosecution of the counterinsurgency operations were alleged to have been diverted to fund the presidential campaign of the former president. The former National Security Adviser Sambo, Sambo Dasuki is still being prosecuted over these allegations. However, the state did not completely jettison the idea as part of its strategy has fed into the "Operation Safe Corridor" (OSC) which is handled by the Chief of Defence Staff.

The "Operation Safe Corridor" was aimed at rehabilitating and reintegrating repentant Boko Haram militants back into their communities after twelve weeks of deradicalisation and vocational training in a secure facility in Gombe. If it succeeds, it may encourage insurgents still in the trenches to surrender and accept the olive branch. The OSC has since graduated its first batch of 95 out of 254 graduates including 20 minors (Leman, 2018). However, the programme has had limited success and drawn a lot of criticisms. First, the emphasis on ex-insurgents at the detriment of victims does not seem to go down well with the communities that are expected to receive the deradicalised. This was a major concern voiced by stakeholders at a meeting convened by the Abuja based Centre for Democracy and Development at Maiduguri, to sensitise affected communities on the importance of the Operation Safe Corridor, in July 2016 (CDD, 2016). This concern was re-echoed at another stakeholder meeting convened by the Modibbo Adama University of Technology Yola in April 2018. Communities' perception that ex-insurgents are favoured over victims and survivors to need to be handled with utmost caution. Second, stakeholders believe it is too early to start reintegrating ex-insurgents as the conflict is still ongoing, they suggested a "ten-year window before defecting members can be reintegrated into local communities" (CDD, 2016, 2). Reintegration is an especially vital component of DDR, however, for this to succeed the communities must be taken along.

An international dimension of the state's counterinsurgency effort is the resuscitation of the regional military alliance Multi-National Joint Task Force (MNJTF) under the auspices of the Lake Chad Basin Commission (LCBC). The Boko Haram threat had become transnational and regional involving all of Nigeria's neighbours to the northeast by 2014. This compelled Niger, Chad, and Cameroon to join the counterinsurgency operations following a little persuasion by the French President Francoise Hollande in March 2014. Thereafter the MNJTF was revamped for deployment into the CT-COIN operations. Established in 1998 to check cross border banditry in their common but porous frontier region, the MNJTF was now deployed to counter the Boko Haram menace. The effective closure of the borders, the involvement of multinational troops in fighting in Nigerian soil, and Nigerian pressure on the insurgents in the Sambisa forest have helped to degrade the insurgency. The MNJTF approach to counterinsurgency operations is similar to the one adopted by individual countries.

Another component of the CT-COIN strategy was the involvement of non-state security actors such as the Civilian Joint Task Force (C-JTF) in Borno and the Hunters Association of Adamawa. The C-JTF was established in June 2013 and structured along military lines with "sectors" led by sector commanders under the direct supervision of local military commanders. This group of young boys and girls was instrumental in ejecting Boko Haram out of its urban bases into the rural areas in mid-2013. Military engagement in the urban areas had caused the military massive loss of support as they brutalised the local inhabitants following Boko Haram attacks since they could not identify the insurgents. Initially made up of repentant Boko Haram members but increasingly drawing many volunteers, the C-JTF provided much needed local human intelligence (HUMINT), an area in which the military lagged Boko Haram. The C-JTF helped to identify and track down insurgents for capture, occasionally fought alongside the military and often took casualties. They provided a much-needed breakthrough for the COIN operations. The strategic importance of this development led an elated President Jonathan to single them out for praise as "new national heroes" (Idris and Sawab, 2013).

In Adamawa state, local hunters joined the counterinsurgency efforts following Boko Haram's occupation of Mubi and sacking of several communities of the state in late 2014. The hunters' knowledge of the local terrain including the nooks and crannies of the forests where Boko Haram had taken refuge, and their ability to identify Boko Haram members in their communities, was of immense help to the military. They often served as trackers and guides but occasionally directly got involved in the fighting. Untrained in modern warfare, wielding outdated weapons but yet eager to get involved in the fight, they had taken heavy casualties including the death of Bukar Jimeta, their fearless and charismatic commander in August 2017 (Anwar, 2017). Among the hunters are young women including Aisha Bakari Gombi who has become their public face, and Hamsatu Hassan (Collyer, 2017). These young women are at the forefront of the fight against insurgency in Adamawa state. These non-state security actors involved in the CT-COIN operations are good examples of community response and successful community policing approach to countering the insurgency.

The downside of the CT-COIN was the excessive force deployed by the military, and to a lesser extent, by the C-JTF. The military according to local and international observers was responsible for massive human rights abuses. According to Amnesty International (2012, 2015), the military is responsible for war crimes including the extra-judicial-judicial killing of 1,200 people; the arrest and detention of 20,000 others; and the consequent death in captivity of 7,000 detainees as a result of torture, "starvation, extreme overcrowding, denial of medical assistance" (AI 2015). The military has consistently denied all accusations labelled against it without success (Ibekwe, 2017). As mentioned earlier, the constant criticism of military excesses and non-observance of its rules of engagement had compelled it to create a Human Rights Desk aimed at strengthening the military's compliance to international standards of human rights, observance of its rules of engagement, and addressing the concerns of citizens in conflict areas (NA 2016, Reliefweb, 2016).

The C-JTF has also engaged in numerous cases of human rights abuses under the close supervision of the military. In some instances, the group has even surpassed the military in its brutality against suspected Boko Haram foot soldiers or their alleged collaborators. However, they did not commit the large-scale indiscriminate attacks on civilian communities for which the military became infamous.

Military CT-COIN has succeeded in substantially degrading the capacity of Boko Haram to launch the mega attacks of 2011 to 2014 when it took the fight to the military including sacking their barracks in Monguno, Baga and Gwoza or chasing them across the border into Cameroon and Niger. They have also succeeded in reclaiming territory earlier lost to the insurgents; however, the insurgents have not been completely defeated as claimed. A complete cessation of conflict leading to the return of normalcy will require more than brute force.

## Prospects of the non-military options in the fight against insurgency

The management of the Boko Haram insurgency was left to the military. This ensured that there was little attempt to use persuasion or dialogue in countering it. Boko Haram itself did not show any enthusiasm towards a peaceful resolution of the conflict. The military leadership of the counterinsurgency operations coupled with the emergence of the hawkish Abubakar Shekau to the leadership of the group ensured the continuation of the conflict as each side stuck to its hardened position. The onus of seeking for non-military solution lay with the state. The complexity of the crisis meant there were other factors that militated against dialogue and non-military solution.

First, the state's understanding of what the insurgency represented was at best shallow. It was beclouded by sectional or partisan considerations and steeped in conspiracy theories. As the state dithered and vacillated, the Boko Haram waxed stronger and became even more violent under the watch of President Jonathan, who had come to power following an acrimonious succession dispute within his party following the death of President Umaru Yar'Adua in May 2010 (Adeniyi, 2011; Abdullahi, 2018). As his contest for the presidency was vehemently opposed by several northern politicians within his political party, arguing that it breached an agreed power rotation arrangement between the north and south of the country and that they will make the country ungovernable should he succeed. Therefore, newly elected President Jonathan, who had emerged victorious in spite of those northern politicians' opposition to his candidature, viewed Boko Haram as his opponents making real their threat to make the country "un-governable" (Abdullahi, 2018, 144). This perception of Boko Haram as a political ploy affected the Federal Government's approach to the insurgency as well as shaped the opinion of residents of communities devastated by the insurgency. Just like the Jonathan administration, the affected communities believed the government was deliberately reluctant in fighting the insurgency, and deploying the military to torture and abuse them, because of their support for opposition candidate Muhammadu Buhari since 2003 (Author's Interview with elders statesmen Ambassador Gaji Galtimari and Bulama Mali Gubio, 2014). This lack of understanding of the dynamics of the insurgency made President Jonathan vacillate on how to deal with the insurgency (Mustapha, 2014, 159). Conspiracy theories continued to thrive and every attempt at apprehending the insurgency was viewed with tinted lenses, thereby politicising, and further complicating an already complex crisis (see Mustapha, 2014:159ff).

By April 2013, the Federal Government had decided to explore other means of dealing with the insurgency. This led to the constitution of a "Committee on Dialogue and Peaceful Resolution of Security Challenges in the North" headed by the Minister of Special Duties, Kabiru Tanimu Turaki. The Turaki Committee was charged with the responsibility of developing a framework for the granting of amnesty, disarmament of combatants, development of a "Victim Support Programme", and suggesting mechanisms for addressing the root causes of the insurgency (Abdullahi, 2018, 178). The Turaki Committee led to the establishment of another committee on a continuous dialogue with the insurgents. All efforts at dialogue were thwarted by the seeming unwillingness of Shekau to negotiate, bogus claims of impostors hoping to fleece the government posing as Boko Haram representatives, the fractious splintering of the insurgents, and the change of government in Nigeria.

There were various attempts at dialoguing with Boko Haram at both state and national levels, but the Turaki Committee was the most high-powered. Before then, there was the Galtimari Committee I and II set up by the Borno state and Federal Government in 2009 and 2012, respectively. There were the Datti Ahmad and Shaykh Dahiru Bauchi committees - both of which attempted to dialogue with Boko Haram to no avail. The reports of the Galtimari and

Turaki committees were not given the seriousness they deserved by the government. Incidentally, Boko Haram did not show any eagerness to embrace the government's dialogue or amnesty carrot either. An indecisive government and a truculent insurgent leader ensured the continuity of military conflict despite attempts at mediation.

While both sides seemed bent on holding onto their hardened positions, the abduction of over 200 schoolgirls at a secondary school in Chibok in April 2014 was to force the two sides to engage a little more seriously. The Chibok incident brought global notoriety and infamy to Boko Haram and put tremendous pressure on the government to find and rescue the girls. The urgency to rescue the girls compelled the two warring sides to talk leading to the release of some of the girls in two batches. Even though the government has denied that ransom was paid nor was prisoners released, it was believed that both took place. A similar incident in Dapchi also led to a negotiated settlement in which Boko Haram could return the girls back to where they were snatched in February 2018. The Dapchi settlement was with the Al-Barnawi and not the Shekau faction. This shows the former faction as more amenable to a negotiated settlement. Clearly the state and Boko Haram had been dialoguing with the assistance of some inter-mediaries, but this has not led to a more comprehensive peace.

The dividing line between terrorism and insurgency is very thin, and under the laws, both are treated as terrorism. Terrorism is a serious criminal offence globally even though what constitutes terrorism is subject to different interpretations. Nigeria had no laws specifically dealing with terrorism until the enactment of the Terrorism Prevention Act in 2011 (hence on TPA) which was amended in 2013. Prior to this period, all activities deemed terroristic were tried under the extant laws: the criminal and penal codes in southern and northern Nigeria respectively (Dakas, 2014:20). The TPA defines what amounts to terrorism and prescribes the death penalty for committing the offence.

The TPA, according to Nigeria's chief law officer, Abubakar Malami will still be amended to "expand the definition of terrorism and create additional sanctions for terrorists and their financiers" (Adesomoju, 2018). The legal framework for dealing with insurgency and terrorism is still a work in progress. Thus, the initial response to the Boko Haram insurgency was primarily the use of military force which turned out to be insufficient and counterproductive quite early in the counterinsurgency operations. Without a legal framework, and the police too indolent to engage in diligent prosecution of many cases before the courts, state officials resorted to extra-judicial-judicial measures. This tarnished the image of the nation abroad and caused it heavily in reputation.

## Concluding remarks

The Boko Haram insurgency with its terrorist tactics and the CT-COIN measures adopted by the Nigerian military were both new. The military had not been confronted by Boko Haram style insurgency and the legal system had not encountered terrorism. It was a first for the Nigerian state at both military and legal angles. Therefore, the Boko Haram insurgency was a first for the Nigerian state and thus the state initially groped in all fronts to address it. The insurgency and the counterinsurgency operations led to massive loss of lives, human rights abuses, and torture, and in the opinion of rights activists, both may have committed war crimes. The Nigerian state securitised the insurgency and prioritised military force over non-military options in responding to the crisis. This prolonged the conflict and made its resolution difficult. For Nigeria to solve its Boko Haram problem, it must adopt a combination of both force and persuasion.

The Boko Haram insurgency and the state's response have exposed the weakness of the Nigerian state in security provisioning, governance, and management of insecurity. This insurgency shows that the state has no functional security architecture to respond to complex insurgencies such as Boko Haram. It groped and dithered allowing the insurgents to take the initiative, grow and become a threat to national and regional security.

The politicisation of the Boko Haram insurgency along religious, ethnic, regional, and partisan lines blocked the political leaders from reaching national consensus and responding patriotically to the insurgency. The insurgency was variously presented as a northern conspiracy against a southern president, or Muslim attempts to derail a Christian president, or Christian conspiracy to destabilise Muslin north, etc. These conspiracy theories were given a fillip by partisan leaders desperate for political power. The Nigerian state should attempt to study and understand the Boko Haram insurgency for what it is, a state threatening insurgency aimed at destabilising the Nigerian state that requires national efforts at containment. The Nigerian state must comprehend the insurgency to apprehend it. This should serve as a road map on how to manage a future crisis.

Military efforts are cardinal to the counterinsurgency efforts, but it requires a multi-dimensional approach to defeat the insurgency. These efforts must include a whole of society efforts aimed to address the root causes of the conflict, building and strengthening governance institutions at all levels but especially at the community level, resettling displaced persons, re-integrating former insurgents, developing peace-building mechanisms and rebuilding ravaged communities. All efforts at rebuilding the communities should be bottom-up rather than we know it all top-down approach preferred by governments in Nigeria.

The Nigerian military should intensify efforts at its hearts and minds campaign by observing its rules of engagement, addressing issues of rights abuses, reduce collateral damage and engage the communities in order to win them over to its side and isolate the insurgents. No military can fight asymmetrical warfare successfully without the support of the populace. The successes so far achieved by working with the C-JTF and local hunters should be consolidated as part of breaching the wide gap between state and society in the counterinsurgency efforts.

## References

Abdullahi, B. (2018). *On a platter of gold: How Jonathan won and lost Nigeria*. Lagos: Kachifo.

Abubakar, R. (2016, April 5). *DHQ establishes camp for repentant Boko Haram members* [Press Release Nigeria].Retrieved from https://prnigeria.com/2016/04/05/dhq-establishes-camp-repentant-boko-haram-members/ Accessed 13.04.18.

Adeniyi, O. (2011). *Power, politics and death: A front row account of Nigeria under the late President Yar'Adua*. Lagos: Kachifo.

Adesomoju, A. (2018). *AGF seeks stiffer sanctions against terrorists, financiers in new bill. Punch newspaper, Lagos*. 10 April. http://punchng.com/agf-seeks-stiffer-sanctions-against-terrorists-financiers-in-new-bill/ Accessed 13.04.18.

Adewumi, A. A. (2014). The battle for the minds: The insurgency and counter-insurgency in Northern Nigeria. *West Africa Insight*, 4( 2), 3–11.

Amnesty International. (2012). *Nigeria: Trapped in a cycle of violence*. London: Amnesty International. https://www.amnesty.org/en/documents/AFR44/043/2012/en/ Accessed September 2017.

Amnesty International. (2015). *Stars on their shoulders, blood on their hands: War crimes committed by the Nigerian military*. London: Amnesty International. http://www.amnesty.org/download/ Accessed 10.04.18.

Anon. (2012). The popular discourses of Salafi radicalism and Salafi counter-radicalism in Nigeria: A case study of Boko Haram. *Journal of Religion in Africa*, 42, 118–144.

Author's Interview with elders statesmen Ambassador Gaji Galtimari and Bulama Mali Gubio held at Maiduguri on 14 June 2014.

Anwar, K. (2017). Boko Haram vs Hunters: Inside Adamawa's other war. *Daily Trust*. 9 August. https://www.dailytrust.com.ng/news/general/boko-haram-vs-hunters-inside-adamawa-s-other-war/210667.html. Accessed 05.05.18.

Care. (2018). *Humanitarian crisis in Nigeria and the Lake Chad Basin*. https://www.care.org/emergencies/global-hunger-crisis/humanitarian-crisis-nigeria-and-lake-chad-basin. Accessed 14.04.18.

CDD. (2016). *Policy brief: Stakeholders' dialogue on government approaches to managing defecting violent extremists*. Abuja: Centre for Democracy and Development, nd. C. 2016.

Collyer, R. (2017). Meet Aisha, a former antelope hunter who now tracks Boko Haram . *The Guardian*. 8 February. https://www.theguardian.com/world/2017/feb/08/antelope-hunter-boko-haram-nigeria. Accessed 05.05.18.

Dakas, C. J. Dakas. (2014). Interrogating Nigeria's counter terrorism strategy through the prism of law and human rights. *West Africa Insight*, 4( 2), 20–24.

Dasuki, S. (2014). Sambo Dasuki: Nigeria's soft approach to countering terrorism: Being a presentation by Sambo Dasuki, National Security Adviser on 18th March 2014 on the roll out of Nigeria's soft approach to countering terrorism held at Abuja, Nigeria. http://dailypost.ng/2014/03/19/sambo-dasuki-nigerias-soft-approach-countering-terrorism/ Accessed 14.04.18.

FGN. (1999). *Constitution of the Federal Republic of Nigeria*. http://www.wipo.int/edocs/lexdocs/laws/en/ng/ng014en.pdf. Accessed 26.04.18.

Higazi, A. (2013). Les Origins et la Transformation de l'Insurrection de Boko Haram dans le Nord Nigeria. *Politique Africaine*, 130, 137–164.

Human Rights Watch. (2012). *Spiraling violence: Boko Haram attacks and security force abuses in Nigeria*. Chicago: Human Rights Watch. https://www.hrw.org/report/2012/10/11/spiraling-violence/boko-haram-attacks-and-security-force-abuses-nigeria. Accessed 13.04.18.

Ibekwe, N. (2017). *Nigerian military accuses Amnesty International of fabricating report of extra judicial killings, torture*. Premium Times. 22 February. https://www.premiumtimesng.com/news/headlines/224261-nigerian-military-accuses-amnesty-international-of-fabricating-report-extrajudicial-killings-torture.html. Accessed 11.04.18.

Idris, H. & Sawab, I. (2013). *Hopes turn to despair over 'Civilian JTF' weekly trust*. 29 June. https://www.dailytrust.com.ng/weekly/index.php/new-news/13113-hopes-turn-to-fears-over-civilian-jtf. Accessed 13.04.18.

Joseph, R. (1983). Class, state and prebendal politics in Nigeria. *Journal of Commonwealth and Comparative Politics*, 21(3), 21–38.

Joseph, R. (2013). *Prebendalism and dysfunctionality in Nigeria*. Africa Plus, July 26. Available: https://africaplus.wordpress.com/2013/07/26/prebendalism-and-dysfunctionality-in-nigeria/, Accessed 13.04.18.

Last, M. (2014). From dissent to dissidence: The genesis and development of reformist Islamic groups in Northern Nigeria. In A.R. Mustapha (Ed.), *Sects and social disorder: Muslim identities and conflicts in Northern Nigeria* (pp. 18–53). Suffolk: James Currey.

Leman, H. (2018). *Operation safe corridor graduates 95 ex –insurgents in Gombe state*. The Herald. http://www.herald.ng/operation-safe-corridor-graduates-95-ex-insurgents-in-gombe-state/ Accessed 26.04.18.

Lubeck, P. (1985). Islamic protests under semi–industrial capitalism: Yan Tatsine explained. *Africa*, 55(4), 369–389.

Mohammed, K. (2014). The message and methods of Boko Haram. In M-A Perouse de Montclos (Ed.), *Boko Haram: Islamism, politics, security and the state in Nigeria* (pp. 9–32). Leiden: African Studies Centre and Institute for French Research in Africa. https://openaccess.leidenuniv.nl/bitstream/handle/1887/23853/ASC-075287668-3441-01.pdf.

Mohammed, Kyari (2018), "The Origins of Boko Haram". Carl Levan & Patrick Ukata (Eds.), *Oxford handbook of Nigerian Politics*. Oxford: Oxford University Press.

Murphy, J. (2015). *Eeben Barlow speaks out (Pt. 1): PMC and Nigerian Strike Force devastates Boko Haram*. SOFPREP News. 4 January.https://sofrep.com/40608/eeben-barlow-south-african-pmc-devestates-boko-haram-pt1/. Accessed 04.05.18.

Mustapha, A. R. (2014). Understanding Boko Haram. In A. R. Mustapha (Ed.), *Sects and social disorder: Muslim identities and conflicts in Northern Nigeria* (pp. 147–198). Suffolk: James Currey.

NA (Nigerian Army). (2016). *Establishment of human rights desk*. Nigerian Army/Official Website. 8 February. http://www.army.mil.ng/establishment-of-human-right-desk/ Accessed 05.05.18.

Osaghae, E. E. (2002). *Crippled giant: Nigeria since independence*. Ibadan: John Archers.

Osaghae, E. E. (2015). *A state of our own: Second independence, federalism and the decolonization of the state in Africa*. Ibadan: Bookcraft.

Perouse de Montclos, M-A. (Ed.). (2014a). *Boko Haram: Islamism, politics, security and the state in Nigeria.* Leiden: African Studies Centre and Institute for French Research in Africa. https://openaccess. leidenuniv.nl/bitstream/handle/1887/23853/ASC-075287668-3441-01.pdf. Accessed 13.04.18.

Perouse de Montclos, M-A. (2014b). *Nigeria's interminable insurgency? Addressing the Boko Haram crisis.* London: Chatham House. September. https://www.chathamhouse.org/publication/nigerias-interminable-insurgency-addressing-boko-haram-crisis Accessed 13.04.18.

Pileggi, Tamar. (2015). US said to block Israeli arms deal with Nigeria. *Times of Israel.* 26 January. https://www.timesofisrael.com/us-said-to-block-israeli-arms-deal-with-nigeria/ Accessed 14.04.18.

Reliefweb. (2016). *Nigeria creates a military human rights desk.* https://reliefweb.int/report/nigeria/nigeria-creates-military-human-rights-desk. Accessed 13.04.18.

Reliefweb. (2017). *Nigeria situation: UNHCR regional update 01 – 31 January.* https://reliefweb.int/report/nigeria/nigeria-situation-unhcr-regional-update-01–31-january-2017. Accessed 05.05.18.

Reliefweb. (2018). *Nigeria: Humanitarian response plan (January – December 2018).* 7 February. https://reliefweb.int/report/nigeria/nigeria-humanitarian-response-plan-january-december-2018. Accessed 05.05.18.

Soriwei, F. (2016). *Boko Haram: US blocks Nigeria from buying aircraft from Brazil. Punch Newspaper.* 13 November. http://punchng.com/boko-haram-us-blocks-nigeria-buying-aircraft-brazil/ Accessed 13.04.18.

Thurston, Alex. (2018). *Boko Haram: The history of an African Jihadist Movement.* Princeton: Princeton University Press.

US. (2013). *Terrorist designations of Boko Haram and Ansaru.* Department of State. 13 November. https://www.state.gov/j/ct/rls/other/des/266565.htm. Accessed 26.04.18.

Tukur, Sani. (2015). *South Africa returns seized $15 million to Nigeria. Premium Times.* 18 July. https://www.premiumtimesng.com/news/top-news/186871-south-africa-returns-seized-15-million-to-nigerian-government.html Accessed 23.04.18.

# 27

# Uganda

## The state and its struggle against the Lord's Resistance Army

*Omona Andrew David and Samuel Baba Ayegba*

## Introduction

This chapter examines Uganda's struggle against the Lord's Resistant Army (LRA). It notes that starting in 1987 under the leadership of Joseph Kony, the LRA waged one of the enduring and protracted conflicts that defined the postcolonial history of Uganda. Starting in northern Uganda, the porosity of borders between Ugandan, Sudan (now South Sudan), and Democratic Republic of Congo (DRC) saw the sustained operation of the LRA in the three countries. After the failed Juba Peace process and a series of mediation efforts, relocating the base in the Garamba forests in the DRC, the Uganda People's Defence Forces (UPDF) launched a military attack on the LRA that saw it spreading its tentacles and eventual base into the Central African Republic, and Sudan (Ochan, 2009: 3–4). In all the places where the LRA operated and had an encounter with the UPDF, the local communities in the areas experienced a lot of untold sufferings. To date, the attempt by the government of Uganda, the local and the international communities have not yielded much in as far as ending the struggle between the government of Uganda and the LRA.

The tumultuous experience during much of Uganda's postcolonial period is the direct opposite of how the country started. The independence from Britain on 9 October 1962 drew a lot of excitement among the local population and gave them the hope that they can run their affairs. To this end, the immediate postcolonial government concentrated on achieving their campaign promises of routing out colonial vestiges; thus, it afforded them to employ qualified Ugandans to take up the helm of administration. To help propel the country forward, schools, hospitals, and road networks were constructed. Given that agriculture is the backbone of the economy, cooperative societies were established to provide technical support to farmers, right from planting to marketing their produce (Rubaihayo, 2006). Unfortunately, the glamour and excitement of independence were distorted by conflicts of all sorts. Of the many insurgent groups that emerged to contest political governance in Uganda, the most prominent ones have been the Uganda National Liberation Army (UNLA), Federal Democratic Movement (FEDEMU), National Resistant Army (NRA), Uganda National Rescue Front I & II (UNRF I & II), Force Obote Back Again (FOBA), Holy Spirit Movement (HSM), and the LRA.

Given that the rebellion that NRA-under the leadership of Yuweri Kaguta Museveni launched in 1981 brought them to power, it created impetus in many rebel groups to think revolution was a sure route to the State House. So, the LRA that emerged to contest the hold of the NRA regime to power. In the sections that follow, we shall concentrate to analysing the emergence, expansion, and effects of the LRA insurgency on the local people and the state; analyse the strategies devised to address the LRA insurgency by local, state and international communities; analyse the lessons learnt from the state and its struggle against the LRA in Uganda; draw a conclusion and then give some practical recommendation for countering insurgent groups whenever they emerge.

## LRA insurgency and power struggle

The LRA insurgency is a continuation of insurgent groups that emerged in Northern Uganda to contest the NRA's capture and hold to power. The take-over by Museveni's forces came after years of turmoil dating back to the regime of Idi Amin in the 1970s (Ochan, 2009: 7). The NRA first launched a rebellion against the government of President Doctor Milton Obote in 1981, purportedly for rigging the 1980 elections. The power struggle within the UNLA that saw Obote's overthrow by General Tito Okello was a blessing in disguise to the NRA. Whereas Tito Okello quickly initiated peace negotiations with Museveni that resulted in a peace agreement signed in Nairobi, the NRA ignored the agreement and marched on Kampala in January 1986 (Kustenbauder, 2010:456). The overthrow of General Lutwa became possible because the NRA rebels used ethnicity to galvanise the people from central and western Uganda and made them see the UNLA government as the government of the people from the north (Atkinson, 2009: 5). The use of ethnicity as an identity marker made almost everyone hailing from the north to be regarded as a killer, even though they committed some of the killings during the NRA bush war. With such intense propaganda against the UNLA forces and the people from northern Uganda in particular, after the overthrew of General Tito Okello Lutwa by the NRA forces, a large contingent of the UNLA forces, whose bulk came from among the Acholi and Lango, had to retreat northwards (Ochan, 2009: 7). Perhaps fearing the repeat of what the Acholi and Langi suffered after Iddi Amin's coup in 1971, many of the former UNLA forces fled to Sudan with their arms and ammunition while others decided to demobilise and settle among the local population (Gersony, 1997).

Whereas the initial extension of the NRA control to northern Uganda was peaceful, such peacefulness was short-lived. The fear of reprisal by some former UNLA soldiers had proved right when errant NRA soldiers started to pillage, rape men and women, torture, steal livestock and other properties, and destroy infrastructure (Ochan, 2009: 7; Piwang-Jalobo, 2006: 35), maim and kill innocent civilians. To protect the local population from the continuation of such virulence by the NRA forces, a group of former UNLA contingent under the command of Brigadier Odong Latek formed the Uganda People's Defence Movement/Army (UPDM/A) (Gersony, 1997: 20–37) decided to challenge the ills committed by the NRA. In a way, this led to the re-emergence of the old North-South conflict that has marked Ugandan politics and society since independence (Komakech, 2011). After a series of encounter with and the continued brutality of the NRA on the local population, the Uganda People's Defence Army (UPDA) were joined by the Holy Spirit Mobile Forces and Holy Spirit Movement (HSMF/ HSM) led by Alice Auma Lakwena (RLP, 2004: 5–6) to continue the fight. The rebellion led by Auma gained momentum to the extent that she marched with her forces up to Jinja, a few miles to Kampala, the capital city of Uganda. The defeat of Auma's forces in Jinja in 1988 (Westbrook, 2000, sects III, VI) and the need to protect the local population from vandalism by the NRA ushered in another insurgency in northern Uganda under the command of Severino Lukoya Kiberu, Auama's father. The rebellion staged by Kiberu's forces was short-lived because he was captured during action and imprisoned by the government. However, the rag tags of Kiberu's and Auma's forces joined another rebel faction under the leadership of Joseph Kony to form the Uganda Peoples Democratic Christian Army (UPDCA) (Dolan, 2000: 4). After a series of change of names, this group finally came to be known as the Lords' Resistance Army (Gersony, 1997) and the conflict generated by their rebellion, at the time of writing this chapter in 2019, was still being felt in parts of Central African Republic, DRC and South Sudan.

A pertinent question now is: why did this conflict continue for so long when Kony the rebel leaders was an untrained military person. According to the Human Rights Peace Centre (HURIPEC) and Liu Institute for Global Security (LIGS) (2003: 11), the answer to this and other related questions is found in the authoritarian character of governance in Uganda, and the militaristic tendencies that reinforced authoritarian rule are responsible factors that explain why the conflict has dragged for a long time. Besides, some people argue "Museveni dislike Northerners right from the beginning". This according to Andrew Mwenda is reflected in his constant abuse of the former leaders of Uganda from northern Uganda as swine, murderers, terrorists (Mwenda, 2006), thugs, and bandits (*The Observer*, 25–31 March 2004). This and other related issues add to the reasons for the persistence of the conflict. Furthermore, the Sudan factor and the proliferation of small arms and light weapons were also factors (Omona, 2015: 94) that contributed to the resilience and insistence of the LRA to continue the rebellion.

Whereas the LRA initially concentrated their operations in the Acholiland's districts of Gulu, Kitgum and Pader, in 1992, they extended their sphere of influence into East Moyo, the present Adjumani District. The attack of East Moyo was strategically meant to divert the attention of the NRA soldiers who were organised into mobile units to hunt the LRA forces in the Acholi sub-region. Given that the LRA attack of East Moyo in 1992 was on a United Nations (UN) facility and Adjumani health centre, it is reasonable to claim that they had gone to fetch food and medical supply for their forces. Around that time, the intensification of the pursuit of the LRA by the government forces made them locate their tactical headquarters to Southern Sudan. While in Sudan, the LRA received overt support from the National Islamic Front (NIF), the national army of Sudan. This support came as part of the Khartoum Government's effort to use the LRA to reduce the strength of the Sudan People's Liberation Army (SPLA) that the Government of Uganda was also supporting. From such safe havens in Sudan, the LRA continued to carry heinous operations inside Uganda in Acholi sub-region to loot foodstuff, medicine and abduct civilians as a way of recruiting to their force (Ochan, 2009:7).

Given, at that time the governments of both Sudan and Uganda were supporting insurgent groups to carry operations in each other's territory a proxy war emerged between Khartoum and Kampala. Each of them accused the other of disorganising their peace and security. However, the increased pressure from the international community in the late 1990s forced the Khartoum Government to stop overt support to the LRA, though covert support continued through other rebel groups that were loyal to the National Salvation Army (NSA). Subsequently, in 1999, the governments of Sudan and Uganda agreed to end aiding each other's insurgent group thus affording them to renew diplomatic relations. The 11 September 2001 attack of the US by the Al-Qaeda further worked to cement this relation; thus, when the US Department of State listed the LRA as a terror group, Khartoum tried as much as possible to distance herself from any deals with them. To the extent in 2002, as part of an effort to improve their international image, the Khartoum government allowed 10,000 Uganda People's Defence Forces (UPDF) to pursue LRA into Southern Sudan. Whereas permission was granted for this operation, it was however on condition that the UPDF does not cross the red-line which is some 100 km north of the Ugandan border along Juba-Torit road.

Unfortunately, in March 2002 when the Uganda People's Defiance Force (UPDF) launched the "Operation Iron Fist I" to flush the LRA from their hideouts, it instead made the LRA

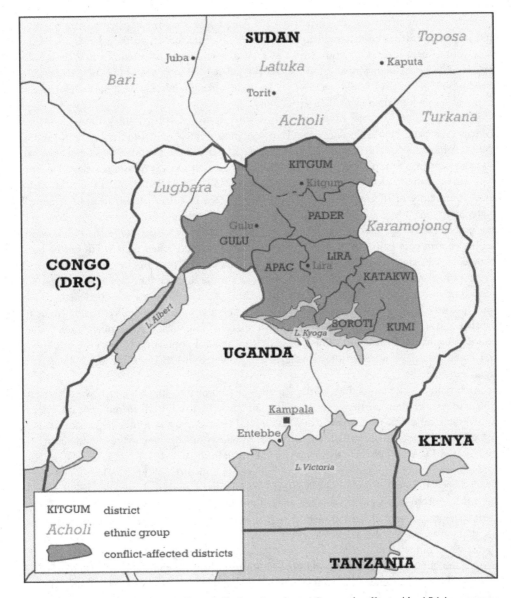

*Figure 27.1* The Conflict Map of Uganda showing the parts mostly affected by LRA Insurgency
Source: http/molg.go.ug/content/images/Uganda

scatter in the jungles of both Southern Sudan and Northern Uganda (Lanz, 2007). Given the unfamiliar terrain, the UPDF could not pursue the LRA swiftly, thus aiding them to increase their attacks on the civilian population and military installations both inside Southern Sudan and Northern Uganda. To prove their discontent to the Khartoum Government for allowing the UPDF to pursue them inside Sudan, in April 2002 the LRA attacked some Sudanese Government controlled villages and military posts near Juba and Sudanese Refugees Camp in Northern Uganda at a place called Acholi Pii. Since the Operation Iron Fist stretched the UPDF so much, they failed to protect the local population from the LRA attacks. To further confuse the UPDF, the LRA extended their operations into Lango and Teso in June 2003.

411

Until the time of writing this paper in 2019, Lango and Teso sub-regions remain peaceful and safe except for occasional incursion of Karimojong cattle rustlers on their far flanks. At the time of this incursion, "Operation Iron Fist I" was at its highest momentum in Acholi Sub-region. The LRA incursion to Lango and Teso sub-regions was probably a plot to create a buffer zone where they could get supplies for their upkeep and also to abduct children and eventually conscript them into their rebel ranks.

The point of entry of the LRA into Teso sub-region was Obalanga sub-county in Amuria District (See Map. 1). The leader of the Teso operation was Tabuley, the third in command of the LRA rebel force. The mission to Teso was superintended by, among others, Vincent Otti, Kamdulu Onen, Dominic Ogwen, and Opio who were all top LRA commanders. The first two weeks of the LRA incursion into Teso was peaceful. They tried to build the trust of the local community of their peacefulness credentials by, for instance, participating in a football match with some locals and young children who they had abducted from other areas. However, this pretence was short-lived. When provoked by the local militia, they unleashed their wrath on the civilian population. In January 2003 when the LRA unleashed their wrath on the local people in Obalanga, they burnt over 115 grass-thatched houses. Besides, they also looted 15 shops in the trading centre and abducted several people to carry their booty of rice, posho, sugar, biscuits, and sodas to their campsite (JRP, 2012: 8). The first time the LRA attacked the local population to kill was on 24 June 2003 when they ambushed a vehicle heading to Obalanga from Soroti. Most of the dead in that attack were civilians. According to the Justice and Reconciliation Project (JRP) field note (2012) the local population blamed the UPDF for not coming to their aid even though the LRA's presence in Obalanga was made known to them earlier on.

After roaming in Amuria for a while, the LRA in their plan to attack Soroti town decided to split into smaller units so they can divert the attention of the UPDF in different directions. When the local militia (the Arrow Boys) saw the UPDF were not proactive to attack the LRA forces, they decided to engage them in fights. Whereas the decision of the local militia to contain the LRA in Teso sub-region was good, it, unfortunately, gave the LRA a leeway to spread from Amuria to Katakwi, Soroti and Kaberamaido districts- abducting, looting foodstuff and killing whoever they found (JRP, 2012: 10). The impressive challenge the UPDF gave to the LRA in Teso sub-region was when they attempted to attack Soroti Flying School. When their attack was repulsed by the UPDF, the LRA were forced to withdraw from the battlefront. Of all the places in the Teso sub-region the LRA left a daunting mark was in Obalanga where there was about 40,000 Internal Displaced People (IDP) camp. The LRA killed over 600 people and abducted over 2000 children. Some of the people who were killed in Obalanga were buried in a mass grave that contained over 265 bodies. In Wera and Asamuk sub-counties of Teso sub-region, 133 people were killed, 230 children were abducted, and nine permanent buildings were destroyed (JRP, 2012: 11). Unfortunately, instead of protecting the civilian population, the UPDF also resorted to kill, loot and bomb the local community using helicopter gunships, a mistake for which they have not apologised to date (JRP, 2012: 19).

The intensification of operation by the UPDF and the Local Defence Forces- the Arrow Boys- in the Teso sub-region saw the LRA forces retreating to Northern Uganda and eventually into Sudan. While in Sudan, about 10,000 contingents of UPDF were deployed to pursue them. Then in 2005 when the government of Sudan signed a comprehensive peace agreement with Sudan's People's Liberation Army (SPLA), the support for the LRA that used to be supplied by the Khartoum government dwindled, thus making them withdraw their operations inside Uganda. The peaceful relations between the Khartoum Government and SPLA also ushered in peaceful relations between Uganda and Sudan. To the extent, the

Uganda government could deploy the UPDF inside Sudan to pursue the LRA rebels (Atkinson, 2009:12).

The RLA moved swiftly to express the need for peace talks, though which did not actualise. After the failed Juba Peace talks, the LRA spread activities spread from northern Uganda to cover an expansive territory including eastern DR Congo, the Central African Republic, and southern Sudan (Komakech, 2011). Since much of this territory is outside the day-to-day control of governments in the region, the LRA forces find it very conducive for their operations. As a lethal force in "endurance mode," the LRA has continued to remain a destabilising factor in the Great Lakes region, with the capability to upset the lives of many people (Komakech, 2011: 4).

## Impact assessment

The LRA insurgency in Northern Uganda has affected both the government of Uganda and the local people. In this sub-section, we shall turn our attention to explain this, starting with the effects of the insurgency on the state and then on the local people.

### Effect of insurgency on the state

In any country when issues of insurgency arise, the State becomes the principal. Whereas some people thought the LRA insurgency was payback for what the people from northern Uganda did to the people of other parts of the country, the State did bare its brunt too. As one looks at the effects of the LRA insurgency on the state, what comes out are the economic and relational costs. Accordingly, Gulu Civil Society Organisations for Peace in Northern Uganda (2006) in over the 20 years, estimated the economic cost of the insurgency on the government to be in excess of Uganda $ 1.7 billion, meaning that during the active periods of the insurgency the government was spending about $ 85 million annually. In other words, the cost of the insurgency was equivalent to Uganda's total annual income from coffee exports. If this money were to be used for service delivery, it could have provided safe, clean drinking water to 3.5 million people per year. Given such expenditure, government efforts to engage in developmental programmes were curtailed.

The insurgency led to mistrust and lost of confidence in the government of Uganda among the population. This was clearly reflected in the voting pattern in 1997, 2001, 2006, and 2011 where the people of northern Uganda overwhelmingly supported the opposition with the hope that things could change for the better if a different government came to power. Besides, the government lost a substantial number of her human resources because of the brutal killing people, and as others ran into exile (Ogenga, 2002). The running of a section of the population to exile, also lead to brain drain when a lot of skilled manpower left the country for other countries where they resorted to offering their services to serving their new-found countries of exile. Some of the people decided to remain in exile to avoid dehumanisation and demonisation attributed to them by some people in government. The constant reference to them as killers, rapists, thugs, and so forth made some of the people to feel they are better off staying in exile than being in their own country where they are not counted as human beings.

The insecurity that ensued because of the insurgency led to wanton destruction of properties and human lives. In the guise of denying the rebel supply, the cramming people in the IDP camps where they lived in squalid conditions retarded economic and social development of people in Northern Uganda (Lamwaka, 2002). Indeed, a huge sum of money was spent during the active phase of the conflict as soldiers who command the operations were given special allowances. If all that were spent were directed to the provision of social services to the people, their lives could have changed for the better. Similarly, the people who were abducted by the rebels have bitter feelings against the government because they were not protected by the UPDF.

## Effect of insurgency on the local people

The effect of the LRA insurgency on the local people, as it was on the State, is well articulated in literature. For instance, the work of Omona (2015) on "Management of postcolonial intrastate conflicts in Uganda: A case of Northern Uganda" and GSCOPNU's (2006) compilation entitled, "Counting the cost: Twenty years of war in northern Uganda," provide insightful data on the subject matter. The key issues identified are internal displacement, high mortality rate, abduction, degeneration of education, lack of access to humanitarian services and the cost of the conflict in terms of the socio-economic is revealed as the major effects of the LRA insurgency to the local population in northern Uganda.

While explaining the senseless killings during the insurgency, Ochola-Onono & Oryem (2000: 1) assert that the series of conflicts left so many people orphaned and destitute with no one to take care of them. Indeed, during the LRA insurgency, a lot of people have lost their loved ones. Unfortunately, some of those who died left young children and elderly people without anyone to provide them with the care they need. Apart from those who were killed during the insurgency, some people died of HIV and AIDS, a situation which Olara Otunnu in a Documentary entitled "LRA conflict" (Stanton, n.d) asserts were used by the NRA government as an instrument of violence during the twenty-one years of insurgency in northern Uganda. Although some of the orphans were taken care of by their relatives, the fact that those who took up the orphans were themselves equally needy, they were not able to meet all the social, educational and physical needs of the orphans. In a way, this further increased the misery of the people of northern Uganda after going through a period of suffering.

The insurgency in Northern Uganda has affected the civilian population. Women and children endured most of the conflict, especially after the death of some men. Thus, leading to the feminisation of poverty since women became the sole providers for the family. Yet women are not as mobile as men, and they do not have ready access to credit facilities and communal resources to engage in self-help endeavours and business ventures. As for children, their conscription into the rebel and government militia ranks imposed a special burden on them. This made them be denied the opportunity to go to school and receive care from their families (Pham et al., 2007). Those who were afraid to join these forces stayed at home or ended up on the streets. Even if some of the children joined the forces willingly or by force, the final analysis is that their physical and mental developments have been impaired, thus immersing them into the culture of violence.

In Northern Uganda in particular, many people went into exile or got displaced within the country. Just like during the 1970s when many people ran to Tanzania and Kenya and in the 1980s some people went to the Sudan and Zaire now DRC, the LRA insurgency sent others beyond the mentioned countries. While in exile, some of the people lived in squalid conditions. Feeding, sanitation, educational facilities, and social services in their places of refuge were extremely poor. To make matters even worse, in the 1990s to mid-2000s, those who could not go to exile were forced into IDP camps that were created across Northern and Eastern Uganda. In a documentary entitled "the LRA conflict," Olara Otunnu argued that when a similar situation started to happen in Burundi around the same time, the International Community forced the Burundi government to disband the IDP camps (Stanton, n.d). They conditioned the Burundi government to let the people go back into their villages. Unfortunately, the same International Community kept quiet when this was happening in northern Uganda. Since the silence of the international community on the plight of the people of northern Uganda made them be exposed to untold suffering; some section of the people of northern Uganda lost hope in the international system (HURIPEC, & LIGI, (2003). While in these IDP camps people tested homelessness, abject poverty and accompanying war distress. This was because they could not meet their basic needs since the crops and farmlands, they depended on were destroyed. The cramming of people into IDP camps without enough sanitary facility led to the outbreak of preventable diseases that killed many people.

The inhuman treatment that was unleashed on the people of Northern Uganda during the periods of LRA insurgency left bitter memories in the minds of the local population. Common among such inhuman treatment was: the rape of women and girls in the presence of their husbands, parents, brothers and children, having sexual relations with men –sodomy in the presence of their family (HURIPEC, & LIGI, 2003). Furthermore, some UPDF defecated in the water pots or food staffs of these powerless people as the LRA concentrated on cutting off body parts like lips, nose, breasts, ears, and arms; and the wounds left after injury. While recounting such a daunting experience in Pader district, Omona asserts:

> A certain man, whose dog tried to bark when the LRA were entering his compound, was forced to tie the dog on his back like a child. Then one of the rebels got firewood that had fire on it and started to burn the anus of the dog. Since it was tied on the owners back, the dog thought its owner was the one inflicting this pain on itself. In its desperate attempt to escape, the dog started biting its owner several times at the back of his head, thus leaving him with multiple wounds on his head (Omona, 2015: 255).

Such sufferings made people look forward to an opportune moment to revenge on the criminals. The conflict also destroyed societal social fabric and coping mechanism. Since civilians were direct targets of both the rebels and government forces, people disperse in different directions for their security. In the process, some of the key cultural value the support provided by the wider family and kinship system were destroyed. Consequently, this exacerbated division between groups and increased intra-group insecurity and hostility. It also acted to disrupt inter-group economic relations (RLP, 2013).

In a way of adding insult to injury, when people were displaced by conflicts, men lost their traditional position of being the breadwinners at home. While in the IDP camps, it was the women who were receiving relief food and other properties. This provision by the UN to families made family respect to cease and everybody started behaving contrary to family norms. After the UN had stopped providing food rations to families, some women resorted to befriending soldiers so as to survive. This exposed them to sexually transmitted diseases like Human Immune Deficiency Virus (HIV) and Acquired Immune Deficiency Syndrome (AIDS). Since men became powerless, the majority resorted to bettering their wives in their attempt to assert their position as men. As a result, a lot of families broke during the time in the camps. In some cases, some of these families have not been able to come together up to today. During the IDP camp life, some families were forced to share small huts with all the members of their household for fear of risking the girl child's life. Through such, children got exposed to sexual practice early in life since some of the parents could not wait but start having sex before the children were asleep.

The LRA insurgency further reduced people of Northern Uganda into abject poverty, especially after losing their livelihood. Quoting from Uganda Bureau of Standard and UNDP's statistics, Robert Senath Esuruku has this to say about the poverty levels in northern Uganda:

> While the national average of Ugandans living in absolute poverty declined from 38.8% in 2002/03 to 31.1% in 2005/6 and to 24.53% in 2009/10, poverty in northern Uganda increased from 2.9 million in 2002/03 to 3.3 million in 2005/06 and decreased to 2.9 million in 2009/10. Despite the overall significant reduction in poverty, the northern Uganda regions remained poorer than other regions…The human development indices (HDIs) and human poverty indices (HPIs) demonstrate that Northern Uganda is lagging behind the rest of the country in regional and district specific breakdowns. (Esuruku, 2012: 149–151).

The assertion of Esuruku (2012) is spot on. Given the gruesome LRA conflict, while the national income per capita is estimated at Uganda shillings (UGX) 570,000 in 2012 few years after the end of the insurgency, the figure for the Northern region stands at a paltry UGX 153,000, which is about 27% of the national average. Putting this in context, Esuruku (2012: 149–151) further argues:

> Although at national level income poverty fell from 56% in 1992 to 31.1% in 2006 and 24.5 in 2009/10, 46.2% of the residents in the northern region have remained. Although the mean consumption expenditure per adult equivalent has increased from UGX 55,092 in 2006 to 62,545 in 2009/10, the expenditure in the north has remained at UGX 38,988.

The state of the poverty level in Northern Uganda, highlighted by Esuruku (2012) has made most people hailing from those ends to think the insurgency was a deliberate ploy by the government to crush their spirit. Due to such level of poverty, many people from northern Uganda have failed to support their families. Instead, some became dependent on food rations from the World Food Programme to the extent that they want to be supported even after the end of the LRA insurgency.

Since people got used to being provided for, some have failed to adjust to the life of hard-working and fending for themselves. The situation is even worse among those who were born in the IDP camps. The dependency syndrome that developed among the local people made several youths to resort to stealing or roaming around in trading centres without any gainful employment. The insurgency has also affected harmonious living in the villages due to land wrangles with relatives. In Gulu, for example, "land crisis led to the burning of a lady with her two daughters in their house near Gulu High School" (Omona, 2015: 259) and also in Lira, a man confessed having killed 12 people from the same family due to land conflicts. The trauma such incidences caused has made some people go mad thus forcing them to kill their own parents, children, or relatives.

According to Wade Snow (2009: 1), the resulting violent conflicts have contributed to the lowest return rate of the former IPDs to their ancestral land in Gulu as compared to other war-affected districts. This is because people fear getting involved in bitter conflicts over land, a usual form of conflict during the post LRA insurgency. In regard to the female fraternity, the effects of the conflict have been: physical/sexual abuse, psychological trauma, the pressure to restore traditional norms, dislocation, additional responsibilities, and often the head of households, low education and discrimination. Those who could not bear such burden have since become helpless.

The destruction of properties and infrastructure of Northern Uganda like roads made Chris Dolan, at a conference presentation on 21 November 2011 to assert "the people of Northern Uganda were exposed to structural violence, an event that one lives to remember for the rest of his/her life." The memories of such bad roads come to mind vividly because people have lost many lives on it. For example, during the 1990s, a lot of people died on the roads in northern Uganda. This has made the people who are still alive to regard the roads in northern Uganda as "the road that kills". The insurgency further led to the creation of income disparity between the people in northern Uganda and other parts of Uganda due to loss of source of income thus subjecting them to abject poverty and starvation. The school drop-out rate during IDP life also shot up. This led to an increase in crime rate in the IDP camps thus making people develop the spirit of violence as a defence mechanism. Consequently, this led to a high prevalence rate of sexual and gender-based violence - which in some instances led to murders of spouses.

The politicisation of the LRA insurgency led to the negative identity of the Acholi by their neighbours. For example, the Acholi were collectively branded as rebels even by their neighbours the Lango and Madi. Such generalisation of a community through stereotype is what brings failing to look at people as individuals but as a community which is not fair. The negative identity attributed to the Acholi made, on 25 May 2003 a peaceful march in Lira town, in protest against the Barlonyo massacre to translate into anti-Acholi sentiments leading to the killing of five people. The killing of the five people made some Acholi youths in Gulu to retaliate on the Langi. Around the same time in Teso, a Member of Parliament urged his people to kill all Acholi who were 18 years old (HURIPEC, & LIGS, 2003). Then in Adjumani District, some people celebrated the death of innocent abductees who were mowed by a UPDF helicopter gunship. Yet not all the Acholi supported the rebellion.

The protracted armed conflict resulted in many people suffering from post-traumatic disorders in northern Uganda. As such, Omona (2009), quoting a respondent who preferred anonymity said: "there are more lunatics in northern Uganda today than before due to their experience during the active phase of the LRA rebellion". After the cessation of hostility, the youths who were targeted for abduction and conscription into the rebel and government militia forces failed to have productive lives on returning home. The attempt by some of these youth to become productive made them resort to early marriages. This was especially true among the girls among whom the highest incidence of this was reported. Some of these girls got married at the tender age of thirteen years and others were impregnated at twelve years old- thus creating a scenario where a child takes care of another child or other children.

Besides the above effect, issues like famine, destruction of properties and social amenities like schools, health centres, and roads, retardation of development, and increase in illiteracy amongst the local people were reported. Furthermore, jealousy by some section of the community towards those who they regard to be better off was also reported. Such negative feeling amongst local people further works to complicate harmonious post-conflict resettlement in northern Uganda.

## Counterinsurgency (COIN) strategies to address the LRA insurgency

There is no doubt that the Ugandan state has struggled over time to curtail the LRA insurgency. This seeming failure cannot be attributed to inaction, as several efforts and strategies have been aggressively pursued, to no avail. These efforts have witnessed the involvement of parties from within and outside of the country. We shall briefly examine the various counterinsurgency (COIN) strategies adopted by local communities, the state, and the international community.

## Local communal counterinsurgency (COIN) initiatives

It has been argued that insurgency does not pose a direct military threat to the authority of the national government in individual states (Tumutegyereize, 2012). Nonetheless, the local population in rural areas are at the receiving end of the insurgents' atrocious activities, which include among others terror, violence, kidnapping, abductions, and rape. This sad development has helped to create a high sense of mistrust and hopelessness in the psyche of the people, towards the national government; making sure that an extensive gap exists between the government and the people, dealing a fatal blow against the needed cohesion and peace required to address the LRA question.

Consequently, with the people feeling let down by their own government- whose statutory role is the preservation of the lives and properties of its citizenry, decided to resort to diverse self-help mechanisms, at the grassroots. Some of these efforts include among others the emergence of civilian defence forces for self-defence; the distribution of leaflets in conjunction with the military and FM Radio broadcasts aimed at encouraging defection of LRA combatants; the involvement of CSOs in the Ugandan Peace Process; advocacy to stave abductions while aiding the return of abductees through newsletters, such as The Voice of Peace, as well as the integration of children born of war (Conciliative Resources, 2012; Woldetsadik, 2017).

Besides, the Traditional Leaders' and Elders' Peace initiative, Acholi Religious Leaders Peace Initiative, District Peace Team, Civil Society Initiatives, and the Umbrella *"Oduru Kuc"* (return peace) (HIRIPEC & LIGS, 2003, pp. 113–121), the *"Kacoke madit"* (big meeting) convened by the Acholi in Diaspora in London in 1997 and 2002, and in Nairobi in 1999 (Nyeko, 2002), in attempt to broker peace but it never gave peace to the people were employed. And within the context of local players, an organisation like the Acholi Religious Leaders Peace Initiative (ARLPI) and other Christian groups in northern Uganda thought alternative justice system, attempted to address the conflict. According to Niringiye (2007), using the alternative justice system was the best way to go because it offers a flexible, accessible and cheap procedure for all; ensure community participation in conflict resolution; promote mutual healing and restoration of broken relationships; ensures satisfaction for both offenders and victims; addresses the concern of the victims through payment of reparation; enhances effective reintegration of combatants into the community; facilitate documentation of crimes committed by the perpetrators; protects against the culture of impunity because perpetrators of crimes that are unwilling to cooperate are subjected to the contemporary justice systems; and guarantees creative collaboration with cultural and religious institutions. (Niringiye, 2007: 17).

Whereas the efforts by the local community to broker peace was gaining momentum, there were some spoilers within the state and rebel group who wish to have the conflict continue for financial gains. So, a lot of frustrations were directed from all corners to frustrate the local initiatives. In an unfortunate event, some elders who were passionate about brokering the peace got killed by the LRA accusing them of spying for the government.

## Ugandan government's counterinsurgency (COIN) strategies

The Uganda government has been criticised by the people for its laidback attitude towards addressing the LRA insurgency. The criticism came about because, whereas Uganda is actively intervening to seek for the peaceful ending of conflicts in other countries within the Great Lakes Region, the government of Uganda is reserved to do so in her own territory. The people might be right in their criticisms and bitterness towards the government, after all; this is so, as the government's official military campaign against the insurgents took about a decade to take-off. The first such operation was the mobile force units, which began right from the time when Alice Auma Lakwena was commanding her HSMF in the Acholi sub-region. When Kony came to the scene, "Operation North/Sim-Sim" in 1998, "Operation Iron Fist I & II" in 2002 and 2004, and then "Operation Lightning Thunder" in 2008 (Omona, 2015, p. 268) were launched by the Uganda People's Defence Forces. The question that readily comes to mind is, why all the dilly-dally since 1987? The unfortunate bit of all these operations were, as noted above, they made the LRA spread and intensify their virulence on the local people in Uganda or in the neighbouring countries of South Sudan and DRC. This same situation was extended to the Central African Republic when in November 2008 the Ugandan government with the backing of the US Government started a COIN campaign that was primarily based on wholesome military tactics. Whereas its main objective was the suppression of LRA activities and the elimination of LRA leader, Joseph Kony from the frontline, and protection of families and communities from LRA attacks but it only came to infuriate the LRA to carry out more atrocious activities against the people with impunity.

At the end of December 2010, following two years of the military campaign, the US government had spent an initial US$23 million, which later rose to US$40 million on military operations, principally in the form of logistics (airlifts, fuel and tracks), and intelligence report. However, this strategy proved too costly and grossly unsuccessful. This prompted a volte-face from the Ugandan government and her ally, the United States, in December 2010. According to Conciliative Resources (2011), the parties admitted that "there is no purely military solution to the LRA threat and impact." In spite of this admittance tactical failure, a hundred US military advisers were later deployed in the northern region, to give impetus to on-going military COIN operations. Regrettably, after all the substantial financial outlay, the LRA's capacity to inflict damage remains intact. This is a clear statement that pure military tactics alone as a strategy for ending the LRA insurgency is unproductive.

Despite the criticism levelled against the Ugandan government for her over-reliance on military strategy for ending the LRA conflict, it is important to note that, the government has at various times, tried the peace option as an alternative strategy. The most notable efforts are the Betty Bigombe peace initiative I & II in 2002 and 2004 respectively and the Juba Peace Process (Omona, 2009). The Betty Bigombe peace process started bearing fruits. It saw a section of the LRA come out of the bush, reported to the military barracks, and were moving freely in the community. However, when President Museveni gave an ultimatum of seven days within which all the remaining LRA forces to come out or he will crush them, even those that came out decided to withdraw back into the bush. Some people, thought reasoned that such an arrogant statement from the president was occasioned by the thinking 'how can a woman of all people lead a successful peace deal when the military genius have all failed'. The unfortunate bit was that the yearned-for peace was not achieved.

The Juba Peace Talks was hosted in the South Sudan Capital, and mediated by the Vice President of South Sudan, Rick Machar was another peaceful means the government was credited for. The peace process, which started in July 2006, saw the involvement of the US, Europe, African Union, and the United Nations, to help keep the belligerents at the table (The Resolve, 2010). Unfortunately, the talks collapsed in 2009, after high expectations for final agreements that would end the conflict, were thwarted by series of walkouts by the LRA, and the refusal of the LRA leader Joseph Kony, to append his signature on the deal; even his meeting with a coalition of Ugandan CSOs representatives, could not convince him to have a change of heart. In fact, LRA's deputy leader, Vincent Otti, was allegedly killed on the orders of Kony, for his dedicated support for the peace process. In all this, the notable undoing of the Juba Peace process was the coming in of the ICC, a group that the government of Uganda after running to them to hunt for Kony is now the very one spearheading negative talk about it.

However, it is pertinent to note that, despite the failure of the peace talks to deliver the expected result, the resultant ceasefire in the period the talks lasted, offered the northern region some respite and some level of "prosperity".

Furthermore, in pursuit of a peaceful strategy to end the crisis, the US government under President Obama, signed into law, the Lord's Resistance Army Disarmament and Northern Uganda Recovery Act in May 2010, committing the US to advance an all-inclusive strategy to end this protracted conflict. But then again, like other peace initiatives before it, this has failed to deliver to the Ugandan people the expected dividends. Nevertheless, following the collapse of the Juba Peace Process and the lull that ensued since 2009, there arose hope in the horizon for peace once again. On the 4 June 2015, various stakeholders met at Pope John Paul II Peace Justice Centre in Uganda, for a national Dialogue on the National Peace Policy project. The objective is to assess the draft Peace Strategy, produce modalities for the formation of the National Peace Policy (CEWIGO, 2015). In the same vein, the Ugandan government in a seemingly desperate move to end the conflict at all cost, relying on the time-tested strategy of offering pardons to insurgents, as a way of ending intractable conflicts, issued amnesties to the LRA leaders. The Amnesty Act of 2000, offered a pardon to all Ugandans engaged or engaging in acts of rebellion against the state since 26 January 1986 (Refugee Law Project, 2005).

## International and regional support to counterinsurgency (COIN) drive in Uganda

Any discussion about counterinsurgency efforts made by the international community to end the LRA insurgency in Uganda must necessarily have as a starting point the efforts by the US and other non-US based organisations and the US Government's contributions in Uganda. The first Rome made such NGO based The Community Sant'Egidio, Equatoria Civic Fund, and the Cater Centre (Obita, 2002). The efforts of all these organisations were frustrated given the economic import of the conflict to some key people in the government and the military.

In connection with the US government's effort, as stated earlier in this chapter, the US government favoured a pure military strategy to end the LRA conflict in Uganda. Thus, it spent several million dollars in that regard. However, following the failure of military means to achieve the stated objective, the US explored the option of peace. Thus, it actively supported the Juba Peace Process, and even enacted into law, the Lord's Resistance Army Disarmament and Northern Uganda Recovery act. The Senate and House of Representatives of the United States of America enacted the Act. It was intended to support stabilisation and enduring peace in Northern Uganda, and other areas affected by LRA insurgency. To this end, a regional development strategy was put in place to sustain multilateral attempts, aimed at protecting civilians and eradicating threats posed by insurgents. Consequently, the US government was mandated to authorise funds in 2010, for humanitarian relief and reconstruction, reconciliation, and transitional justice, and other purposes (Lord's Resistance Army Disarmament and Northern Uganda Act, 2009).

Furthermore, in addition to earlier military support offered to the Ugandan government, the US government has been at the forefront of support for the regional and continental efforts towards ending the conflict. This support is provided via the secondment of 100 armed Special Forces to provide advice in the hunt for Kony and his men. The advisors were not to engage in any military confrontation with the rebels unless needed for self-defence (Shanker & Gladstone, 2011). Their arrival, it has been argued, helped streamline logistical and intelligence support to Uganda's military forces, and brought more penetrating military pressure on LRA groups. However, these efforts have once again failed to bring the LRA to its knees (The Resolve, 2012).

Similarly, efforts at the international level led to the issuance of an international warrant of arrest for Kony and his commanders, over charges of war crimes. It was hoped that, if the LRA leaders were arrested, the insurgency would end or force Kony and his men to embrace the peace process and amnesty offer. But this was not to be (Peacebuildingdata.org, 2010). Additionally, efforts were made at the continental and regional levels to find a lasting solution to the LRA conflict. In this regard, the African Union and members of the International Conference on the Great Lakes Region (ICGLR), with active support from the US government, came together to strengthen and improve coordination of efforts aimed at dismantling the rebel group; a major value is the AU-led Regional Cooperation Initiative for the Elimination of the Lord's Resistance Army (RCI-LRA). This initiative, equally has the backing of the United Nations Security Council, and its being implemented in unification with the Regional Task Force (RTF); the Regional Task Force, is made of 5,000 solders, from the affected countries within the region. The RTF was charged with the responsibility to protect the local population, who are considered most susceptible to LRA attacks; track and combat LRA insurgents; and where the occasion demands, assist in the delivery of humanitarian assistance (South African Foreign Policy Initiative, 2012; Security Council Report, 2012).

## Lessons learnt from the state and its struggle against the LRA

A critical evaluation of the LRA insurgency indicates that its activities do not pose a direct military threat to the authority of the national government in individual states. However, the rural population in the northern region, that have continued to bear the impact of violence, terror and displacements instigated by the insurgency. Similarly, existing counterinsurgency strategies depend worryingly on military means alone, which has over time, failed to shield the civilian population, nor end the conflict. Rather, it has only continued to produce a self-perpetuating sequence of fatalities, anger and vulnerability that continues to fuel the conflict. This has consequently led to a broadening gap between the government and local communities (Tumutegyereize, 2012).

What then is the lesson to draw from this approach for African countries and the international community? Current trends in Counterinsurgency and Counterterrorism (CT-COIN) operations suggest an encompassing strategy, which views CT-COIN operations from both conventional military and non-military perspectives. Hence, CT-COIN operations require the management of both dimensions with equal dynamism and consideration, as the changing pattern of the international security environment has shown that the strategy towards national defence in the 21st Century, goes beyond conventional military tactics (Muni, 1996: 200–201; Ayegba, 2017). According, the LRA conflict is not likely to end by military means alone; this is owing to the failure of military pressure. The LRA remains unwilling to end the conflict in exchange for amnesty from the government. Consequently, the inclusion of civil society, local traditional, religious leaders as prominent actors, is fundamental to the success of the peace process.

## Conclusion

This chapter illuminates the Ugandan state's longstanding struggle against the Lord's Resistance Army. It is noted that the Ugandan state in the post-colonial era provided a ripe ground for several armed conflicts. The emergence and expansion of the LRA insurgency led to a reign of terror that affected not only the state and its armed forces but also local communities. The strategies devised by the local, state and the international community, to address the LRA insurgency appears to be fraught with challenges of coordination and purposeful leadership. Furthermore, the chapter reveals the lessons learnt from the state's struggle in her bid to nip the LRA insurgency in the bud: poor governance and economic exclusion, are the root cause of armed conflicts in Uganda, while the Ugandan defence force and her allies appear to be ill-equipped and under-motivated in dealing with the scourge. Thus, there can be no peace without good governance. Since the LRA insurgency is largely caused by poor leadership, the panacea is located in open participation and political engagement (substantial peace dialogue and public participation), as well as the incorporation of civilian defence forces in the CT-COIN operation (akin to what is being done in the on-going CT-COIN operation against the Boko Haram in Nigeria), and accountable governance; this will pave way for the end of the insurgency, thereby, enhancing individual, group and national peace and security.

Also, in view of contemporary challenges induced by the changes in the international security environment, and the concomitant changes in the nature and character of African conflicts, it is imperative that the Ugandan government, reframe the country's national defence policy and COIN strategies, by fusing military strategy which relies on "stick" manoeuvres of violence, e.g., detention and elimination of individual insurgents, disruption of insurgent support networks, and decapitation of the LRA; and indirect tactic which encompasses political, economic, psychological, and civic agencies designed to enhance the welfare of civilians beyond security concerns, thus winning their hearts and minds, and turning civilians away from insurgency – the questions of human safety and sustainability of livelihoods, are vital to ending the lingering LRA insurgency in Uganda.

# References

ACCORD. (2002). *Protracted conflict, elusive peace: Initiatives to end the violence in Northern Uganda* (updated 2010: The Juba peace process). Online. Available from: http://www.c-r.org/our-work/accord/northern-uganda/ Accessed on 22.05.15.

Atkinson, R. R. (2009). *From Uganda to the Congo and beyond: Pursuing the Lord's Resistance Army.* New York: International Peace Institute.

Ayegba, S. B., & Yerima, H. (2017). Defence and security with human face: Human security and defence transformation in Nigeria. In UA Tar (Ed.), *Defence transformation and the consolidation of democracy in Nigeria.* Kaduna: Academy Publishers Ltd.

Centre for Women in Governance (CEWIGO). (2015). *Peace policy: A new hope for peace processes in Uganda.* Available from www.cewigo.org/blog/2015/08/peace-policy-new-hope-peace-processes-uganda Accessed 16.07.17.

Chris, D. (2011). *Transitional justice in Uganda.* Opening speech at Kitgum- Northern Uganda, Institute for African Transitional Justice.

Dolan, C. (2000). *What do you remember? A rough guide to the war in Northern Uganda 1986 – 2000,* COPE Working Paper no. 33. Kampala: ACORD.

Conciliative Resources. (2011). *When will this end and what will it take? People's perspectives on addressing the Lord's Resistance Army conflict.* Available from www.c-r.org/node/1230 Accessed 18.07.17.

Conciliative Resources. (2012). *Voice of peace: Grassroots news and opinions on LRA Conflict.* Available from c-r.org/resources/voice-peace-grassroots-news-and-opinions-lra-conflict-2012 Accessed 18.07.17.

Esuruku, R. S. (2012). The peace, recovery and development plan for northern Uganda. In C. M. Okello, C. Dolan, U. Whande, N. Mcwebe, L. Onegi & S. Oola (Eds.), *Where law meets reality: Forging transitional justice* (pp. 144–166). Cape Town, Darker, Nairobi & Oxford: Pambazuka Press.

Gersony, R. (1997). *The anguish of Northern Uganda: Results of a field-based assessment of the civil conflicts in Northern Uganda.* Kampala: USAID Mission. Online. Available from https://reliefweb.int/report/uganda/anguish-northern-uganda-introduction Accessed 23.01.19.

Gulu Civil Society Organisations for Peace in Northern Uganda (GSCOPNU). (2006). *Counting the cost: Twenty years of war in northern Uganda.* Gulu: GSCOPNU.

Human Rights and Peace Center (HURIPEC) & Liu Institute for Global Issues (LIGS). (2003). *The hidden war: The forgotten people; war in Acholi and its ramifications for peace and security in Uganda*. Kampala: Faculty of Law, Makerere University, Uganda.

Justice and Reconciliation Project (JRP). (2012). *The day they came: Recounting the LRA's invasion of Teso Sub-Region through Obalanga Sub-County in 2003*. JRP Field Note XIV, January 2012. Available from www.justiceandreconciliation.com Accessed 25.01.19.

Muni, S. (1996). Arms and conflicts in the post-cold war developing world. In L. Van De Goor, K. Rupesinghe & P. Scilarone (Eds.), *Between development and destruction: An inquiry into the causes of conflict in post-colonial states*. London: Macmillan.

Komakech, L. (2011). *Lord's Resistant Army in Uganda*. Kampala: RLP.

Kustenbauder, M. (2010). Northern Uganda: Protracted conflict and structures of violence. In T. Falola & R. C. Njoku (Eds.), *In war and peace in Africa* (pp. 451–482). Durham, NC: Carolina Academic Press.

Lamwaka, C. (2002). The peace process in northern Uganda 1986-1990. In O. Lucima (Ed.), *Protracted conflict, elusive peace initiatives to end the violence in Northern Uganda* (pp. 28–33). London: ACCORD.

Lanz, D. (2007). *The ICC's intervention in Northern Uganda: Beyond the simplicity of peace vs justice*, Medford: The Fletcher School of Law and Diplomacy-Tuft University.

Lord's Resistance Army Disarmament and Northern Uganda Recovery Act of 2009. Available from https://www.govinfo.gov/content/pkg/PLAW-111publ172/html/PLAW-111publ172.htm Accessed 10.02.19.

Mwenda, A. (2006). *Uganda's roadmap to the end of northern region insurgency: Government/ LRA position statement. The Monitor Newspaper*.

Niringiye, Z. (2007). *A framework for dialogue on reconciliation and peace in northern Uganda*. Kampala: Uganda Joint Christian Council Alternative Justice.

Nyeko, P. C. (2002). Kacoke Madit: A diaspora role in promoting peace. In O. Lucima (Ed.), *Protracted conflict, elusive peace initiatives to end the violence in Northern Uganda*. ACCORD. Online. Available from http://www.c-r.org/our-work/accord/northern-uganda/ Accessed 23.05.15.

Obita, J. A. (2002). First International Peace Efforts 1996-1998. In O.Lucima (Ed.), *Protracted conflict, elusive peace initiatives to end the violence in Northern Uganda*. London: Conciliation Resources.

Ocan, A. O. (2011). *Jesus and violence: The study of Matthew 5: 38-48 in relation to violence prevention in Acholi*. MA dissertation. Uganda Christian University.

Ochan, C. (2009). *Assessing Uganda's cross-border pursuit of the Lord's Resistance Army*. Boston: Feinstein International Center.

Ochola-Onono, G., & Oryem, A. (2000). The effects of the war in Northern Uganda in education in Gulu District. Available from http://www.km-net.org.uk/conferences/KM98/deo.htm Accessed 20.01.17.

Omona, A. D. (2009). The peace process in northern Uganda: Why parties involved have failed to reach a compromise. In *Hakimani Jesuit Journal in Eastern African, seeking truth, justice and reconciliation* (Vol. 01/09) (pp. 64–73). Nairobi: Hakimani.

Ogenga, O. (2002). The conflict in northern Uganda: Causes and dynamics. In O. Lucima (Ed.), *Protracted conflict, elusive peace initiatives to end the violence in northern Uganda* (pp. 10–13). London: ACCORD.

Omona, A. D. (2015). *Management of postcolonial conflicts in Uganda: A case of Northern Uganda*. Nairobi: Kenyatta University PhD Thesis.

Peacebuildingdata.org. (2010). *Historical background Northern Uganda*. Online. Available from www.peacebuildingdata.org/research/uganda/backgroundAccessed 19.07.17.

Piwang-Jalobo, G. (2006). "*Is Uganda close to point of no return? Prospects of divine judgement for the agony of the Acholi and northern Uganda*", Open Letter to Gen. Caleb Akandwanaho, a.k.a Salim Saleh Oraba, Minister of State, Micro Finance, Planning and Economic Development, Kampala-Uganda.

Pham, P., Vinck, P., & Stover, E. (2007). *Abducted: The Lord's Resistance Army and forced conscription in Northern Uganda, Berkeley-Tulane Initiative on Vulnerable Populations*. California: Human Rights Centre-University of California and the Payson Centre for International Development- Tulane University.

Refugee Law Project. (2013). *We died long time ago*. Documentary. Kampala: RLP.

Refugee Law Project. (2005). *Peace first, justice later: Traditional justice in Northern Ugandan*. Refugee Law Project Working Paper 17. Online. Available from http://www.refugeelawproject.org/working_papers/RLP.WP17.pdf Accessed 15.07.17.

Refugee Law Project. (2004). *Behind the violence: Causes, consequences and the search for solutions to the war in Northern Uganda*. Working paper no. 11. Kampala: RLP.

Rubaihayo, P. (2006, Wednesday October 26 ). Obote the nationalist: His vision enabled Buganda to remain part of Uganda. *The New Vision*. Online. Available from https://www.newvision.co.ug/new_vision/news/1115310/obote-nationalist Accessed 23.01.19.

Security Council Report. (2012). *June 2012 monthly forecast*. Online. Available from http://www.Securitycouncilreport.org/monthlyforecast/201206/lookup_c_gIKWL.MTIsG_b_8102695.php?print=true Accessed 20.07.17.

Shanker, T., & Gladstone, R. (2011, October 14). Armed US advisers to help fight African renegade group. *The New York Times*. Online. Available from ww.nytimes.com/2011/10/15/world/africa/barack-obama-sending-100-armed-dvisers-to-africa-to-help-fight-lords-resistance-army.html?_r=0 Accessed 17.07.17.

South African Foreign Policy Initiative. (2012, May 10). AA *quick reaction force moulded by Africa's circumstances*. Online. Available from http://www.safpi.org/news/article/2012/quick-reaction-force-moulded-articles-circumctances Accessed 17.07.17.

Stanton, G. (n.d). LRA Conflict, Documentary, Kampala: Genocide Watch.

The Resolve. (2010). *Basic history*. Online. Available from www.theresolve.org/the-lra-crisis/basic-history/ Accessed 20.07.10.

The Resolve. (2012). *Moment of truth: The potential and limits of the US military's counter-LRA deployment*. Resolve June. Online. Available from https://sulsa.democracyinaction.org/0/224/images/RESOLVE%20moment%20Truth%20June%202012.pgf. Accessed 12.07.17.

Tumutegyereize, K. (2012). *What will it take to end the LRA conflict?* Online. Available from www.cr.org/downloads/LRA_Kony201203_kennedytumutegyereize.pdf Accessed 19.07.17.

Wade, S. (2009). *ARLPI pilot land conflict mitigation project in Lamogi*. Online. Available from http://www.arlpi.org/arlpi-pilots-land-conflict-mitigation-project-in-lamogi Accessed 23.01.19.

Westbrook, D. (2000). The torment of Northern Uganda: A legacy of missed opportunities. *OJPCR: The Online Journal of Peace and Conflict Resolution*, *3*(2)|June 2000. Online. Available from http://www.trinstitute.org/ojpcr/p3_2westbrook.htm Accessed 23.01.19.

Woldetsadik, M. A. (2017). *Lessons from Northern Uganda: Post-conflict integration of 'Children Born of War'*. Online. Available from https://www.rand.org/blog/2017/04/lessons-from-northern-uganda-post-conflict-integration.htm Accessed 20.07.17.

# 28

# Somalia

## Al-Shabaab, counterterrorism and counterinsurgency in a recovering failed state

*Mala Mustapha*

## Introduction

In the Horn of Africa, the Somalia-based terrorist group Al-Shabaab remained the most potent threat to regional security, and the group has continued to maintain its allegiance to al-Qaida. This chapter examines the structural causes of Somalia's long-running conflict—analysing the antecedents from its "state collapse" to the rise of Al-Shabaab and the drive to counterterrorism (CT) and counterinsurgency (COIN) interventions. The chapter further examines the current strategies and challenges facing CT-COIN operations against Al-Shabaab in Somalia. It highlights numerous lessons for the newly emerging approaches to CT-COIN in Africa. It argues that lack of legitimate government and coherent plan for CT-COIN, marred by the pursuit of the geostrategic interest of intervening actors such as the United States (US), and AMISOM's contingent pursuing their national interests, remain a severe challenge for countering Al-Shabaab insurgency in Somalia.

The CT-COIN operations in Somalia involved the United Nation's endorsed African Union Mission in Somalia (AMISOM) operations and the US special operations under a tailored engagement strategy (Bruton, 2014; Jones et al., 2016; Reno, 2013). Since 2011, AMISOM's operations recorded major security gains against ISIS cells in Putland and Al-Shabaab "safe havens" in southern Somalia. The AMISOM's earlier mandate was to protect Somalia's fragile transitional government and stabilise the worsening security situation. Still, later its mission emerged to extend beyond traditional peacekeeping to include COIN operations and humanitarian assistance (Bruton, 2014). Despite such progress, the security situation in Somalia remains fragile, both AMISOM and the Somali National Army (SNA) could not degrade Al-Shabaab's capacity for coordinated attacks. The terrorist group is leveraging on clan politics to win local support and foster distrust among local communities towards security forces operating in its enclaves. Al-Shabaab also exploits poor economic conditions to recruit disenchanted populations into its ranks. In 2016, Al-Shabaab used "ungoverned spaces" in northern, central and southern Somali as "safe havens" to conduct operations with impunity. The group has recently overrun Somali and AMISOM bases and inflicted serious damages and casualties on troops. For instance, in June 2015, Al-Shabaab killed nearly 60 Ethiopian troops in the south. Also in the same year, the group killed more than 50 Burundi soldiers in Leego. Similarly, in January 2016, Al-Shabaab terrorists launched an assault on a military base in Al Ade in the south and killed at least 100 Kenyan troops (Roggio, 2017). This chapter interrogates why CT-COIN seems to have failed to counter Al-Shabaab's ferocious attacks in the Horn of Africa.

The chapter is divided into five main parts. The first part conceptualises terrorism, counterterrorism, insurgency and counterinsurgency. It challenged the Critical Terrorism Studies' (CTS) perspective, which focuses on who a terrorist is, and how terrorist activities can be countered? The second part traces the history and dynamics of state collapse in Somalia. The third part is concerned with how state collapse in Somalia provided the fertile ground for the rise of Al-Shabaab. The fourth part outlines the textual CT-COIN strategies employed by regional and international actors to combat insurgency in Somalia. And the final part of the chapter offers a concluding remark highlighting the need for alternative approaches to CT-COIN in Somalia a shift from military strategy to developmental response to terrorist threats.

## Defining terrorism, insurgency, counterterrorism and Counterinsurgency counter in surgency: debating viewpoints

This section attempts to expand our understanding of the term terrorism and insurgency beyond a "value-laden" approach as alluded by Omeje (Chapter 2) and Tar and Ibobo-Eze (Chapter 19) in this volume, and the way most researchers on terrorism tend to construct the concept. It questioned existing definitions as largely drawn from contemporary debates over definition and responses to terrorism and insurgency that dominates CTS. This chapter seeks to place terrorism and insurgency in the wider discourse of epistemological politics of "labelling" or "name-calling" that have been widely ignored in the dominant narratives on terrorism studies. Covering a broad spectrum of existing narratives on terrorism and insurgency it focuses on the politics of "terrorist" label and how such framing compounded the definitional problems of terrorism and insurgency and undermined robust CT-COIN interventions.

Conceptualising terrorism has evaded a widely agreed definition for long in the academic literature (e.g. Richards, 2015; Schmid, 1992). More importantly, terrorism has become a subject that is so much entangled with the politically motivated application and labelling. What is more perplexing is how terrorism achieved ubiquity recently and presented a diverse picture in contrast to the dominant narratives that classically placed it to Islamic terrorism (Blanchard, 2016). When Al-Shabaab militant killed 148 people in an attack on Garissa University College and reportedly singled out Christians and killed them is compared with Boko Haram co-ordinated attack of a mosque in Maiduguri killing 13 Muslim worshippers, the media will quickly attribute such attacks to Islamist terrorism. When numerous coordinated attacks in Paris that killed many innocent people and a stabbing by a man with a reported history of mental illness that left three people wounded at an East London Tube station are analytically merged under "terrorism", it is probably time for a conceptual dismemberment—setting analytical boundaries between terrorism and other forms of political violence. Yet terrorism has become synonymous with "Islamic terrorism" since 9/11 due to the pervasive Global War on Terrorism (GWOT) campaign. Mainstream media has been complicit in creating this framing—the juxtaposition of Islamic symbols with terrorism alongside with a historical narrative of Islam as barbaric (Tipu, 2013). What about other forms of extremism or white supremacist ideology that encourages individuals to commit violent acts against peoples of specific stock? On 22 July 2011, 77 innocent people were murdered and 319 injured in Norway. "Muslims" were quickly blamed but the perpetrator – Anders Breivik – turned out to be right-wing fanatic whose motive was media attention for his far-right ideology. The fact is that if a lone wolf, right-wing fanatic or white supremacist commits acts of violence it must be equated with an extremist Muslim who commits violent acts of terrorism. Both actions should be framed as terrorism with distinct ideological linen. This suggests Islamic terrorism need to be differently conceptualised with right-wing terrorism.

Similarly, while acts such as US drone attacks in Pakistan and Somalia, NATO airstrikes in Libya and Saudi Arabia air bombardment of Yemen can all be labelled as actions against "terrorists", these acts further illuminate the conceptual and empirical ambiguity embedded in the CTS. From this vantage point, how can terrorism be defined? Terror reportage in the media are considered as either "terrorist acts" or "counterterrorism measures" under the (GWOT) were violent in nature, do such acts undermine analytical clarity to the concept of terrorism? There is a common saying that an internationally accepted definition of terrorism cannot be agreed upon; it is argued, "one man's terrorist is another man's freedom fighter". The Arab-Israel conflict is an excellent example in this context. The question of who a terrorist is, according to this claim conceptualising terrorism depends on the subjective outlook of the definer (Ganor, 2010; Schmid, 2011). In most cases, the adoption of a standard definition is simply a matter of convenience—which not only refers to a form of political violence but also used as a pejorative political term of stigmatisation to express moral condemnation in official and public discourse (Schmid, 2011).

Given this conceptual problem, Richards (2015) argues for a broader analytical framework that distinguishes terrorism from other forms of political violence where boundaries and exclusions are established. Richards argues that there is something analytically distinctive about terrorism compared to other forms of political violence. Nevertheless, if terrorism is to be conceptualised as a method as in many academic works of literature, it is analytically irrelevant who uses it and upon whom it is used, just so long as the intent and the motive is to generate a psychological impact is present (Blanchard, 2016; Richards, 2015). Moreover, if utilised as a rhetorical tool, the term terrorism ostensibly becomes a mere invective in political debates where accusations and counter-accusations compete for the moral indignation or approval relevant to the audience, in particular, the mainstream media (Schmid, 2011).

Consequently, the definitions of terrorism often reflect the political interests and the moral judgment of those who define it. In its simplest form, Alex Schmid (2011:40) defined terrorism "as political violence or violence for political purposes." Similarly, Richards (2015: 18) conceptualised it as "the use or threat of violence or force with the primary purpose of generating a psychological impact beyond the immediate victims for a political motive". Some key elements of many conceptualisations also refer to the fact that terrorism is an instrument for the attempted realisation of a political or religious project that perpetrators lacking mass support are seeking, that it generally involves a series of acts of demonstrative public violence accompanied by threats of more to impress, intimidate, or coerce target audiences. Most of these terrorists' actions are also acknowledged by experts to be driven by the presence of political motives underlying them. The reason or intent of such violence might be political, but the act itself is considered criminal in international law (Schmid, 2010: 197). The long tradition of theorising that dominated critical terrorism studies situate the term terrorism in various contexts expressed in shared elements of violence form such as indiscriminate bombings, armed assaults on civilians, focused assassinations, kidnappings, hostage-taking and hijacking are considered as acts of terrorism.

The root causes of terrorism include: social inequality, marginalisation and exclusion, political oppression, extreme poverty and violation of basic rights, deprivation, prejudices, despair for lack of perspectives, alienation of the youth population in situations of economic deprivation and political tension, uncertainty, a sense of injustice and lack of hope, fear; absence of a sense of belonging to the human family and anti-Western domination etc. (Schmid, 2011: 14).

The definitional problem of terrorism also extends to counterterrorism simply because there is no general agreement as to what constitutes terrorism. Is terrorism a form of war, a criminal problem or is it a problem of general insecurity, an issue of national security, a threat to democratic order or a societal problem? Counterterrorism policy-makers did not agree on a specific threat caused by terrorism hence cannot be fought effectively. Fighting terrorism also raises the question of whether it can be fought only by military approach or dealing with the structural causes of terrorism or both? Another definitional challenge is that counterterrorism measures do not stop at states borders as terrorism threat is transnational this blurs the boundaries between domestic and international security, between foreign and domestic policy dimensions. In the abstract, counterterrorism can be defined as a mix of domestic and foreign policies designed to counter the threats and actions of terrorist groups and individuals linked to terrorist organisations in an attempt to protect the general public from violence (Omelicheva, 2007). Counterterrorism measures include freezing financial assets of terrorist organisations, multilateral treaties aimed at addressing different aspects of terrorism. Since 9/11 most of the Western counterterrorism measures encompass practices such as preemptive war, targeted killings, mass surveillance, torture, control orders and de-radicalisation programmes.

Insurgency and counterinsurgency have been conceptualised in many ways and applied to different situations (Brennan, 2005; Rich & Duyvesteyn, 2012). Insurgency is widely considered as a tactic of warfare—often used synonymously with guerrilla warfare. Insurgency is often referred to the means by which, increasingly through the 20th century, the traditional methods associated with the long history of guerrilla and irregular warfare became revolutionary in both intent and practice (Rich & Duyvesteyn, 2012). In this context, social, economic, psychological and political elements are deployed onto traditional hit-and-run or suicide bombings and kidnappings in order to radically change the structure of a state by force carried out by violent non-state actors. The contemporary changing dynamic of insurgency includes pirates, narco gangs and even failed states (Rich & Duyvesteyn, 2012).

When conceptualising insurgency as a tactic, the activity has an extreme pedigree in warfare. Some violent non-state actors work pragmatically together in what (Brennan, 2005) labelled as "federated insurgents complexes" to describe the overlapping and ambiguous nature of the actors whether as insurgents or guerrilla actors. However, despite such conceptual ambiguity, scholars have heatedly debated that insurgent groups are driven by motivations whose context are also subject to change over time. Rich & Duyvesteyn (2012: 12) argued that insurgency motivations have shifted from traditional nationalism, decolonisation, liberation struggles and revolution to most importantly, the Salafist jihad. Until recently, Mackinlay (2009) introduced the concept of post-Maoist insurgency to articulate the idea that contemporary insurgency has metamorphosed from purely national struggles into a global undertaking with transnational linkages and motives. While Maoist insurgencies were characterised by a clear ideology, a national state being the target of violence, post-Moist insurgencies relies on multiple audiences, multiple actors and proliferation of communication and virtual communities (Mackinlay, 2009). However, the increased transnational linkages and nature of modern insurgencies has shifted the conceptual frontiers of insurgency with significant development of new features. For instance, traditionally most insurgency movements operated within their own countries and direct transnational collaboration with external actors was exceedingly rare. Today, transnational networks of insurgent movements have become a key component of insurgency (Rich & Duyvesteyn, 2012: 11).

How does counterinsurgency differ from counterterrorism? Counterinsurgency is a set of tactical tools or alternatively as an overarching strategy to defeat an opponent. It involves military, paramilitary, political, economic, psychological, and civic actions taken by a government to defeat an insurgency (Boyle, 2008). Scholars have argued that traditional approaches to counterinsurgency were a product of the era of decolonisation, when ideas were developed on how to deal with political challenges faced by independence movements. However, from the early part of the 21st century onward, classical counterinsurgency thinking witnessed a dramatic change leading to the emergence of the neo-classical school of thought. Neo-classical thinkers such as Mackinlay, J. (2009), Nagl (2005) and Kilcullen (2005) focused on how differences in the strategic security environment and the complex trans-nationalisation of insurgent actors through a global network warrant a new strategic approach to counterinsurgency.

## State collapse and the rise of insurgency in Somalia

The end of the authoritarian regime of Mohammed Siad Barre in 1991 led to the collapse of the Somali state and opened up space for the emergence of warlord politics—a system of a "strong clan" and "weak state". The post-Barre Somali politics was characterised by warlords competition to occupy "ungoverned spaces" and amassed large-scale war infrastructure for tactical advantage (Tar & Mustapha, 2017:281).

The collapse of state institutions and the subsequent political fragmentation of Somaliland eventually led to the birth of the radical Islamists group known as Al-Shabaab. Al-Shabaab meaning *"the Youth"* in the Arabic language is an al-Qaeda-linked extremist group comprised of far-right Salafist and *Wahhabis* youth fighting for the creation of "theocratic state" or a *Caliphate,* in Somalia. The rise of Al-Shabaab in Somalia has compounded the problems of anarchy in the Horn of Africa. The group, also known as *Harakat Al-Shabaab al Mujahideen* (loosely) translated as "Movement of Striving Youth," held control over Mogadishu and some parts of southern region prior to CT-COIN operations by AMISOM and the US. The actual antecedents of Al-Shabaab's origins are still widely debated among researchers. Several radical figures who later become prominent leaders in the group had already functioned as a small Salafi jihadi cell in Somaliland with links to *Masjid Jaama,* the main Hargeysa Mosque. Others had created enclaves in southern towns of Ras Kambani, and many others had been with either Salafi jihadi groups in Gedo, Bay, Bakol, Galgaduud and Putland strongholds while others remain among the Somali diaspora (Tar & Mustapha, 2017:283). These radical figures gathered in early 2003 at Mogadishu at a time when the resurgent business community showed increased support for the rapid growth of the clan and *Sharia* (Islamic law) Islamic courts as an option to the warlords and militia campaign that had shattered the city since the early 1990s. Al-Shabaab was later formed at a workshop known as "Nasruddin garage" under the protection of the Sharia court (International Crisis Group, 2014: 5).

High profile Islamist figures such as Sheik Hassan Dahir Awey founded the group and commanded the military wing of the *Al-Ittihaad Al-Islami* (AIAI) and subsequently took over the leadership of the Islamic Court Union (ICU). Later in 2006, Awey handed over the military command of Al-Shabaab to Aden Hashi Ayro, a young Somali militant who was subsequently killed by a US missile strike in 2008. Ahmed Abdi Godane took over as the group's leader after the death of Ayro. In September 2014, the US military confirmed it had killed Godane in a coordinated and targeted airstrike in Somalia, and the group's leadership was handed over to Ahmed Umar. Al-Shabaab's terrorist activities focused on targets within Somalia, and it recently has expanded its operations across borders, including suicide bombings in Uganda in 2010, a coordinated attack on Nairobi Westgate Mall in 2013 and the attack on Garissa University on 2 April 2015, killing 148 people. The group's attacks on Kenya are largely in retaliation to Kenya's robust COIN operations in the entire region and its pivotal role in AMISOM (Tar & Mustapha, 2017).

Jones et al. (2016:23) divides the historical evolution of Al-Shabaab into five chronological and transformative phases: (1) ideological and historical origins (the 1960s–2005), (2) proto-insurgent phase (2005–2007), (3) rebirth and rise to organisational maturity (2007–2009), (4) the peak of its territorial control and institutional power (2009–2011), and (5) weakening and devolution to a terrorist group (2011–2016). The first phase from the 1960s to 2005 relates to the ideological and historical origins of Al-Shabaab when Salafi and Wahhabi doctrines were introduced into Somalia from Saudi Arabia and Egypt to challenge the dominance of Sufism. Somalia's early generation of jihadists went to Afghanistan in the early 1990s to join the *Mujahideen* (fighters) against Soviet occupation. Later these fighters become founders of Al-Shabaab who eventually succeeded in spreading Salafist Islamist ideology inspired by people like Abdullah Azzam. In 1983 the Al-Ittihaad al-Islamiya was founded as an early militant group that later constituted the ranks of Al-Shabaab. The group primary aim then was to overthrow the Siad Barre's government and establish an Islamic state in the entire region including Somalia, some parts of Kenya, Ethiopia, and Djibouti. In January 1991, Siad Barre's regime collapsed after two decades in power. The ensuing years in Somalia were characterised by the total collapse of the Somalia state and fragmentation of the society based on inter-clan war and the drumming up of warlords. The emerging "ungoverned spaces" in Somalia gave an opportunity for the second generation of Somali Salafi-jihadist such as Aden Hashi, Farah Ayro to undergo military training in Afghanistan under the Taliban. In 2001 and 2002, many Somalis including prominent jihadi figures and Al-Shabaab leaders such as Aden Hashi Ayro, Mukhtar Robow, Ahmed Godane, Abdullahi Salad, and Ibrahim Haji Jamal al-Afghani travelled to Afghanistan to fight alongside al-Qaeda and Taliban forces (Jones et al., 2016:12).

The second phase was described as the *proto-insurgency 2005–2007* era, which marked the beginning of a dialogue, by extremists for the formation of Al-Shabaab. During this period, the loose network of extremists (jihadi-elements) who returned from the fighting in Afghanistan sought unification that included the Afghan veterans, former AIAI members, some al-Qaeda elements in East Africa. In June 2006, the ICU took over power in Somalia overcoming US-backed group of mostly secular warlords. In August 2006, Al-Shabaab was formerly formed as a splinter group of the ICU hardliners of the Sharia courts (Jones et al., 2016: 13).

In the third phase labelled as the *rebirth and the rise of the Islamists*, 2007–2009, Al-Shabaab focused on strengthening its beleaguered and weakened organisational structure and rearming its units in southern Somalia. This was a result of the death of many of its leaders, Ethiopian forces occupation in the southern part and AMISOM support for the Transitional Federal Government (TFG). To garner support among local communities, Al-Shabaab began a propaganda tactic by establishing Internet presence and recruiting Somali diaspora. In 2007 Al-Shabaab got an internal recruitment boost by deepening clan divisions, widespread opposition to Ethiopia's occupation and growing legitimacy crisis that rocked the TFG whose police force was widely seen as corrupt. By the end of 2007, Al-Shabaab began to resurge again gaining popular support across Somalia. In August 2008, Al-Shabaab in collaboration with allied forces from the Ras Kamboni clan captured Kismayo and later advanced towards Mogadishu (Jones et al., 2016: 14).

The fourth phase from 2009–2011 is considered as *the heyday of Al-Shaabab* when the group expanded its territorial control following Ethiopian withdrawal from southern region in 2009. In early 2009, Al-Shabaab captured Baidoa, the interim capital of the TFG and seized territory north and west of Mogadishu. Subsequently, in 2010 the group continued its territorial expansion by capturing territory under the control of the moderate Sufi paramilitary group the *Ahlu Sunna Wah Jamaa*. During this period, Al-Shabaab also started conducting cross-border attacks into Kenya and issuing a statement to foreign jihadists to launch attacks against Uganda and Burundian embassies worldwide in retaliation for their active participation in AMISOM (Jones et al., 2016:16).

Finally, the fifth phase (2011–2016) is considered as *the period of retreat and adaptation* in which the Africa Union-led AMISOM military campaign has weakened Al-Shabaab. Between February and May 2011, AMISOM conducted multiple onslaughts against Al-Shabaab strongholds in Mogadishu and they suffered colossal territorial losses and its recruitment of fighters declined. In October 2011, Kenyan forces launched a combined air and ground offensive in the southern part of Mogadishu forcing Al-Shabaab to retreat and lost control of occupied territory. The Kenyan military intervention compelled Al-Shabaab to expand its terrorist operations in Kenya including suicide bombings, attack on the Nairobi Westgate Mall in 2013 and the massacre of hundreds of Kenyan citizens during the attack on the Garissa University in April 2015. After losing control of its seaport revenue base, the group began to adapt and adjust by forcefully imposing "taxes" from local businesses and humanitarian organisations to sustain its operations (Jones et al, 2016:21).

Table 28.1 illustrates how Al-Shabaab evolved and transformed from a local jihadist group in Somalia to a regional terrorist group that destabilises the Horn of Africa.

## Somalia's counterterrorism and drive: From post-war reconstruction to national security

In the last couple of years, Somalia has experienced tremendous progress towards the post-war reconstruction of the collapsed state. There have been sustained efforts by the international

*Table 28.1* Selected Indicators of Al-Shabaab's Strength

| Years | Range of Fighters | Number of Terrorist Attacks & Civilian Casualties | Organisational Cohesion | Al-Shabaab's Approximate Areas of Influence (on percentage of Somalia Population) |
|---|---|---|---|---|
| Phase 1:1960s–2005 | 0–30 | 2 attacks (Average: less than 1 per month) 3 killed (Average: less than 1 per month) | Low | 0% |
| Phase 2:2005–2006 | 30–400 | 4 attacks (Average: less than 1 per month) 20 killed (Average: less than 1 per month) | Moderate (as of fall 2006) | 10% |
| Phase 3:2007–2009 | 1,000–7000 | 59 attacks (Average: 2 per month)286 killed (Average: 12 per month) | Moderate (as of fall 2008) | 35% |
| Phase 4:2009–2011 | 5,000–12,000 | 135 attacks Average: 6 per month) 364 killed (Average: 15 per month) | Moderate (as of spring 2010) | 55% |
| Phase 5:2011–2016 | 3,0008,000 | 1,962 attacks (Average; 33 per month)4,233 killed (Average: 71 per month) | Low (as of summer 2016) | 5% |

Source: Jones et al. (2016), Counter-terrorism *and Counter-insurgency in Somalia: Assessing the Campaign against Al-Shabaab*, p.8

431

community to reconfigure the country's path to democracy and sustainable peace. This section contextualises the various CT-COIN approaches deployed by regional and international actors as part of the "state-building" initiatives in Somalia. The point of argument here is that the plethora of national, regional and international response to Al-Shabaab threats in Somalia exemplify and reflects the evolving dynamics of CT-COIN in Africa aimed at addressing the continent's new security challenges—growing threats of Islamist terrorism. The African Union (AU) mission in Somalia AMISOM and US counterterrorism strategy in Somalia will be critically examined.

## African Union counterterrorism-couterinsurgency strategy

The framework for addressing terrorism and violent extremism in Africa predates the growing international campaign against terrorism in the aftermath of the 9/11 attack of the US. National, regional, and continental efforts to CT have been evolving as far back as the early 1990s. The continental framework for CT is largely derived from the 1999 Organisation of African Unity (OAU) Convention on the Prevention and Combating of Terrorism. In 2004, this framework was later modified and expanded after the transition of the OAU to the AU into the Plan of Action on the Prevention and Combating of Terrorism, aimed at addressing Africa's security challenges. Whilst the frameworks outlined earlier provide guidelines on tackling threats of terrorism and violent extremism, in practice, CT-COIN interventions have been carried out primarily in military terms (Ramdeen, 2017).

Somalia presents a good example of AU's CT-COIN interventions to counter transnational terrorism. In 2007, the AU's Peace and Security Council (PSC) established AMISOM to support the transitional government (TFG) of Somalia and to collaborate with the Somali national defence and public safety institutions to counter the threat posed by Al-Shabaab and other extremist groups. In 2014, AMISOM working with the Somali National Army (SNA) through coordinated efforts had successfully recaptured territories seized by Al-Shabaab (Ramdeen, 2017). From an earlier six-month mandate, AMISOM has grown into over ten years as the largest regional peace-support operation in Africa. AMISOM also emerged to represent a multi-layered security architecture through which the UN and other donor agencies provide financial and logistic support to counter the threat of Al-Shabaab. The mission has been hailed as a successful model of CT-COIN collaboration between regional and international organisations (Albrecht & Haelein, 2016).

It is obvious that the Africa Union-led AMISOM military offensive has degraded Al-Shabaab's capability for attacks (Jones et al., 2016; Meservey, 2013). Through its coordinated onslaughts against Al-Shabaab, AMISOM successfully captured Kismayo and Mogadishu and damaged the group's source of income. Whilst some progress has been achieved by AMISOM and the SNA to counterterrorism, Al-Shabaab continues its attacks across the region particularly targeting military operations and bases because they are still well funded, and even though they are degraded as a force, their access of arms and intelligence are not degraded.

## US counterterrorism-couterinsurgency strategy in Somalia

Somalia represents a frontline in the US Global War on Terror (GWOT) because of the potential link between terrorism and state fragility. While initially, the US focused on a dual policy towards building state and at the same time-fighting terror, its subsequent isolationist strategy yielded an opposite result of deepening the existing conflict—encouraged the political polarisation and military radicalisation of the insurgency (Malito, 2015). The US military strategy in

Somalia also focused on combined CT- COIN operations under the auspice of the United State Africa Command (AFRICOM). US revised CT strategy in Somalia involved a tailored engagement strategy which focuses on deploying a small number of US Special Operations Forces to conduct targeted strikes, provide intelligence and build the capacity of local partners to conduct ground operations. This strategy was aimed at working with and supporting the SNA, AMISOM and clan forces which were in the lead on the COIN operations (Jones et al, 2016). The US provides supports to build capacity for AMISOM and the Somali National Army including training, advising, assisting and occasionally accompanying AMISOM and Somali forces to conduct targeted strikes (Jones et al., 2016:47).

The CT-COIN operations largely target Al-Shabaab. The strategy attempts to build capacity and strengthen local social structures to "win hearts and minds" through deradicalisation approach so that local people should stop supporting Al-Shabaab. Counterinsurgency operation is also limited to combat or direct police actions against terrorists or insurgents to build a functioning local community. Thus, the US CT-COIN strategy is geared towards defeating violent non-actors across the spectrum—building up a functioning government and at the same time destroying terrorists' and insurgents' network (Ganon, 2015). For instance, in Somalia the CIA-trained the local commando unit, Alpha Group or Somalia's National Intelligence and Security Agency (NSA) conducting specialised target operations against Al-Shabaab particularly around Gedo region of Southern Somalia (Ganon, 2015).

## Rethinking AU and US CT-COIN strategies in Somalia

In spite of regional and international CT- COIN operations in Somalia the terrorist group Al-Shabaab has continued to thrive. The attack on the Westgate shopping mall in Nairobi illustrates that Al-Shabaab is not yet eliminated and has the capacity for the cross-border attack in the Horn of Africa (Busher, 2014). In February 2016, Al-Shabaab had succeeded in smuggling a bomb onboard a flight from Mogadishu; it has retaken cities in southern Somalia including the important port of Merka. Al-Shabaab had also overrun AMISOM bases and seized weapons (Felbab-Brown, 2016). The question is why are efforts to counter Al-Shabaab failing in Somalia?

Huge challenges for CT-COIN operations remain in Somalia. Critics have argued that both the UN-AU-backed AMISOM and US CT-COIN strategy lack a coherent plan to fight Al-Shabaab and relied heavily on the state system (military solution) as the primary instrument to combat terrorism. Emphasis on strengthening military resulted in ineffectual mechanism for CT (Solomon, 2015). In contrast to Al-Shabaab's rejuvenation, AMISOM operations have stalled. The training of the SNA is stagnating and the national force is torn by clan rivalries and politics. Attacks by the US drone and special operations forces further undermined Al-Shabaab's operations but do not alter the balance of power on the ground (Felbab-Brown, 2016). AMISOM continues to be barricaded in its bases and many of the main roads are under the control of Al-Shabaab. In areas and towns where AMISOM is nominally in control, Al-Shabaab is in charge of control more at night as AMISOM forces conduct sketchy patrol. Similarly, the Somali forces lack the capacity to hold "post-clearing" and secure government offices. There is little coordination, intelligence sharing among the AMISOM contingents (Felbab-Brown, 2016). The Somali government and the SNA forces are weak and poorly trained, and AMISOM countries often turned to clan militias to help fill the political and security vacuum following Al-Shabaab's retreat. AMISOM is largely beset by poor coordination among its troop-contributing countries, and lack logistics, manpower and equipment (Jones et al., 2016: 46).

The major lapse in US counterterrorism policy in Somalia is the failure to assess and co-opt the local conflict dynamics and clan-based politics into its CT-COIN operations. In other words, the gap between the external perception of the Somali conflict and the local reality on the ground creates challenges for a robust CT-COIN operation. Elliot & Holzer (2009) argues that three interrelated external perceptions of the Somali crisis informed the current US policy in Somalia: (i) a post-Cold War narrative of "state building," (ii) a post-9/11 war on terror involving military approach, and (iii) a reloaded vision of state-building as counterterrorism model. These perceptions are derived from an Anglo-Saxon intellectual edifice, detached from the Somali context. In other words, the externally misread internal dynamics of Somali conflict—misplaced factors in the analysis of the conflict dynamics from among the drivers of the conflict including clan, class, nation, religion and the US interpretation of the Somalia situation within the frame of "War on Terror" and state-building narratives created a disjuncture and gap between local reality and CT-COIN policy perception by the US. The implication of this US counterterrorism posture in Somalia is that it has impaired a CT-COIN engagement and failed to prevent Al-Shabaab from operating in Somalia and beyond (Elliot & Holzer, 2009: 4). This problem informed the reason the US has failed to construct a functioning government that can address the root causes of terrorism in Somalia.

Another key challenge is the geopolitics of intervention by both global and regional actors in Somalia. The CT-COIN approaches had been politicised. US-backed warlord politics also played a role in the rise of Al-Shabaab. The US, which declared its "War on Terror" after the 9/11 attacks were to fight Islamic radicalism and sought to take advantage of the Somali situation by funding warlords in Somalia. The implications of this strategic error by the US contributed to institutionalisation of violent extremism and radicalisation of Al-Shabaab. As a result of geopolitics, Al-Shabaab has transformed itself from a local terrorist organisation into a lethal regional violent-non-state actor with anti-Western and anti-US rhetoric (Tar and Mustapha: 291). Similarly, Ethiopia and Kenya still support their favourite Somali proxies. Kenya continues to back its ally Sheik Ahmed "Modobe", a former high-level Al-Shabaab commander who defected to create his Ogadeni anti-Shabaab militias. In collaboration with Madobe and other Ogadeni powerbrokers, Kenyan Defence Forces control the Kismayo port. Like Al-Shabaab, the Kenyan forces have been allegedly illegally taxed smuggled sugar, charcoal, and other goods through the port and southern Kenya (Tar & Mustapha, 2017). Kenya's other interests in Somalia often clash with those of Ethiopia and the Somali national government including over projecting of power off the Somali coast and strengthening local warlords and militias who promise to keep Ogadeni mobilisation in Kenya down (Tar & Mustapha, 2017). Thus, the geostrategic calculation of intervening actors complicates efforts to coordinate counterterrorism activities in Somalia.

In contrast to a military solution, both AU and US counterterrorism strategies in Somalia often tend to ignore the social, political, and economic context for the rise of Al-Shabaab. The spread of militant extremist groups is rooted in the deepening socio-economic inequality, marginalisation of youths and social exclusion arising from the complex process of globalisation. Somalia is today one of the poorest countries in the world where the state collapse that eschewed in 1991 provided the "ungoverned space" for the emergence of violent groups like Al-Shabaab (Tar & Mustapha: 2017:294). Al-Shabaab also exploits these poor economic conditions to recruit disenchanted populations into its ranks. To counter Al-Shabaab's surging threats in the Horn of Africa will require both global and regional efforts to tackle poverty and socio-political inequalities.

The ultimate solution to the Al-Shabaab threats is two folds: first is the long-term project of building a legitimate government. Second AMISOM will remain unable to accomplish its mission in Somalia until it builds a vibrant Somali National Forces capable of securing the country against Islamist insurgents. The fundamental challenge for CT-COIN in Somalia relates to what William Reno (2013) described as "mismatch of the concept and reality of the state". Reno (2013: 15–16) further argued that counterinsurgency rests upon two key principles:

a. "there must be government with the political will and capacity to reform and effectively engage citizens;
b. there must be a cohesive indigenous armed force with the ability to protect the government and provide security to civilians."

Both tenets presuppose that local political actors accept the existence of a state that state collapse is temporary and state restoration is possible. In this context, state-building requires a clear-cut distinction between insurgent and government, subversion, and support, and legal and illegal even if it becomes clear that individuals are often divided by loyalties and multiple motives. On the contrary, key elements of politics in Somalia lack this fundamental logic and illustrate the main difficulties facing counterinsurgency. Local authorities collaborate with insurgents that they fight. Armed group unify and then suddenly split along clan fronts. Political authority, personal honour and social practices of vendetta and protection become wrapped up in what others regards as subversion, infiltration and corruption blurring externally defined boundaries between licit or illicit activities in Somalia (Reno, 2013: 16). These challenges have undermined robust regional and international CT-COIN interventions in Somalia.

## Conclusion

This chapter examined the challenges for effective counterinsurgency measures in Somalia and argued that the current CT-COIN approaches focused on military strategy, which proved counterproductive. The chapter explored how the dissonance and gap between the external perception of the Somali conflict and the local reality create challenges for a robust CT-COIN approach in Somalia. The regional and international CT-COIN strategies in Somalia are unresponsive to the origins, motives, and realities of Islamist group Al-Shabaab. Most African security scholars believe that the current traditional CT-COIN approaches as epitomised in both the AU and the US strategies in Somalia in particular reliance on military engagement often tend to deal only with the symptoms of terrorism and insurgency instead of tackling the root causes of the problem. This illuminates how the AU and Washington analytical framing of the Somali conflict within the GWOT label ignored the complex connections between terrorism and state fragility particularly poverty, social exclusion and local conflict dynamics such as clan politics and the need to deal with through economic development. As illustrated in this chapter, the fractioning and fragmentation of the political space in Somaliland along clan politics and loyalties as well as deepened poverty and inequality undermines the emergence of a viable reformist central government and cohesive indigenous armed force which are key tenet upon which both CT-COIN is found. The Somalia experience highlights the need for a shift from this traditional CT-COIN approaches to include developmental approaches to counterinsurgency with emphasis on building capacity for local institutions of law enforcement and governance, eradicate poverty and foster national cohesion in Somalia.

## References

Albrecht, P., & Haelein, C. (2016). Fragmented peacekeeping: The African Union in Somalia. *The RUSI Journal, 161*(1), 50–61.
Beckett, I. (2012). The historiography of insurgency. In P. Rich & I. Duyvesteyn (Eds.), *The Routledge handbook of insurgency and counterinsurgency* (pp. 23–31). Abingdon: Routledge.
Blanchard, A. (2016). Book Review: "Conceptualising Terrorism by Anthony Richards". (online). http://www.blogs.lse.ac.uk Accessed 15.08.2017.

Boyle, M. (2008). *"Terrorism and Insurgency"*. In C. Snyder (ed), *Contemporary Security and Strategy*, London: Palgrave Macmillan, p. 186.

Brennan, R. (2005). *Future insurgent threats*. Santa Monica: RAND.

Bruton, B. (2014). "Counter-insurgency in Somalia: Lessons Learned from the African Union Mission in Somalia". *The Atlantic Council*.http://www..atlanticcouncil.org Accessed 21.08.2017.

Busher, J. (2014). Introduction: Terrorism and counterterrorism in Sub-Saharan Africa. *Journal of Terrorism Research*, 5(1), 1–7.

Elliot, A., & Holzer, G. S. (2009). The invention of 'terrorism' in Somalia: paradigms and policy in US foreign relations. *South African Journal of International Affairs*, 16(2), 215–244.

Felbab-Brown, V. (2016). "Why are Efforts to Counter Al-Shaabab falling so Flat"? Brookings (online) .http://www.brookings.edu/blog/order-from-chaos/2016/05/why-are-efforts-to-counter-al-shaabab-falling-so-flat. Accessed 09.09.2017.

Ganon, D. (2015). "Somali Special Forces Strike Kills Senior Al-Shaabab Leader", *SOFREP*. (online). http://www.sofref.com Accessed 20.08.2017.

Ganor, B. (2010). Defining terrorism: Is one man's terrorist another man's freedom fighter. *Journal Police Practice and Research*, 3(4), 287–304.

International Crisis Group. (2014). *Somalia: Al-Shaabab–It will be a long war* (Policy Briefing No, 99, pp. 1–23). Brussels: International Crisis Group.

Jones, G. S., Liepman, M., & Chandler, N. (2016). *Counter-terrorism and counterinsurgency in Somalia: Assessing the campaign against Al-Shaabab*. Santa Monica, California: RAND Corporation.

Kilcullen, D. (2005). Countering global insurgency. *Journal of Strategic Studies*, 28, 597–617.

Mackinlay, J. (2009). *The insurgent archipelago*. London: Hurst.

Malito, D. V. (2015). Building terror while fighting enemies: How the Global War on Terror deepened the crisis in Somalia. *Third World Quarterly*, 36(10), 1866–1886.

Meservey, J. (2013). Al-Shaabab's Somali safe havens: A springboard for terror. Atlantic Council.(Online). http://www.atlanticcouncil.org Accessed 08.09.2017.

Nagl, J. (2005). *Learning to eat soup with a knife: Counterinsurgency lessons from Vietnam and Malaya*. Chicago and London: University of Chicago Press.

Omelicheva, Y. M. (2007). Counter-terrorism: The state of scholarship, direction for future data collection and analysis. *Perspective on Terrorism*, 1(2), 1–14.

Ramdeen, M. (2017). "Countering Terrorism and Violent Extremism in Africa". (online). www.accord. org.za Accessed 07.09.2017.

Reno, W. (2013). "Rethinking Counter-insurgency in Somalia". *Combating Terrorism Centre, Sentinel*, 6(4), 15–19.

Richards, A. (2015). *Conceptualising Terrorism*, Oxford: Oxford University Press.

Rich, P., & Duyvesteyn, I. (2012). The study of insurgency and counterinsurgency. In P Rich & I. Duyvesteyn, (Eds.) *The Routledge handbook of insurgency and counterinsurgency* (pp. 1–20). Abingdon: Routledge.

Roggio, B. (2017). "Shaabab gains in Somalia due to lapses in offensive counter-terrorism operations" . (online).http://www.longwarjournal.org Accessed 27.08.2017.

Schmid, P. A. (1992). The response problem as a definition problem. *Terrorism and Political Violence*, 4(4), 7–25.

Schmid, P. A. (2010). Framework for Conceptualisingconceptualising terrorism. *Terrorism and Political Violence*, 16(2), 197–221.

Schmid, P. A. (2011). The definition of terrorism. In P. A. Schmid (Eds.), *The Routledge handbook of terrorism research* (pp. 39–98). London: Routledge.

Solomon, H. (2015). *Terrorism and counterterrorism in Africa: Fighting insurgency from Al-Shaabab, Ansar Dine and Boko Haram*. UK: Palgrave Macmillan.

Tar, A. U., & Mustapha, M. (2017). Al-Shaabab: State collapse, warlords and Islamist insurgency in Somalia. In C. Varin & D. Abubakar (Eds.), *Violent non-state actors in Africa: Terrorists, rebels and warlords* (pp. 227–300). Switzerland: Palgrave Macmillan.

Tipu, G. (2013). "It is Time that Right-Wing Extremist Acts are labelled as Terrorist". *Open democracy*. Available from: http://www.opendemocracy.net/ghazal-tipu/it-is-time-that-right-wing-extremist-acts-are-labelled-as-terrorist Accessed 17.08.2017.

# 29

# Egypt

## Transnational terrorism, counterterrorism and counterinsurgency

*Audu Nanven Gambo*

## Introduction

The end of the historic Cold War in 1989 was greeted with the widespread expectation of enduring peace, security, and stability around the globe. Third World societies heaved a deep sigh of relief from the economic, political, and social burdens imposed on them by a tight bipolar international system. Many Third World countries were used to fight proxy wars for the two leading ideological camps of capitalism and socialism. The capitalist bloc was driven by the United States of America, while the defunct Union of Soviet Socialist Republic (USSR) drove the socialist camp. No sooner had the Cold War ended than conflicts of varying frequency, scope and intensity erupted in different locations, but primarily in Third World countries still in the throes of nation-building. Many of these conflicts were largely identity and resource-based. The experiences of Liberia, Sierra Leone, Sudan, Burundi, Angola, Algeria, Somalia, Rwanda, Central African Republic, Cote D'Ivoire, Democratic Republic of Congo and many more are quite instructive here. The unprecedented explosion in intrastate armed conflicts not only threatened the stability but the survival of many African states (Fawole, 2001). The demise of the Cold War in a fundamental sense widened and heightened the frontiers of the vulnerability of Third World countries to the intrastate form of conflict. Preceding this development, conflicts were interstate and certainly not as pronounced and deadly as the intrastate forms of conflict, especially in Africa.

The Post-Cold War World order is significantly characterised by the emergence of non-state actors on the global scene with comparable capacity and capability as state actors to destabilise the global system. This is, however, not to suggest that before the demise of the Cold War in the late 1980s, non-state actors were not active on the global scene. What made them gain recognition in the Post-Cold War World order is their immense capacity to inflict unspeakable scale of destruction on state actors which are widely recognised as the legitimate custodians of instruments of violence. The harrowing memory of 911 attacks on some parts of the United States of America is still verdant in the memory of humanity. Not only was the foundation of national stability of the United States of America, globally recognised as the leading world power fundamentally threatened, but also the world was awakened to the grim reality of the capacity and capability of non-state actors such as Osama Bin Laden's AL Qaeda terrorist organisation to wreak such havoc of unprecedented magnitude and intensity on the USA. Similarly, on 11 March 2004, there was the bombing of commuter train system of Madrid killing almost 200 people and wounded over 2,000. On 7 July 2005, a "series of suicide bombing attacks on London's public transport system undertaken by four British nationals of Pakistani descent, cost over 50 lives along with about 700 injuries" Jeong (2000). In effect, one can contend that there has been an upsurge in both the tempo and range of global terrorism and insurgencies (Fafowora, 2013). Terrorism and insurgencies, which used to be isolated cases, have now become inextricably linked and widespread. Third World countries have become helplessly vulnerable to subversive and deadly penetration by these non-state actors operating either as terrorists or insurgents.

Terrorism and insurgency are therefore extreme forms of conflicts that are growing in resilience and potency globally despite concerted effort to degrade and defeat these twin social evils. The Boko Haram insurgency in the Northeast, militancy in the Niger Delta region, Movement for the Actualization of Sovereign State of Biafra (MASSOB), Al-Shaabah in Somalia, Taliban in Afghanistan, IRA in Great Britain, AL Qaeda in the Islamic Maghreb (AQIM), Polisario in Western Sahara, Islamic State in Iraq and Syria (ISIS), and a host of others are familiar terrorist and insurgent groups that have dotted the global landscape. There is hardly any continent in the world that is utterly immune to terrorism and insurgency due to globalisation which has made movement easy and pleasurable. Although it may be factually inaccurate to suggest that globalisation is primarily responsible for terrorism, it is a fundamental truth that technologies associated with globalisation have been exploited by terrorists worldwide (Baylis, Smith, & Owens, 2011) to ease their sinister operations. Technologies have assisted terrorists to quickly mobilise and reach out to each other and build vast networks around the globe. This is the sense in which globalisation is seriously implicated in any act of terrorism. One can therefore argue that every country is at risk due to the permeable nature of inter-state borders. This hard reality about terrorism and insurgency demands building strategic partnership not only to check and halt their spread but also to effectively counter them through concerted efforts when and where they rear their ugly heads.

Africa has in the 21st Century been inundated with the twin evils of insurgency and terrorism. These twin evils have found fertile ground across the length and breadth of the continent because of what is commonly referred to in the literature as the deep-seated culture of "catastrophic governance" that is widespread and which has generated groundswell support for the culture of impunity and anomic behaviour in most African states. This point is trenchantly and pungently captured by Umezulike (2015) when he contends that African countries richly blessed with vast arable lands and good climatic conditions for profitable agriculture; huge revenues earned from the exportation of mineral resources, African leaders have failed to develop their countries. Africa has been marred by a multitude of negative or violent conflicts, acute corruption, poor governance, and gross abuse of political power (Gambo, 2014). These are undoubtedly symptoms of bad governance across the length and breadth of the continent.

Egypt is one of the 54 countries in Africa and it is one of those infested with the scourges of insurgency and terrorism. The Egyptian society has historically been politically unstable and is composed of a population that is critically and intensely argumentative, agitated and politically hyperactive. The wind of 2010 Arab Spring blew fiercely across the Egyptian society in January 2011 with far-reaching consequences for the society. Not only did this phenomenon deepen the political consciousness of an average Egyptian citizen, but also in a more fundamental sense, exposed citizens to radical and extremist tendencies. The Chapter interrogates the nature of transnational terrorism and insurgency in Egypt and how these twin evils have been responded to through carefully articulated counterterrorism and counterinsurgency. It is structured into five sections. Section one provides the introductory remarks. Section two focuses on conceptual/theoretical considerations. Section three analyses the internal dynamics of Egyptian society as the foundation for insurgency and terrorism. Section four critically examines the nature of terrorism and insurgency in Egypt. Section five evaluates the response to the twin evils of terrorism and insurgency through counterterrorism and counterinsurgency. Section six articulates alternative strategies for engaging terrorism and insurgency in the Sinai Peninsula of Egypt. Section seven draws a curtain by way of concluding remarks.

## Conceptual/theoretical considerations

The concepts of terrorism and insurgency have intensely been debated by scholars and have hardly yielded themselves to any universally shared viewpoint because of their varied context, form and objective. This Chapter captures a few of some of these contending definitions to give us a sense of the diversity of opinions on the concepts of terrorism and insurgency. One of the leading scholars on terrorism, Hoffman (1998: 43) views terrorism "as involving politically motivated violence or threatened violence, designed to have far-reaching psychological repercussions beyond the immediate victim or target carried out by a sub-national or non-state, non-uniformed organisation." Fundamentally speaking, terrorism is calculatedly targeted at instilling massive fear in a civilian audience with a view to pitching them against the political authority by making them believe that it has lost its responsive capacity and capability. Since the overall goal of terrorism is to bring about a change in political authority or altering its agenda, hitting civilian target sends a strong message about government's apparent weak capacity to provide safety and protection to citizens.

English (2009: 5), one of the notable authorities on terrorism, sees the concept of terrorism as deriving from the Latin word "*terrere*" which means to frighten, terrify, deter, or scare away. Terrorism is targeted at causing extreme fear thereby forcing people to do what they ordinarily would not do. For instance, if there is a bomb explosion in a public place like market square, school or Motor Park, everyone will be scampering for safety. It is what Updike (2006) would describe as "coercive intimidation" aimed at achieving a political objective. Terrorists mostly target a crowd so as to make news headlines. Their primary target is government and since they cannot penetrate the governmental circle easily and directly, they look for the soft target to cause disquiet in the land. Terrorism seeks to break an enemy's will through the exploitation of fear as argued by Gearson (2002). Terrorism is, therefore, a rebellious behaviour motivated by the desire to subvert an existing socio-political order and establish a new one by a sub-national actor, individual or group to reflect their vision, preferences, and expectations. The use of violence to cause widespread fear by terrorists is essentially to "compel those in authority to respond favourably to the demands and expectations of the individual or group behind such violent acts" (Onuaha, 2014:69). Terrorists employ the use of force to draw attention to grievances, secure concessions, change the constitutional order, frustrate the implementation of policies and programmes that may appear repugnant to their sensibilities, etc. (Crenshaw, 2011; Lutz & Lutz, 2011, Alemika, 2013). Naureen and Hamed (2011) observe that terrorist acts are committed by non-state actors and are consciously targeted at non-combatants to influence an audience far beyond the act itself and its victims. The underlying motive of any terrorist act is to cultivate sufficient fear in both government and citizens believing that this can pitch citizens against their government, leading to political change.

Cronin (2002: xi) views terrorism as "violence perpetrated by either individuals or groups against a more powerful opponent, usually a government, the goal of which is to disrupt normal functioning by the dissemination of fear and intimidation thereby forcing a change in the policy or approach of that opponent in the direction of the terrorists' political or social programme or viewpoint." Often, terrorists employ the use of assassination, bombing, kidnapping, hijacking, and the weapons of mass destruction. Any act of terrorism is an expression of fundamental discontent with the existing socio-economic, political, and cultural order. Terrorism is perpetrated by an individual, a group, or the state. A good example of an individual terrorist was the case of Umar Farouk Abdulmutallab, popularly referred to as "Underwear Bomber," who, on the 25 December 2009, attempted to detonate plastic explosives hidden in his underwear while on board Northwest Airlines Flight 253, en route from Amsterdam to Detroit, Michigan. The Boko Haram in Nigeria represents "group terrorism" in the sense that members are united by shared vision and purpose, which is their driving force. Example of state terrorism was the spate of bombings by the state during the days of Nigeria's General Sani Abacha, in response to the strong opposition of National Democratic Coalition (NADECO) to military rule and the unyielding pressure by the group for the resurrection of the annulled 12 June 1993, Presidential election believed to have been won by Chief Moshood Kashimawo Olawale Abiola of the then Social Democratic Party (SDP). State-sponsored terrorism is common where the state is faced with intense opposition at the domestic front. Bombings and assassinations are sponsored by the state and attributed to the domestic opposition group to justify massive clamp down on its members, especially the frontline elements.

The concept of the insurgency, on the other hand, refers to an organised rebellious movement targeted at overthrowing the government of the day by a group feeling extremely dissatisfied with the existing social order. Any movement that uses the instrumentality of violence to overthrow any constituted political authority can be properly regarded as insurgency (Nwala, 2013). In the context of this viewpoint, all non-violent movements such as those of Mahatma Gandhi of India, Martins Luther King of United States of America, Nigeria's nationalist movement, and a host of other examples do not fit into the description of insurgency. Nwala (2013: 34–35) spells out conditions that breed insurgency within any given state. These are:

1. Injustice such as the denial of rights, inequity, persecution, discrimination, marginalisation, exclusion, etc.
2. Illegitimacy of the regime when it comes to power through the seizure of power, electoral fraud, tyranny and abuse of power and denial of human rights, corruption, etc.
3. Longing for freedom and self-determination.
4. Poverty, especially when the regime is deemed to be weak, incompetent, and incapable to protect the poor masses in the midst of plenty.
5. The militarisation of the society due to the long reign of the military as well as the proliferation of insurgency and terrorism in contemporary times is also contributory factors which cannot be ignored.
6. The proliferation of small arms and light weapons in a country could also be responsible for the phenomenon of insurgency, especially amid unemployment.

Insurgencies all over the world use either or a combination of tactics and methods such as cell-networks that maintain secrecy; terrorism is used to foster insecurity among the civil populace and drive them to the insurgents for protection; multifaceted attempts to cultivate support in the general population, often by undermining the new regime; attacks against the government through its institutions; and massive propaganda towards winning the support of the people (Nwala, 2013:36). Steven (2007:1) conceives of "insurgency as an armed rebellion against a constituted authority." This suggests that for any behaviour to qualify as an act of insurgency, it must manifest an element of violence. This may always not be the case because some acts of insurgency may not be violently expressed. Violence becomes a strategic option when the legitimately constituted authority remains impervious to the expressed grievances of the group. For instance, the agitations for self-determination by some Igbo youths have not been violently expressed. They have been mobilising their fellow Igbo, but this has never assumed a violent dimension. Eventually, it may take the path of violence if the Federal Government continues to give the group's struggle blackout. This is when the group may employ the instrumentality of terrorism to give expression to its grievances.

It is instructive to note that terrorism is a method often employed by insurgents to promote their cause. Without the instrumentality of violence, insurgents can hardly make any impact on the polity. Terrorism is therefore adopted by insurgents as a deliberate strategy to gain wide-spread attention. One can therefore contend that where there is insurgency, terrorism is likely to manifest. This is the sense in which the two concepts are described as "twin evils". It is often argued how do terrorists sustain their offensives against the state that is traditionally expected to bear superior instruments of violence to those of the terrorists? The linkage between terrorism and crime is a functional one. Political terrorism does require incredibly enormous resources for the acquisition of arms, logistics, and sustenance and shelter for activists (Gurr, 2006). This explains why terrorists such as the Boko Haram in the Northeast part of Nigeria do engage in criminal activities such as robbery, kidnapping for ransom, extortion, trafficking in drugs and scarce commodities, or consumer goods. They may also receive funds and arms from Diasporas, private sympathisers, and foreign governments (Gurr, 2006:94). Part of their resource generation strategies is forging alliances with other well-established criminal networks across the globe for all tangible and intangible supports.

There is a multitude of theoretical perspectives on insurgency and terrorism. These range from psychopathology, rational choice theory, strategic choice theory, frustration-aggression theory, relative deprivation theory to oppression theory (Crenshaw, 2011; Lutz & Lutz, 2011). All these theoretical perspectives attempt to provide explanations for the phenomena of insurgency and terrorism. Relative deprivation theory is considered as more analytically profitable for our purpose in this Chapter. Our choice of this theory is not because it can explain everything linked to terrorism and insurgency, but more because of its promise of giving us deeper insights into why these twin evils have become so widespread and have no respect for territorial boundaries. Relative deprivation "is defined as actors' perception of discrepancy between their value expectations and their value capabilities" (Jeong, 2011:69). When a wide gap exists between people's perception of what they expect and what is available, it generates a deep sense of discontentment and resentment which could depend on its severity, snowball into rebellious behaviour. Gurr's (1970) argument with respect to why men rebel is intricately linked to the gap expectations and capabilities. He contends that "frustration-aggression is the primary source of the human capacity for violence" (Gurr, 1970:36). The consistent failure of a political system to meet the legitimate demands of citizens could easily provoke their instinct for violence and this is more so in a political environment that is widely believed to have the capacity to respond positively and satisfactorily to such demands.

Generally, rising expectations fuel the feelings of deprivation within society. For example, the Boko Haram in the North-eastern part of Nigeria was widely believed to have been partly engendered by the brazen corrupt behaviour of the political class and the consequent diminishing size of resources needed to make life meaningful and more fulfilling for the ordinary Nigerians. This is the basis of the sect's disdain for western civilisation which they believe has a massive corrupt influence on the society. The political elites in Nigerian society have historically been extremely insensitive to the socio-economic well-being of Nigerians. They are not only self-serving when entrusted with leadership responsibility, but also engage in a brazen act of corruption. Consequently, citizens whose welfare the political elites are expected to minister to are left to wallow in abject poverty and deprivation.

The failure of political systems to consistently meet people's social and material expectations can translate into a negative mood that instigates political action (Jeong, 2011). Once there is a gross imbalance between expectations and fulfilment, it produces a wide level of dissatisfaction among the people. This point is particularly important in the sense that it is not only the material expectations of the people that should be met but even their non-material expectations as well. When citizens expect to have a morally and ethically decent society but are seeing a society immersed in a pool of corruption, this can generate a groundswell sense of hopelessness in them. A robust environment should be put in place to help them meet their expectations with minimum or no stress at all. Citizens expect the government to be sensitive and responsive to their socio-economic and political demands towards making life freer and fulfilling for them. The popular perception of government as uncaring and unresponsive has implications for the legitimacy of the political system generally. This can breed widespread discontent, frustration, and feeling of hopelessness which may stoke popular uprising that may weaken governmental authority if not constructively and productively managed.

The argument that poverty is behind terrorism or insurgency is hardly tenable in the light of the fact that those who initiate the project of terrorism or insurgency are mostly people of considerable means in society. For instance, Osama Bin Laden came from a very wealthy Saudi family and yet was behind the 911 deadly terrorist attacks against the United States of America. Again, Umar Abdulmutallab comes from an incredibly wealthy Nigerian family with sound quality education and yet attempted to bomb a plane en route to Detroit on 25 December 2009. Poverty could be one of the drivers of terrorism and insurgency, but not the root cause. When poverty becomes widespread in society, it becomes easy for terrorists to recruit the poor for their sinister objectives. Deprivation is implicated in terrorism and insurgency only in the sense that it facilitates the process of easy recruitment to swell the membership of these twin social evils in any human society. In a more explicit sense, the phenomenon of poverty serves to animate terrorism and insurgency through conscious mobilisation and recruitment of foot soldiers. Poverty is implicated in insurgency and terrorism to the extent that those who are victims of poverty are more vulnerable to pecuniary influence.

## The internal dynamics of Egyptian society and insurgency/terrorism

The Egyptian society has historically been enlightened, restive, assertive, argumentative, agitated, active and politically dynamic. There has been intense political fragmentation in Egypt since she got her independence from the British in 1922. The curious contradiction that characterises the Egyptian society is the diversity of interests even as a predominantly Muslim country. Egypt as one of the 54 countries in Africa is 90% Muslims and 10% Coptic Christians in composition. Yet, this factor has failed to cultivate or ensure a legacy of robust political stability and enduring social order (Gambo, 2015). Most of Egypt's post-independence socio-political and economic life has been under the authoritarian rule with the fragile legacy of the consensus-driven decision-making process, inclusiveness, the enduring culture of accountability and transparency in governance, tolerance of diversity of interests and healthy and productive culture of opposition.

Democratic rule in Egypt was kept at bay between 1952 and 2011. The reason for this is not farfetched. The British did not prepare the Egyptian society for democratic rule in the post-independence dispensation. The monarchical rule was instituted in place of democratic rule at independence. Mohammed Ali ruled Egypt between 1922 and 1952 as a dynasty (Martin,

2011). It was the 1952 revolution that terminated monarchy through the declaration of Egypt as a republic by Gamal Abdel Nasser. Even with the declaration of Egypt as a republic, autocratic rule continued till 2011 when an unprecedented wind of revolution blew across some Arab states leading to the emergence of new sociopolitical order in some affected states. Egypt was one of the Arab states that yielded to the "Arab Spring" revolutionary wind of political change that swept the Maghreb and North Africa late 2000s. This culminated with the exit of Hosni Mubarak from the corridors of power. Hosni Mubarak who succeeded Anwar Sadat following his brutal assassination in 1981, did not appoint a Vice-President as prescribed by the constitution of the Republic of Egypt until the 25 January 2011 popular uprising which removed him from office. This was obviously brazen constitutional misbehaviour. With a population of 82 million, Egypt is arguably the second most populous African country after Nigeria.

The economy of Egypt is heavily dependent on the Nile which sustains profitable agrarian activities all year round. Egypt is also blessed with many tourist sites that attract tourists from different parts of the world annually. The thriving tourism industry in Egypt and the Diaspora remittances also contribute significantly to the economy. It is instructive to note that Egypt is predominantly a desert which is scarcely supportive of large-scale agricultural production. This geographical factor imposes a severe limitation on the productive capacity of most Egyptians. Consequently, poverty as one of the critical drivers of insurgency and terrorism is widespread in Egypt. Zalman (2015) trenchantly and pungently underscores this point when he observes that "a sense of deprivation helps fuel terrorism." The lamentable material condition of many Egyptians makes them helplessly vulnerable to the manipulative skills of those pursuing a sinister agenda against the state. The common belief among the ordinary Egyptian citizens is that socioeconomic prosperity is limited to major settlements such as Cairo and Alexandria, while most Egyptian settlements including the Sinai Peninsula feel alienated and excluded from the benefit of common patrimony. This feeling of extreme marginalisation among the vast majority of the Egyptian society makes them easy recruits to help drive insurgency and terrorism project in the Sinai Peninsula.

The socio-economic condition of most Egyptians, especially the youths is a telling one. Generally speaking, Egypt is a developing country characterised by a fast-growing population which places acute strain on the economy. The youth component of the population is not only huge but also scarcely considered. The gap between the rich and the poor in Egypt is quite pronounced. The per capita income in Egypt is about $1,200 per year (Ernest, 2015:.85). This amount is grossly inadequate to guarantee decent survival for an average Egyptian citizen. The limited available economic opportunities in Egypt means that the unemployment rate is frightening. Many youths who are energetic and productive are left to drift. Consequently, they become readily available to be mobilised for any subversive agenda. The principle of reciprocity which is a core defining element of the Egyptian political culture has been considerably weakened and this is attributed to the growing inability of the government to fulfil its own part of the social contract in exchange for citizens' habitual obedience and loyalty. There is in a sense, massive loss of faith in the responsive capacity of the government to citizens' legitimate socio-economic and political demands in Egypt and this is really leading to a widespread feeling of discontentment, hopelessness and despair. The January 2011 popular revolution further exaggerated the bad socio-economic condition of Egyptians as many businesses folded up and many others relocating to safer neighbouring countries. Capital flight led to worsening unemployment in Egypt. There is in a sense, a fundamental dislocation in the socio-economic life of citizens engendered by the unprecedented uprising against the autocratic rule of former President Hosni Mubarak and the legacy of poor governance and the attendant crisis of legitimacy in Egypt.

What one can deduce from the preceding concise profile of the internal dynamics of the Egyptian society is the entrenched culture of bad governance from 1952 to date. The key characteristics of bad governance in Egypt include denial of freedom and rights of citizens, limited access to participation in governance, lack of transparency and accountability in the governance process, discrimination, exclusion, marginalisation, lack of inclusive and equitable development, etc. All these have conspired to generate a condition of crippling poverty in the society, a sense of hopelessness among the poor in the society, frequent conflict and instability, growing insecurity, rising unemployment and a strained relationship between the state and society. All these constitute the critical drivers or enablers of terrorism and insurgency in Egypt. Socio-political factors such as denial of freedom of expression, political and economic dissatisfaction bred by the repressive policies of the government are at the heart of radicalisation and terrorist recruitment in Egypt.

## The nature of terrorism and insurgency in the Sinai Peninsula

One of the effects of the post 25 January 2011 popular uprising in Egypt was the expression of terrorism and insurgency in the Sinai Peninsula. The Sinai Peninsula is considered one of the least developed regions in Egypt due to several years of neglect by successive central governments in Cairo. This is possibly due to its transnational status as a settlement in Asia even though under the sovereignty of Egypt. The 2011 uprising brought about a convoluted security environment in Egypt characterised by the availability of large arms in the hands of non-state actors, frequent violent protests, killings of citizens and a host of others (Ernest, 2015). Insecurity in the Egyptian capital, Cairo worsened as millions of young men and women took to the street protesting against former President Hosni Mubarak. Anyone who is closely familiar with the geography of Egypt will know that the Sinai Peninsula, one of the tourist sites of the country is remotely located from Cairo. Sinai continues to serve as an incubator of terrorist groups due to its geographic distance from the capital, Cairo. The weak presence of government in the Peninsula coupled with the underdeveloped nature of the settlement makes it a fertile breeding ground for all kinds of moral malcontents. This explains why the insurgents and terrorists prefer the site to the State capital to perpetuate their sinister activities. A radical Islamist group popularly known as *al-Jihad al-Islami* or Islamic Jihad (IJ) has been the perpetrator of violent extremism in the Sinai Peninsula.

The local Jihadists whose initial targets were "tourists and Israeli during the Presidency of Mohamed Morsi Muslim Brotherhood-affiliated from 2011 to 2013, the ouster of the democratically elected Islamist government of Mohamed Morsi on 3 July 2013 by the military-led to a sudden change in their targets. Angered by this development, the pro-Muslim Brotherhood Jihadists turned against the Egyptian military, police and government officials" with a view to weakening their capacity in providing security for Egyptian citizens. Around this same period, a more deadly group initially known as *Ansar Bayt al-Maqdis* (ABM) emerged in the Sinai Peninsula. This group later rechristened itself *Wilayat Sinai* (Sinai Province) after pledging allegiance to the Islamic State (IS). Many believed that the Sinai Province group is the most organizationally sophisticated and well-armed with deadly weapons in the Peninsula. It has launched series of attacks against both civilian and non-civilian targets including the assassination on 29 June 2015 of Egypt's Chief public Prosecutor, Hisham Barakat in a car bomb attack on his convoy (Leadership Sunday Newspaper, 23 July, 2017, p.67). The Sinai Peninsula has undoubtedly become a sanctuary for terrorists not only because of poor visibility of government in the region, but also the Bedouins who are the main inhabitants of the region have deep-seated grievances against the central government in Cairo. They feel ignored and abandoned by the government for long and therefore show no hope to cooperate with neither the army nor the government in combating terrorism at their backyard. The attitude of Bedouins is quite instructive in the sense that when citizens are denied the benefits of development or are left out of the development process, their sense of emotional attachment to the state is fundamentally weakened. They begin to cultivate the feeling of lack of stake in the survival of Egyptian society. In some extreme cases, they may consider the option of supporting the enemy to overrun the state which has failed to meet their developmental aspirations. This is the inherent danger of neglecting a community developmentally, especially one that is strategically located at a border. Lack of equitable and inclusive development in a segmented society can easily fuel collective anger against the government and the state.

Terrorism in the Peninsula is fuelled by the availability of arms believed to have been smuggled in from Libya following the downfall of Muamar Ghaddafi's regime in 2011. Mohamed (2011) corroborates this claim by observing that the increase in violence in Egypt's Sinai region is also been partially attributed to smuggled Libyan arms into Egyptian territory. The poorly managed security environment in Egypt in the wake of the Arab Spring, especially development in Libya witnessed the free flow of arms from Libya into Egypt and this perhaps, aided and abetted criminal behaviour of the insurgents thereby heightening the level of insecurity in the country, and the Sinai Peninsula in particular. When arms are widely available and in the hands of unauthorised persons or non-state actors, insecurity is inevitably heightened in society. Smuggled arms from Libya emboldened non-state actors to begin to challenge the integrity of the Egyptian society. According to Mohamed (2011), the number of unlicensed weapons in Sinai increased by 50% after the January 2011 popular uprising in Egypt. These weapons were obtained mainly by the Bedouins in the Peninsula for the protection of their families and common heritage which is land. The inadequate presence of government in the region left them with no option than to organise for their collective defence and securing their land against the raging terrorism at their backyard. Terrorism in the Sinai Peninsula is also fuelled and driven by the widespread availability of arms in Egyptian society. Sources of these arms could be traced to Libya, Sudan, and Chad (Mohamed, 2011). These three countries had at varying times witnessed violent and deadly conflicts which might have weakened the capacity of these states to control the inflow and outflow of small arms and light weapons.

The insurgents have been intensely committed to taking over ownership of the territorial space in the Sinai Peninsula against the determined effort of the Egyptian military and other security forces to deter them from doing so. The indiscriminate killing perpetrated by the Egyptian military had forced many inhabitants of the Peninsula, especially the minority Coptic Christians to flee their traditional communities for safety. The hit and run strategy adopted by the insurgents made it difficult for the military to identify who is a terrorist or innocent civilian. The local people in the Sinai have often complained bitterly about their vulnerability to a military response to terrorist attacks. The terrorists would hit the military target and dissolved into the civil populace making it difficult for the military to spot, isolate and deal with them as terrorists. This kind of situation is what is referred to as "collateral damage" in military parlance. As if the long-standing grievances of the local population of the Sinai Peninsula were not enough to cause sleepless nights for the Egyptian government, the frequent military counter-attacks against the insurgents who have mixed up with the local population have led to accusations of insensitivity on the part of the military and massive human rights violations in the course of operations.

## Counterterrorism and counterinsurgency in Egypt

Any country that has become prey to the twin evils of terrorism and insurgency must of practical necessity, articulate a comprehensive approach to tackling the security challenge. Egypt responded to the challenges of terrorism and insurgency by developing far-reaching mechanisms for not only dealing with the threat but also uprooting the source of the menace. The Egyptian approach is a combination of both hard and soft approaches. In a sense, both military and non-military approaches were effectively blended to respond adequately and effectively to the threats of terrorism and insurgency in the Sinai Peninsula. Concerned about the growing threat of terrorism to the territorial integrity and peace and security of Egypt, President Abdel Fattah El-Sissi had to adopt a wide range of measures to counter violent extremism and to combat terrorism in the Sinai Peninsula. The first of this range of anti-terrorism measures were outlawing the Muslim Brotherhood and branding its terrorist organisation. The Egyptian government believed that terrorism was growing in potency and resilience because of the anti-government stance of the Muslim Brotherhood. The overthrow of former President Mohamed Morsi who was a frontline member of the Muslim Brotherhood provoked the hostile reaction of the group. President Abdel Fattah El-Sissi's sensitivity to the opposition of this group might have motivated the decision to outlaw it and brand it a terrorist organisation. All these measures proved counter-productive in the fight against terrorism and insurgency in the Sinai Peninsula. The Islamic State is yet to be vanquished. The Islamic State in North Sinai has killed hundreds of soldiers and police and has increasingly targeted Egypt's minority Christians with frequent Church bombing (Leadership Sunday Newspaper, 23rd July, 2017 edition, p.67). The Islamist insurgency is turning the heat against the minority Coptic Christians in Egypt and this is fast changing the dynamics of the situation in the North Sinai. President El-Sissi is widely accused of human rights violation while combating insurgency and terrorism. This is not healthy for a collective response to the challenge of these twin social evils.

Closely related to the above is a series of policies taken in response to the threat of terrorism in Egypt. For instance, the shutting down thousands of Mosques in February 2014, banning of *Salafi* texts believed to have radicalising impact on adherents in Mosques in June 2014, and banning of preachers from commenting on politics in their sermons in July 2014 (John, 2015) were all targeted at curbing the spread of violent extremism which feeds terrorism and insurgency. Again in August 2014, President Abdel El-Sissi passed a wide-ranging counterterrorism law which established special procedures and courts for trying those suspected of actors in terrorism and insurgency and also expanded the scope of powers of security and law enforcement agencies in their response to the threat of terrorism. This omnipotent law also sought to punish pressmen whose accounts of events or terrorism and insurgency-related news contradicts that of government official records. For instance, exaggerating the figure of casualties in a terrorist-related attack is considered a fundamental breach of this law and prescribed punishment for this would apply. Journalists, both local and foreign were expected to demonstrate utmost sensitivity in their reportage of events in the Sinai Peninsula so as not to unnecessarily inflame passion.

*The Economist* (2017), an influential journal reported that in 2014, President Abdel Fattah El-Sissi had declared a state of emergency in northern Sinai and launched a bloody offensive against the militants which led to the death of hundreds of soldiers and police personnel. Similarly, hundreds of houses have been razed by the Egyptian military leading to the displacement of over 10,000 people. This is enough to prove against excessive reliance on the military in counterterrorism and insurgency. The local population had lost trust in the military as their custodians in the sense that military operations have made life hellish for them. Government's military tactics and actions have not only alienated the local people but also angered them. The indiscriminate bombings and killings of civilians in the course of military operations have turned the locals against the Egyptian government thereby making the military approach counter-productive in the long run. The local people are the repository of intelligence that is critically needed to defeat insurgency and terrorism. If they feel greatly displeased with the tactics and actions of the military and other security forces they may decide not to divulge intelligence information that could be used to weaken the capacity of the insurgents and terrorists. This is one of the fundamental reasons why there should not be any mutual suspicion between the military and the civilians. They must see themselves as critical stakeholders in the fight against insurgency and terrorism in Egypt.

In tackling the menace of terrorism in Egypt, nothing was left to chance. All citizens, both civilians and security personnel were expected to play a complementary role that could lead to the defeat of the twin evils of terrorism and insurgency. It was not limited to the security agencies alone because of the irregular nature of the warfare. While military resources were comprehensively mobilised and deployed in the fight against terrorism and insurgency, civil components were never relegated to the background because of the belief that response to the threat of terrorism and insurgency must be all-inclusive. The counterterrorism strategy of the Egyptian government is aimed at re-establishing an Egyptian society that is stable, tolerance, peaceful, secure, cohesive, and prosperous for citizens to pursue their decent and legitimate means of livelihoods.

## Alternative strategies for engaging terrorism and insurgency in Egypt

Terrorism is no doubt a manifestation of insurgency in any society. Where insurgency expresses itself, terrorism rears its ugly head. Insurgency is an expression of dissatisfaction with the existing social order and the determined effort of a group to rebel against it with a view to changing it. Terrorism is irregular warfare that only a well-trained, equipped, and motivated military can effectively engage with in the field. In addition, it requires careful and diligent mobilisation of all citizens to key into the framework designed for combating terrorism. In another word, all resources (human and material) must be aggregated towards building a strategic platform for fighting terrorism. Against this background, the following strategies are proposed for engaging terrorism in the Sinai Peninsula in Egypt:

1. Building an effective propaganda Machinery: effective propaganda machinery is needed to really portray the movement as a rebellious one essentially motivated by the inordinate ambitions of the drivers of the group. Unless there a good comprehension of the psychology and beliefs of the movement, it will be exceedingly difficult to freeze the minds of the uncritical mass of the deadly beliefs inculcated in them. Application of force may be necessary at a stage but should not be the primary response to violent extremism.
2. Providing quality and emancipatory education: quality education can help free citizens from the pangs of ignorance. The broad philosophy of education must be articulated to include developing the critical and analytical instinct of the citizens in addition to reading for prescribed national examinations. Access to quality education should be broadened and deepened to allow the vast majority acquire it. The government should view education as a strategic weapon for countering violent extremism in any society. For example, one of the grievances of the extremist group in Nigeria is that Muslim faithful should not work for an un-Islamic government using Saudi Arabia as a model. It is only an uncritical minded person who can easily be influenced by this argument because Nigeria and Saudi Arabia are fundamentally different in social contexts. While Nigeria is religiously pluralistic, Saudi Arabia is predominantly a Muslim country. It is foolhardy to expect what is practised in Saudi Arabia to be replicated in Nigeria.
3. In addition to the provision of quality education, effort should also be made to promote technical and vocational education. A developing society needs to boost technical and

vocational education as a conscious strategy of growing a robustly productive population. Technical and vocational education empowers citizens to go into productive ventures that can generate immense prosperity for them. A productive and purposeful population can hardly think of joining an extremist movement in society.

4. The use of covert operations: countering violent extremism entails the use of covert operations to detect and nib in the bud any sinister movement. Covert operations help to identify prospective recruits and how they can be discouraged from doing so. For example, the tragic and strategic blunder committed by the Nigerian security agencies was the capturing and subsequent extra-judicial killing of Mohammed Yusuf, the leader of the movement.

5. The social problem of unemployment should be effectively tackled through creative ways of generating gainful employment opportunities for the growing youth population. Growing the private sector is critical to meeting the employment need of the youth. Any society that neglects and allows its youths to drift is begging for combustible social unrest. They become easy recruits for any group with a sinister agenda against society. The highly inflammable youth constituency should on no account be made to feel neglected and abandoned. Making the youths radiate with happiness and contentment guarantees their strong emotional attachment to the state.

6. There should be good governance that gives everyone a good sense of belonging and inclusion in the mainstream affairs of society. The values of transparency, accountability, inclusiveness, probity, consensus-driven decision-making process, etc. should be diligently cultivated and grown to ensure peace, order, stability, and progress of the society. When the basic needs of the vast majority are sufficiently met, society is most likely to be shielded from the destabilising and subversive activities of some few miscreants. The local population in the Sinai Peninsula should be made to have a robust feeling of a stake in the survival of Egyptian society through the provision of basic social services and other development projects. This is with a view to making other option unattractive to them.

7. The family as the primary unit of the society should be strengthened through deliberate cultivation of values of honesty, discipline, trust, industry, respect, tolerance, the dignity of labour, patriotism, etc. These values are grossly scarce in most societies today including Egyptian society. The scarcity of these critical values which should help in building productive, patriotic, and responsible citizens has created space for moral malcontents in the society. These moral contents are like "tabula rasa" that is receptive to all kinds of subversive ideas and beliefs. Rebuilding the family as the basic unit of the society is a critical imperative for making the society invulnerable to both external and internal subversive forces.

8. The concept and practice of total defence which involves the participation of all and sundry in the enterprise of defence should be adopted by societies that are susceptible to subversive tendencies. Defence in the present times must not be the exclusive preserve of the military and other security forces alone. All citizens must be carefully mobilised to participate actively in the defence of their society. Defence elements must be mainstreamed into government policies and programmes so as to ensure a speedy and comprehensive response to any threat to the national interest. Even the banking sector should be mobilised against the transfer of funds to violent extremist groups.

9. There should be a policy of building women capacity in peacebuilding. Women's potential for peacebuilding is quite enormous and if capacity building workshop is organised for them regularly, it can strengthen their responsiveness to violent extremism. The United Nations Security Council Resolution 1325 provides a fulcrum to this suggestion.

10. Women as caregivers understand the language of peace more than the men and this naturally earns them recognition and inclusion in peace-building processes around the globe. In a study undertaken by Pierson and published in 1987, it was established that women are more sensitive to the use of language in peacebuilding process than the men who care less. On the strength of this finding, women should occupy a primary position in the enterprise of peacebuilding.

11. The Egyptian government should take deliberate steps to empower women by appointing them into key political offices hitherto reserved for men. This is with a view to growing their capacity for enhanced input in policymaking concerning peacebuilding. For instance, nothing should stop a woman from being appointed Minister of Defence, Foreign Affairs, Finance, Trade and Investment, Governor of Central Bank, etc. Apart from gathering useful experience that would help grow and deepen their capacity, it empowers them economically to be self-reliant. This will in the main, promote women's participation, leadership and empowerment, thus equipping them for the challenges of peacebuilding.

12. Women are the primary teachers at the family level and if the language of peace and tolerance should be taught to growing up children, they are readily available to do so. This recognition should really place them at the forefront of peacebuilding in any society. Women have the capacity to promote positive social change in society through the family institution.

13. Women are the repository of intelligence and this has often been overlooked by relevant security agencies. More often than not, they engage with certain gatekeepers who are mostly traditional rulers and in the process, neglect the critical input of women who may have good access to intelligence that can help in countering violent extremism. Women are much closer to the children than men and this makes them assess children behaviour better than the men. They tend to have a better knowledge of the community than the men.

14. The Egyptian government should embark on comprehensive security sector reform with a view to giving women greater visibility in their peace and security architecture. Gender equality should reflect in the recruitment policy into the armed forces and other Para-military institutions so that the untapped resources of women can energise these institutions.

15. Above all, the Egyptian authority should commence building a healthy and productive society where mutual tolerance, accommodation, common prosperity and robust sense of rule of law are the driving factors. Where there is equitable and inclusive development, social frictions would be minimal and are not likely to be subversive of the social order. In a more explicit sense, what the Egyptian society requires to roll back the frontiers of terrorism and insurgency is an established culture of good governance characterised by accountability, transparency, due process, rule of law, broad participation, capacity building, constitutionalism, effectiveness and efficiency of institutions and a host of others. A well-governed society may make the choice of radicalisation and extremism less attractive.

## Concluding remarks

The twin evils of terrorism and insurgency in Egypt have grown significantly in scope and intensity, particularly in the Sinai Peninsula. This unwholesome development is largely attributed to the popular uprising which began on 25 January 2011 and which led to the downfall of the regime of former President Hosni Mubarak. The security conundrum engendered by the popular uprisings against the regime of Hosni Mubarak bred a fertile environment for the emergence of terrorism and insurgency in Egypt. The Sinai based insurgency and terrorism pledged allegiance to the Islamic State of Iraq and Syria (ISIS) for possible support. The implication of this development for counterinsurgency and counterterrorism is that the effort must transcend Egypt to cover countries battling with ISIS. It requires transnational collaboration and strategic partnership to effectively combat the twin evils which appear to be growing in resilience and potency. This Chapter prescribed some strategies towards combating terrorism and insurgency in Egypt. Some of these strategies include building effective propaganda machinery to counter insurgents and terrorists' narratives; provision of quality and emancipatory education; boosting of technical education for self-reliant; security sector reform; cultivating a robust culture of good governance; strengthening family ties, and so many others. The Egyptian government has to take all appropriate measures to tackle the social problems of poverty, unemployment, conflicts and bad governance as drivers of insurgency and terrorism. In a sense, the Egyptian government needs to adopt a balanced approach which includes both soft and hard elements in countering insurgency and terrorism. The use of counter-narratives is particularly effective in deterring potential recruits.

# References

Adamu, A. (2013). Insurgency in Nigeria: The northern Nigerian experience, In Olu and Galadima (Eds.) *Complex insurgencies in Nigeria*. Kuru: National Institute Press.

Alemika, E. E. O. (2013). Insurgencies in Nigeria: Causes and remedies, the sociological dimension. In Olu & H Galadima (Eds.), *Complex insurgencies in Nigeria*. Kuru: National Institute Press.

Baylis, J., Smith, S., & Owens, P. (2011). *The globalization of world politics: An introduction to international relations*. Oxford: Oxford University Press.

Crenshaw, M. (2011). *Explaining terrorism: Causes, processes, and consequences*. London: Routledge.

Cronin, I. (2002). *Confronting fear: A history of terrorism*. New York: Thunder's Mouth Press.

English, R. (2009). *Terrorism: How to respond*. New York: Oxford University Press.

Ernest, A. U. (2015). Politics in Egypt. In C. O. Chris & I. M. Alumona (Eds.), *Comparative politics: An African viewpoint*. Enugu: Rhyce Kerex Publishers.

Fafowora, O. (2013). Understanding insurgencies in Nigeria: Nature, types, dynamics and the way out. In Olu & Galadima (Eds.), *Complex insurgencies in Nigeria*. Kuru: National Institute.

Fawole, W. A. (2001). *Military power and third party conflict mediation in West Africa: The Liberia and Sierra Leone case study*. Ife: Obafemi Awolowo University Press.

Federal Republic of Nigeria. (2014). *National security strategy*. Abuja: Yaliam Press Ltd.

Gambo, A. N. (2013). Insurgency in Nigeria: The plateau experience. In Olu & Galadima (Eds.), *Complex insurgencies in Nigeria*. Kuru: National Institute Press.

Gambo, A. N. (2014). Conflicts and Africa in global strategic calculations in the 21st century. In Amutabi (Ed.), *Africa and the Challenges of Globalization*. Nairobi: Research, Catholic University of Eastern Africa.

Gambo, A. N. (2015). The Plateau crisis in the context of the Nigerian Federation. In Obasanjo, Mabogunje & Okebukola (Eds.), *Towards a new dawn in Nigeria post 2015*. Abeokuta: Olusegun Obasanjo Presidential Library Centre for Human Security.

Gurr, T. (1970). *Why men rebel*. Princeton New Jersey: University Press.

Gurr, T.R. (2006). Economic factors. In Richardson (Ed.), *The roots of terrorism*. New York: Routledge.

Hoffman, B. (1998). *Inside terrorism*. London: Victor Gollancz.

Jenold, M. (2008). *The mind of the terrorist: The psychology of terrorism from the IRA to Al-Qaeda*. New York: Macmillan.

Jeong, H. (2000). *Peace and conflict studies*. Aldershot: Ashgate Publishing Limited.

Jeong, H. (2011). *Understanding conflict and conflict analysis*. Los Angeles: Sage.

John, N. Egypt's Counter Terrorism and Counter Insurgency Strategy: Lessons for Nigeria? University of Jos,. (2015) *Vol. 4(5) Journal of Political Science (UJJPS)*, 23-52.

Kyari, M. (2014). The message and methods of Boko Haram. In Mac-Antoine (Ed.), *Boko Haram: Islamism, politics, security and the state In Nigeria*. Leiden: African Studies Centre.

Leadership Sunday Newspaper (Nigeria). (23 July 2017). *28 sentenced to death in Egypt over 2015 prosecutor killing* (edition.). Abuja: Leadership Group Limited.

Lutz, J., & Lutz, B. (2011). *Terrorism: The basics*. London: Routledge.

Martin, M. (2011). *The state of Africa: A history of the continent since independence*. London: Simon and Schuster.

Mohamed, E. (2011). *Smuggled, stolen and homemade guns flood Egypt's streets*, Independent, June 26, 2011, http://www.egyptindependent.com/news/smuggled-stolen-andhomemade-guns-flood egypt02%E2%80%99s-streets (Retrieved on 8 July 2018).

Mohammed, F. F. (2011). *Egypt's President condemns deadly attacks in Sinai*. CNN, August 8, 2012. http://www.cnn.com/2012/08/06/world/africa/egypt-violence/index.html (Retrieved on 8 July 2018).

Mustapha, R. A. (2014). Understanding Boko Haram. In Mustapha (Ed.), *Sects and social disorder: Muslim identities and conflict in Northern Nigeria*. New York: James Currey.

Naureen, C. F., & Hamed, E. (2011). *Transforming terrorists: Examining international efforts to address violent extremism*. New York: International Peace Institute.

Nwala, U. T. (2013). Insurgency in Nigeria: The MASSOB experience. In Olu & Galadima (Eds.), *Complex insurgencies in Nigeria*. Kuru: National Institute Press.

Onuaha, F. C. (2014). Boko Haram and suicide terrorism in Nigeria: Current mode and extrapolations. In Nwoke & Oche (Eds.), *Contemporary challenges in Nigeria, Africa and the world*. Lagos: Nigeria Institute of International Affairs.

Steven, M. (2007). *Rethinking insurgency*. United States: Army War College.

the Economist, 6 April, 2017, https://www.economist.com/--/201720310 (Retrieved 6 July 2018).

Umezulike, O. (2015). *Africa's economy and its strategic environment*. Jos: Monex Books.

Updike, J. (2006). *Terrorist*. London: Hamish Hamilton.

Zalman, A. (2015). *History of poverty and underdevelopment helps explain terrorism*. Available from http://terrorism.about.com/od/a/TerrorPoverty-2.htm (Retrieved on 8 July 2018).

# 30

# Libya

## Rethinking humanitarian intervention and the dilemmas of counterinsurgency in Africa

*Dauda Abubakar*

## Introduction

The increasing incidence of a humanitarian catastrophe, especially within the context of civil war and insurgency conflicts has opened up a vibrant debate among scholars around issues of international intervention, global security and state sovereignty; and how these could be reconciled with the complex dilemmas of self-determination and civilian protection in armed conflicts (Wheeler, 2000; Duffield, 2006; Mamdani, 2009; Kaldor, 1999; Hehir, 2013; Autesserre, 2014; Prinz & Schetter, 2017; Lamont, 2016; Doyle, 2016; Abrahamsen, 2016). Advocates of neoliberal interventionism (Kaldor, 1999; Thakur, 2006; Weiss, 2007; Bellamy, 2005, Bellamy, Alex, & Williams (2011); Pattisson, 2010; Deng, 1996; ICISS, 2001) assert that with the rising tide of war crimes and crimes against humanity, the principle of sovereign autonomy over internal affairs of the state should be reconstituted in such a manner as to empower the international community to "protect" innocent civilians if the state is unable or unwilling to protect its citizenry. This has led to the emergence of the doctrine of "Responsibility to Protect" (R2P) following the submission of a Report by The International Commission on Intervention and State Sovereignty (ICISS, 2001). However, critiques of the doctrine of R2P (Hehir, 2010; 2012; 2013; Abubakar, 2017; Mamdani, 2010; Kuperman, 2013; De Waal, 2007; Hobson, 2016; Cunliffe, 2016; Wai, 2014) contend that while the notion of civilian protection in armed conflicts may save innocent lives, such intervention should not be instrumentalised as a Trojan horse in pursuit of major power geostrategic and national interests in the global South. More often than not, paternalistic neoliberal intervention in armed conflicts may degenerate into deeper humanitarian tragedy by destroying not only the institutions and infrastructures of the state; but it may, as in the case of Libya, exacerbate internal factional and militant insurgency violence that leads to the displacement of the same civilians that ought to have been protected (Pradella & Rad, 2017; Ronen, 2017; Cunliffe, 2010). Such unintended consequences and the human catastrophe it generates not only reveals the limits of the neoliberal project in post-colonial Africa, but also demonstrates that paternalistic approach to human protection neglects local agency and knowledge; and, more often than not, likely to fail in securing population (Mavelli, 2016; Chandler & Reid, 2016; Kuperman, 2012, 2013; Autesserre, 2012).

The purpose of this Chapter is to critically evaluate North Atlantic Treaty Organisation's (NATO) 2011 humanitarian intervention in Libya and its aftermath, especially the outbreak of violent insurgency and the subsequent rise of the Islamic State (ISIS) in the conflict. I argue that although the intervention was framed within the narrative of R2P and legitimated by the United Nations Security Council Resolution 1973, NATO's use of military force in Libya exceeded its mandate through regime change. By equipping and supporting the rebel movement during the Libyan "Arab Spring", NATO's military intervention facilitated the ultimate capture and assassination of Muammar Qaddafi; as well as the destruction of Libya's socio-economic infrastructure, exacerbation of rival militia insurgency and creating a political vacuum that led to the insertion of Islamic State (ISIS) fighters and a full-blown counterinsurgency conflict. I develop this argument in three related sections. In the section that follows, I outline a conceptual framework of humanitarian intervention as a form of subjectification, drawing on the notions of conditioned state sovereignty as inscribed in the doctrine of R2P, and the biopolitics of neoliberal intervention based on the extant literature (Foucault, 2003, 2010; Prinz & Schetter, 2017; Mavelli, 2016; Kuperman, 2013; Mamdani, 2010; Cunliffe, 2016; Hobson, 2016; Reid, 2010; Mavelli, 2017). Embedded within the notion of post-Cold War humanitarian protection is a subtle imperial logic that the population, as a target, is being "saved" from some form of self-destructive maladaptation and "barbarism" (Mamdani, 2010; Wai, 2014). As the liberal peace narrative goes, Libyan civilians are vulnerable to Qaddafi's imminent atrocities and must, therefore, be protected through international intervention, to avert a repeat of Rwanda (Muller & Wolff, 2014). However, the limitations of this logic, as I will demonstrate in this Chapter, is that it inadvertently removes the democratic rights of citizens to change their government or enact change in accordance with the principle of self-determination and autonomy. In the neoliberal discourse of R2P, state sovereignty is conditional upon fulfilling certain norms and "standards of civilisation" including the capacity to ensure the rule of law, protection of civil and political liberties and the autonomy of the market in state-society relations. "Failed" or so-called "collapsed states" and "ungovernable spaces", so the neoliberal argument goes, are "outside the normative model of a state and its relationship with society" (Prinz & Schetter, 2017; Jabri, 2007; Mavelli, 2016) and constitute an existential threat to Western civilisation and global security (Reid, 2010). As Jabri (2007) rightly puts it, such cosmopolitan neoliberal solidarities are always constituted hierarchically "…not simply in terms of technological and material resource capacity, but in a self-understanding that sees itself in moral terms, constructed in terms of saving others, just warriors engaged in the rescue of other distant populations." Furthermore, such conception of international morality not only demonises the violence of African authoritarian regimes as mass violence that ought to be stopped but confers legitimacy on perpetrators of other forms of structural violence. Such a conception of social change depoliticises violence as a productive agency in the socio-structural transformation of state-society relations in the periphery. As Mamdani (2010) rightly alerts us, the politics of labelling performs a vital function in a hierarchical global order: "It isolates and demonises the perpetrators of one kind of mass violence, and at the same time confers impunity on perpetrators of other forms of mass violence." In the third section, I discuss how NATO's neoliberal project of humanitarian protection in Libya metamorphosed into illegitimate regime change; thereby providing the enabling environment for various militia groups to engage in fratricidal conflict over state power, oil resources and territory (Ronen, 2017; Pradella & Rad, 2017; Doyle, 2016; Jebnoun, 2015). The gradual disintegration of the Libyan state after the elimination of Qaddafi, I argue, provided an opening for ISIS to insert itself into the conflict thereby exacerbating population displacement, extra-judicial killings, and counterinsurgency warfare in Libya. The failure of R2P in Libya, I contend, had an unintended consequence for the continuing insurgency war in Syria where thousands of civilians have been killed and over one million displaced as refugees. Ironically, the same refugees from both Libya and Syria conflicts have been restricted from entering Western European countries over the fear of terrorism. The biopolitics of neoliberalism which unilaterally determines who shall be saved and, therefore, live; or who must die, certainly alerts us to the imperatives of critically re-thinking the implications of humanitarian intervention in Africa. The fourth section of the chapter turns to the counterinsurgency war in Libya and its implications not only for the civilian population in the country but also the ramifications at regional and global levels. The conclusion summarises the key arguments advanced in the Chapter and provides viable solutions for the continuing insurgency conflict in Libya in particular, and postcolonial Africa in general.

## Conditional state sovereignty, "Responsibility to Protect" (R2P) and the biopolitics of intervention

The principle of sovereignty has been an important defining attribute of the international system that regulates the behaviour of state actors in world politics. Sovereignty has two main coordinates: internal control overpopulation within a defined territory, and external autonomy which entails not only recognition by other states in international society, but also the capacity to protect the territory from attack and occupation by other actors. Thus, the original conception of sovereignty grants the sole prerogative for states to control their internal affairs. The principle of "non-interference in the internal affairs" of sovereign states has been sacrosanct, especially for post-colonial countries primarily because of the historical precedence of imperial rule. However, post-Cold War incidence of genocide, ethnic cleansing, war crimes and crimes against humanity as demonstrated in Kosovo, Darfur-Sudan and Rwanda has led to the gradual transformation of the normative principle of sovereignty. This normative shift from sovereignty as internal control and autonomy to "sovereignty as responsibility" as enshrined in the doctrine of Responsibility to Protect (R2P) has opened the Pandora's Box for external intervention in the internal affairs of weak states in the global South. The doctrine of R2P has its origins in the works of Francis Deng (1996) and was sharpened into a global norm through the Report of the International Commission on Intervention and State Sovereignty (ICISS, 2001). It was further refined in the United Nations World Summit Document of 2005, thus entrenching it into a normative doctrine. As the ICISS Report puts it, R2P implies "…a responsibility to react to situations of compelling need for human protection. When a … state is unable or unwilling to redress the situation, then intervention measures by other members of the broader community of states may be required. These coercive measures may include political, economic or judicial measures, and in extreme cases – but only extreme cases – they may include military action." (ICISS, 2001: 29). The use of military force as an instrument in humanitarian protection, therefore, is only a last resort when other options have been exhausted.

R2P rests fundamentally on three pillars: namely, the *responsibility to react* when a situation in a particular country has degenerated beyond the capacity of the state to restore social and political order; second, the *responsibility to protect* innocent civilian populations that may be caught up in the conflict; and, third, the *responsibility to rebuild*, through reconstruction and rehabilitation so that peace and order is restored. However, the normative shift from Westphalian construction of sovereignty to R2P, as Mamdani (2009: 275) cogently argues, "turns the citizens into wards or beneficiaries of external humanitarian order, rather than active agents involved in their own self-defined emancipation as bearers of rights. Humanitarianism inadvertently reinforces dependency by promoting the logic of trusteeship and external control." In Foucauldian biopolitics, the life of those regarded as deserving of survival is bare life. As Mavelli (2017: 6) puts it, biopolitics denotes a modern condition and particular technology of power "...in which the life of individuals and the life of the population as a whole becomes the object of political strategies and intervention. At the heart of this condition is a transformation in the technology of power: from sovereign power to take life to the biopolitical power to make life."

In 2011, when the rebellion broke out against the Qaddafi regime in Benghazi, Western powers – in particular, United States, Great Britain and France – under the rubric of NATO, and with legal clout provided by UN Security Council Resolution 1973, deployed a "No-fly-zone" strategy over Libya with the claim that it is to protect innocent citizens from extermination by their government. Libyan lives are to be protected not by Libyans themselves, but by external patrons under the principle of R2P. The Libyan crisis has indeed redefined sovereignty as a normative principle in international relations because it has shown how an important doctrine may be suspended or made conditional depending upon which state's interests are at stake. However, the biopolitics of intervention, as I will show, in the case of Libya, has several limitations. First, the bio-politicisation of humanitarianism (Reid, 2010) which claims to transform so-called "ungovernable spaces" into governable populations, exorcises the agency of citizens, thereby undermining autonomy, self-determination, and the sovereignty of the state. Second, R2P as a form of the biopolitics of intervention raises the dilemma of selectivity as to which population should be saved and which ones should be left to die. The response of Western powers to the "Arab Spring" clearly reveals this contradiction. As Wai (2014: 492) reminds us, neoliberal interventionism not only "re-territorialises and re-centres global relations within blocks of power through spatial displacement and redefinition of traditional notions of sovereignty..." but also perfects violent logics of hegemony and the subversion of African self-determination; as illustrated in France's use of force against the Laurent Gbagbo regime in Cote d'Ivoire after the disputed 2010 presidential election.

Similarly, the case of Darfur-Sudan in 2003–2005 where the incumbent government of President Omar el-Bashir utilised the *Janjaweed* militia in counterinsurgency warfare against rebel movements culminated in the death of over 250,000 people and the displacement of another 1.5 million as refugees (Mamdani, 2009); but Western powers were not enthusiastic in saving the Dafuri people. Simply put, even in an apparent case of genocide and ethnic cleansing in Darfur-Sudan, there was no robust attempt by Western powers at saving the population in need (Hehir, 2009). Libyan rebels, however, were protected under the umbrella of NATO's "No-fly-zone"; but in the case of Syria, R2P doctrine was not even contemplated as a policy option, and consequently thousands of innocent civilians have been left to be slaughtered by the Free Syrian rebel movement, ISIS insurgents, Russia's air bombardment, and the Assad regime. What leads to these double standards and politics of selectivity in the biopolitics of humanitarian intervention? The geostrategic, economic, and political interests of Western powers, I shall argue, may have been a driving force behind the biopolitics of humanitarianism in Libya, rather than a genuine and neutral effort at resolving the national question. NATO's intervention and subsequent regime change plunged Libya into deeper counterinsurgency conflict and exacerbated the flow of weaponry into the turbulent Sahel-Sahara region. This is the focus of the next section.

## From humanitarianism to regime change: NATO and the overthrow of Qaddafi

The bio-politicisation of the doctrine of R2P in Libya's crisis arose from UN Resolution 1973, which mandated NATO to implement a "No-fly zone" to protect civilians from Qaddafi's forces. However, as I discuss below, NATO's disproportionate use of force in the Libyan conflict exceeded the initial mandate granted by the UN Security Council. There are three key questions I seek to examine: first, does UN Security Council authorisation for humanitarian engagement provide a legitimate basis for supporting rebel movements, disproportionate use of force and regime change in a sovereign state? Second, in what way does the problems of collateral damage and mixed motives during civilian protection in armed conflicts, impact the future legitimacy of R2P doctrine in international society? As I have argued elsewhere (Abubakar, 2017) it is important to note from the outset that the outbreak of the crisis in Libya is part of the larger "Arab Spring" revolt by opposition groups in the Middle East and North African countries, against authoritarian dictatorship; and demand for the democratisation of the political space. Specifically, in North Africa, the "Arab Spring" which began in Tunisia with the self-immolation of one Mohammed Bouzazi, gradually spread to Egypt, Libya, Bahrain, Yemen, Syria, and other Middle Eastern countries. However, unlike Egypt, Syria and Tunisia where there was no external military intervention, the uprising in Libya degenerated into a civil war that prompted foreign intervention by NATO under the doctrine of R2P that culminated into violent regime change (Zoubir & Rozsa, 2012). The rebellion against Qaddafi that started in Benghazi is intricately woven with the history of state formation in Libya. Prior to Italian colonial occupation in 1911, the geographical space that became Libya was composed of three Ottoman provinces of Cyrenaica, Fezzan, and Tripolitania. While Cyrenaica was under the monarchy of King Muhammad Idris Sanusi, the western province of Tripolitania formed the autonomous Tripolitania Republic in 1918 (Ahmida, 2012). The Sanusiyya monarchy based in Cyrenaica and the Tripolitania Republic constituted the bastion of nationalist opposition to Italian colonial occupation. In its brutal campaign against the Libyan people, Italy exterminated about half a million people, while another 60,000 perished in concentration camps (Ahmida, 2012). The three provinces were eventually amalgamated to form the present state of Libya. Between 1943 and 1951, Britain and France administered Libya. After independence in 1951, political power was handed back to the Sanusiyya monarchy which was overthrown by Muammar Qaddafi in the 1969 military coup.

With the ascendance of Qaddafi and the availability of oil wealth in the 1970s, Libya experienced impressive socio-economic transformation, urbanisation, expansion of higher education, health services and the emergence of a middle class. Between 1950 and 2010, Libya's population increased from 1 million to 6.5 million. In Tripoli, the population increased from 130,000 in 1951 to 1.8 million in 2010, while in the eastern city of Benghazi, the population increased from 70,000 to 650,000 (Ahmida, 2012). With abundant wealth from the export of oil and natural gas resources to Europe, the Libyan state-subsidised social services such as health, transportation, and education; thereby improving the livelihood of the citizenry. For example, in 2011 Libya's Human Development Index of 0.760 was ranked at number 54 out of 187 countries which is better than most African and Middle Eastern countries. Between 1980 and 2011 life expectancy increased in Libya from 60.1 years to 74.8 years, while adult literacy rate reached an impressive 88.9%. In 2010, Gross National Income per capita was $15,767 which is far greater than that of all Sub-Saharan African countries (UNDP, Human Development Report 2011).

However, in spite of these impressive accomplishments under Qaddafi, the centralisation of power and restriction of the political space increasingly created dissatisfaction with the ideology of personal rule. For the people of Cyrenaica, the Qaddafi regime that sacked the Sanusi monarchy which hitherto had its headquarters in Benghazi, was fundamentally illegitimate. By the 1990s, there emerged a formidable opposition group called the Libyan Islamic Fighting Group (LIFG- led by Abd al-Hakim Bilhaj, a veteran of the Afghan war) which drew most of its support from eastern cities such as Baida, Darnah and Ajdabiyya in Cyrenaica (Brahimi, 2011). As the base of the Sanusiyya Movement that fiercely fought Italian colonisation through heroes such as Omar Mouktar, Benghazi and the province of Cyrenaica, in general, became the rallying heartland for opposition against Qaddafi's autocracy (Wehrey, 2012; Brahimi, 2011). Qaddafi regime responded to the LIFG through harsh crackdown, and several of its leaders were incarcerated and tortured in the Abu Salim prison in Tripoli. As a result of LIFG uprisings in 1998, the Qaddafi regime conducted aerial bombardments in Cyrenaica and declared a state of emergency in the eastern city of Darnah (Brahimi, 2011). In 1996 a protest in the Abu Salim prison led to the massacre of about 1,200 incarcerated political prisoners. It was a commemorative protest organised on 15 February 2011, by the families of the Abu Salim prison massacre victims in Benghazi, and the arrest of their lawyer Fathi Terbal that triggered a confrontation with Qaddafi's security forces and the subsequent rebellion which metamorphosed into a revolution calling for the overthrow of the regime (Ahmida, 2012). As the confrontation escalated, approximately 10,000 people were killed (Pattison, 2010: 272). The increase in civilian casualties and Qaddafi's threat to wipe out the opposition made the Libyan conflict a challenge for regional organisations as well as the UN. The League of Arab States (LAS) and the AU responded differently to the unfolding civil war and threat of humanitarian catastrophe in Libya.

At the outset of the Libyan crisis, the AU clearly stated its position that since the conflict is an internal political matter in a sovereign state, it should be resolved through a negotiated political settlement. To find a diplomatic solution to the crisis, AU established a High-Level Committee composed of South Africa, Mauritania, Mali, Uganda, and the Republic of Congo. The mandate of the Committee was to: 1) facilitate the cessation of hostilities, 2) ensure that Libyan authorities cooperate in allowing timely delivery of humanitarian assistance, 3) encourage Libyan authorities to protect foreign nationals, including African migrants, and 4) ensure that the Qaddafi regime implements political reforms that would facilitate the resolution of the crisis (AU Peace & Security Council, March 2011). However, AU's proposal for a peaceful negotiated settlement of the conflict was rejected by the Interim National Transition Council (NTC). In a meeting with members of the AU High-level delegation in Benghazi, Mustafa Abdel Jalil (Chair of the TNC) insisted that the AU road map to a negotiated settlement is not acceptable because it did not include the immediate departure of Qaddafi. According to Jalil, "Qaddafi must leave immediately if he wants to survive…" (De Waal, 2007: 2). In its efforts to defuse the mounting violence, the AU at its Extraordinary Summit on May 25 proposed an "inter-positioning force" in Misrata area that would monitor a ceasefire between Qaddafi forces and rebel forces. The ceasefire was to be monitored by the AU, UN, and LAS. However, this option could not materialize because no African country was ready to volunteer troops; and the much-needed funding from EU was delayed (De Waal, 2007). As the rebel forces entered Tripoli, the internal dynamics of the Libyan conflict decisively swung in the TNC's favour. Some African countries such as Ethiopia and Nigeria not only recognised the TNC but also urged the AU to do the same. In the final analyses, AU's strategy of negotiated settlement did not yield significant success because neither Qaddafi nor the TNC was willing to enter a ceasefire. Nonetheless, from the perspective of the doctrine of R2P as elaborated in the ICISS Report (2001), AU's position on the Libya conflict is consistent with the principle that diplomatic and political options must first be explored; and if negotiated settlement fails, then force could be applied as a last resort. While the AU strategy emphasised dialogue and mediation as an appropriate channel for the resolution of the Libyan conflict, the LAS opted for a more coercive approach by calling for the imposition of a "no-fly zone" over Libya's air space.

From the onset of the Libyan conflict, members of the LAS were eager to ensure some form of regime transformation in that country because of Qaddafi's tacit support for Western intervention in Iraq, which led to the overthrow of a Sunni-Arab regime under Saddam Hussein. Furthermore, Libya's attempt in December 2010 to take a dominant financial controlling position in the Bahrain-based Arab Banking Corporation (Pradella & Rad, 2017) may have generated alarm and anxiety among leaders of the Gulf Cooperation Council (GCC). The first major response of LAS in February 2011 was the suspension of Libya's membership from the organisation. Furthermore, during its Extraordinary Ministerial meeting held in Cairo on March 12, 2011, LAS not only urged Libyan authorities to respect international law by ending "...crimes against the Libyan people..."; but also emphatically called on the UN Security Council "...to bear its responsibilities towards the deteriorating situation in Libya and to take the necessary measures to impose immediately a no-fly zone on Libyan military aviation and to establish safe areas in places exposed to shelling as a precautionary measure that allows the protection of the Libyan people and foreign nationals residing in Libya, while respecting the sovereignty and territorial integrity of neighbouring States" (League of Arab States, Resolution number 7360, March 2011). Also, the LAS urged for a coordinated effort by the UN, AU, Organisation of Islamic Conference (OIC), and EU in finding a solution to the Libyan conflict.

Five days after the LAS Ministerial session which called for the imposition of a "No-fly zone" over Libya's airspace, the UN Security Council adopted Resolution 1973 that explicitly authorised a "...ban on all flights in the airspace of the Libyan Arab Jamahiriya to help protect civilians...and civilian populated areas under attack...including Benghazi, while excluding a foreign occupation force of any form on any part of Libyan territory...." (UN Security Council Resolution 1973, March 2011). Two days after the passage of the UN Security Council resolution, NATO military forces began air bombardment against Libya's air defences (Williams, 2011: 248). However, this military operation authorised by the UN Security Council meant that the UN had initiated a war against a sovereign state and the incumbent regime premised primarily on the R2P principle of protecting civilians. According to Kuperman (2013), NATO's intervention and support for Libya's rebel to overthrow Qaddafi extended the duration of the conflict, thereby, increasing the number of civilian casualties. For example, the UN Nations Human Rights Council investigation found that 20 NATO airstrikes killed 60 civilians and injured another 55 (Report of International Commission of Inquiry on Libya 2012). Also, on 8 August 2011, another NATO bomb killed 34 civilians and injured 38 (Human Rights Watch, 2012: 17). By assisting the rebels through airstrikes, rather than seeking a negotiated settlement as proposed by AU, NATO elongated the duration of the Libya conflict, thereby increasing the magnitude of collateral damage to human lives and property. As Kuperman (2013) indicates, "...Repeatedly, NATO would bomb Libyan forces, enabling the rebels to advance on populated areas [such as coastal towns of Misrata, Bani Walid, Sirte and Ras Lanuf], until the government counterattacked – with each round of combat inflicting casualties on both fighters and non-combatants." (UN, 2011a; see also UN, 2011b)

Consequently, estimated casualties in the Libya conflict reached between 8,000 and 11,500 (Kuperman, 2013). Rebels also expelled 30,000 (mostly black), African guest workers, on the grounds that they were "mercenaries" supporting the Qaddafi regime. Furthermore, in April 2012, Human Rights Watch reported that violence against innocent civilians around Misrata persisted and "appear to be so widespread and systematic that they may amount to crimes against humanity" (HRW 2012). NATO's humanitarian intervention in Libya indicates the dilemmas of the R2P doctrine whereby interveners may go beyond the initial intent of UN Security Council resolution to pursue self-serving agenda of regime change. NATO's disproportionate use of force, even when Qaddafi's forces were on retreat, exacerbated collateral damage against both combatants and non-combatants, thereby defeating the initial objective of civilian protection as enunciated in UN Resolution 1973 that authorised the intervention.

The NATO intervention raises some basic questions: in what ways did the overthrow of Qaddafi impact the sovereignty and autonomy of Libya? To what extent did the political vacuum provide an opening for militant groups to exacerbate violence and deepen the disintegration of the Libyan state? First, NATO countries, especially US, Great Britain and France had some grudges against Qaddafi because of his role in sponsoring the 1988 Pan-Am Airline bombing over Lockerbie, Scotland in which about 243 passengers (mostly Americans) perished. Second, Britain and France were interested in regime change not only to open up access for their corporations to Libya's vast oil and gas reserves but also ensure that a new regime in Tripoli would curb the rising tide of illegal migration into Europe. Libya's oil and gas reserves is one of the highest in Africa, and its proximity to Europe meant that it provided a more accessible and reliable source of energy than Russia or other volatile Middle Eastern OPEC countries. Russia's closure of gas supply to Ukraine was perceived as a wake-up call among EU countries. Over the years, oil and gas imports by EU countries were rising steadily as North Sea reserves declined. For example, it is estimated that EU imports about 82% of its oil, and 57% of gas requirements from Libya; and by 2030 this import is projected to increase to 93% and 82% respectively (Lutterbeck, 2009). Another geostrategic significance of Libya's carbon resources to EU's consumption is that in Libya oil recovery cost is low; it's also of high quality with less sulphur content, and closer to EU market (Lutterbeck, 2009). Between 2002–2006, Libya's oil exports to the EU rose from EUR 15 billion to more than EUR 42 billion (Lutterbeck, 2009). Another area of Western economic linkage with Libya is a financial investment in commercial banks and hedge funds. Libya's financial assets under the Libya Investment Authority (LIA)was invested in several US and European banks. For example, it is estimated that of the $53 billion Libyan state assets, $293 million was deposited in HSBC and another $275 million in an HSBC hedge fund; $110 million in Royal Bank of Scotland and $182 in Goldman Sachs accounts; while French Bank Societe Generale had $1.8 billion of Libyan Investment Authority funds.

Furthermore, Japanese bank Nomura had $500 million if LIA's funds invested in the bond portfolio and another $500 million managed by the Bank of New York (BBC, 2011). In 2006, Libya's officials were trying to diversify their holdings of the foreign reserve to ensure greater national control over the investment portfolio. It is, therefore, not surprising that French President Sarkozy declared at the start of the 2011 war against Qaddafi that: "We fight to save the Euro" (Pradella & Rad, 2017). The issue of illegal migration from Sub-Saharan Africa and the Middle East across the Mediterranean Sea into the EU has been a major source of friction between Qaddafi and Europe. EU countries have tried to persuade Qaddafi to crackdown on illegal migration, but he has not taken any serious action in that direction. Qaddafi may have assumed that the open-door policy of Libya towards Sub-Saharan migrants could be used as leverage and influence over AU countries. Third, since the 1980s, Western countries have accused Qaddafi's Libya of being a "state sponsor of terrorism." Hence, Resolution 1973 provided a convenient opportunity for regime change in Tripoli. As for LAS, particularly the Sunni Gulf States such as Saudi Arabia, Qatar, and Kuwait, intervention in the Libya conflict provided the window to unseat Qaddafi who supported the overthrow of Saddam Hussein's Sunni regime in Iraq. In the case of the AU, their position for a negotiated settlement is premised on the principle that the conflict between Qaddafi and the rebels is an internal matter that should be settled through diplomacy rather than the use of force. Furthermore, because of the legacy of colonial domination, African states are generally suspicious of any form of external intervention. As President Jacob Zuma of South Africa stated: "We strongly believe that the resolution [1973] is being abused for regime change, political assassinations and foreign military occupation…" and that the use of force for a humanitarian cause in Libya may hamper the future prospect for the legitimate use of R2P doctrine to save civilians from harm (Kuperman, 2013).

Through the bio-politicisation of humanitarianism in Libya, NATO's disproportionate use of airpower in support of rebellion exacerbated collateral damage and harm to civilians, thereby eclipsing the initial intent of Resolution 1973. NATO's imposition of "No-Fly-zone" in Libya reveals the tensions within the logic of R2P doctrine that make its utilisation as a tool for saving bare life highly problematic. First, is the problem of the mixed-motive whereby state actors may either support or derail humanitarian action based on self-interest motives. Second, the inconsistency problem in which interveners may be enthusiastic in utilising disproportionate force for regime change, as in Libya, while dithering in cases such as Syria where there has been an obvious case of the attack against the innocent civilian population by the Assad regime using chemical weapons. Third, is the collateral damage and conspicuous harm problem by which I refer to the situation where the outcome of humanitarian action leaves behind a trail of continuing violence, political uncertainty, insurgency, and anarchy. Most of the armed militia groups in Libya retained their heavy weapons and have been fighting each other for control of cities, territory, and oil terminals. Five years after the NATO operation in Libya, the country does not have a central government. There are currently two governments in the country – one located in Tripoli and the other in Tobruk. Also, Benghazi remains the site of a fierce battle between the forces of General Khalifa Hafter (the self-proclaimed leader of the Libya National Army – LNA- engaged in *"Operation Dignity"* against jihadist groups) and Ansar-al-sharia militants along with their allies. With the political vacuum created as a result of NATO's regime change in Libya, other external jihadi groups such as ISIS (the Islamic State in Iraq and Syria or *Daesh*) has joined the fight, thereby exacerbating the anarchy. In the words of Pradella & Rad (2017: 2422), "… NATO intervention and civil war exacerbated social divides in Libya, leading to the impoverishment of vast swathes of the population, extreme human rights abuses, and an unprecedented displacement crisis. Because of this socio-economic and political situation, including the rise in racism and racist attacks, the number of immigrants in the country has declined. In contrast, the transit towards Europe of African and Syrian migrants and refugees has increased."

A closely related unintended consequence of NATO's actions in Libya is that several weapons from Qaddafi's stockpiles have spread into Sahelian countries, thereby fuelling violence in Mali and north-eastern Nigeria. Boko Haram terror group in Nigeria may have benefitted from the cache of this weaponry that bolstered its operational capacity in 2013–2015. It is estimated that about 15,000 man-portable surface-to-air missiles (MANPADs), capable of shooting down civilian and military aircraft are unaccounted for after the fall of the Qaddafi regime (Kuperman, 2013). In Libya, international interveners seem to have neglected pillar three of the R2P doctrine that enjoins them to support the state in rebuilding its infrastructures, political inclusion, and the reconstruction of institutions of democratic accountability, good governance, and the rule of law. The failure of liberal peace interventionism in Libya to follow through with the principle of rebuilding state institutions that facilitate socio-economic development exacerbated the chasm between the citizenry and the government, thereby deepening democratic deficit. By refracting sovereignty outwards to the international community rather than inwards to the people within the country, the principle of sovereignty as responsibility in R2P seems to undermine an essential ingredient of popular democratic sovereignty, which historically rests with the people. In the next section, I examine the aftermath of the overthrow of Qaddafi's regime in Libya and the rise of insurgency conflict following the takeover of cities such as Dernah and Sirte by ISIS.

## Regime change and the dilemmas of counterinsurgency in post-Qaddafi Libya

Regime change in Libya arising from NATO's bio-politicisation of humanitarian intervention not only created a political vacuum; but, it also provided an opportunity for the numerous ideologically diverse militia groups to constitute themselves into local law enforcement agencies in many cities, including the capital, Tripoli. The National Transition Council (NTC) was ineptly paralysed by violent militia groups under the umbrella of *Thuwwar* – an amalgam of the rebel groups that overthrew Qaddafi with NATO's support. Since the militia groups were well armed while the NTC lacked any national armed force to rely upon, it devolved local security to the local militia groups that held on to neighbourhoods, cities and territory in Libya. With the destruction of Libya's armed forces, security agencies, prisons and the justice system during NATO's intervention, militia groups quickly transformed themselves into *de facto* structures for the maintenance of law and order. For example, the NTC carved up about 6,000 kilometres of Libyan borders to militia groups, including ports; and recognised militia powers for unilateral detention and incarceration of over 8,000 detainees. As Pelham (2012: 540) puts it, militia commanders "…wielded the powers of policemen, judges, and executioners." While the NTC tried to embark on a process of disarmament, demobilisation and reintegration of rebel forces to rebuild security apparatuses of the Libyan state, *Thuwwar,* which saw itself as the guardians of the revolution rejected any attempt at disarmament. They suspected that the NTC was mainly composed of ex-Qaddafi officials and that if they surrender their weapons, Qaddafi's henchmen will strike back at them. The Misrata Brigade maintained its dominant presence in Tripoli while Zintan militia and their allies held on to the national airport. In the eastern city of Benghazi, renegade General Khalifa Hafter and his Libya National Army (LNA) continued to battle Ansar-al-sharia and other extremist elements of the Muslim Brotherhood.

The Libya Islamic Fighting Group (LIFG) which resisted Qaddafi's regime in the 1990s, changed its name into Libya Islamic Movement for Change (LIMC) and retained its weaponry. Also, a coalition of several militia groups under the rubric of Libya Shield, led by Wissam Ben Hamid, established rapid reaction force that could be deployed to southern parts of the country to ensure control of smuggling routes. "Subsidized petrol, flour and guns went out; alcohol and migrants came in" (Pelham, 2012: 545). In eastern Libya, the bastion of the revolution against Qaddafi, militia groups and government forces clashed over who should maintain law and order, as well as control of oil ports and cities. For example, in May 2012, an NTC-appointed military commander was shot dead at a petrol station in the city of Derna the day before he could take charge (Pelham, 2012). Also, NTC's foreign supporters came under severe attack by militia groups. For example, US and British Consulates, as well as the compound of the International Committee of the Red Cross (ICRC), were attacked in Benghazi. As Ronen (2017: 112) put it, the overthrow of the Qaddafi regime and the absence of a significant functional military and security system dealt a fatal blow to the Libyan state and society as armed militias "…engaged in internecine violence aimed at protecting the interests important to them…. The momentum of the internal war and the terror unleashed stepped up, spilling over into civil war in …2014. Its accelerated disintegration placed Libya in ISIS crosshairs as easy prey, and ISIS …rushed to exploit the military-security void to promote its ends."

In April 2014, the *Bataar* Brigade – a jihadi group affiliated with ISIS in Syria – arrived in the eastern city of Derna. With the support of the local Islamic Youth Council, it established a foothold in the city. With the help of a Salafist group *Ansar –al-Shari'a*, ISIS extended its control into the larger city of Benghazi and later Sirte, the hometown of Muammar Qaddafi. The penetration into Libya's violent post-Qaddafi socio-political space further exacerbated a "war within a war" (Ronen, 2017: 113) by pitting different militia groups against the NTC as well as fighting for the control of strategic oil ports such as Ras Lanuf, Ajdabiyya, Bin Jawad and Misrata – Libya's centre of iron and steel industry, as well as the largest seaport. ISIS's effective consolidation of its support in both Sirte and Misrata derives not only from the fact the Sirte is Qaddafi's hometown and the population were disgruntled with the rebels that assassinated him; but even most importantly, ISIS saw the control of Sirte and Misrata from geostrategic perspective. The control of a large seaport like Misrata along with oil resources will enable the group to secure a stable source of income through the export of crude oil, human smuggling, and extortion.

Most importantly, however, its proximity to Europe. As one Libyan ISIS fighter, Abu Irhim al-Libi stated: "We are knocking on the gates of Rome…. There is nothing between you except this narrow sea and us…. So now you can only wait for your inevitable fate" (Ronen, 2017:114). Another significance of Misrata is that it is strategically located at the crossroads which connect eastern province of Cyrenaica and Tripolitania in the west; while Sirte's commercial ties with the southern province of Fezzan provide ISIS with further access into the Sahel region where it could recruit supporters and expand the Caliphate into West Africa. It is estimated that from 2015–2016, ISIS armed fighters numbered approximately 6,000 in Libya and was growing at an alarming rate (Ronen, 2017). ISIS insurgency warfare in Libya included not only the use of suicide attacks against civilian targets, but it was involved in violent execution of groups which it considers as infidels and those who fail to submit to its strict puritanical interpretation of the Qur'an and Sharia law. For example, in February 2016, ISIS executed at least 49 people in the city of Sirte and outlying areas; and killed another 28 in Misrata (HRW, 2016).In February 2015, ISIS decapitated 21 Egyptian Coptic Christians on the beach near Sirte. It also targeted the Corinthea Hotel in Tripoli killing over 12 guests. ISIS also engaged in terrorist attacks in neighbouring Tunisia killing 38 British tourists in Sousse resort in 2015. Furthermore, in 2016, it targeted a Coast Guard training camp in Zlitan using a truck filled with explosives that killed about 70 cadets. The attacks against civilians as well as state assets by ISIS were meant not only to inflict fear in society but also to deepen its grip over the territory that it had captured in Libya.

In June 2016, the Government of National Accord (GNA) which was cobbled together through UN-sponsored negotiations was able to secure the support of the Misrata militia coalition – Libya Dawn – to launch a counterinsurgency attack, with Western support, against ISIS stronghold of Sirte-Ajdabiyya. In the ensuing fight, approximately 1,700 ISIS militants were killed while the GNA and its allies lost about 700 fighters and another 3,200 wounded. Many ISIS fighters escaped into Libya's vast desert in the west and south while others fled into neighbouring countries such as Tunisia, Egypt, Algeria and Mali. General Hafter's LNA with the support of Egypt and the United Arab Emirates continue with the battle against jihadi groups in Derna and Benghazi areas to ensure control of oil and gas infrastructure as well as Libya's territory in the east. So far, Haftar's forces control most of Libya's oil, especially around the ports of Ras Lanuf, Es-Sidra and Zuetina oil terminal (Ronen, 2017).

The insurgency warfare and counterinsurgency against ISIS and jihadi militants in Libya has exacerbated human displacement, perilous smuggling across the Mediterranean sea, human rights violations by both ISIS and disparate militia groups and regional instability arising from the 2011 NATO intervention and overthrow of the Qaddafi regime. According to the UN High Commission for Refugees, approximately 435,000 Libyans are internally displaced (IDPs), and neighbouring countries such as Tunisia are "…dealing with a deluge after already having sheltered 1.8 million Libyan refugees since the fall of Qaddafi" (Jebnoun, 2015; HRW, 2016). The International Organisation for Migration (IOM) estimates that there are about 771,146 migrants and asylum seekers in Libya; and, the flow into Europe through Italy continues. Also, UNHCR recorded over 342,774 arrivals to Italy by sea, mostly from Libya; and another 4,518 died or went missing while crossing the Mediterranean Sea from Libya to Europe (HRW, 2016). As the counterinsurgency war in Libya intensifies against jihadi groups, more innocent civilians are likely to be displaced and forced into refugee status. Meanwhile, militia groups that may be controlling human smuggling networks, prison cells and illicit trade are likely to resist disarmament and restoration of legitimate statehood. Thus, the bio-politicisation of humanitarianism occasioned through NATO's 2011 intervention in Libya has inflicted more suffering on innocent civilians rather than saving bare life. The bifurcation of Libya into two competing centres of power – the Tripoli-based GNA and the Tobruk based House of Representatives (HoR) with diverse militia groups competing for local power, resources and territory, makes the future of the country uncertain and precarious.

## Conclusion

The insurgency war in Libya which has been raging for the last five years alerts us to the paradox of neoliberal humanitarian intervention which, in the post-Cold War epoch, has been framed within the normative doctrine of R2P. In 2011, as I discussed above, NATO powers, specifically US, Great Britain and France secured a UN Security Council Resolution 1973 to implement a "No-fly-zone" over Libya with the sole purpose of civilian protection. However, these major powers exceeded the mandate of UN Resolution 1973 by not only using excessive force in the destruction of Libya's socio-economic infrastructure and military assets but also enabling the process of regime change that has plunged an African country into violent conflict. NATO's bio-politicisation of humanitarianism in Libya raises several important lessons for African states in the emerging post-Cold War international order. First, Libya (including Syria, Darfur-Sudan and Iraq) alerts us to the precarious transition in the Westphalian myth of sovereignty (Osiender, 2001) in which the supposed core principle of autonomy over internal affairs may be suspended when peripheral state actors fail to comply with the normative orders of powerful states in international society. The responsibility to protect the citizenry from internal and external harm has been the primary function of the state in international society. Democratic theory reminds us that the right to alter government and its powers rests primarily with the people. However, R2P, as implemented in Libya shows how the refraction of self-determination to an external "international community" may inadvertently lead to catastrophic unintended consequences. Although the African Union insisted on a negotiated settlement through diplomacy, its position was not taken seriously by NATO powers that were focused on the use of military force and regime change. The subjection of African state actors as wards by NATO powers in the run-up to the intervention in Libya may set a dangerous precedence in the resolution of conflicts in Africa. Second, the biopolitics of humanitarian intervention in Libya reveals the contradictions and paradox of EU over its cosmopolitan ontology on universalist solidarity of human rights. If NATO, as the narrative goes, intervened to protect Libyan civilians from Qaddafi's atrocities, why not follow through with pillar three of R2P which enjoins interveners to rebuild and restore vital state infrastructure in the aftermath of conflict? For the last five years, Libya has not received significant material assistance to rebuild its infrastructures following the overthrow of Qaddafi. Most support to Libya has been either in the counterinsurgency war against ISIS and allied jihadi groups under the rubric of "Global War on Terror", or training coast guard to curtail migration into EU. Instances of terror-related attacks in European cities such as Paris, Manchester, Barcelona, and Brussels have further complicated the dilemma for innocent civilians in war-torn Libya and Syria. Third, Libya's experience alerts us to the limitations of the Weberian state model in post-colonial formations. As Jebnoun (2015: 840) rightly put it, "The violence of Italian colonialism exerted against nascent pre-colonial indigenous political structures has been followed by the establishment of loosely and flawed post-colonial institutions. These institutions lacked roots in Libyan society and have failed to perform their social, economic, and political functions." UN initiatives in resuscitating the Weberian state model in Libya may need to take seriously the lessons of the past one hundred years by crafting a more inclusive, participatory and locally empowered political arrangement that involves all the peoples of Libya. Finally, Western morality and its distinction between destructive violence that violates the rights of citizens (as alleged in the case of Qaddafi) and its military violence to save innocent lives reveals how misguided and dangerous such neoliberal assumptions of selectivity could be in international affairs. Even after NATO's intervention to "save" Libyans, we know that thousands of innocent civilians continue to die in the festering insurgency conflict.

## Bibliography

Abrahamsen, R. (2016). Africa and international relations: Assembling Africa, studying the world. *African Affairs, 116/462*, 125–139.

Abubakar, D. (2017). Responsibility to protect: The paradox of humanitarian intervention in Africa. In B. Abu Bakarr, *International security and peacebuilding: Africa, the Middle East and Europe*. Bloomington: Indiana University Press.

Autesserre, S. (2012). Dangerous tales: Dominant narratives on the Congo and their unintended consequences. *African Affairs, 111*(444), 202–222.

Autesserre, S. (2014). *Peaceland: Conflict resolution and the everyday politics of international intervention*. New York: Cambridge University Press.

Ahmida, A. (2012). Libya: Social origins of dictatorship and the challenge of democracy. *Journal of the Middle East and Africa, 3*, 70–81.

AU PSC (AU Peace and Security Council (2011). *Community of the 265th Session of the AU Peace Security Council*Issued on 10th March 2011. Available http://www.peaceau.org/uploads/communique-libya-eng.pdf. Accessed: on 04.08.2019.

BBC (British Broadcasting Corporation). (2011, May 26. Revealed: Where Libya invests $53 billion. Available: https://www.bbc.com/news/business-13552364. Accessed on 15.06.2019.

Bellamy, J. A. (2005). Responsibility to protect or Trojan Horse? The crisis in Darfur and humanitarian intervention after Iraq. *Ethics and International Affairs, 19*(2), 31–53.

Bellamy, J. A., & Williams, P. D. (2011). The new politics of protection: Cote d'Ivoire, Libya and responsibility to protect. *International Affairs, 87*(4), 825–850.

Brahimi, A. (2011). Libya's revolution. *Journal of North African Studies, 16*(4), 605–624.

Cunliffe, Philip (2016). The doctrine of the responsibility to protect as practice of political exceptionalism. *European Journal of International Relations, 23*(2), 466–486.

Cunliffe, Philip (2010). Dangerous duties: Power, paternalism and the responsibility to protect. *Review of International Studies, 36*, 79–96.

Chandler, D., & Reid, J. (2016). *The neoliberal subject: Resilience, adaptation and vulnerability*. London: Rowman and Littlefield International.

Doyle, W. M. (2016). The politics of global humanitarianism: The responsibility to protect before and after Libya. *International Politics, 53*(2016), 14–31.

Deng, F. et al. (1996). *Sovereignty as responsibility: Conflict management in Africa*. Washington, DC: Brookings Institution Press.

De Waal, A. (2007). Darfur and the failure of responsibility to protect. *International Affairs, 83*(6), 1039–1054.

De Waal, A. *The African Union and the Libya conflict of 2011*. World Peace Foundation. Online at http://sites.tufts.edu/reinventingpeace/2012.

Duffield, M. (2006). *Global governance and the new wars: The Merging of Development and Security*. London: Zed.

Foucault, M. (2003). In *Society must be defended: Lectures at the College de France, 1975–76* (D. Macey, Trans.). New York: Picador.

Foucault, M. (2010). In *The birth of biopolitics: Lectures at the College de France, 1978–79* (G. Burchell, Trans.). Basingstoke: Palgrave Macmillan.

Hehir, A. (2009). NATO's humanitarian intervention in Kosovo: Legal precedent or aberration? *Journal of Human Rights, 8*, 245–264.

Hehir, A. (2010). The responsibility to protect: Sound and fury signifying nothing. *International Relations, 24*(2), 218–239.

Hehir, A. (2013). *Humanitarian intervention: An introduction*. New York: Palgrave Macmillan.

Hobson, C. (2016). Responding to failure: The responsibility to protect after Libya. *Millennium: Journal of International Studies, 44*(3), 433–454.

HRW (Human Rights Watch). (2016). We Feel Cursed: Life Under ISIS in Sirte, Libya. Available: https://www.refworld.org/docid/573d80a84.html. Accessed on 15.06.2019.

HRW (Human Rights Watch). (2012).*Unacknowledged deaths: Civilian casualties in NATO's air campaign in Libya*. May 2012. Available from www.hrw.org/sites/default/files/reports/Libya Accessed 05.02.13.

ICISS. (2001). *International Commission on Intervention and State Sovereignty report: The responsibility to protect*. Ottawa: International Development Research Centre.

Jabri, V. (2007). Solidarity and spheres of culture: The cosmopolitan and the postcolonial. *Review of International Studies, 33*, 715–728.

Jebnoun, N. (2015). Beyond the mayhem: Debating key dilemmas in Libya's statebuilding. *The Journal of North African Studies, 20*(5), 832–864.

Kaldor, Ma. (1999). *New and old wars*. London: Polity.

Kuperman, J. A. (2008). The moral hazard of humanitarian intervention: Lessons from the Balkans. *International Studies Quarterly, 52*, 49–80.

Kuperman, J. A. (2013). A Model Humanitarian Intervention? Reassessing NATO's Libya campaign. *International Security, 38*( 1 (Summer)), 105–136.

Lamont, K. C. (2016). Contested governance: Understanding justice interventions in post-Qaddafi Libya. *Journal of Intervention and Statebuilding, 10*(3), 382–399.

Lutterbeck, D. (2009). Migrants, weapons and oil: Europe and Libya after the sanctions. *The Journal of North African Studies, 14*(2), 169–184.

Mamdani, M. (2009). *Saviors and survivors: Darfur, politics and the war on terror*. New York: Pantheon books.

Mamdani, M. (2010). The responsibility to protect or the right to punish?". *Journal of Intervention and Statebuilding, 4*(1), 53–67.

Mavelli, L. (2017). Governing populations through the humanitarian government of refugees: Biopolitical care and racism in the European refugee crisis.*Review of International Studies, 43*:1–24.

Mavelli, L. (2016). Governing the resilience of neoliberalism through biopolitics. *European Journal of International Relations, 23*(3), 489–512.

Muller, H., & Wolff, J. (2014). The dial use of an historical event: Rwanda 1994, the justification and critique of liberal interventionism. *Journal of Intervention and Statebuidling, 8*(4), 280–290.

Osiender, A. (2001). Sovereignty, international relations and the Westphalian myth. *International organization, 55*(2), 251–287.

Prinz, J., & Schetter, C. (2017). Conditioned sovereignty: The creation and legitimation of spaces of violence in counter-terrorism operations of the war on terror. *Alternatives: Global, Local, Political, 4*(3), 19–136.

Pattison, J. (2010). *Humanitarian intervention and the responsibility to protect*. Oxford: Oxford University Press.

Pradella, L., & Rad, S. T. (2017). Libya and Europe: Imperialism, crisis and migration.*Third World Quarterly, 38*(11)2411-2427

Pelham, N. (2012). Libya in the shadow of Iraq: The Old Guard vs the Thuwwar in the battle for stability. *International Peacekeeping, 19*(4), 539–548.

Ronen, Y. (2017). Libya: Teetering between war and diplomacy – The Islamic state's role in Libya's disintegration. *Diplomacy and Statecraft, 28*(1), 110–127.

Reid, J. (2010). The biopoliticization of humanitarianism: From saving bare life to securing the biohuman in post-interventionary societies. *Journal of Intervention and Statebuilding, 4*(4), 391–411.

Thakur, R. (2006). The responsibility to protect. In R. Thakur & W. P. S. Sidhu (Eds.), *The Iraq crisis and world order: Structural, institutional and normative challenges*. New York: United Nations University Press.

UNDP. (2011). Human Development Report, 2011. New York: UNDP. Available: http://hdr.undp.org/sites/default/files/reports/271/hdr_2011_en_complete.pdf. Accessed on 15.01.19.

UN United Nations Human Rights Council. (2012). *Report of the International Commission of Inquiry on Libya*. New York: United Nations.

UN (United Nations). (2011a). UN *Security Council Resolution 1973*. New York: United Nations. Available: http://www.securitycouncilreport.org/atf/cf/%7B65BFCF9B-6D27-4E9C-8CD3-CF6E4FF96FF9%7D/Libya%20S%20RES%201973.pdf. Accessed on 15.04.19.

UN (United Nations). (2011b). UN *Security Council Resolution 1970*. New York: United Nations. Available: https://www.securitycouncilreport.org/atf/cf/%7B65BFCF9B-6D27-4E9C-8CD3-CF6E4FF96FF9%7D/Libya%20S%20RES%201970.pdf. Accessed on 15.04.19.

Wehrey, F. (2012). *The struggle for security in Eastern Libya* (pp. 4–28). Washington, D.C.: Carnegie Endowment for International Peace.

Wai, Z. (2014). The empire's new clothes: Africa, liberal intervention and contemporary world order. *Review of African Political Economy*, 41(142), 483–499.

Wheeler, N. (2000). *Saving strangers: Humanitarian intervention in international society*. Oxford: Oxford University Press.

Weiss, T. (2007). *Humanitarian intervention* (2nd ed.). London: Polity.

Williams, P. D. (2011). The road to humanitarian war in Libya. *Global Responsibility to Protect, 3*, 248–259.

Zoubir, Y. H., & Rozsa, E. N. (2012). The end of the Libyan dictatorship: The uncertain transition. *Third World Quarterly, 33*(7), 1267–1283.

# 31

# Tanzania

## Counterterrorism and counterinsurgency in an unstable Region

*Mnyero Janja Ibn Sheikh Gunda and Gambo Maimuna Hammawa*

---

## Introduction

The 1998 terrorist attack and bombardment of the United States (US) Embassy in Dar es Salaam was a foundational threat to Tanzania's peace and security. Such experience did not only espouse terrorist capability of thorough intelligent collection of strategies against their target, use of sophisticated equipment that challenged Tanzania's sovereignty but it also espouses terrorism as an integral part of the ongoing Tanzanian political process traceable to foreign influence and porosity of the Tanzanian border, religious and political sentiment targets (Forest & Giroux, 2011; Shinn, 2003). Remarkably, the experience was a threshold to the Tanzania government responds and adoption of Prevention of Terrorism Act (POTA), 2002 (*Miscellaneous Amendment* in 2016) and Prevention of Terrorism Regulation (POTR), 2014 as legislative measures that prohibit and prevent terrorism.

Counterterrorism and counterinsurgency CT-COIN are efforts by nations to addressing the growing threats of terrorism and insurgency. This chapter explores CT-COIN in Tanzania. The chapter briefly provided an introduction that dwelled on an overview of CT-COIN, it highlighted on Tanzania's insurgency and terrorism, the context and scope of Tanzania's CT-COIN with emphasis on Tanzania's POTA, 2002 (*Miscellaneous Amendment* in 2016) and the POTR, 2014. Lastly, terrain matters counterterrorism and local peculiarities. The paper argued that Tanzania may have given premium to the legislative mechanism and regulatory framework which are presumed vibrant in combating terrorism but the effectiveness of such approaches were constrained by corruption, insufficient resources, narrow focus and competing priorities which made it difficult to meet the peculiarities of Tanzania. Recommendations were therefore advanced.

## Global and regional signposts

The global efforts to deter terrorism and organised violence have focused on addressing the root causes and manifestations of the phenomena. The European Convention on the Suppression of Terrorism (1977), the South Asian Association for Regional Cooperation's (SAARC), Regional Convention on Suppression of Terrorism (1987), the Arab Convention for the Suppression of Terrorism (1998) and the Inter- American Convention against Terrorism (2002) enjoined the adoption of comprehensive convention against terrorism in conformity with the

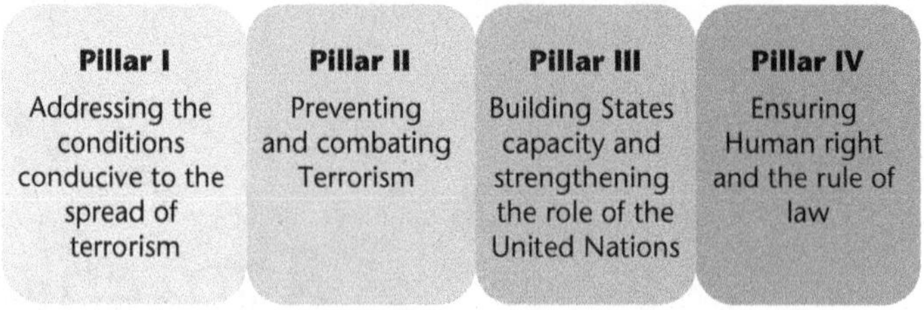

| **Pillar I** | **Pillar II** | **Pillar III** | **Pillar IV** |
|---|---|---|---|
| Addressing the conditions conducive to the spread of terrorism | Preventing and combating Terrorism | Building States capacity and strengthening the role of the United Nations | Ensuring Human right and the rule of law |

*Figure 31.1*   UN Global Counterterrorism Strategy
*Source*: United Nations General Assembly (2012)

UN Security Council Resolution 1373 which prevents and suppresses the financing of terrorist acts, refrain from supporting terrorist act; ratify and conform to international instruments by introducing comprehensive domestic counterterrorism strategies and measures (United Nations Security Council, 2001). With the objectives of respecting and protecting human life, the African Union (AU) established a Convention on the Prevention and Combating of Terrorism in 2002. The convention generally and specifically provided for member state commitment to control drug trafficking, the illicit proliferation of small arms and light weapons. It also provide for combating corruption, money laundering, the establishment of state's institution (police, army and security forces etc.) cooperation and interaction among regional groupings, exchange of information; addressing root causes of terrorism such as poverty and marginalisation (Kimunguyi, 2011; Moshi, 2007). Additionally, the Peace & Security Council (PSC) and the African Centre for the Study and Research on Terrorism (ACSRT) were concurrently established in 2004 to ensure the implementation of AU's policies and to facilitate state capacity building through studying and analysing terrorism and terrorist groups in Africa respectively (Moshi, 2007). Similarly, the UN Global Strategy on Counterterrorism adopted by the UN General Assembly in 2006, enjoins state implementation of the "four pillars strategy" at the national, regional and international level. These are illustrated below.

The four pillars strategy revolve around adopting measures to resolving domestic shortfalls in developing states' capacities in combating terrorism; improving security and protection and as well maintaining effective rule of law-based national criminal justice system that ensures the protection of human right (United Nations, 2012). Although this strategy has several times been reviewed it is generally agreed that combating terrorism cannot be effectively accomplished by merely following the traditional methods of prosecuting criminals. It must be a comprehensive collation of requisite intelligence and investigative skills; promoting international cooperation; developing and implementing national and regional strategic plans (United Nations, 2012).

Though both the UN and AU have demonstrated immense potential in providing international and regional strategies and guidelines respectively against terrorism, the primacy of the state in combating terrorism remains centrally indispensable (Ford, 2011). Apparently, states vary in capacity and encounter with terrorism, a one-size-fit all approach is therefore inappropriate (Fulgence, 2015; Ridley, 2014; Moshi, 2007). Nevertheless, there are minuscule studies on how individual countries, especially African responds to terrorism (Ford, 2011) this study fills the gap from the Tanzanian perspective owing to its reputation of a peaceful country with growing intimidation. This study will be approached in the following sequence:

- Tanzania's insurgency and terrorism
- The context and scope of Tanzania's counterterrorism strategies
- Terrain matters: counterterrorism and local peculiarities

## Tanzania's insurgency and terrorism

East Africa is the most threatened region by indigenous and international terrorism in Sub-Saharan Africa (Ploch, 2010; Shinn, 2003) but Tanzania has been tagged the peaceful and stable country "in a troubled region"(LeSage, 2014:1). Remarkably, this is linked to the pristine doctrine of Ujamaa widely acknowledged to have instilled the practice of peace, equality, freedom, development, democracy and communalism through state corporatism or monolithic state politics, economic and education nationalism (Vittori et al., 2014). However, while Ujamaa upheld and claimed to build a unified nation, some Tanzanians were ostracized (Vittori et al., 2014; Rosenau, 2007), this gradually instilled corruption, state-sponsored repression and paved for high rates of unemployment (LeSage, 2014). Tanzania has since been witnessing resistance especially from the Zanzibaris who incessantly mobilise youth in demand for secession subject to the community's perception of been marginalized from national politics.

Resistance from the public manifest in other varied forms. For instance, a pocket of Tanzanian citizens seek external financial assistance from foreigners especially those from Gulf states to build an educational institution and they relate with regional militants such as Somalia's Al-Shabab and Kenya's Al-Hijra (Lopez-Lucia, 2015; Vittori et al., 2014; LeSage, 2014; Gatsiounis, 2012). In addition, training camps and indoctrination centres were established at Lindi and Tanga to transmit the ideology of the benefactors (Lopez-Lucia, 2015; LeSage, 2014). Currently, Tanzania is experiencing a rising domestic attack in the form of arson, acid attacks, shootings, and bombings, largely predisposed by affiliation to Al Shabab (Mniwasa, 2004). It is reported that for the past five years (2013–2017), Tanzanian has witnessed 41 terrorist incidences in both private and public places with 33 people killed, five taken hostage and 149 injured (Ritchie et al., 2018). The table below illustrates some of these attacks.

It is evident from the above occurrences that Tanzania is experiencing violence manifested in the context of religious delineation perpetrated by both domestic and foreign militant affiliate that intend to achieve a political ambition. In fact, these violent acts

> risks prompting the failure of Tanzania's longstanding tradition of religious tolerance, the rise of sectarian conflicts across the country, the escalation of an independence struggle for Zanzibar and an economic crisis that would damage Tanzania's prospects for development. At the extreme, Tanzania [has become a] regional haven for militants linked to Al Shabab (LeSage, 2014:5).

These occurrences are further compounded by Tanzania's absorbent maritime boundaries [with Comoros and Seychelles], air links with West Southern Africa, Asia [Pakistan and the Gulf States] (LeSage, 2014; Ridley, 2014; Ploch 2010; Mniwasa, 2004) as well as porous land borders with eight countries (Burundi, the Democratic Republic of the Congo [via Lake Tanganyika], Kenya, Malawi, Mozambique, Rwanda, Uganda and Zambia) predominantly marred by domestic strife respectively (Ridley, 2014; Mniwasa,2004; Shinn, 2003).

Notably, Tanzania is lauded as leading in the East African region in countering terrorism (Ford, 2011). It is therefore momentous to explore the context and scope of Tanzanian counterterrorism. This is what the next section would examine.

## The context and scope of Tanzania's counterterrorism strategy

Tanzania has been apt in legislating against crime, terrorism, and organised violence. For instance, it had promulgated the Economic and Organised Crime Control Act of 1984; the

*Table 31.1* Government Responses to Cases of violent Attacks in Tanzania from November 2011–July 2017

| Date | Attacks |
| --- | --- |
| November 2012 | Tanzanian government issues a warning of potential Al-Shabab attacks after ten Tanzanian nationals were arrested on the Kenya- Somalia border attempting to join Al-Shabab. |
| June 2012 | Arrest of Erath Erdogan, a German national who had joined Al-Shabab, at Dar-el-Salam Airport. |
| October 2012 | Tanzanian policeman is hacked to death with matches in Zanzibar. |
| November 2012 | Acid attack on moderate, anti- UAMSHO Muslim Imam in Zanzibar. |
| December 2012 | Shooting of a catholic priest in Zanzibar. |
| February 2012 | -Interfaith rioting in Mwanza area related to Muslim protests against Christian butchery practices lead to beheading of a local priest.<br>- Murder of a Catholic priest and torching of a church in Zanzibar. |
| March 2013 | Rioting by Sheikh Ponda Issa Ponda supporters in Dar-es- Salam. |
| May 2013 | -Hand grenade attack at St Joseph's Church in Arusha, killing 3 and wounding 63 during a celebration by the Vatican nuncio.<br>-Burning a Christian church in Tanga region.<br>-Arrest of five men in Dar-es-Salam in possession of explosives and Improvisedimprovised explosives devise-related materials. |
| July 2013 | Arrest of British terrorism suspect, Hassan Ali Iqbal, in Kyele, Mbeya region, as he tried to cross into Malawi. |
| August 2013 | -Acid attack on two young British women in Zanzibar's stone town.<br>-Homemade petrol bomb attack a Christians church in Dar-es-Salam. |
| September 2013 | Acid attack on a Catholic priest in Zanzibar's Stone Town. |
| November 2013 | Arrest of 69 people running an Al-Shabab child indoctrination camp with over 50 (4–13 years old) children and 39 women in Tanga. |
| January 2014 | Explosive attack at New Year's Eve celebration at Christian church in Arusha. |
| February 2014 | -Three improvised explosive device (IED) attacks in Zanzibar targeting two Christian churches and a restaurant popular with tourists.<br>- Acid attack on moderate Muslim preacher and his son in Arusha. |
| April 2014 | Bombing of a crowded bar popular with tourist in Arusha, injuring 15 people. |
| June 2014 | -Explosives attack on a mosque in Zanzibar's Stone Town, killing one and wounding four people, potentially linked to Islamists' intent to attack an anti-Al-Shabab cleric.<br>-Explosives attack on the private house in Arusha where clerics were gathered.<br>-Explosives attack on an Indian restaurant in Arusha popular with tourist and local residents. |
| January 2015 | - Attack of Kilombero, Morogoro and Ushirombo police post in the Northern Shinyanga Region and assassination of two police officers in Ikwiriri, Pwani Region. |
| April 2015 | Al Shabab killed eight policemen and soldiers |
| May 2015 | -15 masked assailants (Al-Shabab militants) used improvised explosive devices, machetes and axes to attack a mosque in Mwanza. At least three people were killed. |
| August 2015 | Armed assailants attacked a police station where they killed two police officers and stole weapons. |
| April & July 2017 | Masked gunmen killed more than 30 police and local political officials in the Pwani region |

*Source*: Culled from LeSage (2014), Ridley (2014), Sembony (2015) & National consortium for the study of terrorism and responses to terrorism. (2016)

Mutual Assistance in Criminal Matters Act of 1991, the Proceeds of Crime Act of 1991, the Drugs and Illicit Traffic in Drugs Act of 1995, the Extradition Act of 1965, the Banking and Financial Institutions Act of 1991, the Prevention of Corruption Act of 1971, the Armaments Control Act of 1991 and the Ammunition Act of 1991. The 1998 bombing of the US embassy in Dar-es-Salaam spurred a firm resolve between the US and East African countries on the need for a bilateral and multilateral mechanism for the fight against terrorism. However, the currently enacted POTA, 2002 (Miscellaneous Amendment, 2016) and the POTR, 2014 are not only post-AU strategy but encompass significant provisions geared towards combating terrorism, this is why this write-up focuses on them. As discussed below, POTA, 2002 amended in 2016 is a legal framework that prevents, identifies, criminalises support and suppresses terrorism while POTR, 2014 is a regulatory framework that spelt out the approach and responsibilities of the state in terms of response to terrorism. Specifically, the POTR saddles the police and the Financial Intelligence Unit (FIU) with enforcing the law through coordinating information between state institutions, detecting suspected terrorists and defining the procedure for freezing terrorist assets.

## Legislation for CT-COIN

Tanzania's key legislative instruments for CT-COIN include POTA, 2002 (amended in 2016) and the POTR, 2014. The Tanzanian government employed these counterterrorism legislative mechanisms because the victory or botch in combating terrorism is dependent on actions of preventing and prosecuting terrorist activity of national-level laws (Ford, 2011). Both POTA, 2002 (Miscellaneous Amendment in 2016) and POTR, 2014 provisions are to be achieved through an interagency collaboration of security agents in the National Counterterrorism centre (NCTC) (Fulgence, 2015; Adekanye, 2006). The POTA, 2002 (Miscellaneous Amendment in 2016) provides for a number of landmark provisions:

1. The Act provides that terrorism is prohibited for anyone within and Tanzanians outside the country. More so, the Act defines terrorism as serious damage made to a country and or the population. Such acts range from compelling government to act in a particular way; destabilising or destroying the constitution, economic and social structure of the country; false threat, attacking the public, person's life, integrity, property and health through the use of arms or any dangerous substance. Furthermore, any conscious moral, material and financial assistance or support declared for these purposes are tantamount to committing terrorism but the embarkation of protest, demonstration, or stoppage of work unconnected to terrorism are exceptional. In this regard, the Minister is obliged to proscribe any organisation with the said aims. However, the Act failed to provide sentencing guidelines for all crimes. However, through the *Written Laws (Miscellaneous Amendment) (No. 2) Act, 2016*, Tanzania's legislature amended POTA, 2002 Act *to include a* new section that provided for the sentencing of terrorism crimes with harsher punishments of the death penalty on those found guilty of material support to terrorism but it still did not apply specific sentence for membership in a terrorist organization or one who execute a terrorist act. This implies that the penalty would vary.
2. The Act identifies international terrorism as an act connected to a non-citizen. In this regard, the prevention of terrorism Act empowers the Minister to declare any person or group as an international terrorist when such groups are reasonably suspected, linked to an international terrorist group listed by the UN Council or any international instrument or an individual is a "risk to national security" (United Republic of Tanzania Ministry of Finance and Planning

Financial Intelligence Unit, 2002, Para; 12). As a result, the Minister of Home Affairs is obliged to make regulation on such individual or group by freezing fund, financial assets, or economic resources, including those derived from the property directly controlled. Furthermore, the terrorist shall be prevented from entry into the United Republic and be prohibited from direct sale and supply of "weapons, ammunition, military vehicles and equipment, paramilitary equipment, spare parts and related material, and technical advice, assistance or training related to military activities" ( United Republic of Tanzania Ministry of Finance and Planning Financial Intelligence Unit, 2002, Para; 12:5). Any person who contravenes any regulations made under this subsection commits an offence liable to imprisonment with hard labour for a period not exceeding five years ( United Republic of Tanzania Ministry of Finance and Planning Financial Intelligence Unit, 2002).

3. In a related development, terrorist offences as identified by the Act range from funding, provision of property, concealing and harbouring of terrorist, soliciting support for terrorist, recruitment, facilitation and participation in the act, promoting terrorism from foreign state and conspiracy to committing terrorism within and outside the United Republic. Meeting within and outside the country to support terrorist acts carries the least punishment for ten to 15 years. Offences such as direct or indirect provision and collection of the fund with the intention of executing terrorist acts; harbouring, retaining, and concealing a terrorist to impede apprehension, and participation and recruitment in terrorism attract a punishment of not less than 15 and not more than 20 years of imprisonment. Similarly, offences such as direct and indirect provision or collection of properties and allied services for the purpose of facilitating the act of terrorism; utilising property knowingly owned by a terrorist; soliciting for support for a terrorist act and promoting terrorism from outside the United Republic are liable to imprisonment from 20 to 30 years. This Act takes into cognisance terrorist activities not only within the country but also outside the country.

4. Additionally, the power of arrest, investigation, and intelligence gathering and incepting communication, detention of aircraft or vessel and power to seize property used in perpetrating the act of terrorism is vested on any police officer. Furthermore, the Minister can seek information from any communication service provider with regards to preventing, prosecuting, and detecting offences of terrorism. On resistance by the service providers, the court may intercepts on application by the Attorney General order for compliance Similarly, a detention order may be issued by the Inspector General of Police when threats are deemed to have been committed or already committed to properties or persons on board and in case of non-compliance, force may be utilised. However, in case of trial, the offender is handed to the High court.

5. The Act permits the disclosure of any information on terrorism by the Inspector General of Police to any foreign state on request unless if prejudicial for the national security and safety. Financial institution and citizens must also cooperate with the government to disclose relevant information relating to prosecuting and preventing terrorism. In addition, detailed information of aircraft and ships passengers and cargo departing or entering the country must be provided.

In 2014, the Regulations on the enforcement of Prevention of Terrorism 2014 was published, it provides for the declaration of a terrorist, freezing of fund, prohibits dealing with declared person or entity assets, provided for institutional cooperation and exchange of information, review delisting and unfreezing and general provision. Specifically, the Act provided for the following:

a. Disclosing information, transaction and property of terrorist group (s) to the police or the FIU on terrorist activities, failure of which is liable to not less than two years and not exceeding five years of imprisonment.

b. Categorises suspected terrorist taking into consideration the relevant information available to declare terrorist as international terrorists, terrorist within the United Republic and proscription of organisations by the Minister of Home Affair.

c. It formalised the freezing and prohibition in dealing directly or indirectly (military vehicle, ammunition, arms, spare parts technical assistance advise or training) with funds or other assets of declared entities and the prevention of entry into the United Republic.

d. Institutional cooperation among law enforcement agencies and exchange of information on investigation and freezing of funds.

e. Review, unfreezing and delisting of a declared

Evidently, struggles of combating terrorism in Tanzania essentially concentrate on prevention, recruitment and participation in terrorism, money laundering, punishment of offenders and encouraging information disclosure on terrorism. However, Tanzania has dwelled so much on money laundering because "there is an increasing recognition that money laundering is an inherent feature of international and organised crime such as trade in illicit drugs, firearms trafficking, corruption and trafficking in people have become really lucrative" (Mniwasa, 2004; 37–38). However, it is obvious that the government has embarked upon CT. The next section will highlight on Tanzania's CT architecture.

## Institutional design: Tanzania's architecture for CT-COIN

Tanzania's counterterrorism architecture dwells elaborately on approaches of dealing with terrorism alongside mandates of promoting security, this makes the domestic counter terrorism frameworks of POTA 2002 amended in 2016 and POTR, 2014 significant. The framework are embedded in the pioneering role of the Minister of Home Affairs in declaring a terrorist, inter-agency collaboration and foreign cooperation (United Republic of Tanzania Ministry of Finance and Planning Financial Intelligence Unit, 2014). Under this auspice, the declaration of an individual or group as suspect is made on reasonable grounds by the Minister of Home Affairs who also carries the mandate of proscribing an organisation but on the advice of the Inspector General of Police (IGP). In addition, a third-party state request for the declaration of a terrorist is directly made to the Minister of Home Affairs or through the Minister of Foreign Affairs (MOFA). The Minister of Home Affairs in this regard directs the IGP to constitute a Terrorist Declaration Working Group comprising two representatives from the police force, one from MOFA, one from office of the Attorney General, one from the Tanzanian Intelligence and security service, one from the FIU and one from Immigration to conduct an investigation, which may lead to revocation, freezing of account and or prosecution of the suspect. This provides coordination in the declaration of an international terrorist or terrorist group in Tanzania.

In a related development, the Police is central in the counterterrorism struggle. Only the Police has the right to intercept communication of a suspect with the prior consent of the Attorney General and only the Police, immigration officer and member of Tanzania intelligent security service have the authority to arrest a person committing or that has committed an act of terrorism. In addition, the IGP can detain aircraft or vessel and seize any property linked to a suspect. Furthermore, within the country's law enforcement agents, the Police work in conjunction with the MOFA, Office of the Attorney General, the Tanzanian Intelligence and security service, the FIU and the Immigration service to detect and fully prosecute suspected terrorists through investigative forensic techniques while the Director of Public Prosecutions of the Attorney General's Office charges the case to court upon completion of the investigation. The POTR, 2014 provided that the Police similarly work with external law enforcement agencies and other national authorities within the United Republic on investigation and freezing of terrorist financial assets (the United Republic of Tanzania Ministry of Finance and Planning Financial Intelligence Unit, 2014). The Police also work closely with the immigration and NCTC to share information (upon request) on persons entering and leaving Tanzania with foreign state that signed a bilateral agreement with her and a party to United Nation Convention on Counterterrorism and member of INTERPOL (the United Republic of TanzaniaMinistry of Finance and Planning Financial Intelligence Unit, 2014:15) while the request of information by foreign states on terrorist financing is issued by the IGP, the Commissioner of the FIU or anybody authorises by the law. Tanzania's architecture to counterterrorism is a mesh of domestic interagency on one hand and foreign interaction with entities having counterterrorism mandates.

## Bilateral response to counterterrorism

Tanzania's benefitted from the Western strategy against terrorism. There had been considerable "... support for counterterrorism efforts by the wider international community, most notably the USA" (Busher, 2014:1), the United Kingdom (UK) and France demonstrated by their "military presence and security cooperation programs with regional states" (Rabasa, 2009:71). For instance, through the Combined Joint Task Force-Horn of Africa [CJTF-HOA]) established in 2002 to foster "conditions that counter ideological support for terrorism" (Ploch, 2010:15), the regional partnership was built, military and civil affair training were offered to East African countries (Rabasa, 2009). In addition, Tanzania received the assistance of $1billion from the US in 2006 ( Ploch, 2010; Whitaker, 2010) and this aided the country to build its capacity to respond to terrorist threats through improving aviation and border security, support military and police professionalization, improve communications and developed a counter-terrorism training curriculum for civil-military operations (Kimunguyi, 2011; Shinn, 2003). Previously, through the CJTF-HOA the US train the military in East Africa. However, with less involvement of the foreign donors in the activities of the CJTF-HOA, it is currently faced with challenges of ineffective and unsustainable operations due to insufficient national CT specialists, limited resources and obsolete equipment (Rabasa, 2009). However, the State Department through the Terrorist Interdiction Program (TIP) and Personal Identification Secure Comparison and Evaluation System (PISCES) provided the Tanzanian government with computer systems that facilitate immigration processing exchange of information with State Department officials on suspected terrorists attempting to travel (Ploch, 2010). In 2003, the regional US-led programmes (the East Africa Counterterrorism Initiative [EACTI] substituted with the East African Regional Strategic Initiative (EARSI) in 2009 was established and funded to promote regional counterterrorism efforts, build a partnership in the provision of coastal and border security and diminish support for violent extremism among East African countries [Comoros, Djibouti, Eritrea, Ethiopia, Kenya, Mauritius, Seychelles, Somalia, Sudan, Tanzania and Uganda] (Ploch, 2010; Rabasa, 2009). The West has built close tie with Tanzania and have strengthened regional cooperation between and among East African countries in combating terrorism.

The AU efforts of peacekeeping, conflict prevention and crisis management tortuously contributed to counter terrorism in Africa. These "three dimensions of AU peacekeeping engagement are imperative given East Africa's persistent regional tensions and conflicts" (Kimunguyi, 2011:13) which trigger terrorism. In line with the AU bilateral elixir of partnership, Kenya and Tanzania built the Joint Commission for cooperation to scale up war against terrorism and drug trafficking. The Kenyan President (Uhuru Kenyatta) affirmed that "our country has in the past suffered...., in the hands of these merciless individuals... we must use the strongest possible action to stop the unnecessary violence that threatens the safety, security and prosperity of our peoples" ("Kenya, Tanzania to Jointly Fight Terrorism...", 2015: para 4). The Kenyan President further argued that "we have agreed that our security agencies would work closely to fight terrorism share information and experiences (Government of Kenya, 2016:7). Similarly, Tanzania and Israeli collaborates on key defense and security matters such as troops training, cyber and inter-territorial security, sharing vital intelligence information on security threats (Mbashiru, 2018; Chandran, 2018). Tanzania has made ties that have comparatively benefited both Africa and the West in strive against terrorism.

## Terrain matters: counterterrorism and local peculiarities

As part of government effort in arresting culprits, the Tanzania security agents arrested some suspects. For instance, the police in 2016 killed three alleged Al-Shabab-linked terrorists in Northern town of Arusha and recovered army uniforms, ammunition and materials for making explosives but no supporting evidence to their linkage to Al-Shabab were provided (LeSage, 2014). In 2013, 69 suspected Al-Shabab-linked militants were arrested at a military–site training camp and dozens of recruits aged 4–13 were freed at Tanga (Balile, 2013). In the same vein, Mr Juma Abdullah kheri (Tanzanian businessman) was arrested for financing terrorism in Kenya and Tanzania (LeSage, 2014). These arrested were aided by the NCTC fronted community policing program in at-risk areas throughout Tanzania, improving anti-terrorism intelligence through building communication and confidence between security personnel and civilians.

Tanzania's effort to boost its counter terrorism capabilities impelled its interaction with the West. As a result, Tanzania witnessed improvement in its personnel, border and regional interaction and has been described as possessing the most capable militaries, police force and equipment in Sub-Sahara Africa. Sequel to these developments, the Tanzanian Immigration Service employ the US-provided PISCES and collaborate with the East African Police Chiefs' Organization, the Southern African Police Chiefs' Organization and the INTERPOL to ensure efficacy in border control at major ports entry (Bureau of Counterterrorism and Countering Violent Extremism, 2016). These collective effort couple with the efficient use of terrorist watch lists and checking of passports against the paper copies of the list safeguarded border posts (Bureau of Counterterrorism and Countering Violent Extremism, 2016). Similarly, the Tanzania Police officials share information of combating terrorism with police and counter-terrorism officials in Kenya and Uganda, this exposed and aborted two terrorist attacks planned to be executed during the 2013 Kenya's General Elections (BMI Research, 2016). These development have been facilitating cordial relationship between Tanzania and its neighbors. However, despite this progress, Tanzania is unable to maximally benefit from its engagements because of limitations, this is what the next section examines.

### Challenges of CT-COIN in Tanzania

It is certain that crime and its proliferation is globally and nationally motivated by globalisation, liberalisation of the economy and advances in information communication technology. However, Tanzania's peculiarities of violence are instigated by border porosity and religious discrimination manifested in terrorism and instability. Tanzania enacted POTA 2002 (amended in 2016) and the POTR, 2014 to combat terrorism but their applicability can only be adjudged against what has been accomplished in meeting Tanzania's peculiarities. These could be understood in the following

## Corruption

Corruption hampers growth and has devastating effects on the quality and the quantity of public investment. In spite, Africa's historical neopatrimonialism, POTA 2002 (amended 2016) and POTR, 2014 have not identified corruption as a terrorism-related problem in Tanzania. However, the Transparency International reported Tanzania's Corruption Perceptions Index as 100th; 119th and 116th out of 175 countries from 2014 through 2016 respectively (Bureau of Counterterrorism and Countering Violent Extremism, 2016). Tanzanian is an aid dependent nation and was the second-biggest beneficiary of foreign aid in Sub-Saharan Africa in 2013 receiving $3.43bn (£2.19 m) but donors were forced to suspend $490 m in budget support after the disclosure that some Ministers diverted $180 m from the Central Bank (McNeish, 2015). More so, government officials engage in fictitiously and fabricated payments to local companies like the 120 million dollars saga in 2008 which led to the resignation of two ministers (Lindner, 2014). It is been estimated by the Auditor General that 20% or more of the government budget is annually lost to corruption and selective justice that prevents the prosecution of high-level officials (Michael, 2014; Lindner, 2014). In a related development, Tanzanian public sector (specifically the Police) is reported as the most corrupt (Transparency International, 2015) even though this is chiefly attributed to low pay, it implies otherwise that the principal institution responsible for enforcing the rule of law is compromised and the consequences are appalling in the deliverance of justice and security. In a related development Similarly, cases such as Sheik Ponda Issa Ponda and Sheikh Farid Hadi Ahmed in 2012 (Ali-Koor, 2016) have been labelled "blanket criminalization of conservative Islamic groups" (Ali-Koor, 2016) which reflect lack of transparency in prosecution, unfair treatment of Muslims, weak investigation and poorly framed charges. The government must need to perform according to POTR, 2014 provision of declaring a terrorist with evidence. In other words, this demonstrates poor political commitment and response to counterterrorism and security.

## Insufficient resources in combating terrorism

The Tanzanian government is making progressive effort in arresting terrorists, but the fact remains that the government lacks the capacity of combating terrorism especially in border patrol (United States Department of State Publication, 2016). For instance, in larger border posts and airports are few facilities like passport security control and access to watch-lists but rural coastal region borders remain absorbent due to insufficient manpower for patrol; un-reliable electric power and inaccessible communications networks (United States Department of State Publication, 2017). More so, the institutions of FIU and the NCTC lack specialized equipment and staff, basic infrastructure for border security training on intelligence analysis and crime scene investigation, these have encouraged the over-reliance of Tanzania on the US (United States Department of State Publication, 2017: para 6). For instance, when President Bush declared a counterterrorism initiative of $100 million for East Africa and the Horn of Africa in 2003, over 100 Tanzanians' police benefited from its criminal investigation training (BMI Research, 2016), the expectation for further foreign funds and assistance has lost its grip with the glaring higher priority of the US to only promote and protect its interest abroad (Gardner, 2014). Sequel to inadequate resources therefore, there has been no case of terrorist financing investigated or prosecuted despite proliferation in fund transfer and arrest of people like Mr Juma Abdullah Kheri accused of financing terrorism. These are practical realities of limited capacity and political will whose implication is that the government would remain dependent on America and may unlikely achieve its goals

## Prevalence of insecurity

The Tanzanian counterterrorism instruments of POTA, 2002 ( amended in 2016) and POTR, 2014 placed a high priority in money laundering and border security in combating terrorism and the government has partly accelerated progress in strive for border security. For instance, statistics revealed that from the year 2000 to 2015, international immigrants in Tanzania were drastically reduced from 928.200 to 261.200 (United Nations, 2016). However, Table 31.1 illustrates that "Tanzania is facing rising violence executed by citizens influenced by foreign militant Islamists, some of whom are directly associated with al Qaeda and its regional affiliate based in Somalia, al Shabab" (LeSage, 2014:5). Despite this prevalence in insecurity and the conviction that such perpetrated violence in Tanzania is externally influenced, the Tanzanian government is yet to declare a particular group or individual as terrorist in Tanzania. This reveals that the government has not been accordingly providing sentencing to all terrorist act or prosecute offenders (United States Department of State Publication, 2017) and this could be responsible for rising militant's violence. The prevalence of insecurity in Tanzania is stimulated by laxity in the Police.

## Competing priorities

The Tanzanian POTA, 2002 & 2016 and POTR, 2012 & 2014 have given more premium to money laundering and border security while isolating all other significant Tanzanian problems such as pervasive poverty, marginalisation and religious discrimination which are also significant in combating terrorism. It is not inappropriate that the Tanzanian CT-COIN focused on money laundering, considering the fact that the Central Bank has discovered an equivalence of $650 million transferred each month through mobile transfers (United States Department of State Publication, 2015). However, there is need as provided by AU's 2002 Convention on the Prevention and Combating of Terrorism to focus on addressing the root causes of terrorism such as poverty, authoritarianism, and marginalisation. From the above discussion, it is apparent that the efficacy of Tanzania's counterterrorism is undermined by corruption, limited expertise and resources in criminal investigations and other areas of security which have espoused the weakness of POTA 2002 and POTR 2016.

## Conclusion

CT-COIN comprises measures aimed at combating terrorism and insurgency spearheaded by the UN to be domesticated. Tanzania's approach has significantly been a short term legislative and regulatory measures targeted particularly on money laundering and punishment of offenders rather than the long term strategy that hammers on root causes of Tanzanian peculiarities such as marginalisation, border porosity and corruption. Tanzania's counterterrorism responses, therefore, is unlikely to make a prolific impact because it is not shaped by local and national peculiarities. It is therefore recommended that Tanzania should firstly adopt multifaceted actions towards diplomacy in its counterterrorism measures to include balancing interest, promoting results-oriented bilateral and multilateral relation, building mutual trust, communication and understanding with its neighbours. This will go a long way to enhance border management. Secondly, Tanzania should reinvigorate some impeccable features of the Ujamaa doctrine such as inclusivity, self-reliance and communality in all activities and this will aid combating corruption, create intercultural connections improve security, empower the community and reduce over-reliance on the West. Thirdly, Tanzania must fully utilise opportunities offered by the technological revolution to enhance national development, to build its security agents and intelligence. Developed countries have a significant role in counterterrorism and improving the capacities of countries but caution must be made to avoid overreliance of which Tanzania has become a victim.

## References

Adekanye, S. (2006). *African challenges and capacity in countering terrorism regional differences in coordination of counter terrorism efforts regarding the United Nations anti terrorism technical assistance to Africa.* New York: The African- American Institute.

Ali-Koor, A. M. (2016). Islamist extremism in East Africa. *Africa Security Brief, 32,* 1–8.

Balile, D. (2013, November 15). Tanzania dismantles Al-Shabaab child indoctrination camp in Tanga region. Sabahi. Retrieved from https://allafrica.com/stories/201311180387.html.

BMI Research. (2016). *Tanzania: Crime and Security Risk Report Q3 2016.* United Kingdom. Retrieved from www.awex-export.be/.../BMI-Tanzania-Crime-and-Security-Risk-Report-Q3-2016.pdf.

Bureau of Counterterrorism and Countering Violent Extremism. (2016). *Country Reports on Terrorism 2016.* https://doi.org/10.1017/CBO9781107415324.004.

Busher, J. (2014). Introduction: Terrorism and counter-terrorism in Sub-Saharan Africa. *Journal of Terrorism Research, 5*(1), 1–4.DOI: http://doi.org/10.15664/jtr.824.

Kenya, Tanzania to Jointly Fight Terrorism, drug trafficking and poaching (2015, October 05 ). https://nation.africa/kenya/news/politics/kenya-tanzania-to-jointly-fight-terrorism-drug-trafficking-and-poaching-1133838.

Chandran, N. (2018, June 27). *China says it will increase its military presence in Africa.* Retrieved from https://www.cnbc.com/2018/06/27/china-increases-defence-ties-with-africa.html.

Ford, J. (2011, March 01). *African counter-terrorism legal frameworks a decade after 2001.* Retrieved from https://www.africaportal.org/publications/african-counter-terrorism-legal-frameworks-a-decade-after-2001/.

Forest, J., & Giroux, J. (2011). Terrorism and Political Violence in Africa: Contemporary Trends in a Shifting Terrain. *Perspectives on Terrorism, 5,* (3–4). 54-67. doi: 10.1080/10246029.2010.503061. Retrieved from http://www.terrorismanalysts.com/pt/index.php/pot/article/view/152/html.

Fulgence, N. (2015). War on Terrorism in Africa: A Challenge for Regional Integration and Cooperation Organizations in Eastern and Western Africa. *J Pol Sci Pub Aff.* S1: 007, 1-11. https://doi.org/10.4172/2332-0761.S1-007.

Gardner, F. (2014, February 07). *US Military Steps up Operations in the Horn of Africa.* Retrieved 30.07.2017, from http://www.bbc.com/news/world-africa-26078149.

Gatsiounis, I. (2012). After Al-Shabaab. *Current Trends in Islamic Ideology, 14,* 74–89.

Government of Kenya. (2016, October 31). *Presidents Kenyatta, Magafuli support joint Meeting to boost Economic Tie.* Retrieved July 30, 2017, from http://www.president.go.ke/2016/10/31/presidents-kenyatta-magufuli-support-joint-meetings-to-boost-economic-ties/.

Kimunguyi, P. (2011). *Terrorism and counter terrorism in East Africa.* Australia: Global Terrorism Research Centre, Monash University.

LeSage, A. (2014). *The Rising Terrorist Threat in Tanzania: Domestic Islamist Militancy and Regional Threats. Center for Strategic Research, Strategic Forum., 288,* 1-15.

Lindner, S. (2014, March 7). *Tanzania: Overview of corruption and anti-corruption.* Retrieved from https://www.u4.no/publications/tanzania-overview-of-corruption-and-anti-corruption.

Lopez-Lucia, E. (2015, May 18). *Islamist radicalisation and terrorism in Tanzania. governance, social development, humanitarian response and conflict (GSDRC) helpdesk research report 1233.* Birmingham, UK: GSDRC, University of Birmingham.

Mbashiru, K. (2018, March 22). *Tanzania: Dar, Tel Aviv ties under revival. Tanzania Daily News.* Retrieved from https://allafrica.com/stories/201803220817.html.

McNeish, H. (2015, July 29). Rampant corruption in Tanzania keeps fruits of the many in hands of the few. *The Guardian*. Retrieved from https://www.theguardian.com/global-development/2015/jul/29/tanzania-corruption-aid-poster-sellers.

Michael, M. (2014). *Assessing crime prevention by Tanzania Police Force: A case of Chamwino – Dodoma (Unpublished master's thesis)*. The Open University of Tanzania.

Mniwasa, E. E. (2004). Detection and suppression of money laundering in Tanzania. In C. Goredema (Ed.), *Tackling money laundering in East and Southern Africa: An overview of capacity*. Pretoria: Institute for Security Studies.

Moshi, H. P. B. (2007). *Fighting money laundering the challenges in Africa*. South Africa, Pretoria: Institute for Security Studies.

National Consortium for the Study of Terrorism and Responses to Terrorism (2016). "Annex of Statistical Information: Country Reports on Terrorism 2015". *Final report prepared for the United States Department of State. College Park, MD: START, 2016*, (June), 1–15. Retrieved from http://www.state.gov/documents/organization/257738.pdf.

Ploch, L. (2010, November 3). *Countering Terrorism in East Africa: The U.S. Response. Congressional report service R41473*. Retrieved from https://fas.org/sgp/crs/terror/R41473.

Rabasa, A. (2009). *Radical Islam in East Africa*. Santa Monica: Rand Corporation.

Ridley, N. (2014). *Terrorism in East and West Africa: The under-focused dimension*. Cheltenham, United Kingdom: Edward Elgar Publishing Limited.

Ritchie, H., Hassell, J., Appel, C., & Roser, J. (2013). "Terrorism". Published online at OurWorldInData.org. Retrieved from:' https://ourworldindata.org/terrorism' .[Online Resource].

Rosenau, W. (2007). Al Qaida recruitment trends in Kenya and Tanzania. *Studies in Conflict & Terrorism*, *28*(1), 1–10.

Sembony, G. (2015, February 15). Soldiers killed in raid against Al Shabab linked gang. *The Citizen*. Retrieved from https://www.thecitizen.co.tz/News/national/Soldier-killed-in-raid-against-Al-Shabaab-linked-gang/-/1840392/2624512/-/nks3mgz/-/index.html.

Shinn, D. H. (2003). Terrorism in East Africa and the Horn: An overview. *Journal of Conflict Studies*, *23*(2), 1-13. Retrieved from https://journals.lib.unb.ca/index.php/jcs/article/view/218/376.

Transparency International. (2015). *People and Corruption: Africa Survey 2015*. Retrieved from https://www.transparency.org/whatwedo/.../people_and_corruption_africa_survey_20Please provide full details in reference (Transparency International. (2015).

United Nations. (2016). *United Republic of Tanzania:Migration Profile*. Retrieved from https://esa.un.org/miggmgprofiles/indicators/files/Tanzania.pdf.

United Nations. (2012). *United Nations global Counter-Terrorism strategy: Activities of the United Nations system in implementing the strategy: Report of the Secretary-General: Addendum*. A/66/762available at:https://www.un.org/counterterrorism/activities-united-nations-system-implementing-united-nations-global-counter-terrorism-strategy.

United Nations Security Council. (2001). *Security Council resolution 1373 on threats to international peace and security caused by terrorist acts*, 28 September 2001, S/RES/1373 (2001), available at: https://www.refworld.org/docid/3c4e94552a.html [accessed 7 October 2020].

United Republic of Tanzania Ministry of Finance and Planning Financial Intelligence Unit. (2014). The Prevention of Terrorism Regulation, 2014. Retrieved February 27, 2019, from http://www.fiu.go.tz/legislation.asp.

United Republic of Tanzania Ministry of Finance and Planning Financial Intelligence Unit. (2002). *Prevention of Terrorism Act, 2002 (POTA)*. . Retrieved from https://www.fiu.go.tz/POTA.

United States Department of State Publication. (2015). *2015 International Narcotics Control Strategy Report (INCSR)*. Retrieved July 25 2017 from https://2009-2017.state.gov/j/inl/rls/nrcrpt/2015//index.htm.

United States Department of State Publication. (2016). *Country Reports on Terrorism 2015*. Retrieved July 25 2017 from https://www.state.gov/reports/country-reports-on-terrorism-2016/.

United States Department of State Publication. (2017). *Country Reports on Terrorism 2016*. Retrieved July 30, 2017, from https://www.state.gov/reports/country-reports-on-terrorism-2017/.

Vittori, J., Bremer, K., & Vittori, P. (2014). Islam in Tanzania and Kenya: Ally or threat in the War on Terror? *Studies in Conflict & Terrorism*, *32*(12), 1075–1099.

Whitaker, B. (2010). Compliance among weak states: Africa and the counter-terrorism regime. *Review of International Studies (2010)*, *36*, 639–662.

# 32

# Algeria

## The struggle against Al-Qaeda in the Maghreb

*Rasheed Oyewole Olaniyi*

## Introduction

Following historical developments during the 1990s, including post-colonial power structures and the rise of Islamic radicalism, Algeria witnessed a civil war that was characterised by tremendous brutality and in which an estimated 200,000 people lost their lives (Roberts, 2003: 254). Algeria is still struggling with the aftermath of the war and is dealing with persistent threats, such as the presence of Al-Qaeda in the Lands of the Islamic Maghreb (AQIM) on its territory. Domestic terrorism perpetrated by violent Islamists remains Algeria's principal security challenge. Local and regional protests about a diverse range of socio-economic issues have been taking place in Algeria since 2011. However, much of the literature suggests that Algeria was not affected by the protests emerging from the "Arab Spring." The Algerian government has succeeded in preventing protests from escalating to the levels witnessed in neighbouring countries through a number of short-term economic measures. The government revised the annual budget to increase public spending by 25%. This involved increasing spending on subsidies, social housing, public sector wages and employment. In February 2011, political reform included the lifting of state emergency that had been in operation since 1992. Algeria's historical legacy and conflicts in neighbouring countries have also led to a reluctance to engage in violent protest. Algerian terrorists also operate across the southern border in the Sahel and are linked to terrorism abroad. The US State Department listed two Algerian groups as Foreign Terrorist Organisations. The most virulent has been Al Qaeda in the Islamic Maghreb (AQIM), which pledged allegiance to Al Qaeda in 2006 and may increasingly be described as a criminal-terrorist mutation. As the dominant economic and military power in the region, Algeria has attempted to take the lead in developing a regional approach to counterterrorism in the Sahel.

To prevent attacks and bring terrorists to justice is among the core responsibilities of any state. It is both logical and necessary, therefore, that in Algeria as elsewhere national authorities are leading the fight against terrorism. As today's terrorism is both international and domestic, however, no state can defend its citizens effectively unless it works closely with international partners, both bilaterally and multilaterally. For example, (Ammour, 2013: 1–11) describes Algeria as seeking to centralise the war on terror. The country has long favoured a hard-line approach to combatting radical Islam and terrorist groups. As part of its counterterrorism activities, Algeria has also launched a "deradicalisation programme," and it tries to exercise control over the content of religious sermons. The September 11, 2001 attacks in the USA paved the way for a change in world dynamics. The attacks, committed by a terrorist group called al-Qaeda, destroyed the World Trade Center in New York City. Those attacks have become a milestone in international relations. According to some observers, the crucial event marked the beginning of a new age. The lives of migrants and minorities, living in both the United States and Europe, changed because of the attacks. Before the incidents, migrants enjoyed the advantages of multicultural societies. Now, they are contending with the discriminating assimilation policies of the Western world.

It is not possible to see a positive outcome stemming from 9/11, which affected the lives of thousands of innocent people. And it is the first pivotal pillar of the confrontation between the West and the Muslim world during the postmodern era. Although Muslims across the globe condemned the attacks, al-Qaeda militants under Osama bin Laden's leadership have not altered their discourse on jihad. In response, the West re-invoked the idea of "enemies within."

In the aftermath of 9/11, the West has been more suspicious of minorities, migrants, and Muslims. While the migrants living in the US and Europe were dragged into a boiling bowl in the aftermath of the attacks, on the one hand, the state administrations looked for various precautions on the other hand.

## The geography and strategic location of Algeria

Algeria, officially the People's Democratic Republic of Algeria, is a sovereign state in North Africa. President Abdelaziz Bouteflika has been in power since 1999. Algeria's capital and the most populous city is Algiers, located in the country's far north. With an area of 2,381,741 square kilometres (919,595 sq. mi), Algeria is the tenth-largest country in the world, and the largest in Africa (CIA, 2017). Algeria is bordered to the northeast by Tunisia, to the east by Libya, to the west by Morocco, to the southwest by the Western Saharan territory, Mauritania, and Mali, to the southeast by Niger, and to the north by the Mediterranean Sea. The country is a semi-presidential republic consisting of 48 provinces and 1,541 communes (counties). Algeria lies mostly between latitudes 19° and 37°N (a small area is north of 37°), and longitudes 9°W and 12°E. Most of the coastal area is hilly, sometimes even mountainous, and there are a few natural harbours. The area from the coast to the Tell Atlas is fertile. South of the Tell Atlas is a steppe landscape ending with the Saharan Atlas; farther south, there is the Sahara Desert. Algeria, whose economy is reliant on petroleum, has been an OPEC member since 1969. Its crude oil production stands at around 1.1 million barrels/day, but it is also a major gas producer and exporter, with important links to Europe. Hydrocarbons have long been the backbone of the economy, accounting for roughly 60% of budget revenues, 30% of GDP, and over 95% of export earnings.

In January 2016 Algeria's population was an estimated 40.4 million, who are mainly Arab-Berber. Religiously Islam is the predominant religion in the country, with its adherents accounting for 99% of the population. There are about 150,000 Ibadis in the M'zab Valley in the region of Ghardaiand. At the outset of the 20th century, its population was approximately 4 million (Library of Congress Country Studies, 2017). About 90% of Algerians live in the northern, coastal area; the inhabitants of the Sahara Desert are mainly concentrated in oases, although some 1.5 million remain nomadic or partly nomadic. 28.1% of Algerians are under the age of 15.

Algeria's hydrocarbons constitute critical strategic importance to Europe. New exploration and production techniques are seeing proven oil reserves of 9.2 billion barrels being revised upwards, while oil exports, 90% of which go to Western Europe, are also set to increase. Algeria's gas resources are more crucial. Proven reserves of 160 trillion cubic feet (Tcf) are being revised upwards of 200 Tcf, making Algeria one of the world's top gas producers. Exports are by pipeline under the Mediterranean and by LNG (liquid natural gas). A significant contribution to this enhanced gas production will come from the recently discovered gas fields close to In Salah (a metaphorical stone's throw from Arak), where engineering work is expected to begin in 2004. Two of the main contractors are the US-based Halliburton subsidiary Kellogg, Brown, and Root (already engaged at the NASA base at Tamanrasset) and the Bechtel Corporation.

## Islam and radical ideology

Contemporary Islamic movements which have emerged in different parts of the Islamic world for a variety of reasons may appear, given their radical interpretation of Islam, akin to the old phenomenon, stretching all the way back to the Islamic revivalism of the teachings of jurists such as Ibn Hanbal (780–855), Ibn Taimiyya (1263–1328) and Muhammad Abd al Wahhab (1703–92) (Ghaly, 2005/2006: 26). Yet, the modern Islamic movements are not direct continuations of that revivalism: none of the earlier movements, which were suppressed at the time, were mass movements. When Caliph Al Ma'mun in the ninth century brutalised Ibn Hanbal and his followers, he was not faced with a major reaction. When in the 14th century Ibn Taimiyya was constantly sent to jail by the Mongols and Egyptians, and eventually died in captivity, no movement was formed around him. Likewise, when in the 18th century Muhammad Ali, the Viceroy of Egypt, sent an expedition to suppress and eliminate the Wahhabis in Arabia, there were no mass reactions in their favour. Even at the earlier stages of the rise of Islamic fundamentalist movements in the contemporary era, we do not witness any mass movements. When in Egypt Hasan Al-Banna was killed by King Farouk, and later Sayyed Qutb was killed by Nasser, or when in Iran the leaders of the Fedayeen of Islam were executed by the Shah, Mohammad Reza Pahlavi, there were no mass uprisings.

The European expansionism - or the expansion of capitalism and imperialism – reached the regions of Islam in the late 19th century and particularly in the mid-20th century. With the ensuing defeat and humiliation of the Muslim world by the West, Muslim religious leaders apart from the traditional establishment clerics who continued their opportunistic politics followed two other broad strategies. One was to reform and modernise, while the other was to rehabilitate Islam and return to the fundamentals (Meddeb, 2003: 22–40). The creation of nation-states and national identities in these societies was accompanied by both reform efforts and the gradual emergence of militant Islamic movements challenging the political status quo.

Of all the charges against Islam which westerners made in the 19th century, the one who hurts Muslim intellectuals most deeply was the accusation that Islam was incompatible with modernity. At the time, modernity was associated with liberal individualism. In economics, it was linked with the entrepreneurial skills and spirit of private achievement characteristic of the new ethos of industrial capitalism. Islamic reformism gained momentum both in Turkey and in the Arab world. And the direction of change which most intellectual reformers tended to advocate was towards greater similarity with Western norms. In Turkey, the movement finally found a revolutionary climax in the loss of the Ottoman Empire and in the subsequent triumph of Mustapha Kemal Ataturk. With the secular transformation launched by Ataturk, Turkey became less Muslim, and more liberal, in her determination to be more modern. Changes towards secularism in the rest of the Middle East were less spectacular, but Islam was never the same again after the Western impact (Berkes, 1964: 253–324).

It is believed that Islam, under certain conditions, has a propensity to produce both re-bellious leaders and submissive followers (Mazrui, 1969: 147). The militant tradition of re-volutionary leadership and the submissive following has recurrently broken out in Islamic history since then. In various parts of the Muslim world, this is a tradition which can lie dormant for generations. But it is susceptible to outbursts of new life under a particular type of stimulation. Europe's impact on the Islamic world in the nineteenth and twentieth centuries has often crystallised into this kind of motivation. Nor was this a simple case of nationalistic re-sistance. In a sense which does not apply to Buddhism, Hinduism or Confucianism, Islam has a deep-seated defensiveness concerning Christianity.

The phenomenon of Jihadism in Algeria dates to the 1980s. Between 2001 and 2012, 938 terrorist attacks took place within its borders. While the Algerian government has traditionally taken a hard-line approach against terrorism, this strategy appears to have had limited success in recent years, due to a lack of cooperation with neighbouring countries and changing nature of the threat. Algeria and Morocco have conflicting interests, and as such, there has been a long-aged rivalry between the two countries. According to Ammour, one of the main reasons for the fragmented regional response to AQIM and other Islamist groups is the inability of regional governments to define the enemy (Ammour, 2013). MUJAO has also carried out several attacks in Algeria.

In the extant literature, AQIM is increasingly being viewed as a criminal organisation rather than just being perceived through the Islamist terrorist lens (Jesus, 2011; Ammour, 2012). Lacher (2011) states that it is necessary to differentiate between AQIM in northern Algeria and AQIM in the Sahel. AQIM is currently divided into separate cells, with a northern cell based in Kabylia and the Algiers hinterland, and two southern cells operating in the Sahel. According to the UCDP, this division became more evident in 2011. The northern factions of the group have remained more focused on the struggle against the Algerian government and their aim of establishing an Islamic caliphate.

In contrast, the southern cells have increasingly turned to criminal activity (Uppsala Conflict Data Programme). According to the UCDP, Algeria's geographical features, and the region in which AQIM operates, might be the factors behind the split, as the Sahara desert separating the different cells makes it difficult for them to coordinate and cooperate. Ammour notes that the groups sometimes appear to be acting in competition with one another. The changing nature of AQIM has already had an impact on the regional dynamics of the conflict. Countries in the Sahel are keen to prevent increasing cooperation between AQIM and other terrorist organi-sations. Spencer (2012) argues that the northern branch of AQIM has become less important, as the importance of the southern branch has increased.

Some authors argue that the AQIM "phenomenon" is manipulated by the Algerian regime to serve its strategic aims both domestically and in the Sahel. For example, Ammour (2013) states that the Algerian authorities deny the fact that there is a connection between AQIM and domestic terrorist groups. She argues that they view AQIM as a new type of terrorist orga-nisation, which is driven by its extremist ideology, while other governments in the Sahel emphasise the criminal nature of AQIM. AQIM has funds because it collected tolls on trans-border drug smuggling and engages in kidnapping for ransom (Boukhars, 2013). AQIM in Algeria also receives funds from supporters living abroad, especially in Western Europe. A number of sources cite the possibility of links between AQIM and the Nigerian Islamist group Boko Haram. One expert argues that many terrorists are not terrorists because of their con-victions, but due to the money earned.

The growing internationalisation of conflicts in Islamic societies, particularly after 11 September the invasion of Afghanistan and Iraq and their continued disastrous and failed occupations, the continued Israeli occupation of the West Bank, Gaza and East Jerusalem and the unresolved Palestinian situation, have provided new breeding grounds for radical Islamists. The continued political repression imposed on Muslim-majority societies by authoritarian regimes has also pushed many of these radicals out of their home bases. One impact of the heightened confrontations between Islamic radicals and their opponents has been the increased suffering of the majority of people in Muslim-majority countries, and the further deterioration of the social, political and economic conditions of their lives. This situation provides an ideal opportunity for radical Islamists to recruit new followers and propagate their cause. The continued suppression of all other oppositional forces, particularly of secular progressive elements by authoritarian regimes, further enhances the fortunes of Islamic fundamentalist organisations, making them the only effective oppositional force in many Middle Eastern societies and the Northern part of Africa. It seems obvious that the mobilising power and populist appeal of radical Islamists' can be challenged effectively only if the social, economic, and political factors that give rise to these movements in the first place are eliminated.

## The global significance of Algeria

Algeria is the largest country in the Arab world, Africa and the Mediterranean basin. Its 1,200 km coastline gives it a strategic continental location in the hub of the Maghreb. Due to its geographic proximity and colonial legacy, Algeria is a privileged partner of France and, by extension, of the European Union. The country is also a key supplier of oil and gas to the West, with the third-largest conventional oil reserves (12.2 billion barrels) in Africa, and the 10th biggest gas reserves (4.5 trillion cubic metres) in the world. Throughout the past decade, Algeria was able to take advantage of high international oil and gas prices to provide a comfortable financial cushion. In 2013, Algeria's foreign exchange reserves stood at US$201 billion. The revenue from hydrocarbon exports has been used to sustain steady economic growth. In the past three years, the country's economy has grown at an average annual rate of 3%. Thanks to its newfound wealth, Algeria was also able to pay off nearly all of its external debt, which now stands at 2% of GDP.

Finally, Algeria has a strong and modern military. The People's National Army (PNA) has an active frontline force of 512,000 and an active reserve force of 400,000. According to a 2014 SIPRI report, Algeria became the first weapon buyer in Africa with military spending exceeding US$10 billion, which represents an increase of 176% since 2004. Algeria is also among the world's top 10 buyers, moving up in ranking from 24th in 2011 to 6th in 2013. Algeria is also developing its domestic military manufacturing industry by forming joint ventures with firms from several countries: In 2011, three commercial vehicle plants were commissioned by Aabar Investments Fund in the UAE, and Daimler, MTU Friedrichshafen and Deutsch AG in Germany; in the same year, an agreement was reached with Serbian Yugo import to build three production plants for small arms and ammunition for a total of US$400 million. In January 2015, Algeria revealed the first locally assembled Mercedes-Benz Ztros six-wheel-drive military truck (Ghanem-Yazbeck, 2015).

### National politics

After the Arab uprisings of 2011, the Algerian regime has shown a remarkable degree of stability and continuity. The regime adapted to the new local, regional, and international realities. The relative peace and more broadly the regime's longevity can be explained by the combination of elements from both authoritarianism and democracy. The Algerian regime is a hybrid one. To preserve itself while managing democratisation demands, the regime opened up the political arena, allowed for more freedom of association and speech, liberalised (selectively) the economy while continuing to co-opt large and diverse interest groups and personalities and to use coercion to avoid social unrest (Ghanem-Yazbeck, 2015).

Algeria took the first step towards liberal democracy in the Arab world in 1989. We can argue that the experience was short (1989–1991), messy and untidy. Yet, the one-party system ended, civil society bloomed, and competitive elections were held for the first time in the country. Since the advent of the multi-party system, 15 elections have been held regularly, among them five presidential elections. The political arena is mainly divided between nationalist groups, Berbers, democrats, independents, and Islamists who have been integrated into the political game since 1995 (Addi, 1998).

More recently, in 2016, electoral reforms were also adopted to enhance individual and collective freedom, improve voting and women's participation as well as strengthening election oversight with the creation of an independent electoral commission. However, these democratic elements are mixed with authoritarian ones such as the oppression of opposition figures, legal obstacles to party formation and financing as well as restrictions of access to both media and funds. Fraud and gerrymandering stratagems make the elections safe for the regime. Hence, the dominant party of power, the National Liberation Front (FLN), wins most votes and keeps a tight grip on parliament. Nonetheless, opposition parties remain significant in national politics, yet outsized margins are common, but they are more "realistic" to avoid people's disdain. Co-optation, clientelism, patronage is embedded political subterfuges used to maintain the regime and reinforce the status quo.

In essence, the country has been stuck in a state of permanent transition because of the military's predominance. Officially, Algeria is a Republic with a strong presidency, but, in practice, any presidential initiative must be approved by the military. Fifty-three years after independence, the military is still prevailing over the state (Ghanem-Yazbeck, 2015). President Abdulaziz Bouteflika swept into power in 1999 on a platform of peace-making and national reconciliation, beginning a lengthy process of re-engagement with international partners (International Crisis Group Africa Report, 2001). He was already building cooperation with the US and France based on mutual interests in the energy sector when the 11 September 2001 attacks in the US occurred. Claiming that Algeria had long been on the front line in a war on terror that had only just reached American soil, he succeeded in forging stronger security ties with Washington, ending his country's isolation and restoring its international legitimacy. In 2002, the US lifted its ten-year arms embargo against Algeria and began to include it in regional security forums, notably NATO's Mediterranean Dialogue (initiated in 1994) (Ghanem-Yazbeck, 2015). For some, it seemed that this focus on regaining standing in the West came at the expense of Algeria's historic role in Africa and its immediate neighbourhood, notably through the African Union (AU) and its predecessors, where its diplomats have played leading roles.

Bouteflika vowed during his first election campaign not to be "three-fourths of a president" (i.e., not to be a frontman for the military), signalling a willingness to challenge the army's tight grasp on power since the time of President Houari Boumediene (1965–1978) and a succession of weak presidents during the "black decade." Despite sporadic violence and frequent attacks on security forces, the remaining militant threat to the state and society has mostly dissipated on Bouteflika's watch. He was also successful in strengthening a weakened presidency, in part because, by improving the security environment and help produce national reconciliation, he diminished the need for the military and intelligence services in national life.

Nonetheless, despite the integration of opposition parties, including Islamists, in successive national unity governments since the late 1990s, politics remains largely authoritarian and dominated by the presidency and the security services (Crisis Group Middle East and North Africa, 2004: 30). The experience of the 1990s continues to cast a shadow over politics, with many

Algerians (as well as Western officials) convinced that security and stability are closely interwoven with – and perhaps dependent upon – Bouteflika's authoritarian style. The government lifted the nineteen-year state of emergency in March 2011 in response to domestic protests inspired by those in Tunisia and Egypt, even if they never gained momentum. But it also enacted new legislation conferring more massive penalties on protesting, which remains illegal.

Popular and elite anxiety that the Arab uprisings would revive the 1990s turmoil was a reason Algeria did not experience the same unrest as its neighbours; a huge increase in state spending to address socio-economic demands was another. As the situation deteriorated elsewhere, the government pointed to spreading chaos across the region, as well as Algeria's complicated history, as a warning against revolutionary upheaval and justification for the status quo. During the April 2014 presidential elections, in which Bouteflika won a controversial fourth term without campaigning (due to poor health after a crippling stroke in 2013, he turned the crises in Libya, Tunisia and Mali into a domestic political issue. Though he made no public appearances, he received heavily publicised weekly visits from the army chief of staff, Gaid Salah, in which they discussed security and stability. The not-so-subtle message was that given regional turmoil, Algeria could ill afford a leadership transition. Critics argued that the president's re-election strategy amounted to *"chantagesécuritaire"* ("security blackmail"), emphasising the prospect of instability and turmoil in the event the status quo was threatened and the military turned its attention from protecting against external threats to undoing the expansion of presidential powers under his rule.

The security forces, such as the police and the gendarmerie, receive significant material incentives to protect the regime from dissident groups. A crucial player remains the military apparatus that maintains the locus of power in Algeria. It is the most professionalised and organised institution in the country. Despite widespread criticism, most Algerians see it as the *"saviour"* that prevented the radical Islamic Salvation Front (FIS) from seizing power and was able to ensure the stability of the country. The military apparatus capitalises on the population's fear (which is well-founded) of instability and change - especially with the dangerous situation along the borders with neighbouring Tunisia, Libya and the Sahel - to justify, locally and internationally, its grip on power, as the country became a pivotal ally for the US and Europe in the fight against terror.

The military apparatus remains the source of decision-making in Algeria with a firm grip on Algerian society and politics (Shatz, 2003). Even if the older generation is disappearing, it had plenty of time to socialise with and educate recruits to its visions and way of actions. Except in 1989, the military apparatus never went back to their barracks and are unlikely to do so anytime soon. For the aforementioned reasons, the regime is not likely to crumble even if it faces a fragile situation with the succession problem. The succession of Bouteflika is a delicate issue and might introduce a moment of instability, yet the Algerian regime has resources to deal with it. The military "young" Generals, who do not want to antagonise the civil society as they did in the 1990s, seem likely to accept a slow but steady transition that would put a more representative and consensual government and president in place. The political-military elite may be currently trying to organise a consensus around a figure who will preferably be a civilian, a "présidentiable," someone with historical legitimacy and an acceptable level of public support. But again, one cannot be sure about Algeria's political-military apparatus' next step, nor about the durability of Algeria's civil society and political parties' consensus on the need for a peaceful transition.

## Cases of terrorism in Algeria, 2010–2017

Islamist guerrilla warfare broke out in January 1992, after the army cancelled elections won by the Islamic Salvation Front (FIS). Prevented from governing the state, the FIS was banned in

March 1992. A subsequent crackdown drove its moderate wing to re-join the radicals, who resorted to violence after the annulment of the elections. The Islamists targeted military vehicles, barracks, the police, and government buildings. Another Islamist organisation, the Armed Islamic Group (GIA), then appeared and went even further, killing intellectuals, journalists, women, and foreigners and massacring villagers in western Algeria. But the lack of information about the GIA murders bred widespread scepticism about the group's identity. Many observers suspect that the GIA is a product of the state's intelligence service, designed to discredit the Islamists. These suspicions have been heightened by the Algerian government's sharp refusal to allow any international inquiry into the massacres.

By 2010, Al-Qa'ida in the Islamic Maghreb (AQIM) continued to pose a significant terrorist threat in the mountainous areas east of Algiers (Office of the Coordinator for Counterterrorism, 2017). AQIM primarily targeted Algerian security forces, but civilians were also wounded or killed because of AQIM criminal activity. Algerian security forces isolated AQIM in the north, and the group launched fewer successful terrorist attacks but continued to execute suicide attacks, attacks using improvised explosive devices (IED), and ambushes in the areas east of Algiers. 2010 incidents included:

- On 11 June, a suicide truck bomb killed five police and wounded 30 others at a para-military police barracks in Timizar, 30 miles east of Algiers.
- On 14 July, four linked "daisy-chain" IEDs killed four soldiers and wounded 13 others on patrol near Tizi Ouzou, 80 miles east of Algiers. Linking bombs in this fashion was a new technique for AQIM, which has a history of adopting methods of attack used elsewhere by al-Qa'ida or affiliated groups, especially in Iraq.
- On 31 August and 1 September, three attacks took place within 24 hours. Terrorists stormed a mosque near Ain Defla, 60 miles southwest of Algiers, killing one and injuring eight. Near Boumerdes, a suicide bomber drove a pickup truck loaded with explosives into a military convoy 45 miles east of Algiers, killing two soldiers and wounding 30 others. A barrage of homemade rockets caused no injuries when they were fired at the judicial police headquarters 40 kilometres north of Tizi Ouzou.

In 2011, Al-Qa'ida in the Islamic Maghreb (AQIM) remained a significant security threat, primarily in the mountainous areas east of Algiers and in the vast desert regions of the south, near countries on Algeria's southern border: Mali, Mauritania, and Niger (United States Department of State, 2012). AQIM largely targeted Algerian security forces, but civilians were also wounded or killed collaterally. Algerian officials cited links between AQIM and other African terrorist groups, such as al-Shabaab and Boko Haram, and noted criminal links between AQIM and narco-traffickers in the Sahel. AQIM engaged in notable terrorist activities in non-urban areas, including the first major terrorist attack in Western Algeria since July 2009, the first kidnapping of a foreigner in southern Algeria since 2003. The group's repeated attempts to move weapons from Libya into northern Mali and south Algeria were partially stymied by joint Algerian and Nigerien border security operations. As in years past, Algeria experienced a spike in terrorist incidents during the summer and just before the start of Ramadan, which began on 1 August.

- On 2 February, AQIM kidnapped Italian tourist Maria Sandra Mariani near Alidena, marking the first abduction of a foreigner by a terrorist group in southern Algeria since 2003.
- On 15 April, approximately 40 AQIM militants attacked an army post east of Algiers and killed 17 soldiers.

- On 16 July, a pair of suicide bombings near Boumerdes signalled the start of the annual pre-Ramadan uptick in violence. The vehicle-borne IEDs were the first suicide bombings in Algeria since July 2010 and targeted a police station in a small town.
- On 26 August, a double suicide bombing against the Algerian Military Academy of Cherchell, west of Algiers, killed at least 18 people, mostly military officers, and injured as many as 35. The first attacker dressed in an army uniform and the second bomber targeted those who responded to the first explosion.
- On 23 October, an AQIM-affiliated group kidnapped one Italian and two Spanish aid workers from a Polisario-run refugee camp near Tindouf. AQIM was suspected of holding the hostages on Malian soil.

In 2012, The deteriorating security situation in neighbouring northern Mali, the proliferation of weapons smuggled out of Libya, and the emergence of the Mali-based Movement for Unity and Jihad in West Africa (MUJAO), which targeted Algeria on several occasions, all contributed to the terrorist threat to Algeria USAID, 2013. Within Algeria, AQIM remained the most active terrorist threat.

- On 3 March, a vehicle-borne IED was used to attack the military base in the southern city of Tamanrasset. Twenty-three people were injured in the attack. The Mali-based group MUJAO claimed responsibility for that attack.
- On 27 June, a vehicle-borne improvised explosive device (VBIED) was detonated at the gate of the Gendarmerie headquarters in the town of Ouargla, located approximately 50 miles northwest of Hassi Messaoud, situated within Algeria's oilfield area. The attack was significant due to its proximity to oil operations and because it took place in a military exclusion zone. The device detonated at the gate of the base, killing the occupant of the vehicle and one Gendarme.
- In October, the Algerian National Gendarmerie noted that 15 kidnappings had occurred in the northern Kabylie region throughout the year.

By 2013, the AQIM, the al-Mulathamun Battalion (AMB) had become a separate organisation in late 2012 and its sub-battalion, "Those Who Sign in Blood," led by Mokhtar Belmokhtar, claimed responsibility for the January 16, 2013 attack against a gas facility near In Amenas, Algeria (United States Department of State, 2014). In August 2013, the Mali-based Movement for Unity and Jihad in West Africa (MUJAO) and AMB announced that the two organisations merged and adopted the name al-Murabitoun. On 16 January, AMB attacked the Tiguentourine gas facility (a joint venture among Algerian, British, and Norwegian companies) near In Amenas, in southeastern Algeria. Over 800 people were taken hostage for four days, and the attackers killed 39 foreign hostages, including three US citizens. The group's leader, Algerian national Mokhtar Belmokhtar, remained a threat and was at-large in the region, at year's end. In October, Foreign Minister Lamamra said the four Algerian diplomats kidnapped in April 2012 from the Algerian consulate in northern Mali are alive and that the government is fully mobilised to ensure the diplomats' release. MUJAO claimed responsibility for the kidnapping.

In 2014, the terrorist group Jund al-Khilafa fi Ard al-Jazayer (JAK, Soldiers of the Caliphate in Algeria), emerged following a split from AQIM, and swore allegiance to the Islamic State in Iraq and the Levant (ISIL) (United States Department of State, 2015). On April 19, terrorists attacked an Algerian military convoy in Tizi Ouzou province, killing 11 soldiers, and wounding five. AQIM claimed responsibility for the ambush. The Algerian government observed that

AQIM's Ramadan offensive in 2014 was significantly reduced relative to the past decade. On September 21–24, JAK-A abducted and beheaded a French citizen, Hervé Gourdel, in the Kabylie region, east of Algiers.

By 2015, there were more than 62 terrorist acts in 2015 (Bureau of Counterterrorism and Countering Violent Extremism, 2015). Attacks included:

- On 20 June, an IED killed an Algerian colonel and two soldiers near BeniFedala in the Batna province.
- On 6 July, at least two policemen were injured in a shootout in downtown Bouira that started when a terrorist group attacked a patrol of the Mobile Brigade of the Judicial Police.
- On 17 July, AQIM ambushed Algerian soldiers while on patrol in the province of AinDefla. AQIM claimed on 18 July to have killed 14 soldiers in the attack. Still, a press statement from the Algerian Ministry of Defence on 19 July indicated nine soldiers were killed and two others wounded.

By November 2016, 36 terrorist attacks were reported (United States Department of State 2017).

- On 18 March, projectiles struck a gas plant operated by Statoil and BP in Krechba, in the southern Algerian desert. AQIM released a statement claiming the attack, which produced no casualties.
- On 15 April, four soldiers were killed during a combing operation in the Constantine province.
- On 29 October, a policeman was killed in the eastern city of Constantine. ISIS claimed responsibility for the attack via its propaganda arm, Amaq.

On 26 February 2017, a suicide bomber tried to enter the Bab el Kantara Police station in the city of Constantine but was stopped and shot dead by a policeman. His suicide vest detonated, wounding two policemen, but not critically (Roy, 2017). The Islamic State terror group claimed responsibility. By the end of the first quarter of 2017, 35 terrorists were killed and 18 arrested by Algeria's National People's Army (ANP).

## Algeria's counterterrorism and counterinsurgency (CT-COIN) strategies

This Section considers some CT-COIN strategies adopted by the Algerian authorities and International Community (USA, European Union, and France) to tackle terrorism. These are classified into soft and hard approaches or the "stick and carrot" tactics. The "hard" approach is defined as measures that are employed by the state that focuses on the function and role of the security apparatus (primarily the Algerian army and elite forces) and their use of force, which includes, among other things, tactical raids, arrests, infiltration and killings. The "soft" approach, on the other hand, is seen as the function, role and activities of the non-security state apparatus (such as the ministry of education, as well as non-state actors – such as civil society, and zawiyyas, which do not resort to force – in their efforts to address the existential and developmental questions that underpin terrorism in the country.

### The carrot: soft CT-COIN approach

Parallel to its military strategy, the regime developed its "soft" approach by encouraging "repentant" guerrillas to speak out publicly. Their testimonies were broadcast on television at peak hours, and instead of a source of dignity and pride, the former guerrillas described (or were forced to explain) the guerrilla campaign as "hell" explaining their battle as induced by money rather than establishing an Islamic state (Martinez, 2000: 158–159). The young, a potential reservoir for guerrilla fighters, became the centre of the regime's economic policy. The government offered them jobs in the public sector bonuses and assistance in building a house but also contracts with the Ministry of Defence (Martinez, 2000: 161). In 2008, the government began to recruit 100,000 new police and gendarme officers to reinforce borders, augment security at airports, and increase the security presence in major cities. Instead of risking death in the maquis, the regime thus offered young men the certainty of housing and income, a persuasive method that led many to join the army. By establishing this "social net" or network of clientelism, the regime helped ordinary Algerians to escape from material inducements to join an armed Islamist group.

The violence of 1997 and 1998, however, brought about the conditions for reconciliation, both within the army and among Islamist militants. The massacres of 1997–1998 caught the international media's attention and heavily undermined the authority and credibility of the military. In July 1999 Bouteflika introduced the Civil Harmony Law in the People's Assembly. The Civil Harmony Law granted conditional amnesty to radical Islamists who surrendered and renounced violence before 13 January 2000. Islamist insurgents were eligible for amnesty if they had not caused death, committed rape, or used explosives in public places. Insurgents who had committed such crimes would receive reduced prison sentences but not full amnesty. Many violent Islamists were granted amnesty without investigation into their activities.

In 2006, Bouteflika introduced the Charter for Peace and National Reconciliation (CPNR), which contained the same provisions as the Law of Civil Harmony, but explicitly exempted security agents, the military, pro-regime militias, and everyone else who had a role in the civil war, from prosecution. The Charter for Peace and National Reconciliation enjoyed broad support in general, but critics claim that it also created an atmosphere of impunity, not only for terrorist crimes but also by shielding the Algerian army and security services from any inquiry into their possible involvement in the violence. The Charter exempted all individuals, whether Islamists, civilian militiamen, or security forces, from prosecution for crimes committed during the war.

## The stick: hard CT-COIN approach

In response to the increasing violence and in line with its "eradicator" strategy, the government decided in 1993 to task the Directorate-General for National Security (Direction Générale de la Sureté Nationale, DGSN) with waging "total war" against the armed groups. At the same time, the Department of Intelligence and Security (Département du Renseignement et de la Sécurité, DRS), the military intelligence service, was formed, as well as a special interdepartmental force that was tasked with the suppression of terrorism, headed by General Mohamed Lamari. The ultimate goal of the DGSN was to eradicate the armed groups by both infiltrating them and crushing them militarily (Willis, 2012: 118). Between 1994 and 1997, the regime applied a security strategy that was based on the slogan "making fear change sides," thus launching a policy of mass repression.

## Recent "Hybrid" strategies

The Algerian government continued its decade-long push to increase the strength of its military and security forces and to professionalise and modernise them. Following restructuring in September 2013, a June 2014 presidential decree restored some judicial police authority to the

Department of intelligence and security (DRS), Algeria's intelligence service. It created a new Judicial Investigation Service under the jurisdiction of both the DRS and the general prosecutor of the court of appeal's criminal division. A public decree related to DRS affairs could be considered an attempt to bring more transparency to the institution's functioning. The Algerian government underscored that border security remained a top priority to guard against the infiltration of smugglers and terrorists from neighbouring countries. In September, President Bouteflika convened a meeting of the High Council on Security to increase border security, expand search operations to detect and disrupt terrorist activity, increase troops in southern Algeria, and strengthen coordination with neighbouring countries on border security. Measures included increased border security, among them closed military border areas, new observer posts in the east, reinforced protection of energy installations, additional permanent facilities for border control management, new aerial-based surveillance technologies, upgrades to communication systems, and additional 20,000 troops deployed on the borders with Tunisia, Libya, Mali, Mauritania, and Morocco (USDS, 2014). Algerian law enforcement and armed forces increased security cooperation with Tunisian counterparts to reduce the flow of arms. Border security measures included new joint checkpoints and patrols along the frontiers, information sharing, and training and equipment programs.

The government of Algeria closely monitored passenger manifests for inbound and outbound flights and scrutinised travel documents of visitors but did not fingerprint them. Algeria employed biometric screening systems to identify suspect travellers, undertook training, and was equipped to recognise fraudulent documents. The government of Algeria used Interpol channels, alerts, and fusion notices to stay informed on suspicious travellers at land, air, and maritime borders.

## Responses of international allies

This section examines the collaborative response of USA, France, and the European Union to terrorism in Algeria. Following the cancellation of the 1992 elections and the ensuing violent struggle between the Algerian army and Islamic militants, both the US and EU countries have been reluctant to sell arms to Algeria for fear of Islamist reprisals (as experienced in France) and criticism from human right groups. But the 9/11 attack on the World Trade Centre heralded a new era in US-Algerian military relations. In 2005, the United States and Algeria launched a Joint Military Dialogue to foster exchanges, training, and joint exercises. Algeria participates in the US Trans- Sahara Counter Terrorism Partnership (TSCTP). As part of TSCTP, US Special Forces trained, equipped, and aided national forces in fighting the AQIM in southern Algeria and the Sahel. On its part, the Algerian government have shared information regarding terrorists of Algerian origin with the United States. To support Algeria's efforts to combat terrorism, the US Treasury Office of Foreign Assets Control (OFAC) has listed leaders of AQIM, including Droukdel, as Specially Designated Global Terrorists. Algeria also participated in the NATO Mediterranean Dialogue and in NATO naval exercises (Arieff, 2011).

With France's support, Algeria signed an association agreement with the European Union (EU) in 2001 and has participated in the Europe-Mediterranean Partnership (MEDA) since 1995. In March 2009, Algeria enacted a law making it a crime to leave "the national territory in an illegal manner" to address EU concerns about illegal immigration as well as to stop human trafficking. At the same time, Algeria wants Europe to assist with development to strike at the causes of emigration. France's inclusion of Algerians on a list of persons subject to "meticulous inspection" for security purposes at French airports prompted Algiers to demand that Algerians be removed from the list and to cancel, or at least postpone, a January 2010 visit by French Foreign Minister Bernard Kouchner to Algeria. An Algerian official later described UfM as a

"Trojan horse for the normalisation with Israel" and said that Algeria is not interested in it "if its aim is to normalise relations with the Zionist regime. AQIM has kidnapped several French citizens in the Sahel, and the group declared war on President Sarkozy after the failed French attempt to free a hostage in July 2010 resulted in several AQIM casualties. President Sarkozy declared that France was at war with AQIM and has made fighting the group one of his highest priorities, dispatching military and intelligence forces and equipment to the Sahel. He vowed that France would no longer pay ransoms (Bremner, 2010).

## Algeria's assistance to other countries in Africa on war against terrorism

Algeria firmly believes that, as with the fight against terrorism, the fight against violent extremism and the country's efforts toward deradicalisation also require greater attention, and must be the subject of sustained bilateral, regional, and international cooperation. At the regional level, Algeria has promoted the Comité d'état-major opérationnel conjoint (CEMOC), a joint counterterrorism committee in cooperation with Mali, Mauritania and Niger headquartered in the southern Algerian town of Tamanrasset. Last May important steps were taken in cooperation with Tunisia and Libya, in which Algeria has committed to patrolling their common borders. In this context, Algeria has deployed more than 4,000 soldiers at the border with Tunisia, as well as exchanging intelligence information with the Tunis government as a result of the talks between their respective foreign ministries.

Algeria is also in the forefront of raising the awareness of the countries that host Muslim communities regarding the new forms of violent extremism represented by xenophobia and Islamophobia, and the impact of these phenomena on segments of the youth in these communities in terms of their receptiveness to recruiters for violent extremist and terrorist groups. Algeria also participated in various Sahel-Saharan forays to discuss development and security policies, the evolution of regional terrorism, and donor coordination; these included the Nouakchott Process on the Enhancement of Security Cooperation, the Operationalisation of the African Peace and Security Architecture (APSA), and the EU Strategy for Security and Development in the Sahel. Moreover, with a relative degree of success, Algeria has elicited the adherence of Sahel countries to a vision that focuses on the settlement of regional security problems without the involvement of foreign powers, except in sectorial cooperation. It played a leading role in the creation of some regional organisations such as the Common Operational Joint-Chiefs of Staff Committee (CEMOC), located in Tamanrasset, and the Unified Fusion and Liaison (UFL), the intelligence arm of the core countries.

In a leadership role, Algeria sits on the UN Counterterrorism Centre's Advisory Board and hosts the headquarters of AFRIPOL, a pan-African organisation that fosters police training and cooperation in response to security threats such as terrorism, drug trafficking, and cybercrime. Algeria actively participates in the 5 +5 Defence Initiative, which brings together five European and five North African countries to address security issues in the western Mediterranean (USDS, 2015). As a founding member of the GCTF and co-chair of its Sahel Region Capacity Building Working Group, Algeria continued to champion the implementation and development of the Algiers Memorandum on Good Practices on Preventing and Denying the Benefits of Kidnapping for Ransom by Terrorists.

## Policy blueprints: tackling terror menace in Algeria

In light of the foregoing analysis, the following recommendations are offered. First, Western governments should stop paying ransoms to terrorist organisations. There is a strong consensus in the literature and amongst experts that western governments should stop paying ransoms. Both the UK and the AU have supported a ban on the payment of ransoms, but it seems unlikely that France and Spain would agree to such a move. Indeed, (Jesus, 2011, 54) argues that there should also be a ban on the exchange of imprisoned terrorists for the release of hostages. Secondly, there is a need to increase regional cooperation and military capacity building. Increased regional cooperation is considered to be vital in combatting Islamist groups and criminal gangs operating in Algeria and in the wider region. According to (Ammour, 2012: 7) there is a need for the creation of intra-regional battalions to undertake operations in border areas. She adds that the Tuaregs should be involved in any such initiative due to their knowledge of the terrain and the population in target areas. With regard to combatting criminal activity in the region, cooperation should be extended to include Burkina Faso, Senegal, Morocco, Ghana, Guinea, Guinea-Bissau, and Nigeria, as they are all transit points for cocaine. Foreign governments should also provide law enforcement and military capacity building to regional governments.

Thirdly, there is a need to support the diversification of the Algerian economy and employment creation initiatives. According to Achy (2013), a coherent economic strategy is required if Algeria is to avoid the dangers of continued protests and the long-term threat posed by running out of hydrocarbons for export. He argues that complex administrative procedures need to be simplified and the system of universal food and fuel subsidies abolished, in order to target the poor rather than the entire Algerian population. Fourthly, there is a need to avoid short-term focus on counterterrorism. Achy (2013: 23) argues, again, that rather than focusing solely on counterterrorism strategies, the international community needs to help the Algerian leadership understand that "the only way to retain power is to share it." Algeria's international partners should also support efforts to bring about political and economic reform. In this regard, Ammour (2012: 7) emphasises the importance of reducing the role of the military in Algerian politics.

## Conclusion

There is no doubt that Algeria has encountered several terrorist attacks and threats since the 1990s. The Algerian government, her neighbours and the international community must brace up and face the challenges confronting international peace. Al-Qa'ida in the Islamic Maghreb (AQIM) remained a significant security threat, primarily in the mountainous areas east of Algiers and in the vast desert regions of the south, near countries on Algeria's southern border: Mali, Mauritania, and Niger. The Algerian government continued its decade-long push to increase the strength of its military and security forces and to professionalise and modernise them. The government embarked on deradicalisation programmes, economic reforms, and social welfare schemes to promote peace and stability. The government continues to train and equip the military to confront terrorism and minimise their activities. To protect itself, Algerian government-assisted neighbouring countries in West Africa and the Sahel to help eradicate terrorism. The Algerian counterterrorism operations and strategies have been successful in localising terror threats and controlling violence from militant groups.

## References

Abrams, E. (2013, May 22). Is Algeria the next crisis? *Council on Foreign Relations from Pressure Points and Middle East Program.* Available from https://www.cfr.org/blog-post/weekend-reading-iraqs-marshes-lebanons-elites-and-algerias-islamists Accessed 22.07.17.

Abrams, E. (2014, February 27). Algeria, young and old, *Council on Foreign Relations, Pressure Points and Middle East Program.* Available from https://www.cfr.org/blog-post/algeria-young-and-old Accessed 22.07.17.

Achy, L. (2013). The price of stability in Algeria. *Carnegie Endowment for International Peace*. Available from http://carnegieendowment.org/files/price_stability_algeria.pdf.

Addi, L. (1998, July 1). Algeria's army, Algeria's agony. *Le Monde Diplomatique, Council on Foreign Relations*. Available from https://www.foreignaffairs.com/articles/algeria/1998-07-01/algerias-army-algerias-agony Accessed 22.07.17.

Ammour, L. A. (2012). Regional security cooperation in the Maghreb and Sahel: Algeria's pivotal ambivalence (Africa security brief. No.18). *African Center for Strategic Studies*. Available from http://africacenter.org/wp-content/uploads/2012/02/ASB-18-web.pdf.

Ammour, L. A. (2013). Algeria's role in the Sahelian security crisis. *Stability: International Journal of Security and Development, 2*(2), 1–11.

Arieff, A. (2011). *Algeria: Current Issues*. Available from https://fas.org/sgp/crs/row/RS21532.pdf Accessed 05.11.18.

Boukhars, A. (2013). 'What's next for Mali and Algeria?' *Carnegie Endowment for International Peace*. Retrieved from:http://carnegieendowment.org/2013/01/23/what-s-next-for-mali-and-algeria/f4sl.

Berkes, N. (1964). *The development of secularism in Turkey*. Montreal: McGill University Press.

Bremner, C. (2010). *Sarkozy wages Desert War on Terror*. London. The Times. Available from https://www.everycrsreport.com/files/20101122_RS21532_62b994435c161b32c5c33abaf045914e21d7e0ff.pdf Accessed 15.01.19.

Bureau of Counterterrorism and Countering Violent Extremism, *Country Reports on Terrorism 2015Report*, https://2009-2017.state.gov/j/ct/rls/crt/2015/257517.htm.

CIA (Central Intelligence Agency). (2017, July 19). *World Factbook*. Available from https://www.cia.gov/library/publications/the-world-factbook/geos/ag.html Accessed 27.07.17.

Crisis Group Africa Report (2001, July 9). *N°31, The Civil Concord: A peace initiative wasted*.

Crisis Group Middle East and North Africa (2004, July 30). *Report no. 29, Islamism, violence and reform in Algeria: Turning the page*.

Dalia, G. (2015, November 4). Algeria, the sleeping giant of North Africa. *The Broker Online*. Available from http://www.thebrokeronline.eu/Articles/Algeria-the-Sleeping-Giant-of-North-Africa Accessed 27.07.17.

Dalia, G. (2017, May 2). The Algerian enigma. *Italian Institute for International Political Studies*. Available from http://carnegie-mec.org/2017/05/02/algerian-enigma-pub-69845 Accessed on 05.11.18.

Desert Shadows. (2004, February 10). *Africa Confidential, Vol. 45, No. 4*. Available from https://digital.library.unt.edu/ark:/67531/metacrs9133/m1/1/high_res_d/RS21532_2006Apr24.pdf? Accessed 5.11.18.

Ghaly, M. M. I. (2005/2006). Writings on disability in Islam: The 16th century Polemic on Ibn Fahd's 'al-Nukat al-Ziraf. *The Arab Studies Journal, 13/14*, (2/1), 9-38.

Ghanem-Yazbeck, D. (2015). Algeria, the sleeping giant of North Africa. *The Broker. Carnegie Middle East Centre*. Available from http://www.carnagie-mec.org/2015/11/04/Algeria-sleeping-giant-of-north-Africa-pub-61875 Accessed 05.11.18.

International Crisis Group. (2015, October 12). Algeria and its neighbours. *Middle East and North Africa Report N°164*. Available from https://www.crisisgroup.org/middle-east-north-africa/north-africa/algeria/algeria-and-its-neighbours Accessed 22.07.18.

Jesus, C. E. (2011). Terrorism financing: The particular case of Al-Qaida in the Islamic Maghreb (AQIM). *African Journal for the Prevention and Combatting of Terrorism, 2*(1), 39–59. Available from http://www.caert.org.dz/journal-2.pdf Accessed 05.11.18.

Lacher, W. (2011). Organised crime and terrorism in the Sahel: Drivers, actors, options. *Stiftung Wissenschaft und Politik*. Available from http://www.swpberlin.org/fileadmin/contents/products/comments/2011C01_lac_ks.pdf Accessed 05.11.18.

Library of Congress Country Studies. (2017). Available from http://countrystudies.us/algeria/48.htm Accessed 20.07.17.

Martinez, L. (2000). *The Algerian Civil War*. Paris: C. Hurst & Co. Publishers.

Mazrui, A. A. (1969). *Political values and the educated class in Africa*. California: University of California Press.

Meddeb, A. (2003). *The malady of Islam* (English Trans.). New York: Basic Books.

Office of the Coordinator for Counterterrorism; Country Reports on Terror August 18, 2011 https://2009-2017.state.gov/j/ct/rls/crt/2010/170257.htm accessed on 10 October, 2020.

Roberts, H. (2003). *The battlefield: Algeria, 1988–2002, studies in a broken polity*. London.

Roy A. (2017, February 27). *International Business Times*. Available from http://www.ibtimes.co.uk/several-police-officers-injured-suicide-bomb-attack-algerias-constantine-1608704 Accessed 30.07.18.

Shatz, A. (2003, July 3). Algeria's failed revolution. *New York Review of Books*. Available from http://www.nybooks.com/articles/archives/2003/jul/03/algerias-failed-revolution/ Accessed 07.11.18.

Spencer, C. (2012). *Strategic posture review – Algeria (world politics review)*. Chatham House. Available from http://www.chathamhouse.org/sites/default/files/public/Research/Middle%20East/0712wpr_s pencer.pdf Accessed 15.01.19.

United States Department of State, *Country Reports on Terrorism 2011 – Algeria*, 31 July 2012, available at: https://www.refworld.org/docid/501fbcc5c. html [accessed 10 October 2020].

United States Department of State, *Country Reports on Terrorism 2013 – Algeria*, 30 April 2014, available at: https://www.refworld.org/docid/53622a088. html [accessed 10 October 2020].

United States Department of State, *Country Reports on Terrorism 2014 – Algeria*, 19 June 2015, available at: https://www.refworld.org/docid/5587c75c28. html [accessed 10 October 2020].

United States Department of State, *Country Reports on Terrorism 2016 – Algeria*, 19 July 2017, available at: https://www.refworld.org/docid/5981e4571e. html [accessed 10 October 2020].

USDS (United States Department of State). (2011). *Office of the Coordinator for Counter-terrorism;Country reports on terrorism 2010*. Available from https://www.state.gov/documents/organisation/170479.pdf Accessed 29.07.18.

USDS (United States Department of State). (2012). *Bureau of Counterterrorism; Country reports on terrorism 2011*. Available from https://www.state.gov/documents/organisation/195768.pdf Accessed 08.11.18.

USDS (United States Department of State). (2013). *Bureau of Counterterrorism; Country reports on terrorism 2012*. Available from https://www.state.gov/documents/organisation/210204.pdf Accessed on 05.11.18.

USDS (United States Department of State). (2014). *Bureau of Counterterrorism; Country reports on terrorism 2013*. Available from https://www.state.gov/documents/organisation/225886.pdf Accessed 05.11.18.

USDS (United States Department of State). (2015). *Bureau of Counterterrorism; Country reports on terrorism 2014*. Available from https://www.state.gov/documents/organisation/239631.pdf Accessed 02.11.18.

USDS (United States Department of State). (2016). *Bureau of Counterterrorism and Countering Violent Extremism; Country reports on terrorism 2015*. Available fromhttps://www.state.gov/documents/organisation/258249.pdf Accessed on 06.11.18.

USDS (United States Department of State). (2017). *Bureau of Counterterrorism; Country reports on terrorism 2016*. Available from https://www.state.gov/documents/organisation/272488.pdf Accessed 05.11.18.

Uppsala Conflict Data Programme. Available from http://www.ucdp.uu.se/gpdatabase/gpcountry.php?id=3&regionSelect=1-Northern_Africa# Accessed 05.11.2018.

Willis, M. J. (2012). *Politics and power in the Maghreb: Algeria, Tunisia and Morocco from independence to the Arab Spring*. New York: Columbia University Press.

# 33

# Sierra Leone

## Warlordism, complex emergency and counterinsurgency

*Sharkdam Wapmuk*

## Introduction

Sierra Leone represents one of Africa's most tragic failed states that struggled through more than a decade of turmoil and gruesome atrocities perpetrated by warlords (Wahlert, 2009). In Sierra Leone, insurgent movements, particularly the Revolutionary United Front (RUF), waged a campaign of terror against the government and citizens of their own country. The case of Sierra Leone no doubt presents a complex characterisation in Africa's counterterrorism and counterinsurgency (CT-COIN). This is particularly so because while some would classify Sierra Leone's RUF as primarily a rebel movement or an insurgency group (Fortna, 2015:523), the US State Department has named the RUF as a terrorist group, pointing to the violence that characterised their campaign of terror against the weak government in a failed state during the 1990s. Howard (2010:964) has argued that "Regardless of one's position on the appropriate classification of the RUF, the RUF's relationship with Al Qaeda through the diamond smuggling operation, and its harbouring of members of this terrorist organisation within Sierra Leone is well known." Keen and Attree (2015:3) also noted that the RUF in Sierra Leone is among the most prominent and reviled rebel, insurgent group (or "terrorist") "spoilers" in recent years. The interest of the US, on not only Sierra Leone, but Africa as a whole, is not surprising. In the aftermath of the terrorist attacks of 9/11, the West became increasingly concerned with "failed states" in Africa. This concern has important implications for international responses to armed insurgency groups on the African continent (Keen, 2008).

The end of the Cold War did not exactly bring about the much-expected peace to the global environment. Instead, it had other indirect and unforeseen effects on African insurgency groups that were exposed to an illicit international market for small arms. The RUF in Sierra Leone, the various factional rebel groups in the Liberian civil war, and the many insurgency groups, that came to control diamond fields and other mineral-rich areas, used that economic leverage to access the international market for small arms. The availability of blood diamonds which were sold to buy weapons made it lucrative for the RUF to invade Sierra Leone, backed by the governments of Libya, Burkina Faso and Charles Taylor's National Patriotic Front of Liberia (NPFL) in 1991 (Berman & Labonte, 2006). The RUF did not espouse any ideology. At inception, it claimed to be waging war on the corrupt government of Sierra Leone, and demanding free and fair elections, along with social and economic justice for the citizens, but it later waged war on civilians as well. The RUF terrorised civilians by the gruesome killings, looting, raping, and torturing them to create fear. The most dehumanising of its atrocities were cutting-off hands and feet of men, women, and children. The rebels abducted thousands of young boys and girls to join the rebel group, forcing these child soldiers to kill, maim and destroy. Though most girls and women were forced to become sex slaves and rebels' wives, some were actively deployed in combat (Richards, 2005). The war created complex emergencies in the forms of humanitarian problems due to the collapse of the state, and the proliferation of internally displaced persons and refugees in West Africa. The complexity of the situation proofed to be difficult to end even with regional and international bodies such as the UN and ECOWAS as well as the UK playing major roles in seeking peace in Sierra Leone. These included the ECOWAS Monitoring Group (ECOMOG) with about 13,000 soldiers - staffed with principally Nigerian soldiers and two UN operations - United Nations Mission in Sierra Leone (UNAMSIL) and United Nations Observer Mission in Sierra Leone (UNOMSIL) - with an authorised strength of more than 20,000 men. Following the end of the war, several reforms were undertaken, including strengthening national laws and putting in place counterterrorism and counterinsurgency (CT-COIN) measures in conformity with international standards.

This chapter examines the issue of terrorism and insurgency and efforts at counterterrorism and counterinsurgency (CT-COIN) in the context of Sierra Leone. It examines the historical background of the civil war in Sierra Leone and the emergence and development of the RUF into a Violent Non-State Actor (VNSA) and the use of terror in Sierra Leone, and the diamond-terror linkage in the context of Sierra Leone. Finally, it examined the CT-COIN efforts and legislation in post-conflict Sierra Leone.

## Conceptual discourse: key terminologies

It is imperative to clarify certain terms and concepts as used in the context of the chapter. The necessity of such clarification stems from the fact that concepts such as terrorism, insurgency and warlords are often not only contested but also evoke lots of emotions.

### Terrorism

There is no universal consensus regarding the term "terrorism". There are as many definitions as there are scholars working on the evolving phenomenon of terrorism. With the lack of consensus on a definition, the tendency is thus to describe acts of terrorism. For the purpose of this paper, we shall adopt the definition provided by Imobighe (2009:361) that terrorism is the "indiscriminate use of different levels of violence to strike fear on an opponent in an adversarial relationship in order to tailor the action of the latter towards a desired goal." African leaders under the auspices of the Organisation of African Unity (OAU), now African Union (AU), have also attempted to define terrorism from the African context (Ford, 2011). The OAU, now AU, at its Algiers meeting in 1999, defined terrorism as

a. any act which is a violation of the criminal laws of a state party and which may endanger the life, physical integrity or freedom of, or cause serious injury or death to, any person, any member or group of persons or causes or may cause damage to public or private property, natural resources, environmental or cultural heritage and is calculated or intended to:

    i.   Intimidate, put fear, force, coerce or induce any government, body, institution, the general public or any segment thereof, to do or abstain from doing any act, or to adopt or abandon a particular standpoint or act according to certain principles; or

    ii.   Disrupt any public service, the delivery of any essential service to the public or create a public emergency; or

    iii.   Any promotion, sponsoring, contribution to, command, aid, incitement, encouragement, attempts, threats, conspiracy, organising or procurement of any person, with the intent to commit any act referred to in paragraph (a) (i)-(iii) (OAU, 1999: 207).

The 1999 Algiers Convention significantly expanded the 1992 OAU heads of state and government Declaration against Extremism and the Code of Conduct for Inter-African Relations adopted at the 30th Ordinary Assembly in Tunis in 1994, which rejected fanaticism and all forms of extremism (Ford, 2011). Though some have argued that terrorism is essentially the weapon of the weak against the strong, it is evident that both the powerful and the weak, as well as both government and non-state actors within the society have applied terrorism at some point in time. It has been noted that different groups such as freedom fighters, nationalist and ethnic groups, insurgents, rebels and even national armed forces and other state security forces have applied some terrorist tactics at one time or the other. It is on account of these contradictions that some observers have argued that 'one man's terrorist is another man's freedom fighter' (Ganor, 2002).

## Insurgency

The term insurgency is synonymous with a number of other words such as small wars, guerrilla wars, partisan wars, and wars of national liberation. In more clear terms, insurgency refers to the strategic use of violence by armed factions against a state for the purpose of overthrowing the existing political order. It also refers to a rebellion against a recognised and accepted authority. Insurgent warfare is marked by the absence of fixed lines, using secrecy and ambush, and by the competition for the support of the population between the insurgents and their opponents. Insurgency has been the most prevalent type of armed conflict since the creation of organised political communities. In the contemporary era, since World War II, terrorism and guerrilla warfare have been predominant types of political violence. Consequently, to understand terrorism, especially within the context of our study on Sierra Leone, we must also understand insurgency.

## Counterterrorism and counterinsurgency (CT-COIN)

To counter terrorism is to act against or in opposition to terrorism. Hence counterterrorism has also been referred to as anti-terrorism or prevention of terrorism. Keen and Attree (2015) are of the view that counterterrorism consists of military efforts to defeat particular actors who have been designated as 'terrorists' and their sponsors. The term broadly captures broad efforts at national, regional, and global levels to combat or prevent terrorism. Counterterrorism may also include measures to apply law enforcement approaches to disrupt, prevent or punish terrorists. Counterterrorism strategies include attempts to counter the financing of terrorism (Madzima, 2009). Traditional responses to, and policies no, terrorism seek to neutralise terrorist groups through deterrence and dissuading attacks by threats of dire penalties. In such a scenario, the military, police, and intelligence apparatus play an enhanced role, resulting in a militarised counterterrorism policy (Solomon, 2015). Another aspect of counterterrorism is the focus on eliminating the leadership of terrorist groups.

The non-traditional approach focuses on eliminating the root of the problem. It can further involve efforts to stop people joining or identifying with terrorists. This can be done through the promotion of human security and tackling the root causes of terrorism. The idea is that without leadership, these groups will be weakened (Solomon, 2015). However, traditional counterterrorism approach remains the dominant paradigm and overarching strategy of the US with its focus on building regional intelligence capacity and military capacity.

On the other hand, to "counterinsurgency" is to fight, act against or in opposition to insurgency. The term has been defined by the US Department of State (2006) as "those military, paramilitary, political, economic, psychological and civic actions taken by a government to defeat an insurgency" (US Government Counterinsurgency Guide, 2009). There are two schools of thought for counterinsurgency. The first is the direct approach, which assumes that fighting an insurgency operates by the same general logic as fighting a war. Natural methods focus on punishing insurgents by drawing them into open combat and destroying them. The second is the indirect approach, also referred to as "hearts and minds approach" — this approach to prevent insurgency favours winning the support of the population through political concessions and aid. The term "hearts and minds" was coined by Field Marshal Gerald Templar, an officer who served as commander in the Malaya Emergency between 1952 and 1954 (Cloake, 1985:25). He points out that this approach consists of three "oughts". That government ought to secure their population from insurgent coercion; they ought to provide competent, legal and responsive administration that is free from abuse and broader in the domain, scope, and vigour; and, that government ought to meet rising expectations with higher living standards.

## Warlordism

The word warlord would suggest to the reader that it refers to "lord of the war" (McCormick, & Fritz, 2009: 81). However, some have argued that warlords do not only operate in situations of war. Even so, warlords can be described as local strongmen that run in their fiefdom-like locales, autonomous from the state. In most cases, they require a political vacuum and do operate under the use or threatened use violence to secure their military and political position (Freeman, 2015). For this study on Sierra Leone, the term 'warlord' is employed to describe actors operating within conditions of war in Sierra Leone, especially during the war period.

## Complex emergency

Complex emergency has been defined as a situation that disrupts livelihoods and threats to life produced by warfare, civil disturbance and large-scale movements of people, in which any emergency response has to be conducted in a challenging political and security environment. Complex emergencies combine internal conflict with large-scale displacements of people, mass famine or food shortage, and fragile or failing economic, political, and social institutions (Keen, 2008). Often, complex emergencies are also exacerbated by natural disasters. Since the end of the Cold War, the nature of emergencies has changed dramatically. Internal conflicts are increasing, and these are worsened by uneven social and economic development, religious identities, lack of democratic space, and ethnic versus national identity.

## Historical overview of a complex conflict in Sierra Leone

To understand the relationship between the warlords, the RUF and terror unleashed by this Violent Non-State Actor (VNSA) on Sierra Leone, it is necessary to re-examine the historical context of the war. Sierra Leone with a population of 7,075,641 (2015 National Census) and 71,740 km$^2$ in territorial size began its encounter of "outsiders" with the Mane invasions in the mid-16th century. The name Sierra Leone derived from "Serra Lyoa" (meaning Lion Mountains) was first used by Pedro da Cintra, a Portuguese explorer in 1462. The history of this territory was to change in 1787 when 400 freed North American slaves settled in the city of Freetown and became collectively known as Krios. Freetown later became a British Colony in 1808, and throughout the 19$^{th}$ century, it was the administrative headquarters for British West Africa. It was used as a significant source of slave labour from the Trans-Atlantic trade until the British Parliament abolished slavery in 1833 (Vehnämäki, 2002). By 1896, the British also took over the interior region, occupied by ethnic tribes as its protectorate. Apart from the resettlement of the returnee slaves, another major development which altered the future of the territory was the discovery of diamonds on the bank of the Gbobora River in 1930 by a British geologist named JD Pollet (Robbin-Coker, 2005). With the considerable mineral deposit in Sierra Leone, the British colonial regime was able to build railways that connected coastal ports with the interiors.

The returnee slaves, no doubt, altered the population, ethnic composition, and the socio-economic and political relations of the entire society. The ethnic cracks were sown with the introduction of a dual system of government by the British Government. In which case, a separate one was created for the Crown Colony of Free-town area where free slaves were settled, and another for the native hinterland of the tribal population where the British extended rule. For the backcountry, indirect rule was adopted where the government was through the tribal chiefs under the supervision of British district officials or District Commissioners. The occupations of native lands, dominations by the British, were fiercely resisted by the local people, particularly following the introduction of Hut Tax, which resulted in the War of 1898 (Robbin-Coker, 2005). Another major issue between the 1920s and 1930s was the competition over land that pitted farmers now producing cash crops such as coffee and cocoa against British miners who started the exploiting mineral resources such as diamonds. These issues further complicated the social and economic make-up of pre-independent Sierra Leone.

Given these internal dynamics, the people of Sierra Leone were not exactly united when independence was granted in 1961. Even so, independence came with grand expectations of socio-economic transformations and development that will trickle down to the people. It was not too long before the people realised that the post-independence state managers were much more interested in preserving their power base rather than pursuing national development. Milton Marga of Sierra Leone People's Party (SLPP) became Sierra Leone's first Prime Minister after independence in 1961. In 1967, however, the All People's Congress (APC), a party which was formed out of the SLPP in 1957, won the elections and its leader, Siaka Stevens, created a new government and later became the country's first President. Sierra Leone was transformed into a single-party state during his rule, and his regime was also accused of pervasive corruption. Post-colonial Sierra Leone experienced democratic governance interrupted by a series of military juntas that seized power through coups. In the years that followed, domestic politics became increasingly characterised by corruption, mismanagement, and intermitted violence that led to weak civil society, lack of popular participation in governance, and poor performance of essential state institutions including, the education sector (Abdullah, 2004). By 1991, an entire generation of dissatisfied youth became easy targets for recruitment to join RUF in a rebellion that it claimed was to liberate the state from corruption and misrule and to promote social justice.

## Warlords, RUF insurgency and the use of terror in Sierra Leone

When members of the RUF invaded Kailahun District in the Eastern Province of Sierra Leone along the border with neighbouring Liberia on 23 March 1991, the government of Sierra Leone was caught unprepared with a ceremonial army of about 3,000 soldiers, mostly untrained, and exceptionally poorly equipped (Woods & Reese, 2008). The position of the government was that Charles McArthur Ghankay Taylor was behind the attack and the invasion as a spillover from the Liberian civil war. Taylor, by this time, was internationally recognised as a prominent Liberian warlord. He later became the 22nd President of Liberia, serving from 2 August 1997 until his resignation on 11 August 2003. The RUF, a group of rebel fighters, led by a warlord, Foday Sankoh, a Temne and former corporal in the Sierra Leonean army who had received training in Libya's secret-service camp, later stormed into Freetown. The RUF had received external support from the governments of Libya and Burkina Faso and Charles Taylor's National Patriotic Front of Liberia (NPFL) (Berman & Labonte, 2006). Its activities were sustained through the capture, control, exploitation, and sale of mineral wealth, particularly the diamonds, mined in the Eastern Kono district.

President Momoh could not stop or even slow the rebel force as the Sierra Leone Army (SLA) had insufficient supplies, ammunition, and food. The relationship between the Liberian warlords and the RUF in Sierra Leone was key to giving the rebels unlimited access to weapons to wage their vicious war (Hironaka, 2005). Many scholars (Richards, 2005; Keen, 2005; Vehnämäki, 2002; & Robbin-Coker, 2005) have argued that in the case of Sierra Leone, the availability of 'blood diamonds' made the extension of the Liberian war to Sierra Leone by proxy not only feasible but irresistible. This inevitably sustained and prolonged the civil war. Taylor's major grievance against Momoh's government which made him vow to seek revenge was Momoh's interference in the first Liberian civil war (1989–1996). He also accused Momoh of allowing the ECOMOG led by Nigeria to establish a base in Sierra Leone to attack the NPFL's positions. As noted by Weinberg and Eubank (2007) terrorism, which creates fear in the victims, is the only type of violence by which the insurgents seek to achieve their objectives. The RUF's war was characterised by banditry and horrific brutality towards civilians. Rebels terrorised civilians in their homes and out in the fields, killing, looting raping and torturing civilians. Their mark was cutting off the hands and feet of men, women, and children.

The adoption of a new constitution providing for a multiparty system in September 1991 did not appease the rebels and army officers led by Captain Valentine Strasser, ousted President Joseph Momoh in 1992. The military coup was a result of frustration due to government's failure to deal with the rebels. Under international pressure, Strasser announced plans for the first multi-party elections since 1967. Strasser himself was ousted in a military coup led by his defence minister, Brigadier Julius Maada Bio in January 1996. It was in February of the same year that Ahmad Tejan Kabbah was elected president. With the help of Executive Outcomes (EO), the government was able to push back the rebel forces temporarily and later signed peace accord (Abidjan Accord) with Sankoh's rebels in November. The deal was short-lived as the army deposed president Kabbah in May 1997. The coup led by Johnny Paul Koroma, who was in prison and awaiting the outcome of a treason trial, had the support of the Armed Forces Revolutionary Council (AFRC). President Kabbah had to flee to Guinea to seek international aid.

Johnny Paul Koroma and his junta aligned with the RUF and established an Armed Forces Revolutionary Council ((AFRC), chaired by himself and with Sankoh as Vice-Chair. It was at this point that the Nigerian led ECOWAS Monitoring Group (ECOMOG) intervened in June 1997 and again in February 1998 to oust out the rebels and reinstate Kabbah as President. Even so, the RUF and AFRC fighters retreated into the bush, resorting to guerrilla tactics. The RUF continued to receive support from Liberia and Burkina Faso. The alliance between the RUF and AFRC fighters was short-lived as mistrust, and disregard for the command chain weakened the partnership. There is no doubt that the fractionalisation of the fighting forces exacerbated the level of violence in the country. It increased the personalisation of power in the RUF and AFRC. Civilians became easy targets of proxy war of anti-government resentment. Amputations, public and gang rape, and summary executions all increased (Marks, 2013). The reports of violence in 1998 followed the path of the RUF–AFRC's retreat out of the capital into the North and East of the country. The disastrous 6 January siege of Freetown the following year saw a return and increase in the violence. In just two weeks, the RUF–AFRC forces committed over 1,000 reported human rights violations (Kabbah, 2012). The RUF–AFRC forces also embarked on the cruel practice of deliberate mutilation, whereby parts of the body among other things, arms, lips, noses, hands, breasts, and legs were amputated, and eyes gouged out. According to Human Rights Watch, this was deliberately done to Sierra Leoneans "so that they could not vote" (Human Rights Watch,1998). When the rebel and former army forces were again pushed back into the provinces, they remained in territorial control of almost 80% of the country (Kabbah, 2012).

From July 1998, the Security Council set up the UN Observer Mission in Sierra Leone (UNOMSIL) and United Nations Mission in Sierra Leone (UNAMSIL) to monitor the peace and disarmament process (Olonisakin, 2008). This intervention on the part of the international community could not prevent the rebels from continues attacks. Negotiations had to be opened, culminating in the Lomé Agreement, which provided for power-sharing agreement between the government and RUF in a government of national unity under Kabbah as president and Sankoh as Vice-President and Head of the Commission for the Management of Strategic Mineral Resources, National Reconstruction and Development (CMRRD). The reality of Sankoh's and RUF greed became clearer when, under his leadership as Chairman of the CMRRD, he did nothing to stop the flow of diamonds to Liberia. The security situation worsened as Sankoh used his position to engage in illicit trade in diamonds. The RUF also attacked UNAMSIL repeatedly and kidnapped about 500 peacekeepers in May 2000 (Olonisakin, 2008). It took the combined efforts of ECOWAS, UNAMSIL, the Sierra Leone Army, and a British intervention to successful defeat of the RUF. This paved the way for the conclusion of the Abuja Cease-Fire Agreement and the restoration of democracy in the country (Kabbah, 2012). Sankoh was subsequently arrested, and a Special Court for Sierra Leone was established to try him and fellow combatants. Unfortunately, the warlord, Sankoh died before he could be tried by UN-backed war crimes court.

## Complex emergencies of the war in Sierra Leone

The war in Sierra Leone created complex emergency situations that proved difficult to manage in terms of humanitarian response (Keen, 2008). The war caused the deaths of over 70, 000 people, displaced over two million Sierra Leoneans and forced about 500,000 refugees into neighbouring countries in the West African sub-region. The United Nations Office for the Coordination of Humanitarian Affairs (UNOCHA) reported that between 1991 and 1998, refugees in neighbouring countries consisted of 374,000 to Guinea; 177,000 to Liberia; 5,700 to the Gambia; 2,000 to Cote d'Ivoire; and 1,000 elsewhere in the region. Following the renewed fighting in February 1998, approximately 55,000 Sierra Leoneans fled to Liberia and 182,000 to Guinea, and the number continued to rise until the crisis ended. It was reported that refugees arrived in bad physical shape after spending weeks hiding in the bush before reaching neighbouring countries, and many died of exposure, starvation, torture, and war-related injuries. There were three categories of people who desperately needed humanitarian assistance. These were the refugees, internally displaced people and those trapped in rebel-held territories. There were over two and a half million internally displaced persons living in Freetown and safe havens in the Northern, Eastern and Southern parts of the country. The worst affected were the people living in rebel-held areas. These people lacked food, medicines, clothing, and other basic human necessities. With difficulty accessing these basic needs, many were malnourished, sick, and traumatised.

## The diamond-terror linkage in the context of Sierra Leone

Dempsey (2006) argues that transnational terrorist groups often take advantage of the chaos in failed states and use such states to shield themselves from effective counterterrorism efforts by the international community. Failed states are understood to mean countries in which government authority and critical institutions have collapsed; violence has become endemic and characterised by the complete failure of functional governance. Sierra Leone in the 1990s provided a classic example of the conditions described by scholars as that of state failure (Rotberg, 2003:80). Both Howard (2010:964) and Dempsey (2006) have argued that the connection of the Al Qaeda to Sierra Leone occurred during the interregnum that followed the collapse of the state and easy availability of diamonds in Sierra Leone and the black markets. The diamonds were smuggled through Liberia to earn money to buy weapons, particularly the Kalashnikov (AK47) a weapon of choice by the RUF. The Al Qaeda connection to the Sierra Leone diamond trade was captured by the Washington Post in its articles (Rabasa et al., 2006; Farah 2001:A01). The Washington Post wrote that Al Qaeda operatives participated in the illicit diamond trade in Sierra Leone. Yoroms (2008) argued that the illicit trade-in diamonds generated direct profits to support the Al Qaeda's activities, access to weapons, and provided avenues for money laundering to avoid detection and freezing of its assets by Western counterterrorism experts.

During the trials of the terrorists responsible for the bombings of US embassies in Kenya and Tanzania in 1998; and during US congressional hearings on the connection between illicit diamond trade and terrorism; and hearings of the Special Court for Sierra Leone, in October 2004, it was also revealed that the Al Qaeda was using proceeds from the illicit diamond trade with the Revolutionary United Front (RUF) to finance its terrorist operations (Cook, 2003:7). According to Crane (2004:2), Chief Prosecutor for the Special Court for Sierra Leone, rebels and terrorist organisations, including Al Qaeda, were "taking blood diamonds from the mines of eastern Sierra Leone and trading them for cash to buy weapons to sustain the conflicts throughout the region or international terrorism." The United Nations (UN) report of arms smuggling networks in Sierra Leone documented that terrorists may be able to exploit failed state-based finances to tap into the global arms market (United Nations Panel of Experts, December 20, 2000).

It became clear to the UN that the only option was to stop the trade in illicit diamonds. In June 2000, the UN passed a resolution demanding that all states take measures to prohibit the direct or indirect import of rough diamonds from Sierra Leone. The government of Sierra Leone was also mandated to implement a certificate-of-origin system for diamond exports so that diamonds from RUF areas could be distinguished from other diamonds (Dempsey, 2006). However, this was far from a solution as some diamonds from the RUF were still getting certificates within Sierra Leone; and smuggling into Liberia remained lucrative. The sanctions were less than productive due to the failure of some developed countries to apply such sanctions so as to protect their own interest in accessing natural resources in nearby Liberia that was deeply involved with the RUF.

## Rethinking CT-COIN in failed states

The case of the RUF in Sierra Leone does not fit the typical characterisation of terrorist groups that engage in deliberate acts such as the bombing of selected places, hostage-taking, hijacking of planes, assassinations, and many others. Terrorism of this nature has been associated with groups such as the Al Qaeda, Hezbollah, Boko Haram, and many others. Even though the RUF was associated with some terrorist groups such as the Al Qaeda and Hezbollah in the diamonds trade for weapons, it waged war against a failed state and its citizens employing the weapon of terrorism to create fear in its march. This, therefore, calls for a profound rethink of the direct military action or traditional approach to CT-COIN as often emphasised by the West, particularly the USA. The conventional approach or direct military action, which target identified terrorists for elimination, has seen the West engaging in "revenge missions". Examples in this regard include:

> the bombing of Libya in 1986 by the Reagan administration in response to Libyan sponsored terrorist attacks against U.S. targets in Europe; the U.S. cruise missile attacks on targets in The Sudan and in Afghanistan in 1998 in response to the Al Qaeda bombings of U.S. embassies in Kenya and Tanzania; the invasion and occupation of Afghanistan in 2002 in response to the 9/11 attacks; and ongoing U.S. military operations to locate and destroy Al Qaeda cells still operating in eastern Afghanistan (Dempsey, 2006:19).

There is no doubt that the direct military action has been less successful in addressing terrorists operating in failed states as was the case of Somalia in 1993. The failed mission in Somalia was on account of challenges posed by state failures such as lack of infrastructure, the complete absence of state security, criminal justice systems and endemic violence in the state.

An alternative approach to CT-COIN in failed states or those undergoing reconstruction such as Sierra Leone seeks to identify the root causes of terrorism and insurgency. This approach draws largely from the "hearts and minds approach" proposed by Field Marshal Gerald Templar, an officer who served as commander in the Malaya Emergency between 1952 and 1954 (Cloake, 1985:25). This approach is generating growing attention in policy communities and academic circles. It involves 'the task of reducing conditions that can be exploited by terrorists as a goal' (Dempsey, 2006:19) and dealing with fundamental problems such as economic distress, ethnic and religious fissures, fragile governance, weak democracy, and rampant human rights abuses that create an environment in which terrorists thrive (Lyman & Morrison, 2004:75). The Al Qaeda took advantage of the violent and chaotic environment that permeates collapsed states like Sierra Leone. This approach recommends that the developed countries should focus on supporting participatory democracy and promoting recovery from the failed state condition. No doubt addressing the needs of state failure itself will go a long way in removing the situation that furnishes sanctuary and cover to terrorist groups.

Sierra Leone's recent struggle to overcome the Ebola pandemic attests to the fact that the country still grapples with numerous challenges in its efforts to ensure genuine state recovery.

The subsequent intervention efforts of the ECOWAS and UN peacekeeping missions may have put an end to the violent conflict of the 1990s; however, rebuilding and enhancing the state's capacity, especially in the area of CT-COIN requires strong international support. Building local state capacity to combat terrorists within individual nation-states has emerged since the 9/11 attacks as a critical component of US counterterrorism strategy. This element of US strategy has been particularly important in areas of the world characterised by weak or failing states just as it has focused on ensuring capable state security forces in Sub-Saharan Africa. Examples of initiatives to support counterterrorism include the Pan Sahel Initiative (PSI) and the Trans-Sahel Counterterrorism Initiative (TSCTI). The PSI was initiated in 2002 to help countries in the Sahel region improve border security and enhance counterterrorism capabilities. The program intended to strengthen the ability of US partners in Africa to deny the use of their territory to terrorist groups. A follow-on initiative in this regard is the TSCTI, which has provided additional funding and sought to foster regional cooperation among Sahelian states in addressing the regional terrorist threat (Koch, 2004).

## CT-COIN measures and legislation in post conflict Sierra Leone

Terrorism, being a global phenomenon, is not new, and from the onset, international responses have highlighted the role of national-level measures. Since 1963, through the UN and its various specialised agencies, the international community has promulgated a comprehensive set of universal legal instruments to provide a basis for all states that become parties to them, to act to prevent and prosecute terrorists (Ford, 2011). These instruments cover areas such as aircraft hijacking, aviation sabotage, violence at airports, acts against the safety of maritime navigation, acts against the safety of fixed platforms located on the continental shelf, act against internationally protected persons, unlawful taking and possession of nuclear materials, hostage-taking, terrorist bombings, funding the commission of terrorist acts and terrorist organisations, and nuclear terrorism. The objective of the universal scheme is to harmonise all national laws to ensure that they align with the global instruments and sufficient for preventive, punitive and legal measures that constitute the primary resource in counterterrorism strategies.

A starting point for countering terrorism is the country's level of ratification of the various international conventions. According to Ford (2011:43) "one of the most objective and reliable indicators of counterterrorism compliance is the increase in the number of states that ratify the various conventions." The Counterterrorism Committee of the UN Security Council (CTC) has aptly described ratification of the universal counterterrorism instruments as a barometer of international cooperation. This approach, no doubt, provides us with a yardstick to begin to measure post-conflict Sierra Leone's efforts in CT-COIN. In terms of the status of ratification and status of legislative implementation, out of 16 conventions, treaties or protocols identified by Ford (2011), Sierra Leone has ratified not less than (7) universal instruments against terrorism. These include:

1. Convention on Offences and Certain Other Acts Committed on Board Aircraft (1963)
2. Convention for the Suppression of Unlawful Seizure of Aircraft (1970)
3. Convention for the Suppression of Unlawful Acts against the Safety of Civil Aviation (1971)
4. Convention on the Prevention and Punishment of Crimes against Internationally Protected Persons, Including Diplomatic Agents (1973)
5. International Convention against the Taking of Hostages (1979)
6. International Convention for the Suppression of Terrorist Bombings (1997)

7.   International Convention for the Suppression of the Financing of Terrorism (1999)

In its 2003 report to the CTC (S/2003/278), the Government of Sierra Leone stated that it had established a High-Level National Committee on Counterterrorism comprised of re-presentatives from various ministries/agencies involved in the development and coordination of counterterrorism activities. However, in the area of criminal legislation, according to Sierra Leone's report to the CTC (S/2003/278) (Dag Hammarskjold Library, 2004:138), the country has no specific legislation on the prevention and suppression of terrorism. However, Sierra Leone noted, in the same report that several provisions in its Criminal Code and Criminal Procedural Act of 1965 can be used to prosecute acts of terrorism. These provisions explicitly enumerated by the Government in its report are those related to issues of murder, extortion, currency smuggling, illegal possession of firearms and ammunition. In addition to the Criminal Code and Code of Criminal Procedure, the Malicious Damage Act (1861) contains provisions which include some of the acts criminalised by the universal instruments against terrorism. Sierra Leone has submitted several reports to the United Nations Security Council Committees dealing with counterterrorism. These include: report to the CTC (S/2003/278, 3 March 2003; and report (S/AC.37/2005/ (1455)/11 of 29 September 2003) to the Al Qaeda and Taliban Sanctions Committee pursuant to Security Council resolution 1455 (2003) (Dag Hammarskjold Library, 2004:138). So far, Sierra Leone has not yet submitted its terrorist checklist in accordance with Security Council resolution 1617 (2005) (Dag Hammarskjold Library, 2004).

Sierra Leone has presented follow up reports on measures being taken to confront and combat the financing of terrorism. In its May 2010 report, Sierra Leone reported that a National Strategy on anti-money laundering and counter-terrorist financing (AML/CFT) is-sues, which provides a five-year framework or road map to fight against money laundering and terrorism financing offences was developed and approved by Cabinet. The five-year strategic plan is aimed at achieving maximum political will, implementing a comprehensive AML/CFT legislation and regulations, empowering a successful fight against money laundering and ter-rorism financing through effective enforcement and resources to enhance international cooperation and build strategic partnerships.

## Concluding remarks

The chapter has examined the issue of terrorism and insurgency and efforts at CT-COIN in the context of Sierra Leone. It clearly noted that the RUF as Violent Non-State Actor (VNSA), led by a warlord, Foday Sankoh, waged a war of terror in Sierra Leone from 1991 until 2002 when the war was declared over. The group, which took advantage of the weak government in Sierra Leone, was able to sustain its war through the illicit exploitation diamonds, which it sold to terrorist groups such as the Al Qaeda and Hezbollah, which in turn took advantage of the failed state to promote their goals. We conclude by underscoring the point that that though the RUF employed the weapon of terrorism to create fear during the war, it does not fit into the typical characterisation of terrorist groups such as the Al Qaeda, Hezbollah and Boko Haram. Thus, the situation involving the RUF in Sierra Leone was the case where terrorist groups took advantage of state collapse to penetrate through rebel groups and transact trade in illicit diamonds to generate profits to support their activities. Accordingly, were commend that rather than an overemphasis on the traditional approach to CT-COIN which focuses on military action, an alternative approach, which stresses identification of the root causes of terrorism and insurgency in failed states or those undergoing reconstruction such as Sierra Leone is more efficacious in

Africa. The case of Sierra Leone shows the importance of reforming state structures rather than simply focusing on the elimination of a rebel or spoiler and members of the group. The report of the IEP Report (2016) ranked Sierra Leone 130 compared to Liberia 110, and Nigeria 3.This clearly points that what Sierra Leone needs in its current efforts at CT-COIN is international support through capacity building, security reforms and developmental initiatives to ensure that it does not lapse into conditions that can be exploited by terrorist groups who take advantage of failed states to achieve their goals.

## References

Abdullah, I. (2004). Bush path to destruction: The origin and character of the Revolutionary United Front (RUF/SL). In A. Ibrahim (Ed.), *Between the Sierra Leone civil war :Democracy and terror* (pp. 41–65). Dakar: CODESRIA.

Berman, E. G., & Labonte, M. T. C. (2006). Sierra Leone. In E. G. Berman & M.T.C. Labonte (Eds.), *Twenty-first century peace operation*. Washington DC: US Institute of Peace Press.

Cloake, J. (1985). *Templer, tiger, and Malaya: The life of Field Marshal Sir Gerald Templer*. London: Harrap.

Cook, N. (2003, July 16). *CRS report for Congress- diamonds and conflict: Background, policy, and legislation*. Washington DC: Congressional Research Service.

Crane, D. M. (2004). Dancing with the devil- prosecuting West Africa's warlords: Building initial pro-secutorial strategy for an international tribunal after third world armed conflicts. *Case Western Reserve Journal of International Law, 37*(1), 1–11.

Dag Hammarskjold Library (2004). *S/2003/278 Letter, 3 Mar. 2003, From the Chairman of the Security Council Committee established pursuant to Resolution 1373 (2001) Concerning Counter-Terrorism*. Transmits report from Sierra Leone, submitted to the Counter Terrorism Committee pursuant to paragraph 6 of Security Council Resolution 1373 (2001). Index of Proceedings of the Security Council fifty eight year – 2003. New York: United Nations Publication. Available from https://library.un.org/sites/library.un.org/files/.../1430-201211261124424108239_0.pdf.

Dag Hammarskjold Library (2004). *S/Res/1455 (2003) Improving implementation of measures imposed by paragraph 4(b) of Resolution 1333 (2000) and paragraph 1 and 2 of Resolution 1390 (2002) on measures against the Taliban and Al Qaida*. Index of Proceedings of the Security Council fifty eight year – 2003. New York: United Nations Publication. Available from https://library.un.org/sites/library.un.org/files/.../1430-201211261124424108239_0.pdf.

Deen, T. (2005). *Politics: UN Member States Struggle To Define Terrorism*. IPS 25 July 2005. Retrieved from http://www.ipsnews.net/2005/07/politics-un-member-states-struggle-to-define-terrorism/

Dempsey, T. (2006). Counter-terrorism *in African Failed States: Challenges and Potential Solutions*. Retrieved from http://www.StrategicStudiesInstitute.army.mil/.

Farah, D. (2001, November 2). *Al Qaeda Cash Tied To Diamond Trade. Washington Post*. Retrieved from https://www.washingtonpost.com/archive/politics/2001/11/02/al-qaeda-cash-tied-to-diamond-trade/93abd66a-5048-469a-9a87-5d2efb565a62/.

Ford, J. (2011). *African : Legal frameworks a decade after 2001*. Tshwane: Institute for Security Studies.

Fortna, V. P. (2015). Do terrorists win? 'Rebels' use of terrorism and civil war outcomes. *International organisation, 69*(3), 519–556.

Freeman, L. (2015). The African warlord revisited. *Small Wars & Insurgencies, 26*(5), 790–810.

Ganor, B. (2002). Defining terrorism: Is one man's terrorist another man's freedom fighter? *Police Practice and Research: An International Journal, 3*(4), 287–304.

GIABA. (2010, May). *Third follow-up report: Mutual evaluation antimony laundering and combating the finance of terrorism*. Dakar: GIABA.

Hironaka, A. (2005). *Never ending wars: The international community, weak states, and the perpetuation of civil war*. Cambridge: Harvard University Press.

Howard, T. (2010). Failed states and the spread of terrorism in Sub-Saharan Africa. *Studies in Conflict & Terrorism, 33*(11), 960–988.

Human Rights Watch (1998). *Human rights abuses committed by members of the AFRC/RUF*. Available from https://www.hrw.org/legacy/reports98/sierra/Sier988-03.htm.

IEP Report. (2016). *Global Terrorism Index 2016: Measuring and understanding the impact of terrorism*. New York: Institute for Economics and Peace.

Imobighe, T. A. (2009). Challenges in Categorisingcategorizing domestic terrorism. In W. Okumu & A. Botha (Eds.), *Domestic terrorism in Africa: Defining, addressing and understanding its impact on human security*. Pretoria: Institute for Security Studies.

Ipe, J., Cockayne, J., & Millar, A. (September, 2010). *Implementing the UN global counter-terrorism strategy in West Africa*. Washington DC: The Center on Global Counterterrorism Cooperation.

Kabbah, A. T. (2012). *Two decades of conflict and democracy in Sierra Leone: A personal experience*. Tshwane: Institute for Security Studies.

Keen, D. (2005). *Conflict and collusion in Sierra Leone*. Oxford: James Currey.

Keen, D. (2008). *Complex emergencies*. Cambridge: Polity.

Keen, D., & Attree, L. (2015). *Dilemmas of counter-terror, stabilisation and statebuilding: A discussion paper*. London: Saferworld.

Koch, A. (2004, October 6). US *to Bolster Counter-Terrorism Assistance to Africa. Jane's Defence Weekly*.

Lyman, P. N. & Morrison, J. S. (2004). *The terrorist threat in Africa* Retrieved from https://www.foreignaffairs.com/articles/africa/2004-01-01/terrorist-threat-africa

Marks, Z. (2013). Sexual violence inside rebellion: Policies and perspectives of the Revolutionary United Front of Sierra Leone. *Civil Wars, 15*(3), 359–379.

Madzima, J. (2009). *Money laundering and terrorism financing risks in Botswana. ISS Paper 184*. Available from https://issafrica.org/.../money-laundering-and-terrorism-financing-risks-in-botswana.

McCormick, G. H., & Fritz, L. (2009). The logic of warlord politics. *Third World Quarterly, 30*(1), 81–112.

OAU (1999). *OAU Convention on the Prevention and Combating of Terrorism, 1999*. Available from http://www.peaceau.org/uploads/oau-convention-on-the-prevention-and-combating-of-terrorism.pdf.

Olonisakin, F. (2008). *Peacekeeping in Sierra Leone: The story of UNAMSIL*. London: Lynne Rienner Publishers.

Rabasa, A., Chalk, P., Cragin, K., Daly, S. A., Gregg, H. S., Karasik, T. W., O'Brien, K. Al., & Rosenau, W. (2006). *Beyond Al Qaeda-part 2: The outer rings of the terrorist universe*. Santa Monica: RAND Corporation.

Richards, P. (2005). War as smoke and mirrors: Sierra Leone 1991–2; 1994–5; 1995–6. *The Anthropological Quarterly, 78*, 377–402.

Robbin-Coker, C. (2005). *Amputation is forever: Blood diamonds and the civil war in Sierra Leone*. Available from http://ibrarian.net/navon/paper/Amputation_is_forever_blood_diamonds_and_civ.pdf.

Rotberg, R. I. Ed. (2003). *State failure and state weakness in a time of terror*. Washington DC: Brookings Institution Press.

Solomon, H. (2015). *Terrorism and counter terrorism in Africa: Fighting insurgency from Al Shabaab, Ansar Dine and Boko Haram*. London: Palgrave Macmillan.

UNODC. (2009). *A review of the legal regime against terrorism in West and Central Africa*. New York: United Nations.

United Nations Panel of Experts, (2000, December 20). *Letter dated 19 December 2000 from the Chairman of the Security Council Committee established pursuant to Resolution 1132 (1997) concerning Sierra Leone, addressed to the President of the Security Council*, S/2000/1195, para. 87, 20 December 2000.

US Government Counterinsurgency Guide. (2009). Bureau of Political-Military Affairs, US Department of State, Washington, DC. Available from https://www.state.gov/documents/organization/119629.pdf.

Vehnämäki, M. (2002). Diamonds and warlords: The geography of war in the Democratic Republic of Congo and Sierra Leone. *Nordic Journal of African Studies, 11*(1), 48–74.

Wahlert, M. H. (2009). The failed state. In J. J. F. Forest (Ed.), *Countering terrorism and insurgency in the 21st century: International perspectives* (pp. 109–126). Westport: CT, Praeger Security International.

Weinberg, L., & Eubank, W. L. (2007). Twenty-first century insurgencies: Understanding the use of terrorism as a strategy. In J. J. F. Forest (Ed.), *Countering terrorism and insurgency in the 21st century: International perspectives* (*Vols. 1–3*, pp. 80–92). Westport: Praeger Security International Peace Academy.

Wood, L. J., & Reese, T. R. (2008). Military interventions in Sierra Leone: Lessons from a failed state. *The Long War series occasional paper 28*. Fort Leavenworth, Kansas: Combat Studies Institute Press US Army. Combined Arms Center.

Yoroms, G. (2008). Counter-TerrorismCounter-terrorism measures in West Africa. In O. Wafula & A. Botha (Eds.), *Understanding terrorism in Africa: Building bridges and overcoming the gaps*. Pretoria: Institute for Security Studies.

# 34

# Ethiopia

## Counterterrorism and counterinsurgency in Africa's volatile Horn

*Roy Love*

## Introduction

Terrorism and insurgency may come from opposition within a country or external forces. In response, states are often faced with treading a fine line between the enforcement of counterterrorism measures and infringements of civil liberties, with some deliberately swinging the balance in favour of the former, at the expense of the latter, for self-serving political ends. Until early 2018 the Ethiopian government regularly faced accusations of this kind, principally through its use of anti-terrorism and state of emergency legislation to repress opposition, and which, by declaring an opposition group, such as the Oromo Liberation Front (OLF), a terrorist organisation, gave power to the authorities to detain indefinitely a wide range of suspected sympathisers. In 2018, however, following a period of increasing civil discontent, a radical change of leadership in the ruling alliance, the Ethiopian Peoples' Revolutionary Democratic Front (EPRDF), introduced a more inclusive, conciliatory approach to opposition. The primary change was the appointment in April 2018 of a new Prime Minister, Abiye Ahmed, from the Oromo party of the coalition, thus marking a radical change from the past. Early actions then included the release of all political prisoners, unbanning of previously proscribed opposition parties, rapprochement and restoration of diplomatic relations with neighbouring Eritrea, creation of new opportunities for incoming foreign investment, and the formation of a new Cabinet with women comprising 50% of its membership.

At the same time, however, some inter-ethnic conflicts across the country have either persisted or emerged. These include the deep-rooted existing conflict on the border between Oromia and Somali federal regions, displacing, by mid-1918, over a million people; more recent clashes at the Benishangul-Gumuz border region with Oromia, displacing a further 70,000; and Sidama speakers fleeing from Bale in Oromia. In mid-1918 there have also been ethnically driven clashes in Addis Ababa, an attempted grenade attack on Abiye Ahmed as he addressed a large public gathering in the city, and the police discovery of a cache of weapons in a truck entering the city.

While, therefore, the positive nature of the changes has introduced a period of general, if cautious, optimism about the future, several significant threats remain. These include a potential spread of these regional ethnically based conflicts; a reaction from disaffected members of the former government or their allies in the armed forces; civil disorder during the run-up to the planned 2020 national elections; and, relatedly, open divisions appearing within the ruling EPRDF. Externally, the potential terrorist threat from *al Shabaab* in Somalia remains high, bordering as it does with the Somali region of Ethiopia. At the same time, the absence of any regime change in Eritrea leaves considerable uncertainty on how the new relationship will evolve under open borders. In the meantime, existing counterterrorism and other controlling legislation remain in place, although discussions to amend the Anti-terrorism Act have taken place (Ethiopian News Agency 2018), and the risks that events may unfold in such a way as to bring them into play once again are high. The country's record in this respect in recent years has been widely criticised by international human rights observers as having been harshly and indiscriminately implemented in such a way to crush all significant opposition. This raises the more general question of how far the state may infringe on civil and human rights in a context of terrorism and counterterrorism, mostly when the authorities regard opposition within the country as a security threat.

This chapter, therefore, begins with a conceptual note on the degree to which state counterterrorism activities may be allowed to infringe on legitimate political freedoms, as a prelude to a brief historical overview of key elements of the legacy of history in the Ethiopian case. There then follows a summary of post-1991 externally sourced terrorist incidents in the country before moving on to sections on opposition within Ethiopia, regional and Ethiopian counterterrorism response, and the effectiveness of counterterrorism in Ethiopia. The chapter concludes with a look at the continuing challenges of counterterrorism in Ethiopia, ranging from the domestic risks attached to the radical changes introduced in 2018 by the latest Prime Minister, Abiye Ahmed, to the continuing threat from the Islamist group, *al Shabaab* in Somalia, and from conflict in Yemen and the increasing presence of Arabian, Western, Turkish and Chinese bases spread along the Red Sea and Arabian Gulf coastlines of the Horn.

## Terrorism, counterterrorism and internal opposition: a conceptual note

The complex history of Ethiopia's role in the formation of the present state structures in the Horn of Africa, with all their volatile allegiances and propensity for conflict along with ethnic and religious identity, has rendered it highly susceptible to violent acts of opposition, both from internal opponents and by those from neighbouring countries. Where the Ethiopian state has responded to such threats in recent years by what is regarded by many external observers as extreme measures against suspected groups within its population, involving mass detentions, arbitrary arrest, and widespread security monitoring (Brechenmacher 2017), the concept of terrorism by the state itself arises.

As with much of the debate on terrorism and counterterrorism, it is essential to acknowledge the ambiguities of meaning that are often present. A convenient starting point, in this case, is Ruth Blakely's classification of forms of "state terrorism"' First, there are deliberate acts of violence by a state against its citizens or creation of fear of such violence. Second, the acts may be perpetrated by a range of agents on behalf of the state. Third, the intention goes beyond the suppression of the victim of the state-sponsored violence alone, to instil fear into those in the community who are or may be sympathetic to their beliefs. Fourth, that this target group is thereby made to change its behaviour (Blakely, 2010: 12–27). In the case of Ethiopia, as we shall see later, the charge as it has affected groups in the country is rendered more feasible given the ethnic federalist structure of governance. Thus, by clamping down heavily, even brutally, legitimised by anti-terrorist legislation, on those suspected of belonging to, or sympathising with an ethnically based organisation that has in the past used armed opposition, others on the broader group will be deterred through fear, from expressing their opposition to the government by supporting or sympathising with this or any similar party.

On the other hand, it may be argued that if a government intends to target specific members and supporters of a banned organisation which has particular ethnic objectives, and that it is an unintentional side effect of this that fear is instilled among all members of that ethnic group then the *jus in bello* aspect of "just war" theory could be argued to apply, with the primary objective on the target group being seen as morally acceptable in the context (Blakely, 2010: 23). The acts may not then be classed as "state terrorism." This is a slippery slope, however, open to abuse and complacency. Related to this type of argument is the primacy that governments may give to developmental objectives, the achievement of which is argued to be threatened by political instability, which is then defined as a state security threat, a phenomenon sometimes described as the 'securitisation' of development (Gebresenbet 2014). By also classifying certain opposition groups as 'terrorist' organisations, and all that such terms entail, the state is effectively de-politicising their identity, hence undermining their legitimacy as political opposition and justifying extreme forms of repression. (Pointing & Whyte, 2012) The relevance of these debates to the record of the Ethiopian approach to counterterrorism and counterinsurgency will become evident as we proceed. In the meantime, we begin with an account of how contemporary inter-state and intra-state tensions in the region have their origins in the past in a way that has reverberated across succeeding generations up to the present, and which add fuel to current grievances and state responses.

## The legacy of history

As already noted, the year 2018 saw two significant changes from the past: the appointment of a more conciliatory Prime Minister, Abiye Ahmed, from the Oromo group in the coalition government; and a settlement of the Ethiopia-Eritrea border dispute. To understand the full weight of the significant challenges that remain, however, it is essential to appreciate the legacy of history, which continues to colour contemporary politics in the region.

The 19th century saw the emergence of Abyssinia from a period of warring regional princes at the beginning of the century to the consolidation, under Menelik's expansionary conquests, to the country recognisable today as Ethiopia. The declining influence of the Ottoman Empire along the coastal regions of the Red Sea, Arabian Gulf and the Indian Ocean also allowed footholds for West European colonial powers, resulting in the French and Italian colonies of Somaliland, the British protectorate of the same name, and the Italian colony of Eritrea. To the west of Abyssinia was the Anglo-Egyptian Sudan, while in the south were the British colonies of Uganda and Kenya. To the north, east and west of these Coptic Christian highlands were, therefore, numerous local Islamic sultanates and sheikhdoms, mostly under Western colonial jurisdiction, but some of which also came within Menelik's expanded Abyssinian boundaries. Today the population of Ethiopia comprises 43.5% Orthodox Christians and 33.9% Muslims, with the remainder Protestant Christians (18.5%), Traditional (2.6%), plus other (1.3%).

In the aftermath of World War II, Eritrea was eventually incorporated into Ethiopia as a province, leaving a discontent which produced the early Eritrean Liberation Front (ELF) and later Eritrean Peoples' Liberation Front (EPLF) and, in 1991, following the defeat of the socialist regime in Ethiopia, to the establishment of the independent state of Eritrea (in the process rendering Ethiopia totally land-locked) and under sole, and continuing, control of the EPLF. Meanwhile, the former British and Italian Somali colonies were united to become the independent nation of Somalia. French Djibouti became the independent Republic of Djibouti in 1977. Together with North East Kenya and the Ogaden region of Ethiopia, the territory of these three former colonies covers an area of Somali speakers which has been referred to as

'Greater Somalia', symbolised in the five-pointed star of the Somalia flag. The aspiration to unite all five regions produced two significant conflicts between Somalia and Ethiopia in the 20th century: between 1960–1964 a rumbling border dispute and in 1977–1978 a major clash in the Ogaden. The Somalian defeat in the latter contributed to the later collapse of Siad Barre's government in 1991, followed by some years of failed attempts to restore the effective central government, and out of which emerged the militant Islamist group, *al Shabaab*, which continues to occupy the territory as a base for regular armed incursion and suicide drove terrorist actions, principally in Somalia and Kenya. This period also saw the establishment in 1991 of the self-declared, though not internationally recognised, the independent Republic of Somaliland in the north, overlapping with the former British Protectorate boundaries.

On taking power in Ethiopia in 1991 (together with the EPLF), the Ethiopian Peoples' Revolutionary Democratic Front (EPRDF) restructured the governance of the country (without Eritrea) along ethnic federalist lines, while keeping central government under the tight control of the Tigray Peoples Liberation Front (TPLF), chaired by Meles Zenawe, later Prime Minister. As at mid-2018 the EPLF and EPRDF remained in total control of their respective governments, and until July 2018 were in dispute, without diplomatic relations, since their 1998–2000 border war. Although the direct conflict between the two countries had ceased, occasional scares and violent clashes continued (Fente, 2016), and each took opposite sides in their interventions in the Somali civil conflict and hosted each other's, dissident groups. In Ethiopia, the dominance of the TPLF within the EPRDF since 1991, and its methods of control, created increasing resentment amongst other ethnic groups. Mutual acceptance of each other by Coptic Christians and Muslims has generally held together despite occasional local tensions. However, recent years have seen growing concern about the influence of Saudi inspired *wahabbism*.

The legacy of this history is that until mid-2018 (when Ethiopia and Eritrea were reconciled) the four nations of the Horn comprised a fragile web of unresolved conflict: between nations in the case of Ethiopia and Eritrea, and within all four countries to different degrees and in different forms, often with repercussions across borders (Clapham 2017).

## The wider impact

The position of the Horn of Africa on the fringes of the Middle East, separated only by the Red Sea, inevitably brings it into the tensions of that region, currently manifested in the conflict in Yemen, and associated risks relating to Western interest in protecting the supply of oil and other merchant shipping through the nearby Bab el Mandeb Straits and eventually to the Mediterranean. In the Horn, in recent years Ethiopia has been the least unstable, the strongest militarily and the one most amenable to US interests in the wider region. By 2015–2016, the USA was the largest single bilateral aid donor to the country, which, in turn, was the recipient in the same period of more ODA than any other African country (OECD 2018: data updated on 22 December 2017). Djibouti, through whose port most of Ethiopia's surface trade currently passes, is also hosting some Western, Arab, and Asian bases and watching posts. At the same time, Saudi Arabia, UAE and Turkey are present at ports in Eritrea, Somaliland and Somalia. The implications for Ethiopia of this ring of international bases along the Red Sea and Arabian Gulf coasts are explored in the closing section of this chapter.

## Terrorist actions against Ethiopia

The history outlined above has left a legacy of overlapping political, ethnic and border grievances which have fomented numerous incidents of terrorist-type violence, ranging from bombings in Addis Ababa in the 1990s, blamed on the Somali irredentist group *Al Ittihad,* through to an attempted grenade attack on the new Prime Minister at a rally in June 2018.

From 2006, following the entry into Somalia of Ethiopian armed forces to dislodge the Islamic Courts Union from Mogadishu, the Islamic jihadist group *Al Shabaab* has regularly engaged with Ethiopian troops, and was behind the bombing of an Ethiopian restaurant in Uganda in 2010, previously declared allegiance with *Al Qaeda* in 2009, and has since then committed terrorist atrocities in Kenya. In June 2016, *al Shabaab* claimed to have killed 43 Ethiopian soldiers in an attack on a base in Central Somalia (Al Jazeera, 2016).

Following the 1998–2000 war with Ethiopia and until recently, Eritrea was accused of arming and financing any armed group opposing the Ethiopian state, particularly if operating from Somalia, thus continuing the conflict with Ethiopia by proxy (UN Security Council 2016: Section III; Gebrewold, 2009: 179–219).

Other events include bombings in Dire Dawa and Addis Ababa in 2002, the latter blamed by the authorities on the OLF (BBC News, 2002), and a planned bombing of Jan 2011 African Union Summit by the OLF assisted by Eritrea, but foiled by Ethiopian security. In the meantime, the Ogaden National Liberation Front (ONLF) attacked and killed 65 Ethiopians and 9 Chinese oil workers in the Ogaden in 2007. In November 2017, the Ethiopian courts convicted four supposed OLF members for planning a terrorist attack (Africa News 2017a).

In response to these and other perceived threats several counterterrorism programmes have been introduced, which are summarised below.

## Regional counterterrorism response

In 2009, the US-funded Partnership for Regional East Africa Counterterrorism (PREACT) was introduced, designed to *"build counterterrorism capacity and cooperation of the military, law enforcement, and civilian actors across East Africa to counter terrorism"*. Its aims include reducing the operational capacity of terrorist networks, enhancing border security, countering the financing of terrorism, and reducing the appeal of radicalisation and recruitment to violent extremism. This programme also supports the African Union Mission in Somalia (AMISOM) in its fight against *Al Shabaab*. The Horn of Africa is also one of six global regions for the US programme of "Countering and Preventing Terrorist Safe Havens and Recruitment," of which two are African, the other being North-West Africa. This programme also includes the Terrorist Interdiction Program (TIP)/Personal Identification Secure Comparison and Evaluation System (PISCES) which *"provides partner countries border security assistance at airports … to identify, disrupt, and deter terrorist travel"* (US Department of State, undated).

Ethiopia is also a key member of the regional Intergovernmental Authority on Development (IGAD) based in Djibouti, which has a critical role as a regional forum for communication and joint agreements between the countries of the greater Horn. IGAD's counterterrorist architecture has evolved into the current IGAD Security Sector Programme (based in Addis Ababa) with a mandate to counter terrorism, transnational organised crime, and to enhance maritime security and the capacity of security institutions. Within this programme is the Transnational Security Threats Initiative (TSTI), to promote cooperation and coordination within the region (IGAD 2016). In April 2018 IGAD established the Centre of Excellence in Preventing and Countering Violent Extremism (ICEPCVE) with a typical workshop for Young African Leaders in November 2018 (Goobjoob 2018; ICEPCVE 2018), and in August the IGAD Security Sector Programme held a workshop on security threats in the cross-border corridor between Ethiopia, Djibouti and Somaliland (IGAD 2018).

Ethiopia is also a member of the Eastern and Southern Africa Anti-Money Laundering Group (ESAAMLG) and in March 2012 acceded to the International Convention for the

Suppression of the Financing of Terrorism. In 2008 the government created a Financial Intelligence Centre to monitor finance for terrorism and money laundering. In February 2017 a high-level political commitment was made with FATF (Financial Action Task Force) and ESAAMLG to strengthen its AML/CFT (Anti Money Laundering/Counter Financing of Terrorism) effectiveness and the implementation of an action plan on risk assessment and other factors. By February 2018, some progress had been noted, but the commitment remained to be met in full (Financial Action Task Force 2018). The high level of informal businesses, a predominantly cash-based economy and weak regulation make Ethiopia particularly vulnerable to unrecorded monetary transactions, with one estimate that between 2004 and 2013 some $26 billion left the country unlawfully, and that $2 billion is lost every year in illicit financial flows (Berhane 2017). The country may have counterterrorism under control but continues to provide a high-risk money laundering environment.

## Ethiopian state counterterrorism response

The Ethiopian National Defence Force (ENDF), the Ethiopian Federal Police (EFP), Ethiopian intelligence, and regional special police share collective responsibility for preventing attacks by *Al-Shabaab* and other terrorist groups. At federal level is the Ethiopian Task Force for Counterterrorism (ETFC), responsible for overall counterterrorism management and co-ordination, at times with US involvement. A particular focus has been on border security in which PISCES (see the previous section) has provided traveller screening at airports and other points of entry (Mesfin, 2011:20–21). The country's highly organised and "politicised" internal administrative structure extends from regional bodies down to local neighbourhood offices, or *kebeles*, of around 500 households, which effectively brings sensitivity on security matters down to local level.

The powers given to these various bodies are enhanced directly and indirectly by the 2009 Anti-Terrorism Act, with its origins in the period following the 2005 elections together with the rising influence of *Al Shabaab* in Somalia from 2006. The Act gives the authorities wide-ranging powers of investigation, and detention of those suspected of planning or having carried out acts of terrorism, and of having supported such planning or acts in any way. Its actual implementation has been heavily criticised by human rights observers, but the political changes of early 2018 have opened the door to a review of its powers and definitions. A summary of its original powers as at October 2018 follows.

Article 3 of the Act defines terrorist acts as "a group intending to advance a political, religious or ideological cause by coercing the government, intimidating the public or section of the public, or destabilising or destroying the fundamental political, constitutional or, economic or social institutions of the country" and lists six acts that are punishable "with rigorous imprisonment from 15 years to life or with death." These include serious risk to the safety or health of the public or section of the public, serious damage to property, damage to natural resource, environment, historical or cultural heritages, serious interference or disruption of any public service (Federal Democratic Republic of Ethiopia, 2009).

Article 5.1 on "Rendering Support to Terrorism" provides for rigorous imprisonment from 10 to 15 years for "whosoever, knowingly or having reason to know that his deed has the effect of supporting the commission of a terrorist act or a terrorist organisation" and in addition to a number of obvious ways of supporting such acts it includes the provision of a "skill, expertise or moral support or gives advice", and "making available any property in any manner."

Article 6 on "Encouragement of Terrorism" mainly affects journalists, with an all-embracing statement:

Whosoever publishes or causes the publication of a statement that is likely to be under-stood by some or all of the members of the public to whom it is published as a direct or indirect encouragement or other inducement to them to the commission or preparation or instigation of an act of terrorism stipulated under Article 3 of this Proclamation is pun-ishable with rigorous imprisonment from 10 to 20 years.

The Act also allows for the establishment of a National Anti-Terrorism Coordination Committee (NATCC) comprising the heads of the Ministry of Justice, National Intelligence and Security Service and Federal Police, and chaired by Director-General of the National Intelligence and Security Service.

The Act has been widely reviewed and critiqued, particularly on its definitional broadness in key areas, such as the definition of a "terrorist act," which allows for a considerable degree of discretion on the part of the authorities to arrest and detain (Kassa 2014: 371–405). It is difficult to say how much of this was intentional and how much was inadequate drafting, but in practice, it has been useful to the authorities. Other concerns relate to the inclusion of punishment by death in Article 3 which is a matter of concern from a human rights perspective, while reference to a "statement likely to be understood by some or all of the public ..." raises questions of proof. Regarding evidence in court, Article 23(1) allows intelligence reports as evidence without having to disclose the "source or the method it was gathered," thus opening the possibility of torture. However, while broadness is found in some areas, in others, there is a definitional narrowness which could limit the scope for conviction (Kassa 2014).

Alongside the Anti-Terrorism Act, in 2009 the government also introduced a Proclamation for the Registration and Regulation of Charities and Societies, which curtailed NGOs working on human rights only to those local NGOs which were 90% locally funded. The effect has been to forbid all international NGOs from operating in the human rights field and to dramatically cut the funding of local NGOs working in the area (Dupuy, K. E., et al, 2015: 419–456). The preceding year, 2008, also saw Proclamations on Mass Media and Freedom of Information and on Political Parties Registration. Despite its title, the first of these imposed restrictions on journalists' activities, carrying severe penalties any perceived breach, while in 2012 the Telecom Fraud Offences Proclamation appeared, which criminalised the use of the telecommunications network for terrorist purposes. The combined effect of this group of proclamations has been to stifle all effective dissent, both by the threat and fear of arrest and imprisonment and by its subsequent implementation. In 2015 Ethiopia was ranked 4th behind Eritrea, North Korea, and Saudi Arabia of the most censored countries in the world (Committee to Protect Journalists, 2017).

While the impact of this array of measures, together with the politicised network of local government, does appear to have contained internal and externally-originating terrorist actions in the country, they have been widely condemned internationally for the way in which they have been used to suppress political dissent and opposition to the government, which, by implication, has meant (until the changes of early 2018) the TPLF, and giving little concession to the grievances of popular protest (Kassa, 2014: 371–405; Human Rights Watch, 2009 and 2017; The Oakland Institute and Environmental Defender Law Center, 2015; Amnesty International, 2016; US Department of State, 2016). These have included encroachment and dispossession of traditional land, lack of economic opportunities for youth, and deep resentment of the TPLF's reluctance to share power and the widespread belief that party subsidiaries and cadres in the armed forces have used their position for personal and corporate enrichment from the economic development and international aid that has often sponsored it (Clapham, 2017: 99; Vaughan, 2015: 307). This suppressed sense of grievance eventually burst out in August

2015, in a spate of mass anti-government protests in provincial towns and cities, especially in Oromia and Amhara regions, which continued until October 2016. The immediate government response was to allow excessive repression by the security forces, resulting in some 800 violent deaths between November 2016 and the end of that year (Amnesty International, 2016/ 17). The six-month State of Emergency was declared on 8 October 2016 which gave the authorities additional powers to those already in the Anti-Terrorism Proclamation, creating an environment in which "Security forces arbitrarily arrested and detained protesters, … opposition party members and supporters, accusing them of inciting violence." (US Department of State, 2016).

Following a further four-month extension, and a few minor concessions to the protesters, the State of Emergency was lifted on 7 August 2017. The other change, however, was slow. In an apparent sign of the magnitude of the challenge faced by the government, and to the TPLF in particular, the Prime Minister at the time, Hailemariam Desalegn, resigned on 16 February 2018. This prompted a quick and controversial decision by the Parliament to declare a new six month State of Emergency, in the face of increasing demands that the next PM should be from a different ethnic group, such as Oromo. It was only after some five weeks of internal debate among factions of the EPRDF that Abiye Ahmed, from the Oromo Peoples Democratic Organisation in the EPRDF coalition, was appointed on 2 April 2018, who has since taken a more open, conciliatory approach, as discussed below in the section on "Challenges of Ethiopia's Counterterrorism Policies."

## Who is the terrorist?

From the perspective of many of those Ethiopians affected, and in the opinion of many external observers, the manner of the state response to internal opposition until early 2018, as described above, was tantamount to terrorism by the state. In light of the conceptual discussion of this topic at the beginning of the chapter, it is instructive to note two reasons often given as to why the TPLF was so repressive of free democratic participation. The first is that as Ethiopia only emerged in 1991 from a centuries-long history of dictatorship and imperial autocracy to embrace democracy the learning process in adjusting to democratic freedoms must inevitably be slow, especially in a largely uneducated populace who may be readily swayed by what the government perceives as emotive and biased opposition propaganda. Political and economic stability is therefore argued to be more important in ensuring the eventual establishments of a fully democratic society than taking the risk of a sudden leap into the freedom of speech and political participation that is found in the longer-established democracies. It then follows that such actions as are deemed necessary to ensure this stability, including limitations on political expression, are duty and responsibility of the parties which took power in 1991, to ensure that the country does not slide into back into civil war or anarchy (Pausewang et al., 2002:243: De Waal, 2015 passim).

Second, is the adoption by former Prime Minister, Meles Zenawi, of a variation in the concept of the "developmental state" under the necessary guidance of EPRDF, in planning for the national interest in the longer term (Vaughan, 2015). In this scenario, the "securitisation" of development emerges as a response to defining poverty as an existential threat to national prosperity and stability. It thus justifies more sweeping powers for the state to limit what it regards as destabilising political opposition. (Gebresenbet, 2014). As the US government has stated, "The official ideology of the government is 'developmental democracy', a model that prioritises economic development over political rights" (US Department of State, 2017). To a degree, this approach appears to have been vindicated by an average annual growth rate of GDP of 10.8% between 2003/4 and 2014/15 (World Bank 2017), and of significant improvements in infant mortality, child morbidity, education of boys and girls and a number of other human development indicators in recent years.

Yet, the measures taken to protect this objective have entailed a degree of force that has in many respects been unnecessarily excessive and counterproductive, while at the same time allowing the TPLF and its associated business activities to gain a considerable foothold in the financial benefit arising from the economic expansion gained from the security thus obtained, and captured via the mutual benefits of developmental patrimonialism (Clapham, 2017:99; Vaughan & Gebremichael, 2011). That is, the view of the TPLF and EPRDF as responsible public-spirited, guardians of national development was undermined by the consistently high level of violent, and often lawless, the response of the security forces to protest over the years since 1991, creating an ethos of control consistent with Alex de Waal's concept of the "political marketplace" in which "political entrepreneurship can be seen naked, stripped of the flattering wardrobe of democracy, rule of law, and state-building" (De Waal, 2015:17). Although de Waal makes a case for the late Meles Zenawi to be an enlightened exception to this Hobbesian view of African politics the record, especially since the 2005 elections, the consistency over the years of reports by international observers on the extent and brutality of human rights violations in the country, and the extensive involvement of EFFORT (Endowment Fund for the Rehabilitation of Tigre) in the economy seriously undermine the credibility of this view, as indeed acknowledged at one point by Meles (De Waal, 2015 Ch.10).

Given consistent reports over the years by international human rights organisations of widespread arbitrary arrest and detention in harsh conditions of government opponents the argument that these have been unintentional side effects of more specific counterterrorism targeting, as described in the Conceptual Note at the beginning of this chapter, is therefore weak. Yet, a justification based on the securitisation of development may have sufficiently appeased major official donors, such as the USA, which have an interest in stability and gradual change in Ethiopia, amid a wider concern for regional stability in their own geopolitical interests (Matfess, 2017) despite collateral effects. Such an unremitting approach, however, can be counterproductive in that the wider impact may fuel further criticism, as was undoubtedly a factor leading up to the dramatic changes of 2018.

In taking this position the actions of the EPRDF, and TPLF within it, have been consistent with similar historical routes to power elsewhere, in that the winning group in an armed struggle for national control will tend to hold on to power, the ostensible justification being that only through the stability that they see themselves as being able to provide will their country be truly united in the long run (Jackson et al., 2010: 231; Duvall, & Stohl, 1988).

## Effectiveness of counter-terrorist policies in Ethiopia

In recent years the number of major terrorist attacks, as conventionally defined, within Ethiopia has been few, especially when compared with Kenya. It is difficult to assess the degree to which this is owing to the introduction of the Anti-Terrorist Proclamation and other legal measures taken in Ethiopia. It has been suggested, for instance, that Kenyan targets are preferred by *Al Shabaab* because, as a former British colony, they attract more international attention, and hence publicity, than would similar attacks in Ethiopia (Cannon & Pkalya, 2017). Other factors are likely to include the strong intelligence links between the local, regional, and central government in Ethiopia which, with state control over the internet in addition to the powers available to the security services in recent legislation, greatly facilitate intelligence gathering and hence deterrence. In the Ogaden, the paramilitary US-financed police, *Liyu*, has cracked down harshly on villages and communities suspected of supporting the ONLF (Hagmann, 2014:728; The East African, 2016) though this has exacerbated existing tensions in local Oromo-Somali relations. One may also surmise that it has been in *Al Shabaab*'s interest to leave the field in Ethiopia to domestically inspired opposition groups, bearing in mind that the Eritrean armed border crossing into Ethiopia in 1998 led not to the collapse of a divided Ethiopia but to a united national-patriotic response which bolstered the government. Nevertheless, *al Shabaab* does attack those Ethiopian forces which are active in Somalia (ESAT News, 2017) and vice versa (Africa News 2017b).

There is also the fact that many divisions in the country predate the protests of recent years: political marginalisation of the Oromo, Ogadeni and other peoples, the dominance of one ethnic group in government, formerly Amhara and, from 1991 to early 2018, Tigray, the status of the Somali region and the Ogaden, and Ethiopia-Eritrea relations. In this view, the recent anti-terrorism acts legitimised not only what would be happening anyway but were in many respects the latest in a long line of centralised repression as the outcome of "*historically contingent state-formation techniques*" (Hagmann, 2014: 726). At the same time, the unchallengeable control of the EPRDF over domestic politics has helped the USA, EU and other international interests which needed Ethiopian stability as a base for their wider geographic security interests (De Waal, 2015: Chapter 10).

## Challenges of Ethiopia's counterterrorism policy

Until early 2018 the key internal challenge was how to handle the mass displays of social, economic and political discontent that had swept the country since the second half of 2016, and how to deal with these other than through continued repression by means of Counter-Terrorist and State of Emergency legislation, which was clearly counter-productive in any sense of fomenting dialogue and national unity. Externally sourced challenges arose from the propensity of chronic instability in neighbouring countries to provide a platform for regionally sourced terrorism, principally from Somalia and Eritrea. Outside the Horn, risks from being on the periphery of the Middle East and its multiple tensions added to the external challenges.

Since then both categories have seen dramatic changes, potentially for the better. Within the country, the new Prime Minister appointed in April 2018, Abiye Ahmed, has opened up a dialogue with discontented regional groups, freed large numbers of imprisoned protesters, declassified three key opposition groups (OLF, ONLF, Ginbot 7) as terrorist organisations, and opened up major state-owned companies to a degree of private shareholding, domestic or international. Externally, the 2002 international arbitration decision on the border dispute with Eritrea has been accepted and diplomatic and economic relations have been restored. This potentially gives Ethiopia additional access to the Red Sea via the ports of Assab and Massawa, while also eliminating the risk of terrorist attacks resourced from Eritrea.

At the time of writing (October 2018) these changes have still to settle down and a number of challenges remain. First, is the possibility that divisions within the EPRDF, especially in the TPLF, unhappy with the speed of change, the concession to Eritrea, and the threat to their own positions, may intervene, assisted by allies in the armed forces. An early sign of discontent came from a grenade attack aimed at Abiye while addressing a mass rally on 23 June 2018. Intervention by opponents within the EPRDF could also be prompted if the new government fails to control remaining regional dissent, especially on the Somali/Oromo, Gideo/Somali border districts, and around Jigjiga close to the Somalia border (BBC 2018), or spreads to other regions. Relatedly, if the aspirations of the young unemployed are regarded as not being adequately addressed then a resurgence of mass protests could, even though unlikely, result in a repeat of previous patterns of repression which would undermine Abiye's credibility, initiating a return to the *status quo ante*.

Finally, there is the considerable challenge of managing the 2020 national elections peacefully and openly, and whether or not the EPRDF alliance will, for the first time since it came to power in 1991, be prepared to accept any result in which it loses power. This would, of course, mean that the Prime Minister would also be replaced, as his party, the Oromo People's Democratic Organisation (OPDO), is part of the ruling group. Fear of this in the past, particularly by the TPLF, has resulted in severe restrictions on opposition pre-election campaigning, and if these are now to be relaxed, as is widely expected, the agreement and guidelines on responsible electioneering (including in social media) will be essential. For some member parties of the EPRDF the risk of losing power may lead them to question their continued membership, and to either stand-alone or in a new partnership. Most at risk are the TPLF, which, as the party primarily in control since 1991 until recently, is widely unpopular, and, with one of the smaller electoral bases, would be at high risk of being isolated and voted out of power in the event of the break-up of the EPRDF. Given its past influence in the higher levels of the armed forces (Hagmann & Abbink 2011), the potential for serious disruption is considerable, and how this risk is handled by the TPLF itself and by the Prime Minister and his party could have implications for the re-appearance of some form of state terrorism as in the past.

In the wider Horn, the rapprochement between Ethiopia and Eritrea has reduced the threat of terrorism connected with their former dispute, and by opening up the likelihood of Ethiopian use of Eritrea's ports the risk from terrorist attempts to disrupt trade through Djibouti has also reduced. Much will depend, however, on an opening up of internal repression within Eritrea while remaining politically stable, and on the negotiating stance of the Eritrean government on issues of currency and trade. It is notable that during the gap between the resignation of Hailemariam Desalegn and the appointment of Abiy Ahmed the Ethiopian government reported the capture of a weapons convoy crossing the border from Eritrea (Al Jazeera 2018). During the same period, tensions in and around the southern town of Moyale, bordering with Kenya, following the shooting by Ethiopian troops of 21 villagers suspected erroneously of being Oromo terrorists, and triggering a claim by the OLF that it had attacked Ethiopian troops in retaliation (Manek 2018) was a reminder of the nature of the challenges ahead.

In Somalia, Ethiopian troop involvement with AMISOM since January 2014, in countering *al Shabaab*, has entailed regular counter-attacks (Weiss 2018) while the planned withdrawal of AMISOM, originally for December 2020 but extended to December 2021, raises possibilities of an *al Shabaab* revival and hence potential terrorist attacks within Ethiopia itself, a possibility encouraged by recent outrages and tensions between ethnic Somalis in the Somali Region of Ethiopia and their Oromo neighbours. On the other hand, any eventual defeat of *al Shabaab* is likely to see the Somali government turning its attention more forcefully to Somaliland, in whose seaport, Berbera, Ethiopia has been cultivating an interest, in partnership with the UAE, as an alternative to Djibouti.

The entire region is also vulnerable to the considerable peripheral impact of surrounding Arab states, their conflicts, the global geopolitics of the Middle East, and the critical role of the Red Sea both for shipping oil to Europe and for the bulk of Europe-Asia, including China, sea trade. The risks intensified in 2015 when Saudi Arabia and UAE intervened in the conflict in Yemen, and in challenging Qatar on its relationship with Iran, a long-time supporter of the Yemeni opposition, the Houthi. In addition to the US, British, French, Italian, Turkish, and Chinese bases in Djibouti, Saudi Arabia has a naval base in Massawa, UAE in Assab and its Dubai Ports World in Berbera (Somaliland) and Bossaso (Puntland). The latter had also been in Djibouti until the contact was unilaterally cancelled by the Djibouti authorities in February

2018, while China has a stake in a new Free Trade Zone (Financial Times 2018). In the meantime, Turkey has a planned base in Sudan's Red Sea port, Suakin, in response to which Egypt sent troops to a UAE base in Western Eritrea, in addition to concerns about Ethiopia's Grand Renaissance Dam on the Blue Nile close to the border with Sudan (Al Jazeera 2018). Turkey is also in Mogadishu, as is Qatar. The benefit of all this to the countries of the Horn comes from the financial inducements; for infrastructural and commercial investments locally, but requires diligent diplomacy in a context such as the Middle East where the expected return is often personal loyalty (De Waal, 2018). Behind everything is the USA which is not only militarily active in pushing back *al Shabaab* in Somalia but was instrumental behind the scenes in bringing Eritrea and Ethiopia together with the aid of Saudi Arabia and its ally, the UAE. US objectives are now not only confined to suppressing terrorism in the region but to countering the increasing influence of China on the global stage, as indicated herein Chinese development aid and the presence of a military base in Djibouti. Given all this, the regional ramifications of the conflict in Yemen, which at the nearest point is only some 30km from the Djibouti coast, presents the greatest external terrorist risk to the countries of the Horn should their alliance with Saudi Arabia and the UAE prompt the Houthi to resort to external terrorist practices, which would then add to existing threats from *al Shabaab*, though, as a Shia group, the Houthi are unlikely to form links with the Sunni *al Shabaab*.

## Conclusion

In one sense, the country is a victim of geography, located, along with its neighbours in the Horn, on the edges of one of the most volatile regions in the world, namely, the Middle East and its global geopolitics. Added to this is Ethiopia's own dependency on the same major sea channels used for Arabian oil exports, the Red and Arabian Seas, to which the country's lack of direct access exposes a vulnerability to potential terrorist disruption. Historical path dependence also permeates the politics of the present, especially the post-WWII settlement of national boundaries in the Horn, which in effect gave Italian Eritrea to Haile Selassie, and re-instated the British and Italian colonial boundaries as the basis for a new Somalia. Going even further back, the emperor Menelik's southern expansion in the late 19th century has left a long-standing legacy of discontent, often expressed violently over the years and directed both at the central state and between rival ethnicities, and which has only recently been realistically addressed, following the radical change of leadership in 2018. Serious regional challenges remain, however, as the various consequences of the 1974 revolution continue to work themselves out.

As the country approaches elections in 2020 with its first Oromo Prime Minister, it would be not only refreshing to see a generous relaxation of the 'securitisation' of development, as described in this paper, but also productive in the hopes that this would provide to those who have until now been excluded. Early indications are that the Prime Minister, Abiye Ahmed, and his new gender-mixed cabinet, appointed in October 2018, are intent on this. Such actions are also a powerful form of counterterrorism and entail more productive use of national resources.

## Postscript

The COVID-19 pandemic led the Government to postpone planned August 2020 elections until June 2021. The TPLF responded by declaring the government to be illegitimate after the original date had passed, and ran its own election. This and subsequent tensions have led to armed conflict in Tigray (as at end-November 2020) between government and TPLF forces. In January 2020 an amended, more precisely worded anti-terrorism law was introduced.

# References

Africa News, (2017a). Ethiopia jails four over planned terrorist attacks in Oromia state. Online: http://www.africanews.com/2017/11/25/ethiopia-jails-four-over-planned-terrorist-attacks-in-oromia-state/Accessed 01.11.18 at 10.56hrs.

Africa News, (2017b). Ethiopia to help retake strategic Somali town of Leego from Al-Shabaab. Online: http://www.africanews.com/2017/08/06/ethiopia-to-help-retake-strategic-somali-town-of-leego-from-al-shabaab/ Accessed 09.08.17 at 10.25hrs.

Al Jazeera, (2016). Abdirahman Mahdi of ONLF: 'Ethiopia is boiling': Senior leader of Ethiopia's Somali rebel group discusses a growing alliance of groups seeking self-determination. Online: http://www.aljazeera.com/programmes/talktojazeera/2016/05/ethnic-somali-abdirahman-mahdi-onlf-ethiopia-boiling-160507083254836.html. Accessed 29.05.17 at 21.15hrs.

Al Jazeera, (2016). Somalia raid: Al-Shabab says 43 Ethiopian troops killed. Online: http://www.aljazeera.com/news/2016/06/al-shabab-claims-killing-43-soldiers-ethiopian-base-160609061024588.html. Accessed 25.05.17 at 15.43hrs.

Al Jazeera, (2018). Ethiopia accuses Eritrea of trying to destabilise its security. Online: https://www.aljazeera.com/news/2018/03/ethiopia-accuses-eritrea-destablise-security-180318095126111.html. Accessed 25.03.18 at 14.17hrs.

Al Jazeera, (2018). Why are tensions rising in the Red Sea region?. Online: https://www.aljazeera.com/news/2018/01/tensions-rising-red-sea-region-180109064758337.html. Accessed 03.03.18 at 1109hrs.

Al Jazeera, (2018). Why the US is engineering political change in East Africa. Online: https://www.aljazeera.com/indepth/opinion/political-horn-africa-181009105638922.html. Accessed 10.10.2018 at 11.09hrs.

Amnesty International, (2016). Ethiopia: End use of counter-terrorism law to persecute dissenters and opposition members. Online: https://www.amnesty.org/en/latest/news/2016/06/ethiopia-using-counter-terrorism-law-to-persecute-dissenters/. Accessed 14.05.2017 at 1109hrs.

BBC News, (2002). Ethiopia links blast to Oromo rebels. Online: http://news.bbc.co.uk/1/hi/world/africa/2293185.stm. Accessed 29.05.2017 at 1625hrs.

BBC, (2018). Violence as troops deploy in Ethiopia's Somali region. Online: https://www.bbc.co.uk/news/world-africa-45070213. Accessed 20.08.18 at 17.46hrs.

Berhane, S. (2017). EU lists Ethiopia over money laundering" Fortune. Online: https://addisfortune.net/articles/eu-lists-ethiopia-over-money-laundering/. Accessed 21.02.18 at 12.34hrs.

Blakely, R. (2010). State terrorism in the social sciences. In R. Jackson et al. (Eds.), Contemporary state terrorism: Theory and practice. London:Routledge.

Brechenmacher, S. (2017). Civil Society Under Assault: Repression and Responses in Russia, Egypt, and Ethiopia. Chapter 4: Surveillance and State Control in Ethiopia. Washington, DC: Carnegie Endowment for International Peace.

Cannon, B. J. & Pkalya, D. R. (2017). Why al-Shabaab attacks Kenya: Questioning the narrative paradigm, terrorism and political violence. DOI: 10.1080/09546553.2017.1290607. Online: http://dx.doi.org/10.1080/09546553.2017.1290607. Accessed 25.05.17 at 12.17hrs.

Clapham, C. (2017). The Horn of Africa: State formation and decay. London: Hurst & Co.

Committee to Protect Journalists, (2017). Online: https://cpj.org/2015/04/10-most-censored-countries.php. Accessed 02.06.17 at 1945hrs.

De Waal, A. (2015). The Real Politics of the Horn of Africa: Money, War and the Business of Power. Cambridge, UK: Polity Press

De Waal, A. (2018). Beyond the Red Sea: A new driving force in the politics of the Horn. African Arguments, 11 July, 2018. Online: http://africanarguments.org/2018/07/11/beyond-red-sea-new-driving-force-politics-horn-africa/. Accessed 06.08.18 at 16.47hrs.

Dupuy, K. E. et al. (2015). Who survived? Ethiopia's regulatory crackdown on foreign-funded NGOs. Review of International Political Economy, 22(2), 419-456

Duvall, R., & Stohl, M. (1988). Governance by terror. In M. Stohl (Ed.), The politics of terror (3rd ed.). New York: Marke Dekker.

ESAT News, (2017). Al Shabaab ambushes Ethiopian troops. Online: https://ethsat.com/2017/05/al-shabaab-ambushes-ethiopian-troops/. Accessed 09.8.17 at 10.14hrs.

Ethiopian News Agency, (2018). Anti-terrorism law tabled for discussion. Online: https://www.ena.et/en/2018/08/18/anti-terrorism-law-tabled-for-discussion/. Accessed 20.10.18 at 16.54hrs.

Federal Democratic Republic of Ethiopia, (2009). *Anti-Terrorism Proclamation. Proclamation No. 652/2009.* Federal Negarit Gazeta.

Fente, H. (2016). Eritrea says more than 200 Ethiopians killed in border clash, Voice of America 16 June. Online: https://www.voanews.com/a/eritrea-says-more-than-200-ethiopians-killed-in-border-clash/3379175.html. Accessed 15.05.17 at 14.37hrs.

Financial Action Task Force, (2018). Improving global AML/CFT compliance: On-going process. Online: http://www.fatf-gafi.org/countries/a-c/bosniaandherzegovina/documents/fatf-compliance-february-2018.html. Accessed 12.03.18.

Financial Times, (2018). Djibouti row with DP World embodies Horn of Africa power struggle. Online: https://www.ft.com/content/bcaf5452-4f0e-11e8-ac41-759eee1efb74. Accessed 30.10.2018 at 13.04hrs.

Freedom House, Freedom of the Press, (2013). https://freedomhouse.org/report/freedom-ress/2013/ethiopia. Accessed 02.06.17 at 20.17hrs.

Gebresenbet, F. (2014). Securitisation of development in Ethiopia: the discourse and politics of developmentalism. *Review of African Political Economy.* 41(No. S1), S64–S74.

Gebrewold, B. (2009). *Anatomy of Violence: Understanding the Systems of Conflict and Violence in Africa.* Farnham, UK: Ashgate Publishing.

Goobjoob, (2018). IGAD to unveil regional counter terrorism centre. Online: http://goobjoog.com/english/igad-to-unveil-regional-counter-terrorism-centre/. Accessed 17.10.18. at 1300hrs.

Hagmann, T., & Abbink, J. (2011). Twenty years of revolutionary democratic Ethiopia, 1991 to 2011. *Journal of Eastern African Studies,* Vol.5(No.4), 579–595.

Hagmann, T. (2014). *"Punishing the periphery: legacies of state repression in the Ethiopian Ogaden",* Journal of Eastern African Studies . Vol8(No.4). 725-739

Human Rights Watch, (2009). "Analysis of Ethiopia's Draft Anti-Terrorism Law", Online: https://www.hrw.org/news/2009/06/30/analysis-ethiopias-draft-anti-terrorism-law. Accessed 23.06.17 at 1310hrs.

Human Rights Watch, (2017). Ethiopia: Events of 2016. Online: https://www.hrw.org/world-report/2017/country-chapters/ethiopia. Accessed 20.07.17 at 14.27hrs.

ICEPCVE, (2018). YALI Workshop. Amplifying the voices of young African leaders. Online: http://cve.igad.int/news/yali-workshop-13th-to-16th-november-2018-amplifying-the-voices-of-young-african-leaders. Accessed 29.10.18 at 15.50hrs.

IGAD, (2016). Al-Shabaab as a transnational security threat. Online: http://www.igadssp.org/index.php/documentation?task=document.viewdoc&id=4. Accessed 10.07.17 at 11.18 hrs.

IGAD, (2017). Communique of the 57th Extra-ordinary Session of the IGAD Council of Ministers on Djibouti and Eritrea. Online: https://igad.int/communique/1587-communique-of-the-57th-extra-ordinary-session-of-the-igad-council-of-ministers. Accessed on 10.06.17 at 09.59hrs.

IGAD, (2018). Online: https://www.igad.int/divisions/peace-and-security/1928-ethiopia-and-djibouti-meet-to-map-and-analyze-cross-border-security-threats-and-criminal-networks-between-the-dewele-and-tog-wajaale-corridor. Accessed 20.09.18 at 11.25hrs.

Jackson, R.et al. (2010). *Contemporary State Terrorism: Theory and Practice*Series: Critical Terrorism Studies. London:Routledge. .

Kassa, W. D. (2014). *"The Scope of Definition of a Terrorist Act under Ethiopian Law: Appraisal of its Compatibility with Regional and International Counter-terrorism Instruments".* Mizan Law Review, 8(2). December.371-405

Manek, M. (2018). Kenya boosts border security after Ethiopian rebels claim attack. Online: https://www.bloomberg.com/news/articles/2018-03-16/kenya-boosts-border-security-after-ethiopian-rebels-claim-attack. Accessed 29.03.18 at 17.05hrs.

Matfess, H. (2017). Ethiopia: Counter-terrorism legislation in Sub-Saharan Africa. *Small Wars Journal,* April 11, Online: http://smallwarsjournal.com/jrnl/art/ethiopia-counter-terrorism-legislation-in-sub-saharan-africa. Accessed 12.08.17 at 10.50hrs.

Mesfin, B. (2011). The Horn of Africa security complex. In R. Sharamo & B. Mesfin (Eds.), *Regional security in the post-Cold War Horn of Africa* (p. 178). Monograph: Institute for Security Studies.

Newsweek, (2017). Online: http://www.newsweek.com/qatar-crisis-eritrea-saudi-arabia-625356. Accessed 24.06.17 at 16.09hrs.

Oakland Institute and Environmental Defender Law Center, (2015). Ethiopia's anti-terrorism law: A tool to stifle dissent. Online: https://www.oaklandinstitute.org/sites/oaklandinstitute.org/files/OI_Ethiopia_Legal_Brief_final_web.pdf. Accessed 03.08.17 at 09.09hrs.

OECD, (2018). Development aid at a glance. Online: http://www.oecd.org/dac/stats/aid-at-a-glance.htm. Accessed 19.10.18 at 21.18hrs.

Pausewang, S., Tronvoll, K., & Aalen, L. (2002). *Ethiopia since the Derg: A decade of democratic pretension and performance.* London: Zed Books.

Pointing, S. & Whyte, D. (eds). (2012). Introduction: Counter-terrorism and the terrorist state, *Counter-terrorism and state political violence: The 'war on terror' as terror.* London and New York 2012: Routledge: Critical Terrorism Studies.

Reuters, (2017). Online: https://uk.reuters.com/article/uk-gulf-qatar-turkey-saudi-idUKKBN19D0CY. 22.June. Accessed 13.07.17 at 11.01hrs.

Reuters, (2017). Online: https://uk.reuters.com/article/uk-gulf-qatar-turkey-saudi-idUKKBN19D0CY. Accessed 25.07.17 at 21.30hrs.

The East African, (2016). East Africa: West must act to stop the Liyu police terror in Ogaden. Online: http://allafrica.com/stories/201607040435.html. Accessed 27.05.17 at 11.19hrs.

The Guardian (2011). Eritrea planned massive bomb attack on African Union summit, UN says. Online: https://www.theguardian.com/world/2011/jul/28/eritrea-planned-ethopia-bomb-attack. Accessed 29.05.2017 at 17.24hrs.

The Guardian, (2017). Gulf plunged into diplomatic crisis as countries cut ties with Qatar. Online: https://www.theguardian.com/world/2017/jun/05/saudi-arabia-and-bahrain-break-diplomatic-ties-with-qatar-over-terrorism. Accessed 06.06.17 at 16.46hrs.

The National, (2017). P&O Ports to develop in Puntland. Online: http://www.thenational.ae/business/economy/po-ports-to-develop-in-puntland. 6 April. Accessed 06.06.17 at 11.14hrs.

UN Security Council, (2016). "Letter dated 7 October 2016 from the Chair of the Security Council Committee pursuant to resolutions 751 (1992) and 1907 (2009) concerning Somalia and Eritrea addressed to the President of the Security Council. 31/10/2016. Section III."

UN Tribune, (2015). UN Report: UAE, Saudi using Eritrean land, sea, airspace and, possibly, Eritrean troops in Yemen battle. Online: http://untribune.com/un-report-uae-saudi-leasing-eritean-port-using-eritrean-land-sea-airspace-and-possibly-troops-in-yemen-battle/. Accessed 0.06.17 at 16.06hrs.

United States Commission on International Religious Freedom, (2015). USCIRF Condemns Trial Outcome of Ethiopian Muslim Leaders. Online: http://www.uscirf.gov/news-room/press-releases/uscirf-condemns-trial-outcome-ethiopian-muslim-leaders. Accessed 1.06.17 at 12.27hrs.

US Department of State, (2016). *Country reports on terrorism: Ethiopia 2016 (for 2015).* Online: https://www.state.gov/j/ct/rls/crt/267763.htm. Accessed 24.05.17 at 13.57hrs.

US Department of State, (2017). *Annual Report on Assistance Related to International Terrorism Fiscal Year 2016.*

US Department of State, (2017). Bureau of African Affairs. "US Relations with Ethiopia. Fact Sheet". Online: https://www.state.gov/r/pa/ei/bgn/2859.htm. Accessed 06.06.17 at 23.02hrs.

US Department of State (undated), Bureau of Counterterrorism and Countering Violent Extremism (undated). *Programs and Initiatives.* Online: https://www.state.gov/j/ct/programs/index.htm#TSI. Accessed 11.07.17 at 19.09 hrs.

Vaughan, S. (2015). Federalism, revolutionary democracy and the developmental state, 1991–2012. In G. Prunier & E. Ficquet (Eds.), *Understanding contemporary Ethiopia: Monarchy, revolution and the legacy of Meles Zenawi.* London: Hurst & Co.

Vaughan, S., & Gebremichael, M. (2011). *Rethinking business and politics in Ethiopia: The role of EFFORT, the Endowment Fund for the Rehabilitation of Tigray. Africa Power and Politics.* Research Report, August 2011 No.2.

Weiss, C., (2018). Shabaab targets Somali, African Union troops in southern Somalia. Online: https://www.longwarjournal.org/archives/2018/03/shabaab-targets-somali-african-union-troops-in-southern-somalia.php. Accessed 26.03.18 at 16.26hrs.

World Bank, (2017). Ethiopia: Economic Overview. Online: http://www.worldbank.org/en/country/ethiopia/overview. Accessed 12.08.17 at 10.06hrs.

# Part V
# Alternative perspectives

# 35

# Civil society, counterterrorism and counterinsurgency in Africa

*Ben U. Nwosu*

## Introduction

This chapter explores the association between civil society counterterrorism and counterinsurgency in Africa. The contradiction of connecting civil society with counterinsurgency and counterterrorism lies with the reason that the essence of civil society is characteristically at variance with both terrorism and insurgency. More so force applied majorly to counterterrorism and insurgency is far removed from the ideal civil character of civil society. Counterterrorism, just like counterinsurgency, is framed around the containment of two phenomena that are united by the application of violence which banishes civil society. Essentially, the state-centric and force-driven processes of eliminating the two phenomena indicate gaps that invite consideration for the presence of civil society.

While terrorism and insurgency are by no means new phenomena, the post 9/11 period has witnessed their phenomenal rise and extension to regions that did not have much of their prevalence in the past. The Global Terrorism Index (GTI) reports the total number of deaths from terrorism between 2000 and 2015 to be 15,538 (Global Terrorism Index, 2017). Terror is said to be centralised in the Middle East and North African (MENA) region, followed by South Asia and Sub-Saharan Africa. These three regions together constitute 84% of recent terrorist attacks and 95% of deaths. Further, in the global terrorist index, there are 13 African states among the worst affected 30 states in the GTI. While the death toll is reported to be decreasing from terrorism, there is a record of increasing spread of terrorism in Sub-Saharan Africa (see Global Terrorism Index, 2017) especially the lake Chad Basin. Precisely, *Boko Haram* terrorism is spreading beyond the borders of its originating country, Nigeria. Therefore, it is timely to consider a research interest that addresses the relevance of civil society to anti-terrorism and anti-insurgency. This is more so because force-centered, state-driven methods do not address the entire dimensions of terrorism and insurgency.

Containment of terrorism and insurgency with the force of the political state usually leads to a few likely outcomes, among which three stand out. The first is the total destruction of the terrorist insurgency. The second is a partial defeat of terrorism in which the state holds a superior margin of power but could not stop a re-emergence of terrorism/insurgency like the Nigerian case with *Boko Haram*. The third kind of outcome is state failure arising via a triumph of terrorism and or insurgency. Sometimes an insurgent terrorist group could establish a new state having sacked the preceding regime. This was the case in Afghanistan when the *Talibans* defeated the sitting government in Kabul and established a theocratic state and when one of the factions in the Somali conflict achieves military victory over others and momentarily dominates the major cities. The two instances of state failure also go side by side with the abdication of the ethos of civil society. The key thesis of this chapter is that civil society has a contradictory connection with counterinsurgency and counterterrorism because it is open to the forces working to either promote or reverse the two phenomena. Thus, following this introduction, the other sections of the chapter include, a cursory tour of the meaning of civil society to find linkages with insurgency and terrorism; an examination of the two-way connection between civil society, anti-terrorism and anti-insurgency; case presentation of the experiences of civil society in anti-terrorism and anti-insurgency and finally, the conclusion.

## Civil society, counterterrorism and counterinsurgency

Establishing the connection between civil society, anti-terrorism and anti-insurgency warrants another cursory look at the concept of civil society to see possible meeting points. Civil society's meaning presents a tangle of confusion due to the multiplicity of meanings and definitions of the concept (Nwosu, 2014). The structure and agency-centred approaches to civil society will be applied as an analytic framework. The rationale for this approach is that each of the paths to the civil society concept opens essential perspectives to the idea. But the point needs to be made that even in structural views of civil society, it is possible to find elements of the agency-centred perspective. For instance, Young (2000) sees it as an arena where distinct kinds of activities occur across a range of private, political, and civic associations and networks (cited in Hendriks, 2006). Although the arena or structure tends to stand out here, there is equally an effort to show what happens in that arena which draws in the agency in the form of interacting social forces. Adam Ferguson's (1980)*Essay on the History of Civil society* also presents a structural viewpoint on the idea because the human transformation from barbarism to law-governed contract order established a civil order which provides the context of interaction in a framework provided by the law. But the structure or framework is incomplete in thinking about civil society because, in the first place, the creation of that structure is a product of dynamics of social forces (agency) who collectively set up civilised contexts in the form of institutional framework to guide social relations. Not only that the structure is framed by agency, but it is also the agency of social forces that give meaning to the civilised contexts of engagement that they have created. They accord meaning to the institutions by providing them legitimacy and preserving them. When for instance we think about Non-Governmental Organisations, political parties, Faith-Based groups, schools, and other expressions of civil society concept, we know that these are contexts of relations in which social forces seek to reflect the moral essence of society either by enabling preservation of existing ethos or moving the community towards a better standard of civility. Thus, the agency of social forces is as essential as their structure of action.

Alexis de Tocqueville's *Democracy in America* dwells on the importance of social forces (agency-centred approach), one of which finds expression in associational forms of civil society. Such form of civil society supports engagement with the state's political authority for the maintenance of civil society's link with freedom (Tocqueville, 2002). This constructs civil society as one of the intellectual reactions to the dangers of the absolutist state (Ekeh, nd). Similar to the support of associational forms as a bulwark for the defence of freedom is the phenomenon of social capital which Putnam (1995) presented as a facilitator of the ethos of democracy and development using empirical cases from Italian public life. In both Tocqueville and Putnam, the activities of social agents form the pivot of change or preservation in favour of freedom and other moral imperatives of civil society.

Nonetheless, what the writers do not appear to acknowledge, is the character that civil society is likely to bear as times unfold. It was out of the question for them to imagine placing civil society side by side with eruptions of terrorism and insurgency. Thus, a direct answer to how civil society connects to clearly lawless phenomena that could overwhelm the established institutions which are supposed to respond to them is not easy to locate in Tocqueville and Putnam. Essentially, terrorism and insurgency contrast the essence of civil society. But, curiously, some of the terrorist and insurgent activities emanate from faith-based groups which are supposed to be part of the contexts of civil society. A sort of problem arises in thinking about the contrasting relationships of these phenomena. The new thinking in the containment of terrorism advocates the involvement of civil society which provides contexts and narratives that seem to support a breach of security — such a paradox of juxtaposing civil society and terror warrants a discursive engagement.

It is instructive that most of the terror groups in Africa operate from the background of religion. Some of the more notorious ones include *Boko Haram* operating in Nigeria, Cameroon, Niger, Chad and the Northern tip of Central African Republic; Al-Qaeda in the Maghreb (AQIM), which operates in Northern Mali, Mauritania; the Movement for Unity and Jihad in West Africa (MUJAO); the *Janjaweed* of Southern Sudan. The central objective of these terrorist groups is to do away with Western civilisation and restore classical Islam. *Al-Shabaab* and other terror groups are sources of menace to Somalia and the horn of Africa, AQIM threatens peace in North Africa and has links in parts of Sub-Saharan Africa while Boko Haram presents security challenges to the Lake Chad Basin (Nkwi, 2015; Ray, 2016; International Crisis Group, 2017).

In responding to *Boko Haram* terrorism, the Economic Community of West African States (ECOWAS) established the Abuja Commission following a terrorist attack in a Nigerian high school, Government Secondary School Buni Yadi, on 24 February 2014 which led to the death of about 50 students. The commission is to cooperate with all members states of ECOWAS and other partners in the struggle against terror. Lake Chad Basin Commission (LCBC) also declared that the basin is exposed to insecurity because of *Boko Haram*'s grave threat for which a joint action was necessary (see Nkwi, 2015).

The actions of ECOWAS and Lake Chad Basin Commission conform with the spirit of cooperation contained in the United Nation's counterterrorism strategy adopted in 2006 by the General Assembly. The Global strategy of the United Nations aims to integrate different pillars of counterterrorism policies to ensure a comprehensive approach in combating terrorism. The four pillars of the Global strategy include: (1) Measures to address the conditions conducive to the spread of terrorism (2) Measures to prevent and combat terrorism (3) Measures to build state capacity to prevent and combat terrorism and to strengthen the role of the UN system in this regard (4) Measures to ensure respect for human rights for all and the rule of law as the fundamental basis of the fight against terrorism (Ginkel, 2012). Ginkel noted that UN resolutions on countering terrorism do not refer to the importance of cooperation with civil society in countering terrorism. However, one of the four pillars of the Global strategy invites the role of civil society. For the first pillar of Global Strategy, for instance, the range of processes for counter-narratives that support terrorism and assist in de-radicalisation creates a fitting role for civil society. Terrorism and the violence accompanying it can throw up conditions for further growth of the ranks of terror agents. For instance, forceful recruitment and spread of messages that stimulate radicalisation to swell up the ranks of terrorists are common strategies of terrorist groups. This process is critical in the growth of terrorism because violence creates fear and to sustain the conditions that enable terrorist aims to be actualised, victims are brainwashed and coerced into accepting the message of the terrorists to join in actualising their objectives. As Eric Fromm reasoned in *Escape from Freedom*, victims under menace may surrender their individuality and integrity to conform to a life-threatening condition to survive. Yet, they fail to achieve a solution that leads to happiness and positive freedom (Fromm, 1941). It is under this condition that civil society provides an appropriate context for countering narratives of radicalisation to prevent a breakdown of the moral fabric of society. However, there are instances where it has assumed security roles enlarged beyond counter-narratives against terrorism and insurgency. Civil society watchman-ship through vigilantism in the Lake Chad Basin would be an essential empirical presentation in a later section of this chapter.

Hegel had addressed what he called police duties which he assigned to civil society. Hegel's use of the concept of police is broader than the contemporary idea of the concept. Actually, it has to do with 'surveillance' (linked to crime and tort), intervention in the economy in the form of price controls and regulation of major industrial branches and public welfare in the form of education, charity, public works and founding of colonies (Cohen & Arato, 1992, p.104). To Hegel, actualising the right of a particular individual has to do with two factors including removal of all fortuitous hindrances on property and security of individual's subsistence and happiness (see Hegel, 2001a). This formulation implies a level of responsibility by civil society in maintaining socio-economic security of members of the society. Hegel's take on civil society and security was reinforced by Marx's observation that "security is the highest social concept of civil society, the concept of police, expressing the fact that the whole of society exists only to guarantee to each of its members the preservation of his person, his rights and his property. It is in this sense that Hegel calls civil society "the state of need and reason" (Marx, 1844: 12–13). Hegel and Marx carved a clear place for civil society in the security architecture of society.

In a related vein, Gramsci's work which does not directly address the role of civil society around security volunteers implicit support for state civil society coordination for the protection of the state when he argued that where the state and civil society have a proper relation when the state is threatened, a sturdy structure of civil society which acts to protect the state is revealed. According to Gramsci (1971), the state represents only an outer ditch behind which there stands a robust system of fortresses and earthworks. These earthworks in Gramsci's idea are analogous to the norms of civil society that include, among other things, the generalisation of conditions for security. In any moment of stress to the state, social forces in civil society have a duty to act on the side of these norms to complement the state in regaining its major reason for existence is the maintenance of security and support of citizens' freedom. Gramsci's perspective further reflects Hegel's thought in section 249 and 250 of *The Philosophy of Right* that the Universal (state) which is contained in the particularity of civil society (the civic community) is realised and preserved by police duties for the preservation of the private interests that exist in the state (Hegel, 2001b).

The major debate that arises out of a side by side placement of civil society with two major security concerns - insurgency and terrorism has to do with first, whether civil society should be concerned with physical security role instead of actions to promote norms that support security. Secondly, the preceding articulations on civil society tend to project it as being free from the character of the state and society at each point in time whereas the character of the state actually reflects the quality of civil society. In the first point, civil society does not necessarily disappear because of actors in its resort to using physical actions to protect the society from the grave menace. Civic vigilantism which expresses direct involvement in physical security is an important form of direct community action against Boko Haram terrorism. Organised community groups in parts of North-East Nigeria were formed to support conventional security forces. The groups provide useful intelligence and guide soldiers around the local terrains for easy anti-terrorist operations. In some instances, however, they had been allowed to carry arms (International Crisis Group, 2017). A crucial point of concern here is about the import of arms used by a supposedly civic group despite the existence of conventional security forces.

Before we dismiss civility due to the application of physical resistance to insurgent terrorism, there is a need to understand the ecology of insecurity and how it affects civil society in each circumstance. A pertinent reference material to serve as a corollary for addressing the circumstance of civil society in the areas affected by terrorist insurgency is Meagher's (2007) work in another Nigerian situation where security was under significant threat. Meagher's study explained the background to the rise of the vigilante group called the *Bakassi Boys* in Eastern Nigeria. The group was formed to provide security against armed robbery attacks on informal shoe manufacturers in Aba Abia state Nigeria. Bakassi Boys clearly had an anti-crime mandate and rose because "the police and judiciary are no longer able to protect citizens and have therefore lost all respect…" (Harnischfeger, 2003 cited in Meagher, 2007: 90). The story of civic vigilantism in the North East equally rose against the background of graver security issues of terrorism and insurgency. Like the Bakassi Boys story, it could be grounded on the same institutional weakness of the state in guaranteeing security. Communities of the North East were infiltrated and used for refuge and human shields by terrorists so that military actions against the terror group resulted in heavy collateral damages for several communities. Responding to the limitations of the military in protecting their communities, robbery and punitive attacks by the *Boko Haram* members against the communities for assisting the soldiers against the terror group, the communities began to form vigilante actions against *Boko Haram*. For the aspect of occasionally bearing arms, it is almost inevitable considering the level of sophistication of the insurgent terrorists in military engagements. Hence, the form of civic vigilantism in North-East Nigeria against *Boko Haram* does not dissolve civil society.

The second note I made on the discussions above is that civil society is projected as if it lacks original sin, uninvolved in unethical and violent relations. Incidentally, this is one point where a consensus is not possible on the civil society concept. In fact, some writers have like Nwosu (2014), Chambers and Kopstein (2001), Ikelegbe (2001), Hassan (2009), and Fatton (1995) draw attention to the more profound complexity of civil society which requires that it should be understood in its plurality rather than as a homogenous space. These writers see that civil society is not exclusively about the articulation of ethical norms since it is only a space of action by social forces. This space is available to the good, the bad and the ugly. In fact, it has the face of a Janus. Chambers and Kopstein (2001) drew attention to "bad civil" society exemplified with suicidal religious sects and racist groups.

Similar misapplication of civil society includes how it advances the entrenchment of authoritarianism in contestation against democratic forces in civil society (see also Nwosu, 2013, 2014). The same civil society was also the space appropriated by the Nazi party in Germany to articulate racial supremacy that led to a severe human catastrophe in World War II. Other genres in the form of movements of political Islam represent a challenge to the development of society. There is in fact the need to note that the very context explored by Boko Haram and other religion-driven terrorism belongs to civil society. Gramsci (1971) clearly demonstrated that the press, the church, and schools are contexts of civil society for articulating hegemony for the political state. But some of the contexts (especially that of religion), sometimes get overrun by forces which are not only against the state but also against the very norms of the religions they claim to act in its name. Accordingly, civil society is also susceptible to infiltration and is indeed infiltrated by forces working against citizen security, including terrorist groups. In this connection, Howell (2011) remarked about the Middle Eastern experience, that following the post 9/11 global security regime, some charities and NGOs working in the Middle East, conflict countries, Muslim-majority countries and Muslim organisations were singled out for particular attention arising from the fear of their possible connection, promotion and funding of terror groups. The thinking behind this is that the global security climate that trailed 9/11 deepened the fracturing of civil society into 'bad' parts that need to be surveyed, contained and prohibited while the "good" part could be courted and deployed for security purposes. Some of the "bad" features, according to Howell, include those prohibited and put on the terrorist list and those that could be potentially "bad." This trend resonated in Africa because in Kenya, several Muslim charities were closed following the 1998 Kikambala bombings (USIP 2006 cited in Howell, 2011).

To synthesise the relationship of civil society with counterterrorism and counterinsurgency (CT-COIN), it is imperative to note that as much as civil society conveys a sense of civic virtue, it also needs to be understood in its ambiguous nature: the susceptibility of its space to inter-loping non-civic elements. Therefore, civil society is connected to terrorism and insurgency in two different ways – non-civic forces appropriate its space to promote bad outcomes while civil elements organise for good from the same contexts. Hence, counterterrorism and counterinsurgency are related to the activities of groups committed to the promotion of civic virtue and eradication of the insecurity and large-scale violence associated with insurgency and terrorism. For the empirical study of civil society engagement with counterterrorism and counterinsurgency, this chapter examines the on-going case of Boko Haram which though originated in Nigeria, but is a major source of menace to the entire Lake Chad Basin comprising Nigeria, Cameroun, Niger and Chad. The Chapter equally considers the connection of civil society with CT-COIN funding in Africa.

## Civil society and ambivalent connections with counter terrorism and counter insurgency (CT-COIN)

As noted above, two associations are traceable to the sphere of civil society and the phenomena of terrorism and insurgency. The first connection is one which projects the civil character of the civil society illustrated with the commitment of actors in the space to counter both the basis of violence and violence itself which unites insurgency and terrorism. The other connection that sets out the ambivalence of civil society is the appropriation of the space to facilitate insurgency and terrorism.

With regard to how civil society directly engages in CT-COIN initiatives, the reports of the ICG (2017) note that vigilante groups in Nigeria, Cameroon, Niger, and Chad play major roles in the fight against *Boko Haram*. Their contribution in this regard is covered under the rubric of civic vigilantism which is vital in thinking about civil society's security role in states where formal security institutions are too weak to protect the citizens (Pratten, 2008; Meagher, 2007). The six necessary features of vigilantism by Johnston (1996) not only provide a vivid con-ceptualisation but also draw vigilantism into the circuit of civil society discourse, and they include:

> (i) it involves planning and premeditation by those engaging in it; (it) its participants are private citizens whose engagement is voluntary; (iii) it is a form of 'autonomous citizen-ship' and, as such, constitutes a social movement; (iv) it uses or threatens the use of force; (v) it arises when an established order is under threat from the transgression, the potential transgression, or the imputed transgression of institutionalized norms; (vi) it aims to control

crime or other social infractions by offering assurances (or 'guarantees') of security both to participants and to others (Johnston, 1996: 220).

It is instructive that the above conception of vigilantism embraces the social movement idea, the notion of voluntarism, identity with restoration or preservation of certain norms of civil society and of course indicates that it is a place of solidarity of a group for a common cause. Often, most local vigilantism in Africa is formed on Johnston's framework. Regarding the Lake Chad Basin experience on vigilantism, the four countries involved, Nigeria, Cameroun, Niger, and Chad have had a history of local community organising for security. But the culmination of civic action against *Boko Haram* commenced in what could be termed a spontaneous response to a major threat to the lives and livelihoods of local people across various communities. In a detailed account provided by International Crisis Group (ICG International Crisis Group, 2017), the anti-Boko Haram vigilantism has its provenance in Maiduguri Nigeria in early 2013 when Baba Jafar Lawan who is a trader from the Hausari district of Maiduguri town went after a *Boko Haram* militant with a stick, captured and delivered him to the authorities. Subsequently, others joined him in patrolling the Hausari district. Several suspected *Boko Haram* members were handed over to the authorities while crowds brutally killed some. By the middle of 2013, about 500 vigilantes were manning city checkpoints armed with sticks and cutlasses and became known as the Civilian Joint Task Force (CJTF). The name derives from the Joint Task Force (JTF) which is the nomenclature of the coordinated operations of the Police, Army and other security outfits that fight *Boko Haram* in Borno state. CJTF is said to make military operations less blunt and more effective. Despite its contribution to mitigating the Boko Haram menace, vigilantism contributed to turning an insurgency that was basically against the state into a bloodier encounter that pits Boko Haram against communities, thereby increasing the scale of violence.

Local anger against *Boko Haram* was fuelled by several factors. Security officers, government officials and Islamic clerics critical of *Boko Haram* were threatened and assassinated by the jihadists who also extorted wealthier members of the community. The other factor that deepened the anguish of the people and compelled their collective action against terrorism is that security forces were brutal in implementing collective punishment when soldiers and policemen were killed. They burnt homes, carried out a mass arrest of young males and their commanders were not addressing these abuses of rights. In addition, the Federal government-imposed state of emergency that included a shutdown of phone services from May to December 2013. The effect of this was quite harsh on the traders. As a result, the city inhabitants decided to fight *Boko Haram* rather than be killed by soldiers who could not distinguish them from other youths. Army's retaliation that involved collateral damages were said to be a strategy to compel the residents to cooperate in exposing *Boko Haram* insurgents (International Crisis Group, 2017).

The success of CJTF in Maiduguri led the Borno state authorities in helping the spread of its model by encouraging other communities to form vigilante groups. Vigilante forces also spread in other north-eastern states as *Boko Haram* terror continued to spread. In Yola capital of Adamawa state, there was a mobilisation of hunter brotherhoods, and they helped the army take back the cities of Gombe and Mubi in Adamawa state. In the same Adamawa state, the Kanuri minority formed its own 300 men CJTF. The reason was to preserve their lives and livelihood and show that not all Kanuri were *Boko Haram* members despite the top hierarchy and many of the membership drawing from the Kanuri ethnic group (see International Crisis Group, 2017).

The CJTF model also spread to Nigeria's neighbours, Cameroon, and Chad, when *Boko Haram* stepped up activities in those areas. The affected states did not have sufficient security infrastructure and personnel to deal with the crises. About 16,000 vigilantes are said to be on duty in Cameroon's far north (International Crisis Group, 2017). After the attack in Chad's capital N'Djamena, in February 2015, the authorities advised some local villages to create their own vigilantes. We need to take note of the issue of autonomy in civic organising and this would appear to be lost in cases where the state initiates the organising. In the case of Niger Republic, the fear of the potentials for the misuse of the vigilante political purposes and the fuelling of ethnic tensions made the authorities resist it and made use of informant networks. But vigilante groups later formed in some of the insecure areas such as Bagara and Toumour (International Crisis Group, 2017).

The vigilantes are found to have been especially useful operationally given their better understanding of the local terrain (social or physical). They have a better sense of the normal and the abnormal locally and easily detect threats in their environments. Besides, they fill the gap of language skills which could be a setback for the military. Their contributions in CT-COIN campaigns in the Lake Chad Basin have earned them high commendations (International Crisis Group, 2017).

The civil society context presents a feeble platform in terms of counter-radical narratives and de-radicalisation processes. It only has space in a vertical approach of the government that involves a lot of other partners in which the context of religion is targeted for the training of clerics who can provide robust and critical rebuttals of extremist Islamic narratives and ideology (Akilu, 2015). Also, the press, which is another crucial context of civil society provides editorials on the need for de-radicalisation, while the electronic media broadcast anti-terror security caution. In all, there is no systematically developed independent civil society framework with a core mandate that focuses on counter-radicalisation and de-radicalisation processes. Perhaps the inadequacy of the roles of civic groups in this regard is what leaves gaps for narratives that foster the growth of terror. These narratives happen around religious settings, as Omale (2013) observed concerning hate and incendiary preaching in religious places.

The openness of the civic sphere is exploited in other ways that undermine counterterrorism efforts. The associational realm in the form of Non-Governmental Organisations and Charities is quite susceptible in this regard. In a series of investigation and reports by the Financial Action Task Force (FATF) on West Africa, some NGOs were found to have several subtle ways of funding insurgency and terrorism and West Africa. Below is a summary of two few cases:

## Case I: NGO work and dangers of terror connections

An international NGO/Charity with headquarter in the Middle East opened a bank account in Nigeria. While carrying out due diligence in the organisation, the bank discovered that the organisation and one of its directors had been indicted in a case involving terrorist financing in two countries. Further analysis of the organisations bank statements and transactions established that transactions of the NGO were inconsistent with the profiles of its accounts — there had been frequent cash deposits and withdrawals including those from domestic ATMs by individuals with no apparent connection to the organisation and mostly in areas with a high incidence of terrorist activities within Nigeria. Also, the NGO received cash deposits from multiple branches of the same bank while transfers were wired from a country known to be a state sponsor of terrorism and these transfers came from the NGOs headquarters in the Middle East

Investigations equally revealed that the NGO was affiliated with another NGO known to have supported terrorist groups, including *Al-Qaeda, Hamas,* and *Jama' al-Islamiyya,* an Algerian terrorist group. Frequency of withdrawals from the accounts of the NGO in the states known for Boko Haram activities raised concerns about the ultimate use of the funds. At the same time, the organisation claimed to be paying the salaries of itinerant Islamic clerics in Nigeria (Financial Action Task Force, 2013).

## Case II: NGO work and the dangers of terror currency remittance

A Non-Profit Organisation (NPO) based in Bamenda, the capital of the north-west region of Cameroon, received several Western Union transfers from entities in various African countries. Over a period of six months in 2013 and 2014, the NPO received CFA 10 million from a number of ordering customers in African countries. Investigations revealed that the funds were sent to support illegal migrants. But local authorities denied that there were illegal migrants in Bamenda or any associations supporting them. Within this same period, militants of Boko Haram had infiltrated Cameroon through the north-west region claimed to be migrants. Thirty persons that were arrested and detained for suspicion of belonging to Boko Haram carried illegal national identity cards. Also, the promoter of the Non-Profit Organisation was found to have forged Cameroonian national identity card even though he was a Burkinabe. He refused to provide an explanation for the purpose of the remitted funds (Financial Action Task Force, 2016).

Similar FATF reports (2016) from Mali and Niger also point to the use of NPOs for the illicit wiring of funds that service terrorist and insurgency networks. One such instance was found to promote insurgency in Mali. Such use of aspects of civil society shows that as a solitary sphere, it sometimes permits aims which in the end contradict civic virtue.

The analytic imports of the above case studies are that while they can be powerful CT-COIN ally, civil society (NGOs) can also be conduits for terror financing. Thus, civil society can support either civil or uncivil (violence) articulations and outcomes depending on the actors involved and their motives. What stands out here is the ambivalence of civil society in connection with CT – COIN. It is amenable to actors with contrasting objectives, including those that undermine the moral essence of civil society.

## Conclusion

This chapter considered the connection between civil society, counterterrorism and counterinsurgency. The core of its argument is that ambivalence characterises civil society's linkage with counterterrorism and counterinsurgency. The reason is that civil society is bifurcated by the dialectics of engagement between good and bad social forces both of which seek to dominate the space and use it to establish their aims in society. The paper began with reckoning the contrariness civil society, terrorism and insurgency and recognition of the distance between the dominant state-centric force-oriented counterterrorism and counterinsurgency approaches with the norms of civil society. However, it identified the gap in the dominant approaches, which is that force alone can only secure temporary victory in counterinsurgency and counterterrorism efforts. Hence, there arises an inevitable opening for civil society. The opening is at the various points where the soft power of counter-narratives is necessary to dilute messages and conditions that promote radicalisation and swell the ranks of violent extremists and insurgents. Beyond the relevance of civil society for projecting the soft power of counter-narratives against radicalisation, new forms of organising are arising in civil society in response to terrorism and insurgency, namely, civic vigilantism which warrants direct participation of volunteers in community security. A culmination of civic vigilantism is the Civilian Joint Task Force (CJTF) in Nigeria against Boko Haram which comprises a plethora of loosely organised, lightly-armed, semi-autonomous gangs that provide vanguard force for community policing and act as auxiliary and intelligence units for military's CT-COIN campaigns. These groups enjoy partial support of the armed forces in terms of finance, training, and ordinance support. This model is replicated in diverse ways in the other Lake Chad Basin countries of Cameroon, Niger, and Chad.

The appropriation of sinister social forces illustrates the ambivalence of civil society with Non-Governmental Organisations that serve as channels for funding terrorism. Besides, religion as a context that is a target for counter-radicalisation strategies is shown in some instances to continue to be used for disseminating extremist views that could feed terrorism and insurgency.

## References

Akilu, F. (2015). Hope, challenges and opportunity: Nigeria's strategy to counter violent extremism. In K. Khalid & T. Thorp (Eds). *How to prevent extremism and policy options*. Available in http://tonyblairfaithfoundation.org/sites/default/files/How%20to%20Prevent_Global%20Perspectives%20Vol%202_0.pdf. Accessed 11.08.17.

Chambers, S., & Kopstein, J. (2001). Bad civil society. *Political Theory, 29*(6), 837–865.

Cohen, J., & Arato, A. (1992). *Civil society and political theory.* Cambridge: MIT Press.

Ekeh, P. (nd). Civil society and the construction of freedom in African history. Conference keynote address, University of New York at Buffalo. Available in http://www.waado.org/nigerian_scholars/archive/pubs/triatlantic3.htm Accessed 17.06.16.

FATF (Financial Action Task Force). (2013). Terrorist financing in West Africa. *FATF Report*, October. Available in http://www.fatf-gafi.org/media/fatf/documents/reports/tf-in-west-africa.pdf. Accessed 13.08.17.

FATF (Financial Action Task Force). (2016). *Terrorist Financing in West and Central Africa, FATF Report*, October. Available in http://www.fatf-gafi.org/media/fatf/documents/reports/Terrorist-Financing-West-Central-Africa.pdf Accessed 13.08.17.

Fatton, R. Jr. (1995). Africa in the age of democratisation: The civic limitations of civil society. *African Studies Review, 38*(2), 67–99.

Ferguson, A. (1980). *An essay on the history of civil society.* New Brunswick: Transaction Publishers.

Fromm, E. (1941). *Escape from freedom.* New York: Farrar and Rinehart Inc.

Ginkel, B. V. (2012). *Engaging civil society in countering violent extremism: experiences with the UN Global counter-terrorism strategy, Research Paper*, August, International Centre for Counter-Terrorism, The Hague. Available in https://www.icct.nl/download/file/ICCT-Van-Ginkel-Civil-Society-in-CVE-August-2012.pdf Accessed 13.08.17.

Global Terrorism Index. (2017). *Global Terrorism Index 2016.* Sydney: Institute for Economics and Peace. Available in http://economicsandpeace.org/wp-content/uploads/2016/11/Global-Terrorism-Index-2016.2.pdf Accessed 31.07.17.

Gramsci, A. (1971). *Selections from prison notebooks.* London: Lawrence and Wishart.

Hassan, H. A. R. (2009). The state and civil society in Africa: A North African perspective. *African Journal of Political Science and International Relations, 3*(2), 066–076.

Hegel, G. W. F. (2001a). *Philosophy of right.* Kitchener Ontario: Batoche Books. Available in http://www.efm.bris.ac.uk/het/hegel/right.pdf Accessed 16.07.17.

Hegel, G. W. F. (2001b). *The philosophy of history.* Kitchener, Ontario: Batoche Books. Available in http://socserv.mcmaster.ca/~econ/ugcm/3ll3/hegel/history.pdf Accessed 10.07.17.

Hendriks, C. M. (2006). Integrated deliberation: Reconciling civil society's dual role in deliberative democracy. *Political Studies, 54*, 486–508.

Howell, J. (2011). *The securitisations of civil society post-9/11. Draft paper ECPR Joint Session st Gallen.* Available in https://ecpr.eu/Filestore/PaperProposal/c74aeab6-3cff-4d1a-8a1b-25695c776e3d.pdf Accessed 28.06.17.

Ikelegbe, J. (2001). The perverse manifestations of civil society: Evidence from Nigeria. *Journal of Modern African Studies, 39*(1), 1–24.

ICG (International Crisis Group). (2017). *Watchmen of Lake Chad Basic: Vigilante groups fighting Boko Haram, Africa Report* No 244, February. Available in https://www.crisisgroup.org/africa/west-africa/nigeria/244-watchmen-lake-chad-vigilante-groups-fighting-boko-haram Accessed 29.06.17.

Johnston, L. (1996). What is vigilantism? *The British Journal of Criminology, 36*(2), 220–236.

Marx, K. (1844). *On the Jewish Question (1844).* Deutsch-Franzosische Jahrbucher. Available in http://www.marxists.org/archive/marx/works/download/pdf.On%20The%20Jewish%20Question.pdf Accessed 10.07.17.

Meagher, K. (2007). Hijacking civil society: The inside story of Bakassi Boys vigilante group of south-eastern Nigeria. *Journal of Modern African Studies, 45*(1), 89–115.

Nkwi, W. G. (2015). Terrorism in West African History: A 21st century appraisal. *Austral: Brazillian Journal of Strategy & International Relations, 4*(8), 78–99.

Nwosu, B. U. (2014). Two faces of civil society and the military in Nigeria's democratisation. *Research on Humanities and Social Sciences, 4*(13), 153–163.

Nwosu, B. U. (2013). State, civil society and political change: The dialectics of democratisation in Nigeria (Thesis, (PhD)). University of Waikato, Hamilton, New Zealand. Available in http://hdl.handl.net/10289/8636 Accessed 12.04.15.

Omale, D. J. (2013). Terrorism and counter-terrorism in Nigeria: Theoretical paradigms and lessons for public policy. *Canadian Social Science, 9*(3), 96–103.

Pratten, D. (2008). The Politics of protection: Perspectives on vigilantism in Nigeria. *Africa, 78*(1), 1–15.

Putnam, R. (1995). Bowling alone: America's declining social capital. *Journal of Democracy, 6,* 65–78.

Ray, N. (2016). Growing threat of terrorism in Africa: The case of Boko Haram, *Indian Council of World Affairs,* Issue Brief, February. http://icwa.in/pdfs/IB/2014/GrowingThreatofTerrorisminAfricaIB20022016.pdf Accessed 18.07.17.

Tocqueville, A. de (2002). *Democracy in America* (Vols. 1 & 2). Pennsylvania: Pennsylvania State University. Available in http://seas3.elte.hu/coursematerial/LojkoMiklos/Alexis-de-Tocqueville-Democracy-in-America.pdfAccessed 22.07.17.

# 36

# Humanitarian aid and terrorism in the Sahel

## Preventing or fuelling conflicts?

*Marc-Antoine Pérouse de Montclos*

## Introduction

Some analysts see humanitarian aid as a way to "win the hearts and minds" of the people against insurgent and terrorist groups in Africa. However, this chapter shows that their expectations rely on false assumptions and a simplistic understanding of conflict dynamics. First, it is believed that deprivation and illiteracy are the main drivers of terrorism, a hypothesis that needs further investigation. Secondly, it is supposed that foreign aid effectively reduces poverty and ignorance, which is another area of contest. Finally, it is alleged that relief helps secure social peace. Yet foreign aid can exacerbate the competition for resources and prolong conflicts. Moreover, integrated interventions that attempt to combine humanitarian and military operations are quite difficult to implement.

Historically, the use of foreign aid for security purposes came from two main currents of thought that gradually emerged during the 19th century. The first one, which was inspired by philanthropy and liberalism, aims at saving people in danger and supports the concept of armed interventions carried out for the benefit of humanity. The second one, of military origin, developed during the colonial period and aimed at "winning the hearts and minds" of the inhabitants of occupied territories through social actions. It gained momentum during decolonisation, this time in a counterinsurgency effort that was akin to a "psychological war" for the British in Malaysia in the 1940s, the French in Algeria in the 1950s, and the Americans in Vietnam in the 1960s.

These two currents finally met at the end of the Cold War when the UN increased its peacekeeping operations around the world. Following the failures of the international community in Somalia, Angola, and Rwanda in the 1990s, the concept of a "responsibility to protect", or "R2P", then recycled in Libya in 2011 the old principle of a right of humanitarian intervention, which infringed on national sovereignties and permitted the use of force to save lives (Boisson de Chazournes & Condorelli, 2005). The 2001 Al-Qaeda attacks in New York also reframed the civil-military actions of the decolonisation period in terms of a "global war on terror." In Africa, strategies that mix the use of force and social action now target jihadist groups throughout the Sahel, from Somalia to Mali or Northern Nigeria.

However, not everyone agrees on the merits of foreign aid to fight terrorist insurgencies. "Military-cum-humanitarian" interventions are heavily criticised for their combined—or "integrated"—approach. While pacifists condemn any use of force, even to stop massacres, relief organisations that adhere to the ideals of the International Red Cross do not want to compromise their neutrality and they do not accept the principle of killing people in order to save lives. Third world activists also denounce the imperialist motives behind such interventions.[1] As for the military and politicians, they are worried that integrated approaches make the use of force subservient to humanitarian imperatives. Some doubt that aid could promote peace because foreign assistance can in fact worsen the competition between belligerents who try to get their hands-on resources. Instead of "winning the hearts and minds" of the population, aid diversion and the failures of development projects in corrupt states are more likely to foster local frustrations against Western agencies and donors.

The idea that humanitarian action can buy social peace is based on two hypotheses that are analysed in this chapter. The first establishes a clear link between poverty and insurgencies, including terrorist violence. When applied to jihadist movements in the Sahel, this reasoning seems simplistic. Indeed, it does not consider the political grievances of criminal groups that are supposedly motivated by poverty and greed only. It also ignores other causes of rebellion, in particular the weak legitimacy of states and their tendency to handle any conflict with violence. The second illusion about "integrated" approaches is that international aid helps buy social peace when it actually sets competition that can instead exacerbate and prolong conflicts.

## Poverty, Wahhabism and Jihad: some missing links

Using humanitarian aid as part of a counterinsurgency strategy is based on the hypothesis that poverty is the root cause of terrorism. This view assumes that jihadist groups in Africa are the mere result of the economic and moral misery of the people living in the Sahel. Such a hypothesis is supported by fundamentalists when they present Islam as the religion of the poor because of the importance it attaches to charity. Since believers are all equal before God and death, this idea was also propagated by the "socialist" regimes of Muslim African countries who sought to combine Islam and Marxism, like Libya under Muammar Gaddafi, Sudan under Gaafar Nimeiry, and Egypt under Gamal Abdel Nasser. Progressive clerics of the time often mentioned the mythical figure of Abu Dharr al-Ghifari, who was expelled from Medina after the death of the Prophet Muhammad in 632 for having urged the faithful to give up all their earthly possessions (Clarence-Smith, 2006, p. 50).

Historically, there were cases where jihad combined with a revolt of the poor. An early example, from the 1st century of the Hegira, is that of the Kharijites ("dissidents") who accused the fourth caliph of corruption and murdered him in 661. For them, the prophet's successor was to be chosen for his personal qualities and not for his blood ties with the richest families of Mecca. In theory, slaves or individuals with low social status could thus lead the community of believers. The Kharijites challenged the racism and privileges of the Sunni Arabs. The latter considered themselves superior to other Muslims and felt the need to co-opt converts and monopolise positions of power based on clan allegiances. Of course, advocating equality among all believers attracted captives and non-Arab populations, especially Berbers from the Maghreb. From 694 to 695 and from 869 to 893, it also inspired the revolts of the black slaves of Iraq, the Zanj, who used some of its slogans and developed at the same time as the insurgencies of Kharijite rebels who had taken refuge in the swamps of the region (Popovic, 1976, p. 62).

Similar phenomena took place in Africa. The 19th-century Sahelian and Sufi jihads often started as tax-motivated revolts and were carried out by itinerant pastoralists against chiefdoms that exploited an amenable peasantry (Hiskett, 1994, p. 109). Such is the case of Usman dan Fodio (1754–1817), a Fulani and Qadiri imam who took up arms in 1804 and was joined by non-Muslim slaves to overthrow the old Hausa kingdoms and establish a caliphate in Sokoto. His example inspired other jihads in the Sahel (Clarence-Smith, 2006, pp. 153–154). In the Adrar region in the 1810s, Muhammad al-Jaylani (1777–1840), a Tuareg of the Qadiriyya Brotherhood, took up arms to establish an egalitarian society in which nomads could settle down. In the Macina region, Sékou Amadou Lobo (1776–1844), a Fulani and Qadiri marabout, freed the slaves who had joined his cause and participated in the 1818 jihad against the animist kingdoms of the region. In Futa Toro, in 1852, freed slaves started joining the fight of El Hadj Umar Tall (1794–1864), a leader of the Tijaniyya who had condemned enslaving animists in times of peace and selling slaves to infidels, especially if those captives had converted to Islam. Further to the east, in Sudan, the uprising of Muhammad Ahmad ibn Abd Allah (1844–1885) from 1883 also promoted the hope for a better world in which the advent of a saviour, the Mahdi, could be seen as a Millenarian version of the Big Day of the Marxist revolution.

However, the 19th-century jihads of the Sahel did not live up to their promises. The Sudanese Mahdiyya, Usman dan Fodio's caliphate, and El Hadj Umar Tall's Toucouleur Empire all developed thanks to an economy based on predation, raiding, and slavery. Their failure to defend the rights of the poor raises related questions about today's jihadism in the Sahel. The issue is not only to check if Salafism indeed serves as the ideological basis of modern terrorism, another area of contest (see Chapter 6 of this book). It is also to know if Wahhabi-inspired movements truly embody social revolts.

On the one hand, they do challenge the power of the elders and traditional Sufi brotherhoods.[2] Some poor, including a few Christians and "animists", have been attracted to the austerity of the Salafi way of life, its "theology of liberation," the simplicity of its dogma, its egalitarian vision of the world (without distinctions of castes or classes) and its refusal to discriminate Muslims according to their social, ethnic or national origins. On the other hand, it would be difficult to prove that so-called Wahhabis give more care to the destitute than the Sufi brotherhoods in Africa. The situations from one country to another are too different for any definitive conclusions to be drawn.

While the so-called Wahhabis are strong among wealthy traders in the Sahel, for instance, those in Ghana and southern Côte d'Ivoire are not. In Abidjan, they attracted new converts and immigrants from a new suburb, Abobo, where Sufi traditionalists did not have a strong foothold (Miran-Guyon, 1998). In Bamako, on the other hand, "Wahhabism" has spread mostly among the "bourgeoisie" (Amselle, 1985). Indeed, traders grew tired of paying for sacrifices and amulets. As a result, they joined a doctrine that maintained their Muslim legitimacy while condemning marabouts who were always busy extorting money. "Wahhabism" then developed as a puritan, liberal, and capitalist ideology that valued frugality, praised the merits of work, and blamed idleness (Loimeier, 2016, p. 115).

On a global African scale, so-called Salafi movements have not had much success with the rural poor, who have remained faithful to the Sufi brotherhoods. They have been limited, for the most part, to urban middle classes, mainly traders and students, while peasants refused to follow a model that would have deprived them of manpower by forcing their wives to stay at home.[3] Indeed, Salafism is related to the prophet's origins in Medina, the city par excellence. Some specialists even believe Islam is incompatible with a nomadic lifestyle that prevents Bedouins and pastoralists from praying together at the mosque (Planhol 1968, p. 24). From this point of view, Wahhabi-inspired protest movements are very different from peasants' uprising of the wretched of the earth, even if some African urban jihadists did settle in rural hiding spots to continue their struggle, using revolutionary references from the Arab world.

In northern Mali, for example, Al-Qaeda in the Islamic Maghreb (AQIM) did not develop in the poorest parts of the country: in 2011, the poverty rates of Gao and Kidal were below the national average (Institut National de la Statistique du Mali, 2013, p. 31). Similarly, Boko Haram was not born within the most disadvantaged segments of the population. Its initiators were from the city of Maiduguri, and Borno was not the poorest state in Nigeria before the group's insurrection in 2009 (Pérouse de Montclos, 2012). If poverty had been the one determining factor of the revolt, the movement should have emerged from Diffa in Niger or Maroua in Cameroon, the least educated and the poorest region in the country, where three-fourths of the population lived below the poverty line (see Figure 36.1). Only subsequently did poverty drive the youth into the ranks of Boko Haram. In a vicious circle, poverty and

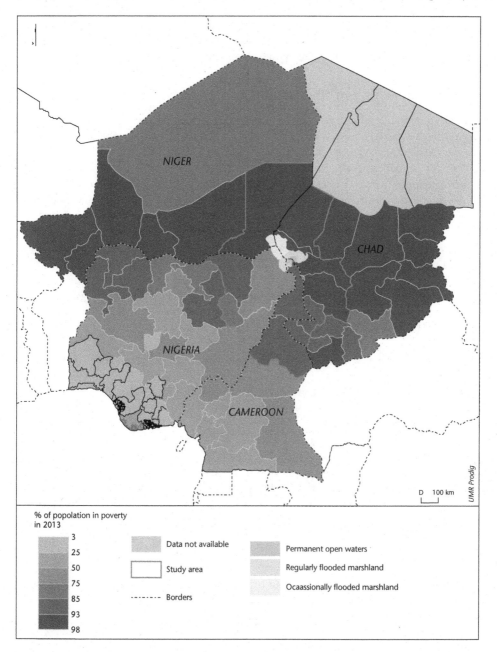

*Figure 36.1* Poverty Rates around Lake Chad, 2013
Source: Magrin, G.& Pérouse de Montclos, M.-A. (2018), Crisis and Development. The Lake Chad Region and Boko Haram, Paris, AFD, p.77.

insurrection then went together as the fighting exacerbated the impoverishment of the people in Borno.

Generally speaking, it is well known that the relationship between rebellion and poverty is extremely complex and ambiguous (Gurr, 1970). We should therefore be careful not to speculate too much on whether international aid could foster economic growth to demobilise combatants and defuse rebellions carried out in the name of the Qur'an (Pérouse de Montclos, 2005). Indeed, periods of economic growth can also generate social tensions. Moreover, mixing humanitarian action and military intervention has not always been successful, far from it.

## Humanitarian aid and military action: no love lost

According to some researchers, for example, social programs funded by the US military in Iraq in the mid-2000s helped to earn the support of the population and reduce violent attacks of the insurgents (Eli, Shapiro, & Felter, 2011). But these conclusions are contested. In Afghanistan after 2003, the Provincial Reconstruction Teams (PRTs), set up by the anti-terrorist coalition, and the Community Development Councils (CDCs), funded by the World Bank, have been the subject of strong criticism. Indeed, they did not prevent the Taliban from winning many battles against a corrupt government supported by Western powers. Instead of being elected and including women, the CDCs did not promote democracy either. On the contrary, they strengthened local chiefdoms and could not solve land disputes which used to be settled by traditional *shuras* ('councils'). Sometimes, they even revived tensions and prompted warlords to rebuild their militias to control structures that became the main recipient of international aid (Brick Murtazashvili, 2016). Being dependent on foreign subsidies and unable to generate their own resources, the CDCs lacked legitimacy because they were not accountable to their communities, but to the NGOs that funded them.

Such shortcomings are not limited to the main countries targeted by the "global" war against terrorism. In the Philippines, development projects designed by the government to win the hearts and minds of the people also exacerbated the conflict with the jihadists of the Moro Islamic Liberation Front and the communist insurgents of the New People's Army (Crost et al., 2014). Funded by the World Bank between 2002 and 2006, their objective was clearly strategic and aimed, among other things, to build roads for the transport of troops. As a result, the insurgents' attacks focused on development projects that were likely to provide jobs for the locals, strengthen social support for the government, and facilitate its repression efforts. Their purpose was not to extort money and get a share of foreign aid, as they occurred before the projects were implemented.

In Africa too, the material and symbolic resources of international aid are a source of competition. As a result, they can prolong hostilities, or exacerbate—and even create—new conflicts (Pérouse de Montclos, 2001). Humanitarian aid is highly fungible. It can be diverted and used to fund military operations, sustain forced displacements, supply guerrillas in refugee camps, reinforce the communication policy of belligerents, and legitimise a political cause by designating on which side the good victims are. In practice, international aid is often captured by dominant groups because it is difficult to reach the poorest segments of the population. In the Sahel, for instance, it favoured elite-controlled NGOs and administrative sectors that were financed by official development assistance (Blundo, 2011).

Many examples in Africa illustrate how international aid can prolong hostilities. Foreign relief reinforced the capacity of the Biafran secessionists against Nigeria's blockade in the 1960s. As his troops were surrounded, the leader of the rebellion knew that he could not secure a military victory. Hence his hope was, according to his own words, to resist long enough to convince the international community about the necessity of independence for the Biafran victims of the blockade, which was presented as a "genocide", even if this meant prolonging the famine and suffering of his own people.[4]

In the same vein, foreign relief was diverted for military purposes in Ethiopia, Sudan, and Somalia. During the famine of 1984–1985, the Marxist dictatorship in power in Addis Ababa restricted international aid to the regions under its control. It forced the people living in northern rebel areas to relocate to the south as part of a "villagisation" program financed by the World Bank, for instance in the province of Gambella (Clay & Holcomb, 1986; Evans, 2013; Rawlence, 2010). In Sudan and Somalia, aid diversion also helped government troops and warlords to continue fighting. In the city of Ed'Dien in Darfur, for example, it was estimated that in 1999, one-quarter of relief ended up in the hands of combatants or chiefs (Loane & Schüme, 2001, p. 66). Humanitarian organisations had in fact assessed the needs for 90,000 people instead of the 30,000 who were displaced and who resold their food rations to repay debts to local moneylenders. As a result, malnutrition persisted despite—or because of—the abundance of relief.

Looting and theft, however, are not the only way for belligerents to divert aid in Africa. Other schemes include overbilling contracts, inflating the number of people in need, or creating fraudulent NGOs.[5] The creation of artificial humanitarian organisations to capture foreign aid is quite efficient indeed because it corresponds to the expectations of Western donors who think that the proliferation of non-profit associations contributes to democratic pluralism and the non-violent resolution of conflicts. Building local capacities also fulfils the communication policy of international NGOs which claim to defend the interests of the victims, yet do not say how much they spend to decentralise their organisation and to support their partners in developing countries (Audet, 2016).

## Are humanitarian workers "Useful Idiots"?

In fact, the diversion of humanitarian aid is an entire system. On the one hand, the belligerents obviously try to make the most of it. On the other hand, the pressure exerted by foreign donors to spend money quickly can lead to fraud because it incites the authorities to circumvent the accounting rules of public expenditure audits, which are temporarily suspended in case of emergency and force majeure. As for international and local NGOs, they often try to minimise the diversion of their aid in order not to lose the support of their donors. Some do not even see that they are manipulated by stakeholders in the conflicts.

Indeed, there is often an element of naivety to the way humanitarian organisations approach African crises. Since they use the media to raise funds from the general public, first, NGOs tend to simplify their message, use stereotypes, and mask the political complexity of armed conflicts so that they can avoid "lengthy explanatory comments" about "a reality deemed too obscure" (Robinet, 2016, p. 228). Many development practitioners also have a technocratic—and even condescending—mindset; they see poverty as resulting from a lack of expertise rather than "a shortage of rights" (Easterly, 2014, p. 7). Their idealism, which leaves no room for introspection, sometimes borders on stubbornness when it denies the military instrumentalisation of aid and blames the failures of development projects on purely technical errors. Like communism or capitalism, humanitarian ideology and faith in progress can thus lead to disaster when it only argues for more intervention, not less (Gray, 2013, p. 75, cited in Menon, 2016, p. 29).

In fact, humanitarian workers have sometimes been described as "useful idiots," a phrase that Vladimir Lenin allegedly coined to mock the blindness of American philanthropists. At the time, the United States was assisting the victims of the 1922 Russian famine. Herbert Hoover, who

543

was Secretary of Commerce from 1921 to 1928, initiated this aid. He was an anti-Bolshevik Quaker who had strongly opposed the establishment of diplomatic relations with the USSR. For him, famine and communism resulted from poverty. Hence foreign aid was supposed to expose the failures of the Soviets, demonstrate the merits of the capitalist model, show America's generosity to the Russian people, and, ultimately, develop commercial outlets for US military food rations that were leftover from the First World War (Cabanes, 2014, p. 195 & 243). However, relief did not bring down the communist regime. On the contrary, it enabled the communists to strengthen their grip on the population by controlling the distribution of food.[6] Hence the phrase "useful idiot," which was later used to criticise the role played by relief organisations during the famines of Biafra in 1968, Ethiopia in 1985, and Somalia in 1992 (Rufin 1986).

From a purely strategic point of view, the humanitarian game could in fact mean that everybody tries to fool everybody. On the one hand, the notion of "useful idiot" highlights the diversion of aid by its recipients. On the other hand, the image of a "Trojan Horse" shows how donors try to use their assistance as an extension of their foreign policy in order to strengthen or weaken a foreign government. Like Herbert Hoover, who wanted to use aid to precipitate the fall of the USSR in 1922, Ronald Reagan tried to instrumentalise American relief to the victims of famine in 1985 to encourage Marxist Ethiopia to have a closer relationship with the West (Minear, 2013, p. 50). The imperialist and colonial powers were actually not the only ones to see humanitarian action as a political or a religious tool of influence.[7] Historically, the understanding of altruism and self-interest has in fact varied a lot from one cultural context to another.

The limits of universal humanitarian ideals have thus generated vivid debates within the NGO community. The French doctors from *Médecins Sans Frontières* (MSF), in particular, conspicuously withdrew from situations where they considered that their assistance exacerbated conflicts and went against the victims' interests (Magone et al., 2011). Such was the case in Ethiopia in 1985 and Zaire in 1995, where aid was captured by belligerents or refugees and used for military purposes to starve rebel areas, to displace populations forcibly, or to attempt to carry on the Rwandan genocide. British NGOs, on the other hand, have more rarely admitted in public the harmful effects of their interventions. For example, Hugo Slim worked for Save the Children (SCF) in the Ethiopian camp of Korem in 1985 when Addis Ababa expelled MSF for denouncing the diversion of aid. According to him, the French doctors were wrong to abandon the victims of famine. He rightly points out that humanitarians do not cause wars. But he goes even further and contests the role of relief in prolonging conflicts. According to him, international aid always does more good than harm, while criticising the work of NGOs masks the responsibilities of the real perpetrators of mass violence (Slim, 2014, p. 185).

## The challenges of the implementation of integrated approaches

Differences of opinion within the humanitarian community can thus complicate coordination and the implementation of integrated approaches as part of peacekeeping operations or counterinsurgency strategies. Some government-funded NGOs accept to follow the deployment of international armed forces, for example, to help demobilise combatants in eastern regions of the Democratic Republic of Congo (Pérouse de Montclos, 2008). But others pay more attention to the values of the International Red Cross and refuse to compromise their neutrality. They argue that the possibility of being mistaken for soldiers put them at risk. Moreover, integrated approaches require humanitarian workers to adopt security procedures, including armed escorts, which limit their freedom of movement, delay their operations, and eventually cut them off from the population. In so doing, NGOs lose their autonomy and the flexibility which, in principle, is their added value compared to the massive bureaucracy of international organisations. Once they are locked up in secure shelters, humanitarian workers find it more challenging to be in touch with the victims, to get first-hand information about the situation, and to check for themselves whether their fears are well-founded (Duffield, 2012; Roth, 2015).

Hence many humanitarian organisations denounce the militarisation and the politicisation of aid in the context of the global war against terrorism. They also complain about the integrated approach of peacekeeping operations that aim at state-building, as in Mali, Somalia, or the Democratic Republic of Congo, especially when troops are allowed to open fire on belligerents under Chapter 7 of the Charter of the United Nations. Humanitarian relief always had a political and military dimension. In the beginning, it focused primarily on soldiers rather than civilians; the first Geneva Convention of 1864 protected only war casualties from government armies. During the First World War, for instance, humanitarian workers on the battlefield were directly supervised by the military, wore uniforms, and had to abide by disciplinary codes (Pérouse de Montclos, 2014). It was also before the end of the Cold War that peacekeeping missions started resorting to the use of force under Chapter 7, like in the Congo in 1961, and adding political agendas to their armed interventions in order to organise independence referendums or get involved in state-building.[8] During the Korean War, for example, relief organisations were asked to "provide such assistance as the Unified Command may request," under a UN Security Council resolution of 31 July 1950.[9]

Undoubtedly, there is a gap between historical facts and current narratives about the alleged novelty of a militarisation of aid which is supposed to explain the problems faced by humanitarian workers today. Changes in the international context since the end of the Cold War do not properly explain structural difficulties in implementing integrated approaches. Some of the problems are also related to cultural misunderstandings. Many volunteers in humanitarian NGOs do not want to cooperate with soldiers, whom they see as brutes and torturers. In the same vein, they consistently seek to bypass the civil servants of developing states, which they perceive as corrupt, selfish, and incompetent gatekeepers. The military and political decision-makers have a similar attitude and often view NGOs as troublemakers that are likely to undermine their authority and legitimacy. The armies deployed to fight insurgencies or to impose peace do not share the same institutional cultures either. While Americans were used to working with NGOs as part of their civil-military actions, for instance in Somalia in the 1990s, Indian and Pakistani peacekeepers were not as keen to cooperate with relief organisations in the Democratic Republic of Congo in the 2000s.

Finally, many developing countries see humanitarian interventions as an attempt to violate their sovereignty. Historically, the colonisation of Africa has often been justified by a moral imperative to put an end to the slave trade. Yet the abolitionist movement in Great-Britain was suspected of harbouring imperialist ambitions to deprive competitors of their manpower, to legitimise territorial conquests, and to take control of the maritime trade on the oceans.[10] As for France, it celebrated its colonial wars as a "humanitarian" and civilising mission, together with the evangelisation of the continent (Bonet-Maury, 1906, p. 294). As late as 1936, a fascist Italian decree also abolished slavery in Ethiopia to legitimise the invasion of the country. This colonial history certainly played a role in today's nationalist reactions against humanitarian interventions.

However, the reservations about integrated approaches also reveal more fundamental incompatibilities between humanitarian and military actors when they are both involved in peacekeeping or counterinsurgency. NGOs argue that, in such a context, relief is no longer determined by the needs of the victims, but by security imperatives, which are sometimes irreconcilable with humanitarian values. Such is the case of military blockades that aim at depriving the enemy of its supply sources and can have a devastating medical, agricultural, and nutritional impact, for example around Lake Chad, where a regional coalition is fighting against Boko Haram since 2015 (Pérouse de Montclos, 2017). For humanitarians, Disarmament, Demobilization, and Rehabilitation (DDR) programs are equally problematic because they give more aid to "former" combatants and thus reward the perpetrators of violence at the expense of civilians.

Beyond the ethical issues raised by integrated approaches, relief organisations complain about the ineffectiveness of military operations, which do not save civilians and sometimes cause extensive collateral damage. The problem is also that such interventions are very political and do not match the altruistic and universalist ideals of humanitarian workers. Indeed, competing states defend their own interest first. Military interventions for humanitarian purposes actually emerged in the 19th century from a paradox, as they violated the sacred principle of national sovereignty at the very moment when the nation-state was at its peak in Europe (Rodogno, 2015). In practice, those interventions were used to dismantle the Ottoman Empire by creating protectorates and concessions for Christians, known as "capitulations" (Rodogno, 2012; Bass, 2008). Imperialist powers thus applied double standards. On the one hand, they intervened selectively to stop the pogroms of Christians committed by Turks, who were accused of not respecting freedom of religion and ignoring the rights of their citizens. On the other hand, they sought to evangelise "pagans" and they massacred "natives" in their African or Indian colonies, all in the name of the civilising mission of the West (Conklin, 1998).

Regardless of the historical and local contexts, we thus have to admit that despite its altruistic and universalist ideals, humanitarian aid is fundamentally political. From this point of view, it represents a military asset for the belligerents. But this does not mean that it could successfully be used to support counterinsurgency strategies to win peace… and not just wars. Indeed, the resources of the aid industry sometimes exacerbate tensions and contribute to prolonging conflicts. Countering terrorist insurgencies and fighting poverty are two separate policies that should not be confused, not only because their modus operandi and objectives are different, but also because their integration to military interventions is based on illusions about the causes of rebellions and the merits of international aid. In general, feelings of frustration, humiliation, oppression, and discrimination play a much more decisive role than does poverty in explaining the dynamics of insurgencies. As for humanitarian aid, it already has a difficult time fighting poverty effectively, let alone preventing or resolving conflicts.

## Notes

1 In the third chapter of his Communist Manifesto, Karl Marx had already described humanitarian workers as agents of the ruling classes and capitalism because they bought social peace in order to contain the revolutionary impulses of the proletariat. This criticism is still present today when NGOs are accused of helping the poor to channel protests and prevent rebellions (Choudry & Kapoor, 2013).
2 See, for example, the case of the Dioula of the city of Korhogo in northern Côte d'Ivoire (Launay, 1992).
3 There are some exceptions, of course. In Nigeria's Middle Belt, Fulani herdsmen from Plateau State, for example, joined the Salafi "Izala" group to escape the authority of Hausa "marabouts," the *mal-lamai*. This process of re-Islamization also helped to mitigate their clan differentiations. I wish to thank my colleague Adam Higazi for this information.
4 Stremlau, 1977, cited in Aaronson, 2013. See also Pérouse de Montclos, 2009.
5 Of course, these tricks can be found in other parts of the world such as Palestine after the 2000 Intifada, where an unpublished UNDP report admitted the deep corruption of the authorities (Benthall, 2015, p. 283).
6 In 1922, for example, a Bolshevik decree requisitioned the property of the Russian Church to finance

the Soviet Union's share of food imports and, in so doing, discredit the Americans in the eyes of the still very religious peasantry.

7 At a world congress in Mecca in 1926, for instance, representatives of Muslim countries developed a religious interpretation of aid to promote Islamic solidarity within the community of believers after the fall of the Ottoman caliphate in 1924. In this case, their "charitable and exclusively humanitarian work" was explicitly aimed at ensuring "the prosperity of the Islamic family and ... of Muslims so that they [would] surpass, Inchallah, other peoples, without any feeling of hostility toward any Muslim or non-Muslim state (Sékaly, 1926)."

8 As early as 1920, the ancestor of the United Nations, i.e. the League of Nations, thus deployed British, Dutch, Italian and Swedish troops to rule the territory of the Saar and eventually organise in 1935 a referendum which gave the inhabitants the choice to opt for reunification to France or Germany or to extend the international mandate (Macqueen, 2016, p. 234).

9 In Korea, international aid, in fact, responded to the immediate needs of the military but did not seek to develop the country in the long term. Quite on the contrary, the US Command ordered the suspension of food distributions to decongest the region of Pusan and force displaced people to return to areas near the front line despite recurrent guerrillas' attacks (Hong, 2015, pp. 85 & 89).

10 At the time, the British abolitionist movement also resulted from internal politics opposing non-conformist churches to the Anglican establishment, which condoned slavery.

# References

Aaronson, M. (2013). The Nigerian Civil War and humanitarian intervention. In B. Everill & J. Kaplan (Eds.), *The history and practice of humanitarian intervention and aid in Africa*. Basingstoke: Palgrave Macmillan.

Amselle, J.-L. (1985). *Le Wahhabisme à Bamako (1945–1985)*. Canadian Journal of African Studies 19:2.345-57

Audet, F. (2016). *Comprendre les organisations humanitaires*. Québec: Presses universitaires du Québec.

Bass, G. J. (2008). *Freedom's battle: The origins of humanitarian intervention*. New York: Alfred Knopf.

Benthall, J. (2015). Religion and humanitarianism. In R. Mac Ginty & J. Peterson Éds., *The Routledge companion to humanitarian action*. New York: Routledge.

Blundo, G. (2011). Une administration à deux vitesses: Projets de développement et construction de l'État au Sahel. *Cahiers d'études africaines, 202-203*, 427–452.

Boisson de Chazournes, L., & Condorelli, L. (2005). *De la Responsabilité de Protéger, ou d'une nouvelle parure pour une notion déjà bien établie. Revue Générale de Droit International Public1* (1), 11–18.

Bonet-Maury, G. (1906). *L'islamisme et le christianisme en Afrique*. Paris: Hachette.

Branch, A. (2011). *Displacing human rights: War and intervention in Northern Uganda*. New York: Oxford University Press.

Brick Murtazashvili, J. (2016). *Informal order and the state in Afghanistan*. Cambridge: Cambridge University Press.

Cabanes, B. (2014). *The Great War and the origins of humanitarianism: 1918–1924*. Cambridge: Cambridge University Press.

Choudry, A., & Kapoor, D. (2013). *NGOization: Complicity, contradictions and prospects*. London: Zed Books.

Clarence-Smith, W. G. (2006). *Islam and the abolition of slavery*. London: Hurst.

Clay, J., & Holcomb, B. (1986). *Politics and the Ethiopian famine, 1984–1985*. Cambridge (Mass.), Cultural Survival, 250p.

Conklin, A. (1998). Colonialism and human rights, a contradiction in terms? The case of France and West Africa, 1895-1914. *American Historical Review, 103*(2), 419–442.

Crost, B., Felter, J., & Johnston, P. (2014). Aid under fire: Development projects and civil conflict. *American Economic Review, 104*(6), 1833–1856.

Duffield, M. (2012). Challenging environments: Danger, resilience and the aid industry. *Security Dialogue, 43*(5), 475–492.

Easterly, W. (2014). *The tyranny of experts. How the fight against global poverty suppressed individual rights*. New York: Perseus.

Eli, B., Shapiro, J., & Felter, J. (2011, August). Can hearts and minds be bought? The economics of counterinsurgency in Iraq. *Journal of Political Economy, 119*(4), 766–819.

Evans, J. (2013). *Abuse-free development. How the World Bank should safeguard against human rights violations.* New York: Human Rights Watch.

Gray, J. (2013). *The silence of animals: On progress and other modern myths.* New York: Farrar, Straus and Giroux.

Gurr, T. R. (1970). *Why men rebel.* Princeton: Princeton University Press.

Hiskett, M. (1994). *The course of Islam in Africa.* Edinburgh: Edinburgh University Press.

Hong, Y.-S. (2015). *Cold War Germany, the third world, and the global humanitarian regime.* New York: Cambridge University Press.

Institut National de la Statistique du Mali. (2013). *Consommation, Pauvreté, Bien-être des Ménages, Avril 2011 - Mars 2012.* Bamako: INSM.

Launay, R. (1992). *Beyond the stream. Islam and society in a West African town.* Berkeley: University of California Press.

Loane, G. & Schüme, T. (Eds.) (2001). *Tracing unintended consequences of humanitarian assistance: The case of Sudan.* Baden-Baden: Nomos Books.

Loimeier, R. (2016). *Islamic reform in 20th century Africa.* Edinburgh: Edinburgh University Press.

Macqueen, N. (2016). Cold War peacekeeping *versus* humanitarian intervention. In F. Klose (Ed.), *The emergence of humanitarian intervention: Ideas and practice from the nineteenth century to the present.* Cambridge: Cambridge University Press.

Magone, C., Neuman, M. & Weissman, F. Éds. (2011). *Agir à tout prix? Négociations humanitaires: l'expérience de Médecins Sans Frontières.* Paris: La Découverte.

Menon, R. (2016). *The conceit of humanitarian intervention.* New York: Oxford University Press.

Minear, L. (2013). Humanitarian action and Politicisation: A review of experience since World War II. In A. Donini(Ed.), *The golden fleece: Manipulation and independence in humanitarian action.* Sterling: Kumarian Press.

Miran-Guyon, M. (1998). *Dynamisme urbain d'un islam réformiste en Côte d'Ivoire contemporaine (1960–1996). Islam et Sociétés au Sud du Sahara*(12), 5–74.

Pérouse de Montclos, M.-A. (2001). *L'aide humanitaire, aide à la guerre?* Bruxelles: Complexes.

Pérouse de Montclos, M.-A. (2005). Etats, ONG et prévention des conflits dans les pays du Sud: quelques éléments de réflexion. In N. Bagayoko-Penone & B. Hours (Éds.), *Etat, ONG et production de normes sécuritaires dans les pays du Sud* (pp. 135–149). Paris: L'Harmattan.

Pérouse de Montclos, M.-A. (2008). L'Afrique et les organisations non gouvernementales (ONG): une contestation du 'monopole' du Nord. In T. Montbrial (de) & P. Moreau Defarges (Éds.), *Ramsès 2009: Turbulences économiques et géopolitique planétaire* (pp. 188–191). Paris: Dunod.

Pérouse de Montclos, M.-A. (2009). Humanitarian aid and the Biafra War: Lessons not learned. *Africa Development, 34*(1), 69–82.

Pérouse de Montclos, M.-A. (2012). *Boko Haram et le terrorisme islamiste au Nigeria: insurrection religieuse, contestation politique ou protestation sociale? Question de Recherche*(40), 1–33.

Pérouse de Montclos, M.-A. (2014). The (De) Militarisation of Humanitarian Aid: A Historical Perspective. *Humanities, 3,* 232–243.

Pérouse de Montclos, M.-A. (2017). *Le Nigeria, Boko Haram et la crise migratoire. Outre-Terre* 51.

Planhol (de), X. (1968). *Les fondements géographiques de l'histoire de l'islam.* Paris: Flammarion.

Popovic, A. (1976). *La révolte des esclaves en Irak au IIIè, IXè siècle.* Paris: Paul Geuthner.

Rawlence, B. (2010). *Development without freedom. How aid underwrites repression in Ethiopia.* New York: Human Rights Watch.

Robinet, F. (2016). *Les médias français à l'épreuve des conflits africains (1994-2015).* Paris: INA.

Rodogno, D. (2012). *Against massacre: Humanitarian interventions in the Ottoman Empire, 1815-1914: The emergence of a European concept and international practice.* Princeton: Princeton University Press.

Rodogno, D. (2015). Humanitarian interventions in the nineteenth century. In A. Bellamy & T. Dunne (Eds.), *Oxford handbook on the responsibility to protect* (pp. 20–37). Oxford: Oxford University Press.

Roth, S. (2015). Aid work as edgework – voluntary risk-taking and security in humanitarian assistance, development and human rights work. *Journal of Risk Research, 18*(2), 139–155.

Sékaly, A. (1926). Les deux congrès islamiques généraux. *Revue du monde musulman, 64,* 181.

Slim, H. (2014). *Humanitarian ethics: A guide to the morality of aid in war and disaster.* London: Hurst.

Stremlau, J. (1977). *The international politics of the Nigerian Civil War, 1967-1970.* Princeton: Princeton University Press.

# 37

# Civil-military cooperation

## Joint military-civilian operations in counterterrorism and counterinsurgency in North-East Nigeria

*Usman A. Tar and Bashir Bala*

## Introduction

Relations between the military and the civilian society have been a longstanding and particular concern of sociologists, political scientists, and historians in one hand and reformers, statesmen and other critical stakeholders. Attention to Civil-Military Cooperation (CIMIC) has enjoyed growing concern as a result of the end of the politics of the Cold War era, the nature of post-Cold War conflicts and the emergence of political leaders who have no military background or experience (Holsti, 2001). The ability of the United States and other advanced democracies to apply lethal force in pursuit of "national interest" has been reduced by the evolution of civil-military relations since the Vietnam War and its aftermath. Transformational changes in such societies have reduced their tendency to inflict unwarranted combat casualties on enemy non-combatant civilians due to enhanced global awareness. Technological change through enhanced telecommunications and civilian access to classified and strategic information has tended to necessitate the need for civic engagement in military operations and defence management. Mass-media applications and internet technology have also given visibility to military commanders, thereby increasing their power, and enhancing their consciousness and sense of operational responsibility in engaging irregular agents of violence (Luttwak, 1999). At the same time, these technologies have exposed military commanders to the gaze of the mass media and digitally connected mass population.

On the other side, in the Sahelian region, combative alliances on the part of Violent Non-State Actors (VNSAs) and religious extremist groups have continued to escalate, both local and regional partnerships. These relationships constitute threats to the various states of the region. Aning and Amedzrator (2014) describe these forms of partnerships in two dimensions. First, they appear to be temporary alliances built on opportunistic grounds to destabilise the state. And second, they are a rallying point for radical extremist groups to collaborate with local and international allies on the one hand, and on the other hand a platform for disgruntled political actors and government officials' to collaborate with these VNSAs to clandestinely carry out their anti-state activities to create opportunities for power. It is these alliances that emboldened the ties between Al-Qaeda in the Islamic Maghreb (AQIM), Movement for Unity and Jihad in

West Africa (MUJWA) and Boko Haram in the Lake Chad Basin region – with disastrous consequences in the Lake Chad Basin.

The emergence of these violent ties have emboldened the Boko Haram and helped in characterising the Lake Chad Basin region, particularly, the northeast of Nigeria as a cesspool of terrorism, insurgency, trans-border crimes, kidnappings, illicit trades in narcotics and human trafficking and more worrisome, the proliferation of Small Arms and Light Weapons (SALWs). These ties, as aptly captured by Onouha (2014), have also provided Boko Haram with funding, arms, and training support and, eventually, helped in sustaining the group's existence and operations. Boko Haram capitalised on the afore-mentioned loopholes to expand its scope of numerical strength and frequency/intensity of attacks by recruiting more fighters from Chad, Cameroon, Mali, Niger, and Libya to cause mayhem. And in 2013, the group extended its lines of offensive operations and laid barefaced challenge on the Nigerian government by destabilising the security environment of three states – Adamawa, Borno and Yobe. This, according to Maiangwa and Audu (2018), has caused a dire humanitarian crisis in the North-eastern part of Nigeria.

The nature of complex humanitarian relief, peacebuilding, and reconstruction missions has fortuitously co-positioned military and civilian actors to operate in the same space thereby pretesting and challenging their capacity to remain professional, neutral, independent and in-terdependent in some respects (Franke, 2006). This is particularly what is tenable in the ongoing Counterterrorism and Counterinsurgency (CT-COIN) operations against Boko Haram in the northeast of Nigeria. The theatre of operation has witnessed a heightened presence and op-erational interface of various critical stakeholders with clear distinction in terms of civilian and military roles coalescing for the benefit of the local population. Despite the visibility of a healthy (and sometimes unhealthy) social relations among the humanitarian actors, the Nigerian military and the civil authority, very few efforts have been placed by policymakers to under-stand the expectations of military commanders on the one hand, and on the other the nature and scope of CIMIC in the strategic, operational and tactical contexts of CT-COIN in the northeast. Against this backdrop, therefore, this chapter attempts to explore the civil-military operations within the morphology of CT-COIN operation in Nigeria. In the long run, this exploration would help to aid the provision of more effective relief, stabilisation, and trans-formation operations. The chapter first examines the conceptual and historical context of civil-military cooperation. It traces back the emergence of the civilian joint task force (CJTF) – a band of lightly armed civilians under the control of the armed forces assembled to confront terrorism and insurgency – as essential stakeholders in defining the ambit of CIMIC in the northeast operations in Nigeria. The chapter further unearths the manifestations and challenges of CIMIC in CT-COIN operations and responsibilities and expectations of both military commanders and CJTF operatives.

## The concept and evolution of civil military (co) operation

The concept of civil-military cooperation has varying extents of conception, ranging from its normative meaning to its institutional perception. However, it is often linked with and mis-taken to mean the same as Civil-Military Relation (CMR). The concept of CMR entails the need for the military of a state to subordinate itself to civil control and authority. The sub-ordination is expected not to undermine and erode the standard of military professionalism in the discharge of its constitutional tasks to the state. The civilian and military levels of interaction further highlight the subjective argument as elucidated by Edet (2017: 40) that the civilian control of the military is more "better, more acceptable and preferred to the military control of the state". Thus, a sharp contrast between the civilian and military components is underpinned by attitude and values as well as political orientation. Huntington (1957: 80) described these attitudes and values as ones held by mostly the conservative military personnel and the liberal civilians. In all, CMR is defined by Gibson (2008:5) as "the delineation of duties among top-level civilian and military leaders". While this definition is apt and more straightforward to comprehend, it is deficient of the more elaborative context upon which the general relationship between two integral segments of the society is presupposed to be perceived.

To overcome this definitional deficit, Welch (1999: 79) defined CMR more appropriately as "the interaction between the armed forces as an institution and sector of the society in which it is embedded". From the definition, it is evident that CMR captures the military on the one hand and the civil society in other with both interacting and performing duties interdependently of each other. For example, in the context of Nigeria, CMR would entail the extant relationship between the hierarchical command of the Nigerian Armed Forces such as the Minister of Defence, Chief of Defence Staff, Chief of Army Staff, Chief of Naval Staff, Chief of Air Staff with their associated and familiar to services' councils and the political leadership of the country on the other front defines the civil-military relation in the Nigerian context.

On the other hand, CIMIC as an institutional concept has been defined, in the operational context of NATO, as the "coordination and cooperation, in support of the mission, between the NATO commander and civil actors, including national population and local authorities, as well as international, national and non-governmental organisations and agencies" (NATO, 2003:1). In its much-attested description, CIMIC encompasses tasks such as coordination between the military force and all the civilian actors in the area of operation, the synergy of support to the civilian environment, and aid to the force in the conduct of their operations. While military aid to civilian governance is geared towards improving the relationship between the military and the civilians in the areas of operation, efficient speciality skills on the part of the military is also needed to enhance and sustain civil-military operations (CMO) (Department of Defence, United States of America, 2003). CMO comprises such activities as those processes and events put in place by a commander in order to establish, influence, sustain and in the long run, exploit the cooperation between the military "outposts", other governmental and non-state establishments and the civilian population in a "friendly, neutral, or hostile operational area" (Department of Defence DoD United States of America, 2018: 2).

The non-combat functions of the NATO and United States Armed Forces (USAF) that involve armed forces undertaking civilian operations and other tasks typically performed by civilian authorities, NGOs or international humanitarian organisations are respectively described as CIMIC and "Civil affairs" (CA). To humanitarian actors, CIMIC and CA can be understood as follows:

i. "It is the interface to facilitate unity of effort between military forces and the relevant civilian entities, including local, national or regional authorities, non-governmental and international organisations;

ii. It serves as the focal point within the military for monitoring and influencing the general and humanitarian situation facing the civilian population;

iii. CIMIC and CA staff play the role of humanitarian diplomats and act as the conscience of their commander, though as a combat support function and not as operational decision-makers;

iv. CIMIC and CA are part of a broader range of non-combat tools that a commander employs to dominate whatever landscape is being faced — the media (national/

international), the civilian population (winning support for his forces/denying support to the enemy), intelligence, and in support of broader political objectives (nation-building, integrated approach, etc.);

v.  Current CIMIC and CA humanitarian projects conducted by armed forces are almost identical in implementation to those of humanitarian organisations. The modus operandi of their teams includes needs assessments, the definition of projects, securing of financing (military or national donors), finding implementing partners or contractors and evaluating the impact of their projects" (Rana, 2004: 574).

The operational dimension to CIMIC is captured more lucidly as an operational function centred on the coordinating relationships between the military force and the civilian actors such as the Non-governmental organisations (NGOs), national development agencies and inter-governmental organisations. The concept also has wider applicability, where it is deployed to achieve the aim of winning the hearts and minds of the local population for force protection and peace and stability. This operational function of CIMIC is operationalised through re-construction and quick impact projects, public announcements and media engagements in-volving the military force and the host population (Johansson, 2011). This definition stresses the need for a synergistic relationship between the military and civilian components as a necessary condition for success in military campaigns and harmonious civil-military activities. Giving the institutional perspective on the concept of CIMIC, NATO questions the needed validity and reliability of this conception. Being a battle-tested organisation with sufficient combat ex-perience in the battle environment and particularly, its integration of the civilian component in its threat assessment, planning and execution of military operations against belligerent forces, NATO's perspective is informed and all-embracing. Suffice it to say that, the definition also captures the ingredients of contending issues in the execution of the ongoing counterinsurgency operation by the Nigerian military in the north east of Nigeria and is thus relevant to this chapter.

The historical context to CIMIC can be established through an analysis of the events since the end of the Cold War. While developed democracies of Europe and North America were in effective control of their security spheres, the situation is quite different in developing economies where abject poverty, squalor, relative unemployment and underemployment, import and export of crimes and atrocities have resulted in a crisis of security – or complex political emergencies – characterised by the rise of civil war and, in extreme cases such as Somalia, state collapse. In such scenarios, armed forces have found it challenging to ensure regime and societal security.

With the heightened vulnerability of the weak states in Africa comes the pressing need for strong efforts to assert and place in the right direction, strengthened international cooperation to ameliorate the scourge of threat to global peace and security (Boutros-Ghali, 1992). In respect of the worldwide effort, initially, three sets of violations to international humanitarian law were identified as obvious flashlights since after the Cold War. These are harm to civilians, con-flicting issues in aid delivery and abuse against humanitarian workers (Adam, 2000). These three variables added to the new perception of security influenced a shift in United Nations (UN) policy. The fundamental human rights and dignity of individuals were accorded more priority over the state's sovereignty and the "society of commonality" advanced a better-improved willingness to intervene in the face of crimes against humanity and human rights violations through such instruments beyond coercive and persuasive diplomacy as well as economic sanctions and embargoes (Rehse, 2004).

With the passage of time and considering the need to evolve an effective strategy to cope with the new security challenges, the UN changed the scope of its peacekeeping missions to include, in addition to military contingent, civilian actors. They are deployed to engage in mediation, reconstruction, and rehabilitation efforts. In contrast, soldiers engage in core military tasks such as the enforcement of humanitarian corridors, sentry, reconnaissance, search, and rescue, and in extreme circumstances combat duties. This paradigm shift led to the transformation of "Peacekeeping" to "Peace Support Operations" (PSOs). PSOs missions thus became a testing ground for the application of CIMIC in UN Peacekeeping requiring cooperation between military and civil components of these missions. And the task entrusted with the peacekeepers was elevated to a more elaborate and complex one. It is in a bid to change the game of peacekeeping operations that the UN was mandated to deploy troops for coercive action under Chapter VII of the UN Charter. In this UN effort, the number of civilians working hand in hand with the military segment of the missions increased as a result of the changing nature of the multi-dimensional peacekeeping, peace enforcement and peacebuilding missions in many corners of the world. These missions moreover accommodate the broader intercourse of military activities and humanitarian aspects of assuaging security threats. It is in this manner that the military shifted more grounds and consequently closed up to embrace more civilian entities into its operations and the relevancies of this interaction is more importantly evidenced by the plethora of good stories in relation to contemporary CIMIC (Rehse, 2004).

It is in this vein that, the enhancement in the level of operational shift in the deployment of troops for operations as a result of the significant changing "conflict scenarios" in the aftermath of the end of Cold War, that the debate on CIMIC was originally triggered (Kasselmann, 2012). The evolution and development of CIMIC were therefore borne out of the core objective of creating a military engagement that would involve a robust synergy between the military and civil actors and institutions in an "effort to meet the challenges posed by unclear confrontation patterns between opposing forces, changing geographical conditions, political and ethnic considerations, and domestic and international factors. It was also rational to consider, at the operational level, the entire spectrum of civil actors and their interaction and effects regarding military mission accomplishment" (Kasselmann, 2012: 18).

## The emergence of the civilian joint task force in North-East Nigeria

The Boko Haram movement started to gain momentum and entrench in the public conscience in North-eastern Nigeria since 1995. Since then the group metamorphosised into a combative violent group due to unhealthy electioneering leading to the 2003 general elections that heated up the Nigerian body polity. During the elections, the state government under Ali Modu Sheriff was alleged to have armed the group with dangerous weapons to carry out onslaught against perceived political enemies under the well-structured leadership. Thereafter, the original founder of the Sect left for further studies in Saudi Arabia and Muhammed Yusuf was selected to head the group by an inner caucus committee of the Sect in 2002. On assumption of the leadership of the group, Yusuf accused the clerics (of the group) of lacking the requisite knowledge to interpret the teachings of the Qur'anic chapters correctly. Subsequently, Yusuf's vocal attacks on state establishments and means of governance added colours to his method of preaching which later garnered him popularity and attracted the attention of unemployed youths in Yobe and Borno States, and equally from the neighbouring countries such as Niger and Chad (Bala & Tar, 2018). The group began massive-scale attacks on Nigerian police and military units and formations in 2009 upward. In March 2015, Boko Haram declared total allegiance to the Islamic State in Syria (ISIS) proclaiming itself the Islamic State in West African Province (ISWAP). As the Islamic State expands its growing followership and subsidiaries, its presence and influence in Libya signalled a dangerous partnership with Boko Haram. The proliferation of small arms and light weapons coupled with the flow of sophisticated weapons from North Africa through Lake Chad's unsecured borders further stepped up the group's ties with other radicalised Islamist group (Tar & Mustapha, 2016).

The Boko Haram insurgency in North-eastern Nigeria emerged in full force in 2009 – but its antecedents date back to earlier decades – as a result of the failure of the state to regulate religious institutions and operational shortcomings of the Nigerian Police Force (NPF) to tackle the problem when the Boko Haram movement was brewing up as a religious group with anti-state posture. What was initially a minor police case quickly escalated into full-blown insurgency necessitating the deployment of the Armed Forces of Nigeria (AFN) for CT-COIN operations. In addition, what started as Nigeria's internal security problem quickly escalated into a regional security challenge in the Lake Chad Basin Commission (LCBC). The deployment of military operations and task forces both the national and regional levels required the cooperation between and civilian components. At the onset of the operations, CIMIC proved difficult as a result of the complex nature of the problem and failure of the AFN to distinguish between its friends and foes: the core insurgents, civilian supporters of the insurgency on the one hand, and on the patriotic civilians who were willing to cooperate with the military in the CT-COIN drive. Thus, combat casualty and collateral damages were high at the initial state of the operations.

Notwithstanding the efforts of the security personnel in containing the insurgency that erupted from the three states (Adamawa, Borno and Yobe) of Nigeria's Northeast Zone which is the vortex of the insurgency, social and economic activities of the citizens have largely collapsed in those areas due to the prevalence of violence. The complexities associated with the conduct of unconventional warfare were the reasons given by the Nigerian military and its public relations and communication experts from the theatre for the slow pace in containing the threat. At the onset of the insurgency, Boko Haram adopted the guerrilla tactics of a hit-and-run where they earmarked specific targets of value and launched attacks with target precision that resulted in a heavy casualty. With the attainment of this level of success, they continued to wreak havoc on Maiduguri before extending that other parts of the region (AlibiDaily Trust, 29 May 2014).

With the escalation of violence especially between 2009 and 2013, effort to identify the perpetrators proved ambivalent and obscured. The then constituted (JTF) and other "security operatives began to point accusing fingers at residents in Maiduguri, in places like Ruwan Zafi, Lawan Bukar, Kasuwar Gwoza, Hausari, Shehuri, Kofa Biyu, Kula Gumna, Zajeri, Lamisula, Gamboru, Budun and other densely populated areas, seeing residents as accomplices to the insurgents who curiously disappear through countless alleys in the neighbourhoods after attacks" (*Daily Trust*, 29 May 2014). The situation deteriorated as innocent civilians, especially those who remained neutral in the combative confrontation between the security forces and Boko Haram members, became targets of extreme violence and needless victims of mass assassination carried out by both the military and insurgents as a contemptuous reaction against civil neutrality. With the passage of time and space, the insurgents kept widening their scope of operations to include not only hostile acts against the state's establishment but also the local populace who happened to be harmless. This led to the imposition of the state of emergency which came with more restrictions on the movement of people, vehicles and materials and mass communication (especially mobile telephones and internet access) in the domain of operations.

This naturally disrupted essential and the provisioning of public utilities as at when due and the populace were left with no option than to bore the brunt.

The potentials of a vigilante response in the fight against Boko Haram were first acknowledged by the security forces, and particularly the army. The military-led (JTF) recognised the imperatives of involving the civilian vigilantes and hence organised the groups and subsumed them into its various deployments with the "sectorisation" (a division of the area for easy and effective command and control) and "sub-sectorisation" (a further subdivision of the area for effective command and control) of Maiduguri. The officers of the military constituted JTF were also involved in the selection of CJTF leaders with a chairman and a secretary for each sector working closely with the Nigerian military in Maiduguri. Afterwards, the CJTF and their activities drew the attention of prominent personalities in Borno State who aspired and projected the remodelling of the CJTF model to reflect a more viable and professional outfit capable of providing the needed support to the military to tamed the waging attacks of Boko Haram. These personalities include the *Shehu of Borno, Abubakar Ibn Umar Garbai El-Kanemi, and Governor Kashim Shettima* (ICC, 2017). Thereafter, in 2013, the Borno Youths Empowerment Scheme (BOYES) which was earlier initiated by the Borno State Government as a developmental initiative was transformed into a platform for civil recruitment in support of the government CT-COIN drive. Young men were selected, screened, vetted, and given basic training to support the armed forces. The State further provided these youth volunteers with uniforms, patrol cars and identification documents (IDs), as well as a monthly allowance (International Crisis Group ICG, 2017). The CJTF soon proved successful and eventually received a wider recognition as an ad hoc unit of the Nigerian Army who has so far given them proper military training consistent with the ethos of military professionalism and the national army.

## Military command and the nature of civil-military operations in the North East

Over the course of 50 years, the participation of the Nigerian military in governance has created a wrong perception of the roles and operations of the military in nation-building. Similarly, the members of the armed forces were viewed with a lot of suspicion by the civil populace, humanitarian agencies, and civil society organisations even after the emergence of a democratically elected government in 1999. The compelling need to rebuild trust, confidence and restore a positive image and integrity of the military particularly the Nigerian Army necessitated the establishment of the Department of Civil-Military Affairs in the Army Headquarters on 6 December 2010 in line with the Nigerian Army Order of Battle, 2010 (Angbazo, 2017). The core strategic mission of the Army Headquarters Department of Civil-Military Affairs (AHQ DCMA) is anchored on improving the credibility and integrity of the Nigerian Army as a critical strategic stakeholder in conflict mediation and resolution in the country and beyond. The Department was equally established to achieve the following subsidiary objectives:

a.   "To underscore the fundamentality of Civil-Military Relations as a strategic national security driver.
b.   To enhance the value and integrity of the NA as an agent, protector and defender of the community and national interests through proactive Civil-Military Relations education and interactions.
c.   To introduce and transmit the core elements of effective Civil-Military Relations in the areas of interpersonal and organisational bonding, rule of law, accountability, communications, liaison, negotiation, and conflict management.

d.   To train officers in these core Civil-Military Relations areas and integrate Civil-Military Affairs into the curriculum, doctrine and training of the Nigerian Army personnel through continuous systematic engagement and practice" (Nigerian Army CIMIC Manual, 2015: 27).

The AHQ DCMA seeks to achieve these general and specific objectives through visits, effective liaison, advisory roles, seminars, workshops, field studies, human rights advocacy, and assessments (Angbazo, 2017). In addition to the foregoing objectives, CIMIC as a national security driver owes its foundation to the 1999 Constitution of the Federal Republic of Nigeria, which provides clear provisions for the relationship between civil authority and military leadership where elected leaders control the armed forces (Gibson, 2008). The seamless nexus between CIMIC and constitutional provisions is however shaped by structure and norms' emphasising the critical role of CIMIC on national decision-making processes. CIMIC thus remains a viable instrument for national security through which national survival could be achieved without discarding the liberal democratic way of life (Urben, 2010; and Recchia, 2015). The CIMIC problematique presents a paradox in which the military as an institution established to protect the polity is been given enormous powers to risk becoming a counter-veiling force threatening the survival of the polity (Burk, 2002). Thus the military exists as an agency to contain the disaster and deter any attack on a nation's sovereignty and there is the need for the institution to be ready for tasks and responsibilities in peace and wartimes (Feaver, 2009). The difference between military and civilians is necessary and desirable in a society based on civil liberty and democratic governance. Also, military institutions must subordinate themselves to civil authority by subjecting them to risk their lives and give up their personal freedoms for mission accomplishment despite the military contempt for civilian culture (Feaver & Kohn, 2001). Understanding this difference, and aspects of concern in relation to civil and military cohabitation are, therefore, necessary for military commanders as they would shape personnel orientation and perspective on civilian roles in military processes.

The mission commanders are expected to ensure inter-organisational and inter-agency coordination to facilitate the achievement of the higher commander's mission. However, the operational commanders are hinged with certain expectations in CIMIC. Some of these expectations as highlighted in the Nigerian Army CIMIC Manual (2015: 28) are:

a.   "Commanders are expected to identify critical or capability gaps that need to be bridged in the civil environment that may affect his mission.
b.   Commanders must positively reflect the image of the Nigerian Army.
c.   Commanders are expected to conduct security meetings with Traditional Rulers and Religious Leaders and other relevant stakeholders within their area of responsibility.
d.   Commanders should carryout community-related projects in the form of Quick Impact Projects.
e.   Commanders should ensure cooperation with other security agencies. Interagency collaboration is critical in the counterinsurgency operation.
f.   Commanders are expected to liaise and cooperate with local community leaders.
g.   As part of CIMIC, commanders should endeavour to conduct outreaches in the form of sanitation exercises and free medical outreaches.
h.   Commanders are also expected to hand over arrests to the civil police in their area of responsibility and as much as possible, avoid detention of such suspects to avoid cases of human rights abuses. However, there are exceptions to cases that bother on national security.
i.   Commanders should always refer media interviews to appropriate superior authority except when directed.
j.   Commanders while enforcing control measures such as curfew during operations should bear in mind the peculiarity of their operating environment.

k.  Commanders should as much as possible minimise civilian interference on military operations while making the protection of civilians their priority.
l.  Commanders should ensure the protection of Internally Displaced Person Camps within their area of responsibilities.
m.  Commanders must always ensure they guide against human right abuses".

Based on the foregoing expectations, in terms of understanding and working on critical gaps, Commanders are to focus on key concerns that create any potential gap of the characteristics, attitudes and beliefs of the military and civilian society. Thus, the implementation of CIMIC in the CT-COIN operations in North-eastern Nigeria has bolstered temperate public perceptions of the threat posed by the insurgency and softened the ground for civilian participation in the CT-COIN both as volunteers for the CJTFs and as agents for intelligence gathering. Thus, the alliance and cooperation between military and civilians for CT-COIN operations appear to be an existential reaction to the overwhelming threats posed by terrorism and insurgency (see also Szayna et al. 2007; Hoffman, 2007; and Rahbek-Clemmensen et al., 2012).

An important factor in CIMIC is the engagement of the media in battle reporting and the military utilisation of "strategic communication" which involves the relay of useful information and feedback from the battlefield to a wide range of stakeholders. Advances in mass media, new social media and internet connectivity have exposed military operations to public scrutiny. In demonstrating the professional and regimental image of the military as a professional fighting force, operational Commanders in the northeast theatre of operations are now faced with the new challenge of commanding their troops in the field and in combat to the full glare of the public as a result of the new media and, in particular, the live streaming of battle errors often based on "informal contents" (for instance, clips of extra-judicial execution) generated by both operatives and civilians on the ground. In the contemporary operating environment, commanders are likely to find themselves exerting command and control of their men and battle resources before a live camera on a global stage. The emergence of 24/7 news networks and the proliferation of satellite technology has created what Belknap (2001) called the "CNN effect" in relation to strategic level decision-making, and how warfighters direct their commands. Belknap further reiterated that commanders must fully understand, completely anticipate, and plan for the dynamics of media to protect and reflect on the image of the military. In the Western militaries, those attitudes of the military towards the media are changing and the relations between the military and the media have attained an unprecedented height. However, certain areas of tension and misunderstanding remain with other factors that characterise the current state of the military-media relationship. In recent military operations around the world, the military has recognised and accommodated the media in operations in Somalia, Haiti, and Bosnia by allowing the media to cover military operations (Venable, 2002; Lovejoy, 2002; and Miracle, 2003). In Nigeria's CT-COIN operation against Boko Haram, the media is recognised is granted limited access to some war-torn regions in the northeast. There are allegations that access is allowed to only friendly media establishments who will report in favourable terms. In addition to allowing access to the media, the relevant public relations units of the Armed Forces also organise regular press briefings to provide the military's side of the story. To ensure that the media does not deviate from its core mandate, the military also regularly organises conferences and workshops to enrich the media coverage and reportage of its operations. These have served as constructive platforms for counter-narrative and mechanisms of psychological operations against the Boko Haram media campaigns of terror.

The battle for hearts and minds constitute a virtual front in the CT-COIN operations in North-East Nigeria. In the area of harmonising supports from traditional and religious rulers, the "legitimate local stakeholder" who are perceived to be critical to CIMIC include tribal leaders, traditional rulers, youth movements, women groups, politicians, retired military and other security agencies. Others also include civil servants, members of state assemblies, businessmen or university professors, freelance journalists and those with traditional influence exercised by their family "emerging as representatives of the local population from among a larger number of elders and notables" (Giustozzi, 2005: 11). These set of stakeholders enjoy a considerable degree of local legitimacy within their own environs and therefore important elements for military engagement in operations. In the North-East Nigeria, the CT-COIN operations have witnessed since 2015 a surge in critical involvement of the traditional rulers, religious leaders, humanitarian aid and relief agencies, members of the civilian joint task force (CJTF) as well as civil society organisations (CSOs) are all carried along at various levels by the Nigerian military. This engagement of critical stakeholders is because of the realization that military force alone cannot win an ideological and ideational battle. These critical stakeholders wield considerable means to serve as the conduit between the state and the masses in brewing and disseminating counter-narratives that will confront the vile messaging of the insurgents.

The CT-COIN drive in North-East Nigeria has exposed in bold relief the concept of Military Operations Other Than War (MOOTW) as an alternative constructive platform for the military to provide the much needed humanitarian support in the theatre of operations. MOOTW has exposed military forces to conduct of humanitarian relief missions – a function erroneously viewed as the exclusive preserve of mandated NGOs. This transition has re-invigorated the reconstruction activities by the military in modern operations. Both the Nigerian Army and Airforce have carried out a number projects to provide support to civilians who are trapped in, or displaced by, the CT-COIN: distribution of food and medical supplies, evacuation of civilians to safety, provision of immunization against child killer diseases, construction of field hospitals in Internally Displaced Person (IDP) camps, and provision of mobile schools for the children of IDPs Reconstruction operations by the military play an enabling role in the wider conduct of a counterinsurgency campaign. In retrospect, the impacts of reconstruction operations are likely to be advantageous to the strategic leadership in the realisation of its end state tactical or non-kinetic operations. It is important to however note that the utility, versatility and capacity of combat forces are not in any way to be relegated to the background as potential insurgent targets of value may be destroyed by the combat firepower. However, the asymmetrical nature and scope of modern insurgency and its critical requirement of a population-centric strength and nature of counterinsurgency "mean that kinetic operations may often play a supporting role for other nation-building activities. The ability of the counterinsurgent to achieve the right balance between precise, discriminate kinetic and non-kinetic actions will have a major impact on how successfully local populations can be influenced" (Ryan 2007: 1). Reconstruction operations led by the military also provide latitude of time and space for domestic activities to be revived and flourished as well see to the backfilling disintegrated military programs and functions while also allowing for the reintegration of humanitarian aid and relief organisations (Ryan, 2007; Rietjens et al, 2009).

A key challenge of the military's contribution to humanitarian support in the theatre of operation is the risk of bifurcation between the military and other humanitarian service providers. The military and humanitarian agencies are guided by different, often conflicting standing operating procedures (SOPs). In addition, both sets of organisations may exhibit territorial tendencies leading to clashes and sabotage of efforts. In conflict intervention and humanitarian support operations, it is essential for the military with its emphasis on humanitarian relief missions to work with the plethora of NGOs as responding agencies in carrying out the primary critical relief functions. These functions in the form of stabilisation operations include but not limited to the provision of security, food/water relief, the shelter of civilians, medical treatment, reconstruction of infrastructure, resettlement of internally displaced persons, and reform and restructuring of government and police functions (Currey, 2003; Heaslip, Mangan & Lalwani, 2007). In the North East Nigeria, the counterinsurgents are engaged in creating quick impacts projects that would see to the post-conflict reconstruction of numerous villages and critical national facilities and infrastructure destroyed by the Boko Haram insurgents. The military is also facilitating the clearance of access for road networks in order to restore the conditions necessary for the conduct of commercial and transport activities in the area. This has therefore explained the centrality of the military engaging in projects that would realise the goals and objectives of population-centric counterinsurgency operations.

Contemporary counterinsurgency strategy requires a comprehensive primary level of humanitarian care as a key strategic tool. However, the degree of humanitarian care and services provided to the local population can result in some controversy thereby putting the surgeons, patients, and medical unit commanders at loggerheads in certain instances. For Commanders to avoid the controversies and pitfalls that usually result in unintended negative consequences of humanitarian care, Woll and Brisson (2013) suggested the following be observed:

i. "Keep expectations low by continually informing the population that our resources were very limited.
ii. Avoid the treatment of chronic problems.
iii. Partner with the local physicians. A hand-written referral commonly accompanied the Afghan patient. Unfortunately, we had scant access to local physicians for reasons that were not completely clear to us. There were other government organizations such as the US Agency for International Development interacting with local physicians in regard to the future of their health care system.
iv. Provide follow-up.
v. Provide some curative interventions such as the treatment of abscesses, appendicitis, SBOs, and wound care.
vi. Probably most important, provide some education and hygiene supplies in our care of wounds".

Education in the form of medical seminars enhanced the sustainability of medical interventions. Furthermore, the education of the local populace improves relationships and promotes interoperability through collaboration between local medical providers and the counterinsurgents as the representatives of the government (Malish et al., 2006; Alderman et al., 2010; Rice & Jones, 2010). This is not also to disregard the intricacies and suspicion associated with the military engagement in medical outreaches and the differed perceptions of the general public. For example, at one time, Major General John Enenche, the then Director Defence Information had to issue a statement in Maiduguri that there was no sinister motive behind the Armed Forces medical outreach exercise due to a smear campaign against the military regarding the Monkey Pox disease outbreak in parts of the country. This the military believes is part of its constitutional responsibility of securing lives and property of Nigerians had been conducting medical outreach during operations and routine training exercises such as the war.

The situation of complex and asymmetric environments in CT-COIN operations in the northeast requires a more cooperative and efficient interagency system to synchronise all elements of national power and ensure execution to success. Inter-agency system is viewed as the broad-based mechanism for ensuring the collective participation of, and collaboration between, the military, para-military agencies and civilian volunteers to ensure that the CT-

COIN is conducted effectively and with minimum damage. Addressing the challenges in the way the different components align their objectives, resources, and strategic thinking is paramount (Boggs, 2007): any failure in so doing could result in limited communication and difficult integration when conducting daily operations to counterinsurgency. The integration of various security agencies into a counterinsurgent force expected to coordinate at different levels with one another required that the different components have a common understanding of and familiarity with each other's institutional culture, rules of engagement and standard operating procedures. This is apparently clear for the fact that insertion of civilian representatives with lack of understanding of the armed forces into a military-dominated operation often results in poor understanding and communication and same for military personnel with poor grounding and experience in joint and combined operations (Hernandorena, 2007).

Deficits in interagency collaboration – in particular lack jointness and interoperability between military and civilian agencies – has arguably resulted in the transmutation of Boko Haram into a more lethal irregular force in the northeast coupled with the concerns about security capability in Nigeria. An enemy needs a breathing space to retreat, regroup and consolidate its cause. Lack of joint doctrine and strategy, in particular, in terms of training and equipment for personnel of the police, the State Security Service (SSS) and the military has created gaps in the CT-COIN drive. For example, the October 2010 50th independence anniversary bomb blast, brought to the fore an awareness and compelling dimensions of response necessary for collaboration of all the security agencies: the military, paramilitary and civil institutions. The event also helped to expose years of rivalry between and among these agencies. This was evident from the impacts of the tragedy, which emerged with the police and the SSS having worked at variance in the immediate investigations and arrest of suspects (Adeniyi, 2012). Over the course of time and with the emergence of new heads of security agencies in Nigeria, the inter-agency rivalry is beginning to be addressed. Though, spokespersons of various security agencies have consistently leveraged on their meeting platforms to collaborate in harmonising security information in order to achieve operational security (Shuaib, 2017). Beyond information sharing and security, commanders are expected to work in close collaboration with their sister security agencies to achieve harmony, consistency, and a sense of direction for the counterinsurgency strategy in the northeast.

## Conclusion

The imminent alliances forged by the Boko Haram with other terrorist networks in Sahelian region, coupled with the group's lethal transformation and trans-nationalisation have necessitated the need for a prompt, realistic, measurable and military response to tame its impacts. This has availed the civilian joint task force as professional guides aiding the military in familiarising with the terrain configuration, the military for kinetic and reconstruction operations and above all, the local populace cum the civil authority in the form of political leadership. In addition, it has unveiled the phenomenal influx of humanitarian actors for aid and relief responsibilities, often under the care of military units and formations. The North East Nigeria a beehive of these critical stakeholders all in effort to contain the lethality and intensity of Boko Haram attacks against key national and state infrastructure as well as military and civilians. The defining moment of the whole CT-COIN operations was the belated population-centric posture of the Nigerian military in its engagement. The enhanced military friendliness and close cooperation and collaboration with the civil society organisations, NGOs and humanitarian agencies is a welcome development. However, the new development is amidst controversies surrounding alleged cases of human rights violations by the military as well as deliberate sabotage on the part of some humanitarian actors. The Nigerian military has made considerable efforts in safeguarding its image and injecting human face in the ongoing joint and combined civil-military operations in the northeast. The establishment of the human rights desk, working relationship with the media in terms of reporting incidences of terrorism and insurgency, various medical outreaches to win the hearts and minds of the civil populace as well as the establishment of a sole Department of Civil-Military Cooperation are giant steps taken to bridge the previously widened gap between military and civil engagement in kinetic and reconstructive operations.

# References

Adam, R. (2000). Humanitarian issues and agencies as triggers for international military action. *International Review of the Red Cross, 839*. Accessed 18.08. 2018 from https://www.icrc.org/en/doc/resources/documents/article/other/57jqqa.htm.

Adeniyi, O. (2012). Terrorism and inter-agency coordination in Nigeria, *Sahara Reporters*. Retrieved on the 15.12.2018 from http://saharareporters.com/2012/11/29/terrorism-and-inter-agency-coordination-nigeria-olusegun-adeniyi.

Alderman, S., Christensen, J., & Crawford, I. (2010). Medical Seminars: A new paradigm for SOF counterinsurgency medical programs. *Journal of Special Operations Medicine: A Peer Reviewed Journal for SOF Medical Professionals, 10*(1), 16–22.

Angbazo, N. E., (Major General and Chief of Civil Military Affairs, Department of Civil Military Affairs Nigerian Army Headquarters Abuja). (2017). *Civil Military Cooperation and the Nigerian Army: Challenges And Prospects*. A Lecture Delivered to Regimental Sergeant Majors in Enugu, Nigeria on 22 August 2017.

Aning, K., & Amedzrator, L. (2014). Security in the Sahel: Linking the Atlantic to the Mediterranean. In R. Alcaro (Ed.), *Transatlantic Security from the Sahel to the Horn of Africa*. Rome: Istituto Affari Internazionali (IAI). Retrieved 13.12.2018 from http://www.iai.it/sites/default/files/iairp_12.pdf.

Aning, K., & Amedzrator, L. (2016). Critical perspectives on transnational criminality in West Africa. *Journal of Military and Strategic Studies, 17*(2), 70–85.

Alibi, I. (29 May 2014) *Lessons from Boko Haram Terror*. Daily Trust Newspaper, https://dailytrust.com/lessons-from-boko-haram-terror.

Bala, B., & Tar, U. A. (2018). Insurgency and military transformation in Nigeria. In U. A. Tar (Ed.), *Defence Transformation and the Consolidation of Democracy in Nigeria*. Kaduna – Nigeria: Academy Publishers.

Belknap, M. H. (2001). *The CNN Effect: Strategic Enabler or Operational Risk?*.Carlisle Barracks: A Publication of the Army War College.

Boggs, J. W. (2007). Introduction. In J. W. Boggs & J. R. Cerami (Eds.), *The Interagency and Counterinsurgency Warfare: Stability, Security, Transition, and Reconstruction Roles*. U.S. Army War College, Strategic Studies Institute.

Boutros-Ghali, Boutros (1992). *An Agenda for Peace – Report of the Secretary General*, UN Doc. A/47/227-S/24111. New York: United Nations.

Burk, J. (2002). Theories of democratic civil-military relations. *Journal of Armed Forces and Society, 29*(1), 7–29. https://doi.org/10.1177/0095327X0202900102.

Currey, C. J. (2003). *A new model for military/nongovernmental organization relations in post-conflict operations*. Carlisle Barracks: Army War College.

Daily Trust (Newspaper). (2017). Who are Borno's civilian JTF. Retrieved on the 2.12.2018 from https://www.dailytrust.com.ng/weekly/index.php/top-stories/16115-who-are-borno-s-civilian-jtf#dRrCOGPfsg1uZQzl.99

Department of Defence, United States of America. (2003). *Joint Publication 3-57.1: Joint Doctrine for Civil Affairs*, Washington: United States Government.

Department of Defense (DoD) United States of America. (2018). Civil military operations. *Joint Publication of 3 – 57*. Accessed 15.01.2019 from https://fas.org/irp/doddir/dod/jp3_57.pdf.

Edet, I. H. (2017). *Civil-military relations: Explaining a misunderstood and misused concept in the Nigerian military*. The Professional Journal of the Nigerian Army Infantry Corps, July- September 2017 Edition, 1 (1), 38–43.

Feaver, P. D., & Kohn, R. H. (2001). The civil-military gap and America's national security, In P. D. Feaver & R. H. Kohn (Eds.), *Soldiers and civilians: The civil-military gap and American national security*. Massachusetts: MIT Press.

Feaver, P. D. (2009). *Armed servants: Agency, oversight, and civil-military relations*. U.S. Harvard: Harvard University Press.

Franke, V. (2006). The peacebuilding dilemma: Civil-military cooperation in stability operations. *International Journal of Peace Studies*, *11*(2), 5–25.

Gibson, C. (2008). *Securing the state*. London: Routledge.

Gibson, C. P. (2008). *Securing the state, reforming the national security decision-making process of the civil mlitary nexus*. Aldershot: Ashgate Publishing.

Giustozzi, A. (2005). *The debate on warlordism: The importance of military legitimacy*. Crisis States Research Centre discussion papers, 13 (13). Crisis States Research Centre, London School of Economics and Political Science, London, UK.

Heaslip, G., Mangan, J., & Lalwani, C. (2007). *Integrating military and non-governmental organisation (NGO) objectives in the humanitarian supply chain: A proposed framework*. United Kingdom: Logistics Research Network, Hull.

Hernandorena, C. (2007). U.S. provincial reconstruction teams in Afghanistan, 2003-2006: Obstacles to interagency cooperation. In J. W. Boggs & J. R. Cerami (Eds.), *The interagency and counterinsurgency warfare: Stability, security, transition, and reconstruction roles*. U.S. Army War College, Strategic Studies Institute.

Hoffman, F. (2007). Bridging the civil-military gap: Rifts between civilians and the armed forces must be healed to avoid further damage to the Republic's ideals and traditions. *Armed Forces Journal (Washington)*, *Vol. 145*(5), 18–46.

Holsti, O. R. (2001). Of chasms and convergences: Attitudes and beliefs of civilians and military elites at the start of a new millenium. In P. D. Feaver & R. H. Kohn (Eds.), *Soldiers and civilians: The civil-military gap and American national security*. Massachusetts: MIT Press.

Huntington, S. (1957). *The soldier and the state: The theory and politics of civil military relations*. New York: Vintage Books.

International Criminal Court (2017) Report on Preliminary Examination Activities (2017)-Nigeria. https://www.icc-cpi.int/Pages/item.aspx?name=2017-otp-rep-PE-Nigeria.

International Crisis Group (ICG). (2017). Watchmen of Lake Chad: Vigilante groups fighting Boko Haram. Report No. 244/Africa. Accessed 14.08. 2018 from https://www.crisisgroup.org/africa/west-africa/nigeria/244-watchmen-lake-chad-vigilante-groups-fighting-boko-haram.

International Crisis Group. (23 February 2017). Watchmen of Lake Chad: Vigilante groups fighting Boko Haram. Report No. 244/Africa. Retrieved on the 2.12.2018 from http://www.crisisgroup.org/africa/west-africa/nigeria/244-watchmen-lake-chad-vigilante-groups-fighting-boko-haram.

Johansson, T. (2011). *The Effectiveness of CIMIC in Peace Operations from the View of the Local People*. Unpublished Master's Thesis in Peace and Conflict Studies Submitted to the Department of Peace and Conflict Research. Uppsala University, Sweden.

Kasselmann, H. J. (2012). Civil-military cooperation: A way to resolve complex crisis situations. *Prism*, *1*(4), 1–29.

Lovejoy, J. K. (2002). Improving media relations. *Military Review*, *82* (1), Accessed online on 13.08.2018 from http://media.leeds.ac.uk/papers/vp014312.html.

Luttwak, E. (1999). From Vietnam to Desert Fox: Civil-military relations in modern democracies. *Survival*, *41*(1), 99–112. 10.1093/survival/41.1.99.

Maiangwa, J. S., & Audu, A. R. (2018). Civilians in Frontlines: Evolving grassroots force for counter-insurgency operations in the Lake Chad region. In U. A. Tar (Ed.), *Defence transformation and the consolidation of democracy in Nigeria*. Nigeria – Kaduna: Academy Publishers.

Malish, R., Scott, J. S., & Rasheed, B. O. (2006). Military-civic action: Lessons learned from a brigade-level aid project in the 2003 war with Iraq. *Prehospital and Disaster Medicine*, *21*(3), 135–138.

Miracle, T. L. (2003). The Army and embedded media. *Military Review*, *83*(5), 41–45.

Mockaitis, T. R. (2004). *Civil-Military Cooperation in Peace Operations: The Case of Kosovo*., U.S. Army War College, 122 Forbes Ave, Carlisle, PA : Strategic Studies Institute, 122 Forbes Ave, Carlisle, PA.

NATO (North Atlantic Treaty Organisation) (2003) *NATO civil-military cooperation (CIMIC) Doctrine*. Available https://www.nato.int/ims/docu/AJP-9.pdf Accessed on 05.06.2019.

Nigerian Army Civil Military Cooperation Manual. (2009). *1*(4) Abuja:Nigerian Army Headquarters.

Nigerian Army (2015). *Civil-Military Cooperation Manual, Vol. 13* Abuja: Nigerian Army Printing Press

Onouha, F. (2014). *A danger not to Nigeria alone – Boko Haram's transnational reach and regional responses*.

Abuja: Friedrich Ebert Stiftung. Retrieved on 11.12.2017 from http://library.fes.de/pdf-files/bueros/nigeria/11066.pdf.

Rahbek-Clemmensen, J., Archer, E. M., Barr, J., Belkin, A., Guerrero, M., Hall, C., & Swain, K. E. (2012). Conceptualizing the civil–military gap: A research note. *Armed Forces & Society*, *38*(4), 669–678.

Rana, R. (2004). Contemporary challenges in the civil-military relationship: Complementarity or incompatibility? *International Review of the Red Cross of the Unit for Relations with Armed and Security Forces at the International Committee of the Red Cross*, *86*(855), 565–597.

Recchia, S. (2015). *Reassuring the reluctant warriors: US civil-military relations and multilateral intervention.* Ithaka United States, Cornell Studies on Security Affairs: Cornell University Press.

Rehse, P. (2004). *CIMIC: Concepts, definitions and practice.* Hamburg: Juni-Heft Publishers.

Rice, M. S., & Jones, O. J. (2010). Medical operations counterinsurgency warfare: Desired effects and unintended consequences. *Military Review*, *90*(3), 47–57.

Rietjens, B., Bollen, M., Khalil, M., & Wahidi, S. F. (2009). Enhancing the footprint: Stakeholders in Afghan reconstruction. *Parameters*, *39*(1), 22–47.

Ryan, M. (2007). The military and reconstruction operations. *Parameters*, *37*(4), 58–71.

Shuaib, Y. A. (2017). Tackling the inter-agency rivalry, *This Day Live*, an electronic article retrieved on the 14.12.2018 from https://www.thisdaylive.com/index.php/2017/06/09/tackling-the-inter-agency-rivalry/.

Szayna, T. S., McCarthy, K. F., Sollinger, J. M., Marquis, J. P., Demaine, L. J., & Steele, B. (2007). *The Civil-Military Gap in The United States: Does it Exist, Why, and Does it Matter?* A Monograph Prepared for the United States Army by RAND Corporation. https://www.rand.org/content/dam/rand/pubs/monographs/2007/RAND_MG379.pdf.

Tar, U.A., & Mustapha, M. (2016). *Emerging Architecture of Regional Security Complex in the Lake Chad Basin.* Being a Paper Presented at the International Conference on Security Regimens in Africa Organised by CODESERIA, Held at Azalai Grand Hotel, Bamako, Mali, 28 – 29 September.

Urben, H. A. (2010). *Civil-Military Relations in a Time Of War: Party, Politics, and the Profession of Arms.* Doctoral Dissertation, Submitted to the Faculty of the Graduate School of Arts and Sciences of Georgetown University.

Vanguardngr. (October 16, 2017). Medical outreach part of Armed Forces' constitutional responsibility – Enenche. Retrieved on the 13.12.2018 from https://www.vanguardngr.com/2017/10/medical-outreach-part-armed-forces-constitutional-responsibility-enenche/.

Venable, B. E. (2002). The Army and the Media. *Military Review*, *82*(1), 66–81.

Welch, C. (1999). *Civil Supremacy of the Military in Namibia: A Retrospect Case Study. SACDI Defence Digest Paper*, 82–33

Woll, M., & Brisson, P. (2013). Humanitarian care by a forward surgical team in Afghanistan. *Military Medicine*, *178*(4), 385–388.

# 38

# Violent non-state actors

## The challenges of counterterrorism and counterinsurgency in Africa

*Caroline Varin*

## Introduction

The African continent has been the operating theatre for a large number of violent non-state actors (VNSAs). These have been categorised as insurgents, terrorists, criminals, rebels, guerrillas, warlords, pirates and so on. The distinctions are based on group size, operational capabilities, tactics, legitimacy, but very often end up being politicised depending on the authority of the central government and their relationship with the VNSA. Part of the challenge to countering violent non-state actors in Africa is defining the appropriate strategy to address the type of violence taking place. The public discourse on violent actors has further conflated all manifestations of political violence into the term "terrorism". However, there are significant differences between terrorism and other types of violence, especially on the continent. While some violence is politically motivated, many VNSAs are driven by economic, ethnic or historical reasons to pick up arms. These require a different strategy depending on whether the population is heavily involved in or victimised by the group.

Furthermore, the local geographical and political landscape has made it easy for VNSAs to work together, merge and adapt, thereby changing their nature as they cross borders and encounter other like-minded groups. This has made it increasingly difficult to organise effective counterinsurgency and counterterrorism strategies, all the more so as most countries on the continent still refuse to invest in intelligence gathering domestically and share their findings regionally.

This chapter will begin by outlining the differences between terrorism and insurgency as defined in the literature. It argues that these labels are important but often politicised and not adapted to the situation in many African conflicts. As a result, it is critical to understand the type of violence taking place in each location and take note of the increasing trend of groups to work together and learn from each other, leading to hybridisation of VNSAs. This makes it all the more difficult to address and counter these combatants, requiring governments and the armed forces to work together and adapt to the threat at hand.

## The difficulty of conceptualizing terrorism and insurgency

This chapter demonstrates that an important conceptual difference is traditionally made when defining terrorism and insurgency, particularly as it relates to the strategy adopted to counter both forms of violence. Duyesteyn and Fumerton define terrorism and insurgency as "two distinct types of *strategies* of irregular war" (in Holmqvist-Jonsäter, Coker, & Henriksen, 2010: 28). As such, it is not a commentary on the difference in the composition and motivation of a terrorist group versus an insurgent group. Rather the key component is in the strategy adopted by the violent actor in pursuit of its goal. Understanding this difference therefore is necessary to adapting the military and policy response to successfully counter the adversary.

Insurgents and terrorists often share a common goal of bringing about political change. The defining goal of an insurgency, according to David Galula, is to exercise political power with "the tacit or explicit agreement of the population or, at worst, on its submissiveness" (Galula, 2006: 4). Insurgents are supported by and are able to mobilise a significant portion of the local population, making them first and foremost a domestic actor. The battle for the population drives the strategic map of an insurgent group. This means that the insurgent will work with and through the population, seeking to occupy and control territory with the objective of exercising political power. As a result, the group leading the insurgency must mobilise a segment of the population, either ideologically or through brute force, to build an army capable of capturing territory from the state (Beckett 2005; Hoffman 2006). The success of the group depends on its ability to mobilise and lead sufficient numbers, its access to weaponry, and the strength or legitimacy of the government (Grey 1999). The size and support base of the group is crucial for terrorism expert Bruce Hoffman, who explains that insurgents refer to a "numerically larger group of armed individuals" than are present in terrorist groups (Hoffman, 2006). Bell and Evans define insurgents as "overtly nationalist, spatially contained and classically defensive (...) designed to liberate a homeland" from a tyrant or an unacceptable way of life (Bell & Evans, 2010).

A terrorist group seeks to undermine the state and provoke a response that further delegitimises the sitting administration. This does not require the cooperation of the population. To the contrary, the strategic application of terror on civilians serves to further the political goals of the terrorist group by publicly denouncing the state as a lame duck, unable to protect its citizens (Hoffman 2006). By reverting to this tactic, "the terrorist (makes sure he) is almost always in a minority (...), they rarely have majority support, let alone some alternative blueprint as to how their vision of a better world will work" (Bell & Evans 2010). Terrorists rarely bring about change, although they can cause a lot of damage in their attempt to do so. This is because the type of violence utilised by the terrorist is a provocation of the state, forcing it to respond with increased violence and repression, thereby alienating the population who is victimised on all sides (Fromkin 1975: 4). The strategy tears away at the social contract, leaving a vacuum to be exploited.

The relationship with the population, therefore, is vital in distinguishing between an insurgency and a terrorist group. The strategy of insurgency includes building territorial enclaves where the members of the group can develop freely without fear of the state thereby creating an enabling environment. Kalyvas (2006) terms these "zones of insurgent control" and argues that they are necessary to expand operations into areas controlled by the government. The group numbers of an insurgency are as a result much higher than those of terrorist organisations that depend on security and discretion and are more discriminating in their recruitment (Crenshaw, 1981). In these territorial enclaves, insurgent groups also play a governing role, establishing their own justice systems and offering public services that would normally be supplied by the state. None of this is typically relevant to a terrorist group.

Both strategic choices, insurgencies and terrorism, may include acts of terror. Terror is a tactic adopted by a wide array of violent non-state actors in pursuit of their strategic goal (Tilly 2005: 21). Considering that any actor may use terror, Duyesteyn and Fumerton warn against the temptation of labelling all such actors as terrorists, as a distinction with insurgent groups nonetheless remains (in Holmqvist Coker & Henriksen, 2010: 31). Who they target is of importance: While insurgents mainly attack the state and its representatives such as the police and the armed forces near their operational base, terrorists tend to include foreign and especially western interests as their top targets causing terror beyond their immediate victim – although most of the time their victims are local inhabitants.

How they wield violence is also relevant. Terrorists have been portrayed in western literature as "nihilistic" or "apocalyptic'" (Ignatieff 2017) due to their recent use of suicide attacks and are therefore stripped of any political legitimacy. However, this is too simplistic. Notwithstanding the use of suicide bombers, every paramilitary movement requires a certain amount of sacrifice. Suicide bombers are unarguably a cost-effective, low-risk strategy that spurs terror among the population. But while some individuals have volunteered for this mission, others have been forced into it, as is increasingly the case in suicide bombings carried out by women and children for Boko Haram (Varin 2016). This method does not in any way erode the deeply political and religious long-term objectives of the group and does not reflect a nihilistic ideology from the leadership. Furthermore, few organisations in history have been simply destructive. While Al-Qaeda, for example, may have started out this way with bin Laden, its local branches have grown on the seeds of social discontent within a population that maintains hope in a better future.

In summary, the literature emphasises the differences in terms of the role played by the population and the control over territory, as "the principle and practice of establishing political-military control over a population and its territory is conspicuously absent in the strategy of terrorism" (Holmqvist-Jonsäter et al. 2010: 31). Insurgents generally aim to exercise some form of sovereign territorial control over a specific geographic space and its population, feeding off social and political discontent. It, therefore, struggles with the state in a contest over land and hearts (Schmitt & Ulmen 2006). Furthermore, terrorism is but one tactic employed by insurgent groups, whereas terror remains the main *modus operandi* of terrorists.

However, these distinctions are often marginal. Insurgent groups may behave like terrorists, using kidnapping and suicide bombings to gain political traction while developing social benefit

*Table 38.1* Characteristics of Terrorists and Insurgents

| Descriptor | Terrorists | Insurgents |
| --- | --- | --- |
| **Numbers** | A minority | Representative of population |
| **Ideology** | Nihilistic | Based on existing grievances |
| **Methods** | Undermine government by causing fear | Territorial and population control to expand and overthrow government |
| **Targets** | Anyone, including foreigners in the country and abroad | The state and its symbols, generally close to the home base |
| **Objectives** | Transnational | Pushing the government out of insurgents' territory |
| **Legitimacy** | None | Local and international recognition |
| **Response** | Hunt and eliminate | Address grievances, deter the use of violence |

*Source:* Adapted from Varin 2016.

programs for the people they command. This was the case of Hezbollah, which employed both terrorist and guerilla tactics against Israel while providing social welfare to the communities under its protection. Likewise, Boko Haram ensures that its combatants receive wives, an important service in a culture where poverty is both rampant and humiliating as young men are not able to support a family. The Islamic State/ISIS made a lot of effort to portray itself as helping to rebuild the community in territories it occupied in Syria and Iraq (Zelin 2017). The Islamic State/ISIS' grand strategy involved conquest and control, much like any insurgency. Its rejection of existing borders decided by the Sykes-Picot Agreement appears to be anti-colonial and defensible, rather than purely abstract or ideological, even if it does erase an established convention a hundred years in the making.

The designation of "terrorist organisation" therefore has been as political as it is problematic for any attempt to categorise and define violent non-state actors. The Tamil Tigers, Hamas and Hezbollah have all received the tag "terrorist" by their respective states and corresponding allies. But they have also gained local and international credibility by mobilising a significant portion of the population and clearly establishing their political goals in opposition too often corrupt and inefficient governments. They have proven their ability to control territory and offer protection and support to the inhabitants, thereby further eroding the legitimacy of the state. One may argue that the real difference between a terrorist and an insurgent, where the actor appears to bridge both categories, is in the outcome and level of success over time. If terrorists are defined as agents of wanton destruction with no real or realistic political agenda, then their failure in the long term is unavoidable.

## The challenge of hybrid VNSAs

Much of the existing literature on terrorism and insurgency is based on a Western-centric experience. As a result, since the 1950s, counterinsurgency has included a strategic mandate to win the hearts and minds of the population in recognition that this is required to defeat an insurgency. However, this does not take into account evidence that insurgencies today, especially in Africa, are less dependent on popular support. Weinstein finds that insurgent groups in Africa often derive revenue from natural resources and external funding, meaning that they need not develop a significant rapport with the local population to ensure their logistical needs (Weinstein 2007). Conversely, assumptions that terrorists do not seek to rule over populations is erroneous today, as renowned terrorist groups in Mali, Nigeria and Somalia have sought to control territory and people as part of their strategy. Counterinsurgency strategies need to understand the local dynamics *and their changes* if they are to have any chance of succeeding.

Violent groups across Africa have benefited from improved networks of communication and transportation inevitably born out of globalisation. Islamist-oriented groups around the continent have sent ambassadors to each other and shared intelligence, ideas and technology. Criminal groups have moved from smuggling to terrorism, as evidenced by Mokhtar Belmokhtar, known as "Mr Marlboro" who orchestrated the Tingantourine attack in 2013 (Lister & Cruickshank 2013). On the other end of the spectrum, rebels with territorial aspirations have become warlords, their political goals tempered by. the easy exploitation of natural resources. A number of notable examples are worth highlighting to illustrate the resulting difficulty of orchestrating an effecting counterterrorism or counterinsurgency strategy.

## Dispelling territorial claims

According to prevalent definitions, the territory is critical to differentiating between an insurgent group and a terrorist group. de la Calle & Sánchez-Cuenca (2012) explain that insurgents hold territory in countries that have a weak state capacity. Governments tend to focus their resources on the city, leaving large swathes of countryside vulnerable to exploitation by non-state actors. As demonstrated previously, insurgents depend on these enclaves of power to develop and prosper. Likewise, warlords orchestrate their strategy around easily extracted resources that depend on their control over the territory. Conversely, terrorist groups have been *identified* by their lack of territorial control.

The playing field was transformed in March 2012 when Al-Qaeda in the Islamic Maghreb (AQIM), a terrorist group that had been operational in the region since 2007, succeeded in defeating state forces and occupying territory in northern Mali. AQIM lorded over a huge part of the country, including the cities of Gao, Timbuktu and Kidal for close to a year until January 2013. During this time, argues Cocodia, the terrorist group, working with other like-minded organisations *Ansar Dine* and *Mouvement pour l'Unification et le Jihad en Afrique de l'Ouest* (MUJAO), established their own political system and enforced Sharia law on the population (Varin & Abubakar 2017). Despite its brief existence, AQIM's rule in Mali was instrumental for two reasons: First, it enabled the free-flow of Islamist radicals from around Africa into the country, where they were able to meet and share knowledge undisturbed, creating a lasting network and acting as a force multiplier for other groups. Second, it created a precedent where, for the first time in the modern era, a non-state actor was allowed to invade and claim sovereignty over a sizeable territory. Evidently this has inspired other Islamist groups to establish their so-called Caliphate in Africa and beyond.

In Nigeria, the Islamist group Boko Haram has been labelled in turn a terrorist group and an insurgent group. Between 2014 and 2015, the group led by Abu Shekau occupied territory in the northeast the size of Belgium. This further served to blur the lines. However, Boko Haram's political goals remain unclear if not undefined, and the group has not actively sought to overthrow the government. Likewise, there is little proof that the militants tried to govern over the occupied population beyond forcing conversions to their version of Islam and arbitrarily imposing their interpretations of Sharia law (Varin 2016). However, there is ample evidence that members of Boko Haram travelled to Mali in 2012 to meet with AQIM, where they also encountered other members of Al-Shabaab and the Islamic State. As a result, Boko Haram adapted their strategy, resorting to kidnap-and-ransom as a source of income and developing a social media strategy that has allegedly benefited from technological know-how from members of ISIS (Cummings 2015).

A similar case can be made for Islamic State/ISIS in Africa. Described near-universally as a terrorist group, ISIS has nonetheless stated its intent to create a Caliphate, and in Libya in 2015, it managed to control territory along the middle coastal belt of the country between Sirte and Bin Jawwad, taking advantage of the civil war and state vacuum in the area (Varin & Abubakar 2017). However, a change of fortunes and competition with other VNSAs has stemmed their ambitions for the time being.

All three organisations have proven and declared affiliations with Al-Qaeda and the Islamic State. They have used terror tactics targeting civilians and foreigners and wielded huge violence against the populations they sought to control. The conundrum for a government's response is whether to use a counterinsurgency (COIN) strategy or a counterterrorism (CT) strategy. These VNSAs have effectively forced government forces out of parts of the country, which they, in turn, occupied, if not governed themselves, resembling an insurgency. The territorial factor must change the discourse as it requires both a military response to dislodge the VNSA from their strongholds and a concerted government policy to address the sufferings and grievances of the population. This has been particularly difficult to achieve in Africa, where civil-military ties are historically strained and the central state often suffers from a lack of legitimacy and capacity.

## Fluid categories and adaptive VNSAs

Although VNSAs are organised into different categories, groups learn from each other and adapt to new opportunities and challenges. In Africa, VNSAs have been known to change their objectives, their membership, their operations and even their territorial claims. Terrorists, rebels and warlords are known to have engaged in and rely on extensive criminal activities locally and internationally with other illegitimate actors. This makes it particularly difficult to determine an effective CT-COIN strategy.

The Allied Democratic Forces (ADF) in the Democratic Republic of Congo (DRC) is one such example of a group that has proven highly adaptive. The ADF has claimed to have Islamist affiliations and is labelled as a terrorist group by the government. Jesper Cullen demonstrates that the operations and objectives of the ADF have become economic rather than political or ideological, evolving from its initial declared goal of overthrowing the government of Uganda (where they originally operated) and replacing it with Islamic rule (Varin & Abubakar 2017). The group has undergone several transformations since its inception in 1993 in response to the political situation in Uganda and DRC and the economic opportunities that have presented themselves. ADF was initially labelled as a rebel movement or insurgent group in Uganda but presently remains in the Beni area of eastern DRC where it prioritises illegal commercial activities, primarily smuggling operations of consumer goods, gold and timber. Today, Cullen describes it as a "Congolese criminal group" (109) and explains that its capability has been reduced thanks to a robust security operation led by the Ugandan state although they remain undeterred in DRC.

A second illustration of the adaptive abilities of VNSAs in Africa is the case of the Lord's Resistance Army (LRA). Led by the warlord Kony, the LRA's objectives have changed from wanting to overthrow the state in Uganda to exploiting the economic opportunities available to the group. Van Wyk explains that Kony, not unlike Islamist terrorist groups, sought to "establish a theocracy through the holy war" but also appeared to have "political, particularly nationalist objectives" that promoted the ethno-nationalist demands of the Acholi (in Varin & Abubakar 2017: 229). In addition, he provided "public goods" to his followers including socio-economic security and social legitimisation (Lilyblad 2014). However, faced with sustained government pressure, the group has transformed its objectives to simple survival, creating economic opportunities through looting, illegal elephant poaching and wildlife trafficking in Central Africa, narcotics smuggling and illegal trading in ivory, diamonds and gold. They have created transit routes through territories they control, once more resembling more a criminal group rather than an organised insurgency. Van Wyk argues that the LRA is an exceptional group that demonstrates the "adaptability, durability and evolution of warlords as violent non-state actors in Africa" (in Varin & Abubakar 2017: 242).

What is interesting in both cases is the government's motivation to drive the insurgents out when they challenged the state's legitimacy, but their relative compliance when the group changed its ambitions from political to economic. It is unclear whether the government simply lacks commitment when its interests are not at stake, or whether it is more difficult to counter warlords on the periphery of a very large country, or perhaps both. Regardless, the existence of these VNSAs, even in small and relatively unthreatening quantities, can reap huge damage on the local population located on occupied territory. Military incursions into warlord territory have been relatively successful, as has the counterterrorist policy of decapitation, which finally put an end to Jonas Savimbi's terror in Angola after nearly forty years of effective warlordism. A counterinsurgency strategy focused on the population would not have succeeded, as demonstrated below.

## Mobilisation, the case against hearts and minds

Former US President Lyndon B. Johnson stated that "the ultimate victory (in Vietnam) will depend upon the hearts and minds of the people who actually live out there" (cited in Williamson 2011: 1036). This was repeated by Former President Barack Obama who claimed that defeating "extremism will not succeed with bullets or bombs alone" (ibid). A hearts and minds campaign has been adopted in modern counterinsurgency strategies that assume that insurgencies are rooted in popular support and thrive on the failures or weakness of the ruling government and associated institutions. Recent studies have shown that the benefits and gratitude originated from humanitarian aid aimed at improving local relations have been "short-lived" however. In any case, this population-centric strategy often falls short when applied to the African continent.

The "winning hearts and minds" approach rests on the ability to convince people that a better life is possible (Mansoor in Rid & Keaney 2010: 82); it includes a component of state-building or state reinforcing to return faith in the government and its ability to provide public services and implement the rule of law. In theory, grievances will, in turn, be addressed by legitimate state structures, thereby removing the incentive for people to support alternative options to the central government (Gompert & GordonI, 2008). This is already a complex problem in most African states, which would be far too long to develop here. Suffice it to say here that the social contract developed in most European states and to an extent in the United States takes on a very different meaning on the African continent where tribal and family ties often supersede the relationship between the politicians and the population.

A second shortcoming of the COIN discourse is the tendency to separate the "people" from the "insurgents". This is impossible in many places where the "people" are the family members of the "insurgents". As explained by Gurman (2013:9) "the 'people' includes not only those who oppose or are victimised by the insurgency (or terrorist group) but those who physically support it, providing their relatives and friends with food, clothing, and shelter". Not only does this approach ignore the importance of kinship, especially in rural places where survival depends on the family, it also presumes the role of ideology or grievance as a mobiliser of insurgents.

It is difficult to distinguish a motive for individuals that join groups of VNSAs. In his survey of youth radicalisation in Nigeria, Onuoha (2014) found that religious belief and education, followed by unemployment and poverty were the biggest motivators for joining Boko Haram. The government's high rate of corruption and neglect of citizens' welfare were also cited as reasons for picking up arms. In addition to social grievances, research has shown that strong affiliation with a religious community, especially one that is perceived to be in conflict with another, is directly related to its willingness to carry out acts of aggression (see Varin 2016: 86). A study by the Cleen Foundation in 2014 revealed that a significant acceptance among the people in Yobe and Borno for the use of violence in order to impose one's religious beliefs.

Although some people may be ideologically or politically motivated, many young men join up simply because there are no other economic alternatives. They are given a gun; they can take what they need from others. This is particularly the case in Africa, where *raison d'être* is a less significant motivator for recruits. A hearts and minds campaign will find it hard if not impossible to address all these grievances/motivators for joining or supporting a VNSA. Reforming the state to make is more accountable is one problem, creating jobs and sustaining employment is another one that most countries haven't fully grasped yet. In addition, the tribal factor cannot be ignored in the behaviour of many VNSAs. The gruesome bloodbaths in Rwanda, Burundi, and Sudan (among others) across ethnic lines demonstrate how political aspirations can take advantage of tribal affiliations to mobilise a following and exercise extreme levels of violence (Lemarchand 2009). This is not something that current counterinsurgency strategies are able to resolve.

As this section shows, poverty and underdevelopment are not the only or even the major sources of mobilisation for VNSAs in Africa. While some people may join or support a terrorist group or an insurgency out of political disillusionment and economic aspirations, others are forced to join by familial ties, out of religious conviction, or simply to survive. Neither a CT nor a COIN strategy will suffice to reverse the trends of violence in these cases. The dynamics of VNSAs in Africa are a lot more complex and require a case-by-case study in order to understand them and subsequently draft a strategy to defeat.

## Obstacles to counterterrorism and counterinsurgency in Africa

The war in Afghanistan was arguably an eye-opener on the complexity of counterterrorism and counterinsurgency. After 15 years, the all-powerful American army is nowhere close to reversing the violence in the country, despite significant investment in studies, technology and experimentation with diverse strategies. The complexity of the situation in most African countries meets, if not exceeds, the conflict in Afghanistan. The hybrid nature of most VNSAs discussed above, the porous borders and the lack of coordination between states today make it difficult for militaries to adapt their strategy.

### Porous borders

Porous borders in Africa remain one of the principal challenges to militarily countering VSNAs. The borders, inherited from colonialism, are enormous and often without natural geographical separation between them. There is limited state security along the borders between most countries and over 100 disputed border areas in Africa, making it difficult for states to cooperate and share resources and intelligence. On the other hand, people divided by artificial borders have no problem moving across the region and coordinating operations.

Mali is such an example. The Tuaregs, split between Mali, Algeria, Niger, Mauritania, Burkina Faso and Libya, have a shared cultural background and aspiration for statehood. They have launched a number of rebellions in Mali and Niger that were defeated, until 2012 when they banded with National Movement for the Liberation of Azawad (MNLA) and AQIM, creating a new type of hybrid threat born out of the opportunity. Part of the reason the groups were able to meet up is that they have been working together smuggling and trading across the Sahel (Smith 2014). The rough terrain and porous borders have made it nearly impossible to defeat them, although for now, the French and Malian troops seem to have pushed the rebels back into the desert.

The porous borders are exacerbated by a lack of cross-border cooperation. Nigeria has over 4,000 kilometres of shared borders with Cameroon, Chad, Niger and Benin, with a known 1,500 illegal border crossings (not counting the tunnels) and 84 legal entry routes into the country (Onuoha 2013: 4). This has facilitated transnational trafficking of goods, weapons and even people. The five countries, however, have been reluctant to commit financially or politically to fighting the enemy together, exacerbating the existing problem. Despite the creation of a multinational joint task force, most of the military operations take place within the borders of a given country, with terrorists and insurgents able to cross the borders unconcerned that their pursuant will follow them (Varin 2016). Yet, it is clear that none of the countries is able or willing to police their own borders, leading to the inevitable failure of government efforts to vanquish Boko Haram (Onuoha 2013).

## Challenges to intelligence sharing

Part of the difficulty with intelligence sharing across borders in many African conflicts is the involvement of neighbours supporting one or other VNSA. Eritrea, for example, has been at war intermittently with Ethiopia since 1998 and at the same time allegedly supporting rebel groups and terrorists according to Addis Ababa. Countries in Africa have been accused of interfering in each other's affairs, exploiting resources and supporting non-state actors since independence. In addition, the cultural and linguistic differences between francophone, lusophone and English-speaking countries have created an environment of distrust as well as increasing costs should they chose to work together. Regional rivalries continue to disrupt efforts by the African Union and the international community to organise a structured communication system in Africa (Cline 2016).

Another problem is the rivalry between agencies within one country. Security agencies compete for funding and influence, often failing to share intelligence among themselves (Cline 2016). While some intelligence sharing does take place, it stops where it might create an opportunity for another agency to gain attention nationally. In Nigeria, one military officer explained that the army had a strong intelligence gathering system but failed to communicate it effectively with troops on the ground (Varin 2016).

While there have been some improvements in intelligence sharing on the continent, often spearheaded by the AU or regional bodies, there are intrinsic limitations that are nearly impossible to overcome. Internal weaknesses, including a lack of investment and an excessive focus on regime survival, have impaired states from systematically and responsibly collecting intelligence domestically, let alone sharing the results among agencies and across borders. ECOWAS has lamented its coordination system, claiming that it suffered from "weak internal coordination, underutilisation and misdirection of human capital as well as the deployment of limited instruments" (ECOWAS Economic Community of West African States, 2008).

The United Nations Office on Drugs and Crime highlights the importance of enhancing border management and fostering international collaboration and exchange of information between countries as a priority for combating VNSAs. Both of these seem to be distant goals that can only be achieved following a considerable investment in building credible domestic institutions, which requires political will.

## Conclusion: Adapting strategies to Africa

As this volume shows, there is no single concept of a successful COIN or CT strategy. States have had to adapt to the challenges of defining the enemy and keeping up with it as it changes over time. VNSAs do share one characteristic; in order to survive, they need to always be a step ahead of the government. This has become easier in a globalised world where information is easily available to all and provides more comprehensive details than ever before (Gardham 2011). Insurgents and terrorists use Google Earth and Street View to conduct reconnaissance and plan their attack. Social media such as Twitter, YouTube and Facebook serve to recruit followers and disseminate their message. PayPal can be used to raise funds and make payments. Drones help with transporting phones, money or drugs over large distances. Each of these makes it easier for VNSAs to operate, and harder for governments and their armies to stop them.

A successful strategy to counter VNSAs, especially in Africa, requires a combination of COIN and CT tactics. A robust military response is necessary to protect the population from falling victim to violence and especially territorial occupation. This requires sufficient investment into the military infrastructure, something that many African leaders have neglected in response to the many military coups that have historically taken place across the continent. The strategy of decapitation has been relatively successful for most insurgent groups in Africa as these are often led by charismatic leaders whose following falls apart when they disappear. Again this requires a strong military intelligence wing but also the cooperation of the population for information about the location and operations of the insurgent group. However, the strategy of decapitation has been less successful in the case of terrorist groups that operate in decentralised networks – although according to one study by Bryan Price, "leadership decapitation may have negative short-term consequences, it significantly increases terrorist group mortality rates" (Price 2012).

Arguably the biggest challenge for African leaders is investing in building the social contract with their citizens. This requires at the very least improvements in political accountability, democratic transitions of power and especially putting serious money into infrastructure to provide basic services to the population, starting with a guarantee of security as the first pillar of state-building. Borrowing from Western-constructed strategies will inevitably fail if the local context and extensive structural weaknesses across the continent are not integrated into a collaborative campaign by African societies to combat the threat of violent non-state actors. So long as states fail to provide security and resources to their citizens, there will be opportunities for competitors who offer hope or forcibly bend the population to their will.

# References

Amony, Evelyn. (2016). *Interview with the British Broadcasting Corporation (BBC)*, 12 January. http://www.bbc.co.uk/programmes/p03f91dm.

Beckett, I. (2005). The future of insurgency. *Small Wars & Insurgencies, 16*(1), 22–36.

Bell, C., & Evans, B. (2010). From Terrorism to Insurgency: Remapping the Postinterventionary Security Terrain. *Journal of Intervention and Statebuilding, 4*(4), 371–390.

Cline, L. (2016). African regional intelligence cooperation: Problems and prospects. *International Journal of Intelligence and CounterIntelligence, 29*(3), 447–469.

Crenshaw, M. (1981). The causes of terrorism. *Comparative Politics, 13*(4), 379.

Cummings, R. (2015). *Boko Haram's pledge to ISIS: Public relations or reality?*. [online] IPI Global Observatory. Available from: https://theglobalobservatory.org/2015/03/boko-haram-pledge-allegiance-isis/ Accessed 16. 08.2017.

de la Calle, L., & Sánchez-Cuenca, I. (2012). Rebels without a territory. *Journal of Conflict Resolution, 56*(4), 580–603.

ECOWAS (Economic Community of West African States). (16 January 2008) *Regulation Msc/Reg.1/01/08, The ECOWAS Conflict Prevention Framework*, 6, https://www.right2info.org/resources/publications/instruments-and-standards/africa_ecowas-regulation_conflct-prevention.

Fromkin, D. (1975). The strategy of terrorism. *Foreign Affairs, 53*(4), 683.

Galula, D. (2006). *Counterinsurgency warfare: Theory and practice*. Greenwood Publishing Group.

Gardham, D. (2011). *Terrorists are harnessing hi-tech communications, government warns*. [online] Telegraph.co.uk. Available from: http://www.telegraph.co.uk/news/uknews/terrorism-in-the-uk/

8633311/Terrorists-are-harnessing-hi-tech-communications-government-warns.html Accessed 18.08.2017.

Gompert, D., & GordonI, J. (2008). *War by other means: Building complete and balanced capabilities for counterinsurgency*. Santa Monica: RAND National Defense Research Institute.

Grey, C. (1999). *Modern strategy*. Oxford University Press.

Gurman, H. (2013). *Hearts and minds*. New York: The New Press.

Hoffman, B. (2006). *Inside terrorism*. Columbia University Press.

Holmqvist-Jonsäter, C., Coker, C., & Henriksen, R. (2010). *The character of war in the 21st century*. London: Routledge.

Ignatieff, M. (2017). *It's war - but it doesn't have to be dirty*. [online] The Guardian. Available from: https://www.theguardian.com/world/2001/oct/01/afghanistan.terrorism9 Accessed 15.08.2017.

Kalyvas, S. (2006). *Logic of violence in civil war*. Cambridge University Press.

Lemarchand, René R. (2009). *The dynamics of violence in Central Africa*. University of Pennsylvania Press.

Lilyblad, C. (2014). Illicit authority and its competitors: The constitution of governance in territories of limited statehood. *Territory, Politics, Governance, 2*(1), 72–93.

Lister, T., & Cruickshank, P. (2013). *'Mr. Marlboro': The veteran jihadist behind the attack in Algeria - CNN*. [online] CNN. Available from: http://edition.cnn.com/2013/01/17/world/meast/algeria-who-is-belmoktar/index.html Accessed 16.08.2017.

Onuoha, F. (2013). *Porous borders and Boko Haram's arms smuggling operations in Nigeria*. Al Jazeera Center for Studies.

Onuoha, F. (2014). *Why do youth join Boko Haram?* United States Institute of Peace.

Price, B. (2012). Targeting top terrorists: How leadership decapitation contributes to counterterrorism. *International Security, 36*(4), 9–46.

Rid, T., & Keaney, T. (2010). *Understanding counterinsurgency warfare*. Milton Park, Abingdon, Oxon, England: Routledge.

Schmitt, C., & Ulmen, G. (2006). *The nomos of the earth in the international law of the jus publicum Europaeum*. New York: Telos.

Smith, A. (2014). *Islamists bankrolled by large-scale African drug-smuggling operation*. [online] The Guardian. Available from: https://www.theguardian.com/world/2014/sep/16/islamist-groups-african-drug-smuggling-operation Accessed 16.08.2017.

Tilly, C. (2005). Terror as strategy and relational process. *International Journal of Comparative Sociology, 46*(1-2), 11–32.

Varin, C. (2016). *Boko Haram and the war on terror*. Praeger ABC Clio.

Varin, C., & Abubakar, A (2017). *Violent non-state actors in Africa: Terrorists, rebels and warlords*. London: Palgrave Macmillan.

Weinstein, J. (2007). *Inside rebellion*. Cambridge: Cambridge University Press.

Williamson, J. (2011). Using humanitarian aid to 'win hearts and minds': a costly failure? *International Review of the Red Cross, 93*(884), 1035–1061.

Zelin, A. (2017). *How the Militants Overrunning Iraq Win Hearts and Minds*. [online] The Atlantic. Available from: https://www.theatlantic.com/international/archive/2014/06/the-isis-guide-to-building-an-islamic-state/372769/ Accessed 15.08.2017.

# 39

# Defence contractors, counterterrorism and counterinsurgency in Africa

*Jonathan S. Maiangwa*

## Introduction

As Africa continues to navigate through the pathway to sustainable development and stable democracy, it still faces severe challenges from the increasing activities of terrorist and insurgent groups. In recent times, the activities of these groups have disrupted socio-political processes and displaced a large number of persons across different regions in the continent which of course have taken away the attention of governments from critical issues of development to mainly security concern of counterterrorism (CT) and counterinsurgency (COIN). This situation has necessitated governments' utilisation of the services of highly organised private entities known as defence contractors against terrorist and insurgent groups. These bodies provide military and police services to deal with a complex conflict situation. Extensive studies on defence contractors or private military and security companies (PMSCs) which include, Foaleng (2007); Zarate (1998); Williamson (2007); Brooks (2002); Henineken and Motzouris (2011); and Gumedze (2011) across different regions reveal the extensive outsourcing in diverse conflict scenarios and the apparent weak or lack of regulations of these merchants of conflict in conflict zones. It is at the heart of this chapter therefore that defence contractors (foreign and local) are viewed as performing dual purposes that is, providing peace and stability through engagement in CT and COIN, and the risk they pose to the security of their host or client states (during and even long after) their engagement. This is exhibited in multifaceted services they provide to diverse groups which include governments, non-governmental organisations, giant corporations as well as rebel groups. In addition to the negative consequence, Ndlovu-Gatsheni (2007) and Roeber (2005) argues that corrupt practices in the defence sector in many countries have posed a greater risk to security as well. In this chapter, both defence contractors and PMSCs will be used interchangeably though refer to the same nomenclature.

Recently the demands for defence contractors in Africa rose astronomically because of increasing violent conflicts, and the speed in which state actors go about to outsource them. Baker (2011:116) attributed the unprecedented explosion of defence contractors to high demand in Iraq which, of course, correlates with the war in Afghanistan and other serious conflicts around developing countries. State actors in Africa outsource PMSCs to perform CT and COIN operations such as fighting wars, crushing terrorists and insurgent movements and defend key locations and installations (Barstow, 2004), protection of strategic national assets such as energy plants, oil sites, communication facilities, equipment and government mineral resources, etc. Similarly, giant multinational corporations also deploy defence contractors to their sphere of investments and to places where they have control over natural resources. Owing to this increasing task and demands over the services of PMSCs in conflict zones as well as their recognition by contracting states, they enjoy privileges and incentives such as tax relief from weak and fragile states in addition to protection from Western countries. This chapter draws attention to the nature, scope, structures, and the debilitating consequences of defence contractors on Africa. The resurgence of conflicts increases in defence expenditures, arms proliferation and creation of multi-dimensional conflict zones and corrupt practices are keys to this discussion.

There is no doubt that arms procurement, intelligence gathering, strategic planning, equipment supply and maintenance and retraining of security personnel in most developing countries have been surrendered to foreign defence professionals especially for countries facing extreme violent conflicts. Mali, Chad, Congo DRC, Iraq, Columbia, and Afghanistan are all notable thresholds of PMSCs today because of the perennial conflicts in those countries. Donor countries also multiply the grief of these countries as they allow "humanitarian services" delivery to be done by defence contractors with devastating impacts on national and regime security. Not only that, countries with poor human rights record and questionable constitutional change of governments often employed foreign military professionals to provide protection to such leaders and in some instances, but local security personnel are also given special training to perform this role. Often defence contractors and other arms suppliers and dealers in Africa are been criticised for their counter security roles, lack of respect to the sovereignty of states, being harbingers of conflicts and seen as promoters of corrupt practices. They are also viewed as "mercenaries" that violate municipal regulations and international laws. Well on the issue of mercenary, Cilliers (1999:1) stresses that mercenaries within international law, are explicitly associated with the process of armed opposition to decolonisation as reflected in the 1977 OAU Convention on the Elimination of Mercenaries in Africa and the 1989 UN International Convention against the Recruitment, Use, Financing and Training of Mercenaries which are quite different from the current PMSCs.

Defence contractors arguably offer attractive services to secure the elites of weak African states- a vital service that even the national armed forces may not be able to provide, especially where the state leadership is at odds with, or suspicious of the defence establishment and are therefore considered as reliable means of dealing with insurgents, rebels and opposition forces. Defence system in many African countries such as Libya, Tunisia, Uganda, Malawi, and Zimbabwe have at different times been weakened by poor leadership, funding deficit, deficient training and infrastructure and persistent conflicts. In these states, the defence has been turned to a "commodity of trade" for leaders that insist to have power over their countries for life. This service is to be supplied by the "highest bidder" amongst competing defence contractors. Leaders like late Umar Bongo of Gabon, Joseph Kabila of Congo DRC, Idris Deby of Chad etc prefer to contract the security of their countries to well-resourced defence contractors in return of their personal protection and safety of their family and clan members. Some analysts have argued that some leaders in Africa deliberately weaken the industrial defence sector of their countries to establish dependence on foreign assistance and arms aid. This is the more reason in some African countries today we have overblown defence expenditure to cater for defence contractors. Conversely, in critical moments of war and terror attacks, weaknesses of leaders in such countries are exposed as they tend to look outward for military support rather than relying inward on their ill-trained and underequipped military forces. In their arguments, Roeber (2005) and Looney (1988) stressed that the defence sector is one of the most; if not the most corrupt in the International arena. According to them the attraction and cooperation of private involvement in security matters have eroded accountability and transparency in defence administration and public sector management. There are three types of corrupt practices in the defence sector: bribery, commissions, and inducements. Both are common in sub-Saharan Africa owing to poor accounting/auditing and secrecy associated with the defence sector. Hartley (2007) ascribed this to weak measures and poor statistics on defence expenditure and arms procurement. Bribery is associated with government official circumventing rules to please their cronies. For example, Tompolo, a militant leader in the Niger Delta region of Nigeria became rich unexpectedly because of his link to former President, Goodluck Jonathan to fight piracy. Tompolo became the owner of the private security company and received a contract from government running to millions of dollars during the regime of his kinsman (Boas, 2014) (*emphasis added*). A study using international treasury and intelligence databases found out that 40% of all corruption in global trade occurred in the defence sector (Roeber, 2005). Similarly, Transparency International estimates that $20bn in defence spending per year is ridden with corruption[1].

Also, in the last couple of decades, political violence has altered the nature and context of African conflicts with implications for the conspicuous and penetration of defence contractors. The threat of international terrorism has been on the increase mostly in the Horn of Africa and the West African region. Terrorists have also built strongholds and support base in parts of North and East Africa and visibly occupying a substantial portion in the Maghreb due to international diffusion and connections to most of their activities. Even though inter-state conflicts have been reduced in the recent decade to the barest minimum because of regional and international interventions, intra-state insurgent movements and terror attacks are on the risk in most African states. Some of the manifestations are due to poor CT and COIN regulations and weak legal frameworks. As a result, Africa as a continent has been repeatedly labelled as an unsecured continent by the West and summarily designated in the Post 9/11 era as a haven and exporter of terrorists to the developed world. Omeje (2008:96) argues for instance, that 9/11 incidents affected America's perspective, perception, and policies in a radical way that security issues from the developing world are no longer treated lightly. In view of that global attention has shifted to Africa as "ground zero" of the "Global War on Terror" (GWOT) with an intensified focus on all sorts of support in the defence of the African state to withstand the scourge of terrorism. Defence contractors have joined the bandwagon by providing contractable services to African armed forces in areas of training, intelligence, technology, and military campaigns. Abrahamsen (2005:65–67) notes that although the negative perception over Africa remains deep, however other primordial reasons attached to this are too strong to ignore. We must also note that CT-COIN support from Western countries to Africa, from Djibouti in the Horn of Africa to North and West Africa precedes 9/11. The terror attacks on the US assets and diplomatic missions in Nairobi, Kenya and Dar-Salam, Tanzania in 1998 are precursor and incentives for CT-COIN support and outpouring of PMSCs to Africa in recent decades.

Though, insurgent movements are not new to Africa, what is new is the speed at which international terrorism is gaining traction on the continent by decimating communities and causing trauma and upsurge of refugees' population in the continent. Poor governance, social injustice, prebendal politics, corrupt practices and political exclusion are the causes of Africa's unstable socio-political conditions. Ethnic and religious groups have expressed deep resentment and disappointment on those that exercise rule and control over them. Too often, anger and hatred from excluded groups are inflamed by their poor material conditions and result to unhealthy outrages which apparently make ways for defence contractors to hijack and provide arms to distressed groups to indulge in armed struggle against the state and other groups.

Jonathan S. Maiangwa

*Table 39.1* Examples, Activities and Users of Defence Contractors

| Defence Contractors | Activities and Services Provided | Main Users of Services |
|---|---|---|
| Executive Outcomes (now defunct), Sandline International, Gurkha Security Guards | Combat and operational support | Governments |
| DSL, MPRI, Silver Shadow, Levdan, Vinnel, BDM | Military advice and training | Governments |
| Executive Outcomes, Sandline International, Levdan | Arms procurement | Governments |
| Control Risk Group, Kroll, Saladin, DynCorp | Intelligence gathering | Governments, MNCs |
| DSL, Lifeguard, Group 4, Control Risk Group, Gurkha Security Guards, Gray Security, Coin Security | Security and crime prevention services | MNCs, humanitarian agencies |
| Brown & Root, DynCorp, Pacific Architects and Engineers | Logistical support | Peacekeeping organisations, humanitarian agencies |

Source: UK House of Commons, "Private Military Companies: Options for Regulation", Green Paper (HCC 577 of 2002), London: HMSO, February 2002 (O'Brien, 2000).[3]

A reflection on public perception and government strategy on CT-COIN acknowledge that arms procurement, military build-up, and "outsourcing" of PMSCs is a component of Africa's occupation of disposing threat. However, in the wake of the fight against terrorist and insurgent movements and extant civil wars in Africa, it is a known fact that the continent has become a potential client to defence contractors (foreign and local) whose avowed interest has provided relative stability, arms proliferation and instability. On the strength of the foregoing, therefore, this chapter analysed CT-COIN measures carried out by PMSCs in Africa by identifying glaring cases across the regions which have significant impacts on peace and security in the continent.

## An overview of foreign and local defence contractors

In today's world, the presence of foreign and local contractors are so visible in combat and conflict zones seemingly due to the numbers of coercive corporate tasks they perform in frontlines and at peace times which include the capacity of rapid deployment and precision in the target. Private contractors are virtually involved in the transportation of weapons, military commodities, intelligence, strategic planning and sometimes procurement of arms for government forces or enemy forces. Faite (nd) stress that some defence contractors have developed a profound connection and unparallel expertise, for instance, the American firm Airscan operates private air reconnaissance, while Ronco, specialises in clearing minefields. Others have been engaged in training security forces in Iraq, flying gunships in Colombia, training civilian police in Bosnia and Kosovo[2]. The table from the UK House of Commons provides an example of critical activities undertaken by defence contractors and indicates that they are currently a critical component of the security architecture in the global arena.

In fact, the phenomenon of private contractors carrying out duties for the armed forces is not new: Article 4 (4) of the Third Geneva Convention explicitly refers to "persons who accompany the armed forces without being members thereof, such as [...] supply contractors, members of labour units or of services responsible for the welfare of the armed forces." Article 4 (4) of the Third Geneva Convention further provides that those persons who have fallen into the power of the enemy shall be a prisoner of war "provided that they have received authorisation from the armed forces which they accompany, who shall provide them for that purpose with an identity card similar to the annexed model." The implications of the official recognition of defence contractors can be so damaging to African security and economy provided that most countries in Africa are not mature to regulate their activities. Similarly, the activities of PMSCs in Africa go unregulated for lack of coherent legislation from states and regional organisations like the African Union (AU). They lacked standing organs to oversee and determine the methods of operation of defence contractors in Africa. On the other hand, since the last decade of the 20th-century defence contractors are well renowned and have commanded exceptional attention due to the increased interest in the role they play in internal conflicts and in the work of international institutions in peace maintenance.[4] Whereas some are directly involved in combat few others have been involved in humanitarian works and the defence of conglomerate investments. Singer (2004:1) associated most of the activities of defence contractors with businesses which have a direct link to warfare'. In short, the arena of war or conflict is a place of business for most non-state actors including defence contractors and arms suppliers or "merchants of death." Schreier & Caparini (2005:16) are of the view that even though they appear to have some goals which is profits making instead of political aims, it is also good to understand them from the context of different services they offer in a warring environment. They argue that private security companies are limited to "provide armed protection, most often for other companies rather than states" unlike, Private Military Companies (PMCs) that deals directly with the state. Therefore, PMCs services are tailored to influence a course of conflict for those that engage them. In summary, defence contractors' attempts are to create a condition that in the future states will no longer dominate in an armed conflict environment.

Even though the defence contractors may not wish to be described as mercenaries but rather considered themselves as outfits offering a legitimate service for peace and the "defence of democracy," yet their potential to fuel conflicts to enable them to sell arms and take over the training of the personnel and the motive to occupy mineral-rich regions in conflict zones as well as support to oppressive regimes and weak and fragile state is so strong. Gumedze (2011) provide examples of PMSCs in such business as Executive Outcome, Sandline International, Mount Everest, Pentagon, Hughes Security etc. The disintegrated Executive Outcome, for example, have been prominent in the Sierra Leone war in the 1990s and recruitment of Ex-militia for security operations in Iraq in 2006, they also featured in Angola crisis in the 1980s and 1990s, equipping and training government forces against the União Nacional para a Independência Total de Angola or National Union for Total Independence of Angola (UNITA) rebels of Jonas Savimbi.

Geneva Centre for the Democratic Control of Armed Forces (DCAF) [5] defines PMCs as businesses that offer specialised services related to wars and conflicts, including combat operations, strategic planning, intelligence collection, operational and logistical support, training, procurement and maintenance (Geneva Centre for the Democratic Control of Armed Forces, 2006:2). It is an industry that operates openly in the global market and is fully organised along corporate lines. Private Security Companies (PSCs) for instance provide reconnaissance, training, security guard, mines clearing; protect food and humanitarian supply in crises zones. Overall, the distinction between PMCs and PSCs are well captured in several documents for further reading.[6]

On the other hand, local defence contractors are indigenous merchants or elites with recognised registered companies that engage in the supply of food, medicine and military hardware for the armed forces with strong links to governments and serve as allies to foreign contractors. They mostly play the role of middlemen and win defence contracts on behalf of their foreign partners. Local contractors usually consist of retired or serving military personnel, politicians, and businessmen with strong international affiliations and local influences. Most local contractors feature prominently in African conflicts in places where violence is privatised by irresponsive and weak governments. Weak leaders privatise violence and outsourced private firms for defence, a situation Reno (1998:9) aptly describes as 'regime innovations for managing' internal threats.

## Defence contractors, counterterrorism and counterinsurgency in conflict zones in Africa

The argument that Africa is a hub of many conflicts is not new in international security phraseology. States have been involved in the outsourcing of contractors for combat and security services to bridge the security gaps created as a result of the ineffectiveness of military and police forces in most conflict areas. In the nascent world, critical components CT-COIN operations have been taken over by the PMSCs in many countries simply through invitation or through the involvement of stronger nations and international organisations. For example, many defence contractors through the US intervention in the Middle East flooded Iraq and Afghanistan in the last two decades to perform military and police services (for example, Vinnel, a subsidiary of Northrop Grumman, Control Risk Group and Blackwater) and likewise in Africa they are visible in all conflict zones, Executive Outcome in Angola, Bralima and Soco Oil in Congo DRC, Saracen, Uganda and Executive Outcome in Sierra Leone. PMSCs have become prominent in this Post 9/11 era where weak states are forced to outsource them not only as an existential strategy but also a means for making money for the ruling and governing elites. PMSCs have also forcefully penetrated "the marketplace" in conflict zones to search for new clients like the case of Executive Outcomes in Sierra Leone in the 1990s and in Papua New Guinea in 1993.

It is germane to note that PMSCs are notable in conflicts that have international connections or linked to natural resources contestation between government and belligerents. Through physical presence, subsidiaries, and direct financing PMSCs can establish an unprecedented presence in weak and fragile states where both the government and rebels make use of the services they offer.

Convincing evidence has shown that since colonial era European powers have expressed greater interest in Africa for economic and strategic reasons. They have also supported and funded a series of wars and military coups in different parts of Africa either directly or using proxy actors. The British battle against the *Mau Mau* revolt in Kenya in the 1950s, French against Algeria (1954–1962) and subsequent counterinsurgency attempts in Angola, Mozambique, and Namibia etc are clear illustrations of foreign interference in the political life of Africa. Likewise, the one-time Royal Niger Company in Nigeria remained a typical example of PMSCs in the colonial era. European interest in Africa was meant to establish a sphere of influence for foreign multinational corporations and the market for finished products from Europe. Since then foreign troops and mercenaries have been active in most African countries as aid workers or military professionals and advisors. The presence of Israeli and Chinese military instructors in Zimbabwe after the 2007 election and the frequency of foreign military

Table 39.2 Major Defence Contractors in Africa

| Defence Contractors | Country of Origin | Profile |
|---|---|---|
| Executive Outcome | South Africa | Operated in Angola in 1980s and Sierra Leone in 1990s and in 2006 no longer bearing name as Executive Outcome |
| Sandline International | Britain | Operated in Sierra Leone |
| Mount Everest, Pentagon, Hughes Security | United States | |
| Bralima and Soco Oil | South Africa | Congo DRC, Angola, Uganda and Sierra Leone |
| Levdan | Israel | Congo-Brazzaville |
| Lifeguard and Hughes Security | United States | |
| Specialised Tasks, Training, Equipment and Protection (STTEP) | South Africa | Operated in Nigeria in 2015 |

Source: Data compiled by author

advisors in Nigeria, Mali, and Burkina-Faso in 2012 and 2016 clearly show the extent of foreign involvement in Africa.

In a more recent related development, some countries around the globe (For example, Britain, France, Canada, Saudi Arabia and Kuwait) supported US "GWOT" unreservedly not for sheer interest to contain the menace but to defend their national interest and strategic investments in other countries. The development has helped in two ways namely, the expansion of the scope of terrorist operation and growing anxiety against terrorist movements in Africa. Secondly, it provided the impetus for active participation of Defence contractors in conflict zones. Regions considered as brewing grounds for terrorists and zones of internecine wars; Angola, Congo DRC, Somalia, Nigeria, Mali, and South Sudan have become flourishing precincts for defence contractors. Most of them gain access to conflict countries through the US and some European countries who are involved in counterinsurgency operations. The supporting role of local elites in striking deals and shadowing personal stake are apparent.

It is observed that Executive Outcomes, which drew heavily on members of South African Special Forces, assisted the Angolan government of Jonah Savimbi against the rebel movement. It also helped the Sierra Leone authorities defeat the Revolutionary United Front (RUF) and restore the elected President Tijani Kaba to power when the latter was ousted by the military.[7] In fact, during the country's civil war the leaders officially invited Executive Outcomes to assist securing the country and the diamond-rich regions against the rebels. They thus became active players in the country's CT-COIN trying to assist the military take over the capital city and repel rebels from establishing a stronghold in key towns like Freetown, Kanima, Pendembu and others. Similarly, Sandline International, a big private security company, was involved in the conflict that pitted President Kabbah of Sierra Leone against the rebels. President Kabbah prevailed eventually to stabilise his country as Sandline International facilitated logistics supply, movement of forces, weapons, and intelligence for the armed forces. There is controversy on the role of PSCs in conflict intervention in Sierra Leone and Africa as a whole. Harker (1998:2) stressed that Sandline International provided weapons and skills to the forces loyal to Kabbah in May 1997 because the country was in dire need of a neutral force especially considering the polarised nature of the military. Doyle (1986) described the development as "imperialism by invitation" and Howe (1998:318) termed it in a more critical form as "recolonisation." These harsh claims about the role of the PSCs underpin the fate of the state as custodian of the coercive machine to ensure law and order. It is most common that leaders in weak states are known for outsourcing for outside assistance to deal with rivals in their countries. For instance, in 1994 the president of Congo-Brazzaville hired a private military provider, Levdan, from Israel to provide security to the country while he was busy dismantling those units loyal to the former president. More worrisome is the fact that Sierra Leonean Office of National Security (ONS), a government agency responsible for the private security sector observed that, over 30 different PSCs that have been operating in Sierra Leone were apparently at the request of the government. Some of the private security companies that feature prominently and continue to serve as the largest employer of labour in Sierra Leone include Mount Everest, Pentagon, Lifeguard and Hughes Security as noted by Abrahamsen and Williams (2005).

It is pertinent to note that PSCs are not always successful in supporting the state or re-inforcing order, they may also compound conflict. In Somalia, Mohamed Aideed managed to sustain himself in power in the early 1990s through the invitation of PSC from South Africa who got involved in counterinsurgency against the Al-Shabaab in Mogadishu, Somalia capital to recover ground for Aideed. Aideed lost the ground and the crisis in the country escalated and institutions of government paralysed. The Somali case which accurately fits into the analysis of failed state thesis and what Tar and Mustapha (2017:279) aptly describe as "weak and dys-functional state." Another poignant example is Liberia, Charles Taylor of Liberia having rea-lised his weak position as President of the country decided to have around him foreign private security guards who were also invited to the country to fight the rebels. Taylor was eventually indicted by the International Criminal Court (ICC) in The Hague for war crime and crime against humanity, a role which PSCs complicit in executing through Taylor's era. While still supporting Taylor of Liberia the same foreign forces were contracted to take control of the machinery of government in the neighbouring state of Sierra Leone for Taylor by using Fode Sanko a rebel leader as allied to Taylor. This allowed Taylor to plunder diamond in Sierra Leone. PMSCs have been involved in counterinsurgency operations in Congo DRC, Guinea Bissau, Ethiopia, Eritrea, Cote d' Ivoire and recently the war in the Central African Republic and South Sudan. Recently a South African defence contractor named, Specialized Tasks, Training, Equipment and Protection (STTEP) has been involved in counterinsurgency op-erations in Nigeria on the side of the government against the Boko Haram group. They have been criticised by the Nigerian public as "mercenary" and "racist" group, yet they have suc-cessfully trained the Nigerian Strike Force which degraded Boko Haram in 2015 and 2016.

## Defence contractors, CT-COIN and African security

Scholars in the field like Gumedze (2011) have argued that in addition to PMSCs direct in-volvement in combat operations in Africa which include counterterrorism and counter-insurgency they are part of the destabilising forces in the continent. PMSCs are described as both short term solution provider as well as sponsors of conflicts. Worse still, as Ndlovu-Gatsheni (2007) argued, most of the PMSCs operate beyond the realm of legal accountability and public oversight, which likewise threaten the state within which they operate, as well as its citizens. The profit motive of PMSCs makes their services ready for everyone for the highest bidder which of course poses a serious threat to African security.

It is worth noting that PMSCs operate freely within the domain of host states with little or less restrained. The implications of this is that they could gain access to vital security in-formation of a country and trade-off or sell out to adversary countries, rebels or even terror organisations. Apart from exposing the security of the contracting states to risk, this scenario provides an avenue for the high and unregulated influx of arms into a country as well as create a dangerous "ground for militarisation" where arms could literally flow into wrong hands. This may cause social disorder and an increase in the crime rate. In 2011 Libya suffered similar experience a heightened case of unregulated arms flows in the country after Gadhafi's exit. Many armed rebel groups came up to contest for political control which they gained access to arms to cause mayhem in the state and some neighbouring countries. Arms from Libya found a swift way into the West African corridors such as Nigeria, Niger, Chad and Mali, and the Central African Republic and Cameroon in the Central African region.

Defence contractors undermine host African states through violation, sabotage of their laws and regulations. In maximising profits, PMSCs by-pass often with the connivance of compromised elites and public servants, extant rules, and regulatory provisions such as tax return, import duties and compliance with tariffs and restriction. In addition, their activities are highly unregulated and, in some cases, their violations are either pardoned or condoned, they violate domestic laws and human rights of citizens especially in combat zones. It is difficult to hold PMSCs accountable or accused them of war crimes because of the freedom and immunity that they enjoy as clandestine agents of the state. They fortuitously benefit from the immunities enjoyed by the elites that they protect.

At the regional and international levels, PMSCs leverage significant privilege and exceptions in their activities in Africa. At the level of the African Union (AU) the activities of the PMSCs are treated with kid-glove in the areas of peacekeeping missions and humanitarian assistance. The OAU Anti-Mercenary Convention of 1977 which has not been updated thus allowed PMSCs to take advantage of the Cold War-era legal framework to carry out their activities in the post-Cold War environment. Similarly, at the level of the United Nations, plans to regulate private military companies were considered but no concrete steps seem to have been effectively taken.[8] Apart from the UN Working Group on the Use of Mercenaries as a Means of Violating Human Rights and Impeding the Exercise of the Right of Peoples to Self-determination which was presumed to serve as a draft to International Convention on the Regulation, Oversight and Monitoring of Private Military and Security Companies, there are no relevant documents in the UN kitty to that effect and the draft has not been adopted by the UN member states either. Activities of the PMSCs are left to contracting countries to regulate and most countries would not want to place legal restraint to the operations of PMSCs because they find them useful and dependable. The subsisting OAU protocol which essentially focused on mercenaries ignores the emerging categories of high-tech PMSCs that are now operating smartly in conflict zones. It is noteworthy, though, that it is only the United States and South Africa that have national legislation covering the provision of PMSCs services in other countries[9] and the Montreux Document signed in Switzerland in 2008 between PMSCs and countries in war zones.[10] Representatives of civil society and of the private military and security industry were consulted as part of the Swiss Initiative.[11,12] Despite the fact that the Montreux Document attempted to provide a legal framework for PMSCs it does not have to provide for organs that could place sanction and discipline violators. Due to these limitations, PMSCs in African countries have disregard to international humanitarian laws and poses danger to civilians in combat zones.

Defence assistance for most weak states usually comes from the developed countries which also allow the flow of PMSCs. By this, defence contractors have flooded the continent and weak states that have been vulnerable begin to outsource them for the protection of leaders who insist on staying in power at the expenses of the sovereignty of their states, for example, Joseph Kabila of Congo DRC (though later handed over power to the opposition in 2019), Paul Kagami of Rwanda and Silva Kir of South Sudan. It is observed that undemocratic leaders have bankrolled foreign forces to subvert democracy and good governance, thus securing their own survival and undermining their peoples' right to self-determination.[13]

Due to their close alliance with power elites, as discussed above, PMSCs are pointed for their involvement in and promotion of high-level corruption in defence procurement and money laundering often under the guide of official transaction. Purchase contracts and long-term maintenance contracts entered into between contracting states and defence contractors are open to manipulation to capture the vested interest of the ruling elites. *Justice Africa* in its report 2014 titled "Defence Procurement, Corruption and Illicit Financial Flow" notes that defence companies can, and sometimes do, inflate the cost of their maintenance contracts, in order to earn additional funds and generate an income stream that can be used for corrupt ends (*Justice Africa, 2014:5-6*). Defence companies can do this easily as the purchasing country becomes heavily dependent on the selling company for spare parts and other technical assistance. The implications of this is that it milks the countries dry of finance capital which can be used to foster development and ensure a better standard of living for the people. In the absence of this, a large portion of the population is left unattended to, with unemployment on the increase and youth restiveness a menace to the society thereby ensuring high crime rates and continues recruitment of young Africans into terror organisations and insurgent groups.

Defence contractors may not be wholly blamed for woes in Africa. Rotberg (2002:127) argues that poor decisions emanating from leaders always paved the way for their entry, a development Doyle (1986:8–12) earlier described. In the views of Ndung'u (2011:24) the international system is now in an era in which the notion of the state as being the main actor is being challenged with the emergence of non-traditional actors such as the international PMSCs who have become significant players in the international arena. He maintains that some of the challenges occasioned by PMSCs' presence are because of the state's abdication of its role as the sole wielder of the legitimate use of violence.

Thus, the presence of PMSCs in mineral-rich parts of Africa to provide protection to multinational corporations, rebel groups and oil thieves like the cases in Sierra Leone and Nigeria tends to undermine the state sovereignty and economy of the host state. The RUF rebels in Sierra Leone and Niger Delta militants in Nigeria have relied on some foreign PMSCs for mining and exploitation of minerals. The cost security outsourcing to secure mining field is often covered in the budget of mining licenses of these joint ventures. Apart from the additional security burdens created it also placed an additional budget burden on the state. In recent times, Nigeria has been defrauded by local contractors in what is commonly referred to as arms contract fraud where key government officials and politicians are involved using fictitious companies to swindle the state. The former National Security Adviser, Col. Sambo Dasuki (rtd) in partnership with some contractors was alleged to have diverted the sum of 1.9$ billion for the purchase of arms. Based on the diversion of resources meant for counterinsurgency in Nigeria the military forces are unable to defeat Boko Haram and the conflict rapidly spread to neighbouring countries, Cameroon, Chad and Niger with attendant devastating consequences and large population displacement around the Lake Chad region.

Furthermore, as conflict continues to escalate in most parts of Africa, the attention of governments is gradually shifting away from the provision of basic social amenities like health care, education, water, and infrastructures to the funding of wars. In the last decades, countries like Cote d'Ivoire, Mali, Nigeria, Kenya, Central African Republic, the Maghreb, and South Sudan mainly focused on how to finance wars and curb civil strife in their domain. In short, a poor accounting system coupled with corrupt practices has complicated the African security challenge. Monies released for security purposes are seldom accounted for by government officials thereby placing unnecessary financial burdens on the people and depriving them access to social amenities. It has become so bad that some African countries, Nigeria, Ghana, Cameroon, among others have to borrow from outside to meet their financial obligations which include financing war, acquisition of military technology and training of personnel. As a matter of fact, apart from South Africa that has functional defence industries, most African countries have remained net recipient of military technology transfer which weigh down the GDP of countries and further dwarf local technology and industry.

## Conclusion

A fertile opportunity and markets for PMSCs have emerged in the destabilising conditions in Africa. This condition will persist so long as Africa's weak states are not salvaged from their position of comparative advantage where greedy leaders have refused to abdicate the seat of power and fail to provide essential services to the people even when they lose out in elections, the legitimacy and the capacity of the state will remain precarious.

Amidst the several conflicts and wars in Africa, defence contractors have become viable actors in Africa's security matters, state actors rely on them for their survival, giant multinational corporations engaged them for the protection of their investments, while organisations employ them to perform both military and police duties. They have been used against terrorist and insurgent groups in most African countries especially those experiencing a severe socio-economic and political crisis. It is argued herein, that defence contractors have the capacity to create stability and anarchy to their advantage. This is ultimately situated within the context of cyclical violence and increasing terrorist threats in Africa which are sometimes provoked by subsidiaries multinational companies which feel threatened by unfriendly government policies and regulations. It is worthy of note, that defence contractors in Africa consist of foreign and local actors who work in partnership in the areas of contract awards and legal procedures to consolidate and reap profit for their investments. Upholding the argument of authors who view PMSCs as actors who use anarchy as an avenue for profit-making and solely hang on to that for their survival, it is the submission of this chapter that the major trigger of conflicts in Africa remains the PMSCs who have the backing of the highly industrialised countries, who are ready to supply weapons for their sustenance.

In addition, the activities of PMSCs in Africa go largely unregulated for lack of coherent legislation from states and regional organisations like the AU. They lacked standing organs to oversee and determine the methods of operation of defence contractors in Africa. Hence there is no regulatory framework to determine their activities it is absolutely difficult to conclude that their participation in conflicts add to the improvement of African security rather it leads to further escalation of violence. It is worthy of note that as foreign troops and PMSCs push hard into the interior of Africa, the military capabilities and security potentials of African states are greatly undermined and their ability to confront terrorist and insurgent groups will continue to diminish. In view of the above issues raised, the need for African states to concentrate on reinforcing the public sector and equipping states security agencies to meet up with the ever-challenging threats from terror and insurgent groups cannot be overemphasised. In addition to local legislation to regulate PMSCs the UN and AU should develop a legal framework to regulate the activities of PMSCs in contracting states that will eliminate impunity in the operations of such actors in conflicts. Furthermore, African states should take it as a matter of necessity to send their security personnel abroad for training to acquire necessary skills so that they can come back home to give same to their comrades, by that enough resources would be saved and channels of finance leakages would be blocked. Finally, African states can counter the counter-veiling effect of PMSCs if they can reposition their ailing defence industries to match modern warfare.

## Notes

1 Transparency International "Government Defence Anti-Corruption Index 2013," http://government.defenceindex.org/sites/default/files/documents/GI-main-report.pdf. Accessed 23.07.17.
2 E. Pape and M. Meyer, 2003, August 25, Training Security Forces in Iraq, *Newsweek*.
3 House of Commons, Private military companies: Options for regulation, Green Paper (HCC 577 of 2002), London: http://www.ssrnetwork.net/uploaded_fi les/3541. pdf; see also Gumedze, S. The privatisation and regulation of security in Africa. In L le Roux (Ed.), *South African Army Vision 2020*, Vol 2: The South African army relevant and ready for future security challenges in Africa, Pretoria/Tshwane: ISS, 197. Website accessed on 12 August 2017.
4 See, for instance, Full Proceedings of the Conference on Engaging Non-State Actors in a Landmine Ban: A Pioneering Conference held on 24 and 25 March 2000 at the International Conference Centre of Geneva. The Proceedings were published by the Conference Organisers in Quezon City in 2001 and comprise 186 pages.
5 The Geneva Centre for the Democratic Control of Armed Forces (DCAF). (2006). *Private actors and security governance:LIT and DCAF*. New Brunswick: Transaction, 12.
6 The Foreign and Commonwealth Office, private military Companies: Options for regulations, also, D. Brooks (2000). Messiahs or mercenaries? The future of international private military services. *International Peacekeeping*,7(winter 4), 129–144; Taulbee (2002). The privatisation of security: Modern conflict, globalisation and weak states. In *Civil wars* (Vol.5 No.2). Franck Cass, p.3.
7 Quoted in Alexandre Faite (n.d.) *Involvement of Private Contractors in Armed Conflict: Implications under International Humanitarian Law*. International Committee of the Red Cross. (1998, June 26) *The Secretary-General reflects on 'intervention' in thirty-fifth annual Ditchley Foundation Lecture, SG/SM/6613*, [Press Release], p 8.
8 The report of the Secretary-General of the UN at the Millennium Summit, 'We the Peoples: The Role of the United Nations in the 21st Century,' (A/54/2000), pt. 212 stated that: "Consideration should also be given to an international convention regulating the actions of private and corporate security firms, which we see involved in internal wars in growing numbers." After the report there has been no concrete documents supporting the regulations of Private armed personnel by the UN.
9 See Bryden, his views apparently approached the privatisation of security from a security governance perspective.
10 Montreux Document on Pertinent International Legal Obligations and Good Practices for States Related to the Operations of Private Military and Security Companies during Armed Conflicts, http://www.un.org/ga/search/view_doc.asp?symbol=A/63/467. Accessed 27.08.17.
11 Swiss Initiative on private military and security companies. In Gumedze, S. (Ed.).(2007). *Private security in Africa: manifestation, challenges and regulation*. ISS Monograph no 139. Pretoria/Tshwane: ISS, November 2007.
12 Viljoen, F. (2007). *International human rights law in Africa*. Oxford: Oxford University Press,p. 295.
13 See Regulation of Foreign Military Assistance Act, 1998, No. 15 of 1998: Government Gazette of the Republic of South Africa Vol. 395, 20 May 1998 (Republic of South Africa 1998).

## References

Abrahamsen, R. (2005). Blair's Africa: The politics of securitisation and fear.*Alternatives* , *30*(1): 55–80.
Abrahamsen, R., & Williams, W. C. (2005). *The Globalisation of Private Security: Country report Sierra Leone*. Aberystwyth: University of Wales.
Baker, Deane-Peter. (2011). *Will global demand for private military services in major conflicts continue?* In S. Gumedze (Ed.), *Merchants of African conflict more than just a pound of flesh*. ISS Monograph 176 (pp. 1–14). South Africa: Institute for Security Studies.
Barstow, D. (2004, April 19). Security companies: Shadow soldiers in Iraq. *New York Times*.
Boas, M. (2014). *"How Seven Norwegian Small Warships Ended up in the Hands of a Former Niger Delta Militant"*, Available: https://matsutas.wordpress.com/2014/12/16/how-seven-norwegian-small-warships-ended-up-in-the-hands-of-a-former-niger-delta-militant-by-morten-boas/. Accessed on 20.8.18.
Brooks, D. (2002). *Protecting people: The private military companies potential: Comments and suggestions for the UK Green paper on Regulating Private Military Services, 25 July, P3*. Available from website of International Peace Operation Association (IPOA) www.ipoaonline.org Accessed 20.08.17.

Brooks, D. (2000). Messiahs or mercenaries? The future of international private military services. *International Peacekeeping*, 7( winter 4), 129–144.

Bryden, A. (2006). Approaching the privatisation of security from a security governance perspective. In A. Bryden & M. Caparini (Eds.), *Private actors and security Governance: LIT and DCAF*. New Brunswick: Transaction.

Cilliers, J. (1999). Private security in war-torn African states. In Cilliers, J., & Mason, P. (Eds.), *Peace, Profit or Plunder? The privatisation of security in war-torn African societies*. Pretoria: Institute for Security Studies. (Out of Print). Available from http://www.issafrica.org/index.php?link_id=3&slink_id= 225&link_type=12&slink_type=12&tmpl_id=3 Accessed 28.08.17.

Doyle, M. (1986). *Empires*. Ithaca: Cornell University Press.

Fallah, K. (2007). *Regulating Private Security contractors in armed conflicts*. In Sabelo Gumedze. (ed) Private Security in Africa Manifestation, Challenges and Regulation. *Institute for Security Studies (ISS)* Monograph Series, No. 139. South Africa: Institute for Security Studies.

Faite, A. (n.d) *Involvement of Private Contractors in Armed Conflict: Implications under International Humanitarian LawDefence Studies, 4*(2). International Committee of the Red Cross. Available from https://www.icrc. org/en/doc/resources/documents/article/other/pmc-article-310804.htm Accessed 15.8.18.

Foaleng, M. H. (2007). Private military and security companies and the nexus between natural resources and civil wars in Africa. In S. Gumedze. (Ed.), *Institute for Security Studies (ISS) Monograph Series, No. 139. Private security in Africa manifestation, challenges and regulation*. Pretoria, South Africa: Institute for Security Studies.

Geneva Centre for the Democratic Control of Armed Forces (DCAF). (2006). *The Privatisation of Security*. Available from http:// www.dcaf.ch/privatisation-security/_index.cfm Accessed 21st 2019.

Gumedze, S. (2011). The Privatisation of Security in African Conflicts. *Institute for Security Studies, 2011*(176): 195.

Harker, B. J. (1998). Private power, public insecurity: The growing reality of security for profit. *The Ploughshares Monitor,19*(3), 1–5.

Hartley, K. (2007). *Military expenditure data for SSA nations: the report for DFID*, Monograph, York, Canada: Centre for Defence Economics, University of York.

Henineken, L., & Motzouris, M. (2011). The effect of Private Security on national armed forces' capacity and capabilities, In G. Sabelo (Ed.), *The privatisation of security in African Conflicts, more than just a pound of flesh*. Pretoria, South Africa.: Institute for Security Studies.

Howe, H. (1998). Private Security Forces and African Stability: the Case of Executive Outcomes. *The Journal of Modern African Studies, 36*(2), 307–331.

Justice Africa Draft Report 'Defence Procurement, Corruption and Illicit Financial Flows' for The TANA High-Level Forum on Security in Africa February 2014. Pp. 5 and 6. Chester House, United Kingdom.

Looney, R. E. (1988) *Third world military expenditure and arms production*. London: The Macmillan Press LTD.

Ndlovu-Gatsheni, S.J. (November 2007). Weak States and the Growth of the Private Security Sector in Africa: Whither the African State?. Private Security in Africa Manifestation, Challenges and Regulation. In Gumedze S.(Ed.), *Institute for Security Studies (ISS)* Monograph Series, No. 139. Pretoria, South Africa.: Institute for Security Studies.

Ndung'u, I. (January 2011). Human Security and Challenges Related to Private Military and Security Companies in Africa. In Gumedze S. (Ed.), *Merchants of African conflict more than just a pound of flesh. Institute for Security Studies (ISS)*. Monograph 176. Pretoria, South Africa: Institute for Security Studies,.

O'Brien, K. (2000). *PMCs, myths and mercenaries: The debate on private military companies. Royal United Services Institute Journal, 145*(1) 59–64.

Omeje, K. (2008). The war on terror and the crisis of postcoloniality in Africa. *African Journal of International Affairs, 11*(2), 89–114. Council for the Development of Social Science Research in Africa (CODESRIA).

Reno, W. (1997). African weak states and commercial alliances. *Africa Affairs, 96*(383) 165–185.

Reno, W. (1998). *Warlord politics and African states*. Boulder: Lynne Rienner.

Republic of South Africa. (1998). Regulation of Foreign Military Assistance Act, 1998 No. 15: Government Gazette of the Republic of South Africa Vol. 395(18912), 20 May 1998.

Roeber, J. (2005). *"Hard Wired for Corruption: The Arms Trade and Corruption"*, Prospect, 28 August.

Rotberg, R. I. (2002). Failed states in a world of terror. *Foreign Affairs, 81*(4), 127–140.

Schreier, F., & Caparini, M. (2005). *Privatizing security: Law, practice and governance of private military and security companies*. Geneva, DCAF Occasional Paper.

Singer, P. W. (2004). *The Private Military Industry and Iraq: What have we learned and where to next?* Geneva, DCAF Policy Paper.

Taulbee, J. L. (2002). The privatisation of security: Modern conflict, globalisation and weak states. *Civil wars* (Vol. 5 No. 2), (pp. 3–26).Franck Cass.

Tar, U., & Mustapha, M. (2017). Al-Shabaab: State collapse, warlords and Islamist insurgency in Somalia. In C. Varin & D. Abubakar (Eds.), *Violent non-state actors in Africa terrorists, rebels and warlords*. Switzerland: Palgrave Macmillan, Springer Nature.

Transparency International. Government Defence Anti-Corruption Index 2013. http://government. defenceindex.org/sites/default/files/documents/GI--main--report.pdf. Accessed 20.08.17.

Viljoen, F.(2007).*International human rights law in Africa*, Oxford: Oxford University Press, p. 297.

Williamson, J. (2007) *Private security companies and private military companies under International Humanitarian Law*. In S.Gumedze (Ed.), *Private Security in Africa manifestation challenges and regulation*. ISS Monograph Series. No 139, November. Pretoria, South Africa: Institute for Security Studies,.

Zarate, J. C. (1998).The emergence of a new dog of war: Private international security companies, international law, and the new world disorder. *Stanford Journal of International Law, 34,*( winter 1), 124.

# 40

# Private Military and Security Companies (PMSCs) and national security in Africa

*Bashir Bala and Usman A. Tar*

## Introduction

The modern-day security environment has witnessed the growth and development of the revolution in the perplexing nature of privatisation in both human and material forms (Edmonds, 1999; Caparini, 2006; and Krahmann, 2010). Privatisation is now beyond the economic dimension as evidenced by the unfolding events in the international system, and tends to encompass the multi-dimensional complexities associated with the human desire for peace and security (Luckham, 2009; Isima, 2009; and Juma, 2011). The state has, since the treaty of Westphalia, remained the primary unit of political organisation and the provision of security (Kruger, 1992; Mabee, 2003; and Crawford, 2006). However, the state is increasingly challenged by subversive elements (Whitton, 1961), agitations for regimes change (Owen, 2013), and existential threats of food (Barrett, 2010), human and national security (Job, 1992) to more eminent volatility in the global security environment. The state often relies on its own defence and security architecture but where that fails it reserves the right to seek alliance and, in an extreme circumstance, hire the capacity to maintain law and order. Therefore, in addition to the traditional method of protection, the states can outsource certain critical capacities for defence and security. Thus, the coming on stage of private establishments to complement the very effort of national forces in the provisioning of security for national defence has become paramount and ingenious. The Private Military and Security Companies (PMSCs) boomed in providing critical requirements for security services in terms of logistical supports, physical security and firepower against elements threatening the corporate existence of the states. They are now operating in places like Afghanistan, Iraq (Schwartz, 2011), the Democratic Republic of Congo and Haiti. Africa is not new to their intervention as history has shown the operations of these companies (Ferguson, J. 2005 in both their corporate and military forms to support auxiliary defence and security functions in most war-torn states in Africa: Somalia, Sudan, South Sudan, South Africa, and Uganda.

In today's Africa, it is evident that the struggle to consolidate power by leaders of weak or fragile states has partly manifested in the employment of the services of the PMSCs to boost the capacity of the state to provide security, and thus contributed in facilitating the evolution of the private security sector in Africa. In the aftermaths of the end of the Cold War, African countries witnessed spike in the volume of civil wars and communal strife which over-stretched the capacity of national police to overcome these challenges thus necessitating the deployment of the armed forces often with dire consequences. In addition, the rise of armed militias and insurgencies following 9/11 has weakened the capacity of the weak African state and their leaders to manage the crisis of governance and state fragility (Gatsheni, 2007: 22). Thus, PMSCs emerged as a strategic supplement in the state's governance framework. In this regard, Howe (1998: 307) articulated four key factors that underpin the rise of PMSCs in Africa. First is the post-Cold War withdrawal of superpowers from patronising their African dependencies. Second is the lack of commitment for intervention by the Western world and the United Nations in the post-Somalia War. Third, are the increased external demands for economic and political reform. And fourth is the transmuting nature of African insurgencies, insurrections and militancy that have destabilised leaders of fragile African states. It is important to note that the private security sector tailored its activities and operations towards meeting the needs of national security, and thus an intricate nexus exists between the state and PMSCs.

This chapter anchors on the assumption that, as private auxiliary pillars of national security, PMSCs have emerged and expanded beyond national and regional boundaries. The chapter attempts to contextualise the framework of issues bordering on the operations, development, and challenges peculiar to the private security sector in Africa. This chapter first argues that the vibrancy of civil society and emergence of violent opposition regimes challenging the prolonged dictatorship of some African politicians in a number of African states have led to the invitation and intervention of the PMSCs; to provide their firepower and professionalism to quench the threats to national security. Secondly, it argues that the lack of capabilities and capacities by national forces to ensure public safety and security in African states has yielded the unprecedented growth and expansion of the services of both the Private Security Companies (PSCs) and the PMSCs[1]. Thirdly, the chapter also argues that a strong regulatory and policy framework is a necessary requisite for checking the activities of PMSCs at the national level, while effective overlapping and interlocking of national, regional as well as international frameworks are needed to impose global control regulation on PMSCs; as the existing laws at an international level are insufficient. Proceeding this section, the chapter starts off by examining the dynamics of the development of the PMSCs from the global to continental and then national levels as the basis upon which to project the advances in defence of the arguments raised in the chapter. The chapter then underscores the various services offered by these companies with a view to understanding the nature of their operations and then looks into the issues bordering on their activities that tend to have one impact or the other on national security in Africa. The chapter further analyses the challenges confronting the PMSCs in Africa and lastly, it concludes that, it has become desirable and essential for the African governments to calibrate the benefits of the PMSCs towards the effective provisioning of national security as the phenomenon of their proliferation has come to stay in Africa as the continent presents some breeding turfs for the companies' market survivability.

## Crisis of security and the imperatives of PMSCs and PSCs in Africa

The evolution and subsequent spread of PMSCs and PSCs signifies a paradigm shift and paramount need to ensure the security and safety of persons and property, as well as intellectual property and sensitive corporate information. Private security officers are responsible for protecting the nation's institutions and critical infrastructure systems, including industries, utilities, transportation, and health and educational facilities (Strom et al., 2010:2-1). As argued earlier, the end of the Cold War has bolstered the proliferation of PMSCs in weak states of the global south. Though several factors that are endemic to the continent provide the context for the efflorescence of PMSCs in Africa, the external contradictions provide the springboard for the development of PSCs in Africa.

With the end of the Cold War support for weak regimes in Africa reduced drastically, thus bringing to the fore the weak structural and institutional structures of the African states (Ayoob 1995). At the end of the War, many African states were left in chaos and weak status consequent upon geo-strategic of superpowers from the continent. In the post-Cold War dispensation, African leaders were suddenly confronted with challenges of civil wars, communal strife and the attendant emergence of "Warlords" who usurped the state of territory which became "ungoverned spaces". At the same time, they faced internal agitations from the masses and civil society for democratic reforms. In the midst of internal insurgencies and civil strife, African states failed to garner external support to eliminate internal threats and consolidate on their power (Gatsheni, 2007: 21–22). With this adverse descent of some African states into "third wave democracy", featured by prolonged stay of African politicians in governance (Gatsheni, 2007: 21), Somalia, Sierra Leone and Liberia experienced the proliferation of various combative groups fighting each other for control of governance and resources. This has disrupted peace and destroyed the very infrastructure of political governance. These countries became failed states characterised by crisis of law and order, and collapse of social services. The heightened desire by regimes in Africa to hang onto power, led some African leaders to establish alliance with foreign powers. The alliance is mainly borne out of the desire to manipulate outsiders' demands, rather than condescend to the "failed state paradigm" (Gatsheni, 2007). Thus, the lack of trust on local military forces in protecting African states against internal armed groups and the acceptable terms of services provided by foreign private outfits altered the security environment in the region; and brought about what Reno (1997: 167) termed as the "intervention of the phenomenon of private security in Africa to fill the so-called capacity gap".

While serving as agents of defence and security, PMSCs are also argued to have exacerbated security threats across the continent. Africa is perceived as an unstable environment, a continent in persistent conflict, though there are parts of the continent where political turbulence is absent (Stead, 2006: 36). Both internal and external actors (of which PMSCs are a part) have played complementary role in Africa's crises of security. And, the crises have assumed transnational dimension. The resurgence and lethality of Boko Haram attacks in Nigeria, Chad, Niger and Cameroon; Al-Shabbab attacks in Somalia, Kenya and Uganda; ISIS threats in North Africa; and attacks from fundamentalist groups in West and East Africa are among the recent and unfolding terrorist activities defining the crisis of security in Africa (Cardoso, 2016). In today's Africa, terrorists and Islamist militants have proliferated in the continent and succeeded in creating a turbulent politico-economic and social disorder in a manner that countries sharing similar international boundaries are vulnerable to trans-border terrorist incursions in the region. A good example of a terror that speedily assumed a transnational dimension is the Boko Haram, an Islamic extremist insurgent group which has been fighting for the Islamization of Nigeria through such violent means as assassinations, bombings, kidnappings and suicide bombings. The Sect emerged as an armed group in 2009. By 2011, it transformed into one of the deadliest terrorist organisations whose scope and intensity of attacks have seriously affected peace and security of lives and property across Nigeria, Cameroon, Niger and Chad (Tar & Bala, 2019).

Aside the large-scale threats of terrorism, there is also the growing security threat from non-terrorism activities like domestic crimes, armed robbery, pipeline vandalisation, hostage taking, cattle-rustling, arsons, brutality and kidnapping. For example, in March 2013, an average of 2,209 serious felonies, including 45 homicides, were committed daily in South Africa and it appears very little has changed over the course of time. In Nigeria, estimates suggest that up to

600 people are kidnapped in the country every year. In this environment of rising insecurity and inadequate public protection, private security outfits are plugging the gap and present a viable option for people and organisations who are determined to protect the lives of their families and employees, "while safeguarding their assets and investments" (The Conversation, 2017).

The foregoing combined threats have compelled the emergence of PMSCs in Africa. In mid-1990s, known as Executive Outcomes, a South African company was hired by the Angolan government to take back oilfields captured by rebels. Executive Outcomes was subsequently hired by the government of Sierra Leone to dislodge from strongholds and push back the violent rebel group the Rebel United Front (RUF), which had "come extremely close to the capital, Freetown. In both cases, Executive Outcomes planned and executed missions in the same way a national army would". In Liberia, Executive Outcome was hired by the UN to disband and reconfigure the Armed Forces of Liberia. A similar company, Sandline International, appeared in the late 1990s, also offering combat services, and was hired in Sierra Leone and in Papua New Guinea (Percy, 2012: 3).

Also, Securico was founded in Zimbabwe by Divine Ndhlukala in 1998 to provide quality private security needs in the emerging private security market in Africa and the company is now the leading security services provider in Zimbabwe. The company provides services on scale of technological interventions, on-site guards, procurement of armoured vehicles, trained guard dogs, onsite banking, and transportation of valuables, employee vetting, private investigations, and security consulting. Over two decades, the company has been collaborating with its customers to expand its service provision beyond the shores of Zimbabwe to satisfy the needs of its internal and external clients. The company is completely women-owned with Divine Ndhlukula as the Founder and Managing Director of the company (Vieews.com, 20 December 2018). In 2016, the African Chief Executive Officers' Forum, dedicated to the development of private sector in Africa, shortlisted her as a nominee for the 2016 CEO of the Year Award in Abidjan, Côte d'Ivoire. Owing to the ubiquity, frequency and preponderance of continuous unabated crisis, the ability of states to rise to the challenge has been weakened and private security companies have been attempting to fill the vacuum (Olaniyan, 2010:5), and thus blossomed in grounds that are in dire need of their services in Africa.

Another dynamic factor that reshaped the progression of the PMSCs in Africa is the *lack of national capacity on the part of the key stakeholders of the national security architecture, including the armed forces* in most African countries, particularly the police. Conventional security forces such as national armies, police and paramilitaries find themselves overstretched with so many calls on their manpower capacity, resources, and cuts to their numbers. As a result, the *Africa Business Magazine* (2012) argues that the privatisation of security has gained momentum in recent years in Africa largely because national police and security establishments have failed to bear on their own the burden of national security. A major source of concern is that national police in most African countries are ill-equipped, understaffed, and underfunded and thus being severely incapacitated to effectively discharge their constitutional roles of being responsible for internal peace and security in Africa. The United Nations recommends one police officer for every 450 citizens (The Conversation, 2017). According to its estimates, Kenya has one police officer for every 1,150 people; Tanzania has one for every 1,298; and Ghana one for every 1,200. Unfortunately, these ratios hold true for several other countries on the continent. Also, in Uganda, the police/ population ratio remains very ineffective and stands at one police officer per 1,473 people. This is below the international ratio of 1:400. This ratio added with the effects of inadequate resources, the police inefficiency and ineffectiveness are glaring. It was in this light that the government felt duty-bound to apportion some police functions to private security organisations. This was done to address the problem of a police force deficit of numerical strength and overstretched. The policy direction was influenced by the paradigm of new managerialism, which started in America in the 1980s – projects de-monopolising the delivery of goods and services by a single bureaucracy as one of the ways of ensuring the efficient provision of goods and services to the public (Kirunda, 2008: 8).

Africa's population of over 1.1 billion and the projection of it to be doubled in size to 2.4 billion over the next 35 years couple with competing demands to fund other critical needs like healthcare, education, food and infrastructure, "it's highly unlikely that the funding or staffing of police forces across the continent will improve with time" (The Conversation, 2017). This particular worrisome assumption is what made the Geneva Centre for the Democratic Control of Armed Forces (DCAF), in a background paper on PMSCs, to corroborate the generalisation that, PMSCs developed to compensate in the event of national capacity and thus spreading their wings across the shores of Africa with the accompanying degrees of states' inefficacies; to discharge social responsibilities. In sum, the failure of the states to provide security has the potency to generate responses from the citizenry, particularly the issue of taking their own security into their hands outside the parameters of the established norms of the state security institutions. This can be devastating and overbearing on the part of the general safety and security of the state.

The fourth wave in the development of the PMSCs in Africa is the *devastating consequences of the global capitalist economy*. Though the conglomerates of the World Bank and the International Monetary Fund (IMF) provides the needed financial relief to African states in the form of soft-loans, debt rescheduling and even debt forgiveness, the support comes with certain prescriptions very unfavourable to the African economic environment. This was observed more scholarly by Mkandawire and Soludo (1999) that, the failure of the economic liberalisation and structural adjustment programmes that were imposed by the Bretton Woods resulted in the weak state capacity and its "decline from the late 1980s onwards and throughout the 1990s" in Africa. The structural and institutional factors produced hardened economic situation accentuated by a high rate of unemployment and also the proliferation of small arms and light weapons which concomitantly cleared the ground for PMSCs in Africa. The consequences of these "phenomena" have led to an acute escalation of violent crimes that are sometimes beyond the capacities of the national security forces (Bearpark and Schulz, 2007: 77). Thus, in the absence of policing capacity to stem security challenges, national armed forces are often been drafted to provide military aid to civil authority (MACA). This has generated controversy. First, it has created a role contradiction between warfighting and crime-fighting. Deploying a warfighter into crime-fighting becomes for a culture-shock for the armed forces: the primary role of the armed forces is to fight against foreign invasion, not fighting local crime. Secondly, the armed forces are professionally trained to apply over-bearing force in confronting the enemy. In confronting local security challenges, the armed forces have often applied overwhelming force as demonstrated in the Odi crisis in Nigeria on 20 November 1999, when the Nigerian Army was drafted to quell a local communal crime: Odi was razed down in flame and most of its inhabitants were fired and killed randomly.

In sum, the crisis of security in Africa – characterised by a deficit of policing and overbearing nature of national armed forces – has led to the imperatives of out-sourcing of PMSCs as an alternative to filling the gaps created by this contradiction. The next section discusses the contending issues surrounding PMSCs in Africa.

## PMSCs in Africa: services and contending issues

PMSCs and particularly the PSCs undertake certain services in Africa ranging from private investigations of facts or personal profiling; and watch, guard, escort, and patrol duties to provide protection against crime and criminality. PSCs are employed by banks to provide routine guard duties and surveillance on their premises. They are used by Bureau de Change agents in escorting money to customers and banks and they are also employed by national governmental organisations. PSCs are specially employed to provide security to people and their homes, properties, and businesses and these are the contracts that are most sought after. Some of these PMSCs, particularly the PSCs use modern search and surveillance equipment. In Africa, they offer secured services such as:

1. *Central station monitoring*: This includes remote site monitoring of CCTV and access systems; alarm monitoring and response service dispatch; satellite tracking systems of vehicles and goods in transit; and a response vehicle fleet of alarm cars.
2. *Radio alarm response services*: All vehicles are electronically monitored for position and status; armoured response for incidents; self-testing digital alarm transmitters equipped with anti-tamper devices; and automatic commercial and domestic alarm systems.
3. *Perimeter protection and access system*: This includes integrated and modular control systems; multiple zoned electric fences; automatic vehicular access barriers; acoustic and microphonic cable perimeter detection systems; external and internal building security hardening; and point of sale and cashiers ballistic protection.
4. *Facilities management*: This involves security vetted ancillary and temporary personnel; background and security vetting services; ID card services and personnel database systems; buildings and grounds maintenance; programmed preventative maintenance scheduling; environmental control equipment maintenance; and security, safety and fire procedural training.
5. *Electronic security systems*: These include automatic intruder alarm systems for commercial and residential applications; cluster alarms with area enunciator for townhouse and flat complexes; fixed and remote panic button systems; anti-hijack and integrated security systems; access control and closed-circuit television surveillance systems; structured cabled installations to certified standards; covert surveillance equipment services; retail security systems and point of sale monitoring; banking, bureau de change and financial institution security systems; and digital incident recording cameras with integral data storage.
6. *Fire alarm and equipment*: This involves fire surveys and consultancy; fire detection and alarm equipment; fire suppression equipment, including gas fire suppression for computer rooms and switchgear; sprinkle systems for new installations and retrofits; and fire escape, fire door and handheld appliances.
7. *Cash-in-transit and cash services*: These include a fully armoured vehicle fleet with armed crew; cash in transit, patrolling and cash services; overnight vaulting and out of hour's collection; and key holding services.
8. *Satellite tracking systems*: These include a 24-hour manned control-room monitoring installed units; capability to monitor and control vehicle functions in real-time; anti-hijack alert, driver ID interface, route monitoring, real-time engine monitoring; logging and reporting of position and operations transgressions in real-time basis; geo-fencing, no-go-area definition; full fleet management reporting systems; and asset tracking and investigation applications
9. *Manned guarding and dog patrols*: These consist of continuous supervision by radio-dispatched

mobile patrols; electronic guard alert systems and electronic attendance/incident reporting; remote site security teams; a diplomatic protection unit; and attack and sniffer trained dogs and incident response (Kirunda 2008: 16).

While PSCs provide above services mainly to private firms and wealthy individuals, the PMSCs offer services to contracting agencies, giant multinational corporations or states in the areas of military advice and training, operational support, logistical support, site/personnel security, crime prevention, and mercenary-styled operations. The bottom line is that a clear-cut assumption of misconception always prevails on the variegated and overlapping levels of security to be provided by both these agencies. This misconception has been already addressed in the second section of this chapter. This section will now address the contending issues in respect of the PMSCs and PSCs.

The peculiar marketization[2] of public security in Africa, which has shifted the role of the state from the traditional provider of security to a complimentary ally in the provisioning of safety nets and security, has led to openings for the establishment of more of these privatised PMSCs. And they are enjoying a huge market base in Africa as a direct consequence of state failure and lack of capacities. The African Union (AU) and Economic Community of the West African States (ECOWAS) as both continental and regional security arrangements have been struggling with the challenge of capacity to contain African's growing security threats from Violent Non-State Actors (VNSAs). The intervention by the French troops in containing Tuaregs rebellion in Mali is a pointer to the fact that both AU and ECOWAS have failed in that regards. Besides the capacity issue, there is also a commitment problem on member states within the AU to deal with the issue of peace and security in the continent. Lack of funding also surfaces and it has continued to setback the operations of AU and made it to be fully dependent on donors, such as USA and EU, to finance its institutional apparatus and running cost of its operations (Wolkanto, 2016). However, the activities and operations of these companies are somehow regulated by law and statutory provisions in most countries they operate; they are still at the centre of global and regional controversies and thus generating issues that have consequences either directly or indirectly on their host bases.

The first issue is that of *the growing economic inequality in Africa that the operations of the PMSCs have continued to heighten.* Kofi Annan, as the then Chair of the African Progress Panel, in a keynote addressing titled "Africa and the Global Security Architecture" held at Bahir Dar, Ethiopia on 16–17 April, submitted that the economic growth in Africa over the last fifteen years; perhaps reasonably impressive has been neither flourishing and adequate nor inclusive (Annan, 2016). In fact, Africa has become the world's second most unequal continent, according to the African Development Bank. Income, consumption, and wealth are the underlying measures of financial inequality and the Gini index is the most widely used yardstick for measuring inequality. South Africa, Namibia and Haiti are among the most unequal countries in terms of the income distribution – based on the Gini index estimates from the World Bank. Alternatively, The Palma ratio focuses on the differences between those in the top and bottom income brackets and on the growing divide between the richest and poorest in society. The ratio takes the richest 10% of the population's share of gross national income (GNI) and divides it by the poorest 40% of the population's share. According to the Palma ratio figures in the UN Human Development Index, South Africa and Botswana as African countries had the starkest inequalities in income, based on the Palma ratio. Furthermore, the World Happiness Report measures real GDP per capita, social support, healthy life expectancy and people's perception of their freedom to make life choices, generosity and perceptions of corruption. It ranks 155 countries from 1 to 10 in terms of happiness; the Central African

Republic, Burundi and Tanzania lag behind with low scores in GDP per capita, social support and people's freedom to makes life choices (Barr, 2017).

In most African countries, the elites have egoistically enriched themselves using state resources, and not enough was spent on infrastructure, health, or education, which would have fostered development. It is "no coincidence that Boko Haram originated in one of the world's poorest and most deprived areas of the continent". Wealth is barely taxed and does not sprinkle down, impoverishing the state of resources needed to provide public services. Africa is not only unequal: but also unfair. The AU estimates that 25% of the GDP of African states, equivalent to $148 billion, is lost to corruption every year on the continent. The African Development Bank (AfDB) estimates corruption costs Africa up to 50% of lost tax revenues and over $30 billion in aid, annually. As a comparison, according to the Organization for European Economic Cooperation and Development (OECD), Africa receives approximately $22.5 billion in development aid from development countries (Gumede, 2016). Development of security remains uneven and the threats today are accompanied by elements of internal and external dimensions. Rebel groups have flourished and created "ungoverned spaces" in the poorest parts of weak states that feel neglected and clear lack of presence by their governments, where the population is often abused by the security forces, or where they do not trust the courts to deliver justice due high sense of inequality in dispensing justice. External forces take advantage of these shortcomings. It is now apparent that unemployed young men are especially willing tools to the "temptations of violence and easily instrumentalised for that purpose (African Leadership Forum Report, 2017: 6)." A World Bank survey in 2011 showed that about 40% of those who join rebel movements say they are motivated by a lack of jobs – which clearly represent the high level of inequality (World Bank, 2014 and African Leadership Forum Report, 2017, Ibid). The downtrodden class cannot afford to enjoy security beyond the basic public security dispensed by the national security outfits, but the governing elite elevates personal and personnel security at the expense of popular security. As the widened gap between the rich and poor continues to expand, more people (both individuals and companies) are hiring the services of private security firms; with the adverse impact that only a small fraction of the general population can afford these private security services at the detriment of the majority of the public. This phenomenon is common across Africa and constitutes the key reason PMSCs and PSCs are mushrooming all over Africa.

The second underlying issue is a *growing competition – both between PMSCs themselves and between state armed forces and PMSCs – as a result of the revolution in security privatisation.* When considering self-regulation of the PSCs, the main hurdle that companies in several African countries may encounter is that of competition and the risk associated with competing trade associations vying for patronage and access to privileges (Bearpark & Schulz, 2007: 84). In Nigeria, with the difficulty to regulate the operations of PSCs, the regulatory standards set for the companies and their modes and methods of operations are likely to impose themselves through increased competition and service delivery rivalry (Bearpark & Schulz, 2007). This is possible particularly as the larger clients like the oil multinational corporations in Nigeria pa-tronise the services rendered professional and organised PSCs for their oil facilities and in some cases vulnerable areas. However, at the same time, most local companies fear the competition of foreign PSCs whose "elevated levels of professionalism" may threaten their own existence (Bearpark & Schulz, 2007: 79). There are all manners of PSCs in the country each pursuing its own mission and driven by the corporate profit motive, and working in line with its agenda even though the agenda may not necessarily be in tandem with the national security re-quirement. The major cause of this is the ineffective regulatory mechanism essential for putting the PSCs in the right track. The competition is, however, good for the security market as it may yield a reasonable number of PSCs that can raise the standard of service and equipped with the expertise to meet up with the national demand. As for the competition of the PMSCs, there are only a few resourceful outfits in Africa some of which boast of platforms that are more sophisticated than the capability of most national armed forces in Africa. This has negative consequences of contributing to the proliferation and stockpiling of armaments in private domains, and the likelihood of the equipment getting into the hands of unregulated violent entities.

Another issue with respect to the PMSCs is *the strategic impact they create in their host client's states*. It is contested that, the superior firepower and extends of capability tools of violence by the PMSCs oftentimes lay a huge impact on the security environment of host countries. Their operations have the potency to de-escalate a crisis and coerce the warring parties into a negotiated settlement and thus the main rationale behind their employment and international appeal for the intervention of PMSCs. In situations where crisis persists unabated and there is a clear unwillingness on the part of the international institutions such as UN and AU, to intervene and contain the graduation of violence, deployment and use of military companies is considered as an alternative for peace enforcement. This is what obtained in Sierra Leone and Angola where the governments employed PMSCs otherwise tagged "mercenaries" then, to fight rebellions and to regain control over diamond-rich areas. However, it should be remembered that PMSCs are not the only military forces at scenes of war, as they are supplemented by the national forces (Foaleng, 2007: 49). The companies they cannot possess the monopoly and surety of success in fighting wars during interventions, but they establish a breeding effort upon which total control can be restored. This was the case in Sierra Leone where the defunct Executive Outcomes' claimed to have restored stability which was short-lived because in May 1997 the newly elected government was overthrown in a military coup d'état staged by the Armed Forces Revolutionary Council (ARFC). When Sandline International intervened "on behalf of the government in exile to fight against the unrecognised ARFC/ Revolutionary United Front military regime, other elements on the scene included forces of the Economic Community of West Africa (ECOWAS), different militia groups and the UN arms embargo that had been put in place. The embargo did not prove effective" (Foaleng 2007: 50). The PMCs have had causes at several fora to defend some Africa countries against near collapse as a result of the activities of indigenous insurrectional groups attempting to wage total war against the state. In Nigeria, at the peak of the Boko Haram insurgency, it was alleged that the then government of Goodluck Jonathan hired South-African and Israeli mercenaries as PMC to collaborate with the Armed Forces of Nigeria (AFN) in the fight against terrorism and insurgency in the north-east part of the country. Their superior firepower, technical and expertise was adjudged to be the best compared to the arsenals of the insurgent group and with the clandestine operations they carried out within the fringes of Sambisa forest, it was allegedly believed that they wreaked havoc on the group and helped in degrading the insurgents' capacity and capability to carry out large attacks (Freeman, 2015 and Smith, 2015). This has therefore justified the notion that, even with the unwillingness of other international bodies to come to the aid of the country, hired PMSCs to play a crucial role in national CT-COIN operations in Africa.

Also, while *the PSCs and the PMCs provide security for purely monetary value as profit-oriented mercantilists on one hand; the PMCs extend this to a point of exploitation of natural resources.* It is clear from the events of history, as Foaleng (2007: 45) rightly observed that violent groups also utilise the illegal possession of natural resources to attract PMCs. This incident happened in Angola where the rebel group *União Nacional para a Independência Total de Angola* (UNITA) applied "the strategy of using rough diamonds rather than cash or bank deposits as the primary and preferred means of stockpiling wealth. Indeed, the rebel group used diamonds exploited in the area under its control to purchase arms, weapons and military equipment as well as to fund military training from foreign actors and from neighbouring countries such as South Africa and Namibia" (Foaleng, 2007: 45). Harnessing wealth and resources of host communities by armed groups is not in new to Africa, as we have witnessed in Nigeria where the Boko Haram engaged in large scale agriculture (farming, fishing and animal husbandry) in the islands of Lake Chad and fringes of Sambisa forest, as well as coordinated acts of robbery, burglary, kidnapping and other heinous operations aimed at gaining more resources to pump into their operations. Similarly, the UNITA in Angola amassed diamond and other natural resources to lure and buy other foreign military fighters into their armed struggles. This happened in most cases where the state apparatus of security are gaining more advantage over the opposing dissident violent group in the execution of violence. Even for Boko Haram, it was fortuitously alleged that enlisted foreign fighters into their ranks and files particularly their snipers and other handlers of sophisticated equipment.

On the other hand, governments generally welcome the presence of PMSCs in situations of civil war when the states' natural resources remain the main source of generating fund to cater for the logistics of prosecuting CT-COIN operations. Legitimate governments make optimal use of natural resources, either in their raw form or as revenues derived from their exploitation, as a medium of exchange with the PMSCs who in reality engage in military actions (Gumedze, 2008). Most often the PMSCs bargain their access to and concessions for the exploitation of natural resources and participate in the game of exploitation the ruins of violence as intermediaries that facilitate contact with both parties to the conflict.

> "Some of the individuals (nationals or foreigners) working for these companies are businesspersons who often supply arms to all sides of the conflict in exchange for access to the revenue from the exploitation of natural resources or who facilitate the transformation of natural resources into financial revenue. The role of these individuals is not always well elucidated because it is not clear if they act as individuals or as employees of those companies" (Foaleng, 2007: 46).

This issue connects with the profit maximisation orientation of the PMSCs through the instrumentality of exploitation. The PMSCs are not mere conglomerates, their operations and sustenance of establishments require the huge commission of resources and therefore, some African countries in turmoil are often compelled to provide the ground for the PMSCs to continue waging what we termed the *economy of opportunities*. Therefore, through the purchasing powers of the states in Africa, PMSCs have flourished and got emboldened to participate in the illegitimate and unequal allocation of resources under the guise of security, preventive operations while waging huge destructions and indiscriminate attacks against the party they are hired to degrade.

## Challenges of PMSCs in Africa

The operations and the procedures guiding the existence of PMSCs in Africa cannot be hitch-free in an environment of social, economic, and political dislocations. Thus, there are several challenges encountered by these companies with peculiarity across the broad spectrum of their areas of establishments. The first challenge is that of the *weak regulatory and policy framework*. The national and international legal framework to regulate the PMSCs include, in addition to municipal legislation of specific countries, the International Humanitarian Law, International Human Rights Law, the Additional Protocols I and II from 1972 to Article 47 of the Geneva

Convention of 1949, and the International Convention against the Recruitment, Use, Financing and Training of Mercenaries, 1949. There are varying reasons why these conventions have not yielded the required result in regulating PMSCs. First, as Christopher (2006: 134) alludes, the original conventions are dated to the cold war era when the private industry was not as commonly and predominantly used by governments and non-state actors as they are in modern time. PMSCs have previously not been performing duties that traditionally have been reserved for the armed forces, but now they are fully engaged in a host of armed CT-COIN activities. Furthermore, these conventions lack clear definitions as to what constitutes mercenaries and PMSCs as well as the dividing line between the two in composition and modalities. With the policy and regulatory deficiency, the PMSCs is found hanging under the guise of ineffective harmonised legal frameworks to check and balance their excesses. The amplification of this challenge is aptly described by Bryden (2006: 10) "existing laws at an international level are insufficient, and national laws are lacking in many countries, creating a legal grey zone".

There is also the challenge of training gap which constraints in terms of training by the various Acts establishing them across the various African countries. This limitation is further reinforced by some provisions of Law. For instance, in Nigeria, Section 18 of the Private Guards Company Decree 33 of 1986 (later amended as the Private Guard Companies Act Cap 367, Decree 33 Law of the Federal Republic of Nigeria 1990) stipulates that no agency licensed under the provision of the Act shall train, or order persons to be trained, except the training syllabus and instruction manual is approved by the Ministry of Internal Affairs through the Nigerian Security and Civil Defence Corps. This gap is considered as a major challenge since the private security agencies require good training to face emerging security challenges. Although multinational companies engage national police in providing in training to their private security operatives, it appears this practice is not backed by the Act. This is contrary to the practice in the developed countries that have put in place well-established with integral facilities for training of PMSCs operatives. Also, in Uganda, the government regulates the training of employees of the PSCs and ensures that the Office of the Inspector General of Police tenders benchmarks on performance and training of the PSCs providing policing functions for private individual and agencies. This training became more essential considering that some of the qualified PSCs are licensed to carry small firearms. This is contrary to what obtain in Nigeria where the PSCs are not allowed to carry firearms. In all, there is a clear manifestation of inadequate professionalism on the part of the PSCs caused by the poor state of training and thus, made it a breeding ground for quacks to have a point of easing nature.

While training is insufficient and in most cases PSCs are restricted from using firearms in Africa aside few exceptions, the PSCs are also challenged by *the volatility of the environment charged by emerging security threats and institutional rivalry in Africa.* Considering the level of insecurity in some African countries, the private security operatives bear great risk especially when the law did not permit them to bear arms. The fact is that in most African countries, private security operatives are paid a pittance as take-home at the end of the month (the exception is private security operatives employed by multinational companies, embassies, telecoms firms and other big players in the economies). In the face of the current harsh economic conditions in Africa, the remuneration package of average private security operatives in Africa is not sufficient enough to cover the existential needs of their personnel and their families – for Nigeria, an average private security operator collects between 15,000-20,000 naira (about 50 USD) per month depending on his condition and place of service.

Also, as a result of institutional rivalry, PSCs' operatives are discriminated, rivalled, and frustrated by other security agencies in Africa especially the national police forces. The police see the private guards as rivals. And this scenario has led to distrust between the police and the in-house private security operatives hired by those organisations. The private security operatives are only complementing the efforts of the police and other security agencies in Nigeria. Besides the discrimination suffered on the hands of security agencies, in Nigeria for instance, Kasali (2011: 2) agreed that there also exists discrimination between the local and foreign private security companies due to the belief that the former is under-engaged because of the preference that most multinational corporations have for the latter in seeking for private security services.

Another challenge confronting the PMSCs is also *the comparative disadvantage in exporting private security services across different states*. In a situation whereby the PMSCs are not deeply connected indigenous interests of a client country, they tend to carry out activities exceeding bounds and limits of indigenous laws and thus, scale prosecution. It is obvious that the impetus to this challenge is the lack of effective across international, regional and national jurisdiction to avert the excesses. As Kenyan experience reveals, the PSCs industry exports private security services to neighbouring countries with scarce inhibitions. Bearpark and Schulz (2007: 80) corroborate that, "because of the comparatively highly developed private security market in Kenya and because of the country's strategic geographical position, Kenya serves as a hub for the export of private security services to the entire Horn of Africa, Sudan and DRC. International agencies as well as the extractive industry are increasingly relying on the services of Kenyan PSCs, which adds weight to the call for regulation". Similarly, the PMCs in South-Africa are also notorious for exporting services to some crisis-ridden countries in Africa, evade domestic laws and operate in daring but profitable terms beyond what can be exercised by the national armies of the client countries.

Another challenge confronting the PMCS particularly is the poor knowledge of the ground against the backdrop of their flamboyant conduct of operations in the host state. The personnel of these companies, though ex-servicemen that are adequately equipped with the needed knowledge to understand the terrain configuration of their area of operation, they are still challenged by the lack of instant understanding of the dynamics in their client state. The insurgents or violent dissidents they are to confront must be in a position of geostrategic advantage with deep foreknowledge of the terrain and, thus they can possibly impose restrictions to the extent of the PMCs operations. Nonetheless, we cannot ignore the fact that modern-day military operations avail sophisticated devices and surveillance equipment that can be of help in familiarising the PMCs' personnel with the Area of Operation (AOR). In a similar manner, theatre briefings are most often conducted by these PMCs to acquaint their personnel with the situation on the ground, but this cannot in any way be compared to the fluidity of operations – one that may involve physical presence and adequate familiarisation with the AOR. This has continued to pose a challenge on the PMCs in most places they operate in Africa.

## Conclusion

PMSCs have become an enduring feature of the African defense and security landscape by virtue of the ubiquity and preponderance of their operations on the continent. The existence of PMSCs have on face value provided weak states of Africa with the opportunity to outsource a ground troop for CT-COIN; however, it has also placed a morbid restriction on the sovereignty of these states. Thus, as a continent riddled with varying degrees of crises, the need has arisen for African states to device better mechanisms of harnessing the potentials of the PMSCs; and converting their inherent threats to regional and, most importantly, national security to the benefit of peace and security. Given the rate at which PMSCs undermine economic progress and expand economic inequality in Africa, to the risk of the resort to violence by the neglected majority, which is likely to destabilise national security, is imminent. To overcome this, more enabling environment ought to be established by African governments where citizens would in the structures of economic progress: applied to PMSCs this would mean placing restrictions of these companies to create local quota and favourable terms of employment and remuneration for local personnel. PMSCs should contribute to effective provisioning of public security by the national institutions in such a way that both the rich and poor would feel a sense of belonging can help to cover up for this wide margin of economic disparity and by implication, sustain peace and national security in African states.

The growing competition created by PMSCs in weak African states as a result of their proliferation and the comparative market advantage is a potential ground for improved service delivery as these companies compete within themselves and with local firms to drive competition. This competition brings out the best services from those companies and each would compete to survive and establish a stronger market base and, in so doing, they would aid in complementing the effort of national forces in restoring and maintaining national security. On the other hand, unhealthy competition can result in replanting the PMSCs industry with all manner of companies that would be ready to break into ranks with all means available – even if it takes compromising the architecture of national security. Therefore, in order to set a limit to the brewing competition in the industry, African states should devise an effective municipal and regional regulatory framework for PMSCs. Reviewing the existing frameworks to reflect current realities and also address the gaps and inconsistencies emanating from the competition would also be a good direction.

Further, the active participation of PMSCs in the plundering and exploitation of natural resources through such measures as providing back-ups to troubled African politicians are inimical to national security. African regimes should promptly recognise the need for the projection of national interest at the expense of personal political aspirations as this could jeopardise the corporate existence of the state. Also, in this vein, African leaders should employ all legitimate local tools for containing violence before resorting to foreign PMCs. In the face of their compelling invitation, African states should clearly define the boundaries of operations for these PMSCs through national regulation and regional diplomacy.

With regards to the resource and training gaps between African security agencies and PMSCs, it is incumbent on host states to ensure that their local forces are well kitted such that PMSCs are only needed as auxiliaries. Though the institutional rivalry between these companies and the national police has been established in this chapter, it would be paramount if the police of African states, rather than the armed forces, are fully involved in the drafting, implementing and regulating of the PSCs' training programmes before and after licensing. This is to be done to achieve a result-oriented structure. It would also be useful to consider setting a benchmark in the requirements for professionalism and training for the PSCs' personnel before been issued license to operate. This would invariably help to check the anomalies of the proliferation of quacks in the PSC's market and identify the critical frontiers for improvement in their service delivery and thus touch base with the national security of African states in a more balanced and equated platform.

## Notes

1    "There is a scholarly debate on whether or not PMSCs are 'mercenaries' in new clothing. The acronym PMSC is a merger of 'private military companies' (PMCs) and what is referred to as 'private security companies' (PSCs). Notionally, the former has a military nature, while the latter has a policing

function. However, the terms are difficult to distinguish as PMSCs often provide more than one type of service. The changeable nature of PMSCs inadvertently plays into definitional and conceptual ambiguities. It is for this reason that the UN Working Group on Mercenaries also tends to use the two terms interchangeably" (Gwatiwa, 2016: 71). In this chapter, the authors, therefore, defined PMSCs as private companies or contractors hired for military and other combat functions while PSCs are solely meant for policing processes not involving actual combat.

2    The concept of marketisation of public security gained influence as a result of the deviation of political wisdom followed by most western governments before the neoliberalist era. This was characterised by a period where certain aspects of public engagement and utilities were kept from the influence of the market. The conventional political thinking increased the range of areas more efficiently governed by market forces of demand and supply than state intervention. Thus, marketisation of former public sectors was believed to deliver better outcomes both for the economy and society at large. The main thrust of marketisation is to create enabling conditions for free market forces, limit government interventions, achieve privatisation and deregulation as well as allow markets to allocate resources more efficiently than governments (Bjønness, 2018).

# References

Abrahamsen, R., & Williams, M. (2005). *The gobalisation of private security: Country report: Nigeria.* Aberystwyth: University of Wales Press.

Africa Business Magazine. (22 November, 2012). Is security taking over Africa. https://africanbusinessmagazine.com/uncategorised/is-private-security-taking-over-africa/.

African Leadership Forum Report 2017. *Peace And Security For An Integrated, United And Sustainable Africa. Report of a Conference Held at Johannesburg*, South Africa from 24th-25th August 2017.

Annan, K. (2016). Africa and the Global Security Architecture. *A Keynote Addressed Delivered as the then Chair of the African Progress Panel Held at Bahir Dar*, Ethiopia on 16–17 April.

Ayoob, M. (1995). *The third world security predicament: State making, regional conflict, and the international system.* Boulder: Lynne Rienner Publishers.

Barr, C. (26 Apr 2017). Inequality index: Where are the world's most unequal countries? *The Guardian.* https://www.theguardian.com/inequality/datablog/2017/apr/26/inequality-index-where-are-the-worlds-most-unequal-countries Accessed on 11.02.2017.

Barrett, C. B. (2010). Measuring food insecurity. *Science, 327*(5967), 825–828.

Bearpark, A., & Schulz, S. (2007). *The Private Security Challenge in Africa: Problems and Options for Regulkation.* In Gumedze S. (Ed.), *The Private Security Sector in Africa*, 73–88. ISS Monograph Country Series, No. 146, Pretoria, South Africa: Institute for Security Studies.

Bearpark, A., & Schulz, S. (2007). *The private security challenge in Africa: Problems and options for regulation.* S. Gumedze(Ed.), *Private Security in Africa: Manifestation, Challenges and Regulation*, Monograph No 139.South Africa: Institute of Strategic Studies.

Bjønness, M. (2018). Marketisation *of security: A critical discourse analysis of the decision making process in the Danish parliament prior to outsourcing of maritime security to private military and security companies.* Peace and Conflict Studies Bachelor's Degree Dissertation. https://muep.mau.se/bitstream/handle/2043/26340/Martine%2CBjonness_BAthesis_15_08%281%29.pdf?sequence=1&isAllowed=y    Accessed    on    13.02.2019.

Bryden, A. (2006). Approaching the privatisation of security from a security governance perspective. In A. Bryden & M. Caparini (Eds.), *Private actors and security governance.* Geneva: Lit & Dcaf Verlag.

Caparini, M.   (2006). Applying a Security Governance Perspective to the Privatisation of Security. In Bryden A., and  Caparini, M. (Eds.), *Private Actors and Security Governance*, 248–263. Geneva: Geneva Centre for the Democratic Control of Armed Forces (DCAF).

Cardoso, N. C. F. (2016). Regional security in the Horn Of Africa: Conflicts, agendas and threats. *Brazilian Journal of African Studies, 1*(2), 131–165.

Christiansen, S.K. (2010). *Private Militaryand Security Companies and the Lack of National Legislation Hired Help or the Way to the Future?* Unpublished Master Thesis Submitted to the Department of Development and International Relations, Aalborg University, Denmark.

Christopher, K. (2006). *Corporate soldiers and international security – the rise of private military companies.* New York: Routledge.

Crawford, A. (2006). Networked governance and the post-regulatory state? steering, rowing and anchoring the provision of policing and security. *Theoretical Criminology, 10*(4), 449–479.

Edmonds, M. (1999). Defence Privatisationprivatisation: From state enterprise to commercialism. *Cambridge Review of International Affairs, 13*(1), 114–129.

Ferguson, J. (2005). Seeing like oil company: Space, security, and global capital in neoliberal Africa. *American Anthropologist, 107*(3), 377–382.

Foaleng, M.H. (2007). *Private Military and Security Companies and the Nexus between Natural Resources and Civil Wars in Africa.* In Gumedze, S. (Ed.), *The Private Security Sector in Africa,* 39–56. ISS Monograph Country Series, No. 146. Pretoria, South Africa.: Institute for Security Studies,

Freeman, C. (10 May, 2015). South African Mercenaries' Secret War on Boko Haram. *The Telegraph.* https://www.telegraph.co.uk/news/worldnews/africaandindianocean/nigeria/11596210/South-African-mercenaries-secret-war-on-Boko-Haram.html Accessed on 11.02. 2019.

Gatsheni, S.J.N. (2007). *Weak States and the Growth of the Private Security Sector in Africa: Wither the African State?.* In Gumed, S. (Ed.), *Private Security in Africa: Manifestation, Challenges and Regulation,* 17–38. Institute of Security Studies Monograph Series, No. 139. Pretoria, South Africa: Institute for Security Studies.

Geneva Centre for the Democratic Control of Armed Forces. (2006). *DAAF backgrounder: Private military companies.* Geneva: DCAF.

Gumede, W. (21 October, 2016). Cleaning up corruption in Africa, Democracy Works Foundation, https://democracyworks.org.za/cleaning-up-corruption-in-africa/.

Gumedze, S. (2008). *Pouring Old Wine into New Bottles? The Debate around Mercenaries and Private Military and Security Companies.* In S. Gumedze(Ed.), *Elimination of Mercenarism in Africa: A Need for a New Continental Approach,* 1–18, Monograph No 147. Pretoria, South Africa: Institute for Security Studies.

Gwatiwa, T. T. (2016). Private military and security companies policy in Africa: Regional policy stasis as agency in international politics. *Scientia Militaria: South African Journal of Military Studies, 44*(2), 68–86.

Howe, H. M. (1998). Private security forces and African stability: The case of Executive Outcomes. *The Journal of Modern African Studies, 36*( 2), 307–331.

Isima, J. (2009). The global marketplace and the privatisation of security. *Institute of Development Studies Bulletin, 40*(2), 113–120.

Job, B. L. (Ed.) (1992). *The insecurity dilemma: National security of third world states.* Boulder: L. Rienner Publishers.

Juma, L. (2011). Privatisation, human rights and security: Reflections on the Draft International Convention on Regulation, Oversight and Monitoring of Private Military and Security Companies. *Law, Democracy & Development, 15*(1), 1–33.

Kasali, M. A. (2011). Analysing the Evolution of Private Security Guards and their Limitations to Security Management in Nigeria. *African Journal of Criminology and Justice Studies: AJCJS, Vol.5,* No., 1–2.

Kirunda, S.W. (2008). *Private and Public Security in Uganda.* In Gumedze, S. (Ed.), *The Private Security Sector in Africa,* 1–34. ISS Monograph Country Series, No. 146. Pretoria, South Africa: Institute for Security Studies.

Krahmann, E. (2010). *States, citizens and the privatisation of security.* Cambridge University Press.

Kruger, J. J. (1992). *State provision of social security: Some theoretical, comparative and historical perspectives with reference to South Africa* (Doctoral dissertation). Stellenbosch University, Stellenbosch.

Luckham, R. (2009). Introduction: Transforming security and development in an unequal world. *Institute of Development Bulletin, 40*(2), 1–10.

Mabee, B. (2003). Security studies and the security state: Security provision in historical context. *International Relations, 17*(2), 135–151.

Mkandawire, P. T., & Soludo, C. (1999). *Our continent, our future: African perspectives on structural adjustment.* Dakar: Council for the Development of Social ScienceResearch in Africa.

Olaniyan, A. O. (2010). *Unorthodox peacekeepers and responses in Africa .* In Gumedze, S. (Ed.), *From market for force to market for peace: Private military and security companiesin peacekeeping operations,* 5–12, Institute for Security Studies. Monograph 183. Pretoria, South Africa: Institute for Security Studies.

Owen, R. (2013). *State, power and politics in the making of the modern Middle East.* London/New York: Routledge.

Percy, S. (2012). Regulating the private security industry: A story of regulating the last war. *InternationalReview of the Red Cross, 94*(887), 941–960.

Private Guard Companies Act. (1986). *Cap 367 Laws of the Federal Republic of Nigeria.* Abuj: Federal Government of Nigeria.

Remarks at the Tana high-level forum on security in Africa in Bahir Dar, Ethiopia on 16–17 April 2016, Kofi Annan, Chair of the Africa Progress Panel, *Africa and the Global Security Architecture*. Retrieved 20.10.2017.http://www.africaprogresspanel.org/tana-high-level-forum-on-security-in-africa/?gclid=EAIaIQobChMIv8Hn34yR1wIVNCjTCh32Wwv-EAAYASAAEgLKbPD_BwE.

Reno, W. (1997). African weak states and commercial alliances. *Africa Affairs*, *96*, 165–185.

Schwartz, M. (May, 2011). *The Department of Defense's use of private security contractors in Afghanistan and Iraq: Background, analysis, and options for Congress*. Library of Congress Washington DC Congressional Research Service.

Smith, D. (4 April, 2015). South Africa's ageing White mercenaries who helped turn tide on Boko Haram, *The Guardian*. Accessed on 14.02.2019 from https://www.theguardian.com/world/2015/apr/14/south-africas-ageing-white-mercenaries-who-helped-turn-tide-on-boko-haram.

Stead, S. (2006). The role of external tools to manage African conflicts. In T McNamee (Ed.), *African security, commodities and development*. London: Royal United Services Institute for Defence Studies.

Strom, K., Berzofsky, M., Shook, B., Barrick, K., Daye, C., Horstmann, N., & Kinsey, S. (2010). *The Private Security Industry: A Review of the Definitions, Available Data Sources, and Paths Moving Forward*. This document was prepared by Bureau of Justice Statistics (BJS) under International Cooperative Agreement Number 2009–BJ–CX–K045 f. https://www.ncjrs.gov/pdffiles1/bjs/grants/232781.pdf. Accessed on 5.9.2019.

Tar, U.A., & Bala, B. (2019). Terrorism, insurgency and the challenges of peace-building in the Lake Chad Basin. In K. C. Omeje (Ed.), *Peacebuilding in contemporary Africa: In search of alternative strategies*. London: Routlegde.

The Conversation. (2017, 26 October). Private Security in Africa: Time to Regulate the Bad and Harness the Good. Retrieved 19 October 2017 from http://theconversation.com/private-security-in-africa-time-to-regulate-the-bad-and-harness-the-good-85793.

The Guardian Newspaper. (26 February 2016). The Africa CEO Forum Awards 2016 to honour astounding CEOs' companies https://guardian.ng/news/the-africa-ceo-forum-awards-2016-to-honour-astounding-ceos-companies/ Accessed 12.02.2019.

2018 Vieews. com. (20 December, 2018). Meet the market leader in Zimbabwe's security industry, Securico. http://www.vieews.com/securico-quality-security-oriented-company/ Accessed on 13.02.2019.

Whitton, J. B. (1961). "Subversive Propaganda" reconsidered. *American Journal of International Law*, *55*(1), 120–122.

Wolkanto, N. A. (2016). Responsibilities and challenges of the African Union in maintaining continental peace and security: A case study of the Malian crisis. *Arts Social Science Journal*, *7*(4), 1–25. 10.4172/2151-6200.1000205.

World Bank. (2014). Realising Africa's youth potential: Africa needs investors to create jobs for its youth, and develop skills http://blogs.worldbank.org/developmenttalk/realizing-africas-youth-potential-africa-needs-investors-create-jobs-its-youth-and-develop-skills. Accessed on 8.02.2019.

# 41

# Civilians in the frontline of counterinsurgency operations

## The Civilian Joint Task Force in the war against the *Boko Haram* in Northeast Nigeria

*Hussaini Jibrin*

## Introduction

One fundamental issue that retards progress in Africa, despite decades of independence from colonial hegemony, has been the recurrence of different kinds of conflicts. In fact, as a result of the volume of conflicts on the continent, the entire region has thus become a market of small arms and light weapons due to the local arms markets as against the commodity markets which the continent used to be during pre-colonial and colonial periods. Although Nigeria has witnessed different types of armed conflicts ranging from resource control to ethnoreligious clashes, the *Boko Haram* (BH) insurgency in the northeast has brought dire consequences on the state and society.

The war of *Boko Haram* with its complex nature has resulted in the incorporation of thousands of youths in the affected areas who volunteered in assisting the armed forces at the battlefields. Known as the Civilian Joint Task Forces (CJTFs), youth volunteers are known to have mastered both the language of the terrorists for intelligence gathering and of the terrain of counterinsurgency operations. It has also resulted in the recruitment of civilian volunteers to confront the armed insurgents with the view of defeating them. This chapter attempts to explore the role played by the CJTF in counterterrorism operations against the BH insurgency. The youth group includes different vigilante elements such as hunters, traditional-sword-men (*YanTauri*), blacksmiths among others who emerged out of the circumstances that were about to make the city of Maiduguri a failed-state-capital in Nigeria. The chapter is divided into subsections: introduction, historicising the emergence and development of *Boko Haram* insurgent group, a prelude to ending *Boko Haram* Insurgency in the Northeast Nigeria, Formation of Civilian Joint Task Force, the CJTF in the War against the Insurgency and Conclusion.

## Historicizing the emergence of the *Boko Haram* insurgency

Like most terrorist groups, *Boko Haram* emerged from the faultiness of the crisis of governance and public regulation of religion that characterise the post-colonial state in Nigeria. The violent fundamentalist sect which calls itself *Jama'atahlulsunna lid-da'awatiwal-Jihad* (People Committed to the Propagation of Prophetic Tradition and Jihad) but popularly known by the public, media, and the international community as *Boko Haram*, meaning, the forbidders of a western type of education (Perouse-de-Montclos, 2014: 2). Many writers such as Kyari (2014), Loimeier (2014) and Brigaglia (2015) have written extensively on the emergence and development of *Boko Haram* insurgent group in Northern Nigeria. The key argument of these scholars is that the insurgency is bred by the failure of the state to provide existential goods to the society which, in return, seeks solace in the religious space. The rise of *Boko Haram* is caused by the desire of impressionable youth and other aggrieved adherents – often under the guidance of anti-establishment clergy – to use the religious space to bring about a theocratic-developmental state. This seems problematic in a secular plural state like Nigeria, but *Boko Haram* operatives are hell-bent on achieving this goal.

With regards to the evolution and transformation of the *Boko Haram* within which conventional studies on the group are categorized, there are two phases that define the Sect: clandestine phase (1999–2009) and guerrilla phase (2009 to date). The clandestine phase marked the evolution of the group through the mobilisation of the youths in Yobe and Borno states and the commencement of urban warfare and hit-and-run in some rural outposts. Around that period, their movement was first identified when they clashed with the Police at Kanama, Yobe state, where they later retreated claiming to shun "corrupt" public life. It was during this encounter they lost their first leader Muhammad Ali (Walker, undated:3). The movement of the group from Kanama back to Maiduguri and subsequent regrouping of its members further radicalized the group to adopt a more militant posture in dealing with the Nigerian state with vengeance. Throughout the first phase, the group conducted their activities in open space (mosques and lecture sessions). But towards the end of this phase, they changed more to the terror-oriented group using very harsh words and condemnation against the rest Muslims that boycotted them. This is what made them be rejected by the main Sunni Muslims of Nigeria. In Maiduguri, they re-established themselves under a new leader Muhammad Yusuf. The leader built a new mosque named *Markas Ibn Taimiyya* (Ibn Taimiyya Memorial Islamic Centre) located at Railways Quarters Area on the outskirt of Maiduguri where they conducted their activities. The mosque became the centre of gravity for Muhammad Yusuf's debates and indoctrination. In the words of Kyari (2014), the period of 2003–2005 marked the phase of intensive proselytisation, recruitment, indoctrination, and radicalisation of the followers of Mohammed Yusuf. The lectures, *Tafsir* and other theological rhetoric of the leader of the group had been characterised by a rejection of the employment in the civil service, western education, the traditional authority, and use of modern technological gadgets. Loimieir describes the worldview of the group in the following words:

> Muhammad Yusuf rejected the modern Islamic schools ...and Nigeria's secular system of education and summarized this specific position as *Boko Haram* (Hausa: western education is forbidden). He also turned against the Nigerian state and criticized the arbitrariness of Nigerian institutions--- in particular, the police and security forces. He refused to recognize the Sultan of Sokoto as the nominal head of all Nigerian Muslims and called him "Sarkin Sokoto" (Hausa: King of Sokoto). Central to Muhammed Yusuf's argumentation was a text written by a Saudi Arabian Wahabbi-oriented scholar, Abubakar b. Abdullah Abu Zayd (d. 2008), titled *al-madadis al-alamiyya al-ajnabiyyaal-isti'mariyya:ta'rikhuhawa-makhatiruha* (The Secular, Foreign and Colonialist Schools: Their History and Dangers). This text specifically served as the theological basis for his rejection of natural science-based (western and secular) view... (Loimeier, 2014:149)

The followers of Mohammad Yusuf became convinced about the ideological orientation of the group and gradually became radicalized. Loimeier (2014), also describes the Sect's rejection of modernization and technological products as "modernization shock" (Loimeier, 2014). In spite of the Sect's condemnation of the modern world, its members contradictorily used mobile phones, video cameras, DVDs, YouTube, chemical explosives, automatic weapons, and cars which are by-products of modern technology (Walker, 2012:7). The views and ideology of this group attracted the attention of the Nigerian security apparatuses, especially State Security Services and Police Force. The radicalization of the group and its encounter with the police in 2009 resulted in the insurgency that ravaged Northeast and some Northwest Nigerian states of Borno, Yobe, Adamawa, Bauchi, Kano and Kaduna. According to the findings of the Administrative Committee of Inquiry, the immediate factor that triggered violence and constant attacks on Nigerians by *Boko Haram* are:

> On 11 June, 2009, Muhammad Yusuf's followers were going to Gwange cemetery to bury some of their members who died in a motor accident when their attention was drawn to the Operation Flush II (a security patrol team) disciplining one of their members. The group stopped to rescue the man and tried to dispose the soldiers of their guns. In self-defence, the men of Operation Flush II opened fire, targeting them in the legs. In the process 17 of them were injured and later taken to the University of Maiduguri Teaching Hospital for treatment. When Muhammad Yusuf learned of the foregoing incident, he was enraged and threatened revenge. Subsequently, on 12th June, 2009, at the Da'ifatul Mansura Mosque, UnguwarDoki, he issued a stern warning in what he tagged an "Open letter" to the Nigerian president, Governor, etc...(Anonymous, ny 128)

The second phase, 2009–2015, underlined the sudden metamorphosis of the group into a covert terrorist organization under their new leader Abubakar Shekau. This followed the July 2009 uprising when its second leader Muhammad Yusuf was killed and had over 900 of its members extra-judicially killed by Nigerian security agents (Loimeier, 2014: 19). It can be understood that, the clash between members of this group and the security forces sow the seeds of the insurgency that terrorized some parts of northern Nigeria. After the clash, they disappeared for a while to draw strategies and tactics for vengeance against the security personnel. On 26 July 2009, violence broke out when 60 members of *Boko Haram* attacked DutsenTanshi Police station in Bauchi. It was reported that about fifty people died because of the attack. The following day, the violence escalated and spread to Borno, Kano Katsina and Yobe producing more than one hundred casualties and release of many prisoners (Comolli, 2015:54). These events made the Bauchi government to crack down the group, arresting more than seven hundred of their members. The police besieged their mosque in Maiduguri but the majority escaped. According to Walker, several them went to the insurgents' training camps in Algeria, while others received training in Tuareg rebel camps in Mali. (Walker, 2012: 6)

In 2010, *Boko Haram* launched a series of attacks on security forces, churches, mosques, schools, and other public gathering places. Between 2010 and 2012, the group extended its attacks to some parts of Northcentral Nigeria such as in Niger, Abuja, and Plateau states. For instance, on 20 January 2012, *Boko Haram* launched coordinated attacks on the Police Headquarters (Zone-I), the office of the Immigration Service and the State Security Service in Kano killing about 250 people. The group also continued to launch sporadic attacks in Kano killing hundreds of people. A fatal attack on Kano occurred in November 2014 when suicide bombers killed over two hundred congregants at Kano Central Mosque while observing Juma'at prayers. (Daily Trust:2014)

In Northeast Nigeria which is the dominant home of the BH especially Borno and Yobe states, the activities of the insurgents led to the enormous destruction of lives and properties worth billions of Naira. This is evident as thousands of people lost their capitals which adversely increased the rate of unemployment that has for decades bedevilled the region. It also led to the displacement of thousands of innocent citizens from their ancestral homelands to new areas throughout Northern Nigeria in search of shelter and food.[1]

Boko Haram's extension of its terror activities beyond the Nigerian territories of the Chad Basin (such as Niger, Chad, and Cameroon) resulted in the trans-nationalisation of the insurgency. At this time, the US officials stated that the insurgents allied with other terror groups in other parts of the world, such as *Al Qaeda* of North Africa, *Al-Shabab* in Somalia and the Islamic State of the Middle East (ISIL) (Akinfala, Akinbode, and Kemmer, 2014:5). By 2012, the government declared a state of emergency in Borno and Yobe states. Later, the emergency rule was extended to Adamawa State. In 2015, when Nigeria's general elections were about to commence, the activities of the insurgents increased up to some areas under the federal capital territory, Abuja. This is what led to the postponement of the elections from18 February which was earlier scheduled to 28th, the same month and from 28 March to 11 April same year, respectively. The war of counterterrorism in Nigeria around that period was overly complex so much so that, the defence sector was categorized with full corruption. Funds allocated for procurement of modern weapons were squandered. Military units were overrun, and soldiers were easily mowed down by the insurgents as a result of lack of sophisticated weapons and the terrorists were day-by-day taking towns and villages. There was the collapse of *spirit de corps* among the three arms of the military and other security operatives in intelligence report gathering and operations. It was estimated that the *Boko Haram* insurgency in Nigeria has claimed the lives of over 15,000 Nigerian since the beginning of the insurgency in 2009.

The foregoing analysis reveals the following: first, that the conflict has resulted in a situation of tensions and uncertainties in the affected areas. There was an absence of stability and an increase in the number of unemployed youths. Secondly, it reveals the lack of synergy and corruption within the Nigerian Defence sector. Third, it exposes, the great demand of the civilian population to contribute to whatever form in dealing with the insurgents.

## Politics and counterinsurgency in Nigeria

One catastrophic feature of the *Boko Haram* insurgency in Nigeria is the politicization of the conflict by the country's politicians. For instance, with extra-judicial killing of the group's leader, Muhammed Yusuf, by the Nigeria Policemen and subsequent terror activities of the BH as vengeance, the Nigerian government under President Goodluck Ebele Jonathan declared that the conflict was just a Trojan Horse crafted and amplified by the opposition in order to ridicule his regime's popularity in Northeast Nigeria. On the other hand, the opposition parties (especially the All Peoples Party, APP), in their rallies, campaigned against the incumbent government of failure to end the insurgents who were increasingly inflicting severe damages on the population, worship centres and public places.

The 2015 general elections in Nigeria was an epoch in Nigeria's history. It was the first time when an opposition party, All Progressives Congress (APC) won the presidential seat against the incumbent president, Goodluck Ebele Jonathan of the Peoples' Democratic Party (PDP). The election brought a retired Army General and longstanding opposition politician, Muhammadu Buhari, as the new President of the Federal Republic of Nigeria. President Buhari won the 2015 elections against the backdrop of popular frustration with the failure of the Jonathan Government to end the Boko Haram insurgency. President Buhari's tripod campaign agenda included: (1) fighting corruption (2) economic renaissance and (3) ending insecurity throughout the country. In its bid to quickly counter terrorist activities, the new government appointed a well-trained and professional Army General in the person of Lieutenant Tukur Yusuf Buratai as the new Chief of Army Staff. Under General Buratai's leadership style, the Nigerian Army in collaboration with the Nigerian Air Force and the Civilian Joint Task Force (CJTF) inflicted defeats after defeats on the terrorists that greatly reduced their influences and were able to establish a base at Sambisa Forest, their stronghold.

## Formation of the Civilian Joint Task Force (CJTF)

The Civilian Joint Task Force (CJTF) is a group of civilian youth that emerged as combatant groups under the tutelage, training and guidance of the Nigerian Army personnel out of the circumstances that gave rise to the *Boko Haram* (BH) terrorism in Northeast Nigeria. Between 2009 and 2013, BH insurgents operated as a sleeper urban terror cell carrying out hit and run against military and police units and formations. At this stage, the operatives found shelter within the city of Maiduguri. As a result of the catastrophic impact of the terrorism war on civilian population[2] at the midst of the conflict, in June 2013, a group of youth at Hausari quarters in Maiduguri decided to take the bull by the horn of identifying real members of the BH to the security personnel. This group was later named as the Civilian Joint Task Force (CJTF). They decided to henceforth attack any terrorist that paroled any place around the Monday Market and Babbban Layi to detonate explosives and/or shoot innocent civilians (Dan-Azumi and Azeez,2018).

As their exercise gained momentum, the youth volunteers sought to collaborate with the Nigerian Army in search of lasting peace in their fatherland. They converged at the main stadium of Maiduguri city and were addressed by Colonel Sagir Musa, the then spokesperson of the Joint Task Force before the inauguration of the current 7 Division of the Nigerian Army in Maiduguri. Colonel Musa, on behalf of the Federal Government, appreciated their individual sacrifice and efforts. This has no doubt boosted their morale on the one hand, and, on the other hand, immensely reinforced the government's counterinsurgency troops (military and para-military).[3]

With this development, the CJTF, who were majority Muslims, adopted a binding strategy and tactics by making all interested volunteers swear with holy Qur'an not to "… betray the government's troops either by leaking out information of attack or any other act of sabotage, may the curse of Allah befall them." The process of this indoctrination was so effective and akin to the military oath of allegiance, the leader of the CJTF would stay at the middle and new volunteers circled him at the centre, after the oath of allegiance to the government troops with the holy book, then be commissioned as real accredited members of the CJTF. When the activities of CJTF yielded fruits in the city of Maiduguri, other towns and villages that experienced attacks of the BH – initially in Borno but later in Adamawa and Yobe States – also started establishing CJTF for the same purpose. In this process, the leaders of the CJTF in Maiduguri travelled to those areas, initiate new volunteers and appointed a leader to them who in most cases a son of the soil or someone that was very familiar with the area. Simultaneously, this exercise extended to other Northeast states that suffered the same crisis (Haruna, 2016).

It is important to state that, the appointment of leaders among the CJTF group was based on merit largely by obtaining some magical or spiritual powers. In other words, the members of CJTF group being mostly drawn from a different specialised group of people in the society such as hunters, traditional-sword-men (*Yantauri*), vigilante groups, guards and the likes, they possessed some magical qualities that were needed in a war against terrorism. Members assigned to lead a team were the best fearless and in possession of large charms. In Maiduguri, they were and are still known as *Obarol*, meaning "Over All in Bravery." Thus, *Obarol* became a badge of honour for the CJTF operatives.

Simultaneously, a centralized structure emerged in the formation of the CJTF group which probably had to do with the initial training and assistance they received from the Nigerian Army that assisted to shape the outlook of the group. For instance, given the large volume of volunteers seeking enlistment into the CJTF, they were screened in their immediate towns and villages using standards army recruitment – such as aptitude test, psychological profiling, and medical test after which those who are fit are transported to Maiduguri where they were trained in combat skills[4] known as "removal of civilian mentality in their heads" as the soldiers called it. The Borno state government responded positively to the recruitment exercise by giving a significant amount of money drawn from the State's Security Vote as an allowance to the group members. All men that passed through enlistment list from their towns were contained in the government's records, therefore, enjoyed the State government's allowance under Borno Youth Empowerment Service (BOYES). As time went on, due to having limited resources to sustain the volunteers, it became difficult for people to get enlisted easily. In this situation, a large number of interested youth brought themselves to the training ground in Maiduguri for training without the allowance. (Dan-Azumi and Azeez, 2018).

## The CJTF in the war against the insurgency

In an attempt to trace the role played by the CJTF toward the intermittent successes of the Nigerian Military in counterterrorism in North-east Nigeria, it was noted that the initiative was initially well-received in different parts of the crisis areas. Due to the successes of the joint operations of the army units and CJTF, the *Boko Haram* was defeated in Maiduguri city. The core leadership and remnants of the Sect were forced by the excruciating defeat to seek refuge in the Sambisa Forest. Before the migration to Sambisa Forest, the CJTF exposed the insurgents to the security personnel and, through this exercise, thousands of them and their sympathisers were arrested. Many of them were allegedly shot to death extra-judicially (Author's Interview with Buikar, CJTF volunteer held at Biu, 15/08/2017).

They also assisted the security personnel in language interpretation during the interrogation of suspected *Boko Haram* operatives held in detention. In the same vein, they helped in exonerating non-members of the BH who were kidnapped by the insurgents. Further, they provided intelligence for identifying *Boko Haram* who abandoned militancy and escaped into the community, often tracking, arresting, and transporting them to the military barracks for detention and interrogation. During several encounters, the CJTF fought gallantly against the terrorists. For instance, the recapture of Mungonu, Kukawa, Baga, and DoronBagain February 2015 testified to this claim. The operation to recapture of the above-mentioned towns was organized at Old Shagari Low-cost Housing Estate, Baga Road, Maiduguri where the officers and soldiers of both the 5 Brigade Monguno and 7 Brigade Baga who were dislodged were camped. The Nigerian Army troops with about 15 Hilux vehicles belonging to the CJTF started advancement from this area on the 17 February 2015. The contingents met stiff resistance from the enemy so much so that they could not secure the Headquarters of the Multinational Task Force Baga until 22 February 2015. During the operations, for easy command and control, the CJTF were organized into sectors under the control of the Army officers. The CJTF volunteers displayed unprecedented bravery with few of them in possession of only locally made hunting-guns and the majority with swords, daggers, machetes, and sticks. They committed fully using their vehicles in the evacuation of dead bodies and wounded comrades and soldiers to the hospital of the 7 Division in Maiduguri. It is interesting to note that, during the operations, the morale of the CJTF men were high that at a point where a particular member killed or sustained a serious injury, another man would replace it.

The CJTF caught many BH members with bare hands and handed them over to the authority. At a time when their activities of CJTF against the BH became enormous, the latter started disguising as the former to launch attacks in many places of the former. When this was discovered, members of the CJTF were alerted and took charge against it. As a result of the war difficulties and firepower experienced by the CJTF in the theatres of the war, it made some of them to become bold enough and had on many occasions challenged some soldiers openly, "that without our efforts you could not defeat the BH boys." (Author's Interview with Sergeant Mukhtar Musa, Veteran in the battle to capture Baga town, held in Katsina, 15/03/2016). This might be true considering the role they played. Before achieving this development, the CJTF were not fully trusted by the Nigerian Armed Forces. They were restricted to move in the midst of the soldiers freely due to fear of soft attacks. Later, their roles were fully appreciated and involved in sensitive security meetings. As such, they exposed some of the traditional rulers that have hands in the BH conflicts.

However, the involvement of civilians in counterinsurgency operations is not free of controversy. Though CJTF has so far proved useful for the CT-COIN drive of the government in Nigeria, the involvement of civilians in warfare – as volunteers rather than trained reservists – comes with dire consequences. These are untrained or poorly indoctrinated civilians who are barely lettered in the laws of armed conflict and therefore susceptible to war crimes. In 2016, for instance, the CJTF was listed on the annexes of the UN Secretary General's Annual Report for Children and Armed Conflict for recruitment and use of children in terrorism. Similarly, in line with the UN Security Council resolutions of 1539 (2004), 1612 (2005), 1882 (2009), 1998 (2011) and 2225 (2015), on children and armed conflicts, the UN in collaboration with the CJTF authority signed an action plan in September 2017 as part of efforts in counterterrorism war in Northeast Nigeria. They also progressively enlarged their counterterrorism activities in security operations and provision of security on camps for internally displaced populations.

## Conclusion

The foregoing analysis reveals that in the zones of conflict in Africa, the civilian population has a role to play either on the side of the government actively and passively to contain the crisis or to side with the enemy and sabotage the restoration of law and order. It also informs us that, if the civilians in the line of defence actively participate in a war and become exposed to combat skills, they should be given the necessary incentives and equipment to discharge their responsibilities. They should also be given the care both in the course of the counterinsurgency and afterwards: those of them that sustained various degrees of injuries in the course of service are not well taken care of after been discharged from military hospitals. In other words, they should not be abandoned to take care of their ill-health situations without proper follow up from the side of the government. As at 2018, it is estimated that there were about 26,000 CJTF in the city of Maiduguri only, out of which only 600 received a salary (Author's Interview with Buikar, CJTF volunteer held at Biu, 15/08/2017). This ineptitude attitude may further culminate to another fresh security challenges to the country during the post-insurgency periods. Therefore, there is a need for fresh research to be undertaken that could deeply deal with how to address the challenges that might arise out of this insensitivity.

The state should create a way of professionalising and mainstreaming the CJTF into the armed forces as a "reserve force" with specific terms and conditions of service, regular remuneration and a stable supply of consumables and hardware. They should also be adequately trained in the laws of armed conflict, military aid to civil authority and democratic norms and ethos. Finally, they should be exposed to vocational training and formal education to enable them to become useful members of society, especially in the aftermaths of the CT-COIN operations. The task of rehabilitation of members of CJTF should rest squarely on the Nigerian Army (NA), the Presidential Initiative for the North East (PINE) and the newly established Northeast Development Commission (NEDC).

## Notes

1 Around this period, as a result of the *Boko Haram* terror activities, many people of the Northeast region especially Borno state natives were found all over the states of Northern Nigeria, begging as internally displaced persons.
2 At this period, the natives of the city of Maiduguri suffered double agonies of the conflict. On the one hand, in the course of investigation/arrest of the members of the *Boko Haram,* a large number of innocent people became victims of the circumstance. On the other hand, members of the *Boko Haram* started attacking the innocent civilian population for refusal to support their actions against the Government.
3 See, Nigerian Newspapers March-December 2013. However, *Daily Trust* and *The Nation* newspapers have widely covered events of the period under discussion.
4 They were not given military weapons, rather, used their local weaponry such as swords, bow and arrows, spears, local-hunting-guns and so on.

## References

Akinfala, Akinbode, and Kemmer (2014). Boko Haram and Terrorism in Northern Nigeria: (A Psychological Analysis), *British Journal of Arts and Social Sciences*, 17(1), 117–118.
Umar, M.S. (2012). The Popular Discourses of Salafi Radicalism and Salafi Counter-Radicalism in Nigeria: A Case Study of Boko Haram, *Journal of Religion in Africa*, 42(2), 118–144.
Comolli, V., (2015). *Boko Haram: Nigeria's Islamist insurgency*, London: Hurst & Company.
Dan-Azumi, D. J. and Azeez, A, (2018). 'The Intervention of Civilian Joint Task Force (CJTF) in the War against Boko Haram in the North East Nigeria: A Theoretical Approach' in *Journal of Research in Humanities and Social Science*, 6(5), 40–48.
Daily Trust Newspaper, November 28, 2014.
Haruna, Kabiru Isa (2016). Religion and Society: A historical study of intra-faith relations in Kano, Unpublished PhD thesis, Sokoto, NIgeria: Usmanu Danfodio University.
Interview with Aliyu Bukar (Dan Gora), member of CJTF in Miaduguri, 45 years, held Id at Biu, 15th/08/2017.
Interview with Major Iliyasu Muhammed, Commander in the Nigerian Army during counterterrorism war with Boko Haram, 47 years, Biu, 15th /08/2017.
Interview with Haruna Goni, a CJTF member in Maiduguri, 33 years, held ld at Maiduguri, 12/04/2016.
Interview with some soldiers of the Nigerian Army who served under Multi-National Joint Task in Baga border town and preferred anonymity on 3rd July, Abuja Nigeria.
Interview with Sergeant Mukhtar Musa, Veteran in the battle to capture Baga town, held in Katsina, 15/03/2016.
Kyari, M. (2014) The message and methods of Boko Haram in M. Perouse-de-Montclos(Ed.) , *Boko Haram: Islamism, politics, security and the state in Nigeria*, Netherlands: Ipskamp Drukkers.
Loimeier, R. (2014) "Boko Haram: The Development of a Militant Muslim Movement in Nigeria", *Annual Review of Islam in Africa*, Centre for Contemporary Islam, University of Cape Town, Issue No. 12. 99–117.
Perouse-de-Montclos, M. (ed.) (2014), *Boko Haram: Islamism, Politics, Security and the State in Nigeria*, Netherlands: Ipskamp Drukkers.
The Nation Newspapers, (2012–2016) covered lot of issues on the subject matter.
Walker, A. (undated) *Special Report*, United States Institute of Peace (www.usip.org).
Walker, A. (2012) *What is Boko Haram?* Special Report by the United States Institute of Peace.
Wikipedia (2019) 'Joint Civilian Task Force', https://en.n.wikipedia.org, retrieved on 29/01/2019.

# 42

# Child soldiers, counterterrorism and counterinsurgency in Africa

## Usman A. Tar, Al-Hassan Conteh, and Emmanuel Ukhami

## Introduction

The history of Africa has been characterised by various kinds of wars, conflicts, insurgency, and terrorism. The conflict caused by different reasons, which may include ethnic rivalry, land/communal dispute, religious reason and even struggle for political power and economic resources. Some of these conflicts degenerate into wars, terrorism, and insurgency, with grave consequences. The civilians/non-combatant groups are usually at the receiving end of conflicts. Their human rights are constantly being breached and outrightly disregarded of such groups are the children, who are innocent, naïve, easily influenced, fearful of authority and lacking the maturity to make a sound judgement.

Unfortunately, Africa has provided the largest number of conflicts in the world (Barnitz 1999) and children have been recruited, as child soldiers to be at the centre of some of these armed conflicts. According to Wessels (1997), throughout history, and in many cultures, children have been extensively involved in armed conflicts even when such practices were against cultural morals. According to Norman (2004), in World War I, in Great Britain, 250,000 boys under 18 were conscripted to join the army. In World War II, as put by Achvarina and Reich (2006), child soldiers fought throughout Europe. Still, Africa has witnessed a steady increase of young children joining the ranks of terror organisations and executing horrendous acts of violence. The involvement of child soldiers in conflicts, insurgency and terrorism has increased over the years. The situation has degenerated so severely that children from the age of seven years are recruited continuously as child soldiers into government armed forces, whether or not an armed conflict exists. As of 2006, an estimated 300,000 child soldiers are involved in armed conflicts in Africa.

According to the International Action Network on Small Arms, Safer World and Oxfam International, in Kakhuta-Banda (2014), "between 1990 and 2005, 23 African nations have been involved in armed conflicts where child soldiers have been used. Some of the countries involved include Sierra Leone, Burundi, Liberia, Rwanda, Angola, Uganda, and Democratic Republic of Congo (DRC), just to mention a few." In Nigeria for instance, Boko Haram terrorist group recruit boys and girls as a child soldier. They are trained to handle and use sophisticated ammunitions, suicide bombings and all heinous acts. Furthermore, the Coalition to Stop the Use of Child Soldiers (2000), noted that about 120,000 children were active in Africa at the beginning of the 21$^{st}$ century, making Africa, the largest single continent in terms of child soldier usage and the fastest-growing region in terms of child soldiers in recent years followed by East Asia and the Pacific.

The use and concept of child soldiers have been a significant concern in the act of terrorism insurgency and more massive wars. Counterterrorism and counterinsurgency (CT-COIN) operations have contributed to the continuance of the use of child soldiers during CT-COIN operations. Children are usually recruited by some African government to act like soldiers and fight against rebel groups during war, counterinsurgency and terrorism operations. Unfortunately, this negates the phrase "children are the leaders of tomorrow," as their normal lives activities are truncated, to becoming soldiers of today, with no hope for the future. To what extent has counterterrorism and counterinsurgency been an enabler of child soldiers? What measures have been taken by African countries to annihilate this menace or trend? What is the effect of the menace of child soldiers on development in Africa?

The chapter is divided into seven subsections which include the introduction, theoretical framing of child soldiers and conceptual clarifications, historical development of child soldiers, causes and effects of child soldiering, eradication of child soldiers in Africa, and conclusion.

## Child soldiers and children in war-conceptual and theoretical framing

The phenomenon of child soldiers and children in war has attracted scholarly attention for quite some time. Several scholars such as Michael Wessells, Alcinda Honwana, Rachel Brett and Irma Specht have debated on the issue of child soldiers and have placed the subject in diverse trajectories to understand why children are drafted into, or become victims of war, conventional or asymmetric. In this section, the Human Security theory are recalled evaluating the concept of child soldiers and children in war.

*The Human Security Theory* provides a people-centred paradigm to the phenomenon of child soldiers and children in war. The theory stresses the material and existential factors behind wars in general and, in particular, the "paediatricisation of war" through the recruitment of children as an endemic feature of conflicts caused by the crisis of underdevelopment. Thus, states are expected to put in place developmental governance systems that will make war and child soldiering needless and counter-productive. The human security theory posits that the solution is to provide a genuine development that will dis-incentivise violence and deny a breathing space to child recruiting agencies.

Human security emphasisesses the individual's rights and interests which are often ignored by the state and the international community. This theory can be used to analyse the problem of child soldiers in that some of the reasons' children join armed groups is so that they can get food. Armed groups entice children with the food they rob off people. Some children join for economic reasons where they feel they are better off economically as a child soldier than to languish in poverty at home or in IDP camps. Armed groups have often pledge handsome reward to children as an incentive for joining armed groups.

This theory is demonstrated in the writings of Wessells that children join armed forces in search of security, food, and health care. These are the factors that push children who have been orphaned or girls escaping forced marriages. They want to fill the void left by their parents or caregivers. Other children are pulled into joining armed forces to be with an older sibling or an uncle or father by joining the company of an older relative in a militant organisation. In addition, the occultic and hypnotic recruitment of children to cause mayhem is reported in the literature. Wessells (2005:363) points out that "LRA tactics of isolation, physical beatings and intimidation are used to force children into obedience."

The human security theory is yet to achieve a significant mileage in the discourse of war, conflict management and peacebuilding. Fox (2003:474) explain that "… the human security paradigm is a building that is still under construction and has been the object of much criticism as well as praise." In his criticism, Paris (2001), points to the "broad sweep and definitional elasticity of most formulations of human security," the theory unable to generate a viable mechanism of ending the conflict. According to McRae (2001), while human security can bring a much-needed shift in emphasis and become "the new measure of success for international security and the international system" through equality and inclusive development, its potency in theorising war and child soldiers remain weak.

In sum, human security theory highlights the key role the society plays in the emergence or not of child soldiers. The theory stresses the role of the state and society in moulding the child and protect him from situations that lead to them joining armed groups. Who is a child soldier?

The Convention on the Rights of the Child (Convention on the Rights of the Child, 1989) defines a child soldier as any combatant under the age of 18 who is or who has been recruited or used by an armed force or armed group. According to World Health Organisation (WHO, 2009), a child soldier can be described as any person under 18 years of age who is compulsorily, forcibly, or voluntarily recruited or used in hostilities by any kind of armed forces or groups in any capacity, including but not limited to soldiers, cooks, porters, messengers and informants. It includes girls recruited for sexual purposes and forced marriage. It does not, therefore, refer exclusively to a child who bears arms. Unfortunately, children are recruited by the government, insurgency, and terrorist groups to either be part of counterterrorism, counterinsurgency or even terrorism in a post-conflict situation. It depends on whose side they belong. The practice threatens the future of millions of children in some of the most underdeveloped and poverty-stricken areas of the world.

## Terrorism and insurgency

The concept of terrorism and its operationalisationsation defies one universally accepted definition. Since the September 11, 2001 attacks in the US, the concept of terrorism is more problematic to conceptualisese, because of too many ideological interpretations. One of such interpretations, that either give credence to terrorism or put it in a negative light is the concept "one man's terrorism, is another man's freedom fighter." However, Akpotor and Oromareghake (2013) surmise that the concept "terrorism" is etymologically derived from a Latin and French word: terrere, meaning "to frighten," and "state rule by terror" respectively. According to Stibli (2010), terrorism is an act of using unconventional tactics to achieve political goals through the use of violence, sabotage or threat to the state, organisationsation or social group against civilians with the sole motive of producing psychological fear and intimidation.

Annan (2005) described terrorism as an act "intended to cause death or serious bodily harm to civilians or non-combatants with the purpose of intimidating a population or compelling a government or an international organisationsation to do or abstain from doing any act."

Though insurgency and terrorism have contrasting objectives and strategies, both still employ fear and terror outcomes to make popular their demands. Initially, acts of insurgency may be location-specific with clear threat signals to the nation (Akpuru-Aja Mbachu 2013). In the lexicon of military studies, the insurgency has often been used interchangeably, and imprecisely, with "irregular warfare," "unconventional warfare," "revolutionary warfare," "guerrilla warfare," and even "terrorism." Similarly, insurgents have been called "guerillas," "terrorists," "revolutionaries," extremists," and "irregulars" (Osakwe & Ubong, 2013).

Insurgency is a condition of violent revolt against constituted authority or established leadership through sabotage and harassment in order to undermine its authority. In other words, insurgency becomes latent when a group of persons use violent methods to resist the enforcement of the law or the group opposed the running of organised governance through bloody violent and insurrection. In the Nigerian constitutional context, an insurgency is defined within the active framework and physical activities of the following; attack on the defenceless civilians resulting in the massive loss of lives and properties; prevention of the flourishing domestic and foreign investments and investors and its linkages to murder, genocide and indeed, treasonable felony (Okene & Olawale, 2013). The extreme extension and aggravation of insurgency and threat to security lead to terrorism which is a systematic use of violence, destructive acts and coercive methods to intimidate individuals, population and constituted government (Okene & Olawale, 2013). In summary, according to the US Department of Army Field Manual (2014), an insurgency is defined as an organised, protracted politico-military struggle designed to weaken the control and legitimacy of an established government, occupying power or other political authority while increasing insurgent control.

## Counterterrorism and counterinsurgency (CT-COIN)

The concept of counterterrorism and counterinsurgency emanate as a result of the emergence of terrorism and insurgency. The new realities of insecurity and terrorism in the international system has brought up new ideas to mitigate, reduce or eliminate its effects. Hence, there are concepts like counterterrorism and counterinsurgency. According to Moore (2007), counterterrorism incorporates the practice, military tactics, techniques, and strategy that government, military, law enforcement, business and intelligence agencies use to combat or prevent terrorism. It includes the strategies to counter the financing and ideological spread of terrorism. The most common definition of counterterrorism is the practices, tactics, techniques, and strategies that governments, militaries, police departments and corporations adopt in response to terrorist threats and/or acts, both real and imputed. Counterterrorism according to Stepanova (2003) implies a heavy reliance on the specialisedsed capabilities of the works of intelligence and counterintelligence sector. Its central goals are always the prevention, description and pre-emption of terrorist activities and networks.

The term "counterinsurgency," suffers from imprecision and confusion. In the lexicon of military studies. It has frequently been given a euphemistic colouration and used interchangeably with stability operation, "internal defence" "internal security," "counter guerrilla operations" and "countering irregular threat." Theoretically, counterinsurgency is a term used to explain the various techniques that relate to the prevention and suppression of armed insurgencies. As such, it is a response to the insurgency. Counterinsurgency is defined as "those military, paramilitary, political, economic, psychological and civic actions taken by a government to defeat an insurgency." According to Moore (nd), counterinsurgency is "an integrated set of political, economic, and social structures and resolve the underlying causes of an insurgency in order to establish and sustain the condition necessary for lasting stability." According to Nwanne (2016), counterinsurgency strategies are designed to help save the affected population from insurgent violent, reinforce the legitimacy and capacity government institutions, in addition to eliminating the insurgents' influence over a region.

Africa has had its experience of insurgency, terrorism and government adopting strategies and tactics to counter it. Some African countries like Nigeria, Somalia, Tanzania, Kenya, just to mention a few have in recent years been battling with insurgency and terrorism. In Nigeria, for instance, the Boko Haram insurgency has continually wreaked havoc on the security and stability of the country, causing the destruction of lives and properties, abducting young girls and boys who later become sex slaves, suicide bombers and generally, child soldiers. The government have continually adopted various strategies and tactics to counter the activities of the sect and to bring their activities to an end.

## Historical evolution of child soldiers

The use of child soldiers in armed conflict is not a recent phenomenon in the history of man. According to Smith (2002), the history of child soldiers date-back many centuries, although it has been portrayed as a current phenomenon. Brocklehurst (2007) traced the use of child soldiers, far back as the 17th century, though they were not considered as true combatants in those days. Child soldiers were used to arming and maintaining the knights of medieval Europe as well as carrying ammunition to cannon crews. At that time, they were not considered as true combatants or legitimate targets though they were part of armies. However, the most known and early use of "child soldiers" occurred during the 1212 children's crusade. This was a march of thousands of unarmed boys from northern France and Western Germany who thought they might take back the Holy land by the sheer power of their faith. Although, many never left Europe. Ellis & Clapham (1998) claimed that large numbers of its 30,000 child crusaders were sold into slavery and many more drowned in the Mediterranean Sea. In modern history, it has been suggested that Napoleon's army in the early 19th century featured several 12 years old boy combatants.

This historical precedent notwithstanding, the post Second World War period has become known as the "era of the child soldier" (Jeannette, 2002). Modern conflicts are characterisedsed by the proliferation of small arms and light weapons such as grenades and AK-47s as opposed to the nuclear and biological weapons of the cold war era. The development of the light weapons trade "takes the child soldier from the margins to the very heart of modern conflict" (Alcinda, 1999). The incessant spread of conflicts in Africa witnessed the use of child soldiers, especially immediately after the countries in the continent gained political independence. A lot of African countries like Somalia, Rwanda, Uganda, Chad, Democratic Republic of Congo, Liberia, Libya, Sierra Leone, Sudan, and even Nigeria faced some form of conflicts, civil wars, ethnic rivalry and religious crisis. Children affected by any of these crises, including insurgency and terrorism, are often deprived of basic social amenities like food, shelter, clothing, clean and good water, and medical attention. Given the scourge of deprivation and depression, they are subjected to, children affected by war are easy prey for recruitment as child soldiers, as a survival strategy. The heavy use of child soldiers according to Jézéquel (2006), constitutes one of the principal characteristics of these post-cold war African crises. Indeed, the image of the African childbearing a Kalashnikov bigger than himself has come to symbolisese a typically African brand of violence to western eyes barbaric violence beyond the bounds of the acceptable and the rational.

Non-Governmental Organisations (NGOs) such as Human Rights Watch, Save the Children, or the Coalition to Stop the Use of Child Soldiers have led active campaigns against the use of child soldiers. Though, these organisations have drawn attention to the participation of children in conflicts from Latin America (Columbia) to the Near East (Palestine) and even Asia (Burma), Africa is often presented as the continent hardest hit by this "unacceptable practice" (Jézéquel, 2006). Thus, based on the foregoing, a number of points are pertinent. First, children constitute both the target and instruments for the perpetuation of war. Secondly, the use and volume of child soldiers have grown over the past five decades. Thirdly, child soldiers are used by both government and rebel forces. However, rebels and militias use child soldiers more than conventional forces. Finally, existing international instruments for combating child soldiering seem to have failed due to lack of solid mechanisms for enforcement and adjudication.

## Child soldiers, counterterrorism and counterinsurgency in Africa

The heightened rate of insurgency and terrorism in Africa and even globally has consequently led to the development of new and sophisticated ways, weapons and tactics to counter insurgency and terrorism. Counterinsurgency and terrorism operations are often described as a "war of attrition," but in its soft forms such as de-radicalisation and civil-military relations – it can spill over to non-military and governance issues. During CT-COIN, there is often gross human rights violation including the rights of children and other vulnerable subjects. During operations, children are usually maimed, killed, sexually molested, and used as child soldiers. According to The Coalition to Stop the Use of Child Soldiers (2001), the use of children in violent conflicts is a serious problem that continues to plague both the African continent and the international community as a whole. More than 300,000 children under the age of 18 serve as child soldiers with government armed forces and armed opposition groups worldwide, with over 120,000 of them located in Sub-Saharan Africa alone. In some of these countries, according to Kalis (2002), it is common to even find 7 and 8-year-olds engaged in battle.

In Africa, on the part of the government, armed forces have involved children as child soldiers to assist them in the fight against insurgents. Children are often recruited to carry guns, cook, act as a spy, carrying out killings and obeying instructions from their commanders. While some are forced often at gunpoint to join armed forces, others join voluntarily, sometimes because they see it as a means to escape from poverty, or in order to seek revenge over the killing of their loved ones. In some African countries, the state armed forces are guilty of using child soldiers during counterinsurgency operations. Government of countries such as Angola, South Sudan, Democratic Republic of Congo (DRC), and Somalia have been constantly accused especially by international organisations of recruiting child soldiers to serve in military units and assist armed forces during wars. In the Angola civil war 1970s – 1990s, according to Child Soldiers Global Report (2004), child soldiers were used extensively during the civil war by both government armed forces and the armed opposition group, UNITA (National Union for the Total Independence of Angola). Human Right Watch (2003) claimed that up until 2002 ceasefire, thousands of child soldiers were used in government forces. After full-scale conflict broke out again in 1998, children had been rounded up in recruitment drives in government-held areas and forced to fight. The Coalition to Stop the Use of Child Soldiers (2001) estimates that 7,000 children served with UNITA and government forces, Angola Armed Forces (Forcas, Armadas Angolanas, FAA).

The most recent conflict in South Sudan, beginning in December 2013, has had a severe impact on children, with an estimated 19,000 children associated with armed forces and groups, according to UNICEF (2017). Human Rights Watch lamented that: "South Sudanese government forces are actively recruiting boys as young as 13, often by force, as soldiers in Malakal, Upper Nile State. Both parties to South Sudan's conflict have recruited and used child soldiers, which is a war crime when children are under 15" (Human Rights Watch, 2015).

The Democratic Republic of Congo (DRC) is one of those countries in the African continent plagued by armed national and foreign groups and forces for over 20 years (from 1995-till date). Children have also been recruited in various armed groups either as terrorist/insurgents or counterterrorist and COIN in the conflict. According to Ngera (2009), in the DRC, an estimate 7,000 child soldiers were recruited and remained in government forces and armed groups, including foreign armed groups, mostly found in the eastern provinces of Equateur, Ituri, Kotanga, North and South Kivu, and Maniema. Children were used as combatants, porters, guards, and sex slaves. Children were recruited from refugee camps in Rwanda and used by armed groups in North Kivu. The BBC reported the following from a respondent: "When they came to my village, they asked my elder brother whether he was ready to join the militia. He was just 17 and he said no; they shot him in the head. Then they asked me if I was ready to sign, so what could I do, I did not want to die, so I joined" (Child Soldiers Global Report, 2008). Similarly, a former child soldier from DRC said: "They gave me a uniform and told me that now I was in the army. They even gave me a new name: 'Pisco'. They said that they would come back and kill my parents if I didn't do as they said" (Child Soldiers Global Report, 2008).

In 2003, armed political groups continued to recruit child soldiers, who constituted more than 40% of their forces in some instance (Child Soldiers Global Report, 2004). In Somalia, a country is considered another hotbed for violent crisis and insurgency, the figures of child solider are depressing. In 2002, the UN Independent Expert on Somalia noted large numbers of child soldiers with factional militias in Mogadishu and Baidoa, and reported that "often young boys carrying weapons were riding with larger groups of armed men on anti-aircraft or similar vehicles" (United Nations, 2002). Over 200,000 children were estimated to have carried a gun or been involved with militias over a 14-years period (United Nations, 2004). Boys as young as 14 or 15 allegedly participated in militia attacks, and many youths were members of marauding gangs known as *moryan* (maggots) (US Department of State, 2003). In the Liberian armed conflict from 2000, which intensified in 2002, child soldiers were also recruited by all parties of the conflict. The use of child soldiers was a deliberate policy at the highest levels of government and the two-armed opposition groups. According to Human Right Watch (2004), the use of child soldiers by government forces was systematic, widespread, and endorsed at the highest level. Commanders of child soldiers in government units such as the Small Boy Units (SBUs) were as young as 12. As the conflict intensified in 2002, the government stepped up conscription of former combatants in the capital, Monrovia, recruiting former child soldiers and other children into the armed forces, the paramilitary Anti-Terrorist Unit (ATU) and associated militias. Further recruitment, often forcible, occurred in response to the emergence of the movement for Democracy in Liberia (MODEL) in 2003 and again as the conflict intensified in the months before Charles Taylor's departure as Liberians United for Reconciliation and Democracy (LURD) advanced towards Monrovia.

In the Sri Lanka CT-COIN campaign (1983–2009), children were often used as key players in the Liberation Tigers of Tamil Eelam (LTTE) strategy along with other numerous atrocities such as kidnapping and murder committed by the Sri Lanka government. In the beginning, children or young adults joined the LTTE "out of altruistic reasons to save their group identity from being eclipsed. In time, however, the older youths matured enough to become disillusioned with the way the struggle was being directed" (Somasundaram, 2002). The account of child soldiers' engagement in Africa, is inexhaustible. Hence, very few examples are mentioned. Conflicts, insurgency, terrorism, CT-COIN in Nigeria, Kenya, Chad, and some other African Countries also drew attention to the use of child soldiers.

## Causes of child soldiering in Africa

Many factors have been adduced to be the cause of child soldiers in Africa, considering that Africa since the beginning of a post-colonial era, has been a hotbed for conflict, insurgency and terrorism; as a result of the land and communal dispute, political contestation, economic interest, intra- and interstate rivalry, religious extremism, corruption and weak governance. Thus, the use of child soldier. This is particularly true about Somalia, South Sudan, Nigeria, Liberia, and Congo. Twum-Danso (2000), argued that "the use of children in numerous armed conflicts across the continent has led some commentators to infer that it is a legitimate African tradition and thus an inherent part of the culture."

There are many reasons why children join violent conflicts. First, children are susceptible to manipulation because of their level of moral vulnerability and inability to make a sound judgement. According to Cohn & Goodwin (2003), "children are influenced to join the war by religion, ideology and indoctrination, social, community and family values, peer pressure, feeling of helplessness, feeling of vulnerability, the desire of revenge and identity formation. No doubt, working on the mind of children through indoctrination and making them believe in an ideology, can make a child, want to die for a cause. For instance, children that are often used as suicide bombers in Nigeria, by the Boko Haram sect been programmed to believe that if they die in the process, they have died for a good cause. And that, God will reward them.

Poverty can be "arguably," a factor motivating a child to join armed force or groups. The child is at least assured that his basic needs, and those of his relatives at home or in the camps, would be provided. Child Soldiers Global Report (2004) considers poverty and a lack of alternative employment as critical "push factors" in the recruitment of children. Achvarina and Reich (2006) had argued that "research by intergovernmental organisations, activists and academics reveal that poverty has been identified as the main factor in trying to explain the participation of child soldiers in conflicts in Africa. For example, rich countries generally do not use child soldiers in armed conflict as compared to poor countries. Moreover, many former child soldiers have given poverty as the reason for joining conflict when interviewed." Also, some parents who are poor, give their children as child soldiers to either the government or the rebels, in the hope that they would be taken care of. Granting consent for children to be recruited into war or CT-COIN is a function of chronic poverty.

Violent crises situation, often time leaves a bad impression on the mind of people when loved ones are lost in the process. Children who witnessed their parents being killed or a sister being raped or a family member being murdered in times of war may be motivated to join armed forces or groups in a bid to revenge or in an effort to play their part in defending the community. Also, the spread of violence, as one of the consequences of militarisationsation, creates conditions under which a child is more eager to volunteer to be a fighter. As shown by Massey (2000), after experiencing violence (executions, disappearances, killings, rape, torture), many children often develop the desire for revenge. Wessells, in a US State Department Report, quotes a girl from the Republic of Congo, as she describes her ordeal after joining a rebel group at 12 years of age:

> One day rebels attacked my village where I lived. I hid and watched as they killed my relatives and raped my mother and sisters. I thought if I joined, I would be safe… I was trained to use a gun and I performed guard duty. I was often beaten and raped by the other soldiers. One day the commander wanted me to become his wife so I tried to escape. They caught me, whipped me, and raped me every night for many days. When I was just 14, I had a baby. I don't even know who his father is. I ran again but I have nowhere to go and no food for the baby. I am afraid to go home (Wessells, 2006).

Conflict-induced vulnerability is a "natural" environment to nourish and encourage the recruitment of child soldiers. According to Tynes, the "weak states" developing countries are more vulnerable in the face of child recruitment. When a weak state is pulled into armed conflict, multiple variables increase the likelihood that youths will volunteer, or will be forcefully recruited to fight (Tynes, 2011). Though, not every conflict involves child soldiers.

Technological developments and the proliferation of small and light weapons (SALWs) is found to be one of the underlying causes that make child soldiering possible. With the advances of technology, guns became lighter in a way that even children are able to carry and operate them. The feeling of handing a gun for security purpose, make some children volunteer to be part of child soldiers' recruitment. According to Nagle (2011), modern weapons for the infantry are easy to use and operate even in poor conditions. This ease of arming children, coupled with the drugs, alcohol, and magical potions given to children by militating leaders, convert these children into ruthless combatants.

Most often, wars could lead to loss of lives (including loss of parent or children, or both), and displacement of families. Children who are disjointed from families and loved ones could naturally be vulnerable to any kind of association or recruitment. According to Singer and de Haan (2007), children without parents lack parental guidance or care and are easily attracted to the war incentives or being threatened to join. They may be lured by the promise of food, protection, or glory, or coerced by the threat of punishment or death. If they are guaranteed that this is the only way to have regular meals, clothing, or medical attention, they may end up joining any group that promises them that. DiCicco (2009) added that not all children join willingly as some are abducted from homes, schools, hospitals and market places; and are later forced to attack men, women and other children in order to desensitisese them to violence. Child soldiers who do not attack on command are executed or beaten; therefore, most children commit unspeakable acts when ordered by their commanders.

Finally, there is no legal mechanism put in place to avoid the recruitment of children as child soldiers or even law to punish those who recruit children into armed forces and groups. Also, there is a failure of states to secure Children's Rights, even though there is a number of international policies that are aimed to protect children from violence, abuse, recruitment, and harmful labour. The main document regarding children's right is the "Convention for the Rights of the Child" (International Convention for the Rights of the Child), which is the most widely ratified document in the world. However, international treaties or policies only have persuasive effect in any nation. That is, the state is under no obligation to make such treaty legally binding. For example, in Nigeria, section 12 of the 1999 constitution of the Federal Republic of Nigeria, as amended, provides that international treaties have no legal effect until they are made into law by the National Assembly.

## Effects of child soldiering in Africa

It is undisputed fact that children have been used in African armed conflicts and as such have contributed to the political end state in a number of wars. The problem of child soldiers is widespread and the numbers are hard to find. The turmoil and destruction caused by war make it difficult to keep accurate records of children involved in the conflict (Brett & McCallin, 1996). During CT-COIN operations, vulnerable groups in society, such as women and children are usually affected the most. Generally, any form of war affects every facet of a child's growth and development.

The risk of child soldiers is huge, and the aftereffect could last a lifetime. Child soldiers often find it difficult to adjust to the normal day to day activities compared to normal children of their age. They are sometimes rejected by their families and communities. According to one account (2001), an aid worker in Sierra Leone said, "families don't want a rebel child" (ReliefWeb, 2001; see also *The New Humanitarian*, 2001 for experience from Burundi). It is worst for girl soldiers. Specht and Attree (2006) put it that, "it is not uncommon for girl soldiers to have a child or children while they are in the bush. They often become mothers at an incredibly young age and frequently contract sexually transmitted diseases. Culturally conceived ideas about sexual activities may lead these girls to withdraw from any former community or family for fear of rejection" Some of them often meet an empty house on their return or escape; their families might have been wiped out or displaced. Child soldiers often go through ex-cruciating experiences that change their attitude to life and behaviour in any society they find themselves, except they are properly taken care of after their ordeal. An article entitled, "Boy Soldiers" published in Newsweek as a special report in August 1995, stated:

> Even if they survive the rigors of combat, it's often too late to salvage their lives. un-relenting warfare transforms them into preadolescent sociopaths, fluent in the languages of violence but ignorant of the rudiments of living in a civil society (Newsweek, 1995).

Wessells points out that the Lord's Resistance Army in Uganda uses children to abduct other children and to terrorise villages. By terrorisingsing villages, the children break the bonds be-tween them and the community. Cases of use of alcohol and drugs on children being forcefully recruited have been reported (Wessells, 2005). Denov highlights such incidences as happened in Sierra Leone that "the apparent abundance of alcohol and hallucinating drugs deliberately and unquestionably contributed to the creation of efficient and effective soldiers. The drugs were effective and engendered feelings of strength and a readiness to pick up their weapons and kill." (Denov, 2010).

Children who are child soldiers are usually exposed to elevated levels of violence, such as killings, bombings, raiding villages and others. Child soldiers are programmed to exhibit the higher and morbid trait of hostility over time. Their involvement in wars is usually toxic to their psychological and social well-being. Upon their dis-engagement from armed forces and groups, they show symptoms of depression and are often traumatisedsed. According to Dodge and Raundalen (1991) research in Uganda, Sudan and Mozambique, identified Post Traumatic Stress Disorder (PTSD) in children and argue that the psychological effects of war on children can be described in terms of "psychological reaction patterns ranging from aggression and revenge (an aspect we think is exaggerated) to anxiety, fear, grief and depression." Furthermore, child soldiering could lead to low self-esteem, feeling of guilt, violent behaviour, as well as lack of trust and confidence in the society. Thus,

> A 10-year-old who had been abducted by RENAMO, subjected to brutal training and ultimately forced to kill civilians and soldiers before escaping and finding refuge in a Maputo orphanage, was found to be suspicious of adults and suffering from "flashbacks" in which events from the past would come flooding back at unexpected moments to haunt him (Cohn & Goodwin, 2003).

According to the former UN Secretary-General, Mr Kofi Annan, "if there is any lesson that we can draw from the experience of the past decade, it is that the use of child soldiers is far more than a humanitarian concern; that its impact lasts far beyond the time of actual fighting; and that the scope of the problems vastly exceeds the numbers of children directly involved" (Annan, 2002). Annan's poignant position is supported by the French Foreign Minister, Philippe Douste-Blazy, in a keynote speech at a 2007 Child Soldiering Conference held at Paris, warned that child soldiers are "a time bomb that threatens stability and growth." They are "lost chil-dren": lost for peace and lost for the development of their countries (BBC, 2007). Using children as child soldiers reduce the human resource of any nation. Ordinarily, children are meant to grow into responsible and productive youths that should contribute reasonably to the political, social, and economic growth of a nation.

Labour force performance suffers due to the abduction of children. Abducted children who later become youth show lower skills at work, they go for jobs of little capital intensity due to their lack of good education or vocational training. In Uganda, a research was carried out on child soldiers, former and present and it revealed that abducted male youths attain 0.75 fewer years of education, a 10% reduction relative to the average non-abducted youth's 7.6 years of education. This schooling loss corresponds closely to the average length of abduction – 8.9 months, 0.74 of a year. The abducted are also 15 percentage points less likely to report being functionally literate (able to read a book or newspaper), implying that abductees are nearly twice as likely to be illiterate than non-abductees... such traumatic events can disrupt children's development, staying with them for the rest of their lives. It was also reported that abducted youth, are five percentage points (43%) less likely than non-abducted youth to be engaged in skilled and capital intensity work (Blattman & Annan, 2007).

No doubt, in summary, the effects of child soldiering is numerous. Child soldiering has negative consequences not only on the children, but on their families, communities, and society as a whole. The effect is also evident on the economic, social, and political development of any nation. Children's development, health and wellbeing are disrupted when they are drawn into militating organisations and rebel groups. Recruited children, particularly those used in armed violence, run a high risk of being killed or maimed, and of suffering serious psychological and social problems afterwards, thus reducing the man-power percentage of any nation and increasing the number of socially imbalanced citizens who become a burden and nuisance to the government.

## Eradication of child soldiering in Africa

Since the use of child soldiers in war or crises situation depletes moral and normal societal value, measures have been taken to eradicate child soldiering; even though little or no success has been recorded. Communities, international organisations, civil society organisations, and NGOs have played huge roles in ensuring it is completely eradicated. Some of these organisations that have been actively involved in proffering ways and carrying out projects that would help eradicate child soldiering in Africa include United Nations (UN), United Nations Children Funds (UNICEF) Oxfam, Save the Children and Child Soldier International.

Some of them have partnered with the government of different states, they have functioned well in the areas of creating awareness, making government sign agreement promising to eradicate child soldiering in the different countries, agitating for the enforcement of international laws and treaties that protect children. Okon & Okeke (2015) pointed out that the 1989 UN Convention on the Rights of the Child (UNCRC) contains 50 Articles which could be broken into three broad categories: *Provision Articles, Protection Articles* and *Participation Articles*. The Provision Article include the rights of children to minimum standards of health, education, social security, physical care, family life, culture and leisure. Protection articles identify the rights of children to be safe from discrimination, physical and sexual abuse, exploitation, cruelty, injustice, including the right to special protection in times of war and protection from abuse in the criminal justice system. While participation articles include civil and political rights, such as the right of children to freedom to express their opinions and to have a say in matters affecting their social, economic, religious, cultural, and political life. Despite the ratification of the UNCRC and widespread approval under international law affirming the rights of children, too many children still experience acts of cruelty - killings, severe physical beating, deprivations, rape, child abuse and neglect. These abuses are a violation of article 6 of the UNCRC, which provides that every child has an inherent right to life.

According to Child Soldiers Newsletter (2008), in 1999, Sudan agreed to cease sponsorship of the LRA, the rebel group in northern Uganda notorious for the abduction of children for use in combat, in return for Uganda's promise to stop support of insurgents in Sudan. This bilateral cooperation produced the disarmament of hundreds of Ugandan children that had been abducted into the Southern region of Sudan. Bilateral mechanisms to end the use of child soldiers have also been included in peace agreements. The 1999 Lome Peace Accord between the government of Sierra Leone and the RUF was the first peace accord to incorporate special protection for child soldiers. Many of the demolition and reintegration strategies have utilised multilateral action between international institutions, governments, and NGOs. In 2002, the World Bank partnered with international government donors and UN peacekeeping forces to establish the multi-country demobilisationsation and reintegration program (MDRP) to demobilisese combatants in the Great Lakes region of Africa. Although this programme focuses on combatants generally, it has successfully demobilised over 3,000 children from armed groups in the DRC and over 3,000 child soldiers from Burundi.

In Liberia also, following the 2003 peace agreement, some of the estimated 21,000 child soldiers demobilised by the UN mission in Liberia eventually migrated to the Buduburam Refugee Camp in Accra, Ghana, to make the reintegration process a positive step in the lives of approximately 200 Liberian children (Amnesty International, 2004).

In 2014, the United Nations started a campaign to end recruitment of child soldiers, the campaign was spearheaded by UN Special Representatives jointly with United Nations Children Funds (UNICEF). The United Nations stated that it listed 55 parties that recruit child soldiers. Among them are 46 non-state actors and eight governments, including those of Afghanistan, Burma, Chad, the Democratic Republic of Congo, Somalia, South Sudan, Sudan, and Yemen. It mentioned that out of the eight states listed, six already signed the action plan with the United Nations and two (Yemen and Sudan) remaining were in the process of finalising their action plan to end these violations and to prevent them from occurring in the future (Schlein, 2014).

Apart from UNICEF, other NGOs such as the Alliance Save the Children and World Food Programme (WFP) also assisted in the process. In Angola, Civil Society Organisations played a key role in regard to the child soldiers. Organisations like the Coalition to Stop the Use of Child Soldiers assisted in the identification of child soldiers who served with UNITA and government forces. The Human Rights Watch focused on human rights abuses while UNICEF provided psychological support to former child soldiers. Other international organisationssations provided basic foods and medical care to residents in many of the quartering areas (Human Rights Watch, 2003).

Efforts have been made in all other African countries that are facing this problem, however, the child soldier phenomenon is still prevalent and a lot more needs to be done to ensure that children enjoy their childhood and live a normal life that would be beneficial to them, their families, communities and the society at large when they become adults. The social aspects of reintegration include the permanent role of the child's family and key community members. Their roles and capacity to support and advice the demobilisedsed children is more important in the reintegration process than the role of NGOs. The roles of family and local community are critical in the follow-up.

## Conclusion

Ultimately, all issues concerning human rights focus on the alleviation of human suffering. The concept of child soldiers is not new. However, until recently in Africa, the rate at which children were used as soldiers was minimal, compared to what is presently obtainable. Child soldiering is a dangerous practice that has compounded the misery of war and plagued the growth and development of the continent. Stakes are high for child soldiers in Africa, especially as the number of intra-state conflicts, insurgency and terrorism increase the risk of child soldiering to produce "a scarred generation among those who would be expected to become the leaders (and) drivers of economic well-being and the future of the continent (of Africa)" is eminent (Gislesen, 2006). Even though the inhumane use of children in violent conflict continues to result in much suffering and devastation to many African nations, efforts to stop the crisis are more determined than ever. International awareness of the problem and its causes is constantly increasing and there seems to be a growing consensus that something must be done before it is too late (Mwangi, 2001).

Government of African nations where insurgency and terrorism are prevalent have employed every means, tactics, and strategies to annihilate the menace completely, including the use of child soldiers, without achieving much-desired results. In as much as terrorism and insurgency continue, there would be government's counter operations, however, these operations should not involve children. They are naïve and innocent and should not be exposed to such violent activities and being robbed of having a normal childhood. Governments of African nations should endeavour to leave children out of the fight against insurgency and terrorism and develop better strategies to counter it.

Child soldiers should be completely shunned and eradicated. Although, without wars, insurgency and terrorism, there would be no need to recruit children to serve in armed forces, thus governments should endeavour to tacitly fight insurgency and terrorism and intensify its efforts toward countering it. Child soldiers should be seen as a bane to development, hence, legal mechanisms that punish child recruiters should be put in place and effectively enforced. African countries that have ratified the United Nation Convention on Child Rights should be enforced, and campaigns against child soldiering should be frequently conducted. There should be sanctions for parents and family members who willingly give their children to armed forces and rebel groups and subtle sanctions for children who volunteer to join armed forces and rebel groups for one reason or the other. Frequent and proper scrutiny should be conducted in the armed forces to help identify child soldiers and remove or retire them. Poverty and unemployment should be reduced to the barest minimum and education should be free, or at least affordable for all and sundry.

## References

Achvarina, V., & Reich, F. S. (2006). No place to hide: Refugees, displaced persons, and the recruitment of child soldiers. *International Security, 31*(1), 127–164.

Akpotor, A. S., & Oromareghake, P. B. O. (2013). Terrorism and insecurity in the Nigerian State: The challenge. In O. Mbachu & M. U. Bature (Eds.), *Internal security management in Nigeria: A study in terrorism and counter terrorism*. Kaduna: Medusa Academic Publishers Limited.

Akpuru-Aja, A., & Ibebanjo, O. B. (2013). Combating a new decade of insurgency in Nigeria: A new perspective. In O. Mbachu & M. U. Bature (Eds.), *Internal security management in Nigeria: A study in terrorism and counter terrorism*. Kaduna: Medusa Academic Publishers Limited.

Alcinda, H. (1999). *Negotiating Post-War Identities: Child Soldiers in Mozambique and Angola*. Available: https://www.medico.de/download/report26/ps_honwana_en.pdf accessed on 15/06.2019.

Amnesty International (2004). *Liberia: The Promise of Peace for 21,000 Child Soldiers, AFRM 34/006/2004*, London: Amnesty International.

Annan, K. (2002, May 7). *Use of child combatants will carry consequences*. United Nations [Press Release] .

Annan, K. (2005). *Conference on combating terrorist financing Vienna*. United Nations Office of Drugs and Crime, November 9.

Barnitz, L. (1999). *Child soldiers: Youth who participate in armed conflicts*. Washington: Youth Advocate Program International.

BBC. (2007). *Child soldiers are a time bomb [Electronic Version]. BBC News*. Retrieved from http://news.bbc. co.uk/go/pr/fr/-/2/hi/europe/6330503.stm Accessed on 25.08.17.

Blattman, C., & Annan, J. (2007). The consequences of child soldiering. *Households in conflict Network, The Institute of Development Studies*. Brighton: University of Sussex, Falmer.

Brett, R., & McCallin, M. (1996). *Children: The invisible soldiers*. Sweden: Swedish Save the Children, Vaxjo.

Brocklehurst, H. (2007). Child soldiers. In C. Allan (Ed.), *Contemporary security studies*. New York: Oxford University Press.

Child Soldiers Global Report. (2004). *Child Soldier*. London: Coalition to stop the Use of Child Soldiers.

Child Soldiers Newsletter. (2008). Published by *International Action Network on Small Arms, Coalition to Stop the Use of Child Soldiers and Human Security Programme at Foreign Affairs*, Canada: March 3.

Child Soldiers Global Report. (2008). *To Stop the Use of Child Soldiers*, Childsoldiers//globalreport.org.

Coalition to Stop the Use of Child Soldiers. (2000). *The use of children as soldiers in Africa: A country analysis of child recruitment and participation in armed conflict*. Available from http://www.reliefweb.int/library/documents/chilsold.htm Accessed 30.05.13.

Coalition to Stop the Use of Child Soldiers. (2001). *Global report on child soldiers*, June 12.

Cohn, I., & Goodwin, G. S. (2003). *The role of children in armed conflict*. Oxford University Press.

Convention on the Rights of the Child. (1989), Article 3 (1).

Denov, M. (2010). *Child soldiers, Sierra Leone's Revolutionary United Front*. Cambridge: Cambridge University Press.

DiCicco, L. (2009). *Former child soldiers face psychological battle*. Available from http://www.thestar.com/printArticle/627688 Accessed 01.04.13.

Dodge, C., & Raundalen, M. (1991). *Reaching children in war: Sudan, Uganda and Mozambique* (p. 21). Uppsala and Bergen: Sigma Forlag and the Scandinavian Institute of African Studies.

Ellis, S. (1998). Liberia warlord insurgency. In Clapham, C. (Ed.), *African guerrillas*. Oxford: James Currey.

Fox (2003). Refernece awiated ...

Gislesen, K. (2006). *A Childhood Lost? The Challenges of Successful Disarmament, Demobilisation and Reintegration of Child Soldiers: The Case of West Africa*. Oslo, Norwegian Institute of International Affairs.

Human Right Watch. (2004 February). *How to fight, how to kill: Child soldiers in Liberia*. http://www.hrw.org.

Human Right Watch HRW. (April 2003). *Forgotten fighters: Child soldiers in Angola* .

Human Rights Watch. (2015). *South Sudan: Government forces recruiting child soldiers*. Available fromhttps://www.hrw.org/news/2015/02/16/south-sudan-government-forces-recruiting-child-soldiers Accessed on 28.08.17.

Jeannette, E. (2002). *The Sierra Leone conflict and its impact on girls*. Paper delivered at the *Learning for Change Conference on Youth and Conflict Avoidance in West Africa*, 18–20th November, Otta, Ogun State.

Jézéquel, Jean-Herve. (2006). *Child soldiers in Africa: A singular phenomenon: On the necessity of a historical perspective*. http://www.diplomatie.gouv.fr/fr/IMG/pdf/0605-JEZEQUEL-UK-2.pdf Accessed on 11.07.13.

Kakhuta-Banda, F. B. (2014). *The use of child soldiers in African armed conflicts: A comparative study of Angola and Mozambique*. A research report submitted to the Faculty of Humanities and Social Sciences in Fulfilment of the requirements for the degree of Master of Arts (MA) in International Relations at the University of the Witwatersrand, Johannesburg.

Kalis, M. (2002). *Child soldiers in Africa: Solutions to a complex dilemma*. African Centre for the Constructive Resolution of Dispute.

McRae, B., (2001). *Human Security and the New Diplomacys*, McGill-Queen's University Press, Montreal.

Massey, C. M. (2000). Child soldiers: Theory and reality of their existence: The question of international protection. *Available to them in contemporary times*. PhD thesis. University of Nottingham.

Moore, R. S. (nd). *The basics of counterinsurgency*. Washington, D.C.: U.S. Joint Forces Command, J9, Joint Urban Operations Office (n.d.), 14. Available from http://smallwarsjournal.com/documents/moorecoinpaper.pdf.Internet Accessed 10.11.07.

Mwangi, George (2001). *Child soldiers in Sudan lifted to safety. The Times Educational Supplement*, 2 March 2001, section news.

Nagle, E. L. (2011). Child soldiers and the duty of nations to protect children participation in armed conflict. *Cardozo Journal of International and Comparative Law, 19*(1), 1–58.

Ngera, P. K. (2009). *Child soldiers and "Volunteerism" in civil wars in Africa: The case of Somalia, 1991-2011.* A research project submitted in partial fulfilment of the requirement for the award of Master Degree in Armed Conflict and Peace Studies in the Department of History, University of Nairobi, Unpublished Project.

Norman, D. (2004). *Rising '44: The battle for Warsaw.* Pan Books.

Nwanne, D. (2016). Junior leaders in counterinsurgency and complex military operations: A case study of North East Nigeria. In C. C. C. Osakwe (Ed.), *Leadership and complex military operations.* Kaduna: Defence Academy Publishing.

Okene, A. A., & Olawale, I. (2013). National security and insurgency in Nigeria, 1999-2012: A preliminary assessment of Federal Government Strategy of Containment. In O. Mbachu & M. U. Bature (Eds.), *Internal security management in Nigeria: A study in terrorism and counter-terrorism.* Kaduna: Medusa Academic Publishers Limited.

Okon, E., & Okeke, V. O. S. (2015). *The Right of the Child and the Phenomenon of Child Soldiering in Africa. Developing Studies, 5*(3): 1–9.

Osakwe, C., & Ubong, E. U. (2013). The military and counter insurgency operations in Nigeria. In O. Mbachu & M. U. Bature (Eds.), *Internal security management in Nigeria: A study in terrorism and counter terrorism.* Kaduna: Medusa Academic Publishers Limited.

ReliefWeb (2001, July 19). Sierra Leone: IRIN focus on children with an uncertain future. Aviable: https://reliefweb.int/report/sierra-leone/sierra-leone-irin-focus-children-uncertain-future Accessed on 21/06/2019.

Rosen, D. M. (2005). *Armies of the young: Child soldiers in war and terrorism.* New Brunswick: Rutgers University Press.

Schlein, I. (2014). *UN campaigns to end recruitment of child soldiers.* VOA, March 13.

Singer, E., de Haan, D. (2007). *The Social Lives of Young Children.* SWP Publishing, Amsterdam.

Smith, M. (2002). *End of an era for little drummer boys and the powder monkeys. Daily Telegraph,* March 29.

Somasundaram, D. (2002). Child Soldiers: Understanding the Context. *British Medical Journal, 324*(7348), 1268–1271.

Specht, I., & Attree, L. (2006). *The Reintegration of Teen-aged Girls and Young Women Intervention, 4*(3): 219–228.

Stepanova, E. (2003). *Anti-Terrorism and Peace Building and After Conflict.* Stockholm: : Stockhom International Peace Research Institute.

Stibli, F. (2010). Terrorism in the context of globalisation. *AARMS Journal, 9*(1), 1–17.

*The New Humanitarian* (2001). IRIN in Focus – containing the crisis: Available: https://www.thenewhumanitarian.org/report/22705/burundi-irin-focus-%E2%80%93-containing-crisis *accessed on 21 June, 2019.*

Twum-Danso, A. (2000). *The limits of individualism: What constitutes an effective form of the reintegration and rehabilitation of child soldiers into society after civil war. MSC Development Studies Dissertation.* LSE.

Tynes, R. M. (2011). *Child soldiers, armed conflicts, and tactical innovations* (p. 344). State University of New York at Albany, ProQuest Dissertations and Theses.

UNICEF. (2017). *Childhood under attack: The staggering impact of South Sudan's crisis on children.* Reliefweb, December 15.

United Nations. (2002). *Report of the UN Independent Expert on Somalia,* UN Doc. EC/CN.4/2002/119, 14 January 2002. http://www.ohchr.org.

United Nations. (2004). *Report of the UN Independent Expert on Somalia,* UN Doc. E/CN.4/2004/103, 30 November 2003, drawing on UNICEF Somalia, "From perception to reality: A study on child protection in Somalia", *A benchmark to measure progress.*

US Department of Army Field Manual. (2014). *Insurgencies and countering insurgencies* (p. 2). Washington D.C.: Department of the Army.

US Department of State. (2003). *Country reports on human rights practice,* March. http://www.state.gov/g/dri/hr/ci470.htm.

Wessells, M. (2005). *Child Soldiers, Peace Education, and Post Conflict Reconstruction for Peace Theory into Practice. Peace Education, 44*(4): 363–369.

Wessells, M. (2006). *Child soldiers: From violence to protection* (p. 59). Cambridge: Harvard University Press.

Wessels, M. (1997). Child soilders. *Bulletin of the Atomic Scientists, 53*(4), 32.

WHO, (2009). Healing child soldiers. *87:* 330–331.

# 43

# Gender, counterterrorism and counterinsurgency in North-East Nigeria

*Nachana'a Alahira David and Muhammad Sanusi Lawal*

## Introduction

Africa has over the years been a fertile ground for both domestic and transnational terrorist groups and other forms of violent criminal organisations. Since the 9/11 terrorist attacks on the United States (US) and the subsequent declaration of "Global War on Terror" (GWOT), the operations of terrorist groups like Al-Shabaab, Al-Qaeda in the Maghreb (AQIM) and, more recently, the Boko Haram (BH) have become prominent in the continent. These are security challenges not just for their local operational base but impacting directly or indirectly on the global community in terms of the political and socio-economic interchange. The vulnerabilities of African countries like porous borders and inadequate capacity for border controls, poverty, communal clashes, ethnic and religious strife, high rate of unemployment, marginalisation, corruption, lack of good governance etc have been exploited by terrorist groups. State failure has emboldened terrorist groups in Africa. For instance, the BH in Northeast Nigeria has been responsible for 136 out of 978 terrorist attacks in the whole of Africa in 2011 (Solomon, 2013). It has caused the death of over 100,000 people and displaced 2,152,000 persons as well as the destruction of properties worth billions of Naira since it began its campaign of terror in 2009 (Sani, 2017).

Furthermore, between 2013 and 2014, the BH sect invaded and occupied 15 Local Government Areas in Borno, Yobe, and Adamawa States and, on 14 April 2014, it abducted over 270 girls from a female Boarding School in Chibok town in Borno BH State. BH activities have equally spread into neighbouring African countries of Cameroon, Chad and Niger and with serioussevere consequences. Counterterrorism and counterinsurgency (CT-COIN) strategies for combating the menace of BH have significantly impacted greatly on the general population and more so on women. This chapter brings to fore the gendered construction of CT-COIN, and implications for women in Northeast Nigeria.

# Conceptual, discourse: gender, terrorism, insurgency, and CT-COIN

## Gender

The concept of gender has several meanings depending on the author's orientation and context within which it is being applied. For the feminists, gender is basically a set of socially and culturally constructed characteristics that vary across time and place. Characteristics such as power, autonomy, rationality, and the public are often associated with masculinity or what it means to be a 'real man'. On the other hand, characteristics like weakness, dependence/connection, emotionality, and privacy, are linked to femininity (Tickner, 2011: 265). Gender, therefore, denotes inequality and is a mechanism for the unequal distribution of social benefits, marginalisation, exploitation, deprivation, insecurity, and social justice. The perception of gender from this line of argument provides the basis for establishing the link between war and masculinity. For instance, militaries work hard to turn men into soldiers or "killer beings" who must go into combat. Military training depends on the denigration of anything considered feminine or civil, and to act like a soldier means to exhibit macho characteristics. However, the association of masculinity with war has helped to render women invisible and only equate women with tools required by men for the execution of war (gender is an instrument of war). BH's ideology clearly demonstrates this gender construct by casting men in hyper-masculine combat roles, and their duty to violently oppose the west and anything related to it. This gender norm permits Gender-Based Violence (GBV) to serve as a display of power (Jacob & Pearson, 2014:44). This has been demonstrated in the offensive confrontation between the Nigerian government and BH sect.

## Terrorism

Terrorism is a complex and subjective term, and its definition varies widely. Kiras (2011) sees terrorism as characterised by the use of using violence to impose an ideological worldview on an otherwise unwilling population or political system, and the tactics of violence take many forms and often indiscriminately targets non-combatants. The United Nations (UN) referred to terrorism as criminal acts intended or calculated to provoke a state of terror in the general public whatever the considerations of political, ideological, ethnic, religious, or others that may be invoked to justify them (Egbue, Uche, & Alichie, 2015; Ishtiaq, 2012: 5). While the Nigerian National Terrorism Prevention Act of 2013 as amended sees it as an act deliberately done to harm or cause damage with the intent to intimidate, destabilise or negatively influence a group of people, organisation or government in order to achieve a political, religious, economic or social goal (National Counter Terrorism Strategy (NACTEST), 2014).

## Counterterrorism (CT)

CT implies the art, craft, practice, military tactics, techniques, and strategies that government, individuals, military, law enforcement, business, and intelligence agencies use to prevent and combat terrorism in a nation or geographical location. This includes a strategy to counter the financing of terrorism. The various definitions of terrorism show that act of terrorism can be committed by both state and non-state actors. Logically, this means that CT can be carried out both by the state, to neutralise terror perpetrated by individuals or groups against it – and equally so, by individuals or groups against the violence perpetrated by the state against such individuals or groups (Stigall, Miller & Donatucci, 2019).

## Insurgency

Insurgency according to National Counter Terrorism Strategy (NACTEST) (2014:1) is an organised armed struggle by a group aimed at weakening or usurping the authority of the state. Egbue *et al.* (2015) see it as an armed rebellion against constituted authority recognised by the United Nations. According to Younkyoo and Stephen (2013:919) the US Department of Defence defines COIN as "those military, paramilitary, political, economic, psychological and civic actions taken by a government to defeat an insurgency." This simply means the range of military, political and socio-economic measures adopted by a state or body in response to the outbreak of insurgency.

## Counterterrorism and counterinsurgency (CT-COIN)

The post-Cold War era has witnessed among other fundamental changes in the identities of parties engaged in warfare as the role of other actors has become increasingly prominent. These include groups united by extreme religious or ethnic identity conducting war by means of terrorism. According to Younkyoo and Stephen (2013:917) the most outstanding trend in contemporary conflicts has been the fusion of the threats from terrorism and insurgency. Counterterrorism and counterinsurgency (CT-COIN), are models of warfare that tend to interrogate the role of force, the importance of winning support among the local population, and the imperative of building a strong and representative government to counter contemporary threats and terror posed by non-state violent movements, organisations, groups in the security architecture. This chapter draws from the theoretical postulation of the "New Wars" scholars views.

The proponents of the "new wars" theory – Kaldor, Corn, and Meilinger criticise the traditional approach to warfare in which the work of the Prussian strategist Karl von Clausewitz is prominent. A central tenet of the 'new wars' thinking is that the fundamental characteristics of war are subject to change, making it possible for armed conflict to develop through several distinct phases. This proposition Bart (2014) notes stands in direct contradiction to the work of Clausewitz and that 'new wars' theorist attempt to do away with the Prussian strategist to validate their own findings. This chapter does not attempt to engage itself in the debate on fundamental works of scholars of warfare (strategist or new wars) rather; it draws from views that are of relevance in her interrogation of gender, CT-COIN in northeast Nigeria.

The "new wars" scholars maintained that what is termed new wars are not new, rather the Cold War period clouded scholarly ability to analyse small wars or low-intensity wars that many of the characteristics of new wars associated with weak states can be found in the modern period (see Kaldor, 2005). By terming the contemporary form of warfare as it relates to the role of states and non-state actors as 'new wars' is to demonstrate that old approaches are not really appropriate and effective in the post-cold war era. The increase in terrorism and insurgency as well as the CT –COIN strategies just goes to show that these are wars with their own logic and which is different from old wars, and which dictates a very different research strategy and policy responses (Kaldor, 2013).

Meilinger (2007) maintains that the wholesale application of the Clausewitz paradigm was a mistake that the United States of America made in Iraq and the result has been disastrous as over 3000 Americans and tens of thousands of Iraqis lost their lives. The American–led invasion of Iraq, Jason (2010) argues, not only diverted attention away from the 9/11 attacks and the perpetrators but gave rise to a new wave of research and analysis on insurgency and COIN warfare globally (Al Qaeda networks, Al Shabaab and Boko Haram in Africa). Jason (2010) notes these as classical counterinsurgency strategies aimed at "winning the hearts and minds" of the people. This is the contemporary reality for successful CT-COIN strategies.

In the context of northeast Nigeria, CT-COIN is linked to the emerging arguments "new wars": contemporary CT-COIN derives have employed conventional and non-conventional means of warfare ranging from multinational cooperation, joint military engagement and the engagement of the population in the battlefield. The CT-COIN in northeast Nigeria witnessed more reliance on intelligence, the deployment of a Multi-national Joint Task Force (MJTF), local involvement in the form of Civilian Joint Task Force (CJTF), local (CJTF), local vigilante and, in particular, the inclusion of women as battle-auxiliaries in areas of operation. Women have been and are still active in CT-COIN as members of the CJTF (more than 300 women are members superintended by the Nigerian Armed Forces. As Abba notes, CJT came into being as a child of necessity to protect the civilian population and to combat the insurgency. The involvement of CJTF in which women have been active in contracts to non-inclusion of women in local or community security and warfare engagement in pre-BH insurgents activities clearly demonstrate the view of the 'new wars' theorist that contemporary warfare has changed with regard to actors, goals and methods.

## Background: terrorism and insurgency in Africa

Terrorism and insurgency are historical features of contemporary African countries which have, over the years, transmuted into new forms of threat. For example, in Egypt, the Muslim Brotherhood (MB) is noted to have laid the foundation for the religiously motivated violence that has been expressed in contemporary terrorist movements and Al-Qaeda has been identified as a typical example (James and Giroux, 2011) In addition, there are ideologically inspired violent non-state groups that have carried out a periodic spate of terrorist attacks: Al Shabaab in Somalia or AQIM, BH in Nigeria (Okereke, 2010). Severe socio-economic and political conditions in Africa have helped to produce grievances that have been used by militant groups to justify their recourse to terrorism. Also, the rough physical terrain in Africa – from the Sahel savannah to the rain forests - is strategically vital to terrorist and insurgent groups in perpetrating violent activities. Previous studies show that in Uganda, the Allied Democratic Forces (ADF) took advantage of the terrain and local context to set up rear bases in neighbouring Congo and then began its recruitment and training of fighters promising in return financial benefits and social development. The range of activities also include the use of brute force, assaults, kidnapping, and hostage taking.

In post-Cold War era, African countries not only struggle against domestic terror entities, but they also have to face transnational terrorist groups that have used the continent as a base to carry out attacks against both domestic and international targets. For instance, the 2002 bombing of Israeli-owned hotel and aeroplane by al-Qaeda, attacks against UN buildings in Algeria in 2007, and of 2010 in Nigeria by BH demonstrate the networked and coordinated nature of terrorist organisations. Between 1990 and 2002, Africa recorded 6,177 casualties from 296 attacks from AQIM (the group traces its provenance to Algeria's civil war in the 1990s and has in the past decades become an al-Qaeda affiliate with regional ambitions). Worthy of note is the 2007 merger of Algeria's Salafist Group for Preaching and Combat (*Groupe Salafiste Pour La Prechication el le Combat, GSPC*) with Al-Qaeda to become AQIM. Similarly, BH based in northern Nigeria declared allegiance to the Islamic States of Iraq and Syria as its province – Islamic States West African Province (ISWAP) (Salisu, Mohammed, & Abdullahi, 2015).

At this point, it is imperative to focus on a particular terrorist organisation to explore the human, ideological and political dynamics of terrorism and insurgency in Africa. The Boko Haram Sect in ~~North eastern~~ North-eastern Nigeria is used here as our BH study. BH was founded in 1995 by Abubakar Lawan from Kano as *Jama'atuAhlisSunnaLidda'awatiWal-jihad* meaning "People Committed to the Propagation of the Prophet's Teachings and Jihad" and in 2002 late Mohammed Yusuf became the leader (Olomojobi, 2013; Andrew, 2012:2). Yusuf reorganised the movement in line with his ideology of waging a religious war and went out to totally condemn western education thus giving the group the current nomenclature BH. His popularity increased as all categories of adherents who were disenchanted with the state – the illiterates, semi-educated, unemployed, as well as educated persons, gladly joined the sect. The mission of the sect was to implement true Shari'ah in Nigeria and in this regard began to openly preach for jihad to change the socio-political order. Membership of the sect cut across social strata of the society but especially the down trodden. (Abdulkareem, 2010; Olomojobi, 2013).

Late Mohammed Yusuf's militant orientation has been traced to teachings of the ~~hard liner~~ hardliner Ibn Taymiyyah who called for Muslims' return to the puritanical fundamentals of Islam (1263–1328) (Olojumobi, 2013 and Abdulkareem, 2010). The BH which Yusuf built has links with Al-Qaeda: evidence shows that before the crisis of July 2009, Yusuf was charged to court (in 2006) for receiving funds from an Al Qaeda linked organizations, but he was granted bail and the case was dismissed as a result of his alleged connections to highly placed Nigerian elites. BH transformed from unarmed Islamic movement to a Violent Non-State Actor in 2009 after the extrajudicial killings of Yusuf and Foi by the Nigerian Police. In March, 2010, AQIM with an operational base in North Africa offered to assist BH with training in order to destabilize the Nigerian State. It has been established that most of the militants are local Kanuri, Hausa, Fulani and Egbira youths among others supported by a mixture of foreign elements from Chad, Somalia and Sudan (Olomojobi, 2013: 82; Seteolu, 2011).

In order to contain and defeat BH, a Counter Terrorism Department (CTD) in the Office of the National Security Adviser (ONSA) was established in 2011 to focus exclusively on the emerging insurgency posed by the BH militants and other terrorist groups. The CTD was granted the responsibility for coordinating the NACTEST. It is also responsible for ensuring that analysis of intelligence from other agencies by the Joint Terrorism Analysis Bureau (JTAB), strategic communication in association with foreign partners for capacity building and at the same time ensures that oversight operations by the security and intelligence agencies are optimally used. However, this has not been the case.

First, African countries lack the capacity to combat the threat posed by domestic as well as transnational terrorism. CT-COIN operations are affected by a crisis of governance, as well as technical failure on the part of the military and security agencies. This allows terrorist groups to find sanctuary in African countries and the porous borders make it easy for terrorist groups to migrate and spread into other countries. Secondly, terrorism, insurgency and CT-COIN are socially constructed: they tend to affect people differently. The gendered dimension of CT-COIN is pursued in the following section.

## Gendered construction of CT and COIN in North-Eastern Nigeria: women and girls as perpetrators and victims

Terrorism, insurgency, and related acts of violence are not new forms of warfare: states and non-state actors alike have in the course of history deployed either of these to advance economic, political, and other interests. Terrorism has been used by states not only to deal with adversaries, but to dethrone political leaders, and to expand political and economic powers (Michael & Gunarata, 2007). In March 2015, BH leader Abubakar Shekau pledged his allegiance to Islamic State's self-acclaimed Caliph Abubakar al-Baghadadi, the two terrorist groups have experienced a change in their (mis)fortunes. In March 2015, BH's allegiance resulted in the sect's renaming itself as Islamic State West Africa Province (ISWAP). However, in June 2014, BH had introduced a tactical manoeuvre in contrast to both al-Qaeda central and Islamic State principle and practice: Female Suicide Terrorism (FST). By late 2015, the intensity of BH female suicide attacks was already globally unprecedented (Pearson, 2018). BH used its first FST in an attack on a military base in Gombe State in June 2014, and as of February 28 2018, a recorded 469 FST, have been deployed or arrested in 240 accidents, and they have killed more than 1,200 people across four countries: Nigeria, Niger, Chad and Cameroon (Jason & Matfess, 2017). Available figures show that most FST incidents affect Nigeria (197, 75% of attacks), with the majority of those in Borno State (133, 55% of attacks). The FST areis scarcely identified by name in the press, nor are their basic bio-databiobiodata provided. There is very extraordinarily little academic data on the reasons why women become FST. It is quite obvious that, most were coerced, with many accounts from women and girls who have refused to detonate devices (Guardian, 2017). Primary data on BH FST is minimal, and literature on female participation in the group is slowly coming to light. becoming known. Studies indicate that BH has slowly engaged in GBV, abusing, and harassing both Muslim and Christian women in north eastern north-eastern Nigeria. BH has systematically used women and young girls before the use of FST, in order to recruit, propagate, and smuggle arm. (Barkindo, Gudaku, & Wesley, 2013). There is concrete evidence of the use of coercion on females into becoming FST: reports from NGO's and women liberated from BH camps, government officials' narratives, and interviews with women who refuse to self-detonate attest to that. While operatives of the CJTF and *Operation Lafiya Dole* command argued that, both hypnotism and drugs were used to force women to become suicide bombers. The argument here is that BH's use of FST is different from that of any other terrorist group because BH did not accord these FST any symbolic status for carrying out their dastardly acts.

Looking at FST via different prism locates BH's female operations as being more related to other African terror organisations than to Islamic State modus operandi. These forms of women abuse stems from the radical Salafi interpretation of the Shari'ah– which allows the use of female as instruments of war –and most likely from established patriarchal legal and social structures in the northeast, which socially marginalised women, even though women also feel they benefited from other aspects of Islam (Pearson, 2018). In northeast Nigeria, as well as in other countries in Africa, GBV is sanctioned by religious norms, traditional beliefs, and practices. With the emergence of BH, there was an increase in GBV against women and children in all the states of the northeast region. It is worth noting that, these violent attacks were committed either directly by BH members, or indirectly as a result of the conflict, and mostly motivated by the Sunni Salafi ideology that always relegates women, especially Christian women, as justifiable targets or collaterals of Jihad. There was straightforward evidence of kidnapping, forced marriages, and forceful conversion of abductees to Islam. It is important to point out that, the negative interplay of education, politics, religion, and other socioeconomic factors contribute into explaining the nature of this GBV. The Nigerian office of the British Council states that most structurally motivated GBV emanate from social norms which define what constitutes an abuse of women both at the private and public levels (British Council Report, 2012). Therefore, GBV occurs in both public and domestic environments and sometimes also committed by the state through policies or the actions of agents of the state such as the police, military, or other agencies.

## Gendered construction of insurgency, counterinsurgency: Boko Haram during the state of emergency

The adoption of the CT-COIN strategy by the armed forces and, the lateral involvement of the CJTF in 2012 eventually succeeded in dislodging BH from Maiduguri capital of Borno State and dispersal of its armed units to other parts of the state, and neighbouring states of Yobe and Adamawa – which lie within the ecology of the Sambisa Forest. From the safety of the Forest, BH planned and carried out daring attacks on Maiduguri and outlying local government areas dislodging the structures in at least 16 local government areas of Northern Borno. Between 2013 and 2014, BH was able to lay claim to and occupy more than 15 local government areas in some states in the north east. (Abadam, Bama, Shani, Chibok, Dambowa, BuniYadi, Gwoza, Konduga, Mobba, Kukawa, Uba, Madagali, Michika, and Mubi North and Mubi South). BH abducted/kidnapped women and children to be used as sex slaves or FST. For instance, the 14 April 2014 Chibok town abduction of over 270 female students in a Government Secondary School attracted national and international condemnations and then the social media campaign #Bring Back Our Girls (BBOG) that went international. However, there are other instances of abduction that did not receive the same attention.

The foregoing prompted the federal government to take, in 2013, some decisive actions such as the declaration of a state of emergency; creation of a new army formation (7 Division) in Maiduguri; the passage of the Anti-Terrorism Act for legal backing to CT; formation of the CJTF comprising youths, vigilante groups, and local hunters to complement the efforts of security agencies; offer of strategic dialogue with terrorist sect; and ban on the use of the motorcycle.

In conflict situations such as BH insurgency, the impact on women and girls are always aggravated. With the declaration of a state of emergency in Borno State, women and girls became defenceless victims of the collapsed moral and social order that accompanied these circumstances. Women and girls were therefore exposed to more physical/emotional abuse and exploitation, human trafficking, rape, forced marriages, deprivation of resources needed for physical and psychological well-being and abandonment. The adoption of this initiative by the government clearly shows that new strategies are imperative to combat terrorism and insurgency as put forward by the "new wars" theorist. There are observed successes in this regard and they include: decrease in a spate of terrorist drive-by-shooting using a motorcycle and easy detection and interception of BH operatives through physical search and intelligence tracking.

As noted earlier, the BH insurgency affected women and other vulnerable people in severe ways not least internal displacement and physical abuse. The impact of BH was initially restricted to Nigeria, at least before 2013. The realisation that Nigeria was not the only country affected by the activities of BH necessitated the security cooperation of the countries of the Lake Chad Basin Commission (LCBC) to resuscitate the MNJTF which was established in the 1990s to combat cattle rustling and low-intensity conflict and expanded the task force's mandate to combat the menace of BH insurgents in the region. MNJTF comprises military units from five countries: Benin, Cameroon, Chad, Niger and Nigeria and its engagement with BH began after the attack on Baga in 2015, the headquarters of the force. As noted earlier, MNJTF has been in existence before 2015 as the task force was first established as solely Nigerian force in 1994 during the military regime of late General Sani Abatcha to combat banditry and to facilitate free movements of humans and goods along Nigeria's northern border.

The force was however expanded in 1998 to include units from neighbouring Chad and Niger with the purpose of dealing with common cross border security threats in the Lake Chad Region. But with BH threat, the force mandate expanded in 2012 to encompass CT operations while the number of troops increased from 7,500 to 10,000. The Operation Headquarter was relocated to N'Djamena in Chad and the operation of the MNJTF came under the supervision of the LCBC. With regard to the command structure, Nigeria has the responsibility of providing the Commander for the operation, while Cameroon provides the Deputy Commander and a Chadian to serve as Chief of Staff (Adewumi, 2016; Abdullahi, 2016).

As a result of the concerted CT-COIN drive at both national and regional levels, BH was dislodged from all the local government areas that were hitherto under their control. However, this success is not without cost as BH has now reorganised and trying to retake some of the liberated areas. The predominance of the cash economy, without controls, is conducive to terrorist groups funded by extortion, charitable donations, smuggling, remittances, and kidnappings (Ejere, 2018). This tends to validate the opinion of those who believe that ransom paid for the release of the 100 Dapchi schoolgirls has further increased the terrorist's ability to buy more sophisticated weapons.

## Engendering CT-COIN: females as instruments of war

To meet their end of the social contract, states are expected to establish a legal and institutional framework to protect non-combatants and innocent civilians during any form of violent confrontation including CT-COIN operations. Given the complex nature of asymmetric warfare, combating terrorism and insurgency is a difficult task for any government to handle and, in particular, it is even more daunting for countries with poor technological capacity for tracking and detecting terrorist activities. One of the key features of BH insurgency in recent times has been the instrumental use of women – their abduction, incarceration, and abuse – as a weapon of war. Between 2013 and 2017, BH abducted and kidnapped more than 1000 women and over 5000 women were made widows as a result of losing their husbands and male relatives (Sani, 2017). Among those abducted are the 276 female students of Chibok in Borno State (57 managed to escape their captors). Even though the Nigerian government negotiated the release of 103 of these females (21 on 14 October 2016 and 82 on 7 May 2017, respectively), 116 of them are still in captivity.

Furthermore, females are not only vectors of a suicide mission, but constitute the bulk of the victims – double jeopardy. FST target public places and settlements populated by women, markets, bus stops, kerosene surface tank peddlers and camps where women form 53% IDPs. The reported instances of death and injuries in bomb attacks do not illuminate the gender profile of victims. It is argued that since more women patronise most public places, more women die in such attacks. Worse still, the BH exploits Nigerian Islamic culture prohibiting a man to conduct a bodily search on a woman not only for suicide bomb attacks but to smuggle weapons and bombs on their bodies (Ania, 2015).

The use of FST by BH is a tactic of choice in asymmetrical warfare. This is because FST is considered a minimal risk in terms of detection and apprehension. The abduction of women means that women are "plentiful" resource and extremely dispensable for use to advance the cause and goals of BH. Record of suicide bomb attacks indicates that 434 suicide bombings were carried out by BH since 2011, and 244 of the 338 attacks in which the bomber's gender was established were carried out by women. The potency that gender offers in raising the global profile of BH is a clear indication of their use as instruments of terror and negotiation in the CT-COIN in northeast Nigeria.

## The impact of insurgency and CT-COIN on the livelihood of women

Insurgency and CT-COIN affect the livelihood of women in adverse ways than their male counterparts. This is by virtue of economic and cultural restrictions that instrumentally see women as spouses and dependents and diminish the desire of "independent" women from asserting their autonomy. This Sections present results of interviews conducted with 38 sampled individuals (30 women; 8 men) to examine the impact of insurgency and CT-COIN on women. It was established that hundreds of women have since 2009 to 2017 lost their sources of livelihood; this is in addition to the loss of family breadwinners as a result of CT-COIN through extra-judicial killing or due to crossfire. In addition, women and young girls who have been raped, impregnated, and left traumatised find it difficult, even impossible, to return to normal life, get married or engage in productive activities. Security and health operatives interviewed submitted that as at 2018 about 400 pregnant women and girls were rescued from BH and sheltered in secured military institutions between November 2014 and June 2015. While 15 women lamented that they lost their husbands to BH violent activities. One of the victims – Hauwa, a widow in her 40s –confessed that she suffered "double tragedy" of losing her husband to BH invasion of her village, and death of her son two months later who was fleeing to safety from Chibok. She has become a destitute relying solely on hand-outs from the government and relief agencies. Similarly, three women – Christiana Bulus, Martha Nuhu, and Comfort Markus from Shindufu and Shafah area of Adamawa and Borno State lost their husbands and breadwinners. Most of these victims are left stranded with vulnerable children and the elderly to look after. Given the near-collapse of economic activities in North-eastern Nigeria, most have ended up as IDPs. Where women are themselves the victims of killing, the consequences on the bereaved and society can be equally dire. Between 29 October 2014 and January 2015 when BH attacked and took over Mubi town of Adamawa state many female students of the Adamawa State University were killed. In addition to the blow on family members, the state's health care infrastructures have been overwhelmed as a result of many injured victims. In summary, field data reveals the following: (1) women tend to suffer the impact of insurgency and CT-COIN far worse than their male relatives (b) as it has caused general fear, anxiety and apprehension amongst women and girls in the affected communities (c) it further damaged the educational, social and health sectors of the economy.

### Impact of CT–COIN on Women

Women have played a significant role in the CT-COIN efforts in northeast Nigeria. Women are used by the armed forces of Nigeria as agents of CT-COIN both in "formal" and "informal" capacities: Formally, female constitutes a significant proportion of the members of the armed forces, even though they are clearly quarantined to the support units – such as intelligence, education and catering corps. Female officers and personnel have deployed to Northeast by the Nigerian armed forces for combat operations and non-combatant functions (operation "Lafiya Dole"). But when female became the target for rape and abduction by BH, the decision to deploy female personnel for a combat operation was reviewed. As such their deployment is now restricted to non-combat operations/functions (administrative and Medical team). A female Lieutenant Colonel in the Nigerian Army Medical Corps served in this capacity for 4 years while over 15 other female personnel served in an administrative capacity. Currently, there are more than 14 female personnel serving in non-combat functions. In addition, civilian women have been active as members of the CJTF Elder Abba (25 January 2019) the Borno State Coordinator of the CJTF, said there are 350 women of the 26000 CJTF members scattered across the northeast. The social and economic lives of these women have been shattered by CT-COIN (either widows or sisters of those killed) between 2009 and 2012 in Maiduguri. They are active in intelligence gathering and identification of suspected BH members. Informally, female are conscripted as members of the CJTF providing auxiliary support to the male-dominated units both during combat operations and in the routine mounting of checkpoints to monitor vehicular movements of persons: this has proved useful in detecting the infiltration of insurgents into population centres and IDP camps. Presently, the CJTF boast between 25,000 to 36,000 members including men and women and currently have between 50–100 female members (Peace Direct, 2017).

## The use of female as combatants

BH has used women to advance its reign of terror in the northeast and beyond. The record shows that BH captured and radicalised women as an instrument for suicide missions, so as to demonstrate their capacity to exert terror both on government and civilian targets. Examples are the attack on 301 Battalion Barracks of Nigerian Army in Gombe on 8 June 2014 by a middle-aged woman who detonated explosive concealed under a female garment "hijab" killing herself and a soldier; the Maiduguri phone market attack of 11 January 2015, carried out by two FST; the Adamawa State, bomb attacks carried out in Madagali market place by two females on 22 June 2015, and that of 11 September 2015 in a tent at Yola South IDP Camp. Around 45 persons were killed in Madagali and three persons in the Yola South IDP Camps. While 33 and 9 persons sustained injuries in the two locations respectively; the 11 February 2016 attacks on Dikwa IDP camp that killed 56 people; the 15 March 2017 at Usmanti area of Maiduguri attack in which , four female suicide bombers blew themselves up near a bus station; the 16 June 2018 attacks on Shuwari and Abbachari communities in Damboa local government area in which 32 people were killed, while 84 people sustained injuries when FST detonated their Improvised Explosive Devices (IED) (*Punch,* Dec 11 2016; and Vanguard, 2018).

There is scarce information about the presence of women and girls in the ranks of BH. While former abductees interviewed by the Human Rights Watch (HRW) described the presence of hundreds of women and children in BH camps (HRW, 2013), it was not clear if they had been abducted or had voluntarily joined their family members involved in BH. However, there is concrete evidence of the use of coercion on females into becoming FST from many accounts from women and girls who have refused to detonate devices (*Daily Trust*, 2017). Reports from Non-Governmental Organisations (NGO)'s and women liberated from BH camps, government official's narratives, and interviews with women who refuse to self-detonate attest to that. However, operatives of the CJTF and Operation Lafiya Dole command argue that both hypnotism and drugs were used to force women to become suicide bombers (KII, Yola, 2017).

The BH insurgency and CT-COIN have adverse effects on the socio-economic activities of the region, and this is more so on women. BH insurgency has disrupted agricultural and commercial activities in the north-eastern region. Note that up to 53% of women in Internally Displaced Person (IDP) camps were engaged in agricultural and other commercial activities before being displaced (Salisu et al. 2015). This has deepened the limitation on women who had to cater to the family in the absence of the family head.

BH insurgency and CT-COIN has negatively impacted the lives of women and girls in northeast Nigeria. Many have been targeted for instrumental purposes: as targets to violence, sex slaves and hypnotised carriers of IEDs. Women have been on the forefront of those impacted by BH insurgency as a result of the increasing feminisation of violence by BH in different ways: the employment of girls as both victims and vectors of violence (Onuoha & George, 2015). They were not only physically harassed but sexually violated. Apart from being raped, as victims, they were also at risk of being divorced by their husbands thus further increasing their vulnerability in their communities. Field data gathered shows that, GBV was more pronounced in the extra-judicial killings of Christian women and children, the destruction of shops belonging to women, and the abduction and rape of Christian girls in tertiary institutions (KII, Yola, 2017).

From the government side, HRW has reported the widespread abuses carried out by government security agents in responding to the attacks by BH (HRW, 2013). Since 2009, security forces and CJTF have used excessive force, burned homes, engaged in physical and sexual abuses, and extra-judicially killed those suspected of supporting BH. In addition, the 2016 Participatory Protection Assessment Report (PPAR) on Adamawa state in northeast shows that sexual exploitation of women and girls, rape and physical risk from bombings were reported in all displacement and returnees location (PPAR July 9–15, 2016:3).

## Conclusion

The chapter examined the gendered construction of CT-COIN in north-eastern Nigeria. It established that effort to combat the menace of BH insurgents by the Nigerian government have used both conventional and non-conventional approach. The initial approach was enemy centric but achieved limited success, and then population centred CT-COIN in line with the contemporary global strategy for combating new forms of threat from non-state actors (terrorist and insurgents' group). These CT-COIN strategies have impacted on the population in northeast Nigeria, but more so on women. Socio-economic activities like agriculture have been put on hold and 53% of women that constitute the bulk of IDPs across northeast were active in this social endeavour. Scores of women and girls have been abducted, raped, abused, exploited and some have been radicalised into FST. It is recommended that the government and other stakeholders should intensify efforts to rescue those still in captivity and to improve security in recaptured communities. This can be achieved by strengthening their collaboration with the international community in further decimating the BH insurgency. The government should also ensure that issues of corruption, poverty, inequality, and bad governance are properly dealt with.

## References

Abdulkareem, M. (2010). *The paradox of Boko Haram*. Kaduna: Espee Printing and Advertising.

Abdullahi, K. A. (2016, February 2). Boko Haram have no difficulty entry heavily guarded camps for displaced. *BBC*. http://www.bbc.com/news/world-Africa-35543996 Accessed 08.17, 2019 at 5:52 pm.

Adewumi, J. F. (2016). *Countering Boko Haram group in Nigeria: The relevance of hybrid doctrine*. http://www.smallwarsjournal.com/junl/art/countering-boko-haram-group Accessed 08.08.17 at 2:07 pm.

Andrew, W. (2012). *What's Boko Haram?* United States Institute of Peace Special Report 308 (pp. 1–15). www.usip.org Accessed 27.01.19 at 5.30 pm.

Ania, Skinner. (2015). The Rising Trend of Female Suicide Bombers in Nigeria: Fund for Peace-Global Square Blog, accessed at www.fundforpeace.org on 14.01.2019.

David, N. A. & Lawal, S. M., "*Transcript from an interview of a young female Boko Haram bomber*",*Author's interview*, 2017, 1-3.

Barkindo, A., Gudaku, B., & Wesley, C. (2013). *Our bodies, their battleground: Boko Haram and gender based violence against Christian women and children in North-Eastern Nigeria since 1999*. Open Doors International.

Bart, W. S. (2014). *Clausewitz and the 'New Wars' scholars*. https://www.researchgate.net/publication/267637446 Accessed 29.01.19 at 10.00 pm.

British Council Report. (2012). *Gender in Nigeria report 2012: Improving the lives of girls and women in Nigeria*. http://www.britishcouncil.org.ng/gender2012 Accessed 02.08.13.

Chothia, F. (2014, August 6). Boko Haram crisis: Nigeria's female bombers strike. *BBC Africa*.

Constitution Federal Republic Nigeria. (1999 with amendments 2011) Abuja: Federal Ministry of Information. accessed at www.wipo.int>lexdocs>laws on 17.01.2019.

Olatunji, Omirin. (2017). *Army Parades 3 Female Bombers, 8 Foreigners:* Daily Trust News paper March 2.

Kalli, K. A. (2017). *Coordinator CJTF Northeast Nigeria*. Interview 25.01.17. KII.

Egbue, G. N., Uche, N. I., & Alichie, B. O. (2015). Curbing Boko Haram terrorist insurgence in Nigeria: Imperative of quadruple action package of limited military response, improved social services, conflict resolution initiative and modified pacifism. *British Journal of Arts and Social Sciences*, *20*(1), 13–29.

Ejere, E. (2018) *Nigerians worried the increase in Boko Haram attacks*. http://realnewsmagazine.net/resurgence-of-boko-haram-attacks-in-nigeria/ Accessed 20.01.19.

Elizabeth, G. P. (2015). *Boko haram and Nigeria's female suicide bombers*, Royal United Services Institute (RUSI), London UK.

Ruth, Maclean (2017), "Dressed for death: the women Boko Haram sent to blow themselves up", The Guardian News paper accessed at www.theguardian.com/world/2017/may/05/dressed-for-death-the-women-the-boko-haram-sent-to-blow-themselves-up on 18.02.2019.

Human Rights Watch. (2013). *Nigeria: Turning blind eye to mass killings*. http://www.hrw.org/news/2013/12/12/nigeria-turning-blind-eye-mass-killings Accessed 10.01.16.

Hart, B. (2015). *Boko Haram attack BabbanGida Town, Yobe state*. https://www.naij.com>localnews Accessed 12.03.18.

Ishtiaq, A. (2012). Terrorism: A conceptual framework. In U. Kumar & M. K. Mandal (Eds.), *Countering terrorism* (pp. 3–25). New Delhi: Sage Publications.

Jacob, Z., & Pearson, E. (2014). Women gender and evolving tactics of Boko Haram. *Journal of Terrorism Research*, *5*, (1) (February special issue), 46–57.

James, J. F. Forest & Giroux, Jennifer. "Terrorism and political violence in Africa: contemporary trends in a shifting terrain" (2011), *Vol.5*, 3-4, *Journal of the Terrorism Research Initiative*, pp.5-18.

Jason, W., & Matfess, H. (2017). *Exploding stereotypes: The unexpected operational and demographic characteristics of Boko Haram's suicide bombers*. West Point, NY: Combating Terrorism Centre.

Jason, Rineheart. (2010). *Counterterrorism and Counter-insurgency in Perspectives on Terrorism*, vol. 4(No. 5), 31–47 Terrorism Research Initiative; https://www.scholar.google.com accessed 22 01 2019 22.03 pm.

Kaldor, M. (2013). In defence of new wars stability. *International Journal of Security and Development*. Available from http://eprints.Ise.ac.uk/49500/ in LSE Research. Accessed 29.01.19.

Kaldor, M. (2005). Elaborating the new wars thesis in Duyvesteyn. In Isabelle and J., Angstrom (Eds.), *Rethinking the nature of war* (pp. 212–221). New York: Frank Cass.

Kaldor. (1996). *cosmopolitan response to new wars: peace review* Vol. 8, No. 4, accessed at www.tandfonline.com>doi>abs on 18.01.2019 505–514.

Kabiru, R. A. (2016, March 24). Boko Haram abducts 16 women in Madagali. *Daily Trust*.

Kiras, J. D. (2011). Terrorism and globalisation. In J. Baylis, S. Smith & O. Patricia (Eds.), *The globalisation of world politics* (pp. 366–378). New York: Oxford University Press.

Maclean, Ruth, "*Dressed for Death: The Women Boko Haram Sent to Blow Themselves Up*," Guardian, May 5, 2017.

Manu, Y. A. (2016). terrorism and national security in Nigeria. In U. A. Tar, M. EU. Tedheke & E. B. Mijah (Eds.), *Readings on globalisation and development in Africa*. Kaduna: NDA Press.

Chandler, Michael & Gunaratna, Rohan. (2007). *Countering terrorism: can we meet the threat of global violence?* London: Reaktion Books.

Michael, F. & Hy, R. (2011). *Gangs and guerrillas: Ideas from counter-insurgency and counterterrorism*. Monterey, Califonia: Department of Defence Analysis Naval Post graduate School.

Mijinyawa, Ahmed. (2015, March 1) Mob burns woman to death. *Premium Times*. https://www.premiumtimesng.com Accessed 20.08.18 at 6.00 pm.

Meilinger, P. S (2007). Busting the icon: Restoring balance to influence of Clausewitz. *Strategic Studies Quarterly*, Vol. 1 No. 1, accessed at www.galeacademiconefile.com on 18.01.2019.

Mukhi, H. RR (2006). *Political thought*. Nai Sarak Delhi: SBD Publishers Distributors.

National Security Strategy of the Federal Republic of Nigeria (2014). Office of the National Security Adviser, Federal Republic of Nigeria Abuja. Yaliam Press Ltd, Abuja 08037222209, 08054356202.

Olanrewaju, F. O., Olarewaju, A., Loromeke, E. R. & Joshua, S. (2017). Implications of the release of Chibok girls on Nigeria's war on terrorism. *Covenant University Journal of Politics and International Affairs*, 5(1 June 2017), 40–59.

Okereke, C. Nna-Emeka., "Combating terrorism and transnational organized crimes (TOTs) in West Africa" (2010), *Vol. 36*, No. 2, *Nigerian Journal of International Affairs*, 9-32.

Onuoha, F. C., & George, T. A. (2015). *Boko Haram's use of female suicide bombing in Nigeria*. Aljezeera Centre for Studies, 2. Available from www.studies.aljazeera.net Accessed 20.01.19.

Participatory Protection Assessment Report. (2016). *Adamawa state a publication of Protection Sector Working Group Nigeria*, July 9-15, www.globalprotectioncluster.org Accessed 20.07. 18.

Peace Direct. (2017). *The role of women in countering violent extremism: The Nigerian experience with Boko Haram*. https://reliefweb.int>report>nigeria.

Pearson, E. (2018).Wilayat Shahidat: Boko Haram, Islamic state, and the question of the female suicide bomber. In J. Zenneds (Ed.), *Boko Haram beyond the headlines: Analyses of Africa's enduring insurgency*. West Point:Combating Terrorism Centre.

Pulse. (2014, December 19) *Two female students of Federal University of Technology Minna were nearly lynched*. https://www.pulse.ng Accessed 20.10.18.

Punch Newspaper, (11 December, 2016). "Boko Haram invades Borno villages abducts 18 girls and four women" www.punchng.com accessed on 14.01.2019.

Ross, M. (1993). *The management of conflict: Interpretation and interest in comparative perspectives*. New Haven: Yale University Press.

Salisu, S. S., Mohammed, A. S., & Abdullahi, Y. S. (2015). The impact of Boko Haram insurgency on Nigerian national security. *International Journal of Academic Research in Business and Social Sciences*, 5(6), 254–266.

Sani, Tukur. (2017, August 14). Shocking revelation: 100,000 killed, two million displaced by Boko Haram insurgency in Borno State. *Premium Times*.

Seteolu, D. (2011). Terrorism in the Sahel Region. *Nigerian Journal of International Affairs*, 37(3), 3–15.

Solomon, E. (2013). *Boko Haram: Developing new strategies to combat terrorism in Nigeria*. College Research Paper, United States Army War College.

Stigall, D. E., Miller, C. & Donnatucci, L., (2019) *The 2018 U.S. National Strategy for counterterrorism: A synoptic overview, Am. U. Nat'l Sec. L. Brief*, accessed at www.papers.ssrn.comon 19 October, 2019.

Stiwala, I. N. (2017). Terrorism and counter-insurgency in Africa- The failure of Africa's political leadership keynote address. Presented at the *First International Conference*, Nwafor Orizu College of Education, Nsukka, Anambra State, Nigeria.

UNO Global Counterterrorism Implementation Task Force. Accessed at http://www.un.org>unglobal-co on 13 August, 2017.

Tickner, J. A. (2011). Gender in world politics in John Baylis. In S. Smith & P. Owens (Eds.), *Globalisation of world politics* (pp. 262–275). New York: Oxford University Press.

Vanguard. (2013, June 30). *Vigilante arrest two women with assault rifle, IEDs, in Maiduguri*. http://www.vanguard.com/2013/06/vigilante-arrests-2-women-with-assault-weapons-ied-in-maiduguri Accessed 28.07.17 at 10.00 am.

Vanguard. (2018, June 16). How 6 female bombers killed 32 in Borno. https://www.vanguardngr.com Accessed 18.08.2018 6.30 pm.

Vanguard Newspaper (June 17, 2018). "How 6 female bombers kill 32 in Borno" www.vanguardngr.com accessed on 14.01.2019.

Yinka, Olomojobi. (2013). *Islam and Conflict in Northern Nigeria*. Malthouse Press Limited Lagos.

Younkyoo, Kim, & Stephen, Blank. (2013). *Insurgency and Counter-insurgency in Russia: Contending Paradigms and Current Perspectives, Studies in Conflict and Terrorism*, Rutledge Taylor and Francis Group, 917–932. https://doi.org/10.1080/1057610X. 2013. 832115 accessed 25/01/2019.

# Index